W9-CNJ-774

# www.wadsworth.com

*wadsworth.com* is the World Wide Web site for Wadsworth Publishing Company and is your direct source to dozens of online resources.

At *wadsworth.com* you can find out about supplements, demonstration software, and student resources. You can also send e-mail to many of our authors and preview new publications and exciting new technologies.

**wadsworth.com**
Changing the way the world learns®

# Ethical Theory and Moral Problems

### HOWARD J. CURZER

*Texas Tech University*

**Wadsworth Publishing Company**

I(T)P® An International Thomson Publishing Company

Belmont, CA • Albany, NY • Boston • Cincinnati • Johannesburg • London • Madrid
Melbourne • Mexico City • New York • Pacific Grove, CA • Scottsdale, AZ • Singapore • Tokyo • Toronto

This book is dedicated to my parents, Abe and Ruth Curzer;
to my wife, Anne Epstein;
and to my daughter, Mirah Curzer.

*Philosophy Editor:* Peter Adams
*Assistant Editor:* Kerri Abdinoor
*Editorial Assistant:* Mindy Newfarmer
*Marketing Manager:* Dave Garrison
*Print Buyer:* Stacey Weinberger
*Permissions Editor:* Robert Kauser

*Production:* Matrix Productions Inc.
*Copy Editor:* Connie Day
*Cover Design:* Lisa Langhoff
*Cover Image:* PhotoDisk®
*Compositor:* TBH Typecast, Inc.
*Printer:* Webcom Limited

COPYRIGHT © 1999 by Wadsworth Publishing Company
A Division of International Thomson Publishing Inc.

I(T)P® The ITP logo is a registered trademark under license.

Printed in Canada
1  2  3  4  5  6  7  8  9  10

For more information, contact Wadsworth Publishing Company, 10 Davis Drive, Belmont, CA 94002, or electronically at
http://www.wadsworth.com

International Thomson Publishing Europe
Berkshire House
168-173 High Holborn
London, WC1V 7AA, United Kingdom

International Thomson Editores
Seneca, 53
Colonia Polanco
11560 México D.F. México

Nelson ITP, Australia
102 Dodds Street
South Melbourne
Victoria 3205 Australia

International Thomson Publishing Asia
60 Albert Street
#15-01 Albert Complex
Singapore 189969

Nelson Canada
1120 Birchmount Road
Scarborough, Ontario
Canada M1K 5G4

International Thomson Publishing Japan
Hirakawa-cho Kyowa Building, 3F
2-2-1 Hirakawa-cho, Chiyoda-ku
Tokyo 102, Japan

International Thomson Publishing Southern Africa
Building 18, Constantia Square
138 Sixteenth Road, P.O. Box 2459
Halfway House, 1685 South Africa

All rights reserved. No part of this work covered by the copyright hereon may be reproduced or used in any form or by any means—graphic, electronic, or mechanical, including photocopying, recording, taping, or information storage and retrieval systems—without the written permission of the publisher.

**Library of Congress Cataloging-in-Publication Data**

Ethical theory and moral problems / [edited by] Howard J. Curzer.
    p.  cm.
  ISBN 0-534-52974-7 (alk. paper)
    1. Ethics.   2. Social ethics.   3. Ethical problems.    I. Curzer, Howard J.
BJ1012.E88347   1998
170—dc21                                                    98-39126

# Contents

## PART III   CARE AND JUSTICE   277

## PART IV   MORAL PROBLEMS   385

# PREFACE

*Of the tree of the knowledge of good and evil, thou shalt not eat of it; for in the day that thou eatest thereof thou shalt surely die.*

GOD

*Ye shall not surely die; for God doth know that in the day ye eat thereof, then your eyes shall be opened, and ye shall be as God, knowing good and evil.*

THE SERPENT

*Behold, the man is become as one of us, knowing good and evil.*

GOD

Part I of *Ethical Theory and Moral Problems* removes obstacles to ethics and builds foundations to ethics. Part II exposes students to Utilitarian, Kantian, and Aristotelian ethical theories while Part III discusses justice and care. Part IV then applies all of these ethical theories to moral problems. The first three parts of this anthology (especially when combined with primary sources) contain ample material for a "pure theory" course. The fourth part of this anthology contains enough articles addressing enough different issues for a "pure problems" course. However, *Ethical Theory and Moral Problems* emphasizes the *connections* between theory and problems. The range of selections is designed to provide the instructor with the flexibility to bring out these connections in manifold ways. For example, courses contrasting the practical implications of different moral theories, or integrating the ethics of justice and the ethics of care, or tracing egoistic and religious strands of thought within ethics could easily be constructed from the material in this anthology. Courses might be organized around themes such as freedom and responsibility, or happiness and sexuality, or benevolence and self-interest.

No background in philosophy is presupposed by this anthology, so it would be suitable for a very basic Introductory Ethics course. On the other hand, many of the articles are rich enough to stimulate even strong, sophisticated philosophy students, so this anthology would be suitable for a high-powered course, too. Although there is occasional cross-referencing, each section of the anthology is independent of the others. The sections can be read in any order.

## Distinctive Features of this Anthology

(1) Focuses on applying ethical theories to moral problems
(2) Incorporates feminist perspectives on problems of particular interest to women
(3) Contains interesting and exotic essay questions
(4) Introduces each section in a clear, comprehensive, challenging manner
(5) Provides an unusually large number of articles per topic
(6) Presents a brief history of ethics
(7) Treats topics in innovative ways
(8) Includes commentary on, rather than selections from, Mill, Kant, and Aristotle

(1) Many Introductory Ethics courses begin by sketching Utilitarian, Kantian, and perhaps Aristotelian ethical theories and then spend the bulk of the course treating moral problems through contemporary journal articles. This approach faces two difficulties. First, a brief treatment leaves the student with only a tenuous and superficial grasp of the theories. Second, the articles typically do not straightforwardly apply an ethical theory to a moral problem. Instead, the theory hovers in the background, implicitly assumed, but not explicitly invoked. Students find it difficult to knit the theories and the problems together. To address this difficulty, I have carefully chosen many articles that straightforwardly apply Utilitarian, Kantian, and Aristotelian ethical theories to particular moral problems. The section introductions and the essay questions also help students to apply these theories to particular problems. The choice of articles, the structure of the section introductions, and the focus of the essay questions help broaden, deepen, and strengthen the student's grasp of the theories while clarifying the relationship between the theories and the problems.

(2) This anthology includes the contributions of several feminists and emphasizes the problems of gender. My aim is to expose large numbers of people to moderate feminism. The anthology reflects this goal in the following ways:

(a) More than one third of the articles were written by women.
(b) The moral problems I have chosen are all problems of particular relevance to women.
(c) The "moral problems" sections contain articles addressing the problems from feminist perspectives as well as articles utilizing more traditional lines of thought.

(d) The section introductions discuss feminist approaches to the problems alongside the more standard approaches.

(e) The anthology includes a section on the ethics of care, a feminist approach to ethics.

(3) Creating new, stimulating, challenging, comprehensive essay questions year after year can become a chore. Yet such questions are necessary for many reasons, not the least of which is that the answers to standard essay questions are now readily available commercially. I want to share the bank of essay questions that I have been developing and refining for two decades. These are not puny, two-sentence questions, but rather they are detailed, thought-provoking, lively questions that lead the student through a series of philosophical moves. The questions ask students to apply theories to problems, compare and contrast articles, defend and attack theories, and so on. My hope is that these essay questions will intrigue instructors and make essay writing and class discussions more interesting for students.

(4) I have struggled to make the section introductions easy to read and to the point. They are not cluttered with scholarly apparatus such as extensive references to the professional literature or excessive precision about trivial matters. The introductions are aimed at the student rather than at the instructor. On the other hand, the introductions will challenge even the advanced student. Although they are brief, the introductions are detailed and thorough. They present most of the standard arguments as well as some non-standard arguments on each topic. The introductions also suggest implications and criticisms of these arguments.

(5) Coverage is comprehensive within each section. For example, instead of two or three articles on abortion, this anthology includes six articles. Throughout the anthology the articles range from the simple to the challenging, from the plain to the exciting, from the obviously relevant to the meta-ethical, and from the classic to the recent. They present a variety of different points of view within each section. I chose depth rather than breadth to give instructors a wider range of options of articles to assign on each topic and to provide students with a multi-sided approach to each topic. Depth has an additional advantage. If the instructor does not assign all the essays within a section, the remaining articles constitute built-in further reading for students who wish to pursue a topic beyond the assigned essays.

(6) The general introduction to this anthology includes several items of value to students:

(a) a description of the difficulties and rewards of philosophy,
(b) some advice on reading and writing philosophy,
(c) a few remarks on the nature of ethics, and
(d) a brief account of the history of ethics.

The point of this last item is to situate various ethical theories within an intellectual-historical context. The sketch of the history of ethics enables the students to connect their Introductory Ethics course with their Western

Civilization course. That is, it strives to convey some of the relationships between various ethical theories, on the one hand, and important past events on the other. It also offers students a sense of the development of ethics, a slice of the fascinating, trans-temporal conversation among philosophers.

(7) The section topics are traditional rather than gimmicky, but the section introductions expound on some of the topics in unconventional ways. I shall just mention a few examples. The "Morality and Religion" section introduction does not simply debunk divine command theory; it actually introduces the student to some methods and perils of scriptural interpretation and also to some strands of ethical thought within both the Jewish and the Christian traditions. Second, not only the theory but also the application of virtue ethics is displayed throughout the anthology. Finally, although poverty is now well established as a feminist issue, the "Euthanasia, Suicide, and Futility" section introduction brings out some surprising ways in which life-ending decisions are viewed from a feminist perspective.

(8) Formidable cultural, intellectual, and linguistic barriers hinder contemporary students attempting to comprehend the thought of Mill, Kant, and Aristotle. This anthology thus contains some desperately needed commentary on the works of these difficult philosophers. Because instructors are rarely happy with another person's abridgement of a classic text, and because the classics are readily available, this anthology does not contain selections of classic texts. Citations to the works of Mill, Kant, and Aristotle are parenthetical page numbers in the section introductions. For Mill, citations are to *Utilitarianism*, edited by G. Sher (Indianapolis: Hackett, 1979). For Kant, citations are to both *Grounding for the Metaphysics of Morals*, translated by J. Ellington (Indianapolis: Hackett, 1981), and the standard Akademie edition of Kant's collected works. For Aristotle, citations are to both *Nicomachean Ethics*, translated by D. Ross (Oxford England: Oxford University Press, 1925) and the standard Bekker edition of Aristotle's collected works.

### Acknowledgments

I am grateful to the following people for making many useful suggestions about differing portions of the manuscript: Deborah Achtenberg, Anne Epstein, John Moskop, William Nelson, Walter Schaller, and Mark Webb. I also wish to thank the following reviewers: Earl Conee, University of Rochester; Daniel Farrell, Ohio State University, Columbus; Robert Hollinger, Iowa State University, Ames; Paulette Kidder, Seattle University; and Anita Silver, San Francisco State University.

# INTRODUCTION

*I'd like to see people, instead of spending so much time on the ethical problem, get after the problems that really affect the people of this country.*

RICHARD NIXON

## Difficulties and Rewards of Doing Philosophy

"Philosophy begins in wonder," says Plato. Philosophers are seekers after certain sorts of truth. But philosophers want their beliefs not only to be true but also to be somehow justified or supported or explained. Thus philosophers are obsessed with *arguments.* I do not mean that philosophers shout at each other. By "arguments" I mean inferences from some statements to others. Arguments consist of premises offered in support of conclusions. If the conclusion follows logically from the premises, then the argument is called *valid.* If the argument is valid and the premises are true, then the argument is called *sound.* Why do philosophers care about arguments? Why is mere truth not enough? True beliefs are easily lost when challenged by passion, sophistry, or even just long periods of time. Moreover, true beliefs alone cannot persuade others. One must have good reasons for one's true beliefs, and these reasons are arguments.

However, the arguments of philosophers create confusion in various ways. For example, after philosophers state their views and argue for them, they usually go on to play devil's advocate. They raise potential objections to their own views and then rebut these objections with counter-objections. They may even present counter-counter-objections and then rebut them with counter-counter-counter-objections. By this time, you, the reader, are lost.

Then again, sometimes philosophers rely on assumptions that you do not share. This would not be problematic if all premises were explicit, but implicit premises are rampant. Thus you often find yourself being led to a conclusion that you do not like by an argument whose hidden assumptions you would reject if they were clearly stated. You come away from the argument feeling duped but are unable to put your finger on the trick.

People have very different beliefs, but these differences are typically shrouded by the shared conventions and routines of everyday life. Philosophy, however, bares these differences by inquiring into things usually taken for granted. You may discover to your dismay that you disagree over fundamental matters with loved ones, peers, authority figures, and the like.

Worse yet, you may find that you disagree with yourself. Philosophers often make claims that seem false or even weird at first, but then they go on to bolster their claims with oddly persuasive arguments. Your reason is convinced and it urges you to accept these claims despite your intuition, your common sense, your desires, or some other aspect of yourself. You find yourself profoundly conflicted.

Even when there is no conflict, philosophy demands that, in order to justify previously unquestioned assumptions, you defend beliefs that earlier seemed obvious. This can be a traumatic task. If you fail to find reasonable reasons to hold on to your fundamental beliefs, then you come away feeling shaken, uprooted, disoriented. You used to be confident about your opinions, but now you do not know what to think.

There are no vaccines against these and other perils of philosophy. Philosophy, therefore, requires a certain sort of character. Because philosophy undermines peace of mind, it requires a sort of *inner strength* or *balance*. It is not for the psychologically fragile. Philosophy also requires you to be *industrious*. You must go over and over the text, the idea, the argument. You must turn things around in your mind, thinking about them this way, that way, and the other way to see which way makes the most sense, which way is most plausible, which way seems best. Philosophy demands *integrity*. You cannot alter your views, accept some position, or become persuaded by an argument just because it is convenient to do so. Nor can you comfortably believe one way while speaking and/or acting another. Your thoughts, words, and deeds must be in harmony. Philosophy also demands *open-mindedness.* You must be willing to change your mind and abandon firm convictions about very important matters. You must value truth above peace of mind, above winning the argument, above fitting in with other people, above practically everything. Philosophers must be *generous*. They must give the benefit of the doubt to the ideas of others, for truth is found in unlikely places. Ideas that seem silly at first turn out, upon reflection, to be profound. Philosophy requires *courage*. It is not enough to understand or even challenge other people's views; you must propose your own. And once you state your own view, either aloud or on paper, your view is open to criticism. Philosophy requires other virtues, too. Clearly, philosophy is not for everyone.

Philosophy is not all struggle and strength of character, though. It has a bright side. Philosophy will transform you. Your beliefs will change, and you will experience the world in new ways. After you have done a fair amount of philosophy, you will find yourself confused about things you used to take for granted, but you will also discover the excitement of penetrating hazy clouds of words or worries straight to the heart of issue after issue. In general, philosophy will make simple things complicated and complicated things simple.

People around you will notice the change. Some will appreciate it; others will not. You, however, will cherish the change in yourself. You will treasure the enlightenment that philosophy brings, even if that enlightenment is no more than a recognition of how much you do not know.

Philosophy is pursued not only for the sake of pure knowledge. Because philosophy investigates the underlying issues of every field of activity and inquiry, the study of philosophy makes you well rounded and better grounded. Philosophy will improve your odds of success at whatever you choose to do. For example, both artists and art appreciators benefit from studying philosophy of art. Scientists, lawyers, doctors, and members of the clergy find philosophy of science, law, medicine, and religion useful in their respective endeavors.

This is an ethics book. What will ethics do for you? As Aristotle says, we study ethics "not in order to know what virtue is, but in order to become good" (30, 1103b). By itself, the study of ethics is not guaranteed to make you into a moral person leading a happy life. It will help, however. Indeed, ethics may be a prerequisite. Moreover, almost everyone who reads this book will eventually have and raise children. Do you want to be able to guide your children toward becoming morally good adults? Do you want to be able to answer their questions about right and wrong? Do you want them to grow up in a moral environment? Do you want them to inherit a moral world? The study of ethics will help you reach these goals.

## Reading Philosophy

Philosophy texts are surprisingly different from texts of other disciplines. When you read a piece of philosophy for the first time, you may have the following strange experience. All of the words and sentences make sense, but after you have finished the article, you find that you have only a dim and confused idea of what it was about. If this happens, do not panic. It is not a sign of stupidity or inattention. This is a very common experience. Philosophy does not lend itself to casual perusal. Most people must read each philosophy passage at least twice before it makes any sense at all. You cannot simply read philosophy; you need to work through it slowly, carefully, and repeatedly.

Read with a pencil as well as with your eyes. You will find that philosophers often say confusing and outrageous things as well as stimulating and insightful things. Make a note of all such things as you encounter them. As you are reading and afterwards, questions, amplifications, examples, and objections, will come to mind. (If you do not find the article thought-provoking, something has gone wrong.) Write them down as they occur to you. A philosophy journal may be helpful if the margin of this book proves insufficient.

After you have finished reading an article, try to state the author's main claims and arguments as clearly as you can in your own words. Then ask yourself whether you agree with the author, and ask yourself why or why not. Unless you do this, the time spent reading will have all been wasted. The article will be just a jumble of words, soon forgotten.

### Writing Philosophy

Philosophy courses are more like carpentry courses than chemistry courses. The objective of a philosophy course is not just to master a body of data but also to develop and practice certain techniques. No one becomes a good carpenter merely by reading books about carpentry. You must get out of your comfortable chair and build things. The first table you build will wobble, and the first birdhouse will leak. You will hammer your thumbs and get splinters in your fingers, but with practice you will improve. Similarly, no one learns philosophy just by reading books—and especially not by skimming them the night before exams. Of course, you must read the books and read them carefully, but you must also practice the techniques of philosophy. You must think about everything in new, philosophical ways. You must learn to ask philosophical questions, develop philosophical answers, and support your answers with philosophical arguments. Your early questions, answers, and arguments may be simplistic or silly. You may bruise your ego or shatter a cherished belief. But keep on trying and you will improve. As in carpentry, proficiency in philosophy comes with practice.

Philosophy papers are not research papers. The objective is not just to report what someone else said but rather to think through a problem for yourself. You must state your own theory or interpretation *clearly* and (this is the most important part) explain *why* you think your theory or interpretation is true. As I said earlier, philosophy is a quest for both true beliefs and rational arguments. If you are unsure about how to proceed, try following these instructions.

A. Read the essay question carefully.
   1. What is the question asking? Explain the question to yourself until it makes sense.
   2. What are several possible answers?
   3. Which of these is your answer? Take a clear stand.
   4. Your goal is to convince the reader that your answer is right. What strategies for explaining and justifying your answer will you use?
B. Construct an outline using complete sentences.
   1. The outline should consist of explanation and argumentation.
   2. What assumptions are you making?
   3. Are these assumptions simple and self-evident? If not, you will have to explain and/or defend them.
   4. Try to think of objections someone might raise against particular points or against your outline in general. Then decide how you will defend your claim against these objections.
   5. If you find yourself unable to defend your claim, then you will have to revise your claim or abandon it and start over.
   6. If you are able to defend your claim, add the objections and your refutation of the objections to the outline.
C. Write the opening paragraph.
   1. Get to the point right away. Meandering introductions are out of fashion these days.

2. Include a thesis sentence or two that express your main point, the conclusion of your central argument.

D. Write the body of the paper by elaborating the outline.

1. Most of the sentences of the outline should become topic sentences of separate paragraphs in the body of the paper.

2. Try stating each point three different times in three very different ways. This may bring out connections and implications that you might otherwise have missed.

3. Each non-obvious point in your exposition will require some elaboration. Clarify and explain your points. Give examples, applications, analogies, and so on.

4. Each non-obvious premise or step in your argument will require some justification. The more controversial a point is, the more effort you need to put into convincing your reader.

5. Write a lot. There is an enormous amount to say about any philosophical issue. Thus short papers are usually superficial. If your paper is short, you are probably omitting important points.

6. On the other hand, don't just repeat yourself or include superfluous material.

E. Write the closing paragraph.

1. Summarize what you have shown and how you have shown it.

2. Your conclusion should match the thesis sentence(s) in your introduction. Otherwise, you set out to prove one thing and ended up proving another.

F. Reexamine the paper that you have written.

1. Have you established the main point, the thesis sentence(s)?

2. Have you answered all parts of the question?

3. Have you made all parts of your argument explicit? Sometimes a point that seems to you to follow directly from something that you have already said will seem *to the reader* to be coming out of nowhere. You may have been unconsciously assuming some crucial connecting thesis. You must explain the connection between your ideas, even if the connection seems clear to you. Make sure, then, that you have not omitted a crucial sentence or paragraph.

G. Write your second draft.

1. No one thinks or writes well enough to hand in a first draft, so plan to write at least two drafts.

2. Don't let your second draft be merely a grammatically and stylistically improved version of the first draft. Your second draft should be substantively different from your first draft.

3. Important new ideas will occur to you in the process of writing and reviewing the first draft. These ideas should be included in the second draft.

4. The flaws in some of your original ideas will also become apparent. Naturally, these ideas should be omitted from the second draft.

5. Proofread the paper. Then read the paper *out loud*. Your ear tends to catch awkward sentences that your eye tends to miss.

H. Watch out for common mistakes.
1. Pace yourself. Don't spend lots of time polishing the first page of your paper before you get the rest of the paper written.
2. Focus your paper. Don't just blurt out everything you know about the general topic, whether all the details are relevant or not. Answer the specific question asked.
3. Beware of the tendency to drift into a digression and never return to the main point.
4. Beware of slogans. They are usually vague and offer only the illusion of meaning.
5. Beware of vagueness. *You* may know what you mean, but it is your responsibility to make sure *the reader* knows what you mean.
6. Beware of the fallacy of begging the question by assuming as a premise what you are trying to prove.
7. Don't just express your opinions. Bolster your opinions with arguments.
8. Using other people's words or ideas without giving them credit is plagiarism. Therefore, if you quote someone's words or use her or his ideas, provide a reference that includes author, title of the book or article, and page number. If you are in doubt about whether a citation is necessary, err on the side of caution and include a citation.
9. If you are using a word processor, save your work frequently in both soft and hard copy. Computer malfunctions, printer deaths, and the like should be setbacks, not tragedies.
10. Professors sometimes lose papers, so keep a copy of your paper.

## What Is Ethics? What Is Morality?

These are difficult questions to answer because philosophers disagree about the methods, goals, and subject matter of ethics and morality. It is probably safe to say that *morality* is a code of conduct or system of values providing guidance about right and wrong actions as well as the passions, desires, beliefs, words, character traits and other such things related to these actions. Morality tells us which options to choose in a wide range of different situations and why these choices are right and others are wrong. *Ethics* is more complicated. (a) Sometimes ethics simply means morality. The terms "ethical" and "moral" can be used interchangeably. (b) Sometimes ethics is taken to be a theory providing guidance not just about right and wrong but about all aspects of life. In this sense, ethics includes morality and much more. (c) Finally, ethics is sometimes thought of as the study of morality, a theoretical investigation of morality.

Morality is not the only code of conduct or system of values purporting to provide guidance about action. How is morality to be distinguished from law, etiquette, custom, prudence, religion, aesthetics, and other systems of values? The statement "You should not steal this car" might be a moral claim, or it might spring from any one of these other value systems.

Perhaps morality is just a part of, or is deduced from, another set of values. A surprising number of people say that morality arises from culture. Presumably, the value system of a culture is embedded in the law, etiquette, and customs of the culture, so in this sense morality is a set of corollaries to these other systems. But some cultures endorse acts and practices that are clearly immoral. Slavery has been endorsed by many past cultures, for example. [See the "Morality and Knowledge" section.] One version of Egoism says that morality can be deduced from the injunction to promote our own happiness. In this view, morality is a part of prudence. But the morally right thing to do does not always seem to be in the agent's overall, long-term best interest. For example, I have a moral duty to grade papers fairly. However, as all know but few admit, fair grading is difficult, boring, and time-consuming. It is in my best interest, therefore, to assign grades more or less arbitrarily. (Few students will challenge the grades they receive, and if any do, I can then go on to read the paper and assign the correct grade.) [See the "Morality and Happiness" section.] The Divine Command Theory says that moral acts are moral because God endorses them. Thus our moral duties are primordially religious duties. But sometimes a moral principle may even seem to conflict with a religious principle. When God told Abraham to kill his son, Abraham presumably believed himself to be facing such a dilemma. [See the "Morality and Religion" section.] Thus it seems that morality is not deduced from, or even a component of, these other value systems.

To return to the original question, what is morality and how is it distinguished from other value systems? One traditional answer is that morality is the value system that always has priority in any conflict. Moral values are the highest values. But this seems to beg an important question. Surely, we should not just *assume* that morality takes precedence over other values. The priority of morality stands in need of justification.

Many other accounts of morality also beg important questions. For example, some philosophers maintain that moral injunctions are rules that apply to everyone regardless of inclinations. Rules such as "Thou shalt not wear striped pants, a plaid shirt, and a paisley tie together (except in a few, rather odd situations)" apply to people who want to look fashionable, but they are irrelevant to people who are indifferent to fashion. On the other hand, rules such as "Thou shalt not steal (except in a few, rather odd situations)" apply to everyone, whether they like it or not. Even so, the claim that moral rules apply universally is not universally accepted among philosophers. Like the priority of morality, the universality of morality requires argumentation, so we should not simply stipulate that universality is the defining characteristic of morality.

Perhaps the best way to investigate the essence of morality is to scan the history of morality—to examine past moral theories. Of course, this approach assumes that we can already distinguish moral theories from non-moral value theories, and that past moral theorists were more or less right about what morality is. On the other hand, the history of morality is intrinsically interesting and may prove to be a helpful orientation for the contemporary study of morality. The following survey is quite sketchy and is, unfortunately, limited to thinkers within the Western European tradition.

## Highlights of the History of Morality

Perhaps the earliest documents in the ancient world that were recognizably concerned with morality were the first five books of the *Bible,* known to the Jews collectively as the *Torah* (compiled ca. 450 BCE). The antecedent Babylonian creation myth, *Enuma Elis* (ca. 2000 BCE) was a religious document starring capricious and amoral Gods. But from the very beginning, the God of the *Bible* exemplifies and enforces moral standards. God rewards and punishes people according to the morality of their actions rather than some other criterion, such as the costliness of their sacrifices. The Israelites are the chosen people not because of frivolous favoritism but rather because of a contract between the Israelites and God. The Mesopotamian *Code of Hammurabi* (ca. 1700 BCE) was a legal document consisting of a list of rules and the penalties for disobedience. However, the *Torah* contains not only rules and penalties but also an account of how these rules chart a way of life. Of course, most of our basic moral rules derive from this part of the *Bible.* It contains the ten commandments, the injunction to love your neighbor as you love yourself, and many other familiar moral rules. It embodies the radical idea that all people, rich or poor, noble or commoner, friend or stranger, are equal before the moral law and advances the equally radical idea that people have a duty to be kind to the disadvantaged, the widow and the orphan, the disabled and the elderly, the poor and the stranger. These are the foundations of our contemporary concepts of justice and benevolence. The sanctity of all human life and the idea that everyone, even servants and animals, deserves a day of rest were also revolutionary ideas at the time. But the *Bible* is also an epic of a people becoming increasingly morally sophisticated within a cosmos whose laws are moral as much as physical. It can be read, therefore, as an account of moral development within a moral context. In the *Torah* the rules of morality are intermingled with rules of ritual and sacrifice. But the Israelite *prophets* (ca. 750–450 BCE) de-emphasized the latter, thus forging a religion with morality as its fundamental requirement. Moreover, the prophets proclaimed that the Israelites were to set an example for other peoples, thus applying the moral rules to all peoples rather than just to the Israelites. As the circumstances of the Jews changed, they worked out increasingly detailed interpretations and applications of the moral rules to cover a myriad of cases, rather than relying on the possibly capricious or biased judgments of individuals. This reliance on detailed, impartial principles became a model for contemporary Anglo-American law.

Meanwhile, the ancient Greek poet *Homer* (ca. 800 BCE) presented a different sort of moral theory in the *Iliad* and the *Odyssey.* These poems painted a picture of an ideal person, a role model, a set of good character traits or virtues built around the virtue of courage. Of course, epics in other cultures painted pictures of role models, too, but the Greek epics were the beginning of a tradition of virtue ethics. For hundreds of years the Greeks strove to emulate the Homeric heroes and acquire the character traits they displayed. However, as Greece entered its golden age (ca. 500 BCE), the consensus that the Homeric heroes represented the right ideal and that their character traits really were virtues began to break down. Changes in the Greek economy brought wealth and power to merchants and producers who scorned the traditional, aristocratic values. Moreover, advances in sciences, technology, arts, and philosophy were undermining traditional beliefs. Morality was in crisis. *Tragedians* wrote plays about unfortunate people torn by conflicts between different moral ideals and between morality and religion, law, tradition, nature, rationality, passions, and so on. *Aristocrats* who favored the old values were challenged by *Sophists,* who advocated a new paradigm. These itinerant teachers of rhetoric, who were patronized predominantly by the *nouveau riche,* used the tool of persuasion to outmaneuver the aristocracy in political conflicts. The Sophists justified this use of rhetoric by denying the existence of a universal standard of value. If truth is an illusion, then the ultimate virtue is the ability to manipulate people—that is, rhetoric.

Many cultures revere particular individuals who themselves write nothing but inspire everyone they meet and are known to us through the writings of disciples. These figures are moral revolutionaries who lead exemplary lives in times of moral crisis. However, when they try to inspire others to do the same, they engender fatal hostility. *Socrates* (470–399 BCE) was such a person. He attacked the Aristocrats by showing that they did not understand or believe their own slogans, their own Homeric quotations, their own pious platitudes. Socrates attacked the Tragedians by showing that what seem to be conflicts of different sorts of values are really conflicts between real value and the mere illusion of value. Socrates attacked the Sophists by forcing them to admit that they did not accept the radical implications of their own relativism. Knowledge is available (contrary to the relativist Sophists) but you must seek it yourself (contrary to the rely-on-authority Aristocrats). Socrates debunked the self-proclaimed experts' claims to knowledge, as well as common-sense views about morality, by using a question-and-answer technique called the elenchus. However, Socrates was more than a mere critic. He propounded his own moral theory, which was that all virtue is a sort of knowledge. This knowledge, consisting of understanding of moral terms such as "courage" and "justice," is quite rare. But people who possess this knowledge would be able to recognize which acts are right and which are wrong. Indeed, such people would always act rightly and live happily (contrary to the happiness-depends-on-luck Tragedians), for such knowledge cannot be lost through confusion or overcome by passion or desire. Because wisdom is virtue, Socrates presented the philosopher rather than the warrior or the rhetorician as the ideal person.

Our picture of Socrates comes predominantly from his extraordinary student *Plato* (427–347 BCE), who wrote dialogues (starring Socrates) of questionable historical accuracy but unquestionable philosophical brilliance. Whereas Socrates criticized the intellectual positions of his day, Plato synthesized and transmuted them. The Traditionalists are right, said Plato. There are unchanging, absolute values. But they are not the old values passed down by tradition. Instead, they are values that we come to know through a process of rational inquiry sometimes called dialectic. The Sophists are right. Values do vary. But they do not vary from state to state. Instead, the application of the unchanging values differs from situation to situation. The Tragedians are right. There are conflicts among values. But the conflicts are not among true, real values but rather are among illusory, merely apparent values (the things that different people mistakenly take to be valuable). Thus misfortune cannot really destroy a person's happiness. Socrates is right. Knowledge (or at least true beliefs about morality) is essential to moral action, and both common sense and the so-called experts are seriously confused about morality. But virtue requires more than knowledge. One's passions and desires must be shaped according to the dictates of reason to avoid wrong action. Plato claimed that this harmony within the soul, which he called justice, is achieved through a multi-step process of moral development culminating in a method of thought called dialectic. Dialectic yields a mathematics-like grasp of moral ideals. For Plato, the paradigmatic person is a philosopher engaged in moral activity (such as Socrates). In a perfect state, such a person would reluctantly renounce pure philosophy in order to serve the state by becoming a philosopher-ruler, but in an imperfect state, such a person would choose the philosophical life over the corrupt political life, as Socrates did.

Plato's best student and worst critic was *Aristotle* (384–322 BCE). Rather than trying to define virtues and vices in terms of relationships among mental faculties, Aristotle simply defined the virtues as dispositions or habits of moderate action and passion conforming to rational principles. Aristotle focuses on describing these dispositions and their acquisition. Rather than thinking of each virtue as the opposite of some vice, Aristotle maintained that each virtue is bracketed by two vices—two general failure modes. Courage lies between cowardice and rashness, for example. Thus Aristotle's paradigmatic virtue is not Homeric courage or Socratic wisdom or Platonic justice. Instead, it is moderation. Rather than allow his ideal person to be torn between philosophy and politics, Aristotle described two ideals: the detached, intellectual life focused on theoretical reasoning and the moral life of involvement in one's community informed by practical reasoning. Rather than rejecting common sense and empirical observation in favor of Socratic elenchus and Platonic dialectic, Aristotle accepted common sense and the sciences as legitimate starting points for ethical investigation. Right action depends on human nature, which is discovered by biology and psychology. Rather than maintaining that luck either determines or is irrelevant to happiness, Aristotle argued that our happiness depends largely on our own choices but partially on the goods of fortune such as wealth, beauty, friends, and the like. [See the "Aristotle" section.]

After Aristotle, mainstream Greek moral thought divided over the question of what the ideal person was like. The *Epicureans* maintained that the ideal person pursues pleasure. However, the Epicureans were not recommending the short-term, intense bursts of what we call sensual pleasure. Epicurean pleasure is the tranquility produced by the absence of the pain of unsatisfied desire. Desires are of two sorts: natural desires that cannot be expunged and non-natural desires over which we have control. Pleasure is produced by satisfying natural desires through moderate indulgence of appetites, intellectual exercise, and a generally relaxed way of life. The claim that pleasure is the goal of life suggests that the Epicureans advocated self-centered amoralism. But the Epicureans believed that both friendship and virtue are natural desires. Thus the Epicureans advocated the pursuit of both friendship and virtue, for happiness requires the satisfaction of natural desires. Pleasure is also produced by satisfying some non-natural desires and eliminating those non-natural desires that cannot be satisfied. Because most unhappiness arises from unfulfilled non-natural desires, and because we have the power to rid ourselves of these desires, the Epicureans maintained that happiness is primarily a function of our choices rather than a function of luck.

The *Stoics* were also concerned to reduce the pain of unsatisfied desire. But they could not recommend that people act to satisfy some desires and rid themselves of others because the Stoics were determinists. Happily, although people cannot control their actions or desires, people can choose their attitudes. Thus the Stoics recommended that people train themselves to be indifferent to the pain of unsatisfied desire. The Stoic strategy for "becoming philosophical" about suffering is to transcend one's own personal point of view and see oneself as part of a larger whole—to see oneself as part of humankind or even part of the cosmos. This perspective enables one to be impartial, to have no more concern for one's own interests than for the interests of others. Indeed, one's own interests lose significance, so personal setbacks do not produce pain. Thus, like the Epicureans, the Stoics believed happiness to be independent of luck. Similarly, because the Stoics were determinists, they believed that virtue consists not in performing certain acts but rather in performing the predetermined act with the right attitude. What is the right attitude? The Stoics maintained that people should act according to nature. Reason is the distinctive aspect of human nature, so acting according to nature is acting from rational principles of conduct rather than from passion, desire, or anything else. This is duty.

Aristotle's most brilliant student, however, was neither an Epicurean nor a Stoic. In fact, he was not even a philosopher. He was Alexander the Great (356–323 BCE), who conquered the world of the Mediterranean and then extended his empire all of the way to India in just a few years. Yet Alexander's influence on moral philosophy was enormous, for he brought Greek ideas wherever he went. In particular, Alexander brought Greek moral theory to the Near East, where it combined with the morality-as-a-list-of-rules tradition to produce several new theories. The moral theory embedded in the *Gospels,* for example, was a synthesis of the Near Eastern rules tradition and the Greek virtue tradition. So was the philosophy of *Philo* (20 BCE–50 CE). The Rabbis whose compiled rulings became the *Talmud* (ca. 200 BCE–500 CE) used Greek philosophical techniques to interpret the *Bible* and apply it to both moral and non-moral issues of everyday life. In general, Greek reason combined fruitfully with Jewish revelation to produce several related yet different moral theories.

Alexander's empire fell into three pieces at his death and was eventually consumed by the Roman Empire (ca. 50 BCE–400 CE), the dominant moral philosophies of which were Epicureanism and Stoicism. As Rome waned and the Middle Ages began, *St. Augustine* (354–430) attempted to combine Christian thought with Plato's philosophy. Augustine lived in an era of increasing chaos and catastrophe. The fall of the Roman Empire left Europe torn by war and economic collapse, haunted by panic and poverty, despair and disaster. Small wonder that Augustine rejected the Greek injunction to seek happiness in this world by acting virtuously according to reason. Instead, Augustine saw this world as punishment for original sin and urged people to strive for salvation in the next world through faith.

After Augustine, moral theory, like most other intellectual pursuits, stagnated for hundreds of years among Christians (although it flourished among Jews and Moslems). Only a tiny fraction of the Christian population could even read or afford the luxury of intellectual pursuits, and these people were preoccupied with faith and salvation. Much of the learning of the Greco-Roman period was lost. Late in the Middle Ages the Crusaders brought Aristotle's manuscripts to Europe from the Moslem empire, where they had been preserved. These manuscripts excited the imagination of European intellectuals. Aristotelian philosophy was combined with Jewish thought by *Moses Maimonides* (1135–1204) and with Christian thought by *St. Thomas Aquinas* (1225–1274).

Following Talmudic tradition, Maimonides proposed three versions of morality: a minimal standard for non-Jews, a higher standard for ordinary Jews, and an even higher standard for Jewish scholars. Following Aristotle, Maimonides maintained that the actions and passions of ordinary Jews should be moderate. Jewish scholars, however, should avoid some passions (such as pride and anger) completely rather than feeling them moderately. According to Maimonides, humanity's ultimate goal is to love and imitate God. But metaphysics and revelation can tell only what God is not; they cannot provide any of the positive attributes of God. The best we can do is study God's works. Foreshadowing the Renaissance, Maimonides thus endorsed the rational, scientific investigation of nature.

Aquinas was more optimistic about this world than Augustine but more pessimistic about reason than Maimonides. He maintained that human nature is part of the divine plan and that reason and conscience are part of human nature. Reason's role is to discover divinely created laws of nature, and conscience prompts us to act in conformity with these natural laws. Thus science and ethics are legitimate enterprises. However, faith trumps reason, according to Aquinas. That is, when science or ethics conflict with religious doctrine, the scientific or ethical claim must be wrong. (This view had a somewhat stifling effect on science, as Galileo's later conflict with the Church over astronomy illustrates.) Thus Aquinas tinkered with Aristotle's ethics to make it harmonize with religious doctrine. He added theological virtues of faith, hope, and charity to Aristotle's list of moral virtues.

The Middle Ages (ca. 400–1400) faded into the Renaissance (ca. 1400–1517), which was a great burst of creativity and optimism in every field of human endeavor. Moral theorists, like other intellectuals, turned away from the medieval Christian picture of humans as pitiful, sinful creatures dependent on God for aid and redemption and embraced a much more upbeat and secular picture. The Renaissance emphasized the tremendous potential of humanity, especially humanity's ability to understand and control nature. Renaissance art, for example, focused on healthy, powerful human bodies and rich, individual personalities. Toward the end of the Renaissance, however, *Niccolo Machiavelli* (1469–1527) sounded a cynical note. He pointed out that effective rulers act only in their own interests, rather than according to theology or morality. For effective rulers, everything is a means to gaining and maintaining power.

The Renaissance was followed by the intellectual, political, and social turmoil of the Reformation (1517–1618) and the Thirty Years War (1618–1648). However, the subsequent Enlightenment (1648–1789) yielded enormous advances in the theory and application of the arts and sciences. These advances, together with the explosion of commerce and industry, the discovery of the Americas, the rise of modern nation-states, and many other changes generated a widespread confidence in humankind's ability to solve its own problems through reason, science, and cooperation. Scientific investigation of human nature and people's agreements with each other replaced scriptural revelation as the foundation of morality. According to *Thomas Hobbes* (1588–1679), science tells us that our primary drive is self-preservation. Hobbes concludes from this that in nature people may stomp on others in order to achieve their own interests. The state of nature is a "war of all against all." On the other hand, in a well-organized state the citizens cede their stomping freedom to the sovereign in order to maintain peace. This agreement to renounce the use of force legitimizes the government and endows the citizens of a state with rights. Thus for Hobbes, kings rule by the consent of the governed rather than by divine right. Moreover, rights are not natural; they derive instead from the social contract.

On the other hand, a cluster of thinkers, including *John Locke* (1632–1704) and *Jean Jacques Rousseau* (1712–1778), forcefully presented the view that all people, just because they are people, have the rights to life, liberty, and property even in a state of nature. These Enlightenment thinkers took natural rights to be expressions of moral laws built into the structure of the universe, by analogy with the newly discovered laws of physics and chemistry. (Note that moral equality and intrinsic cosmic morality are ideas that go back to the first books of the *Bible*.) Moral laws are not invented by people (by custom or by kings); rather, they are discovered by reason and science. The Enlightenment concepts of secular progress and human rights profoundly influenced democratic revolutionaries in Europe and America. They shaped the discourse surrounding the American revolution (1776) and the French revolution (1789), and they continue to shape much of our contemporary moral discourse.

*David Hume* (1711–1776), however, raised doubts about the Enlightenment's rationalism. Hume maintained that just as God's existence can be shown neither by logical deduction nor by sense perception, so moral principles cannot be conjured out of definitions or extracted from experience. They are neither time-less truths of reason nor natural truths discovered by science. According to Hume, because all truth must be derived either tautologously or empirically, the propositions of morality are ungrounded. Moral judgments simply express our feelings of approval or disapproval. Moreover, Hume argued that reason cannot motivate people to act rightly because reason cannot motivate people at all. People are moved only by passion. Luckily, human nature includes both sympathy, which informs us of the passions of others, and moral sensibility, which leads to consensus about which judgments and actions are moral.

The crowning figure of the Enlightenment, *Immanuel Kant* (1724–1804), accepts Hume's claim that moral principles cannot be established by defini-tion or by experience, but Kant finds a third way to determine the truth of moral principles. Indeed, Kant purports to have discovered a criterion for moral evaluation of action. Kant thus rejects Hume's moral skepticism. Simi-larly, Kant accepts Hume's claim that theoretical reason cannot motivate peo-ple, but he finds another sort of reason (practical reason) that generates a passion (respect for the moral law), which in turn inspires people to act morally. Reason both grounds and motivates morality. Like the Stoics, Kant maintains that the moral perspective is a universal, impartial point of view independent of one's particular desires, passions, beliefs, and so on. Morally wrong acts are acts that are incompatible with this perspective and make a special exemption for one person or some people. For example, if I give myself permission to steal while believing that stealing is wrong for others, then I am not acting from an impartial perspective. Often I do not recognize my hypocrisy until someone asks me, "Would it be OK with you if others stole—in particular, if others stole from you?" Kant formalizes this test. He demands that we ask ourselves whether our acts are universalizable, espe-cially when they rebound upon ourselves. Thus one way to put Kant's ulti-mate moral principle (which he calls the categorical imperative) is to say that acts are morally right only if they can be universally thought and willed with-out contradiction. Kant proposes an alternative approach to morality, too. Like other Enlightenment philosophers, he asserts that all humans—indeed all rational beings—deserve to be treated with a certain sort of respect because of their ability to make free, rational choices. Acts that subvert or ignore this ability and treat people as un-free, non-rational things are immoral acts. We should not do things to others (or to ourselves) when consent is impossible. Deception is wrong, for example, because people cannot consent to be deceived. Moreover, we cannot morally adopt a policy of not helping people develop and/or maintain their rational agency. Thus another way to put Kant's ultimate moral principle is that we should respect the autonomy of people (including ourselves). Finally, Kant thinks that the best sort of person (the person with a good will) is a person who makes an overall, long-term commitment to try to perform right acts not because they will pay off but rather because they are right. This is Kant's secularized version of the idea that salvation consists in making an unconditional commitment to God and goodness, just as his first formulation of the categorical imperative is his ver-sion of the Golden Rule and his second formulation of the categorical imperative is his version of the idea that people are priceless because they can choose between good and evil. [See the "Kant" section.]

The post-Enlightenment nineteenth century was a time of tumultuous social change. Industrialization, urbanization, pollution, the development of mass culture, the rise of the middle class, the restructuring of the family—all inflicted enormous stress on society as a whole and on each of its members. People became increasingly alienated from nature, God, work, and each other. Reason, science, and cooperation had failed to solve all of humanity's problems. Many social and intellectual movements sprang up in response. Spasms of utopian socialism, romanticism, religious fundamentalism, nihilism, downright madness, and revolution swept through Europe in every generation. The ideology of the haves, *Social Darwinism*, pictured history as a struggle of all against all in which the talented would rise and the weak would perish. The ideology of the have-nots, *Communism*, pictured history as a struggle of classes in which the oppressed masses would eventually overthrow their tyrannical, capitalist bosses. The ideology of the group, *Nationalism*, pictured history as a struggle of peoples who share common languages and traditions against multinational states that artificially divided them. The ideology of the individual, *Existentialism*, pictured history as a struggle of individuals against passionless conformity and alienation. Social Darwinists such as *Herbert Spencer* (1820–1903), Communists such as *Karl Marx* (1818–1883), and Existentialists such as *Sören Kierkegaard* (1813–1855) and *Friedrich Nietzsche* (1844–1900) were all shrill critics of establishment churches, states, traditions, and moralities.

The Enlightenment was not completely extinguished by the problems of the nineteenth century. One vestige of the Enlightenment was *Utilitarianism*, the moral theory championed by *Jeremy Bentham* (1748–1832) and *John Stuart Mill* (1806–1873). Bentham proposed a quantitative method for morally evaluating action. All actions are motivated by the desire for pleasure and the absence of pain, he said. This psychological claim, reminiscent of Epicureanism, enabled Bentham to settle all moral questions simply. In every situation, the morally best option is the one that produces "the greatest good for the greatest number." That is, one should maximize pleasure and minimize pain not just for oneself but rather for all concerned. Each person's interests should count equally.

Mill was also a Utilitarian. He agreed with Bentham that our moral duty is to maximize pleasure and minimize pain in the world. However, Mill found Bentham's proposal too simple. He observed that whereas some pleasures differ from each other in quantity, others differ in quality. Moreover, Mill seemed to say that rather than making decisions on a case-by-case basis, we should follow those rules that, when generally followed, maximize pleasure and minimize pain. Armed with their hedonistic calculus, Bentham and Mill set out to solve various social problems in true Enlightenment fashion: rationally, scientifically, cooperatively. Yet Mill was not immune to the nineteenth-century awareness of social conflict. Mill pictured history as a struggle of ideas or ways of life. He recognized that the conformist pressures of the times tended to crush individuality, self-actualization, and minority views. Thus

Mill strongly endorsed freedom of expression and action. He maintained that neither individuals nor government may justifiably restrict people's liberty, except insofar as this is necessary for self-protection. Freedom is socially valuable because it allows experiments in living. In a free marketplace of ideas, the best notions about how to live gain adherents, and unsuccessful notions die out. [See the "Mill" section.]

As early twentieth-century arts and literature came to concentrate on their own practices, traditions, and media, thus moving further and further away from the understanding and concerns of the non-specialist, so early twentieth-century Anglo-American philosophy came to concentrate on the practices, traditions, and media of the philosophical enterprise. There was much discussion of the nature of language in general and, in particular, of the meaning of moral terms. However, during the upheavals of the 1960s, moral philosophy turned dramatically away from this meta-ethics and began to address the myriad of moral problems thrown up by changes in science and technology, war and peace, race and gender relations, etc. Articles and books on abortion, euthanasia, pornography, sex roles, and the like proliferated. Moral philosophers attempted more or less explicitly to use Utilitarian, Kantian, and (more recently) Aristotelian and feminist moral theories to solve these and other moral problems. This phase of moral philosophy continues today with no end in sight. Indeed, the very anthology you hold is a part of this late twentieth-century trend.

# PART I

# OBSTACLES AND BEGINNINGS

# Morality and Knowledge: Relativism and Realism

*What is truth?*

PONTIUS PILATE

**M**any people call themselves *Relativists* these days. Slogans like "What is right for me is not necessarily right for you" are often wielded like incantations to ward off accusations of wrongdoing or to smash the pretensions of moralizers. Yet such slogans are ambiguous. Understood in some ways, such relativistic slogans say nothing about morality. They might merely mean "Because different people find themselves in different situations with different goals and abilities, the best way for you to achieve your goals is not necessarily the best way for me to achieve my goals." This is true, but it is a matter of prudence rather than morality.

Of course, the relativistic slogans might mean "Different people have different moral duties because they are in different situations." For example, I have the duty to ensure that my daughter is fed, clothed, and cared for, but you have no such duty because you have no children. So understood, these slogans are claims about morality, but they are uncontroversial claims.

Alternatively, the relativistic slogans might mean that different people have conflicting beliefs about morality and that people disagree about what one should do in certain situations. Such disagreement is an indisputable fact about our fractious world, but by itself such disagreement does not tell us anything about how we should act. In particular, it does not automatically settle the crucial question of whether different people in similar situations ought to do different things.

Understood yet another way these slogans directly challenge the project of ethics—the search for and the study of the correct moral theory. Ethics seeks *absolute moral rules*, rules that in some sense apply to everyone. But these slogans might mean "Different people have different moral obligations even in the same situation, because different people have different beliefs, belong to different cultures, and so on." I have the duty to care for my daughter, but you do not have a duty to care for your daughter even though there are no relevant differences in our respective situations. The relativistic slogans may imply that there are no absolute moral rules—that ethics is a quixotic quest.

Once the term "Relativism" and its associated slogans are divested of ambiguity it may turn out that most Relativists are committed to some innocuous version of Relativism rather than to the sort of Relativism that opposes the project of ethics. Yet the anti-ethics Relativists must also be addressed. Of course, the best way to defend the project of ethics against the Relativist challenge would be to provide a proof of an absolute moral rule. It would do no good to show that an intermediate moral rule follows from a higher-level moral rule, because if Relativists deny the absoluteness of the one, then they will also deny the absoluteness of the other. Thus a defender of ethical theory must provide a proof of an *ultimate moral rule*, a rule that does not depend on some other moral rule. This would establish morality upon some non-moral foundation. Mill, Kant, and Aristotle all present arguments grounding their ultimate moral rules, but I shall not consider their arguments here. Indeed, the project of justifying ultimate moral rules is too large to undertake in this section. Instead, after isolating the sort of Relativism that is antithetical to the project of ethics, I shall show that most common arguments for this sort of Relativism are flawed and that such Relativism conflicts with the core beliefs of almost everyone.

## Arguments against Absolutism

*Absolutism*, Relativism's opposite, is the view that there are absolute moral rules. Many people think of themselves as Relativists not because of a straightforward commitment to Relativism but rather because they find Absolutism repugnant for one reason or another. I shall try to make Absolutism more palatable by refuting several arguments that might be raised by critics of Absolutism, beginning with the following argument: Morality is clearly contextual. That is, one's moral duty depends on the facts of one's situation. Abortion is OK for some women but is wrong for others because they are in different situations. Lying is morally wrong in some situations, morally acceptable in others, and morally required in yet others. But Absolutism seems to say that the facts of the situation are irrelevant, and this is absurdly rigid.

### Argument (A)

(1) Moral rules have exceptions.
(2) If rules have exceptions, then they do not apply to everyone.
(3) Therefore, no moral rules apply to everyone.

In order to clarify argument (A), I shall distinguish between two sorts of Absolutism.

> *Normative Absolutism:* Different people (cultures) morally should do different things in different situations, but they should do the same things when they are in the same situations. Thus you and I have the same duties when we are in the same situation but different duties in different situations.
> *Extreme Absolutism:* Different people (cultures) morally should do the same things whether their situations are the same or different. Thus you and I always have the same duties no matter what our situations are.

Argument (A) attacks Extreme Absolutism. But almost no Absolutists are Extreme. (Kant is sometimes thought to be an Extreme Absolutist, but sophisticated, contemporary Kantians are not.) Nor does ethical theory need an Absolutism as strong as Extreme Absolutism. The project of ethical inquiry is compatible with the weaker, more plausible doctrine of Normative Absolutism, which concedes that moral rules do have exceptions. However, legitimate exceptions are situational rather than personal, according to Normative Absolutism. Whether you are entitled to an exception depends on the situation in which you find yourself, but not on who you are, what your beliefs are, or what your culture is. For example, "Do not kill," is shorthand for "It is wrong to kill people under ordinary circumstances, but it is OK to kill them in situations of self-defense and just wars." Thus moral rules apply to everyone in the following sense: No one has a personal exemption from a moral rule. No one has a license to kill. Everyone must follow the rule, but the rule has situational variations built into it.

This fact allows Normative Absolutists to distinguish between justifications and excuses. Suppose I perform an act that seems wrong. A *justification* is an explanation of why my act is not really wrong. An *excuse* is an admission that the act really is wrong, together with an explanation of why I should be forgiven. Justifications often arise in cases that seem to generate conflicts of duties. There are situations where the shorthand version of one moral rule says, "Do X," whereas the shorthand version of another moral rule says, "Don't do X." Some people think that in cases like these there is no right choice. Others think that in cases like these there is a right choice and that it is to obey the higher-priority moral rule. This does not constitute a violation of the lower-priority rule, because the full version of the lower-priority rule contains an exception for conflict-of-duty situations. Consider the following example: Suppose I am very late for a lunch date because on the way to the restaurant I stopped to render aid to the victims of a traffic accident. If I admit that I have broken a promise, but I claim that I did nothing wrong, then I am offering a justification for being late. I am claiming that the rule concerning promises is not "Keep your promises no matter what," but rather is "Keep your promises except when your duty to help others takes precedence." On the other hand, if I explain that I am late because I got absorbed in an exciting book and lost track of the time, then I am offering an excuse for being late. I acknowledge that I did something wrong, but I am asking forgiveness because my sin was minor and familiar.

*

Even a quick glance at history reveals that enormous harm has been done by various people (cultures) who believed that there were absolute moral rules, were sure that they knew what these rules were, and went on to impose their values on others at a terrific cost in human suffering. Unfortunately, many such people (cultures) are still busy bullying others. The intellectual arrogance and individual (cultural) imperialism of these authoritarian dogmatists give Absolutists a bad name—and give rise to the following argument.

### Argument (B)

(1) If moral rules apply to everyone, then these rules should be enforced.
(2) People (cultures) should not interfere with what other people (cultures) do, even if these acts seem morally wrong. I should not force you to do what I think you morally should do (the *Principle of Tolerance*).
(3) Therefore, no moral rules apply to everyone.

One problem with argument (B) is that premise (1) is false. Premise (1) says that Normative Absolutism is incompatible with the Principle of Tolerance. It may derive from an analogy between moral and legal rules. However, the fact that laws are enforced provides no reason to believe that moral rules should also be enforced. Normative Absolutism and the Principle of Tolerance are compatible. Anthropologists have made us aware of the pervasiveness of ethnocentrism and other sorts of bias. Many Normative Absolutists accept the Principle of Tolerance because they are aware of their own ignorance or fallibility. Although they believe that there are absolute moral rules, they are not sure enough of what these rules are to justify imposing their own views on others. Other Normative Absolutists are confident that they know what the absolute moral rules are, but they accept the Principle of Tolerance because they believe that trying to force people to obey these rules is

morally wrong and/or generally counter-productive. In fact, if you believe that we have a moral duty to be tolerant, then you believe that there is at least one absolute moral rule, the Principle of Tolerance itself. Thus you are already a Normative Absolutist.

Relativists may, at this point, feel cheated. They may acknowledge that the Principle of Tolerance is compatible with Normative Absolutism, but they may maintain that we should adopt the Principle of Tolerance not because of our uncertainty or because of the drawbacks of using force, but rather because everyone's beliefs about ethics are merely unjustified prejudices absorbed from their own society. The "proofs" of moral rules provided by Normative Absolutists are mere rationalizations, according to the Relativists, so no one is qualified or entitled to create and enforce rules for others. Relativists may ask rhetorically, "Who is to say what is right and what is wrong?" And the answer is "no one," for there are no "moral experts." Everyone's moral beliefs are equally unjustified.

Note that the Relativists are *assuming* that values are stipulated rather than discovered. It is this assumption that allows the Relativists to assert that everyone's beliefs are mere unjustified prejudices. However, this assumption begs the question, and Normative Absolutists reject it. Normative Absolutists agree that no person (culture) says what is right and what is wrong in the sense of arbitrarily stipulating rules of morality. Instead, philosophers "say" what the rules of ethics are in the same way that physicists "say" what the laws of physics are and mathematicians "say" what the laws of mathematics are. Philosophers explain the discoveries of ethics just as physicists and mathematicians explain the discoveries of physics and mathematics. Thus, just as there can be experts in physics and mathematics even though the laws of physics and mathematics are discovered rather than stipulated, so there can be experts in ethics even though the rules of ethics are not laid down by those experts.

*

The very idea of consulting ethics experts is repugnant to some people. They believe that people should make their own decisions about ethical questions. This belief seems to require the rejection of Absolutism *via* the following argument.

### Argument (C)

(1) If moral rules apply to everyone, then people (cultures) need not and should not decide for themselves about right and wrong. They should simply follow the rules.
(2) People (cultures) should decide for themselves what acts are right and what acts are wrong. I should not rely on you to tell me what I should do.
(3) Therefore, no moral rules apply to everyone.

Premise (2) of argument (C) is true and important. Indeed, the main point of ethics classes is to help and encourage people to decide for themselves what acts are right and what acts are wrong. The problem with argument (C) is that premise (1) is false. First, according to Normative Absolutism, the absolute moral rules are contextual. They tell us to do different things in different situations. Thus Normative Absolutism does not require people simply to follow general rules. Instead, the general rules must be applied to concrete situations. Naturally, to apply general rules correctly to a situation, one must be knowledgeable about that situation. Because people are typically (though not always) most knowledgeable about the features of their own situations, people themselves should apply the general moral rules to their own situations. Second, people should make their own moral choices because their doing so builds character and sustains democratic institutions. People should make it a habit to think for themselves, especially about important matters, and with practice they will get better and better at it. Of course, just as in physics and mathematics, people are more likely to get to the truths of morality if they take into account the opinions of experts. Thus the existence of absolute moral rules and even the existence of experts in morality are perfectly compatible with the possibility and desir-

ability of making one's own decisions about how to act.

\*

David Hume distinguishes two sorts of propositions.[1] *Relations of Ideas* are true by definition, contentless, necessarily true, and known by reason alone (an example is "All bachelors are unmarried"). *Matters of Fact* are non-trivial, non-tautological, contingent on what exists, and cannot be known without experience (an example is "The sun is shining today"). Moral propositions do not seem to be Relations of Ideas. Propositions such as "Torturing animals is wrong" are not true by definition. Yet moral propositions do not seem to be Matters of Fact, either. We certainly cannot perceive rightness or wrongness with our five senses. If a gang of hoodlums lights a gasoline-doused cat in front of me, I see the cat, smell the burning fur, and hear the scream, but I do not see, smell, or hear the wrongness of the act. Thus J. L. Mackie maintains that in order to know moral truths, we would need some special faculty different from the ordinary perception. And the objects of this special faculty—moral properties, objective moral values—would have to be very queer objects if they exist at all. But if the propositions of morality are neither Relations of Ideas nor Matters of Fact, then they are not true. And if paradigmatic moral propositions such as "Torturing animals is wrong," are not true, then there are no absolute moral truths.

### Argument (D)

(1) There are two sorts of truths: Relations of Ideas and Matters of Fact.
(2) Moral propositions are neither Relations of Ideas nor Matters of Fact.
(3) Therefore, moral propositions are not true. No moral rules apply to everyone.

Kant denies premise (1) of argument (D). He develops an account of propositions that are neither Relations of Ideas nor Matters of Fact. Kant explains that these *synthetic, a priori propositions* are known to be true through a rational investigation of our modes of perception and categories of thought. Kant then argues that both the propositions of mathematics and the foundations of science, as well as the propositions of morality, are synthetic, *a priori* propositions. How do we know that the proposition "7 + 5 = 12" is true? It is not true by definition, for the concept of 12 contains more than merely the concepts of 5, 7, and +. It is not known by experience, either. Any child will tell you that "7 drops + 5 drops = 1 big drop," and "7 rabbits + 5 rabbits = lots more than 12 rabbits." That is, we do not derive the proposition "7 + 5 = 12" from experience, because experience tells us that this proposition is false. Instead, we believe the proposition "7 + 5 = 12" on some non-empirical basis, and we explain away experiences that do not conform to this belief. Similarly, the proposition "Every event has a cause" is neither true by definition nor empirical. Thus premise (1) of argument (D) seems to be false.[2] Kant's next step is to argue that the propositions of morality belong in the class of synthetic, *a priori* propositions along with the propositions of mathematics and the foundations of science. Unfortunately, Kant's argument is beyond the scope of this section.

David Brink denies premise (2) of argument (D). He argues that the propositions of morality are based on experience. They are Matters of Fact. Of course, rightness and wrongness are not directly experienced. We do not see rightness in the way that we see redness. Instead, we infer rightness and wrongness from things we perceive in a way that is quite similar to many other, less controversial properties. For example, we do not see, hear, smell, touch, or taste the happiness or the teenager-hood of the hoodlums setting fire to the cat. We see their faces and subconsciously deduce that they are happy teenagers. Similarly, we extrapolate from physical facts of the situation to the moral properties of cruelty and wrongness. We subconsciously deduce the cruelty and wrongness of the act. Moral properties supervene upon physical properties in just the same way that mental properties such as happiness, or even complex properties such as being-a-teenager, supervene upon physical properties. The claim that "Those

people are cruel and wicked" is no stranger than the claim that "Those are people are happy teenagers." So contrary to Mackie, moral properties are not queer sorts of entities, and we need not postulate new modes of perception in order to explain how moral propositions can be Matters of Fact.

## The Cultural Differences Argument

The greatest impetus for rejecting Absolutism is probably the dramatically different value judgments of different people (cultures). The slogan "What is right for me is not necessarily right for you" may mean simply that you and I have different beliefs. That is, the phrase *is right for* may mean *seems right to*. On the other hand, the slogan may mean that you and I have different duties if the phrase *is right for* is taken to mean *is morally optional for*. Thus there are at least two versions of Relativism.

> *Descriptive Relativism:* Different people (cultures) believe that they morally should do different things when they are in the same situation. Thus, if you and I are in the same situation, we might have different beliefs about what our duties are.
> *Normative Relativism:* Different people (cultures) really morally should do different things when they are in the same situation. Thus, if you and I are in the same situation, we might have different duties.

Descriptive Relativism is a claim about *beliefs*, whereas Normative Relativism is a claim about *duties*. These are different claims. Descriptive Relativism is clearly true, but it is Normative Relativism that is the opposite of Normative Absolutism. Many people cite some dramatic difference(s) between the moral beliefs of different people (cultures) and immediately infer that different people (cultures) have different duties. That is, they assume that Descriptive Relativism directly implies Normative Relativism.

*Argument (E)*

(1) Different people (cultures) have very different beliefs about which actions are right and which are wrong in the same situation (Descriptive Relativism).

(2) If different people (cultures) have very different beliefs about which actions are right and which are wrong in the same situation, then there are no absolute right and wrong.

(3) Therefore, there are no absolute right and wrong. Different people (cultures) in the same situation have different duties (Normative Relativism).

It does not simply follow, in general, from the fact that different people (cultures) have different beliefs about something that there is no truth about that thing. Some or all of the disagreeing people (cultures) might simply be mistaken. After all, people (cultures) disagree about the shape of the earth and about the sum of 7 + 5. But it would be an odd person who maintained that the earth is flat for the members of the Flat Earth Society. (They must be careful not to fall off the edge, but the rest of us can relax.) Nor does anyone think that 7 + 5 = 11 for people allergic to arithmetic. (Their checkbooks balance under conditions that cause our checks to bounce.) Similarly, that fact that some people (cultures) think wife beating is OK does not immediately imply that wife beating is morally optional for them but wrong for the rest of us. Indeed, without further argument, the fact that some people disagree about moral rules seems totally irrelevant to the question of whether there are absolute moral rules. Premise (2) of argument (E) begs the question.

\*

Mackie provides an argument for moving from Descriptive Relativism to Normative Relativism. He maintains that the best explanation of the individual (cultural) diversity of moral beliefs is that there are no moral facts but only opinions. If there really were an absolute truth about how people should act in certain situations, then people could and would settle moral disputes by appeal to the truth.

*Argument (F)*

(1) Different people (cultures) have very different beliefs about which actions are right and what actions are wrong (Descriptive Relativism).

(2) The best explanation of these different beliefs is that there are no moral facts, no values built into the nature of the universe.

(3) Therefore, no moral rules apply to everyone. Different people (cultures) in the same situation have different duties (Normative Relativism).

Brink and Martha Nussbaum object to premise (2) of argument (F). They offer several explanations of the disagreements between people (cultures) that are compatible with Normative Absolutism. First, Nussbaum observes that many disputes evaporate when it becomes clear that the parties are discussing different situations. For example, Eskimos formerly believed that it was OK to allow elderly relatives to die when they could no longer contribute to the welfare of the tribe, but Texans considered abandoning unproductive elderly relatives to be morally wrong. Although this seems to have been a moral disagreement, it was not. Eskimos and Texans were talking about different situations. Eskimo tribes lived on the edge of survival. A few extra mouths to feed would bring the society down, so unproductive people could not be tolerated. Eskimos were applying the principle that individuals may be sacrificed in order to preserve the society. Texans also accepted this principle, as their support for the draft showed. But Texas society was affluent. Texans did not need to abandon their elderly relatives to die, so they disapproved of this practice. Thus what seemed to be a disagreement about moral rules turned out to be a difference of situation.

Second, Brink observes that many disagreements that seem to be about moral rules are really disputes about non-moral facts. For example, Communists and Capitalists disagree about which economic system is more just. But this dispute hinges on non-moral issues such as whether human beings are intrinsically competitive. We need not assume that there are no moral facts in order to explain such disagreements.

Third, Normative Absolutism does not require that there be only one correct act for each situation, says Nussbaum. There might be several different moral rules and several different virtuous character traits governing the same matters. A disagreement between two people (cultures) might arise if one side holds to one rule or virtue while the other side holds to a different, equally good rule or virtue. Such disagreements arise from having too many moral facts rather than from having no moral facts.

Fourth, Brink explains that Normative Absolutism does not imply that all disputes are resolvable. If *some* disputes about morality are resolvable, then there are *some* absolute moral rules. Indeed, we might use resolvability to delimit the boundary of morality. Those disputes that are not resolvable may be relegated to etiquette, esthetics, prudence, or some other nonmoral system of rules.

My own contribution to this list of explanations of disputes is this. Many people (cultures) stubbornly cling to doctrines and practices even after they have been refuted by good arguments. It is common to see people (cultures) still arguing and resisting change even after reasonable people would have acknowledged their error and changed their ways. For this reason as well as the ones mentioned by Nussbaum and Brink, we need not assume that there are no absolute moral rules in order to explain the differences of moral beliefs among individuals (cultures).

\*

Nussbaum considers a cultural differences objection that is not based on Descriptive Relativism. She puts it in terms of virtues, but it can easily be expressed in terms of rules. The Normative Absolutist claims that for each sphere of human life there are virtues or rules about how to act, feel, desire, and think. For example, temperance is the virtue governing sensual pleasure in food, drink, and sex; courage is the virtue governing risk of death, wounds, and pain, and so on. Now the Normative Relativist challenge is that different people (cultures) not only have different beliefs about which character traits are virtues and what the moral rules are but also have different conceptions of the spheres. People (cultures) disagree about what counts as sex or death. Is a goodbye kiss on the cheek a type of sex? Is being "born again" a type of death? People (cultures) even have different conceptual schemes that divide human life into different sets of spheres. Aristotelian liberality includes buying, spending, receiving, and donating money and material goods, whereas non-monetary items are in different spheres governed by different virtues. Other virtue theorists might consider buying and spending to be governed by one virtue (frugality?), receiving both monetary and non-monetary items to be governed by another virtue (gratitude?), and donating both monetary and non-monetary items to be governed by yet a third virtue (benevolence?). The reason for these different conceptions of the spheres is that we never perceive things simply the way they are in themselves. If someone surgically implanted rose-colored lenses on your eyes at birth, you would always see the world as rosy without even suspecting a distortion and without hope of seeing the world as it really is. Similarly, our culture and language permanently implant in us certain ways of perceiving and understanding the world. We cannot apprehend the world except through the distorting lens of our categories of perception and thought. These differ from person (culture) to person (culture). Some feminists claim that men and women apprehend the world through different categories, too. Thus we are doomed to disagree not only about the moral rules and virtues but also about the subject matter of the rules and virtues, because we cannot get at the truth. We cannot remove our implanted lenses—our culturally and linguistically implanted worldviews—to see the world as it really is. The Normative Absolutist hope of resolving moral disputes by discovering the truth about morality founders.

### Argument (G)

(1) Each virtue or moral rule is about how to act, feel, desire, and/or think with respect to some sphere of human life.

(2) Different people (cultures) have different conceptions of the spheres of human life because of their different worldviews.

(3) People (cultures) cannot apprehend the world except through the lenses of their worldviews.

(4) Therefore, even if there are moral rules that apply to everyone, we cannot have objective, unbiased knowledge of them.

Nussbaum finds promising common ground among the different conceptions of different people (cultures). Because all people share in human nature, their worldviews grow from this common source. Although there are differences, there is a fundamental similarity among the conceptions of the spheres of human life because they are all spheres of *human* life. In particular, Nussbaum says that because all humans die, have a body, experience pleasure and pain, reason theoretically and practically, develop from babies, affiliate with others, and have a sense of humor, each of these must constitute a sphere of human life.

Unfortunately, the Relativist might reply that the appearance of common ground is illusory. For example, believers in reincarnation may deny the existence of death. For them, human life never ends. Similarly, people (cultures) who believe in ghosts may deny that all humans have a body. And so on.

Nussbaum produces evidence against this claim of basic individual (cultural) disagreement. We understand the people, the practices, the literature, the art, and many other facets of other cultures. Moreover, people (cultures) communicate these days. They do not develop alternative worldviews in a vacuum. Thus, although there certainly are cultural differences, they are not overwhelming obstacles to communication. Premise (2) of argument (G) is true, but it does not imply that people (cultures) have *completely* and *incorrigibly* different conceptions of the spheres of human life. And upon the similarities we may build consensus about some moral issues.

Of course, the die-hard Relativist may maintain that even if we achieve consensus, we may still be wrong. Perhaps we all wear the same distorting lenses, preventing us from seeing the world as it really is. Perhaps, as Kant says, these lenses are part of human nature. Perhaps Martians will use radically different categories and see the world very differently.

On the other hand, even if argument (G) is sound, it does not prove that Normative Absolutism is false. At worst, it implies that we cannot achieve *certainty* about the absolute moral rules. People, cultures, and even species may differ on the terms of the debate, but some may be right and some wrong here, too. Even if there is no agreement, there may be truth.

## Objections to Normative Relativism

Normative Relativism conflicts with the deeply held beliefs of most people. It is, for example, clearly incompatible with mainstream Judaism and Christianity, for these religions quite explicitly maintain that there are moral and immoral ways to act in certain circumstances. Adultery, for example, is simply immoral, and if you think it is OK, then you are mistaken, according to these religions. In general, Judaism and Christianity assert that there is one right way to live. If you are living differently, then whatever your beliefs, you are living wrongly.

Moreover, Normative Relativism makes it impossible to praise or blame other people (cultures). If there is no right way to act, then people (cultures) cannot be commended for acting rightly or criticized for acting wrongly. The force of this objection may not be apparent if you focus only on controversial contemporary moral problems such as abortion and affirmative action. But turn to the moral problems that have been solved, the problems that no longer even seem to be moral problems because their solutions now seem obvious, and you will see that judging the acts of other people (cultures) is important and necessary. What will you say about the practice of slavery in early nineteenth-century America, for example? What will you say when you see your neighbor beating a child mercilessly? Surely you want to say more than merely "These people (cultures) may believe they are acting rightly, but I do not act this way." Most people want to say "Whether they realize it or not, these people are acting wrongly." But you cannot say this unless you abandon Normative Relativism and accept Normative Absolutism. [By the way, examples like these suggest that the Principle of Tolerance in argument (B) is implausible as it stands. It should be amended to say something like "People (cultures) should not interfere with others, except to prevent horribly immoral acts."]

Another problem with Normative Relativism concerns the size of the value-determining group. *Cultural Relativism* is a version of Normative Relativism that says that different values are right for different cultures. Each culture sets a different standard for what is right and what is wrong so that if you and I are members of different cultures, then we have different duties. "X is the morally right thing for me to do," means "X is endorsed by my culture." But how large is a culture? Cultural Relativism seems to presuppose that there are large groups of people who share roughly the same values. But this seems false. Certainly there is no consensus among Americans about what the moral rules are. Nor is there such a consensus among Texans. I doubt that there is such a consensus even among black, female, twenty-five-year-old Texans living on the east side of Lubbock. Almost any two people disagree somewhat about what is right and what is wrong. Normative Relativists seeking a homogeneous culture are driven to smaller and smaller subcultures until finally they arrive at the limiting case of Cultural Relativism, the "culture" consisting of one person.

This view is really no longer Cultural Relativism. It is a different version of Normative Relativism that might be called *Individualism*. It is the view that moral statements are reports of individual attitudes. "X is the morally right thing for me to do" means "X is approved of by me." Unfortunately, according to Individualism, every honest moral statement is true, and moral statements made by different people never conflict. Suppose I say that abortion is always wrong. Unless I am trying to deceive you, my statement is true because it is a report of my beliefs. Suppose that you honestly say that abortion is always OK. Your statement is true, too, and we are not disagreeing. Yet we may exhibit every symptom of disagreement. We may try to persuade each other, get angry over the issue, and so on. Individualism's denial that this is an argument seems implausible.

Some people opt for the view that moral statements are expressions rather than reports of individual attitudes. On this view, "X is the morally right thing for me to do" does not mean "My culture endorses X" or even "I believe I should do X." Instead it means something like "Hurrah for X!" This view is called *Emotivism*. Unfortunately, it is just as counter-intuitive as Individualism. According to Emotivism, rationality has no place in moral discussions. But common sense says that reason plays a central role in moral discussions. Thus Emotivism, like the other versions and offshoots of Normative Relativism, has implausible implications.

## The Appeal of Normative Relativism

Some Normative Relativists are victims of equivocation. As I have already mentioned, slogans such as "What is right for me is not necessarily right for you" have several meanings. It is easy to slip from Descriptive Relativism or the Principle of Tolerance to Normative Relativism, for example.

Some people adopt Normative Relativism because it pays. It offers a ready reply to criticism and restriction. ("Maybe living together before marriage was wrong for you, Mom and Dad, but it is not wrong for me because people's values have changed.") Normative Relativism also offers a way to feel superior to others. ("Those poor, deluded fools think they know the truth about ethics, but actually there is no truth to know.") Of course, some people adopt Normative Absolutism because of psychological payoffs, too. Normative Absolutism offers security and power in an increasingly uncertain world. ("Now that I know the truth about ethics, I can tell those people just how wrong they are.")

Some people turn to Normative Relativism out of revulsion for Normative Absolutists. Many Normative Absolutists simply accept, without reasons or reflection, the values of their parents, society, or religion. This is bad enough. Watching people cling unquestioningly to dimly understood values does not inspire confidence that there are rational ways to determine absolute values. On the other hand, most people probably believe that the earth is round because someone told them it was round, but that does not mean that there are no good reasons for believing that the earth is round. Similarly, although many people are Normative Absolutists for no reason or no good reason, Normative Absolutism may still be true.

Many Normative Absolutists are also tyrannical or hypocritical or both. It is repulsive to watch dogmatists impose their values on others through rhetorical trickery or coercion, all the while holding themselves to standards lower than those to which they hold others. Even worse, it is often perfectly clear to an unbiased observer that some Normative Absolutists unconsciously adopt the values they do as a way of coping with their own psychological problems. Timid people, afraid of change and difference, elevate the values of the establishment into absolute truths. Much of the energy that fuels the condemnation of various acts (such as adultery, homosexuality, and theft) derives from repressed desires to perform these very acts or from guilt over having performed these acts. Nietzsche is suspicious of Absolutist moral theories for these reasons (among others). [See the "Morality and Happiness" section.] However, it is important to keep in mind that the merits of a doctrine do not depend on the behavior or the (conscious or unconscious) motives of its adherents. Twisted people have massacred in the name of God, but this does not prove that religion endorses massacre.

People sometimes come to Normative Relativism through despair. A person may work on some contemporary moral problem for a while, fail to find a satisfactory solution, and then jump to the conclusion that the problem has no solution. It is all relative. When this line of thought is stated explicitly, however, the Relativist's attitude appears absurd. After all, there is no reason to expect the project of ethics to be easy. Interesting problems in other disciplines take a long time to solve, and ethics is similar to other disciplines in this respect. We should not move from "Moral problems have no simple solutions" to "Moral problems have no solutions."

A more sophisticated mistake is to note that there is no consensus on contemporary moral problems, even among "moral experts," and then to conclude that there is no solution. It is all relative. Again, the Relativist seems to be jumping to conclusions. After all, we recognize that there are both solved and unsolved problems in other disciplines. Why not in ethics? Moreover, the Relativist is ignoring all of the moral progress that has already been made. Typically, people do not recognize a solved moral problem as a moral problem. For example, child sacrifice was an unsolved moral problem in Biblical times, and women's suffrage was an unsolved moral problem in the nineteenth century, yet now that consensus on these problems has been reached, we do not even consider them problems. Moral progress is still going on. Only recently has our society recognized that informed consent is generally required before treatment begins or that women deserve the same pay as men for the same work. Perhaps I am being too optimistic, but I believe that in 50 years some of the problems we now find difficult will no longer even seem to be moral problems because their solutions will be obvious.

## Notes

1. D. Hume, *An Inquiry Concerning Human Understanding* (Indianapolis: Bobbs-Merrill, 1955), p. 40.

2. I. Kant, *Critique of Pure Reason*, trans. N. K. Smith (New York: St. Martin's Press, 1965), pp. 41–55.

# 1    A Defense of Ethical Relativism

## RUTH BENEDICT

Modern social anthropology has become more and more a study of the varieties and common elements of cultural environment and the consequences of these in human behavior. For such a study of diverse social orders primitive peoples fortunately provide a laboratory not yet entirely vitiated by the spread of a standardized worldwide civilization. Dyaks and Hopis, Fijians and Yakuts are significant for psychological and sociological study because only among these simpler peoples has there been sufficient isolation to give opportunity for the development of localized social forms. In the higher cultures the standardization of custom and belief over a couple of continents has given a false sense of the inevitability of the particular forms that have gained currency, and we need to turn to a wider survey in order to check the conclusions we hastily base upon this near-universality of familiar customs. Most of the simpler cultures did not gain the wide currency of the one which, out of our experience, we identify with human nature, but this was for various historical reasons, and certainly not for any that gives us as its carriers a monopoly of social good or of social sanity. Modern civilization, from this point of view, becomes not a necessary pinnacle of human achievement but one entry in a long series of possible adjustments.

These adjustments, whether they are in mannerisms like the ways of showing anger, or joy, or grief in any society, or in major human drives like those of sex, prove to be far more variable than experience in any one culture would suggest. In certain fields, such as that of religion or of formal marriage arrangements, these wide limits of variability are well known and can be fairly described. In others it is not yet possible to give a

generalized account, but that does not absolve us of the task of indicating the significance of the work that has been done and of the problems that have arisen.

One of these problems relates to the customary modern normal-abnormal categories and our conclusions regarding them. In how far are such categories culturally determined, or in how far can we with assurance regard them as absolute? In how far can we regard inability to function socially as diagnostic of abnormality, or in how far is it necessary to regard this as a function of the culture?

As a matter of fact, one of the most striking facts that emerge from a study of widely varying cultures is the ease with which our abnormals function in other cultures. It does not matter what kind of "abnormality" we choose for illustration, those which indicate extreme instability, or those which are more in the nature of character traits like sadism or delusions of grandeur or of persecution, there are well-described cultures in which these abnormals function at ease and with honor, and apparently without danger or difficulty to the society.

The most notorious of these is trance and catalepsy. Even a very mild mystic is aberrant in our culture. But most peoples have regarded even extreme psychic manifestations not only as normal and desirable, but even as characteristic of highly valued and gifted individuals. This was true even in our own cultural background in that period when Catholicism made the ecstatic experience the mark of sainthood. It is hard for us, born and brought up in a culture that makes no use of the experience, to realize how important a role it may play and how many individuals are capable of it, once it has been given an honorable place in any society. . . .

Cataleptic and trance phenomena are, of course, only one illustration of the fact that those whom we regard as abnormals may function ade-

*Journal of General Psychology,* 10 (1934), 59–82 with omissions. Reprinted with permission of the Helen Dwight Reid Educational Foundation. Published by Heldref Publications, 1319 Eighteenth St. N. W. Washington, D.C. 20036-1802. Copyright © 1934.

quately in other cultures. Many of our culturally discarded traits are selected for elaboration in different societies. Homosexuality is an excellent example, for in this case our attention is not constantly diverted, as in the consideration of trance, to the interruption of routine activity which it implies. Homosexuality poses the problem very simply. A tendency toward this trait in our culture exposes an individual to all the conflicts to which all aberrants are always exposed, and we tend to identify the consequences of this conflict with homosexuality. But these consequences are obviously local and cultural. Homosexuals in many societies are not incompetent, but they may be such if the culture asks adjustments of them that would strain any man's vitality. Wherever homosexuality has been given an honorable place in any society, those to whom it is congenial have filled adequately the honorable roles society assigns to them. Plato's *Republic* is, of course, the most convincing statement of such a reading of homosexuality. It is presented as one of the major means to the good life, and it was generally so regarded in Greece at that time.

The cultural attitude toward homosexuals has not always been on such a high ethical plane, but it has been very varied. Among many American Indian tribes there exists the institution of the berdache, as the French called them. These men-women were men who at puberty or thereafter took the dress and the occupations of women. Sometimes they married other men and lived with them. Sometimes they were men with no inversion, persons of weak sexual endowment who chose this role to avoid the jeers of the women. The berdaches were never regarded as of first-rate supernatural power, as similar men-women were in Siberia, but rather as leaders in women's occupations, good healers in certain diseases, or, among certain tribes, as the genial organizers of social affairs. In any case, they were socially placed. They were not left exposed to the conflicts that visit the deviant who is excluded from participation in the recognized patterns of his society.

The most spectacular illustrations of the extent to which normality may be culturally defined are those cultures where an abnormality of our culture is the cornerstone of their social structure. It is not possible to do justice to these possibilities in a short discussion. A recent study of an island of northwest Melanesia by Fortune describes a society built upon traits which we regard as beyond the border of paranoia. In this tribe the exogamic groups look upon each other as prime manipulators of black magic, so that one marries always into an enemy group which remains for life one's deadly and unappeasable foes. They look upon a good garden crop as a confession of theft, for everyone is engaged in making magic to induce into his garden the productiveness of his neighbors'; therefore no secrecy in the island is so rigidly insisted upon as the secrecy of a man's harvesting of his yams. Their polite phrase at the acceptance of a gift is, "And if you now poison me, how shall I repay you this present?" Their preoccupation with poisoning is constant; no woman ever leaves her cooking pot for a moment untended. Even the great affinal economic exchanges that are characteristic of this Melanesian culture area are quite altered in Dobu since they are incompatible with this fear and distrust that pervades the culture. They go farther and people the whole world outside their own quarters with such malignant spirits that all-night feasts and ceremonials simply do not occur here. They have even rigorous religiously enforced customs that forbid the sharing of seed even in one family group. Anyone else's food is deadly poison to you, so that communality of stores is out of the question. For some months before harvest the whole society is on the verge of starvation, but if one falls to the temptation and eats up one's seed yams, one is an outcast and a beachcomber for life. There is no coming back. It involves, as a matter of course, divorce and the breaking of all social ties.

Now in this society where no one may work with another and no one may share with another, Fortune describes the individual who was regarded by all his fellows as crazy. He was not one of those who periodically ran amok and, beside himself and frothing at the mouth, fell with a knife upon anyone he could reach. Such behavior they did not regard as putting anyone outside the pale. They did not even put the individuals who were known to be liable to these attacks under any kind of control. They merely fled when they saw the attack coming on and kept out of the way. "He would be all right tomorrow." But there was one man of sunny, kindly disposition who liked work and liked to be helpful. The compulsion was too strong for him to repress it in favor of the opposite tendencies of his culture. Men and women never spoke of him without laughing; he was silly and simple and definitely crazy. Nevertheless, to the ethnologist used to a culture that has, in Christianity, made his type the model of all virtue, he seemed a pleasant fellow. . . .

. . . Among the Kwakiutl it did not matter whether a relative had died in bed of disease, or by the hand of an enemy, in either case death was an affront to be wiped out by the death of another person. The fact that one had been caused to mourn was proof that one had been put upon. A chief's sister and her daughter had gone up to Victoria, and either because they drank bad whiskey or because their boat capsized they never came back. The chief called together his warriors, "Now I ask you, tribes, who shall wail? Shall I do it or shall another?" The spokesman answered, of course, "Not you, Chief. Let some other of the tribes." Immediately they set up the war pole to announce their intention of wiping out the injury, and gathered a war party. They set out, and found seven men and two children asleep and killed them. "Then they felt good when they arrived at Sebaa in the evening."

The point which is of interest to us is that in our society those who on that occasion would feel good when they arrived at Sebaa that evening would be the definitely abnormal. There would be some, even in our society, but it is not a recognized and approved mood under the circumstances. On the Northwest Coast those are favored and fortunate to whom that mood under those circumstances is congenial, and those to whom it is repugnant are unlucky. This latter minority can register in their own culture only by doing violence to their congenial responses and acquiring others that are difficult for them. The person, for instance, who, like a Plains Indian whose wife has been taken from him, is too proud

to fight, can deal with the Northwest Coast civilization only by ignoring its strongest bents. If he cannot achieve it, he is the deviant in that culture, their instance of abnormality.

This head-hunting that takes place on the Northwest Coast after a death is no matter of blood revenge or of organized vengeance. There is no effort to tie up the subsequent killing with any responsibility on the part of the victim for the death of the person who is being mourned. A chief whose son has died goes visiting wherever his fancy dictates, and he says to his host, "My prince has died today, and you go with him." Then he kills him. In this, according to their interpretation, he acts nobly because he has not been downed. He has thrust back in return. The whole procedure is meaningless without the fundamental paranoid reading of bereavement. Death, like all the other untoward accidents of existence, confounds man's pride and can only be handled in the category of insults.

Behavior honored upon the Northwest Coast is one which is recognized as abnormal in our civilization, and yet it is sufficiently close to the attitudes of our own culture to be intelligible to us and to have a definite vocabulary with which we may discuss it. The megalomaniac paranoid trend is a definite danger in our society. It is encouraged by some of our major preoccupations, and it confronts us with a choice of two possible attitudes. One is to brand it as abnormal and reprehensible, and is the attitude we have chosen in our civilization. The other is to make it an essential attribute of ideal man, and this is the solution in the culture of the Northwest Coast.

These illustrations, which it has been possible to indicate only in the briefest manner, force upon us the fact that normality is culturally defined. An adult shaped to the drives and standards of either of these cultures, if he were transported into our civilization would fall into our categories of abnormality. He would be faced with the psychic dilemmas of the socially unavailable. In his own culture, however, he is the pillar of society, the end result of socially inculcated mores, and the problem of personal instability in his case simply does not arise.

No one civilization can possibly utilize in its mores the whole potential range of human behavior. Just as there are great numbers of possible phonetic articulations, and the possibility of language depends on a selection and standardization of a few of these in order that speech communication may be possible at all, so the possibility of organized behavior of every sort, from the fashions of local dress and houses to the dicta of a people's ethics and religion, depends upon a similar selection among the possible behavior traits. In the field of recognized economic obligations or sex tabus this selection is as nonrational and subconscious a process as it is in the field of phonetics. It is a process which goes on in the group for long periods of time and is historically conditioned by innumerable accidents of isolation or of contact of peoples. In any comprehensive study of psychology, the selection that different cultures have made in the course of history within the great circumference of potential behavior is of great significance.

Every society, beginning with some slight inclination in one direction or another, carries its preference farther and farther, integrating itself more and more completely upon its chosen basis, and discarding those types of behavior that are uncongenial. Most of those organizations of personality that seem to us most uncontrovertibly abnormal have been used by different civilizations in the very foundations of their institutional life. Conversely the most valued traits of our normal individuals have been looked on in differently organized cultures as aberrant. Normality, in short, within a very wide range, is culturally defined. It is primarily a term for the socially elaborated segment of human behavior in any culture; and abnormality, a term for the segment that that particular civilization does not use. The very eyes with which we see the problem are conditioned by the long traditional habits of our own society.

It is a point that has been made more often in relation to ethics than in relation to psychiatry. We do not any longer make the mistake of deriving the morality of our locality and decade directly from the inevitable constitution of human nature. We do not elevate it to the dignity of a first princi-

ple. We recognize that morality differs in every society, and is a convenient term for socially approved habits. Mankind has always preferred to say, "It is a morally good," rather than "It is habitual," and the fact of this preference is matter enough for a critical science of ethics. But historically the two phrases are synonymous.

The concept of the normal is properly a variant of the concept of the good. It is that which society has approved. A normal action is one which falls well within the limits of expected behavior for a particular society. Its variability among different peoples is essentially a function of the variability of the behavior patterns that different societies have created for themselves, and can never be wholly divorced from a consideration of culturally institutionalized types of behavior.

Each culture is a more or less elaborate workingout of the potentialities of the segment it has chosen. In so far as a civilization is well integrated and consistent within itself, it will tend to carry farther and farther, according to its nature, its initial impulse toward a particular type of action, and from the point of view of any other culture those elaborations will include more and more extreme and aberrant traits.

Each of these traits, in proportion as it reinforces the chosen behavior patterns of that culture, is for that culture normal. Those individuals to whom it is congenial either congenitally, or as the result of childhood sets, are accorded prestige in that culture, and are not visited with the social contempt or disapproval which their traits would call down upon them in a society that was differently organized. On the other hand, those individuals whose characteristics are not congenial to the selected type of human behavior in that community are the deviants, no matter how valued their personality traits may be in a contrasted civilization.

The Dobuan who is not easily susceptible to fear of treachery, who enjoys work and likes to be helpful, is their neurotic and regarded as silly. On the Northwest Coast the person who finds it difficult to read life in terms of an insult contest will be the person upon whom fall all the difficulties of the culturally unprovided for. The person who does not find it easy to humiliate a neighbor, nor to see humiliation in his own experience, who is genial and loving, may, of course, find some unstandardized way of achieving satisfactions in his society, but not in the major patterned responses that his culture requires of him. If he is born to play an important role in a family with many hereditary privileges, he can succeed only by doing violence to his whole personality. If he does not succeed, he has betrayed his culture; that is, he is abnormal.

I have spoken of individuals as having sets toward certain types of behavior, and of these sets as running sometimes counter to the types of behavior which are institutionalized in the culture to which they belong. From all that we know of contrasting cultures it seems clear that differences of temperament occur in every society. The matter has never been made the subject of investigation, but from the available material it would appear that these temperament types are very likely of universal recurrence. That is, there is an ascertainable range of human behavior that is found wherever a sufficiently large series of individuals is observed. But the proportion in which behavior types stand to one another in different societies is not universal. The vast majority of individuals in any group are shaped to the fashion of that culture. In other words, most individuals are plastic to the moulding force of the society into which they are born. In a society that values trance, as in India, they will have supernormal experience. In a society that institutionalizes homosexuality, they will be homosexual. In a society that sets the gathering of possessions as the chief human objective, they will amass property. The deviants, whatever the type of behavior the culture has institutionalized, will remain few in number, and there seems no more difficulty in moulding the vast malleable majority to the "normality" of what we consider an aberrant trait, such as delusions of reference, than to the normality of such accepted behavior patterns as acquisitiveness. The small proportion of the number of the deviants in any culture is not a function of the sure instinct with which that society has built itself upon the fundamental sanities, but of the universal fact that, happily, the majority of mankind quite readily take any shape that is presented to them. . . .

# 2   Ethical Relativism

## PAUL W. TAYLOR

One of the most commonly held opinions in ethics is that all moral norms are *relative* to particular cultures. The rules of conduct that are applicable in one society, it is claimed, do not apply to the actions of people in another society. Each community has its own norms, and morality is entirely a matter of conforming to the standards and rules accepted in one's own culture. To put it simply:

Reprinted by permission of Wadsworth Publishing Co. from *Principles of Ethics: an Introduction* (Dickenson Publishing Company, 1975), 13–29, with omissions.

What is right is what my society approves of; what is wrong is what my society disapproves of.

This view raises serious doubts about the whole enterprise of normative ethics. For if right and wrong are completely determined by the given moral code of a particular time and place, and if moral codes vary from time to time and place to place, it would seem that there are no unchanging cross-cultural principles that could constitute an ideal ethical system applicable to everyone. Since the purpose of normative ethics is to construct and defend just such a universal system of principles, belief in the relativity of moral norms denies the possibility of normative ethics. . . .

## Descriptive Relativism

Certain facts about the moral values of different societies and about the way an individual's values are dependent on those of his society have been taken as empirical evidence in support of the claim that all moral values are relative to the particular culture in which they are accepted. These facts are cited by the relativist as reasons for holding a general theory about moral norms, namely, that no such norms are universal. This theory is what we shall designate "descriptive relativism." It is a factual or empirical theory because it holds that, as a matter of historical and sociological fact, no moral standard or rule of conduct has been universally recognized to be the basis of moral obligation. According to the descriptive relativist there are no moral norms common to all cultures. Each society has its own view of what is morally right and wrong and these views vary from society to society because of the differences in their moral codes. Thus it is a mistake to think there are common norms that bind all mankind in one moral community.

Those who accept the position of descriptive relativism point to certain facts as supporting evidence for their theory. These facts may be conveniently summed up under the following headings:

(1) The facts of cultural variability.
(2) Facts about the origin of moral beliefs and moral codes.
(3) The fact of ethnocentrism.

(1) The facts of cultural variability are now so familiar to everyone that they need hardly be enumerated in detail. We all know from reading anthropologists' studies of primitive cultures how extreme is the variation in the customs and taboos, the religions and moralities, the daily habits and the general outlook on life to be found in the cultures of different peoples. But we need not go beyond our own culture to recognize the facts of variability. Historians of Western civilization have long pointed out the great differences in the beliefs and values of people living in different periods. Great differences have also been discovered among the various socioeconomic classes existing within the social structure at any one time. Finally, our own contemporary world reveals a tremendous variety of ways of living. No one who dwells in a modern city can escape the impact of this spectrum of different views on work and play, on family life and education, on what constitutes personal happiness, and on what is right and wrong.

(2) When we add to these facts of cultural and historical variability the recent psychological findings about how the individual's values reflect those of his own social group and his own time, we may begin to question the universal validity of our own values. For it is now a well-established fact that no moral values or beliefs are inborn. All our moral attitudes and judgments are learned from the social environment. Even our deepest convictions about justice and the rights of man are originally nothing but the "introjected" or "internalized" views of our culture, transmitted to us through our parents and teachers. Our very conscience itself is formed by the internalizing of the sanctions used by our society to support its moral norms. When we were told in childhood what we ought and ought not to do, and when our parents expressed their approval and disapproval of us for what we did, we were being taught the standards and rules of conduct accepted in our society. The result of this learning process (sometimes called "acculturation") was to ingrain in us a set of attitudes about our own conduct, so that even when our parents were no longer around to guide us or to blame us, we would guide or blame ourselves by thinking, "This is what I ought to do": "That would be wrong to do"; and so on. If we then did something we believed was wrong we would feel guilty about it, whether or not anyone caught us at it or punished us for it.

It is this unconscious process of internalizing the norms of one's society through early childhood training that explains the origin of an individual's moral values. If we go beyond this and ask about the origin of society's values, we find a long and gradual development of traditions and customs which have given stability to the society's way of life and whose obscure beginnings lie in ritual magic, taboos, tribal ceremonies, and practices of religious worship. Whether we are dealing with the formation of an individual's conscience or the development of a society's moral code, then, the origin of a set of values seems to have little or nothing to do with rational, controlled thought. Neither individuals nor societies originally acquire their moral beliefs by means of logical reasoning or through the use of an objective method for gaining knowledge.

(3) Finally, the descriptive relativist points out another fact about people and their moralities that must be acknowledged. This is the fact that most people are ethnocentric (group centered). They think not only that there is but one true morality for all mankind, but that the one true morality is their own. They are convinced that the moral code under which they grew up and which formed their deepest feelings about right and wrong—namely, the moral code of their own society—is the only code for anyone to live by. Indeed, they often refuse even to entertain the possibility that their own values might be false or that another society's code might be more correct, more enlightened, or more advanced than their own. Thus ethnocentrism often leads to intolerance and dogmatism. It causes people to be extremely narrow-minded in their ethical outlook, afraid to admit any doubt about a moral issue, and unable to take a detached, objective stance regarding their own moral beliefs. Being absolutely certain that their beliefs are true, they can think only that those who disagree with them are in total error and ignorance on moral matters. Their attitude is: We are advanced, they are backward. We are civilized, they are savages.

It is but a short step from dogmatism to intolerance. Intolerance is simply dogmatism in action. Because the moral values of people directly affect their conduct, those who have divergent moral convictions will often come into active conflict with one another in the area of practical life. Each will believe he alone has the true morality and the other is living in the darkness of sin. Each will see the other as practicing moral abominations. Each will then try to force the other to accept the truth, or at least will not allow the other to live by his own values. The self-righteous person will not tolerate the presence of "shocking" acts which he views with outraged indignation. Thus it comes about that no differences of opinion on moral matters will be permitted within a society. The ethnocentric society will tend to be a closed society, as far as moral belief and practice are concerned.

The argument for descriptive relativism, then, may be summarized as follows. Since every culture varies with respect to its moral rules and standards, and since each individual's moral beliefs—including his inner conviction of their absolute truth—have been learned within the framework of his own culture's moral code, it follows that there are no universal moral norms. If a person believes there are such norms, this is to be explained by his ethnocentrism, which leads him to project his own culture's norms upon everyone else and to consider those who disagree with him either as innocent but "morally blind" people or as sinners who do not want to face the truth about their own evil ways.

In order to assess the soundness of this argument it is necessary to make a distinction between (a) specific moral standards and rules, and (b) ultimate moral principles. Both (a) and (b) can be called "norms," and it is because the descriptive relativist often overlooks this distinction that his argument is open to doubt. A specific moral standard (such as personal courage or trustworthiness) functions as a criterion for judging whether and to what degree a person's character is morally good or bad. A specific rule of conduct (such as "Help others in time of need" or "Do not tell lies for one's own advantage") is a prescription of how people ought or ought not to act. It functions as a criterion for judging whether an action is right or wrong. In contrast with specific standards and rules, an ultimate moral principle is a universal proposition or statement about the conditions that must hold if a standard or rule is to be used as a criterion for judging *any* person or action. Such a principle will be of the form: Standard S or rule R applies to a person or action if and only if condition C is fulfilled. An example of an ultimate moral principle is that of utility. The principle of utility may be expressed thus: A standard or rule applies to a person or action if, and only if, the use of the standard or rule in the actual guidance of people's conduct will result in an increase in everyone's happiness or a decrease in everyone's unhappiness.

Now it is perfectly possible for an ultimate moral principle to be consistent with a variety of specific standards and rules as found in the moral codes of different societies. For if we take into account the traditions of a culture, the beliefs about reality and the attitudes toward life that are part of each culture's world-outlook, and if we also take into account the physical or geographical setting of each culture, we will find that a standard or rule which increases people's happiness in one culture will not increase, but rather decrease, people's happiness in another. In one society, for example, letting elderly people die when they can no longer contribute to economic production will be necessary for the survival of everyone else. But another society may have an abundant economy that can easily support people in their old age. Thus the principle of utility would require that in the first society the rule "Do not keep a person alive when he can no longer produce" be part of its moral code, and in the second society it would require a contrary rule. In this case the very same kind of action that is wrong in one society will be right in another. Yet there is a single principle that makes an action of that kind wrong (in one set of circumstances) and another action of that kind right (in a different set of circumstances). In other words, the reason why one action is wrong and the other right is based on one and the same principle, namely utility.

Having in mind this distinction between specific standards and rules on the one hand and ultimate moral principles on the other, what can we say about the argument for descriptive relativism given above? It will immediately be seen that the facts pointed out by the relativist as evidence in support of his theory do not show that ultimate moral principles are relative or culture-bound. They show only that specific standards and rules are relative or culture-bound. The fact that different societies accept different norms of good and bad, right and wrong, is a fact about the standards and rules that make up the various moral codes of those societies. Such a fact does not provide evidence that there is no single ultimate principle which, explicitly or implicitly, every society appeals to as the final justifying ground for its moral code. For if there were such a common ultimate principle, the actual variation in moral codes could be explained in terms of the different world-outlooks, traditions, and physical circumstances of the different societies.

Similarly, facts about ethnocentrism and the causal dependence of an individual's moral beliefs upon his society's moral code do not count as evidence against the view that there is a universal ultimate principle which everyone would refer to in giving a final justification for his society's standards and rules, if he were challenged to do so. Whether there is such a principle and if there is, what sort of conditions it specifies for the validity of specific standards and rules, are questions still to be explored. . . . But the facts cited by the descriptive relativist leave these questions open. We may accept those facts and still be consistent in affirming a single universal ultimate moral principle.

## Normative Ethical Relativism

The statement, "What is right in one society may be wrong in another," is a popular way of explaining what is meant by the "relativity of morals." It is usually contrasted with "ethical universalism," taken as the view that "right and wrong do not vary from society to society." These statements are ambiguous, however, and it is important for us to be mindful of their ambiguity. For they may be understood either as factual claims or as normative claims, and it makes a great deal of difference which way they are understood. . . .

When it is said that what is right in one society may be wrong in another, this may be understood to mean that what is *believed* to be right in one society is *believed* to be wrong in another. And when it is said that moral right and wrong vary from society to society, this may be understood to mean that different moral norms are adopted by different societies, so that an act which fulfills the norms of one society may violate the norms of another. If this is what is meant, then we are here being told merely of the cultural variability of specific standards and rules, which we have already considered in connection with descriptive relativism.

But the statement, "What is right in one society may be wrong in another," may be interpreted in quite a different way. It may be taken as a normative claim rather than as a factual assertion. Instead of asserting the unsurprising fact that what is believed to be right in one society is believed to be wrong in another, it expresses the far more radical and seemingly paradoxical claim that what *actually is* right in one society may *actually be* wrong in another. According to this view, moral norms are to be considered valid only within the society which has adopted them as part of its way of life. Such norms are not to be considered valid outside that society. The conclusion is then drawn that is is not legitimate to judge people in other societies by applying the norms of one's own society to their conduct. This is the view we shall designate "normative ethical relativism." In order to be perfectly clear about what it claims, we shall examine two ways in which it can be stated, one focusing our attention upon moral judgments, the other on moral norms.

With regard to moral judgments, normative ethical relativism holds that two *apparently* contradictory statements can both be true. The argument runs as follows. Consider the two statements:

(1)  It is wrong for unmarried women to have their faces unveiled in front of strangers.

(2)  It is not wrong for . . . (as above).

Here it seems as if there is a flat contradiction between two moral judgments, so that if one is true the other must be false. But the normative ethical relativist holds that they are both true, because the statements as given in (1) and (2) are incomplete. They should read as follows:

(3)  It is wrong for unmarried women *who are members of society S* to have their faces unveiled in front of strangers.
(4)  It is not wrong for unmarried women *outside of society S* to have their faces unveiled in front of strangers.

Statements (3) and (4) are not contradictories. To assert one is not to deny the other. The normative ethical relativist simply translates all moral judgments of the form "Doing act X is right" into statements of the form "Doing X is right when the agent is a member of society S." The latter statement can then be seen to be consistent with statements of the form "Doing X is wrong when the agent is not a member of society S."

The normative ethical relativist's view of moral norms accounts for the foregoing theory of moral judgments. A moral norm, we have seen, is either a standard used in a judgment of good and bad character or a rule used in a judgment of right and wrong conduct. Thus a person is judged to be good insofar as he fulfills the standard, and an action is judged to be right or wrong according to whether it conforms to or violates the rule. Now when a normative ethical relativist says that moral norms vary from society to society, he does not intend merely to assert the fact that different societies have adopted different norms. He is going beyond descriptive relativism and is making a normative claim. He is denying any universal validity to moral norms. He is saying that a moral standard or rule is correctly applicable only to the members of the particular society which has adopted the standard or rule as part of its actual moral code. He therefore thinks it is illegitimate to judge the character or conduct of those outside the society by such a standard or rule. Anyone who uses the norms of one society as the basis for judging the character or conduct of persons in another society is consequently in error.

It is not that a normative ethical relativist necessarily believes in *tolerance* of other people's norms. Nor does his position imply that he grants others the *right* to live by their own norms, for he would hold a relativist view even about tolerance itself. A society whose code included a rule of tolerance would be right in tolerating others, while one that denied tolerance would be right (relative to its own norm of intolerance) in prohibiting others from living by different norms. The normative ethical relativist would simply say that *we* should not judge the tolerant society to be any better than the intolerant one, for this would be applying our own norm of tolerance to other societies. Tolerance, like any other norm, is culture-bound. Anyone who claims that every society has a *right* to live by its own norms, provided that it respects a similar right in other societies, is an ethical universalist, since he holds at least one norm valid for all societies, namely, the right to practice a way of life without interference from others. And he deems this universal norm a valid one, whether or not every society does in fact accept it. . . .

The most frequent argument given in defense of normative ethical relativism is that, if the facts pointed out by the descriptive relativist are indeed true, then we must accept normative ethical relativism as the only position consistent with those facts. For it seems that if each person's moral judgments are formed within the framework of the norms of his own culture and historical epoch, and if such norms vary among cultures and epochs, it would follow necessarily that it is unwarranted for anyone to apply his own norms to conduct in other societies and times. To do so would be ethnocentrism, which is, as the descriptive relativist shows, a kind of blind, narrow-minded dogmatism. To escape the irrationality of being ethnocentric, we need but realize that the only norms one may legitimately apply to any given group are the ones accepted by that group. Since different peoples accept different norms, there are no universal norms applicable to everyone throughout the world. Now, to say that there are no universal norms applicable worldwide is to commit oneself

to normative ethical relativism. Thus, the argument concludes, normative ethical relativism follows from the facts of descriptive relativism.

Is this a valid argument? Suppose one accepts the facts pointed out by the descriptive relativist. Must he then also accept normative ethical relativism? Let us examine some of the objections that have been raised to this argument. In the first place, it is claimed that the facts of cultural variability do not, *by themselves,* entail normative ethical relativism. The reason is that it is perfectly possible for someone to accept those facts and deny normative ethical relativism without contradicting himself. No matter how great may be the differences in the moral beliefs of different cultures and in the moral norms they accept, it is still possible to hold that some of these beliefs are true and others false, or that some of the norms are more correct, justified, or enlightened than others. The fact that societies differ about what is right and wrong does not mean that one society may not have better reasons for holding its views than does another. After all, just because two people (or two groups of people) disagree about whether a disease is caused by bacteria or by evil spirits does not lead to the conclusion that there is no correct or enlightened view about the cause of the disease. So it does not follow from the fact that two societies differ about whether genocide is right that there is no correct or enlightened view about this moral matter.

A similar argument can be used with regard to the second set of facts asserted by the descriptive relativist. No contradiction is involved in affirming that all moral beliefs come from the social environment and denying normative ethical relativism. The fact that a belief is learned from one's society does not mean that it is neither true nor false, or that if it is true, its truth is "relative" to the society in which it was learned. All of our beliefs, empirical ones no less than moral ones, are learned from our society. We are not born with any innate beliefs about chemistry or physics; we learn these only in our schools. Yet this does not make us skeptical about the universal validity of these sciences. So the fact that our moral beliefs come from our society and are learned in our homes and schools has no bearing on their universal validity. The origin or cause of a person's *acquiring* a belief does not determine whether the *content* of the belief is true or false, or even whether there are good grounds for his accepting that content to be true or false.

If it is claimed that our moral beliefs are based on attitudes or feelings culturally conditioned in us from childhood, the same point can still be made. Suppose, for example, that a person who believes slavery is wrong feels disapproval, dislike, or even abhorrence towards the institution of slavery. His negative attitude, which has undoubtedly been influenced by the value system of his culture, may be contrasted with a positive stance (approval, liking, admiring) of someone brought up in an environment where slave owning was accepted. Here are positive and negative attitudes toward slavery, each being causally conditioned by the given cultural environment. It does not follow from this that the two are equally justified, or that neither can be justified. The question of whether a certain attitude toward slavery is justified or unjustified depends on whether good reasons can be given *for* anyone taking the one attitude and *against* anyone taking the other. This question requires the exercise of our reasoning powers. Exactly how we can justify attitudes, or show them to be unjustified, is a complex problem that will be dealt with in later chapters of this book. But the mere fact that the attitudes which underlie moral beliefs are all learned from the social environment leaves open the question of what attitudes an intelligent, rational, and well-informed person would take toward a given action or social practice.

The same kind of argument also holds with respect to the third fact of descriptive relativism: ethnocentrism. People who are ethnocentric *believe* that the one true moral code is that of their own society. But this leaves open the question, Is their belief true or false? Two people of different cultures, both ethnocentric but with opposite moral beliefs, may each think his particular moral norms are valid for everyone; however, this has no bearing on whether either one—or neither one—

is correct. We must inquire independently into the possibility of establishing the universal validity of a set of moral norms, regardless of who might or might not believe them to be universally true.

It should be noted that these various objections to the . . . argument for normative ethical relativism, even if sound, are not sufficient to show that normative ethical relativism is false. They only provide reasons for rejecting one argument in support of that position. To show that the position is false, it would be necessary to give a sound argument in defense of ethical universalism. . . .

## Ethical Absolutism

When someone asks, "Are moral norms relative or absolute?" there is often an ambiguity in his question, not only with respect to the word "relative" but also with respect to the word "absolute." We have seen that "relative" can mean, among other things, "causally dependent on variable factors in different cultures" (descriptive relativism); *or* "validly applicable only within the culture which accepts the norm" (normative ethical relativism) . . . Let us now examine an important ambiguity in the term "absolute" as it is applied to moral norms. For unless this ambiguity is cleared up, we cannot give a straightforward answer to the question of whether moral norms are relative or absolute.

That moral norms (that is, specific moral rules and standards) are "absolute" can mean either of two things. It can mean that at least some moral norms are justifiable on grounds that can be established by a cross-cultural method of reasoning and that, consequently, these norms correctly apply to the conduct of all human beings. This, we have seen, is ethical universalism. It entails the denial of normative ethical relativism. . . . Hence, in this first sense of the term "absolute," ethical absolutism may simply be equated with ethical universalism.

The second meaning of the term "absolute" is entirely different from the first. According to the second meaning, to say that moral norms are "absolute" is to say that they *have no exceptions.* Thus, if the rule "It is wrong to break a promise" is an absolute moral norm in this second sense, then one must never break a promise no matter what the circumstances. It follows that it is our duty to keep a promise, even if doing so brings suffering to innocent people. It means, for example, that a hired gunman who promises his boss to murder someone should commit the murder. It signifies that, if we have promised a friend to go to a movie with him on Saturday night, we must do so even if our parents are injured in an automobile accident Saturday afternoon and desperately need our help. Extreme cases like these show that, at least in our ordinary unreflective moral judgments, the rule "Do not break promises" has exceptions and that consequently, ethical absolutism in the second sense of the term is not true of that particular moral rule.

Are there *any* rules of conduct that are "absolute" in the second sense? The reader should try to work out his own answer to this question for himself. What is important for present purposes is to notice the *logical independence* of the two meanings of "ethical absolutism."

According to the first meaning, an ethical absolutist holds that there are moral norms that apply to everyone, no matter what norms are actually accepted in a given society. According to the second meaning, an ethical absolutist is one who claims that at least some moral norms allow for no legitimate or justifiable exceptions. It is clear that the first meaning of ethical absolutism does not necessarily entail the second. In other words, it is possible to be an ethical absolutist in the first sense but not in the second. For it may be that all moral norms valid for everyone in any society are norms that allow for legitimate exceptions in special circumstances, *whenever* those circumstances occur. Let us consider an example.

Suppose we think that in almost all situations of life it is wrong for one person to take the life of another. Suppose, further, that we hold the rule "Thou shalt not kill" to be a universal moral norm, believing that it applies to all persons in all societies (even if a certain group of people in a given

society do not accept the rule). Thus, with respect to this rule we are ethical universalists. Now suppose that we also think that there are very unusual conditions which, when they occur, make it permissible for one person to kill another. For instance, we might think that if a person's only means of defending his life or the lives of his children against the attack of a madman is to kill him, then it is not wrong to kill him. Or we might think that killing is permissible when such an act is necessary to overthrow a totalitarian government carrying out a policy of systematic genocide. If we hold these cases to be legitimate exceptions to the rule "Thou shalt not kill," are we contradicting our position of ethical universalism with regard to that rule? The answer is no, since we may be willing to consider these exceptions legitimate whenever they occur, no matter whether a given society accepts them as legitimate exceptions or not. In this case the *full* statement of our rule against killing would be expressed thus: It is wrong for anyone, in any society, to take the life of another, except when such an act is necessary for self-defense or the prevention of systematic genocide.

When a moral rule is stated in this manner, it encompasses its own exceptions. In other words, the complete rule stipulates all the kinds of situations in which an action of the sort *generally* forbidden by the rule is right. If we then accept the rule in its complete form, *including the list of exceptions,* as validly applicable to all human beings, we are ethical universalists (and hence ethical absolutists in the first sense of the term) with respect to this rule. However, we are not ethical absolutists in the second sense of the term, since we hold that the simple rule "Thou shalt not kill" does have legitimate exceptions. . . .

The main point of this discussion may now be indicated. When an ethical universalist says that there are moral norms applicable to everyone everywhere, he does not mean that the application of these norms to particular circumstances must determine that one kind of action is always right (or that it is always wrong). He means only that, whenever the norms do apply, they apply regardless of whether a given society may have accepted them in its actual moral code and another society may have excluded them from *its* moral code. The (normative) ethical relativist, on the other hand, claims that what makes an act right is precisely its conformity to the accepted norms of the society in which it occurs, while its violation of such accepted norms makes it wrong. Consider, then, two acts of the very same kind done in the very same sort of circumstances, but each occurring in a different society. One can be right and the other wrong, according to the relativist, since the moral norms of the two societies may disagree concerning the behavior in question. The ethical universalist (or "absolutist" in the first sense), however, would say that if one act is right the other is too and if one is wrong so is the other. For both are acts of an identical kind per-

formed in identical circumstances. Therefore a rule which required or prohibited the one would also require or prohibit the other, and only one rule validly applies to such actions performed in circumstances of that sort. Thus the universalist holds that the rightness and wrongness of actions do not change according to variations in the norms accepted by different societies, even though (contrary to what the "absolutist" in the second sense says) the rightness and wrongness of actions do vary with differences in the sorts of circumstances in which they are performed.

If we keep this distinction between the two meanings of ethical absolutism clearly in mind, we call then see that it is possible to be an absolutist in one sense and not in the other.

# 3   Non-Relative Virtues: An Aristotelian Approach

## MARTHA C. NUSSBAUM

*All Greeks used to go around armed with swords.*

> THUCYDIDES,
> *History of the Peloponnesian War*

*The customs of former times might be said to be too simple and barbaric. For Greeks used to go around armed with swords; and they used to buy wives from one another; and there are surely other ancient customs that are extremely stupid. (For example, in Cyme there is a law about homicide, that if a man prosecuting a charge can produce a certain number of witnesses from among his own relations, the defendant will automatically be convicted of murder.) In general, all*

*human beings seek not the way of their ancestors, but the good.*

> ARISTOTLE, *Politics* 1268a39 ff.

*One may also observe in one's travels to distant countries the feelings of recognition and affiliation that link every human being to every other human being.*

> ARISTOTLE,
> *Nicomachean Ethics* 1155a21–22

I

. . . The purpose of this paper is to establish that Aristotle does indeed have an interesting way of connecting the virtues with a search for ethical objectivity and the criticism of existing local

From *Midwest Studies in Philosophy,* Volume XIII, ed. Peter A. French, Theodore E. Uehling, Jr., and Howard K. Wettstein, p. 36–53, with omissions. Copyright © 1988 by the University of Notre Dame Press. Used by permission of the publisher.

norms, a way that deserves our serious consideration as we work on these questions. Having described the general shape of the Aristotelian approach, we can then begin to understand some of the objections that might be brought against such a non-relative account of the virtues, and to imagine how the Aristotelian could respond to those objections.

## II

The relativist, looking at different societies, is impressed by the variety and the apparent non-comparability in the lists of virtues she encounters. Examining the different lists, and observing the complex connections between each list and a concrete form of life and a concrete history, she may well feel that any list of virtues must be simply a reflection of local traditions and values, and that, virtues being (unlike Kantian principles or utilitarian algorithms) concrete and closely tied to forms of life, there can in fact be no list of virtues that will serve as normative for all these varied societies. It is not only that the specific forms of behavior recommended in connection with the virtues differ greatly over time and place, it is also that the very areas that are singled out as spheres of virtue, and the manner in which they are individuated from other areas, vary so greatly. For someone who thinks this way, it is easy to feel that Aristotle's own list, despite its pretensions to universality and objectivity, must be similarly restricted, merely a reflection of one particular society's perceptions of salience and ways of distinguishing. At this point, relativist writers are likely to quote Aristotle's description of the "great-souled" person, the *megalopsuchos,* which certainly contains many concrete local features and sounds very much like the portrait of a certain sort of Greek gentleman, in order to show that Aristotle's list is just as culture-bound as any other.[1]

But if we probe further into the way in which Aristotle in fact enumerates and individuates the virtues, we begin to notice things that cast doubt upon the suggestion that he has simply described what is admired in his own society. First of all, we notice that a rather large number of virtues and vices (vices especially) are nameless, and that, among the ones that are not nameless, a good many are given, by Aristotle's own account, names that are somewhat arbitrarily chosen by Aristotle, and do not perfectly fit the behavior he is trying to describe.[2] Of such modes of conduct he writes, "Most of these are nameless, but we must try . . . to give them names in order to make our account clear and easy to follow" (*NE* 16–19). This does not sound like the procedure of someone who is simply studying local traditions and singling out the virtue names that figure most prominently in those traditions.

What *is* going on becomes clearer when we examine the way in which he does in fact, introduce his list. For he does so, in the *Nicomachean Ethics,*[3] by a device whose very straightforwardness and simplicity has caused it to escape the notice of most writers on this topic. What he does, in each case, is to isolate a sphere of human experience that figures in more or less any human life, and in which more or less any human being will have to make *some* choices rather than others, and act in *some* way rather than some other. The introductory chapter enumerating the virtues and vices begins from an enumeration of these spheres (*NE* 2.7); and each chapter on a virtue in the more detailed account that follows begins with "Concerning X . . ." or words to this effect, where "X" names a sphere of life with which all human beings regularly and more or less necessarily have dealings.[4] Aristotle then asks: What is it to choose and respond well within that sphere? What is it, on the other hand, to choose defectively? The "thin account" of each virtue is that it is whatever it is to be stably disposed to act appropriately in that sphere. There may be, and usually are, various competing specifications of what acting well, in each case, in fact comes to. Aristotle goes on to defend in each case some concrete specification, producing, at the end, a full or "thick" definition of the virtue.

Table 1 lists the most important spheres of experience recognized by Aristotle, along with the names of their corresponding virtues.[5]

There is, of course, much more to be said about this list, its specific members, and the names Aristotle chooses for the virtue in each case, some of which are indeed culture bound. What I want, however, to insist on here is the care with which Aristotle articulates his general approach, beginning from a characterization of a sphere of universal experience and choice, and introducing the virtue name as the name (as yet undefined) of whatever it is to choose appropriately in that area of experience. On this approach, it does not seem possible to say, as the relativist wishes to, that a given society does not contain anything that corresponds to a given virtue. Nor does it seem to be an open question, in the case of a particular agent, whether a certain virtue should or should not be included in his or her life—except in the sense that she can always choose to pursue the corresponding deficiency instead. The point is that everyone makes some choices and acts somehow or other in these spheres: if not properly, then improperly. Everyone has *some* attitude and behavior toward her own death; toward her bodily appetites and their management; toward her property and its use; toward the distribution of social goods; toward telling the truth; toward being kindly or not kindly to others; toward cultivating or not cultivating a sense of play and delight; and so on. No matter where one lives one cannot escape these questions, so long as one is living a human life. But then this means that one's behavior falls, willy nilly, within the sphere of the Aristotelian virtue, in each case. If it is not appropriate, it is inappropriate; it cannot be off the map altogether. People will of course disagree about what the appropriate ways of acting and reacting in fact *are*. But in that case, as Aristotle has set things up, they are arguing about the same thing, and advancing competing specifications of the same virtue. The reference of the virtue term in each case is fixed by the sphere of experience—by

**Table 1**

| Sphere | Virtue |
| --- | --- |
| 1. Fear of important damages, esp. death | courage |
| 2. Bodily appetites and their pleasures | moderation |
| 3. Distribution of limited resources | justice |
| 4. Management of one's personal property, where others are concerned | generosity |
| 5. Management of personal property, where hospitality is concerned | expansive hospitality |
| 6. Attitudes and actions with respect to one's own worth | greatness of soul |
| 7. Attitude to slights and damages | mildness of temper |
| 8. "Association and living together and the fellowship of words and actions" | |
|    a. truthfulness in speech | truthfulness |
|    b. social association of a playful kind | easy grace (contrasted with coarseness, rudeness, insensitivity) |
|    c. social association more generally | nameless, but a kind of friendliness (contrasted with irritability and grumpiness) |
| 9. Attitude to the good and ill fortune of others | proper judgment (contrasted with enviousness, spitefulness, etc.) |
| 10. Intellectual life | the various intellectual virtues (such as perceptiveness, knowledge, etc.) |
| 11. The planning of one's life and conduct | practical wisdom |

what we shall from now on call the "grounding experiences." The thin or "nominal definition" of the virtue will be, in each case, that it is whatever it is that being disposed to choose and respond well consists in, in that sphere. The job of ethical theory will be to search for the best further specification corresponding to this nominal definition, and to produce a full definition.

## III

. . . Aristotle's ethical and political writings provide many examples of how such progress (or, more generally, such a rational debate) might go. We find argument against Platonic asceticism, as the proper specification of moderation (appropriate choice and response vis-à-vis the bodily appetites) and the consequent proneness to anger over slights, that was prevalent in Greek ideals of maleness and in Greek behavior, together with a defense of a more limited and controlled expression of anger, as the proper specification of the virtue that Aristotle calls "mildness of temper." (Here Aristotle evinces some discomfort with the virtue term he has chosen, and he is right to do so, since it certainly loads the dice heavily in favor of his concrete specification and against the traditional one.)[6] And so on for all the virtues.

In an important section of *Politics* II, part of which forms one of the epigraphs to this paper, Aristotle defends the proposition that laws should be revisable and not fixed, by pointing to evidence that there is progress toward greater correctness in our ethical conceptions, as also in the arts and sciences. Greeks used to think that courage was a matter of waving swords around; now they have (the *Ethics* informs us) a more inward and a more civic and communally attuned understanding of proper behavior toward the possibility of death. Women used to be regarded as property, bought and sold; now this would be thought barbaric. And in the case of justice as well we have, the *Politics* passage claims, advanced toward a more adequate understanding of what is fair and appropriate. Aristotle gives the example of

an existing homicide law that convicts the defendant automatically on the evidence of the prosecutor's relatives (whether they actually witnessed anything or not, apparently). This, Aristotle says, is clearly a stupid and unjust law; and yet it once seemed appropriate—and, to a tradition-bound community, must still be so. To hold tradition fixed is then to prevent ethical progress. What human beings want and seek is not conformity with the past, it is the good. So our systems of law should make it possible for them to progress beyond the past, when they have agreed that a change is good. (They should not, however, make change too easy, since it is no easy matter to see one's way to the good, and tradition is frequently a sounder guide than current fashion.)

In keeping with these ideas, the *Politics* as a whole presents the beliefs of the many different societies it investigates not as unrelated local norms, but as competing answers to questions of justice and courage (and so on) with which all the societies (being human) are concerned, and in response to which they are all trying to find what is good. Aristotle's analysis of the virtues gives him an appropriate framework for these comparisons, which seem perfectly appropriate inquiries into the ways in which different societies have solved common human problems.

In the Aristotelian approach it is obviously of the first importance to distinguish two stages of the inquiry: the initial demarcation of the sphere of choice, of the "grounding experiences" that fix the reference of the virtue term; and the ensuing more concrete inquiry into what appropriate choice, in that sphere, *is*. Aristotle does not always do this carefully, and the language he has to work with is often not helpful to him. We do not have much difficulty with terms like "moderation" and "justice" and even "courage," which seem vaguely normative but relatively empty, so far, of concrete moral content. As the approach requires, they can serve as extension-fixing labels under which many competing specifications may be investigated. But we have already noticed the problem with "mildness of temper," which seems to rule out by fiat a prominent contender for the appropriate disposition concerning anger. And much the same thing certainly seems to be true of the relativists' favorite target, *megalopsuchia,* which implies in its very name an attitude to one's own worth that is more Greek than universal. (For example, a Christian will feel that the proper attitude to one's own worth requires understanding one's lowness, frailty, and sinfulness. The virtue of humility requires considering oneself *small,* not great.) What we ought to get at this point in the inquiry is a word for the proper behavior toward anger and offense and a word for the proper behavior toward one's worth that are more truly neutral among the competing specifications, referring only to the sphere of experience within which we wish to determine what is appropriate. Then we could regard the competing conceptions as rival accounts of one and the same thing, so that, for example, Christian humility would be a rival specification of the same virtue whose Greek specification is given in Aristotle's account of *megalopsuchia,* namely, the proper way to behave toward the question of one's own worth.

And in fact, oddly enough, if one examines the evolution in the use of this word from Aristotle through the Stoics to the Christian fathers, one can see that this is more or less what happened, as "greatness of soul" became associated, first, with Stoic emphasis on the supremacy of virtue and the worthlessness of externals, including the body, and, through this, with the Christian denial of the body and of the worth of earthly life.[7] So even in this apparently unpromising case, history shows that the Aristotelian approach not only provided the materials for a single debate but actually succeeded in organizing such a debate, across enormous differences of both place and time.

Here, then, is a sketch for an objective human morality based upon the idea of virtuous action—that is, of appropriate functioning in each human sphere. The Aristotelian claim is that, further developed, it will retain virtue morality's immersed attention to actual human experiences, while gaining the ability to criticize local and traditional moralities in the name of a more inclusive account of the circumstances of human life, and of the needs for human functioning that these circumstances call forth.

## IV

The proposal will encounter many objections. The concluding sections of this paper will present three of the most serious and will sketch the lines along which the Aristotelian conception might proceed in formulating a reply. To a great extent these objections are not imagined or confronted by Aristotle himself, but his position seems capable of confronting them.

The first objection concerns the relationship between singleness of problem and singleness of solution. Let us grant for the moment that the Aristotelian approach has succeeded in coherently isolating and describing areas of human experience and choice that form, so to speak, the *terrain* of the virtues, and in giving thin definitions of each of the virtues as whatever it is that consists in choosing and responding well within that sphere. Let us suppose that the approach succeeds in doing this in a way that embraces many times and places, bringing disparate cultures together into a single debate about the good human being and the good human life. Different cultural accounts of good choice within the sphere in question in each case are now seen not as untranslatably different forms of life, but as competing answers to a single general question about a set of shared human experiences. Still, it might be argued, what has been achieved is, at best, a single discourse or debate about virtue. It has not been shown that this debate will have, as Aristotle believes, a single answer. Indeed, it has not even been shown that the discourse we have set up will have the form of a *debate* at all, rather than that of a plurality of culturally specific narratives, each giving the thick definition of a virtue that corresponds to the experience and traditions of a particular group. . . .

The Aristotelian proposal makes it possible to conceive of a way in which the virtues might be non-relative. It does not, by itself, answer the question of relativism.

The second objection goes deeper. For it questions the notion of spheres of shared human experience that lies at the heart of the Aristotelian approach. The approach, says this objector, seems to treat the experiences that ground the virtues as in some way primitive, given, and free from the cultural variation that we find in the plurality of normative conceptions of virtue. Ideas of proper courage may vary, but the fear of death is shared by all human beings. Ideas of moderation may vary, but the experiences of hunger, thirst, and sexual desire are (so the Aristotelian seems to claim) invariant. Normative conceptions introduce an element of cultural interpretation that is not present in the grounding experiences, which are, for that very reason, the Aristotelian's starting point.

But, the objector continues, such assumptions are naive. They will not stand up either to our best account of experience or to a close examination of the ways in which these so-called grounding experiences have in fact been differently constructed by different cultures. In general, first of all, our best accounts of the nature of experience, even perceptual experience, inform us that there is no such thing as an "innocent eye" that receives an uninterpreted "given." Even sense-perception is interpretive, heavily influenced by belief, teaching, language, and in general by social and contextual features. There is a very real sense in which members of different societies do not see the same sun and stars, encounter the same plants and animals, hear the same thunder.

. . . It is all the more plainly true, the objector claims, in the area of the human good. Here it is only a very naive and historically insensitive moral philosopher who would say that the experience of the fear of death or the experience of bodily appetites is a human constant. Recent anthropological work on the social construction of the emotions,[8] for example, has shown to what extent the experience of fear has learned and culturally variant elements. When we add that the object of the fear in which the Aristotelian takes an interest is death, which has been so variously interpreted and understood by human beings at

different times and in different places, the conclusion that the "grounding experience" is an irreducible plurality of experiences, highly various and in each case deeply infused with cultural interpretation, becomes even more inescapable.

Nor is the case different with the apparently less complicated experience of the bodily appetites. Most philosophers who have written about the appetites have treated hunger, thirst, and sexual desire as human universals, stemming from our shared animal nature. Aristotle himself was already more sophisticated, since he insisted that the object of appetite is "the apparent good" and that appetite is therefore something interpretive and selective, a kind of intentional awareness. But he does not seem to have reflected much about the ways in which historical and cultural differences could shape that awareness. The Hellenistic philosophers who immediately followed him did so reflect, arguing that the experience of sexual desire and of many forms of the desire for food and drink are, at least in part, social constructs, built up over time on the basis of a social teaching about value that is external to start with, but that enters so deeply into the perceptions of the individual that it actually forms and transforms the experience of desire. Let us take two Epicurean examples. People are taught that to be well fed they require luxurious fish and meat, that a simple vegetarian diet is not enough. Over time, the combination of teaching with habit produces an appetite for meat, shaping the individual's perceptions of the objects before him. Again, people are taught that what sexual relations are all about is a romantic union or fusion with an object who is seen as exalted in value, or even as perfect. Over time, this teaching shapes sexual behavior and the experience of desire, so that sexual arousal itself responds to this culturally learned scenario.

This work of social criticism has recently been carried further by Michel Foucault in his *History of Sexuality*.[9] This work has certain gaps as a history of Greek thought on this topic, but it does succeed in establishing that the Greeks saw the problem of the appetites and their management in an extremely different way from the way of twentieth-century Westerners. To summarize two salient conclusions of his complex argument, the Greeks did not single out the sexual appetite for special treatment; they treated it alongside hunger and thirst, as a drive that needed to be mastered and kept within bounds. Their central concern was with self-mastery, and they saw the appetites in the light of this concern. Furthermore, where the sexual appetite is concerned, they did not regard the gender of the partner as particularly important in assessing the moral value of the act. Nor did they identify or treat as morally salient a stable disposition to prefer partners of one sex rather than the other. Instead, they focused on the general issue of activity and passivity, connecting it in complex ways with the issue of self-mastery.

Work like Foucault's—and there is a lot of it in various areas, some of it very good—shows very convincingly that the experience of bodily desire, and of the body itself, has elements that vary with cultural and historical change. The names that people call their desires and themselves as subjects of desire, the fabric of belief and discourse into which they integrate their ideas of desiring, all this influences, it is clear, not only their reflection about desire, but also their experience of desire itself. Thus, for example, it is naive to treat our modern debates about homosexuality as continuations of the very same debate about sexual activity that went on in the Greek world. In a very real sense there was no "homosexual experience" in a culture that did not contain our emphasis on the gender of the object, our emphasis on the subjectivity of inclination and the permanence of appetitive disposition, our particular ways of problematizing certain forms of behavior.

If we suppose that we can get underneath this variety and this constructive power of social discourse in at least one case—namely, with the universal experience of bodily pain as a bad thing—even here we find subtle arguments against us. For the experience of pain seems to be embedded in a cultural discourse as surely as the closely related experiences of the appetites; and significant variations can be alleged here as well. The Stoics already made this claim against the Aristotelian virtues. In order to establish that bodily pain is not

bad by its very nature, but only by cultural tradition, the Stoics had to provide some explanation for the ubiquity of the belief that pain is bad and of the tendency to shun it. This explanation would have to show that the reaction was learned rather than natural, and to explain why, in the light of this fact, it is learned so widely. This they did by pointing to certain features in the very early treatment of infants. As soon as an infant is born, it cries. Adults, assuming that the crying is a response to its pain at the unaccustomed coldness and harshness of the place where it finds itself, hasten to comfort it. This behavior, often repeated, teaches the infant to regard its pain as a bad thing —or, better, teaches it the concept of pain, which includes the notion of badness, and teaches it the forms of life its society shares concerning pain. It is all social teaching, they claim, though this usually escapes our notice because of the early and non-linguistic nature of the teaching.

These and related arguments, the objector concludes, show that the Aristotelian idea that there is a single non-relative discourse about human experiences such as mortality or desire is a naive idea. There is no such bedrock of shared experience, and thus no single sphere of choice within which the virtue is the disposition to choose well. So the Aristotelian project cannot even get off the ground.

Now the Aristotelian confronts a third objector, who attacks from a rather different direction. Like the second, she charges that the Aristotelian has taken for a universal and necessary feature of human life an experience that is contingent on certain non-necessary historical conditions. Like the second, she argues that human experience is much more profoundly shaped by non-necessary social features than the Aristotelian has allowed. But her purpose is not simply, like second objector's, to point to the great variety of ways in which the "grounding experiences" corresponding to the virtues are actually understood and lived by human beings. It is more radical still. It is to point out that we could imagine a form of human life that does not contain these experiences—or some of them—at all, in any form. Thus the virtue that consists in acting well in that sphere need not be included in an account of the human good. In some cases, the experience may even be a sign of *bad* human life, and the corresponding virtue, therefore, no better than a form of non-ideal adaptation to a bad state of affairs. The really good human life, in such a case, would contain neither the grounding deficiency nor the remedial virtue.

This point is forcefully raised by some of Aristotle's own remarks about the virtue of generosity. One of his points against societies that eliminate private ownership is that they have thereby done away with the opportunity for generous action, which requires having possessions of one's own to give to others.[10] This sort of remark is tailor-made for the objector, who will immediately say that generosity, if it really rests upon the experience of private possession, is a dubious candidate indeed for inclusion in a purportedly non-relative account of the human virtues. If it rests upon a "grounding experience" that is non-necessary and is capable of being evaluated in different ways, and of being either included or eliminated in accordance with that evaluation, then it is not the universal the Aristotelian said it was.

Some objectors of the third kind will stop at this point, or use such observations to support the second objector's relativism. But in another prominent form this argument takes a non-relativist direction. It asks us to assess the "grounding experiences" against an account of human flourishing, produced in some independent manner. If we do so, the objector urges, we will discover that some of the experiences are remediable deficiencies. The objection to Aristotelian virtue ethics will then be that it limits our social aspirations, getting us to regard as permanent and necessary what we might in fact improve to the benefit of all human life. This is the direction in which the third objection to the virtues was pressed by Karl Marx, its most famous proponent.[11] According to Marx's argument, a number of the leading bourgeois virtues are responses to defective relations of production. Bourgeois justice, generosity, etc. presuppose conditions and structures that are non-ideal and that will be eliminated when communism is achieved. And it is not only the current *specification* of these virtues

that will be superceded with the removal of deficiency. It is the virtues themselves. It is in this sense that communism leads human beings beyond ethics.

Thus the Aristotelian is urged to inquire into the basic structures of human life with the daring of a radical political imagination. It is claimed that when she does so she will see that human life contains more possibilities than are dreamed of in her list of virtues.

## V

. . . At this point, however, we can make four observations to indicate how the Aristotelian might deal with some of the objector's concerns here. First, the Aristotelian position that I wish to defend need not insist, in every case, on a single answer to the request for a specification of a virtue. The answer might well turn out to be a disjunction. The process of comparative and critical debate will, I imagine, eliminate numerous contenders—for example, the view of justice that prevailed in Cyme. But what remains might well be a (probably small) plurality of acceptable accounts. These accounts may or may not be capable of being subsumed under a single account of greater generality. Success in the eliminative task will still be no trivial accomplishment. For example, if we should succeed in ruling out conceptions of the proper attitude to one's own human worth that are based on a notion of original sin, this would be moral work of enormous significance, even if we got no further than that in specifying the positive account.

Second, the general answer to a "What is X?" question in any sphere may well be susceptible of several or even of many concrete specifications, in connection with other local practices and local conditions. For example, the normative account where friendship and hospitality are concerned is likely to be extremely general, admitting of many concrete "fillings." Friends in England will have different customs, where regular social visiting is concerned, from friends in ancient Athens. And yet both sets of customs can count as further spec-ifications of a general account of friendship that mentions, for example, the Aristotelian criteria of mutual benefit and well-wishing, mutual enjoy-ment, mutual awareness, a shared conception of the good, and some form of "living together." Sometimes we may want to view such concrete accounts as optional alternative specifications, to be chosen by a society on the basis of reasons of ease and convenience. Sometimes, on the other hand, we may want to insist that this account gives the only legitimate specification of the virtue in question for that concrete context; in that case, the concrete account could be viewed as a part of a longer or fuller version of the single normative account. The decision between these two ways of regarding it will depend upon our assessment of its degree of nonarbitrariness for its context (both physical and historical), its relationship to other non-arbitrary features of the moral conception of that context, and so forth.

Third, whether we have one or several general accounts of a virtue, and whether this account or these accounts do or do not admit of more con-crete specifications relative to ongoing cultural contexts, the particular choices that the virtuous person, under this conception, makes will always be a matter of being keenly responsive to the local features of his or her concrete context. So in this respect, again, the instructions the Aristotelian gives to the person of virtue do not differ from one part of what a relativist would recommend. The Aristotelian virtues involve a delicate balancing between general rules and the keen awareness of particulars, in which process, as Aristotle stresses, the perception of the particular takes priority. It takes priority in the sense that a good rule is a good summary of wise particular choices and not a court of last resort. Like rules in medicine and in navigation, ethical rules should be held open to modification in the light of new circumstances; and the good agent must therefore cultivate the ability to perceive and correctly describe his or her situation finely and truly, including in this per-ceptual grasp even those features of the situation that are not covered under the existing rule. . . .

What I want to stress here is that Aristotelian particularism is fully compatible with Aristotelian objectivity. The fact that a good and virtuous deci-sion is context-sensitive does not imply that it is right only *relative to,* or *inside,* a limited context, any more than the fact that a good navigational judgment is sensitive to particular weather condi-tions shows that it is correct only in a local or rela-tional sense. It is right absolutely, objectively, from anywhere in the human world, to attend to the particular features of one's context; and the person who so attends and who chooses accordingly is making, according to Aristotle, the humanly cor-rect decision, period. If another situation ever should arise with all the same morally relevant features, including contextual features, the same decision would again be absolutely right.

Thus the virtue-based morality can capture a great deal of what the relativist is after and still lay claim to objectivity. In fact, we might say that the Aristotelian virtues do better than the relativist virtues in explaining what people are actually doing when they scrutinize the features of their context carefully, looking at both the shared and the non-shared features with an eye to what is best. For as Aristotle says, people who do this are usually searching for the good, not just for the way of their ancestors. They are prepared to defend their decisions as good or right, and to think of those who advocate a different course as disagree-ing about what is right, not just narrating a differ-ent tradition.

Finally, we should point out that the Aris-totelian virtues, and the deliberations they guide, unlike some systems of moral rules, remain al-ways open to revision in the light of new circum-stances and new evidence. In this way, again, they contain the flexibility to local conditions that the relativist would desire, but, again, without sacri-ficing objectivity. Sometimes the new circum-stances may simply give rise to a new concrete specification of the virtue as previously defined; in some cases it may cause us to change our view about what the virtue itself is. All general accounts are held provisionally, as summaries of correct decisions and as guides to new ones. This flexibility, built into the Aristotelian procedure, will again help the Aristotelian account to answer the questions of the relativist, without relativism.

## VI

We must now turn to the second objection. Here, I believe, is the really serious threat to the Aristotelian position. Past writers on virtue, including Aristotle himself, have lacked sensitivity to the ways in which different traditions of discourse, different conceptual schemes, articulate the world, and also to the profound connections between the structure of discourse and the structure of experience itself. Any contemporary defense of the Aristotelian position must display this sensitivity, responding somehow to the data that the relativist historian or anthropologist brings forward.

The Aristotelian should begin, it seems to me, by granting that with respect to any complex matter of deep human importance there is no "innocent eye"—no way of seeing the world that is entirely neutral and free of cultural shaping. . . .

Even where sense-perception is concerned, the human mind is an active and interpretive instrument and . . . its interpretations are a function of its history and its concepts, as well as of its innate structure. The Aristotelian should also grant, it seems to me, that the nature of human world-interpretations is holistic and that the criticism of them must, equally well, be holistic. Conceptual schemes, like languages, hang together as whole structures, and we should realize, too, that a change in any single element is likely to have implications for the system as a whole.

But these two facts do not imply, as some relativists in literary theory and in anthropology tend to assume, that all world interpretations are equally valid and altogether non-comparable, that there are no good standards of assessment and "anything goes." The rejection of the idea of ethical truth as correspondence to an altogether uninterpreted reality does not imply that the whole idea of searching for the truth is an old-fashioned

error. Certain ways in which people see the world can still be criticized exactly as Aristotle criticized them: as stupid, pernicious, and false. The standards used in such criticisms must come from inside human life. (Frequently they will come from the society in question itself, from its own rationalist and critical traditions.) And the inquirer must attempt, prior to criticism, to develop an inclusive understanding of the conceptual scheme being criticized, seeing what motivates each of its parts and how they hang together. But there is so far no reason to think that the critic will not be able to reject the institution of slavery or the homicide law of Cyme as out of line with the conception of virtue that emerges from reflection on the variety of different ways in which human cultures have had the experiences that ground the virtues.

The "grounding experiences" will not, the Aristotelian should concede, provide precisely a single language—neutral bedrock on which an account of virtue can be straightforwardly and unproblematically based. The description and assessment of the ways in which different cultures have constructed these experiences will become one of the central tasks of Aristotelian philosophical criticism. But the relativist has, so far, shown no reasons why we could not, at the end of the day, say that certain ways of conceptualizing death are more in keeping with the totality of our evidence and with the totality of our wishes for flourishing life than others; that certain ways of experiencing appetitive desire are for similar reasons more promising than others.

Relativists tend, furthermore, to understate the amount of attunement, recognition, and overlap that actually obtains across cultures, particularly in the areas of the grounding experiences. The Aristotelian in developing her conception in a culturally sensitive way, should insist, as Aristotle himself does, upon the evidence of such attunement and recognition. Despite the evident differences in the specific cultural shaping of the grounding experiences, we do recognize the experiences of people in other cultures as similar to our own. We do converse with them about matters of deep importance, understand them, allow ourselves to be moved by them. When we read Sophocles' *Antigone,* we see a good deal that seems strange to us; and we have not read the play well if we do not notice how far its conceptions of death, womanhood, and so on differ from our own. But it is still possible for us to be moved by the drama, to care about its people, to regard their debates as reflections upon virtue that speak to our own experience, and their choices as choices in spheres of conduct in which we too must choose. Again, when one sits down at a table with people from other parts of the world and debates with them concerning hunger or just distribution or in general the quality of human life, one does find, in spite of evident conceptual differences, that it is possible to proceed as if we are all talking about the same human problem; and it is usually only in a context in which one or more of the parties is intellectually committed to a theoretical relativist position that this discourse proves impossible to sustain. This sense of community and overlap seems to be especially strong in the areas that we have called the areas of the grounding experiences. And this, it seems, supports the Aristotelian claim that those experiences can be a good starting point for ethical debate.

Furthermore, it is necessary to stress that hardly any cultural group today is as focused upon its own internal traditions and as isolated from other cultures as the relativist argument presupposes. Cross-cultural communication and debate are ubiquitous facts of contemporary life. Our experience of cultural interaction indicates that in general the inhabitants of different conceptual schemes do tend to view their interaction in the Aristotelian and not the relativist way. A traditional society, confronted with new technologies and sciences, and the conceptions that go with them, does not, in fact, simply fail to understand them or regard them as totally alien incursions upon a hermetically sealed way of life. Instead, it assesses the new item as a possible contributor to flourishing life, making it comprehensible to itself and incorporating elements that promise to solve problems of flourishing. Examples of such assimilation, and the debate that surrounds it,[12] suggest that the par-

ties do, in fact, recognize common problems and that the traditional society is perfectly capable of viewing an external innovation as a device to solve a problem that it shares with the innovating society. The parties do, in fact, search for the good, not the way of their ancestors; only traditionalist anthropologists insist, nostalgically, on the absolute preservation of the ancestral.

And this is so even when cross-cultural discourse reveals a difference at the level of the conceptualization of the grounding experiences. Frequently the effect of work like Foucault's, which reminds us of the non-necessary and non-universal character of one's own ways of seeing in some such area, is precisely to prompt a critical debate in search of the human good. It is difficult, for example, to read Foucault's observations about the history of our sexual ideas without coming to feel that certain ways in which the Western contemporary debate on these matters has been organized, as a result of some combination of Christian morality with nineteenth-century pseudo-science, are especially silly, arbitrary, and limiting, inimical to a human search for flourishing. Foucault's moving account of Greek culture, as he himself insists in a preface,[13] provides not only a sign that someone once thought differently, but also evidence that it is possible for *us* to think differently. Foucault announced that the purpose of his book was to "free thought" so that it could think differently, imagining new and more fruitful possibilities. And close analysis of spheres of cultural discourse, which stresses cultural differences in the spheres of the grounding experiences, is being combined, increasingly, in current debates about sexuality and related matters, with the critique of existing social arrangements and attitudes, and with the elaboration of a new norm of human flourishing. There is no reason to think this combination incoherent.

As we pursue these possibilities, the basic spheres of experience identified in the Aristotelian approach will no longer, we have said, be seen as spheres of *uninterpreted* experience. But we have also insisted that there is much family relatedness and much overlap among societies. And certain areas of relatively greater universality can be specified here, on which we should insist as we proceed to areas that are more varied in their cultural expression. Not without a sensitive awareness that we are speaking of something that is experienced differently in different contexts, we can nonetheless identify certain features of our common humanity, closely related to Aristotle's original list, from which our debate might proceed.

1. *Mortality.* No matter how death is understood, all human beings face it and (after a certain age) know that they face it. This fact shapes every aspect of more or less every human life.

2. *The Body.* Prior to any concrete cultural shaping, we are born with human bodies, whose possibilities and vulnerabilities do not as such belong to one culture rather than any other. Any given human being might have belonged to any culture. The experience of the body is culturally influenced; but the body itself, prior to such experience, provides limits and parameters that ensure a great deal of overlap in what is going to be experienced, where hunger, thirst, desire, the five senses are concerned. It is all very well to point to the cultural component in these experiences. But when one spends time considering issues of hunger and scarcity, and in general of human misery, such differences appear relatively small and refined, and one cannot fail to acknowledge that "there are no known ethnic differences in human physiology with respect to metabolism of nutrients. Africans and Asians do not burn their dietary calories or use their dietary protein any differently from Europeans and Americans. It follows then that dietary requirements cannot vary widely as between different races."[14] This and similar facts should surely be focal points for debate about appropriate human behavior in this sphere. And by beginning with the body, rather than with the subjective experience of desire, we get, furthermore, an opportunity to criticize the situation of people who are so persistently deprived that their *desire* for good things has actually decreased. This is a further advantage of the Aristotelian approach, when contrasted with approaches to choice that stop with subjective expressions of preference.

3. *Pleasure and pain.* In every culture, there is a conception of pain; and these conceptions, which overlap very largely with one another, can be plausibly seen as grounded in universal and pre-cultural experience. The Stoic story of infant development is highly implausible; the negative response to bodily pain is surely primitive and universal, rather than learned and optional, however much its specific "grammar" may be shaped by later learning.

4. *Cognitive capability.* Aristotle's famous claim that "all human beings by nature reach out for understanding"[15] seems to stand up to the most refined anthropological analysis. It points to an element in our common humanity that is plausibly seen, again, as grounded independently of particular acculturation, however much it is later shaped by acculturation.

5. *Practical reason.* All human beings, whatever their culture, participate (or try to) in the planning and managing of their lives, asking and answering questions about how one should live and act. This capability expresses itself differently in different societies, but a being who altogether lacked it would not be likely to be acknowledged as a human being, in any culture.

6. *Early infant development.* Prior to the greatest part of specific cultural shaping, though perhaps not free from all shaping, are certain areas of human experiences and development that are broadly shared and of great importance for the Aristotelian virtues: experiences of desire, pleasure, loss, one's own finitude, perhaps also of envy, grief, gratitude. One may argue about the merits of one or another psychoanalytical account of infancy. But it seems difficult to deny that the work of Freud on infant desire and of Klein on grief, loss, and other more complex emotional attitudes has identified spheres of human experience that are to a large extent common to all humans, regardless of their particular society. All humans begin as hungry babies, perceiving their own helplessness, their alternating closeness to and distance from those on whom they depend, and so forth. Melanie Klein records a conversation with an anthropologist in which an event that at

first looked (to Western eyes) bizarre was interpreted by Klein as the expression of a universal pattern of mourning. The anthropologist accepted her interpretation.[16]

7. *Affiliation.* Aristotle's claim that human beings as such feel a sense of fellowship with other human beings, and that we are by nature social animals, is an empirical claim, but it seems to be a sound one. However varied our specific conceptions of friendship and love are, there is a great point in seeing them as overlapping expressions of the same family of shared human needs and desires.

8. *Humor.* There is nothing more culturally varied than humor, and yet, as Aristotle insists, some space for humor and play seems to be a need of any human life. The human being was not called the "laughing animal" for nothing; it is certainly one of our salient differences from almost all animals, and (in some form or other) a shared feature, I somewhat boldly assert, of any life that is going to be counted as fully human.

This is just a list of suggestions, closely related to Aristotle's list of common experiences. One could subtract some of these items and/or add others. But it seems plausible to claim that in all these areas we have a basis for further work on the human good. We do not have a bedrock of completely uninterpreted "given" data, but we do have nuclei of experience around which the constructions of different societies proceed. There is no Archimedean point here, and no pure access to unsullied "nature"—even, here, human nature—as it is in and of itself. There is just human life as it is lived. But in life as it is lived, we do find a family of experiences, clustering around certain foci, which can provide reasonable starting points for cross-cultural reflection.

# VII

The third objection raises, at bottom, a profound conceptual question: What is it to inquire about the *human* good? What circumstances of exis-

tence go to define what it is to live the life of a *human being,* and not some other life? Aristotle likes to point out that an inquiry into the human good cannot, on pain of incoherence, end up describing the good of some other being, say a god, a good, that on account of our circumstances, it is impossible for us to attain (cf. *NE* 1159a10–12, 1166a18–23). Which circumstances then? The virtues are defined relatively to certain problems and limitations, and also to certain endowments. Which ones are sufficiently central that their removal would make us into different beings, and open up a wholly new and different debate about the good? This question is itself part of the ethical debate we propose. For there is no way to answer it but ask ourselves which elements of our experience seem to us so important that they count, for us, as part of who we are. I discuss Aristotle's attitude to this question elsewhere, and I shall simply summarize here.[17] It seems clear, first of all, that our mortality is an essential feature of our circumstances as human beings. An immortal being would have such a different form of life, and such different values and virtues, that it does not seem to make sense to regard that being as part of the same search for good. Essential, too, will be our dependence upon the world outside of us: some sort of need for food, drink, the help of others. On the side of abilities, we would want to include cognitive functioning and the activity of practical reasoning as elements of any life that we would regard as human. Aristotle argues, plausibly, that we would want to include sociability as well, some sensitivity to the needs of and pleasure in the company of other beings similar to ourselves.

But it seems to me that the Marxian question remains, as a deep question about human forms of life and the search for the human good. For one certainly can imagine forms of human life that do not contain the holding of private property—and, therefore, not those virtues that have to do with its proper management. And this means that it remains an open question whether these virtues ought to be regarded as virtues, and kept upon our list. Marx wished to go much further, arguing that communism would remove the need for justice, courage, and most of the bourgeois virtues. I think we might be skeptical here. Aristotle's general attitude to such transformations of life is to suggest that they usually have a tragic dimension. If we remove one sort of problem—say, by removing private property—we frequently do so by introducing another—say, the absence of a certain sort of freedom of choice, the freedom that makes it possible to do fine and generous actions for others. If things are complex even in the case of generosity, where we can rather easily imagine the transformation that removes the virtue, they are surely far more so in the cases of justice and courage. And we would need a far more detailed description than Marx ever gives us of the form of life under communism, before we would be able even to begin to see whether this form of life has in fact transformed things where these virtues are concerned, and whether it has or has not introduced new problems and limitations in their place.

In general it seems that all forms of life, including the imagined life of a god, contain boundaries and limits. All structures, even that of putative limitlessness, are closed to something, cut off from something—say, in that case, from the specific value and beauty inherent in the struggle against limitation. Thus it does not appear that we will so easily get beyond the virtues. Nor does it seem to be so clearly a good thing for human life that we should.

# VIII

The best conclusion to this sketch of an Aristotelian program for virtue ethics was written by Aristotle himself, at the end of his discussion of human nature in *Nicomachean Ethics* I:

So much for our outline sketch for the good. For it looks as if we have to draw an outline first, and fill it in later. It would seem to be open to anyone to take things further and to articulate the good parts of the sketch. And time is a good discoverer or ally in such things.

That's how the sciences have progressed as well: it is open to anyone to supply what is lacking. (*NE* 1098a20–26)[18]

# Notes

1. See, for example, Williams, *Ethics and the Limits*, 34–36; Stuart Hampshire, *Morality and Conflict* (Cambridge, Mass., 1983), 150 ff.

2. For "nameless" virtues and vices, see *NE* 1107b1–2, 1107b8, 1107b30–31, 1108a17, 1119a10–11, 1126b20, 1127a12, 1127a14; for recognition of the unsatisfactoriness of names given, see 1107b8, 1108a5–6, 1108a20a ff. The two categories are largely overlapping, on account of the general principle enunciated at 1108a16–19, that where there is no name a name should be given, unsatisfactory or not.

3. It should be noted that this emphasis on spheres of experience is not present in the *Eudemian Ethics*, which begins with a list of virtues and vices. This seems to me a sign that that treatise expresses a more primitive stage of Aristotle's thought on the virtues—whether earlier or not.

4. For statements with *peri,* connecting virtues with spheres of life, see 1115a6–7, 1117a29–30, 1117b25, 27, 1119b23, 1122a19, 1122b34, 1125b26, 1126b13; and NE 2.7 throughout. See also the related usages at 1126b11, 1127b32.

5. My list here inserts justice in a place of prominence. (In the *NE* it is treated separately, after all the other virtues, and the introductory list defers it for that later examination.) I have also added at the end of the list categories corresponding to the various intellectual virtues discussed in *NE* 6, and also to *phronesis* or practical wisdom, discussed in 6 as well. Otherwise the order and wording of my list closely follows 2.7, which gives the program for the more detailed analyses of 3.5–4.

6. See 1108a5, where Aristotle says that the virtues and the corresponding person are "pretty much nameless," and says "Let us call . . ." when he introduces the names. See also 1125b29, 1126a3–4.

7. See John Procope, *Magnanimity* (1987); also R.-A. Gauthier, *Magnanimité* (Paris, 1951).

8. See, for example, *The Social Construction of the Emotions,* edited by Rom Harré (Oxford, 1986).

9. M. Foucault, *Histoire de la sexualité,* vols. 2 and 3 (Paris, 1984).

10. *Politics* 1263b11 ff.

11. For a discussion of the relevant passages, see S. Lukes, *Marxism and Morality* (Oxford, 1987). For an acute discussion of these issues I am indebted to an exchange between Alan Ryan and Stephen Lukes at the Oxford Philosophical Society, March 1987.

12. C. Abeysekera, paper presented at Value and Technology Conference, WIDER 1986.

13. Foucault, *Histoire,* vol. 2, preface.

14. C. Gopalan, "Undernutrition: Measurement and Implications," paper prepared for the WIDER Conference on Poverty, Undernutrition, and Living Standards, Helsinki, 27–31 July 1987, and forthcoming in the volume of Proceedings, edited by S. Osmani.

15. *Metaphysics* 1.1.

16. M. Klein, in Postscript to "Our Adult World and its Roots in Infancy," in *Envy, Gratitude and Other Works 1946–1963* (London, 1984), 247–63.

17. "Aristotle on Human Nature and the Foundations of Ethics," forthcoming in a volume of essays on the work of Bernard Williams, edited by R. Harrison and J. Altham (Cambridge). This paper will be a WIDER Working Paper.

18. This paper was motivated by questions discussed at the WIDER conference on Value and Technology, summer 1986, Helsinki. I would like to thank Steve and Frédérique Marglin for provoking some of these arguments, with hardly any of which they will agree. I also thank Dan Brock for his helpful comments, and Amartya Sen for many discussions of these issues.

# 4   The Subjectivity of Values

## J. L. MACKIE

## The Argument from Relativity

The argument from relativity has as its premiss the well-known variation in moral codes from one society to another and from one period to another, and also the differences in moral beliefs between different groups and classes within a complex community. Such variation is in itself merely a truth of descriptive morality, a fact of anthropology which entails neither first order nor second order ethical views. Yet it may indirectly support second order subjectivism: radical differences between first order moral judgements make it difficult to treat those judgements as apprehensions of objective truths. But it is not the mere occurrence of disagreements that tells against the objectivity of values. Disagreement on questions in history or biology or cosmology does not show that there are no objective issues in these fields for investigators to disagree about. But such scientific disagreement results from speculative inferences or explanatory hypotheses based on inadequate evidence, and it is hardly plausible to interpret moral disagreement in the same way. Disagree-

ment about moral codes seems to reflect people's adherence to and participation in different ways of life. The causal connection seems to be mainly that way round: it is that people approve of monogamy because they participate in a monogamous way of life rather than that they participate in a monogamous way of life because they approve of monogamy. Of course, the standards may be an idealization of the way of life from which they arise: the monogamy in which people participate may be less complete, less rigid, than that of which it leads them to approve. This is not to say that moral judgements are purely conventional. Of course there have been and are moral heretics and moral reformers, people who have turned against the established rules and practices of their own communities for moral reasons, and often for moral reasons that we would endorse. But this can usually be understood as the extension, in ways which, though new and unconventional, seemed to them to be required for consistency, of rules to which they already adhered as arising out of an existing way of life. In short, the argument from relativity has some force simply because the actual variations in the moral codes are more readily explained by the hypothesis that they reflect ways of life than by the hypothesis that they express perceptions, most of

Reprinted with permission of the publisher from *Ethics: Inventing Right and Wrong* (Penguin, 1977), 36–39, 41–42, with omissions.

them seriously inadequate and badly distorted, of objective values.

But there is a well-known counter to this argument from relativity, namely to say that the items for which objective validity is in the first place to be claimed are not specific moral rules or codes but very general basic principles which are recognized at least implicitly to some extent in all society—such principles as provide the foundations of what Sidgwick has called different methods of ethics: the principle of universalizability, perhaps, or the rule that one ought to conform to the specific rules of any way of life in which one takes part, from which one profits, and on which one relies, or some utilitarian principle of doing what tends, or seems likely, to promote the general happiness. It is easy to show that such general principles, married with differing concrete circumstances, different existing social patterns or different preferences, will beget different specific moral rules; and there is some plausibility in the claim that the specific rules thus generated will vary from community to community or from group to group in close agreement with the actual variations in accepted codes.

The argument from relativity can be only partly countered in this way. To take this line the moral objectivist has to say that it is only in these principles that the objective moral character attaches immediately to its descriptively specified ground or subject: other moral judgements are objectively valid or true, but only derivatively and contingently—if things had been otherwise, quite different sorts of actions would have been right. And despite the prominence in recent philosophical ethics of universalization, utilitarian principles, and the like, these are very far from constituting the whole of what is actually affirmed as basic in ordinary moral thought. Much of this is concerned rather with what Hare calls "ideals" or, less kindly, "fanaticism." That is, people judge that some things are good or right, and others are bad or wrong, not because—or at any rate not only because—they exemplify some general principle for which widespread implicit acceptance could be claimed, but because something about those things arouses certain responses immediately in them, though they would arouse radically and irresolvably different responses in others. "Moral sense" or "intuition" is an initially more plausible description of what supplies many of our basic moral judgements than "reason." With regard to all these starting points of moral thinking the argument from relativity remains in full force.

## The Argument from Queerness

Even more important, however, and certainly more generally applicable, is the argument from queerness. This has two parts, one metaphysical, the other epistemological. If there were objective values, then they would be entities or qualities or relations of a very strange sort, utterly different from anything else in the universe. Correspondingly, if we were aware of them, it would have to be by some special faculty of moral perception or intuition, utterly different from our ordinary ways of knowing everything else. These points were recognized by Moore when he spoke of nonnatural qualities, and by the intuitionists in their talk about a "faculty of moral intuition." Intuitionism has long been out of favour, and it is indeed easy to point out its implausibilities. What is not so often stressed, but is more important, is that the central thesis of intuitionism is one to which any objectivist view of values is in the end committed: intuitionism merely makes unpalatably plain what other forms of objectivism wrap up. Of course the suggestion that moral judgements are made or moral problems solved by just sitting down and having an ethical intuition is a travesty of actual moral thinking. But, however complex the real process, it will require (if it is to yield authoritatively prescriptive conclusions) some input of this distinctive sort, either premises or forms of argument or both. When we ask the awkward question, how we can be aware of this authoritative prescriptivity, of the truth of these distinctively ethical premises or of the cogency of this distinctively ethical pattern of reasoning, none of our ordinary accounts of sensory perception or intro-spection or the framing and confirming of ex-planatory hypotheses or inference or logical construction or conceptual analysis, or any com-bination of these, will provide a satisfactory answer; "a special sort of intuition" is a lame answer, but it is the one to which the clearheaded objectivist is compelled to resort.

Indeed, the best move for the moral objectivist is not to evade this issue, but to look for compan-ions in guilt. For example, Richard Price argues that it is not moral knowledge alone that such an empiricism as those of Locke and Hume is unable to account for, but also our knowledge and even our ideas of essence, number, identity, diversity, solidity, inertia, substance, the necessary exis-tence and infinite extension of time and space, necessity and possibility in general, power, and causation. If the understanding, which Price defines as the faculty within us that discerns truth, is also a source of new simple ideas of so many other sorts, may it not also be a power of immedi-ately perceiving right and wrong, which yet are real characters of actions?

This is an important counter to the argument from queerness. The only adequate reply to it would be to show how, on empiricist foundations, we can construct an account of the ideas and beliefs and knowledge that we have of all these matters. I cannot even begin to do that here, though I have undertaken some parts of the task elsewhere. I can only state my belief that satisfac-tory accounts of most of these can be given in empirical terms. If some supposed metaphysical necessities or essences resist such treatment, then they too should be included, along with objective values, among the targets of the argument from queerness. . . .

Another way of bringing out this queerness is to ask, about anything that is supposed to have some objective moral quality, how this is linked with its natural features. What is the connection between the natural fact that an action is a piece of deliberate cruelty—say, causing pain just for fun—and the moral fact that it is wrong? It cannot be an entailment, a logical or semantic necessity. Yet it is not merely that the two features occur

together. The wrongness must somehow be "con-sequential" or "supervenient"; it is wrong because it is a piece of deliberate cruelty. But just what *in the world* is signified by this "because"? And how do we know the relation that it signifies, if this is something more than such actions being socially condemned, and condemned by us too, perhaps through our having absorbed attitudes from our social environment? It is not even sufficient to postulate a faculty which "sees" the wrongness: something must be postulated which can see at once the natural features that constitute the cru-elty, and the wrongness, and the mysterious con-sequential link between the two. Alternatively, the intuition required might be the perception that wrongness is a higher order property belonging to certain natural properties; but what is this belong-ing of properties to other properties, and how can we discern it? How much simpler and more com-prehensible the situation would be if we could replace the moral quality with some sort of sub-jective response which could be causally related to the detection of the natural features on which the supposed quality is said to be consequential.

It may be thought that the argument from queerness is given an unfair start if we thus relate it to what are admittedly among the wilder prod-ucts of philosophical fancy—Platonic Forms, non-natural qualities, self-evident relations of fitness, faculties of intuition, and the like. Is it equally forceful if applied to the terms in which everyday moral judgments are more likely to be expressed —though still, with a claim to objectivity—"you must do this," "you can't do that," "obligation," "unjust," "rotten," "disgraceful," "mean," or talk about good reasons for or against possible actions? Admittedly not; but that is because the objective prescriptivity, the element a claim for whose authoritativeness is embedded in ordinary moral thought and language, is not yet isolated in these forms of speech, but is presented along with relations to desires and feelings, reasoning about the means to desired ends, interpersonal de-mands, the injustice which consists in the viola-tion of what are in the context the accepted standards of merit, the psychological constituents of meanness, and so on. There is nothing queer about any of these, and under cover of them the claim for moral authority may pass unnoticed. But if I am right in arguing that it is ordinarily there, and is therefore very likely to be incorporated almost automatically in philosophical accounts of

ethics which systematize our ordinary thought even in such apparently innocent terms as these, it needs to be examined, and for this purpose it needs to be isolated and exposed as it is by the less cautious philosophical reconstructions.

# 5   Moral Realism and the Skeptical Arguments from Disagreement and Queerness

## DAVID BRINK

## The Argument from Disagreement

Mackie claims that the best explanation of inter- and intra-societal ethical disagreement is that there simply are no moral facts, only differences of attitude, commitment, or decision. (*E:* pp. 36–7)[1] Of course, disagreement does not entail scepticism. Mackie recognises that we do not infer from the fact that there are disagreements in the natural sciences that the natural sciences are not objective disciplines. Nor do we make what might appear to be the more modest inference from the fact that there is a specific dispute in some subject that there is no fact of the matter on the particular issue in question. For example, no one concluded from the apparently quite deep disagreement among astronomers a short while ago about the existence of black holes that there was no fact of the matter concerning the existence of black holes. Mackie's claim is that disagreement in ethics is somehow more fundamental than disagreement in other disciplines. In particular, realism about a discipline requires that its disputes be resolvable at least in principle, and, while most scientific disputes do seem resolvable, many moral disputes do not.

Mackie imagines the moral realist replying that moral disputes are resolvable, because deep moral disagreements are not really cases of disagreement. Rather, they are cases in which "dis-

putants" apply antecedently shared moral principles under different empirical conditions. (*E:* p. 37) The resulting moral judgments are about different action types, so the "disagreements" in question are really only apparent.

Mackie issues two rejoinders to this realist reply. His first rejoinder is that this realist response commits the realist to (a) claiming that necessity can only attach to general moral principles and (b) accepting the following counterfactual: ". . . if things had been otherwise, quire different sorts of actions would have been right." (*E:* p. 37) (a) and (b), Mackie claims, imply that many action types will be right or wrong only contingently.

Although this rejoinder does raise some interesting questions about the modal status of moral facts, it in no way threatens moral realism. First, certainly some moral facts are contingent, and, even if this realist reply requires the contingency of some moral facts, this shows nothing about how many moral facts the realist must regard as contingent. But, secondly and more importantly, Mackie's modal issue is a red herring. The truth of moral realism turns on the existence of moral facts, not their modal status.

Mackie's second rejoinder to the realist reply is simply that some moral disputes are real disputes. Not all putative moral disagreements can be explained away as the application of antecedently shared moral principles in different circumstances. (*E:* p. 38)

Mackie is right that many moral disputes are genuine, and, if the realist had no account of these

Reprinted by permission of the author and publisher from *Australasian Journal of Philosophy*, 62 (1984), 111–125, with omissions.

disputes, Mackie would have a strong argument against moral realism. But the realist can account for moral disputes.

As we have seen, not every apparent moral disagreement is a genuine dispute. But the realist need not maintain even that all genuine moral disputes are resolvable. He can maintain that some moral disputes have no uniquely correct answers. Moral ties are possible, and considerations, each of which is objectively valuable, may be incommensurable. So the moral realist need only maintain that most genuine moral disputes are resolvable.

Indeed, the realist can plausibly maintain that most genuine moral disputes are in principle resolvable. Mackie's discussion of the realist's reply shows that Mackie thinks moral disagreement is resolvable if and only if *antecedent* agreement on general moral principles obtains. This claim presupposes a one-way view of moral justification and argument according to which moral principles justify particular moral judgments but not vice versa. However, this view of moral justification is defective. As Goodman, Rawls, and other coherentists have argued, justification proceeds both from general principles to particular cases and from particular cases to general principles. Just as agreement about general moral principles may be exploited to resolve disagreement about particular moral cases, so agreement about particular moral cases may be exploited to resolve disagreement about general moral principles. Ideally, trade-offs among the various levels of generality of belief will be made in such a way as to maximise initial commitment, overall consistency, explanatory power, etc. A coherentist model of moral reasoning of this sort makes it much less plausible that disagreements over moral principles are in principle unresolvable.

Moreover, a great many moral disagreements depend upon disagreements over the non-moral facts. First, many disagreements over the non-moral facts result from culpable forms of ignorance of fact. Often, for moral or non-moral reasons, at least one disputant culpably fails to assess the non-moral facts correctly by being insufficiently imaginative in weighing the consequences for the relevant people of alternative actions or policies. This sort of error is especially important in moral disputes, since thought experiments (as opposed to actual tests) play such an important part in the assessment of moral theories. Thought experiments play a larger role in moral methodology than they do in scientific methodology, at least partly because it is often (correctly) regarded as immoral to assess moral theories by realising the relevant counterfactuals.

Secondly, many moral disagreements result from reasonable but nonetheless resolvable disagreements over the non-moral facts. The correct answers to moot moral questions often turn on certain non-moral facts about which reasonable disagreement is possible and which may in fact be known by no one. Correct answers to moral questions can turn at least in part upon correct answers to non-moral questions such as "What (re)distribution of a certain class of goods would make the worst-off representative person in a particular society best-off?" "Would public ownership of the means of production in the United States lead to an increase or decrease in the average standard of living?" "What is the correct theory of human personality?" and "What kind of life would my severely mentally retarded child lead (if I brought the pregnancy to term and raised the child), and how would caring for him affect my family and me?" However difficult and controversial these questions are, the issues which they raise are in principle resolvable. Moral disputes commonly do turn on disagreement over issues such as these, and, insofar as they do, moral disputes are clearly resolvable in principle.

Mackie argues that if moral realism were true, all moral disputes should be resolvable, and since many seem irresolvable, he concludes that moral realism is false. But the moral realist need only claim that *most genuine* moral disputes are in *principle* resolvable. Not all apparent moral disagreements are genuine, because some apparent moral disputes merely reflect the application of antecedently shared moral principles under different circumstances. Not every genuine moral dispute need be even in principle resolvable, since moral ties are possible and some objective moral values may be incommensurable. Of those genuine moral disputes which the realist is committed to treating as in principle resolvable, some depend upon antecedent disagreement over moral principles, while others depend upon disagreement over the non-moral facts. The realist can claim that antecedent disagreement over moral principles is in principle resolvable by coherence arguments and that disagreement over the non-moral facts is always in principle resolvable. The moral realist gives a plausible enough account of moral disagreement for us to say that Mackie has not shouldered the burden of proof for his claim that the falsity of moral realism is the best explanation of the nature of moral disagreement.

## The Argument from Queerness

. . . There are two limbs to the argument from queerness: one metaphysical, one epistemological. (*E:* p. 38) I turn to the metaphysical branch of the argument first. Mackie thinks that moral realism is a metaphysically queer doctrine, because he believes that moral facts or properties would have to be ontologically simple or independent. (*E:* p. 38) The assumption is that moral properties would have to be *sui generis,* that is, ontologically independent of natural properties with which we are familiar. Although it is not inconceivable that there should be *sui generis* moral properties, we have very good *a posteriori* evidence for the truth of materialism and for the falsity of ontological pluralism.

However, Mackie's crucial assumption that moral facts and properties would have to be *sui generis* is false; moral realism does not require ontological pluralism. The moral realist has at least two options on the assumption that materialism is true: he can claim that moral properties are identical with certain physical properties, or he can claim that moral properties supervene upon certain physical properties. Because moral properties and their instances could be realised in non-physical as well as a variety of physical ways, neither moral properties nor their instances should be identified with physical properties or their instances. For this reason, it is best for the moral

realist to claim that moral properties supervene upon physical properties.

Mackie recognises the realist's claim about the supervenience of moral facts and properties on physical facts and properties but claims that the alleged supervenient relation is also metaphysically queer:

> Another way of bringing out this queerness is to ask about anything that is supposed to have some objective moral quality, how this is linked with its natural features. What is the connection between the natural fact that an action is a case of deliberate cruelty—say, causing pain just for fun—and the moral fact that it is wrong? It cannot be an entailment, a logical or semantic necessity. Yet it is not merely that the two features occur together. The wrongness must somehow be "consequential" or "supervenient"; it is wrong because it is a piece of deliberate cruelty. But just what *in the world* is signified by this "because"? (*E:* p. 41)

Although I do not think that Mackie has really motivated a metaphysical worry about moral supervenience, I shall defend moral realism against the charge of metaphysical queerness by adopting the strategy which Mackie mentions of finding partners in guilt—although once it is clear what sort of company the realist is keeping it would only be perverse to regard them as partners in *guilt.* I shall argue that the supervenient relation which the realist claims obtains between moral properties and natural or physical properties is neither uncommon nor mysterious.

Although it is an interesting question what the precise relation is between property identity and supervenience, it is fairly clear that one property can supervene upon another without those two properties being identical. A supervenient relation obtains between two properties or sets of properties just in case the one property or set of properties is causally realised by the other property or set of properties; the former property or set of properties is the supervening property or set of properties, and the latter property or set of properties is the base property or set of properties. Supervenience implies that no change can occur in the supervening property without a change occurring in the base property, but it also asserts a claim of ontological dependence. Assuming, as Mackie does, that materialism is true, all properties ultimately supervene on material or physical base properties. Physical properties are basic then in the sense that all other properties are nothing over and above physical properties. Biological, social, psychological, and moral properties are all realised physically; they are simply different *kinds* of combinations and arrangements of matter which hang together explanatorily.

Supervenience is a relation of causal constitution or dependence. There is nothing strange and certainly nothing unique about the supervenience of moral properties on physical properties. Assuming materialism is true, mental states supervene on physical states, yet few think that mental states are metaphysically queer (and those that do do not think that supervenience makes them queer). Social facts such as unemployment, inflation, and exploitation supervene upon physical facts, yet no one supposes that social facts are metaphysically queer. Biological states such as being an organism supervene on physical states, yet no one supposes that organisms are queer entities. Macroscopic material objects such as tables supervene on microscopic physical particles, yet no one supposes that tables are queer entities. In short, it is difficult to see how the realist's use of supervenience in explaining the relationship between moral and physical properties makes his position queer. Moral properties are not ontologically simple or independent; but then neither are mental states, social facts, biological states, or macroscopic material objects. It is unlikely that moral properties are identical with physical properties; moral properties could have been realised non-materially. But there is every reason to believe that in the actual world moral properties, like other natural properties, are realised materially.

This realist account of supervenience discharges any explanatory obligation which the argument from metaphysical queerness imposes. The details of the way in which moral properties supervene upon other natural properties are worked out differently by different moral theories. Determination of which account of moral supervenience is best will depend upon determination of which moral theory provides the best account

of all our beliefs, both moral and non-moral. Although I obviously cannot do here what is needed to defend a particular account of moral supervenience, I will now offer a *model* specification of the moral realist's metaphysical claims.

When trying to determine the way in which moral properties supervene upon other natural properties, one might start by looking at plausible theories about other kinds of properties. Functional theories provide plausible accounts of a wide variety of kinds of properties; the nature of biological, psychological, social, and economic properties is profitably viewed in functional terms. Consider functionalist theories of mind as an example. Although functionalism is not without its critics, it is fair to say that there are no rival *theories* in the philosophy of mind today. What is essential to any particular mental state type, according to functionalism, is the causal role which that mental state plays in the activities which are characteristic of the organism as a whole. Mental states are identified and distinguished from other mental states in terms of the causal relations which they bear to sensory inputs, behavioural outputs, and other mental states. To take a hoary example, functionalist theories of mind claim that pain is identified and distinguished from other mental states by virtue of its tendency to result from tissue damage, to produce an injury-avoidance desire, and to issue in the appropriate injury-avoidance behaviour. The physical states which realise this functional state are the physical states upon which pain supervenes.

Similarly, the moral realist might claim that moral properties are functional properties. He might claim that what is essential to moral properties is the causal role which they play in the characteristic activities of human organisms. In particular, the realist might claim that moral properties are those which bear upon the maintenance and flourishing of human organisms. Maintenance and flourishing presumably consist in necessary conditions for survival, other needs associated with basic well-being, wants of various sorts, and distinctively human capacities. People, actions, policies, states of affairs, etc. will bear good-making moral properties just insofar as they contribute to the satisfaction of these needs, wants, and capacities. People, actions, policies, states of affairs, etc. will bear bad-making moral properties just insofar as they fail to promote or interfere with the satisfaction of these needs, wants, and capacities. The physical states which contribute to or interfere with the satisfaction of these needs, wants, and capacities are the physical states upon which, on this functionalist theory, moral properties ultimately supervene.

Although I cannot and do not need to defend here this functionalist model, it is worth pointing out how this model addresses two issues of concern to Mackie, namely, the justifiability and the decidability of moral disputes. . . . If this functionalist account of moral value which I have proposed as a realist model is plausible, then there is reason to think that moral facts will at least typically provide agents with reasons for action. Everyone has reason to promote his own well-being, and everyone has reason to promote the well-being of others at least to the extent that his own well-being is tied up with theirs. Presumably, any plausible theory of human needs, wants, and capacities will show that the satisfaction of these desiderata for any given individual will depend to a large extent on the well-being of others. People have needs and desires for friendship and love and for the benefits of cooperative activity; they also have capacities for sympathy, benevolence, and social intercourse. In order to satisfy these social needs, desires, and capacities, agents must develop and maintain stable social dispositions, and this means that they will often have reason to benefit others even when they do not otherwise benefit by their action. So, although there may be cases in which maintaining or promoting human well-being involves no benefit to the agent, there is good reason to suppose that human well-being and agent well-being will by and large coincide. As this functionalist theory of value illustrates, externalism allows a strong justification of morality.

This functionalist theory of moral value also helps to explain the nature of moral disagreement. Common sense and attention to the argument from disagreement tell us that moral disputes can be extremely difficult to resolve. This functionalist specification of moral realism explains why many

moral disputes which are in principle resolvable are nonetheless so difficult to resolve even under favourable conditions. Because facts about human well-being and flourishing depend at least in part upon facts in such complex and controversial empirical disciplines as economics, social theory, and psychology, even disputants who share something like the functionalist theory of value and are well informed will often disagree about what morality requires.

In addition to the metaphysical complaint about "what in the world" a supervenient relation is, Mackie lodges an epistemological complaint about how we could know when the appropriate supervenient relation obtains. (*E:* p. 41) We may know that certain natural facts or facts under a non-moral description obtain, but how do we know or go about finding out whether these physical facts realise any moral facts and, if so, which? Mackie claims that we could gain this kind of moral knowledge only if we had special faculties for the perception of moral facts of the sort ethical intuitionism ensures. But, Mackie argues, although moral intuitionism could have been true, there are good *a posteriori* grounds for believing that no such faculties exist. Therefore, barring the cognitive inaccessibility of moral facts, moral realism must be false. (*E:* pp. 38–9)

The epistemological belief that moral realism is committed to intuitionism rests at least in Mackie's case on the mistaken metaphysical assumption that moral values would have to be ontologically *sui generis*. If and only if moral facts were queer kinds of entities would we need some special faculty for cognitive access to them. But the realist denies that moral facts are *sui generis*; moral facts supervene on natural facts. One goes about discovering which natural facts moral facts supervene on by appeal to moral theories. (Of course, appeal to a particular moral theory is justified only if that theory coheres well with other moral and non-moral beliefs we hold.) For example, if the functionalist account of moral value sketched above can be defended, then we do know how to set about ascertaining which if any moral facts supervene on a particular set of natural facts. We ascertain whether the natural facts in question contribute to, interfere with, or are neutral with respect to the maintenance and promotion of human well-being. Granted, in many cases this will be no easy task, since completion of the task will depend in part upon answers to controversial empirical questions in such fields as economics, social theory, and psychology. But all this shows is that moral knowledge is sometimes hard to come by, not that it is queer or mysterious.

Mackie might complain that both acceptance and application of moral theories must be guided by other moral commitments. Not only does acceptance of the functionalist theory of value depend upon its coherence with, among other things, other moral beliefs, but also the findings of such disciplines as economics, sociology, and psychology cannot fully determine the extension of "human well-being and flourishing." Even if the special sciences can tell us something about human needs, wants, and capacities, and the effective ways of realising them, these sciences cannot rank these components of the good or adjudicate conflicts among them. Some irreducibly normative questions must be answered in determining what constitutes human well-being and flourishing.

But if the fact that some or all of our moral judgments are theory-dependent in this way is supposed to present a genuine epistemological problem for the moral realist which is not simply the result of applying general sceptical considerations to the case of morality, Mackie must claim that theory-dependence is a feature peculiar to moral methodology. Is this claim at all plausible?

Here, as before, the moral realist can find quite respectable partners in "guilt." It is a commonplace in the philosophy of science that scientific methodology is profoundly theory-dependent. Assessments of theoretical simplicity and theory confirmation as well as standards of experimental design and instrument improvement require appeal to the best available background theories in the relevant disciplines. For example, in theory confirmation there is an ineliminable comparative component. Theories count as well confirmed only if they have been tested against relevant rivals, and determination of which alternative theories are relevant or worth considering requires

appeal to background bodies of accepted theory. Acceptance of normal scientific observations and judgments, as well as application of general methodological principle, is also theory-laden. For example, judgments about the acidity or alkalinity of a substance which are based on the results of litmus paper tests presuppose belief in the normality of the test conditions and acceptance of the relevant chemical theories explaining how litmus paper detects pH and how pH reflects acidity and alkalinity.

The fact that scientific method is heavily theory-dependent shows that science and ethics are on a par in being theory-dependent. Thus, the fact that moral commitments must be appealed to in the acceptance and application of moral theories poses *no special* epistemological problem for moral realism. Of course, although most of us do not draw non-realist conclusions from the theory-dependence of scientific method, one may wonder how the profoundly theory-dependent methodologies in science and ethics can be *discovery* procedures. The answer is that theory-dependent methodologies are discovery procedures just in case a sufficient number of background theories in the disciplines in question are approximately true. And I have been arguing that Mackie has provided no good reason for doubting that some of our moral background theories are approximately true.

Mackie might respond that the moral and scientific cases are not in fact on a par and that there is reason to doubt the approximate truth of our moral theories, because while there is a good deal of consensus about the truth of the scientific theories appealed to, say, in the making of pH judgments, there is a notable lack of consensus about which moral theories to appeal to in making moral judgments. There are at least three reasons, however, for dismissing this response. First, this response probably overstates both the degree of consensus about which scientific theories are correct and the degree of disagreement about which moral theories are correct. Secondly, the response probably also overstates the amount of antecedent agreement necessary to reach eventual moral agreement. Finally, this response just raises from a different perspective the argument from disagreement, and we saw that the moral realist has a plausible account of moral disputes.

These considerations show that moral realism is committed to nothing metaphysically or epistemologically queer. The realist holds that moral facts supervene upon other natural facts and that moral knowledge is acquired in the same theory-dependent way that other knowledge is. Moral realism is plausible enough both metaphysically and epistemologically to allow us to say that Mackie has again failed to shoulder the burden of proof.[2]

## Notes

1. J. L. Mackie, *Ethics: Inventing Right and Wrong* (New York: Penguin Books, 1977) (hereinafter *E*). Mackie further discusses a number of features of these two arguments in *Hume's Moral Theory* (Boston: Routledge & Kegan Paul, 1980) (hereinafter *HMT*) and *The Miracle of Theism* (New York: Oxford University Press, 1982) (hereinafter *MT*). Parenthetical references in the text to *E, HMT,* or *MT* are to pages in these books.

2. I would like to thank Tom Arner, Richard Boyd, Norman Dahl, T. H. Irwin, David Lyons, John McDowell, Alan Sidelle, Nicholas Sturgeon, and readers for the *Australasian Journal of Philosophy* for helpful comments on earlier versions of this paper.

## Questions

1. *Psychiatric Relativism* says, "What is crazy for you is not necessarily crazy for me," and "Who's to say what behavior is crazy and what behavior is sane?" *Normative Psychiatric Relativism* says, "Verbal and physical behaviors in a certain situation that constitute more or less conclusive evidence of mental illness when they occur in one culture do not necessarily constitute more or less conclusive evidence of mental illness when they occur in another culture." Are you a Normative Psychiatric Relativist? If so, list the best arguments *against* Normative Psychiatric Relativism and show why they fail. If not, list the best arguments *for* Normative Psychiatric Relativism and show why they fail.

2. Hinduism says that different lives are right for different people. Some people ought to live according to moral principles; others ought to live according to religious principles; still others ought to make the pursuit of truth their ultimate aim in life; and so on. Let us call this view *Life-choice Relativism.*

   Explain the difference between Normative and Descriptive Relativism. What is the relationship between Normative and Life-choice Relativism? Are they compatible? If not, why not? If so, can one logically accept one doctrine without accepting the other?

   What is the relationship between Normative Egoism and Life-choice Relativism? Are they compatible? If not, why not? If so, can one logically accept one doctrine without accepting the other?

   If you are a Normative Relativist, do you think that the arguments in favor of Normative Relativism also justify Life-choice Relativism? Why or why not? If you are not a Normative Relativist, do you think that the arguments against Normative Relativism also refute Life-choice Relativism? Why or why not?

   Whether or not different lives are right for different people, how do I decide which life is right for me? Is my choice purely arbitrary or are there principles according to which I can make a rational choice?

3. The Principle of Tolerance says that no culture should try to impose its beliefs and practices on other cultures by force. It is morally wrong to force others to live by your rules. Call a person who believes this principle a *Tolerator.* The Principle of Intolerance says that if you think a certain act is morally wrong, then you have a moral obligation to prevent others from performing that act. If necessary, you should use force to prevent others from violating moral rules. Call a person who subscribes to this principle an *Intolerator.*

   Can a person be a Normative Relativist without being a Tolerator? Can a person be a

Tolerator without being a Normative Relativist? Can a person consistently be both a Tolerator and a Normative Relativist? Can a person be a Normative Absolutist without being an Intolerator? Can a person be an Intolerator without being a Normative Absolutist? Can a person consistently be both a Tolerator and a Normative Absolutist?

Suppose that Ivan Intolerator thinks abortion is morally wrong and forcibly prevents Mary from getting an abortion. Would Tommy Tolerator think that Ivan's act is morally wrong? Suppose Tommy tells Ivan that his act is morally wrong. Has Tommy violated his own principle? Suppose Tommy forcibly prevents Ivan from preventing Mary from obtaining an abortion. Has Tommy violated his own principle? Would Ivan think that Tommy's act is morally wrong?

Annie Anti-Hypocrite says, "I am against hypocrisy. Thus I think that people (or cultures) that believe in the Principle of Tolerance should be tolerant, whereas people (or cultures) that believe in the Principle of Intolerance should be intolerant. If you believe in the Principle of Intolerance, then you are morally justified in forcing others to live by your rules." Would Annie think Ivan's act is morally wrong? Would Annie think that Tommy's act is morally wrong?

Cathy Compromiser says, "Both the Principle of Tolerance and the Principle of Intolerance are too inflexible. We should tolerate some practices. For example, if some Arabs think that women should wear veils, we should not force them to change that custom. On the other hand, there are some practices that we should not tolerate. For example, some Indians think that when a husband dies, his dutiful wife should kill herself. And if she doesn't do so, someone else should kill her. It would be OK for us to try to stamp out this practice." Help Cathy out by formulating a defensible principle that is a compromise between the Principle of Tolerance and the Principle of Intolerance. Cathy's Principle of Compromise should tell us when we should be tolerant and when we should be intolerant.

4. One version of Normative Relativism says that what makes an act morally right is that the act is approved of by society. And what makes an act morally wrong is that the act is disapproved of by society. State and explain the best argument against this version of Normative Relativism. Divine Command Theory says that what makes an act morally right is that the act is approved of by God and what makes an act morally wrong is that the act is disapproved of by God. State and explain the best argument against Divine Command Theory. [See the "Morality and Religion" section.] Choose *one* of the following tasks.

   a. If you think that Normative Relativism is correct, explain why the best argument against Normative Relativism fails.
   b. If you think that Divine Command Theory is correct, explain why the best argument against Divine Command Theory fails.
   c. If you think that neither Normative Relativism nor Divine Command Theory is correct, consider the following combination: NR/DCT says that what makes an act morally right is that the act is approved of either by society or by God (or by both) and what makes an act morally wrong is that the act is disapproved of both by society and by God. Do the arguments against Normative Relativism and those against Divine Command Theory also refute the NR/DCT combination? Why or why not?

5. Consider the following dialogue between an Absolutist and a Relativist.

   *A:* "Don't steal!" is a universal moral rule. It applies to every person. All thefts are immoral acts no matter what the thief or his society think about theft.

   *R:* Do you really believe this "universal moral rule" razzmatazz? Do you really think it is wrong to steal a loaf of bread from a wealthy person in order to feed your starving child?

*A:* No, of course not. "Defense of others" is an exception. You see, "Don't steal!" really stands for "Don't steal except in self-defense, or defense of others, or in a just war, and so on." It is the full rule, including exceptions, that applies to everyone.

*R:* Oh, I see. It is OK to steal if it is a matter of life and death, or if you are a soldier in a just war, or if you are Robin Hood, or if you are a Communist (who does not believe in private property), or if you are a fifteen-year-old member of the To-Fu tribe (which has the tribal custom that on the first night of the full moon in a person's fifteenth year, that person must steal the hood ornament of a police car in order to be considered an adult).

*A:* Whoa! Stealing to save a life or in a just war are real exceptions, but being Robin Hood, being a Communist, and being a To-Fu kid are not real exceptions.

*R:* Why not?

If you were A, how would you answer R's question?

*A:* One disgusting aspect of your view is that it sanctions Egoism. Egoists are Relativists. Everyone thinks different things will make them happy, so Egoism says that different people should do different things even in the same situation.

*R:* Relativists have a duty to do whatever their culture believes is right, whether or not they believe it will make them happy. Thus Egoists are not Relativists.

*A:* Not so fast. Cultural Relativists have a duty to follow their society, but individual Relativists are free to do as they please. So Relativism still sanctions one sort of Egoism.

If you were R, how would you defend yourself against A's criticism?

6. Consider the following dialogue between an Absolutist and a Relativist.

*A:* "Don't commit adultery!" is a universal moral rule. It applies to every person. Sex between a married person and someone who is not that person's spouse is an immoral act no matter what the two people or their society think about adultery.

*R:* Do you really believe this "universal moral rule" razzmatazz? Do you really think it is wrong for a married woman to consent to sex with someone who is threatening to kill her unless she consents?

*A:* No, of course not. "Self-defense" is an exception. You see, "Don't commit adultery!" really stands for "Don't commit adultery except in self-defense, or defense of others, and so on." It is the full rule, including exceptions, that applies to everyone.

*R:* Oh, I see. It is OK to commit adultery if it is a matter of life and death, or if God tells you to commit adultery, or if you are named James Bond, or if you are a member of a tribe that considers it the duty of a host to offer his wife to male guests, or . . .

*A:* Whoa! Adultery to save a life is a real exception. Probably there are other real exceptions, too. I am not sure about being ordered to commit adultery by God. But being named James Bond and being a member of a tribe that endorses adultery are not real exceptions.

*R:* Why not?

If you were A, how would you answer R's question?

*R:* Adultery is OK when it is endorsed by one's religion, isn't it?

*A:* No religion endorses adultery. And even if some religion did endorse adultery, adultery would still be wrong.

*R:* The patriarchs had multiple wives and concubines, so the *Bible* endorses adultery. Moreover, the Buddha says that people should be moderate. This means that they should eat, drink, and commit adultery in moderate amounts. Thus Buddhism endorses adultery.

*A:* You are misinterpreting the *Bible* and the Buddha.

*R:* What is wrong with my interpretation? And if some religion did endorse adultery, how could adultery still be wrong for believers of that religion?

If you were A, how would you answer R's questions?

7. Although Aristotle never mentions it, contemporary Aristotelians might construct a virtue governing a person's stance toward the practices of other people and cultures in the following way: A person with the virtue of *tolerance* is not typically repelled by the practices of others. Instead, he or she tries to understand the reason for these practices. The *tolerant* person seldom imposes his or her own beliefs or practices on other people and cultures. On the other hand, the *intolerant* person imposes his or her own beliefs or practices on other people and cultures too quickly and too often, whereas the *passive* person imposes his or her own beliefs or practices too slowly and too seldom. The tolerant person tolerates the right practices, the intolerant person tolerates too few practices, and the passive person tolerates too many practices.

State precisely the rule specifying which practices the tolerant person should tolerate and which he or she should try to change. Is the virtue of tolerance compatible with the virtue of justice? State precisely the definitions of a Normative Relativist, a Normative Absolutist, a Divine Command Theorist, and a Rule Utilitarian. Which of the following are consistent possibilities?

   a. Tolerant Normative Relativist
   b. Intolerant Normative Relativist
   c. Tolerant Normative Absolutist
   d. Intolerant Normative Absolutist
   e. Tolerant Divine Command Theorist
   f. Intolerant Divine Command Theorist
   g. Tolerant Rule Utilitarian
   h. Intolerant Rule Utilitarian

8. The role of common sense in ethics is controversial. In what ways (if any) does Utilitarianism seem to run counter to common sense? In what ways (if any) does the Sermon on the Mount seem to run counter to common sense? In what ways (if any) does Normative Relativism seem to run counter to common sense?

   For each point of ostensible disagreement between these moral theories and common sense, explain why common sense is wrong, or why the moral theory is wrong, or why there is really no disagreement between common sense and the moral theory.

9. Aristotle, Mill, and Kant all try to refute Normative Relativism by proving their ultimate moral principle. Some scholars think these proofs succeed; others think they fail. Choose *one* of these proofs and state it as clearly as you can. (*Hint:* It will probably be helpful to identify and number the premises and conclusion.) If you think your chosen proof fails, what is wrong with it? Can you suggest a better proof for the principle? If you think your chosen proof succeeds, defend the proof from the best attack you can imagine.

   a. Mill tries to prove the Greatest Happiness Principle (34).
   b. Kant tries to prove the second formulation of the Categorical Imperative (35–36, A 427–429).
   c. Aristotle tries to prove that the "human good turns out to be [rational] activity of the soul exhibiting excellence . . . in a complete life" (14, 1098a).

# Morality and Happiness: Egoism and Common Sense

*A person's virtues are called good not with regard to the effects they produce for himself, but with regard to the effects we suppose they will produce for us and for society. . . . For otherwise it must have been seen that virtues (such as industriousness, obedience, chastity, piety, justness) are mostly injurious to their possessors. . . . If you possess a virtue you are its victim! . . . One's "neighbor" praises selflessness because he derives advantage from it!*

NIETZSCHE

## Psychological Egoism

Like "relativism," the term "egoism" is ambiguous. Sometimes it refers to *Psychological Egoism*, the view that all people always choose an option they believe to be in their own interest. Psychological Egoism is an obstacle to the project of ethics because it is a sort of determinism. If Psychological Egoism is true, then a person cannot make choices except among self-interested options. Of course we seem, even to ourselves, to be making non–self-interested choices, but according to Psychological Egoism, this is an illusion. Now the main point of ethics is to make morally correct choices. Thus the project of determining which acts are morally required, which neutral, and which prohibited presupposes that our will is free—that we can choose among acts. This point is expressed by the slogan "Ought implies can." However, if everyone in every situation is going to choose what he or she believes is likely to advance his or her own happiness, then there is no point in trying to determine what morality requires. We ought to stop kidding ourselves or fooling others about moral choices and simply get on with the business of enjoying ourselves. Thus, just as the point of seeking *universal* principles of moral choice presupposes the rejection of Normative

Relativism, so the project of seeking universal principles of moral *choice* presupposes the rejection of Psychological Egoism.

Note that Psychological Egoism is a very strong claim. It predicts almost every choice of every person in every situation. If we can find only one person who once acted unselfishly, we will disprove Psychological Egoism. At first glance, self-sacrificing acts and self-destructive acts seem to be obvious counter-examples to Psychological Egoism. But the Psychological Egoist maintains that if we look hard enough, we will find that at some level, the people performing such acts really believe that the acts are in their interest. Jill gives money to charity in order to savor the warm glow of giving. Jack braves the fire because he believes the fun of raising his child is worth the risks of rescue. Aladdin skips class because he thinks that watching the soaps will be more fun; Jasmine shoots heroin to forget her troubles. The Psychological Egoist makes the following argument.

### Argument (A)

(1) Any action can be explained in terms of a hypothetical (possibly unconscious) self-interested motive.
(2) If an action can be explained by a self-interested motive, then it must be motivated by self-interest.
(3) Therefore, all actions are motivated by self-interest.

Premise (2) embodies a naive view of explanation. It illicitly assumes that if an account of some event explains the data adequately, then that account must be true. However, for many events, several incompatible explanations may be given. Jane's sneezing may be explained by demonic possession or by cold germs. Similarly, many acts can be explained by self-interested and non–self-interested motives. Perhaps Jill helps others from duty; Jack saves his child out of love; Aladdin skips class because he is afraid to be called on; and Jasmine shoots up because she has a death wish. So premise (2) is false.

The Psychological Egoist could avoid this objection by replacing premise (2) with the following statement: (2') If an action can *best* be explained by a self-interested motive, then it must be motivated by self-interest. However, it is far from obvious that statement (2') is true. Many acts seem, on the surface, to be non–self-interested and can be reconciled with Psychological Egoism only by postulating an unobserved, unacknowledged, unconscious self-interested motive. As Rachels points out, this makes Psychological Egoism an untestable theory. When you were little, your parents probably fascinated you by proposing the following hypothesis: "All of your toys come to life when you are asleep and dance around the room, but they magically return to their places just before you wake up so that you can never catch them frolicking." Now, presumably, you are quite skeptical about this hypothesis, even though it cannot be disproved. Indeed, you are now skeptical of this hypothesis partially *because* it cannot be disproved. For similar reasons, I suggest that mature stances toward Psychological Egoism range from agnosticism to extreme skepticism.

Many people resist this conclusion. Self-interest just seems to them to be the more plausible explanation. From where does this cynicism about human nature come? Perhaps it springs from the doctrine of original sin. Or perhaps it derives from the following argument.

### Argument (B)

(1) If any randomly chosen act is self-interested, then every act is self-interested. Consider Joy's act.

(2) Joy *chose* the act.

(3) No one ever does what he or she does not want to do.

(4) Therefore, Joy chose the act because she thought it was in her own interest. (from 2 and 3)

(5) Therefore, people always chose what they believe is in their own interest. (from 1 and 4)

The problem with this argument is that the term "want" in premise (3) is ambiguous. If "want" means "chose," then premise (4) does not follow from premise (3). On the other hand, if "want" means "believes is in her own interest," then premise (3) is equivalent to conclusion (5), and the argument begs the question. We always act on our desires, but the object of our desires is not always our own interest. Psychological Egoism remains unlikely at best.

## Common Sense, Happiness, and Morality: Kant

If Psychological Egoism may be bracketed or rejected, if people are free to choose non–self-interested options, then ethical inquiry is not futile. Whew, my life's work is not a waste! But are there occasions when we must choose between happiness and morality, between the happy life and the moral life? Kant has a common-sense view about happiness, morality, and their relationship. Along with common sense, Kant maintains that a person's happiness is basically the satisfaction of whatever desires remain after self-destructive desires are eliminated and conflicts among desires are resolved. Kant thinks that the common-sense conception of morality is basically right, too, although it needs philosophical clarification and systematization. The traditional moral life is the true moral life. Is common sense right about the relationship between happiness and morality? Kant believes that the morally correct action is usually in our interest but that occasionally these diverge and we must choose between happiness and morality. It is not hard to think of occasions when common sense says that the morally right thing to do is not in one's interest. For example, the morally right thing for your teacher to do is to grade your papers fairly. However, as all know but few admit, fair grading is difficult, boring, and time-consuming. It is in your teacher's interest to assign grades more or less arbitrarily and spend the time he or she saves in publishing or partying. After all, few students challenge the grades they get, and these few are easily mollified with grade concessions. At various points, then, the person whose ultimate aim is happiness and the person whose ultimate aim is moral action will make different choices. The life aimed at happiness and the life aimed at morality are different. The following equation expresses the common-sense view.

> Common-sense happy life = true happy life ≠ true moral life = traditional moral life

Should we choose the moral life, the happy life, or some other type of life? Existentialists would say that there is no principled way to choose among different types of life. To accept a type of life is to accept certain assumptions as well as certain goals, and no reason can be given for preferring one type of life to another without utilizing the assumptions of one or the other types of life. Whether to choose the moral life is not a question that morality can settle. It is a question that precedes all moral questions. It is an issue that transcends worldviews rather than an issue within the moral worldview. We must choose arbitrarily (though after we have chosen, we will be able to justify our choice on the basis of the assumptions of the life we have chosen). Common sense, Kant, and many other philosophers have maintained that we should choose the moral life. They say that morality takes priority over all other values. I shall call the view that morality should be rejected *Immoralism*. According to Immoralism, the right life is not the moral life but some other life. There are many different versions of Immoralism. Because Sören Kierkegaard thinks the moral life and the religious life conflict, he takes advocates of the religious life to be Immoralists.[1] According to some interpretations of the *Republic*, Plato thinks that intellectuals must choose between the pure pursuit of knowledge (contemplation of the Forms) and the moral life of the administrator (returning to the cave).[2] Thus "ivory tower" academics are Immoralists! The view that the right life is the happy life rather than the moral life is another sort of Immoralism. I shall label it *Egoistic Immoralism* because the term "egoism" sometimes refers to this view. According to Egoistic Immoralism, we should always act in our own interest, even if doing so is immoral.

Another alternative to the common-sense view is to deny that the happy life and the moral life are different and hence to avoid the terrible choice. Sometimes the term "egoism" refers to *Ethical Egoism*, the view that all people always morally should do what they believe is in their own interest. Although Psychological Egoism and Ethical Egoism are easily and often conflated because they sound very similar, they are really quite different doctrines. They differ in just the way that Descriptive and Normative Relativism differ. Psychological Egoism is a descriptive claim, a claim about how people *actually do* behave, whereas Ethical Egoism is a normative claim, a claim about how people morally *should* behave. Indeed, Psychological Egoism and Ethical Egoism are incompatible. Psychological Egoism says that you have no choice but to do what you think is in your interest. Ethical Egoism says that you do have a choice and that you morally should choose the self-interested option. Let me emphasize that Ethical Egoism is a moral theory, although it is an unusual moral theory. The word "should" expresses moral obligation. People who choose not to advance their own interests, whether because of self-destructive motives or altruistic motives or indifference or whatever, are acting immorally according to Ethical Egoism. They are exploiting themselves.

## Critique of Traditional Morality: Nietzsche

Both Egoistic Immoralists and Ethical Egoists reject traditional morality. One of the most influential critics of traditional morality is the nineteenth-century German iconoclast Friedrich Nietzsche. No one is lukewarm about Nietzsche. To begin with, his flamboyant and aphoristic style, his martial and sexist metaphors, his unsystematic and cynical approach fascinate some and repel others. The content of his thought is even more controversial. Nietzsche approaches morality as a social scientist studying an institution or practice. He does not ask whether the particular claims of traditional morality are true.

Instead, he asks other questions: What sort of people tend to make such claims? What are their motives? What do they gain and lose? What is the history of traditional morality? How does it function now? Whom does it benefit and whom does it harm? In general, what are the causes and effects of traditional morality? Like Karl Marx, Kierkegaard, and other nineteenth-century thinkers reacting to political and social upheavals such as romanticism, urbanization, industrialization, and mass culture, Nietzsche comes to the conclusion that traditional morality is an invention that enables one group of people to dominate another (although these thinkers disagree among themselves about who is using traditional morality to dominate whom). The more plausible Nietzsche's account of the origins and workings of traditional morality is, the more seriously we must take his critique.

Nietzsche's first step as a social scientist is to distinguish between two opposite types of people—two ends of a spectrum. He observes that most people tend to cluster near one end, whereas only a few are found near the other end. These few, whom Nietzsche calls *the noble*, are stronger, smarter, and generally more talented than the rest. They are creative, powerful, winners who excel at everything they do; they are self-sufficient, individualistic, and self-actualizing. Thus they are proud of themselves and their achievements and are filled with joy, for they are generally able to achieve their goals. They are at peace with themselves. By comparison, the masses, whom Nietzsche calls *the base*, are weak, stupid, and talentless. Most folks are dull, hapless losers, unable to develop or deploy their mediocre abilities. Because they need and desire to be helped, they tend to herd together. Because they are basically frustrated failures, they are miserable, self-despising, and humble. And because they are not at peace with themselves, they are characterized by jealousy, resenting and fearing those who are more successful. Nietzsche adds the intriguing suggestion that cultures as well as individuals may be classified as either noble or base. He also observes that sometimes there are both noble and base ele-

ments within a culture and even within a single person.

Nietzsche's second step is to observe that the noble and the base are drawn to different moral theories. The moral theory of the noble, which Nietzsche somewhat misleadingly calls *master morality*, takes the characteristics of the noble to be good. Pride, joyfulness, self-sufficiency, internal harmony, and the like are virtues, their opposites vices. The moral theory of the base, *slave morality*, is a sour grapes morality. Because they cannot achieve success on their own, the base resent those who can and go on to praise cooperation. Because they are not proud of themselves, they say that pride is a sin and humility is a virtue. Because they are weak and stupid, they say things like "The meek shall inherit the earth" and "Ignorance is bliss." Because they are unable to satisfy their sensual desires, they say that the body is evil and sensual desires are to be fought. Thus the base end up maintaining that people should not be at peace with their animal nature but should be frustrated and unnatural instead. In general, the moral theory of the base arises as a reaction of resentment and fear of the noble. It labels the characteristics and acts of the noble as evil, and the characteristics and acts of the base end up as good by contrast. Slave morality enables the base to feel good about themselves, although at some level the base still recognize the superiority of the noble and yearn to be numbered among them. See Table 2.

Aristotle's moral theory is a master morality. Aristotle denies that human nature is sinful or that natural desires are wicked. Instead, each aspect of human nature should be enjoyed, although exercising moderation is important to preserving balance and harmony in one's life. According to Aristotle, a good person is one with the wisdom and character and resources to achieve this sort of life. Such a person's attitude toward the rest of mankind should be *noblesse oblige*. A good person recognizes her or his own superiority to others and is proud of it yet does not lord it over inferior people. Unlike insecure people, good people have no need to boast or subordinate others in order to boost their own self-esteem. With a modicum of luck, a good person will be happy living a life that is basically the traditional moral life. But a good person will not be happy leading the life that common sense takes to be the happy life. Thus common sense is right about morality but wrong about happiness.

> Common-sense happy life ≠ true happy life
> = true moral life = traditional moral life

Christianity is Nietzsche's paradigm example of slave morality. In one interpretation, Jesus urges us to treat everyone like family; to help everyone, friend and foe alike; to love even our enemies. People are not to be treated and valued differently according to their ability. Losers are as good as winners. (According to the Beatitudes, losers are even better than winners.) Christianity tells us that pride is sinful because success without divine help is impossible. Similarly, psychic harmony is impossible (unless we reject our human nature), because natural sensual desire is sinful. (This is one aspect of the doctrine of original sin.) Jesus thinks that common sense is wrong about everything. The common-sense view of happiness is that it consists of worldly success, but true happiness is otherworldly. The common-sense conception of morality is that it consists primarily of avoiding evil action (no stealing, no killing, etc.), but true morality demands substantial self-sacrifice, too. ("Give to all who beg from you. Lend without expecting repayment." And so on.) Common

sense says that morality and happiness conflict, yet through God, the true moral life is the most rewarding life.

> Common-sense happy life ≠ true happy life
> = true moral life ≠ traditional moral life

Nietzsche's third observation as a social scientist studying traditional morality is that although the base cannot defeat the noble, they manipulate the noble into defeating themselves by getting them to internalize slave morality. Because slave morality equates evil with the characteristics of the noble, noble people who accept slave morality come to loathe themselves. They become ashamed rather than proud of the way they are. They exchange their joy for misery and their internal peace for discord as they set about repressing and distorting their true nature. Instead of ignoring or pitying the base, the duped noble people admire and struggle to emulate and serve the base. Naturally, this *transvaluation of values*, wherein the value system that exalts the base becomes the dominant morality, greatly benefits the base. They subordinate the noble whom they resent and fear, and they harness the energy and creativity of the noble to achieve what the base alone could not accomplish.

But how do the base get the noble to internalize slave morality? This is accomplished through the postulation of God's existence. The base say to the noble, "By comparison with God you are not great, wonderful, or successful. We are all

**Table 2**

|  | Master Morality | Slave Morality |
| --- | --- | --- |
| *The noble:* strong, smart, talented, creative, powerful, winners, excelling, self-sufficient, individualistic, self-actualizing, proud, joyful, psychic peace, confident | good | evil |
| *The base:* weak, stupid, talentless, dull, hapless, losers, mediocre, need help, herd together, self-despising, miserable, humble, frustrated, failures, jealous, resentful, fearful | bad | good |

humble, miserable, impotent wimps compared to God, so you ought to adopt our slave morality." Once the noble accept God's existence, they naturally go on to accept slave morality and destroy themselves. Thus Nietzsche exposes traditional morality (and its ally, religion) as hypocrisy. These are mere devices used by the base to obtain power over the noble and acceptance of themselves. Traditional morality is a psychic defense and offense mechanism.

Is Nietzsche right about traditional morality? Do people tend to cluster into a small group of highly talented people and a large group of mediocre people, as his first observation says? Do these groups naturally gravitate toward the value systems Nietzsche describes in his second observation? Does the mediocre group tend to subordinate the talented group by religious indoctrination, as stated in Nietzsche's third observation? If Nietzsche is right, we would expect to find most noble types repressing their natural tendencies, becoming neurotically miserable while laboring for the sake of others, or feeling terribly guilty because they are not repressed and self-sacrificing. We would expect to find most base types using morality and religion to rationalize their failures and flaws as well as to humble and exploit the talented. They would be using morality and religion as crutches and as weapons.

Consider the sphere of sexuality. Nietzsche would say that although some fervent advocates of chastity for singles and monogamy for married people are motivated by principle alone, most of these people advocate chastity and monogamy because they are pathologically repelled by sex, too disgusting to attract sexual partners, too timid to seek sexual satisfaction, or inadequate in some other way. In general, Nietzsche would say that, consciously or subconsciously, they advocate unnatural sexual behavior because they are sexual losers. On the other hand, people who are able and eager to attract sexual partners either restrain themselves and become miserable, because of their unsatisfied desire, or indulge their natural desires and feel guilty, because they have been indoctrinated

since their youth with the doctrine that extramarital sex is evil. In general, Nietzsche would say that this doctrine comforts the neurotic losers and degrades the talented winners.

Similarly, Nietzsche would say that although some advocates of altruism and cooperation are sincere, most hypocritically advocate benevolence and sharing because they are incapable of succeeding on their own and themselves need help. Consciously or subconsciously, they disparage selfishness and competition because they have little to lose and much to gain from a morality of self-sacrifice. It is in the best interest of the incompetent to convince the competent that everyone has a duty to be helpful. On the other hand, Nietzsche would say that successful people either share their labor and ideas with others and feel exploited or refuse to share and feel guilty because they have been taught since their youth that selfishness is wicked. In general, Nietzsche would say that this ideology helps the lazy and incompetent take advantage of the hardworking and talented.

Some find Nietzsche's critique of traditional morality quite persuasive; others find it completely wrong-headed. Note that Nietzsche does not argue that the claims of traditional morality are false. His claim is merely (merely!) that the advocates of traditional morality are hypocrites and that traditional morality subordinates and destroys the talented while comforting and benefiting the incompetent.

Although it is clear that Nietzsche rejects traditional morality, it is far from clear what life Nietzsche proposes instead. Although Nietzsche is sympathetic with the noble, he does not endorse master morality. He is no Ethical Egoist, for he believes that we should place certain sorts of progress ahead of our own interests. Confused by his metaphors and terminology (such as the term "overman" and the phrase "will to power"), and viewing him through the distorting lens of their own preconceptions, the Nazis took Nietzsche to be endorsing a racially tinged pursuit of power over others. But the Nazi reading of Nietzsche is clearly a misinterpretation. Nietzsche's overmen overcome themselves (their own flaws and hang-ups) rather than over-coming others. Overmen seek power over their world, the power to discover and create, rather than power over others. Some contemporary interpreters take Nietzsche to be endorsing the creative life, the life dedicated to progress in the arts and sciences. At any rate, whatever value system Nietzsche endorses is so different from traditional morality that it seems more accurate to call it an alternative to morality than to call it a very non-traditional morality.

## Ethical Egoism: Rand

I shall offer a rather controversial reading of Ayn Rand, a twentieth-century novelist and popular proponent of Ethical Egoism. My interpretation is that Rand agrees with the main lines of Nietzsche's critique of traditional morality, though not with all of the details. She joins Nietzsche in railing at traditional morality for demanding self-sacrifice. Sacrificing one's interests for other people, for God, for anything at all is simply wrong, according to Rand. On the other hand, Rand does not follow Nietzsche in rejecting morality altogether. Her view is that after reject-ing traditional morality, which is approximately Nietzsche's slave morality, we should go on to adopt the true morality. Because Rand more or less accepts the common-sense view of happi-ness, and because she believes that there is no conflict between the pursuit of morality and the pursuit of happiness, Rand's view is this:

Common-sense happy life = true happy life
= true moral life ≠ traditional moral life

The title of one of her books, *The Virtue of Self-ishness*, may leave the misimpression that Rand is an Immoralist. But by maintaining that selfish-ness is a virtue, Rand is not saying that we should disregard morality or forgo caring rela-tionships in order to pursue our own interests. She is not saying that it is good to exploit others or to avoid others. She believes that people have

rights and that love and friendship are impor-tant goods. She is merely saying, in a provoca-tive way, that the self-sacrifice prescribed by Kant and Christianity is immoral. Why? One reason is that according to Rand, self-sacrifice harms not only the sacrificer but also the benefi-ciary. Instead of becoming independent, self-reliant people enjoying the development and exercise of their abilities and taking pride in their accomplishments, beneficiaries shrivel into de-pendent parasites, afraid that the people they come to rely on will one day desert them and angry at being reminded of their inadequacy.

A similar dialectic occurs at the level of the society as a whole. Rand applies Nietzsche's distinctions to modern economic alternatives. She takes Communism (and Utilitarianism) to exemplify some aspects of slave morality. Com-munism says that people should cooperate and help each other rather than competing. If a few misfit individuals need to be expelled from or exploited by society for the sake of the many, so what? The important thing is the good of the whole. Conversely, Rand takes Capitalism to exemplify some aspects of master morality. Here success, individualism, creativity, and power are prized, and the masses who cannot or do not succeed are simply ignored. If a few lazy or incompetent people suffer or die, so what? The important thing is the accomplishments of the natural elite that rises to the top of society. Like the parent who "does everything" for the child, liberals support the poor with charity (and even force others to support the poor by imposing taxes to pay for welfare). Like the overindulged child, the poor become dependent, ungrateful, and unhappy. If liberals would simply stop helping, then people would learn to support themselves and gain self-esteem. Almost every-one would be happier. Thus Rand thinks that moral theories such as Kantianism, Christianity, Utilitarianism, and Communism cause much harm by convincing people that they have a duty to sacrifice themselves for the sake of oth-ers. This line of thought leads some people, though not Rand herself, to make the following argument.

### Argument (C)

(1) If everyone always pursued his or her own happiness, then the world would be a better place.
(2) People should do whatever will make the world a better place.
(3) Therefore, everyone should always pursue his or her own happiness.

There are two problems with argument (C). First, premise (1) seems blatantly false. Self-sacrifice does cause some harm, but it also produces a great deal of good in the world. Moreover, selfishness does produce some good, but it also causes a great deal of harm in the world. Even if self-sacrifice is, on balance, harmful, it seems to be much less harmful than self-interest. Second, premise (2) of argument (C) is a rough statement of Utilitarianism. Thus, rather than proving that Ethical Egoism is the correct moral theory, the argument merely recommends self-interested action as a means to achieving the goals of Utilitarianism.

Rand has another reason for thinking that the sacrifice of one's own interests for the sake of something or someone else is immoral.

### Argument (D)

(1) Rational life is the only possible ultimate goal, the point of all rational choices.
(2) Only things that sustain a person's rational life have value.
(3) Thus it is wrong to subordinate your own interests to others or to subordinate their interests to yours.
(4) Therefore, your own happiness should be your ultimate value.

Defenders of Rand have tried various maneuvers to fill the gaps in this argument. Eschewing that project, I shall simply suggest that Rand's core idea seems to be the Kantian notion that people have intrinsic value. Slavery is wrong because it treats people as though they were merely instrumentally valuable, as though they were valuable only in the way that tools are valuable. Similarly, to sacrifice my interests is to treat myself as though I were merely instrumentally valuable, as though I were merely useful to someone else.

### Argument (E)

(1) People are ends, not mere means.
(2) Self-sacrifice—not doing what is in one's interests—is always treating oneself merely as a means for achieving the interests of someone else.
(3) Therefore, self-sacrifice is wrong.

Let me now turn from exposition to discussion of Rand's ideas.

Like Normative Relativism, Ethical Egoism is a counter-intuitive doctrine with many adherents. Naturally, some people embrace Ethical Egoism as a rationalization for disregarding the constraints of traditional morality. They camouflage their immoralism by espousing Ethical Egoism. But Ethical Egoism appeals to sincere people too, presumably because premise (1) is true and because premise (2) identifies a common form of injustice. Sadly, people often treat themselves as mere tools to be used by other people. One of the goals of assertiveness training is to learn to avoid this common trap—to learn to say "no" to unjustified demands to serve others. Moreover, Rand's observation that some people think it is their duty to serve others is quite right. However, self-sacrifice is *not always* treating oneself merely as a means. Premise (2) of argument (E) is important, but it is not quite true as it stands. Moreover, although traditional morality does sometimes require the sacrifice of important interests, it does not demand that people treat themselves merely as a means.

Actually, traditional morality requires us to sacrifice our own interests only to respect the rights of others and (less definitively) to help others who critically need help when we can do so with little effort or risk. Rand also thinks we should respect the rights of others and (perhaps) render aid in emergencies. She agrees that people who perform these acts are not treating themselves merely as a means. Although she might disagree a bit with traditional morality about what rights people have and what counts as an emergency (traditional morality is somewhat vague on these matters), the main dispute is that Rand thinks that respecting rights and rendering emergency aid is not self-sacrifice. According to Rand, it is always in everyone's interest to do these things. (Why?) Thus Rand ends up denying implicitly what she explicitly affirms. Notwithstanding her reputation as an iconoclast, Rand manages to equate the happy life with the moral life not by espousing a radically non-traditional morality but rather by denying implicitly that the traditional moral rules require self-sacrifice! Her controversial claim is not really her definition of morality but rather her assertion that the moral life is the happy life. Thus, if common sense is right to maintain that respecting rights and rendering aid (a) are not self-exploitive acts and (b) are self-sacrificial acts, then premise (2) of argument (E) is false.

Rand's treatment of love and friendship as exchanges motivated by self-interest is also problematic. In Rand's view, I should do things for my wife because I gain happiness from her existence and her happiness. I should do things for her for my sake. But this will produce a cold, calculating business relationship rather than love or friendship. In her eagerness to assign a dominant role to reason, Rand has undervalued passion. (In general, I think Rand has not sufficiently acknowledged the pleasure of helping others.) A healthy relationship is not simply a free, rational exchange of goods (although this is a minimal condition of a non-exploitive relationship). People do nice things for lovers and friends not because it pays but rather because they care for the other person. The acts of lovers and friends are often self-sacrificing acts, yet they are hardly self-exploitive acts. Thus sacrifices for love and friendship also constitute counter-examples to premise (2).

## Notes

1. S. Kierkegaard, *Fear and Trembling*, trans. W. Lowrie (Princeton, NJ: Princeton University Press, 1941).

2. Plato, *Republic*, trans. D. Lee (London: Penguin, 1953).

# 6  Psychological Egoism

## JAMES RACHELS

### Is Unselfishness Possible?

Morality and psychology go together. Morality tells us what we *ought* to do; but there is little point to it if we are not *able* to do as we ought. It may be said that we should love our enemies; but that is empty talk unless we are capable of loving them. A sound morality must be based on a realistic conception of what is possible for human beings.

Reprinted from *The Elements of Moral Philosophy* (Random House, 1986), 53–64.

Almost every system of morality recommends that we behave unselfishly. It is said that we should take the interests of other people into account when we are deciding what to do: we should not harm other people; in fact, we should try to be helpful to them whenever possible—even if it means forgoing some advantage for ourselves.

But are we capable of being unselfish? There is a theory of human nature, once widely held among philosophers, psychologists, and economists, and still held by many ordinary people, that says we are not capable of unselfishness. According to this theory, known as *Psychological Egoism,* each person is so constituted that he will look out only for his *own* interests. Therefore, it is unreasonable to expect people to behave "altruistically." Human nature being what it is, people will respond to the needs of others only when there is something in it for themselves. Pure altruism is a myth—it simply does not exist.

If this view is correct, people are very different from what we usually suppose. Of course, no one doubts that each of us cares very much about his own welfare. But we also believe that we care about others as well, at least to some extent. If Psychological Egoism is correct, this is only an illusion—in the final analysis, we care nothing for other people. Because it so contradicts our usual conception of ourselves, this is a shocking doctrine. Why have so many believed it to be true?

## The Strategy of Reinterpreting Motives

Psychological Egoism seems to fly in the face of the facts. It is tempting to respond to it by saying something like this: "*Of course* people sometimes act unselfishly. Jones gave up a trip to the movies, which he would have enjoyed very much, so that he could contribute the money for famine relief. Brown spends his free time doing volunteer work in a hospital. Smith rushed into a burning house to rescue a child. These are all clear cases of unselfish behavior, and if the psychological egoist thinks that such cases do not occur, then he is just mistaken."

Such examples are obvious, and the thinkers who have been sympathetic to Psychological Egoism were certainly aware of them. Yet they have persisted in defending the view. Why? Partly it is because they have suspected that the "altruistic" explanations of behavior are too superficial—it *seems* that people are unselfish, but a deeper analysis of their motives might tell a different story. Perhaps Jones gives money for famine relief because his religion teaches that he will be rewarded in heaven. The man who works as a hospital volunteer may be driven by an inner need

to atone for some past misdeed, or perhaps he simply enjoys this work, as other people enjoy playing chess. As for the woman who risks her life to save the child, we all know that such people are honored as heroes; perhaps she is motivated by a desire for public recognition. This technique of reinterpreting motives is perfectly general and may be repeated again and again. For any act of apparent altruism, a way can always be found to eliminate the altruism in favor of some more self-centered motive.

Thomas Hobbes (1588–1679) thought that Psychological Egoism was probably true, but he was not satisfied with such a piecemeal approach. It is not theoretically elegant to deal with each action separately, "after the fact." If Psychological Egoism *is* true, we should be able to give a more general account of human motives, which would establish the theory once and for all. This is what Hobbes attempted to do. His method was to list the possible human motives, concentrating especially on the "altruistic" ones, and show how each could be understood in egoistic terms. Once this project was completed, he would have systematically eliminated altruism from our understanding of human nature. Here are two examples of Hobbes at work:

1. *Charity.* This is the most general motive that we ascribe to people when we think they are acting from a concern for others. *The Oxford English Dictionary* devotes almost four columns to "charity." It is defined variously as "The Christian love of our fellowman" and "Benevolence to one's neighbors." But for the psychological egoist, such neighborly love does not exist, and so charity must be understood in a radically different way. In his essay "On Human Nature," Hobbes describes it like this:

There can be no greater argument to a man, of his own power, than to find himself able not only to accomplish his own desires, but also to assist other men in theirs: and this is that conception wherein consisteth *charity*.

Thus charity is a delight one takes in the demonstration of one's powers. The charitable man is demonstrating to himself, and to the world, that he is more capable than others. He can not only take care of himself, he has enough left over for others who are not so able as he. He is really just showing off his own superiority.

Of course Hobbes was aware that the charitable man may not *believe* that this is what he is doing. But we are not the best judges of our own motivations. It is only natural that we would interpret our actions in a way that is flattering to us (that is no more than the psychological egoist would expect!), and it is flattering to think that we are "unselfish." Hobbes's account aims to provide the *real* explanation of why we act as we do, not the superficial flattering account that we naturally want to believe.

2. *Pity.* What is it to pity another person? We might think it is to sympathize with them, to feel unhappy about their misfortunes. And acting from this sympathy, we might try to help them. Hobbes thinks this is all right, as far as it goes, but it does not go far enough. The *reason* we are disturbed by other people's misfortunes is that we are reminded that the same thing might happen to us! "Pity," he says, "is imagination or fiction of future calamity to ourselves, proceeding from the sense of another man's calamity."

This account of pity turns out to be more powerful, from a theoretical point of view, than it first appears. It can explain very neatly some peculiar facts about the phenomenon. For example, it can explain why we feel greater pity when a good person suffers than when an evil person suffers. Pity, on Hobbes's account, requires a sense of identification with the person suffering—I pity you when I imagine *myself* in your place. But because each of us thinks of himself or herself as a good person, we do not identify very closely with those we think bad. Therefore, we do not pity the wicked in the same way we pity the good—our feelings of pity vary directly with the virtue of the person suffering, because our sense of identification varies in that way.

The strategy of reinterpreting motives is a persuasive method of reasoning; it has made a great many people feel that Psychological Egoism might be true. It especially appeals to a certain cynicism in us, a suspicion that people are not nearly as noble as they seem. But it is not a conclusive method of reasoning, for it cannot *prove* that Psychological Egoism is correct. The trouble is, it only shows that it is *possible* to interpret motives egoistically; it does nothing to show that the egoistic motives are deeper or truer than the altruistic explanations they are intended to replace. At most, the strategy shows that Psychological Egoism is possible. We still need other arguments to show it is true.

## Two Arguments in Favor of Psychological Egoism

Two general arguments have often been advanced in favor of Psychological Egoism. They are "general" arguments, in the sense that each one seeks to establish at a stroke that *all* actions, and not merely some limited class of them, are motivated by self-interest. As will be seen, neither argument stands up very well under scrutiny.

1. The first argument goes as follows. If we describe one person's action as selfish and another person's action as unselfish, we are overlooking the crucial fact that in both cases, assuming the action is done voluntarily, *the person is merely doing what he most wants to do.* If Jones gives his money for the cause of famine relief rather than spending it on the movies, that only shows that he wanted to contribute to that cause more than he wanted to go to the movies—and why should he be praised for "unselfishness" when he is only doing what *he* most wants to do? His action is being dictated by his own desires, his own sense of what *he* wants most. Thus he cannot be said to be acting unselfishly. And since exactly the same may be said about *any* alleged act of altruism, we can conclude that Psychological Egoism must be true.

This argument has two primary flaws. First, it rests on the premise that people never voluntarily do anything except what they want to do. But this is plainly false; there are at least two kinds of actions that are exceptions to this generalization. One is actions that we may not want to do but that we do anyway as a means to an end that we want to achieve—for example, going to the dentist to stop a toothache. Such cases may, however, be regarded as consistent with the spirit of the argument, because the ends mentioned (such as stopping the toothache) are wanted.

Still, there are also actions that we do not because we want to nor even because they are means to an end we want to achieve, but because we feel that we *ought* to do them. For example, someone may do something because she has promised to do it, and thus feels obligated, even though she does not want to do it. It is sometimes suggested that in such cases we do the action because, after all, we want to keep our promises; so even here we are doing what we want. However, this will not work. If I have promised to do something and I do not want to do it, then it is simply false to say that I want to keep my promise. In such cases we feel a conflict precisely because we do *not* want to do what we feel obligated to do. If our desires and our sense of obligation *were* always in harmony, it would be a happier world. Unfortunately, we enjoy no such happy situation. It is an all too common experience to be pulled in different directions by desire and obligation. Jones's predicament may be like this: he *wants* to go to the movies, but he feels he *should* give the money for famine relief instead. Thus if he chooses to contribute the money, he is not simply doing what he wants to do. If he did that, he would go to the movies.

The argument has a second flaw. Suppose we were to concede, for the sake of argument, that all voluntary action is motivated by desire, or at least that Jones is so motivated. Even if this were granted, it would not follow that Jones is acting selfishly or from self-interest. For if Jones wants to do something to help starving people, even when it means forgoing his own enjoyments, that is precisely what makes him *un*selfish. What else could unselfishness be, if not wanting to help others, even at some sacrifice to oneself? Another way to put the point is to say that it is the *object* of a want that determines whether it is selfish or not. The

mere fact that I am acting on *my* wants does not mean that I am acting selfishly; it depends on *what it is* that I want. If I want only my own good and care nothing for others, then I am selfish; but if I also want other people to be happy and I act on *that* desire, then my action is not selfish.

Therefore, this argument goes wrong in just about every way that an argument can go wrong: the premises are not true, and even if they were true, the conclusion would not follow from them.

2. The second general argument for Psychological Egoism appeals to the fact that so-called unselfish actions produce a sense of self-satisfaction in the person who does them. Acting "unselfishly" makes people *feel good* about themselves. This has often been noted and has been put in various ways: "It gives him a clear conscience" or "He couldn't sleep at night if he had done otherwise" or "He would have been ashamed of himself for not doing it" are familiar ways of making the same point. This sense of self-satisfaction is a pleasant state of consciousness, which we desire and seek. Therefore, actions are "unselfish" only at a superficial level of analysis. If we dig deeper, we find that the *point* of acting "unselfishly" is really to achieve this pleasant state of consciousness. Jones will feel much better about himself for having given the money for famine relief—if he had gone to the movies, he would have felt terrible about it —and that is the real point of the action.

According to a well-known story, this argument was once advanced by Abraham Lincoln. A nineteenth-century newspaper reported that

> Mr. Lincoln once remarked to a fellow-passenger on an old-time mud coach that all men were prompted by selfishness in doing good. His fellow-passenger was antagonizing this position when they were passing over a corduroy bridge that spanned a slough. As they crossed this bridge they espied an old razor-backed sow on the bank making a terrible noise because her pigs had got into the slough and were in danger of drowning. As the old coach began to climb the hill, Mr. Lincoln called out, "Driver, can't you stop just a moment?" Then Mr. Lincoln jumped out, ran back, and lifted the little pigs out of the mud and water and placed them on the bank. When he returned, his companion remarked: "Now, Abe, where does selfishness come in on this little episode?" "Why, bless your soul, Ed, that was the very essence of selfishness. I should

have had no peace of mind all day had I gone on and left that suffering old sow worrying over those pigs. I did it to get peace of mind, don't you see?"

Lincoln was a better President than philosopher. His argument is vulnerable to the same sorts of objections as the previous one. Why should we think, merely because someone derives satisfaction from helping others, that this makes him selfish? Isn't the unselfish person precisely the one who *does* derive satisfaction from helping others, whereas the selfish person does not? If Lincoln "got peace of mind" from rescuing the piglets, does this show him to be selfish or, on the contrary, doesn't it show him to be compassionate and good-hearted? (If a person were truly selfish, why should it bother his conscience that others suffer—much less pigs?) Similarly, it is nothing more than sophistry to say, because Jones finds satisfaction in giving for famine relief, that he is selfish. If we say this rapidly, while thinking about something else, perhaps it will sound all right; but if we speak slowly and pay attention to what we are saying, it sounds plain silly.

Moreover, suppose we ask *why* Jones derives satisfaction from contributing for famine relief. The answer is, it is because Jones is the kind of person who cares about other people: even if they are strangers to him, he doesn't want them to go hungry, and he is willing to take action to help them. If Jones were not this kind of person, then he would take no special pleasure in assisting them; and as we have already seen, this is the mark of unselfishness, not selfishness.

There is a general lesson to be learned here, having to do with the nature of desire and its objects. If we have a positive attitude toward the attainment of some goal, then we may derive satisfaction from attaining it. But the *object* of our attitude is *the attainment of that goal;* and we must want to attain the goal *before* we can find any satisfaction in it. We do not first desire some sort of "pleasurable consciousness" and then try to figure out how to achieve it. Rather, we desire all sorts of different things—money, a new car, to be a better chess player, to get a promotion in our work, and so on—and because we desire these things, we derive satisfaction from getting them. And so if

someone desires the welfare and happiness of other people, he will derive satisfaction from helping them; but this does not mean that those good feelings are the *object* of his desire. *They* are not what he is after. Nor does it mean that he is in any way selfish on account of having those feelings.

These two arguments are the ones most commonly advanced in defense of Psychological Egoism. It is a measure of the weakness of the theory that stronger arguments have not been forthcoming.

## Clearing Away Some Confusions

One of the most powerful theoretical motives is a desire for simplicity. When we set out to explain something, we would like to find as *simple* an explanation as possible. This is certainly true in the sciences—the simpler a scientific theory, the greater its appeal. Consider phenomena as diverse as planetary motion, the tides, and the way objects fall to the surface of the earth when released from a height. These appear, at first, to be very different; it would seem that we would need a multitude of different principles to explain them all. Who would suspect that they could all be explained by a single simple principle? Yet the theory of gravity does just that. The theory's ability to bring diverse phenomena together under a single explanatory principle is one of its great virtues. It makes order out of chaos.

In the same way, when we think about human conduct, we would like to find one principle that explains it all. We want a single simple formula, if we can find one, that would unite the diverse phenomena of human behavior, in the way that simple formulas in physics bring together apparently diverse phenomena. Since it is obvious that self-regard is an overwhelmingly important factor in motivation, it is only natural to wonder whether all motivation might not be explained in terms of it. And so the idea of Psychological Egoism is born.

But, most philosophers and psychologists would agree today, it is stillborn. The fundamental idea behind Psychological Egoism cannot even be expressed without falling into confusion; and once these confusions have been cleared away, the theory no longer seems even plausible.

The first confusion is between selfishness and self-interest. When we think about it, the two are clearly not the same. If I see a physician because I am feeling poorly, I am acting in my own self-interest, but no one would think of calling me "selfish" on account of it. Similarly, brushing my teeth, working hard at my job, and obeying the law are all in my self-interest, but none of these are examples of selfish conduct. This is because selfish behavior is behavior that ignores the interests of others, in circumstances in which their interests ought not to be ignored. The concept of "selfishness" has a definite evaluative flavor; to call people selfish is not just to describe their action but to criticize it. Thus you would not be called selfish for eating a normal meal in normal circumstances (although this would surely be in your self-interest); but you would be called selfish for hoarding food while others are starving.

A second confusion is between self-interested behavior and the pursuit of pleasure. We do lots of things because we enjoy them, but that does not mean we are acting from self-interest. The man who continues to smoke cigarettes even after learning about the connection between smoking and cancer is surely not acting from self-interest, not even by his own standard—self-interest would dictate that he quit smoking at once—and he is not acting altruistically either. He *is*, no doubt, smoking for the pleasure of it, but this only shows that undisciplined pleasure seeking and acting from self-interest are very different. This is what led Joseph Butler, the leading eighteenth-century critic of egoism, to remark, "The thing to be lamented is, not that men have so great regard to their own good or interest in the present world, for they have not enough."

Taken together, the last two paragraphs show (a) that it is false that all actions are selfish and (b) that it is false that all actions are done from self-interest. When we brush our teeth, at least in normal circumstances, we are not acting selfishly; therefore not all actions are selfish. And when we smoke cigarettes, we are not acting out of self-interest; therefore not all actions are done from self-interest. It is worth noting that these two points do not depend on examples of altruism; even if there were no such thing as altruistic behavior, Psychological Egoism would, according to these arguments, *still* be false!

A third confusion is the common but false assumption that a concern for one's own welfare is incompatible with any genuine concern for others. Since it is obvious that everyone (or very nearly everyone) does desire his or her own well-being, it might be thought that no one can really be concerned for the well-being of others. But again, this is surely a false dichotomy. There is no inconsistency in desiring that everyone, including oneself *and* others, be happy. To be sure, it may happen on occasion that our interests conflict with the interests of others, in the sense that both cannot be satisfied. In these cases we have to make hard choices. But even in these cases we sometimes opt for the interests of others, especially when the others are our friends and family. But more important, not all cases are like this. Sometimes we are able to promote the welfare of others when our own interests are not involved at all. In those circumstances, not even the strongest self-regard need prevent us from acting considerately toward others.

Once these confusions are cleared away, there seems little reason to think Psychological Egoism is a plausible theory. On the contrary, it seems decidedly implausible. If we simply observe people's behavior with an open mind, we find that much of it is motivated by self-regard, but by no means all of it. There may indeed be one simple formula, as yet undiscovered, that would explain all of human behavior—but Psychological Egoism is not it.

## The Deepest Error in Psychological Egoism

The preceding discussion may seem relentlessly negative—even objectionably so. "If Psychological Egoism is so obviously confused," you may ask, "and if there are no plausible arguments in its favor, why have so many intelligent people been attracted to it?" It is a fair question. Part of the answer, I think, is the almost irresistible urge toward theoretical simplicity; another part is the attraction of what appears to be a hard-headed, deflationary attitude toward human pretensions. But there is a deeper reason: Psychological Egoism was accepted by many thinkers because it appeared to them to be *irrefutable*. And in a certain sense, they were right. Yet in another sense, the theory's immunity from refutation is its deepest flaw.

To explain, let me first tell a (true) story that might appear to be far from our subject.

A few years ago a group of investigators led by Dr. David Rosenham, professor of psychology and law at Stanford University, had themselves admitted as patients to various mental institutions. The hospital staffs did not know there was anything special about them; the investigators were thought to be simply patients. The investigators' purpose was to see how they would be treated.

The investigators were perfectly "sane," whatever that means, but their very presence in the hospitals created the assumption that they were mentally disturbed. Although they behaved normally—they did nothing to feign illness—they soon discovered that everything they did was interpreted as a sign of some sort of mental problem. When some of them were found to be taking notes on their experiences, entries were made in their records such as "patient engages in writing behavior." During one interview, one "patient" confessed that although he was closer to his mother as a small child, he became more attached to his father as he grew older—a perfectly normal turn of events. But this was taken as evidence of "unstable relationships in childhood." Even their protestations of normalcy were turned against them. One of the real patients warned them: "Never tell a doctor that you're well. He won't believe you. That's called a 'flight into health.' Tell him you're still sick, but you're feeling a lot better. That's called insight."

No one on the hospital staffs ever caught on to the hoax. The real patients, however, did see through it. One of them told an investigator, "You're not crazy. You're checking up on the hospital." And so he was.

What the investigators learned was that *once a hypothesis is accepted, everything may be interpreted to support it.* The hypothesis was that the pseudopatients were mentally disturbed; once that became the controlling assumption, it did not matter how they behaved. Everything they did would be construed so as to fit the assumption. But the "success" of this technique of interpretation did not prove the hypothesis was true. If anything, it was a sign that something had gone wrong.

The hypothesis that the pseudopatients were disturbed was faulty because, at least for the hospital staffs, it was *untestable*. If a hypothesis purports to say something about the world, then there must be some conditions that could verify it and some that conceivably could refute it. Otherwise, it is meaningless. Consider this example: suppose someone says "Kareem Abdul-Jabbar cannot get into my Volkswagen." We know perfectly well what this means, because we can imagine the circumstances that would make it true and the circumstances that would make it false: to test the statement, we take the car to Kareem, invite him to step inside, and see what happens. If it turns out one way, the statement is true; if it turns out the other way, the statement is false. The problem with the hypothesis about the pseudopatients' mental health, as it was applied within the hospital setting, was that nothing could have refuted it. Such hypotheses may be immune from refutation, but their immunity is purchased at too dear a price —they no longer say anything significant about the world.

Psychological Egoism is involved in this same error. All our experience tells us that people act from a great variety of motives: greed, anger, lust, love, and hate, to name only a few. Sometimes, people think only of themselves. At other times, they do not think of themselves at all and act from a concern for others. The common distinction between self-regard and unselfishness gets its meaning from this contrast. But then Psychological Egoism tells us that there is *really* only one motive, self-regard, and this seems a new and fascinating revelation. We must have been wrong. But as the theory unfolds, it turns out that we were not wrong at all. The psychological egoist does not deny that people act in the variety of ways they have always appeared to act in. In the ordinary sense of the term, people are still, sometimes, unselfish. In effect, the psychological egoist has only announced his determination to *interpret* people's behavior in a certain way, *no matter what they do.* Therefore, *nothing that anyone could do could possibly count as evidence against the hypothesis.* The thesis is irrefutable, but for that very reason it turns out to have no factual content. It is not a new and fascinating revelation at all.

I am not saying that the hypothesis of the pseudopatients' mental illness or the hypothesis of Psychological Egoism are meaningless in themselves. The trouble is not so much with the hypotheses as with the people who manipulate the facts to fit them. The staffs of the mental institutions, and the estimable Hobbes, *could* have allowed some facts to count as falsifying their assumptions. Then, their hypotheses would have been meaningful but would have been seen to be plainly false. That is the risk one must take. Paradoxically, if we do not allow some way in which we might be mistaken, we lose all chance of being right.

# 7 Critique of Traditional Morality

**FRIEDRICH NIETZSCHE**

## On the Virtuous

Slack and sleeping senses must be addressed with thunder and heavenly fireworks. But the voice of beauty speaks gently: it creeps only into the most awakened souls. Gently trembled and laughed my shield today; that is the holy laughter and tremor of beauty. About you, the virtuous, my beauty laughed today. And thus its voice came to me: "They still want to be paid."

You who are virtuous still want to be paid! Do you want rewards for virtue, and heaven for earth, and the eternal for your today?

And now are you angry with me because I teach that there is no reward and paymaster? And verily, I do not even teach that virtue is its own reward.

Alas, that is my sorrow: they have lied reward and punishment into the foundation of things, and now also into the foundation of your souls, you who are virtuous. But like the boar's snout, my words shall tear open the foundation of your souls: a plowshare will I be to you. All the secrets of your foundation shall come to light; and when you lie uprooted and broken in the sun, then will your lies also be separated from your truths.

For this is your truth: you are too *pure* for the filth of the words: revenge, punishment, reward, retribution. You love your virtue as a mother her child; but when has a mother ever wished to be paid for her love? Your virtue is what is dearest to you. The thirst of the ring lives in you: every ring strives and turns to reach itself again. And like a dying star is every work of your virtue: its light is always still on its way and it wanders—and when will it no longer be on its way? Thus the light of your virtue is still on its way even when the work has been done. Though it be forgotten and dead, the ray of its light still lives and wanders. That your virtue is your self and not something foreign, a skin, a cloak, that is the truth from the foundation of your souls, you who are virtuous.

Yet there are those for whom virtue is the spasm under the scourge, and you have listened to their clamor too much.

"On the Virtuous," from *The Portable Nietzsche* by Walter Kaufmann, ed., transl. By Walter Kaufmann. Translation copyright © 1954 by The Viking Press, renewed © 1982 by Viking Penguin, Inc. Used by permission of Viking Penguin, a division of Penguin Books USA Inc. Reprinted with permission of the publisher from *A Nietzsche Reader,* trans. R. Hollingdale (Penguin, 1977), selections.

And there are others who call it virtue when their vices grow lazy; and when their hatred and jealousy stretch their limbs for once, then their "justice" comes to life and rubs its sleepy eyes.

And there are others who are drawn downward: their devils draw them. But the more they sink, the more fervently glow their eyes and their lust for their god. Alas, their clamor too has reached your ears, you who are virtuous: "What I am not, that, that to me are God and virtue!"

And there are others who come along, heavy and creaking like carts carrying stones downhill: they talk much of dignity and virtue—they call their brake virtue.

And there are others who are like cheap clocks that must be wound: they tick and they want the tick-tock to be called virtue. Verily, I have my pleasure in these: wherever I find such clocks, I shall wind and wound them with my mockery, and they shall whir for me.

And others are proud of their handful of justice and commit outrages against all things for its sake, till the world is drowned in their injustice. Oh, how ill the word virtue comes out of their mouths! And when they say, "I am just," it always sounds like "I am just—revenged." With their virtue they want to scratch out the eyes of their enemies, and they exalt themselves only to humble others.

And then again there are such as sit in their swamp and speak thus out of the reeds: "Virtue—that is sitting still in a swamp. We bite no one and avoid those who want to bite; and in all things we hold the opinion that is given to us."

And then again there are such as love gestures and think that virtue is some kind of gesture. Their knees always adore, and their hands are hymns to virtue, but their heart knows nothing about it.

And then again there are such as consider it virtue to say, "Virtue is necessary"; but at bottom they believe only that the police is necessary.

And some who cannot see what is high in man call it virtue that they see all-too-closely what is low in man: thus they call their evil eye virtue.

And some want to be edified and elevated, and they call that virtue, while others want to be bowled over, and they call that virtue too.

And thus almost all believe that they have a share in virtue; and at the very least everyone wants to be an expert on good and evil.

Yet Zarathustra did not come to say to all these liars and fools: "What do *you* know of virtue? What *could* you know of virtue?"

Rather, that you, my friends, might grow weary of the old words you have learned from the fools and liars.

Weary of the words: reward, retribution, punishment, and revenge in justice.

Weary of saying: what makes an act good is that it is unselfish.

Oh, my friends, that your self be in your deed as the mother is in her child—let that be *your* word concerning virtue!

Verily, I may have taken a hundred words from you and the dearest toys of your virtue, and now you are angry with me, as children are angry. They played by the sea, and a wave came and carried off their toy to the depths: now they are crying. But the same wave shall bring them new toys and shower new colorful shells before them. Thus they will be comforted; and like them, you too, my friends, shall have your comfortings—and new colorful shells.

Thus spoke Zarathustra.

[*Thus Spoke Zarathustra, On the Virtuous*]

*

## Good and Evil, Good and Bad

The slave revolt in morality begins when *ressentiment* itself becomes creative and gives birth to values: the *ressentiment* of creatures to whom the real reaction, that of the deed, is denied and who can indemnify themselves only through an imaginary revenge. While every noble morality develops from a triumphant affirmation of itself, slave morality from the outset says No to what is "outside," what is "different," what is "not itself": and *this* No is its creative act. This reversal of the value-creating view—this *necessary* directing of the eye outwards instead of back to oneself—pertains precisely to *ressentiment*: in order to come into existence, slave morality always first requires a contrary and outer world, it requires, in the language of physiology, an external stimulus in order to act at all—its action is from the very bottom reaction. The opposite is the case with the noble mode of valuation: it acts and grows spontaneously, it seeks its antithesis only so as to affirm itself more gratefully and joyously—its negative concept "low," "common," "bad" is only a subsequently produced pale contrasting image in comparison with its positive basic concept, saturated through and through with life and passion, "we noble, we good, we beautiful, we happy!" [ . . . ] The "well born" *feel*  themselves to be the "happy"; they do not first have to construct their happiness artificially, or if need be convince themselves of it, *lie* themselves into it (as all men of *ressentiment*  are accustomed to do), by gazing on their enemies; and as whole men, overcharged with strength and therefore *necessarily* active, they likewise do not know how to sever themselves from the happiness of acting—to be active is with them necessarily a part of happiness (whence *eu prattein* takes its origin)—all this very much in contrast to "happiness" on the level of the powerless, the oppressed, those festering with poisonous and inimical feelings, with whom it appears essentially as narcosis, stupefaction, rest, peace, "Sabbath," relaxation of the heart and stretching of the limbs, in short *passively*. While the noble man lives in trust and openness with himself (*gennaios*, "nobly born," underlines the nuance "upright" and probably also "naive"), the man of *ressentiment* is neither upright nor naive, or honest and straightforward with himself. His soul *squints:* his spirit loves hiding-places, secret paths and back doors, everything covert strikes him as *his* world, *his* security, *his* refreshment; he knows how to keep silent, how not to forget, how to wait, how to make himself provisionally small and humble. A race of such men of *ressentiment* will necessarily end up *cleverer* than any noble race, it will also hold cleverness in an altogether higher degree of honour: namely, as a condition of its existence of the first order; while with noble men cleverness can easily acquire a slight flavour of luxury and *raffinement*—here it is not nearly so essential as the perfect functioning of the regulatory *unconscious* instincts or even a certain lack of cleverness, perhaps a brave recklessness in face of danger or in face of the enemy, or that enthusi-

astic impetuosity in anger, love, reverence, gratitude and revenge by which noble souls have in all ages recognized one another. When the noble man does feel *ressentiment* it consummates and exhausts itself in an immediate reaction, it therefore does not *poison:* on the other hand, it simply fails to appear in countless instances in which it would inevitably do so with the weak and powerless. An inability to take their enemies, their misfortunes, even their *misdeeds* seriously for long— that is a sign of strong, full natures in which there is an excess of plastic, formative, curative power, and also the power of forgetting. [ . . . ] Such a man shakes from himself with a *single* shrug much vermin which would bore its way into others; here alone, too, is there possible, if it is possible on earth at all—actual "love of one's enemies." How much respect for his enemies does a noble man already feel!—and such respect is already a bridge to love . . . For he wants his enemy for himself, as his distinction, he can indeed endure no enemy but one in whom there is nothing to despise and *very much* to honour! Picture, on the other hand, "the enemy" as the man of *ressentiment* conceives him—and here precisely is his deed, his creation: he has conceived "the evil enemy," *"the Evil One,"* and this indeed is his basic conception from which he then evolves, as a corresponding and opposing figure, a "good one"—himself! . . .

This is, then, quite the contrary of what the noble man does, who conceives the basic conception "good" spontaneously, out of himself, and only then creates from that an idea of "bad"! This "bad" of noble origin and that "evil" out of the cauldron of unsatisfied hatred, [. . .] how different these words "bad" and "evil" are, although they are both apparently the opposite of the same concept "good." But it is *not* the same concept "good": one should ask rather precisely *who* is "evil" in the sense of the morality of *ressentiment*. The answer is, in all strictness: *precisely* the "good man" of the other morality, precisely the noble, powerful man, the ruler, only recoloured, reinterpreted and seen differently by the poisoned eye of *ressentiment*. Let us here deny one thing least of all: he who gets to know these "good men" only as enemies gets to know only *evil enemies,* and the same men who are held so strictly in bounds *inter pares* by custom, respect, usage, gratitude, even more by mutual watchfulness, by jealousy, and who on the other hand show themselves so inventive in consideration, self-control, sensitivity, loyalty, pride and friendship in their relations with one another—with respect to what lies outside, where the strange and the stranger begin, these men are not much better than beasts of prey let loose. There they enjoy a freedom from all social constraint; they indemnify themselves in the wilderness for the tension which a protracted imprisonment and enclosure within the peace of the community produces; they *go back* to the innocence of the beast-of-prey conscience, as rejoicing monsters who perhaps make off from a hideous succession of murders, conflagrations, rapes and torturings in high spirits and equanimity of soul as if they had been engaged in nothing more than a student prank, and convinced that the poets now again have something to sing about and praise for a long time to come. One cannot fail to see at the core of all these noble races the animal of prey, the splendid *blond beast* prowling about avidly in search of spoil and victory; this hidden core needs to erupt from time to time, the animal has to get out again and go back to the wilderness: the Roman, Arabian, Germanic, Japanese nobility, the Homeric heroes, the Scandinavian Vikings—they all shared this need. It is the noble races which have left behind them the concept 'barbarian' wherever they have gone [ . . . ]

[ . . . ] To require of strength that it should *not* express itself as strength, that it should *not* be a desire to conquer, a desire to subdue, a desire to become master, a thirst for enemies and resistances and triumphs, is just as absurd as to require of weakness that it should express itself as strength. A quantum of force is an equivalent quantum of drive, will, operation—or, rather, it is nothing whatever other than this driving, willing, operating itself, and only under the misleading influence of language (and the fundamental errors of reason fossilized in it), which understands and misunderstands all operation as conditioned by an operator, by a "subject," can it seem otherwise. For just as the people separates the lightning from its flash and takes the latter as an *action,* as an operation on the part of a subject called lightning,

so popular morality separates strength from expressions of strength, as if there were a neutral substratum behind the strong man which was *free* to express strength or not to do so. But there is no such substratum; there is no "being" behind doing, operating, becoming; "the door" is merely added to the deed—the deed is everything. [ . . . ] When the oppressed, downtrodden, despoiled say to themselves in the revengeful cunning of impotence: "let us be different from the evil, namely good! and good is everyone who does not despoil, who injures no one, who does not attack, who does not requite, who leaves vengeance to God, who lives in obscurity as we do, who avoids everything evil and demands little from life in general, like us, the patient, humble and just"—this, heard coldly and without prepossession, really meant nothing more than: "we weak are after all weak; it would be a good thing to do nothing *for which we are insufficiently strong*"; but this austere fact, this prudence of the lowest sort which even insects possess (who, when there is danger, pretend to be dead so as not to do "'too much"") has, thanks to that false-coinage and self-deluding of impotence, clothed itself in the finery of the virtue of renunciation and silent waiting, as if the weakness of the weak man itself—and that means his *essence,* his actions, his whole, sole, inevitable, irredeemable actuality—were a voluntary achievement, something willed, chosen, a *deed, meritorious.* [ . . . ]

[*On the Genealogy of Morals,*
"Good and Evil," "Good and Bad"
sections 2, 4, 5, 10, 11, 13]

*

## Origin of Justice

Justice (fairness) originates between parties of approximately *equal power,* as Thucydides correctly grasped (in the terrible colloquy between the Athenian and Melian ambassadors): where there is no clearly recognizable superiority of force and a contest would result in mutual injury producing no decisive outcome the idea arises of coming to an understanding and negotiating over one another's demands: the characteristic of *exchange* is the original characteristic of justice. Each satisfies the other [ . . . ] Justice is thus requital and exchange under the presupposition of an approximately equal power position: revenge therefore belongs originally within the domain of justice, it is an exchange. Gratitude likewise.— Justice goes back naturally to the viewpoint of an enlightened self-preservation, thus to the egoism of the reflection: "to what end should I injure myself uselessly and perhaps even then not achieve my goal?"—So much for the *origin* of justice. Since, in accordance with their intellectual habit, men have *forgotten* the original purpose of so-called just and fair actions, and especially because children have for millennia been trained to admire and imitate such actions, it has gradually come to appear that a just action is an unegoistic one: but it is on this appearance that the high value accorded it depends; and this high value is, moreover, continually increasing, as all valuations do: for something highly valued is striven for, imitated, multiplied through sacrifice, and grows as the worth of the toil and zeal extended by each individual is added to the worth of the valued thing.—How little moral would the world appear without forgetfulness! A poet could say that God has placed forgetfulness as a doorkeeper on the threshold of the temple of human dignity.

[*Human, All Too Human,* section 92]

*

## To the Teachers of Selflessness

A person's virtues are called *good,* not with regard to the effects they produce for himself, but with regard to the effects we suppose they will produce for us and for society—praise of virtue has always been very little "selfless," very little "unegoistic"! For otherwise it must have been seen that virtues (such as industriousness, obedience, chastity, piety, justness) are mostly *injurious* to their possessors, as drives which rule in them too fervently and demandingly and will in no way allow reason to hold them in equilibrium with the other drives. If you possess a virtue, a real whole virtue (and not merely a puny drive towards a virtue!)—you

are its *victim*! But that precisely is why your neighbour praises your virtue! [ . . . ] Praise of the selfless, sacrificing, virtuous—that is to say, of those who do not expend all their strength and reason on *their own* preservation, evolution, elevation, advancement, amplification of their power, but who live modestly and thoughtlessly, perhaps even indifferently or ironically with regard to themselves—this praise is in any event not a product of the spirit of selflessness! One's "neighbour" praises selflessness because *he derives advantage from it!* [ . . . ] Herewith is indicated the fundamental contradiction of that morality which is precisely today held in such high esteem: the *motives* for this morality stand in antithesis to its *principle*! That with which this morality wants to prove itself it refutes by its criterion of the moral! [ . . . ]

[*The Gay Science,* section 21]

*

## Master Morality and Slave Morality

In a tour of the many finer and coarser moralities which have ruled or still rule on earth I found certain traits regularly recurring together and bound up with one another: until at length two basic types were revealed and a basic distinction emerged. There is *master morality* and *slave morality*—I add at once that in all higher and mixed cultures attempts at mediation between the two are apparent and more frequently confusion and mutual misunderstanding between them, indeed sometimes their harsh juxtaposition—even within the same man, within *one* soul. The moral value-distinctions have arisen either among a ruling order which was pleasurably conscious of its distinction from the ruled—or among the ruled, the slaves and dependents of every degree. In the former case, when it is the rulers who determine the concept "good," it is the exalted, proud states of soul which are considered distinguishing and determine the order or rank. The noble human being separates from himself those natures in which the opposite of such exalted proud states finds expression: he despises them. It should be noted at once that in this first type of morality the antithesis "good" and "bad" means the same thing as "noble" and "despicable"—the antithesis "good" and "*evil*" originates elsewhere. The cowardly, the timid, the petty, and those who think only of narrow utility are despised; as are the mistrustful with their constricted glance, those who abase themselves, the dog-like type of man who lets himself be maltreated, the fawning flatterer, above all the liar—it is a fundamental belief of all aristocrats that the common people are liars. [ . . . ] It is immediately obvious that designations of moral value were everywhere first applied to *human beings,* and only later and derivatively to *actions:* which is why it is a grave error when moral historians start from such questions as "why has the compassionate action been praised?" The noble type of man feels *himself* to be the determiner of values, he does not need to be approved of, he judges "what harms me is harmful in itself," he knows himself to be that which in general first accords to honour things, he *creates values.* Everything he knows to be part of himself, he honours: such a morality is self-glorification. In the foreground stands the feeling of plenitude, of power which seeks to overflow, the happiness of high tension, the consciousness of a wealth which would like to give away and bestow—the noble human being, too, aids the unfortunate but not, or almost not, from pity, but more from an urge begotten by superfluity of power. The noble human being honours in himself the man of power, also the man who has power over himself, who understands how to speak and how to keep silent, who enjoys practising severity and harshness upon himself and feels reverence for all that is severe and harsh. [ . . . ] Deep reverence for age and the traditional—all law rests on this twofold reverence—belief in and prejudice in favour of ancestors and against descendants, is typical of the morality of the powerful; and when, conversely, men of "modern ideas" believe almost instinctively in "progress" and 'the future' and show an increasing lack of respect for age, this reveals clearly enough the ignoble origin of these "ideas." A morality of the rulers is, however, most alien and painful to contemporary taste in the severity of its principle that one has duties only towards one's equals; that towards beings of a lower rank, towards everything alien, one may act as one wishes or "as the heart dictates" and in any case "beyond good and evil": it is here that pity and the like can have a place. The capacity for and the duty of protracted gratitude and protracted revenge—both only among one's equals—subtlety in requital, a refined conception of friendship, a certain need to have enemies (as conduit systems, as it were, for the emotions of envy, quarrelsomeness, arrogance—fundamentally so as to be able to be a good *friend*): all these are typical marks of noble morality [ . . . ] It is otherwise with the second type of morality, *slave morality.* Suppose the abused, oppressed, suffering, unfree, those uncertain of themselves and weary should moralize: what would their moral evaluations have in common? Probably a pessimistic mistrust of the entire situation of man will find expression, perhaps a condemnation of man together with his situation. The slave is suspicious of the virtues of the powerful: he is sceptical and mistrustful, *keenly* mistrustful, of everything "good" that is honoured among them—he would like to convince himself that happiness itself is not genuine among them. On the other hand, those qualities which serve to make easier the existence of the suffering will be brought into prominence and flooded with light: here it is that pity, the kind and helping hand, the warm heart, patience, industriousness, humility, friendliness come into honour—for here these are the most useful qualities and virtually the only means of enduring the burden of existence. Slave morality is essentially the morality of utility. Here is the source of the famous antithesis "good" and "*evil*"—power and danger were felt to exist in evil, a certain dreadfulness, subtlety and strength which could not admit of contempt. Thus, according to slave morality the "evil" inspire fear; according to master morality it is precisely the "good" who inspire fear and want to inspire it, while the "bad" man is judged contemptible. The antithesis reaches its height when, consistently with slave morality, a breath of disdain finally also comes to be attached to the "good" of this morality—it may be a slight and benevolent disdain—because within the slaves' way of thinking the good man has in any event to be a *harmless* man: he is good-natured, easy to deceive, perhaps a bit stupid, *un bonhomme.* Wherever slave morality comes to predominate, language exhibits a tendency to bring the words "good" and "stupid" closer to each other.—A final fundamental distinction: the longing for *freedom,* the instinct for the happiness and the refinements of the feeling of freedom, belong just as necessarily to slave morality and morals as the art of reverence and devotion and the enthusiasm for them are the regular symptom of an aristocratic mode of thinking and valuating.—This makes it clear without further ado why love *as passion*—it is our European specialty—absolutely must be of aristocratic origin: it was, as is well known, invented by the poet-knights of Provence, those splendid, inventive men of the *"gai saber"* to whom Europe owes so much and, indeed, almost itself.

[*Beyond Good and Evil,* section 260]

*

## The Heaviest Burden

What if a demon crept after you one day or night in your loneliest solitude and said to you: "This life, as you live it now and have lived it, you will have to live again and again, times without number; and there will be nothing new in it, but every pain and every joy and every thought and sigh and all the unspeakably small and great in your life must return to you, and everything in the same series and sequence—and in the same way this spider and this moonlight among the trees, and in the same way this moment and I myself. The eternal hour-glass of existence will be turned again and again—and you with it, you dust of dust!"— Would you not throw yourself down and gnash your teeth and curse the demon who thus spoke? Or have you experienced a tremendous moment in which you would have answered him: "You are a god and never did I hear anything more divine!" If this thought gained power over you it would, as you are now, transform and perhaps crush you; the question in all and everything: "do you want

this again and again, times without number?" would lie as the heaviest burden upon all your actions. Or how well disposed towards yourself and towards life would you have to become to have *no greater desire* than for this ultimate eternal sanction and seal?

[*The Gay Science,* section 341]

*

## What Our Cheerfulness Signifies

The greatest recent event—that "God is dead," that belief in the Christian God has become unbelievable—is already beginning to cast its first shadows over Europe. For the few, at least, whose eyes, the *suspicion* in whose eyes is strong and subtle enough for this spectacle, it seems as though some sun had just gone down, some ancient profound trust had been turned round into doubt: to them our old world must appear daily more crepuscular, untrustworthy, stranger, "older." On the whole, however, one has to say that the event itself is much too great, too distant, too remote from the comprehension of many for news of it even to have *arrived* yet; not to speak of many knowing already *what* has really taken place— and what, now that this belief has been undermined, must now fall in because it was built on this belief, leaned on it, had grown into it: for example, our entire European morality. This protracted abundance and succession of demolition, destruction, decline, overturning which now stands before us: who today could divine enough of this to feel obliged to be the teacher and herald of this tremendous logic of terror, the prophet of a darkening and eclipse of the sun such as there has probably never yet been on earth? . . . Even we born readers of riddles, who wait, as it were, on the mountains, set between today and tomorrow and yoked to the contradiction between today and tomorrow, we first-born and premature-born of the coming century, to whom the shadows which must soon envelop Europe *ought* already to have come into sight: why is it that even we lack any real participation in this darkening, above all behold its advent without any care or fear for *our-*

*selves*? Do we perhaps still stand too much within the *immediate consequences* of this event—and these immediate consequences, its consequences for *us,* are, conversely from what one could expect, in no way sad and darkening but, rather, like a new, hard to describe kind of light, happiness, alleviation, encouragement, dawn . . . We philosophers and "free spirits" in fact feel at the news that the "old God is dead" as if illumined by a new dawn; our heart overflows with gratitude, astonishment, presentiment, expectation—at last the horizon seems to us again free, even if it is not bright, at last our ships can put out again, no matter what the danger, every daring venture of knowledge is again permitted, the sea, *our* sea again lies there open before us, perhaps there has never yet been such an "open sea."

[*The Gay Science,* section 343 (1887)]

*

## Improving Mankind

One knows my demand of philosophers that they place themselves *beyond* good and evil—that they have the illusion of moral judgement *beneath* them. This demand follows from an insight first formulated by me: *that there are no moral facts whatever.* Moral judgement has this in common with religious judgement, that it believes in realities which do not exist. Morality is only an interpretation of certain phenomena, more precisely a *mis*interpretation. Moral judgement belongs, as does religious judgement, to a level of ignorance at which even the concept of the real, the distinction between the real and the imaginary, is lacking [ . . . ] To this extent moral judgement is never to be taken literally: as such it never contains anything but nonsense. But as *semeiotics* it remains of incalculable value: it reveals, to the informed man at least, the most precious realities of cultures and inner worlds which did not *know* enough to "understand" themselves. Morality is merely sign-language, merely symptomatology [ . . . ]

A first example, merely as an introduction. In all ages one has wanted to "improve" men: this above all is what morality has meant. But one

word can conceal the most divergent tendencies. Both the *taming* of the beast man and the *breeding* of a certain species of man has been called "improvement": only these zoological *termini* express realities [ . . . ] To call the taming of an animal its "improvement" is in our ears almost a joke. Whoever knows what goes on in menageries is doubtful whether the beasts in them are "improved." They are weakened, they are made less harmful, they become *sickly* beasts through the depressive emotion of fear, through pain, through injuries, through hunger.—It is no different with the tamed human being whom the priest has "improved." In the early Middle Ages, when the Church was in fact above all a menagerie, one everywhere hunted down the fairest specimens of the "blond beast"—one "improved," for example, the noble Teutons. But what did such a Teuton afterwards look like when he had been "improved" and led into a monastery? Like a caricature of a human being, like an abortion: he had become a "sinner," he was in a cage [ . . . ] There he lay now, sick, miserable, filled with ill-will towards himself; full of hatred for the impulses towards life, full of suspicion of all that was still strong and happy. In short, a "Christian" . . . In physiological terms: in the struggle with the beast, making it sick *can* be the only means of making it weak. This the Church understood: it *corrupted* the human being, it weakened him—but it claimed to have "improved" him . . .

[Twilight of the Idols,
*The "Improvers" of Mankind*]

*

## Twofold Prehistory of Good and Evil

The concept good and evil has a twofold prehistory: *firstly* in the soul of the ruling tribes and castes. He who has the power to requite, good with good, evil with evil, and also actually practises requital—is, that is to say, grateful and revengeful—is called good; he who is powerless and cannot requite counts as bad. As a good man one belongs to the "good," a community which has a sense of belonging together because all the individuals in it are combined with one another through the capacity for requital. As a bad man one belongs to the "bad," to a swarm of subject, powerless people who have no sense of belonging together. The good are a caste, the bad a mass like grains of sand. Good and bad is for a long time the same thing as noble and base, master and slave. On the other hand, one does not regard the enemy as evil: he can requite. In Homer the Trojan and the Greek are both good. It is not he who does us harm but he who is contemptible who counts as bad. [ . . . ] *Then* in the soul of the subjected, the powerless. Here every *other* man, whether he be noble or base, counts as inimical, ruthless, cruel, cunning, ready to take advantage. Evil is the characterizing expression for man, indeed for every living being one supposes to exist, for a god, for example; human, divine mean the same thing as diabolical, evil. Signs of goodness, benevolence, sympathy are received fearfully as a trick, a prelude with a dreadful termination, a means of confusing and outwitting, in short as refined wickedness. When this disposition exists in the individual a community can hardly arise, at best the most rudimentary form of community: so that wherever this conception of good and evil reigns the downfall of such individuals, of their tribes and races, is near.—Our present morality has grown up in the soil of the *ruling* tribes and castes.

[*Human, All Too Human,* section 45]

*

## Preserver of the Species

It is the strongest and most evil spirits who have up till now advanced mankind the most: they have again and again re-ignited the slumbering passions—all ordered society makes the passions drowsy—they have awoken again and again the sense of comparison, of contradiction, of joy in the new, daring, untried, they have compelled men to set opinion against opinion, model against

model. Most of all by weapons, by overturning boundary stones, by wounding piety: but also by new religions and moralities! The same "wickedness" is in every teacher and preacher of the *new* as makes a conqueror infamous [ . . . ] The new, however, is under all circumstances the *evil*, as that which wants to conquer and overturn the old boundary stones and the old pieties; and only the old is the good! The good men of every age are those who bury the old ideas in the depths of the earth and bear fruit with them, the agriculturalists of the spirit. But that land will at length become exhausted, and the ploughshare of evil must come again and again.—There is nowadays a fundamentally false theory of morality which is especially celebrated in England: according to this theory the judgements "good " and "evil" are the summation of experiences of "useful" and "not useful"; that which is called "good" is that which preserves the species, that which is called "evil" is that which injures the species. In truth, however, the evil impulses are just as useful, indispensable and preservative of the species as the good:—only their function is different.

[*The Gay Science,* section 4]

*

## Content of the Conscience

The content of our conscience is everything that was during the years of our childhood regularly *demanded* of us without reason by people we honoured or feared. It is thus the conscience that excites that feeling of compulsion ('I must do this, not do that') which does not ask: *why* must I?—In every case in which a thing is done with "because" and "why" man acts *without* conscience; but not yet for that reason against it.— The belief in authorities is the source of the conscience: it is therefore not the voice of God in the heart of man but the voice of some men in man.

[*The Wanderer and His Shadow,* section 52]

# 8 The Virtue of Selfishness

AYN RAND

## The Objectivist Ethic

. . . The standard of value of the Objectivist ethics —the standard by which one judges what is good or evil—is *man's life,* or, that which is required for man's survival *qua* man.

Since reason is man's basic means of survival, that which is proper to the life of a rational being is the good; that which negates, opposes or destroys it is the evil.

Since everything man needs has to be discovered by his own mind and produced by his own effort, the two essentials of the method of survival proper to a rational being are: thinking and productive work.

If some men do not choose to think, but survive by imitating and repeating, like trained animals, the routine of sounds and motions they learned from others, never making an effort to understand their own work, it still remains true that their survival is made possible only by those who did choose to think and to discover the motions they are repeating. The survival of such mental parasites depends on blind chance; their unfocused minds are unable to know *whom* to imitate, *whose* motions it is safe to follow. *They* are the men who march into the abyss, trailing after any destroyer who promises them to assume the responsibility they evade: the responsibility of being conscious.

If some men attempt to survive by means of brute force or fraud, by looting, robbing, cheating or enslaving the men who produce, it still remains true that their survival is made possible only by their victims, only by the men who choose to think and to produce the goods which they, the looters, are seizing. Such looters are parasites incapable of survival, who exist by destroying those who *are* capable, those who are pursuing a course of action proper to man.

The men who attempt to survive, not by means of reason, but by means of force, are attempting to survive by the method of animals. But just as animals would not be able to survive by attempting the method of plants, by rejecting locomotion and waiting for the soil to feed them—so men cannot survive by attempting the method of animals, by rejecting reason and counting on productive *men* to serve as their prey. Such looters may achieve their goals for the range of a moment, at the price of destruction: the destruction of their victims and their own. As evidence, I offer you any criminal or any dictatorship.

Man cannot survive, like an animal, by acting on the range of the moment. An animal's life consists of a series of separate cycles, repeated over and over again, such as the cycle of breeding its young, or of storing food for the winter; an animal's consciousness cannot integrate its entire lifespan; it can carry just so far, then the animal has to begin the cycle all over again, with no connection to the past. *Man's* life is a continuous whole: for good or evil, every day, year and decade of his life holds the sum of all the days behind him. He can alter his choices, he is free to change the direction of his course, he is even free, in many cases, to atone for the consequences of his past—but he is not free to escape them, nor to live his life with impunity on the range of the moment, like an animal, a playboy or a thug. If he is to succeed at the task of survival, if his actions are not to be aimed at his own destruction, man has to choose his course, his goals, his values in the context and terms of a lifetime. No sensations, percepts, urges or "instincts" can do it; only a mind can.

"The Objectivist Ethics" and "The Ethics of Emergencies" from *The Virtue of Selfishness* by Ayn Rand. Copyright © 1961, 1964 by Ayn Rand. Used by permission of Dutton Signet, a division of Penguin Putnam Inc., 23–48, with omissions.

Such is the meaning of the definition: that which is required for man's survival *qua* man. It does not mean a *momentary* or a merely *physical* survival. It does not mean the momentary physical survival of a mindless brute, waiting for another brute to crush his skull. It does not mean the momentary physical survival of a crawling aggregate of muscles who is willing to accept any terms, obey any thug and surrender any values, for the sake of what is known as "survival at any price," which may or may not last a week or a year. "Man's survival *qua* man" means the terms, methods, conditions and goals required for the survival of a rational being through the whole of his lifespan—in all those aspects of existence which are open to his choice. . . .

Man must choose his actions, values and goals by the standard of that which is proper to man—in order to achieve, maintain, fulfill and enjoy that ultimate value, that end in itself, which is his own life.

*Value* is that which one acts to gain and/or keep—*virtue* is the act by which one gains and/or keeps it. The three cardinal values of the Objectivist ethics—the three values which, together, are the means to and the realization of one's ultimate value, one's own life—are: Reason, Purpose, Self-Esteem, with their three corresponding virtues: Rationality, Productiveness, Pride.

Productive work is the central *purpose* of a rational man's life, the central value that integrates and determines the hierarchy of all his other values. Reason is the source, the precondition of his productive work—pride is the result.

Rationality is man's basic virtue, the source of all his other virtues. Man's basic vice, the source of all his evils, is the act of unfocusing his mind, the suspension of his consciousness, which is not blindness, but the refusal to see, not ignorance, but the refusal to know. Irrationality is the rejection of man's means of survival and, therefore, a commitment to a course of blind destruction; that which is anti-mind, is anti-life.

The virtue of *Rationality* means the recognition and acceptance of reason as one's only source of knowledge, one's only judge of values and one's only guide to action. It means one's total commit-ment to a state of full, conscious awareness, to the maintenance of a full mental focus in all issues, in all choices, in all of one's waking hours. It means a commitment to the fullest perception of reality within one's power and to the constant, active expansion of one's perception, *i.e.*, of one's knowledge. It means a commitment to the reality of one's own existence, *i.e.*, to the principle that all of one's goals, values and actions take place in reality and, therefore, that one must never place any value or consideration whatsoever above one's perception of reality. It means a commit-ment to the principle that all of one's convictions, values, goals, desires and actions must be based on, derived from, chosen and validated by a process of thought—as precise and scrupulous a process of thought, directed by as ruthlessly strict an application of logic, as one's fullest capacity permits. It means one's acceptance of the respon-sibility of forming one's own judgments and of liv-ing by the work of one's own mind (which is the virtue of Independence). It means that one must never sacrifice one's convictions to the opinions or wishes of others (which is the virtue of Integrity) —that one must never attempt to fake reality in any manner (which is the virtue of Honesty)—that one must never seek or grant the unearned and undeserved, neither in matter nor in spirit (which is the virtue of Justice). It means that one must never desire effects without causes, and that one must never enact a cause without assuming full responsibility for its effects—that one must never act like a zombie, *i.e.*, without knowing one's own purposes and motives—that one must never make any decisions, form any convictions or seek any values out of context, *i.e.*, apart from or against the total, integrated sum of one's knowl-edge—and, above all, that one must never seek to get away with contradictions. It means the rejec-tion of any form of *mysticism, i.e.*, any claim to some nonsensory, nonrational, nondefinable, supernatural source of knowledge. It means a commitment to reason, not in sporadic fits or on selected issues or in special emergencies, but as a permanent way of life.

The virtue of *Productiveness* is the recognition of the fact that productive work is the process by which man's mind sustains his life, the process that sets man free of the necessity to adjust himself to his background, as all animals do, and gives him the power to adjust his background to himself. Productive work is the road of man's unlimited achievement and calls upon the highest attributes of his character: his creative ability, his ambitiousness, his self-assertiveness, his refusal to bear uncontested disasters, his dedication to the goal of reshaping the earth in the image of his values. "Productive work" does not mean the unfocused performance of the motions of some job. It means the consciously chosen pursuit of a productive career, in any line of rational endeavor, great or modest, on any level of ability. It is not the degree of a man's ability nor the scale of his work that is ethically relevant here, but the fullest and most purposeful use of his mind.

The virtue of *Pride* is the recognition of the fact "that as man must produce the physical values he needs to sustain his life, so he must acquire the values of character that make his life worth sustaining—that as man is a being of self-made wealth, so he is a being of self-made soul." (*Atlas Shrugged.*) The virtue of Pride can best be described by the term: "moral ambitiousness." It means that one must earn the right to hold oneself as one's own highest value by achieving one's own moral perfection—which one achieves by never accepting any code of irrational virtues impossible to practice and by never failing to practice the virtues one knows to be rational—by never accepting an unearned guilt and never earning any, or, if one *has* earned it, never leaving it uncorrected—by never resigning oneself passively to any flaws in one's character—by never placing any concern, wish, fear or mood of the moment above the reality of one's own self-esteem. And, above all, it means one's rejection of the role of a sacrificial animal, the rejection of any doctrine that preaches self-immolation as a moral virtue or duty.

The basic *social* principle of the Objectivist ethics is that just as life is an end in itself, so every living human being is an end in himself, not the means to the ends or the welfare of others—and, therefore, that man must live for his own sake,

neither sacrificing himself to others nor sacrificing others to himself. To live for his own sake means that *the achievement of his own happiness is man's highest moral purpose. . . .*

Happiness is that state of consciousness which proceeds from the achievement of one's values. If a man values productive work, his happiness is the measure of his success in the service of his life. But if a man values destruction, like a sadist—or self-torture, like a masochist—or life beyond the grave, like a mystic—or mindless "kicks," like the driver of a hotrod car—*his* alleged happiness is the measure of his success in the service of his own destruction. It must be added that the emotional state of all those irrationalists cannot be properly designated as happiness or even as pleasure: it is merely a moment's *relief* from their chronic state of terror.

Neither life nor happiness can be achieved by the pursuit of irrational whims. Just as man is free to attempt to survive by any random means, as a parasite, a moocher or a looter, but not free to succeed at it beyond the range of the moment—so he is free to seek his happiness in any irrational fraud, any whim, any delusion, any mindless escape from reality, but not free to succeed at it beyond the range of the moment nor to escape the consequences.

I quote from Galt's speech: "Happiness is a state of noncontradictory joy—a joy without penalty or guilt, a joy that does not clash with any of your values and does not work for your own destruction. . . . Happiness is possible only to a rational man, the man who desires nothing but rational goals, seeks nothing but rational values and finds his joy in nothing but rational actions."

The maintenance of life and the pursuit of happiness are not two separate issues. To hold one's own life as one's ultimate value, and one's own happiness as one's highest purpose are two aspects of the same achievement. Existentially, the activity of pursuing rational goals is the activity of maintaining one's life; psychologically, its result, reward and concomitant is an emotional state of happiness. It is by experiencing happiness that one lives one's life, in any hour, year or the whole of it. And when one experiences the kind of pure happiness that is an end in itself—the kind that makes one think: "*This* is worth living for"—what one is greeting and affirming in emotional terms is the metaphysical fact that *life* is an end in itself. . . .

The Objectivist ethics proudly advocates and upholds *rational selfishness*—which means: the values required for man's survival *qua* man—which means: the values required for *human* survival—not the values produced by the desires, the emotions, the "aspirations," the feelings, the whims or the needs of irrational brutes, who have never outgrown the primordial practice of human sacrifices, have never discovered an industrial society and can conceive of no self-interest but that of grabbing the loot of the moment.

The Objectivist ethics holds that *human* good does not require human sacrifices and cannot be achieved by the sacrifice of anyone to anyone. It holds that the *rational* interests of men do not clash—that there is no conflict of interests among men who do not desire the unearned, who do not make sacrifices nor accept them, who deal with one another as *traders,* giving value for value.

The principle of *trade* is the only rational ethical principle for all human relationships, personal and social, private and public, spiritual and material. It is the principle of *justice.*

A trader is a man who earns what he gets and does not give or take the undeserved. He does not treat men as masters or slaves, but as independent equals. He deals with men by means of a free, voluntary, unforced, uncoerced exchange—an exchange which benefits both parties by their own independent judgment. A trader does not expect to be paid for his defaults, only for his achievements. He does not switch to others the burden of his failures, and he does not mortgage his life into bondage to the failures of others.

In spiritual issues—(by "spiritual" I mean: "pertaining to man's consciousness")—the currency or medium of exchange is different, but the principle is the same. Love, friendship, respect, admiration are the emotional response of one man to the virtues of another, the spiritual *payment* given in exchange for the personal, selfish pleasure which one man derives from the virtues of

another man's character. Only a brute or an altruist would claim that the appreciation of another person's virtues is an act of selflessness, that as far as one's own selfish interest and pleasure are concerned, it makes no difference whether one deals with a genius or a fool, whether one meets a hero or a thug, whether one marries an ideal woman or a slut. In spiritual issues, a trader is a man who does not seek to be loved for his weaknesses or flaws, only for his virtues, and who does not grant his love to the weaknesses or the flaws of others, only to their virtues.

To love is to value. Only a rationally selfish man, a man of *self-esteem,* is capable of love—because he is the only man capable of holding firm, consistent, uncompromising, unbetrayed values. The man who does not value himself, cannot value anything or anyone.

It is only on the basis of rational selfishness—on the basis of justice—that men can be fit to live together in a free, peaceful, prosperous, benevolent, *rational* society. . . .

The basic political principle of the Objectivist ethics is: no man may *initiate* the use of physical force against others. No man—or group or society or government—has the right to assume the role of a criminal and initiate the use of physical compulsion against any man. Men have the right to use physical force *only* in retaliation and *only* against those who initiate its use. The ethical principle involved is simple and clear-cut: it is the difference between murder and self-defense. A holdup man seeks to gain a value, wealth, by killing his victim; the victim does not grow richer by killing a holdup man. The principle is: no man may obtain any values from others by resorting to physical force.

The only proper, *moral* purpose of a government is to protect man's rights, which means: to protect him from physical violence—to protect his right to his own life, to his own liberty, to his own *property* and to the pursuit of his own happiness. Without property rights, no other rights are possible.

I will not attempt, in a brief lecture, to discuss the political theory of Objectivism. Those who are interested will find it presented in full detail in

*Atlas Shrugged.* I will say only that every political system is based on and derived from a theory of ethics—and that the Objectivist ethics is the moral base needed by that politico-economic system which, today, is being destroyed all over the world, destroyed precisely for lack of a *moral,* philosophical defense and validation: the original American system, *Capitalism.* If it perishes, it will perish by default, undiscovered and unidentified: no other subject has ever been hidden by so many distortions, misconceptions and misrepresentations. Today, few people know what capitalism is, how it works and what was its actual history.

When I say "capitalism," I mean a full, pure, uncontrolled, unregulated laissez-faire capitalism—with a separation of state and economics, in the same way and for the same reasons as the separation of state and church. A pure system of capitalism has never yet existed, not even in America; various degrees of government control had been undercutting and distorting it from the start. Capitalism is not the system of the past; it is the system of the future—if mankind is to have a future. . . .

It is not men's *immorality* that is responsible for the collapse now threatening to destroy the civilized world, but the kind of *moralities* men have been asked to practice. The responsibility belongs to the philosophers of altruism. They have no cause to be shocked by the spectacle of their own success, and no right to damn human nature: men have obeyed them and have brought their moral ideals into full reality.

It is philosophy that sets men's goals and determines their course; it is only philosophy that can save them now. Today, the world is facing a choice: if civilization is to survive, it is the altruist morality that men have to reject.

## The Ethic of Emergencies

. . . "Sacrifice" is the surrender of a greater value for the sake of a lesser one or of a nonvalue. Thus, altruism gauges a man's virtue by the degree to which he surrenders, renounces or betrays his values (since help to a stranger or an enemy is regarded as more virtuous, less "selfish," than help

to those one loves). The rational principle of conduct is the exact opposite: always act in accordance with the hierarchy of your values, and never sacrifice a greater value to a lesser one.

This applies to all choices, including one's actions toward other men. It requires that one possess a defined hierarchy of *rational* values (values chosen and validated by a rational standard). Without such a hierarchy, neither rational conduct nor considered value judgments nor moral choices are possible.

Love and friendship are profoundly personal, selfish values: love is an expression and assertion of self-esteem, a response to one's own values in the person of another. One gains a profoundly personal, selfish joy from the mere existence of the person one loves. It is one's own personal, selfish happiness that one seeks, earns and derives from love.

A "selfless," "disinterested" love is a contradiction in terms: it means that one is indifferent to that which one values.

Concern for the welfare of those one loves is a rational part of one's selfish interests. If a man who is passionately in love with his wife spends a fortune to cure her of a dangerous illness, it would be absurd to claim that he does it as a "sacrifice" for *her* sake, not his own, and that it makes no difference to *him,* personally and selfishly, whether she lives or dies.

Any action that a man undertakes for the benefit of those he loves is *not a sacrifice* if, in the hierarchy of his values, in the total context of the choices open to him, it achieves that which is of greatest *personal* (and rational) importance to *him.* In the above example, his wife's survival is of greater value to the husband than anything else that his money could buy, it is of greatest importance to his own happiness and, therefore, his action is *not* a sacrifice.

But suppose he let her die in order to spend his money on saving the lives of ten other women, none of whom meant anything to him— as the ethics of altruism would require. *That* would be a sacrifice. Here the difference between Objectivism and altruism can be seen most clearly: if sacrifice is the moral principle of action, then that husband *should* sacrifice his wife for the sake of ten other women. What distinguishes the wife from the ten others? Nothing but her value to the husband who has to make the choice—nothing but the fact that *his* happiness requires her survival.

The Objectivist ethics would tell him: your highest moral purpose is the achievement of your own happiness, your money is yours, use it to save your wife, *that* is your moral right and your rational, moral choice.

Consider the soul of the altruistic moralist who would be prepared to tell that husband the opposite. (And then ask yourself whether altruism is motivated by benevolence.)

The proper method of judging when or whether one should help another person is by reference to one's own rational self-interest and one's own hierarchy of values: the time, money or effort one gives or the risk one takes should be proportionate to the value of the person in relation to one's own happiness.

To illustrate this on the altruists' favorite example: the issue of saving a drowning person. If the person to be saved is a stranger, it is morally proper to save him only when the danger to one's own life is minimal; when the danger is great, it would be immoral to attempt it: only a lack of self-esteem could permit one to value one's life no higher than that of any random stranger. (And, conversely, if one is drowning, one cannot expect a stranger to risk his life for one's sake, remembering that one's life cannot be as valuable to him as his own.)

If the person to be saved is not a stranger, then the risk one should be willing to take is greater in proportion to the greatness of that person's value to oneself. If it is the man or woman one loves, then one can be willing to give one's own life to save him or her—for the selfish reason that life without the loved person could be unbearable.

Conversely, if a man is able to swim and to save his drowning wife, but becomes panicky, gives in to an unjustified, irrational fear and lets her drown, then spends his life in loneliness and misery—one would not call him "selfish"; one would condemn him morally for his treason to himself and to his own values, that is: his failure to

fight for the preservation of a value crucial to his own happiness. Remember that values are that which one acts to gain and/or keep, and that one's own happiness has to be achieved by one's own effort. Since one's own happiness is the moral purpose of one's life, the man who fails to achieve it because of his own default, because of his failure to fight for it, is morally guilty.

The virtue involved in helping those one loves is not "selflessness" or "sacrifice," but *integrity*. Integrity is loyalty to one's convictions and values; it is the policy of acting in accordance with one's values, of expressing, upholding and translating them into practical reality. If a man professes to love a woman, yet his actions are indifferent, inimical or damaging to her, it is his lack of integrity that makes him immoral.

The same principle applies to relationships among friends. If one's friend is in trouble, one should act to help him by whatever nonsacrificial means are appropriate. For instance, if one's friend is starving, it is not a sacrifice, but an act of integrity to give him money for food rather than buy some insignificant gadget for oneself, because his welfare is important in the scale of one's personal values. If the gadget means more than the friend's suffering, one had no business pretending to be his friend.

The practical implementation of friendship, affection and love consists of incorporating the welfare (the *rational* welfare) of the person involved into one's own hierarchy of values, then acting accordingly.

But this is a reward which men have to earn by means of their virtues and which one cannot grant to mere acquaintances or strangers.

What, then, should one properly grant to strangers? The generalized respect and good will which one should grant to a human being in the name of the potential value he represents—until and unless he forfeits it. . . .

It is on the ground of that generalized good will and respect for the value of human life that one helps strangers in an emergency—*and only in an emergency*.

It is important to differentiate between the rules of conduct in an emergency situation and the rules of conduct in the normal conditions of human existence. This does not mean a double standard of morality: the standard and the basic principles remain the same, but their application to either case requires precise definitions.

An emergency is an unchosen, unexpected event, limited in time, that creates conditions under which human survival is impossible—such as a flood, an earthquake, a fire, a shipwreck. In an emergency situation, men's primary goal is to combat the disaster, escape the danger and restore normal conditions (to reach dry land, to put out the fire, etc.).

By "normal" conditions I mean *metaphysically* normal, normal in the nature of things, and appropriate to human existence. Men can live on land, but not in water or in a raging fire. Since men are not omnipotent, it is metaphysically possible for unforeseeable disasters to strike them, in which case their only task is to return to those conditions under which their lives can continue. By its nature, an emergency situation is temporary; if it were to last, men would perish.

It is only in emergency situations that one should volunteer to help strangers, if it is in one's power. For instance, a man who values human life and is caught in a shipwreck, should help to save his fellow passengers (though not at the expense of his own life). But this does not mean that after they all reach shore, he should devote his efforts to saving his fellow passengers from poverty, ignorance, neurosis or whatever other troubles they might have. Nor does it mean that he should spend his life sailing the seven seas in search of shipwreck victims to save.

Or to take an example that can occur in everyday life: suppose one hears that the man next door is ill and penniless. Illness and poverty are not metaphysical emergencies, they are part of the normal risks of existence; but since the man is temporarily helpless, one may bring him food and medicine, *if* one can afford it (as an act of good will, not of duty) or one may raise a fund among the neighbors to help him out. But this does not mean that one must support him from then on, nor that one must spend one's life looking for starving men to help.

In the normal conditions of existence, man has to choose his goals, project them in time, pursue

them and achieve them by his own effort. He cannot do it if his goals are at the mercy of and must be sacrificed to any misfortune happening to others. He cannot live his life by the guidance of rules applicable only to conditions under which human survival is impossible.

The principle that one should help men in an emergency cannot be extended to regard all human suffering as an emergency and to turn the misfortune of some into a first mortgage on the lives of others.

Poverty, ignorance, illness and other problems of that kind are not metaphysical emergencies. By the *metaphysical* nature of man and of existence, man has to maintain his life by his own effort; the values he needs—such as wealth or knowledge—are not given to him automatically, as a gift of nature, but have to be discovered and achieved by his own thinking and work. One's sole obligation toward others, in this respect, is to maintain a social system that leaves men free to achieve, to gain and to keep their values. . . .

## Questions

1. Consider the following dialogue.

*A:* You admit that the multinational corporation for which you work is significantly damaging the environment and causing a serious famine in a third world country. Aren't you afraid the damage and the famine will be bad for business?

*B:* No. We don't employ or sell to citizens of that country. We just get the raw materials there and manufacture and market our product elsewhere.

*A:* Do you believe in Ethical Egoism?

*B:* Heavens no! Sometimes an act which is in my interest is an unethical act. In such cases the right thing to do is the Ethical act, not the prudent one.

*C:* I am an Ethical Egoist. I believe that each person should pursue his or her own interest except when this would violate someone's rights. Such conflicts will occur, of course.

*D:* I am an Ethical Egoist. I believe that each person should do what is actually in his or her own interest. What people think is in their own interest sometimes violates the rights of others, but what is actually in their interest does not.

*E:* I am an Ethical Egoist. I believe that each person should pursue his or her own interest because if everyone did this, the world would be a happier place.

*F:* I am an Ethical Egoist. I intend to pursue my own interest because if I don't look out for number 1, who will? Of course, if you get in my way, I'll stomp on your face.

*A:* But isn't it unethical to damage the environment significantly and cause a serious famine?

*B:* Well, corporations and individuals have different moral duties. In fact, Ethical Egoism is OK for corporations even though it is wrong for individuals. Thus damaging the environment significantly and causing a serious famine would be unethical for individuals but ethical for corporations.

Do B, C, D, E, and/or F have a correct understanding of Ethical Egoism? Why or why not? Do you agree with B's last statement? Why or why not?

2. List the three weirdest statements you have found in Nietzsche's writings. Explain how all of these statements are systematically interrelated. (Do *not* say that they are not interrelated.) Now explain why each statement is correct. (Do *not* say that they are incorrect.)

3.     *H:* Do you think that it is OK for the Federation to support the Cardassians?

*R:* Sure! The Federation needs Cardassia's natural resources and its strategic position.

*H:* I see. You think that the Federation should support Cardassia because it is in our interest to do so.

*R:* Right.

*H:* How would you characterize the present government of Cardassia?

*R:* Well, it is an incredibly totalitarian and repressive government, ideologically opposed to democracy and freedom.

*H:* By supporting the government of Cardassia, the Federation is acting as an accomplice to totalitarianism and repression, isn't it?

*R:* Yes, I guess so.

*H:* Do you believe in Ethical Egoism?

*R:* Heavens no! It is morally wrong to violate the rights of others even if doing so would be in my own best interest.

*H:* Aren't you suggesting that the Federation should help the Cardassian government violate the rights of its people because it is in the Federation's best interest to do so?

*R:* Well, Ethical Egoism is morally OK for states even though it is morally wrong for individuals.

Do you agree with R's last statement? Why or why not? (Do not waste your time arguing about whether supporting Cardassia is in the best interest of the Federation or whether supporting Cardassia involves totalitarianism, repression, and rights violations. The specific question here is *"If* supporting Cardassia is in the best interest of the Federation, and *if* supporting Cardassia involves totalitarianism, repression, and rights violations, *then* should the Federation support Cardassia?" The general question, of course is *"If* certain practices are morally wrong for individuals, *then* could these practices be morally OK for states?")

4. Ethical Egoism and Utilitarianism are, in a certain way, parallel. [See the "Utilitarianism" section.] Ethical Egoism says that one person should sacrifice the welfare of many other people if necessary to procure his own best interest. Utilitarianism says that a group of people should sacrifice the welfare of one person if necessary to procure the group's best interest. This sacrificial parallel suggests the following questions.

   a. Sketch the best arguments you can think of against Ethical Egoism. Do modified versions of these arguments defeat Utilitarianism as well? Why or why not?

b. Sketch the best arguments you can think of against Utilitarianism. Do modified versions of these arguments defeat Ethical Egoism as well? Why or why not?

c. We found that Rule Utilitarianism was more sophisticated and plausible than Act Utilitarianism. Using the distinction between Act Utilitarianism and Rule Utilitarianism as a model, define Act Ethical Egoism and Rule Ethical Egoism. Is Rule Ethical Egoism more sophisticated and plausible than Act Egoism? Why or why not?

5. In the nineteenth century, two opposing ways of looking at the origin and effects of both Christianity and the state appear. Nietzsche says that both Christianity and the state were more or less invented by the base to overcome the noble. At least, the base benefit from these institutions, and the noble are hindered. Marx, on the other hand, suggests that both Christianity and the modern state were more or less invented by the owners of the means of production in order to control the workers. At least, the owners benefit from these institutions, and the workers are hindered. Are these accounts of the origin and effects of Christianity and the state compatible? Is either or both of these accounts true?

6. *Tom:* I believe that I should pursue my own happiness except when this pursuit would interfere with someone else's rights. Therefore, I am an Egoistic Immoralist.

*Dick:* No! An Egoistic Immoralist pursues his or her own happiness whether or not it interferes with someone else's rights. If someone happened to get in the way of an immoralist's happiness, the immoralist would stomp on his or her face.

*Harry:* Me too! Me too!

*Dick:* Now I am an Ethical Egoist. I happen to believe that if I pursue my own happiness *rationally*, then I will not interfere with other people's rights. It will never be prof-

itable for me to stomp on anyone. It is not in my interest to steal or lie, for example, because conscience and society punish these things severely.

*Harry:* Wrong! Wrong! Wrong! Society punishes only the fools who get caught, and if you make a habit of ignoring your conscience it will eventually go away and stop bothering you. Thus it often pays to steal, lie, and stomp on others. It is in your best interest to *seem* to respect the rights of others but not *really* to respect their rights. Nice guys finish last.

*Tom:* I agree. And when I must choose between pursuing my own happiness and acting morally, I always act morally. I guess I am a Moral Immoralist.

*Harry:* I act morally, too. But because I am an Ethical Egoist, acting morally means doing whatever I want to do.

*Dick:* I pursue my own happiness rationally.

*Tom:* What is this "pursue my own happiness rationally" razzmatazz? Do you guys do whatever you want to do, or not?

*Harry:* Of course I do what I want to do. Everyone wants what he or she thinks is in his or her own interest.

*Tom:* Oh, so you are a Psychological Egoist, too.

*Harry:* Certainly not!

*Dick:* I'm not a Psychological Egoist either. People do not always do what they believe to be in their interest. They sometimes engage in self-destructive behavior. However, if everyone were rational, then Psychological Egoism would be true.

*Tom:* This is too complicated for me. Luckily, I don't have to think about it. I simply obey God's rules. This ends up maximizing my happiness, especially when the next life is taken into account. I guess I am a Religious Egoist.

*Dick:* Simply obeying God's rules is very different from "pursuing your own happiness except when this pursuit would interfere with someone else's rights." Anyhow, do you obey God's rules in order to pursue your happiness or do you pursue your happiness in order to obey God's rules?

*Tom:* What is the difference?

*Dick:* Well, a person who obeys God's rules in order to pursue happiness is an Ethical Egoist, but a person who obeys God's rules for their own sake, whether or not doing so produces happiness, is not an Ethical Egoist.

*Harry:* No one ever obeys God's rules for their own sake. The only possible reason a person could have for obeying God's rules is that the person believes that obeying God's rules will pay.

*Tom:* That statement proves that you are a Psychological Egoist.

*Harry:* No it doesn't! No it doesn't!

*Tom:* Yes it does! Yes it does!

Which of the claims made by Tom, Dick, and Harry are correct? Which are incorrect?

7. Kant, Aristotle, Jesus, and Rand hold the following views.

*Kant:* common-sense happy life = true happy life ≠ true moral life = traditional moral life

*Aristotle:* common-sense happy life ≠ true happy life = true moral life = traditional moral life

*Jesus:* common-sense happy life ≠ true happy life = true moral life ≠ traditional moral life

*Rand:* common-sense happy life = true happy life = true moral life ≠ traditional moral life

Because common sense denies that the happy life is the moral life, there are only three remaining possibilities. Devise and describe a position corresponding to *one* of these three possibilities.

a. common-sense happy life ≠ true happy life ≠ true moral life = traditional moral life

b. common-sense happy life = true happy life ≠ true moral life ≠ traditional moral life

c. common-sense happy life ≠ true happy life ≠ true moral life ≠ traditional moral life

8. One important question concerning the metaphysics of morals is "Who or what makes right acts right?" Divine Command Theory says that what makes an act morally right is that the act is approved of by God. [See the "Morality and Religion" section.] Normative Relativism says that what makes an act morally right is that the act is approved of by society. [See the "Morality and Knowledge" section.] Utilitarianism says that what makes an act morally right is that the act maximizes the overall amount of happiness in the universe. [See the "Utilitarianism" section.] Egoism says that what makes an act morally right is that the act maximizes the overall amount of happiness of the agent.

State in your own words the main argument against Divine Command Theory. Can this argument be modified so as to work against Normative Relativism? Can it be modified so as to work against Utilitarianism? Can it be modified so as to work against Egoism? In each case, if the argument can be successfully modified, do so. If not, explain why not.

9. Nietzsche's view of morality is very complex. Sometimes he approaches morality like a scientist. He tries to study the phenomenon of morality. For example, he distinguishes between slave morality and master morality while giving a historical and psychological account of the origin of morality. Sometimes he sheds the objectivity of science and takes an evaluative stance toward morality. He mocks and criticizes the teachers of virtue and the practitioners of virtue. On the other hand, Nietzsche himself is a teacher of virtue. He often tells us how we should behave. Does Nietzsche have a consistent view of morality? If so, what is it?

# Morality and Religion:
# The Bible and Divine Command Theory

*Faith is believing what you know ain't so.*

MARK TWAIN

One obstacle to doing ethics is the belief that ethics has already been done. It is all in the *Bible*. Rather than working out a moral theory on our own, we should just apply the *Bible*'s moral theory. Moreover, we need not subject Biblical texts to philosophical analysis because their meaning is obvious. We should simply obey God's rules. Other people reply that we must understand the texts in order to obey the rules and that the meaning of Biblical texts is not obvious. The *Bible* must be interpreted and perhaps even supplemented and corrected through common sense, reason, the observations of later thinkers, and other sources of insight. I suggest that even if the *Bible*'s moral theory were clear and complete, simply using it as a reference would be a bad idea. Just as people do not come to understand and internalize math by looking up the answers to the problems in the back of the book, so people do not come to understand and internalize ethics by looking up the answers in the *Bible*. Indeed, people may be more likely to understand the *Bible* by doing ethics than to understand ethics by reading the *Bible*. I suggest that we try to comprehend, compare, and apply several moral theories in addition to that of the *Bible*. Eventually, we will be able to go back and forth among the several moral theories, using each theory to improve our understanding of the others. This process will enable us to come closer and closer to the truth about ethics—and to understand it when we find it.

In the process, we must beware of the temptation to read our own beliefs into the text and thus make the *Bible* (or any other text) say what we want to hear. There are many ways to do this. One way is to deny the plain meaning of a passage in order to make it fit in with one's preconceptions. Another way is to take very seriously or literally some passages, while ignoring or taking metaphorically other passages with equivalent claims. For example, some people take seriously the passages that prohibit homosexuality and theft while ignoring the passages that prohibit wearing clothing made of mixed fabrics and working on the Sabbath. Intellectual honesty demands not only that we avoid deceiving others but also that we avoid deceiving ourselves. On the other hand, we must be aware that philosophy is dangerous and potentially painful because it is in the business of challenging people's deepest beliefs. Philosophy demands an open mind—a willingness to give up ideas or interpretations when philosophical reflection reveals that they are false. Yet there is a tension between open-mindedness and faith, for faith demands a willingness to hold on to certain doctrines and interpretations no matter what. Thus philosophy is threatening to believers. As we read sacred texts philosophically, we must strike a balance between closed-minded dogmatism on the one hand and strident apostasy on the other.

We must also beware of anachronistic interpretations. The *Bible* was written thousands of years ago for people of the ancient Near East. It was not written by contemporary college professors for readers of philosophy journals. Nevertheless, in this section I shall treat Biblical texts as a moral system that purports to apply to us rather than as documents of anthropological, historical, or religious interest. I shall sketch partial interpretations of a few passages to illustrate how to extract and examine a moral theory from the *Bible*—or from any other text, for that matter. I shall also make a few remarks and raise a few questions about ethics in general.

Like most complex texts, one cannot completely grasp the meaning of parts of the *Bible* unless one already understands the whole, but one cannot comprehend the whole unless one has already mastered the parts. To resolve this paradox, begin with a provisional interpretation of the parts; use this as a basis for a first interpretation of the whole, use this understanding of the whole to revise the initial interpretation of the parts, use this new understanding of the parts to revise the previous interpretation of the whole, and so on. Of course, we can only begin this cycle here.

A good interpretation of any text, including the *Bible*, strives for consistency. Other things being equal, interpretations that make the text consistent with itself and with the rest of the *Bible* are preferable to interpretations that make the text contradict itself.

Generally, we should use common sense as a touchstone. An interpretation that makes the text sound plausible seems preferable to an interpretation that makes the text sound wild and crazy. An interpretation that has God making unreasonable demands and preposterous claims should be rejected if a more common-sense interpretation that is equally true to the text is available. On the other hand, there may be good reason to believe that certain texts are deliberately rejecting common sense. In that case, using common sense as a basis for interpretation would obviously be a mistake.

## The Ten Commandments and The Holiness Code

There is surprising disagreement over how to divide the collection of commandments into *ten*. To bypass that dispute, I offer the following list.

1. I am the Lord your God.
2. Do not have other Gods besides Me.
3. Do not carve idols.
4. Do not worship idols.
5. Do not take the Lord's name in vain.
6. Do not work on the Sabbath.
7. Honor your father and mother.
8. Do not kill.
9. Do not commit adultery.
10. Do not steal.
11. Do not bear false witness against your neighbor.

12. Do not covet your neighbor's house.
13. Do not covet your neighbor's wife.
14. Do not covet your neighbor's slave, ox, ass, or anything else that belongs to him.

The Jews bundle together (2), (3), and (4) into one commandment and (12), (13), and (14) into another. Catholics and Lutherans combine (1), (2), (3), and (4) into one commandment and (13) and (14) into another. Most Protestants combine (1) and (2) into one commandment, (3) and (4) into another commandment, and (12), (13), and (14) into yet another. Numbering the commandments is a trivial issue, of course, but it presages more substantive interpretive disputes down the line. Traditionally, the first group of commandments is thought to concern people's relationship with God, whereas the second group concerns people's relationship with each other. In this section I shall ignore the former group in order to focus on the latter.

Many moral rules are not mentioned in the Ten Commandments passage ("Do not assault people," "Give to the needy."). It should come as no surprise that the Ten Commandments are not a complete list of moral rules. If they were complete, then the rest of the *Bible* would be superfluous from a moral point of view. The Ten Commandment passage is incomplete in other ways, too. It provides no mechanisms for resolving conflicts of duties or determining exceptions. Nor does the text specify boundary conditions—statements of when the commandments do and do not apply. Finally, the text provides no priority ranking, no guidance for cases where two commandments conflict.

Some people might respond that there is no need for a way to resolve conflicts because conflicts cannot arise, no need for boundary conditions because the commandments apply in all situations, and no priority ranking because all sins are equal before God. I think this is too simple. For example, if honoring includes obedience, and if your parents tell you to murder your sister, there is a conflict between the rule "Honor your father and mother" and the rule "Do not kill." Conflict may be avoided if each commandment contains implicit exceptions. If "Honor your father and mother" is really shorthand for some more complex rule such as "Honor your father and mother except when they order you to violate a moral rule," then there is no conflict. Of course, the conflict could also be avoided if, buried within the commandment "Do not kill" is the clause "except when ordered to kill by a parent." We need a priority principle to know how to flesh out the moral rules.

Once it is conceded that commandments are abbreviated versions of longer rules, other motivation for expanding the commandments will tempt us. Perhaps the commandments include exceptions designed to avoid conflicts with common sense, too. If your parents order you to marry someone you despise, do you have a duty to honor their order? Perhaps "Honor your father and mother except when they order you to violate a moral rule or common sense" is closer to the truth about honoring parents. On the other hand, once the game of amending rules begins, we risk twisting the rules to suit our whims. Surely the rule is not "Honor your father and mother except when you do not want to do so."

For this and other reasons, some people take the commandments to be exceptionless. God says, "Do not steal," and that is the whole truth about stealing. It is always wrong to steal. However, both common sense and the rest of the Bible suggest that exceptions must be made. Stealing is at least permissible and perhaps required in self-defense, defense of others, and so on. Surely, it is OK to seize the attacker's gun without his or her permission. One common suggestion is that in such situations stealing is wrong but is the lesser evil. Thus stealing is what you morally should do in such situations, yet you should feel guilty when you do it. But could you really have a moral duty to perform an immoral act? Another view is that if stealing is what you should do in some situation, then it is the right thing to do. Therefore, you should feel sorrow, but not guilt, when you do it. The problem with this view is that it trivializes the tragedy of situations where no morally acceptable options seem available.

As for the equality of sin, it contravenes common sense to say that killing a person is the equivalent of stealing a pencil, but an easy resolution is ready to hand. Murder and theft are both sins against God as well as transgressions against particular people. We might break the wrongness of each sin into two components (using "w" as the unit of wrongness)

> 10 w against God + 8 w against a person = 18 w for murder
>
> 10 w against God + 2 w against a person = 12 w for theft

The "against God" component of every sin is equal to that of every other sin, for every offense against God is an offense of disobedience, but all sins are not equally wrong, overall.

\*

In the *Exodus* version of the Ten Commandments, people and animals are prohibited from working on the Sabbath because God rested on the Sabbath. The passage suggests that we should refrain from work in order to honor God and creation. In the *Deuteronomy* version of the Ten Commandments, the Israelites are told to rest on the Sabbath "because you were slaves in the land of Egypt." The passage reminds the people of how they were exploited as an explanation of why they should refrain from overworking their servants, slaves, and animals (and themselves). The passage introduces sympathy for others as a tool of moral understanding and development. It suggests that one should use one's own experiences as a guide for treating others. In the first version, "Do not work on the Sabbath" is a religious duty, whereas in the second version, it is a moral duty to treat people and animals justly. Of course, there is nothing incompatible about these versions. We simply have two different reasons for obeying this commandment. Do other commandments also have both religious and moral justifications? Are religious and moral duties always compatible?

\*

"Do not covet" demands that we avoid a certain psychological state. We are not only forbidden to commit theft and adultery, but we are also told to avoid the desires that might lead to these acts. This is an example of a general principle of Jewish ethics, "Build a fence around wrongdoing." If something is morally wrong, one should not only refrain from doing it but should not even get close to it. For example, God tells Adam and Eve not to eat the fruit of the Tree of Knowledge, but Eve tells the serpent that she is forbidden even to touch the fruit. The problem is that fences tend to multiply. At first, the fence keeps us a safe distance from wrongdoing, but as time passes, people tend to treat the fence itself as wrongdoing. Then they build a second fence around the first fence. Then they build a third fence. And so on. Perhaps at first "Do not covet" was merely a fence around the wrongdoing of theft and adultery. Later, coveting itself came to be thought of as wrong, and a new fence was erected. Women should dress modestly so as to avoid encouraging covetous thoughts. (Note that at this point, women lose certain freedoms in order to keep men from wrongdoing.)

Do we really have moral obligations to avoid certain psychological states? Suppose I commit no adultery, but I just cannot get my neighbor's wife out of my head. I continue to lust after her and have sexual fantasies about her even though I have taken hundreds of cold showers, paid thousands of dollars in therapy fees, prayed desperately and sincerely for help, and so on. I have done everything I can think of, but I am still preoccupied with her. Common sense says that morality requires of us only what is within our power. This principle is sometimes abbreviated by the slogan "Ought implies can." Can we control our psychological states? Am I responsible for my obsessive desire for my neighbor's wife? Aristotle thinks that people can change their desires and that they are, therefore, generally responsible for their desires, although acquiring right desires and jettisoning wrong desires can be a long and difficult process. Kant, on the other hand, thinks that our desires are beyond our control. We simply cannot eliminate bad desires. The best we can do is to refrain from acting on whatever wrong desires we have. If Aristotle is right, then by lusting after my neighbor's wife I have violated the commandment against coveting, and I should feel guilty. On the other hand, if Kant is right, then morality cannot really require that I refrain from coveting. The commandment is either wrong or hyperbolic. Perhaps "Do not covet" really means something like "Try your best not to covet." On this interpretation, I have discharged my duty by taking the showers and so on. I should not feel guilty about my obsessive desires, for I have done nothing wrong.

\*

Whether *honor* means "obey," "respect," or something else, "Honor your father and mother" says that children have special obligations to their parents. We are not instructed to honor everyone, but only our parents. Extrapolation suggests that we have many duties to our family and friends, fewer duties to our fellow citizens, and even fewer duties to our fellow humans. We even have duties to animals (such as not making them work on the Sabbath.) However, this common-sense view that different relationships involve different levels of duties seems to be substantially repudiated in the Holiness Code.

\*

The Holiness Code contains several moral rules not found in the Ten Commandments passage. First, the Holiness Code orders farmers to harvest only part of their crops so that poor people and strangers can take the rest. Several important general principles are illustrated by this rule. First, we have a duty to give to the needy. Benevolent action is not supererogatory but rather is morally required. Second, the giving should be done in a way that allows the recipients to retain as much self-respect as possible. (Because they harvest the crops themselves, the poor can feel that they work for what they receive. It is no handout. Moreover, because the crops can be harvested at twilight, the poor need not reveal their poverty.) Third, it is up to the recipients, not the giver, to determine how much they need. Fourth, we have a duty to help not only our needy relatives, friends, and fellow citizens but also needy strangers.

Indeed, our duties to people beyond our immediate circle are surprising. A bit later on, the Holiness Code contains the statement "thou shalt love thy neighbor as thyself." Even later it states, "The stranger that sojourneth with you shall be unto you as the homeborn among you, and thou shalt love him as thyself." (In the Good Samaritan Parable, Jesus is giving a commentary on these passages rather than breaking new ground.) Presumably, the point is not just that we should love neighbors and strangers but also that we should treat them as well as we treat our relatives and friends. Here the Holiness Code clashes with common sense, for it lumps nearly all relationships into one type of relationship.

*

Justice of several sorts is a high priority in the Holiness Code. First, the Holiness Code requires that judges show no favoritism. People should get no special treatment because they are rich or because they are poor or because they are white, black, male, female, or whatever. The general principle illustrated here is that all people are equal before the law. This principle seems obvious now, for it has become the foundation of all of our present conceptions of justice, but at the time it was revolutionary. Second, merchants are commanded not to cheat customers with deceptive scales. Again, the text invites extrapolation. Presumably, merchants should not cheat customers at all. The Holiness Code rejects the principle of *caveat emptor* ("Let the buyer beware"). In general, both representatives of the state and private individuals should act justly.

## Sermon on the Mount

The Sermon on the Mount contains the following moral rules.

1. (It is said, do not kill.) Do not be angry.
2. (It is said, do not commit adultery.) Do not lust.
3. (It is said, do not divorce without giving a "bill.") Do not divorce.
4. (It is said, do not swear falsely.) Do not swear.
5. (It is said, retaliate proportionately. An eye for an eye, etc.) Do not resist aggression.
6. Turn the other cheek.
7. If someone sues you over your tunic, give him your cloak, too.
8. If someone forces you to go one mile, go two miles.
9. Give and lend to whoever asks of you.
10. (It is said, love your neighbor and hate your enemy.) Love your enemy.
11. Pray for those who persecute you.
12. Do not perform good deeds and pray and fast publicly in order to win praise.
13. Forgive others.
14. Do not be devoted to money or material goods.
15. Do not judge others.
16. Remove the beam from your own eye before you remove the splinter from someone else's eye.
17. Do not throw pearls before swine.
18. Do to others whatever you would have them do to you.

Notice that Jesus uses the principle of fence building. We should not only avoid swearing falsely; we should avoid swearing altogether. We should not only avoid killing; we should also avoid anger, presumably because anger might lead to killing. We should not only refrain from harming our enemies; we should not even resist their aggression. We should "Turn the other cheek." This was a radical doctrine in Jesus' time, and indeed it still is. The traditional Greek view, for example, was that a good person helps his friends and harms his enemies. Plato challenged this traditional view around 350 BCE, arguing in the *Gorgias* that it is better to be harmed than to harm an enemy. But Plato's argument was not widely accepted. The Jewish tradition rejected vengeance long before Jesus' day. "An eye for an eye" never meant that you could put someone's eye out if that person had put your eye out. It meant only that if someone had caused you to lose the sight in one eye, then you were entitled to damages amounting to the value of an eye. However, the Jewish tradition did not go so far as to prohibit self-defense, and neither has contemporary common sense.

But Jesus asks us to go even further. We should not only refrain from resisting aggression but also do nice things for our enemies. "If someone sues you over your tunic, give him your cloak, too." Ultimately, we should love our enemies. Of course, Jesus does not think that we should love only our enemies while feeling luke-warm about everyone else. He is urging us to love everyone, from friends to enemies. Here Jesus is doing more than building more fences around the rule "Do not kill." The requirement to love our enemies is also the next fence around the Holiness Code rule "Love the stranger." The process of building fence after fence around rule after rule has gotten to the point where the same fence surrounds two different rules. Indeed, the principle "Love everyone" may encompass all moral rules concerning others. But it is a problematic principle.

The two basic interpretations of this principle correspond to two global interpretations of the Sermon on the Mount. According to the *literal interpretation*, Jesus is saying that we should act and feel toward everyone, even our enemies, in the way that we act and feel toward ourselves and our loved ones. On this interpretation, Jesus literally demands things such as: "If someone forces you to go one mile, go two miles" and "Give and lend to whoever asks of you." Moreover, Jesus wants us to do such things not out of prudence or even duty, but out of love.

If you saw a burglar making off with your stereo, would you run after the burglar with love in your heart in order to offer your TV, too? Following Jesus' teaching would require a radical change in the way we behave and an even more radical change in the way we feel. According to the literal interpretation, Jesus is calling for a moral revolution. The literal interpretation raises the question of whether Jesus is asking too much. Some people will answer, "Jesus is asking more than people can do. The moral theory of the Sermon is therefore flawed." Other people will answer, "Jesus is asking more than people can do. But this does not invalidate the Sermon's moral theory because God forgives us when we fail." However, surely God would not demand that we do something beyond our abilities and then consider us guilty when we fail. A parent who demands that a four-year-old sit still for two hours is a poor parent, whether he or she punishes the child for not obeying or simply makes the child feel guilty and "mercifully" remits the punishment. A third group of people will answer, "Jesus is not asking more than people can do. With God's help we really can manage to love everyone, even our enemies. It is hard, but then being a Christian is supposed to be hard."

Many people find it difficult to accept the possibility, let alone the duty, of loving everyone, even our enemies. At the risk of distorting the text, they cling to the view that Jesus is more moderate, closer to common sense. On the *metaphorical interpretation*, Jesus is not really demanding that we love everyone, even our enemies. He is asking for something less. Perhaps

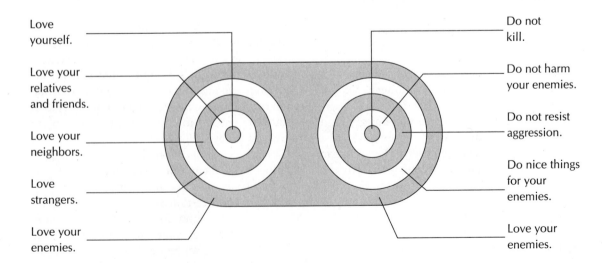

Love yourself.

Love your relatives and friends.

Love your neighbors.

Love strangers.

Love your enemies.

Do not kill.

Do not harm your enemies.

Do not resist aggression.

Do nice things for your enemies.

Love your enemies.

"Love everyone" is a moral recommendation rather than a requirement, an ideal to work toward rather than a rule to follow. Thus we should feel proud insofar as we succeed, but we should not feel guilty insofar as we fail. Or perhaps loving everyone *is* a requirement, but not the requirement it seems to be. By "Love your enemies" Jesus may mean "Do not hate your enemies" or "Accord your enemies some basic respect." In each of these variations of the metaphorical interpretation, Jesus is still asking a lot, but he is not a moral revolutionary.

The problem with the metaphorical interpretation, of course, is that it makes Jesus mean what he does not say and say what he does not mean. Jesus gives no hint that he is speaking metaphorically rather than literally. Thus the metaphorical interpretation seems suspiciously like an attempt to tone Jesus down, to make Christianity less demanding and easier to live with, to turn Jesus' message into what people want to hear.

*

After Jesus exhorts us to help others, he goes on to specify that we should perform good deeds (and pray and fast) privately rather than publicly. We should not be show-offs. We should not only act rightly but also have the right motive. It is not enough to help others for the sake of praise or other worldly goods; we should help others for the sake of heavenly rewards, instead. This rule, like the rules about coveting and loving, raises the issue of whether morality should concern itself with our states of mind. Is it not enough to do the right thing? Must we have the right passions, desires, and motives, too? Do we even have control over and responsibility for our passions, desires, and motives? Moreover, is Jesus right about what our motives should be? Shouldn't we do the right thing because it is right, rather than for some worldly *or* otherworldly reward? A person who acts rightly in order to get into heaven or avoid divine punishment is no less self-interested than a person who acts rightly in order to get money and fame or to avoid jail and censure.

How can we know what the motives and feelings of others are? Jesus replies, "by their fruits you will know them. . . . Every good tree bears good fruit, and a rotten tree bears bad fruit. A good tree cannot bear bad fruit, nor can a rotten tree bear good fruit." In other words, we can infer the motives and feelings of others from their actions. Here Jesus assumes a strong correlation between mental states and actions. Is Jesus assuming that you respect or love a person if and only if you reliably act in a respectful or loving manner toward that person? This assumption seems obviously false. People often act benevolently toward those they despise and malevolently toward those they love. Perhaps Jesus is making the weaker claim that if a person reliably acts in a just, kind, and loving manner, then that person is probably a just, kind, loving person on the inside. Although we cannot be certain about the motives and feelings of others, we can use their actions as a basis for making judgments about their character. This claim is still controversial, but at least it is not ludicrous.

Moreover, why does Jesus advise us on making judgments about the character of others and then issue the command "Do not judge"? What does Jesus mean by this, anyway? Does Jesus really mean that we should refrain from saying "Fred is a liar" when we know that Fred has told lie after lie year after year? Perhaps Jesus is cautioning us not to jump to conclusions. We should make judgments only when we have solid evidence. Maybe Jesus means that we should not sum up Fred's *overall* character. We should not ignore the possibility that Fred may have other redeeming qualities or that Fred may reform. We should not pronounce *final* judgment on Fred. Perhaps by "judging" Jesus means meting out appropriate punishments. Then his point would be that instead of giving Fred the punishment he deserves, we should give Fred forgiveness and kindness even though Fred does not deserve it. We should adopt a stance of mercy rather than justice toward Fred. Jesus actually says, "Judge not lest you be judged." This seems strange because he thinks we will all eventually be judged by God, anyway. We cannot avoid being judged.

The prohibition against judging is contextually linked to the injunction "Remove the beam from your own eye before you remove the splinter from someone else's eye." Presumably, this odd metaphor is telling us to reform ourselves before trying to reform others. Does Jesus really think that there is something wrong with helping others improve morally before one has achieved moral perfection oneself? Perhaps his point is that we are not fit to judge others to be in need of improvement until we have subjected ourselves to the same scrutiny, measured ourselves against the same standard. But people can sometimes be of great help to others even if they have not yet cured or even confronted their own moral failings. Drug addicts who caution others not to try drugs are often very influential, for example. Perhaps Jesus' point is that we should not use the need for improvement in others as an excuse to avoid trying to improve ourselves.

*

Around the time of Jesus, many people were struggling to state a general principle (or a few general principles) that would encompass all moral rules. For example, Rabbi Shimon said, "The world stands on three things, on truth, on judgment, and on peace." Rabbi Hillel, a contemporary of Jesus, summed up Jewish ethics of the day with what is sometimes called the *Silver Rule*, "What is hateful to you, do not do to your neighbor. That is the entire *Torah*. The rest is commentary. Go and learn it."[1] The point of seeking an ultimate moral principle is not just to package the moral rules compactly so that non-scholars can get a handle on the vast, complex business. An ultimate moral principle would also substantially solve both the interpretation problem and the priority problem mentioned above. If all moral rules are theorems of an ultimate moral principle, then we can use this general principle to help us understand the many particular rules and to adjudicate conflicts among them.

The ultimate moral principle proposed by Jesus has two components: an account of how people should feel toward others and an account of how people should act toward others. These components are linked by Jesus' doctrine that the outer reflects the inner—that acts express feelings. The general principle of feeling is, of course, that you should love others just as you

love yourself. The correlate principle of conduct is the *Golden Rule*, "Do to others whatever you would have them do to you." Like much of what Jesus says, the Golden Rule seems straightforward when you say it fast but becomes puzzling when you think about it carefully with the T.V. off. What does the Golden Rule mean? It cannot mean "If you do nice things for others, then they will do nice things for you," for that claim is simply false. Sometimes others reciprocate; sometimes they ignore or even exploit generous acts.

Parents often reason with their children in the following way. "Because you want to play with other kids' toys, you should share your own toys with other kids." Generalizing this yields the most common interpretation of the Golden Rule: "You should use your own desires as a guide for treating others. You should help others to obtain the things that you want." But this interpretation cannot be right, for people's desires are very different. On this interpretation of the Golden Rule, if you like chocolate ice cream, you should inflict chocolate ice cream on me, even if chocolate gives me hives. If Greg is a masochist, then he should torture others. If Jenny does not want to play with other kids' toys (perhaps because Jenny's wealthy parents provide her with everything she wants), then she need not share her own.

Perhaps the Golden Rule means, "Just as you would like to have others help you satisfy your own desires, so you should help others satisfy their desires." On this interpretation, the Golden Rule tells us to figure out what other people want and then help them obtain it. This is an improvement over the previous naive interpretation. But what if the other person's desires are self-destructive or evil or simply trivial? Surely, we should not simply try to satisfy whatever desires the other person happens to have; instead, we should pick and choose. We should try to satisfy only the morally acceptable, reasonably important, and beneficial desires. But if we are to choose the beneficial desires, then the Golden Rule is telling us to paternalistically presume that we know better than other people what is in their best interest. Worse yet, if we are to choose only the morally right desires, then the Golden Rule presupposes a prior standard of morality. It is not the ultimate moral principle.

Perhaps the intermediate rules can be used as tools for interpreting the Golden Rule because they are supposed to be its theorems. "If someone sues you over your tunic, give him your cloak, too" tells us what the Golden Rule means to a victim of robbery. "Give and lend to whoever asks of you" tells us what the Golden Rule means to a wealthy person. And so on. However, part of the point of finding an ultimate moral principle was to provide a tool for interpreting the intermediate rules. This interpretation strategy yields a vicious circle.

\*

Neither the Jewish nor the Christian ethical tradition calcified when the *Bible* was codified. Both continued to grow and change throughout history and on into modern times. By now, neither Jewish ethics nor Christian ethics is a monolithic moral theory. Instead, each consists of interwoven strands of thought. Each strand emphasizes different aspects, and some strands are even incompatible with others. Moreover, even though Christian ethics began as a strand within Jewish ethics, the two have now grown so far apart that the term "Judeo-Christian ethics" is now somewhat misleading, for it suggests more commonality than there is.

For example, one point of divergence is this. Post-Biblical Jewish ethical thought takes human nature to be basically good and the world to be perfectible. Jewish ethics combines this upbeat view with a detailed extrapolation of the duties of justice and kindness stated in the Holiness Code and arrives at the following claim: People, especially the Jews, have been assigned the task of making the world better by acting justly, benevolently, and in general morally. Thus Jewish ethics has focused on social action.

Jesus' exhortation to love one's enemy and to return good for evil has led Christian ethics in a different direction. This demand seems far beyond the capacity of almost everyone. Rather than denying the legitimacy of Jesus' demand, Christian ethics concludes that people are flawed. This is the doctrine of original sin. People have a sinful nature, so they can be moral only with God's help. But God helps only those with the right sort of faith, and the help often comes only after death. Thus the focus of Christian ethics becomes one's beliefs and the next world, as well as one's acts in this world. As for healing the world, that is a task beyond human abilities; only God can heal the world.

## Divine Command Theory

Many moral theories consist of an ultimate moral principle, many intermediate-level principles, and many particular applications of these intermediate-level principles. Each higher-level principle explains why the lower-level principles are true and why we should obey them. For example, robbing a convenience store is wrong, and we should not do it because theft is wrong. Theft is wrong, and we should not do it because it violates the Ultimate Moral Principle. The Ultimate Moral Principle is the principle by which all other moral principles are justified and motivated. If it is a corollary of some even higher-level principle, that principle cannot be a moral principle. There is no consensus on what the Ultimate Moral Principle is. Jesus seems to think it is the Golden Rule, Mill thinks it is the Greatest Happiness Principle, Kant thinks it is the Categorical Imperative, and so on. Surprisingly, there *is* a consensus that the Ultimate Religious Principle is something like "Do what is pleasing to God and avoid what is displeasing to God." (Of course, the consensus evaporates when we ask the question "What is pleasing and what is displeasing to God?" But let us bracket that question for now.) Here are some theoretically possible relationships between the Ultimate Moral Principle and the Ultimate Religious Principle.

a. The Ultimate Moral Principle and the Ultimate Religious Principle are the same principle.
b. The Ultimate Moral Principle and the Ultimate Religious Principle are different principles with the same corollaries.
c. The Ultimate Moral Principle and the Ultimate Religious Principle are different yet

compatible principles. Neither has all of the corollaries of the other.

d. The Ultimate Religious Principle is one of several corollaries of the Ultimate Moral Principle.

e. The Ultimate Moral Principle is one of several corollaries of the Ultimate Religious Principle.

f. The Ultimate Moral Principle and the Ultimate Religious Principle are incompatible. One demands acts prohibited by the other.

We can winnow these possibilities by considering the quite plausible claim that *God is pleased by all moral acts and displeased by all immoral acts*. If (c) the Ultimate Moral Principle and the Ultimate Religious Principle are different yet compatible principles, or if (d) the Ultimate Religious Principle is one of several corollaries of the Ultimate Moral Principle, then some moral rules are not corollaries of the Ultimate Religious Principle. Thus God is indifferent to these moral rules. God does not care whether we violate them or not. But if God is pleased by all moral acts and displeased by all immoral acts, then we must reject possibilities (c) and (d).

If (a) the Ultimate Moral Principle and the Ultimate Religious Principle are the same Principle, or if (e) the Ultimate Moral Principle is one of several corollaries of the Ultimate Religious Principle, then all moral rules are corollaries of the Ultimate Religious Principle. Possibilities (a) and (e) are versions of a widely held view misleadingly named the *Divine Command Theory*, which says that what makes an act morally right is that God is pleased by the act. We should perform morally right acts because they please God.

Arthur, following Plato, argues that the Divine Command Theory must be mistaken. The argument goes like this. Suppose act X is morally right. Does God have a reason for being pleased by act X? If God has no reason, then God is whimsical and might have preferred the opposite of act X (if the coin had landed differently). But an irrational God is not worthy of worship. Thus God must have a reason for being pleased by act X. What could that reason be? Surely the

reason must be that act X is morally right. Thus (1) God is pleased by act X because act X is morally right. Now recall that Divine Command Theory says that (2) act X is morally right because God is pleased by act X. Claims (1) and (2) cannot both be true, because combining them yields a very small circle: God is pleased by act X because God is pleased by act X. This is no explanation at all. Thus we must reject the Divine Command Theory. Claim (2) is false. God knows which acts are right, of course, but God does not make right acts right. The Ultimate Moral Principle is neither (a) the same as, nor (e) a corollary of, the Ultimate Religious Principle.

The Divine Command Theory says that God sets the standard of moral value. "Jane is a morally good person" means that God is pleased by Jane. No problem so far. However, the sentence "God is morally good" ends up meaning nothing more than "God is pleased by God." Yet surely "God is morally good" has more content than this. Some people are uncomfortable with the idea that the standard of morality is independent of God. Yet unless God is separate from this standard, we cannot meaningfully say that God meets this standard.

Yet another reason for rejecting the Divine Command Theory is that the *Bible* gives a different reason for obeying God's moral rules. The Divine Command Theory says that we should perform act X because act X pleases God. We should be moral because God wants us to be moral. But both the Ten Commandments and the Sermon on the Mount say that we should perform act X because God will reward us if we do and will punish us if we do not. The *Bible's* answer to "Why be moral?" is "Because morality pays," not "Because God wants us to be moral."

If (b) the Ultimate Moral Principle and the Ultimate Religious Principle are different principles with the same corollaries, then we know empirically, by observing what God says and does, that God is pleased by all moral acts and displeased by all immoral acts. Unfortunately, God's words and deeds do not at all support the claim that God prefers morality. God does not seem to be pleased by all moral acts and displeased by all immoral acts. We observe that the wicked often prosper while the righteous go unrewarded. Indeed, the God of the *Bible* sometimes demands the performance of immoral acts, such as the Joshua's genocidal slaughter of the inhabitants of the Promised Land and Satan's torturing of Job. Thus it seems that we must reject possibility (b).

Indeed, God's behavior suggests that (f) the Ultimate Moral Principle and the Ultimate Religious Principle are incompatible. This is Sören Kierkegaard's view.[2] Possibility (f) says that God is not pleased by all moral acts and displeased by all immoral acts. The Ultimate Moral Principle and the Ultimate Religious Principle not only are different but also are incompatible because pleasing God sometimes requires immoral action. Although one can go for a long time—often a lifetime—without having to face this conflict explicitly, occasions do arise where one must choose between leading an ethical life and leading a religious life. Abraham faced such a choice when God ordered him to kill his son, Isaac. If Abraham had chosen to lead the ethical life, to follow the Ultimate Moral Principle, then he would have refused to murder Isaac. He might have tried to convince God not to demand Isaac's death, just as he earlier tried to convince God not to destroy Sodom and Gomorrah. However, Abraham chose to lead the religious life, to follow the Ultimate Religious Principle. He was willing to obey God without question, even though God asked him to violate one of the most important moral rules.

Some people try to avoid this unsavory implication by maintaining that Abraham knew all along that Isaac would not end up dead. Thus there was no real conflict between obeying morality and obeying God. But this interpretation smacks of desperation. The whole point and poignancy of the story is that Abraham was willing to give up the two things he valued most, Isaac and the conception of God as a moral be-

ing, in order to obey God. Abraham is admired because of his willingness to sacrifice everything for God. But if Abraham had known all along that he would have to give up nothing, then there would have been nothing admirable about his choice to sacrifice Isaac. Abraham would just have been going through the motions.

Of course, one can avoid this problem by denying that the *Bible* presents an accurate picture of God's preferences. One may take the position that the *Bible* is just a bunch of stories. The real God is pleased by all moral acts and displeased by all immoral acts. The Ultimate Moral Principle and the Ultimate Religious Principle are compatible. The ethical life and the religious life never conflict.

If the Divine Command Theory is false—if the Ultimate Moral Principle is independent of (or even incompatible with) the Ultimate Religious Principle—does this invalidate the moral principles found in the *Bible*, including those contained in the Ten Commandments, the Holiness Code, and the Sermon on the Mount? No, they may be fine moral principles even if they are not ultimately justified by God's endorsement. The Divine Command Theory purports to explain the truth of morality by deducing the Ultimate Moral Principle from the Ultimate Religious Principle. If the Divine Command Theory is false, then perhaps morality may be grounded in some other way. Perhaps the Ultimate Moral Principle may be deduced from a different principle, or perhaps it need not be deduced at all.

## Notes

1. *Babylonian Talmud*, tractate "Shabbat," 31a, quoted in *Pirke Avot: A Modern Commentary on Jewish Ethics*, ed. L. Kravitz and K. Olitzky (New York: UAHC Press, 1993), p. 8.

2. S. Kierkegaard, *Fear and Trembling*, trans. W. Lowrie (Princeton; NJ: Princeton University Press, 1941).

# 9   The Ten Commandments and The Holiness Code

**MOSES**

## Exodus 20

God spoke all these words,[1] saying:

[2]I the LORD am your God who brought you out of the land of Egypt, the house of bondage: [3]You shall have no other gods besides Me.

[4]You shall not make for yourself a sculptured image, or any likeness of what is in the heavens above, or on the earth below, or in the waters under the earth. [5]You shall not bow down to them or serve them. For I the LORD your God am an impassioned God, visiting the guilt of the parents upon the children, upon the third and upon the fourth generations of those who reject Me, [6]but showing kindness to the thousandth generation of those who love Me and keep My commandments.

[7]You shall not swear falsely by the name of the LORD your God; for the LORD will not clear one who swears falsely by His name.

[8]Remember the sabbath day and keep it holy. [9]Six days you shall labor and do all your work, [10]but the seventh day is a sabbath of the LORD your God: you shall not do any work—you, your son or daughter, your male or female slave, or your cattle, or the stranger who is within your settlements. [11]For in six days the LORD made heaven and earth and sea, and all that is in them, and He rested on the seventh day; therefore the LORD blessed the sabbath day and hallowed it.

[12]Honor your father and your mother, that you may long endure on the land that the LORD your God is assigning to you.

[13]You shall not murder.

You shall not commit adultery.

Your shall not steal.

You shall not bear false witness against your neighbor.

[14]You shall not covet your neighbor's house: you shall not covet your neighbor's wife, or his male or female slave, or his ox or his ass, or anything that is your neighbor's.

## Leviticus 19

The LORD spoke to Moses, saying: [2]Speak to the whole Israelite community and say to them:

You shall be holy, for I, the LORD your God, am holy.

[3]You shall each revere his mother and his father, and keep My sabbaths: I the LORD am your God.

[4]Do not turn to idols or make molten gods for yourselves: I the LORD am your God.

[5]When you sacrifice an offering of well-being to the LORD, sacrifice it so that it may be accepted on your behalf. [6]It shall be eaten on the day you sacrifice it, or on the day following; but what is left by the third day must be consumed in fire. [7]If it should be eaten on the third day, it is an offensive thing, it will not be acceptable. [8]And he who eats of it shall bear his guilt, for he has profaned what is sacred to the LORD; that person shall be cut off from his kin.

[9]When you reap the harvest of your land, you shall not reap all the way to the edges of your field, or gather the gleanings of your harvest. [10]You shall not pick your vineyard bare, or gather the fallen fruit of your vineyard; you shall leave them for the poor and the stranger: I the LORD am your God.

[11]You shall not steal; you shall not deal deceitfully or falsely with one another. [12]You shall not swear falsely by My name, profaning the name of your God: I am the LORD.

[13]You shall not defraud your fellow. You shall not commit robbery. The wages of a laborer shall not remain with you until morning.

Reprinted with permission of the publisher from *Tanakh: The Holy Scriptures* (Jewish Publication Society, 1985), 15–16, 185–186, footnotes omitted.

¹⁴You shall not insult the deaf, or place a stumbling block before the blind. You shall fear your God: I am the LORD.

¹⁵You shall not render an unfair decision: do not favor the poor or show deference to the rich; judge your kinsman fairly. ¹⁶Do not deal basely with your countrymen. Do not profit by the blood of your fellow: I am the LORD.

¹⁷You shall not hate your kinsfolk in your heart. Reprove your kinsman but incur no guilt because of him. ¹⁸You shall not take vengeance or bear a grudge against your countrymen. Love your fellow as yourself: I am the LORD.

¹⁹You shall observe My laws.

You shall not let your cattle mate with a different kind; you shall not sow your field with two kinds of seed; you shall not put on cloth from a mixture of two kinds of material.

²⁰If a man has carnal relations with a woman who is a slave and has been designated for another man, but has not been redeemed or given her freedom, there shall be an indemnity; they shall not, however, be put to death, since she has not been freed. ²¹But he must bring to the entrance of the Tent of Meeting, as his guilt offering to the LORD, a ram of guilt offering. ²²With the ram of guilt offering the priest shall make expiation for him before the LORD for the sin that he committed; and the sin that he committed will be forgiven him.

²³When you enter the land and plant any tree for food, you shall regard its fruit as forbidden. Three years it shall be forbidden for you, not to be eaten. ²⁴In the fourth year all its fruit shall be set aside for jubilation before the LORD; ²⁵and only in the fifth year may you use its fruit—that its yield to you may be increased: I the LORD am your God.

²⁶You shall not eat anything with its blood. You shall not practice divination or soothsaying. ²⁷You shall not round off the side-growth on your head, or destroy the side-growth of your beard. ²⁸You shall not make gashes in your flesh for the dead, or incise any marks on yourselves: I am the LORD.

²⁹Do not degrade your daughter and make her a harlot, lest the land fall into harlotry and the land be filled with depravity. ³⁰You shall keep My sabbaths and venerate My sanctuary: I am the LORD.

³¹Do not turn to ghosts and do not inquire of familiar spirits, to be defiled by them: I the LORD am your God.

³²You shall rise before the aged and show deference to the old; you shall fear your God: I am the LORD.

³³When a stranger resides with you in your land, you shall not wrong him. ³⁴The stranger who resides with you shall be to you as one of your citizens; you shall love him as yourself, for you were strangers in the land of Egypt: I the LORD am your God.

³⁵You shall not falsify measures of length, weight, or capacity. ³⁶You shall have an honest balance, honest weights, an honest *ephah,* and an honest *hin.*

I the LORD am your God who freed you from the land of Egypt. ³⁷You shall faithfully observe all My laws and all My rules: I am the LORD.

# 10   The Ten Commandments and The Holiness Code: A Modern Commentary

## GUNTHER PLAUT

## The Ten Commandments

### The First Commandment (verse 2)

Verse 2 lays down the foundation of what follows, it is preamble, yet more than preamble: God is, and He is the One who gave Israel its existence as a nation. He brought it into history, for His own purposes—for Israel is to achieve through service to Him what the whole of mankind, even after the Flood, proved incapable of doing. Israel was redeemed by God so that it might redeem humanity.

The first commandment establishes at once that Israel's is a historical religion, anchored in the people's experience and validated by their free acceptance of the divine will. It is a religion directed to the individual as part of a people in history. The reference to Egypt is thus not a geographic but a spiritual notation: having traversed the road from slavery to freedom Israel can now fulfill its destiny, and it is the duty of each individual Israelite to do his share. The first commandment is in fact a confessional credo: Israel acknowledging that God delivered it from Egypt.

For not only humanity depends on Israel, God —in a manner of speaking—does also. A midrash expresses this thought in memorable fashion. It interprets the first commandment to imply: "I am the Lord (if I am) your God," that is, I can be Myself only if you acknowledge Me. In midrashic language If you do My will I am YHVH, the Merciful One, but if not I will be Elohim, the dispenser of stern justice. Israel is dependent on God, and God depends on Israel to bring His redemptive plans to fruition. Thus seen, the first of the Words

is both preamble and charter, the cornerstone of Israel's covenant and mankind's salvation.

### The Second Commandment (verses 3–6)

Targum Jonathan, one of the Aramaic translations of the Torah, expands on this commandment by saying that these words came forth like storms, lightning, and flames. The first Word established the duty to acknowledge God, the second demands recognition of His singularity and forbids His presentation in any forms of sculptured image. The commandment is not argumentative: it does not refute polytheism but simply indicates that the gods of others are not for Israel. The commandment by itself takes no stand on whether or not such other deities actually exist, its subject matter is the faith of Israel. In a world filled with myriads of deities which were worshiped by men, the stark and simple truth of God's lordship over Israel is here proclaimed and its acknowledgment demanded—nothing more, but also nothing less. Whatever other nations may do or believe, for Israel there is no compromise and, although it took some centuries to root this belief firmly amongst the people, it became in time the cornerstone of their spiritual existence and engaged their unshakable adherence under even the most trying conditions.

The prohibition of sculptured images for purposes of adoration stresses the incorporeality of God. "You saw no shape when the Lord your God spoke to you at Horeb out of the fire," Deuteronomy 4:15 reminds the people. The worship of images is proscribed in the most urgent and vivid terms: nothing, but absolutely nothing, is permitted that might lead to idolatry. This is no prohibition of the plastic arts as such but only of their misuse. This meant, however, that, in ages when the arts served primarily the goals of religion,

Reprinted with permission of the publisher from *The Torah: A Modern Commentary* (Union of American Hebrew Congregations, 1981), 541–543, 556–558, 889–893, with omissions.

sculpture and painting found no fertile soil amongst the Jewish people. Instead, Judaism directed its creative powers toward the inner life, the vision of the soul rather than the eye, the invisible rather than the visible, the intangible rather than the sensual. Prayer became life's great dimension, while the visual arts were denied their place of eminence.

The rigor of the commandment was emphasized through a large promise of both reward and punishment by a God who is described as "impassioned." Critics of the Torah have made much of contrasting a purportedly unrelenting, monstrously stern, and jealous God with one who is filled with mercy, kindness, and forebearance. Such a contrast—used frequently to show the "primitive" nature of the Jewish faith—does gross injustice to both the nature of monotheism and the range of the biblical view. To the Torah, belief in God by the people He chose as His servants is a condition of life itself. To have met Him at Sinai was awesome and fraught with incalculable consequences. Not tolerance is here at stake but Israel's spiritual existence. Further, the very same Book of Exodus tells the questing Moses that the Lord is "compassionate and gracious, slow to anger, rich in steadfast kindness" (34:6); and, in the commandment itself, love by far outlasts the judgment of evil: a thousand generations for the former are compared to three or four for the latter. The text expresses the principle of retribution in terms of ancient society, with its close familial patterns, where children were indeed part of their parents' ambiance, where deeds or misdeeds of one member of the family involved the whole family. The commandment should therefore not be understood as providing for individual retribution; nor does it address itself to questions of criminal law. In that regard the Torah sets forth a different rule: "Parents shall not be put to death for children, nor children be put to death for parents" (Deut. 24:16; see also Ezek. 18:20). Furthermore, it should be noted that the threat of God's wrath, vivid and uncompromising though it is, pales ultimately before the promise of His abiding love. The second commandment ends on a note of

hope: a faithful Israel will inherit a glorious future in the presence of a faithful God.

## The Third Commandment (verse 7)

The second of the Words dealt with the misuse of images, the third turns to the misuse of God's name—a transition from the visual to the verbal. Both image and name are aspects of identity, and man must take care lest he infringe on the sanctity of God in any manner. As noted before, the commandment intends most likely more than a prohibition of false oaths; its wider scope forbids man in every respect to use God's name wrongly or in vain. According to Ibn Ezra, this prohibition is more important than those that follow. For murder, adultery, and theft are circumscribed by opportunity and fear, but misuse of God's name, once it becomes a habit, will proliferate "and in the end one's every assertion will be preceded by using the Name." The result is a devaluation of awe and respect, and in time the holiness of God has no further meaning. Society is deeply affected by such deterioration, as was already reported by Philo who in his second-century C.E. Alexandria deplored that people held the prohibition to swear in small regard.

. . . The commandment does more than forbid profanity and sacrilegious oath-taking; it covers as well irresponsible, loose exclamations as "dear God," "good Lord," "by God," and the like. Whether the commandment forbids false swearing by God's name, or prohibits all wrong or vain usage, the basic intent remains: to safeguard His name from erosion and to maintain the sense of His holiness among His children.

## The Fifth Commandment (verse 12)

Jewish tradition has underscored the importance of one's duty to honor father and mother by listing it among the commandments on the first tablet. It is thus seen as concluding the catalog of man's basic obligations to God. Parents are God's representatives and partners in the rearing of their children, and children who fail to respect this special position are offending against God as well. Even as the penalty of death is prescribed for blasphemy (Lev. 24:15, 16), so it is also for striking, cursing—some say even insulting—one's parents (Exod. 21:15, 17; Lev. 20:9). No difference is made between father and mother. The order of naming one before the other is of no consequence, as Lev. 19:3 makes amply clear, where the mother is named first. In the Code of Hammurabi the striking of a father is made an offense, but the mother is not mentioned. . . .

## The Sixth to Tenth Commandments (verses 13–14)

*"You shall not murder"*

The Rabbis gave this commandment great emphasis by stipulating that it was obligatory for all men.

As indicated above, only unauthorized homicide is meant by the text, and the older translation "You shall not kill" was too general and did not represent the more specific meaning of *tērza*. Hence the claims of pacifists, who would see this command as a prohibition of all killing including that legitimized by the state during warfare, cannot be sustained. The same is true for the abolition of capital punishment. Laudable as these objectives are, they find no warranty in the text itself, which has been used to legitimize other prohibitions as well. Thus, the Church Father Augustine held that the commandment forbade not only the taking of other peoples' lives but of one's own as well, and many countries to this day make suicide a criminal offense. Jewish tradition, while it too frowned on suicide, deriving the prohibition from Gen. 9:5, did not include it in the catalogue of punishable crimes. Although according to the Torah murder was punishable by death, the Rabbis proceeded nonetheless to make a judicial conviction, which would render the penalty mandatory, more and more difficult. Thus in the second century C.E. capital punishment was decried by most Sages, and it has been abolished in modern Israel.

*"You shall not commit adultery"*

The command is directed to both the man and the woman, and both are to be executed when found guilty (Lev. 20:10). Purity of family life is another pillar of society as envisaged by the Bible. In time it became a distinguishing aspect of Israel's social structure, complementing the honor rendered to parents and the sense of responsibility felt for all members of the family.

In biblical days men were permitted to marry more than one wife, and concubinage—the acquisition of lesser-status wives—was also practiced. Jacob had two full-status wives and two concubines, and Solomon was said to have married a thousand, that is to say, very many women (I Kings 11:3). Nowhere in the Torah or the rest of the Bible is monogamy established as a rule or even a desirable principle, although in the course of time polygamy became the exception rather than the rule. Jews who lived among Moslems (who themselves were permitted multiple marriages) frequently continued to practice polygamy into the present age, while the majority who lived in Christian lands adopted the custom of their environment and practiced monogamy. This latter practice was given legal status by an enactment of Rabbenu Gershom (about 1000 C.E., in Germany). While the decree expired technically in the (Jewish) year 5000, that is, 1240 in the civil reckoning, it was generally considered as continuing in force in all countries where monogamy was the rule. In modern Israel monogamy is established in law, but an exception may be made by special permission of the Chief Rabbinate, and immigrants who came with several wives from lands where polygamy was permitted have been allowed to maintain such status.

*"You shall not steal"*

The commandment appears to cover both property and people—kidnaping being already an ancient practice for which Exod. 21:16 specifically provides the penalty of death. (However, the Rabbis interpreted the commandment to refer to persons and Lev. 19:11 to property only. Quite clearly, the right to private property is protected by the Torah, and no earthly ruler could deprive the owner of his property against his will. This principle is demonstrated with particular force in the story of Naboth's vineyard, which was desired by the king but which he could not legally acquire over the proprietor's objection (I Kings 21). Real property was meant to be kept in the family's and tribe's permanent possession, and if it was alienated by sale it would return to the original owners in the jubilee year (Lev. 25:10). We do not know how successfully this ideal was ever implemented, and it appears that, in any case, the law became inoperative after the Babylonian exile (586 B.C.E.).

### "You shall not bear false witness"

The prohibition covers not only the act of witnessing but goes further: It addresses itself to the character of a person. The Hebrew text does not speak of false testimony but of a false testifier. The liar infects both himself and the social fabric, and, when he practices his deceit in court, the damage is doubly destructive. "Everything in the world was created by God," says a midrash, "except the art of lying."

### "You shall not covet"

The commandment, directed as it is to the heart, is primarily a warning that greed unchecked will likely lead to actual transgression. The intent of the command became an issue in the Christian church. Was inward desire to be reckoned as a sin (for which forgiveness needed to be asked) even if it did not lead to any outward act? Pope Pius V, in a rare act of official interpretation by the Church of a biblical text, ruled in 1567 that it was not. Only overt action was to be considered sinful, but not the mere desire.

## The Life of Holiness

The constant theme here is *holiness*. We have already encountered this concept, chiefly in reflections of its ancient and primitive form. Here, after summarizing such material, we shall move on to more advanced and mature conceptions of holiness, and we shall consider their implications for our own life. It will, moreover, be proper to

make use of Hebrew terminology, for the word *kadosh* (plural *kedoshim)* is only roughly, but not exactly, equivalent to the English "holy.". . . .

a. *Kadosh* is the adjective regularly applied to divinity and divinities. In the Book of Daniel (4:5f.), the Babylonian king speaks of the "holy gods" (Aramaic *elahin kadishin).* Other biblical writings refer to angelic beings as *kedoshim* (Zech. 14:5; Ps. 9:8; Job 5:11). The God of Israel is often characterized as *kadosh,* especially by Isaiah.

b. This term, conventionally associated with deity, is also applied to places, times, objects, and procedures connected with deity. A place of worship is called *mikdash.* The innermost Shrine is *Kodesh Kodashim.* "Holy of Holies"—more exactly, "highest level of holiness." All sacrifices are holy, but some are designated as *Kodesh Kodashim.*

As the deity was regarded anciently as set apart and dangerous to approach, so it was often with places and things that were his special possession. In some Bible passages, *kadosh* has the same force as the Polynesian word *taboo.* In such cases, holiness was conceived as a physical force which can pass from one object to another like an electric current with potentially destructive power.

*Kodesh* does not necessarily indicate an absolute taboo. The sacred places may be approached, sacred food may be eaten, but only if special rules, especially those of ceremonial purity, are strictly observed. Disregard of these rules, intentional or otherwise, is a desecration that may lead to disastrous results.

c. This mechanical concept of "holiness" was embodied in practices treated in the earlier chapters of this book—practices that survived even after the ideas they expressed had been supplanted by a more mature concept of *kedushah.* For *kadosh* gradually came to indicate, not the physical separation of God and man, but the spiritual gap between human inadequacy and divine perfection.

. . . Most remarkable of all, our chapter summons the Israelites to imitate God and so become holy themselves.

d. This last point requires special stress in view of the great influence exercised on a generation or more of religious thinkers by the book, *The Idea of the Holy*. The author, Rudolf Otto, a Protestant theologian, was disturbed by the tendency of liberals to reduce religion to ethics. He sought to prove that man's nature has a religious aspect that was originally independent of the ethical. It is that part of us which responds to the mysterious and awesome—to the reality, at once overwhelming and fascinating, that cannot be adequately understood or rationalized. The word "holy" and its equivalents, says Otto, point to the experience of the "numinous," of a divine reality that evokes fear, awe, and submission. This experience, in its cruder and more primitive forms, is that of the uncanny, ghostly, and hair-raising. Later, as concepts of divinity are purified and elevated, ethical elements are introduced into the idea of holiness, and awe is evoked, not only by the frightening mystery, but also by the divine perfection.

It is striking that Otto, a pious Lutheran, made no mention of this chapter of Leviticus in his book. He spoke only of holiness as an emotional experience, not of *kedushah* as aspiration and task to be approached through a disciplined life. In his zeal to give religion a unique character, Otto reduced the ethical component of holiness to a mere "extra." This is not the Jewish view of the subject, as is plain from the text before us, and also from the recurrent declaration in our prayers and benedictions that God "sanctifies us through His commandments." In Judaism, religion and ethics, though not identical, are inseparable.

e. Chapters 18 through 20 give a clear account of holiness in life.

The prime emphasis is ethical. And the moral laws of this chapter are not mere injunctions of conformity. They call for just, humane, and sensitive treatment of others. The aged, the handicapped, and the poor are to receive consideration and courtesy. The laborer is to be promptly paid. The stranger is to be accorded the same love we give our fellow citizens. The law is concerned, not only with overt behavior, but also with motive: vengefulness and the bearing of grudges are condemned.

Among ethical duties, that of sexual decency is singled out for particular emphasis. The Torah demands the control, not the suppression of the sexual instinct. Life is sacred. The physical process by which life is generated is to be treated responsibly.

The ethical injunctions of chapter 19 are interspersed with ritual commandments. Some of these are directed against pagan and superstitious practices deemed incompatible with biblical religion. The intent of others is not so plain. To the biblical author, these ceremonial rulings are divine ordinances with the same authority as the ethical commandments. Traditional Judaism regarded them as "royal decrees," to be observed whether or not we comprehend them (see introduction to Lev. 11:1–23).

The Jewish modernist cannot agree with this. But he can recognize that worship and ceremony, undertaken thoughtfully and reverently, can elevate personal and family life. Though he may reject older views as to the origin and authority of ritual, he may still benefit from the practice of ritual. In holy living, the ethical factor is primary, but it is not the only one. In combining moral and ceremonial commandments, the authors of the Holiness Code displayed sound understanding.

f. Such are the components of the way of life called *kadosh*. Our chapter begins with the startling declaration that by these means we can and should try to be holy like God. The same Torah that stresses the distance between His sublime perfection and our earthy limitations urges us to strive to reduce that distance. The task is endless, but it is infinitely rewarding. Rabbi Tarfon said: "Do not avoid an undertaking that has no limit or a task that cannot be completed. It is like the case of one who was hired to take water from the sea and pour it out on the land. But, as the sea was not emptied out or the land filled with water, he became downhearted. Then someone said to him, 'Foolish fellow! Why should you be downhearted as long as you receive a dinar of gold every day as your wage?'" The pursuit of the unattainable can be a means of fulfillment.

g. The Law of Holiness is not addressed to selected individuals. It is addressed to the entire community of Israel. Its objective is not to produce a few saints, withdrawn from the world in contemplative or ascetic practices. Rather, does the Torah aim to create a holy people which displays its consecration to God's service in the normal day-to-day relations of farming, commerce, family living, and community affairs (cf. Exod. 19:6).

h. Characteristic of [the Law of Holiness] is the notion of the holy land. Though God rules the whole world, He is uniquely attached to, and present in, the land of Canaan, which is to be the Land of Israel. Hence, heathen practices that are tolerable elsewhere will lead to expulsion from the Land of Israel (18:24, 28: 20:22ff.). The law of the Sabbath year is imposed not only on the people but on the soil itself; failure to observe the law will have to made up for through years of desolation (below, 26:34).

The notion that sanctity should attach to a particular geographic area may seem strange to us. Yet many find it natural for Jews to expect more of themselves than of others, to believe that a Jewish community should be a model community, and a Jewish state different from, and better than, other national states.

The idea of holiness implies that what we do and what we make of our lives matters not only to us as individuals, not only to society, but to the entire cosmos. A divine purpose runs through all existence. We can ally ourselves to it or oppose it —or, perhaps worse, we can ignore it. This climactic chapter of the Torah deserves, not only careful reading and study, but continuing reflection on its astonishing implications.

### Sanctifying and Profaning the Name

We have already noted the statement (18:21) that one who offers his offspring to Molech profanes the name of God. The same expression appears in chapter 19, verse 12, in connection with swearing falsely. In these contexts, the phrase seems to require no explanation. But its fuller meaning emerges elsewhere. To profane the name of God means to impair His reputation in the non-Israelite world.

Thus, Ezekiel (who, we have seen, shows affinity to the Holiness Code) declares that, when the people of Judah brought the punishment of exile upon themselves, they profaned the name of God. For the Gentiles regarded the defeat of Judah as a

defeat for Judah's God as well. They supposed the people were in exile because their God was not strong enough to protect them. Therefore, to retrieve His reputation, God would purify and restore Israel. When they were back on their own soil, strong and prosperous, God's name would be "sanctified in the sight of all the peoples"—that is, the nations would recognize His power and understand that the exile was not evidence of His impotence, but of His unswerving justice (Ezek. 36:16ff.).

This concept was transformed in Rabbinic Judaism from a questionable theological proposition into a powerful moral challenge. The prestige of Israel's God among the Gentiles—the Rabbis taught—is not God's worry, it is humankind's responsibility. Jews must so live and act as to win for their God the respect of all mankind. Any behavior that brings public disgrace on Jews and Judaism is *chilul ha-Shem,* profanation of the divine Name; any action that enhances the dignity and honor of Judaism is *kiddush ha-Shem,* sanctification of the Name.

Robbing a Gentile is doubly sinful, since it adds to the sin of robbery the further sin of *chilul ha-Shem.* A Jew should accept martyrdom rather than publicly violate a commandment and thus profane the name of God.

*Kiddush ha-Shem* has no connection with what we now call "public relations." It does not mean currying favor with the Gentiles. It requires us to deserve the approbation of others, whether we actually obtain it or not. The highest act of *kiddush ha-Shem* is to die for one's faith.

### The Golden Rule

The culmination of this climactic chapter is verse 18: "Love your neighbor as yourself." It is one of several versions of what in modern times has been called "the golden rule." (We do not know when or by whom the phrase was coined.) It appears in various forms, positive and negative: but all of them demand for others the same kind of treatment we want for ourselves.

Our passage is apparently the oldest written version of the principle. When Hillel, at the beginning of the Christian era, was asked to sum up the entire Torah briefly, he replied: "What is hateful to you, do not do to your fellow." (This negative form of the golden rule was apparently proverbial in Hillel's time for it appears in practically the same words in the apocryphal book of Tobit.) Jesus of Nazareth, Hillel's younger contemporary, declared that the commandment of Leviticus 19:18 is second in importance only to the command to love God (Mark 12:28ff.). In the following century, Rabbi Akiba declared it to be "the great principle of the Torah" (*Sifra*).

Confucius is credited with having taught the golden rule in its negative form [11]. A more abstract version of the principle is Kant's categorical imperative: "Act only on the maxim whereby thou canst at the same time will that it should become a universal law."

Some Christian apologetes have argued that the negative form of the golden rule is spiritually inferior to the positive form ascribed to Jesus: "All that you would wish that men should do unto you, do ye also unto them" (Matthew 7:12). In their zeal, they forgot that the positive form occurs first in the Torah! But, actually, there is virtually no difference in meaning between the two versions. The golden rule, it has been remarked, is an instrument of criticism. It enables us to judge a proposed course of action, but it does not provide us the means of proposing a course of action; that always requires an effort of creative imagination. Regarded as a standard of judgment, the golden rule is equally effective in negative or positive form.

Some Christians have also tried to show that the saying of Jesus is more truly universal and inclusive than that of Leviticus. They argue that "neighbor" in Leviticus (19:18) means "fellow Israelite" which is true enough; but they apparently overlook the commandment of verse 34 which requires us to show the same love to a foreigner resident in the land. There is no evidence that Jesus had a broader outlook.

Such theoretical distinctions would in any case not be important. Our opportunity to practice the golden rule is chiefly in our relations to those who are physically near to us, our literal neighbors. In ancient times, most people had little awareness of events beyond their immediate vicinity. They had no share in major political and economic decisions. They rarely knew even of major occurrences until the results came upon them in the form of invasion, deportation, new tax demands, and the like. Only in recent centuries, especially in our own, has the average person had the knowledge, the opportunity, and the obligation to apply the golden rule on a global scale. Today, indeed, we must consider what duties we owe to the Vietnamese, the Biafrans, the Bengalis; but that is something new. And it does not make the question of our relationships with those nearer home any less compelling.

# 11   Sermon on the Mount

**JESUS**

## Matthew
## Chapter 5

¹When he saw the crowds, he went up the mountain, and after he had sat down, his disciples came to him. ²He began to teach them, saying:

Reprinted with permission of the United States Catholic Conference from *New American Bible* (Thomas Nelson Inc., 1987), 1067–1072.

## The Beatitudes

³Blessed are the poor in spirit, for theirs is the kingdom of heaven.
⁴Blessed are they who mourn, for they will be comforted.
⁵Blessed are the meek, for they will inherit the land.
⁶Blessed are they who hunger and thirst for righteousness, for they will be satisfied.

[7]Blessed are the merciful, for they will be shown mercy.

[8]Blessed are the clean of heart, for they will see God.

[9]Blessed are the peacemakers, for they will be called children of God.

[10]Blessed are they who are persecuted for the sake of righteousness, for theirs is the kingdom of heaven.

[11]Blessed are you when they insult you and persecute you and utter every kind of evil against you [falsely] because of me. [12]Rejoice and be glad, for your reward will be great in heaven. Thus they persecuted the prophets who were before you.

**The Similes of Salt and Light.** [13]"You are the salt of the earth. But if salt loses its taste, with what can it be seasoned? It is no longer good for anything but to be thrown out and trampled underfoot. [14]You are the light of the world. A city set on a mountain cannot be hidden. [15]Nor do they light a lamp and then put it under a bushel basket; it is set on a lampstand, where it gives light to all in the house. [16]Just so, your light must shine before others, that they may see your good deeds and glorify your heavenly Father.

**Teaching about the Law.** [17]"Do not think that I have come to abolish the law or the prophets. I have come not to abolish but to fulfill. [18]Amen, I say to you, until heaven and earth pass away, not the smallest letter or the smallest part of a letter will pass from the law, until all things have taken place. [19]Therefore, whoever breaks one of the least of these commandments and teaches others to do so will be called least in the kingdom of heaven. But whoever obeys and teaches these commandments will be called greatest in the kingdom of heaven. [20]I tell you, unless your righteousness surpasses that of the scribes and Pharisees, you will not enter into the kingdom of heaven.

**Teaching about Anger.** [21]"You have heard that it was said to your ancestors, 'You shall not kill; and whoever kills will be liable to judgment.' [22]But I say to you, whoever is angry with his brother will be liable to judgment, and whoever says to his brother, 'Raqa,' will be answerable to the Sanhedrin, and whoever says, 'You fool,' will be liable to fiery Gehenna. [23]Therefore, if you bring your gift to the altar, and there recall that your brother has anything against you, [24]leave your gift there at the altar, go first and be reconciled with your brother, and then come and offer your gift. [25]Settle with your opponent quickly while on the way to court with him. Otherwise your opponent will hand you over to the judge, and the judge will hand you over to the guard, and you will be thrown into prison. [26]Amen, I say to you, you will not be released until you have paid the last penny.

**Teaching about Adultery.** [27]"You have heard that it was said, 'You shall not commit adultery.' [28]But I say to you, everyone who looks at a woman with lust has already committed adultery with her in his heart. [29]If your right eye causes you to sin, tear it out and throw it away. It is better for you to lose one of your members than to have your whole body thrown into Gehenna. [30]And if your right hand causes you to sin, cut it off and throw it away. It is better for you to lose one of your members than to have your whole body go into Gehenna.

**Teaching about Divorce.** [31]"It was also said, 'Whoever divorces his wife must give her a bill of divorce.' [32]But I say to you, whoever divorces his wife (unless the marriage is unlawful) causes her to commit adultery, and whoever marries a divorced woman commits adultery.

**Teaching about Oaths.** [33]"Again you have heard that it was said to your ancestors, 'Do not take a false oath, but make good to the Lord all that you vow.' [34]But I say to you, do not swear at all; not by heaven, for it is God's throne; [35]nor by the earth, for it is his footstool; nor by Jerusalem, for it is the city of the great King. [36]Do not swear by your head, for you cannot make a single hair white or black. [37]Let your 'Yes' mean 'Yes,' and your 'No' mean 'No.' Anything more is from the evil one.

**Teaching about Retaliation.** [38]"You have heard that it was said, 'An eye for an eye and a tooth for a tooth.' [39]But I say to you, offer no resistance to one who is evil. When someone strikes you on [your] right cheek, turn the other one to him as well. [40]If anyone wants to go to law with you over your tunic, hand him your cloak as well. [41]Should anyone press you into service for one mile, go with him for two miles. [42]Give to the one who asks of you, and do not turn your back on one who wants to borrow.

**Love of Enemies.** [43]"You have heard that it was said, 'You shall love your neighbor and hate your enemy.' [44]But I say to you, love your enemies, and pray for those who persecute you, [45]that you may be children of your heavenly Father, for he makes his sun rise on the bad and the good, and causes rain to fall on the just and the unjust. [46]For if you love those who love you, what recompense will you have? Do not the tax collectors do the same? [47]And if you greet your brothers only, what is unusual about that? Do not the pagans do the same? [48]So be perfect, just as your heavenly Father is perfect.

# Chapter 6

**Teaching about Almsgiving.** [1]"[But] take care not to perform righteous deeds in order that people may see them; otherwise, you will have no recompense from your heavenly Father. [2]When you give alms, do not blow a trumpet before you, as the hypocrites do in the synagogues and in the streets to win the praise of others. Amen, I say to you, they have received their reward. [3]But when you give alms, do not let your left hand know what your right is doing, [4]so that your almsgiving may be secret. And your Father who sees in secret will repay you.

**Teaching about Prayer.** [5]"When you pray, do not be like the hypocrites, who love to stand and pray in the synagogues and on street corners so that others may see them. Amen, I say to you, they have received their reward. [6]But when you pray, go to your inner room, close the door, and pray to your Father in secret. And your Father who sees in secret will repay you. [7]In praying, do not babble like the pagans, who think that they will be heard because of their many words. [8]Do not be like them. Your Father knows what you need before you ask him.

**The Lord's Prayer.** [9]"This is how you are to pray:

Our Father in heaven,
hallowed by your name,
[10]your kingdom come,
your will be done,
on earth as in heaven.
[11]Give us today our daily bread;
[12]and forgive us our debts,
as we forgive our debtors;
[13]and do not subject us to the final test,
but deliver us from the evil one.

[14]If you forgive others their transgression, your heavenly Father will forgive you. [15]But if you do not forgive others, neither will your Father forgive your transgressions.

**Teaching about Fasting.** [16]"When you fast, do not look gloomy like the hypocrites. They neglect their appearance, so that they may appear to others to be fasting. Amen, I say to you, they have received their reward. [17]But when you fast, anoint your head and wash your face, [18]so that you may not appear to be fasting, except to your Father who is hidden. And your Father who sees what is hidden will repay you.

**Treasure in Heaven.** [19]"Do not store up for yourselves treasures on earth, where moth and decay destroy, and thieves break in and steal. [20]But store up treasures in heaven, where neither moth nor decay destroys, nor thieves break in and steal. [21]For where your treasure is, there also will your heart be.

**The Light of the Body.** [22]"The lamp of the body is the eye. If your eye is sound, your whole body will be filled with light; [23]but if your eye is bad, your whole body will be in darkness. And if the light in you is darkness, how great will the darkness be.

**God and Money.** [24]"No one can serve two masters. He will either hate one and love the other, or be devoted to one and despise the other. You cannot serve God and mammon.

**Dependence on God.** 25"Therefore I tell you, do not worry about your life, what you will eat [or drink], or about your body, what you will wear. Is not life more than food and the body more than clothing? 26Look at the birds in the sky; they do not sow or reap, they gather nothing into barns, yet your heavenly Father feeds them. Are not you more important than they? 27Can any of you by worrying add a single moment to your life-span? 28Why are you anxious about clothes? Learn from the way the wild flowers grow. They do not work or spin. 29But I tell you that not even Solomon in all his splendor was clothed like one of them. 30If God so clothes the grass of the field, which grows today and is thrown into the oven tomorrow, will he not much more provide for you, O you of little faith? 31So do not worry and say, 'What are we to eat?' or 'What are we to drink?' or 'What are we to wear?' 32All these things the pagans seek. Your heavenly Father knows that you need them all. 33But seek first the kingdom [of God] and his righteousness, and all these things will be given you besides. 34Do not worry about tomorrow; tomorrow will take care of itself. Sufficient for a day is its own evil.

# Chapter 7

**Judging Others.** 1"Stop judging, that you may not be judged. 2For as you judge, so will you be judged, and the measure with which you measure will be measured out to you. 3Why do you notice the splinter in your brother's eye, but do not perceive the wooden beam in your own eye? 4How can you say to your brother, 'Let me remove that splinter from your eye,' while the wooden beam is in your eye? 5You hypocrite, remove the wooden beam from your eye first; then you will see clearly to remove the splinter from your brother's eye.

**Pearls before Swine.** 6"Do not give what is holy to dogs, or throw your pearls before swine, lest they trample them underfoot, and turn and tear you to pieces.

**The Answer to Prayers.** 7"Ask and it will be given to you; seek and you will find; knock and the door will be opened to you. 8For everyone who asks, receives; and the one who seeks, finds; and to the one who knocks, the door will be opened. 9Which one of you would hand his son a stone when he asks for a loaf of bread, 10or a snake when he asks for a fish? 11If you then, who are wicked, know how to give good gifts to your children, how much more will your heavenly Father give good things to those who ask him.

**The Golden Rule.** 12"Do to others whatever you would have them do to you. This is the law and the prophets.

**The Narrow Gate.** 13"Enter through the narrow gate; for the gate is wide and the road broad that leads to destruction, and those who enter through it are many. 14How narrow the gate and constricted the road that leads to life. And those who find it are few.

**False Prophets.** 15"Beware of false prophets, who come to you in sheep's clothing, but underneath are ravenous wolves. 16By their fruits you will know them. Do people pick grapes from thornbushes, or figs from thistles? 17Just so, every good tree bears good fruit, and a rotten tree bears bad fruit. 18A good tree cannot bear bad fruit, nor can a rotten tree bear good fruit. 19Every tree that does not bear good fruit will be cut down and thrown into the fire. 20So by their fruits you will know them.

**The True Discipline.** 21"Not everyone who says to me, 'Lord, Lord,' will enter the kingdom of heaven, but only the one who does the will of my Father in heaven. 22Many will say to me on that day, 'Lord, Lord, did we not prophesy in your name? Did we not drive out demons in your name? Did we not do mighty deeds in your name?' 23Then I will declare to them solemnly, 'I never knew you. Depart from me, you evildoers.'

**The Two Foundations.** 24"Everyone who listens to these words of mine and acts on them will be like a wise man who built his house on rock. 25The rain fell, the floods came, and the winds blew and buffeted the house. But it did not collapse; it had been set solidly on rock. [26]And everyone who listens to these words of mine but does not act on them will be like a fool who built his house on sand. [27]The rain fell, the floods came, and the winds blew and buffeted the house. And it collapsed and was completely ruined."

[28]When Jesus finished these words, the crowds were astonished at his teaching, [29]for he taught them as one having authority, and not as their scribes.

# 12　The Sermon on the Mount (5:1–7:29)

**FRANK STAGG**

## 1. Introduction (5:1–2)

### The Sermon's Intention

Apart from detailed exegesis is the question of how the sermon is to be heard. A dozen or more distinct approaches have been suggested. Some sentimentalists boast that the only religion they want is the Sermon on the Mount. Have they read it? Others, awed or frightened by its heavy demands, give up in despair, concluding that it is unrealistic or impossible. A few have actually undertaken to follow it literally, even to self-mutilation (5:29 f.). Some have termed it an interim ethic, intended for a brief period just before an expected end of the world. Others have held that the sermon applies only to the clergy and not to the laity or only to relationships within the church but not in the world, though Jesus never endorsed such double standards. The great danger is that less than justice be done to either the awesome demands or the merciful gifts or to both.

Our proposal is that the Sermon on the Mount is best understood when seen in its setting, seen as God's ultimate and absolute demand addressed to sinners who are also offered acceptance upon the basis of mercy and forgiveness. The demands are not to be toned down or explained away, not even the awesome, "You, therefore, must be perfect, as

your heavenly Father is perfect" (5:48). God's claims, i.e., the demands of the kingdom (reign) of God as it confronts us in Christ (anointed to rule), are ultimate and absolute. They are ultimate in that they are final. They are absolute in the sense that God does not divide his authority with any other. To enter into the kingdom of God is to acknowledge his right to rule as full and final.

This does not mean that any person, except Jesus, has lived up to this demand. But it does mean that to be a Christian is to live under that claim, however far he falls short of living up to it. God does not ask for 50 percent or 99 percent obedience. His will is that we be perfect.

On the other hand, the Sermon on the Mount is addressed to sinners (7:11) who are wholly dependent upon his mercy and forgiveness (cf. 5:3–7; 6:12,14 f.). At no point does the Sermon on the Mount assume that we are sinless or perfect. The sermon is in a setting of mercy. It is preceded by a summary statement of Jesus' ministry of teaching, preaching, and healing (4:23 f.), and it is followed by ten stories of merciful healing and care (8:1–9:34) and with a touching picture of the compassion of Jesus for the neglected multitudes (9:35–38). God's demands are always preceded by his gifts. Just as the Mosaic law arose out of the Exodus, God's merciful act of delivering Israel from Egyptian bondage, so the Sermon on the Mount is couched in God's merciful acts of deliverance. The high demand of Christ (5:1–7:28) comes from one who offers unlimited succour

Reprinted with permission of the Baptist Sunday School Board from *Broadman Bible Commentary* (Broadman Press, 1969), 102–123, with omissions.

(4:23 f.; 8:1–9:34). The sermon is set in a framework of healing and pity.

The Sermon on the Mount leaves us no hope except in the mercy of God, and at the same time it places us under moral, ethical, and other personal demands which are absolute and ultimate. The Christian cannot escape this "tension" between God's gift and his demand. Neither is to be blunted. A righteousness exceeding that of the scribes and Pharisees is demanded of sinners who daily are to forgive and seek forgiveness. The Sermon on the Mount takes seriously man's infinite need of mercy and his infinite moral and ethical possibilities. Of himself man can achieve nothing, but Christ can bring about a new kind of existence in those who are willing to be accepted on the grounds of mercy and to acknowledge God's right to rule. The Sermon on the Mount excludes the pride, superficiality, and deception of legalism and also the moral and ethical irresponsibility and escapism of antinomianism.

It is not moral achievement which brings man into proper relationship with God, but the new relationship is itself God's gift, offered on the basis of mercy; and this new relationship with God first opens to us the possibility for the moral behavior demanded. The one who commands is also the one who forgives, saves, and sustains. In a sense, the Sermon on the Mount confronts us with law and gospel, but it must be remembered that God's law itself is an expression of love and mercy, for what he demands belongs to our true needs and nature. His law consists not of arbitrary rules but of principles without which we miss our true existence. God's kingdom comes to us in Jesus Christ not as a set of rules but as the rule of one who loves enough to give and demand.

### The Mountain

*Seeing the crowds,* Jesus *went up on the mountain.* The mountain is not identified, but probably the reference is to a place west of Lake Galilee and in the vicinity of Capernaum (8:5). That Matthew sees a parallel between the Sermon on the Mount and the giving of the law at Mount Sinai is possible but far from conclusive. He draws no analogies between Moses' receiving the law at Sinai and Jesus' teaching *on the mountain.* Luke (6:12, 17) comes closer to paralleling Exodus 19 than does Matthew, for Luke sees Jesus as descending from the mountain to teach, as did Moses. In Matthew, Jesus ascended to teach. To Matthew, Jesus is not a new Moses giving a new law but the fulfiller of the Law and the Prophets.

## 2. The Beatitudes (5:3–12)

### The Poor in Spirit (v. 3)

Luke's "you poor" (6:20) is likely to be more primitive than Matthew's "poor in spirit." Two views can be traced in ancient Judaism, one seeing wealth as a sign of God's favor, with adversity as a sign of divine judgment. The other view identifies wealth with wickedness and poverty with piety (cf. James 2:5; 5:1). Luke's Beatitude reflects the latter pattern, "the poor," possibly identified with "the people of the land." The Semitic term behind the Greek designates the pious in Israel, chiefly but not exclusively identified with the materially poor. Matthew removes the ambiguity by adding "in spirit," recognizing that material or social poverty alone is not a mark of faith or piety.

The Beatitudes stress the striking contrast between outward appearance and inner reality. The kingdom of heaven belongs not to those who by the world's standards are rich and mighty. They alone reign with God who surrender all claims to that end. Neither material nor spiritual poverty is blessed, but one's honest and humble acknowledgment of his impoverishment (cf. Isa. 61:1) opens the way for the reception of God's blessings. It is precisely when man sees his own nothingness that God can give out of his own fulness. Some argue that *poor in spirit* refers to those who voluntarily accept material poverty or even sell their possessions and give to the poor (19:21), thus finding in Matthew the same emphasis upon outward poverty as in Luke. So understood, Matthew stresses the blessedness of freedom from the tyranny of outward things, living under the rule of heaven rather than the rule of earthly goods (cf. 6:19–34).

## Those Who Mourn (v. 4)

Not all mourning is blessed and much sorrow finds no comfort. This Beatitude echoes Isaiah 61:1; and from the context, reference may be to the grief that follows one's realization of his spiritual impoverishment. But the meaning cannot be confined to sorrow over sin. Probably the reference is to the comfort that is found now and in the final judgment by those who mourn now, whether over the hurts and the hardships of life or over their sins and those of the world.

## The Meek (v. 5)

This verse echoes Psalm 37:11. The meek are not the weak or cowardly. They are those who under the pressures of life have learned to bend their wills and to set aside their own notions as they stand before the greatness and grace of God. They are characterized by humble trust rather than arrogant independence. The earth does not belong to the self-trusting or self-assertive who seek to possess it but to "the poor in spirit" who are willing to lose all for the kingdom. This paradox belongs to the larger teaching which sees that one lives by dying, receives by giving, and is first precisely when willing to be last.

## Hunger and Thirst for Righteousness (v. 6)

This Beatitude did not arise among people whose problem was overweight. It speaks of a craving for righteousness comparable to such physical hunger and thirst as is known only in lands where people die for want of food or water. Blessed are they who yearn for the victory of right over wrong, in their own lives and in the world. These are assured that God's righteousness will prevail.

The verse is eschatological, looking to fulfilment in the future consummation of the kingdom; but righteousness is also a goal for the present (3:15; 5:10,20; 6:1,33; 21:32). Righteousness and kingdom belong together (6:33). Where God reigns, he reigns in righteousness. Both kingdom and righteousness await eschatological fulfilment, but both are also present realities.

## The Merciful (v. 7)

In mercy and forgiveness (6:12,14 f.; 18:21–35), receiving is bound up with giving. It is not that one earns mercy by being merciful, for then it would not be mercy but reward. It is not that one earns forgiveness by forgiving, for again that would be reward for merit. Neither is it that Jesus set up arbitrary requirements for receiving mercy or forgiveness. It is rather that in the nature of mercy and forgiveness there cannot be receiving without giving. The personal condition of the unmerciful or unforgiving is such that they are incapable of receiving. That in one which renders him incapable of being merciful or forgiving also renders him incapable of receiving mercy or forgiveness.

## The Pure in Heart (v. 8)

*Pure* translates *katharos,* the term for cleansing; and purity in heart contrasts with ritual cleansing of hands or body. By various groups within Judaism, a sharp distinction was made between what was ritually clean and what was unclean. Jesus brushed this aside in the interest of real purity, that of *heart* (cf. 15:1–20; 23:25). The heart stood for the whole inner self, mind as well as feeling. Purity of heart is simplicity or integrity as against duplicity. It is the concentration of the whole self upon God. The Beatitude seemingly draws upon Psalm 24:3 f., but also recalls Psalm 51:10. Although the emphasis here is upon inner purity or integrity as contrasted with outward, ritual cleansing, there is no indifference to the outward life of words and deeds. Purity of heart and wholeness go together, the outward life reflecting the inner purity.

## The Peacemakers (v. 9)

Jesus is the "Prince of Peace" (Isa. 9:6). He is our peace (Eph. 2:13 f.). Peacemaking is positive and active, not passive. Jesus plunged into the midst of human life to bring order out of chaos, reconciliation out of estrangement, love in the place of hate. Israel had been designated "son" of God (Hos. 11:1). Jesus taught that God's sons are those who are joined together with him in his work of peace-making. To *be called* is to be, for the name reflects the nature. Although peace includes the ending of war and strife, it is more. It is harmony with man through harmony with God.

### Persecuted for Righteousness' Sake (vv. 10–12)

Persecution or abuse as such is not a blessing, but here is blessing for Christians in their suffering for Christ (Phil. 1:29). The blessedness holds only when one suffers in the service of Christ and righteousness and when the charges of evil doing are false. One may be opposed because he is wrong, wicked, or simply a disturber. For those who, like the prophets, suffer for truth and right, there is *reward in heaven.* There is no assurance of vindication or reward among men now. The reward belongs with certainty to the future, but even now as seen in heaven, those who thus suffer are in a blessed condition. The assurance belongs to those who suffer for what must ultimately prevail.

## 3. Salt, Light, and a City Set on a Hill (5:13–16)

*Salt* was a major food preservative as well as a seasoning. Apart from Christ we are corrupt and corrupting, but in Christ we are to be a saving factor in a perishing world. Pure salt, as we know it today, cannot lose its saltiness; but the salt taken from the Dead Sea in Jesus' time was a mixture of salt and other matter. Exposed to weather, the salt could be lost, leaving only what had the appearance of salt. Commercial salt could be adulterated, the weakened mixture having little or no taste. A strong possibility is that Jesus intended to picture the absurdity of "saltless" salt, physically impossible. No less absurd than saltless salt is savorless Christianity that is not a saving force in the world. Nothing is more despised.

It is possible that salt stands for wisdom. This would agree with the clause which literally reads, "if the salt [wisdom] should become foolish."

Apart from Christ we are darkness; he is the true light (4:16). But Christ declared his people to be *the light of the world.* Jesus taught that his followers ought to shine and would shine. He did not say that *a city set on a hill* (mountain) should not but could not be hidden. He did not say that men should not but do not *light a lamp* and then *put it under a bushel.* One lights a lamp that he may place it *on a stand, and it gives light to all in the house.* Apart from Christ, we are unlighted lamps; but he lights his lamps that they may give light to all men.

It is significant that Jesus commands us to let good works be seen and also warns against proud or self-seeking display in almsgiving, prayer, and fasting (6:4,6,18). He offers no easy way. The Christian is commanded to live in open goodness and service before the world, but he is warned against so doing except to the glory of God.

## 4. Jesus and the Law (5:17–20)

Verses 17–18 could be a reply both to Pharisaic charges that Jesus was destroying *the law and the prophets* (the two oldest parts of the OT) and the antinomian claim that freedom in Christ meant the abolishment of the Law. To both is the warning that one is not to begin to think (so the force of the Greek) that Jesus came to destroy Law or Prophets. He came not to destroy but to fulfil. By fulfilment is meant not just the carrying out of predictions but the accomplishment of the intention of the Law and the Prophets. In contrast to the Pharisees, Jesus brought out the true and deeper meaning of the Law, and he actually lived up to its intention.

The antinomians were warned that *not an iota* (smallest letter of the Greek alphabet) nor *a dot* (probably a stroke forming a part of a Hebrew letter) would pass away, but that the whole Law would be fulfilled. Verse 18 is not to be so interpreted as to contradict Jesus' own refusal to be bound by a wooden, literal reading of Scripture. This verse may best be understood as his protest against the disposition to set aside the Law. Jesus made what appears to be an extreme statement. His own actions and teachings demonstrate that he always took Scripture seriously but not always literally. To literalize may be to trivialize. Jesus is not a neo-legalist, making the letter of the Law supreme. His own *I say to you* shows that he stood above the Law, not it above him. Significantly, his first "I say to you" appears in this verse.

## 5. The Intention of the Law (5:21–48)

These six antitheses seemingly set Jesus' *I say to you* over against the Law. Actually, it is Jesus' interpretation of the Law which is set over against that of the Pharisees. Jesus did not give a new law, but rather he uncovered the intention of the old and brought it to its fullest expression.

### (1) The Essence of Murder (5:21–26)

Jesus traced sin back to disposition, attitude, or intention. The overt act of murder has its roots in anger, hostility, or contempt for another. Jesus cited anger ("without cause" in some manuscripts is probably a scribal gloss), insulting one's brother (*raca* is a term of contempt, but its exact meaning is uncertain), and calling another *fool* (*mōre*, also a term of contempt, may refer to one as stubborn or insubordinate) as being crimes for which one is brought before the *court* (local court of 23 persons), the Sanhedrin (highest ruling body of the Jews), or for which he is liable to Gehenna. No court seeks to convict a person on the grounds of feeling or attitude, but feelings of anger or contempt are as dangerous as are the outward crimes for which one is brought into the courts or considered liable to hell.

Jesus' words are not to be turned into a new legalism. They are to be understood as radical protests and warnings against wrong feeling toward another. This is not to say that it is just as bad to murder as to have ill feeling or ill will toward another. The victim would prefer being hated to being murdered, and it is better to bring hatred under control before it issues in murder than to let it run its course.

That Jesus had his own community in mind is reflected in the recurrence of *his brother,* a term reserved in Matthew for a Christian brother. Anger and contempt are not only self-destructive but destroy the fellowship of the church.

Verse 23 envisions not a synagogue but the Temple. It is better to interrupt or leave the Temple service in order to seek reconciliation than to try to worship God while estranged from one's brother. Jesus never permits one to isolate his relationship with God from that with his fellowman. One cannot compel his brother to join him in reconciliation before God's altar, but one has no access to God unless he seeks to come before God with his brother.

Verses 25–26 urge that reconciliation be sought outside the courts, with the warning that if one chooses otherwise, he can then only let the courts run their course. Christians are urged to work out their difficulties in direct relationship with one another (18:15–20; 1 Cor. 6:1–11).

### (2) Lust and Adultery (5:27–30)

Jesus saw adultery as sin against any woman, as something destructive to the offender, to the offended, and to marriage, and as first of all a matter of attitude or intention. Adultery may occur apart from the overt act. Jesus did not say that to look with lust is as evil as to commit the overt act, for the overt act continues the sin already in one's heart and extends the damage to other people. It is more destructive to all concerned to yield overtly to lust than to bring it under some measure of control. The point made is that it is not enough simply to refrain from the overt act. Freedom from lust is the divine demand.

The New Testament does not equate temptation with sin. Jesus was tempted but did not sin. The teaching is that sin begins at the point of consent, not with the temptation itself and not first in the overt act.

Obviously, lust cannot be controlled merely by plucking out the *right eye* or cutting off the *right hand.* Lust could be implemented through the remaining eye or hand or with no physical eyes or hands at all. Jesus is saying that not only is sexual lust a form of adultery but that the threat of lust is so strong and its dangers so great that a price comparable to the removal of eye or hand is not too great to pay as one seeks freedom from it. Implied, too, is that radical discipline is required for the life free of this evil.

"Gehenna" derives from Hinnom, a valley west of Jerusalem, scene of sacrifice to Molech and later the place where refuse from Jerusalem was burned. The term came to symbolize the place of judgment for the wicked. The description presupposes bodily existence after death.

## (3) The Damage in Divorce (5:31–32)

Discussion of this passage usually centers around the clause *except on the ground of unchastity* and ignores the real problem of the husband who first divorces his wife. Since the "except clause" is not in Mark 10:11–12 or Luke 16:18, it is widely held that Matthew has added the exception to make the teaching more workable in the church of his day. But the removal of this clause does not solve the problem of the passage. The real question is why, as commonly understood, the judgment falls on the divorced woman (who may be an innocent wife without the "except clause" and necessarily so with it) and the second husband, in the event of her remarriage. To say that the passage teaches that divorce is equated with adultery would make superfluous any reference to remarriage.

Freest from difficulty is the interpretation which retains the "except clause," fixes attention on the first husband as the person under judgment, and observes the passive voice of verbs employed. So understood, Jesus says that for a husband to divorce an innocent wife is to victimize her and her second husband should she remarry. It is to treat an innocent woman the way an adulteress is treated and to force a stigma upon her and her subsequent marriage.

What Jesus said may best be understood against the background of a man-centered world in which a husband could boast that in giving a rejected wife a bill of divorce he protected her rights. Jesus demolished these claims, showing that an innocent woman's rights are protected only if she is respected as a wife. A divorce certificate does not secure her against damage. The "except clause" recognizes that the guilty wife is responsible for her own ruin.

## (4) Teaching about Oaths (5:33–37)

This paragraph is a call for the simple honesty which makes oaths unnecessary and excludes casuistry (manipulation of an oath or of Scripture in such way as to mislead others and cover up one's own lack of integrity). The scribes found many ways to get around an oath while pretending to keep it. They made an oath binding or not, depending upon its wording. To swear by the gold on the altar was considered binding, but to swear by the altar itself was said not to be binding. Their idea was that an oath is binding if God is involved. The wording of the oath would involve God or not. But this overlooks the fact that the whole world is God's, and he is already concerned. We do not import him into our affairs. Jesus protests not so much against oaths as against the dishonesty which would hide behind legal fictions. Of course, he taught that for the honest person, one's word itself requires no oath, for his yes means yes and his no means no. This passage is not concerned with profanity or with civil oaths today but with perjury and casuistry, the dishonesty which tries to hide behind clever wording of an oath.

## (5) Overcoming Evil with Good (5:38–42)

The law of *an eye for an eye and a tooth for a tooth* was introduced to restrain from greater evil. Just as a divorce certificate was required to give some measure of protection to the wife who otherwise would be defenseless, so the *eye for an eye* law first intended to restrict unlimited retaliation (cf. Ex. 21:23–25; Lev. 24:19–21; Deut. 19:21). But Jesus penetrated behind this law of controlled or equal retaliation and repudiated the whole idea of revenge.

"Not to resist with evil" may be a better translation than *do not resist one who is evil.* Jesus resisted evil, and that is the Christian's business. One is not to resist with evil but overcome evil with good (cf. Rom. 12:21). Few Christians today ever suffer a physical blow on the cheek, but the principle of "turning the other cheek" may be applied daily in terms of self-exposure to the insults, misunderstandings, resentments, or other harm as one tries to relate redemptively or constructively to others.

In Jewish law one could sue for another's coat, long undergarment with sleeves; but he could not sue for the *cloak,* an outer garment serving the poor as a cover by night (Ex. 22:26 f.). Roman soldiers and officers were permitted to force natives to carry their supplies or baggage for one mile (cf. 27:32, where Simon of Cyrene is compelled to carry the cross). Jesus admonished his followers to go beyond what could be taken or required by law, giving freely to undeserving people, and not to turn away from those who would beg or borrow.

One may protest that many do not deserve such generous treatment. But merit is not the basis for decision. If some do not "deserve" to be helped, neither do we deserve to be in position to help. The Christian's question is never, "Does the other deserve my help?" but "How can I help?" Love sometimes must withhold, but Christian response is to be controlled by the needs of the other, not his merit or one's own "rights." Although an enlightened conscience, must decide how to serve the other, love has already decided that one must serve.

### (6) Love for Enemies (5:43–48)

Christians are seen to be *sons of [their] Father who is in heaven* when they embody his love. God's love does not discriminate but pours itself out upon friends and enemies alike. It is not motivated by our merit. It is governed by its own character, which is ever self-denying and self-giving. God's love seeks to relate to friend or foe for his good without counting the cost. The Greek word *agapē* does not of itself mean a certain kind of love. The *tax collectors* can also love. What is meant by *love* is not to be derived from a Greek word but from what we see of God revealed in Jesus Christ.

The love commended is that which became incarnate in Jesus.

Some of God's gifts, like his sun and rain, can be given regardless of the character or attitude of the recipients. Higher gifts like forgiveness and newness of life can only be offered; in their nature they cannot be imposed. But God does not give as a bargainer, hoping to receive. Giving which is calculated to gain return is not God's love but rather is pagan.

God demands perfection, even though he accepts persons on the ground of mercy, not merit. Within the gift of salvation is absolute demand. Man rebels against this, preferring either the legalism in which he feels that he has earned his salvation or the libertinism in which he assumes that grace is all gift and no demand. Jesus calls us to the narrow way which escapes both legalism and antinomianism. Salvation is gift that is never earned, and the Christian is yet a sinner who needs daily forgiveness. One is never farther from goodness than when he thinks that he is good. On the other hand, following Jesus begins with conversion to the kingdom (rule) of God, submission to a claim that is ultimate and absolute. The demand for perfection is never met, but it is there to be met.

## 6. Motive in Religious Life (6:1–18)

The primacy of motive in religious life is illustrated in the areas of almsgiving, prayer, and fasting. Jesus esteemed all three and assumed that his followers would practice them. His point was that the motive behind religious expression gives it its meaning. Religion as performance designed to impress God, other people, or self is false and futile.

The proposition developed in the three illustrations is set forth in verse 1. *Practicing your piety* is to think of righteousness as outward performance. The fallacy stems from failure to recognize that moral, ethical, or spiritual value is not inherent in things done or said. Outward doing and saying can come from pagan motive as well as Christian. No deed or word is of itself good or bad; it takes on moral quality from motive, intention, context, and other factors. A shove, for example, may be of itself neither good nor bad. It may be a brutish act of self-assertion or a heroic act, as when one at the risk of his own life shoves another from the path of an oncoming car. A kiss may express love and trust, or cowardly betrayal as when Judas kissed Jesus. Almsgiving, prayer, and fasting may be significant expressions of authentic religion. They may also be performances calculated to gain selfish advantage.

### (1) Almsgiving (6:1–4)

*Alms* translates the Greek *eleēmosunēn,* a term for acts of mercy more inclusive than almsgiving. Here the special reference is to charitable gifts. Whether or not Jesus meant that some literally blew a trumpet to call attention to their acts of charity, the ulterior motive is exposed through this picture. Trumpets were blown during fasts in times of drought. "Hypocrite" translates a word used in drama for an actor, one playing a part. God is not impressed by religious acts designed to impress him. If one performs religiously to win men's praise he may succeed, but this praise is the most for which he can hope. *They have their reward* (vv. 2,5,16) employs a commercial term for giving a receipt (*apechein*). Almsgiving, prayer, or fasting as a performance can attract attention; but when one is so recognized, he may as well turn in his receipt, for he has gotten all he will get from his performance.

The command, *do not let your left hand know what your right hand is doing,* is not to be interpreted apart from other teachings of Jesus, e.g., that one's light is to shine and his good works to be seen of men to the glory of God (5:16). Each verse is balanced by the other. To try to reduce these teachings to a rigid system is to miss their intention. From the presence of such verses as 5:16 and 6:3, side by side in the same sermon, emerges the important principle that Scripture is to be interpreted by Scripture. The whole truth can never be captured in a single statement. In 5:16 the teaching is that one is to share with others what he has received from God, doing it to man's good and God's glory. In 6:3 is the warning that self-seeking vitiates religious acts. The lamp is to give forth its light (5:16), but it is not to display itself (v. 3).

*Reward* is promised for almsgiving, prayer, and fasting done *in secret* (vv. 4,6,18). The secrecy commanded is not to be absolutized. Jesus publicly did acts of mercy, prayed, and fasted. The warning is to be interpreted in context. Secrecy is prescribed for one whose temptation Is to perform for others. Religious expression can be open and honest. To "do good" in secret can be an obsession as hypocritical and selfish as openly to parade one's religion. The promise of reward is itself both a blessing and a peril. Genuine service carries its reward, but the reward is proportionate to one's freedom from the seeking of reward. Those receiving the highest rewards in the judgment will be unaware that they had engaged in meritorious service (cf. 25:37 f.). The word "openly" after *your Father who sees in secret will reward you* (vv. 4,6,18) probably is spurious, although found in some early manuscripts.

### (2) Prayer (6:5–15)

The strophe 6:5–6 develops with respect to prayer the same ideas brought out with respect to almsgiving: the bad example of the *hypocrites,* the temptation to display one's piety in the synagogues or on the streets, the desire to be seen of men, the warning that such motivation gains nothing more than men's praise for which a "receipt in full" may as well be given, and the admonition to pray in secret with the assurance of reward from the Father.

**The Model Prayer (vv. 9–13).** The Model Prayer in Matthew is paralleled by Luke 11:2–4. The Lukan form is shorter and on the whole more primitive, although Matthew may preserve some older forms in the petitions for bread and forgiveness. The simple address "Father" in Luke represents a most significant practice and teaching of Jesus. Judaism already knew God as Father, but the direct, childlike address (*Abba* in Aramaic) represents something new in the practice and teaching of Jesus. *Abba* (cf. Rom. 8:15 f.; Gal. 4:6) was a child's way of addressing his father, not the more formal "the father" or "our father," but the intimate and simple word "Father." Jesus knew God as Father and came to enable us so to know him. Matthew's *our Father* is adapted to congregational usage and stresses the fact that we cannot exclude others as we come before God (5:23 f.).

Matthew's *who art in heaven* preserves the balance between recognizing the nearness and transcendence of God. With the family-like intimacy, God may be addressed as Father, but he remains the transcendent God, always to be approached in awe and reverence. The paradox of nearness and transcendence is never lost in biblical revelation.

### (3) Fasting (6:16–18)

Jesus sometimes fasted and expected his followers to do so. What he rejected was fasting for display. The Mosaic Law did not explicitly require fasting, but Leviticus 16:31 was understood to require it for the Day of Atonement. The Pharisees fasted twice a week (Luke 18:12) and made it a test of piety. Jesus refused to be governed by a calendar. He fasted as a normal thing in times of crisis (cf. 4:2), finding it meaningful when spontaneous in situations of sorrow or crisis (cf. 9:14–17). Abstinence may be a private means of freeing oneself of certain preoccupations (e.g., food, sleep, play, or work) in favor of concentration upon something which for the time at least represents a higher claim (cf. 1 Cor. 7:5). Anointing was a symbol of joy, forbidden on the Day of Atonement or other times of fasting or sorrow; but Jesus proposed that one *anoint* his head when he fasted, thus to avoid any display of "humility."

## 7. Freedom from Tyranny of Things (6:19–34)

This section seems to be governed by the theme of freedom from the tyranny of material things. The alternative is the kingdom of God (v. 33). One's choice is between finding his ultimate values in the treasures which perish or those which endure (vv. 19–22), between the stinginess which leaves one in darkness or the generosity which gives one light (vv. 22–23), between the worship of mammon or God (vv. 25–34).

### Treasures in Heaven (vv. 19–21)

The warning is twofold: (1) treasures on earth are perishable and (2) one shares the fate of that to which he gives his heart. There is no ultimate security in material things. *Moth, rust,* and *thieves* illustrate some of the threats to such "security." The warning against trust in the material is not given to the rich alone. The house "where thieves dig through" may be the poor man's house of mud brick.

The word rendered rust (*brōsis*) probably should be translated "eating," with a possible reference to the devouring of stored clothing or food by mice or other vermin.

One does not understand the teaching of Jesus unless he sees that he was both deeply concerned that people have the material necessities of life and that they be free from the tyranny of things. Jesus was not ascetic and required no withdrawal from corporal living. He healed the sick, fed the hungry, and made our attention to the material needs of other people the test of our relationship to him (25:31–46). At the same time, he warned against making material values the object of our trust or affection. Jesus gave bread to the hungry but warned that man cannot live by bread alone. One's *heart* is where his *treasure* is, and he shares the fate or destiny of that to which he gives himself—whether to the perishable or imperishable.

### The Lamp of the Body (v. 22–23)

This parable is built upon the analogy to the *sound eye* that can bring objects clearly into focus and the bad eye that cannot. The eye serves as a *lamp* for the body, giving it light or leaving it in darkness. Applied to the problem of material possessions, the lesson may be that if one divides his attention between God and the material, he may have neither in proper focus. The parable teaches that the generous person (sound eye) walks in light but the stingy person (unsound eye) walks in darkness.

Another approach is to see the sound eye as representing openness or receptivity to God, the unsound eye representing the distrust which shuts one out of God's world of light. So understood, this parable agrees with that of the sower (see 13:1–9,18–23) in teaching that one with no openness to God is blind.

### God and Mammon (v. 24)

This parable can be understood only against the background of slavery, where a master held legal title to a slave and had complete authority over him and where experiments in dual ownership of a slave ran into the difficulty that a slave could not give himself totally to two owners. One cannot belong to God and mammon at the same time. *Mammon* is of uncertain derivation. It may designate something hidden or stored up or something trusted. Here it represents money or material possessions. Jesus warned in the parable of the rich farmer (Luke 12:13–21) that one may be owned by what he thinks he owns. So here, Jesus warns against the tyranny of things. The only escape from the rule of things is submission to the rule of God (v. 33).

*Hate* and *love* are best understood here as "reject" and "accept." The lesson is that God must have exclusive claim upon us. It is significant that Jesus makes money, not Satan, the rival to God's claim upon us. Jesus was concerned about what we do with money (cf. 25:31–46), but his first concern was for what it does to us. It can blind (unsound eye), enslave (mammon), and thus destroy us. Money is not evil, for it can be made to serve God and man; but the love of money is the root of all kinds of evil (1 Tim. 6:10).

### Distraction over Things (vv. 25–34)

*Do not be anxious* is a better translation for *me merimnate* than "take no thought" (KJV), but "be not distracted" may be yet nearer its intention. Jesus did not prescribe indifference to material things nor encourage idleness (cf. 2 Tim. 3:1–12). Idleness is for neither the Christian nor the birds. Birds exemplify not idleness but freedom from anxiety. Far from being idle, Jesus' brief life was full and active. In John 4:6 he is pictured as being so wearied from a journey that he sat exhausted on the curb of a well at Sychar. Sometimes his concern was such that he went without sleep or food. His warning is against distraction or anxiety over things, not concern or effort with respect to legitimate problems and needs. The Greek word *merimnate* is built on a word for "a part," and it could be translated, "Don't go to pieces," or "Don't be distracted."

Anxiety over things like food and clothing is unnecessary, unprofitable, and evil. If God cares for the *birds of the air*, he can be trusted to care for us. If he gives life, he can sustain it. Anxiety is unprofitable, for thereby one does not *add one cubit to his span of life*. Although cubit is a linear measure (about eighteen inches), the term may refer to length of life. Anxiety is more likely to shorten life than lengthen it. The heaviest charge against anxiety over food and clothing is not that it is unnecessary and unprofitable but that it is evil. It reflects lack of faith in God: *O men of little faith!* Striving for material things is "pagan," a better translation than Gentiles.

## 8. Judging Others (7:1–6)

Judgment is the dominant theme throughout chapter 7, although cohesiveness is less apparent than in chapter 5 or 6. Logical bonds are not always apparent as transition is made from one subject to another.

### The Speck and the Log (vv. 1–5)

Forming judgments is an inescapable function of the mind, but expressing them is subject to control. One does not escape being judged by assuming the role of judge, but on the contrary makes certain the fact of his own judgment and determines its measure. Foremost in this teaching is the warning that when we presume to judge others, we bring upon ourselves the judgment of God. Further, when we engage in merciless judgment we deny to ourselves God's mercy. God is not arbitrary in this (cf. 5:7; 6:12,14 f.), but when we deny mercy to others, we deny it to ourselves.

Either we take our stand on the mercy of God or we do not. We cannot have it both ways, mercy for ourselves but not for others. It is also true that one is judged in the very act of judging. In each judgment one reveals his own standards and values.

The hypocrisy of condemning in others what we tolerate in ourselves is set forth in the analogy of *the speck* and *the log*. Jesus deliberately drew the ludicrous picture of a man with a log in his eye trying to remove a speck from another's eye! Much of our judging of others is that absurd. If one is sincere, he will first bring himself under judgment, removing the log from his own eye.

Jesus is not saying that we are to ignore *the speck* in our brother's eye. It is our business to try to free a brother from the speck which impairs his vision. But one is in position for this ministry only after *the log* is out of his *own eye*. It is not a matter of speck or log. Both must be removed, but the log first. Only after one has known the shame or agony of coming under judgment and of having the log removed from his own eye will he understand the need and the feeling of the brother. Only then can he *see clearly to take the speck* from his *brother's eye*.

Even so, God alone has the knowledge and integrity to render final judgment; and, happily, final judgment belongs to him and not us (1 Cor. 4:3–5). Although minds are so made that they cannot escape the function of judging, we can at least remember that we have not been appointed to the bench as judge; and we can remember our fallibility, marred by our own sins, never having all the truth about that which we judge, and always subject to bias or prejudice.

### Pearls before Swine (v. 6)

Dogs and swine were despised by the Jews, both considered unclean. Jesus is not alluding to Gentiles but to any person who is unable or unwilling to distinguish between *what is holy* and what is not, or between *pearls* and what is valueless. This saying sounds harsh, but it must be heard. Jesus did not arbitrarily exclude anyone, but he recognized that there were times when there was no

opening for the gospel or for his ministry (cf. 26:63).

Although it is the Christian's business to share *what is holy* or his *pearls* with any who will receive, there are times when he can only remain silent or try to bring about a better climate for a later sharing. What is holy and pearls may here refer to one's discernments, judgments, or message. Three dangers threaten the Christian witness or minister who does not discern when to speak and when to keep silence: he may further damage the one he tries to help; he may try to force himself or his values upon another; and he may unnecessarily imperil himself and others.

## 9. Ask, Seek, Knock (7:7–12)

What may the Christian do in the face of the responsibility of removing the speck from his brother's eye and of sharing what is holy and his pearls, knowing his personal inadequacy for either ministry? He must look to higher wisdom and resources than his own. He must *ask, seek, and knock.* Surely, this admonition goes beyond the needs arising out of this ministry of judging and sharing, but this is included.

By *ask, seek,* and *knock* is meant primarily an openness to God for his instruction, guidance, or gifts. It does not follow that one may get what he wants simply by praying for it. Jesus prayed thrice for the possible removal of the cup awaiting him (26:39–44). He did not demand its removal and it was not removed. He did receive the strength to drink it. One may not receive what he requests, he may not find what he seeks, and the door upon which he knocks may not be the one opened; but the assurance is that where there is asking there will be receiving, where there is seeking there will be finding, and where there is knocking God will open a door.

### The Golden Rule (v. 12)

In a negative form, this proverb was widely known among Jews (Tobit 4:15; Philo; Hillel) and

Gentiles. Jesus gave it positive form, and termed it the essence of the Law and the Prophets. The Golden Rule presupposes discipleship, submission to the rule of God. It is not a sufficient rule for everyone. In a pagan life the "rule" would be experienced in terms of pagan values, for pagan wishes come from a pagan heart. The intention of the Golden Rule, presupposing discipleship, is that one is to be as concerned for the other person's good as for his own (cf. 22:39 f.).

## 10. Perils to Righteousness and Life (7:13–27)

It is difficult to trace the movement of thought or find the principle of cohesion for this large block of material. The danger of a neat outline is that it forces upon the material a system foreign to it. Some continuity may be seen in the warning against the easy way (vv. 13–14), the false prophets (vv. 15–20), profession without obedience (vv. 21–23), and building on the wrong foundation (vv. 24–27). There is also the positive side, stressing the way that leads to life, the good tree that produces good fruit, and the rock foundation which will not give way; but the strong warnings in verses 13,15,21,26 are so important that they cannot be over-emphasized. Matthew seems to have the antinomian threat in mind as he brings together these teachings of Jesus.

### (1) The Two Ways (7:13–14)

The Father who is in heaven gives good gifts to men who at best are yet evil (v. 11), and he offers the kingdom to the poor in spirit, the meek, and the merciful; but within the gift of salvation is also demand. Matthew knows no salvation through human merit, but neither a salvation which releases man from God's demands. *The way* which *leads to life* is entered through a *narrow gate,* and *the way* itself *is hard,* i.e., afflicted, anguished, or torturous. It is a way of decision, commitment, and obedience to God. In a wicked world it is a lonely road, traveled with a few companions.

Although there is no explicit reference to either legalism or antinomianism, it may not be farfetched to think of the narrow, torturous way as running between the two, avoiding both. Religion easily becomes a rigid, legalistic system, stressing attainable goals or rules, whether ritual, doctrinal, ascetic, or whatever. It just as easily becomes a loose way of license in the name of liberty or grace, morally and ethically irresponsible. Jesus calls us to the narrow, hard way that is neither legalistic nor libertine.

### (2) A Tree Known by Its Fruit (7:15–20)

The *false prophets* who come in *sheep's clothing* but who *inwardly are ravenous wolves* are not Pharisees or Sadducees, for neither claimed to prophesy. These are persons within the Christian community who pose as prophets but who are false. In the next paragraph (v. 23), closely related to this one, may be found a clue in the employment of the word lawlessness (evil-doers in RSV). These may be the antinomians who stress grace, the Spirit, and prophecy, but who prove to be false. Posing as sheep, they prove to be ravenous wolves who divide and destroy.

*Fruit* is a major term in the New Testament, never equated with outward works (see 3:8; John 15:1–10; Gal. 5:22). In verses 17 f., *bad tree* is a better translation than "corrupt tree" (KJV). *Sapron* does not designate a rotten tree, but the wrong kind. This word is used in the parable of the net (13:48). The bad fish are not diseased but the wrong kind, inedible. False prophets produce bad fruit, the wrong kind. What the fruit is, is not specified here; but in Galations 5:22 "the fruit of the Spirit is love, joy, peace, patience, kindness, goodness, faithfulness [or fidelity], gentleness, self-control."

### (3) Saying without Doing (7:21–23)

It may seem that this paragraph offers a simple choice between saying and doing, but that is not the case. Those rejected in the judgment were both sayers and doers! They said, "Lord! Lord!" and they did many religious works: prophesy, casting out demons, and mighty works. The doing required is the doing of *the will* of God and not merely religious deeds, however impressive.

### (4) Hearing and Doing (7:24–27)

Both Matthean and Lukan sermons conclude with the parable of the two foundations. The parable and its embodiment in some form of the sermon are earlier than both Gospels. For the Gospel of Matthew it represents a major concern, stressing the obedience indispensable to discipleship. It also reflects Jesus' sense of having the right to make ultimate claims upon men and his position that their destiny is bound up with their obedience to him.

# 13   Religion, Morality and Conscience

## JOHN ARTHUR

My first and prime concern in this paper is to explore the connections, if any, between morality and religion. I will argue that in fact religion is not necessary for morality. Yet despite the lack of any logical or other necessary connection, I will claim, there remain important respects in which the two are related. In the concluding section I will discuss the notion of moral conscience, and then look briefly at the various respects in which morality is "social" and the implications of that idea for moral education. First, however, I want to say something about the subjects: just what are we referring to when we speak of morality and of religion?

## 1. Morality and Religion

A useful way to approach the first question—the nature of morality—is to ask what it would mean for a society to exist without a social moral code. How would such people think and behave? What would that society look like? First, it seems clear that such people would never feel guilt or resent-ment. For example, the notions that I ought to remember my parent's anniversary, that he has a moral responsibility to help care for his children after the divorce, that she has a right to equal pay for equal work, and that discrimination on the basis of race is unfair would be absent in such a society. Notions of duty, rights, and obligations would not be present, except perhaps in the legal sense; concepts of justice and fairness would also be foreign to these people. In short, people would have no tendency to evaluate or criticize the behavior of others, nor to feel remorse about their own behavior. Children would not be taught to be ashamed when they steal or hurt others, nor would they be allowed to complain when others treat them badly. (People might, however, feel regret at a decision that didn't turn out as they had hoped; but that would only be because their expectations were frustrated, not because they feel guilty.)

Such a society lacks a moral code. What, then, of religion? Is it possible that people lacking a morality would nonetheless have religious beliefs? It seems clear that it is possible. Suppose every day these same people file into their place of worship to pay homage to God (they may believe in many gods or in one all-powerful creator of heaven and earth). Often they can be heard pray-ing to God for help in dealing with their problems

Copyright © 1995 by John Arthur. Reprinted by permission. This is a somewhat revised version of a paper which originally appeared in *Contemporary Readings in Social and Political Ethics* ed. Brodsky, Troyer, and Vance (Prometheus, 1984).

and thanking Him for their good fortune. Frequently they give sacrifices to God, sometimes in the form of money spent to build beautiful temples and churches, other times by performing actions they believe God would approve such as helping those in need. These practices might also be institutionalized, in the sense that certain people are assigned important leadership roles. Specific texts might also be taken as authoritative, indicating the ways God has acted in history and His role in their lives or the lives of their ancestors.

To have a moral code, then, is to tend to evaluate (perhaps without even expressing it) the behavior of others and to feel guilt at certain actions when we perform them. Religion, on the other hand, involves beliefs in supernatural power(s) that created and perhaps also control nature, the tendency to worship and pray to those supernatural forces or beings, and the presence of organizational structures and authoritative texts. The practices of morality and religion are thus importantly different. One involves our attitudes toward various forms of behavior (lying and killing, for example), typically expressed using the notions of rules, rights, and obligations. The other, religion, typically involves prayer, worship, beliefs about the supernatural, institutional forms and authoritative texts.

We come, then, to the central question: What is the connection, if any, between a society's moral code and its religious practices and beliefs? Many people have felt that morality is in some way dependent on religion or religious truths. But what sort of "dependence" might there be? In what follows I distinguish various ways in which one might claim that religion is necessary for morality, arguing against those who claim morality depends in some way on religion. I will also suggest, however, some other important ways in which the two are related, concluding with a brief discussion of conscience and moral education.

## 2. Religious Motivation and Guidance

One possible role which religion might play in morality relates to motives people have. Religion,

it is often said, is necessary so that people will *do* right. Typically, the argument begins with the important point that doing what is right often has costs: refusing to shoplift or cheat can mean people go without some good or fail a test; returning a billfold means they don't get the contents. Religion is therefore said to be necessary in that it provides motivation to do the right thing. God rewards those who follow His commands by providing for them a place in heaven or by insuring that they prosper and are happy on earth. He also punishes those who violate the moral law. Others emphasize less self-interested ways in which religious motives may encourage people to act rightly. Since God is the creator of the universe and has ordained that His plan should be followed, they point out, it is important to live one's life in accord with this divinely ordained plan. Only by living a moral life, it is said, can people live in harmony with the larger, divinely created order.

The first claim, then, is that religion is necessary to provide moral motivation. The problem with that argument, however, is that religious motives are far from the only ones people have. For most of us, a decision to do the right thing (if that is our decision) is made for a variety of reasons: "What if I get caught? What if somebody sees me—what will he or she think? How will I feel afterwards? Will I regret it?" Or maybe the thought of cheating just doesn't arise. We were raised to be a decent person, and that's what we are—period. Behaving fairly and treating others well [are] more important than whatever we might gain from stealing or cheating, let alone seriously harming another person. So it seems clear that many motives for doing the right thing have nothing whatsoever to do with religion. Most of us, in fact, do worry about getting caught, being blamed, and being looked down on by others. We also may do what is right just because it's right, or because we don't want to hurt others or embarrass family and friends. To say that we need religion to act morally is mistaken; indeed it seems to me that many of us, when it really gets down to it, don't give much of a thought to religion when making moral decisions. All those other reasons are the ones which we tend to consider, or else we just don't consider cheating and stealing at all. So far, then, there seems to be no reason to suppose that people can't be moral yet irreligious at the same time.

A second argument that is available for those who think religion is necessary to morality, however, focuses on moral guidance and knowledge rather than on people's motives. However much people may want to do the right thing, according to this view, we cannot ever know for certain what is right without the guidance of religious teaching. Human understanding is simply inadequate to this difficult and controversial task; morality involves immensely complex problems, and so we must consult religious revelation for help.

Again, however, this argument fails. First, consider how much we would need to know about religion and revelation in order for religion to provide moral guidance. Besides being sure that there is a God, we'd also have to think about which of the many religions is true. How can anybody be sure his or her religion is the right one? But even if we assume the Judeo-Christian God is the real one, we still need to find out just what it is He wants us to do, which means we must think about revelation.

Revelation comes in at least two forms, and not even all Christians agree on which is the best way to understand revelation. Some hold that revelation occurs when God tells us what he wants by providing us with His words: The Ten Commandments are an example. Many even believe, as evangelist Billy Graham once said, that the entire *Bible* was written by God using 39 secretaries. Others, however, doubt that the "word of God" refers literally to the words God has spoken, but believe instead that the *Bible* is an historical document, written by human beings, of the events or occasions in which God revealed Himself. It is an especially important document, of course, but nothing more than that. So on this second view revelation is not understood as *statements* made by God but rather as His *acts* such as leading His people from Egypt, testing Job, and sending His son as an example of the ideal life. The *Bible* is not itself revelation, it's the historical account of revelatory actions.

If we are to use revelation as a moral guide, then, we must first know what is to count as reve-lation—words, given us by God, historical events, or both? But even supposing that we could somehow answer those questions, the problems of relying on revelation are still not over since we still must interpret that revelation. Some feel, for example, that the *Bible* justifies various forms of killing, including war and capital punishment, on the basis of such statements as "An eye for an eye." Others, emphasizing such saying as "Judge not lest ye be judged" and "Thou shalt not kill," believe the *Bible* demands absolute pacifism. How are we to know which interpretation is correct? It is likely, of course, that the answer people give to such religious questions will be influenced in part at least by their own moral beliefs: if capital punishment is thought to be unjust, for example, then an interpreter will seek to read the *Bible* in a way that is consistent with that moral truth. That is not, however, a happy conclusion for those wishing to rest morality on revelation, for it means that their understanding of what God has revealed is itself dependent on their prior moral views. Rather than revelation serving as a guide for morality, morality is serving as a guide for how we interpret revelation.

So my general conclusion is that far from providing a short-cut to moral understanding, looking to revelation for guidance often creates more questions and problems. It seems wiser under the circumstances to address complex moral problems like abortion, capital punishment, and affirmative action directly, considering the pros and cons of each side, rather than to seek answers through the much more controversial and difficult route of revelation.

## 3. The Divine Command Theory

It may seem, however, that we have still not really gotten to the heart of the matter. Even if religion is not necessary for moral motivation or guidance, it is often claimed, religion is necessary in another more fundamental sense. According to this view, religion is necessary for morality because without God there could *be* no right or wrong. God, in other words, provides the foundation or bedrock on which morality is grounded. This idea was expressed by Bishop R. C. Mortimer:

"God made us and all the world. Because of that He has an absolute claim on our obedience. . . . From [this] it follows that a thing is not right simply because we think it is. It is right because God commands it."[1]

What Bishop Mortimer has in mind can be seen by comparing moral rules with legal ones. Legal statutes, we know, are created by legislatures; if the state assembly of New York had not passed a law limiting speed people can travel, then there would be no such legal obligation. Without the statutory enactments, such a law simply would not exist. Mortimer's view, the *divine command theory,* would mean that God has the same sort of relation to moral law as legislature has to statutes it enacts: without God's commands there would be no moral rules, just as without a legislature there would be no statutes.

Defenders of the divine command theory often add to this a further claim, that only by assuming God sits at the foundation of morality can we explain the objective difference between right and wrong. This point was forcefully argued by F. C. Copleston in a 1948 British Broadcasting Corporation radio debate with Bertrand Russell.

**Copleston:** . . . The validity of such an interpretation of man's conduct depends on the recognition of God's existence, obviously. . . . Let's take a look at the Commandant of the [Nazi] concentration camp at Belsen. That appears to you as undesirable and evil and to me too. To Adolph Hitler we suppose it appeared as something good and desirable. I suppose you'd have to admit that for Hitler it was good and for you it is evil.

**Russell:** No, I shouldn't go so far as that. I mean, I think people can make mistakes in that as they can in other things. If you have jaundice you see things yellow that are not yellow. You're making a mistake.

**Copleston:** Yes, one can make mistakes, but can you make a mistake if it's simply a question of reference to a feeling or emotion? Surely Hitler would be the only possible judge of what appealed to his emotions.

**Russell:** . . . You can say various things about that; among others, that if that sort of thing makes that sort of appeal to Hitler's emotions, then Hitler makes quite a different appeal to my emotions.

**Copleston:** Granted. But there's no objective criterion outside feeling then for condemning the conduct of the Commandant of Belsen, in your view. . . . The

human being's idea of the content of the moral law depends certainly to a large extent on education and environment, and a man has to use his reason in assessing the validity of the actual moral ideas of his social group. But the possibility of criticizing the accepted moral code presupposes that there is an objective standard, that there is an ideal moral order, which imposes itself. . . . It implies the existence of a real foundation of God.[2]

Against those who, like Bertrand Russell, seek to ground morality in feelings and attitudes, Copleston argues that there must be a more solid foundation if we are to be able to claim truly that the Nazis were evil. God, according to Copleston, is able to provide the objective basis for the distinction, which we all know to exist, between right and wrong. Without divine commands at the root of human obligations, we would have no real reason for condemning the behavior of anybody, even Nazis. Morality, Copleston thinks, would then be nothing more than an expression of personal feeling.

To begin assessing the divine command theory, let's first consider this last point. Is it really true that only the commands of God can provide an objective basis for moral judgments? Certainly many philosophers have felt that morality rests on its own perfectly sound footing, be it reason, human nature, or natural sentiments. It seems wrong to conclude, automatically, that morality cannot rest on anything but religion. And it is also possible that morality doesn't have any foundation or basis at all, so that its claims should be ignored in favor of whatever serves our own self-interest.

In addition to these problems with Copleston's argument, the divine command theory faces other problems as well. First, we would need to say much more about the relationship between morality and divine commands. Certainly the expressions "is commanded by God" and "is morally required" do not *mean* the same thing. People and even whole societies can use moral concepts without understanding them to make any reference to God. And while it is true that God (or any other moral being for that matter) would tend to want others to do the right thing, this hardly shows that being right and being commanded by God are the same thing. Parents want their children to do the right thing, too, but that doesn't mean parents, or anybody else, can make a thing right just by commanding it!

I think that, in fact, theists should reject the divine command theory. One reason is what it implies. Suppose we were to grant (just for the sake of argument) that the divine command theory is correct, so that actions are right just because they are commanded by God. The same, of course, can be said about those deeds that we believe are wrong. If God hadn't commanded us not to do them, they would not be wrong.

But now notice this consequence of the divine command theory. Since God is all-powerful, and since right is determined solely by His commands, is it not possible that He might change the rules and make what we now think of as wrong into right? It would seem that according to the divine command theory the answer is "yes": it is theoretically possible that tomorrow God would decree that virtues such as kindness and courage have become vices while actions that show cruelty and cowardice will henceforth be the right actions. (Recall the analogy with a legislator and the power it has to change law.) So now rather than it being right for people to help each other out and prevent innocent people from suffering unnecessarily, it would be right (God having changed His mind) to create as much pain among innocent children as we possibly can! To adopt the divine command theory therefore commits its advocate to the seemingly absurd position that even the greatest atrocities might be not only acceptable but morally required if God were to command them.

Plato made a similar point in the dialogue Euthyphro. Socrates is asking Euthyphro what it is that makes the virtue of holiness a virtue, just as we have been asking what makes kindness and courage virtues. Euthyphro has suggested that holiness is just whatever all the gods love.

**Socrates:** Well, then, Euthyphro, what do we say about holiness? Is it not loved by all the gods, according to your definition?
**Euthyphro:** Yes.
**Socrates:** Because it is holy, or for some other reason?

**Euthyphro:** No, because it is holy.
**Socrates:** Then it is loved by the gods because it is holy: it is not holy because it is loved by them?
**Euthyphro:** It seems so.
**Socrates:** . . . Then holiness is not what is pleasing to the gods, and what is pleasing to the gods is not holy as you say, Euthyphro. They are different things.
**Euthyphro:** And why, Socrates?
**Socrates:** Because we are agreed that the gods love holiness because it is holy: and that it is not holy because they love it.[3]

This raises an interesting question: Why, having claimed at first that virtues are merely what is loved (or commanded) by the gods, would Euthyphro so quickly contradict this and agree that the gods love holiness *because* it's holy, rather than the reverse? One likely possibility is that Euthyphro believes that whenever the gods love something they do so with good reason, not without justification and arbitrarily. To deny this, and say that it is merely the gods' love that makes holiness a virtue, would mean that the gods have no basis for their attitudes, that they are arbitrary in what they love. Yet—and this is the crucial point—it's far from clear that a religious person would want to say that God is arbitrary in that way. If we say that it is simply God's loving something that makes it right, then what sense would it make to say God wants us to do right? All that could mean, it seems, is that God wants us to do what He wants us to do; He would have no reason for wanting it. Similarly "God is good" would mean little more than "God does what He pleases." The divine command theory therefore leads us to the results that God is morally arbitrary, and that His wishing us to do good or even God's being just mean nothing more than that God does what He does and wants whatever He wants. Religious people who reject that consequence would also, I am suggesting, have reason to reject the divine command theory itself, seeking a different understanding of morality.

This now raises another problem, however. If God approves kindness because it is a virtue and hates the Nazis because they were evil, then it seems that God discovers morality rather than inventing it. So haven't we then identified a limitation on God's power, since He now, being a good

God, must love kindness and command us not to be cruel? Without the divine command theory, in other words, what is left of God's omnipotence?

But why, we may ask, is such a limitation on God unacceptable? It is not at all clear that God really can do anything at all. Can God, for example, destroy Himself? Or make a rock so heavy that He cannot lift it? Or create a universe which was never created by Him? Many have thought that God cannot do these things, but also that His inability to do them does not constitute a serious limitation on His power since these are things that cannot be done at all: to do them would violate the laws of logic. Christianity's most influential theologian, Thomas Aquinas, wrote in this regard that "whatever implies contradiction does not come within the scope of divine omnipotence, because it cannot have the aspect of possibility. Hence it is more appropriate to say that such things cannot be done than that God cannot do them."[4]

How, then, ought we to understand God's relationship to morality if we reject the divine command theory? Can religious people consistently maintain their faith in God the Creator and yet deny that what is right is right because He commands it? I think the answer to this is "yes." Making cruelty good is not like making a universe that wasn't made, of course. It's a moral limit on God rather than a logical one. But why suppose that God's limits are only logical?

One final point about this. Even if we agree that God loves justice or kindness because of their nature, not arbitrarily, there still remains a sense in which God could change morality even having rejected the divine command theory. That's because if we assume, plausibly I think, that morality depends in part on how we reason, what we desire and need, and the circumstances in which we find ourselves, then morality will still be under God's control since God could have constructed us or our environment very differently. Suppose, for instance, that he created us so that we couldn't be hurt by others or didn't care about freedom. Or perhaps our natural environment [was] created differently, so that all we have to do is ask and anything we want is given to us. If God had created either nature or us that way, then it seems likely our morality might also be different in important ways from the one we now think correct. In that sense, then, morality depends on God whether or not one supports the divine command theory.

## Notes

1. R.C. Mortimer, *Christian Ethics* (London: Hutchinson's University Library, 1950) pp. 7–8.
2. This debate was broadcast on the "Third Program" of the British Broadcasting Corporation in 1948.
3. Plato, *Euthyphro,* trans. H.N. Fowler (Cambridge, MA: Harvard University Press, 1947).
4. Thomas Aquinas, *Summa Theologica,* Part I, Q. 25, Art. 3.

# 14   A Modified Divine Command Theory of Ethical Wrongness

## ROBERT MERRIHEW ADAMS

### I

. . . The modified divine command theory clearly conceives of believers as valuing some things

Reprinted by permission of the author.

independently of their relation to God's commands. If the believer will not say that it would be wrong not to practice cruelty for its own sake if God commanded it, that is because he values kindness, and has a revulsion for cruelty, in a way that is at least to some extent independent of his belief that God commands kindness and forbids cruelty. This point may be made the basis of both philosophical and theological objections to the modified divine command theory, but I think the objections can be answered.

The philosophical objection is, roughly, that if there are some things I value independently of their relation to God's commands, then my value concepts cannot rightly be analyzed in terms of God's commands. According to the modified divine command theory, the acceptability of divine command ethics depends in part on the believer's independent positive valuation of the sorts of things that God is believed to command. But then, the philosophical critic objects, the believer must have a prior, nontheological conception of ethical right and wrong, in terms of which he judges God's commandments to be acceptable—and to admit that the believer has a prior, nontheological conception of ethical right and wrong is to abandon the divine command theory.

The weakness of this philosophical objection is that it fails to note the distinctions that can be drawn among various value concepts. From the fact that the believer values some things independent of his beliefs about God's commands, the objector concludes, illegitimately, that the believer must have a conception of ethical right and wrong that is independent of his beliefs about God's commands. This inference is illegitimate because there can be valuations which do not imply or presuppose a judgment of ethical right or wrong. For instance, I may simply like something, or want something, or feel a revulsion at something.

What the modified divine command theorist will hold, then, is that the believer values some things independently of their relation to God's commands, but that these valuations are not judgments of ethical right and wrong and do not of themselves imply judgments of ethical right and wrong. He will maintain, on the other hand, that such independent valuations are involved in, or even necessary for, judgments of ethical right and wrong which also involve beliefs about God's will or commands. The adherent of a divine command ethics will normally be able to give reasons for his adherence. Such reasons might include: "Because I am grateful to God for His love"; "Because I find it the most satisfying form of ethical life"; "Because there's got to be an objective moral law if life isn't to fall to pieces, and I can't understand what it would be if not the will of God." As we have already noted, the modified divine command theorist also has reasons why he would not accept a divine command ethics in certain logically possible situations which he believes not to be actual. All of these reasons seem to me to involve valuations that are independent of divine command ethics. The person who has such reasons wants certain things —happiness, certain satisfactions—for himself and others; he hates cruelty and loves kindness; he has perhaps a certain unique and "numinous" awe of God. And these are not attitudes which he has simply because of his beliefs about God's commands. They are not attitudes, however, which presuppose judgments of moral right and wrong. . . .

## II

This version of the divine command theory may seem *theologically* objectionable to some believers. One of the reasons, surely, why divine command theories of ethics have appealed to some theologians is that such theories seem especially congruous with the religious demand that God be the object of our highest allegiance. If our supreme commitment in life is to doing what is right just because it is right, and if what is right is right just because God wills or commands it, then surely our highest allegiance is to God. But the modified divine command theory seems not to have this advantage. For the modified divine command theorist is forced to admit, as we have seen, that he has reasons for his adherence to a divine command ethics, and that his having these reasons implies that there are some things which he values independently of his beliefs about God's commands. It is therefore not correct to say of him that he is committed to doing the will of God *just* because it is the will of God; he is committed to doing it partly because of other things which he values independently. Indeed it appears that there are certain logically possible situations in which his present attitudes would not commit him to obey God's commands (for instance, if God commanded cruelty for its own sake). This may even suggest that he values some things, not just independently of God's commands, but more than God's commands.

We have here a real problem in religious ethical motivation. The Judeo-Christian believer is supposed to make God the supreme focus of his loyalties; that is clear. One possible interpretation of this fact is the following. Obedience to whatever God may command is (or at least ought to be) the one thing that the believer values for its own sake and more than anything and everything else. Anything else that he values, he values (or ought to) only to a lesser degree and as a means to obedience to God. This conception of religious ethical motivation is obviously favorable to an *un*modified divine command theory of ethical wrongness.

But I think it is not a realistic conception. Loyalty to God, for instance, is very often explained, by believers themselves, as motivated by gratitude for benefits conferred. And I think it is clear in most cases that the gratitude presupposes that the benefits are valued, at least to some extent, independently of loyalty to God. Similarly, I do not think that most devout Judeo-Christian believers would say that it would be wrong to disobey God if He commanded cruelty for its own sake. And if I am right about that I think it shows that their positive valuation of (emotional/volitional pro-attitude toward) doing *whatever* God may command is not clearly greater than their independent negative valuation of cruelty.

In analyzing ethical motivation in general, as well as Judeo-Christian ethical motivation in particular, it is probably a mistake to suppose that there is (or can be expected to be) only one thing that is valued supremely and for its own sake, with nothing else being valued independently of it. The motivation for a person's ethical orientation in life is normally much more complex than that, and involves a plurality of emotional and volitional attitudes of different sorts which are at least partly independent of each other. At any rate, I think the

modified divine command theorist is bound to say that that is true of his ethical motivation.

In what sense, then, can the modified divine command theorist maintain that God is the supreme focus of his loyalties? I suggest the following interpretation of the single-hearted loyalty to God which is demanded in Judeo-Christian religion. In this interpretation the crucial idea is *not* that some one thing is valued for its own sake and more than anything else, and nothing else valued independently of it. It is freely admitted that the religious person will have a plurality of motives for his ethical position, and that these will be at least partly independent of each other. It is admitted further that a desire to obey the commands of God (*whatever* they may be) may not be the strongest of these motives. What will be claimed is that certain beliefs about God enable the believer to integrate or focus his motives in a loyalty to God and His commands. Some of these beliefs are about what God commands or wills (contingently —that is, although He could logically have commanded or willed something else instead).

Some of the motives in question might be called egoistic; they include desires for satisfactions for oneself—which God is believed to have given or to be going to give. Other motives may be desires for satisfaction for other people; these may be called altruistic. Still other motives might not be desires for anyone's satisfaction, but might be valuations of certain kinds of action for their own sakes; these might be called idealistic. I do not think my argument depends heavily on this particular classification, but it seems plausible that all of these types, and perhaps others as well, might be distinguished among the motives for a religious person's ethical position. Obviously such motives might pull one in different directions, conflicting with one another. But in Judeo-Christian ethics beliefs about what God does in fact will (although He could have willed otherwise) are supposed to enable one to *fuse* these motives, so to speak, into one's devotion to God and His will, so that they all pull together. Doubtless the believer will still have some motives which conflict with his loyalty to God. But the religious ideal is that these should all be merely momentary desires and impulses, and kept under control. They ought not to be allowed to influence voluntary action. The deeper, more stable, and controlling desires, intentions, and psychic energies are supposed to be fused in devotion to God. As I interpret it, however, it need not be inconsistent with the Judeo-Christian ethical and religious ideal that this fusion of motives, this integration of moral energies, depends on belief in certain propositions which are taken to be contingent truths about God.

Lest it be thought that I am proposing unprecedented theological positions, or simply altering Judeo-Christian religious beliefs to suit my theories, I will call to my aid on this point a theologian known for his insistence on the sovereignty of God. Karl Barth seems to me to hold a divine command theory of ethics. But when he raises the question of why we should obey God, he rejects with scorn the suggestion that God's *power* provides the basis for His claim on us. "By deciding for God [man] has definitely decided not to be obedient to power as power." God's claim on us is based rather on His grace. "God calls us and orders us and claims us by being gracious to us in Jesus Christ." I do not mean to suggest that Barth would agree with everything I have said about motivation, or that he offers a lucid account of a divine command theory. But he does agree with the position I have proposed on this point, that the believer's loyalty is not to be construed as a loyalty to God *as* all powerful, nor to God *whatever* He might conceivably have willed. It is a loyalty to God *as* having a certain attitude toward us, a certain will for us, which God was free not to have, but to which, in Barth's view, He has committed Himself irrevocably in Jesus Christ. The believer's devotion is not to merely possible commands of God as such, but to God's actual (and gracious) will.

### III

The ascription of moral qualities to God is commonly thought to cause problems for divine command theories of ethics. It is doubted that God, as an agent, can properly be called "good" in the moral sense if He is not subject to a moral law that is not of His own making. For if He is morally good, mustn't He do what is right *because* it is right? And how can He do that, if what's right is right because He wills it? Or it may be charged that divine command theories trivialize the claim that God is good. If "X is (morally) good" means roughly "X does what God wills," then "God is (morally) good" means only that God does what He wills—which is surely much less than people are normally taken to mean when they say that God is (morally) good. In this section I will suggest an answer to these objections.

Surely no analysis of Judeo-Christian ethical discourse can be regarded as adequate which does not provide for a sense in which the believer can seriously assert that God is good. Indeed an adequate analysis should provide a plausible account of what believers do in fact mean when they say, "God is good." I believe that a divine command theory of ethical rightness and wrongness can include such an account. I will try to indicate its chief features.

(1) In saying "God is good" one is normally expressing a favorable emotional attitude toward God. I shall not try to determine whether or not this is part of the meaning of "God is good"; but it is normally, perhaps almost always, at least one of the things one is doing if one says that God is good. If we were to try to be more precise about the type of favorable emotional attitude normally expressed by "God is good," I suspect we would find that the attitude expressed is most commonly one of *gratitude*.

(2) This leads to a second point, which is that when God is called "good" it is very often meant that He is *good to us,* or *good to* the speaker. "Good" is sometimes virtually a synonym for "kind." And for the modified divine command theorist it is not a trivial truth that God is kind. In saying that God is good in the sense of "kind," one presupposes, of course, that there are some things which the beneficiaries of God's goodness value. We need not discuss here whether the ben-

eficiaries must value them independently of their beliefs about God's will. For the modified divine command theorist does admit that there are some things which believers value independently of their beliefs about God's commands. Nothing that the modified divine command theorist says about the meaning of ("right" and) "wrong" implies that it is a trivial truth that God bestows on His creatures things that they value.

(3) I would not suggest that the descriptive force of "good" as applied to God is exhausted by the notion of kindness. "God is good" must be taken in many contexts as ascribing to God, rather generally, qualities of character which the believing speaker regards as virtues in human beings. Among such qualities might be faithfulness, ethical consistency, a forgiving disposition, and, in general, various aspects of love, as well as kindness. Not that there is some definite list of qualities, the ascription of which to God is clearly implied by the claim that God is good. But saying that God is good normally commits one to the position that God has some important set of qualities which one regards as virtues in human beings.

(4) It will not be thought that God has *all* the qualities which are virtues in human beings. Some such qualities are logically inapplicable to a being such as God is supposed to be. For example, aside from certain complications arising from the doctrine of the incarnation, it would be logically inappropriate to speak of God as controlling His sexual desires. (He doesn't have any.) And given some widely held conceptions of God and his relation to the world, it would hardly make sense to speak of Him as *courageous*. For if He is impassible and has predetermined absolutely everything that happens, He has no risks to face and cannot endure (because He cannot suffer) pain or displeasure. . . .

(5) If we accept a divine command theory of ethical rightness and wrongness, I think we shall have to say that *dutifulness* is a human virtue which, like sexual chastity, is logically inapplicable to God. God cannot either do or fail to do His duty, since He does not have a duty—at least not in the most important sense in which human beings have a duty. For He is not subject to a

moral law not of His own making. Dutifulness is one virtuous disposition which men can have that God cannot have. But there are other virtuous dispositions which God can have as well as men. Love, for instance. It hardly makes sense to say that God does what He does *because* it is right. But it does not follow that God cannot have any reason for doing what He does. It does not even follow that He cannot have reasons of a type on which it would be morally virtuous for a man to act. For example, He might do something because He knew it would make His creatures happier.

(6) The modified divine command theorist must deny that in calling God "good" one presupposes a standard of moral rightness and wrongness superior to the will of God, by reference to which it is determined whether God's character is virtuous or not. And I think he can consistently deny that. He can say that morally virtuous and vicious qualities of character are those which agree and conflict, respectively, with God's commands, and that it is their agreement or disagreement with God's commands that makes them virtuous or vicious. But the believer normally thinks he has at least a general idea of what qualities of character are in fact virtuous and vicious (approved and disapproved by God). Having such an idea, he can apply the word "good" descriptively to God, meaning that (with some exceptions, as I have noted) God has the qualities which the believer regards as virtues, such as faithfulness and kindness. . . .

## Questions

1. List all of the ways in which the Sermon on the Mount seems, at first glance, to clash with common sense. Does the Sermon, when correctly interpreted, really clash with common sense at all of these points?

   For each point, if you think the Sermon really does not clash with common sense, explain how to interpret the Sermon so that it is compatible with common sense. That is, give a moderate interpretation of Jesus' view. Provide textual justification for your interpretation.

If you think the Sermon really does clash with common sense at certain points, explain how Jesus might try to convince a person holding the common-sense view to change his or her mind. That is, what arguments might Jesus use to persuade people with common sense to adopt his radical moral theory? (*Hint:* Do not say that people should adopt Jesus' view because He is God or because God rewards people who adopt His view. These are not the sorts of arguments for which we are looking.)

2. Let us make the following definitions. *Rules of morality* govern people's relationship to each other. *Rules of religion* govern people's relationship to God. *Rules of prudence* govern people's relationship to happiness. *Rules of manners* govern people's relationship to custom. A moral system is *complete* insofar as it contains all of the rules of morality. A moral system is *consistent* insofar as its rules do not conflict with each other. A moral system is *plausible* insofar as its rules do not conflict with common sense. To *compare two moral systems* is to say which moral system is more nearly complete, which is more consistent, which is more plausible, and which is better overall. Choose *one* of the following tasks.

   a. List all the rules of morality found in the Holiness Code. Do not list rules of religion, prudence, or manners. Compare the moral system of the Holiness Code to the moral system of the Ten Commandments *or* the moral system of the Sermon on the Mount.

   b. List all the rules of morality found in *Exodus* 22–23. Do not list rules of religion, prudence, or manners. Compare the moral system found in this passage to the moral system of the Ten Commandments *or* the moral system of the Sermon on the Mount.

   c. List all the rules of morality found in *Romans* 12–13. Do not list rules of religion, prudence, or manners. Compare the moral

system found in this passage to the moral system of the Ten Commandments *or* the moral system of the Sermon on the Mount.

   d. List all of the rules of morality found in *Exodus* 22–23 and in *Romans* 12–13. Do not list rules of religion, prudence, or manners. Compare the moral systems found in these passages.

3. Pick a person who loves you. Is "being loved by that person" an essential or an incidental property of you? In other words, is "being loved by that person" part of who you are, or not?

   Is "being loved by God" an incidental or an essential property of moral acts? (I am *not* asking whether God loves such acts. I am asking whether God's love *makes* the acts moral. Would the acts be moral if God didn't love them?) Are the two cases analogous? Why or why not?

   Does God want us to do moral acts because they are moral, *or* are moral acts moral because God wants us to do them? Is this question the same as the preceding one? Explain.

4. Answer any *two* of the following questions.

   a. America maintains a large military force and has participated in wars and other military actions. Is this incompatible with the rules "Do not kill," "Love your enemy," and "Turn the other cheek"? Why or why not?

   b. Several years ago someone stole my stereo. I asked the police to try to get my stereo back. The police tried to apprehend, convict, and sentence the thieves. Did my action violate the rule "If a man takes what is yours, do not demand it back"? Were the police and the courts violating the rule "Do not judge"? Why or why not?

   c. My neighbor has an extremely nice house and drives an extremely nice car. I have often said to myself, "I would love to have both." Does my attitude constitute a violation of the rule "Do not covet anything that belongs to your neighbor"? Why or why not?

d. In various ways the U.S. government has advised third-world nations to balance their budgets, yet the U.S. budget deficit is huge. Is the United States violating the rule "Remove the beam from your own eye before you remove the splinter from someone else's eye"? Why or why not?

e. Several weeks ago while I was walking in an airport, I was approached by an unsavory looking fellow who asked me for spare change. I was also asked to donate to a cause I do not believe in. I refused both requests. Did I violate the rule "Give to all who beg from you"? Why or why not?

f. Several years ago a friend of mine stole some money from me. I went to him and demanded that he give it back. He refused. I did not call in the police, but I resolved not to trust him with money again. Did my request violate the rule "If a man takes what is yours, do not demand it back"? Did my decision to not trust him with money again violate the rule "Do not judge"? Why or why not?

g. Many people tell their children that Santa Claus exists. Politicians often say true but misleading things about their opponents in order to deceive voters. Do these activities violate the commandment that prohibits lying? Why or why not?

h. Many stores are now open seven days each week. Does this violate the commandment that prohibits working on the Sabbath? If not, why not? If so, is a person who shops in such a store on the Sabbath an accessory to the violation?

i. The Holiness Code says that one should not show bias or favoritism. Everyone should be judged according to the same rules. Does this contradict Jesus' rule "Do not judge"? Why or why not?

j. When I left home and got my first full-time job, my parents advised me again and again not to spend all of my money at once, but rather to budget my money so that I would not run out before the end of the month. They also advised me to build and maintain a savings account for emergencies. But in the Sermon on the Mount, Jesus says, "Do not worry about your life, what you will eat or drink, or about your body, what you will wear. . . . Do not worry about tomorrow, for tomorrow will take care of itself." Is Jesus counseling me to disregard the advice of my parents? Why or why not?

k. Jesus says, "If someone forces you to go one mile, go two miles." Does this imply that if I am drafted and forced to do military service for some period of time, then I should enlist for another term of equal length after my first term expires? If I am kidnapped and forced to do slave labor for five years, must I volunteer to work for my kidnappers for another five years after they release me? Why or why not?

l. Danny and Denny have been married for 30 years. At first their marriage was wonderful, but now that the kids have grown up and left, Danny and Denny find that they have gradually fallen out of love with each other. In fact, each loves someone else. Bobby beats his wife Becky black and blue. Bobby has resisted all attempts to get him to stop. He sees nothing wrong with his behavior and intends to keep it up. Tommy's wife Tammy suffered extensive brain damage in a car crash. She has been a psychotic for years, and the doctors say there is no hope that she will recover. Jesus says, "Whoever divorces his wife (unless the marriage is unlawful) causes her to commit adultery, and whoever marries a divorced woman commits adultery." Is Jesus really saying that Danny and Denny, Bobby and Becky, and Tommy and Tammy should not get divorced. Why or why not?

m. Jill is a kind, loving, but depressed and anxious person. Many misfortunes have befallen her, and her life is unhappy. James is a selfish, nasty person who gives a lot of money to charity and usually treats people very well—all because he wants to get a reputation for being a generous, nice guy. This reputation enables him to stab others in the back more effectively. Jan is a well-intentioned but bumbling person. Her attempts to do good often backfire and make the problem she is working on worse instead of better. Jack is an intelligent and morally good parent and teacher. However, his children and many of his students have turned out quite badly. Jesus says, "Every good tree bears good fruit, and a rotten tree bears bad fruit. A good tree cannot bear bad fruit, nor can a rotten tree bear good fruit." Are Jill, James, Jan, and/or Jack counter-examples to this claim? Why or why not?

5. Here are the basic principles of a new moral theory (*Theory X*) that combines aspects of the Ten Commandments, the Sermon on the Mount, Ethical Egoism, and Normative Relativism.

(A) Each person has no duties toward non-citizens.

(B) Each person should do no harm to fellow citizens.

(C) Each person should do a little good for his or her friends and relatives as long as doing so does not violate principle (B).

(D) Each person should maximize good for himself or herself as long as doing so does not violate principle (B) or (C).

Apply the principles of Theory X to any *one* of the following questions. Next apply the principles of the Sermon on the Mount to the same question. Explain and defend your answers.

a. You are the teacher of a Sunday school class. Your child is a student in your class. One of the other children needs substantial extra help in order to master the material, but if you give that student extra help, your child will be bored and frustrated. Should you give the other student extra help?

b. While traveling in another country, you see an opportunity to steal some money from a large department store. You plan to keep most of the money and share the rest with your needy buddies. Should you steal the money?

c. You are an unmarried woman who enjoys having sex with a wide variety of men. You always takes precautions against sexually transmitted diseases (STDs) and pregnancy. From time to time, your male friends ask to sleep with you. Do you have a duty to agree?

d. Toys are now sold in your town at the manufacturer's suggested retail price. You plan to open a new toy store and sell toys at a 10% discount until the other stores go out of business. Then, once you have achieved a toy monopoly, you plan to sell toys at twice the manufacturer's suggested retail price. Is there anything morally wrong with your plan?

e. Sue, an unmarried woman, enjoys having sex with a wide variety of men. She always takes precautions against STDs and pregnancy. Is it morally OK for her to take a job as a prostitute?

f. Bill's company makes an insecticide that has just been banned in the United States because it causes cancer. Bill plans to market it in the third world. Is this morally OK?

g. Joe's five-year-old child has a serious birth defect. A series of medical treatments could substantially increase the child's quality of life over the next seventy years, but Joe would have to take a second job and work long, hard hours for two years to pay for the treatments. Is Joe morally required to do so?

h. Because it is convenient, Jane often parks in spaces reserved for the disabled even though she is not disabled. Is this morally OK?

6. You are a doctor. A man brings his sick, five-year-old son to you. You say, "I have exam-

ined your son. He needs a certain operation. Without this operation he will almost certainly die. With the operation he will almost certainly live. I cannot operate unless you sign this consent form, for you are the boy's legal guardian."

"Will the operation require a transfusion?" asks the father.

"Yes," you answer.

"Then I cannot allow you to operate," says the father. "I am a Jehovah's Witness. My religion prohibits transfusions under any circumstances. To sign that form would be to violate God's commandments as I understand them. And I will not listen to any alternative interpretations of Scripture."

"Monster!" you say. "Don't you love your son?"

"I love my son dearly," says the father, "but God's commands have top priority. Don't be so quick to judge me. You, too, may someday find yourself in a situation where you must choose between following God's commandments as you understand them and preventing the death of an innocent loved one. After all, it happened to Abraham."

Is it really possible that you might someday find yourself forced to choose between obeying God and saving an innocent loved one? That is, would God ever ask a person to let an innocent loved one die? If your answer is "no," why not? How do you interpret the story of Abraham's near-sacrifice of Isaac? If your answer is "yes," are you claiming that God occasionally asks people to do immoral acts? Is a being who occasionally asks people to do immoral acts worthy of worship?

7. One of the Ten Commandments is "Do not kill." This means, I assume, that I have a moral obligation (a duty) to refrain from killing people (except perhaps in relatively rare cases such as self-defense, defense of others, and just wars). It doesn't mean that refraining from killing people is morally optional. If I am the kind of person who goes around killing people, then I am an immoral person.

In the Sermon on the Mount, Jesus says a number of things about how to treat the poor. He says, for example, "Give to all who beg from you." Does Jesus mean that I have a moral obligation to help the poor, or does Jesus mean that helping the poor is merely morally optional? Is helping the poor a duty, or is it above and beyond the call of duty? In the Sermon on the Mount, is Jesus giving us rules for how we must live in order to be moral, or is He presenting an ideal for how to be saintly? If I am the kind of person who follows all of the other rules but does *not* help the poor, am I an immoral person, or am I a moral but not saintly person?

If you think that I *do* have a duty to help the poor, consider this: If I have a duty not to kill you (except perhaps in cases such as self-defense, defense of others, and just wars) and everyone else also has a similar duty not to kill you, then you have a *right* not to be killed. "You have a right to life" is just a shorthand way of saying that everyone has a duty to not kill you. If I have a duty to help the poor, does that mean that every poor person has a *right* to be helped by me?

If you think that I do *not* have a duty to help the poor, explain what your reason is for thinking that the command "Do not kill" imposes a duty and a corresponding right, whereas the command "Give to all who beg from you" does not.

8. Answer any *two* of the following questions.

   a. The Ultimate Philosophic Principle is "Be Reflective! Think about whatever you do, say, feel, and believe. Be open-minded! Be willing to accept whatever claim is best supported by reasoning and evidence." To lead the contemplative life is to try to live up to the Ultimate Philosophic Principle. What is the relationship between the Ultimate Philosophic Principle and the Ultimate Moral Principle? (Is the Ultimate Philosophic Principle a corollary of the Ultimate Moral Principle, for example?) What is the relationship between the contemplative life and the moral life? Are the two lives compatible? If not, why not? If so, should we be contemplative in order to be moral, or should we be moral in order to be contemplative, or neither?

b. What is the relationship between the Ultimate Philosophic Principle and the Ultimate Religious Principle? What is the relationship between the contemplative life and the religious life? Are the two lives compatible? If not, why not? If so, should we be contemplative in order to be religious, or should we be religious in order to be contemplative, or neither?

c. The Ultimate Egoistic Principle is "Everyone always ought to do what he or she believes is in his or her own long-term best interest." To lead the egoistic life is to try to live up to the Ultimate Egoistic Principle. What is the relationship between the Ultimate Egoistic Principle and the Ultimate Moral Principle? (Is the Ultimate Egoistic Principle a corollary of the Ultimate Moral Principle, for example?) What is the relationship between the egoistic life and the moral life? Are the two lives compatible? If not, why not? If so, should we be egoistic in order to be moral, or should we be moral in order to be egoistic, or neither?

d. The Ultimate Aesthetic Principle is "Maximize the creation and appreciation of beauty in the world." To lead the aesthetic life is to try to live up to the Ultimate Aesthetic Principle. What is the relationship between the Ultimate Aesthetic Principle and the Ultimate Moral Principle? What is the relationship between the aesthetic life and the ethical life? Are the two lives compatible? If not, why not? If so, should we be aesthetic in order to be ethical, or should we be ethical in order to be aesthetic, or neither?

9. Consider the following synthesis of Divine Command Theory and Utilitarianism (DCT&UTIL).

(A) If X is good, then what makes X good is that God loves X.

(B) If X is morally good, then what makes X morally good is that God loves X *and* X maximizes overall happiness.

This synthesis has the following implications.

(C) X is good if and only if God loves X.

(D) X is morally good if and only if God loves X *and* X maximizes overall happiness.

(E) If God loves X *but* X does not maximize overall happiness, then X is good, but X is not morally good. For example, suppose going to church on Sunday does not maximize happiness. People might be happier if they slept in on Sunday mornings, but God wants people to go to church, so churchgoing is a religious requirement but not a moral requirement.

(F) If God does not love X *but* X maximizes overall happiness, then X is not morally good or even good. For example, exploiting a few people might increase the overall happiness of society, but God does not love exploitation, so this practice is morally wrong.

The main objection to Divine Command Theory is this. Common sense says that (g) If X is morally good, then God loves X because X is morally good. Otherwise God is arbitrary. Divine Command Theory says that (h) If X is morally good, then X is morally good because God loves X. Because (g) and (h) cannot be combined, we must abandon (h). We must reject Divine Command Theory.

The main objection to Utilitarianism is this. Utilitarianism says that (i) If X maximizes happiness, then X is morally good. Common sense says that some things that maximize happiness are clearly morally wrong. For example, exploiting a few people in order to increase the overall happiness of society is clearly wrong. Thus we must abandon (i). We must reject Utilitarianism.

One problem with both Divine Command Theory and Utilitarianism is that information crucial to the use of both theories is difficult to obtain. In the case of Divine Command Theory, how are we supposed to know what, exactly, God commands? Whence comes the voice of authority? And because different people have different beliefs about God's commands, Divine Command Theory seems to become some sort of relativism. In the case of Utilitarianism, how are we supposed to know, exactly, how many Jollies each policy will produce? And because different people have different beliefs about the Jolly value of each policy, Utilitarianism seems to become some sort of relativism.

Does the synthesis DCT&UTIL avoid these objections to Divine Command Theory and to Utilitarianism? Is DCT&UTIL vulnerable to other objections to which Divine Command Theory and Utilitarianism are not vulnerable? Overall, is DCT&UTIL a better theory than Divine Command Theory? Is DCT&UTIL a better theory than Utilitarianism?

# PART II

# ETHICAL THEORIES

# Utilitarianism: Mill

*"Imagine that you are creating a fabric of human destiny with the object of making men happy . . . but that it was essential to torture to death only one tiny creature—that baby beating its breast with its fist, for instance . . . would you consent to be the architect on those conditions?"*

*"No, I wouldn't consent," said Alyosha softly.*

*"And can you admit the idea that men for whom you are building it would agree to accept their happiness on the foundation of the unexpiated blood of a little victim? And accepting it would remain happy for ever?"*

*"No, I can't admit it, Brother" said Alyosha suddenly, with flashing eyes.*

DOSTOEVSKY

Utilitarianism is a *teleological* theory. It holds, in other words, that the rightness and wrongness of acts are a function solely of the goodness and badness of their consequences. What distinguishes Utilitarianism from other teleological theories is that Utilitarians define "good consequences" to be the maximization (or increase) of happiness in the universe. An Egoist, by contrast, defines "good consequences" to be the maximization (or increase) of *his or her own* happiness. There are many versions of Utilitarianism. Probably the best-known proponent of Utilitarianism is the nineteenth-century British philosopher John Stuart Mill, but it is far from clear which version of Utilitarianism Mill would endorse. Some of the distinctions among the versions were drawn explicitly only after Mill's death, so Mill's works are vague at crucial points. For expository reasons, in this chapter I shall present four versions of Utilitarianism, each a more complex moral theory than the one before.

Utilitarians disagree among themselves about the definition of happiness. Some take happiness to be the satisfaction of desires. However, there are desires whose fulfillment makes one miserable. As the saying goes, "Be careful what you ask for, because your request may be granted." Indeed, self-destructive desires are rather common. Moreover, as Plato observes, if happiness is merely the satisfaction of desires, then the happiest people are those who cultivate and satisfy desire after desire, who are always itching and scratching.[1] But this is not an enviable way of life. Other Utilitarians take happiness to be the satisfaction of *rational* desires. However, sometimes people are not made happy by what reason says should make them happy, and they *are* made happy by what reason says should not make them happy. Moreover, it is not perfectly clear which desires are rational desires.

Mill says that "by happiness is intended pleasure and the absence of pain" (7). Although Mill's account of happiness is actually much more complicated, let me begin by taking happiness to be simply pleasure. Combining Utilitarianism with this hedonistic definition of happiness yields the thesis that our moral duty is to maximize (or increase) pleasure in the universe. Now humans are not the only creatures capable of feeling pleasure and pain. Thus our moral duty is to maximize (or increase) pleasure for all sentient beings (creatures able to feel pleasure and pain).

## Act Utilitarianism

A phrase coined by Francis Hutcheson and championed by one of the founders of Utilitarianism, Jeremy Bentham,[2] tells us that we should seek "the greatest good for the greatest number." However, this guideline is somewhat vague. Some Utilitarians think we should maximize the number of happy people. Others think we should maximize people's average happiness. The simplest sort of Utilitarianism, which I will call *Act Utilitarianism*, says that we should maximize the overall amount of happiness. According to this view there is only one moral principle:

*Greatest Happiness Principle:* In every situation, choose the option that you believe to be most likely to produce the greatest possible happiness (or least possible unhappiness) for the universe.

(Unfortunately, this terminology is somewhat confusing because Mill calls his own, much more complex ultimate moral principle the Greatest Happiness Principle, too). Act Utilitarianism applies this principle directly to all of our acts on a case-by-case basis. In each situation, the right choice is the one that produces more happiness (or less unhappiness) in the universe than any of the other options. All of the other choices in that situation are wrong.

Let us work through an example. Suppose that Angela is a seventeen-year-old, unmarried, pregnant, middle-class Act Utilitarian. The father will not marry Angela or pay child support. Angela is trying to decide among three options: abort the fetus, give the child up for adoption, or keep the child. First, Angela lists all of the people who would be affected by her decision and determines the number of (positive or negative) jollies each option will produce for each person. Second, she determines the likelihood that these jollies will be produced. Third, she multiplies people-affected times jollies-per-person times likelihood-of-jollies and adds up the results. Finally, she chooses the option that produces the most jollies. This four-step process is called the *hedonistic calculus.* Having read some sociological studies, Angela recognizes that her life will probably be happier if she does not keep the child, because she will have a much better chance of finishing her education and embarking on a career if she is not a single parent. The studies also show that giving a child up for adoption is typically more traumatic for the mother than abortion. Angela knows that the happier she is, the happier her family and friends will be. On the other hand, Angela acknowledges that if she gives birth to Freddie Fetus and then gives him up for adoption, he

will almost certainly have a life well worth living, even if he grows up in an orphanage. Over the years, that life represents lots and lots of pleasure. Freddie will be even happier if she keeps him, though. Angela ignores people who are only marginally affected, such as medical personnel who will make some money on the abortion. She then constructs the Utilitarian argument shown in the table on page 156.

So far, keeping the child seems to be the morally right choice for Angela because the number of jollies generated (104,400) seems highest. However, Angela will probably have the same number of children in her life whether or not she has an abortion now. If she has an abortion now, Freddie will be replaced by Francie, a child born after Angela graduates from college and gets married. Francie will get a better start in life than Freddie, so Francie's life will probably be even happier than Freddie's life.[3] On the other hand, if lots of women have abortions, then respect for human life within the society may diminish. People might become callous about killing other people. This would, of course, produce all sorts of horrible consequences. The practice of abortion might be the first step on a *slippery slope* that leads eventually to some sort of genocide. If Angela gets an abortion, then she might be contributing to this process, giving society a tiny nudge down the slippery slope. Thus declining an abortion would slightly reduce the chances of genocidal jolly loss. Angela believes, however, that it is highly unlikely that the practice of abortion undermines people's respect for human life to any significant degree. The slope is not very slippery at all. Angela's revised chart appears on page 157. Because the number of jollies generated by the adoption option exceeds the numbers generated by the other two options, according to Act Utilitarianism, Angela is morally required to give Freddie up for adoption.

This example brings out several aspects of Act Utilitarianism. First, Act Utilitarianism provides a clear method for determining what each person should do in each situation. Second, it is a method based on contingent facts about the world rather than on conceptual relationships or categorical schemes. If the world were different, then the hedonistic calculus would yield different answers. Act Utilitarianism is empirical rather than *a priori*. This is a strength of Act Utilitarianism, for it would be counter-intuitive to deny that facts about the world are relevant. Third, everyone's jollies count equally. Angela's jollies count neither more nor less than the jollies of her friends and family or the jollies of strangers. Similarly, the jollies of good people count neither more nor less than the jollies of bad people. Indeed, the jollies of people count neither more nor less than the jollies of animals, inasmuch as animals also feel pleasure and pain. Utilitarianism is radically impartial. Fourth, future jollies, even if experienced by people who do not yet exist, count just as much as present jollies, although their probability may well be lower because we are typically less certain about the future. Fifth, the morality of an act turns on the future consequences of the act rather than on its past causes. Act Utilitarianism is forward-looking, not backward-looking. Sixth, the morality of an act turns on the expected consequences of the act rather than on the act's actual consequences. If Freddy turns out to start World War III, Angela's decision not to abort him will not be proved wrong.

\*

Act Utilitarianism's clear, empirical methodology is a welcome advance over vagueness, intuitionism, and mysticism, but performing a complex calculation before every choice is cumbersome at best. If infinitely many choices are available in some situations, then finding the choice that maximizes happiness is impossible. Act Utilitarians might reply that no situation offers infinitely many choices and that the calculations are not burdensome if one follows rules of thumb. Initially, Act Utilitarians invest some time and energy working out what to do in a variety of common situations. Then they extrapolate to a broad range of similar cases. After this, Act Utilitarians need to perform calculations only in unusual cases.

Another problem with Act Utilitarianism is that necessary data are often unavailable. How does Angela know, for example, that her 20 rela-

**Argument A**

| Group of People Affected | Number of People | | Jollies per Person | | Probability of Gain or Loss | | Total Jollies |
|---|---|---|---|---|---|---|---|
| **Abortion** | | | | | | | |
| Angela | 1 | x | 10,000 | × | 90% | = | 9,000 |
| Family and friends | 20 | × | 100 | × | 90% | = | 1,800 |
| Freddie Fetus | 1 | × | 0 | × | 100% | = | 0 |
| Grand total | | | | | | | 10,800 |
| **Adoption** | | | | | | | |
| Angela | 1 | × | 7,500 | × | 90% | = | 6,750 |
| Family and friends | 20 | × | 75 | × | 90% | = | 1,350 |
| Freddie Fetus | 1 | × | 50,000 | × | 99% | = | 49,500 |
| Grand total | | | | | | | 57,600 |
| **Keep Child** | | | | | | | |
| Angela | 1 | × | 5,000 | × | 90% | = | 4,500 |
| Family and friends | 20 | × | 50 | × | 90% | = | 900 |
| Freddie Fetus | 1 | × | 100,000 | × | 99% | = | 99,000 |
| Grand total | | | | | | | 104,400 |

tives and friends will feel an average of 100 jollies per person if she has an abortion? In particular, the remote consequences of one's acts are often very large and impossible even to estimate. How does Angela know that the devaluation of human life would cost 800 lives and that it is only 0.00001% likely? Act Utilitarians might reply that one must just make decisions on the basis of one's best guess.

Act Utilitarianism's impartiality is a welcome advance over prejudice, favoritism, and egoism, but it conflicts with the common-sense view of duties within family and friend relationships. Suppose my child will benefit less from piano lessons than the child of an impoverished stranger, and I have the resources to provide lessons for only one child. According to Act Utilitarianism, I am morally required to buy piano lessons for the other child rather than for my own.

Act Utilitarianism leaves insufficient room for morally optional acts. Common sense says that in most situations, several acts are morally acceptable even if some are better than others, but Act Utilitarianism denies this. It says the act that is expected to generate the most jollies in a situation is morally required, and the other acts are morally wrong. We are free to choose among acts only when the acts generate equal jollies. Common sense says that I morally may open a conversation with my colleague by commenting on the weather, or by telling a joke, or by asking a question, but Act Utilitarianism says I must begin by complimenting him on his new haircut because, knowing my colleague, I am confident that that opening remark will produce the greatest pleasure overall. Worse yet, note that the same calculation that tells Angela to give Freddie up for adoption also tells her to get pregnant again and give the next child up for adoption,

**Argument B**

| Group of People Affected | Number of People | | Jollies per Person | | Probability of Gain or Loss | | Total Jollies |
|---|---|---|---|---|---|---|---|
| **Abortion** | | | | | | | |
| Angela | 1 | × | 10,000 | × | 90% | = | 9,000 |
| Family and friends | 20 | × | 100 | × | 90% | = | 1,800 |
| Freddie Fetus | 1 | × | 0 | × | 100% | = | 0 |
| Francie Fetus | 1 | × | 120,000 | × | 99% | = | 118,800 |
| Slippery slope | 800 | × | −100,000 | × | 0.00001% | = | −800 |
| Grand total | | | | | | | 128,000 |
| **Adoption** | | | | | | | |
| Angela | 1 | × | 7,500 | × | 90% | = | 6,750 |
| Family and friends | 20 | × | 75 | × | 90% | = | 1,350 |
| Freddie Fetus | 1 | × | 50,000 | × | 99% | = | 49,500 |
| Francie Fetus | 1 | × | 120,000 | × | 99% | = | 118,800 |
| Grand total | | | | | | | 176,400 |
| **Keep Child** | | | | | | | |
| Angela | 1 | × | 5,000 | × | 90% | = | 4,500 |
| Family and friends | 20 | × | 50 | × | 90% | = | 900 |
| Freddie Fetus | 1 | × | 100,000 | × | 99% | = | 99,000 |
| Francie Fetus | 1 | × | 0 | × | 100% | = | 0 |
| Grand total | | | | | | | 104,400 |

too. Indeed, because each child Angela brings into the world substantially increases the number of jollies, Act Utilitarianism says that Angela is morally required to breed like a bunny! But this is wildly counter-intuitive.

One aspect of this problem is of particular interest. Common sense says that some morally optional acts are *supererogatory*. They are above and beyond the call of duty. People who perform such acts are deserving of praise, but people who do not perform such acts are not deserving of blame. Rushing into a burning building to save a stranger and giving away all of your money to help the poor are examples of supererogatory acts. However, Act Utilitarianism does not have room for supererogation; it *requires* us to maximize happiness. It holds that people who rush into burning buildings and people who donate all of their money are merely doing their duty, not going beyond it. Worse yet, according to Act Utilitarianism, the rest of us who lead ordinary, non-heroic lives are shirking our duty.

## Non-Maximizing Act Utilitarianism

These and other problems may be avoided in various different ways without giving up Act Utilitarianism. One way is to abandon the demand to *maximize* happiness. Mill defines morally right and wrong acts in the following way: "actions are right in proportion as they tend to promote happiness, wrong as they tend to produce the reverse of happiness" (7). He seems to be making the following claims.

All acts expected to increase happiness are morally acceptable. The greater the increase, the better the act. All acts expected to decrease happiness are morally wrong. The greater the decrease, the worse the act. (Situations where there is no way to avoid producing unhappiness are exceptions. In such situations, the act which minimizes unhappiness is morally right, and the rest are morally wrong.)

This leaves room for lots of morally acceptable acts alongside the act that produces maximal happiness. Non-maximizing Act Utilitarianism does not require people to perform the best act in each situation, so complex calculations and precise information are typically unnecessary. Moreover, the set of optional acts is much larger, and it includes supererogatory acts. Because providing piano lessons for my daughter and telling my colleague a joke are good acts, I may do them even though there are morally better alternatives. Rushing into burning buildings and donating all of my money are very good acts but not morally required acts.

*

Serious problems remain, however. Non-maximizing Act Utilitarianism may require the correct set of acts, but some of its *recommendations* are counter-intuitive. Although Angela is not morally required to breed under Non-maximizing Act Utilitarianism, breeding is still *better* than not breeding because it produces more jollies. Similarly, although I am not required to subsidize the piano lessons of a strange child, Non-maximizing Act Utilitarianism considers doing so to be better than subsidizing the piano lessons of my own child.

Both varieties of Act Utilitarianism conflict with the common-sense belief that people have rights. Suppose Ned is a nasty person with no relatives or friends who spends his time making life miserable for others through gossip. Ned is hated by everyone in his small town. Act Utilitarianism seems to say that it is good, or even morally required, to kill Ned, for the overall benefit will be very large and the drawbacks small. Common sense, however, says that it is wrong to kill such people no matter how nasty they are, because people have the right to life.

Similarly, both varieties of Act Utilitarianism conflict with the common-sense view of justice. Act Utilitarianism seems to say that teachers should give A's to those who will be greatly pleased by receiving them and that judges should sentence criminals only when doing so will produce more pleasure than pain. According to common sense, however, justice requires teachers to give A's to all and only those people who do excellent work, and justice requires judges to sentence criminals in proportion to their crime.

## Rule Utilitarianism

Utilitarians respond to these criticisms in different ways. Some try to show that Act Utilitarianism only *seems* to conflict with common sense. Others acknowledge that the conflict is real and go on to reject common sense. Still others adopt a variant of Utilitarianism called Rule Utilitarianism that promises to reduce the conflict. Like the Act Utilitarian, the Rule Utilitarian believes that we should try to maximize happiness in the universe. However, the Rule Utilitarian does not believe that happiness will be maximized by seeking the greatest possible happiness on a case-by-case basis. Instead, the Rule Utilitarian proposes that people act on moral rules derived by performing certain thought experiments.

Let us work through an example. Suppose Ruth, a pregnant Rule Utilitarian, is trying to decide whether she should have an abortion. To find out, she needs to determine the moral rule concerned with killing. She begins by imagining the world in which almost everyone adopts the rule "Killing is always OK." She contrasts this world to the world in which almost everyone adopts the rule "Killing is always wrong." Obviously, the second world would be the happier world, so "Killing is always wrong" is closer to the truth than "Killing is always OK." Next she contrasts the second world with the world in which almost everyone adopts the rule "Killing is always wrong except in self-defense." Because the third world is happier than the second world, the rule "Killing is always wrong except in self-defense" is closer to the truth than "Killing is always wrong." This tells Ruth that an abortion would not be immoral killing (murder) if it were done in self-defense. If her case is not a case of self-defense (that is, if her life or well-being is not being threatened by continuation of

the pregnancy), then she must go on to consider other possible exceptions to the prohibition against killing. Eventually, Ruth will achieve a fairly precise approximation to the truth about killing. Using this approximation, she will be able to determine whether an abortion in her situation would violate the rule governing killing. This is not the end of the process, however. Even if abortion would not be murder in her case, it might be wrong for some other reason. Abortion might constitute promise breaking, for example. Thus Ruth must determine what the rule concerned with promise breaking says, using the same *world-comparison procedure* that she used to determine the rule concerned with killing. She must determine whether her case counts as a legitimate exception to the general prohibition of promise breaking. After Ruth has worked out all of the possible rules that abortion might violate, she will know whether an abortion in her situation would be morally permissible. She will also have made considerable progress toward the goal of listing all of the moral rules of Rule Utilitarianism.

This example brings out several aspects of Rule Utilitarianism. First, The Rule Utilitarian rejects the Greatest Happiness Principle. For the Rule Utilitarian,

> An act is right if and only if the act follows from a rule whose adoption by almost everyone would maximize happiness.

Second, note that Ruth never asks whether the real world would be happier if she obtained an abortion. That is not relevant to a Rule Utilitarian, although it would be relevant to an Act Utilitarian. Ruth follows the rules that, if universally followed, would maximize happiness in general, whether or not these rules do so in her case. Third, the rules of Rule Utilitarianism are *not* derived from common sense, from the laws or mores of society, from the *Bible*, or from anywhere else except the world-comparison procedure. The acts of Rule Utilitarians may *turn out* to conform to common sense, to laws, and so on. Indeed, Rule Utilitarians believe that these acts will so conform, and they consider this conformity to be one of the advantages of Rule Utilitarianism. But they do not simply adopt rules from non-Utilitarian sources.

Rule Utilitarianism has an account of rights and justice. This account begins with the concept of enforcing a rule. Whenever society prohibits a certain type of act (punishes a type of act with legal or social sanctions), there is a cost. Jollies are lost by those who impose the punishment (they must pay for police, jails, and so on), those who are blocked from performing acts they desire, those who are punished, and so on. Sometimes society gains more than it loses, of course. Now Mill says, "When we call anything a person's right, we mean that he has a valid claim on society to protect him in the possession of it, either by the force of law, or by that of education and opinion" (52). That is, if it is in the best interest of society to protect Gloria's possession of X, then Gloria has a *right* to X. On the other hand, if punishing people who deprive Gloria of X costs society more jollies than it gains, then Gloria does not have a right to X. For example, prohibiting theft obviously produces enough security and stability to outweigh the cost of enforcing the moral rule against theft. Thus people have a right to property. But society would lose more than it would gain by punishing infidelity, because only a very intrusive police force could reliably detect infidelity. Thus people do not have a right to fidelity.

Rule Utilitarians claim that their account of rights solves the main problems of Act Utilitarianism. For example, a Rule Utilitarian would not kill Ned, the nasty. Even though killing Ned might produce more happiness than not killing him, Ned has a right to life because it is in society's interest to punish murder. Similarly, a Rule Utilitarian would not give out undeserved A's or jail sentences. Even though in some individual cases, undeserved rewards or punishments might produce maximal happiness, people have a right to have such things distributed according to desert, because it is in society's interest to punish alternative distributions.

Rule Utilitarian *justice* consists in respecting rights. But Rule Utilitarianism includes more

than justice. Mill distinguishes between *perfect duties*, which we have toward particular, identifiable people, and *imperfect duties*, which we have toward no particular person. My duty to repay my debt is a perfect duty, for I owe it not to just anyone but rather to my debtor. My duty not to kill is owed not just to the people of my choice but rather to every person. My duty to help others, on the other hand, is not owed to any particular person. Rights generate perfect duties. That is, if I have a right to X, then someone has a perfect duty not to deprive me of X. For example, if Sarah has a right to be paid $5.00 by me, then I have a duty to pay Sarah $5.00. If I have a right to life, then everyone has a duty not to deprive me of life. But all imperfect duties and some perfect duties lack correlate rights. Thus morality, according to Rule Utilitarianism, demands that people do more than respect each other's rights. (Note that Rule Utilitarians and Kantians define perfect and imperfect duties somewhat differently.) [See the "Kant" section.]

Rule Utilitarianism aims to maximize happiness. Does it block morally optional acts and morally partial acts as the maximizing version of Act Utilitarianism does? The answer is unclear. Note, for example, that Rule Utilitarianism would *not* require or even encourage Ruth to have child after child. This is because a world in which almost everyone followed the rule "Have as many children as possible" would be an overpopulated, miserable world. Similarly, Rule Utilitarianism would not require or encourage me to provide piano lessons for a stranger rather than for my child. A world in which people neglected family and friendship claims would be an unhappy world.

*

Following Bentham, I have been assuming that all pleasures are commensurable. All pleasures can be expressed in terms of a single "common denominator," which I have called jollies. This assumption is necessary if there is to be a hedonistic calculus and if the Rule Utilitarian, world-comparison procedure is to be possible. However, Bentham's assumption is controversial. Some pleasures seem incommensurable. For example, the pleasure of eating an ice cream cone seems neither more nor less than the pleasure of solving a math problem. They are simply different sorts of pleasures.

So far I have been assuming that all pleasures count equally. Intellectual pleasures and sensual pleasures are on an equal footing. The sadistic pleasures of the wicked count for no less than the altruistic pleasures of the good. And so on. But common sense maintains that some pleasures should count for more than others and that some should not count at all. The pleasures of child molesters should not figure at all into the calculation of whether child molestation is right or wrong. Similarly, John Rawls objects that Rule Utilitarianism takes people's tastes as given and simply caters to them instead of discounting or changing people's tastes. It aims to maximize the satisfaction of already-existing desires. But the satisfaction of certain desires is obviously a bad thing.[4]

The main objection to Act Utilitarianism was that it endorsed the exploitation of individuals whenever a net gain of jollies would result. Rule Utilitarianism blocks this exploitation, for it allows society to punish people who break rules even in cases where violating the rule would maximize happiness. However, this is only a partial protection of the individual. According to common sense, rights are supposed to protect the individual not only against other individuals but also against society itself. Even if it is in society's best interest to take X away from an individual, society may not do so if the individual has a right to X. To use Ronald Dworkin's metaphor, rights are trumps that prevent society from exploiting individuals. But Rule Utilitarianism seems to endorse the exploitation of individuals so long as one can formulate a rule for doing so that will produce a net gain of jollies. That is, if following a certain rule will both exploit some people and maximize happiness, then according to Rule Utilitarianism, these people have no right not to be exploited. And such rules may be formulated. Carefully circumscribed slavery might well produce a maximally happy world. The increased leisure and wealth of a large majority might produce enough happiness to outweigh the unhappiness of a small

number of slaves. Thus a rule mandating such slavery would be OK, and the enslaving would violate no one's rights. Indeed, exploitation-justifying rules may easily be formulated by highly specific framing. For example, the world probably would be happier if everyone adopted the complex rule "Do not kill anyone except nasty persons with no relatives or friends who make life miserable for others" than if everyone adopted the simpler rule "Do not kill anyone." Hence it seems that the Rule Utilitarian is committed to this complex rule and, therefore, to the counter-intuitive killing of Ned, the nasty. Thus Rule Utilitarian rights are not the same as common-sense rights, for Rule Utilitarian rights allow the sacrifice of some people for the sake of the overall happiness of society.

Rule Utilitarians might reject such complex rules because they are insufficiently general. After all, if the rules become too specific, we end up with Act Utilitarianism. But how are we to determine where to draw the line between appropriate and excessive detail? What counts as "too specific"? Moreover, even if Rule Utilitarians can reject complex, overly specific rules, the main problem remains. Rule Utilitarian rights do not offer adequate protection when the interests of the individual conflict with the interests of society.

## Revised Rule Utilitarianism

To answer these challenges, the Rule Utilitarian must deploy a more sophisticated conception of happiness. Let us once more look to Mill for a suggestion about how to proceed. First of all, Mill denies that the satisfaction of desire is always pleasant or that all pleasure arises from the satisfaction of desire. Second, Mill denies that different sorts of pleasures are incommensurable. He does not abandon the hedonistic calculus and the world-comparison procedure. Third, although Mill believes that all pleasures are valuable, he denies that all pleasures are *equally* valuable with respect to happiness. "It is quite compatible with the principle of utility to recognize the fact that some kinds of pleasure are more desirable and more valuable than others" (8). Mill provides a method for determining which pleasures have greater weight. "Of two pleasures, if there be one to which all or almost all who have experience of both give a decided preference, irrespective of any feeling of moral obligation to prefer it, that is the more desirable pleasure" (8). Thus if pleasure of type A is preferred to pleasure of type B by an overwhelming majority of people who have sampled both and who are not biased by their moral feelings, then A is a higher-quality pleasure. Although many people might disagree, Mill is confident that the intellectual pleasures will turn out to be more valuable than the sensual ones, and the virtuous pleasures more valuable than the vicious ones, because of his view of happiness and human nature. According to Mill's view, happiness is a composite good consisting of pleasures grounded in our nature as human beings as well as pleasures arising out of the satisfaction of acquired desires. To be happy is not simply to amass lots of jollies. Instead, it is to achieve a certain combination of types of pleasure. The different types of pleasure are interrelated in complex ways, some blocking others, some sustaining and enhancing others, and so on. To gain certain types, one must forgo others. To increase certain types, one must combine them with certain others. Now the natural pleasures are fundamental. They are necessary preconditions for certain other types of pleasure. They are necessary for happiness. Moreover, the intellectual and virtuous pleasures are (or promote and enhance) the natural pleasures, whereas the sensual and vicious pleasures block or inhibit the natural pleasures. This is why the intellectual and virtuous pleasures are more valuable than the sensual and vicious pleasures.

Thus Revised Rule Utilitarianism does not assume that all pleasures count equally. Instead, in conformity with common sense, it gives greater weight to the intellectual and virtuous pleasures. Because it does not put all pleasures on an equal footing, Revised Rule Utilitarianism does not simply accept people's desires as given. Instead, it encourages the acquisition and satisfaction of desires compatible with human nature rather than desires that clash with human nature.

Fred Berger maintains that grounding happiness upon human nature enables Mill to rebut the accusation that Utilitarianism endorses the exploitation of some people for the sake of the overall good. According to Mill, people naturally need self-respect, respect for others, and benevolence in order to achieve happiness. But these virtues are not compatible with exploitation.

＊

I am somewhat skeptical about Berger's solution. It seems to me that people often maintain various virtues while exploiting other people. The exploiters simply happen to be ignorant of morally relevant facts. If you really believe that blacks are better off as slaves, that Ned is better off dead, that women are better off "protected" from employment outside of the home, and the like, then you may be a self-respecting, other-respecting, benevolent, happy exploiter. Exploitation may produce a net increase in happiness in a society with the right false beliefs.

Bernard Williams argues that all versions of Utilitarianism involve a counter-intuitive view of (a) responsibility for acts and (b) the virtue of integrity. Suppose Pedro will shoot twenty innocent people unless Jim agrees to shoot one. Utilitarianism says that Jim *should* shoot one. If he does not, then he is responsible for the deaths of the nineteen people he could have saved. But Williams says that (a) if Jim declines to shoot, then it is obviously Pedro rather than Jim who is responsible for the twenty deaths. Moreover, (b) if Jim is the sort of person for whom shooting would be absolutely abhorrent, incompatible with his deepest commitments, then a moral theory that requires him to shoot must be wrong.

A Utilitarian might reply to Williams as follows: (a) If Jim does not shoot, then *both* he and Pedro are fully responsible for the twenty deaths. There is no "Law of Conservation of Responsibility." (Pedro is also responsible for setting up the situation, of course.) Moreover, (b) there is nothing sacred about integrity. It is perfectly possible for a person to build a life around morally flawed ideals that *should* be violated in certain situations. Huck Finn was committed to the institution of slavery, for example. Nevertheless, he had a moral duty to help his enslaved friend escape. Jim may be committed to the ideal of never taking human life, but that commitment does not absolve him from killing when killing is morally required. His ideal, though hardly as bad as slavery, is morally flawed. Jim is too squeamish.

Finally, an Act Utilitarian might object, "You Rule Utilitarians are hypocrites. If you really believed in maximizing happiness, then you would try to do so in every case." A Rule Utilitarian might reply, "Trying to maximize happiness in every case is too cumbersome, and moreover, doing so conflicts with common sense." However, the Act Utilitarian might answer, "Adopt rules of thumb or reject common sense."

Do not give up on Utilitarianism merely because it is imperfect. As we will see, every moral theory is burdened with difficulties. Unlike many other moral theories, Utilitarianism, at least in principle, has an algorithm for solving moral problems. And that is extremely valuable. We often find ourselves approaching real moral problems from a Utilitarian perspective. For all of its drawbacks, Utilitarianism may be the best game in town.

## Notes

1. Plato, *Gorgias*, trans. W. Helmbolt (Indianapolis, IN: Bobbs-Merrill, 1952), pp. 60–65.
2. J. Bentham, *An Introduction to the Principles of Morals and Legislation* (London, 1789).
3. D. Parfit, *Reasons and Persons* (Oxford, England: Oxford University Press, 1984), pp. 358–359.
4. J. Rawls, *A Theory of Justice* (Cambridge, MA: Harvard University Press, 1971), p. 31.

# 15   Rule-Utilitarianism

## JOHN HOSPERS

1. In order to receive a high enough grade average to be admitted to medical school, a certain student must receive either an A or a B in one of my courses. After his final examination is in, I find, on averaging his grades, that his grade for the course comes out to a C. The student comes into my office and begs me to change the grade, on the ground that I have not read his paper carefully enough. So I reread his final exam paper, as well as some of the other papers in the class in order to get a better sense of comparison; the rechecking convinces me that his grade should be no higher than the one I have given him—if anything, it

should be lower. I inform him of my opinion and he still pleads with me to change the grade, but for a different reason. "I know I didn't deserve more than a C, but I appeal to you as a human being to change my grade, because without it I can't get into medical school, which naturally means a great deal to me." I inform him that grades are supposed to be based on achievement in the course, not on intentions or need or the worthiness of one's plans. But he pleads: "I know it's unethical to change a grade when the student doesn't deserve a higher one, but can't you please make an exception to the rule just this once?" And before I can reply, he sharpens his plea: "I appeal to you as a utilitarian. Your goal is the greatest happiness of everyone concerned, isn't it? If you give me only the grade I deserve, who will be happier? Not I, that's sure. Perhaps you will for a

*Rule-Utilitarianism* Excerpt from *Human Conduct: An Introduction to the Problem of Ethics* by John Hospers, 311–323, 325–328, with omissions, copyright © 1961 by Harcourt Brace & Company, Inc. and renewed © 1989 by John Hospers. Reprinted by permission of the publisher.

little while, but you have hundreds of students and you'll soon forget about it; and I will be ever so much happier for being admitted into a school that will train me for the profession I have always desired. It's true that I didn't work as hard in your course as I should have, but I realize my mistake and I wouldn't waste so much time if I had it to do over again. Anyway, you should be forward-looking rather than backward-looking in your moral judgments, and there is no doubt whatever that much more happiness will be caused (and unhappiness prevented) by your giving me the higher grade even though I fully admit that I don't deserve it."

After pondering the matter, I persist in believing that it would not be right to change the grade under these circumstances. Perhaps you agree with my decision and perhaps you don't, but *if* you agree that I should not have changed the grade, and *if* you are also a utilitarian, how are you going to reconcile such a decision with utilitarianism? *Ex hypothesi,* the greatest amount of happiness will be brought about by my changing the grade, so why shouldn't I change it?

Of course, if I changed the grade and went around telling people about it, my action would tend to have an adverse effect on the whole system of grading—and this system is useful to graduate schools and future employers to give some indication of the student's achievement in his various courses. But of course if I tell no one, nobody will know, and my action cannot set a bad example to others. This in turn raises an interesting question: If it is wrong for me to do the act publicly, is it any the less wrong for me to do it secretly?

2. A man is guilty of petty theft and is sentenced to a year in prison. Suppose he can prove to the judge's satisfaction that he would be happier out of jail, that his wife and family would too (they depend on his support), that the state wouldn't have the expense of his upkeep if he were freed, and that people won't hear about it because his case didn't hit the papers and nobody even knows that he was arrested—in short, everyone concerned would be happier and nobody would be harmed by his release. And yet, we feel,

or at least many people would, that to release him would be a mistake. The sentence imposed on him is the minimum permitted by law for his offense, and he should serve out his term in accordance with the law.

3. A district attorney who has prosecuted a man for robbery chances upon information which shows conclusively that the man he has prosecuted is innocent of the crime for which he has just been sentenced. The man is a wastrel who, if permitted to go free, would almost certainly commit other crimes. Moreover, the district attorney has fairly conclusive evidence of the man's guilt in prior crimes, for which, however, the jury has failed to convict him. Should he, therefore, "sit on the evidence" and let the conviction go through in this case, in which he knows the man to be innocent? We may not be able to articulate exactly *why,* but we feel strongly that the district attorney should not sit on the evidence but that he should reveal every scrap of evidence he knows, even though the revelation means releasing the prisoner (now known to be innocent) to do more crimes and be convicted for them later.

*X:* It seems to me that some acts are right or wrong, not *regardless* of the consequences they produce, but *over and above* the consequences they produce. We would all agree, I suppose, that you should break a promise to save a life but not that you should break it whenever you considered it probable (even with good reason) that more good effects will come about through breaking it. Suppose you had promised someone you would do something and you didn't do it. When asked why, you replied, "Because I thought breaking it would have better results." Wouldn't the promisee condemn you for your action, and rightly? This example is quite analogous, I think, to the example of the district attorney; the district attorney might argue that more total good will be produced by keeping the prisoner's innocence secret. Besides, if he is released, people may read about it in the newspaper and say, "You see, you can get by with anything these days" and may be encouraged to violate the law themselves as a result. Still, even though it would do more total good if the man were to remain convicted, wouldn't it be wrong to do so in view of the fact that he is definitely innocent of *this* crime? The law punishes a man, not necessarily because the most good will be achieved that way, but because he has committed a crime; if we don't approve of the law, we can do our best to have it changed, but meanwhile aren't we bound to follow it? Those who execute the law are sworn to obey it; they are *not* sworn to produce certain consequences.

*Y:* Yes, but remember that the facts *might* always come out after their concealment and that we can never be sure they won't. If they do, keeping the man in prison will be far worse than letting the man go; it will result in a great public distrust for the law itself; nothing is more demoralizing than corruption of the law by its own supposed enforcers. Better let a hundred human derelicts go free than risk that! You see, *one* of the consequences you always have to consider is the effect of *this* action on the *general practice* of lawbreaking itself; and when you bring in *this* consequence, it will surely weigh the balance in favor of divulging the information that will release the innocent man. So utilitarianism will still account quite satisfactorily for this case. I agree that the man should be released, but I do so on utilitarian grounds; I needn't abandon my utilitarianism at all to take care of this case.

*X:* But your view is open to one fatal objection. You say that one never can be sure that the news *won't* leak out. Perhaps so. But suppose that in a given case one *could* be sure; would that really make any difference? Suppose you are the only person that knows and you destroy the only existing evidence. Since you are not going to talk, there is simply no chance that the news will leak out, with consequent damage to public morale. Then is it all right to withhold the information? You see, I hold that if it's wrong not to reveal the truth when others might find out, then it's equally wrong not to reveal it when *nobody* will find out. You utilitarians are involved in the fatal error of making the rightness or wrongness of an act depend on whether performing it will ever be publicized. And I hold that it is immoral even to consider this condition; the district attorney

should reveal the truth regardless of whether his concealing it would ever be known.

*Y:* But surely you aren't saying that one should *never* conceal the truth? not even if your country is at war against a totalitarian enemy and revealing truths to the people would also mean revealing them to the enemy?

*X:* Of course I'm not saying that—don't change the subject. I am saying that *if* in situation S it is wrong to convict an innocent man, then it is equally wrong whether or not the public knows that it is wrong; the public's knowledge will certainly have bad consequences, but the conviction would be wrong anyway even *without* these bad consequences; so you can't appeal to the consequences of the conviction's becoming public as grounds for saying that the conviction is wrong. I think that you utilitarians are really stuck here. For you, the consideration "but nobody is ever going to know about it anyway" is a relevant consideration. It has to be; for the rightness of an act (according to you) is estimated in terms of its total consequences, and its total consequences, of course, include its effects (or lack of effects) on other acts of the same kind, and there won't be any such effects if the act is kept absolutely secret. You have to consider *all* the consequences relevant; the matter of keeping the thing quiet is one consequence; so you have to consider this one relevant too. Yet I submit to you that it isn't relevant; the suggestion "but nobody is going to know about it anyway" is not one that will help make the act permissible if it wasn't before. If anything, it's the other way round: something bad that's done publicly and openly is not as bad as if it's done secretly so as to escape detection; secret sins are the worst. . . .

*Y:* I deny what you say. It seems to me worse to betray a trust in public, where it may set an example to others, than to do so in secret, where it can have no bad effects on others.

*X:* And I submit that you would never say that if you weren't already committed to the utilitarian position. Here is a situation where you and practically everyone else would not hesitate to say that an act done in secret is no less wrong than when done in public, were it not that it flies in the face of a doctrine to which you have already committed yourself on the basis of quite different examples.

4. Here is a still different kind of example. We consider it our duty in a democracy to vote and to do so wisely and intelligently as possible, for only if we vote wisely can a democracy work successfully. But in a national election my vote is only one out of millions, and it is more and more improbable that *my* vote will have any effect upon the outcome. Nor is my failure to vote going to affect other people much, if at all. Couldn't a utilitarian argue this way: "My vote will have no effect at all—at least far, far less than other things I could be doing instead. Therefore, I shall not vote." Each and every would-be voter could argue in exactly the same way. The result would be that nobody would vote, and the entire democratic process would be destroyed.

What conclusion emerges from these examples? If the examples point at all in the right direction, they indicate that there are some acts which it is right to perform, even though by themselves they will not have good consequences (such as my voting), and that there are some acts which it is wrong to perform, even though by themselves they would have good consequences (such as sitting on the evidence). But this conclusion is opposed to utilitarianism as we have considered it thus far. . . .

## Rule-Utilitarianism and Objections to It

The batter swings, the ball flies past, the umpire yells "Strike three!" The disappointed batter pleads with the umpire, "Can't I have four strikes just this once?" We all recognize the absurdity of this example. Even if the batter could prove to the umpire's satisfaction that he would be happier for having four strikes this time, that the spectators would be happier for it (since most of the spectators are on his side), that there would be little dissatisfaction on the side of the opposition (who might have the game clinched anyway), and that there would be no effect on future baseball

games, we would still consider his plea absurd. We might think, "Perhaps baseball would be a better game—i.e., contribute to the greatest total enjoyment of all concerned—if four strikes were permitted. If so, we should change the rules of the game. But until that time, we must play baseball according to the rules which are now the accepted rules of the game."

This example, though only an analogy, gives us a clue to the kind of view we are about to consider—let us call it *rule-utilitarianism*. Briefly stated (we shall amplify it gradually), rule-utilitarianism comes to this: Each act, in the moral life, falls under a *rule;* and we are to judge the rightness or wrongness of the act, not by *its* consequences, but by the consequences of its universalization—that is, by the consequences of the adoption of the *rule* under which this act falls. This . . . interpretation of Kant's categorical imperative . . . differs from Kant in being concerned with consequences, but retains the main feature which Kant introduced, that of universalizability.

Thus: The district attorney may do more good in a particular case by sitting on the evidence, but even if this case has no consequences for future cases because nobody ever finds out, still, the general policy or *practice* of doing this kind of thing is a very bad one; it uproots one of the basic premises of our legal system, namely that an innocent person should not be condemned. Our persistent conviction that it would be wrong for him to conceal the evidence in this case comes *not* from the conviction that concealing the evidence will produce less good—we may be satisfied that it will produce more good in this case—but from the conviction that the *practice* of doing this kind of thing will have very bad consequences. In other words, "Conceal the evidence when you think that it will produce more happiness" would be a bad rule to follow, and it is because this *rule* (if adopted) would have bad consequences, not because *this* act itself has bad consequences, that we condemn the act.

The same applies in other situations: . . . perhaps I can achieve more good, in this instance, by changing the student's grade, but the consequences of the general practice of changing students' grades for such reasons as these would be very bad indeed; a graduate school or a future employer would no longer have reason to believe that the grade-transcript of the student had any reference to his real achievement in his courses; he would wonder how many of the high grades resulted from personal factors like pity, need, and irrelevant appeals by the student to the teacher. The same considerations apply also to the voting example: if Mr. Smith can reason that his vote won't make any difference to the outcome, so can Mr. Jones and Mr. Robinson and every other would-be voter; but if everyone reasoned in this way, no one would vote, and this *would* have bad effects. It is considered one's duty to vote, not because the consequences of one's not doing so are bad, but because the consequences of the general practice of not doing so are bad. To put it in Kantian language, the maxim of the action, if universalized, would have bad consequences. But the individual act of *your* not voting on a specific occasion—or of any *one* person's not voting, as long as *others* continued to vote—would probably have no bad consequences.

There are many other examples of the same kind of thing. If during a water shortage there is a regulation that water should not be used to take baths every day or to water gardens, there will be virtually no bad consequences if only *I* violate the rule. Since there will be no discernible difference to the city water supply and since my plants will remain green and fresh and pleasant to look at, why shouldn't I water my plants? But if everyone watered his plants, there would not be enough water left to drink. My act is judged wrong, not because of *its* consequences, but because the consequences of everyone doing so would be bad. If I walk on the grass where the sign says, "Do not walk on the grass," there will be no ill effects; but if everyone did so it would destroy the grass. There are some kinds of act which have little or no effect if any one person (or two, or three) does them but which have very considerable effects if everyone (or even just a large number) does them. Rule-utilitarianism is designed to take care of just such situations.

Rule-utilitarianism also takes care of situations which are puzzling in traditional utilitarianism,

. . . namely, the secrecy with which an act is performed. "But no one will ever know, so my act won't have any consequences for future acts of the same kind," the utilitarian argued; and we felt that he was being somehow irrelevant, even immoral: that if something is wrong when people know about it, it is just as wrong when done in secret. Yet this condition *is* relevant according to traditional utilitarianism, for if some act with bad consequences is never known to anyone, this ignorance does mitigate the bad consequences, for it undeniably keeps the act from setting an example (except, of course, that it may start a habit in the agent himself). Rule-utilitarianism solves this difficulty. If I change the student's grade in secret, my act is wrong, in spite of its having almost no consequences (and never being known to anyone else), because if I change the grade and don't tell anyone, how do I know how many other teachers are changing their students' grades without telling anybody? It is the result of the *practice* which is bad, not the result of my single action. The result of the practice is bad whether the act is done in secret or not: the result of the practice of changing grades in secret is just as bad as the results of the practice done in full knowledge of everyone; it would be equally deleterious to the grading system, equally a bad index of a student's actual achievement. In fact, if changing grades is done in secret, this in one way is worse; for prospective employers will not know, as they surely ought to know in evaluating their prospective employees, that their grades are not based on achievement but on other factors such as poverty, extra-curricular work load, and persuasive appeal.

*Rule-utilitarianism* is a distinctively twentieth-century amendment of the utilitarianism of Bentham and Mill, often called *act-utilitarianism.* . . . Since this pair of labels is brief and indicates clearly the contents of the theories referred to, we prefer these terms to a second pair of labels, which are sometimes used for the same theories: *restricted utilitarianism* as opposed to *unrestricted* (or extreme, or *traditional) utilitarianism.* (Whether or not Mill's theory is strictly act-utilitarianism is a matter of dispute. Mill never made the distinction between act-utilitarianism and rule-utilitarianism.

. . . Some of Mill's examples, however, have to do not with individual acts but with general principles and rules of conduct. Mill and Bentham were both legislators, interested in amending the laws of England into greater conformity to the utilitarian principle; and to the extent that Mill was interested in providing a criterion of judging rules of conduct rather than individual acts, he may be said to have been a rule-utilitarian.)

Much more must be said before the full nature of the rule-utilitarian theory becomes clear. To understand it better, we shall consider some possible questions, comments, and objections that can be put to the theory as thus far stated.

1. Doesn't the . . . problem arise here . . . of *what* precisely we are to universalize? Every act can be put into a vast variety of classes of acts; or, in our present terminology, every act can be made to fall under many different general rules. Which rule among this vast variety are we to select? We can pose our problem by means of an imaginary dialogue referring back to Kant's ethics and connecting it with rule-utilitarianism:

*A:* Whatever may be said for Kant's ethics in general, there is one principle of fundamental importance which must be an indispensable part of every ethics—the principle of universalizability. If some act is right for me to do, it would be right for all rational beings to do it; and if it is wrong for them to do it, it would be wrong for me too.

*B:* If this principle simply means that nobody should make an exception in his own favor, the principle is undoubtedly true and is psychologically important in view of the fact that people constantly do make exceptions in their own favor. But as it stands I can't follow you in agreeing with Kant's principle. Do you mean that if it is wrong for Smith to get a divorce, it is also wrong for Jones to do so? But this isn't so. Smith may be hopelessly incompatible with his wife, and they may be far better off apart, whereas Jones may be reconcilable with his wife (with some mutual effort) and a divorce in his case would be a mistake. Each case must be judged on its own merits.

*A:* The principle doesn't mean that if it's right for one person, A, to do it, it is therefore right for B

and C and D to do it. It means that if it's right for one person to do it, it is right for anyone *in those circumstances* to do it. And Jones isn't in the same circumstances as Smith. Smith and his wife would be better off apart, and Jones and his wife would be better off together.

*B:* I see. Do you mean *exactly* the same circumstances or *roughly* the same (similar) circumstances?

*A:* I think I would have to mean exactly the same circumstances for if the circumstances were not quite alike, that little difference might make the difference between a right act (done by Smith) and a wrong act (done by Jones). For instance, if in Smith's case there are no children and in Jones' case there are, this fact may make a difference.

*B:* Right. But I must urge you to go even further. Two men might be in exactly the same *external* circumstances, but owing to their *internal constitution* what would be right for one of them wouldn't be for the other. Jones may have the ability to be patient, impartial, and approach problems rationally, and Smith may not have this ability; here again is a relevant difference between them, although not a difference in their external circumstances. Or: Smith, after he reaches a certain point of fatigue, would do well to go fishing for a few days—this would refresh and relax him as nothing else could. But Jones dislikes fishing; it tries and irritates and bores him; so even if he were equally tired and had an equally responsible position, he would not be well advised to go fishing. Or again: handling explosives might be all right for a trained intelligent person, but not for an ignorant blunderbuss. In the light of such examples as these, you see that under the "same circumstances" you'll have to include not only the external circumstances in which they find themselves but their own internal character.

*A:* I grant this. So what?

*B:* But now your universalizability principle becomes useless. For two people never *are* in exactly the same circumstances. Nor can they be: if Smith were in exactly the same circumstances as Jones, including all his traits of character, his idiosyncrasies, and his brain cells, he would *be* Jones. You see, your universalizability principle is inapplicable. It would become applicable only under conditions (two people being the same person) which are self-contradictory—and even if not self-contradictory, you'll have to admit that two exactly identical situations never occur; so once again the rule is inapplicable.

*A:* I see your point; but I don't think I need go along with your conclusion. Smith and Jones should do the same thing only if their situation or circumstances are the same in certain *relevant respects.* The fact that Jones is wearing a white shirt and Smith a blue one, is a difference of circumstances, but, surely, an *irrelevant* difference, a difference that for moral purposes can be ignored. But the fact that Smith and his wife are emotionally irreconcilable while Jones and his wife could work things out, would be a morally relevant circumstance.

*B:* Possibly. But how are you going to determine which differences are relevant and which are not?

Kant . . . never solved this problem. He assumed that "telling a lie" was morally relevant but that "telling a lie to save a life" was not; but he gave no reason for making this distinction. The rule-utilitarian has an answer.

Suppose that a red-headed man with one eye and a wart on his right cheek tells a lie on a Tuesday. What rule are we to derive from this event? Red-headed men should not tell lies? People shouldn't lie on Tuesdays? Men with warts on their cheeks shouldn't tell lies on Tuesdays? These rules seem absurd, for it seems so obvious that whether it's Tuesday or not, whether the man has a wart on his cheek or not, has nothing whatever to do with the rightness of his action—these circumstances are just *irrelevant.* But this is the problem: how are we going to establish this irrelevance? What is to be our criterion?

The criterion we tried to apply . . . was to make the rule more *specific:* instead of saying, "This is a lie and is therefore wrong," . . . we made it more specific and said, "This is a lie told to save a life and is therefore right." We could make the rule more specific still, involving the precise circumstances in which this lie is told, other than the

fact that it is told to save a life. But, now it seems, the use of greater specificity will not always work: instead of "Don't tell lies," suppose we say, "Don't tell lies on Tuesdays." The second is certainly more specific than the first, but is it a better rule? It seems plain that it is not—that its being a Tuesday is, in fact, wholly irrelevant. Why?

"Because," says the rule-utilitarian, "there is no difference between the effects of lies told on Tuesdays and the effects of lies told on any other day. This is simply an empirical fact, and because of this empirical fact, bringing in Tuesday is irrelevant. If lies told on Tuesdays always had good consequences and lies told on other days were disastrous, then a lie's being told on a Tuesday would be relevant to the moral estimation of the act; but in fact this is not true. Thus there is no advantage in specifying the subclass of lies, 'lies told on Tuesdays.' The same is true of 'lies told by redheads' and 'lies told by persons with warts on their cheeks.' The class of lies can be made more specific—that is no problem—but not more *relevantly* specific, at least not in the direction of Tuesdays and redheads. (However, the class can be made more relevantly specific considering certain other aspects of the situation, such as whether the lie was told to produce a good result that could not have been brought about otherwise.)"

Consider by contrast a situation in which the class of acts can easily be made relevantly more specific. A pacifist might argue as follows: "I should never use physical violence in any form against another human being, since if everyone refrained from violence, we would have a warless world." There are aspects of this example that we cannot discuss now, but our present concern with it is as follows. We can break down violence into more specific types such as violence which is unprovoked, violence in defense of one's life against attack by another, violence by a policeman in catching a lawbreaker, violence by a drunkard in response to an imaginary affront. The effects of these subclasses of violence do differ greatly in their effects upon society. Violence used by a policeman in apprehending a lawbreaker (at least under some circumstances, which could be spelled out) and violence used in preventing a would-be murderer from killing you, do on the whole have good effects; but the unprovoked violence of an aggressor or a drunkard does not. Since these subclasses do have different effects, therefore, it *is* relevant to consider them. Indeed, it is imperative to do so: the pacifist who condemns *all* violence would probably, if he thought about it, not wish to condemn the policeman who uses violent means to prevent an armed madman from killing a dozen people. In any event, the effects of the two subclasses of acts are vastly different; and, the rule-utilitarian would say, it is accordingly very important for us to consider them—to break down the general class of violent acts into more specific classes and consider separately the effects of each one until we have arrived at subclasses which cannot *relevantly* be made more specific.

How specific shall we be? Won't we get down to "acts of violence to prevent aggression, performed on Tuesdays at 11:30 P.M. in hot weather" and subclasses of that sort? And aren't these again plainly irrelevant? Of course they are, and the reason has already been given: acts of violence performed on Tuesdays, or at 11:30 P.M., or by people with blue suits, are no different in their effects from acts-of-violence-to-prevent-aggression done in circumstances other than these; and therefore these circumstances, though more specific, are not relevantly more specific. When the consequences of these more specific classes of acts differ from the consequences of the more general class, it is this specific class which should be considered; but when the consequences of the specific classes are not different from those of the more general class, the greater specificity is irrelevant and can be ignored.

The rule, then, is this: we should consider the consequences of the general performance of certain classes of actions only if that class contains within itself no subclasses, the consequences of the general practice of which would be either better or worse than the consequences of the class itself.

Let us take an actual example of how this rule applies. Many people, including Kant, have taken the principle "Thou shalt not kill" as admitting of no exceptions. But as we have just seen, such principles can be relevantly made more specific.

Killing for fun is one thing, killing in self-defense another. Suppose, then, that we try to arrive at a general rule on which to base our actions in this regard. We shall try to arrive at that rule the general following of which will have the best results. Not to kill an armed bandit who is about to shoot you if you don't shoot him first, would appear to be a bad rule by utilitarian standards; for it would tend to eliminate the good people and preserve the bad ones; moreover, if nobody resisted aggressors, the aggressors, knowing this, would go hog-wild and commit indiscriminate murder, rape, and plunder. Therefore, "Don't kill except in self-defense" (though we might improve this rule too) would be a better rule than "Never kill." But "Don't kill unless you feel angry at the victim" would be a bad rule, because the adoption of this rule would lead to no end of indiscriminate killing for no good reason. The trick is to arrive at the rule which, if adopted, would have the very best possible consequences (which includes, of course, the absolute minimum of bad consequences). Usually no simple or easily statable rule will do this, the world being as complex as it is. There will usually be subclasses of classes-of-acts which are relevantly more specific than the simple, general class with which we began. And even when we think we have arrived at a satisfactory rule, there always remains the possibility that it can relevantly be made more specific, and thus amended, with an increase in accuracy but a consequent decrease in simplicity.

To a considerable extent most people recognize this complexity. Very few people would accept the rule against killing without some qualifications. However much they may preach and invoke the rule "Thou shall not kill" in situations where it happens to suit them, they would never recommend its adoption in all circumstances: when one is defending himself against an armed killer, almost everyone would agree that killing is permissible, although he may not have formulated any theory from which this exception follows as a logical consequence. Our practical rule against killing contains within itself (often not explicitly stated) certain *classes of exceptions:* "Don't kill *except* in self-defense, in war against an aggressor nation, in carrying out the verdict of a jury recommending capital punishment." This would be a far better rule—judged by its consequences—than any simple one-line rule on the subject. Each of the classes of exceptions could be argued pro and con, of course. But such arguments would be empirical ones, hinging on whether or not the adoption of such classes of exceptions into the rule would have the maximum results in intrinsic good. (Many would argue, for example, that capital punishment achieves no good effects; on the other hand, few would contend that the man who pulls the switch at Sing Sing is committing a crime in carrying out the orders of the legal representatives of the state.) And there may always be other kinds of situations that we have not previously thought of, situations which, if incorporated into the rule, would improve the rule—that is, make it have better consequences; and thus the rule remains always open, always subject to further qualification if the addition of such qualification would improve the rule.

These qualifications of the rule are not, strictly speaking, *exceptions* to the rule. According to rule-utilitarianism, the rule, once fully stated, admits of no exceptions; but there may be, and indeed there usually are, numerous classes of exceptions *built into the* rule; a simple rule becomes through qualification a more complex rule. Thus, if a man kills someone in self-defense and we do not consider his act wrong, we are not making him an exception to the rule. Rather, his act *falls under* the rule—the rule that includes killing in self-defense as one of the classes of acts which is permissible (or, if you prefer, the rule that includes self-defense as one of the circumstances in which the rule against killing does not apply). Similarly, if a man parks in a prohibited area and the judge does not fine him because he is a physician making a professional call, the judge is not extending any favoritism to the physician; he is not making the physician an exception to the rule; rather, the rule (though it may not always be written out in black and white) includes within itself this recognized class of exceptions—or, more accurately still, the rule includes within itself a reference to just this kind of situation, so that the action of the judge in exonerating the physician is just as much an application of the rule (not an

exception to it) as another act of the same judge in imposing a fine on someone else for the same offense.

We can now see how our previous remarks about acts committed in secret fit into the rule-utilitarian scheme. On the one hand, the rule "Don't break a promise except (1) under extreme duress and (2) to promote some very great good" is admittedly somewhat vague, and perhaps it could be improved by still further qualification; but at least it is much better than the simple rule "Never break promises." On the other hand, the rule "Don't break a promise except when nobody will know about it" is a bad rule: there are many situations in which keeping promises is important . . . situations in which promises could not be relied on if this rule were adopted. That is why, among the circumstances which excuse you from keeping your word, the fact that it was broken in secret is not one of them—and for a very good reason: if this class of exceptions were incorporated into the rule, the rule's adoption would have far worse effects than if it did not contain such a clause. . . .

Rule-utilitarianism and act-utilitarianism are alike with regard to relativism. They are *not* relativistic in that they have one standard, one "rule of rules," one supreme norm, applicable to all times and situations: "Perform that act which will produce the most intrinsic good" (act-utilitarianism), "Act according to the rule whose adoption will produce the most intrinsic good" (rule-utilitarianism). But within the scope of that one standard, the recommended rules of conduct may well vary greatly from place to place. . . . In a desert area the act of wasting water will cause much harm and is therefore wrong, but it is not wrong in a region where water is plentiful. In a society where men and women are approximately equal in number, it will be best for a husband to have only one wife; but in a society in which there is great numerical disparity between the two, this arrangement may no longer be wise. So much for act-utilitarianism; the same goes for rule-utilitarianism. The rule "Never waste water" is a good rule, indeed an indispensable rule, in a desert region but not in a well-watered region. Monogamy seems to be the best possible marital system in our society but not necessarily in all societies—it depends on the conditions. What are the best acts and the best rules at a given time and place, then, depends on the special circumstances of that time and place. Some conditions, of course, are so general that the rules will be much the same everywhere: a rule against killing (at least within the society) is an indispensable condition of security and survival and therefore must be preserved in all societies.

The situation, then, is this: Rule or Act A is right in circumstances $C_1$, and rule or Act B is right in circumstances $C_2$. In X-land circumstances $C_1$ prevail, so A is right; and in Y-land circumstances $C_2$ prevail, so B is right. Perhaps this is all the relativism that ethical relativists will demand.

4. Can't there be, in rule-utilitarianism, a conflict of rules? Suppose you have to choose between breaking a promise and allowing a human life to be lost. . . . What would the rule-utilitarian say? Which rule are we to go by?

No rule-utilitarian would hold such a rule as "Never break a promise" or "Never take a human life." Following such rigid, unqualified rules would certainly not lead to the best consequences —for example, taking Hitler's life would have had better consequences than sparing him. Since such simple rules would never be incorporated into rule-utilitarian ethics to begin with, there would be no conflict between these rules. The rule-utilitarian's rule on taking human life would be of the form, "Do not take human life except in circumstances of types A, B, C . . ." and these circumstances would be those in which taking human life *would* have the best consequences. And the same with breaking promises. Thus, when the rules in question are fully spelled out, there would be no conflict.

In any event, if there were a conflict between rules, there would have to be a second-order rule to tell us which first-order rule to adopt in cases of conflict. Only with such a rule would our rule-utilitarian ethics be *complete*, i.e., made to cover every situation that might arise. But again such a second-order rule would seldom be simple. It would not say, "In cases of conflict between preserving a life and keeping a promise, always preserve the life." For there might always be kinds of cases in which this policy would not produce the best consequences: a president who has promised something to a whole nation or who has signed a treaty with other nations which depend on that treaty being kept and base their own national policies upon it, would not be well advised to say simply, "In cases of conflict, always break your word rather than lose one human life." In cases of this kind, keeping the promise would probably produce the best results, though the particular instance would have to be decided empirically. We would have to go through a detailed empirical examination to discover which rule, among all the rules we might adopt on the matter, would have the best consequences if adopted.

5. Well then, why not just make the whole thing simple and say, "Always keep your promises except when breaking them will produce the most good," "Always conserve human life except when taking it will produce the most good"? In other words, "In every case do what will have the best consequences"—why not make this the Rule of Rules? To do so is to have act-utilitarianism with us once again; but why not? It there anything more obvious in ethics than that we should always try to produce the most good possible?

"No," says the rule-utilitarian, "not if this rule means that we should always do the individual *act* that produces the most good possible. We must clearly distinguish rules from acts. 'Adopt the rule which will have the best consequences' is different from 'Do the act which will have the best consequences.' (When you say, 'Always do the most good,' this is ambiguous—it could mean either one.)" The rule-utilitarian, of course, recommends the former in preference to the latter; for if everyone were to do acts which (taken individually) had the best consequences, the result would *not* in every case be a policy having the best consequences. For example, my not voting but doing something else instead may produce better consequences than my voting (my voting may have no effect at all); your not voting will do the same; and so on for every individual, as long as most *other* people vote. But the results would be very bad, for if each individual adopted the policy of not voting, nobody would vote. In other words, the rule "Vote, except in situations where not voting will do more good" is a rule which, if followed, would *not* produce the best consequences.

Another example: The rule "Don't kill except where killing will do the most good"—which the act-utilitarian would accept—is not, the rule-utilitarian would say, as good a rule to follow as "Don't kill except in self-defense . . ." (and other classes of acts which we discussed earlier). That is, the rule to prohibit killing except under special kinds of conditions specified in advance would do more good, if followed, than the rule simply to refrain except when not refraining will do more good. The former is better, not just because people will rationalize themselves into believing that what they want to do will produce the most good in a particular situation (though this is very important), but also because when there are certain

standard classes of exceptions built into the rule, there will be a greater *predictability* of the results of such actions; the criminal will know what will happen if he is caught. If the law said, "Killing is prohibited except when it will do the most good," what could you expect? Every would-be killer would think it would do the most good in his specific situation. And would you, a potential victim, feel more secure or less secure, if such a law were enacted? Every criminal would think that he would be exonerated even if he were caught, and every victim (or would-be victim) would fear that this would be so. The effects of having such a rule, then, would be far worse than the effects of having a general rule prohibiting killing, with certain classes of qualifications built into the rule.

There is, then, it would seem, a considerable difference between act-utilitarianism and rule-utilitarianism.

# 16  Mill's Theory of Justice

## FRED BERGER

A brief survey of the problems of justice that have been posed for utilitarians is in order, for it is in this area that many believe that definitive objections to utilitarian theories are to be found. The objections all stem from the fact that utilitarian theories are "consequentialist," that is, they judge the rightness or wrongness of acts by their consequences. Duties of justice, however, appear to have bases in considerations other than consequences, or in considerations other than that good consequences have been maximized or not.

Consequentialist theories are said to be "aggregative" theories; they require amassing goods through action. The chief duty (it is alleged) for a consequentialist is to produce the greatest amount

From Fred Berger, *Happiness, Justice, and Freedom: The Moral and Political Philosophy of John Stuart Mill* (University of California Press, 1984), 124–126, 131–133, 159–163, 167–171, with omissions. Used by permission of the University of California Press.

of happiness, or pleasure, or whatever else is taken as good in the theory of value. . . . Since it is the *amount* of good that is produced, and that alone, the consequentialist must be indifferent toward distributions of utilities except insofar as distributions affect the total produced. In a great many cases, then, the utilitarian seems to be required to act in ways that are unjust because they ignore principles that require certain distributions of good.

The most glaring of these problems concern rights. To assert that someone has a right does not entail that his acting in the way protected by the right will produce the best consequences, nor does the statement that the person's right should be respected entail anything about the consequences of doing so. If you agree to pay me for a service I perform, it would be wrong of you to sit down to calculate the consequences of paying me or not when payment time arrives (except in very unusual circumstances). Here, the duty is based on a "backward-looking" consideration—the fact that you made an agreement with me to pay for the service. The existence of the duty does not depend on the calculation of probable future consequences. I have a *right* to your payment which should constrain how you *distribute* goods in the future through your action.

Moreover, if maximizing good is one's overall duty, considerations of fairness seem to go by the boards. A distribution of the economic pie, for example, that concentrated it in the hands of a privileged few would be preferred to a more fair distribution if, by so concentrating it, a larger "pie" was thereby produced. At the extreme, it has been claimed that utilitarianism permits sacrificing the liberty of some for the greater good of others.[1] In addition, duties of fairness in cooperative ventures seem to be inexplicable in utilitarian terms. If a group of people are engaged in a mutually beneficial scheme that requires following rules or otherwise restricting behavior, it is held by some to be a violation of "fair play" not to do one's part when it comes one's turn.[2] The basis of such a duty seems to reside in the fact that one has received benefits from the sacrifices of others, *not* on the basis of a calculation of future utility to be produced by cooperation in the particular case. The person who takes benefits but fails to do his or her part is said to be a "freeloader" on the scheme—an epithet of disapprobation.

These problems of distribution appear to present especial embarrassment for hedonistic and eudaemonistic utilitarians since enormous increases in certain frivolous or even degraded pleasures would warrant deprivations of important rights of others. Thus, if a great many persons derive great enjoyment from seeing a person humiliated on stage,[3] doing so seems not only right, but a duty on the part of those who have it within their power to bring this about. If pushpin is as good as poetry, then suppress poetry if that will vastly increase the total amount of enjoyment obtained from pushpin and few get any pleasure from poetry. It is easy to see that a wide range of injustices in daily life might be generated in this way. A teacher assigning grades would distribute them, not according to the merits of performance, but according to the contribution to happiness that different grades would make; a judge dealing with litigants in court would no longer determine statuses and treatment in accord with the legal rights and duties applicable to the case, but in accord with what decision will be most productive of pleasure, happiness, and so on.

Finally, the utilitarian conception of morality has been thought to treat persons as mere receptacles of pleasure and pain, or "units" of happiness and unhappiness. Two defects are thought to spring from this. In the first place, the view ignores the "separateness" of persons; it results in overlooking respect for persons as such and their "inviolability" as persons.[4] Thus, persons are treated as means to be used for the ends of others, not as ends in themselves. The second alleged defect in the utilitarian conception of persons and morality is that since it is concerned with producing a maximum of pleasure or happiness, it can give no role to *desert* in allocating the good. But the notion of *desert* is crucial to retributive justice—only the guilty deserve punishment. A utilitarian scheme, however, could, in theory at least, permit punishing innocent people if that would thereby maximize the general well-being.

*If* these charges can be sustained, I think few philosophers would be willing to hold to utilitarianism as an acceptable theory. Except for certain of the details, all of these criticisms were made against utilitarianism in Mill's day, or were conceived of by him. He believed these either not to be consequences of his theory, or not defects if they did, indeed, follow. I shall attempt to reconstruct his account of justice and outline some of the chief defenses he could or did make to the objections. . . . Mill thought of duties of justice as given by rules, and . . . at a certain point in his analysis he introduced reference to rules as part of the very idea of justice. That he should have been led to think in terms of rules at this stage of his discussion is easy enough to explain in light of two points: (1) he placed great stress on the need for rules in practical morality; (2) he maintained that justice protects our interest in security, hence, conformity to rule would further promote it.

In another place, however, Mill made a stronger point about the relation of rules and justice that not only capitalizes on the points just mentioned, but . . . also explains his reference to rules as part of the idea of justice. In a letter to George Grote, he said:

human happiness, even one's own, is in general more successfully pursued by acting on general rules, than by measuring the consequences of each act; and this is still more the case with the general happiness, since any other plan would not only leave everybody uncertain what to expect, but would involve perpetual quarrelling: and hence general rules must be laid down for people's conduct to one another, or in other words rights and obligations must, as you say, be recognised; and people must, on the one hand, not be required to sacrifice even their own less good to another's greater, where no general rule has given the other a right to the sacrifice; while when a right *has* been recognised, they must, in most cases, yield to that right even at the sacrifice, in the particular case, of their own greater good to another's less. These rights and obligations are (it is of course implied) reciprocal. And thus what each person is held to do for the sake of others is more or less definite, corresponding to the less perfect knowledge he can have of their interests, taken individually; and he is free to employ the indefinite residue of his exertions in benefitting the one person of whom he has the principal charge, and whose wants he has the means of learning the most completely.[5]

Several points of importance are made in the letter. General rules are needed in order to achieve most successfully the end of happiness, and this is due, in part, to difficulties of knowledge and the need for regularity of conduct. The rules of justice, then, are a device for achieving the end of happiness. But the rules of justice are of a special kind—they specify rights and reciprocal obligations. Thus, for the most part, in determining what one should do, one would base action on the rights that bear on the case. Rights, then, should play an important role in ordinary reasoning about morality.

It is extremely important to stress the conceptual connection between rights and rules. For many of the objections to a utilitarian theory of justice can be met by stressing this point, together with other points made by Mill in the letter to Grote. For example, act-utilitarian theories seem to make the existence of a right depend on the consequences of acts in the particular case. But this is not how right claims are supported. Also, the act-utilitarian appears committed to overriding a right whenever it is perceived that greater utility will thereby be produced, even if the gain is quite small. Rights, however, cannot be overridden in this way if they are to be taken seriously. Mill's theory . . . has neither of these untoward consequences. The possession of a right (either recognized or claimed) is a matter of the rules of justice that are applicable, not a matter of the utilities of the particular case. Although rights in a particular case can be overridden, only very unusual circumstances could justify this, since the device of rights is meant to forestall calculation in each case, and the security they protect would be endangered if the belief that small gains would be obtained by violation were taken as ground for ignoring a right. . . .

It is useful at this stage to give a summary statement of the necessary and sufficient conditions for someone to have a right according to Mill's theory of justice. I believe the following captures Mill's conception of a right: A person has a right to *X* (i.e., perform some act, be treated by others in a certain way, to have some thing, and so on), if, and only if, there is, or ought to be, a recognized moral rule that requires society not to interfere with, and to protect, the person's exercise of, enjoyment of, possession of *X*. Society's "protection," for Mill, consists in providing some means of punishment, legal or social (e.g., in the form of public opinion), for violations. It follows from this conception of a right, together with the Principle of Utility, that someone can (truly) claim a moral right to some mode of behavior or treatment if, and only if, it is something that it is in the general social interest to protect as a matter of recognized rule. If, on the other hand, it is *not* something the systematic, general protection of which would be useful, then it is not something the person can claim as a right.

In all of his discussions of justice, Mill referred to the "rules of justice," and he discussed a number of these rules in various places.[6] For the most part, however, he was concerned with arguing in these places that there are a number of such rules, all of which in some circumstances appear sacred and inviolable, but that contrary rules can be cited which appear equally compelling, and, hence, that utility must be consulted to resolve the conflicts. A consequence of Mill's special concern with justice is that we are not left with a very clearly articulated substantive theory of justice—an account of which principles Mill would hold, under what conditions, for what reasons, or *how* utility is to decide among them. Fortunately, Mill wrote on substantive moral issues, and from these writings it is possible to ferret out a somewhat systematic set of principles and values that constitute the elements of Mill's substantive theory of justice. . . .

I want to show that Mill held what I shall term a "baseline" conception of equality. This conception can be summarized in four propositions:

1. Substantive inequalities of wealth, education, and power are *prima facie* wrong, and require justification.
2. Substantive inequalities must not permit any to "go to the wall"; redistribution to provide subsistence must be guaranteed.
3. Inequalities must not undermine the status of persons as *equals*. In concrete terms, this means that inequalities must not result in some gaining complete power over the lives of others, or in some persons being degraded.
4. Only *certain* kinds of grounds serve to justify inequality—that the inequality will make no one worse off, or that it is the result of rewarding according to desert. Advantages must be *earned* through voluntary effort.

These propositions imply that inequalities must not be permitted to push anyone below a certain "baseline": minimum means to happiness must be guaranteed as a right to all; status as a full-fledged participant in the common social life must be guaranteed as a right. Furthermore, as I shall try to show below, Mill did not have an "overriding" commitment to property, or even to the principle of desert; he was willing to interfere with both in order to preserve "baseline" equality. Though no "welfare-statist," he certainly had no absolutist objections to income transfers or redistributive taxation in order to preserve the equality I have described.

The four propositions define a conception of equality in the sense that they specify minimal conditions for distributions that would guarantee status as equals. Adherence to these propositions would secure for everyone a share in the goods needed to preserve dignity and independence. Power and wealth would be restricted so that one would not be subjected to the arbitrary will of others. On the other hand, the conception specifies grounds for departures from strict equality that do not necessarily undercut equal status. Inequalities that do not violate the other conditions can be justified if they have been earned. Thus, these propositions provide a conception of what it is to have the moral status of an equal of others in a complex society. . . .

The first important argument for equality involves Mill's claim that modern life, and civilization itself, increasingly require equality. Mill maintained that a definitive feature of civilization is the extent to which cooperation takes place. Joint efforts for common goals are spurred by increasing civilization. Cooperation spurs greater productivity, and one result is an increase in capital accumulation and its spread to the masses.[7] An increase in cooperation, and the concomitant division of labor, create a greater interdependence among persons. Indeed, he held that in modern life, the most crucial elements of, or conditions for, happiness are secured by society:

As civilization advances, every person becomes dependent, for more and more of what most nearly concerns him, not upon his own exertions, but upon the general arrangements of society. In a rude state, each man's personal security, the protection of his family, his property, his liberty itself, depend greatly upon his bodily strength and his mental energy or cunning: in a civilized state, all this is secured to him by causes extrinsic to himself.[8]

Historically speaking, increased literacy has resulted, along with a corresponding increase in the powers of communication among the masses. As property, intelligence, and the "power of combination" are all sources of power, the lower classes have, and will continue to, gain power as against that of the higher classes.[9] These levelling tendencies inherent in civilization will result in a feeling among the working classes against all inequalities, and, he held, "the only way of mitigating that feeling is to remove all inequalities that can be removed without preponderant disadvantages."[10] Mill also maintained that there are certain prerequisites for societal cohesion and permanence. Among these is that there be a source of allegiance or loyalty for members of the society, and, for the reasons given, the only such sources likely to be successful in the future are "the principles of individual freedom and political and social equality, as realized in institutions which as yet exist nowhere, or exist only in a rudimentary state."[11]

A second reason to be found in Mill's writing in favor of equality is that inequality has harmful effects on those at the lower end of the scale. He wrote that great inequalities of "wealth and social rank" have a "demoralizing effect" on the disadvantaged.[12] He also maintained that the state has a duty to compensate for natural inequalities, for "in the race of life all do not start fair," so that if the state fails to act "the unfairness becomes utterly crushing and dispiriting."[13] While we may question on what basis it should be judged at the outset that the failure of the state to act is "unfair," at the very least it is indeed plausible to argue that those left behind at the starting line will be "crushed and dispirited" if not assisted. In addition, Mill maintained that everyone is stimulated to greater exertion when "all start fair," thus citing a further consequential ground for compensating natural disadvantage.[14]

Other bad effects were cited by Mill as resulting from those inequalities that leave some in "abject poverty." A laboring class kept in such status is likely to be kept in a state of subjection, unable to have an autonomous role in the common social and political life.[15] One of the chief elements in a happy life is utterly defeated.

Even the wage relationship was condemned by Mill for its inherent inequalities and the bad consequences for laborers. The wage relationship creates a social arrangement in which the parties have hostile interests, and one party—the laborer —is left in a position of dependency on the capitalist. Again, the central value of autonomy is defeated, and Mill insisted that the aim of improvement should be to enable people to work with or for one another "in relations not involving dependence."[16]

A third reason Mill gave for promoting equality was that inequality has bad effects on those who are *favored*. In a social situation marked by large inequalities of means and power, those who rule have a tendency to underestimate the interests of those less well off, and to give greater emphasis to the interests of those with whom they identify. In his own society, he believed that a result of inequality was that the sense of obligation was "lamentably unequal." Consequently:

The comfort and suffering of one man, on the foreknowledge of which all rational sense of obligation towards him is based, counts in general estimation for something infinitely more than that of another man in a different rank or position. The great mass of our labouring population have no representatives in Parliament, and cannot be said to have any political station whatever; while the distribution of what may be called social dignity is more unequal in England than in any other civilized country of Europe, and the feeling of communion and brotherhood between man and man more artificially graduated according to the niceties of the scale of wealth. Assuming perfect rectitude of intentions on the part of a statesman, it is hardly possible that his moral calculations should not be more or less vitiated by the impurities of such an atmosphere.[17]

At times, Mill put his point more strongly, by emphasizing that the exercise of power over others, especially when the power has not been earned, morally corrupts those who are so favored. Large-scale inequalities of wealth and social status were both implicated on these grounds. It is not the *amount* of wealth that corrupts, but inequality itself, especially when it is not merited and has been obtained without personal exertion.[18] The relation of superiors to inferiors, he wrote, "is the nursery of these [selfish] vices of character, which, wherever else they exist, are an overflowing from that source."[19] Among these vices are pride, wilfulness, overbearingness, arrogance, self-indulgence; if left unrestrained, unearned indulgence of power can lead to actual physical cruelty.[20] Though some of these last points were made in connection with the marriage relationship, it is clear that Mill thought the points can be generalized. He described the marriage relationship as one example of "the corrupting influence of power," and wrote that it is true of servitude "except when it actually brutalizes," that it is corrupting to both but "less so to the slaves than to the slave-masters."[21]

Unearned luxury has the further effect, according to Mill, of deadening and enervating the mind. Contrary to those who claim pleasure has this effect, he insisted that the impetus to exercise one's intellect and talents is lessened when one's fortunes are secure and unquestioned without personal effort. . . .[22]

## Basic Principles

The most basic principle of economic justice in Mill's work is the principle that economic rewards should be proportioned to one's labor, or exertions. In several places, he criticized the economic arrangements of his day for permitting some to "be born to the enjoyment of all the external advantages which life can give, without earning them by any merit or acquiring them by any exertion of their own."[23] Throughout his work, we see some economic arrangement or other condemned or supported by appeal to its inconsistency or congruence with this principle.

I know of no argument by Mill to support this principle. He did refer to it as an "acknowledged" principle of justice,[24] and there is no question that he believed the principle to be accepted by the socialists and capitalists of his day. He depicted the former group as *standing* on this principle as a basis for criticizing contemporary social arrangements, and, he described the injustice of a scheme that violates the principle as "obvious."[25] . . .

What seems most likely to me is that Mill thought the basic principle of economic reward to be a part of "natural justice," that is, it is one of those natural reactions to the efforts of ourselves and others within an economic framework to desire that those efforts be met with reward. He described the principle of private property as a

"natural impression of justice," and he most likely thought of the more general principle in the same way. Indeed, he described the "socialist" principle that all should be born to equal advantages as also a "natural impression." The "natural impressions" of justice must be adjudicated by appeal to utility —"the tendency of things to promote or impede human happiness."[26] If I am right, then the general account of desert as being based on natural feelings produced by conduct fits Mill's account of economic justice as well.

A second important principle of economic (and political) justice that Mill employed requires that the distribution of economic goods must not permit some to gain unrestrained power or control over the lives of others. It should be recalled that part of Mill's argument for what I termed "baseline equality" involved this principle. I pointed out that he condemned the wage relationship partly because it involves objectionable relations of dependence. Further, he consistently argued that the state has the right to regulate the accumulation and use of land (which he contrasted with "movable property"), partly on the ground that control of land in excess of that needed for personal subsistence results in some having power over others, and in ways that affect "their most vital interests."[27]

Given the great value attributed to individual autonomy in Mill's theory of value, it is almost axiomatic that there should be a right to autonomy, at least in the sense of imposing a duty on society not to interfere with autonomous behavior except for self-protection. Mill's theory of liberty was, in fact, a branch of his theory of justice, and is best understood as an extended argument for a right to act as an autonomous agent. It would follow that if society permits economic accumulation that results in the destruction of autonomy, it fails to protect a basic right (and a basic element of happiness), and thus is unjust.

In addition, Mill believed that governmental power in a community tends to mirror the real power in a society.[28] Economic power can be crucial, especially if inequalities reach a state where some are kept in abject poverty. Such a state results in being kept under subjection by the privileged classes, and autonomy is impossible.[29] We should expect, then, that Mill would endorse a corollary to the principle opposing economic distribution that permits domination. The corollary would, at the least, require redistributive efforts to guarantee at least a minimal level of subsistence. I argued earlier that such a principle played a role in Mill's conception of "baseline" equality, and he did favor redistribution—in the form of taxation exemptions and the Poor Laws—that would maintain minimal support levels.

Mill did not stop short at favoring redistribution to rectify unjust socially induced inequality. As we saw earlier, he used the analogy of "the race of life," in arguing that the state must act so that some are not left behind at the starting point, and he described the failure to redress natural inequalities as "unfair."[30] He condemned greater taxation of the poor and weak because they derive protection from the state they otherwise could not provide themselves as "the reverse of the true idea of distributive justice, which consists not in imitating but in redressing the inequalities and wrongs of nature."[31]

To be sure, the analogy of "the race of life" is misleading. As Robert Nozick correctly points out: "life is not a race in which we all compete for a prize which someone has established; there is no unified race, with some person judging swiftness"; but then, neither is "life" as Nozick has described it:

there are different persons separately giving other persons different things. Those who do the giving (each of us, at times) usually do not care about desert or about the handicaps labored under; they care simply about what they actually get. No centralized process judges people's use of the opportunities they had; that is not what the processes of social cooperation and exchange are *for.*[32]

Indeed, life is not a race in the literal sense Nozick describes. Still, some people, *as things exist,* are permitted to accumulate goods, or the means to goods, that others, *due largely to matters of birth,* cannot obtain because the existing "processes of social cooperation and exchange" permit distribution to ignore need and desert. While Mill wrote of inequalities of "nature," a nat-

ural feature of a person, *in a social setting,* is a handicap or inequality only to the extent that that natural feature is a basis for disadvantage, or makes it more difficult to achieve a basis for reward. The "processes of social cooperation and exchange" are not *for* any purpose outside of the social ends to which they are put. Thus, life *is* somewhat racelike in that there is a measure of competition for things, and the terms of social and economic interchange can impose penalties on some by virtue of natural features of persons. Whether any natural feature is a "handicap" in getting one's needs met depends on how society *chooses* to require or permit distributions of things,[33] as well as on the things valued in that society.[34]

Finally, there is a negative corollary to the principles already picked out, to which Mill systematically appealed. This principle states that it is wrong to *penalize* industry and thrift, or unnecessarily interfere with liberty. The previously stated principles directly entail this principle, of course, but Mill sometimes appealed to it directly, citing the utilitarian grounds which support it, and the more general principles from which it follows. For example, in *Considerations on Representative Government,* he argued that a taxation scheme that "does not impede the industry, or unnecessarily interfere with the liberty, of the citizen" both preserves and promotes the increase of community wealth, while encouraging "a more active use of the individual faculties."[35]

Before I embark on showing how these basic principles of economic justice were employed by Mill, it is important that I clarify their status. These principles are extremely general and have been formulated in abstract, even vague terms. For example, I have stated the first principle as basing reward on "merit or exertion." Mill used these terms himself. But he used others as well, such as "industry," "sacrifice," "contribution," and "effort." Not all of these are equivalent, and where they do not coincide in meaning, there can arise conflicts that raise serious problems of justice. As an instance, in a cooperative venture, there can be conflicting demands on the benefits produced based on the actual contribution as opposed to the actual sacrifice on the part of workers. While there are good utilitarian reasons to reward those with greater skill when they actually employ it in production, the skills themselves may involve "natural" advantages to which the workers are born, and which they have not earned or merited. Mill was aware of such subtleties, and he did not suppose that abstract principles of the sorts I have enunciated can alone resolve such conflicts.[36]

There is a further problem in formulating the rights that can be claimed are correlated with these "principles" of justice. What, specifically, is entailed by the principle that natural inequalities are to be redressed? Do people have a right that their physical appearance will play no role in determining their life prospects? In what *areas* of life could such a right be asserted: job hiring? choice of marriage partners? Of course, some of the rights that would be needed to realize some of the principles given could require taking things or income, or demanding labor from others. What limits must be observed here, and what would justify doing *any* of these things at all? While I do not think these are insuperable problems that show there cannot *be* rights that correlate with principles such as those I have attributed to Mill, these difficulties show at least that I have not adequately formulated definitive principles.

In these respects, it may be claiming too much to call the formulations I have given "principles." It may be better to regard them as stating important, relevant, considerations in determining the justice of economic arrangements. This attitude is, perhaps, underscored, when one considers that Mill thought all such principles require utilitarian justification in their application.

## Notes

1. John Rawls, *A Theory of Justice* (Cambridge, Mass.: Harvard University Press, 1971), p. 26. Robert Nozick carries the point a step further and maintains that utilitarianism permits the total sacrifice of persons for the greater good of all. See Robert Nozick, *Anarchy, State, and Utopia* (New York: Basic Books, Inc. 1974), pp. 30–33.

2. H. L. A. Hart, "Are There Any Natural Rights?" *The Philosophical Review* 64 (1955), 185. A similar view is

maintained by Rawls (*A Theory of Justice,* p. 112). Later in his book, Rawls elaborates important qualifications, and distinguishes the principle of fairness from a "natural" duty to support and further just institutions (pp. 333–335).

3. I have based the example on an actual case in which an "artist" arranged a "show" of a mentally retarded man sitting unmoving in a chair. I mention this in case the reader should think the suggestion too bizarre to be worth taking up.

4. There are claims of this sort to be found in Rawls, *A Theory of Justice,* pp. 22–27, and in Nozick, *Anarchy, State and Utopia,* pp. 30–33.

5. *The Later Letters, CW* XV:762.

6. Most notably in chapter 5 of *Utilitarianism,* which I have been discussing, and in his review, "Thornton on Labour and Its Claims," *CW,* V:631–668.

7. "Civilization," pp. 123–125. The same points are made in his essay on *Democracy in America,* where he argued that de Tocqueville had mistakenly attributed these consequences to advancing democracy, rather than to the greater degree of civilization in modern life ("De Tocqueville on Democracy in America [II]," *CW,* XVIII:192).

8. "Civilization," p. 129.

9. "De Tocqueville on Democracy in America [II]," p. 163.

10. "The Savings of the Middle and Working Classes," *CW,* V:419.

11. "Coleridge," *CW,* X:134.

12. Ibid., p. 123.

13. "Centralisation," p. 591.

14. Ibid., p. 591.

15. "De Tocqueville on Democracy in America [II]," p. 166.

16. *Principles of Political Economy,* pp. 766–769.

17. "Taylor's Statesman," pp. 636–637. These bad effects on the judgment of wielders of power were reiterated in *Considerations on Representative Government,* pp. 444–445.

18. "Use and Abuse of Political Terms," *CW,* XVIII:12.

19. *The Subjection of Women,* in *Essays on Sex Equality,* ed. Alice S. Rossi (Chicago: The University of Chicago Press, 1970), p. 165.

20. Ibid., pp. 163–164.

21. Ibid., p. 213.

22. "The Spirit of the Age," in *Essays on Politics and Culture,* ed. Gertrude Himmelfarb (Garden City, NY: Doubleday & Company, Inc., 1962), pp. 25–27.

23. "Vindication of the French Revolution", pp. 388–389; also: *Autobiography,* p. 239; and "Newman's Political Economy," *CW,* V:443; *Principles of Political Economy,* pp. 207–208.

24. *Autobiography,* p. 239.

25. "Newman's Political Economy," pp. 443–444.

26. "Newman's Political Economy," pp. 443.

27. "Coleridge," pp. 157–158.

28. Ibid., p. 154.

29. "De Tocqueville on Democracy in America [II]," p. 166.

30. "Centralisation," p. 591.

31. *Principles of Political Economy,* p. 808.

32. Nozick, *Anarchy, State, and Utopia,* pp. 235–236.

33. The point that "natural disadvantage" is not an expression that is neutral with respect to social context is extremely important in a variety of contexts. Richard Wasserstrom has pointed out that we can so construct our physical environment that people who cannot walk can nevertheless lead a normal life involving access to buildings, seating at concerts, movies, lectures, and so on. The effect of natural features of persons depends on how we structure the natural and social environment. Wasserstrom uses this point to argue that natural differences between the sexes need not be a basis for imposing social disadvantage (see "Racism and Sexism," in *Philosophy and Social Issues* [Notre Dame, Ind.: University of Notre Dame Press, 1980], pp. 32–33).

34. Actually, Nozick acknowledges some force to the claim that there is a duty on society to make the competitive aspects of economic life fairer. He provides two counterexamples to such a principle, however (both of which seem to me irrelevant to any formulation of such a principle for which anyone wants to argue). His major objection, however, is that rights to "equality of opportunity, life, and so on," require material things and actions to which others may have rights. This "substructure of particular rights," Nozick contends, forms a barrier against the assertion of any general rights of the kind needed for equalizing the competition; "no rights exist in conflict with this substructure of particular rights" (Nozick, *Anarchy, State, and Utopia,* p. 238). Mill would reject this notion that such rights are inviolable, especially when they *avowedly* do not turn on desert or merit. There is little by way of argument by Nozick for his extraordinary claim, anyway.

35. *Considerations on Representative Government,* p. 387.

36. In the *Chapters on Socialism,* for example, he canvassed the various sorts of desert bases that might be claimed in a communist economic arrangement, using the points made as a basis for holding that there would be need of a "dispensing power" or authority for apportioning work. He thought that competition would spring up for the management positions, which could result in dissension (*Chapters on Socialism,* pp. 743–745). A similar discussion of the difficulties of determining desert bases is found in *Principles of Political Economy,* pp. 206–207.

# 17   A Critique of Utilitarianism

## BERNARD WILLIAMS

(1) George, who has just taken his Ph.D. in chemistry, finds it extremely difficult to get a job. He is not very robust in health, which cuts down the number of jobs he might be able to do satisfactorily. His wife has to go out to work to keep them, which itself causes a great deal of strain, since they have small children and there are severe problems about looking after them. The results of all this, especially on the children, are damaging. An older chemist, who knows about this situation, says that he can get George a decently paid job in a certain laboratory, which pursues research into chemical and biological warfare. George says that he cannot accept this, since he is opposed to chemical and biological warfare. The older man replies that he is not too keen on it himself, come to that, but after all George's refusal is not going to make the job or the laboratory go away; what is more, he happens to know that if George refuses the job, it will certainly go to a contemporary of George's who is not inhibited by any such scruples and is likely if appointed to push along the research with greater zeal than George would. Indeed, it is not merely concern for George and his family, but (to speak frankly and in confidence) some alarm about this other man's excess of zeal, which has led the older man to offer to use his influence to get George the job . . . George's wife, to whom he is deeply attached, has views (the details of which need not concern us) from which it follows that at least there is nothing particularly wrong with research into CBW. What should he do?

(2) Jim finds himself in the central square of a small South American town. Tied up against the wall are a row of twenty Indians, most terrified, a

From *Utilitarianism: For and Against* (Cambridge University Press, 1973), 97–118 with omissions. Reprinted with the permission of Cambridge University Press.

few defiant, in front of them several armed men in uniform. A heavy man in a sweat-stained khaki shirt turns out to be the captain in charge and, after a good deal of questioning of Jim which establishes that he got there by accident while on a botanical expedition, explains that the Indians are a random group of the inhabitants who, after recent acts of protest against the government, are just about to be killed to remind other possible protestors of the advantages of not protesting. However, since Jim is an honoured visitor from another land, the captain is happy to offer him a guest's privilege of killing one of the Indians himself. If Jim accepts, then as a special mark of the occasion, the other Indians will be let off. Of course, if Jim refuses, then there is no special occasion, and Pedro here will do what he was about to do when Jim arrived, and kill them all. Jim, with some desperate recollection of school-boy fiction, wonders whether if he got hold of a gun, he could hold the captain, Pedro and the rest of the soldiers to threat, but it is quite clear from the set-up that nothing of that kind is going to work: any attempt at that sort of thing will mean that all the Indians will be killed, and himself. The men against the wall, and the other villagers, understand the situation, and are obviously begging him to accept. What should he do?

To these dilemmas, it seems to me that utilitarianism replies, in the first case, that George should accept the job, and in the second, that Jim should kill the Indian. Not only does utilitarianism give these answers but, if the situations are essentially as described and there are no further special factors, it regards them, it seems to me, as *obviously* the right answers. But many of us would certainly wonder whether, in (1), that could possibly be the right answer at all; and in the case of (2), even one who came to think that perhaps that was the answer, might well wonder whether it was obviously the answer. Nor is it just a question of the rightness or obviousness of these answers. It is also a question of what sort of considerations come into finding the answer. A feature of utilitarianism is that it cuts out a kind of consideration which for some others makes a difference to what they feel about such cases: a consideration involv-

ing the idea, as we might first and very simply put it, that each of us is specially responsible for what *he* does, rather than for what other people do. This is an idea closely connected with the value of integrity. It is often suspected that utilitarianism, at least in its direct forms, makes integrity as a value more or less unintelligible. I shall try to show that this suspicion is correct. . . .

. . . I want to consider now two types of effect that are often invoked by utilitarians, and which might be invoked in connexion with these imaginary cases. The attitude or tone involved in invoking these effects may sometimes seem peculiar; but that sort of peculiarity soon becomes familiar in utilitarian discussions, and indeed it can be something of an achievement to retain a sense of it.

First, there is the psychological effect on the agent. Our descriptions of these situations have not so far taken account of how George or Jim will be after they have taken the one course or the other; and it might be said that if they take the course which seemed at first the utilitarian one, the effects on them will be in fact bad enough and extensive enough to cancel out the initial utilitarian advantages of that course. Now there is one version of this effect in which, for a utilitarian, some confusion must be involved, namely that in which the agent feels bad, his subsequent conduct and relations are crippled and so on, *because he thinks that he has done the wrong thing*—for if the balance of outcomes was as it appeared to be *before* invoking this effect, then he has not (from the utilitarian point of view) done the wrong thing. So that version of the effect, for a rational and utilitarian agent, could not possibly make any difference to the assessment of right and wrong. However, perhaps he is not a thoroughly rational agent, and is disposed to have bad feelings, whichever he decided to do. Now such feelings, which are from a strictly utilitarian point of view irrational—nothing, a utilitarian can point out, is advanced by having them—cannot, consistently, have any great weight in a utilitarian calculation. I shall consider in a moment an argument to suggest that they should have no weight at all in it. But short of that, the utilitarian could reasonably say that such feelings should not be encouraged, even if we accept their existence, and that to give them a lot of weight is to encourage them. Or, at the very best, even if they are straightforwardly and without any discount to be put into the calculation, their weight must be small: they are after all (and at best) one man's feelings.

That consideration might seem to have particular force in Jim's case. In George's case, his feelings represent a larger proportion of what is to be weighed, and are more commensurate in character with other items in the calculation. In Jim's case, however, his feelings might seem to be of very little weight compared with other things that are at stake. There is a powerful and recognizable appeal that can be made on this point: as that a refusal by Jim to do what he has been invited to do would be a kind of self-indulgent squeamishness. That is an appeal which can be made by other than utilitarians—indeed, there are some uses of it which cannot be consistently made by utilitarians, as when it essentially involves the idea that there is something dishonourable about such self-indulgence. But in some versions it is a familiar, and it must be said a powerful, weapon of utilitarianism. One must be clear, though, about what it can and cannot accomplish. The most it can do, so far as I can see, is to invite one to consider how seriously, and for what reasons, one feels that what one is invited to do is (in these circumstances) wrong, and in particular, to consider that question from the utilitarian point of view. When the agent is not seeing the situation from a utilitarian point of view, the appeal cannot force him to do so; and if he does come round to seeing it from a utilitarian point of view, there is virtually nothing left for the appeal to do. If he does not see it from a utilitarian point of view, he will not see his resistance to the invitation, and the unpleasant feelings he associates with accepting it, *just* as disagreeable experiences of his; they figure rather as emotional expressions of a thought that to accept would be wrong. He may be asked, as by the appeal, to consider whether he is right, and indeed whether he is fully serious, in thinking that. But the assertion of the appeal, that he is being self-indulgently squeamish, will not itself answer that question, or even help to answer it,

since it essentially tells him to regard his feelings just as unpleasant experiences of his, and he cannot, by doing that, answer the question they pose when they are precisely not so regarded, but are regarded as indications of what he thinks is right and wrong. If he does come round fully to the utilitarian point of view then of course he will regard these feelings just as unpleasant experiences of his. And once Jim—at least—has come to see them in that light, there is nothing left for the appeal to do, since *of course* his feelings, so regarded, are of virtually no weight at all in relation to the other things at stake. The "squeamishness" appeal is not an argument which adds in a hitherto neglected consideration. Rather, it is an invitation to consider the situation, and one's own feelings, from a utilitarian point of view.

The reason why the squeamishness appeal can be very unsettling, and one can be unnerved by the suggestion of self-indulgence in going against utilitarian considerations, is not that we are utilitarians who are uncertain what utilitarian value to attach to our moral feelings, but that we are partially at least not utilitarians, and cannot regard our moral feelings merely as objects of utilitarian value. Because our moral relation to the world is partly given by such feelings, and by a sense of what we can or cannot "live with," to come to regard those feelings from a purely utilitarian point of view, that is to say, as happenings outside one's moral self, is to lose a sense of one's moral identity; to lose, in the most literal way, one's integrity. . . .

## Integrity

The [two] situations have in common that if the agent does not do a certain disagreeable thing, someone else will, and in Jim's situation at least the result, the state of affairs after the other man has acted, if he does, will be worse than after Jim has acted, if Jim does. The same, on a smaller scale, is true of George's case. I have already suggested that it is inherent in consequentialism that it offers a strong doctrine of negative responsibility: if I know that if I do $X$, $O_1$ will eventuate, and if I refrain from doing *X*, $O_2$ will, and that $O_2$ is worse than $O_1$, then I am responsible for $O_2$ if I refrain voluntarily from doing *X*. "You could have prevented it," as will be said, and truly, to Jim, if he refuses, by the relatives of the other Indians. . . . [But] what occurs if Jim refrains from action is not solely twenty Indians dead, but *Pedro's killing twenty Indians*. . . . That may be enough for us to speak, in some sense, of Jim's responsibility for that outcome, if it occurs; but it is certainly not enough, it is worth noticing, for us to speak of Jim's *making* those things happen. For granted this way of their coming about, he could have made them happen only by making Pedro shoot, and there is no acceptable sense in which his refusal makes Pedro shoot. If the captain had said on Jim's refusal "you leave me with no alternative," he would have been lying, like most who use that phrase. While the deaths, and the killing, may be the outcome of Jim's refusal, it is misleading to think, in such a case, of Jim having an *effect* on the world through the medium (as it happens) of Pedro's acts; for this is to leave Pedro out of the picture in his essential role of one who has intentions and projects, projects for realizing which Jim's refusal would leave an opportunity. Instead of thinking in terms of supposed effects of Jim's projects on Pedro, it is more revealing to think in terms of the effects of Pedro's projects on Jim's decision. . . .

Utilitarianism would do well . . . to acknowledge the evident fact that among the things that make people happy is not only making other people happy, but being taken up or involved in any of a vast range of projects, or—if we waive the evangelical and moralizing associations of the word—commitments. One can be committed to such things as a person, a cause, an institution, a career, one's own genius, or the pursuit of danger. . . .

On a utilitarian view . . . [t]he determination to an indefinite degree of my decisions by other people's projects is just another aspect of my unlimited responsibility to act for the best in a causal framework formed to a considerable extent by their projects.

The decision so determined is, for utilitarianism, the right decision. But what if it conflicts with some project of mine? This, the utilitarian will say, has already been dealt with: the satisfaction to you of fulfilling your project, and any satisfaction to others of your so doing, have already been through the calculating device and have been found inadequate. Now in the case of many sorts of projects, that is a perfectly reasonable sort of answer. But in the case of projects of the sort I have called "commitments," those with which one is more deeply and extensively involved and identified, this cannot just by itself be an adequate answer, and there may be no adequate answer at all. For, to take the extreme sort of case, how can a man, as a utilitarian agent, come to regard as one satisfaction among others, and a dispensable one, a project or attitude round which he has built his life, just because someone else's projects have so structured the causal scene that that is how the utilitarian sum comes out?

The point here is not, as utilitarians may hasten to say, that if the project or attitude is that central to his life, then to abandon it will be very disagreeable to him and great loss of utility will be involved. . . . On the contrary, once he is prepared to look at it like that, the argument in any serious case is over anyway. The point is that he is identified with his actions as flowing from projects and attitudes which in some cases he takes seriously at the deepest level, as what his life is about (or, in some cases, this section of his life—seriousness is not necessarily the same as persistence). It is absurd to demand of such a man, when the sums come in from the utility network which the projects of others have in part determined, that he should just step aside from his own project and decision and acknowledge the decision which utilitarian calculation requires. It is to alienate him in a real sense from his actions and the source of his action in his own convictions. It is to make him into a channel between the input of everyone's projects, including his own, and an output of optimistic decision; but this is to neglect the extent to which *his* actions and *his* decisions have to be seen as the actions and decisions which flow from the projects and attitudes with which he is most closely identified. It is thus, in the most literal sense, an attack on his integrity.

[T]he immediate point of all this is to draw one particular contrast with utilitarianism: that to reach a grounded decision . . . should not be regarded as a matter of just discontinuing one's reactions, impulses and deeply held projects in the face of the pattern of utilities, nor yet merely adding them in—but in the first instance of trying to understand them.

Of course, time and circumstances are unlikely to make a grounded decision, in Jim's case at least, possible. Very often, we just act, as a possibly confused result of the situation in which we are engaged. That, I suspect, is very often an exceedingly good thing.

## Questions

1. Choose any *two* of the following statements. Explain what the two statements mean. Why does Mill think that they are true? Do you agree with Mill? Why or why not?

   a. "The objectors to utilitarianism . . . say it is exacting too much to require that people shall always act from the inducement of promoting the general interest of society. But this is to mistake the very meaning of a standard of morals and confound the rule of action with the motive of it. It is the business of ethics to tell us what are our duties, or by what test we may know them; but no system of ethics requires that the sole motive of all we do shall be a feeling of duty" (17).

   b. "The only proof that a sound is audible is that people hear it. . . . In a like manner, I apprehend, the sole evidence it is possible to produce that anything is desirable is that people actually desire it. No reason can be given why the general happiness is desirable, except that each person, so far as he believes it to be attainable, desires his own happiness. . . . But it has not, by this alone, proved itself to be the sole criterion. To do that, it would seem necessary to show, not only that people desire happiness, but that they never desire anything else. . . . But does the utilitarian doctrine deny that people desire virtue, or maintain that virtue is not a thing to be desired? The very reverse. . . . The ingredients of happiness are very various and each of them is desirable in itself. . . . [B]esides being means, they are a part of the end. Virtue according to the utilitarian doctrine, is not naturally and originally part of the end, but it is capable of becoming so" (34).

   c. "It is better to be a human being dissatisfied than a pig satisfied; better to be Socrates dissatisfied than a fool satisfied. And if the fool, or the pig, are of a different opinion, it is because they only know their own side of the question. The other party to the comparison knows both sides" (10).

   d. "Again, defenders of utility often find themselves called upon to reply to such objections as this—that there is not time, previous to action, for calculating and weighing the effects of any line of conduct on the general happiness. This is exactly as if anyone were to say that it is impossible to guide our conduct by Christianity because there is not time, on every occasion on which anything has to be done, to read through the Old and New Testaments. . . . Nobody argues that the art of navigation is not founded on astronomy because sailors cannot wait to calculate the Nautical Almanac. Being rational creatures, they go to sea with it ready calculated; and all rational creatures go out upon the sea of life with their minds made up on the common questions of right and wrong" (23–24).

2. You are the sheriff in a small Texas town. A brutal rape/murder has been committed. There is no clue to who the murderer is, but somehow a rumor that the murderer is black has spread throughout the town. An ugly mob has formed. It is on the verge of rampaging through the black section of town, killing everyone in its path. You cannot reason with the mob, and you do not have the power to stop the mob. Indeed your only deputy is hiding under his bed. Things look grim!! Suddenly, an idea occurs to you. You grab the

first black male you see and present him to the mob, saying, "Here is the murderer." The mob does exactly what you expect. They lynch him and disperse. You have saved many lives. Are you proud of yourself? Are the Act Utilitarians proud of you? Are the Rule Utilitarians proud of you? Why or why not?

3. Let us invent another sort of Utilitarian theory parallel to Rule Utilitarianism called *Virtue Utilitarianism*. The Virtue Utilitarian holds that happiness will be maximized by performing acts that flow from moral virtues derived by performing certain thought experiments. First, for each particular moral problem the Virtue Utilitarian lists the various possible relevant character traits. Second, for each character trait the Virtue Utilitarian imagines a world in which almost everyone possesses that character trait. Third, the Virtue Utilitarian compares these worlds. The right character trait is the one that corresponds to the happiest world. The Virtue Utilitarian thus generates a collection of virtues. Finally, the Virtue Utilitarian uses these virtues to determine what to do in particular cases. Thus, for the Virtue Utilitarian, what makes an act right is that the act flows from a character trait whose adoption by almost everyone would maximize happiness. Would the Virtue Utilitarian agree with Aristotle about what the virtues of a good person are? (That is, would they agree about which character traits belong on the list of virtues?) Would the Virtue Utilitarian agree with Aristotle about how to define each of the virtues of a good person?

4. Now that we have completed our study of Rule Utilitarianism, it is time for a final, critical assessment. Answer the following questions about the rules of Rule Utilitarianism. Defend your answers.

Do these rules form a *consistent* moral system? That is, do any of them conflict with each other? If so, explain Rule Utilitarianism's mechanism for resolving such conflicts. That is, explain how Rule Utilitarianism assigns priorities to rules. Does Rule Utilitarianism assign the right priorities to its rules?

Do these rules form a *complete* moral system? That is, are there any rules that you believe to be rules of morality and that are not among the rules of Rule Utilitarianism? If so, could you amend Rule Utilitarianism to include the missing rules while preserving the "flavor" of Utilitarianism?

Do these rules form a *plausible* moral system? That is, do the rules conflict in some way with common sense? If so, could you amend Rule Utilitarianism so as to bring it into harmony with common sense while preserving the "flavor" of Utilitarianism?

5. Explain the distinction between Act Utilitarianism and Rule Utilitarianism. Give an Act Utilitarian analysis *and* a Rule Utilitarian analysis of *one* of the following questions.

a. Some professors penalize late papers; others do not even accept them. (If the paper is not accepted, the student gets an F for that paper, of course.) Should I penalize late papers or should I not even accept them?

b. Sally is HIV+. If a potential sexual partner asks about her HIV status, then Sally tells the truth, but if a potential sexual partner does not ask, then Sally does not volunteer the information. Is Sally's practice of keeping silent morally OK?

c. The board of directors of your church, synagogue, or mosque is considering giving a substantial amount of money to a charitable organization that sends food and medicine to people in famine-stricken countries. Do they have a moral duty to vote for this gift?

d. Suppose that a bill banning pornography is being considered in the legislature. Do the legislators have a moral duty to vote for it? To vote against it?

e. Recently the Supreme Court ruled that it is legally permissible for high school principals to censor student newspapers. Suppose that your university newspaper is about to print an important news story that would seriously offend a few people and would mildly offend about a third of its readers. Does the university president have a moral duty to censor the story? Not to censor the story?

f. At present, it is legal to allow patients to die if they want to, even if there is some high-tech way of prolonging their life (passive euthanasia). But it is not legal to kill them, even if they beg for death (active euthanasia). Should we legalize active euthanasia?

g. My child has a cold. Do I have a moral duty to send her to school anyway? Do I have a moral duty to keep her out of school and stay home to care for her? Or neither?

h. Last week I found a nice pair of gloves on the ground. Is it morally OK for me to keep them, or must I turn them in to the Lost and Found?

i. Some hotels provide guests with small wrapped bars of soap every day during their stay. When I leave the hotel, is it morally OK for me to take bars of soap that I have not unwrapped?

j. In 1998 in Texas, a woman on welfare with two children receives a maximum of $188.00 per month from the Temporary Assistance Fund and $321.00 per month in food stamps. If she gives birth to another child, she will receive an additional $38.00 per month from the fund and an additional $87.00 per month in food stamps in order to defray some of the cost of raising the additional child. A bill that would deny these extra benefits to women on welfare who give birth to children has been debated in Congress. Do the legislators have a moral duty to vote for this bill? To vote against it?

k. Joe puts a Confederate flag bumper-sticker and a swastika bumper-sticker on his pickup truck. Of course, this offends some people. Is Joe's act morally OK?

l. Sam, who is married, purchases sex from a prostitute several times each year. Is Sam's practice morally OK?

6. If Socrates had met Mill on the courthouse steps, Socrates might have asked, "Are moral acts right because they make people happy or do they make people happy because they are right, or neither?" (In other words, is "making people happy" an essential property, an incidental property, or not always a property of moral acts?) How would Mill answer this question? How would Kant answer this question? How would you answer this question?

7. Choose any *one* of the following practices. Give a Utilitarian argument showing that the practice is moral, *and* give a Utilitarian argument showing that the practice is immoral. (*Hints:* Do not give arguments for and against two different practices. Use the very same practice in both arguments. You might try giving an Act Utilitarian argument for one side and a Rule Utilitarian argument for the other. Remember that any Utilitarian argument is a list of pros and cons plus a statement of which outweighs which. Thus your answer should include two lists: pros and cons. Remember that a Rule Utilitarian argument involves a rule.)

   a. Tenure at universities

   b. Cloning humans

   c. Plagiarism

   d. Making and selling pornographic movies

   e. Raising cows for food

8. Choose any *two* of the following rules. What exceptions to these two rules would a Rule Utilitarian consider legitimate? (List all of the legitimate exceptions that you can.) How would a Rule Utilitarian justify these exceptions?

   a. Give approximately 10% of your net income to the truly needy.

   b. If you and another person are sharing a house, do approximately 50% of the housework.

   c. Universities should admit people solely according to their academic ability.

   d. Obey the law.

   e. Do to others whatever you would have them do to you.

   f. When someone strikes you on your cheek, turn the other one to him as well.

   g. Do not lie.

   h. Do not abort fetuses.

i. Pay your taxes.

j. Assign TA-ships in the philosophy department according to ability to do philosophy.

k. Do not kill people.

l. Reform yourself before trying to reform others.

m. Punish criminals in proportion to the seriousness of their crimes.

n. Keep your promises.

o. Legalize pornography.

What exceptions to these *two* rules would a person who based his or her moral theory *solely* on the Sermon on the Mount consider legitimate? (List all of the legitimate exceptions that you can.) How would such a person justify these exceptions?

9. Mill says, "In the golden rule of Jesus of Nazareth, we read the complete spirit of the ethics of utility. 'To do as you would be done by,' and 'to love your neighbor as yourself,' constitute the ideal perfection of utilitarian morality" (16–17). Answer *one* of the following questions.

a. Are the rules of Rule Utilitarianism the same as the corollaries of the golden rule?

b. Are the acts required by Act Utilitarianism the same as the acts required by the golden rule?

10. Mill says,

> The sole end for which mankind are warranted, individually or collectively, in interfering with the liberty of action of any of their number is self-protection. . . . His own good, either physical or moral, is not a sufficient warrant. . . . This doctrine is meant to apply only to human beings in the maturity of their faculties. We are not speaking of children. . . . Those who are still in a state to require being taken care of by others must be protected against their own actions as well as against external injury. (9)

How would Mill respond to the following argument? It is not the age of a child that makes it legitimate to act paternalistically toward him. Rather it is his lack of maturity. Indeed it is legitimate to act paternalistically toward any person with the maturity of a child. Now maturity is a variable trait. A single person can be mature about some things while being immature about other things. Driving without a seat belt is an incredibly stupid thing to do. Anyone who drives without a seat belt is demonstrating his own immaturity with respect to the matter. Therefore it is OK to act paternalistically toward seat belt avoiders. It is OK to force them to wear seat belts for their own good.

11. Mary orders some merchandise from a catalog. When the bill arrives she realizes that the company has charged her $10.00 too little. She does not inform the company of this but merely goes ahead and pays the amount requested by the company. The company has about 1000 shareholders. Mary calculates that her act will result in the company paying each of its shareholders $.01 less this year. Mary's roommate, Jerry, has borrowed $25.00 from Mary, but Mary misremembers the amount and asks Jerry to repay $15.00. Jerry does not correct Mary's misimpression and merely pays her $15.00. Jerry's boyfriend, Terry, simply takes $10.00 out of Jerry's wallet. Answer any *four* of the following questions.

a. Would an Act Utilitarian consider the acts of these three people to be morally equivalent? Why or why not?

b. Would a Rule Utilitarian consider the acts of these three people to be morally equivalent? Why or why not?

c. Would a Kantian using Categorical Imperative 1 consider the acts of these three people to be morally equivalent? Why or why not?

d. Would a Kantian using Categorical Imperative 2 consider the acts of these three people to be morally equivalent? Why or why not?

e. Would you consider the acts of these three people to be morally equivalent? Why or why not?

12. Choose *one* of the following rules.

a. Do not commit suicide.

b. Do not make lying promises.

c. Develop your talents.

d. Help others.

Would a sophisticated Rule Utilitarian accept this rule? Why or why not? What exceptions to this rule would a sophisticated Rule Utilitarian accept? List as many exceptions as you can. How would a sophisticated Rule Utilitarian justify these exceptions?

13. Kant thinks that we have a duty to develop our talents (31, A 423 and 37, A 430). Aristotle thinks that we should exercise all of our essential abilities (13–14, 1197b–1198a). Mill thinks we should employ our higher faculties (9–10). In what ways are these three philosophers saying the same thing? In what ways are they saying different things? In what ways are their reasons for making these claims the same? In what ways are their reasons different? In what ways do you agree with what these three philosophers are saying? In what ways do you disagree?

14. Choose *two* of the following practices. Give Utilitarian, Kantian, and Aristotelian arguments in excruciating detail for or against the morality of the two practices you have chosen.

   a. Self-mutilation (such as cutting off your own little toe)

   b. Getting drunk regularly (for example, drinking a fifth of whiskey per day)

   c. Giving only $10.00 to charity while earning $100,000.00 per year

   d. Raping prostitutes

   e. Stealing a loaf of bread to feed your starving children

   f. Giving misleading information to high school students in order to scare them away from drugs

   g. Allowing homosexuals to serve in the military

   h. Saving your own child from a burning building instead of saving two other children

15. For many years, our nuclear weapons policy was to aim our missiles at Soviet cities rather than merely at military targets. The Soviets knew that if they launched a first strike at us, we could destroy their nation, and this knowledge presumably deterred them from launching a first strike. This policy (which is known as Mutually Assured Destruction, or MAD) has been called immoral by many people. Critics compared MAD to the act of holding a gun on an innocent hostage in order to ensure cooperation from someone else. The critics called MAD a kind of terrorism. For even if the Soviet *leaders* were power-hungry, evil fiends who would stop at nothing to achieve world domination, presumably the Soviet *people* are just like people everywhere else; some are very good, some are very bad, and most are somewhere in between. (One way to reply to these critics would be to say that moral rules apply to individuals but not to states. States should act egoistically. They should always try to maximize their best interest. Since it was in our best interest to adopt the policy of MAD, MAD was a good policy for us. But let us assume, for the sake of argument, that moral rules *do* apply to states as well as to individuals.)

Would an Act Utilitarian think that MAD was an immoral policy? Why or why not?

Would a Rule Utilitarian think that MAD was an immoral policy? Why or why not?

Would a Kantian using Categorical Imperative 1 think that MAD was an immoral policy? Why or why not?

Would a Kantian using Categorical Imperative 2 think that MAD was an immoral policy? Why or why not?

Do you think MAD was an immoral policy? Why or why not?

16. Choose any *one* of the following pairs. Give a Rule Utilitarian analysis that shows that one of the practices is moral and the other is immoral. (*Hints:* Remember that any Utilitarian argument is a list of pros and cons plus a statement of which outweighs which. Remember that a Rule Utilitarian argument involves a rule.)

   a. Giving scholarships to students because they are athletes; giving scholarships to students because they are members of minority groups

b. Going door to door trying to sell encyclopedias; going door to door trying to convert people

c. Using placebos in treatment; telling your date that she looks nice when she really looks awful

d. Capital punishment; killing very defective infants (such as infants born with unfixable holes in their hearts)

e. Affirmative action in admission to medical school; affirmative action in hiring

f. Prostitution; marriage of convenience

# Deontology: Kant

*Within the ranks of the great philosophers, there are a few whose insight into the most profound problems goes so deep that it seems to outreach their capacity for clear, coherent exposition and argument. Kant is such a philosopher.*

ROBERT PAUL WOLFF

**M**any people who try to read the works of Immanuel Kant bounce off. They find that the words and even the sentences make sense, but after reading a page, they have no idea what the page said. There are several reasons for this. One is that Kant is a systematic philosopher. His ethical theory is only one part of a comprehensive philosophy that deals with everything from the possibility of knowledge to the nature of beauty. And as with any systematic work, you cannot fully understand any part without a grasp of the whole. We shall have to settle for a partial understanding of Kant's ethical theory, for I shall not explore the ties between Kant's ethical theory and the rest of his philosophy. For example, I will not discuss Kant's solution to the problem of free will and determinism.

Another complication is that Kant's theory is couched in such general terms that it is hard to fill in the details. I shall present one line of interpretation. My interpretation is plagued with problems, but so are all the others. I shall not try to argue for my interpretation against all of the other interpretations; that would be too esoteric a project for an introductory text. However, I shall point out some of the problems with Kant's theory as I interpret it.

## The Good Will and Moral Worth

Ethics these days usually focuses on the evaluation of acts—on determining which acts are morally required, which acts are morally op-

tional, and which acts are immoral. Kant devotes to this endeavor the second section of his brilliant, though infuriating, little book *Grounding for the Metaphysics of Morals*, but in the first section he focuses on persons rather than acts. He tries to say what makes a person morally good.

Kant thinks that there are only two kinds of motives: the motive of duty (trying to do what is right because it is right) and the various motives of inclination (trying to do what we are inclined, by our desires and passions, to do). Acts motivated solely by duty are said to be done *from duty*. Acts that are morally right are said to be *in accord with duty*. Naturally, acts that are in accord with duty may be motivated either by duty or by inclination. I may give a customer the correct change either because it is the right thing to do or because shortchanging customers is bad for business. Now if I performed an act that I was inclined to perform, then I must have done it, at least partially, *because* I was inclined to do it. Inclinations cannot be present without having an effect on the act. Thus my act can be from duty (motivated solely by duty) only if I am not at all inclined to perform the act. (This is one of the more controversial aspects of my interpretation of Kant.)

Because there are only two motives, Kant thinks that there are only two basic approaches to life. People who resolve to do their duty throughout life are said to have a *good will*. This unconditional commitment to morality is what makes a person morally good. However, people with good wills do not always act in accord with duty. Kant recognizes that it is possible for a person with a good will to act immorally from inclination on many occasions. Such a person is said to have a *good but frail will*. People whose highest priority is the satisfaction of their inclinations are said to have an *evil will*. They do not always act immorally, of course. They may act rightly most of the time. They may even act rightly more often than people with good but frail wills. However, Kant says that they have evil wills because they act rightly only when it pays and only because it pays. When acting rightly does not gratify their inclinations (either in the short term or in the long term), people with evil wills do not act rightly.

An act has *moral worth* if and only if the act is evidence of a good will. Naturally, an act exhibits a good will—an unconditional commitment to morality—if and only if it is from duty. And my act can be from duty only if I am not at all inclined to perform the act. So my act has moral worth if and only if I am either indifferent to performing the act or disinclined to perform it. Thus, Kant says,

To preserve one's life is a duty; and, furthermore everyone has also an immediate inclination to do so. But on this account the often anxious care taken by most men for it has no [moral worth]. They preserve their lives, to be sure, in accordance with duty, but not from duty. On the other hand, if adversity and hopeless sorrow have completely taken away the taste for life, if an unfortunate man . . . wishes for death and yet preserves his life without loving it—not from inclination or fear, but from duty—then his maxim indeed has a moral content. (10, A 397–398)

Of course, Kant is not saying that there is anything wrong with preserving your own life when you want to live. He is merely saying that doing so lacks moral worth because you are motivated, at least partially, by inclination. You want to live, so you are not acting from duty. Your act is not evidence that you have a good will. On the other hand, the choice to refrain from suicide when you desire to die could only be motivated solely by duty. And because this choice is from duty, it does provide evidence that you have a good will. It does have moral worth.

The poet Friedrich Schiller raises the following objection: If we like our friends, then our friendly acts will be motivated by inclination. They will be morally worthless. But if we hate our friends, then our friendly acts will be motivated by duty and will have moral worth. Thus Kant's view seems to imply that we should try to hate our friends so that we can be nice to them from duty. In general, Schiller's objection is that Kant gives credit for overcoming evil inclina-

tions (or indifference) but not for having good inclinations.

Although Schiller's criticism is cute, it is misguided. Kant is not urging us to perform morally worthy acts so that we can earn "morality points." Kant is not giving credit for overcoming temptation. A morally worthy act is not morally more right than other acts that accord with duty. The morally worthy act simply exhibits a good will, whereas the other acts exhibit nothing. People who do the right thing because they want to do it may also have a good will, but until they are in a situation where duty does not coincide with inclination, we do not know what sort of will they have.

Sören Kierkegaard's criticism seems sounder. He takes Kant's division between the motives of duty and inclination to indicate that there are only two basic approaches to life. People who resolve to try to obey God throughout life have a third approach, according to Kierkegaard, because sometimes God's commands conflict with both duty and inclination. For example, when God orders Abraham to sacrifice Isaac, a person motivated by duty would say "no," and so would a person motivated by inclination. Yet a religious person would say "yes." Thus there must be a third motive and a corresponding third sort of will. [See the "Morality and Religion" section.] And perhaps there are yet other sorts of wills. Aristotle, for example, considers the contemplative life to be different from both the life of hedonism and the life of moral virtue.

## Categorical Imperative— First Formulation

In the second section of the *Grounding*, Kant presents three rather different approaches to ethics. Each approach is based on a different cluster of fundamental insights, has a different ultimate moral principle, and utilizes a different decision procedure. Kant believes that these three approaches are equivalent. He describes the three ultimate moral principles as different "formulations" of a single principle called the *categorical imperative.* However, contemporary Kantians believe that the approaches are not equivalent. They yield different answers to a variety of moral questions. I shall present only the first two approaches.

Unfortunately, Kant uses the term *categorical imperative* to refer not only to the ultimate moral principle but also to every moral principle. That is, in one sense there is one categorical imperative (with several "formulations") at the top of the hierarchy of moral rules, but in another sense there are lots of categorical imperatives ("Killing is wrong," "Making lying promises is wrong," etc.). Kant defines categorical imperatives of the latter sort by contrast with hypothetical imperatives. A hypothetical imperative is a statement about what people ought to do if they have certain goals—for example, "If you want to stay dry, you ought to take an umbrella." The "if" clause is the hypothesis. Note that hypothetical imperatives do not apply to all possible people, but only to the people who share the goals named in the hypothesis. If you do not want to stay dry, then the hypothetical imperative just mentioned is not telling you to do anything. By contrast, a categorical imperative is a statement about what people ought to do no matter what their goals are. "(No matter what you want), you ought not to kill people" is a categorical imperative. It does not have an "if" clause, so it commands categorically. It applies to all possible people. Kant maintains that all moral rules are categorical imperatives because if there are any moral rules at all, they must apply to everyone. They cannot apply only to people with certain goals and not to others. Thus Kant believes that he has found the essence of morality, the logical form shared by all moral rules. And this gives him the first formulation of his ultimate moral principle. "Act only according to that maxim whereby you can at the same time will that it should become a universal law" (30, A 421). I paraphrase this formulation of the categorical imperative, which I shall call CI#1, as follows:

CI#1: Act only on universalizable maxims.

The *maxim* of any action is the general principle the agent would take himself or herself to be act-

ing on if he or she thought about it. Each maxim identifies an agent and describes an act, situation, and goal from the agent's point of view. The same physical act can be performed under different maxims, so I cannot be sure of what your maxim is when you act (or even what mine is when I act), although I can make an educated guess. A *universalizable maxim* is a maxim that would yield no contradictions in a world where everyone followed it. Thus CI#1 says that we may perform only acts that could consistently be performed by everyone. Acts that could not consistently be performed by everyone are immoral. Let me illustrate by working through one of Kant's own examples.

A man in need finds himself forced to borrow money. He knows well that he won't be able to repay it, but he sees also that he will not get any loan unless he firmly promises to repay it within a fixed time.... Suppose that he decides to do so. The maxim of his action would then be expressed as follows: when I believe myself to be in need of money, I will borrow money and promise to pay it back, although I know that I can never do so.... He then sees at once that such a maxim could never hold as a universal law of nature and be consistent with itself, but must necessarily be self-contradictory. For the universality of a law which says that anyone believing himself to be in difficulty could promise whatever he pleases with the intention of not keeping it would make promising itself and the end to be attained thereby quite impossible, inasmuch as no one would believe what was promised him but would merely laugh at all such utterances as being vain pretenses. (31, A 422)

**Step 1: Maxim** Suppose I want to know whether the act of making a lying promise to pay back the money is morally wrong. The maxim of the action is something like this. "I, needing money and being unable to repay it, shall promise to repay it in order to get the loan." There are notorious difficulties with framing the maxim. Make the maxim too narrow and the maxim will not generalize. Make the maxim too broad and no contradiction can result. But let us ignore these problems for now.

**Step 2: Universalized Maxim** To universalize the maxim, replace proper names and pronouns with *anyone* and make other appropriate changes. Thus the universalized version of my original maxim is "Anyone needing money and being unable to repay it will promise to repay it in order to get the loan." Now we must see whether there is a contradiction—whether the maxim of the act is truly universalizable.

**Step 3: Contradiction-in-Conception Test**
The first two steps were relatively straightforward, but the third step is complex. Here we must perform a thought experiment. Imagine a world just like ours except that the universalized maxim is (or is believed to be) true. In this world people frequently make lying promises in order to get loans. Could the goal of the original maxim be achieved in such a world? No! The goal is to gain a loan, but this goal would be frustrated in the world of lying promisers. We might expresses this point by saying that there is a *contradiction in conception* between the world of the universalized maxim and the goal of the original maxim. It is inconceivable that the goal could be achieved in the world of the universalized maxim. As we have noted, a maxim is said to be universalizable if it can be universalized without contradiction. In the lying-promise case, the maxim is not universalizable. CI#1 says that one should perform acts only if they are universalizable, so one should not perform this act. Making this lying promise is immoral.

It is not clear exactly how the contradiction arises. Perhaps the idea is that if everyone felt free to make lying promises to obtain money, then money lenders would demand more than promises before lending. Thus in a world of lying promisers, the agent could not achieve the goal of the original maxim. However, as Feldman observes, if lying promises were rare and money lenders gullible, the agent *could* get a loan. Another interpretation, suggested by Kant's statement that "promising itself" would become impossible, is this. The concept of promising includes a commitment to keeping the promise. If everyone felt free to make lying promises, the practice of promising would no longer exist, and the agent could not achieve his or her goal. However, although this may work in

cases where the action violates the rules of a practice, it does not seem to work in cases where no practice is involved. Why, for example, is killing people generally wrong?

There is also some doubt about the scope of Kant's method. Is Kant saying that lying is always wrong, that making lying promises is always wrong, that making lying promises in order to gain a loan is always wrong, or what? On the basis of remarks made by Kant elsewhere, some people take Kant to be saying that lying is always wrong, that general moral rules such as "Lying is wrong" have no exceptions. That is, they take Kant to be an Extreme Absolutist. However, by the interpretation I am advancing, Kant is saying something much narrower. He is saying only that making lying promises is wrong when your goal is to gain a loan and your situation is that you need money but cannot repay it. To determine whether making lying promises is wrong under different circumstances, we would have to go through the three-step process again with a different maxim. To determine whether lying is always wrong we would have to go through the three-step process for every case of lying in every situation. On my interpretation, Kant is not committed to the extreme claim that lying is always wrong—that moral rules are exceptionless. Instead, he is committed only to the more moderate claim that exceptions to general rules must be situational and not personal. That is, I take Kantianism to be a version of Normative Absolutism. [See the "Morality and Knowledge" section.]

Why does Kant think that this three-step procedure works? Why does the existence of a contradiction in conception tell us that the act is immoral? The basic idea is this. Kant thinks the essence of evil is to make a special exception for yourself to a moral rule. If I am considering a lying promise, I do not want lying promises to be OK for everyone, for then I could not achieve my goal. What I want is for no one except me to make lying promises. I want others to be morally required to keep their promises whereas I have license to break mine, even though my situation and the situations of others are not morally different. Kant's three-step procedure is a formalized way of finding out whether any maxim implicitly involves holding others to a higher standard than that to which I hold myself.

CI#1 is reminiscent of the Silver Rule ("Do not do unto others what you would not have them do unto you"). One difference is that CI#1 applies even when others are not involved. It generates duties to oneself as well as to others. However, in cases where others are involved, both principles require that you imagine a world in which the act you are thinking of doing to another person rebounds somehow upon yourself. But the Silver Rule says that you should use your preferences as a guide for action on the assumption that others share your preferences, whereas CI#1 is independent of preferences. CI#1 is merely a matter of contradictions, of logic. According to the Silver Rule, I should not make a lying promise to others because I do not want people to make lying promises to me. But according to CI#1, I should not make a lying promise to get a loan because if everyone did that, I could not get a loan.

Kant thinks that moral rules, unlike other rules such as rules of prudence or etiquette, are universal and necessary. That is, they apply to every rational being in all possible worlds. No matter who you are or what your preferences are, you should not make a lying promise to get a loan. Thus moral rules do not depend on the facts of our world, which could have been different. Because morality does not depend on the contingent facts about our world, the rules of morality are discoverable through reason alone. They are not even partially based on information gathered through the senses. This is roughly what Kant means when he says that categorical imperatives are *a priori* (independent of experience).

In general, Kant believes that he has transformed moral problems into logical problems. The hard, moral question of whether an act is moral has been reduced to the easy, logical question of whether two statements contradict each other. Unfortunately, Kant has not fully reduced moral problems to logical problems, for quite a

bit of judgment and knowledge seems to be required for his method even to get off the ground. The contradictions do not exactly jump out at you. CI#1 is not just a matter of logic, and it is not exactly *a priori*.

Note that although both Kant and the Rule Utilitarians utilize the thought experiment technique to imagine worlds where certain acts are widely performed, this similarity is purely superficial. The Rule Utilitarian asks about the happiness level of the imaginary world, but Kant asks whether the agent can achieve his or her goal in that world. If the goal is achievable, then the maxim passes Kant's test even if its associated world would be a perfectly miserable world. According to the Rule Utilitarian, I should not make a lying promise to get a loan because if everyone did that, the world would not be a very happy place. But according to CI#1, I should not make a lying promise to get a loan because if everyone did that, I could not get a loan. The procedures of Kant and the Rule Utilitarian are very different. [See the "Utilitarinaism" section.] After all, Kant is a *deontologist* rather than a *teleologist*. Utilitarians think that what makes an act right (or wrong) is simply the goodness (or badness) of the consequences of the act or of the related rule. But for Kant, the rightness (or wrongness) of acts is a function of logical consistency rather than consequences. Some acts are wrong even if their consequences are wonderful, because their maxims cannot be consistently universalized.

\*

Kant believes that we have *duties to ourselves* as well as *duties to others*. This is a fairly straightforward distinction, although the claim that we have duties to ourselves is somewhat controversial. Kant also makes a trickier distinction. *Perfect duties* "admit of no exceptions in the interests of inclination," but presumably *imperfect duties* do admit of such exceptions. If I have a *perfect duty* to express gratitude when someone has done me a favor, then within certain limits I have the freedom to decide how to express my gratitude (say "thank you," write a thank-you letter, return the favor, etc.), but I do not have the option of simply *not* expressing gratitude (on occasions when

I do not wish to do so, toward people I detest, when I am too busy, etc.). I must adopt a principle and cultivate a habit of always expressing gratitude somehow or another. On the other hand, if I have an *imperfect duty* to express gratitude, then I must commit myself to the principle of usually expressing gratitude and become a grateful person. But I need not express gratitude on every single occasion when I am the recipient of a favor. Of course, if I seldom express gratitude, then there will be reason to doubt the sincerity of my commitment to the principle, but it is up to me not only how, but also whether, to express gratitude at particular times, toward particular people, and so on. Thus, according to Kant, there is more to morality than merely discharging our particular obligations to particular other people. It is possible to satisfy my perfect duties to others yet neglect my imperfect duties and/or my duties to myself. And despite the connotations of the terms, Kant does not think that perfect duties are more important than imperfect duties. Some perfect duties are trivial, whereas some imperfect duties have a very high priority. Moreover, I have both perfect and imperfect duties to myself as well as to others. Kant's two distinctions enable him to divide duties into four classes (see table), and he provides one example of each class. (Feldman is quite critical of Kant's examples. He does not think that Kant correctly applies his own method.)

Some people (such as Nozick) deny that we have any duty to help others. Helping others is morally optional, above and beyond the call of duty. Other people (such as Singer and, on some interpretations, Jesus) think that we have a perfect duty to help others. If a person needs help that we can provide, then we are morally obliged to help that person. Kant positions himself between these two extreme views. Although Kant

thinks we have a duty to help others, he thinks it is an imperfect duty. He does not specify how much time, energy, or resources we should expend to help others or which others we should help. Kant allows us some flexibility to decide whom to help and how.

The contradiction-in-conception test tells us only whether an act violates a perfect duty. If a certain maxim contradicts itself when universalized, and if we are to act only on maxims that can be universalized without contradiction, then it is never OK to act on that maxim. There can be no exceptions based on inclination. Kant deploys another test, the contradiction-in-will test, to determine whether acts violate imperfect duties. Consider the question of whether I must help others.

A man finds things going well for himself but sees others (whom he could help) struggling with great hardships; and he thinks: what does it matter to me? . . . But even though it is possible that a universal law of nature could subsist in accordance with that maxim, still it is impossible to will that such a principle should hold everywhere as a law of nature. For a will which resolved in this way would contradict itself, inasmuch as cases might often arise in which one would have need of the love and sympathy of others. (32, A 423)

**Step 1: Maxim**    The maxim under consideration is not perfectly clear, but it might be something like this. "I, being well off, shall, in order to conserve my resources, not help others."

**Step 2: Universalized Maxim**    "Anyone who is well off will not help others in order to conserve his or her resources."

**Step 3: Contradiction-in-Conception Test** There is no contradiction between the world of the universalized maxim and the goal of the original maxim. I can achieve my goal in this world

|  | Perfect Duties | Imperfect Duties |
|---|---|---|
| **Duties to Self** | no suicide | develop talents |
| **Duties to Others** | no lying promises | help others |

of uncharitable people. Thus the act of not helping others passes the contradiction-in-conception test. I have no perfect duty to help others.

**Step 4: Contradiction-in-Will Test** Nevertheless, there is a different sort of contradiction here, a contradiction between a goal shared by all humans and the world of the universalized maxim. Kant thinks that all rational beings aim at their own happiness. He also thinks that because we are finite beings, it is reasonable to assume that at some points in our lives, each of us will need help to achieve this goal. Willing the end implies willing the means, so rational finite beings will that others help them. In a world where no one helped anyone, the goal of the original maxim, not helping anyone, could be achieved. But the goal of being happy could not. The universalized maxim can be conceived by finite rational beings, but it could not be willed, because it would contradict another maxim that they also will, the maxim of being helped by others. Thus the original maxim cannot be universalized because it fails the contradiction-in-will test. Kant thinks this test tells us what our imperfect duties are. Thus the act of not helping others violates an imperfect duty.

\*

Kant's method sometimes yields results that would certainly have shocked the very proper eighteenth-century Prussian philosopher. Consider the following example. Suppose I am wondering whether I may engage in premarital sex. The maxim under consideration is this.

**Step 1: Maxim**  "I, being unmarried, shall have sex with Sue, who is also unmarried and who is willing to have sex with me, in order to obtain sexual pleasure."

**Step 2: Universalized Maxim**  "Any unmarried, willing people will have sex with each other in order to obtain sexual pleasure."

**Step 3: Contradiction-in-Conception Test** There seems to be no contradiction between the world of the universalized maxim and the goal of the original maxim. I can achieve my goal of sexual pleasure in this world of promiscuous singles. Thus the act passes the contradiction-in-conception test. I have no perfect duty to avoid premarital sex.

**Step 4: Contradiction-in-Will Test** Similarly, there seems to be no contradiction between the world of the universalized maxim and the goal of all rational beings. I can achieve happiness in this promiscuous world. Thus the act passes the contradiction-in-will test. I have no imperfect duty to avoid premarital sex.

If a maxim can be universalized, then according to CI#1, we may act on it. If an act passes both tests, then it is not immoral. It seems that premarital sex is OK! At this point, some people will reject Kant's method, or suspect that we have somehow misapplied Kant's method. But suppose, for the sake of argument, that premarital sex is OK. There are two sorts of acts that are not immoral: morally required acts and morally optional acts. Thus a further question arises. Is premarital sex morally optional or morally required? To use Kant's method to answer this question, note that an act is morally required if and only if its opposite is immoral. Hence the next task is to use Kant's method to determine whether the opposite act, no premarital sex with Sue, is immoral. Presumably, Kant's method will not tell us that premarital abstinence is immoral! But let us go through the motions in order to illustrate the remainder of the method. The next step is to formulate the maxim of not having sex with Sue.

**Step 5: Opposite of the Original Maxim**  "I, being unmarried, shall *not* have sex with Sue, who is also unmarried and who is willing to have sex with me, in order to obtain sexual pleasure." The idea here might be to enhance sexual pleasure after marriage by refraining from premarital sex. Or it might be to enhance the sexual pleasure of kissing, dancing, and the like. Or it might be some other thing.

**Step 6: Universalized Opposite of the Original Maxim**  "Any unmarried, willing people will *not* have sex with each other in order to obtain sexual pleasure."

**Steps 7 and 8: Contradiction-in-Conception and Contradiction-in-Will Tests**    There seems to be no contradiction in conception or will. It is logically possible for me to obtain my goals of enhanced postmarital sexual pleasure and happiness in a world of premarital abstinence. Thus I have no duty to practice premarital sex. Combining this result with the results of steps 3 and 4, we may conclude that premarital sex is neither morally prohibited nor morally required. It is morally optional.

## Categorical Imperative— Second Formulation

Kant divides the entities of the universe into two categories: persons and things. Persons are free, rational beings; everything else is a thing. Normal, adult human beings are paradigmatic persons, but Kant recognizes the possibility that there may be non-human persons, too. If it turns out that chimps, androids, and Martians are able to make free, rational choices, then everything Kant says about persons will apply to them as well. The essence of immorality, according to Kant's second approach to morality, is to treat persons as though they were things. That is, we should not deny or subvert the ability of a person to make free, rational choices. Kant calls this ability *autonomy*. Thus our fundamental duty is to respect the autonomy of persons. Now we are in a position to understand, at least roughly, a Kantian justification for morality—a Kantian answer to the question of why we should be moral. To be immoral is to make a fundamental mistake about the universe. It is to conflate people and things.

A more complicated Kantian justification for morality goes like this. Things have value, but only instrumental value. Hammers are valuable for pounding nails, pots are valuable for cooking, and so on. Things are valuable merely as means to the achievement of some further goal. If X is valuable merely as means to Y, then X gets its value from Y. Now all value could not possibly be instrumental value. If X is valuable merely

as means to Y, and Y is valuable merely as means to Z, and so on indefinitely, then ultimately nothing is valuable. There must be something that is valuable for its own sake in order to anchor the chain of value. There must be something of *intrinsic* value. There must be some source of value. The chains of means and ends do not exist in the world itself, but rather they are projected onto the world by free, rational choices. That is, something is valuable only because someone chooses it. But my choice can confer value on something only if I already have value to confer on it. Ultimately, the only thing that is intrinsically valuable is a projector of value—a free, rational being, an autonomous being. Thus all persons and only persons are intrinsically valuable. Persons should therefore be treated as possessors of intrinsic value. Let me summarize this line of thought:

*Argument (A)*

(1) Things have instrumental value.
(2) If something has instrumental value, then something else has intrinsic value.
(3) Items of intrinsic value must be projectors of value.
(4) A projector of value is a free, rational being.
(5) Therefore, all persons and only persons are intrinsically valuable.
(6) It is a mistake to treat an intrinsically valuable entity, a person, as though he or she were merely instrumentally valuable. That is, we should treat persons as intrinsically valuable entities, not merely as instrumentally valuable entities.

If we use the word "end" to mean "intrinsically valuable entity" and use the word "means" to mean "instrumentally valuable entity," then we get the second formulation of the categorical imperative. "Act in such a way that you treat humanity, whether in your own person or in the person of another, always at the same time as an end and never simply as a means" (36, A 429). I paraphrase this as follows:

CI#2: Treat persons as ends, not merely as means.

This formulation breaks into two parts. "Treat people not merely as means" defines our perfect duties. *To treat people as means* is to use them to accomplish one's goals, and there is nothing wrong with this. When I buy shoes, I use the salesperson as a means to my goal of obtaining shoes. What makes it morally OK to use the salesperson in this way is that he or she has consented to be so used. On the other hand, *to treat people merely as means* is to exploit them, to use them to accomplish one's goals without even the possibility that they might consent. Or, as Mappes puts it, treating a person merely as a means is doing something without the possibility of that person giving informed consent. It is to this that Kant objects. Kant thinks that our perfect duties consist solely in not treating people merely as means. To avoid treating persons merely as means, I must ensure that the persons are able to consent to the fundamental aspects of the act and that dissent is practical for them. In particular, I must avoid (a) coercion, (b) deception, (c) coercive offers, and (d) paternalism and patronization.

Coercion means simply the use of force or threat of force. Destroying, damaging, enslaving, or thwarting the rational capacities of people (either oneself or others) is immoral. Deception means simply lying or withholding crucial information. Preventing people from making informed decisions is immoral. It seems that a person cannot, even in principle, consent to being coerced or deceived. How could I consent to be lied to, for example? If I say, "Go ahead and tell me a lie," I will not be fooled by the lie you tell. Thus to coerce or deceive someone is to violate her or his autonomy, to treat the person merely as a means. In general, we should not manipulate people but should instead leave them free to exercise their own reason. Hence lying promises turn out to be wrong according to the second formulation as well as the first formulation of the categorical imperative.

Does this mean that I should *never* use force or fraud? May I use force to defend others from attack, for example? A Kantian might analyze this as a case of conflict of duties. I have a duty to refrain from using force, but I also have a duty to help others. In this case, although the duty to abjure force is a perfect duty, the imperfect duty to help others has a higher priority, so it is OK for me to use force against the attacker. My duties are all *prima facie* duties. Why does my duty to help others have a higher priority? Kant provides no method for ranking duties, but O'Neill suggests that because Kant assigns intrinsic value to autonomy, we can rank duties in terms of maximizing the possibility for autonomous action. Famine relief has a higher priority than support for the arts, because famine relief does more to enhance people's ability to act autonomously. In general, the more autonomy enhancement an action provides, the higher is its priority. This seems to turn Kantians into teleologists who take ability to express autonomy rather than happiness to be the goal of morality, but perhaps that is OK.

Is it really impossible to consent to coercion or deception? When I sign a contract, am I not agreeing in advance to be coerced if I fail to fulfill my obligations? When I agree to participate in certain sociological experiments, am I not agreeing in advance to be lied to?

The meaning of a coercive offer is somewhat complicated. Mappes begins by distinguishing between offers and threats. If a person's statement boils down to "Do as I ask; decline and I will make your situation worse," then you are being threatened. On the other hand, if a person says, "Do as I ask and I will make your situation better; decline and I will not make your situation worse," then you are being made an offer. A coercive offer is an offer, not a threat. But it is an offer with strings attached, made to a person in such desperate straits that the person cannot reasonably refuse. It is taking advantage of a desperate situation. For example, if I announce that for a price of $1,000.00 I will throw you a life preserver, then I am making an offer. If you are a non-swimmer and the waters are shark-infested, then the offer is coercive. In general, if one party to a transaction is terribly vulnerable, then the transaction ceases to be a business deal and becomes exploitation, a coercive offer. A person cannot reasonably be said to consent to a coercive offer, because the person had no real choice. Thus to make someone a coercive offer is to violate his or her autonomy—to treat the person merely as a means.

On the other hand, the coercive offer does not diminish the desperate person's overall ability to express autonomy. Indeed, the offer typically enhances it. Of course, it is rather slimy of me to take advantage of the fact that a non-swimmer has fallen into shark-infested waters. It would be decent of me to throw the life preserver for free. But throwing the life preserver for $1,000.00 gives the non-swimmer more ability to express autonomy than not throwing it at all, so perhaps Kantians should not object to coercive offers.

Someone might protest that I have a duty to help people get out of desperate situations. If this were true, then there would be no such thing as a coercive offer. If I make the non-swimmer pay $1,000.00 for something to which he or she is already entitled, then I am actually threatening the non-swimmer. However, because helping others is an imperfect duty, the non-swimmer is not entitled to the life preserver. Assuming I have already discharged my duty to help others by giving at the office, I have no duty to rescue the non-swimmer.

The fourth sort of act we must avoid is a bit different from the other three. Kant recognizes that some humans are immature or irrational. Thus it is OK to force young children to do things because they are not yet persons. They are not yet fully rational beings. Kant also recognizes that we sometimes treat normal adults as though they were children. For example, we sometimes decline to take them seriously or to hold them responsible for their actions. "This argument isn't really about whose turn it is to do the dishes. It's just your PMS again, isn't it?" To treat people paternalistically or patronizingly is to deny that they are persons. It is to refuse to respect their autonomy. Therefore, paternalism and patronizing are other ways of treating a person merely as a means. Paternalism treats a person merely as a means to his or her own happiness. Patronizing exploits a person for the sake of the patronizer.

*

The other part of CI#2, "treat people as ends," defines our imperfect duties. But there are two rather different ways to spell out this injunction, corresponding to two different conceptions of autonomy. Autonomy is freedom of the will. It is the ability to choose without being determined by desire or emotion—even the ability to choose ends one does not desire (negative freedom). It is also the ability to commit oneself rationally to principles of action that might override one's deepest inclinations (positive freedom). Kant's rigid separation between completely autonomous persons and totally non-autonomous things suggests that *autonomy is not a matter of degree*. On his view, nearly all sane adults and children possess autonomy, though some do not express their autonomy in their actions as much as others. Thus nearly all people are worthy of the same level of respect and possess the same basic rights. The injunction to "treat people as ends," then, requires us to help others achieve their morally acceptable goals, perhaps by increasing their range of choices. We should develop our talents in ways that enable us to help others as well as ourselves.

However, the very great differences in rationality and self-control between young children (and childish adults) and mature adults suggests that *autonomy is a matter of degree*. The more a person is able to weigh reasons and make his or her own decisions about ends and principles, independent of his or her desires, emotions, and various social pressures, the more autonomy that person has. Persons and things are not the only sorts of entities. Instead, they are merely the extremes of a continuum. Young children, addicts, lunatics, and perhaps conformists are not fully autonomous; they are not full-fledged persons. However, they do not seem to be mere things, either. They have some rights, though not as many rights as the fully autonomous. Even animals seem to have some rights, at least the right not to be tortured. Thus the injunction to "treat people as ends" requires us to help others gain, maintain, and increase as well as express their autonomy. We are not simply to help others achieve their goals. Instead, we are to help them become and remain full-fledged persons. Perhaps we increase rationality by education and increase freedom by providing assertiveness training. Similarly, we are not simply to develop the talents of our choice. Instead, we are to develop those talents that enhance our personhood.

Should Kant acknowledge that autonomy is a matter of degree, that there is a range of entities between persons and things? On the one hand, it is naive to maintain that young children are either persons or things. On the other hand, the idea of partial autonomy is problematic in several respects. Suppose Kant says that A has more autonomy than B if A has more rationality and/or more freedom than B. Does more ratio-

nality mean higher IQ, better logical skills, or what? Does more freedom mean fewer, weaker inclinations, less social pressure, or what? Moreover, if there are degrees of autonomy, then different entities are worthy of different degrees of respect and rights. Smart, clear-thinking, self-controlled people are surely not entitled to more respect and more rights than the rest of us. Surely, we do not want to say that it is OK to exploit children, but only to some degree. Acknowledging partial autonomy would further complicate Kant's already quite complicated moral theory, but that is probably for the best. Because everything that has to do with people is terribly complicated, a moral theory that is not terribly complicated is probably wrong.

# 18   Kant's Ethical Theory: Exposition and Critique

## FRED FELDMAN

Kant formulates his main principle in a variety of different ways.[1] All of the members of the following set of formulations seem to have a lot in common:

I ought never to act except in such a way that I can also will that my maxim should become a universal law.[2]

Act only on that maxim through which you can at the same time will that it should become a universal law.[3]

Act as if the maxim of your action were to become through your will a universal law of nature.[4]

We must be able to will that a maxim of our action should become a universal law—this is the general canon for all moral judgment of action.[5]

Before we can evaluate this principle, which Kant calls the *categorical imperative,* we have to devote some attention to figuring out what it is supposed to mean. To do this, we must answer a variety of questions. What is a maxim? What is

meant by "universal law"? What does Kant mean by "will"? Let us consider these questions in turn.

## Maxims

In a footnote, Kant defines *maxim* as "a subjective principle of volition."[6] This definition is hardly helpful. Perhaps we can do better. First, however, a little background.

Kant apparently believes that when a person engages in genuine action, he always acts on some sort of general principle. The general principle will explain what the person takes himself to be doing and the circumstances in which he takes himself to be doing it. For example, if I need money, and can get some only by borrowing it, even though I know I won't be able to repay it, I might proceed to borrow some from a friend. My maxim in performing this act might be, "Whenever I need money and can get it by borrowing it, then I will borrow it, even if I know I won't be able to repay it."

From *Introductory Ethics* by Fred Feldman. Copyright © 1978, 99–114, with omissions. Reprinted by permission of Prentice-Hall, Inc., Upper Saddle River, NJ.

Notice that this maxim is *general.* If I adopt it, I commit myself to behaving in the described way *whenever* I need money and the other conditions are satisfied. In this respect, the maxim serves to formulate a general principle of action rather than just some narrow reason applicable in just one case.[7] So a maxim must describe some general sort of situation, and then propose some form of action for the situation. To adopt a maxim is to commit yourself to acting in the described way whenever the situation in question arises. . . .

For our purposes, it will be useful to introduce a concept that Kant does not employ. This is the concept of the *generalized form* of a maxim. Suppose I decide to go to sleep one night and my maxim in performing this act is this:

$M_3$: Whenever I am tired, I shall sleep.

My maxim is stated in such a way as to contain explicit references to me. It contains two occurrences of the word "I." The generalized form of my maxim is the principle we would get if we were to revise my maxim so as to make it applicable to everyone. Thus, the generalized form of my maxim is this:

$GM_3$: Whenever anyone is tired, he will sleep.

In general, then, we can represent the form of a maxim in this way:

$M$: Whenever I am ———, I shall ———.

Actual maxims have descriptions of situations in the first blank and descriptions of actions in the second blank. The generalized form of a maxim can be represented in this way:

$GM$: Whenever anyone is ———, she will ———.

So much, then, for maxims. Let us turn to our second question, "What is meant by universal law?"

## Universal Law

When, in the formulation of the categorical imperative, Kant speaks of "universal law," he seems to have one or the other of two things in mind. Sometimes he seems to be thinking of a *universal law of nature,* and sometimes he seems to be thinking of a *universal law of freedom.*

A *law of nature* is a fully general statement that describes not only how things are, but how things always *must* be. Consider this example: If the temperature of a gas in an enclosed container is increased, then the pressure will increase too. This statement accurately describes the behavior of gases in enclosed containers. Beyond this, however, it describes behavior that is, in a certain sense, necessary. The pressure not only *does* increase, but it *must* increase if the volume remains the same and the temperature is increased. This "must" expresses not logical or moral necessity, but "physical necessity." Thus, a law of nature is a fully general statement that expresses a physical necessity.

A *universal law of freedom* is a universal principle describing how all people ought to act in a certain circumstance. It does not have to be a legal enactment—it needn't be passed by Congress or signed by the president. Furthermore, some universal laws of freedom are not always followed—although they should be. If in fact it is true that all promises ought to be kept, then this principle is a universal law of freedom: If anyone has made a promise, he keeps it. The "must" in a statement such as "If you have made a promise, then you must keep it" does not express logical or physical necessity. It may be said to express moral necessity. Using this concept of moral necessity, we can say that a universal law of freedom is a fully general statement that expresses a moral necessity.

Sometimes Kant's categorical imperative is stated in terms of universal laws of nature, and sometimes in terms of universal laws of freedom. We will consider the "law of nature" version, since Kant appeals to it in discussing some fairly important examples.

## Willing

To will that something be the case is more than to merely wish for it to be the case. A person might wish that there would be peace everywhere in the world. Yet knowing that it is not within his power to bring about this wished-for state of affairs, he might refrain from willing that there be peace everywhere in the world. It is not easy to say just what a person does when he wills that something be the case. According to one view, willing that something be the case is something like commanding yourself to make it be the case. So if I will my arm to go up, that would be something like commanding myself to raise my arm. The Kantian concept of willing is a bit more complicated, however. According to Kant, it makes sense to speak of willing something to happen, even if that something is not an action. For example, we can speak of someone willing that everyone keep their promises.

Some states of affairs are impossible. They simply cannot occur. For example, consider the state of affairs of your jumping up and down while remaining perfectly motionless. It simply cannot be done. Yet a sufficiently foolish or irrational person might will that such a state of affairs occur. That would be as absurd as commanding someone else to jump up and down while remaining motionless. Kant would say of a person who has willed in this way that his will has "contradicted itself." We can also put the point by saying that the person has willed inconsistently.

Inconsistency in willing can arise in another, somewhat less obvious way. Suppose a person has already willed that he remain motionless. He does not change this volition, but persists in willing that he remain motionless. At the same time, however, he begins to will that he jump up and down. Although each volition is self-consistent, it is inconsistent to will both of them at the same time. This is a second way in which inconsistency in willing can arise.

It may be the case that there are certain things that everyone must always will. For example, we may have to will that we avoid intense pain. Anyone who wills something that is inconsistent with something everyone must will, thereby wills inconsistently.

Some of Kant's examples suggest that he held that inconsistency in willing can arise in a third way. This form of inconsistency is a bit more complex to describe. Suppose a person wills to be in Boston on Monday and also wills to be in San Francisco on Tuesday. Suppose, furthermore, that because of certain foul-ups at the airport it will be impossible for her to get from Boston to San Francisco on Tuesday. In this case, Kant would perhaps say that the person has willed inconsistently.

In general, we can say that a person wills inconsistently if he wills that $p$ be the case and he wills that $q$ be the case and it is impossible for $p$ and $q$ to be the case together.

## The Categorical Imperative

With all this background, we may be in a position to interpret the first version of Kant's categorical imperative. Our interpretation is this:

> $CI_1$: An act is morally right if and only if the agent of the act can consistently will that the generalized form of the maxim of the act be a law of nature.

We can simplify our formulation slightly by introducing a widely used technical term. We can say that a maxim is *universalizable* if and only if the agent who acts upon it can consistently will that its generalized form be a law of nature. Making use of this new term, we can restate our first version of the categorical imperative as follows:

> $CI_1'$: An act is morally right if and only if its maxim is universalizable.

As formulated here, the categorical imperative is a statement of necessary and sufficient conditions for the moral rightness of actions. Some commentators have claimed that Kant did not intend his principle to be understood in this way. They have suggested that Kant meant it to be understood merely as a necessary but not sufficient condition for morally right action. Thus, they would prefer to formulate the imperative in some way such as this:

> $CI_1''$: An act is morally right only if its maxim is universalizable.

Understood in this way, the categorical imperative points out one thing to avoid in action. That is, it tells us to avoid actions whose maxims cannot be universalized. But it does not tell us the distinguishing feature of the actions we should perform. Thus, it does not provide us with a criterion of morally right action. Since Kant explicitly affirms that his principle is "the supreme principle of morality," it is reasonable to suppose that he intended it to be taken as a statement of necessary and sufficient conditions for morally right action. In any case, we will take the first version of the categorical imperative to be $CI_1$ rather than $CI_1''$.

It is interesting to note that other commentators have claimed that the categorical imperative isn't a criterion of right action at all. They have claimed that it was intended to be understood as a criterion of correctness for *maxims*.[8] These commentators might formulate the principle in this way:

$CI_1'''$: A maxim is morally acceptable if and only if it is universalizable.

This interpretation is open to a variety of objections. In the first place, it is not supported by the text. Kant repeatedly states that the categorical imperative is the basic principle by which we are to evaluate actions.[9] Furthermore, when he presents his formulations of the categorical imperative, he generally states it as a principle about the moral rightness of action. Finally, it is somewhat hard to see why we should be interested in the principle such as $CI_1'''$. For it does not constitute a theory about right action, or good persons, or anything else that has traditionally been a subject of moral enquiry. $CI_1$, on the other hand, competes directly with act utilitarianism, rule utilitarianism, and other classical moral theories. . . .

## Kant's Four Examples

In a very famous passage in Chapter 11 of the *Groundwork*, Kant presents four illustrations of the application of the categorical imperative.[10] In each case, in Kant's opinion, the act is morally wrong and the maxim is not universalizable. Thus,

Kant holds that his theory implies that each of these acts is wrong. If Kant is right about this, then he has given us four positive instances of his theory. That is, he has given us four cases in which his theory yields correct results. Unfortunately, the illustrations are not entirely persuasive.

Kant distinguishes between "duties to self" and "duties to others." He also distinguishes between "perfect" and "imperfect" duties. This gives him four categories of duty: "perfect to self," "perfect to others," "imperfect to self," and "imperfect to others." Kant gives one example of each type of duty. By "perfect duty," Kant says he means a duty "which admits of no exception in the interests of inclination."[11] Kant seems to have in mind something like this: If a person has a perfect duty to perform a certain kind of action, then he must *always* do that kind of action when the opportunity arises. For example, Kant apparently holds that we must always perform the (negative) action of refraining from committing suicide. This would be a perfect duty. On the other hand, if a person has an imperfect duty to do a kind of action, then he must at least *sometimes* perform an action of that kind when the opportunity arises. For example, Kant maintains that we have an imperfect duty to help others in distress. We should devote at least some of our time to charitable activities, but we are under no obligation to give all of our time to such work.

The perfect/imperfect distinction has been drawn in a variety of ways—none of them entirely clear. Some commentators have said that if a person has a perfect duty to do a certain action, *a,* then there must be someone else who has a corresponding right to demand that *a* be done. This seems to be the case in Kant's second example, but not in the first example. Thus, it isn't clear that we should understand the concept of perfect duty in this way. Although the perfect/imperfect distinction is fairly interesting in itself, it does not play a major role in Kant's theory. Kant introduces the distinction primarily to insure that his examples will illustrate different kinds of duty.

Kant's first example illustrates the application of $CI_1$ to a case of perfect duty to oneself—the alleged duty to refrain from committing suicide. Kant describes the miserable state of the person contemplating suicide, and tries to show that his categorical imperative entails that the person should not take his own life. In order to simplify our discussion, let us use the abbreviation "$a_1$" to refer to the act of suicide the man would commit, if he were to commit suicide. According to Kant, every act must have a maxim. Kant tells us the maxim of $a_1$: "From self-love I make it my principle to shorten my life if its continuance threatens more evil than it promises pleasure."[12] Let us simplify and clarify this maxim, understanding it as follows:

$M(a_1)$: When continuing to live will bring me more pain than pleasure, I shall commit suicide out of self-love.

The generalized form of this maxim is as follows:

$GM(a_1)$: Whenever continuing to live will bring anyone more pain than pleasure, he will commit suicide out of self-love.

Since Kant believes that suicide is wrong, he attempts to show that his moral principle, the categorical imperative, entails that $a_1$ is wrong. To do this, of course, he needs to show that the agent of $a_1$ cannot consistently will that $GM(a_1)$ be a law of nature. Kant tries to show this in the following passage:

. . . a system of nature by whose law the very same feeling whose function is to stimulate the furtherance of life should actually destroy life would contradict itself and consequently could not subsist as a system of nature. Hence this maxim cannot possibly hold as a universal law of nature and is therefore entirely opposed to the supreme principle of all duty.[13]

The general outline of Kant's argument is clear enough:

## Suicide Example

1. $GM(a_1)$ cannot be a law of nature.
2. If $GM(a_1)$ cannot be a law of nature, then the agent of $a_1$ cannot consistently will that $GM(a_1)$ be a law of nature.
3. $a_1$ is morally right if and only if the agent of $a_1$ can consistently will that $GM(a_1)$ be a law of nature.
4. Therefore, $a_1$ is not morally right.

In order to determine whether Kant really has shown that his theory entails that $a_1$ is not right, let us look at this argument more closely. First of all, for our purposes we can agree that the argument is valid. If all the premises are true, then the argument shows that the imagined act of suicide would not be right. $CI_1$, here being used as premise (3), would thus be shown to imply that $a_1$ is not right.

Since we are now interested primarily in seeing how Kant makes use of $CI_1$, we can withhold judgment on the merits of it for the time being.

The second premise seems fairly plausible. For although an irrational person could probably will almost anything, it surely would be difficult for a perfectly rational person to will that something be a law of nature if that thing could not be a law of nature. Let us grant, then, that it would not be possible for the agent to consistently will that $GM(a_1)$ be a law of nature if in fact $GM(a_1)$ could not be a law of nature.

The first premise is the most troublesome. Kant apparently assumes that "self-love" has as its function, the stimulation of the furtherance of life. Given this, he seems to reason that self-love cannot also contribute sometimes to the destruction of life. Perhaps Kant assumes that a given feeling cannot have two "opposite" functions. However, if $GM(a_1)$ were a law of nature, self-love would have to contribute toward self-destruction in some cases. Hence, Kant seems to conclude, $GM(a_1)$ cannot be a law of nature. And so we have our first premise.

If this is Kant's reasoning, it is not very impressive. In the first place, it is not clear why we should suppose that self-love has the function of stimulating the furtherance of life. Indeed, it is not clear why we should suppose that self-love has any function at all! Second, it is hard to see why self-love can't serve two "opposite" functions. Perhaps self-love motivates us to stay alive when continued life would be pleasant, but motivates us to stop living when continued life would be unpleasant. Why should we hold this to be impossible?

So it appears that Kant's first illustration is not entirely successful. Before we turn to the second illustration, however, a few further comments may be in order. First, some philosophers would say that it is better that Kant's argument failed here. Many moralists would take the following position: Kant's view about suicide is wrong. The act of suicide out of self-love, $a_1$, is morally blameless. In certain circumstances suicide is each person's "own business." Thus, these moralists would say that if the categorical imperative did imply that $a_1$ is morally wrong, as Kant tries to show, then Kant's theory would be defective. But since Kant was not entirely successful in showing that his theory had this implication, the theory has not been shown to have any incorrect results.

A second point to notice about the suicide example is its scope. It is important to recognize that in this passage Kant has not attempted to show that suicide is always wrong. Perhaps Kant's personal view is that it is never right to commit suicide. However, in the passage in question he attempts to show only that a certain act of suicide, one based on a certain maxim, would be wrong. For all Kant has said here, other acts of suicide, done according to other maxims, might be permitted by the categorical imperative.

Let us turn now to the second illustration. Suppose I find myself hard-pressed financially and I decide that the only way in which I can get some money is by borrowing it from a friend. I realize that I will have to promise to repay the money, even though I won't in fact be able to do so. For I foresee that my financial situation will be even worse later on than it is at present. If I perform this action, $a_2$, of borrowing money on a false promise, I will perform it on this maxim:

$M(a_2)$: When I need money and can get some by borrowing it on a false promise, then I shall borrow the money and promise to repay, even though I know that I won't be able to repay.

The generalized form of my maxim is this:

$GM(a_2)$: Whenever anyone needs money and can get some by borrowing it on a false promise, then he will borrow the money and promise to repay, even though he knows that he won't be able to repay.

Kant's view is that I cannot consistently will that $GM(a_2)$ be a law of nature. This view emerges clearly in the following passage:

. . . I can by no means will a universal law of lying; for by such a law there could properly be no promises at all, since it would be futile to profess a will for future action to others who would not believe my profession or who, if they did so over-hastily, would pay me back in like coin; and consequently my maxim, as soon as it was made a universal law, would be bound to annul itself.[14]

It is important to be clear about what Kant is saying here. He is not arguing against lying on the grounds that if I lie, others will soon lose confidence in me and eventually won't believe my promises. Nor is he arguing against lying on the grounds that my lie will contribute to a general practice of lying, which in turn will lead to a breakdown of trust and the destruction of the practice of promising. These considerations are basically utilitarian. Kant's point is more subtle. He is saying that there is something covertly self-contradictory about the state of affairs in which, as a law of nature, everyone makes a false promise when in need of a loan. Perhaps Kant's point is this: Such a state of affairs is self-contradictory because, on the one hand, in such a state of affairs everyone in need would borrow money on a false promise, and yet, on the other hand, in that state of affairs no one could borrow money on a false promise—for if promises were always violated, who would be silly enough to loan any money?

Since the state of affairs in which everyone in need borrows money on a false promise is covertly self-contradictory, it is irrational to will it to occur. No one can consistently will that this state of affairs should occur. But for me to will that $GM(a_2)$ be a law of nature is just for me to will that this impossible state of affairs occur. Hence, I cannot consistently will that the generalized form of my maxim be a law of nature. According to $CI_1$, my act is not right unless I can consistently will that the generalized form of its maxim be a law of nature. Hence, according to $CI_1$, my act of borrowing the money on the false promise is not morally right.

We can restate the essentials of this argument much more succinctly:

### Lying-Promise Example

1. $GM(a_2)$ cannot be a law of nature.
2. If $GM(a_2)$ cannot be a law of nature, then I cannot consistently will that $GM(a_2)$ be a law of nature.
3. $a_2$ is morally right if and only if I can consistently will that $GM(a_2)$ be a law of nature.
4. Therefore, $a_2$ is not morally right.

The first premise is based upon the view that it would somehow be self-contradictory for it to be a law of nature that everyone in need makes a lying promise. For in that (allegedly impossible) state of affairs there would be promises, since those in need would make them, and there would also not be promises, since no one would believe that anyone was really committing himself to future payment by the use of the words "I promise." So, as Kant says, the generalized form of the maxim "annuls itself." It cannot be a law of nature.

The second premise is just like the second premise in the previous example. It is based on the idea that it is somehow irrational to will that something be the case if in fact it is impossible for it to be the case. So if it really is impossible for $GM(a_2)$ to be a law of nature, then it would be irrational of me to will that it be so. Hence, I cannot consistently will that the generalized form of my maxim be a law of nature. In other words, I cannot consistently will that it be a law of nature that whenever anyone needs money and can get some on a false promise, then he will borrow some and promise to repay, even though he knows he won't be able to repay.

The third premise of the argument is the categorical imperative. If the rest of the argument is acceptable, then the argument as a whole shows that the categorical imperative, together with these other facts, implies that my lying promise would not be morally right. This would seem to be a reasonable result.

Some readers have apparently taken this example to show that according to Kantianism, it is always wrong to make a false promise. Indeed, Kant himself may have come to this conclusion. Yet if we reflect on the argument for a moment, we will see that the view of these readers is surely not the case. At best, the argument shows only that one specific act of making a false promise would be wrong. That one act is judged to be wrong because its maxim allegedly cannot be universalized. Other acts of making false promises would have to be evaluated independently. Perhaps it will turn out that every act of making a false promise has a maxim that cannot be universalized. If so, $CI_1$ would imply that they are all wrong. So far, however, we have been given no reason to suppose that this is the case.

Other critics would insist that Kant hasn't even succeeded in showing that $a_2$ is morally wrong. They would claim that the first premise of the argument is false. Surely it could be a law of nature that everyone will make a false promise when in need of money, they would say. If people borrowed money on false promises rarely enough, and kept their word on other promises, then no contradiction would arise. There would then be no reason to suppose that "no one would believe he was being promised anything, but would laugh at utterances of this kind as empty shams."[15]

Let us turn, then, to the third example. Kant now illustrates the application of the categorical imperative to a case of imperfect duty to oneself. The action in question is the "neglect of natural talents." Kant apparently holds that it is wrong for a person to let all of his natural talents go to waste. Of course, if a person has several natural talents, he is not required to develop all of them. Perhaps Kant considers this to be an imperfect duty partly because a person has the freedom to select which talents he will develop and which he will allow to rust.

Kant imagines the case of someone who is comfortable as he is and who, out of laziness, contemplates performing the act, $a_3$, of letting all his talents rust. His maxim in doing this would be:

$M(a_3)$: When I am comfortable as I am, I shall let my talents rust.

When generalized, the maxim becomes:

GM(a₃): Whenever anyone is comfortable as he is, he will let his talents rust.

Kant admits that GM(a₃) could be a law of nature. Thus, his argument in this case differs from the arguments he produced in the first two cases. Kant proceeds to outline the reasoning by which the agent would come to see that it would be wrong to perform as:

He then sees that a system of nature could indeed always subsist under such a universal law, although (like the South Sea Islanders) every man should let his talents rust and should be bent on devoting his life solely to idleness, indulgence, procreation, and, in a word, to enjoyment. Only he cannot possibly *will* that this should become a universal law of nature or should be implanted in us as such a law by a natural instinct. For as a rational being he necessarily wills that all his powers should be developed, since they serve him, and are given him for all sorts of possible ends.[16]

Once again, Kant's argument seems to be based on a rather dubious appeal to natural purposes. Allegedly, nature implanted our talents in us for all sorts of purposes. Hence, we necessarily will to develop them. If we also will to let them rust, we are willing both to develop them (as we must) and to refrain from developing them. Anyone who wills both of these things obviously wills inconsistently. Hence, the agent cannot consistently will that his talents rust. This, together with the categorical imperative, implies that it would be wrong to perform the act, a₃, of letting one's talents rust.

The argument can be put as follows:

### Rusting-Talents Example

1. Everyone necessarily wills that all his talents be developed.
2. If everyone necessarily wills that all his talents be developed, then the agent of a₃ cannot consistently will that GM(a₃) be a law of nature.
3. a₃ is morally right if and only if the agent of a₃ can consistently will that GM(a₃) be a law of nature.
4. Therefore a₃ is not morally right.

This argument seems even less persuasive than the others. In the quoted passage Kant himself presents a counterexample to the first premise. The South Sea Islanders, according to Kant, do not will to develop their talents. This fact, if it is one, is surely inconsistent with the claim that we all necessarily will that all our talents be developed. Even if Kant is wrong about the South Sea Islanders, his first premise is still extremely implausible. Couldn't there be a rational person who, out of idleness, simply does not will to develop his talents? If there could not be such a person, then what is the point of trying to show that we are under some specifically moral obligation to develop all our talents?

Once again, however, some philosophers may feel that Kant would have been worse off if his example had succeeded. These philosophers would hold that we in fact have no moral obligation to develop our talents. If Kant's theory had entailed that we have such an obligation, they would insist, then that would have shown that Kant's theory is defective.

In Kant's fourth illustration the categorical imperative is applied to an imperfect duty to others—the duty to help others who are in distress. Kant describes a man who is flourishing and who contemplates performing the act, a₄, of giving nothing to charity. His maxim is not stated by Kant in this passage, but it can probably be formulated as follows:

M(a₄): When I'm flourishing and others are in distress, I shall give nothing to charity.

When generalized, this maxim becomes:

GM(a₄): Whenever anyone is flourishing and others are in distress, he will give nothing to charity.

As in the other example of imperfect duty, Kant acknowledges that GM(a₄) could be a law of nature. Yet he claims once again that the agent cannot consistently will that it be a law of nature. He explains this by arguing as follows:

For a will which decided in this way would be in conflict with itself, since many a situation might arise in which the man needed love and sympathy from others, and in which, by such a law of nature sprung from his own will, he would rob himself of all hope of the help he wants for himself.[17]

Kant's point here seems to be this: The day may come when the agent is no longer flourishing. He may need charity from others. If that day does come, then he will find that he wills that others give him such aid. However, in willing that $GM(a_4)$ be a law of nature, he has already willed that no one should give charitable aid to anyone. Hence, on that dark day, his will will contradict itself. Thus, he cannot consistently will that $GM(a_4)$ be a law of nature. This being so, the categorical imperative entails that $a_4$ is not right.

If this is Kant's reasoning, then his reasoning is defective. For we cannot infer from the fact that the person *may* someday want aid from others, that he in fact already is willing inconsistently when he wills today that no one should give aid to anyone. The main reason for this is that that dark day may not come, in which case no conflict will arise. Furthermore, as is pretty obvious upon reflection, even if that dark day does arrive, the agent may steadfastly stick to his general policy. He may say, "I didn't help others when they were in need, and now that I'm in need I don't want any help from them." In this way, he would avoid having inconsistent policies. Unless this attitude is irrational, which it does not seem to be, Kant's fourth example is unsuccessful. . . .

## Notes

1. Kant's *Grundlegung zur Metaphysik der Sitten* (1785) has been translated into English many times. All references here are to Immanuel Kant, *Groundwork of the Metaphysic of Morals,* translated and analysed by H. J. Paton (New York: Harper & Row, 1964).
2. Kant, *Groundwork,* p. 70.
3. *Ibid.,* p. 88.
4. *Ibid.,* p. 89.
5. *Ibid.,* p. 91.
6. *Ibid.,* p. 69n.
7. In some unusual cases, it may accidentally happen that the situation to which the maxim applies can occur only once, as, for example, in the case of successful suicide. Nevertheless, the maxim is general in form.
8. See, for example, Robert Paul Wolff, *The Autonomy of Reason* (New York: Harper & Row, 1973), p. 163.
9. This is stated especially clearly on p. 107 of the *Groundwork.*
10. Kant, *Groundwork,* pp. 89–91.
11. *Ibid.,* p. 89n.
12. *Ibid.,* p. 89.
13. *Ibid.*
14. *Ibid.,* p. 71.
15. *Ibid.*
16. *Ibid.*
17. *Ibid.,* p. 91.

## 19  Humanity as an End in Itself

**THOMAS HILL**

Few formulas in philosophy have been so widely accepted and variously interpreted as Kant's injunction to treat humanity as an end in itself. For some it is a specific antidote to utilitarianism, prohibiting all kinds of manipulation and exploitation of individuals for selfish or even altruistic ends. For others it is a general reminder that "people count," that no one's interests should be disregarded. Sometimes the formula is viewed as a principle of benevolence. The fact that the formula seems so adaptable for the expression of different ideas may, in fact, explain some of its appeal. Without denying that there are elements in Kant's writing which suggest alternative interpretations, I shall reconstruct what seems to me the main line of his thought about humanity as an end in itself. The interpretation I propose enables Kant to meet many of the objections that critics have raised against his formula, but it also reflects

From *Ethics* 91 (1980): 84–90, with omissions. Reprinted by permission of The University of Chicago Press.

an extreme moral stand that few of us, I suspect, could accept without modification.

# I

Kant's principle, the second formulation of the Categorical Imperative, is introduced as follows: "Act in such a way that you always treat humanity, whether in your own person or in the person of any other, never simply as a means but always at the same time as an end" (G 96 [429]). The first problem of interpretation is to see what is meant by the phrase "humanity *in* a person." On the usual reading this is treated as a quaint way of saying "a human person." That is, treating humanity in persons as an end is just to treat human beings as ends. "Humanity," on this view, refers to the class of human beings, and what is meant is simply that each member of the class is to be treated as an end. This reading is a natural one, for Kant does speak of persons and "rational beings" as ends in themselves (G 97 [430]; 104 [436]; 105 [437]), and human beings are the only persons and rational beings we know. Translators sometimes encourage this interpretation by rendering "*Menschheit*" as "man" instead of "humanity." There is no temptation to think of "man" as referring to something in a person, or a characteristic of a person, though "humanity" can be so understood, for example, when we contrast a person's animality with his humanity or when a theologian contrasts the divinity of Jesus with his humanity.

A review of Kant's repeated use of "humanity in a person" in *The Metaphysics of Morals* and elsewhere strongly suggests that, contrary to the usual reading, Kant thought of humanity as a characteristic, or set of characteristics, of persons. . . .

First, humanity includes the capacity and disposition to act on principles or maxims, at least in the broad sense which encompasses all acting for reasons (G 80 [412]). Second, humanity includes the capacity and disposition to follow rational principles of prudence and efficiency, that is, hypothetical imperatives, at least so far as these do not conflict with more stringent rational principles (G 82–83 [414–15]). Third, as a "power to set

any end whatsoever," humanity is thought to include a kind of freedom which lower animals lack—ability to foresee future consequences, adopt long-range goals, resist immediate temptation, and even to commit oneself to ends for which one has no sensuous desire (G 114–16 [446–49]). Fourth, humanity as rational nature necessarily (though not analytically) includes acceptance ("legislating to oneself") of certain unconditional principles of conduct, that is, categorical imperatives, independently of fear of punishment and promise of reward (G 83–84 [416], 108 [440]). This implies that anyone who has humanity has a capacity and disposition to follow such principles; but since his rationality may be imperfect or counteracted by other features, he may not always follow these principles (G 81 [413–14]). Fifth, as rational nature encompasses theoretical as well as practical reason, humanity must also include some ability to understand the world and to reason abstractly.

Humanity, so conceived, is attributed by Kant to even the most foolish and depraved persons (LE 197; DV 133 [463]; MPV 128). Although he sometimes writes as if certain acts amount to "throwing away" one's humanity, he repeatedly implies that a person's humanity remains, and so must be respected, even though he defiles, abases, violates, dishonors, or rejects it.[1] With a confidence difficult to maintain in the present age, Kant held that the spark of goodness, and therefore of rationality, is inextinguishable in us (R 41 [45]; LE 197; DV 134 [463]; MPV 129).

# II

Kant's formula, in effect, has two parts, namely: (1) Act in such a way that you never treat humanity simply as a means; and (2) act in such a way that you always treat humanity as an end. The first seems to have an instant intuitive appeal, but it cannot, I think, be understood independently of the second. To treat something *simply* as a means is to fail to treat it in some other appropriate way while one is treating it as a means. But (1), by itself, does not indicate what the appropriate treatment in question is. Obviously for Kant the answer is supplied by (2). One treats humanity simply as a means if and only if one treats it as a means but not as an end. The meaning of (1), then, depends upon the meaning of (2), and (1) will always be satisfied if (2) is satisfied.

Furthermore, (2) goes beyond (1). That is, the requirement to treat humanity as an end demands more than the requirement to avoid treating humanity merely as a means. This is suggested by the fact that Kant's discussion of the examples of the imperfect duties of developing one's talents and giving aid to the needy does not refer to the idea of using someone as a means (G 97–98 [430]). The point is confirmed in *The Metaphysics of Morals* when Kant says explicitly that being indifferent to someone satisfies the command not to use humanity merely as a means but fails to meet the requirement to treat humanity as an end (DV 55–56 [395]; MPV 54).

There are good reasons, then, to focus attention on (2) rather than (1). The crucial question is, What is it to treat humanity as an end? The question is especially puzzling because "humanity," as a set of rational capacities and dispositions, is not the sort of thing which is an end, or goal, in the ordinary sense. Kant acknowledges this when he says that it is not an end to be pursued but a "self-existent" end. Everyone has humanity, and the moral imperative is not to produce more of it but something else. But what?

The natural temptation at this point is to ignore the text and supply intuitive answers. Kant uses "as an end" as a technical term for the appropriate additional ways to treat humanity when using it as a means. So we naturally fill in the gap as we feel it should be filled. The point, some say, is to take everyone's interests into account. Thus, for example, a person fails when he employs a servant at the lowest possible wage without regard for the servant's welfare. But taking the individual's interests *into account* may seem insufficient, for it often seems inappropriate to use a person, or his humanity, as a means to some larger social ends which might be thought to override the individual interest. The injunction not to use humanity merely as a means seems to condemn not just self-

ish disregard of others' interests but also utilitarian manipulation of individuals for the general welfare. "I will not be used" is not always a defense against selfishness; it can also oppose abuse of the individual for altruistic purposes. In fact the charge "He is using me as a mere means, an object, a thing" often complains of neglect of one's unique qualities as an individual, as if the agent viewed one as expendable, replaceable by anyone who could serve similar functions.[2]

Whatever the merits of these intuitive reflections in general, they are no substitute, if the aim is to understand Kant, for examination of the puzzling details of Kant's texts. Let us review, then, what Kant says about *ends* in the sense in which humanity is regarded as an end.

(1) Humanity is not a "relative end" but an "objective end" or an "end in itself" (G 95 [427–28]). Relative ends are ends which individuals have because they like, want, and hope for various things as sensuous beings. Objective ends, or ends in themselves, are ends "valid for all rational beings." Their value is contrasted with that of relative ends, which "provide no universal principles, no principles valid and necessary for all rational beings and also for every volition" (G 95 [427]). This does not tell us exactly in what sense humanity is an end, but it does imply that humanity is not an end because it is something desired and that its being an end implies principles which should be recognized by all rational beings.

(2) An end, in general, is defined as "what serves the will as the (subjective) ground of its self-determination" (G 95 [427]). In the typical case this would be some future state of affairs for the sake of which one sets oneself to do something, for example, being financially secure as a goal for which a person might work and save. But humanity is not an end of this sort. In calling it an end, or "ground of self-determination," Kant evidently had in mind something more general, beyond the ordinary use of "end," namely, a reason for acting. This is, to acknowledge that something, such as humanity, is an end is to grant that one has a "ground" for choosing, or "determining oneself," to do or refrain from doing various things. But what, specifically, one has reason to do is not yet clear.

(3) Humanity is a "self-existent" end, not an end to be produced (G 105 [438]). The point, apparently, is that whenever humanity exists it is an end by virtue of what it is and that to say that humanity is an end is not to say that something which does not yet exist should be produced or that the quantity of something desirable should be increased.

(4) Humanity, as an objective end, is one "such that in its place one can put no other end to which (it) should serve simply as a means . . ." (G 6 [428]). Construing "ends" in the broad sense of "reasons for choosing," we may understand this as saying that when a person's humanity gives one a reason for doing or refraining from something, whatever this may be, that reason takes precedence over other reasons; for example, even if neglecting, impairing, or dishonoring a person's humanity were to cause many people pleasure, this would not be a rational exchange.

(5) Objective ends are "a supreme condition limiting the use of every means," "a condition limiting all merely relative and arbitrary ends," and "a limit on all arbitrary treatment" of rational beings (G 105 [438], 104 [436], 96 [428]). Thus the fact that humanity is an end in itself is supposed to set a rational and moral limit to the ways we may treat people in the pursuit of our relative ends, but just what this limit is remains to be seen.

(6) Objective ends are to be "conceived only negatively—that is, as an end against which we should never act . . ." (G 105 [437]). This remark is puzzling. There is no problem if it is merely a reiteration of point (3) above, that to say that humanity, or a rational being, is an end in itself is not to name some goal to be achieved. However, if it means, as it seems to, that treating humanity as an end in itself requires only restraint, a "hands-off" attitude, rather than positive effort to help others, then it flatly contradicts what Kant says elsewhere, for example, that one must "agree positively" with humanity as an end in itself. "For the ends of a subject who is an end in himself must, if this conception is to have its full effect in me, be also, so far as possible, my ends" (G 98 [430]). At least at this point Kant is definite that, though humanity is not itself a goal to be achieved, the

contention that it is an end in itself is meant to have the consequence that we ought to promote the ends of others.

(7) In his second example Kant implies that one at least partially satisfies the requirement to treat humanity as an end if one treats persons as "beings who must themselves be able to share in the end of the very same action." A lying promise is wrong, for example, because "the man whom I seek to use for my own purposes by such a promise cannot possibly agree with my way of behaving to him, and so cannot himself share the end of the action" (G 97 [429]). This seems at first to imply that one should never do anything to a person that he does not want done, but Kant makes clear in a footnote that he does not intend such an absurdly extreme principle. Even the similar principle "Don't do unto others what you don't want done to yourself," if unqualified, is said to be unacceptable because it gives the criminal a basis for disputing with the judge who (justly) punishes him (G 97 [430]).

It would be obviously absurd to say that one cannot use a person's services unless that person, quite literally, shared all of one's ends in doing so —for example, to say that carpenters employed to build an opera house must have among their goals the increased enjoyment of opera. The point is that, insofar as they are used as means, they must *be able* to adopt the agent's end, under some appropriate description, without irrational conflict of will. If the carpenters are in need of work and are decently paid, they can without irrationality adopt the immediate end of building an opera house, whether they care for opera or not. Similarly, at least in Kant's opinion, the criminal can rationally—though he may not—adopt the ends of deterrence and even retribution for which he may be punished. What is relevant is not whether the person who is treated as a means happens to like the ends in question or could psychologically bring himself to value them all for their own sakes; it is rather that the maxim on which the agent acts ("Do this for the sake of that") is such that there is no irrationality in anyone's willing it as a universal law. The first formula of the Categorical Imperative asks us to test maxims from the agent's point of view; the second, insofar as the remarks about shared ends indicate, asks us to consider maxims from the point of view of those who are treated in accord with the maxims. But the main question is the same: Is the maxim one which any human being can, without irrational conflict of will, accept when applied to oneself and to everyone else?

Several considerations favor this interpretation. First, Kant was thinking of the "beings who must be able to share in the end" as rational beings, for he says: "For then it is manifest that a violator of the rights of man intends to use the person of others merely as a means without taking into consideration that, *as rational beings,* they ought always at the same time to be treated as ends—that is, only as beings who must themselves be able to share in the end of the very same action" (G 97 [430]).

Second, in the *Critique of Practical Reason* Kant states as the condition of treating a person as an end that his autonomy as a rational being be subjected to no purpose unless it is in accord with a law that might arise from the will of the person affected (CPrR 90 [87]). Here the restriction on the purposes or ends to which a person may be subordinated is more explicitly the compatibility of such purposes with laws which the affected person, as a rational being, could accept. Third, the present reading helps to make understandable (though not entirely correct) Kant's belief that the first and second formulas of the Categorical Imperative are equivalent, at least for practical purposes (G 103 [436]). Fourth, the more literal alternative readings yield obviously absurd conclusions.

Although Kant's remarks about the ability to share ends do give a sense to his second formula, it would be a mistake, I think, to suppose that it represents his whole understanding of the matter —or even his most dominant line of thought. The remarks occur in a discussion of only one example, and they have little to do with his use of the idea of humanity as an end in *The Metaphysics of Morals.* Moreover, the requirement that the recipient of an act must be able to share its end is subject to all the familiar, even notorious, problems

that can be raised to the first formula of the Categorical Imperative. Until a maxim, including the appropriate description of the end of an act, is specified, the test cannot be used; and, while there are no adequate rules for characterizing the maxim, how one does so makes all the difference in the results of the test. Moreover, it is difficult, if not impossible, to explain the sort of irrational conflict of will in question such that the test condemns just those maxims which morally should be condemned, and not others. For these reasons, I think, it is well to look further for clues regarding what it means to treat humanity as an end.

## III

In describing a "kingdom of ends" Kant distinguishes (relative) personal ends from ends in themselves by saying that the latter have *dignity* whereas the former have only price (G 102 [434]). This idea, repeated in various ways elsewhere,[3] may be a key to understanding the sense in which humanity is supposed to be an end in itself.

Dignity is attributed by Kant to things which are related but of different types: (1) humanity (rational nature, human nature[4]); (2) morality (moral law—references at G 93 [425], 102 [435]; CPrR 152 [147]); (3) persons (rational beings—references at G 105 [436]; MPV 96–97 [433–34]); (4) persons who conform to duty (G 107 [439–40], 102 [434]); and (5) moral disposition (to do duty for duty's sake—reference at G 103 [435]). The attribution of dignity to dutiful persons (4) and moral disposition (5) might suggest that one acquires dignity only by conforming to moral law and so that only morally good people have dignity. But other passages make clear that humanity in each person has dignity, no matter how immoral the person may be (DV 99 [435]; MPV 97; LE 196–97; DV 45 [387]). Autonomy is said to be the ground of dignity, and this is a property of the will of every rational being, namely, the property of legislating to oneself universal (moral) laws without the sensuous motives of fear, hope for reward, and the like (G 103 [436], 108 [440]). Dignity is repeatedly ascribed to "every rational being" and "rational nature" (G 103 [436], 105 [438], 106 [439]). As far as human beings are concerned, this amounts to saying that humanity in persons has dignity; and, as we have seen, Kant does not think that one loses one's humanity when one acts immorally.

Dignity is characterized as "an unconditional and incomparable worth" (G 103 [436]). The first point, that dignity is an unconditioned worth, is that it is a value not dependent upon contingent facts. Thus, for example, whatever has dignity has value independently of any effects, profit, or advantage which it might produce. In Kant's terms, it has value regardless of any *market price* which it may have, that is, regardless of what one could get from others in exchange for it on account of its ability to satisfy universal needs and inclinations. Its value is also independent of *fancy price,* that is, independent of what one could get in exchange for it on account of someone's happening to want it quite apart from its utility in satisfying universal human needs and inclinations (G 102 [434–35]). What has dignity has value whether in fact valued by anyone or not. Thus when Kant speaks of dignity as an "intrinsic value" he does not imply that, as a matter of fact, people value what has dignity for its own sake. The point is rather that a perfectly rational person would so value it.

The second point, not entailed by the first, is that dignity is an "incomparable" worth, "exalted above all price," and "admits of no equivalent" (G 102 [434–35]). This means at least that whenever one must choose between something with dignity and something with mere price one should always choose the former. No amount of price, or value dependent on contingent needs and tastes, can justify or compensate for sacrifice of dignity. We may express this by saying that what has dignity is *priceless.*

While it is clear that Kant thought that dignity should always take precedence over price, it is not so obvious whether he took a more extreme position. That is, did he hold that what has dignity is *irreplaceable* in the sense that there are no legitimate trade-offs among things which have dignity?

Is his view, for example, that there are two scales of value, price and dignity, such that things can be ranked comparatively on each scale even though nothing on the scale of dignity can be overweighed by any amount of value on the scale of price? This would allow that some things may have more dignity than others, and that the sacrifice of dignity in one sphere might be justified by its enhancement in another. This is compatible with the claim that dignity is above all price. Or, alternatively, is Kant's view that dignity is something that cannot be quantified, so that it does not make sense to say that dignity of humanity in one person can fairly and reasonably be exchanged for the sake of a greater amount of dignity elsewhere? On this view to say that something has dignity is to say that it can never be sacrificed for anything with mere price, but it tells us nothing about what to do if one must choose between dignity in one sphere and dignity in another.

The first interpretation may well be more congenial to most readers because it obviously allows the sacrifice of humanity in one person for the sake of humanity in many persons in extreme circumstances. One can imagine a spy story, for example, in which suicide, the use of brain-damaging drugs, and contemptuous mockery of another human being, all of which Kant regards as contrary to the dignity of humanity, are necessary means to the prevention of a holocaust. In such a case, admittedly rare, many people would readily grant that it is justified to sacrifice the humanity of one person for the preservation of life, prevention of misery, and even furtherance of rationality in many persons. The second interpretation, however, seems to be implied by what Kant says. The definition of *price* is that "something else can be put in its place as an equivalent," and *dignity,* by contrast, "admits of no equivalent." Strictly construed, this must mean that what has dignity cannot morally or reasonably be exchanged for anything of greater value, whether the value is dignity or price. One cannot, then, trade off the dignity of humanity in one person in order to honor a greater dignity in two, ten, or a thousand persons. This may seem to imply that there can never be a justification for impairing the rationality or sacrificing the life of any human being, but this is not necessarily so. What is implied, strictly, is only that one may not sacrifice something with dignity *in* exchange for something of greater value. Thus, if the sacrifice of something with dignity is ever justified, the ground for this cannot be "this is worth more than that" or "a greater quantity of value is produced by doing so." Kant in fact takes a quite rigoristic stand regarding acts contrary to the dignity of humanity in a single person; for example, suicide, drunkenness, and mockery are said to be violations of "perfect," that is, exceptionless, duties. To say that one should never, for any reason, damage the rational capacities of any person would probably not come hard for one who held that it is wrong to tell a lie to save a friend from murder. However, the thesis that humanity has an incomparable worth which "admits of no equivalent" does not, strictly speaking, commit Kant to such a view. One cannot trade off a person's rational capacities for anything alleged to be more valuable, but comparisons of quantities of value may not be the only justifications. When we turn to Kant's more specific moral opinions, especially regarding the preservation of human life, we find that Kant sometimes even demands the destruction of a person with humanity of incomparable worth.

## IV

What are the practical implications of the thesis that humanity in persons has an unconditional and incomparable worth? Since humanity is our rationality and capacity to set ends, it seems natural to suppose that one would acknowledge its special value in the following ways. First, and most obviously, one would refuse to do anything which damages or impairs a person's rational capacities, whether the person is oneself or another. For example, drugs or frontal lobotomies that render a criminal nonviolent at the cost of making him permanently cowlike would be for-

bidden. Even temporary impairment of reason through drugs, at least in one who had a viable alternative to use reason, would be suspect. Second, one who sufficiently valued persons' rational capacities would presumably not want to destroy the persons themselves. Thus killing human beings seems to be ruled out. Third, if rational capacities have an incomparable value, then surely one should try to develop them and improve them in oneself and others. Fourth, it seems equally obvious that one should strive to exercise these capacities as far as possible. Thus if, as Kant thought, acting from respect for the moral law is a use of reason, then one should try to do so. And, more surprisingly, even prudence is required so far as it is compatible with unconditional rational principles of morality. Fifth, since the exercise of rationality is something to be cherished, in trying to influence others one should appeal to their reason rather than try to manipulate them by nonrational techniques. Sixth, valuing highly the setting and rational pursuit of ends even in other persons, one should leave them freedom to set and pursue their ends in a rational (moral and prudential) way, subject only to whatever further constraints reason imposes. Finally, certain attitudes and symbolic gestures, and avoidance of others, may be required. If humanity is of incomparable value, it should be honored and respected or at least not mocked, dishonored, or degraded. This is especially suggested by the term dignity (*Würde*), which is Kant's label for this special value.

Kant's own use of the idea of humanity as an end is for the most part in line with these natural applications, and at least some of the discrepancies can be explained as a result of certain special beliefs he held. Let us consider Kant's view on each point in turn.

(1) Kant does not discuss lobotomy and other means of causing permanent brain damage, but he does condemn drunkenness and the use of opium as making one temporarily animal-like, with a weakened "capacity to use his powers purposively" (MPV 88 [427]). Even gluttony is prohibited because it leaves one "temporarily

incapacitated for activities which require adroit-ness and deliberation in the use of one's powers" (MPV 88 [427]). The principle behind these con-clusions, as well as the requirements to develop one's natural talents, is: "it is one's duty to raise himself out of the crudity of his nature, out of his animality . . . more and more to humanity, by which alone he is capable of setting himself ends" (MPV 44–45 [387]).

(2) In both the *Groundwork* and *The Meta-physics of Morals* Kant argues that suicide is wrong because it reflects an undervaluation of humanity in one's own person. He does not, how-ever, draw the general conclusion that killing human beings is always wrong. Execution for murder is said to be a requirement of justice, and killing in a just war is regarded as permissible at least in certain stages of history (MEJ 102 [333], 122–23 [349]). Thus if Kant was consistent, he understood the incomparable value of humanity in persons in a sense that does not imply that the life of every person with humanity must always be preserved. In fact the argument against suicide does not imply that *life* is irreplaceable. What is at issue is suicide for the purpose of ending a painful existence or "as a mere means to some end of one's own liking," and this is said to be wrong not because it destroys something priceless and irre-placeable but because it "degrades" humanity in one's own person. That is, suicide for such rea-sons reflects an attitude that devalues humanity (G 97 [429], 89 [421–22]; MPV 84 [423]) and counts lesser things as more important. Although suicide contravenes a "perfect duty," still Kant leaves open "casuistic questions," for example, whether it is wrong to kill oneself in anticipation of an unjust death sentence, or in order to save one's country, or to escape an impending madness resulting from the bite of a rabid dog (MPV 84–85 [423–24]).

Kant's view, I think, may be best reconstructed as follows. First, to take the life of someone with humanity for the sake of something of mere price is always wrong, an undervaluation of humanity. Pleasure and pain, and the particular goals one has because of what one desires to achieve, are thought to have only conditioned value, or price,

and so suicide or the killing of others for the sake of increasing pleasure, diminishing pain, or achieving any contingently desired goal is wrong. Second, the proper attitude about humanity is not that each bit of it has a value which one can weigh against the value of other bits to calculate reasonable trade-offs. One should not try to de-termine what to do by calculating whether destroying or degrading humanity in one case is warranted by its consequences of preserving or developing it in another. But nevertheless, third, the fact that such calculation is inappropriate does not imply that there is no reason, ever, for ending the life of a being with humanity. Analogously, perhaps, a parent of three children faced with the awful choice of saving two or one might on some ground choose to save the two without having to grant that two are *worth* more than one, that the reason is that the quantity of something valuable in the world has been maximized. What the ground could be would need to be explained by other formulas of the Categorical Imperative, despite Kant's (mistaken) belief that the formulas are equivalent; but I expect that the intuition here is not uncommon.

(3) As we would expect, Kant argues for a duty to develop one's rational capacities, "powers of the spirit" (e.g., in mathematics, logic, and meta-physics of nature) and "powers of the mind" (e.g., memory, imagination, and the like), and again the general ground seems to be "the worth of human-ity in his own person, which he should not degrade" (MPV 109–10 [445–46]). The duty is regarded as an "imperfect" one, but the point is not that one may choose to neglect these powers but only that the principle in question does not specify "the kind and degree" of action needed to satisfy it. Kant does not, however, conclude that it is a duty to develop the rational powers of others. The reason is not that the development of their perfection is unimportant or less important but rather that, in Kant's opinion, such development can only be achieved by the person himself (MPV 44 [386]). As the old quip has it, "you can lead a youth to college, but you can't make him think." The idea that one should at least help to provide opportunity for others' rational development is not

discussed, though in his own life Kant was obviously committed to it.

(4) To strive to exercise reason in moral contexts, Kant implies, is a duty, but to use it to promote one's own happiness, barring special circumstances, is not a duty. Kant says that it is a duty to strive for moral perfection, which consists of a disposition to do one's duty from a sense of duty, which in turn is supposed to be a disposition to act from pure reason as opposed to sensuous inclination (MPV 110 [446]). Despite the incomparable value of rationality, however, Kant does not conclude that the exercise of prudential reason in normal contexts is a duty (even when compatible with other moral principles). The explanation is not that such use of reason is unimportant or that the idea of humanity as an incomparable value fails to commend it; it is rather that human beings are so disposed by nature to pursue their own happiness that it is inappropriate to speak of a "duty" to do so. "Duty" implies constraint, possible disinclination and failure to comply (MPV 43 [385–86]). Thus, though rational prudence is not demeaned, the only *duty* to promote one's own happiness is indirect and concerns special circumstances; that is, the duty, strictly speaking, is to avoid unnecessary pain, adversity, and poverty insofar as these are temptations to vice rather than a general duty to maximize one's (morally permissible) satisfactions (MPV 46 [388]).

(5) The idea that one should try to reason with others rather than to manipulate them by nonrational techniques is manifest in Kant's discussion of the duty to respect others. No matter how stupid a person may appear, it is wrong to censure him "under the name of absurdity, inept judgment, and the like," and no matter how immoral he may seem, one must not treat him as worthless or incapable of improvement (MPV 128 [463–64]). Moral education—as illustrated in Kant's sample moral catechism—is to be by a rational process of question and answer, never by citing examples to emulate (MPV 145–53 [477–84]).

(6) One of the most significant consequences of placing a special value on a human being's capacity to set and rationally pursue ends is that there is a strong prima facie case for allowing individuals freedom to form and pursue their own life plans subject only to the constraint that others be allowed a similar freedom. This is essentially Kant's "universal principle of justice," the foundation of his treatment of rights and juridical duties (MEJ 35 [230–31]). Even in the private sphere the duty of respect for persons is one which requires us to reject arrogance and make room for others; in contrast with beneficence, it is a negative duty and requires that even friends "halt at a suitable distance from one another" (MPV 113–14 [449–50], 130 [464–65], 136 [470]). Thus not only must we allow others "external" freedom but we should also leave even the best of friends a certain private space. We should value not only their happiness but that they set their own ends and pursue them in a rational way.

Valuing someone's rational pursuit of his own ends is not the same as wanting him to have what he desires, or what he will most enjoy, by any (morally permissible) means. The latter is general beneficence, and it is noteworthy that in *The Metaphysics of Morals* Kant's argument for general beneficence has nothing to do with the dignity of humanity (MPV 116–18 [450–54]). Indeed it is hard to see how such a duty would follow from the principle to treat humanity as an end, despite Kant's remark in the *Groundwork* that to accept fully humanity in others as an end one must regard their ends as one's own. If one could paternalistically give another pleasure and diminish his pain by ignoring his own life plan and thwarting his own rational pursuit of his ends, then this would be placing something with mere price (e.g., his comfort) over something with dignity (his capacity to set and rationally pursue ends). If our interpretation is right, what the dignity of humanity should require is that one should help others to set their own ends and rationally pursue them rather than try to make their lives pleasant independently of their own goals. This might well involve removing obstacles, providing opportunities, and all manner of "positive" activity distinct from a passive "hands-off" attitude. In fact Kant's example of beneficence in the *Groundwork* really has to do with helping someone in need rather than with general beneficence, and one is urged to be concerned with his ends, not with what one believes will make him best off (G 90 [423], 98 [430]; MPV 46 [388]). In respecting the dignity of humanity in a person, one is to value another's achievement of a (morally permissible) end because it is an end *he* adopted rather than because one expects it will bring him pleasure or something regarded as intrinsically valuable apart from his choice.

(7) Kant's arguments in *The Metaphysics of Morals* also accord with the final natural application of the idea of the dignity of humanity in persons, namely, that human rationality is to be honored in word and gesture as well as in deed. Kant is unusual, at least compared to moral philosophers today, in stressing the moral importance of attitude and gesture aside from their consequences. Mockery is opposed, whether or not it is effective for the purpose of reform or deterrent, because it reflects a disrespectful attitude toward the humanity of others (MPV 132 [467]). Servility, as often revealed in groveling, flattery, simpering, and self-disparagement, is condemned because it symbolizes an attitude which does not place the dignity of one's own humanity above all price (MPV 96–98 [434–36]).

## V

My purpose has not been to defend Kant but to understand him. Nevertheless, it is worth noting that, if my account is more or less correct, certain objections to Kant's formula regarding humanity as an end turn out to be off the mark. For example, it is sometimes said that this formula is "empty," having no implications independently of other formulations of the Categorical Imperative.[5] Although fine questions about the relations among the formulations must await proper interpretation of each, my reconstruction of Kant's second formulation certainly appears to be independent of others and, in fact, to go beyond the famous first formula, as the usual interpretations would have it, in declaring a rather substantive value judgment with significant practical implications. An-

other objection that has been raised to the second formula is that it prohibits what is impossible, namely, treating oneself merely as a means.[6] On the present account, however, a person can, and too often does, treat humanity in his person merely as a means; for this means, among other things, being willing to trade or sacrifice his rational capacities for something of value merely because he happens to want it. Again, it has been objected that Kant's formula prohibits noble self-sacrifice for the improvement of the human condition as, for example, when a medical researcher undergoes dangerous experiments in hopes of finding a cure for a disease that kills hundreds of thousands.[7] As I understand Kant, however, such self-sacrifice is not necessarily wrong. The second formula condemns sacrifice of life for what has mere price (for example, money, fame, and even cessation of pain) and more controversially, it forbids quantitative calculation of value among things with dignity, but it does not unequivocally prohibit the sacrifice of one's life. Another objection has been that Kant's principle leads to irreconcilable moral dilemmas, as when a typhoid carrier who has done no wrong must be quarantined for the safety of many other people.[8] Treating the individual as an end, it has been alleged, is incompatible with treating other people as ends. Possible conflicts of duties may remain a problem, but the situation in question is not a definitive example. Liberty is a high priority according to the second formula, but it is limited by a concern for the liberty and rational development of all. It should not be curtailed for the sake of anything of minor value or even the highest value by the measure of price, but that does not entail that there is never a reason to limit it.

A more serious worry about Kant's formula is that it places a comparatively higher value on rational capacity, development, control, and honor than most morally conscientious and reasonable people are prepared to grant. Kant has arguments for his view, which I have not considered; and common opinion is hardly decisive. Nevertheless, the striking implications of Kant's view, as I understand it, should not be ignored and his rationale deserves critical scrutiny. Hedonistic utilitarians surely must recoil; for Kant's view implies that pleasure and the alleviation of pain, even gross misery, have mere price, never to be placed above the value of rationality in persons. Kant apparently had faith that unequivocal commitment to this ranking of values would lead, in some indescribable world, to the deserved happiness of every conscientious person; but those of us who do not believe this must question his ranking, however strong its intuitive appeal in particular cases.

## Abbreviations for Kant's Works

CPrR    *Critique of Practical Reason,* trans. Lewis White Beck (New York: Macmillan/Library of Liberal Arts, 1985).

DV    *The Doctrine of Virtue,* trans. Mary Gregor (New York: Harper & Row, 1964).

G    *Groundwork of the Metaphysic of Morals,* trans. H. J. Paton (New York: Harper & Row, 1964).

LE    *Lectures on Ethics,* trans. Louis Infield (New York: Harper & Row, 1963).

MEJ    *Metaphysical Elements of Justice,* trans. John Ladd (Indianapolis: Bobbs-Merrill, 1965).

MPV    *Metaphysical Principles of Virtue,* trans. James Ellington (Indianapolis: Bobbs-Merrill, 1964).

R    *Religion within the Limits of Reason Alone,* trans. T. M. Greene and H. H. Hudson (New York: Harper & Row, 1960).

Page numbers in brackets refer to the appropriate volumes of *Kant's gesammelte Schriften,* herausgegeben von der Königlichen Preussischen Akademie der Wissenschaften, 23 volumes (Berlin: Walter de Gruyter, 1902). Kant's *Grundlegung zur Metaphysik der Sitten* (abbreviated "G") is in volume IV, pp. 387–463. *Kritik der praktischen Vernunft* (abbreviated "CPrR") is in volume V, pp. 1–164. *Die Metaphysik der Sitten* is in volume VI, pp. 203–494. (MEJ is a translation of the first part of *Die Metaphysik der Sitten* and can be found in volume VI, pp. 203–372; DV and MPV are alternative translations of the second part of this work and can be found in the same volume, pp. 375–491.) *Die Religion innerhalb der Grenzen der blossen Vernunft* (abbreviated "R") is in volume VI, pp. 1–202.

## Notes

1. DV 85 [422], 87 [424], 88 [425], 92 [428], 113 [463], 143 [471], 122 [454]; MPV 83, 85, 86, 89, 128, 137, 118.

2. Note that Kant's view, as should be clear in what follows, is quite different from this; he urges us not to value a person's individuality but rather something which he has in common with others, his "humanity."

3. For example, MPV 97 [434], 127 [462]. In the first passage Kant explicitly identifies being an end in itself and having dignity.

4. G 102 [435], 103 [436], 106 [436]; MPV 80 [420], 90 [429], 97 [435], 98 [436], 124 [459], 127 [462].

5. See, for example, M. G. Singer, *Generalization in Ethics* (New York: Knopf, 1961), p. 235.

6. Ibid., p. 236.

7. C. D. Broad, *Five Types of Ethical Theory* (New York: Harcourt, Brace, 1930), p. 132.

8. Ibid.

# 20   Consistency in Action

## ONORA O'NEILL

## Consistency without Universalizing

This account of acting on a maxim shows at least how action can be construed in a way that makes consistency and inconsistency possible, and provides some grounds for thinking that a focus on maxims may avoid some of the difficulties that have arisen in attempts to apply universality tests unrestrictedly to principles of action of all sorts. This opens the way for showing how action on a nonuniversalizable maxim is inconsistent and for considering whether such inconsistency constitutes a criterion of moral unworthiness. Before dealing with these topics it will be useful to run over some of the many ways in which action on a maxim may reveal inconsistency even when universalizing is not brought into the picture.

It is of course true that any act that is performed is possible, taken in itself. But it does not follow that the intentions that are enacted are mutually consistent. There are two sorts of possibilities here: In the first place there may be an internal inconsistency within an agent's maxim; in the second place there may be contradictions between the various specific intentions an agent adopts in pursuit of that maxim, or between some of these specific intentions and the agent's maxim. These two sorts of contradiction correspond closely to the two types of contradiction that Kant thinks may arise when attempts to universalize maxims fail, and that he characterizes as involving, respectively, "contradictions in conception" and "contradictions in the will" (*G*, IV, 424). Since I am also interested in charting the inconsistencies that can arise independently of attempts to universalize, as well as in those that arise when universalizing fails, I shall use the rather similar labels *conceptual inconsistency* and *volitional inconsistency* to distinguish these two types of incoherence in action. A consideration of the different types of incoherence that maxims may display even when the question of universalizability is not raised provides a useful guide to the types of incoherence that nonuniversalizable maxims display.

A maxim of action may in the first place be incoherent simply because it expresses an impossible aspiration. An agent's maxim might be said to involve a conceptual inconsistency if the underlying intention was, for example, both to be successful and to be unworldly, or alternatively, to be both popular and reclusive, or both to care for others and always to put his or her own advantage first, or both to be open and frank with everybody and to be a loyal friend or associate, or both to keep a distance from others and to have intimate personal relationships. Agents whose underlying maxims incorporate such conceptual inconsistencies do not, of course, succeed in performing impossible acts; rather, the pattern of their actions appears to pull in opposite directions and to be in various ways self-defeating. At its extreme we may regard such underlying incoherence in a person's maxim, and consequent fragmentation of the person's action, as tragic or pathological (and perhaps both), since there is no way in which he or she can successfully enact the underlying intention. In other cases we may think of the pattern of action that results from underlying conceptual incoherence as showing no more than ambivalence or presenting conflicting signals to others, who are consequently at a loss about what they should expect or do, finding themselves in a "double bind."

However, not all cases of disjointed action constitute evidence of an internally inconsistent maxim. For it may well be that somebody adopts some accommodation of the potentially inconsis-

Reprinted with kind permission from Kluwer Academic Publishers from *Universality and Morality: Essays on Ethical Universalizability,* ed. N. Potter and M. Timmons (Reidel, 1985), 159–186 with omissions, footnotes renumbered.

tent aspects of an underlying intention. For example, somebody may adopt the maxim of being competitive and successful in public and professional life but of disregarding such considerations in private life; or of being obedient and deferential to superiors but overbearing and exacting with all others. Provided such persons can keep the two spheres of action separated, their underlying intentions can be internally consistent. Hence one cannot infer an inconsistency in someone's underlying intentions merely from the fact that he or she exhibits tendencies in opposing directions. For these tendencies may reflect a coherent underlying intention to respond or act differently in different types of context or with different groups of people. A nonuniversalizable maxim embodies a conceptual contradiction only if it *aims* at achieving mutually incompatible objectives and so cannot under any circumstances be acted on with success.

A focus on maxims that embody contradictions in conception pays no attention to the fact that maxims are not merely principles that we can conceive (or entertain, or even wish) but principles that we *will* or intend, that is to say, principles that we adopt as *principles of action*. Conceptual contradictions can be identified even in principles of action that are never adopted or acted upon. But a second and rather different type of incoherence is exhibited in some attempts to will maxims whose realization can be quite coherently envisaged. Willing, after all, is not just a matter of wishing that something were the case, but involves committing oneself to doing something to bring that situation about when opportunity is there and recognized. Kant expressed this point by insisting that rationality requires that whoever wills some end wills the necessary means insofar as these are available.

Who wills the end, wills (so far as reason has decisive influence on his actions) also the means which are indispensably necessary and in his power. So far as willing is concerned, this proposition is analytic: for in my willing of an object as an effect there is already conceived the causality of myself as an acting cause—that is, the use of means; and from the concept of willing an end the imperative merely extracts the concept of actions necessary to this end. (*G*, IV, 417)

This amounts to saying that to will some end without willing whatever means are indispensable for that end, insofar as they are available, is, even when the end itself involves no conceptual inconsistency, to involve oneself in a volitional inconsistency. It is to embrace at least one specific intention that, far from being guided by the underlying intention or principle, is inconsistent with that intention or principle.

Kant, however, explicitly formulates only *one* of the principles that must be observed by an agent who is not to fall into volitional inconsistency. The Principle of Hypothetical Imperatives, as expressed in the passage just quoted, requires that agents intend any indispensable means for whatever they fundamentally intend. Conformity with this requirement of coherent intending would be quite compatible with intending no means to whatever is fundamentally intended whenever there is no specific act that is indispensable for action on the underlying intention. Further reflection on the idea of intending the means suggests that there is a *family* of Principles of Rational Intending, of which the Principle of Hypothetical Imperatives is just one, though perhaps the most important one. The following list of further Principles of Rational Intending that coherent intending (as opposed to mere wishing or contemplating) apparently requires agents to observe may not be complete, but is sufficient to generate a variety of interesting conclusions.

First, it is a requirement of rationality not merely to intend all *indispensable* or *necessary* means to that which is fundamentally intended but also to intend some *sufficient* means to what is fundamentally intended. If it were not, I could coherently intend to eat an adequate diet, yet not intend to eat food of any specific sort on the grounds that no specific sort of food is indispensable in an adequate diet.

Second, it is a requirement of rationality not merely to intend all necessary and some sufficient means to what is fundamentally intended but also to seek to make such means available when they are not. If it were not, I could coherently claim to intend to help bring about a social revolution but do absolutely nothing, on the grounds that there is no revolutionary situation at present, settling instead for rhetoric and gesture rather than politics. But if I do this, I at most wish for, and do not intend to help to bring about, a social revolution.

Third, it is a requirement of rationality not merely to intend all necessary and some sufficient means to whatever is fundamentally intended but also to intend all necessary and some sufficient *components* of whatever is fundamentally intended. If it were not, I could coherently claim to intend to be kind to someone to whom, despite opportunity, I show no kindness in word, gesture or deed, merely because acting kindly is not the sort of thing that requires us to take means to an end, but the sort of thing that requires that we act in some of the ways that are *constitutive* of kindness.[1]

Fourth, it is a requirement of rationality that the various specific intentions we actually adopt in acting on a given maxim in a certain context be mutually consistent. If it were not, I could coherently claim to be generous to all my friends by giving to each the exclusive use of all my possessions.

Fifth, it is a requirement of rationality that the foreseeable results of the specific intentions adopted in acting on a given underlying intention be consistent with the underlying intention. If it were not, I could coherently claim to be concerned for the well-being of a child for whom I refuse an evidently life-saving operation, on the grounds that my specific intention—perhaps to shield the child from the hurt and trauma of the operation—is itself aimed at the child's well-being. But where such shielding foreseeably has the further consequence of endangering the child's life, it is clearly an intention that undercuts the very maxim that supposedly guides it.

There may well be yet further principles that fully coherent sets of intentions must observe, and possibly some of the principles listed above need elaboration or qualification. The point, however, is to reveal that once we see action as issuing from a complex web of intentions, many of which are guided by and ancillary to certain more fundamental intentions or principles under particular conditions, the business of intending coherently and avoiding volitional inconsistency becomes a demanding and complex affair.

Reflection on the various Principles of Rational Intending reveals a great deal about the connections between surface and underlying intentions to which a rational being must aspire. Underlying intentions to a considerable extent express the larger and longer-term goals, policies and aspirations of a life. But if these goals, policies and aspirations are willed (and not merely wished for), they must be connected with some set of surface intentions that express commitment to acts that, in the actual context in which agents find themselves, provide either the means to or some components of any underlying intentions, or at least take them in the direction of being able to form such intentions, without at any point committing them to acts whose performance would undercut their underlying intentions. Wherever such coherence is absent we find an example of intending that, despite the conceptual coherence of the agent's maxim, is volitionally incoherent. In some cases we may think the deficiency cognitive—agents fail despite available information to appreciate what they need to do if they are indeed to act on their maxims (they may be stupid or thoughtless or calculate poorly). In other cases we might think of the deficiency as primarily volitional: agents fail to intend what is needed if they are to will their maxims and not merely to wish for them to be realized. Each of these types of failure in rationality subdivides into many different sorts of cases. It follows that there are very many different ways in which agents whose intentions are not to be volitionally inconsistent may have to consider their intentions.

Perhaps the most difficult of the various requirements of coherent willing is the last, the demand that agents not adopt specific intentions that in a given context may undercut their own maxims. There are many cases in which agents can reach relatively clear specific intentions about how they will implement or instance their maxims, yet the acts they select, though indeed selected as a means to or component of their underlying intentions, backfire. It is fairly common for agents to adopt surface intentions that, when enacted, foreseeably will produce results that defeat their own deeper intentions. Defensive measures generate counterattack; attempts to do something particularly well result in botched performances; decisive success in battle is revealed as Pyrrhic victory. It is perhaps unclear how long a view of the likely results of their action agents must take for us not to think action that leads to results incompatible with its underlying intention is irrational. But at the least the standard and foreseeable results of an action should not undercut the underlying intention if we are to think of an agent as acting rationally. Somebody who claims to intend no harm to others, and specifically merely intends to share a friendly evening's drinking and to drive others home afterward, but who then decides on serious drinking and so cannot safely drive, cannot plausibly claim to intend merely the exuberant drinking and bonhomie and not the foreseeable drunkenness and inability to drive safely. Given standard information, such a set of intentions is volitionally incoherent. For it is a normal and foreseeable result of exuberant drinking that the drinker is incapable of driving safely. One who intends the drinking also (given normal intelligence and experience) intends the drunkenness; and hence cannot coherently also intend to drive others home if the underlying intention is to harm nobody.[2]

This brief consideration of various ways in which agents' intentions may fail to be consistent shows that achieving consistency in action is a difficult matter even if we do not introduce any universality test. Intentions may be either conceptually or volitionally incoherent. The demand that the acts we perform reflect conceptually and volitionally coherent sets of intentions therefore constitutes a powerful constraint on all practical reasoning. This conclusion provides some reason for thinking that when these demands for consistency are extended in the way in which the second aspect of Kant's Formula of Universal Law requires, we should expect to see patterns of reasoning that, far from being ineffective or trivial, generate powerful and interesting results.

## Inconsistency in Universalizing

The intuitive idea behind the thought that a universality test can provide a criterion of moral acceptability may be expressed quite simply as the thought that if we are to act as morally worthy beings, we should not single ourselves out for special consideration or treatment. Hence whatever we propose for ourselves should be possible (note: not "desired" or "wanted"—but at least *possible*) for all others. Kant expresses this commonplace thought (it is, of course, not his argument for the Categorical Imperative) by suggesting that what goes wrong when we adopt a nonuniversalizable maxim is that we treat ourselves as special:

whenever we transgress a duty, we find that we in fact do not will that our maxim should become a universal law—since this is impossible for us—but rather that its opposite should remain a law universally: we only take the liberty of making an *exception* to it for ourselves (or even just for this once). . . . (G, IV, 424)

It is evident from this understanding of the Formula of Universal Law that the notion of a plurality of interacting agents is already implicit in the Formula of Universal Law. It is not the case that Kant introduces these notions into his ethics only with the Formula of the Kingdom of Ends, which would imply that the various formulations of the Categorical Imperative could not be in any way equivalent. To universalize is from the start to consider whether what one proposes for oneself *could* be done by others. This seems to many too meager a foundation for ethics but not in itself an implausible constraint on any adequate ethical theory.

Clearly enough, whatever cannot be consistently intended even for oneself also cannot be consistently intended for all others. The types of cases shown to be conceptually or volitionally inconsistent by the methods discussed in the previous section are *a fortiori* nonuniversalizable. This raises the interesting question whether one should think of certain types of cognitive and volitional failure as themselves morally unworthy. However, I shall leave this question aside in order to focus on the types of failure in consistent intending that are *peculiar* to the adoption of nonuniversalizable intentions.

I shall therefore assume from now on that we are considering cases of maxims that are in themselves not conceptually incoherent, and of sets of underlying and surface intentions that are not themselves volitionally inconsistent. The task is to pinpoint the ways in which inconsistency emerges in some attempts to universalize such internally consistent intentions. The second part of Kant's Formula of Universal Law enjoins action only on maxims that the agent can at the same time will as universal laws. He suggests that we can imagine this hypothetical willing by working out what it would be like "if the maxim of your action were to become through your will a universal law of nature." To universalize maxims agents must satisfy themselves that they can both adopt the maxim and simultaneously will that others do so. In determining whether they can do so they may find that they are defeated by either of the two types of contradiction that, as we have already seen, can afflict action even when universalizing is not under consideration. Kant's own account of these two types of incoherence, either of which defeats universalizability, is as follows:

We must *be able to will* that a maxim of our action should become a universal law—this is the general canon for all moral judgement of action. Some actions are so constituted that their maxim cannot even be *conceived* as a universal law of nature without contradiction, let alone be *willed* as what *ought* to become one. In the case of others we do not find this inner impossibility, but it is still impossible to *will* that their maxim should be raised to the universality of a law of nature, because such a will would contradict itself (*G*, IV 424)

Kant also asserts that those maxims that when universalized lead to conceptual contradiction are the ones that strict or perfect duty requires us to avoid, whereas those that when universalized are conceptually coherent but not coherently willable are opposed only to wider or imperfect duties.[3] Since we probably lack both rigorous criteria and firm intuitions of the boundaries between perfect and imperfect duties, it is hard to evaluate this claim. However, it is remarkably easy to display contradictions that arise in attempts to universalize maxims that we might think of as clear cases

of violations of duties of justice and self-respect, which Kant groups together as perfect duties; and it is also easy to show how contradictions emerge in attempts to universalize maxims that appear to exemplify clear violations of duties of beneficence and self-development, which Kant groups together as imperfect duties. By running through a largish number of such examples I hope to show how groundless is the belief that universality tests need supplementing with heteronomous considerations if they are to be action-guiding.

## Contradictions in Conception

A maxim that may lead to contradictions in conception when we attempt to universalize it often does not contain any conceptual contradiction if we merely adopt the maxim. For example, there is no contradiction involved in adopting the maxim of becoming a slave. But this maxim has as its universalized counterpart—the maxim we must attempt to "will as a universal law"—the maxim of everybody becoming a slave. But if everybody became a slave, there would be nobody with property rights, hence no slaveholders, and hence nobody could become a slave. Consider alternatively a maxim of becoming a slaveholder. Its universalized counterpart would be the maxim of everybody becoming a slaveholder. But if everybody became a slaveholder, then everybody would have some property rights; hence nobody could be a slave; hence there could be no slaveholders. Action on either of the nonuniversalizable maxims of becoming a slave or becoming a slaveholder would reveal moral unworthiness: It could be undertaken only by one who makes of himself or herself a special case.

Contradictions in conception can also be shown to arise in attempts to universalize maxims of deception and coercion. The maxim of coercing another has as its universalized counterpart the maxim that all coerce others; but if all coerce others, including those who are coercing them, then each party both complies with others' wills (being coerced) and simultaneously does not comply with others but rather (as coercer) exacts their compliance. A maxim of coercion cannot coherently be universalized and reveals moral unworthiness. By contrast, a maxim of coordination can be consistently universalized. A maxim of deceiving others as convenient has as its universalized counterpart the maxim that everyone will deceive others as convenient. But if everyone were to deceive others as convenient, then there would be no trust or reliance on others' acts of communication; hence nobody could be deceived; hence nobody could deceive others as convenient.

An argument of the same type can be applied to the maxim that is perhaps the most fundamental for a universality test, namely the maxim of abrogating judgment. One whose maxim it is to defer to the judgment and decisions of others—to choose heteronomy—adopts a maxim whose universalized counterpart is that everyone defer to the judgments and decisions of others. But if everyone defers to the judgments and decisions of others, then there are no decisions to provide the starting point for deferring in judgment; hence it cannot be the case that everybody defers in judgment. Decisions can never be reached when everyone merely affirms, "I agree." A maxim of "elective heteronomy" cannot consistently be universalized.

Interpreters of Kant have traditionally made heavier weather of the contradiction in conception test than these short arguments suggest is necessary. There have perhaps been two reasons why. One is clearly that Kant's own examples of applications of the Categorical Imperative are more complex and convoluted than these short arguments suggest. But even if detailed analysis of these examples is necessary for an evaluation of Kant's theory, it is clarifying to see whether a contradiction in conception test works when liberated from the need to accommodate Kant's particular discussion of examples.

But a second reason why the contradiction in conception test has seemed problematic to many of Kant's commentators is perhaps of greater importance for present concerns. It is that whereas many would grant that we can detect contradictions in attempts to universalize maxims simply of slaveholding or coercing or deceiving or deference, they would point out that no contradiction emerges if we seek to universalize more circumspect maxims, such as "I will hold slaves if I am in

a position of sufficient power" or "I will deceive when it suits me and I can probably get away with it" or "I will defer in judgment to those I either admire or fear." Still less do contradictions emerge when we aim to universalize highly specific intentions of deception or deference, such as "I will steal from Woolworths when I can get away with it" or "I will do whatever my parish priest tells me to do."

However, the force of this objection to the claim that the contradiction in conception test can have significant moral implications is undercut when we remember that this is a test that applies to agents' maxims, that is, to their underlying or fundamental intentions or principles, and that as a corollary it is a test of moral worth. For what will be decisive is what an agent's fundamental intention or principle in doing a given act really is. What counts is whether the expression of falsehood expresses a fundamental attempt to deceive, or whether agreement with another (in itself innocent enough) expresses a fundamental refusal to judge or think for oneself. For an agent cannot truthfully claim that an underlying intent, plan or principle was of a very specific sort unless the organization of other, less fundamental, intentions reveals that it really was subject to those restrictions. Precisely because the Categorical Imperative formulates a universality test that applies to *maxims,* and not just to any intention, it is not rebutted by the fact that relatively specific intentions often can be universalized without conceptual contradiction. Conversely, further evidence for the interpretation of the notion of a maxim presented in the section entitled "Maxims and moral categories" is that it leads to an account of the Categorical Imperative that is neither powerless nor counterintuitive. However, for the same reason (that it applies to maxims and not to intentions of all sorts) the Categorical Imperative can most plausibly be construed as a test of moral worth rather than of outward rightness, and must always be applied with awareness that we lack certainty about what an agent's maxim is in a given case. This is a relatively slight difficulty when we are assessing our own proposed maxims of action, since we at least can do no better than to probe and test the maxim on which we propose to act (but even here we have no guarantee against self-deception). But it means that we will always remain to some extent unsure about our assessment of others' acts. Kant after all insists that we do not even know whether there *ever* has been a truly morally worthy act. But that is something we do not need to know in order to try to perform such acts. Self-deception may cloud our knowledge of our own maxims; but we are not powerless in self-guidance.

## Contradictions in the Will

Just as there are maxims that display no conceptual incoherence until attempts are made to universalize them, so there are maxims that exhibit no conceptual incoherence even when universalized, but that are shown to be volitionally inconsistent when attempts are made to universalize them. Such maxims cannot be "willed as universal laws"; attempts to do so fail in one way or another to meet the standards of rationality specified by the group of principles that I have termed Principles of Rational Intending. For to will a maxim is, after all, not just to conceive the realization of an underlying intention; that requires no more than speculation or wishing. Willing requires also the adoption of more specific intentions that are guided by, and chosen (in the light of the agent's beliefs) to realize, the underlying intention, or, if that is impossible, as appropriate moves toward a situation in which such specific intentions might be adopted. Whoever wills a maxim also adopts more specific intentions as means to or constituents of realizing that underlying intention, and is also committed to the foreseeable results of acting on these more specific intentions. Since intending a maxim commits the agent to such a variety of other intentions, there are various different patterns of argument that reveal that certain maxims cannot be willed as universal laws without contradiction.

Clearly the most comprehensive way in which a maxim may fail to be willable as a universal law is if its universal counterpart is inconsistent with the specific intentions that would be necessary for its own realization. Universalizing such a maxim would violate the Principle of Hypothetical Imperatives. The point is well illustrated by a Kantian example. If I seek to will a maxim of nonbeneficence as a universal law, my underlying intention is not to help others when they need it, and its universalized counterpart is that nobody help others when they need it. But if everybody denies help to others when they need it, then those who need help will not be helped, and in particular I will not myself be helped when I need it. But if I am committed to the standards of rational willing that constitute the various Principles of Rational Intending, then I am committed to willing some means to any end to which I am committed, and these must include willing that if I am in need of help and therefore not able to achieve my ends without help, I be given some appropriate help. In trying to universalize a maxim of nonbeneficence I find myself committed simultaneously to willing that I not be helped when I need it and that I be helped when I need it. This contradiction, however, differs from the conceptual contradictions that emerge in attempts to universalize maxims such as those considered in the last section. A world of nonbenevolent persons is conceivable without contradiction. Arguments that reveal contradictions in the will depend crucially upon the role of the various Principles of Rational Intending —in this case on the Principle of Hypothetical Imperatives—in constraining the choice of specific intentions to a set that will implement all underlying intentions. It is only because *intending* a maxim of nonbeneficence as a universal law requires commitment to that very absence of help when needed, to which all rational intending requires assent, that nonbeneficence cannot coherently be universalized.

A second Kantian example,[4] which provides an argument to volitional incoherence, is a maxim of neglecting to develop any talents. A world of beings who develop no talents contains no conceptual incoherence. The maxim of an individual who decides to develop no talents, though imprudent, reveals no volitional inconsistency. For it is always *possible* that others fend for the imprudent, who will then find means available for at least some action. (It is not a fundamental requirement of practical reason that there should be means available to whatever projects agents adopt, but only that they should not have ruled out all action.) However, an attempt to universalize a maxim of neglecting talents commits one to a world in which no talents have been developed, and so to a situation in which necessary means are lacking not just for some but for any sort of complex action. An agent who fails to will the development, in self or others, of whatever minimal range of talents is required and sufficient for a range of action, is committed to internally inconsistent sets of intentions. Such agents intend both that action be possible and that it be undercut by neglect to develop even a minimal range of talents that would leave some possibility of action. This argument shows nothing about the development of talents that may be required or sufficient for any *specific* projects, but only points to the inconsistency of failing to foster such talents as are needed and sufficient for action of some sort or other. It is an argument that invokes not only the Principle of Hypothetical Imperatives but also the requirement that rational beings intend some set of means sufficient for the realization of their underlying intentions or principles.

These two examples of arguments that reveal volitional inconsistencies show only that it is morally unworthy to adopt maxims either of systematic nonbeneficence or of systematic neglect of talents. The duties that they ground are relatively indeterminate duties of virtue. The first of these arguments does not specify whom it is morally worthy to help, to what extent, in what ways or at what cost, but only that it would be morally unworthy to adopt an underlying intention of nonbeneficence. Similarly, the second argument does not establish which talents it would be morally worthy to develop, in whom, to what extent or at what cost, but only that it would be morally unworthy to adopt an underlying intention of making no effort to develop any talents. The person who adopts a maxim either of nonbeneficence or of nondevelopment of talents cannot coherently universalize the maxim, but

must either make an exception of himself of herself, and intend, unworthily, to be a free rider on others' beneficence and talents, or be committed to some specific intentions that are inconsistent with those required for action on the maxim.

Another example of a maxim that cannot consistently be willed as a universal law is the maxim of refusing to accept help when it is needed. The universalized counterpart of this underlying intention would be the intention that everyone refuse to accept help when it is needed. But rational beings cannot consistently commit themselves to intending that all forgo a means that, if ever they are in need of help, will be indispensable for them to act at all.

A further example of a nonuniversalizable maxim is provided by a maxim of ingratitude, whose universalized counterpart is that nobody show or express gratitude for favors received. In a world of non-self-sufficient beings a universal maxim of ingratitude would require the systematic neglect of an important means for ensuring that help is forthcoming for those who need help if they are to realize their intentions. Hence in such a world nobody could coherently claim to will that those in need of help be helped. Yet we have already seen that to will that all in need of help be refused help is volitionally inconsistent. Hence, willing a maxim of ingratitude also involves a commitment to a set of intentions not all of which can be consistently universalized. The volitional inconsistency that overtakes would-be universalizers of this maxim arises in two stages: The trouble with ingratitude is that, practiced universally, it undercuts beneficence; the trouble with nonbeneficence is that it cannot be universally practiced by beings who have at least some maxims, yet (lacking self-sufficiency) cannot guarantee that their own resources will provide means sufficient for at least some of their projects.

The hinge of all these arguments is that human beings (since they are adopters of maxims) have at least some maxims or projects, which (since they are not self-sufficient) they cannot always realize unaided, and so must (since they are rational) intend to draw on the assistance of others, and so must (if they universalize) intend to develop and foster a world that will lend to all some support of others' beneficence and talents. Such arguments can reveal the volitional inconsistencies involved in trying to universalize maxims of entirely neglecting the social virtues—beneficence, solidarity, gratitude, sociability and the like—for beings who are rational yet not always able to achieve what they intend unaided. It follows from this point that the social virtues are very differently construed in Kantian and in heteronomous ethics. An ethical theory for nonheteronomous agents sees the social virtues as morally required, not because they are desired or liked but because they are necessary requirements for action in a being who is not self-sufficient. The content of the social virtues in this framework cannot be spelled out in terms of the provision of determinate goods or services or the meeting of certain set needs or the satisfaction of a determinate set of desires. Rather, the content of these virtues will always depend on the various underlying maxims and projects, both individual and collaborative, to which agents commit themselves. What will constitute beneficence or kindness or care for others will depend in great part on how others intend to act.

## Contradictions in the Will and Further Results

The patterns of argument that can be used to show underlying antisocial intentions morally unworthy make use of various Principles of Rational Intending in addition to the Principle of Hypothetical Imperatives. In particular they draw on the requirements that rational agents intend not merely necessary but also sufficient means to or components of their underlying intentions or maxims, and that they also intend whatever means are indirectly required and sufficient to make possible the adoption of such specific intentions. However, the particular features of the fifth Principle of Rational Intending—the Principle of Intending the Further Results—have not yet been displayed. Attempts to evade this Principle of Rational Intending lead to a peculiar sort of volitional inconsistency.

Good examples of arguments that rely on this principle can be developed by considering cases of maxims that, when universalized, produce what are frequently referred to as "unintended consequences." For example, I can adopt the underlying intention of improving my economic well-being, and the specific intention of doing so by competing effectively with others. The maxim of my action can be consistently universalized: There is no conceptual contradiction in intending everyone's economic position to improve. The specific intention of adopting competitive strategies is not inconsistent with the maxim to which it is ancillary; nor is universal action on competitive strategies inconsistent with universal economic advance (that indeed is what the invisible hand is often presumed to achieve). But if an agent intends his or her own economic advance to be achieved solely by competitive strategies, this nexus of intentions cannot consistently be willed as universal law, because the further results of universal competitive activity, by itself, are inconsistent with universal economic advance. If everyone seeks to advance by these (and no other) methods, the result will not put everybody ahead economically. A maxim of economic progress combined with the specific intention of achieving progress merely by competitive strategies cannot be universalized, any more than the intention of looking over the heads of a crowd can be universally achieved by everyone in the crowd standing on tiptoes. On the other hand, a maxim of seeking economic advance by means of increased production can be consistently universalized. It is merely the particular specific intention of advancing economically by competitive strategies alone that leads to volitional inconsistency when universalized. Competitive means are inherently effective only for some: Competitions must have losers as well as winners. Hence, though it can be consistent to seek individual economic advance solely by competitive methods, this strategy cannot consistently be universalized. Once we consider what it would be to intend the consequences of universal competition—the usually *unintended* consequences—we can see that there is an inconsistency not between universal competitive activity and universal economic progress, but between the *further results of intending only universal competitive activity and universal economic progress.* Economic progress and competitive activity might each of them consistently be universal; indeed, it is possible for them to coexist within a certain society. (Capitalist economies do experience periods of general economic growth.) Nevertheless, there is a volitional inconsistency in seeking to achieve universal economic growth *solely by way* of universal adoption of competitive strategies.

This argument does not show that either the intention to advance economically or the intention to act competitively cannot be universalized, but only that the composite intention of pursuing economic advance solely by competitive tactics cannot be universalized. It does not suggest that either competition or economic progress is morally unworthy, but only that an attempt to achieve economic progress solely by competitive methods and without aiming at any productive contribution is not universalizable and so is morally unworthy.

Similarly, there is no inconsistency in an intention to engage in competitive activities of other sorts (e.g., games and sports). But if such competition is ancillary to an underlying intention to win, then the overall intention is not universalizable. Competitive games must have losers. If winning is not the overriding aim in such activities, if they are played for their own sake, the activity is consistently universalizable. But to play competitively with the fundamental intention of winning is to adopt an intention that makes of one's own case a necessary exception.

## Conclusions

The interest of a Kantian universality test is that it aims to ground an ethical theory on notions of consistency and rationality rather than upon considerations of desire and preference. Kant's universality test meets many of the conditions that any such universality test must meet. In particular it focuses on features of action that are appropriate candidates for assessments of coherence and incoherence, namely the maxims or fundamental

intentions that agents may adopt and the web of more specific ancillary intentions that they must adopt in a given context if their commitment to a maxim is genuine. Although Kant alludes specifically to conceptual inconsistencies and to those volitional inconsistencies that are attributable to nonobservance of the Principle of Hypothetical Imperatives in attempts to universalize intentions, there is in addition a larger variety of types of volitional inconsistency that agents who seek to subject their maxims to a universality test (and so not to make an exception of their own case) must avoid. A universality test applied to maxims and their ancillary, more specific, intentions can be action-guiding in many ways without invoking any heteronomous considerations.

However, precisely because it applies to intentions or principles, a universality test of this sort cannot generally provide a test of the rightness or wrongness of the specific outward aspects of action. It is, at least primarily, and perhaps solely, a test of the inner moral worth of acts. It tells us what we ought to avoid if we are not to act in ways that we can know are in principle not possible for all others. Such a test is primarily of use to agents in guiding their own moral deliberations, and can only be used most tentatively in assessing the moral worth of others' action, where we are often sure only about specific outward aspects of action and not about the maxim. This point will not be of great importance if we do not think it important whether an ethical theory enables us to pass judgment on the moral worth of others' acts. But specific outward aspects of others' action are unavoidably of public concern. The considerations discussed here do not reveal whether or not these can be judged right or wrong by Kant's theory. Kant no doubt thought that it was possible to derive specific principles of justice from the Formula of Universal Law; but the success of this derivation and of his grounding of *Rechtslehre* is beyond the scope of this chapter.

The universality test discussed here is, above all, a test of the mutual consistency of (sets of) intentions and universalized intentions or principles. It operates by showing some sets of proposed intentions to be mutually inconsistent. It does not thereby generally single out action on any one set of specific intentions as morally required. On the contrary, the ways in which maxims can be enacted or realized by means of acts performed on specific intentions must vary with situation, tradition and culture. The specific acts by which we can show or fail to show loyalty to a friend or respect to another or justice in our dealings with the world will always reflect specific ways of living and thinking and particular situations and relationships. What reason can provide is a way of discovering whether we are choosing to act in ways (however culturally specific) that we do not in principle preclude for others. The "formal" character of the Categorical Imperative does not entail either that it has no substantive ethical implications or that it can select a unique code of conduct as morally worthy for all times and places. Rather than presenting a dismal choice between triviality and implausible rigorism, a universality test can provide a rational foundation for ethics and maintain a serious respect for the diversity of content of distinct ethical practices and traditions.

## Notes

1. Kant's discussions of duties of virtue in any case suggest that he would count the necessary constituents or components of an end, and not merely the instrumentally necessary acts, as means to that end.

2. The fifth requirement of rational intending clearly deals with the very nexus of intentions on which discussions of the Doctrine of Double Effect focus. That doctrine claims that agents are not responsible for harm that foreseeably results from action undertaken with dutiful intentions, provided that the harm is not disproportionate, is regretted, and would have been avoided had there been a less harmful set of specific intentions that would have implemented the same maxim in that situation. (The surgeon foresees, and regrets, the pain unavoidably inflicted by a lifesaving procedure). Although the Doctrine of Double Effect holds that agents are not to be held responsible for such action, it allows that they do, if "obliquely" rather than "directly," intend it. It is compatible with the Doctrine of Double Effect to insist that an agent whose oblique intention foreseeably undercuts the action for the sake of which what is directly intended is done, acts irrationally. Where the fundamental intention is so undercut by a supposedly ancillary aspect of

action, proportionality is violated, and the attribution of the fundamental intentions may be called in question.

3. *G*, IV, 424; *MM*, IV, Introduction; *DV*, VI, especially 389.

4. Cf. *DV*, VI, 443–7, for discussion of the duty not to neglect to develop talents (the "duty to seek one's own perfection"). "Talents" here are to be understood not as any particularly unusual accomplishments, but as any human powers that (unlike natural gifts) we can choose either to cultivate or to neglect. Kant tends to think the most important talents are second-order ones (e.g., self-mastery, self-knowledge) and that we can do little to develop these in others. Both restrictions seem to me unnecessary. See Onora O'Neill, *Faces of Hunger: An Essay on Poverty, Development and Justice*, Chap. 8, for development of these thoughts.

## Questions

1. Choose any *two* of the following statements. Explain what the two statements mean. Why does Kant think they are true? Do you agree with Kant? Why or why not?

   a. "There is no possibility of thinking of anything at all in the world, or even out of it, which can be regarded as good without qualification, except a *good will*. . . . A good will is good not because of what it effects or accomplishes, nor because of its fitness to attain some proposed end; it is good only through its willing, i.e., it is good in itself" (7, A 394).

   b. "To be beneficent where one can is a duty; and besides this, there are many persons who are so sympathetically constituted that, without any further motive of vanity or self-interest, they find an inner pleasure in spreading joy around them and can rejoice in the satisfaction of others as their own work. But I maintain that in such a case an action of this kind, however dutiful and amiable it may be, has nevertheless no true moral worth" (11, A 398).

   c. "Some actions are so constituted that their maxims cannot without contradiction even be thought as a universal law of nature, much less be willed as what should become one. In the case of others this internal impossibility is indeed not found, but there is still no possibility of willing that their maxim should be raised to the universality of a law of nature, because such a will would contradict itself. There is no difficulty seeing that the former kind of action conflicts with strict or narrow [perfect] (irremissible) duty, while the second kind conflicts only with broad [imperfect] (meritorious) duty" (32, A 424).

d. "[T]he man who contemplates suicide will ask himself whether his action can be consistent with the idea of humanity as an end in itself. If he destroys himself in order to escape from a difficult situation, then he is making use of his person merely as a means so as to maintain a tolerable condition till the end of his life. Man, however, is not a thing and hence is not something to be used merely as a means; he must in all his actions always be regarded as an end in himself. Therefore, I cannot dispose of man in my own person by mutilating, damaging, or killing [myself]" (36, A 429).

e. "The ends which a rational being arbitrarily proposes to himself as effects of this action (material ends) are all merely relative, for only their relation to a specially constituted faculty of desire in the subject gives them their worth. Consequently, such worth cannot provide any universal principles, which are valid and necessary for all rational beings and, furthermore, are valid for every volition, i.e., cannot provide any practical laws. Therefore, all such relative ends can be grounds only for hypothetical imperatives.

But let us suppose that there were something whose existence has in itself an absolute worth, something which as an end in itself could be a ground of determinate laws. In it, and in it alone, would there be the ground of a possible categorical imperative, i.e., of a practical law.

Now I say that man, and in general every rational being, exists as an end in

himself and not merely as a means to be arbitrarily used by this or that will" (35, A 427–428).

2. Compare and contrast the different roles played by reason *or* happiness *or* human nature in the ethical theories of Aristotle, Kant, and Mill.

3. Compare and contrast the different roles that freedom (or autonomy) plays in the ethical theories of Mill, Kant, and Aristotle.

4. Consider the following dialogue between Aristotle and Kant.

*Kant:* Moral worth depends solely on motive. (13, A 399–400)

*Aristotle:* I disagree. Whether or not a person has a good character depends on what she desires and enjoys as well as on her motive. Suppose Sandy, Candy, and Brandy all refrain from theft from duty. Sandy wants to steal but would not enjoy stealing. Candy would enjoy stealing but does not want to steal. Brandy neither wants to steal nor would she enjoy stealing. I think Sandy and Candy are morally worse than Brandy, even though all three act from duty.

*Kant:* There are only two motives: duty and happiness.

*Aristotle:* I disagree. A person who is motivated by duty alone is too narrow. The good person is motivated not only by the virtue of dutifulness but also by a whole range of virtues, such as courage, temperance, justice, etc.

*Kant:* Because there are only two motives, each action exhibits either positive moral worth or no moral worth.

*Aristotle:* I disagree. Surely there are more than two levels of character. I think that there are at least four levels. *Virtuous people* (people who choose to act from virtue and who desire to do the right thing) are better than merely *continent people* (people who choose to act from virtue in spite of their desire to do the wrong thing). Continent people are better than *incontinent people* (people who choose to act from virtue but fail because they are overcome by their desire to do the wrong thing). Incontinent people are better than *vicious people* (people who choose to act from vice in order to satisfy their desire to do the wrong thing).

*Kant:* Because sympathy is an inclination, actions done from sympathy have no moral worth. (11, A398)

*Aristotle:* I disagree. Suppose Ann is sick and her acquaintances Jan and Fran visit her to cheer her up. Ann realizes that Jan is motivated solely by sympathy and Fran is motivated solely by duty. Clearly, Jan's visit will help, but Fran's visit will just depress Ann further. Thus there are some good actions that will succeed if they are done from inclination but not if they are done from duty.

Explain Kant's doctrine of moral worth. Defend it against any *two* of Aristotle's criticisms. (*Hint:* You might need to modify Kant's doctrine a bit in order to defend it adequately.)

5. Explain Kant's doctrine of moral worth. Defend it against any *two* of the following criticisms. [The first three criticisms are taken from W. Schaller, "Kant on Virtue and Moral Worth," *Southern Journal of Philosophy,* 25 (1987), pp. 560–561.]

   a. On certain occasions, something like sympathy or compassion, not duty, is the appropriate motive for one person's helping another. People are often comforted by the fact that someone sympathizes with them, and this is a good that cannot be provided by someone acting from the motive of duty but only by an individual who feels sympathy or compassion.

   b. Because only actions motivated by duty have moral worth, Kant's doctrine seems to reward the lack of virtue. The person who lacks the virtues of sympathy and benevolence, and who therefore can act beneficently only from duty, is more likely to perform actions correctly than the person who possesses those virtues.

   c. Kant claims that only actions done solely from duty can have moral worth. Con-

duct that has several motives—sympathy and duty, for example—appears to be denied any moral value.

   d. Because there are only two levels of moral worth, positive and zero, there are only two sorts of character, good and neutral. But we all know that there are evil characters.

   e. Because moral worth depends solely on motive, the conduct of a person who is horribly confused about what is right and what is wrong and who acts from duty (such as a sincere Nazi who really thinks he has a duty to commit genocide for reasons of eugenics) will end up having positive moral worth. But that is weird.

6. Suppose that an agent has only two options. X is the morally right choice, and Y is the morally wrong choice. Suppose further that the agent has an immediate inclination to perform either X or Y but not both. Finally, suppose that the agent believes that either X or Y, but not both, is in his or her own best interest (Kant calls this a *selfish purpose*). In this situation Kant's account yields the chart on the following page.

   Each letter from A to P represents one combination of choice, immediate inclination, selfish inclination, and type of motive. For example, H stands for a choice to do Y from inclination (sixth column) when the agent's immediate inclination is to do X and the agent believes that Y is in his or her best interest (second row). Kant describes the following cases (10–12, A 397–399):

   a. prudent merchant
   b. lover of life
   c. rejector of suicide
   d. friend of man
   e. unsympathetic person
   f. gouty patient
   g. lover of neighbor
   h. lover of enemy
   i. lying promiser

Under which category in the chart does each of these cases fall? Explain your answers.

| Agent Has Selfish Inclination to Perform Act | Agent Has Immediate Inclination to Perform Act | Agent Chooses to Perform Act X from Duty | Agent Chooses to Perform Act Y from Duty | Agent Chooses to Perform Act X from Inclination | Agent Chooses to Perform Act Y from Inclination |
|---|---|---|---|---|---|
| X | X | A | B | C | D |
| Y | X | E | F | G | H |
| X | Y | I | J | K | L |
| Y | Y | M | N | O | P |
| none | none | Q | R | S | T |

7. Give an analysis based on CI#1 *and* an analysis based upon CI#2 of *one* of the following activities.

   a. Fran's 22-year-old son has joined a cult dedicated to peace, love, and the sharing of all property and tasks. Fran arranges for her son to be kidnapped and deprogrammed.
   b. Jan is a high school teacher who gives false information to her students in order to scare them away from drugs.
   c. Ann hires a black woman with good credentials instead of a white man with excellent credentials because she thinks that the black woman has probably been disadvantaged in the past.
   d. Fred views pornography in private for sexual stimulation.
   e. Jed makes sexually provocative remarks to women in elevators because he savors their embarrassment and discomfort.
   f. Ed harasses pregnant women on their way into abortion clinics in order to prevent them from obtaining abortions.
   g. Susan says to her college professor, "I know my essays were not very good, but I worked on each of them for days and days. And I need a B in this class to stay in school. Being a single parent is really tough." The professor believes what she says and raises her grade from a D to a B.
   h. Jason and Julie are both 21-year-old, middle-class, unmarried college students. They have been dating for about a year and are thinking about getting married.

They decide to live together for a year to see whether they are compatible.
   i. Mary is invited to a party that she does not wish to attend by a man she does not wish to date. In order to avoid hurting his feelings, Mary says that she has another engagement, although this is a lie.
   j. Two parents who believe that homosexuality is immoral learn that their 25-year-old son is a homosexual. They disown and disinherit their son, saying to him, "You are no kin to us. Our son is dead."
   k. Bill refuses to do his share of the housework, knowing that his wife will do it because she loves him so much.
   l. Linda's child asks, "Mommy, does Santa Claus really fly from the North Pole in a sleigh pulled by reindeer, delivering toys to good children?" Linda answers, "Yes, he does."

8. Choose any *one* of the following practices. Give a Kantian argument showing that this practice is moral, *and* give a Kantian argument showing that this practice is immoral. Which argument is closer to Kant's real view? Which argument do you find more persuasive? Defend all of your answers. (*Warning:* Do not describe two slightly different practices and say that Kantians would sanction one but not the other. Give Kantian arguments for and against exactly the same practice.)

   a. Active, voluntary euthanasia (*Hint:* Consider Kant's discussion of suicide and of helping others.)

b. Insanity defense and reduced penalties for minors (*Hint:* Consider Kant's discussion of autonomy.)

c. Using placebos in treatment (*Hint:* Consider Kant's discussion of false promising and of helping others.)

d. Free riding (*Hint:* Consider Kant's discussion of developing your talents and of helping others.)

9. Feldman raises several objections to Kant's examples. Choose *two* of the following objections and explain how Kant would rebut them. (*Hint:* He certainly would not merely repeat what he has already said.)

a. Objection to the suicide example: "Kant apparently assumes that 'self-love' has as its function, the stimulation of the furtherance of life. . . . In the first place, it is not clear why we should suppose that self-love has the function of stimulating the furtherance of life. Indeed, it is not clear why we should suppose that self-love has any function at all! Second, it is hard to see why self-love can't serve two 'opposite' functions. Perhaps self-love motivates us to stay alive when continued life would be pleasant, but motivates us to stop living when continued life would be unpleasant."

b. Objection to the lying-promise example: "Kant hasn't succeeded in showing that [borrowing money on a false promise] is morally wrong. . . . Surely it could be a law of nature that everyone will make a false promise when in need of money. If people borrowed money on false promises rarely enough and kept their word on other promises, then no contradiction would arise."

c. Objection to the developing-talents example: "Kant himself presents a counterexample to the [thesis that everyone necessarily wills that all his talents be developed.] The South Sea Islanders, according to Kant, do not will to develop their talents. . . . Even if Kant is wrong about the South Sea Islanders, . . . couldn't

there be a rational person who, out of idleness, simply does not will to develop his talents? If there could not be such a person, then what is the point of trying to show that we are under some specifically moral obligation to develop all our talents?"

d. Objection to the helping-others example: "The agent may steadfastly stick to his general policy [of helping no one]. He may say, "I didn't help others when they were in need, and now that I'm in need I don't want any help from them. In this way, he would avoid having inconsistent policies."

10. Jesus' Golden Rule (GR), Mill's Greatest Happiness Principle (GHP), Kant's first formulation of the Categorical Imperative (CI#1), Kant's second formulation of the Categorical Imperative (CI#2), and Aristotle's Doctrine of the Mean (DM) all seem to be different principles. Let us say that two moral principles are *equivalent* if a person acting on the basis of one of them would, in every situation, perform the same acts as a person acting on the basis of the other. Answer any *two* of the following questions. In each case justify your answer.

a. Are GR and GHP equivalent?
b. Are GR and CI#1 equivalent?
c. Are GR and CI#2 equivalent?
d. Are GR and DM equivalent?
e. Are GHP and CI#1 equivalent?
f. Are GHP and CI#2 equivalent?
g. Are GHP and DM equivalent?
h. Are CI#1 and CI#2 equivalent?
i. Are CI#1 and DM equivalent?
j. Are CI#2 and DM equivalent?

(*Hint:* If you think two principles are *not* equivalent, then you can justify your answer by providing a situation where these two principles tell people to do different things. However, providing a situation where two principles tell people to do the same thing is *not* a justification for the claim that these two principles *are* equivalent, for these two principles might tell people to do different things in some other situation. To justify the claim that two principles *are* equivalent, you must somehow show that these two principles tell people to do the same thing in *every* situation.)

11. Horton replied, "I meant what I said and I said what I meant. An elephant's faithful one hundred percent." [Dr. Seuss, *Horton Hatches an Egg*] Why does a sophisticated Kantian think that it is wrong to lie? Kant may have believed that all moral rules are exceptionless. Sophisticated Kantians, however, do not believe this. What exceptions to the moral principle against lying would a sophisticated Kantian accept? (List as many different sorts of exceptions as you can think of.) How would a sophisticated Kantian justify these exceptions?

Why do you think that it is wrong to lie? What exceptions to the moral principle against lying would you accept? (List as many different sorts of exceptions as you can think of.) How would you justify these exceptions?

12. Anne's neurotic, 75-year-old patient comes into the hospital complaining of abdominal pain. Tests reveal that he has an untreatable but slow-growing cancer that is probably causing his pain. While Anne is trying to decide what to say, the patient sighs and says, "Well, I guess I've got indigestion again. Do you think cutting down the number of jalapeno peppers I eat for breakfast would help?" Anne makes no reply and does not tell him the results of the tests.

Fran's neurotic, 75-year-old patient also comes into the hospital complaining of abdominal pain. Tests reveal that he too has an untreatable but slow-growing cancer that is probably causing his pain. While Fran is trying to decide what to say, the patient sighs and says, "Well, I guess it's that old piece of shrapnel acting up again, isn't it?" Fran replies, "Yes, it probably is."

Would a Kantian using CI#1 consider the acts of these two people morally equivalent? Why or why not?

Would a Kantian using CI#2 consider the acts of these two people morally equivalent? Why or why not?

Do you consider the acts of these two people morally equivalent? Why or why not?

13. Fred believes that he is fighting a just war. His small, third-world country has been invaded by the army of a superpower. Fred believes that the only way to evict this army in the foreseeable future is through a series of terrorist bombings. He estimates that the bombings will kill 1,000–2,000 innocent people and will have a 75% chance of convincing the superpower to withdraw its army. (You may think of Fred as a Afghan "freedom fighter" or as a member of the Viet Cong.)

Ted believes that he is fighting a just war. He believes that the only way to end the war in the foreseeable future is through a series of aerial terror bombings, bombings not aimed at military targets but rather designed to break the will of the enemy to resist. He estimates that the bombings will kill 1,000–2,000 innocent people and will have a 75% chance of ending the war. (You may think of Ted as a member of the U.S. air force thinking about bombing Hiroshima or as a member of the Luftwaffe thinking about bombing London.)

Would a Kantian using CI#1 consider the acts of these two people morally equivalent? Why or why not?

Would a Kantian using CI#2 consider the acts of these two people morally equivalent? Why or why not?

Do you consider the acts of these two people morally equivalent? Why or why not?

14. Now that we have completed our study of Kant, it is time for a final, critical assessment. Answer the following questions about the rules generated by the Categorical Imperative. Defend your answers.

Do these rules form a *consistent* moral system? That is, do any of them conflict with each other? If so, what mechanism might Kant use to resolve such conflicts? That is, explain how Kant might assign priorities to rules. Would these mechanisms assign the right priorities to these rules?

Do these rules form a *complete* moral system? That is, are there any rules that you believe to be rules of morality but are not among the rules generated by the Categorical Imperative? If so, could you amend Kant's system to include the missing rules while preserving the "flavor" of Kant's theory?

Do these rules form a *plausible* moral system? That is, do the rules conflict in some way with common sense? If so, could you amend Kant's system to bring it into harmony with common sense while preserving the "flavor" of Kant's theory?

15. How would Kant respond to *one* of the following criticisms?

   a. Kant promised to refute the relativist by providing absolute moral principles. But CI#1 says only that P is an absolute moral principle if and only if P has categorical form. That is like saying that U is a unicorn if and only if U is a horny horse. The statement might be true, but it does not prove that unicorns exist. CI#1 tells us what the form of an absolute moral principle would be if there were absolute moral principles, but it does not show that there *are* absolute moral principles.

   b. CI#1 seems to come to the wrong answer quite often. For example, suppose I want to go for a joy ride. My maxim might be this. "I, lacking a bicycle, ought to steal a bicycle so that I can ride it around for a couple of hours." This ought to be a violation of a perfect duty, but it seems to pass the contradiction-in-conception test. I could achieve my objective in a world where everyone was stealing bicycles for joy rides.

16. Choose *one* of the following rules. Explain Kant's justification for this rule. What exceptions to this rule would a sophisticated Kantian accept? List as many exceptions as you can. How would a sophisticated Kantian justify these exceptions?

   a. Do not commit suicide.
   b. Do not make lying promises.
   c. Develop your talents.
   d. Help others.

(You may use CI#1 or CI#2. Remember that for Kant, an exception to the imperfect duty "Help others" is not a situation where you need not help some particular person but rather is a situation where you need not help anyone. Exceptions to the imperfect duty "Develop your talents" are similarly described.)

# Virtue Ethics: Aristotle

*A woman can never be too rich or too thin.*

ANONYMOUS

## The Happy Life

Aristotle's *Nicomachean Ethics* begins and ends with the broad question "What is the best type of life for a human being to live? What is the best type of person to be?" Aristotle presupposes that there is one type of life that all human beings should lead, but he is not denying individual differences and advocating a boring, regimented world. There is room for a great deal of individual variation within each type of life. Aristotle mentions, for example, the life of money making, which is the life aimed at acquiring wealth. It is possible to lead this life while being a fire fighter or a senator, married or single, well-read or illiterate, U.S. citizen or Albanian, and so on. The choice of life type is actually a choice of what is important, how to see the world, and what principles to live by. To lead the life of money making is to be the sort of person who values money and the goods money can buy, who tends to notice financial opportunities and bargains, who pigeonholes people by economic class, who lives according to such principles as "buy low; sell high," and so on. Similarly, to lead the ethical life is to be an ethical person, to concern oneself with ethical problems, to guide oneself by ethical values, and so on.

Aristotle's method for determining the best type of life is to list the types of life that have a claim to being the best life and then to eliminate lives, one by one, until only one type of life remains. Aristotle characterizes lives in two ways. First, he observes that the well-organized life has an ultimate aim. An *ultimate aim* is a good that is desirable solely for its own sake. Moreover, all other goods are desirable either solely or partially for the sake of the ultimate aim (1–2, 1194a). Two types of life differ if and only if their ultimate aims differ. Everyone agrees, says Aristotle, that the ultimate aim of the best life is *eudaimonia* (a Greek word meaning "happiness" or "flourishing"). If someone asks why you want to go to college, buy a car, or get a divorce, it makes sense to answer that you are doing these things as part of a long-term plan to achieve happiness. But if someone asks why you want to be happy, there is no answer because happiness is not a means to anything further. Happiness is valuable solely for its own sake. The claim that everything else is valued for the sake of happiness is somewhat more controversial. Mill would agree with Aristotle, but Kant thinks that duty is desirable solely for its own sake. And there is much disagreement about what happiness is. Some people think happiness is sensual pleasure; others think it is wealth, honor, good action, or contemplation (6–7, 1195b–1196a).

Aristotle also characterizes lives by the abilities they exercise. Two types of life differ if and only if the abilities that are their focus differ. Of course, people have many different abilities. They can write poetry, make babies, ice skate, and so on. But Aristotle is thinking of very broad types of abilities, such as the ability to desire, the ability to sense, and the ability to reason. And he narrows his search drastically by assuming that the happy life is a life that appropriately exercises all essential human abilities. In this sense, the happy life is the natural life. Thus Aristotle needs a list of the abilities that make someone a human being—an account of human nature.

According to Aristotle, plants are characterized by the abilities to take nourishment, grow, and reproduce. Animals have the abilities of plants plus the higher-level abilities to desire, move, and sense. Humans are rational animals, so humans have all of the animal abilities plus rationality. Now reason has two aspects. *Practical reason* is the ability to do means-ends reasoning, to work out the best way to accomplish one's goals, and *theoretical reason* is the ability to do rule-case reasoning, to understand things by subsuming them under general principles. Thus Aristotle works with the picture of human nature shown in Table 1. Higher-level abilities infuse and transform lower-level abilities. Reproduction in animals is different from reproduction in plants because animal reproduction is guided by the abilities of desire, motion, and sensation. Similarly, human desires are not simply brute urges. They are channeled and transmuted by reason. And so on. Combining Aristotle's picture of human nature with the views of "the many and the wise" about happiness yields Table 2. If you think Aristotle's list is incomplete, you might wish to consider other candidates for the happy life (see Table 3).

Aristotle assumes that happiness has certain features, and he rejects some of the lives listed here because they do not match these features of happiness. For example, as we have already seen, Aristotle assumes that happiness is desirable solely for its own sake. It is intrinsically valuable. This enables Aristotle to reject the life of money making. He observes that money cannot be the ultimate end of the happy life because it is only instrumentally valuable. It is desirable only because of what it can buy (7, 1196a). Similarly, the tyrannical life can be dismissed because power is only instrumentally valuable.

Aristotle rejects the political life for several reasons. Honor depends on the bestowers of honor and is easily lost, whereas happiness, according to Aristotle, does not depend on the fickle opinions of others and is not easily lost. Moreover, people can be honored even if they do little or nothing and even if they suffer great misfortunes, but happiness, according to Aristotle, requires activity and precludes tragedy. Because honor is not happiness, the political life is not the happy life (6–7, 1195b).

The life of enjoyment is not the happy life either. As we have already seen, Aristotle assumes that the happy life appropriately exercises all essential human abilities. Although the life of enjoyment exercises the abilities we share with

**Table 1**

theoretical reason
practical reason
desire, motion, sensation
nourishment, growth, reproduction

**Table 2**

| Type of Life | Aim or Goal | Abilities Exercised |
|---|---|---|
| life of enjoyment | sensual pleasure | desire for sensual pleasure |
| money-making life | money | desire for money or material goods |
| political life | honor | desire for honor |
| ethical life | virtuous activity | practical reason and desire |
| contemplative life | contemplation | theoretical reason |

**Table 3**

| tyrannical life | power | desire for power |
|---|---|---|
| religious life | love and obey God | soul |
| creative life | novelty | imagination |

animals, it does not appropriately exercise our rational abilities. (Yes, Don Juan uses his practical reason to arrange seductions, but Aristotle would not consider that an appropriate use of practical reason because it is basically desire guiding reason rather than reason guiding desire. Reason should not be a mere slave of the passions.) Aristotle does not think a human being can be happy living the life of an animal, and that is what the life of enjoyment is (6, 1195b).

But now Aristotle is in trouble, for none of his listed lives appropriately exercises all essential human abilities. Perhaps we should consider combinations such as those shown in Table 4.

The combination of the ethical and money-making lives does not stand a chance. This combination does not exercise all essential human abilities, of course. But the combination has another problem, too. There are times in life when one must choose between profitable and moral paths. Should I spread lies about my competitor to get the job or not? Should I spend my weekend grading my students' exams conscientiously, or should I grade them quickly and spend most of the weekend counterfeiting money with my new color printer? My ultimate aim should provide consistent answers to such questions, but if my ultimate aim is the combination of virtuous activity and money, it will not give me the guidance I need.

The combination of the ethical and religious lives seems more promising. After all, how could a conflict arise between virtuous activity and obeying God? Yet Kierkegaard argues that such conflicts do arise. Kierkegaard's example is God's order to Abraham to kill Isaac. (Another example is God's order to Joshua to commit genocide in the promised land.) If Abraham is leading the religious life, he will say, "OK." If he is leading the moral life, he will say, "No" and try to argue with God as he does in the earlier Sodom and Gomorrah incident. But if Abraham is leading the combination of the ethical and religious lives, he will not know what to say. [See the "Morality and Religion" section.]

The combination of the ethical and contemplative lives looks like the best bet. It exercises all essential human abilities. And probably there are no serious conflicts between the goals of virtuous activity and contemplation (although Aristotle is notoriously unclear about what he means by contemplation). This life seems to be Aristotle's candidate, too. All through the *Nicomachean Ethics*, Aristotle discusses the moral virtues of the ethical life, the intellectual virtues of the contemplative life, and the complex interrelationships among these two sets of virtues. However, when Aristotle returns to the question at the end of the *Nicomachean Ethics*, he seems to ignore the combination of the ethical and contemplative lives. Aristotle seems to say in Book X that the supremely happy life is the contemplative life and that the secondarily happy life is the ethical life (263–269, 1177a–1179a). Hence it is not clear what Aristotle's view really is.

If Aristotle is right to maintain that the happy life is or includes the ethical life, then he has an answer to the question "Why be moral?" Aristotle can say that we should acquire and exercise the moral virtues because they are the character traits most likely to make us happy. Aristotle thinks that happiness depends partially, though

**Table 4**

| ethical life and money-making life | virtuous activity and money | practical reason and moral virtue and desire for money |
|---|---|---|
| ethical life and religious life | virtuous activity and love and obey God | practical reason and moral virtue and soul |
| ethical life and contemplative life | virtuous activity and contemplation | practical reason and moral virtue and theoretical reason |

not primarily, on luck. Therefore, he cannot guarantee that a virtuous person will be happier than a vicious person. For example, the courageous person may volunteer for a risky task and get killed, whereas the coward who shirks the task may lead a long, full life. Aristotle can say, however, that the courageous person's odds of being happy are better than the coward's odds, other things being equal. Thus one should try to become courageous rather than cowardly. In general, a person trying to decide which type of life to lead and which sort of person to be should strive to become a virtuous person and lead a life aimed, at least partially, at virtuous activity. This seems to make Aristotle into an Egoist, but not a simple-minded Egoist. He does not say that you should perform whatever act is in your best interest in each situation. Instead, Aristotle's view is that you should choose to develop the character traits that are in your overall, long-term best interest. These character traits will, in turn, lead you to act in certain ways. In most situations they will lead you to perform acts that are in your best interest, but in some situations they will lead you to perform acts that are quite detrimental. The just person will act justly even when he or she would clearly benefit from performing an unjust act, for example.

\*

People living the lives Aristotle rejects (such as the life of enjoyment) often *think* they are happy. How can Aristotle maintain that these lives are not the happy life? Part of the answer is that for Aristotle, the happy life is not a life filled with feelings of pleasure but is instead a life wherein you act well and things go well for you. Moreover, Aristotle would remind us that people can be mistaken about various aspects of what is going on in their heads and in their lives. People are often confused about their motives, their feelings, their relationships with others, and even their own happiness. We understand what is meant by remarks like "I did not know how happy I was until you left me, dear." Thus Aristotle can maintain that people who claim to be happy while living lives other than Aristotle's happy life are simply mistaken.

Why should we accept Aristotle's claim that the happy life is a life that appropriately exercises all essential human abilities? Why can't people who live less-than-human lives be happy? In Book I Aristotle offers the following complex argument (13–14, 1097b–1098a).

*Argument (A)*

(1) A lyre player and a good lyre player have generically the same goal or end: lyre playing. The difference is that the lyre player just produces lyre playing, whereas the good lyre player produces excellent or virtuous lyre playing. (Excellence and virtue are alternative translations of the Greek word *arete*.)

(2) In general, if X has a goal or end E, then something is a good X if and only if it produces excellent or virtuous E. (from 1)

(3) The goal or end of X is the activity or activities peculiar to X. For example, the goal or end of an oak tree is to grow, put out leaves and acorns, photosynthesize, and so on, which is very different from the goal or end of a rabbit.

(4) Rational activity is the activity peculiar to humans.

(5) Rational activity is the human goal or end. (from 3 and 4)

(6) P is a good human if and only if P produces excellent or virtuous rational activity. (from 2 and 5)

(7) The human good, happiness, is the goal or end of a good human in a complete life.

(8) Happiness is excellent or virtuous rational activity in a complete life. (from 6 and 7)

(9) The element of the soul possessing a rational principle has two components: one possesses and exercises a rational principle (reason), and the other obeys a rational principle (desire and passion).

(10) Happiness is the excellent or virtuous activity of reason and desire and passion in a complete life. (from 8 and 9)

(11) If there are several different kinds of excellent or virtuous rational activity, then happiness is the "best and most complete" kind

of excellent or virtuous rational activity in a complete life.

One problem with this argument is that Aristotle seems to move between three senses of "good person": healthy specimen, happy person, and moral person. Does Aristotle's claim that the moral life is the natural life boil down to the following argument?

### Argument (B)

(1) If X is unnatural, then X is immoral.
(2) X is unnatural.
(3) Therefore, X is immoral.

I hope not. Although this argument is often used to condemn practices from contraception to women working outside the home, it is a bad argument because there is no definition of "unnatural" that makes the argument sound. If "unnatural" means "artificial" or "uncommon" or "not found among the animals" or "used in a way not intended by nature," then premise (1) is false. For example, ear lobes were not intended by nature to hold up earrings, yet the wearing of earrings is not immoral. Premise (2) is also false for many practices attacked by this argument. Homosexual acts, for example, are not artificial or uncommon. They are performed by a wide variety of animals, and for all we know, they were intended by nature.

Some people would argue that Aristotle has the wrong conception of human nature. He has left out something essential or included some non-essential ability. For example, Aristotle seems to have omitted creativity. And although there is a sense in which reproduction is part of our nature, it seems counter-intuitive to say that childless people are not living happy lives.

## The Nature of Virtue

Because in Aristotle's view the happy life involves the exercise of virtue, Aristotle turns to a detailed discussion of the nature of moral virtue and virtuous action. Socrates recommends that one first say what virtue is and then say how it is acquired.[1] But Aristotle reverses this. He first sketches the way in which people become virtuous and then uses his account of moral development to generate an account of virtue. According to Aristotle, people who have been properly raised to have the right attitudes become morally better by performing virtuous acts. They acquire habits of virtuous action, passion, desire, thought, and so on. If virtuous acts could be performed only by virtuous people, then one could not *become* virtuous by performing virtuous acts. Luckily, virtuous acts can be performed by non-virtuous people. Continent people force themselves to stand fast in battle despite their fear; swindlers are scrupulously fair at first in order to gain a good reputation (34–35, 1105a–1105b).

But although non-virtuous people can perform virtuous acts, they cannot perform these acts in the way that virtuous people perform them. Aristotle's description of the virtuous way to perform virtuous acts provides a preliminary list of the characteristics of the virtuous person.

The agent also must be in a certain condition when he does [virtuous acts]; (a) in the first place he must have knowledge, (b) secondly he must choose the acts, and choose them for their own sakes, and (c) thirdly his actions must proceed from a firm and unchangeable character (34, 1105a).

(a) A virtuous act done virtuously obviously requires knowledge of the relevant facts of the situation. But Aristotle's virtuous person also has the knowledge of which acts are virtuous and the knowledge of why these acts are virtuous. That is, in each situation the virtuous person can distinguish the appropriate acts from the inappropriate ones. He or she acts virtuously not through some sort of intuition or appeal to authority or luck, but rather through a rational application of first principles to particular situations. Aristotle calls the ability to do this *practical wisdom* and considers it one of the intellectual virtues.

(b) Choice is deliberate desire. That is, a virtuous person's choice to perform a virtuous act consists of a reasoning process called deliberation leading to the formation of a desire to perform a certain virtuous action (58, 1113a). The virtuous person performs the act "for its own sake." That is, the virtuous person takes the act *qua* virtuous, rather than *qua* something else, to be intrinsically rather than instrumentally choiceworthy. By contrast, an act performed despite a desire to do otherwise or solely for the sake of impressing someone else is not evidence of virtue.

(c) Aristotle describes several sorts of character (see Table 5). The *virtuous* person has right passions and desires, makes right choices based on the right principles, and reliably performs right acts. The *vicious* person has wrong passions and desires, makes wrong choices based on the wrong principles, and reliably performs wrong acts. The *continent* person overcomes temptation by will power. That is, he or she has wrong passions and desires but makes right choices and performs right acts. The *incontinent* person fails to overcome temptation because of weakness of will. That is, he or she has wrong passions and desires and makes right choices but performs wrong acts (175, 1150a15).

Aristotle also mentions *heroic virtue* (supererogatory virtue, acting and feeling even better than ordinary virtuous people) and *brutishness* (which we would call mental illness, acting and feeling even worse than ordinary, vicious people) (159 and 171, 1145a and 1148b). The line between vice and brutishness is fuzzy, but it can be drawn. People who give too little to charity and those who run from battle are morally flawed; people who hoard every penny and those who run from mice are sick. We respond differently to vice, to brutishness, and to incontinence. The stingy and cowardly are criticized and punished; the miserly and phobic are pitied and offered therapy; people who are incontinent

about money and fear are urged to try harder and given self-help books. Aristotle's classificatory scheme is more complex and more enlightening than some of the simpler schemes often used today. Whereas many people today classify all those with drinking problems as alcoholics and take alcoholism to be an illness, Aristotle would say that only some problem drinkers are brutish. Others are vicious, and still others are incontinent.

When Aristotle says that a virtuous person's virtuous acts proceed from a firm character, he means to distinguish virtue from these other sorts of character. First, the acts of a virtuous person do not arise out of some quirk of circumstances. A virtuous person's acts are typical of that person. They are not out-of-character acts. The virtuous person can be counted on to perform such acts. Second, the acts are not the result of outside pressure or persuasion but come instead from within the person. A cowardly person might stand fast in battle because he or she fears the commanding officer more than the enemy, but this is not a display of courage. Third, the act should not be performed by an effort of will against temptation. The virtuous person is not conflicted—not pulled one way by desire and another by duty. He or she is in harmony with himself or herself. Thus even though a continent person is reliably good and internally motivated, his or her act does not "proceed from a firm character."

Aristotle goes on to characterize virtue further in the following way.

Virtue, then, is (d) a state of character (e) concerned with choice, (f) lying in a mean, i.e. (g) the mean relative to us, (h) this being determined by a rational

Table 5

| Character | Passions, Desires | Principles, Choices | Acts |
|---|---|---|---|
| heroically virtuous | very right | very right | very right |
| virtuous | right | right | right |
| continent | wrong | right | right |
| incontinent | wrong | right | wrong |
| vicious | wrong | wrong | wrong |
| brutish | very wrong | very wrong | very wrong |

principle, (i) that principle by which the man of practical wisdom would determine it. (39, 1106b–1107)

(d) A state of character is a set of habits of passion, desire, pleasure, thoughts, and the like. Thus to say that virtue is a state of character is to say that a virtuous person not only reliably performs virtuous acts but also feels the right passions, desires the right objects, enjoys the right things, and holds the right beliefs in each situation. For example, a courageous person will not only stand fast in battle but will also feel the right amount of fear and confidence and have the right goals. He or she will not be thinking, "I can't run because I am so terrified that my legs are off-line, and besides if I stand fast, I may get to appear on national TV." Instead, he or she will be thinking, "The situation is perilous, but I have a reasonable chance of surviving if I keep alert, and besides I must stand fast to help keep my city free. It is the brave thing to do." Similarly, at a party a temperate person will not only consume the right amount of alcohol but will also desire and enjoy the right amount of alcohol for the right reasons. A liberal person will not have to overcome stingy reluctance but will freely give the right amount to the right charities, not solely to gain a good reputation, but primarily to help others. And so on. Is Aristotle demanding an unreasonably high level of perfection from his virtuous person? Well, virtue is a matter of degree, and Aristotle is sketching perfect virtue. He is describing an ideal person so that we can have a mark at which to aim and a standard for judgment. A person can be substantially less than ideal and still be a virtuous person.

(e) Some people believe that you are stuck with whatever passions and desires you happen to have. If you have virtuous passions and desires, then you are lucky, but if you have vicious passions and desires, then the best you can do is to overcome them by an effort of will and thus act rightly. Aristotle, however, believes that unless you are hopelessly wicked, your passions and desires are under your control. He does not believe that you can change them easily or quickly, but he does believe that over time you can modify your passions and desires. In

fact, Aristotle says that you should use your reason to determine which passions and desires to have and then go on develop these passions and desires. You should cultivate a taste for virtue, just as some people cultivate a taste for opera (59–63, 1113a–1114b).

(f) One view about the relationship between virtues and vices is that each virtue corresponds to a single vice. Cowardice is the opposite of courage. Self-indulgence is the opposite of temperance. And so on. But Aristotle's view is that each virtue lies between two opposite character traits: an excess and a deficiency. Courage, for example, lies between cowardice and rashness, temperance is bracketed by self-indulgence and insensibility. And so on. Thus Aristotle's favorite fairy tale character is Goldilocks because she likes her porridge not too hot or too cold, but just right; her bed not too soft or too hard, but just right; and so on. Aristotle suggests that it is easy to miss the fact that each virtue lies between two vices because for each virtue, one of the vices is more common and worse than the other. It is easy to ignore the rare, not-so-bad vice and assume that each virtue has only one opposite.

Virtue is a mean in a second sense as well. To be virtuous is to get a number of parameters right. Good temper, for example, is being angry at the right people, to the right degree, for the right duration, over the right objects, and on the right occasions (96–98, 1125b–1126a). Being typically excessive with respect to any parameter is one vice; being typically deficient with respect to any parameter is the other vice. Thus virtuous action and passion is medial with respect to each parameter. Think of the five parameters as continua forming axes (see the figure on page 244). Imagine two "five-dimensional spheres" centered on the point where these axes intersect. The interior of the smaller sphere represents virtue. That part of the larger sphere that is outside the small sphere represents vice. The area beyond the larger sphere represents brutishness. Shade the spheres as shown. The shaded volume represents too little of each parameter; the unshaded volume between the spheres represents too much. Now every possible sort of anger can be represented as a point in five-dimensional

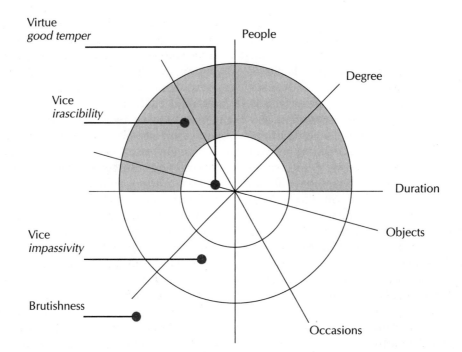

Virtue
*good temper*

People

Degree

Vice
*irascibility*

Duration

Objects

Vice
*impassivity*

Brutishness

Occasions

space. Note that a person may be excessive with respect to one parameter while being medial or even deficient with respect to another. For example, a person might get angry with too few people but stay angry with each of them for too long. As Aristotle notes, some people are a mixture of rashness and cowardice (66, 1115b).

(g) Although Aristotle remarks that the mean is "relative to us," he is no relativist. Instead, he is declaring himself to be a Normative Absolutist rather than a Wild Absolutist. [See the "Morality and Knowledge" section.] What he really means is that the right thing to do, feel, and desire depends on the situation. A passion that is medial in one situation may be extreme in another (37, 1106a–1106b). For example, giving $1,000 per year to charity would be too much (prodigal) if you were a single parent earning $10,000 per year, but it would be too little (stingy) if you were earning $100,000. Similarly, if you intentionally jostle me as we are getting into an elevator, I ought to get mildly irritated. It would be extreme to fly into a rage. On the other hand, if you intentionally burn down my house, rage may well be perfectly appropriate, and mild irritation would be inappropriate. (Thus Jesus'

doctrine that one should love one's enemies is vicious according to Aristotle's doctrine of the mean!)

(h) But how should we determine what are the right acts, passions, desires, and so on? How do we determine the mean for each parameter of each virtue? Aristotle does not think this should be determined by intuition or by feeling or by chance. Instead we should use a rational principle. Thus, to be virtuous is to act, feel, and desire in a mean relative to the situation in accordance with the right rational principle. But which rational principle is the right one?

(i) Aristotle's answer is that we ought to use the principle used by a person with the intellectual virtue of practical wisdom. But this is not very helpful. How can we distinguish between the practically wise and the phonies unless we already know the principles of virtue? In some cases Aristotle gives us the rational principle. It is temperate to indulge in food, drink, and sex so long as doing so is not unhealthy, deconditioning, unaffordable, or ignoble. It is just to distribute goods to people in proportion to their contribution or effort or talent. [See the "Economic Justice" section.] But Aristotle does not state the principle for most of the virtues. Perhaps he thinks these principles are ineffable or too complicated to state. Perhaps he leaves them as an exercise for the reader. Perhaps he simply does not know what these principles are. Perhaps we should use the descriptions Aristotle gives of the different virtues as a guide to finding a person of practical wisdom and then model ourselves on that person, trying to act, feel, desire, and think as that person does. The role model need not be a real person. It could be a combination of several people or a literary figure, for example. Nor need the role model remain constant throughout life. Perhaps you choose an initial role model on the basis of a preliminary conception of virtue. After imitating this role model for a while, you refine your conception of virtue. Then, on the basis of the new conception, you choose a new role model. And so on.

## List of Virtues

How does Aristotle know which traits are virtues? Some people have accused him of uncritically adopting and codifying the standards and values of his time. But that accusation is clearly mistaken. Aristotle is quite critical of certain institutions within his society (such as slavery), and he is also quite willing to state that certain character traits are virtues or vices even though they have not previously been identified as such by his society.

Aristotle says that a character trait is a virtue if and only if it is conducive to leading the happy life. Because the happy life is (or includes) the moral life, the virtues are character traits conducive to moral action. Aristotle derives his list of virtues by dividing the good human life into spheres and then maintaining that acting and feeling right within each sphere is a virtue. For example, because we are beings that may be killed, injured, or pained, there are right and wrong ways of thinking, acting, desiring, and feeling with respect to danger. The right ways constitute a virtue that Aristotle names courage. Similarly, because we hunger, thirst, and lust, there are right and wrong ways of dealing with food, drink, and sex. The right ways constitute the virtue of temperance. And so on. Thus Aristotle arrives at the moral virtues and vices shown in Table 6 (40–43, 1107a–1108b). (I shall not discuss the intellectual virtues.)

**Table 6**

| Virtue | Excess | Deficiency | Sphere |
| --- | --- | --- | --- |
| courage | rashness | cowardice | danger |
| temperance | self-indulgence | insensibility | sensual pleasure |
| liberality | prodigality | stinginess | money |
| magnificence | vulgarity | penny pinching | great wealth |
| pride | vanity | humility | honor and self-respect |
| right ambition | overly ambitious | lack of ambition | honor |
| good temper | impassivity | irascibility | insult |
| ready wit | buffoonishness | boorishness | humor |
| truthfulness about oneself | boastfulness | modesty | self-description |
| friendliness | obsequiousness | quarrelsomeness | social association |
| shame | bashfulness | shamelessness | wrongdoing |
| righteous indignation | spite | envy | fortunes of others |
| justice | greed | ? | scarce goods |

Contemporary common sense is basically in agreement with Aristotle about some of the virtues on this list (courage, temperance, liberality, magnificence, good temper, truthfulness, and justice). Others (appropriate ambition, ready wit, friendliness, and shame) seem, to contemporary common sense, to be good character traits but not moral virtues. Yet others (pride and righteous indignation) seem to be vices. And some traits that contemporary common sense takes to be virtues (such as benevolence, gratitude, and industriousness) do not seem to show up on Aristotle's list at all. Of course, Aristotle does not claim that his list is complete. If you are inclined to supplement or modify his list, you might find it useful to compare Aristotle's list of the virtues with other lists. For example, in addition to being prepared, Boy Scouts are supposed to be trustworthy, loyal, helpful, friendly, courteous, kind, obedient, cheerful, thrifty, brave, clean, and reverent. Although there is some convergence between these two lists, the amount of divergence is noteworthy. Aristotle does not mention loyalty, courtesy, obedience, cleanliness, or reverence. And helpfulness, kindness, and thriftiness are treated only as aspects of liberality. On the other hand, the absence of temperance, right ambition, ready wit, pride, and justice from the Boy Scout list is surprising. Perhaps part of the explanation is that the Boy Scout list is an attempt to capture the virtues of a youngster rather than an adult. Obedience, for example, is a character trait valued more in children than in adults. (Are the virtues of children really different from those of adults?) One traditional list of Christian virtues is this: fortitude, justice, prudence, temperance, faith, hope, and charity. The vices are pride, covetousness, lust, gluttony, envy, sloth, and anger. Although Aristotle takes pride to be a virtue, whereas the Christian list takes it to be a vice, this difference is terminological rather than substantive. The Christian vice of pride is basically having and acting on an overly high estimation of one's own abilities, accomplishments, and deserts, and this is roughly what Aristotle means by the vice of vanity. What Aristotle means by pride is having and acting on a correct estimation of oneself, and

this is essentially Christian humility. Other differences between the Aristotelian and Christian lists may not be so easily resolvable, however. And of course there are other lists.

Aristotle sketches each of the virtues on his list except righteous indignation, but he devotes a great deal of the *Nicomachean Ethics* to the virtue of justice. Justice has two senses. General justice consists simply of those aspects of the other virtues that are concerned with other people, but particular justice is a separate virtue (108–109, 1129b–1130a). O'Connor argues that Aristotelian justice does not consist in respecting the rights and deserts of other people but rather in correctly valuing scarce goods such as money, honor, and safety. The unjust person is not someone with the wrong attitude toward other people but someone with the wrong attitude toward these goods. Aristotle certainly does think that the unjust person excessively desires various goods. But Aristotle also recognizes that justice involves what people deserve. He discusses our obligations toward our fellow citizens in his book *The Politics*, and his extensive discussion of friendship includes detailed accounts of what family members, business partners, acquaintances, and close friends owe to each other. (Aristotle's discussion of friendship is an interesting synthesis of the justice and care perspectives.) [See the "Ethics of Care" section.]

## Other Virtue Theories

Contrasting Aristotle's virtue theory with some other theories might clarify and situate Aristotle's account. Like many others, Aquinas and Foot believe that human beings are subject to various natural tendencies to go wrong. To each of these temptations or deficiencies there corresponds an ability to resist the temptation or make up the deficiency. Each of these wrong tendencies is a vice, and each corresponding, corrective ability is a virtue. For example, the temptation to sensual overindulgence is intemperance, and the corrective virtue of will power is temperance. The vices of indifference to the needs and rights of others are stinginess and injustice, and the corrective virtues are benevolence and justice.

Aristotle rejects this picture. First of all, he does not think that virtues correspond to natural temptations or deficiencies. Instead, they correspond to spheres of life. In each sphere there are many different ways to go wrong, but they are not natural. Humans are neither good by nature, as Rousseau maintains, nor bad by nature, as the Christian doctrine of original sin implies. Second, Aristotle does not think each virtue is opposed to a single vice. Instead, each virtue is a mean between two vices, an excess and a deficiency. Third, Aristotle thinks the disposition to overcome temptation is continence, not virtue. The virtuous person has right desires and passions and so is not tempted. Our long-term goal should not be to strengthen our will power in order to triumph over our bad desires, but rather our goal should be to replace whatever bad desires we have with good ones.

A common view endorsed by various philosophers is that a virtue is simply a disposition to follow a moral rule. To each rule there corresponds a virtue, and to each virtue there corresponds a rule. And the value of virtues is simply that they produce rule-following behavior.

Aristotle disagrees. First, there may be virtues without rules. Perhaps the rules of some virtues cannot be stated in sufficient detail. Knowing what to do may be a matter of having the right rational perception, the right gestalt grasp of the situation. Second, several different dispositions will reliably produce rule-following behavior, but Aristotle does not consider all of these to be virtues, and neither do we. People who reliably act justly because they are too timid to break the law are not just people, for example. People who refrain from adultery, yet still covet their neighbor's spouses, are not temperate. Simply following the rules is not enough. A virtuous person has the right passions, thoughts, and desires, too. Third, the proposal that virtues are dispositions to follow rules gets priorities wrong. It suggests that the important thing is to follow the rules, and it defines virtues derivatively as states of character disposing people to follow the rules. But Aristotle would say that the goal is to have and express the virtue so as to lead the happy life. Rules, if used at all, are mechanisms for gaining, maintaining, and exercising virtues.

Socrates (but not Plato) maintains that to be virtuous is to have a certain sort of knowledge. If people have this knowledge, then they reliably act rightly because this knowledge is so compelling. To know the good is to do it; incontinence is impossible. If people reliably act rightly, then they have this knowledge. People who lack this knowledge might act rightly some of the time, but they cannot be counted on to do so. Even people with true belief are easily confused and distracted. Because people reliably act rightly if and only if they have this knowledge, to become virtuous is to acquire this knowledge.[2]

Against Socrates, Aristotle argues that incontinence is not only possible but common. People often know what is right but do something else because they are distracted or overpowered by wrong passions or desires (165–166, 1147a–1147b). Virtue is not a purely intellectual matter. Becoming virtuous requires the habituation of desire, passion, and the like, as well as the education of practical reason. Ethics classes alone do not suffice to make people virtuous; practice is necessary, too. You must not only teach your children what to do; you must also make them do it. At first, they act virtuously because they hope for reward and/or fear punishment. Later, they internalize the values and force themselves to act virtuously because they think they should. Eventually, they act virtuously without internal struggle because they "develop a taste" for virtuous action.

## Use of Virtue Theory

Suppose we could determine which traits are virtues and then go on to describe each virtue, the sphere it governs, the passions it involves, the actions it calls for, the principles it follows, and the vices with which it contrasts. How would we use virtue ethics to guide us in life? And how would this help us to evaluate social practices such as prostitution and abortion?

One answer is that Aristotle and virtue ethics have no pretensions to solving moral problems and evaluating practices. The aim of virtue ethics is to describe how to be, not how to act— how to become good, not how to do good. But being and doing are not so easily separated. A good person acts rightly as well as feeling, desiring, and thinking rightly, and we become good by doing good. Virtue ethics must have something to say about which acts and practices are moral and which are not.

Perhaps when we wonder in general what sort of person to be, what sort of life to live, and how to raise our children, we should strive to acquire, maintain, exhibit, and inculcate the virtues. But when we come to a moral quandary, we should use rules rather than virtues. Perhaps Aristotle's ethics is aimed not at the rare crisis but at the common, day-to-day life. This suggestion gives virtue ethics a role in moral decision making, but it is a puzzling role. How could virtue ethics be useful in everyday decisions but useless in quandaries?

Perhaps the idea is simply that when we wonder whether to perform a certain act, we should ask ourselves whether a virtuous person in our situation would perform such an act. Instead of finding principled solutions, we should live life by following a role model. But this suggestion is open to a number of objections, not the least of which is "How does the role model know how to act?"

Here is a more complex suggestion for using virtue ethics to evaluate social practices. A good citizen, says Aristotle, is a person who has the character traits conducive to making an appropriate contribution to the goal of the state. These character traits are the virtues of a citizen. Because different states have different goals, a person who is a good citizen in one state might be a poor citizen in another.[3] For example, a person who vigilantly watches the state for violations of human rights and vigorously protests such violations when they occur may be a good citizen of a democratic, open society but would be a bad citizen of a totalitarian dictatorship. Similarly, a good doctor is a person who has the character traits appropriate to performing the function of a doctor—to doing well what a doctor should do. These character traits are the virtues of a doctor. Of course, we could go on to define the virtues of a lawyer, a parent, a soldier, a student, and so on. Because different practices have different goals, the virtues of different roles within different practices may differ, just as the virtues associated with different states vary along with the goals of the states. For example, a person who has the virtues of a lawyer might lack some of the virtues of a soldier, and vice versa.

The virtues of a particular role are not always the same as the moral virtues that constitute the character of a good person. To be good at a role might require all of the moral virtues plus other character traits. Thus when the Wizard of Oz claims to be "a very good man but a very bad wizard," he is claiming to have all of the moral virtues but to lack some of the wizardly virtues. (Actually, his behavior toward Dorothy and her friends reveals that he is a good wizard but a bad man.) However, some role virtues might not be moral virtues, and some moral virtues might not be role virtues. Indeed, role virtues might be moral vices, and vice versa. The competitiveness that makes individuals good entrepreneurs might make them bad people, for example, and the moral virtue of liberality might be a marketplace vice. Moreover, a character trait may occupy different places in the constellations of moral virtues and role virtues. Courage, for example, has a higher priority as a military virtue than as a moral virtue.

Now Aristotle believes that a good person can be a good citizen only in a good state. Thus we could use the moral virtues as a touchstone for evaluating states. We could say that a state in which a good person cannot be a good citizen is a corrupt state. And the more they differ, the more corrupt the state. Similarly, we might say that insofar as the virtues of a role are incompatible with the virtues that characterize the good person, the practice is corrupt. There is something twisted about such a practice and the people who are good at it. And the more incompatible the role virtues and moral virtues are, the more corrupt the practice. This line of thought suggests that there is something corrupt about the practice of prostitution, because in order to be a good prostitute, a person must be sexually intemperate. Temperance seems to be a vice rather than a virtue of the practice of prostitution. Similarly, there is something corrupt about our legal system, because a good trial lawyer must be manipulative and deceptive. And so on.

## Notes

1. Plato, *Meno,* trans. G.M.A. Grube (Indianapolis, IN: Hackett Publishing Co., 1976), p. 20 (86d)

2. Plato, *Protagoras,* trans. S. Lombardo and K. Bell (Indianapolis, IN: Hackett, 1992), pp. 49–55 (352a–357e).

3. Aristotle, *Politics,* trans. C. Lord (Chicago: University of Chicago Press, 1984), p. 90 (1276b).

# 21   Aristotle, *Nicomachean Ethics*

## ROSALIND HURSTHOUSE

. . . [Aristotle maintains that] If you want to flourish/be happy/successful you should acquire and exercise the virtues—courage, temperance, liberality, patience, truthfulness, friendship, justice. . . . Or, as we might say, be a morally virtuous person.[1] With this answer we are clearly back in the business of doing ethics—but how could this have come about when we started with the self-seeking or egoistic question?

The claim that is basic to Aristotle's view is that it comes about because *qua* human beings we naturally have certain emotions and tendencies and that it is simply a brute fact (made up of a vastly complex set of other facts) that *given* that we are as we naturally are we can only flourish/be happy/successful by developing and exercising those character traits that are called the virtues—courage, justice, benevolence and so on. For reasons that I shall go into later, Aristotle does not in fact give the argument for each such character trait, but it is worth briefly considering some examples as an illustration of (roughly) how the argument goes and what sorts of facts are relevant.

Take one of the simplest cases for us—generosity. Here are some of the relevant facts: we are naturally sociable creatures who like to have friends and want to be loved by friends and family. We also like and love people who do things

for us rather than always putting themselves first. We also are not merely sympathetic but empathetic—the pleasure of others is pleasurable to us. Given that this is how we are, someone who is mean and selfish is unlikely to be liked and loved and hence likely to be lonely and unhappy; someone who is generous is likely to enjoy the benefits of being liked and loved and, moreover, in the exercise of their generosity will find much added enjoyment, for the pleasures of those they benefit will be pleasures to them.

Take another—honesty. Amongst the relevant facts there are some similar to the preceding ones—that we want friends, want them to be trustworthy, want them to trust us—and some that are rather different, for instance that there are likely to be occasions in our lives when we need to be believed—as the many fables on the theme of crying "wolf" too often illustrate. Folk wisdom also contains the adage that "honesty is the best policy" and the conviction that "the truth will out" to the discomfort of those who have lied about it. The exercise of this virtue is not as immediately enjoyable as the exercise of generosity, but the honest person has the advantage of not having to keep a constant guard on her tongue and has peace of mind thereby. One should also note that the honest person can tell the truth effortlessly in circumstances in which doing so would be embarrassing, frightening, unpleasant or unfortunately impossible for the person who lacks the virtue. Literature abounds with scenes in which a

From Rosalind Hursthouse, "Aristotle, *Nicomachean Ethics,*" *Philosophers Ancient and Modern,* ed. Vesey (Cambridge University Press, 1986), with omissions. Reprinted by permission of Cambridge University Press.

character desperately needs to tell the truth for if she does not a profound relationship in her life is going to be destroyed—she will lose her lover, or her closest friend will feel betrayed, or her son will turn in bitterness from her, or she will put herself in the hands of the blackmailer or . . . to her subsequent irremediable regret and misery. But the truth in question is one of those truths it is hard to own up to—and she can't bring herself to do so. But had she armed herself with the virtue of honesty she would have been able to. Much more could be said here too about the harm one does oneself through self-deception and how difficult it is to be simultaneously ruthlessly honest with oneself but dishonest to other people.

Even more than honesty, courage is a character trait one needs to arm oneself with given that we are the sorts of creatures we are—subject to death and pain and frightened of them. It is not so much that we need courage to endure pain and face death as ends in themselves, but that we are likely to have to face the threat of pain or danger for the sake of some good that we shall otherwise lose. I read of someone who had the opportunity to save someone's life by donating bone marrow; one might see this as a wonderful opportunity but lack the courage to do it, to one's subsequent bitter regret. And how much worse the regret would be if one's cowardice led to the death of someone one loved. If I have managed to make myself courageous I am ready to save my child from the burning house at whatever risk to myself, to stand up to the terrorists who threaten my friends' lives and to my racist neighbors who are trying to hound me and my family from our home. In a society in which cancer has become one of the most common ways to die we also need courage to enable us to die well, not only so that we may not waste the last years or months of our lives but also for the sake of the people we love who love us.

All the above is schematic. I do not pretend to have shown conclusively that generosity, honesty and courage are necessarily part of flourishing or living well, and of course much of what I have said is open to detailed disagreement. I cannot go through many of the details here, but I will discuss one pair of objections that spring very naturally to mind, since the responses to them form part of the further exposition.

The two objections one wants to make are that, contrary to what has been claimed, the virtues are surely neither sufficient nor necessary for living well. Not sufficient because my generosity, honesty and courage (for example) might, any one of them, lead to my being harmed or indeed to my whole life being ruined or ended. Not necessary because, as we all know, the wicked may flourish like the green bay tree.

How do we envisage that my virtue might lead to my downfall? It is not quite right to say that it is obviously the case that, having the virtue of generosity I might fall foul of a lot of people who exploit me or find myself poverty-stricken. For built into each concept of a virtue is the idea of getting things *right*. (This is what distinguishes full virtue from natural virtue—see 1144b1–17.) In the case of generosity this involves giving the right things or amount for the right reasons on the right occasions to the right people. The *right amount,* in many cases, would be *an amount I can afford* or *an amount I can give without depriving someone else.* So, for instance, I do not count as mean, or even ungenerous when, being relatively poor, or fairly well off but with a large and demanding family, I do not give lavish presents to richer friends at Christmas. *The right people* do not include the exploiters for I do not count as mean or ungenerous if I refuse to let people exploit me; moreover generosity does not require me to help support someone who is simply bone lazy, nor to finance the self-indulgence of a spendthrift. Any virtue may contrast with several vices or failings, and generosity is to be contrasted not only with meanness or selfishness but also with being prodigal, too open-handed, a sucker.[2]

Once this point is borne in mind, examples in which I may suffer because of my virtue are harder to find. Nevertheless, there are some; sudden financial disaster might befall many of us, leaving the generous in dire straits where the mean do much better. Just as, in the past, people have been burnt at the stake for refusing to lie about what they believed, so now, under some regimes, people are shut in asylums and subjected to enforced drugging for the same reason while the hypocrites remain free. My courage may lead me to go to the defense of someone being attacked in the street to no avail and with the result that I am killed or maimed for life while the coward goes through her life unscathed. Given these possibilities, how can anyone claim that the question "How am I to flourish?" is to be honestly answered by saying "Be virtuous"?

There are two possible responses to this. The first is to grit one's teeth and deny that the virtuous person can be harmed by her possession of virtue. To be virtuous *is* to flourish, to be (truly) happy or successful. Nothing counts as being harmed except doing evil, and nothing counts as a genuine benefit, or advantage, or being better off than doing what is right. There is more than a grain of truth in this view, to which I shall return later on, but, on the face of it, it is, as a response to the sorts of examples we have envisaged, simply absurd. As Aristotle says, "Those who maintain that, provided he is good, a man is happy (*eudaimon*) on the rack, or when fallen amongst great misfortunes are talking nonsense. . . ." (NE1153b17) (The point of these examples is that I become unable to exercise virtue, either because I am dead, or because I have become physically, mentally or materially incapable of doing so.)

The second response is to deny that the answer to the question was ever supposed to offer a guarantee. If I ask my doctor "How am I to flourish physically/be healthy?" she gives me the right answer when she says "Give up smoking, don't work with asbestos, lose weight, take some exercise. . . . " Even if, despite following her advice I subsequently develop lung cancer or heart disease, this does not impugn its correctness; I can't go back to her and say "You were wrong to tell me I should give up smoking, etc." She and I both know that doing as she says does not guarantee perfect health; nevertheless, if perfect health is what I want, the only thing I can do to achieve it is follow her advice. Continuing to smoke, work with asbestos, etc, is asking for trouble—even though, it is agreed, I may be lucky and live to be a hearty ninety.

Similarly, the claim is not that being virtuous guarantees that one will flourish. It is, rather, probabilistic—"true for the most part" (1094b21–22). Virtue is the only reliable bet; it will probably bring flourishing—though, it is agreed, I might be unlucky and, because of my virtue, wind up on the rack.[3] So virtue is not being made out to be guaranteed sufficient for flourishing.

But now we move to the second objection. Is it not being made out to be necessary? It was just said to be the *only* reliable bet, as if, as in the medical case, making no effort to acquire the virtues was asking for trouble. But don't the wicked, as we said above, flourish? In which case virtue can't be necessary. The two possible responses to this objection are elaborations on the two that were given to the other. The first denies that the wicked ever do flourish, for nothing counts as having an advantage or being well off or . . . except doing what is right. The second, continuing to pursue the medical analogy, still insists that virtue is the only reliable bet and, agreeing that occasionally the non-virtuous flourish, maintains that this is, like fat smokers living to be ninety, rare and a matter of luck. So, for instance, it is usually true that people who are entirely selfish and inconsiderate miss out on being loved—but such a person might be lucky enough to be blessed with particular beauty or charm, or by lucky chance come across someone else very loving who just fell for them in the mysterious way that sometimes happens. But, the claim is, we can all recognize that this *is* a matter of luck—one could never rely on it.

However, many people may feel that this response is implausible. Surely it is not simply by pure chance and luck that the non-virtuous flourish. Isn't power just as good a bet as virtue, if not a better one, for flourishing? If one has power, people do, as a matter of fact, love one for that; one is respected and honored, people treat one with special concern and consideration—and all despite the fact that in order to get and maintain power one will undoubtedly have to be selfish, dishonest, callous, unjust . . . to a certain extent. So the answer to "How am I to flourish?" should not be "Acquire virtue" but "Acquire power." This objection can be seen as a form of one of the oldest, and still current, debates in moral philosophy. In Plato's *Republic* it takes on a form specifically related to the virtue of justice—if injustice is more profitable than justice to the man of strength, then practicing injustice is surely the best way of life for the strong. Its most modern version is entirely general—"What reason have I to be moral?" One very important question it brings up is whether morality, or moral judgments, give reasons for acting to everyone. If some action ought not to be done (because, say, it is dishonest or unjust) does this mean that everyone has a reason not to do it, or is it open to the powerful to say truly that there is no reason for them to refrain?

What then, should be said about this old, but still hotly debated issue? When we were considering how "success" could work as a translation of *eudaimonia,* we noted that one could be successful in a materialistic sense—wealthy and powerful—while still counting one's life not a success but a failure, because, say, one felt lonely and unfulfilled. Now let us consider someone who is (a) successful in the materialistic sense, (b) non-virtuous—they have acquired their power by cheating and lying, ruthlessly sacrificing people when it suited them, but (c) perfectly happy—they don't feel guilty, or lonely, or unfulfilled or worried about what would happen to them if they lost their power, or that their life is a failure in any sense. The question we then ask ourselves is—do we find this person's life enviable or desirable? And part of the truth I said was contained in the view that nothing counts as a genuine advantage or being better off than doing what is right is that many of us are going to say "No." We may be hard put to explain *why* we say "No"; perhaps we cannot say anything more than that we couldn't live like that, or that we wouldn't want to have cheated our friends or to have let our parents or children down. But our inability to say more than this does not matter; all that matters is that we can view a life containing every apparent benefit and advantage as one that we don't want because it contains having acted wrongly in various ways.

To anyone who thinks this way, Aristotle's answer to "How am I to flourish?" is going to

emerge as the only possible answer. "Acquire power" was, in any case, an answer that could only recommend itself to the minority who thought they could achieve this, and it now appears that even if I count myself as part of this minority, I may still not regard the acquisition of power through the abandonment of virtue as something that will give me the sort of life I want.

But now we encounter a new difficulty. In what way is Aristotle's answer an answer to a question that anyone who thinks this way is genuinely open-minded about? If what you think already is that the wicked do not really flourish; that, viewed as calling for acting wrongly, power and its attendant benefits are not really desirable at all, of course you will reject the answer "Acquire power." And if, seeing the world this way, you already regard acting virtuous as incomparably rewarding of course you will agree with Aristotle's answer. But then he will have been preaching to the converted. And if he has, all along, been preaching to the converted then we may be seized with a qualm about whether his answer has any objective correctness about it. For what appeared to give it some claim to objectivity, namely its grounding in facts about the human condition, is now revealed to be strictly irrelevant. The virtuous do not need to consider facts about the human condition to convince them that living well is practicing the virtues; they already think of living well in those terms—which is exactly why they say that the wicked do not really flourish. . . .

Aristotle's lectures are addressed [to] people old enough to be interested in the question, but young enough to be not (yet) virtuous but not thereby vicious. It is important, Aristotle tells us, that such people have been well brought up for without such training they will not be able to grasp "the starting-point" (1095b4–8). This amounts to his acknowledgement of the point I mentioned above—that his account of flourishing cannot be made out to those who have become so corrupt that they can see pleasures and benefits only in the lives of the very wealthy and self-indulgent. To have been well brought up is to have been trained in some way from infancy to find enjoyment and pain in the right things

(1104b13). So, for example, we may take it that the well brought up . . . do recognize some goods that the vicious do not—they know, for instance, what it is to enjoy a friendship with someone who is neither rich nor glamorous but generous, and to take pleasure in sharing their own possessions with such a friend. They know what it is to feel ashamed about lying to people who trust them and to find relief in confessing. But they also still feel the pull towards the lives of the wicked and are far from being fully virtuous—they still do lie and say cruel things and act selfishly.

So now our question is—can Aristotle's answer recommend itself not only to the fully virtuous but also to them? Can the life of the virtuous be represented to everyone as the flourishing life—i.e. as the most enjoyable, containing real benefits or advantages and the only one worth going for? Or are its pleasures and advantages only recognizable by the virtuous—from the inside as it were?

There is a charming Thurber cartoon which depicts a riotously drunk woman in a flowery hat and low cut gown (perhaps connoting somewhat loose sexual morals) who is clearly having a whale of a time; she is being contemplated with frosty disapproval by a dour man in a dog-collar who is saying "Unhappy woman!" Now part of what makes this funny, I take it, is not so much that describing this obviously cheerful woman as unhappy is completely inappropriate, for it makes good sense to pity someone who habitually gets very drunk, no matter how much they may enjoy themselves at the time. What is inappropriate is that the man who calls her unhappy so obviously never enjoys himself in any way at all. If she may truly be described as unhappy, so may he. If it was the case that the virtuous were bound to be like Thurber's man—virtue was so much a matter of suppressing or eliminating our natural desires and tendencies that the virtuous life did not characteristically contain much recognizable satisfaction—then it would indeed seem impossible for the virtuous to represent their lives as flourishing to anyone but themselves. But Aristotle's promise is that this is not how things are. Although virtue is about things that are difficult for man, we are constituted by nature to receive the virtues (1103a24–26).

Our natural desires and tendencies are such that they can be brought into complete harmony with our reason, so that doing what we know to be right is doing what we enjoy doing (cf. 1099a15–22, 1102b12–29, 1166a13–15). And surely Aristotle's promise is met. The virtuous are not characteristically like Thurber's man; he is not a good example of a virtuous man at all. The virtuous, as they eat, drink and make love with healthy gusto, rejoice in the love, trust and support of their friends and families, cheerfully make the best of the sorts of bad jobs that befall anyone, look forward serenely to their futures, delight in their work and intellectual pursuits, are people who can be seen to be enjoying themselves and possessing advantages and benefits. . . .

Just as the virtuous have to give some reason for saying that Thurber's woman is unhappy in the teeth of the fact that she is clearly enjoying herself so the wicked would (in theory) have to give some reason why the lives of the virtuous are pitiable. If such lives are manifestly being enjoyed and contain *some* things recognized to be goods to the sort of animal we naturally are, such as friends and family, love, respect, independence, leisure, enjoyment itself, some justification has to be given for describing such lives, intelligibly, as pitiable. Presumably what could be said is that people enjoying such lives are content with too little, and that such goods as their lives contain have been bought at too high a price—as Nancy Mitford claimed that she valued independence as a good but not at the price of having to put away her own underclothes instead of having servants to do it. Just as the virtuous say of the wicked happy man that he is content with too little in friends bought with power and respect prompted by fear and that he has gained his (admitted) advantages at the intolerably high price of degradation, so the wicked may say of the virtuous that, for instance, they are degraded by having to cook for themselves and content with too little in always having sex with the same old partner. But is their disagreement solely about what counts as "degradation" and "a good friend" and "the best sexual partner" and "enjoyment" and . . . i. e. a disagreement about the application of "value" terms which amounts to irreconcilable views of what flourishing consists in? . . .

I should like to suggest that the belief that we are so constituted that the virtuous characteristically flourish (so the failures are due to bad luck) while the wicked do not (so their failures are just what was to be expected) is part of virtue itself. It used to be called the belief in providence, and to doubt it while still believing that one must do as virtue requires is to fall into the vice of despair. To doubt it while not yet believing that one must do as virtue requires (because one is unsettled and not yet virtuous) is to be (still) in the grip of a number of beliefs that are corrupting and to which the above belief is the proper corrective. . . .

## Notes

1. The translation of some of Aristotle's terms for virtues makes them sound a little odd, and they are best understood by noting what vices they are opposed to. So, for instance, "temperance" is not a matter of eschewing alcohol, but having the right disposition in respect of alcohol and food and sex—being neither an alcoholic, nor a glutton, nor sexually licentious. Of the virtue called, in translation, "patience," Aristotle himself remarks that it doesn't really have a name, but we can readily grasp it by seeing that it is opposed to the vices of being bad tempered in various ways on the one hand, and poor spirited on the other. It is also important to realize that the term we translate as "virtue" (*arete*) has not specifically moral overtones and is better translated as "excellence." So it should come as no surprise to us that Aristotle's list contains non-moral virtues or excellences such as wittiness. But we need not even take many of these very seriously as excellences, for in his other ethical work, the *Eudemian Ethics*, Aristotle makes a point of denying that they are excellences (of character) on the grounds that they do not involve choice (EE1234a25). Finally, we should note that Aristotle's list is open-ended—he nowhere claims that it is exhaustive—so it is open to us to add to it virtues with which we are more familiar, e.g. benevolence, compassion, honesty, kindness. . . .

2. Cf., for example, 1106b1–22 and 1109a20–29. Note in the latter passage the comparison with finding the center of a circle, which is a better image than finding a midpoint ("mean") between just two opposing vices.

3. It is important to note that the only similarity I am claiming between the two cases is on this point. Giving up smoking, etc., is not constitutive of flourishing physically the way exercising the virtues is constitutive of flourishing as a human being, and there are other disanalogies too.

## 22    Excellence of Character

### J. O. URMSON

One of the main topics discussed in Plato's ethical dialogues, notably the *Meno*, is how excellence (or virtue, as the translations usually say) is acquired. Especially the question asked is whether it can be taught. Aristotle begins Book II of the *Nicomachean Ethics* with a dogmatic, but clearly correct, answer to the question which well illustrates his very frequent way of solving problems by making distinctions. Excellences of intelligence, he says, are largely acquired by teaching; excellences of character, being nonrational, cannot be taught but are acquired by training (the translations often say by "habituation," but excellence of character is not a mere matter of habit, such as putting on one sock before another when dressing). We have, of course, to be born with the relevant capacities if we are to acquire excellences, whether of character or of intelligence, as most men to some degree are, but the excellence has to be developed.

We must not misunderstand this. Aristotle does not mean that we are born bad, antisocial, creatures of original sin, and that training will convert us from being bad into being good. Aristotle believes that we are born without any character at all. If we are normal human beings and not naturally incapacitated by some abnormal defect, then

Reprinted with permission of Blackwell Publishers, UK, from *Aristotle's Ethics* (Basil Blackwell, 1988), 25–37.

whether we acquire a good or a bad character depends on the kind of upbringing we get. He is evidently more impressed by the effects of environment than those of heredity, though in Book X he acknowledges that we can be better or worse disposed to respond to good training, as different soils better or worse nourish the seed (1179b 20–26).

Aristotle compares acquiring a good character with acquiring a skill. Paradoxical though it may sound, one learns to play the piano by playing the piano, and to ride a bicycle by riding one. Before one has acquired the art or skill one acts in accordance with the instructions of a teacher, who tells us what to do, and one does it with effort. Gradually, by practice and repetition, it becomes effortless and second nature. In the same way, one is trained as a child (if lucky in one's parents and teachers) to become truthful, generous, fair and the like by being told how to behave well and encouraged to do so. Parents supply the intelligence and experience that one has not yet developed, and with practice and repetition it becomes easier and easier to follow their counsel. A child who has been trained to share his toys with his friends finds it easier and easier to do so; the child who has not been so trained will find it hard and will resent having to do so. Such is Aristotle's view, and surely he is right. At the same time, he believes, one's practical intelligence will develop so that one will less and less need parents and guardians to tell one how to behave in various circumstances; one will come to see for oneself. Aristotle also echoes Plato, mentioning him by name (1104b 12), in insisting that correct training is not coercion. If properly trained one comes to enjoy doing things the right way, to want to do things the right way, and to be distressed by doing things wrongly.

We must now notice a very important sentence from Chapter 3 of Book II, first in a typical translation, then in my own. It is the passage from 1104b I P 13–16:

If the virtues are concerned with actions and passions, and every passion and every action is accompanied by pleasure and pain, for this reason also virtue will be concerned with pleasures and pains.
(Ross)

If excellences are concerned with actions and emotions, and every emotion and every action involves liking or dislike, for this reason excellence will be concerned with one's likes and dislikes.
(J. O. U.)

Ross's translation is not, of course, wrong, but it can mislead the unwary. What Aristotle is saying is that whether one has an excellent character or not depends not merely on what one does but also on what one likes doing. If a person acts generously there may be many explanations, some discreditable; if one regularly acts generously because one likes acting generously, if one is emotionally inclined towards generosity, then one has an excellent character in this area of action. So character depends rather on what one likes doing, what one enjoys doing, what one wants to do, than merely on what one does. The man of excellent character will act effortlessly in the correct way; he will not have to make himself so act.

Here we have one more reason for preferring to talk of excellence of character rather than of moral virtue. An illustration will help to make the point clear. Let us suppose that Brown is a strong, healthy extrovert, full of self-confidence. He is at a meeting where a course of action which he believes to be wrong is very popular with the majority; he speaks out against the policy and has no difficulty in doing so. Let us suppose that Smith, a shy, retiring, hesitant person, is also at the meeting and also disapproves of the popular view. He can bring himself to speak out against it only by a great and very disagreeable effort of will. Perhaps we may agree that Smith is the man who has displayed the moral virtue of courage; if you were to compliment Brown on his courage he would not have the faintest idea what you were talking about. But for Aristotle, Brown is the man who has excellence of character; he is the man who acts effortlessly and as he wants to act, without any internal friction. Aristotle is not making a hopelessly wrong judgment about moral virtue; he is raising a different sort of question. The excellent character is that which a man will have who lives the most *eudaemon* life, the most choiceworthy life. If we were to ask, not for what sort of person do we feel most moral respect, but what sort of person we should wish a child of ours to be, we shall be nearer to Aristotle's viewpoint. He thinks a parent should aim to train his or her children to behave properly without effort.

Another way in which the rendering of Aristotle's text as saying that moral virtue is concerned with pleasures and pains is liable to mislead is this. There is, indeed, one area of excellence of character which is properly concerned with pleasure, temperance, and one concerned with pain, endurance. The temperate man enjoys, likes, wants sensual pleasure (food, drink, sex) only to the degree appropriate and the man of endurance does not flinch from pain when the situation demands that he endure it. No doubt it is going too far to say that he enjoys it (remember that Aristotle is speaking generally and in outline), but he does not want to act otherwise in spite of the pain; there is no internal conflict. So on the whole we are less liable to misinterpret Aristotle if we use the language of likes, enjoyment, wants, and their contraries rather than that of pleasure and pain when talking of excellence of character in general and not specifically of temperance.

But, the reader may well ask, surely it is possible for us, like the imaginary Smith voicing unpopular views with difficulty, to act properly when we do not want to, and has Aristotle forgotten this? Aristotle has not forgotten this, and there is a careful discussion of this possibility in Book VII. Perhaps Aristotle would have been more helpful to us had he not postponed his discussion of this possibility to so late in the work—if indeed the arrangement of the work is his.

So excellence of character is a settled disposition to want to act and to act in a way appropriate to the situation. What way is appropriate must, of course, be determined by reason; excellence of character can merely ensure willing compliance with the requirements of practical thinking. But Aristotle has more to tell us about excellence of character; most importantly, there is his celebrated doctrine of the mean, which is part of his definition of excellence of character, and it is to the doctrine of the mean that we shall now turn our attention.

Few philosophical theories have been more frequently and more grossly misunderstood, in my opinion, than the doctrine of the mean. Readers are therefore warned that the exposition that they find here will most probably differ greatly from those they will find in other commentaries; they should read Aristotle's text and decide for themselves who is right in their understanding of it. Most conspicuously, the doctrine of the mean has been interpreted as being a doctrine of moderation—the thesis that extremes are to be avoided and that the middle way is the safest. Unless Aristotle is guilty of a very serious mistake, basic and not in detail, this interpretation must be totally wrong. For Aristotle, as he repeatedly makes clear, excellence of character is a willingness to act in whatever way practical reason requires, and the doctrine of the mean is part of Aristotle's formal definition of excellence of character. But the doctrine of moderation, however interpreted in detail, is clearly a principle determining what action is appropriate on each occasion; as such, it is clearly, if correct, a deliverance of practical thinking and not an attribute of character. Thus, if the doctrine of the mean were a thesis of moderation, it would be guilty of confusing excellence of character with that practical wisdom which, Aristotle repeatedly says, must guide our deliberations and our actions.

Moreover, the doctrine of moderation, while reasonable enough at a crude practical level (like "keep your cool" or "don't fly off the handle"), if not taken literally, is hard to interpret to make philosophical sense. Surely we are not supposed to exhibit a moderate amount of fear, anger and every other emotion whenever we act? Clearly the right amount of most emotions to display on most occasions is zero. Does it, then, say that when a display of anger is appropriate we should always be moderately angry? But the suggestion that we should be moderately angry when faced with a trivial slight and when witnessing wanton cruelty is absurd; there are occasions on which we cannot be too angry, just as there are occasions when, at most, a slight degree of annoyance is in order.

So the thesis of moderation, or any other account of the doctrine of the mean that makes it a device for deciding how to act, can have nothing to do with the Aristotelian view put forward in the

*Ethics.* We must look for another interpretation, which is not hard to find if we take Aristotle to mean what he says.

The doctrine of the mean is part of the definition of excellence of character. Though Aristotle holds that the aim of his ethical work is practical and not to discover what excellence of character is (1108b 27), he clearly thinks that theoretical understanding contributes to that practical end, for in Chapter 5 of Book II he raises the question "What is excellence of character?" This is the regular formula for a demand for a definition of the Aristotelian type. A definition of this type should be constructed by first determining the genus of the thing to be defined, or, less technically, by determining to what wide class of things it belongs and then determining its specific difference, or, less technically, by determining how what is to be defined differs from everything else in the genus. Thus the famous Aristotelian definition of man as a rational animal places man in the genus *animal* and then differentiates him from all other sorts of animal by his rationality. We shall find that Aristotle gives a definition of excellence of character strictly in accordance with this theory.

Having asked the question what excellence of character is, Aristotle has little difficulty in showing that it is a disposition or settled state. Moreover in Chapter 5 he has told us that it is a settled disposition with regard to the feeling and displaying of emotions. Any action that displays character at all, he holds, will involve the display of some emotion, such as "desire, anger, fear, confidence, envy, joy, friendliness, hatred, longing, emulation, pity" (1105b 20–21); no doubt he would agree that actions undertaken as part of a long chain of means will often display emotion only indirectly, but there must always be the basic emotional drive. Anger, or any other emotion, is not in itself either an excellence or a defect of character, but a settled state with regard to exhibiting it will be an excellence if it is a disposition to act in a way directed by sound practical wisdom, a defect if it is a disposition towards improper action. The states of character are distinguished as being specific excellences or defects according to the emotion involved: bravery and

cowardice are an excellence and a defect displayed in relation to the emotion fear, even and hot temper are so related to anger, temperance and gluttony to appetite for food, and so on. Excellences and defects are distinguished by the emotions they display.

"So we have stated to what genus excellence of character belongs" (1106a 13); it is a settled state or disposition. But there are many settled states, and not a few settled states of character with regard to the emotions, of which excellence of character is only one. So, not surprisingly, Aristotle immediately recognizes that he must go on to say how excellence of character differs from other states of character. "But we must not merely say that it is a disposition, but also what sort of disposition" (1106b 14–15); Aristotle must complete the definition by stating the difference. The doctrine of the mean provides this completion.

It will be helpful if we know in advance what other states of character Aristotle recognizes; if he were to recognize only one—badness of character —it could be very simply distinguished from excellence; but in fact he recognizes many more. Unfortunately, Aristotle has not yet mentioned any of these other states of character except in passing, which is perhaps a defect in his order of exposition. But he does give a list at the beginning of Book VII, where he distinguishes six states, divisible into three contrary pairs. One of the pairs if formed by, on the one hand, a super-human excellence which might be called heroic, and is attributable only to the gods; a subhuman beastliness indicative of disease or madness—the sort of state which in modern times might lead to the criminal lunatic asylum rather than the prison. As super-human and sub-human, these are perhaps not really states of human character at all, and I shall say no more about them. Aristotle himself says very little about these conditions. Another of these contrary pairs is excellence of character and badness of character. But there is also a third pair of contraries, one of which might be called strength of will or self-control, the other weakness of will or lack of self-control. These states characterize the man who needs and tries to make himself act properly, unlike the man of excellent character who acts properly without any difficulty; the one who succeeds in making himself so act is the strong-willed man, and the one who tries and fails is weak willed.

Thus, if we may neglect the super- and subhuman in studying human excellence, we have four states of character that need to be distinguished from one other. In order of decreasing merit, they are:

1. Excellence of character: the state of the man who wants to act appropriately and does so without internal friction.
2. Strength of will: the state of the man who wants to act improperly but makes himself act properly.
3. Weakness of will: the state of the man who wants to act improperly, tries to make himself act properly, and fails.
4. Badness of character: the state of the man who wants to act improperly, who thinks it an excellent idea so to do, and does so without internal friction.

We can illustrate the situation with [the table below]. Thus these four states can be distinguished from each other in so far as no two display the same merit in . . . the emotional want, [in] the aim or choice settled on after deliberation, and in action. The four states could get a modern illustration from the even-tempered man who has no difficulty in waiting coolly in a traffic jam, the hot-tempered man who successfully restrains himself, the hot-tempered man who tries to remain calm but cannot, and the man who curses and hoots at all and sundry with complete self-approval.

So it appears that Aristotle thinks that no emotion is, in itself, either good or bad; what is good or bad is a disposition to display emotions appropriately or inappropriately. It would be foreign to Aristotle's teleological view of nature to allow that we are naturally endowed with emotions that should never be exhibited or felt. What we still need is some further clarification of the notion of propriety, and that is what Aristotle gives us in the doctrine of the mean. Aristotle holds that excellence of character is a disposition to feel and display the right degree of emotion on each occasion and as the occasion demands, and that this disposition is in a mean between being too much disposed and too little disposed to feel and display each emotion. In the mean one will feel and display each emotion at the right times and not too often or too infrequently, with reference to the right matters, towards the right people, for the right reason and in the right way. To be inclined to excess will involve such errors as feeling and displaying an emotion in season and out of season, in inappropriate situations, towards people indiscriminately, without good cause and in inappropriate ways. A similar account can be given of being inclined to deficiency.

The abbreviated account of excess and deficiency is simply "too much" and "too little"; it is this that has most probably led readers to interpret the doctrine as one of moderation, a view that one must avoid extremes of emotion and action on every occasion. But plenty of passages prove this to be a mistake. Here is one: "Fear and confidence and appetite and anger and pity and in general likes and dislikes may be felt both too much and too little, and in both cases not well; but to feel them at the right time, with reference to the right objects, towards the right people, with the right motive, and in the right way, is what is both intermediate and best, and this is characteristic of excellence" (1106b 19–23).

|  | Want | Aim | Act |
|---|---|---|---|
| Excellence | Good | Good | Good |
| Strength | Bad | Good | Good |
| Weakness | Bad | Good | Bad |
| Badness | Bad | Bad | Bad |

Thus there will be, in the traditional terminology, two vices correlated with each virtue, or two types of bad character correlated with each excellence of character, not just one. Aristotle does not think we should accept this just on the basis of the general considerations so far adduced, but should consider the individual excellences and see whether we can find two defects going with each excellence (1107a 28–29). In the *Nicomachean Ethics* he refers us to a table that is missing from the text (1107a 33) but does discuss briefly a few cases. However, a fairly long list is given in the *Eudemian Ethics,* which is reproduced below for convenience. Not all these examples will be convincing to the modern reader without more ado, but they illustrate the general contention.

We should note, to dispel the ghost of moderation, that excellence of character is explicitly said to be an intermediate disposition towards action (1106b 31) and not a disposition to intermediate action. Extreme action will on some occasions be appropriate and carried out by the man of excellent character. Thus the man whose temper is good will be mildly angry about trifles and enraged by outrages, whereas the irascible man will be excessively angry over trifles and the placid or impassive man may be little or only moderately angered by the worst excesses. To give another modern example: the hot-tempered man will also be liable to rage at the helpless telephonist as well as at the person responsible for letting him down, while the overplacid man will just shrug his shoulders. These are illustrations of the many ways in which both excess and deficiency can be exhibited. Simply being too angry or not angry enough on a given occasion [is] only one way in which excess and deficiency can be exhibited.

It is commonly said that the doctrine of the mean argues that to every virtue there correspond two vices. But, whereas some of the states of character exhibiting excess or defect might be reasonably, if somewhat archaically, called vices, such as intemperance, others could not; some, while flaws in a person's make-up, are barely, if at all, of moral significance. No doubt a person is to some degree badly adjusted if he has no enjoyment in even the simple food necessary for health, of if he is overplacid in temperament, or is too self-effacing; but these are not vices nor even moral misdemeanours. Aristotle is considering that states of character do or do not conduce to the *eudaemon* life, whereas to call a character trait a vice is, in modern English, a moral condemnation. We must also be careful about our understanding of the expressions "bad character" and "good character." For Aristotle, a bad character is one which detracts from eudaemonia, not because he has no conception of or no interest in wrong-doing, but because wrong-doing is not what he is at this stage concerned to discuss.

So Aristotle can arrive at his final definition of excellences of character. "It is a settled state of choice, in a mean relative to us, which mean is determined by reason as the wise man determines it" (1106b 36–1107a 2). The notion of choice and the part played by reason will, of course, require further elucidation, by Aristotle and in this book.

| | | |
|---|---|---|
| irascibility | impassivity | even temper |
| foolhardiness | cowardice | bravery |
| shamelessness | touchiness | modesty |
| intemperance | insensibility | temperance |
| envy | (nameless) | fair-mindedness |
| gain | disadvantage | justice |
| prodigality | meanness | liberality |
| boastfulness | mock modesty | truthfulness |
| flattery | churlishness | friendliness |
| servility | disdain | dignity |
| vanity | mean spirit | pride |
| ostentation | unworldliness | magnificence |

By saying that the mean is relative to us Aristotle is making it clear that he is not using any mathematical notion, such as those of an arithmetical or geometrical mean, but that the mean is determined by, is relative to, all the circumstances in which the choice of actions has to be made.

The statement that excellence of character is in a mean and that this serves to differentiate it from other human dispositions and settled states perhaps requires some justification. To say that excellence of character is in a mean is to say that the emotions that are its domain can be experienced and displayed in action both too much and too little. Let us, anticipating a little our discussion of theoretical excellence, contrast excellence of character with one excellence of theoretical intelligence which Aristotle tells us is concerned with grasping basic truths. But there is no possibility of grasping basic truths too much, too frequently, et cetera; there is only one fault corresponding to the excellence—intellectual dullness, inability to grasp these truths.

In this way, and because, also, excellence of character is the only human disposition concerned with choice at all, the thesis that it is differentiated by choice in a mean, can serve to differentiate excellence of character from other human excellences. Aristotle, of course, realizes, and indeed claims, that intermediates can often be best in other areas. Thus, in relation to health, one can take too much or too little exercise and eat too much or too little food. Here, too, the mean is relative to us, since different people with different occupations will need different quantities and types of food and exercise. Aristotle does not need to claim that only the thing defined exhibits the specific difference; he needs to claim only that it is the one thing within the genus that exhibits the feature. Similarly, God is rational, but Aristotle can define man as a rational animal since God is not an animal. His claim is that exhibiting mean choice applies only to those settled human dispositions that are excellences of character, and that it characterizes all of these.

We have seen that the whole of this account of excellence of character, including the doctrine of the mean, is theoretical, not practical, since it has been devoted to the discovery of a definition. Its theoretical character becomes more obvious by contrast with the very end of Book II, where Aristotle does offer some directly practical advice. There he notes that it is not easy to be sure what action will on each occasion exhibit a mean disposition, so that when in doubt one should veer towards the extreme which is less pernicious than the other and also away from the one that one is more inclined to lean towards. If, for example, one were inclined to be too meek, one should, when in doubt, aim towards the side of self-assertiveness, while, if being too angry were worse than not being as angry as the occasion warrants, one should, for that reason also, tend towards mildness. Aristotle also notes that one cannot in practical matters ever determine exactly where the mean lies and how far one has to depart from it before one is deserving of blame, nor can one lay down precise rules for determining the mean. "The decision rests with perception" says Aristotle (1109b 23), by which laconic remark he does not mean that one sees, intuits, in some ineffable way how to behave, but that you need to be present in the particular situation to judge, and no general principle can be comprehensive enough to take account of the values of all the variables to be taken account of. In the same way, he notes, only the man on the spot can decide whether the bread is properly cooked (1113a 1).

This whole approach to the problems of action is in striking contrast to such modern ethical doctrines as regard certain kinds of action as invariably right in themselves and others as invariably wrong; Kant claimed, for example, that lying, promise breaking and suicide were of their own nature wrong. Others would claim that some emotions are in themselves evil and a mark of the depravity of human nature. But Aristotle is aware of the possibility of such views, and explains that the difference between them and his is more apparent than real. Thus, he agrees that the emotional state called shamelessness is in itself always and inevitably bad (1107a 11): but this is because shamelessness is the name given to an emotion only when in excess, the same emotion being called modesty when in a mean."Some things are named with their worthlessness included" (1107a

10), but these are already extremes. Such principles as "Never display excess or deficiency of an emotion" are, no doubt, true, but are empty. In the same way, some actions are always wrong, such as adultery and murder, which are named with their worthlessness included. But adultery will usually be a manifestation of excessive sexual desire, excessive in this case because towards the wrong person; homicide, similarly, is only called murder when unjustified. Murder will frequently exhibit an excess of anger or greed. Aristotle is clearly to some degree successful in dealing with these apparent exceptions to his view. But there do remain disagreements with such views as those of Kant, for it is not clear how Aristotle could claim that lying and suicide, for example, could be defined in an evaluative way which made their condemnation universal but empty.

Finally, here is a summary of the main points of Aristotle's account of excellence of character:

1. All action directly or indirectly exhibits some emotion.

2. For each specific excellence of character there will be some specific emotion whose field it is.

3. In the case of each such emotion it is possible to be disposed to exhibit it to the right degree; this is excellence of character.

4. In the case of each such emotion it is possible to be disposed to exhibit it too much or too little, and each of these dispositions is a defect of character.

5. "Too much" includes "on too many occasions" and similar possibilities as well as "too violently"; "too little" includes "on too few occasions" and similar possibilities as well as "too weakly."

6. The right amount has to be determined by reason.

7. So excellence can be defined as being a settled disposition of choice in a mean relative to us, such as the wise man would determine it.

8. There is no emotion that no one should ever exhibit.

# 23   Aristotelian Justice as a Personal Virtue

## DAVID K. O'CONNOR

Justice has not fared well in the revival of virtue ethics. In the first place, justice seems more at home in debates about public policy and social institutions than in descriptions of the moral strengths and weaknesses of individuals. We are much more likely to commend a policy than a person for being just. And when we do praise individuals for justice, they are often being singled out for their performance of specialized roles as judges or arbitrators. To describe a potential colleague as always honest, witty, gracious, tenacious, insightful, helpful, dependable: all of these and many more are specific ways of recommending someone, and conjure up specific expectations about his or her conduct. But except for some special contexts (tenure review, for example), I am more likely to puzzle than enlighten if I prepare you to meet someone by saying, "Professor So-and-So is always just." How often, after all, *can* we be just? Justice does not seem to characterize us in the way other virtues do. Justice may be the primary virtue of social institutions, but it seems a distinctly derivative one of individuals, perhaps being nothing other than a settled resolve to promote and support just institutions and the policies issuing from them. From this point of view, there is little independent interest in justice as a personal virtue.

But even when justice has been of interest within virtue ethics, it has often suffered in

From *Midwest Studies in Philosophy, Vol. XIII,* edited by Peter A. French, Theodore E. Uehling, Jr., and Howard K. Wettstein, p. 417–427. Copyright © 1988 by the University of Notre Dame Press. Used by permission of the publisher.

comparisons to virtues like love, compassion, and care. Such virtues, with their direct and natural concern for other human beings, can seem to correct or at least complement the indirect and artificial respect required by justice. Justice, it might be thought, is too entangled with a dubious conception of the autonomous individual to reflect the interdependence that is central to (at least some kinds of) moral experience. Justice seems a virtue fit only for cold and distant strangers, like the characters in a Western; and its demands like the verdicts of a hanging judge, cruel but fair. An account of the virtues that looks to forming members of a moral community would naturally be uneasy with a virtue that seems designed for mere co-existence.

Perhaps justice is simply obsolete as a personal virtue, and virtue ethics can get along without it, or at least without giving it a very exalted role. But there is something surprising about this conclusion, and I want to explore a way of understanding justice that avoids it. Where can we look for an account of justice that avoids the two objections that (1) justice is primarily a virtue of social institutions and policies and only derivatively of individual persons, and (2) justice is as a virtue definitely in tension with and probably inferior to directly altruistic virtues such as love and compassion? I will turn for a helpful model to the founding father of virtue ethics, Aristotle himself. Aristotle was certainly concerned with the institutions that embody justice in different kinds of political regime, but his analysis in the fifth book of the *Nicomachean Ethics* is primarily concerned with justice as a psychic state (*hexis*) of individuals. He describes this psychic state independently of his account of just political institutions, and so provides an account that avoids the first objection. Furthermore, Aristotle was not only unaware of a sharp divide between the virtues of justice and love (*philia*), but makes a point of their near-identity.[1] We should then expect his account of justice to have exactly the sort of resources we need to rehabilitate justice as a personal virtue.

But things are not so simple, and in our eagerness to exploit the father's resources we must beware of squandering the patrimony. The Aristotelian model does not provide a direct answer to our questions about the status of justice as a personal virtue. Aristotle's questions are different from ours, and we can learn more by seeing this difference than by precipitously making him address our concerns. I will be more concerned to bring out the framework within which Aristotelian justice finds its place than to exploit Aristotle's views for answers to questions raised from our framework. His questions are interesting and explore parts of moral life that we might otherwise overlook.

I will emphasize two aspects of the Aristotelian account of justice that distinguish it from most contemporary accounts, whether or not within virtue ethics. First, the vice that provides the primary temptation to injustice is not the same in Aristotle and contemporary accounts. Aristotle disagrees with us about the "enemy" that justice must overcome. I will describe this by saying that Aristotle offers an alternative account of the *corrective* aspect of justice. Second, the exercise of Aristotelian justice expresses a kind of personal excellence in social interaction different from the kinds contemporary accounts emphasize. This disagreement over the particular capacity that justice perfects concerns what I will call the *expressive* aspect of justice. The corrective aspect of justice is the virtue's negative side, telling us what it guards against, while its expressive aspect tells us the positive side of what human capacities it brings into play and perfects.

After examining the corrective and expressive aspects of Aristotelian justice, we will be better able to see how Aristotle treats justice as a personal virtue, and why it is closely connected by him to love. Aristotelian justice is primarily concerned with a part of moral life different from what our understanding of justice would lead us to expect, and the problems and rewards of justice are correspondingly different. I will try to illustrate how Aristotelian justice focuses on a kind of selfishness quite different from the egoistic partiality at the heart of our conception of injustice. I will conclude by considering the resources of the alternative Aristotle offers to virtue ethics, and the change in emphasis that this alternative would require.

## A. The Corrective Aspect of Justice

What distinctive moral defect does justice oppose and correct? Philippa Foot has given a lucid description of the typical contemporary answer to this question:[2]

Virtues such as justice . . . correspond not to any particular desire or tendency that has to be kept in check [as do virtues like temperance and courage] but rather to a deficiency of motivation; and it is this that they must make good. If people were as much attached to the good of others as they are to their own good there would no more be a general virtue of benevolence than there is a general virtue of self-love. And if people cared about the rights of others as they care about their own rights no virtue of justice would be needed to look after the matter.

This picture of justice and its relation to the other virtues implies a fundamental division of virtue into two different kinds. On the one hand, *interpersonal* virtues like justice and benevolence make good our vicious tendency to be partial to our own desires and prerogatives to the detriment of others. On the other, there are *intrapersonal* virtues that moderate and channel various sorts of desires and emotions. For example, the virtue of temperance moderates and controls our desires for bodily pleasures, while courage controls the effect of fear on our actions. These latter virtues confront a set of temptations very different from those connected with justice and the other interpersonal virtues: the intrapersonal virtues are not essentially "other-regarding" and are not opposed primarily by the threat of egoistic partiality. They are instead concerned with the intensity of various desires and the relative priority of the ends reflected in these desires.

In contrast, Aristotelian justice does not primarily involve the control or correction of egoistic motives. Instead, it is like the intrapersonal virtues in opposing misorientation toward or overvaluing of the various sorts of inferior ends. Justice is, of course, concerned with how our actions affect other people.[3] But in Aristotle's picture, what tempts a human being to fall short of a virtue like temperance or courage is just what leads him to be unjust; Aristotle sees no special role even in the interpersonal virtues for egoism and its control. Consider Aristotle's discussion of the motives of unjust people in the following passage:[4]

The reasons people choose to harm [others] and do base things contrary to the law are vice and incontinence. For when people have either one vice or many, they are unjust with regard to whatever they are vicious. For example, an illiberal person [is unjust] with regard to money, a licentious person with regard to bodily pleasures, a soft person with regard to taking it easy, a coward with regard to dangers (for because of fear he deserts those in danger with him), an honor-lover [*philotimos*] because of honor, a sharp-tempered person because of anger, a victory-lover because of victory, a bitter person because of revenge, a thoughtless person because he is deceived about the just and unjust, a shameless person because of contempt for reputation. In the same way with other [causes of vice], a particular person [is unjust] with regard to a particular underlying [cause of vice].

It is clear here that Aristotle understands injustice to have the same underlying causes as vices we would usually think of as intrapersonal. He sees no fundamental division of virtue because he does not believe that injustice is the result of unrestrained egoism so much as of misorientation.[5]

In the passage above, Aristotle is discussing what in the *Nicomachean Ethics* he calls "universal" or "inclusive" justice. But his discussion of the narrower virtue of "particular" or "partial" justice again shows that misorientation, not egoism, is the threat to justice. The special type of misorientation that characterizes particular injustice is the desire for the pleasure that comes from gain, especially gain concerning the external goods of wealth and honor.[6] Aristotle names the vicious overvaluing of such goods *pleonexia*. As he understands this virtue, a person who is just (in the narrow sense of particular justice) is opposed not to the egoist or the partial person, but to the money-grubber or the ruthlessly ambitious person. With regard to what it opposes and corrects, then, particular justice is much like liberality and magnificence (concerning wealth) or magnanimity and proper pride (concerning honors).[7] There is once again no fundamental division between the focus of interpersonal and intrapersonal virtue.

There are two interesting consequences of taking Aristotle's perspective and treating misorientation rather than unrestrained egoism as the root of injustice. First, the Aristotelian account will not categorize the same set of actions under injustice as the contemporary account with egoism at its core. Bernard Williams' criticisms of Aristotle's account provide a striking illustration of this. Williams has a conception of the virtue of justice very much like Foot's. Injustice is distinguished from other vices, says Williams, by the fact that "this vice, unlike others, does not import a special motive, but rather the lack of one," namely, a lack of concern with promoting just distributions.[8] An act can be characterized as unjust whenever it displays this sort of indifference, whatever else its motives may be. "There are acts that are unjust . . . which are the products of fear, jealousy, desire for revenge, and so on."[9] Williams criticizes Aristotle's claim that an action must be motivated by *pleonexia,* an overvaluing of wealth or honor, to count as unjust. The corrective aspect of justice essentially involves overcoming our tepid commitment to fairness rather than our voracious appetite for external goods.

Given this account of what justice opposes and corrects, Williams will not count some cases Aristotle considers paradigmatic of injustice as injustice at all, and similarly an Aristotelian will not count some of Williams' cases. I will illustrate this by considering two hypothetical cases involving a pair of vicious men, Greedy Greg and Lascivious Larry. The first has a misdirected interest in

money, the second too much devotion to the rites of Aphrodite.

For the first case, suppose Greg and Larry are both guilty of seducing a wealthy colleague's wife. Following his lascivious ways, Larry commits adultery out of lust, aiming at sexual pleasure. But true to his name, Greedy Greg aims not so much at the physical pleasure as at the monetary gifts the wife will bestow on him, or perhaps the blackmail she will pay him to keep the affair quiet. On Aristotle's view, Greg is here a paradigm case of an unjust man.[10] His misorientation toward money—and thus his *pleonexia*—has led him to harm another person. Though Larry has also done harm, his motive was not the type that characterizes injustice. Intemperate yes, unjust no. On the other hand, Williams would not count either Greg or Larry as unjust. While both are vicious, neither has displayed injustice's characteristic insensitivity to fairness.

For the second case, suppose both men are judges or arbitrators in a dispute involving the distribution of goods. Greedy Greg accepts a monetary bribe to favor one party in the dispute, while Lascivious Larry accepts sexual inducements. In this case, Williams' view of the virtue of justice implies that both men suffer from the same moral failure: the actions of both display the indifference to fair claims that characterizes injustice. On the Aristotelian view, however, only Greedy Greg displays the vice of injustice: the misorientation behind his action, but not the misorientation behind Lascivious Larry's action, falls within the vice of *pleonexia* that justice opposes.[11]

We can summarize these different ways of categorizing unjust actions in the following table. We see an important disagreement here about which

|  |  | Motive | |
|---|---|---|---|
|  |  | **Greed** | **Lust** |
| **Action** | Misdistribution | A  W | W |
|  | Seduction | A |  |

A = Case of Aristotelian injustice
W = Case of Williams' injustice

cases should receive a unified explanation and which cannot. From Williams' point of view, the Aristotelian account wrongly separates the acts of misdistribution of Greg and Larry, for both display a special kind of insensitivity to just distributions. Furthermore, it also mistakenly unifies Greg's misdistributing and his seducing, since only the former act involves this special insensitivity. From the Aristotelian view, Williams fails to see that one and the same psychic flaw—an overvaluing of money—is operative both in Greg's accepting the bribe and in his mercenary sexual adventures, albeit in different contexts. Nor would an Aristotelian believe that there is a special indifference that Greg and Larry share when they accept their quite different bribes. He or she would doubt that there is any more of a unified, motivationally relevant "indifference to just distributions" in both misdistribution cases than there is an analogous unified, motivationally relevant "indifference to sexual licitness" in both seduction cases. Either of these special types of indifference looks to the Aristotelian like an empty cause postulated to explain an incidental unity.

This disagreement over the underlying psychic causes of injustice brings us to the second consequence of Aristotelian justice's focus on misorientation rather than egoism: its alternative view of the task of moral education. On the view of justice that Foot and Williams share, the strategy for educating people in the interpersonal virtues will be quite different from the strategy for educating them in virtues like temperance, courage, liberality, and magnanimity. These intrapersonal virtues do not depend on the development of the particular sensitivity to fair claims that justice requires. It is quite possible on this view for the two kinds of virtue to be developed independently: the lustful man or the materialistic man may well be a just man, and the temperate man or the man who does not overvalue money may still fail to be sensitive to the just claims of others. It is no guarantee of justice that we have internalized the proper hierarchy of ends, for high-minded injustice is injustice all the same.

The Aristotelian view is entirely at odds with this. It sees injustice as the interpersonal result of an intrapersonal misorientation. More specifically, the psychic root of injustice is overvaluing the external goods of money and honor, treating them as if they were constituents of happiness rather than the mere equipment of it. The human being whose interest in such goods is not delimited by his orientation to the end of virtuous activity will naturally be led to harm others in his futile and misguided search for satisfaction. For this reason, Aristotle calls external goods like money and honor "goods people fight over" (*perimachêta*).[12] The education required to combat the temptation to greed and ambition must then focus directly on promoting a devotion to virtuous activity, a devotion that will put wealth and honor in their place and prevent them from becoming divisive motives for injustice. For the Aristotelian, the man of liberality and magnanimity will be the just man; and the misorientation of the greedy and overly ambitious makes them at least potentially unjust. There is no causally independent sensitivity to fair claims that can anchor justice in a sea of disordered interests.

Aristotle's approach is manifest in a passage of the *Politics* where he discusses the institutions required to prevent injustice and civil conflict (*stasis*) from arising in a community.[13] He criticizes one Phaleas of Chalcedon for suggesting that equality of property would remove the causes of civil conflict: "Even if one were to institute moderate property for all, it would not help. One ought to level desires rather than property, . . . for if people's desires go beyond necessities, they will commit injustice to satisfy them." The only effective cure for civil conflict, claims Aristotle, is public education that corrects people's tendency to be grasping (*pleonektein*) of money and honors. Such correction depends mainly on changing people's orientation from valuing money and honors for their own sake to valuing them only for their contribution to virtuous activity. In itself "the nature of desire is without limit," and only by providing a limit in the life of virtue can the pursuit of external goods be prevented from becoming a source of conflict and injustice. Development of the proper orientation, not the development of a sensitivity to fair claims, is the heart of education in justice.

In summary, we can say that Aristotelian justice takes aim at a different kind of moral failing from what we would expect of justice. The unjust man has not lapsed into egoistic partiality, and he will not be improved primarily by becoming more responsive to others. Instead, he needs to re-order his interests, putting first things first. Then he will not be tempted by those goods that prove so divisive when pursued as ends themselves. His injustice is but the outward manifestation of a psychic misorientation, and the cure for the underlying moral disease of misorientation will also clear up the symptom of unjust treatment of others. The corrective aspect of justice is not on this Aristotelian view essentially different from the corrective aspect of the intrapersonal virtues; and so there is not the sharp distinction between the psychic bases of interpersonal and intrapersonal virtues that exists in most contemporary treatments.

## B. The Expressive Aspect of Justice

Justice is not a virtue characterized merely by the particular kinds of temptation it holds down. An account of justice that spoke only of its corrective aspect would be as incomplete as an account of excellence in swimming that told us only how not to drown. Such accounts will also typically have a more positive side that shows us what psychic capacities justice engages and perfects. This expressive aspect of justice has not, I believe, had as unified a treatment in contemporary moral philosophy as its corrective aspect, so the contrast with the Aristotelian account is somewhat less clear. But a sketch of two approaches within the contemporary perspective will provide a basis for comparison.

One approach might follow Kant in focusing on justice as an expression of autonomy. The idea here would be that acting on a universalizable principle allows the agent to rise above his empirically given desires and drives. By so escaping from the grubbiness of pathology, the agent exercises his capacity for true freedom. Just action expresses this freedom from empirical determination. For the metaphysically less daring, a stripped down version of this idea could focus on rational consistency rather than autonomy.[14] Here the idea would be that rational consistency requires action to conform to certain standards of impartiality, so that failure to live up to the standards convicts one of inconsistency. On this version, the just agent escapes from a practical analogue of fallacy rather than from pathology, and the capacity that finds expression in just action is simply rationality rather than freedom. But either way, the expressive aspect of justice would focus on the capacity for practical rationality, whether or not this is linked with freedom from empirical determination.

A second approach could stress the human capacity for mutuality and reciprocity, focusing more on equality with others than freedom for oneself. Justice might on this view be understood to depend on the ability to see oneself as merely one source of valuation among others. The just person would exercise his or her capacity to be party to a reasonable consensus, and to express [a] particularly *moral* interest in fairness.[15] Alternatively, the capacity perfected by justice might be more Humean, linked to emotional or sentimental response to the good of others (e.g., through sympathy), though this link would typically be distinguished from the more direct link displayed by benevolence or love. In either case, justice would express a special human capacity for identification and involvement with others' conceptions of the good.

I believe that these two approaches to the expressive aspect of justice, one emphasizing rationality, one mutuality, cover most contemporary conceptions. Either could complement the sort of account of justice's corrective aspect seen in Foot and Williams. But if Aristotelians see no such special capacity, linked to justice and independent of the capacities exercised and perfected in the intrapersonal virtues, how will they explain the positive side of justice? There seems on this model nothing to explain how the praise of an action as just adds to its characterization by an intrapersonal virtue like liberality or magnanimity. The worthwhile human capacities seem to have been exhausted by the intrapersonal virtues, leaving justice with no special excellence of its own to express.

In a way this description of the expressive aspect of justice is true. As there was no type of misorientation peculiar to injustice, so too there is no special type of proper orientation that makes justice valuable. Just actions simply *are* actions of liberality or magnanimity, grounded in the same psychic states and aiming at the same ends. But in praising an action for its justice, the Aristotelian does not focus primarily on the fact of proper orientation. Instead, he or she will focus on the excellence of the action as a contribution to a *common* pursuit of the good, to its fitting into a context of shared life. It is true that when an action is criticized as unjust from the Aristotelian perspective, we can be sure that it is motivated by an inordinate attachment to money or honor. But it is not this attachment which is being criticized so much as the effect this attachment has of making the greedy or ambitious person a bad partner or colleague. Justice has its primary and clearest application within the context of communities pursuing a shared conception of the good.

Aristotelian justice does not directly express, then, a human capacity for altruism or impartiality, but for partnership or collegiality. It applies primarily to our interactions with others conceived as partners (though not necessarily equals[16]), sharing in our conception and pursuit of the good, not to our confrontations with others conceived as independent sources of valuation. One way to appreciate this contrast is to consider the different way that selfishness becomes a threat to and is overcome by justice when conceived as expressing on the one hand a capacity for altruism and on the other a capacity for partnership. On the altruism model, selfishness is caused by a poorly developed sensitivity to the independent good of others, and it is overcome by appealing directly to this capacity for justice. On the Aristotelian model, selfishness is the effect in interpersonal life of misorientation toward divisive goods, and its cure depends on reorienting the agent to higher goods, the successful pursuit of which requires and fosters partnership.

To illustrate these differences, consider an analogy with a case of selfishness on an athletic team. Suppose you are the coach of a girls' grade school basketball team. Most of your players are at about the same skill level, but one is much better than the others. This star athlete can run faster, jump higher, dribble and shoot much more effectively than anyone else on the team. When you watch her working out in the gym by herself, she appears to have mastered all the skills that go into making a fine basketball player. But as soon as you see her in an *interpersonal* context, this rosy picture is destroyed. Like many gifted but immature athletes, your star doesn't use her talents to benefit the team effort. On fast breaks she outruns her teammates and spoils the pattern; on defense she wanders from her own assignment and horns in on someone else's. But worst of all, on offense your "star" hogs the ball, dribbling too much and shooting too often; and when she does bother to pass, she befuddles her slower, less coordinated teammates by bouncing rockets off their shins and foreheads. In short, Coach, you have a selfish basketball player on your hands.

How do you go about turning this playground prima donna into a good basketball player? You might try appealing to her capacities for altruism or impartiality. Perhaps you could take her aside and explain that she should give the other girls a chance, even if they aren't much good. Or you could ask her how she would like it if a more talented girl embarrassed her by throwing passes she couldn't handle, going after her latent regard for the categorical imperative. But I think these approaches have an inappropriate conception of selfishness behind them. Her problem is not that her egoism leads her to ignore the needs and desires of her teammates (though she may do this too). You don't cure her selfishness by developing her sensitivity to the fair claims of others. Instead, you need to change her understanding of success, of excellence in basketball.

Part of this will usually consist simply in getting her to think more about *team* success, about outscoring other teams, and less about how many points she scores herself. Teach her to enjoy winning, and she will probably be less tempted to dominate the action, since this usually hurts a team. But if she is far enough above the level of her teammates, the team might actually win *more* games when she dominates and her teammates simply stay out of the way. Your team may well score more points if on every possession she drives the length of the court and fires away. Your star's increased concern for the team's winning could exacerbate her selfish play rather than cure it.

This puts you in a delicate position as a coach. If all you care about is winning grade school basketball games, then you will let her dominate. But if you want to develop your star's excellence as a basketball player—excellence that might be fully exploited by teammates and rewarded with victories only at the high school level and beyond—you will attack her selfishness in another way.[17] You must go beyond making this talented athlete care about team success and change her understanding of what *individual* excellence is in basketball. The skills she perfects and exhibits in her private workouts, she must learn, do not yet make her a fine basketball player. Until she learns to use these individual skills as a member of a team, they are not excellences of a basketball player, but only of a gym rat. An excellent basketball player, as opposed to someone skilled merely at dribbling or shooting or throwing the ball behind her back, uses these skills in ways that respect the limitations of her teammates and exploit their strengths.

This sensitivity to her teammates may look at first to your star like a *sacrifice* of excellence, as if she were to play down to their level. But this is wrong. An exquisite sensitivity to their teammates is very much a part of what makes Magic Johnson and Larry Bird great players, for example: it makes *them* better *individual* basketball players, and not merely their teams better teams. But this kind of sensitivity to one's teammates is quite different from the sensitivity recommended in the contemporary approaches to justice. It is sensitivity to others *as partners* in the pursuit of a shared goal.

Of course, this "interpersonal" excellence would be useless without the developed repertoire of "intrapersonal" skills that your star has developed in the gym. But when at last you can praise her as a fine basketball player, and not merely as a fancy dribbler or accurate shooter, what you have primarily in mind will be something besides these skills. You will have cured her selfishness by helping to change her conception of athletic success from scoring many points and dominating the action to contributing to team success with and through her teammates.

In an analogous way, Aristotelian justice is the virtue of a human being who is a good partner in the pursuit of some worthwhile goal, especially the goal of virtuous action within the context of a political community. The greedy person and the overly ambitious person will not make good partners in this pursuit any more than an athlete bent on scoring as many points as she can makes a good teammate. But their failing, though it involves a type of selfishness, is not primarily a failure of fairness, an indulgence in partiality. Aristotelian justice is more akin to the virtues that make for a good colleague than those that make for a good judge, more directly opposed to the love of honor that leads some academics to monopolize conversations, or stack departments with supporters, than with the indifference to strangers that lets the poor starve. Not that Aristotelians should be indifferent to starving strangers, but that is not the part of moral life with which justice is most concerned.

Given this focus of justice on excellence in partnership or collegiality, it should no longer be surprising that Aristotle links justice closely with friendship. For he thinks of friendships precisely as partnerships in the pursuit of some good, whether pleasure or utility or virtuous activity. In this respect, Aristotle's conception of friendship is quite different from ours, emphasizing the ties of close collaboration rather than of emotional intimacy.[18] It is in the shared life of friendship that the correction of misorientation is most crucial and the expression of partnership most rewarding. Because justice and friendship correct the same vices and express the same excellence (though friendship does so in a tighter and denser nexus of shared activity),[19] there is no hint in the Aristotelian perspective of the Humean distinction between the direct, natural concern for others embodied in benevolence and the indirect, artificial concern for others embodied in justice. For the Aristotelian, love is the perfection of justice, not a modification of it.

We have seen that the Aristotelian approach to justice differs in two important ways from most contemporary approaches. First, it takes a different view of the enemy to be overcome by justice, emphasizing misorientation to inappropriate ends rather than egoistic insensitivity to fair claims. Second, it emphasizes collegial excellence in shared pursuit of a common vision of the good, rather than the respect appropriate between human beings who confront each other as independent sources of value and valuation. As a consequence of these emphases, Aristotelian justice combats selfishness and perfects our interpersonal lives in contexts unlike those most prominent in the contemporary accounts. We are rather unused to confronting in theory the question, "What is required of me and what may I expect as a colleague or partner of others?" even though we confront it often in practice. But the Aristotelian approach gives such questions center stage, and is more concerned in interpersonal life with the quality of the peace than the restraint of war, so to speak.

Some may respond that if this account of Aristotle is right, his approach to interpersonal virtue has little interest for us. For if we think that the most pressing and important moral questions—at least concerning interpersonal virtues—have to do with allowing for and respecting diverse conceptions of the good, Aristotelian interests will seem peripheral, cliquish. and perhaps somewhat elitist. But I prefer to think of Aristotle as pointing toward a part of our moral lives that has great importance for making and unmaking human excellence, perhaps more central than what contemporary accounts point to. For Aristotle locates justice not at the extremities of community, but at its beating heart. Aristotelian justice can charac-

terize a human being in the way that being a good colleague can, because it focuses on our excellence in pursuit of what we hold highest. The shared life of virtuous activity is neither so trivial nor so easy that it cannot profitably be the focus of ethical inquiry into human excellence.[20]

## Notes

1. See *NE* 8.1.1155a22–28.
2. Philippa Foot, "Virtues and Vices," in *Virtues and Vices* (Berkeley, 1978), 9.
3. This is why Aristotle says that justice is virtue considered "in relation to others" (*pros heteron*). See, e.g., *NE* 5.1.1130a12–13; 5.2.1130b1–2.
4. *Rhetoric* 1.10.1368b12–24.
5. I have discussed the interpretive issues at length in "The Aetiology of Justice," in *The Foundations of Aristotelian Political Science,* edited by Carnes Lord and Paul Vander Waerdt, (Berkeley, University of California Press, 1991), 136–166.
6. See, e.g., *NE* 1130b4.
7. I discuss the relation between particular justice and the virtues of liberality and magnanimity in "The Aetiology of Justice."
8. Bernard Williams, "Justice as a Virtue," in *Essays on Aristotle's Ethics,* edited by Amelie Rorty (Berkeley, 1980), 198.
9. Ibid., 192.
10. Aristotle uses the contrast between a man who commits adultery for sexual pleasure and a man who commits adultery for gain to show the distinctive character of particular justice at *NE* 5.2.1130a22–28.
11. Aristotle's view is reflected, I believe, by the different attitudes we have to judges corrupted by sexual favors and judges who accept monetary bribes. We are more likely to describe the first as morally weak than as unjust.
12. See *NE* 9.8.1169a20–22; *EE* 8.3.1248b27.
13. *Politics* 2.7.
14. I have in mind Alan Gewirth's approach, for example.
15. I am thinking of the John Rawls of the Dewey Lectures, for example.
16. Aristotle's accounts of both justice and friendship are much concerned with the different obligations of partners who are peers and partners who are unequal in some relevant respect. If the inequality is too great (as, e.g., between human and god), no partnership is possible, and hence there is neither justice nor friendship in such relationships either. See, e.g., *NE* 8.7.1159a4–5.
17. If the star athlete can bring a team more success as a selfish dominator than as a sensitive partner even at the *highest* level of competition, can we still say he or she

would attain greater basketball excellence by becoming less selfish? In this case, there seems to be no (actual, at least) level of competition to support a preference for unselfishness; yet many will still feel an "aesthetic" preference. The interminable debates about whether Wilt Chamberlain (the dominator) or Bill Russell (the team player) was the greater player seem to me to reflect this issue. Aristotle himself discusses a very similar issue when he explores the legitimacy of a man of outstanding virtue becoming a king rather than taking his turn in a system of rotating rule. See *Politics* 3.14–17.

18. I have defended this interpretation of Aristotle's treatment of friendship (*philia*), and explored the contrast between his approach focused on partnership and our usual conception focused on intimacy, in "Two Ideals of Friendship," a paper delivered in shortened form at the Eastern Division of the American Philosophical Association, December 1987.

19. To say that justice and friendship share *identical* corrective and expressive aspects is not quite true, since on Aristotle's view justice but not friendship has an intrinsic relation to lawabidingness. But this complication does not affect the point at issue here.

20. I would like to thank the University of Notre Dame's Institute for Scholarship in the Liberal Arts for a Junior Faculty Summer Research Grant in support of research on this paper. I would also like to thank Arnold Davidson and W. David Solomon for discussions of some of the main ideas of the paper.

## Questions

1. Choose any *two* of the following statements. Explain what the two statements mean. Why does Aristotle think that they are true? Do you agree with Aristotle? Why or why not?

   a. "We must take as a sign of states of character the pleasure or pain that supervenes upon acts; for the man who abstains from bodily pleasures and delights in this very fact is temperate, while the man who is annoyed at it is self-indulgent, and he who stands his ground against things that are terrible and delights in this or at least is not pained is brave, while the man who is pained is a coward. . . . Hence we ought to have been brought up in a particular way from our very youth, as Plato says, so as both to delight in and to be pained by the things that we ought" (31–32, 1104b).

   b. "Actions, then, are called just and temperate when they are such as the just or the temperate man would do; but it is not the man who does these that is just and temperate, but the man who also does them *as* just and temperate men do them" (35, 1105b).

   c. "Both fear and confidence and appetite and anger and pity and in general pleasure and pain may be felt both too much and too little, and in both cases not well; but to feel them at the right times, with reference to the right objects, towards the right people, with the right motive, and in the right way, is what is both intermediate and best, and this is characteristic of virtue. Similarly with regard to actions also there is excess, defect, and the intermediate. . . . Therefore virtue is a kind of mean, since, as we have seen, it aims at what is intermediate" (38, 1106b).

   d. "He who aims at the intermediate must first depart from what is most contrary to it. . . . For of the extremes one is more erroneous, one is less so. . . . But we must consider the things toward which we ourselves also are easily carried away; for some of us tend to one thing, some to another; and this will be recognizable from the pleasure and the pain we feel. We must drag ourselves away to the contrary extreme, for we shall get into the intermediate state by drawing well away from error, as people do in straightening sticks that are bent" (46, 1109a–1109b).

   e. "We deliberate not about ends but about means" (56, 1112b).

   f. "[C]hoice will be deliberate desire of things in our own power; for when we have reached a judgment as a result of deliberation, we desire in accordance with our deliberation" (58, 1113a).

   g. "[T]hat which is in truth an object of wish is an object of wish to the good man, while any chance thing may be so to the bad man . . . since the good man judges each class of things rightly" (58–59, 1113a).

h. "Therefore, virtue also is in our own power, and so too vice" (59, 1113a).

i. "Now someone may say that all men aim at the apparent good, but have no control over the appearance, but the end appears to each man in a form answering to his character. We reply that if each man is somehow responsible for his state of character, he will also be himself somehow responsible for the appearance. . . ." (62, 1114a).

j. "The friend is another self" (228, 1166a). "The good man should be a lover of self" (237, 1169a).

2. State the problem of incontinence Aristotle tries to solve in Book VII (163–167, 1146a–1147b). Does Aristotle give one solution or more than one? If you think he gives only one solution, defend the consistency of Book VII. If you think he gives more than one solution, explain why he does so.

3. Answer *two* of the following questions.

a. Some critics of Aristotle have accused him of being a Normative (ethical) Egoist. Exactly what is Normative Egoism? What does Aristotle say that might lead a reader to think that he *is* a Normative Egoist? What does Aristotle say that might lead a reader to think that he is *not* a Normative Egoist? Is Aristotle a Normative Egoist?

b. Some critics of Aristotle have accused him of being a Normative (ethical) Relativist. Exactly what is Normative Relativism? What does Aristotle say that might lead a reader to think that he *is* a Normative Relativist? What does Aristotle say that might lead a reader to think that he is *not* a Normative Relativist? Is Aristotle a Normative Relativist?

c. Let S stand for the sentence "Whatever is natural is good and whatever is unnatural is bad." I have argued that there is no way to define "natural" such that S is true. What does Aristotle say that might lead a

reader to think that he *does* believe S? What does Aristotle say that might lead a reader to think that he *does not* believe S? Does Aristotle believe S?

d. Instead of providing a universal moral principle, Aristotle merely presents the elitist prejudices of his age. He is an apologist for the status quo. He assumes that those character traits valued by his contemporaries are virtues. To what extent is this criticism justified? How would Aristotle defend himself?

e. Aristotle tries to derive an "ought" from an "is." He argues illegitimately from facts to values—from premises about the way the world is to conclusions about the way the world should be. To what extent is this criticism justified? How would Aristotle defend himself?

4. "Meno: Tell me, Socrates, can virtue (excellence) be taught? Or is it not teachable but the result of practice (habit), or is it neither of these, but men possess it by nature (innately) or in some other way (e.g. luck)?" (Plato, *Meno*, 70a) What is Aristotle's answer to this question? What is your answer? Do ethics classes really make people more moral?

5. Aristotle characterizes the lives he discusses in terms of their ultimate goal and in terms of the abilities that they appropriately exercise. Has Aristotle correctly matched the ultimate goals with the exercised abilities? In particular, is it true that the mixed life is the only life that appropriately exercises all essential human abilities? (For example, could a person exercise all of his or her essential, human abilities while ultimately aiming at money rather than contemplation?) Is it true that the type of life that ultimately aims at virtuous action appropriately exercises all essential human abilities except theoretical reason? (For example, might a person who ultimately aims at virtuous action also exercise his or her theoretical reason while pursuing a hobby of astronomy? Could a person who exercises his or her practical reason do so without seeking to be a virtuous person?)

Has Aristotle considered all of the plausible candidate lives or should he add other lives to his chart? In general, should Aristotle's chart of lives be modified somehow?

6. Aristotle says that "Justice is a kind of mean, but not in the same way as the other virtues, but because it relates to an intermediate amount, while injustice relates to the extremes" (121, 1133b). Compare and contrast justice with the other virtues. In what ways is justice a kind of mean? In what ways is justice not a kind of mean?

7. Now that we have completed our study of Aristotle, it is time for a final, critical assessment. Consider Aristotle's theory of the golden mean and the virtues that Aristotle lists.

    Do these virtues form a *consistent* moral system? That is, do any of them conflict with each other? If so, what mechanism might Aristotle use to resolve such conflicts? That is, explain how Aristotle could assign priorities to virtues.

    Do these virtues form a *complete* moral system? That is, are there any character traits that you believe to be moral virtues but that are not among the virtues Aristotle lists?

    Do these virtues form a *plausible* moral system? That is, does Aristotle's theory conflict in some way with common sense?

8. Aristotle makes the following claims:

    (A) There is one type of life that is best for each person. It is in the best interest of each person to lead this type of life. Let us call this the happy life.

    (B) The happy life is the life that appropriately exercises all essential aspects of a human being (all aspects of human nature).

    (C) The happy life turns out to be the life that aims at morally virtuous activity.

    Answer any *one* of the following questions.

    a. Hinduism seems to deny claim (A). It says that different lives are right for different people. Some people ought to live according to ethical principles, others ought to

live according to religious principles, still others ought to make the pursuit of truth their ultimate aim in life, and so on. Let us call this view *Life-choice Relativism*. What is the relationship between Normative Relativism and Life-choice Relativism? Are they compatible? If not, why not? If so, can one logically accept one doctrine without accepting the other? Do the arguments against Normative Relativism also refute Life-choice Relativism? Why or why not?

    b. Existentialism seems to deny claim (B). It says that there is no such thing as human nature or essential human abilities. What is essential to a person depends on the choices he or she has made and will make in life. Because my interpretations of my past and my projects for the future differ from yours, you and I have different essences. The life that appropriately exercises my essential abilities differs from life that appropriately exercises your essential abilities. If Aristotle accepted this Existentialist claim, in what ways would his moral theory change? What aspects of his moral theory would remain the same? Would these changes improve or worsen Aristotle's theory?

    c. One strand of common-sense thought seems to deny claim (C). Many people think that "nice guys finish last" and "virtue doesn't pay," etc. Even Aristotle seems to deny claim (C) when he maintains that the contemplative life, rather than the life that aims at morally virtuous activity, is the supremely happy life. Is the life that aims at morally virtuous activity a happy life? Is it the happiest life?

9. Aristotle's account of courage has been criticized in several ways. Select *two* of the following criticisms and explain how Aristotle might rebut them. (*Hint:* Aristotle would certainly not simply repeat what he has already said.)

    a. Aristotle seems to say that courage can be displayed only in life-threatening circumstances on the battlefield (64, 1115a). But surely people can display courage in other life-threatening circumstances and even in circumstances where their lives are not at risk.

b. Aristotle has been accused of conflating what should be separate virtues governing fear and confidence. Urmson says, "[Aristotle] has failed to distinguish the triad concerned with fear of the dangerous—cowardice, bravery and . . . foolhardiness—from another triad the members of which might be called overconfidence, caution, and overcautiousness."

c. The difference between the virtuous and the merely continent is that virtuous people perform virtuous acts without internal struggle, whereas continent people must overcome temptation. Now a person who must struggle against fear in order to perform a courageous act seems merely continent. Aristotle says that the courageous person feels fear. Is Aristotle conflating the courageous person and the person who is merely continent?

d. Aristotle says, "We must take as a sign of states of character the pleasure or pain that supervenes on acts; for . . . he who stands his ground against things that are terrible and delights in this or at least is not pained is brave, while the man who is pained is a coward" (31–32, 1104b). Here Aristotle seems to be saying that a courageous person performing a courageous act feels pleasure or at least feels no pain. Yet later Aristotle says, "Death and wounds will be painful to the brave man and against his will, but he will face them because it is noble to do so or because it is base not to do so. And the more he is possessed of virtue in its entirety and the happier he is, the more he will be pained at the thought of death. . . . It is not the case, then, with all the virtues that the exercise of them is pleasant, except in so far as it reaches its end" (71–72, 1117b). Here Aristotle seems to be saying that even though achieving the goal of a

courageous act is pleasant for the courageous person, the courageous act, itself, is typically painful to perform and even to contemplate. Is Aristotle contradicting himself on the question of whether courageous acts are pleasant for courageous people?

10. Aristotle says that practical wisdom "is not supreme over philosophic wisdom, i.e. over the superior part of us, any more than the art of medicine is over health; for it does not use it but provides for its coming into being; it issues orders, then, for its sake, but not to it" (158, 1145a). At first glance one might think that Aristotle is saying that we should use our practical wisdom in order to maximize the quantity and quality of contemplative interludes. But this cannot be right, for practical wisdom tells us to acquire and exercise moral virtues. And morally virtuous activity does not seem to be a reasonable means to contemplative interludes. What is the relationship between practical wisdom and philosophic wisdom?

11. Urmson says, "[T]he doctrine of the mean has been interpreted as being a doctrine of moderation—the thesis that extremes are to be avoided and that the middle way is the safest. Unless Aristotle is guilty of a very serious mistake, basic and not in detail, this interpretation must be totally wrong." Urmson also says, "We should note, to dispel the ghost of moderation, that excellence of character is explicitly said to be an intermediate disposition toward action (1106b31) and not a disposition to intermediate action." Explain Urmson's claim. Explain why he is mistaken.

12. Discuss the role played by the concept of nature in Aristotle's ethical theory. Relevant passages may include (a) the *ergon* argument (12–14, 1097b–1098a), (b) Aristotle's assertion that "neither by nature nor contrary to nature do the virtues arise in us; rather we are adapted by nature to receive them, and are made perfect by habit" (28, 1103a), and (c) Aristotle's remark that "we ourselves tend more naturally to pleasures and hence are

more easily carried away toward self-indulgence than toward propriety" (45, 1109a).

13. "Aristotle remarks [in VIII.2] that not every case of liking something occurs within the context of a friendship: one can like wine, for example, but this is not evidence of a friendship between oneself and wine, because (1) the wine does not like you back, and (2) you don't wish well to the wine. Thus, he goes on, a friendship exists only where you wish to the other party what is good for him, for his own sake, and this well-wishing is reciprocated. . . . On the other hand, Aristotle repeatedly contrasts the two derivative types of friendship with the basic type by emphasizing the self-centeredness of pleasure- and advantage-friends. This seems to suggest that in pleasure- and advantage-friendships each party is concerned *solely* with his own good, and this would mean that they could not have the sort of concern for one another that Aristotle seems in VIII.2 to attribute to friends. . . . Which is Aristotle's considered view? Or is he simply inconsistent on this point?" [J. Cooper, "Aristotle on Friendship," *Essays on Aristotle's Ethics*, ed. A. O. Rorty (Berkeley: University of California Press, 1980), pp. 304–305.]

14. In Book I and Book X Aristotle seems to argue for the following equations:

> Supremely happy life = natural life = contemplative life
> Secondarily happy life = natural life = political life

Explain Aristotle's arguments in excruciating detail. What are the three most troubling flaws in his argument? How might Aristotle fix these flaws? (*Hint:* He would not fix them by merely repeating what he has already said.)

15. Aristotle's advice about becoming virtuous might be criticized in several ways. Defend Aristotle from any *two* of the following criticisms.

   a. A virtuous person acts with knowledge and chooses virtuous acts for their own sakes. Aristotle says that we become virtuous by performing virtuous actions (34, 1105a). But performing virtuous actions does not seem to provide a person with knowledge, and it does not seem to induce people to choose virtuous acts for their own sakes.

   b. Aristotle says we acquire the habit of performing virtuous actions by performing vicious actions on the opposite extreme to those we are tempted to perform (46, 1109a–1109b). (For example, if we tend to be stingy, then we should perform prodigal actions.) But this contradicts the claim that we become virtuous by performing virtuous actions, and it will not work, anyhow.

   c. Aristotle says that we should avoid pleasure because pleasure leads us astray (46, 1109b). But his overall theory does not say that the virtuous person should avoid pleasure. Instead his theory rightly says that we should cultivate our desires so that we will desire (and, therefore, be pleased by) the right things and not desire (and, therefore, not be pleased by) the wrong things.

16. Early in Book V Aristotle seems to define injustice as an excessive desire for gain. Presumably, he thinks that justice is a medial desire for gain (109–110, 1130a). Later in Book V, however, Aristotle seems to define justice as a disposition to perform just acts. Presumably, he thinks that injustice is a disposition to perform unjust acts (121, 1133b–1134a). However, some just acts and some unjust acts do not seem to be motivated by a desire for gain. There seem to be both just and unjust acts that bring no profit to the agent. There seems to be a mismatch between his two accounts of justice. Aristotle tries to address this problem with his suggestion that a distributor who judges unjustly but seems to get nothing out of it is really "aiming at an excessive share either of gratitude or of revenge" (131, 1136b–1137a). Does this suggestion resolve the mismatch objection?

17. Magnificence is concerned with part of the same subject matter as liberality, the spending and giving of wealth, but it "surpasses liberality in scale" (85, 1122a) Exactly what is the relationship between liberality and magnificence? Define and discuss a virtue parallel to magnificence with respect to one of the following virtues: courage, temperance, justice, or good temper. (For example, define and discuss a virtue that is concerned with some aspect of fear and confidence and that surpasses courage in scale in the same way that magnificence surpasses liberality in scale.) Or explain why it is impossible to do so.

18. In *Pride and Prejudice* Jane Austin focuses her penetrating gaze on the character trait of pride, but she comes to some puzzling conclusions. For example,

> *Mr. Darcy:* As a child, I was given good principles, but left to follow them in pride and conceit. . . . [My parents allowed] me to be selfish and overbearing—to care for none beyond my own family circle, to think meanly of all the rest of the world . . . (ch. 58)
> *Elizabeth:* [Mr. Darcy] has no improper pride. (ch. 59)

Describe the Aristotelian virtue of pride. Does Mr. Darcy have this character trait? Is Aristotle right to call this character trait a virtue? (*Warning:* Do not attempt to answer this question unless you are familiar with *Pride and Prejudice*.)

19. Aristotle presents an argument for the unity of virtue that involves the relationships among cleverness, practical wisdom, natural virtue, and proper virtue (155–158, 1144a–1145a). State and explain this argument. Do you find Aristotle's argument convincing? If so, defend it from the best criticisms you can think of. If not, explain why not. Repair the argument if you can.

20. Aristotle seems to make the following claim. That which appears to be a pleasure to a good person really is a pleasure, whereas that which appears to be a pleasure to a bad person really is not a pleasure, except to the bad person (260, 1176a). In what sense is something that appears to be a pleasure to a bad person really not a pleasure? What is Aristotle trying to say here? Is this claim consistent with the other things he says about pleasure? Is this claim right?

21. Explain what Aristotle means by liberality. Aristotle considers liberality a virtue. Would Kant agree that liberality (as described by Aristotle) is a virtue? Would Mill agree that liberality (as described by Aristotle) is a virtue? Would Jesus agree that liberality (as described by Aristotle) is a virtue? Do you agree that liberality (as described by Aristotle) is a virtue?

22. Aristotle says some puzzling things about the virtue of temperance. Explain how Aristotle might rebut *two* of the following challenges.

   a. Aristotle says, "Temperance and self-indulgence are concerned with . . . touch and taste" (73, 1118a). Why does Aristotle restrict temperance to touch and taste? After all, people can be intemperate with respect to music, heroin, and gambling, can't they?

   b. Aristotle says, "In the natural appetites few go wrong and only in one direction, that of excess" (75, 1118b). What are the natural appetites? Is it true that only few go wrong with respect to the natural appetites? If people go wrong only in one direction, isn't temperance a counter-example to Aristotle's doctrine of the mean?

   c. Aristotle says, "While the people who are "fond of so-and-so" are so-called because they delight either in the wrong things, or more than most people do, or in the wrong way, the self-indulgent exceed in all three ways" (75, 1118b). Why isn't a person who goes wrong in just one or two ways called self-indulgent? After all, such a person is not temperate because he or she is going wrong. Indeed, a person who delights in the right things in the right way, but indulges in too much of it, seems to be a paradigm self-indulgent person.

d. According to the passage quoted above, a person who delights in the right things in the right way but "more than most people do" is not temperate. But Aristotle should use the virtuous person rather than the majority as his standard, shouldn't he? Moreover, this claim says that there is something wrong with you if you enjoy sensual pleasure too much. But if someone told you to try to get less pleasure out of your food or your sexual activity, wouldn't you find that quite odd?

e. Aristotle says, "the things that, being pleasant, make for health or for good condition [the temperate person] will desire moderately and as he should, and also other pleasant things if they are not hindrances to these ends or contrary to what is noble, or beyond his means" (76, 1119a). Thus Aristotle says that the temperate person desires not only healthful things but also other pleasant things. However, shouldn't Aristotle have said that the temperate person desires only healthful things?

# PART III

# CARE AND JUSTICE

# Ethics of Care: Gilligan and Noddings

*Happiness is having a large, loving, caring, close-knit family in another city.*

GEORGE BURNS

Psychologist Lawrence Kohlberg's research suggests that moral development proceeds in six stages. Boys and girls both move from the "good is doing what you are told" stage to the "good is what is good for me" stage. The third stage is the "good is what others consider good" stage. Here children are concerned about their character and reputation. They try to gain self-respect and the approval of others by trying to please others. They build personal relationships based on trust and helpfulness. They develop a true conscience consisting of the internalized values of others. Girls tend to become fixated at this third stage, according to Kohlberg, and they carry this orientation on into adulthood. However, boys tend to progress to the fourth stage. Here to be good is to be a good member of a social system, a good citizen, good church member, and the like. Different social groups impose different standards on their members, and there is no higher standard by which one might evaluate the standards of the groups. In the fifth stage, "good is following the social contract except when society would benefit from bending the rules." A few children go on to the "respect the rights of the individual" stage. In this final stage, self-chosen, abstract, universal, rational principles guide action.[1] Very roughly speaking, moral development looks like Figure 1.

Kohlberg's description of the stages of moral development is based on his studies of *boys'* moral development. Kohlberg assumes that girls develop along the same path. But boys travel further, so Kohlberg concludes that men are typically more morally sophisticated than women. Carol Gilligan, an apostate student of Kohlberg, maintains that boys and girls develop along different paths and end up with different ways of thinking about morality. Gilligan maintains that girls and boys part company after the second stage. Girls enter a self-sacrificing stage where "good is pleasing others at all costs to oneself." Many remain fixated here and become the self-sacrificers against whom Ayn Rand rails. [See the "Morality and Happiness" section.] But some go on to the fourth and final stage of the female developmental path, as shown in Figure 2. The fourth stage is a synthesis of the second and third stages. Gilligan calls it the *Ethics of Care*. Here to be good is to balance one's own needs and integrity with the responsibilities arising out of the relationships one has with others. In some ways Gilligan's third and fourth stages are similar to Kohlberg's third stage (remember that Kohlberg thinks girls remain fixated at his third stage). Gilligan maintains that the female moral development pathway and its endpoint are just as good as the male moral development pathway and endpoint. Moreover, boys and girls get equally close to their respective goals, so women and men are equally morally sophisticated.

From the moment it appeared, Gilligan's book, *In a Different Voice*, resonated with the experience of many women. It was soon followed by *Caring: A Feminine Approach to Moral Education* by philosopher Nel Noddings, a book that works out the Ethics of Care somewhat more philosophically. Of course, the Ethics of Care is just one of several feminist approaches, and not all feminists endorse the Ethics of Care.

## Utilitarianism, Deontology, and the Ethics of Care

Like many movements in the history of ideas, the Ethics of Care begins by defining itself as the negation of the preceding, prevailing views. Gilligan, Noddings, and their followers rebel against twentieth-century Utilitarians and Deon-

278

**Figure 1**

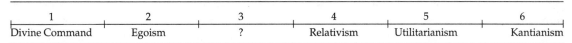

| 1 | 2 | 3 | 4 | 5 | 6 |
|---|---|---|---|---|---|
| Divine Command | Egoism | ? | Relativism | Utilitarianism | Kantianism |

**Figure 2**

| 1 | 2 | 3 | 4 |
|---|---|---|---|
| Divine Command | Egoism | Altruism | Ethics of Care |

tologists (though not exactly against Mill or Kant), especially insofar as these twentieth-century ethicists concern themselves with rules, rights, and rationality. The Ethics of Care distinguishes itself from Utilitarianism and Deontology in three major ways. It is particularist, partialist, and passionate. Proponents of the Ethics of Care characterize the mainstream ethical tradition against which they are rebelling as *Rule Ethics, Justice Ethics,* or *Rationalistic Ethics,* depending on which contrast they wish to emphasize. Rather than singling out one of these contrasts, I shall employ the term *Mainstream Ethics* for now.

Mainstream Ethics is primarily concerned with general moral rules. Both Utilitarians and Deontologists devote nearly all their energy to the tasks of formulating, interrelating, and fine-tuning these rules. Mainstream Ethics works with abstract, hypothetical situations, abstractly formulated problems, and even abstract, interchangeable individuals. Of course, Mainstream Ethics acknowledges that people in different situations have different duties. Thus correctly applying moral rules requires detailed knowledge of the situation. But the Ethics of Care observes that this is merely a perfunctory proviso. The overwhelming emphasis on general rules leaves the twin impressions that (a) getting the general rules right is the central task of ethics, and (b) applying the general rules to particular situations is usually a trivial matter, which can safely be left as an exercise for the reader.

According to the Ethics of Care, each person and each situation is so different from others that general rules provide little or no guidance. The Ethics of Care begins with and focuses on particular people in the midst of life with particular moral problems arising out of particular relationships. Indeed, for the Ethics of Care an individual is a nexus of relationships. The relationships are essential to the person. Mainstream Ethics assumes that individuals are primordially independent, forming relationships by voluntarily relinquishing their autonomy. They are able to make and break relationships at will without being affected in any essential way. But for the Ethics of Care, individuals are primordially related. They are always already in the midst of relationships. Each addition, subtraction, or transformation of a relationship is an essential change for the individual. Who you are is at least partially a function of those to whom you are related and of how you are related to them.

Mainstream Ethics is suspicious of relationships because they threaten objectivity and impartiality. Relationships bias our perceptions, our judgments, our desires, and ultimately our decisions. This is a serious problem, according to Mainstream Ethics, because the most common and paradigmatic moral task is to adjudicate conflicts among the rights of independent strangers justly rather than to fulfill special obligations to friends and relatives. Of course, Mainstream Ethics may be extrapolated to the domain of relationships between non-strangers. It allows us to favor some people if we have already made some sort of commitment to these people. For example, I have a duty to feed my child before feeding yours because she is my child. And what makes her my child is that I have assumed responsibility for her. Thus Mainstream Ethics ends up analyzing relationships in terms of implicit promises.

But the Ethics of Care says that this is backwards. Our relationships to our relatives and friends are not constituted by promises we made to them or by responsibilities we have assumed. Instead, our different responsibilities grow out of our different relationships to other people. Our duties to people are a function of our relationship to them, not the other way around. The Ethics of Care takes morality primarily to be about people already in relationships with each other, with commitments already in place. Morality is not primordially about strangers, but rather it is about parents and children, married couples, groups of friends, and so on. The moral questions concerning the special obligations that arise out of our different relationships are the most commonly asked and the most important moral questions. In general, one should strive to fulfill the responsibilities one has toward particular people within one's relationship network. One should strive to preserve these relationships, as well as one's own integrity, without exploiting or harming others. Thus the Ethics of Care tells us to treat others differently according to how we are related to them, rather than being impartial toward others and treating everyone the same.

Mainstream Ethics is suspicious of emotional attachments to others and to ourselves. Of course, Mainstream Ethics says that we should not be indifferent to the fate of others. We should not violate their autonomy. Moreover, we should aid people and not merely refrain from exploiting them. However, Mainstream Ethics does not require us to be emotionally attached to others. Dispassionate benevolence is perfectly possible. We need not make any emotional commitment to people as individuals. We must merely respect them as persons, and we must respect all persons equally. Indeed, we should try to bracket our emotional attachments lest they prevent us from acting justly, either by distorting our perceptions and judgments or by tempting us to favoritism. Emotions undermine objectivity.

They tend to block us from gaining knowledge of ourselves and others. Love is blind. Moreover, Mainstream Ethics expects us to be motivated by duty rather than by emotion. Because our emotional attachments are likely to bias us toward those we care about, and especially toward ourselves, we should act from duty or at least use duty to trump any wayward emotions. In general, Mainstream Ethics tends to divide people into a mental, rational component and a bodily component that is the seat of the passions. Reason is the better, more valuable component and should control the corrupt, bodily, passionate urges. Society mirrors the individual in this respect. Rational people should rule emotional ones. When this claim is combined with the widespread belief that men are more rational and women are more emotional, Mainstream Ethics draws the conclusion that the family should be run by the husband. Thus Mainstream Ethics understands individual, social, and familial relationships in terms of domination and subordination.

One strand of Christianity accepts (and may be partially responsible for) this bifurcation into the good, rational, objective mental and the bad, passionate, biasing bodily, which the former should control. Nevertheless, there is another strand of Christianity that demands emotional attachment to others. At the other end of the spectrum from dispassionate Mainstream Ethics is the Christian doctrine that we should love all people equally and very much. We should love everyone just as we love our family and ourselves. [See the "Morality and Religion" section.]

Gilligan and Noddings take an intermediate position on emotional attachment to others. They maintain that morality begins with caring for different people to different degrees. We should not strive for dispassionate objectivity. On the other hand, the Ethics of Care denies that we have a duty to love all people. A person who loves only some people is not morally deficient. Love is reserved for a small group of intimate friends and family members. We may have lesser degrees of attachment to other people. We may be devoted to our friends, fond of our acquaintances, and merely neutral toward strangers. Moreover, we should care for people not impersonally, not because of their humanity, but rather because of the individual facts about them—facts about their history, character, situation, and relationships, who they are, and what they have done. We should love people as individuals. Thus, the Ethics of Care positions itself between the unemotional, uncaring Mainstream Ethics view and the extremely caring Christian view.

Care leads us to recognize and respond to the needs of others and our own needs. Understanding people is necessary for ethics and is best done when one cares for the people. In fact, care is a practical prerequisite for adequate knowledge of other people. Perhaps in theory one could dispassionately come to understand someone, but typically, we do not make the effort unless we care about that person. Similarly, care motivates people to help others more effectively than duty. Moreover, sometimes people wish to be helped out of care rather than duty. Other things being equal, would you rather be visited in the hospital by someone motivated by duty or by someone who cares about you as an individual? In general, the Ethics of Care does not divide individuals, families, or communities into a better, controlling part and a worse, controlled part. Instead, the Ethics of Care takes a more holistic, cooperative, and egalitarian stance.

Generality, impartiality, and reason are linked to each other and to the public realm in Mainstream Ethics just as their opposites, particularism, partialism, and passion, are linked to each other and to the private realm in the Ethics of Care. Mainstream Ethics considers morality to be paradigmatically concerned with policy decisions in a public realm among autonomous strangers of roughly equal power. The primary moral problem within this realm is injustice caused by bias, particularly bias in favor of oneself. Morality consists primarily of acting justly by being impartial. Everyone, including oneself, should be treated equally. When one thinks or acts impartially, one applies general principles to interchangeable people in equivalent situations. Each individual has the same rights, duties, and

moral value. Now acting impartially is acting as though one is not emotionally involved; it is being objective, dispassionate, detached. Detachment is not a necessary condition of impartiality. It is possible, though difficult, to be fair even when you care for one of the interested parties in a dispute.[2] Of course, acting as though one is detached is easiest when one really is detached. In general, according to Mainstream Ethics one should act impartially in accordance with general rules by avoiding or ignoring emotional attachments and aversions.

The Ethics of Care, on the other hand, considers morality to be paradigmatically concerned with decisions in the private realm among people of unequal power within ongoing relationships. The primary moral problem within this realm is unkind action caused by insufficient compassion. Morality consists primarily of kindness motivated by caring. Everyone within one's relationship network, including oneself, should be treated in the caring manner appropriate to his or her place in that network. One's responsibilities to other people differ because people differ and because one's relationships to different people differ. The particular facts about people and situations are crucial. Attachment is not a necessary condition of caring action. It is possible, though difficult, to be kind even when you do not care for someone. Of course, acting as though one cares is easiest when one really does care. In general, according to the Ethics of Care, one should act partially (rather than impartially) according to one's passion (rather than just one's reason) for particular people (rather than for people in general).

## Gender and the Ethics of Care

Aristotle notoriously maintains that men and women develop toward somewhat different sets of virtues, or at least toward somewhat different versions of certain virtues. He says, "A man would be held a coward if he were as courageous as a courageous woman, and a woman talkative if she were as modest as the good man."[3] This follows from his claim that women have different natures from men.

Gilligan and Noddings also maintain that men and women develop along different paths toward somewhat different modes of morality, though not for Aristotle's reasons. (This claim is parallel to a number of other recent claims about male/female differences. For example, it has recently been argued that women use language differently, do science differently, and so on.) Gilligan suggests a neo-Freudian explanation for the male/female differences in moral development. Women are overwhelmingly the primary caregivers of young children. Girls do not have to separate emotionally from their primary caregivers, but boys do. Thus girls come to view separation and impartiality as problematic, and they consider relationships, attachment, and cooperation as good. Conversely, boys view entanglements and attachments as problematic and consider independence, objectivity, and competitiveness as good. Thus, boys develop toward Mainstream Ethics and girls toward the Ethics of Care because of their different early-childhood experiences.

Other feminists offer a different explanation for the differences between male and female approaches toward morality. Men have traditionally been at home in the workplace, whereas women have been at home at home. Men have tended to focus on moral issues in the public realm, whereas women have focused on moral issues in the private realm. Not surprisingly, men and women have developed different moral approaches based on their different experiences and needs. These are transmitted to the next generation through socialization, so that even though women are now moving into the public realm, they retain the Ethics of Care.

A Nietzschian might offer an explanation based on differences in power rather than differences in nature, nurture, or culture. Presently, society channels girls into positions of dependence, so women need to build relationships with powerful people and with each other to accomplish their goals. Boys, on the other hand,

are channeled into positions of relative independence, so relationships are less crucial (and may even be hindrances) to men. Emotional attachment fosters and bolsters relationships. Thus emotional attachment is a boon to women but a threat to men. Small wonder that women value care, cooperation, and relationships, whereas men view these with suspicion. Similarly, women emphasize meeting needs, sympathy for others, and fulfilling responsibilities because, being relatively powerless and needy, they reap a net benefit when people (especially the relatively powerful men) act in these ways. On the other hand, men emphasize respecting rights and justice for all (understood as everyone keeping what they already have) because, being in a relatively powerful position already, men reap a net benefit when people preserve the status quo. If this Nietzschian suggestion is right, then an ethic grounded in relationships is a perversion resulting from the subordination of women. Women adopt the Ethics of Care because they are oppressed. The Ethics of Care is a coping mechanism, a slave morality. [See the "Morality and Happiness" section.] Rather than taking pride in the Ethics of Care, women should eliminate the need for it. Women should refrain from endorsing the twisted values and perspectives that have been forced on them by oppression.

There is a political danger lurking in the Ethics of Care. Given our society's tendency to take advantage of women, it seems politically unwise to say that women are specialists in caring, for that promotes the view that women *should* be the caregivers. To accept the claim that the Ethics of Care is women's moral theory risks perpetuating the existing division of labor. Women are dealt the nurturing roles in the private sphere because they are good at nurturing, whereas men go out into the public world and make policy. Philosophers, like scientists, cannot bury themselves in the pursuit of truth while remaining oblivious to the social consequences of their research. We need to be mindful of the ways in which philosophical theories are likely to be used. On the other hand, we cannot bury the truth, either. A delicate balance is necessary.

Do boys and girls really develop along different paths toward different ends? The research by Kohlberg, Gilligan, and others indicating that there is a difference between the moral development of boys and that of girls is somewhat controversial. Perhaps women are not more cooperative than men but instead compete about different things in different ways than men. Perhaps women are not more concerned about relationships than are men, but rather men and women are equally concerned about different sorts of relationships. Perhaps women seem to use general rules less than men because women are more sensitive to exceptions and to qualifications of general rules. Perhaps women are not more emotional about ethics, but rather women are more aware of and willing to express the emotional considerations in their moral thinking. Does the fact that the Ethics of Care strikes a chord among many women support the claim that it models women's moral thinking better than Mainstream Ethics? Perhaps. But sometimes theories appeal to people for the wrong reasons. Perhaps the Ethics of Care seems true to many women because it tells women what they want to hear.

## Using the Ethics of Care

You are the supervisor of a group of children rehearsing a skit. You come upon your ten-year-old daughter engaged in a shoving match with another child. You separate the children. For Mainstream Ethics the crucial question is "Who started it?" because Mainstream Ethics seeks to apply the general rule "Punish unjustified aggression." Facts about relationships are irrelevant at best. Indeed, the fact that one of the children is your daughter is an obstacle, because Mainstream Ethics directs you to be impartial.

For the Ethics of Care, on the other hand, the situation is much more complex. Many more facts about the case are relevant. One of the children is *your daughter*, after all. You love her dearly. Moreover, she is passing through a stressful time right now. She is unusually fragile these days, and she needs to have your support for her affirmed. She needs to know that you are on her side. You scolded her for something else a little while ago, and she is still resentful. Perhaps quasi-consciously she even pushed the other child in order to test you. On the other hand, she has a manipulative streak, and you have been working hard lately to discourage manipulative behavior. The other child is the child of acquaintances you would like to turn into friends. They have trusted you with their child. And their child trusts you to be impartial. Here she is telling you her side and expecting you to be fair. But actually you don't like her at all. She is an obnoxious bully. Of course, you understand why. She feels embarrassed by the fact that she is older than the others in her class. Her resentment manifests itself as bullying behavior. Several other children have clustered around, waiting to see what you will do, watching to determine what sort of a person you are, and wondering what they can get away with. All are on edge because the skit's performance date is coming up. Perhaps a good scolding would set an example and quell the bothersome bickering for a while so that the kids could make some progress on learning their lines. This skit means a lot to them and their parents. You, too, are tense. Moreover, the Tylenol you took earlier is wearing off, and you could use a break from the bickering. And so on. The Ethics of Care asks you to choose an action that takes into account the various relationships and balances the various needs in this situation. From the Care perspective these nuances and feelings are central to this moral issue. But the Ethics of Care provides no rule or formula for determining what to do. Each situation is too different.

Some people might maintain that the "relationship facts" are morally irrelevant. Others might agree that these facts are relevant but might subsume them under general rules. As Lawrence Blum says, these positions effectively dismiss the Ethics of Care. Other people might consider the relationship facts to be morally relevant but still to be less significant considerations than the facts required by Mainstream Ethics.

These positions assign inferior status to the Ethics of Care. Gilligan, Noddings, and their followers claim that the Ethics of Care is an equally viable alternative to Mainstream Ethics. That is, the Ethics of Care is a new, equally good approach to ethics—a whole different way of doing ethics or of being ethical, a "different voice." Care Ethics and Mainstream Ethics include different ways of perceiving situations. They pick out different features as salient. Whereas Mainstream Ethics focuses on people's rights and duties, the Ethics of Care focuses on people's needs and feelings. Mainstream Ethics and the Ethics of Care have different values and different priorities. Whereas Mainstream Ethics values the person, independence, and desert, the Ethics of Care values the relationship, inter-dependence, and nurturing. Gilligan suggests that every situation can be looked at from either perspective. She uses the metaphor of a duck-rabbit to describe the fact that most people use both the Ethics of Care and Mainstream Ethics, although only one perspective may be used at a time. Men tend to use Mainstream Ethics more, whereas women tend to favor the Ethics of Care. Some unfortunate people can use only one of these orientations. However, several serious objections arise from taking Mainstream Ethics and the Ethics of Care to be full-blown, alternative moral theories.

## Objections

Although it is impossible to see both duck and rabbit simultaneously, it seems possible (and perhaps necessary) to integrate both the perspectives of Mainstream Ethics and the Ethics of Care into a single analysis of certain situations. Surely making the right choice in the example sketched above requires knowing *both* who began the shoving match *and* the relationship facts. This suggests that Mainstream Ethics and the Ethics of Care are aspects of a single, unified approach to moral problems rather than alternative moral theories.

How should Mainstream Ethics and the Ethics of Care be unified? George Sher objects that Gilligan and Noddings are attacking a straw man. Mainstream Ethics incorporates, or at least does not exclude, the points made by the Ethics of Care. The Ethics of Care is simply part of an appropriately fleshed-out Mainstream Ethics.[4] Cheshire Calhoun replies that even if Mainstream Ethics could accommodate the insights of the Ethics of Care, it has not yet done so. At least it has not allocated sufficient resources to working out these insights. By underemphasizing these insights, Mainstream Ethics creates the impression that they are not important. Thus Mainstream Ethics undervalues women's moral theory and is gender-biased.[5] Yet even if the negligence of Mainstream Ethics has allowed misconceptions to flourish, perhaps Mainstream Ethics could subsume the Ethics of Care. And even if that is impossible, the perspectives of Mainstream Ethics and the Ethics of Care might still be compatible. They may reflect merely a (dramatic) difference of emphasis. Mainstream Ethics and the Ethics of Care may each be insufficient on its own, yet each may offer some aspects of an adequate evaluation of some situations.

Moreover, adequate moral assessment of many situations seems to require us to go beyond both perspectives. Some situations may demand yet other approaches in addition to or instead of Mainstream Ethics and the Ethics of Care. If so, Mainstream Ethics and the Ethics of Care are neither mutually exclusive nor jointly inclusive moral theories.

\*

Noddings breaks care down into three components: motivational engrossment and displacement in another person, feeling with the other person, and actual caretaking. *Motivational engrossment* is suspending evaluation of the other person, avoiding "being judgmental." *Motivational displacement* is taking the other person's goals as one's own, helping the other person achieve his or her goals. Both are risky if the other person is evil or has evil goals, cautions Victoria Davion. It is one thing to suspend disbelief while reading a novel, quite another to suspend moral judgment. You should not commit yourself to participating in a project until you have cleared it with your conscience. Thus motivational engrossment should be avoided or at least narrowly circumscribed.

Motivational displacement should also be limited. If you see that the other person is aiming at evil, and you cannot persuade the other person to change his or her goals, then surely you should quit the relationship rather than become an accomplice to evil. For example, if a woman enables her husband to exploit others (perhaps even herself) by regularly cooking his dinner and stroking his ego, then she is partially responsible for that exploitation. She has a *prima facie* duty to end either the exploitation or the relationship. Of course, this may be overwhelmingly difficult, or other considerations may override this duty. Noddings says that ending the relationship is justified only if the relationship impairs one's ability to care, but surely there are other legitimate justifications for severing relationships. Otherwise we would exist only to relate. This would reduce people to mere servants of relationships. Davion says that by taking people to be mere relationship nodes, the Ethics of Care devalues people and overvalues relationships so that people can be sacrificed to relationships.

To avoid such problems, Davion recommends supplementing care with integrity, the virtue of being true to oneself. This would justify the refusal to turn a blind eye and lend a helping hand to projects incompatible with one's own values. However, integrity can be just as dangerous as care. If you are basically good, integrity will prevent you from ignoring or assisting evil, but if you are basically bad, integrity will make you worse. You will discard the discordant good qualities in your attempt to be true to yourself— in your quest for consistency. I recommend that care be supplemented not with integrity but with justice, especially justice to oneself.

*

The minimal criteria for an adequate ethical theory include completeness and (arguably) some degree of conformity to common sense

(being careful not to restrict common sense to male common sense). The Ethics of Care seems either incomplete or counter-intuitive. At first glance, the Ethics of Care seems to have nothing much to say about dealing with people to whom we are not emotionally attached: strangers and perhaps unsavory acquaintances. Noddings uses the metaphor of chains to extend the Ethics of Care into the public domain. I care about some strangers because they are my friend's friends. Thus I am linked to people beyond my own circle of friends. Moreover, although I cannot care for unlinked strangers, I must stand ready to care for them because I might become related to them.

But Noddings' attempt to extend the Ethics of Care conflicts seriously with common sense. As Claudia Card reminds us, strangers deserve more from us than mere readiness to care. They deserve justice. Teachers must develop and implement grading policies that are fair; lawmakers must pass and police enforce fair laws; and so on.[6]

Not only does the Ethics of Care omit our duties to strangers, it even sometimes conflicts with those duties. Noddings, for example, says that when push came to shove, she would stand behind the barricades along with the racist relative she cares for rather than storming the barricades along with the blacks who are right. This is indeed what the Ethics of Care would say if it were forced to say something about this ethical problem, but it is a *reductio ad absurdum* of the claim that the Ethics of Care has something to say about this problem. Ironically, whereas Mainstream Ethics overemphasizes justice and devalues care, Noddings reduces morality to care and ignores justice.

Just as Mainstream Ethics seems better suited to the public realm than to family and friends, so the Ethics of Care seems promising (though not problem-free) with respect to the private realm but problematic when applied to strangers. Should we say that Mainstream Ethics governs the public realm, where we deal with strangers, and the Ethics of Care governs the private realm, where we deal with relationships? No. Private actions and relationships can be just or unjust. Public practices and institutions can be caring or uncaring. Historically, the distinction between public and private has been used to shield the family from the demands of justice. Husbands have exploited their wives and defended their unjust actions by claiming that justice does not apply within the family. "A man's home is his castle." Similarly, the public/private distinction has been used to shield governments and corporations from the demands of care. These institutions have acted ruthlessly and defended their callous policies by claiming that care is inappropriate in public contexts.

*

Is care always appropriate in public contexts? Sher argues for the compatibility of Mainstream Ethics and the Ethics of Care. Davion points out the perils of caring in personal relationships. Card describes the inadequacy of the Ethics of Care with respect to strangers. Howard Curzer (that's me!) lists several drawbacks of caring in professional relationships such as the physician/patient relationship. For various reasons being the object of care is not always desirable. For example, being cared for imposes burdens one may not wish to assume and may hinder others from saying or doing what the person cared for would like. Moreover, in professional relationships, emotional attachment tends to produce burnout in the caregiver, undermine professional distance, generate injustice, and lower efficiency.

## Virtue Ethics and the Ethics of Care

Virtues are associated with spheres of human life. Courage, for example, is a disposition to act and feel correctly with respect to danger. A person who tried to elevate courage into an ethical theory—to use nothing but courage as a guide to action and passion—would have a radically incomplete ethical theory. Such a theory would get some things right but would have nothing to say (or worse, silly things to say) about the many ethical issues that are not matters of courage. No

virtue, by itself, covers all of the moral territory. Aristotle might say that Utilitarians, Kantians, and various political philosophers have mistakenly elevated the virtues of benevolence, conscientiousness, and justice, respectively, into ethical theories. I suggest that the Ethics of Care makes a similar error. It elevates the virtue of care into an ethical theory. Conceiving of justice and care as virtues rather than as full-blown, incompatible moral theories may solve all of the problems noted here. If care and justice are virtues, then each alone is insufficient. Each alone says nothing or silly things about many situations. Like unconstrained justice, unconstrained care will lead a person to tolerate or even perform vicious acts, as Davion, Card, and Curzer contend. Justice and care must be combined with and limited by each other (together with all the rest of the virtues) in order to help us arrive at appropriate decisions about how to act and feel.

Noddings objects that the Ethics of Care not only involves a statement of which actions and passions are right in certain situations but also includes a description of whole sets of attitudes, whole modes of perception, and whole ways of relating to people. Thus care is more than a virtue.

This objection fails because it presupposes an impoverished conception of virtue. Virtues involve not just actions and passions but also attitudes and values, perceptual modes and strategies, relationships and interactions. It is part of the virtue of courage, for example, to value goods correctly (to know which goods are worth which risks), to perceive correctly any danger within a situation, to balance the likelihood of avoiding the danger with the likelihood of achieving a worthwhile goal, and so on. Similarly, it is part of the virtue of care to form and maintain the right caring relationships with the right people at the right times for the right reasons. Thus the fact that the Ethics of Care has more to say than merely "These are the right actions and passions for those situations" does not imply that the Ethics of Care is more than merely an account of the virtue of care.

Gilligan and Noddings do not spell out answers to several questions: "Who are the right people?" "What are the right relationships?" and so on. Presumably, Gilligan and Noddings believe that the answers cannot be expressed in general terms but must be context-specific. Aristotle says something like this, too (47, 1109b). But Aristotle also spends one-fifth of the *Nicomachean Ethics* describing the quasi-virtue of friendship, which shares many features with care. Here Aristotle does give rough answers to these questions.

\*

Sher's suggestion that Mainstream Ethics could subsume the Ethics of Care can be understood as the claim that Rule Ethics could subsume the Ethics of Care. If we reject the grandiose claim that the Ethics of Care is an ethical theory in favor of the claim that care is a virtue, then the question of how the Ethics of Care is related to Rule Ethics becomes a small part of the large question of how Virtue Ethics is related to Rule Ethics. Could the relationship be simply "Each virtue is a disposition to follow a moral rule"? Unlikely. Virtue Ethics has a broader view of the moral sphere than Rule Ethics. Some virtues (for example, wittiness) are not morally relevant for Rule Ethics. Moreover, within the sphere of each virtue, some matters cannot be subsumed under rules because they are too contextual, too situation-specific.

If the Ethics of Care and the Ethics of Justice are both simply accounts of virtues, then the relationship between them is a small part of the large question of how different virtues are related to each other. In particular, do the virtues conflict? We need to draw a few distinctions to answer this question. Aristotle distinguishes between *natural virtue*, the proto-virtue of acting and feeling more or less right without knowing why, and *proper virtue*, the fully developed virtue consisting of natural virtue plus practical wisdom (156–157, 1144b). For example, *natural justice* is being a fair-minded person who has just instincts and a passion for justice, but *proper justice* is reliably being pleased by justice and pained by injustice and acting justly through an understanding of justice. Noddings makes a similar distinction between *natural care*, being a caring person, habitually acting and feeling in

caring ways, and *proper care* (Noddings calls this "ethical care"), feeling and expressing care for the right people, at the right times, in the right ways, for the right reasons. I suggest that natural justice and natural care conflict, but proper justice is compatible with proper care. Natural justice tells us that we have an equal duty to help friends and strangers. It tells us to support the right cause no matter what. Natural care tells us to favor our loved ones. It tells us to not hurt our racist aunt. Practical wisdom tells us to adjust the way we act and feel toward people for whom we care so that we remain in conformity with justice and to recognize that we have special duties toward those for whom we care. Thus proper justice and proper care tell us to express our opposition to racial discrimination forcefully in ways that will be minimally offensive to our racist aunt, or convert her to a just point of view, and so on. Now the Ethics of Care and the Ethics of Justice seem jointly incompatible and individually inadequate because they respectively represent natural care and natural justice—that is, care and justice unmodified by the acknowledgement of other virtues with other spheres, perspectives, and values. However, if these two Ethics are brought into dialogue with each other through the mediation of practical wisdom, then a harmonious combined theory will emerge.

Aristotle's theory also suggests an account of the relationship between the Ethics of Care and Rationalistic Ethics. For Aristotle, reason shapes the passions, but it is itself shaped *by* the passions. The influence is reciprocal. Reason has the authority to overrule the passions in the heat of the moment, and reason also tells us which passions to acquire and details the shape of these passions. However, passion influences the principles we choose. Like other virtues, the virtue governing the application of reason to action has two forms: *natural practical wisdom* (Aristotle calls this "cleverness"), which is a proto-virtue, and *proper practical wisdom*, which is the fully developed virtue consisting of natural practical wisdom plus all of the natural virtues (156–157, 1144b). Natural care clashes with natural practical wisdom, but proper care and proper practical wisdom are compatible. Now the Ethics of Care and Rationalistic Ethics seem jointly incompatible and individually inadequate because they respectively represent natural care and natural practical wisdom. But if natural practical wisdom and natural care (and all of the other natural virtues) temper each other, then again a harmonious combined theory will emerge.

To summarize, the objections to the Ethics of Care vanish when the Ethics of Care renounces its pretensions to being a complete moral theory. I have suggested that Care is simply one of many virtues. This proposal has the additional advantage of clarifying the relationship between the Ethics of Care on the one hand and Virtue Ethics, Rule Ethics, the Ethics of Justice, and Rationalistic Ethics on the other hand.

## Notes

1. L. Kohlberg, "Indoctrination v. Relativity in Value Education," in *The Philosophy of Moral Development*, vol. 1 (New York: Harper & Row / Chicago: University of Chicago Press, joint publication, 1971).

2. R. Kyte, "Moral Reasoning as Perception: A Reading of Carol Gilligan," *Hypatia* 11 (1996), 106–110.

3. Aristotle, *Politics*, trans. C. Lord (Chicago: University of Chicago Press, 1984), p. 92.

4. G. Sher, "Other Voices, Other Rooms?: Women's Psychology and Moral Theory," in *Women and Moral Theory*, ed. E. Kittay and D. Meyers (Totowa, NJ: Rowman and Littlefield, 1987), pp. 178–189.

5. C. Calhoun, "Justice, Care, Gender Bias," *Journal of Philosophy* 85 (1988), 451–463.

6. C. Card, "Caring and Evil," *Hypatia* 5 (1990), 101–108.

# 24   Women, Relationships, and Caring

## CAROL GILLIGAN

## Woman's Place in Man's Life Cycle

"It is obvious," Virginia Woolf says, "that the values of women differ very often from the values which have been made by the other sex" (1929, p. 76). Yet, she adds, "it is the masculine values that prevail." As a result, women come to question the normality of their feelings and to alter their judgments in deference to the opinion of others. In the nineteenth century novels written by women, Woolf sees at work "a mind which was slightly pulled from the straight and made to alter its clear vision in deference to external authority." The same deference to the values and opinions of others can be seen in the judgments of twentieth century women. The difficulty women experience in finding or speaking publicly in their own voices emerges repeatedly in the form of qualification

and self-doubt, but also in intimations of a divided judgment, a public assessment and private assessment which are fundamentally at odds.

Yet the deference and confusion that Woolf criticizes in women derive from the values she sees as their strength. Women's deference is rooted not only in their social subordination but also in the substance of their moral concern. Sensitivity to the needs of others and the assumption of responsibility for taking care lead women to attend to voices other than their own and to include in their judgment other points of view. Women's moral weakness, manifest in an apparent diffusion and confusion of judgment, is thus inseparable from women's moral strength, an overriding concern with relationships and responsibilities. The reluctance to judge may itself be indicative of the care and concern for others that infuse the psychology of women's development and are responsible for what is generally seen as problematic in its nature.

Thus women not only define themselves in a context of human relationship but also judge

Reprinted by permission of the publisher from *In a Different Voice* by Carol Gilligan, Cambridge, MA: Harvard University Press. Copyright © 1982 by Carol Gilligan.

themselves in terms of their ability to care. Women's place in man's life cycle has been that of nurturer, caretaker, and helpmate, the weaver of those networks of relationships on which she in turn relies. But while women have thus taken care of men, men have, in their theories of psychological development, as in their economic arrangements, tended to assume or devalue that care. When the focus on individuation and individual achievement extends into adulthood and maturity is equated with personal autonomy, concern with relationships appears as a weakness of women rather than as a human strength (Miller, 1976).

The discrepancy between womanhood and adulthood is nowhere more evident than in the studies on sex-role stereotypes reported by Broverman, Vogel, Broverman, Clarkson, and Rosenkrantz (1972). The repeated finding of these studies is that the qualities deemed necessary for adulthood—the capacity for autonomous thinking, clear decision-making, and responsible action—are those associated with masculinity and considered undesirable as attributes of the feminine self. The stereotypes suggest a splitting of love and work that relegates expressive capacities to women while placing instrumental abilities in the masculine domain. Yet looked at from a different perspective, these stereotypes reflect a conception of adulthood that is itself out of balance, favoring the separateness of the individual self over connection to others, and leaning more toward an autonomous life of work than toward the interdependence of love and care.

The discovery now being celebrated by men in mid-life of the importance of intimacy, relationships, and care is something that women have known from the beginning. However, because that knowledge in women has been considered "intuitive" or "instinctive," a function of anatomy coupled with destiny, psychologists have neglected to describe its development. In my research, I have found that women's moral development centers on the elaboration of that knowledge and thus delineates a critical line of psychological development in the lives of both of the sexes. The subject of moral development not only provides the final illustration of the reiterative

pattern in the observation and assessment of sex differences in the literature on human development, but also indicates particularly why the nature and significance of women's development has been for so long obscured and shrouded in mystery.

The criticism that Freud makes of women's sense of justice, seeing it as compromised in its refusal of blind impartiality, reappears not only in the work of Piaget but also in that of Kohlberg. While in Piaget's account (1932) of the moral judgment of the child, girls are an aside, a curiosity to whom he devotes four brief entries in an index that omits "boys" altogether because "the child" is assumed to be male, in the research from which Kohlberg derives his theory, females simply do not exist. Kohlberg's (1958, 1981) six stages that describe the development of moral judgment from childhood to adulthood are based empirically on a study of eighty-four boys whose development Kohlberg has followed for a period of over twenty years. Although Kohlberg claims universality for his stage sequence, those groups not included in his original sample rarely reach his higher stages (Edwards, 1975; Holstein, 1976; Simpson, 1974). Prominent among those who thus appear to be deficient in moral development when measured by Kohlberg's scale are women, whose judgments seem to exemplify the third stage of his six-stage sequence. At this stage morality is conceived in interpersonal terms and goodness is equated with helping and pleasing others. This conception of goodness is considered by Kohlberg and Kramer (1969) to be functional in the lives of mature women insofar as their lives take place in the home. Kohlberg and Kramer imply that only if women enter the traditional arena of male activity will they recognize the inadequacy of this moral perspective and progress like men toward higher stages where relationships are subordinated to rules (stage four) and rules to universal principles of justice (stages five and six).

Yet herein lies a paradox, for the very traits that traditionally have defined the "goodness" of women, their care for and sensitivity to the needs of others, are those that mark them as deficient in moral development. In this version of moral development, however, the conception of maturity is derived from the study of men's lives and reflects the importance of individuation in their development. Piaget (1970), challenging the common impression that a developmental theory is built like a pyramid from its base in infancy, points out that a conception of development instead hangs from its vertex of maturity, the point toward which progress is traced. Thus, a change in the definition of maturity does not simply alter the description of the highest stage but recasts the understanding of development, changing the entire account.

When one begins with the study of women and derives developmental constructs from their lives, the outline of a moral conception different from that described by Freud, Piaget, or Kohlberg begins to emerge and informs a different description of development. In this conception, the moral problem arises from conflicting responsibilities rather than from competing rights and requires for its resolution a mode of thinking that is contextual and narrative rather than formal and abstract. This conception of morality as concerned with the activity of care centers moral development around the understanding of responsibility and relationships, just as the conception of morality as fairness ties moral development to the understanding of rights and rules.

This different construction of the moral problem by women may be seen as the critical reason for their failure to develop within the constraints of Kohlberg's system. Regarding all constructions of responsibility as evidence of a conventional moral understanding, Kohlberg defines the highest stages of moral development as deriving from a reflective understanding of human rights. That the morality of rights differs from the morality of responsibility in its emphasis on separation rather than connection, in its consideration of the individual rather than the relationship as primary, is illustrated by two responses to interview questions about the nature of morality. The first comes from a twenty-five-year-old man, one of the participants in Kohlberg's study:

[*What does the word morality mean to you?*] Nobody in the world knows the answer. I think it is recognizing the right of the individual, the rights of other individu-

als, not interfering with those rights. Act as fairly as you would have them treat you. I think it is basically to preserve the human being's right to existence. I think that is the most important. Secondly, the human being's right to do as he pleases, again without interfering with somebody else's rights.

[*How have your views on morality changed since the last interview?*] I think I am more aware of an individual's rights now. I used to be looking at it strictly from my point of view, just for me. Now I think I am more aware of what the individual has a right to.

Kohlberg (1973) cites this man's response as illustrative of the principled conception of human rights that exemplifies his fifth and sixth stages. Commenting on the response, Kohlberg says: "Moving to a perspective outside of that of his society, he identifies morality with justice (fairness, rights, the Golden Rule), with recognition of the rights of others as these are defined naturally or intrinsically. The human's being right to do as he pleases without interfering with somebody else's rights is a formula defining rights prior to social legislation" (pp. 29–30).

The second response comes from a woman who participated in the rights and responsibilities study. She also was twenty-five and, at the time, a third-year law student:

[*Is there really some correct solution to moral problems, or is everybody's opinion equally right?*] No, I don't think everybody's opinion is equally right. I think that in some situations there may be opinions that are equally valid, and one could conscientiously adopt one of several courses of action. But there are other situations in which I think there are right and wrong answers, that sort of inhere in the nature of existence, of all individuals here who need to live with each other to live. We need to depend on each other, and hopefully it is not only a physical need but a need of fulfillment in ourselves, that a person's life is enriched by cooperating with other people and striving to live in harmony with everybody else, and to that end, there are right and wrong, there are things which promote that end and that move away from it, and in that way it is possible to choose in certain cases among different courses of action that obviously promote or harm that goal.

[*Is there a time in the past when you would have thought about these things differently?*] Oh, yeah, I think that I went through a time when I thought that things were pretty relative, that I can't tell you what to do and you can't tell me what to do, because you've got your conscience and I've got mine.

[*When was that?*] When I was in high school. I guess that it just sort of dawned on me that my own ideas changed, and because my own judgment changed, I felt I couldn't judge another person's judgment. But now I think even when it is only the person himself who is going to be affected, I say it is wrong to the extent it doesn't cohere with what I know about human nature and what I know about you, and just from what I think is true about the operation of the universe, I could say I think you are making a mistake. [*What led you to change, do you think?*] Just seeing more of life, just recognizing that there are an awful lot of things that are common among people. There are certain things that you come to learn promote a better life and better relationships and more personal fulfillment than other things that in general tend to do the opposite, and the things that promote these things, you would call morally right.

This response also represents a personal reconstruction of morality following a period of questioning and doubt, but the reconstruction of moral understanding is based not on the primacy and universality of individual rights, but rather on what she describes as a "very strong sense of being responsible to the world." Within this construction, the moral dilemma changes from how to exercise one's rights without interfering with the rights of others to how "to lead a moral life which includes obligations to myself and my family and people in general." The problem then becomes one of limiting responsibilities without abandoning moral concern. When asked to describe herself, this woman says that she values "having other people that I am tied to, and also having people that I am responsible to. I have a very strong sense of being responsible to the world, that I can't just live for my enjoyment, but just the fact of being in the world gives me an obligation to do what I can to make the world a better place to live in, no matter how small a scale that may be on." Thus while Kohlberg's subject worries about people interfering with each other's rights, this woman worries about "the possibility of omission, of your not helping others when you could help them."

The issue that this woman raises is addressed by Jane Loevinger's fifth "autonomous" stage of ego development, where autonomy, placed in a context of relationships, is defined as modulating an excessive sense of responsibility through the recognition that other people have responsibility for their own destiny. The autonomous stage in

Loevinger's account (1970) witnesses a relinquishing of moral dichotomies and their replacement with "a feeling for the complexity and multifaceted character of real people and real situations" (p. 6). Whereas the rights conception of morality that informs Kohlberg's principled level (stages five and six) is geared to arriving at an objectively fair or just resolution to moral dilemmas upon which all rational persons could agree, the responsibility conception focuses instead on the limitations of any particular resolution and describes the conflicts that remain. . . .

## Images of Relationship

. . . Two eleven-year-old children, a boy and a girl, see, in the same dilemma, two very different moral problems. . . .

The dilemma that these eleven-year-olds were asked to resolve was one in the series devised by Kohlberg to measure moral development in adolescence by presenting a conflict between moral norms and exploring the logic of its resolution. In this particular dilemma, a man named Heinz considers whether or not to steal a drug which he cannot afford to buy in order to save the life of his wife. In the standard format of Kohlberg's interviewing procedure, the description of the dilemma itself—Heinz's predicament, the wife's disease, the druggist's refusal to lower his price— is followed by the question, "Should Heinz steal the drug?" The reasons for and against stealing are then explored through a series of questions that vary and extend the parameters of the dilemma in a way designed to reveal the underlying structure of moral thought.

Jake, at eleven, is clear from the outset that Heinz should steal the drug. Constructing the dilemma, as Kohlberg did, as a conflict between the values of property and life, he discerns the logical priority of life and uses that logic to justify his choice:

For one thing, a human life is worth more than money, and if the druggist only makes $1,000, he is still going to live, but if Heinz doesn't steal the drug, his wife is going to die. (*Why is life worth more than money?*) Because the druggist can get a thousand dollars later from rich people with cancer, but Heinz can't get his wife again. (*Why not?*) Because people are all different and so you couldn't get Heinz's wife again.

Asked whether Heinz should steal the drug if he does not love his wife, Jake replies that he should, saying that not only is there "a difference between hating and killing," but also, if Heinz were caught, "the judge would probably think it was the right thing to do." Asked about the fact that, in stealing, Heinz would be breaking the law, he says that "the laws have mistakes, and you can't go writing up a law for everything that you can imagine."

Thus, while taking the law into account and recognizing its function in maintaining social order (the judge, Jake says, "should give Heinz the lightest possible sentence"), he also sees the law as man-made and therefore subject to error and change. Yet his judgment that Heinz should steal the drug, like his view of the law as having mistakes, rests on the assumption of agreement, a societal consensus around moral values that allows one to know and expect others to recognize what is "the right thing to do."

Fascinated by the power of logic, this eleven-year-old boy locates truth in math, which, he says, is "the only thing that is totally logical." Considering the moral dilemma to be "sort of like a math problem with humans," he sets it up as an equation and proceeds to work out the solution. Since his solution is rationally derived, he assumes that anyone following reason would arrive at the same conclusion and thus that a judge would also consider stealing to be the right thing for Heinz to do. Yet he is also aware of the limits of logic. Asked whether there is a right answer to moral problems, Jake replies that "there can only be right and wrong in judgment," since the parameters of action are variable and complex. Illustrating how actions undertaken with the best of intentions can eventuate in the most disastrous of consequences, he says, "like if you give an old lady your seat on the trolley, if you are in a trolley crash and that seat goes through the window, it might be that reason that the old lady dies."

Theories of developmental psychology illuminate well the position of this child, standing at the juncture of childhood and adolescence, at what

Piaget describes as the pinnacle of childhood intelligence, and beginning through thought to discover a wider universe of possibility. The moment of preadolescence is caught by the conjunction of formal operational thought with a description of self still anchored in the factual parameters of his childhood world—his age, his town, his father's occupation, the substance of his likes, dislikes, and beliefs. Yet as his self-description radiates the self-confidence of a child who has arrived, in Erikson's terms, at a favorable balance of industry over inferiority—competent, sure of himself, and knowing well the rules of the game—so his emergent capacity for formal thought, his ability to think about thinking and to reason things out in a logical way, frees him from dependence on authority and allows him to find solutions to problems by himself.

This emergent autonomy follows the trajectory that Kohlberg's six stages of moral development trace, a three-level progression from an egocentric understanding of fairness based on individual need (stages one and two), to a conception of fairness anchored in the shared conventions of societal agreement (stages three and four), and finally to a principled understanding of fairness that rests on the free-standing logic of equality and reciprocity (stages five and six). While this boy's judgments at eleven are scored as conventional on Kohlberg's scale, a mixture of stages three and four, his ability to bring deductive logic to bear on the solution of moral dilemmas, to differentiate morality from law, and to see how laws can be considered to have mistakes points toward the principled conception of justice that Kohlberg equates with moral maturity.

In contrast, Amy's response to the dilemma conveys a very different impression, an image of development stunted by a failure of logic, an inability to think for herself. Asked if Heinz should steal the drug, she replies in a way that seems evasive and unsure:

Well, I don't think so. I think there might be other ways besides stealing it, like if he could borrow the money or make a loan or something, but he really shouldn't steal the drug—but his wife shouldn't die either.

*Is she not rising to situation, or choosing a different alternative*

Asked why he should not steal the drug, she considers neither property nor law but rather the effect that theft could have on the relationship between Heinz and his wife:

If he stole the drug, he might save his wife then, but if he did, he might have to go to jail, and then his wife might get sicker again, and he couldn't get more of the drug, and it might not be good. So, they should really just talk it out and find some other way to make the money.

Seeing in the dilemma not a math problem with humans but a narrative of relationships that extends over time, Amy envisions the wife's continuing need for her husband and the husband's continuing concern for his wife and seeks to respond to the druggist's need in a way that would sustain rather than sever connection. Just as she ties the wife's survival to the preservation of relationships, so she considers the value of the wife's life in a context of relationships, saying that it would be wrong to let her die because, "if she died, it hurts a lot of people and it hurts her." Since Amy's moral judgment is grounded in the belief that, "if somebody has something that would keep somebody alive, then it's not right not to give it to them," she considers the problem in the dilemma to arise not from the druggist's assertion of rights but from his failure of response.

As the interviewer proceeds with the series of questions that follow from Kohlberg's construction of the dilemma, Amy's answers remain essentially unchanged, the various probes serving neither to elucidate nor to modify her initial response. Whether or not Heinz loves his wife, he still shouldn't steal or let her die; if it were a stranger dying instead, Amy says that "if the stranger didn't have anybody near or anyone she knew," then Heinz should try to save her life, but he should not steal the drug. But as the interviewer conveys through the repetition of questions that the answers she gave were not heard or not right, Amy's confidence begins to diminish, and her replies become more constrained and unsure. Asked again why Heinz should not steal the drug, she simply repeats, "Because it's not right." Asked again to explain why, she states again that theft would not be a good solution, adding lamely "if he took it, he might not know how to give it to his wife, and his wife might still die." Failing to see the dilemma as a self-contained problem in moral logic, she does not discern the internal structure of its resolution; as she constructs the problem differently herself, Kohlberg's conception completely evades her.

Instead, seeing a world comprised of relationships rather than of people standing alone, a world that coheres through human connection rather than through systems of rules, she finds the puzzle in the dilemma to lie in the failure of the druggist to respond to the wife. Saying that "it is not right for someone to die when their life could be saved," she assumes that if the druggist were to see the consequences of his refusal to lower his price, he would realize that "he should just give it to the wife and then have the husband pay back the money later." Thus she considers the solution to the dilemma to lie in making the wife's condition more salient to the druggist or, that failing, in appealing to others who are in a position to help.

Just as Jake is confident the judge would agree that stealing is the right thing for Heinz to do, so Amy is confident that, "if Heinz and the druggist had talked it out long enough, they could reach something besides stealing." As he considers the law to "have mistakes," so she sees this drama as a mistake, believing that "the world should just share things more and then people wouldn't have to steal." Both children thus recognize the need for agreement but see it as mediated in different ways—he impersonally through systems of logic and law, she personally through communication in relationship. Just as he relies on the conventions of logic to deduce the solution to this dilemma, assuming these conventions to be shared, so she relies on a process of communication, assuming connection and believing that her voice will be heard. Yet while his assumptions about agreement are confirmed by the convergence in logic between his answers and the questions posed, her assumptions are belied by the failure of communication, the interviewer's inability to understand her response.

Although the frustration of the interview with Amy is apparent in the repetition of questions and its ultimate circularity, the problem of interpretation is focused by the assessment of her response. When considered in the light of Kohlberg's definition of the stages and sequence of moral development, her moral judgments appear to be a full stage lower in maturity than those of the boy. Scored as a mixture of stages two and three, her responses seem to reveal a feeling of powerlessness in the world, an inability to think systematically about the concepts of morality or law, a reluctance to challenge authority or to examine the logic of received moral truths, a failure even to conceive of acting directly to save a life or to consider that such action, if taken, could possibly have an effect. As her reliance on relationships seems to reveal a continuing dependence and vulnerability, so her belief in communication as the mode through which to resolve moral dilemmas appears naive and cognitively immature.

Yet Amy's description of herself conveys a markedly different impression. Once again, the hallmarks of the preadolescent child depict a child secure in her sense of herself, confident in the substance of her beliefs, and sure of her ability to do something of value in the world. Describing herself at eleven as "growing and changing," she says that she "sees some things differently now, just because I know myself really well now, and I know a lot more about the world." Yet the world she knows is a different world from that refracted by Kohlberg's construction of Heinz's dilemma. Her world is a world of relationships and psychological truths where an awareness of the connection between people gives rise to a recognition of responsibility for one another, a perception of the need for response. Seen in this light, her understanding of morality as arising from the recognition of relationship, her belief in communication as the mode of conflict resolution, and her conviction that the solution to the dilemma will follow from its compelling representation seem far from naive or cognitively immature. Instead, Amy's judgments contain the insights central to an ethic of care, just as Jake's judgments reflect the logic of the justice approach. Her incipient awareness of

the "method of truth," the central tenet of nonviolent conflict resolution, and her belief in the restorative activity of care, lead her to see the actors in the dilemma arrayed not as opponents in a contest of rights but as members of a network of relationships on whose continuation they all depend. Consequently her solution to the dilemma lies in activating the network by communication, securing the inclusion of the wife by strengthening rather than severing connections.

But the different logic of Amy's response calls attention to the interpretation of the interview itself. Conceived as an interrogation, it appears instead as a dialogue, which takes on moral dimensions of its own, pertaining to the interviewer's uses of power and to the manifestations of respect. With this shift in the conception of the interview, it immediately becomes clear that the interviewer's problem in understanding Amy's response stems from the fact that Amy is answering a different question from the one the interviewer thought had been posed. Amy is considering not *whether* Heinz should act in this situation ("*should* Heinz steal the drug?") but rather *how* Heinz should act in response to his awareness of his wife's need ("Should Heinz *steal* the drug?"). The interviewer takes the mode of action for granted, presuming it to be a matter of fact; Amy assumes the necessity for action and considers what form it should take. In the interviewer's failure to imagine a response not dreamt of in Kohlberg's moral philosophy lies the failure to hear Amy's question and to see the logic in her response, to discern that what appears, from one perspective, to be an evasion of the dilemma signifies in other terms a recognition of the problem and a search for a more adequate solution.

Thus in Heinz's dilemma these two children see two very different moral problems—Jake a conflict between life and property that can be resolved by logical deduction, Amy a fracture of human relationship that must be mended with its own thread. Asking different questions that arise from different conceptions of the moral domain, the children arrive at answers that fundamentally diverge, and the arrangement of these answers as successive stages on a scale of increasing moral maturity calibrated by the logic of the boy's response misses the different truth revealed in the judgment of the girl. To the question, "What does he see that she does not?" Kohlberg's theory provides a ready response, manifest in the scoring of Jake's judgments a full stage higher than Amy's in moral maturity; to the question, "What does she see that he does not?" Kohlberg's theory has nothing to say. Since most of her responses fall through the sieve of Kohlberg's scoring system, her responses appear from his perspective to lie outside the moral domain.

Yet just as Jake reveals a sophisticated understanding of the logic of justification, so Amy is equally sophisticated in her understanding of the nature of choice. Recognizing that "if both the roads went in totally separate ways, if you pick one, you'll never know what would happen if you went the other way," she explains that "that's the chance you have to take, and like I said, it's just really a guess." To illustrate her point "in a simple way," she describes her choice to spend the summer at camp:

I will never know what would have happened if I had stayed here, and if something goes wrong at camp, I'll never know if I stayed here if it would have been better. There's really no way around it because there's no way you can do both at once, so you've got to decide, but you'll never know.

In this way, these two eleven-year-old children, both highly intelligent and perceptive about life, though in different ways, display different modes of moral understanding, different ways of thinking about conflict and choice. In resolving Heinz's dilemma, Jake relies on theft to avoid confrontation and turns to the law to mediate the dispute. Transposing a hierarchy of power into a hierarchy of values, he defuses a potentially explosive conflict between people by casting it as an impersonal conflict of claims. In this way, he abstracts the moral problem from the interpersonal situation, finding in the logic of fairness an objective way to decide who will win the dispute. But this hierarchical ordering, with its imagery of winning and losing and the potential for violence which it contains, gives way in Amy's construction of the dilemma to a network of connection, a

web of relationships that is sustained by a process of communication. With this shift, the moral problem changes from one of unfair domination, the imposition of property over life, to one of unnecessary exclusion, the failure of the druggist to respond to the wife. . . .

The contrast between a self defined through separation and a self delineated through connection, between a self measured against an abstract ideal of perfection and a self assessed through particular activities of care, becomes clearer and the implications of this contrast extend by considering the different ways these children resolve a conflict between responsibility to others and responsibility to self. The question about responsibility followed a dilemma posed by a woman's conflict between her commitments to work and to family relationships. While the details of this conflict color the text of Amy's response, Jake abstracts the problem of responsibility from the context in which it appears, replacing the themes of intimate relationship with his own imagery of explosive connection [see the table on page 296].

Again Jake constructs the dilemma as a mathematical equation, deriving a formula that guides the solution: one-fourth to others, three-fourths to yourself. Beginning with his responsibility to himself, a responsibility that he takes for granted, he then considers the extent to which he is responsible to others as well. Proceeding from a premise of separation but recognizing that "You have to live with other people," he seeks rules to limit interference and thus to minimize hurt. Responsibility in his construction pertains to a limitation of action, a restraint of aggression, guided by the recognition that his actions can have effects on others, just as theirs can interfere with him. Thus rules, by limiting interference, make life in community safe, protecting autonomy through reciprocity, extending the same consideration to others and self.

To the question about conflicting responsibilities, Amy again responds contextually rather than categorically, saying "it depends" and indicating how choice would be affected by variations in character and circumstance. Proceeding from a premise of connection, that "if you have a responsibility *with* somebody else, you should keep it,"

| Jake | Amy |
|------|-----|

---

*(When responsibility to oneself and responsibility to others conflict, how should one choose?)*

---

| | |
|---|---|
| You go about one-fourth to the others and three-fourths to yourself. | Well, it really depends on the situation. If you have a responsibility with somebody else, then you should keep it to a certain extent, but to the extent that it is really going to hurt you or stop you from doing something that you really, really want, then I think maybe you should put yourself first. But if it is your responsibility to somebody really close to you, you've just got to decide in that situation which is more important, yourself or that person, and like I said, it really depends on what kind of person you are and how you feel about the other person or persons involved. |

*(Why?)*

---

| | |
|---|---|
| Because the most important thing in your decision should be yourself, don't let yourself be guided totally by other people, but you have to take them into consideration. So, if what you want to do is blow yourself up with an atom bomb, you should maybe blow yourself up with a hand grenade because you are thinking about your neighbors who would die also. | Well, like some people put themselves and things for themselves before they put other people, and some people really care about other people. Like, I don't think your job is as important as somebody that you really love, like your husband or your parents or a very close friend. Somebody that you really care for—or if it's just your responsibility to your job or somebody that you barely know, then maybe you go first—but if it's somebody that you really love and love as much or even more than you love yourself, you've got to decide what you really love more, that person, or that thing, or yourself. (*And how do you do that?*) Well, you've got to think about it, and you've got to think about both sides, and you've got to think which would be better for everybody or better for yourself, which is more important, and which will make everybody happier. Like if the other people can get somebody else to do it, whatever it is, or don't really need you specifically, maybe it's better to do what you want, because the other people will be just fine with somebody else so they'll still be happy, and then you'll be happy too because you'll do what you want. |

*(What does responsibility mean?)*

---

| | |
|---|---|
| It means pretty much thinking of others when I do something, and like if I want to throw a rock, not throwing it at a window, because I thought of the people who would have to pay for that window, not doing it just for yourself, because you have to live with other people and live with your community, and if you do something that hurts them all, a lot of people will end up suffering, and that is sort of the wrong thing to do. | That other people are counting on you to do something, and you can't just decide, "Well, I'd rather do this or that." (*Are there other kinds of responsibility?*) Well, to yourself. If something looks really fun but you might hurt yourself doing it because you don't really know how to do it and your friends say, "Well, come on, you can do it, don't worry," if you're really scared to do it, it's your responsibility to yourself that if you think you might hurt yourself, you shouldn't do it, because you have to take care of yourself and that's your responsibility to yourself. |

she then considers the extent to which she has a responsibility to herself. Exploring the parameters of separation, she imagines situations where, by doing what you want, you would avoid hurting yourself or where, in doing so, you would not thereby diminish the happiness of others. To her, responsibility signifies response, an extension rather than a limitation of action. Thus it connotes an act of care rather than the restraint of aggression. Again seeking the solution that would be most inclusive of everyone's needs, she strives to resolve the dilemma in a way that "will make everybody happier." Since Jake is concerned with limiting interference, while Amy focuses on the need for response, for him the limiting condition is, "Don't let yourself be guided totally by others," but for her it arises when "other people are counting on you," in which case "you can't just decide, 'Well, I'd rather do this or that.'" The interplay between these responses is clear in that she, assuming connection, begins to explore the parameters of separation, while he, assuming separation, begins to explore the parameters of connection. But the primacy of separation or connection leads to different images of self and of relationships.

Most striking among these differences is the imagery of violence in the boy's response, depicting a world of dangerous confrontation and explosive connection, where she sees a world of care and protection, a life lived with others whom "you may love as much or even more than you love yourself." Since the conception of morality reflects the understanding of social relationships, this difference in the imagery of relationships gives rise to a change in the moral injunction itself. To Jake, responsibility means *not doing* what he wants because he is thinking of others; to Amy, it means *doing* what others are counting on her to do regardless of what she herself wants. Both children are concerned with avoiding hurt but construe the problem in different ways—he seeing hurt to arise from the expression of aggression, she from a failure of response.

If the trajectory of development were drawn through either of these children's responses, it would trace a correspondingly different path. For Jake, development would entail coming to see the other as equal to the self and the discovery that equality provides a way of making connection safe. For Amy, development would follow the inclusion of herself in an expanding network of connection and the discovery that separation can be protective and need not entail isolation. In view of these different paths of development and particularly of the different ways in which the experiences of separation and connection are aligned with the voice of the self, the representation of the boy's development as the single line of adolescent growth for both sexes creates a continual problem when it comes to interpreting the development of the girl.

Since development has been premised on separation and told as a narrative of failed relationships—of pre-Oedipal attachments, Oedipal fantasies, preadolescent chumships, and adolescent loves—relationships that stand out against a background of separation, only successively to erupt and give way to an increasingly emphatic individuation, the development of girls appears problematic because of the continuity of relationships in their lives. Freud attributes the turning inward of girls at puberty to an intensification of primary narcissism, signifying a failure of love or "object" relationships. But if this turning inward is construed against a background of continuing connection, it signals a new responsiveness to the self, an expansion of care rather than a failure of relationship. In this way girls, seen not to fit the categories of relationships derived from male experience, call attention to the assumptions about relationships that have informed the account of human development by replacing the imagery of explosive connection with images of dangerous separation.

# References

Broverman, L, Vogel, S., Broverman, D., Clarkson, F., and Rosenkrantz, P. "Sex-role Stereotypes: A Current Appraisal." *Journal of Social Issues 28* (1972): 59–78.

Edwards, Carolyn P. "Societal Complexity and Moral Development: A Kenyan Study." *Ethos* 3 (1975): 505–527.

Freud, Sigmund. *The Standard Edition of the Complete Psychological Works of Sigmund Freud,* trans. and ed. James Strachey. London: The Hogarth Press, 1961.

————. "On Narcissism: An Introduction" (1914). Vol. XIV.

Holstein, Constance. "Development of Moral Judgment: A Longitudinal Study of Males and Females." *Child Development* 47 (1976): 51–61.

Kohlberg, Lawrence. "The Development of Modes of Thinking and Choices in Years 10 to 16." Ph.D. Diss., University of Chicago, 1958.

————. "Continuities and Discontinuities in Childhood and Adult Moral Development Revisited." In *Collected Papers on Moral Development and Moral Education.* Moral Education Research Foundation, Harvard University, 1973.

————. *The Philosophy of Moral Development.* San Francisco: Harper and Row, 1981.

Kohlberg, L., and Kramer, R. "Continuities and Discontinuities in Child and Adult Moral Development." *Human Development* 12 (1969): 93–120.

Loevinger, Jane, and Wessler, Ruth. *Measuring Ego Development.* San Francisco: Jossey-Bass, 1970.

Miller, Jean Baker. *Toward a New Psychology of Women.* Boston: Beacon Press, 1976.

Piaget, Jean. *The Moral Judgment of the Child* (1932). New York: The Free Press, 1965.

————. *Structuralism.* New York: Basic Books, 1970.

Simpson, Elizabeth L. "Moral Development Research: A Case Study of Scientific Cultural Bias." *Human Development* 17 (1974): 81–106.

Woolf, Virginia. *A Room of One's Own.* New York: Harcourt, Brace and World, 1929.

# 25    An Ethic of Caring

## NEL NODDINGS

## From Natural to Ethical Caring

David Hume long ago contended that morality is founded upon and rooted in feeling—that the "final sentence" on matters of morality, "that which renders morality an active virtue"— ". . . this final sentence depends on some internal sense or feeling, which nature has made universal in the whole species. For what else can have an influence of this nature?"[1]

What is the nature of this feeling that is "universal in the whole species"? I want to suggest that morality as an "active virtue" requires two feelings and not just one. The first is the sentiment of natural caring. There can be no ethical sentiment without the initial, enabling sentiment. In situations where we act on behalf of the other because we want to do so, we are acting in accord with natural caring. A mother's caretaking efforts in

behalf of her child are not usually considered ethical but natural. Even maternal animals take care of their offspring, and we do not credit them with ethical behavior.

The second sentiment occurs in response to a remembrance of the first. Nietzsche speaks of love and memory in the context of Christian love and Eros, but what he says may safely be taken out of context to illustrate the point I wish to make here:

There is something so ambiguous and suggestive about the word love, something that speaks to memory and to hope, that even the lowest intelligence and the coldest heart still feel something of the glimmer of this word. The cleverest woman and the most vulgar man recall the relatively least selfish moments of their whole life, even if Eros has taken only a low flight with them.[2]

This memory of our own best moments of caring and being cared for sweeps over us as a feeling—as an "I must"—in response to the plight of the other and our conflicting desire to serve our own interests. There is a transfer of feeling analogous to transfer of learning. In the intellectual domain, when I read a certain kind of mathematical puzzle, I may react by thinking, "That is like

From Nel Noddings, *Caring: A Feminine Approach to Ethics and Moral Education* (University of California Press, 1984) 79–95, 109–110, with omissions. Reprinted by permission of the University of California Press.

the sailors, monkey, and coconuts problem," and then, "Diophantine equations" or "modulo arithmetic" or "congruences." Similarly, when I encounter an other and feel the natural pang conflicted with my own desires—"I must—I do not want to"—I recognize the feeling and remember what has followed it in my own best moments. I have a picture of those moments in which I was cared for and in which I cared, and I may reach toward this memory and guide my conduct by it if I wish to do so.

Recognizing that ethical caring requires an effort that is not needed in natural caring does not commit us to a position that elevates ethical caring over natural caring. Kant has identified the ethical with that which is done out of duty and not out of love, and that distinction in itself seems right. But an ethic built on caring strives to maintain the caring attitude and is thus dependent upon, and not superior to, natural caring. The source of ethical behavior is, then, in twin sentiments—one that feels directly for the other and one that feels for and with that best self, who may accept and sustain the initial feeling rather than reject it.

We shall discuss the ethical ideal, that vision of best self, in some depth. When we commit ourselves to obey the "I must" even at its weakest and most fleeting, we are under the guidance of this ideal. It is not just any picture. Rather, it is our best picture of ourselves caring and being cared for. It may even be colored by acquaintance with one superior to us in caring, but, as I shall describe it, it is both constrained and attainable. It is limited by what we have already done and by what we are capable of, and it does not idealize the impossible so that we may escape into ideal abstraction. . . .

## Obligation

There are moments for all of us when we care quite naturally. We just do care; no ethical effort is required. "Want" and "ought" are indistinguishable in such cases. I want to do what I or others might judge I ought to do. But can there be a "demand" to care? There can be, surely, no demand for the initial impulse that arises as a feeling, an inner voice saying "I must do something," in response to the need of the cared-for. This impulse arises naturally, at least occasionally, in the absence of pathology. We cannot demand that one have this impulse, but we shrink from one who never has it. One who never feels the pain of another, who never confesses the internal "I must" that is so familiar to most of us, is beyond our normal pattern of understanding. Her case is pathological, and we avoid her.

But even if I feel the initial "I must," I may reject it. I may reject it instantaneously by shifting from "I must do something" to "Something must be done," and removing myself from the set of possible agents through whom the action should be accomplished. I may reject it because I feel that there is nothing I can do. If I do either of these things without reflection upon what I might do in behalf of the cared-for, then I do not care. Caring requires me to respond to the initial impulse with an act of commitment: I commit myself either to overt action on behalf of the cared-for (I pick up my crying infant) or I commit myself to thinking about what I might do. In the latter case, as we have seen, I may or may not act overtly in behalf of the cared-for. I may abstain from action if I believe that anything I might do would tend to work against the best interests of the cared-for. But the test of my caring is not wholly in how things turn out; the primary test lies in an examination of what I considered, how fully I received the other, and whether the free pursuit of his projects is partly a result of the completion of my caring in him.

But am I obliged to embrace the "I must"? In this form, the question is a bit odd, for the "I must" carries obligation with it. It comes to us as obligation. But accepting and affirming the "I must" are different from feeling it, and these responses are what I am pointing to when I ask whether I am obliged to embrace the "I must." The question nags at us; it is a question that has been asked, in a variety of forms, over and over by moralists and moral theorists. Usually, the question arises as part of the broader question of justification. We ask something of the sort: Why must I (or should I) do what suggests itself to reason as "right" or as needing to be done for the sake of some other? We might prefer to supplement "reason" with "and/or feeling." This question is, of course, not the only thorny question in moral theory, but it is one that has plagued theorists who see clearly that there is no way to derive an "I ought" statement from a chain of facts. I may agree readily that "things would be better"—that is, that a certain state of affairs commonly agreed to be desirable might be attained—if a certain chain of events were to take place. But there is still nothing in this intellectual chain that can produce the "I ought." I may choose to remain an observer on the scene.

Now I am suggesting that the "I must" arises directly and prior to consideration of what it is that I might do. The initial feeling is the "I must." When it comes to me indistinguishable from the "I want," I proceed easily as one-caring. But often it comes to me conflicted. It may be barely perceptible, and it may be followed almost simultaneously by resistance. When someone asks me to get something for him or merely asks for my attention, the "I must" may be lost in a clamor of resistance. Now a second sentiment is required if I am to behave as one-caring. I care about myself as one-caring and, although I do not care naturally for the person who has asked something of me—at least not at this moment—I feel the genuine moral sentiment, the "I ought," that sensibility to which I have committed myself.

Let me try to make plausible my contention that the moral imperative arises directly. And, of course, I must try to explain how caring and what I am calling the "moral imperative" are related. When my infant cries in the night, I not only feel that I must do something but I want to do something. Because I love this child, because I am bonded to him, I want to remove his pain as I would want to remove my own. The "I must" is not a dutiful imperative but one that accompanies the "I want." If I were tied to a chair, for example, and wanted desperately to get free, I might say as I struggled, "I must do something; I must get out of

these bonds." But this "must" is not yet the moral or ethical "ought." It is a "must" born of desire.

The most intimate situations of caring are, thus, natural. I do not feel that taking care of my own child is "moral" but, rather, natural. A woman who allows her own child to die of neglect is often considered sick rather than immoral; that is, we feel that either she or the situation into which she has been thrust must be pathological. Otherwise, the impulse to respond, to nurture the living infant, is overwhelming. We share the impulse with other creatures in the animal kingdom. Whether we want to consider this response as "instinctive" is problematic, because certain patterns of response may be implied by the term and because suspension of reflective consciousness seems also to be implied (and I am not suggesting that we have no choice), but I have no difficulty in considering it as innate. Indeed, I am claiming that the impulse to act in behalf of the present other is itself innate. It lies latent in each of us, awaiting gradual development in a succession of caring relations. I am suggesting that our inclination toward and interest in morality derives from caring. In caring, we accept the natural impulse to act on behalf of the present other. We are engrossed in the other. We have received him and feel his pain or happiness, but we are not compelled by this impulse. We have a choice; we may accept what we feel, or we may reject it. If we have a strong desire to be moral, we will not reject it, and this strong desire to be moral is derived, reflectively, from the more fundamental and natural desire to be and to remain related. To reject the feeling when it arises is either to be in an internal state of imbalance or to contribute willfully to the diminution of the ethical ideal.

But suppose in a particular case that the "I must" does not arise, or that it whispers faintly and disappears, leaving distrust, repugnance, or hate. Why, then, should I behave morally toward the object of my dislike? Why should I not accept feelings other than those characteristic of caring and, thus, achieve an internal state of balance through hate, anger, or malice?

The answer to this is, I think, that the genuine moral sentiment (our second sentiment) arises from an evaluation of the caring relation as good, as better than, superior to, other forms of relatedness. I feel the moral "I must" when I recognize that my response will either enhance or diminish my ethical ideal. It will serve either to increase or decrease the likelihood of genuine caring. My response affects me as one-caring. In a given situation with someone I am not fond of, I may be able to find all sorts of reasons why I should not respond to his need. I may be too busy. He may be undiscerning. The matter may be, on objective analysis, unimportant. But, before I decide, I must turn away from this analytic chain of thought and back to the concrete situation. Here is this person with this perceived need to which is attached this importance. I must put justification aside temporarily. Shall I respond? How do I feel as a duality about the "I" who will not respond?

I am obliged, then, to accept the initial "I must" when it occurs and even to fetch it out of recalcitrant slumber when it fails to awake spontaneously. The source of my obligation is the value I place on the relatedness of caring. This value itself arises as a product of actual caring and being cared-for and my reflection on the goodness of these concrete caring situations.

Now, what sort of "goodness" is it that attaches to the caring relation? It cannot be a fully moral goodness, for we have already described forms of caring that are natural and require no moral effort. But it cannot be a fully nonmoral goodness either, for it would then join a class of goods many of which are widely separated from the moral good. It is, perhaps, properly described as a "premoral good," one that lies in a region with the moral good and shades over into it. We cannot always decide with certainty whether our caring response is natural or ethical. Indeed, the decision to respond ethically as one-caring may cause the lowering of barriers that previously prevented reception of the other, and natural caring may follow.

I have identified the source of our obligation and have said that we are obligated to accept, and even to call forth, the feeling "I must." But what exactly must I do? Can my obligation be set forth in a list or hierarchy of principles? So far, it seems that I am obligated to maintain an attitude and, thus, to meet the other as one-caring and, at the same time, to increase my own virtue as one-caring. . . .

Let me say here, however, why it seems preferable to place an ethical ideal above principle as a guide to moral action. It has been traditional in moral philosophy to insist that moral principles must be, by their very nature as moral principles, universifiable. If I am obligated to do *X* under certain conditions, then under sufficiently similar conditions you also are obligated to do *X*. But the principle of universifiability seems to depend, as Nietzsche pointed out, on a concept of "sameness."[3] In order to accept the principle, we should have to establish that human predicaments exhibit sufficient sameness, and this we cannot do without abstracting away from concrete situations those qualities that seem to reveal the sameness. In doing this, we often lose the very qualities or factors that gave rise to the moral question in the situation. That condition which makes the situation different and thereby induces genuine moral puzzlement cannot be satisfied by the application of principles developed in situations of sameness. . . .

A and B, struggling with a moral decision, are two different persons with different factual histories, different projects and aspirations, and different ideals. It may indeed be right, morally right, for A to do *X* and B to do not-*X*. We may, that is, connect "right" and "wrong" to faithfulness to the ethical ideal. This does not cast us into relativism, because the ideal contains at its heart a component that is universal: Maintenance of the caring relation. . . .

There is a legitimate dread of the proximate stranger—of that person who may ask more than we feel able to give. We saw there that we cannot care for everyone. Caring itself is reduced to mere talk about caring when we attempt to do so. We must acknowledge, then, that an ethic of caring implies a limit on our obligation.

Our obligation is limited and delimited by relation. We are never free, in the human domain, to abandon our preparedness to care; but, practically, if we are meeting those in our inner circles adequately as ones-caring and receiving those linked to our inner circles by formal chains of relation, we shall limit the calls upon our obligation quite naturally. We are not obliged to summon the "I must" if there is no possibility of completion in the other. I am not obliged to care for starving children in Africa, because there is no way for this caring to be completed in the other unless I abandon the caring to which I am obligated. I may still choose to do something in the direction of caring, but I am not obliged to do so. . . .

We cannot refuse obligation in human affairs by merely refusing to enter relation; we are, by virtue of our mutual humanity, already and perpetually in potential relation. Instead, we limit our obligation by examining the possibility of completion. In connection with animals, however, we may find it possible to refuse relation itself on the grounds of a species-specific impossibility of any form of reciprocity in caring.

Now, this is very important, and we should try to say clearly what governs our obligation. On the basis of what has been developed so far, there seem to be two criteria: the existence of or potential for present relation, and the dynamic potential for growth in relation, including the potential for increased reciprocity and, perhaps, mutuality. The first criterion establishes an absolute obligation and the second serves to put our obligations into an order of priority.

If the other toward whom we shall act is capable of responding as cared-for and there are no objective conditions that prevent our receiving this response—if, that is, our caring can be completed in the other—then we must meet that other as one-caring. If we do not care naturally, we must call upon our capacity for ethical caring. When we are in relation or when the other has addressed us, we must respond as one-caring. The imperative in relation is categorical. When relation has not yet been established, or when it may properly be refused (when no formal chain or natural circle is present), the imperative is more like that of the hypothetical: I must if I wish to (or am able to) move into relation.

The second criterion asks us to look at the nature of potential relation and, especially, at the capacity of the cared-for to respond. The potential for response in animals, for example, is nearly static; they cannot respond in mutuality, nor can the nature of their response change substantially. But a child's potential for increased response is enormous. If the possibility of relation is dynamic—if the relation may clearly grow with respect to reciprocity—then the possibility and degree of my obligation also grows. If response is imminent, so also is my obligation. This criterion will help us to distinguish between our obligation to members of the nonhuman animal world and, say, the human fetus. We must keep in mind, however, that the second criterion binds us in proportion to the probability of increased response and to the imminence of that response. Relation itself is fundamental in obligation.

I shall give an example of thinking guided by these criteria, but let us pause for a moment and ask what it is we are trying to accomplish. I am working deliberately toward criteria that will preserve our deepest and most tender human feelings. The caring of mother for child, of human adult for human infant, elicits the tenderest feelings in most of us. Indeed, for many women, this feeling of nurturance lies at the very heart of what we assess as good. A philosophical position that has difficulty distinguishing between our obligation to human infants and, say, pigs is in some difficulty straight off. It violates our most deeply cherished feeling about human goodness. This violation does not, of course, make the position logically wrong, but it suggests that especially strong grounds will be needed to support it. In the absence of such strong grounds . . . we might prefer to establish a position that captures rather than denies our basic feelings. We might observe that man (in contrast to woman) has continually turned away from his inner self and feeling in pursuit of both science and ethics. With respect to strict science, this turning outward may be defensible; with respect to ethics, it has been disastrous.

Now, let's consider an example: the problem of abortion. Operating under the guidance of an ethic of caring, we are not likely to find abortion in general either right or wrong. We shall have to inquire into individual cases. An incipient embryo is an information speck—a set of controlling instructions for a future human being. Many of these specks are created and flushed away without their creators' awareness. From the view developed here, the information speck is an information speck; it has no given sanctity. There should be no concern over the waste of "human tissue," since nature herself is wildly prolific, even profligate. The one-caring is concerned not with human tissue but with human consciousness—with pain, delight, hope, fear, entreaty, and response.

But suppose the information speck is mine, and I am aware of it. This child-to-be is the product of love between a man deeply cared-for and me. Will the child have his eyes or mine? His stature or mine? Our joint love of mathematics or his love of mechanics or my love of language? This is not just an information speck; it is endowed with prior love and current knowledge. It is sacred, but I—humbly, not presumptuously—confer sacredness upon it. I cannot, will not destroy it. It is joined to loved others through formal chains of caring. It is linked to the inner circle in a clearly defined way. I might wish that I were not pregnant, but I cannot destroy this known and potentially loved person-to-be. There is already relation albeit indirect and formal. My decision is an ethical one born of natural caring.

But suppose, now, that my beloved child has grown up; it is she who is pregnant and considering abortion. She is not sure of the love between herself and the man. She is miserably worried about her economic and emotional future. I might like to convey sanctity on this information speck; but I am not God—only mother to this suffering cared-for. It is she who is conscious and in pain, and I as one-caring move to relieve the pain. This information speck is an information speck and that is all. There is no formal relation, given the breakdown between husband and wife, and with the embryo, there is no present relation; the possibility of future relation—while not absent, surely

—is uncertain. But what of this possibility for growing response? Must we not consider it? We must indeed. As the embryo becomes a fetus and, growing daily, becomes more nearly capable of response as cared-for, our obligation grows from a nagging uncertainty—an "I must if I wish"—to an utter conviction that we must meet this small other as one-caring.

If we try to formalize what has been expressed in the concrete situations described so far, we arrive at a legal approach to abortion very like that of the Supreme Court: abortions should be freely available in the first trimester, subject to medical determination in the second trimester, and banned in the third, when the fetus is viable. A woman under the guidance of our ethic would be likely to recognize the growing possibility of relation; the potential is clearly dynamic. Further, many women recognize the relation as established when the fetus begins to move about. It is not a question of when life begins but of when relation begins.

But what if relation is never established? Suppose the child is born and the mother admits no sense of relatedness. May she commit infanticide? One who asks such questions misinterprets the concept of relatedness that I have been struggling to describe. Since the infant, even the near-natal fetus, is capable of relation—of the sweetest and most unselfconscious reciprocity—one who encounters the infant is obligated to meet it as one-caring. Both parts of this claim are essential; it is not only the child's capability to respond but also the encounter that induces obligation. There must exist the possibility for our caring to be completed in the other. If the mother does not care naturally, then she must summon ethical caring to support her as one-caring. She may not ethically ignore the child's cry to live.

The one-caring, in considering abortion as in all other matters, cares first for the one in immediate pain or peril. She might suggest a brief and direct form of counseling in which a young expectant mother could come to grips with her feelings. If the incipient child has been sanctified by its mother, every effort must be made to help the two to achieve a stable and hopeful life together; if it has not, it should be removed swiftly and mercifully with all loving attention to the woman, the conscious patient. Between these two clear reactions is a possible confused one: the young woman is not sure how she feels. The one-caring probes gently to see what has been considered, raising questions and retreating when the questions obviously have been considered and are now causing great pain. Is such a view "unprincipled"? If it is, it is boldly so; it is at least connected with the world as it is, at its best and at its worst, and it requires that we—in espousing a "best"— stand ready to actualize that preferred condition. The decision for or against abortion must be made by those directly involved in the concrete situation, but it need not be made alone. The one-caring cannot require everyone to behave as she would in a particular situation. Rather, when she dares to say, "I think you should do X," she adds, also, "Can I help you?" The one under her gaze is under her support and not her judgment.

One under the guidance of an ethic of caring is tempted to retreat to a manageable world. Her public life is limited by her insistence upon meeting the other as one-caring. So long as this is possible, she may reach outward and enlarge her circles of caring. When this reaching out destroys or drastically reduces her actual caring, she retreats and renews her contact with those who address her. If the retreat becomes a flight, an avoidance of the call to care, her ethical ideal is diminished. Similarly, if the retreat is away from human beings and toward other objects of caring—ideas, animals, humanity-at-large, God—her ethical ideal is virtually shattered. This is not a judgment, for we can understand and sympathize with one who makes such a choice. It is more in the nature of a perception: we see clearly what has been lost in the choice.

Our ethic of caring—which we might have called a "feminine ethic"—begins to look a bit mean in contrast to the masculine ethics of universal love or universal justice. But universal love is illusion. Under the illusion, some young people retreat to the church to worship that which they

cannot actualize; some write lovely poetry extolling universal love; and some, in terrible disillusion, kill to establish the very principles which should have entreated them not to kill. Thus are lost both principles and persons.

## Right and Wrong

How are we to make judgments of right and wrong under this ethic? First, it is important to understand that we are not primarily interested in judging but, rather, in heightening moral perception and sensitivity. But "right" and "wrong" can be useful.

Suppose a mother observes her young child pulling the kitten's tail or picking it up by the ears. She may exclaim, "Oh, no, it is not nice to hurt the kitty," or, "You must not hurt the kitty." Or she may simply say, "Stop. See—you are hurting the kitty," and she may then take the kitten in her own hands and show the child how to handle it. She holds the kitten gently, stroking it, and saying, "See? Ah, ah, kitty, nice kitty. . . ." What the mother is supposing in this interaction is that the realization that his act is hurting the kitten, supplemented by the knowledge of how to avoid inflicting hurt, will suffice to change the child's behavior. If she believes this, she has no need for the statement, "It is wrong to hurt the kitty." She is not threatening sanctions but drawing dual attention to a matter of fact (the hurting) and her own commitment (I will not hurt). Beyond this, she is supposing that her child, well-cared-for himself, does not want to inflict pain.

Now, I am not claiming through use of this illustration that moral statements are mere expressions of approval or disapproval, although they do serve an expressive function. . . .

But is this all we can say about right and wrong? Is there not a firm foundation in morality for our legal judgments? Surely, we must be allowed to say, for example, that stealing is wrong and is, therefore, properly forbidden by law. Because it is so often wrong—and so easily demonstrated to be wrong—under an ethic of caring, we may accede that such a law has its roots *partly* in morality. We may legally punish one who has stolen, but we may not pass moral judgment on him until we know why he stole. An ethic of caring is likely to be stricter in its judgment, but more supportive and corrective in following up its judgment, than ethics otherwise grounded. For the one-caring, stealing is almost always wrong:

Ms. A talks with her young son. *But, Mother,* the boy pleads, *suppose I want to make you happy and I steal something you want from a big chain store. I haven't hurt anyone, have I?* Yes, *you have,* responds his mother, and she points to the predicament of the store managers who may be accused of poor stewardship and to the higher prices suffered by their neighbors. *Well, suppose I steal from a rich, rich person? He can replace what I take easily, and . . . Wait,* says Ms. A. *Is someone suffering? Are you stealing to relieve that suffering, and will you make certain that what you steal is used to relieve it . . . But can't I steal to make someone happy?* her son persists. Slowly, patiently, Ms. A explains the position of one-caring. *Each one* who comes under our gaze must be met as one-caring. When I want to please X and I turn toward Y as a means for satisfying my desire to please X, I must now meet Y as one-caring. I do not judge him for being rich—for treasuring what I, perhaps, regard with indifference. I may not cause him pain by taking or destroying what he possesses. *But what if I steal from a bad guy—someone who stole to get what he has?* Ms. A smiles at her young son, struggling to avoid his ethical responsibility: *Unless he is an immediate threat to you or someone else, you must meet him, too, as one-caring.*

The lessons in "right" and "wrong" are hard lessons—not swiftly accomplished by setting up as an objective the learning of some principle. We do not say: It is wrong to steal. Rather, we consider why it was wrong or may be wrong in this case to steal. We do not say: It is wrong to kill. By setting up such a principle, we also imply its exceptions, and then we may too easily act on authorized exceptions. The one-caring wants to consider, and wants her child to consider, the act

itself in full context. She will send him into the world skeptical, vulnerable, courageous, disobedient, and tenderly receptive. The "world" may not depend upon him to obey its rules or fulfill its wishes, but you, the individual he encounters, may depend upon him to meet you as one-caring. . . .

Ms. A recounts an experience she had as a graduate student. The time was the late sixties, a time of antiwar sentiment and strong feeling for civil rights at home. A problem concerning the rights and education of blacks arose, and the only black student in class spoke eloquently of the prevailing injustice and inhumanity against blacks, of his growing despair. He spoke of "going to the barricade." Ms. A was nearly moved to tears. He was clearly right in condemning the treatment of his people and in demanding something better. But the barricade, guns, violence—must it come to this? Perhaps. But if it does, what then: what would I do? Ms. A asked. She saw clearly what she would do, would really do. I could not, she said, ever—not ever oppose my bigoted old father or my hysterical Aunt Phoebe with physical violence. I do not agree with either. Aunt Phoebe! Imagine a person in this day who would actually say (and demonstrate her statement by fainting at the thought) "Ah would just die if a niggah touched me!" Oh, she is wrong, and my father is wrong. But there are years of personal kindness. They must count for something, must they not? My father and the delight in his eyes as he shared *my* delight with a new bicycle; Aunt Phoebe staying up half the night to refashion a prom dress for me; the chocolate cakes for parties; the cold cloths and baking soda pastes for measles. Would I shoot them? Ever? No. You see, if it came to the barricades, and I had to be on this side or that, I would stand beside my dad and Aunt Phoebe. Oh, I would curse them, and try to undo it, and try to bring peace, but I would fight to protect them. I know I could not fight—really fight on the other side. And what now of the black man, Jim, who is, after all, "right"? If my sights picked him out, says Ms. A, I would note that it was Jim and pass on to some other target.

## Notes

1. David Hume, "An Enquiry Concerning the Principles of Morals," in *Ethical Theories,* ed. A. I. Melden (Englewood Cliffs, N.J.: Prentice-Hall, Inc., (1967), p. 275.

2. Friedrich Nietzsche, "Mixed Opinions and Maxims," in *The Portable Nietzsche,* ed. by Walter Kaufmann (New York: The Viking Press. Inc., 1954), p. 65.

3. Friedrich Nietzsche, *The Will to Power,* trans. Walter Kaufmann (New York: Random House, 1967), pp. 476, 670.

## 26    Gilligan and Kohlberg: Implications for Moral Theory*

### LAWRENCE A. BLUM

Carol Gilligan's body of work in moral development psychology is of the first importance for moral philosophy.[1] At the same time certain philosophical commitments within contemporary ethics constitute obstacles to appreciating this importance. Some of these commitments are shared by Lawrence Kohlberg, whose work provided the context for Gilligan's early (though not current) work. I will discuss some of the implicit and explicit philosophical differences between Gilligan's and Kohlberg's outlooks and will then defend Gilligan's views against criticisms which, drawing on categories of contemporary ethical theory, a Kohlbergian can and does make of them.

Gilligan claims empirical support for the existence of a moral outlook or orientation distinct from one based on impartiality, impersonality, justice, formal rationality, and universal principle. This *impartialist* conception of morality, as I will call it,[2] in addition to characterizing Kohlberg's view of morality, has been the dominant conception of morality in contemporary Anglo-American moral philosophy, forming the core of both a Kantian conception of morality and important

Reprinted with permission of the publisher, University of Chicago Press, from *Ethics,* 98 (1988), 472–491.

*A portion of this paper was originally delivered at the twentieth annual Chapel Hill colloquium, University of North Carolina, Chapel Hill, North Carolina, October 1986, as a comment on Carol Gilligan's (and Grant Wiggins's) "The Origins of Morality in Early Childhood Relationships." I wish to thank Owen Flanagan and Marcia Lind for comments on an earlier draft, and the editors of *Ethics* for comments on a later one.

strands in utilitarian (and, more generally, consequentialist) thinking as well.

Recently impartialism has come under attack from several quarters. Bernard Williams's well-known critique takes it to task for leaving insufficient room for considerations of personal integrity and, more broadly, for the legitimacy of purely personal concerns.[3] Thomas Nagel, though rejecting Williams's general skepticism regarding impartialist morality's claim on our practical deliberations, follows Williams's criticism of impartialism; Nagel argues that personal as well as impersonal (or impartial) concerns are legitimate as reason-generating considerations.[4]

Gilligan's critique of Kohlberg and of an impartialist conception of morality is not at odds with these criticisms of impartialism, but it is importantly distinct from them. For personal concerns are seen by Nagel and Williams as legitimate not so much from the standpoint of *morality,* but from the broader standpoint of practical reason. By contrast Gilligan argues—drawing on the conceptions of morality held by many of her largely (but by no means exclusively) female respondents—that care and responsibility within personal relationships constitute an important element of morality itself, genuinely distinct from impartiality. For Gilligan each person is embedded within a web of ongoing relationships, and morality importantly if not exclusively consists in attention to, understanding of, and emotional responsiveness toward the individuals with whom one stands in these relationships. (Gilligan means this web to encompass all human beings and not only one's circle of acquaintances. But how this extension to all persons is to be accomplished is not made clear in her writings, and much of Gilligan's empirical work is centered on the domain of personal relations and acquaintances.) Nagel's and Williams's notions of the personal domain do not capture or encompass (though Nagel and Williams sometimes imply that they are meant to) the phenomena of care and responsibility within personal relationships and do not explain why care and responsibility in relationships are distinctively moral phenomena.[5]

Thus Gilligan's critique of Kohlberg raises substantial questions for moral philosophy. If there is a "different voice"—a coherent set of moral concerns distinct both from the objective and the subjective, the impersonal and the purely personal—then moral theory will need to give some place to these concerns.

Gilligan does not suggest that care and responsibility are to be seen either as *replacing* impartiality as a basis of morality or as encompassing *all* of morality, as if all moral concerns could be translated into ones of care and responsibility. Rather, Gilligan holds that there is an appropriate place for impartiality, universal principle, and the like within morality and that a final mature morality involves a complex interaction and dialogue between the concerns of impartiality and those of personal relationship and care.[6]

## Kohlberg and Gilligan: The Major Differences

One can draw from Gilligan's work seven differences between her view of morality and Kohlberg's impartialist conception. The subsequent discussion will explore the nature and significance of these apparent differences.

1. For Gilligan the moral self is radically situated and particularized. It is "thick" rather than "thin," defined by its historical connections and relationships. The moral agent does not attempt to abstract from this particularized self, to achieve,

as Kohlberg advocates, a totally impersonal standpoint defining *the* "moral point of view." For Gilligan, care morality is about the particular agent's caring for and about the particular friend or child with whom she has come to have this particular relationship. Morality is not (only) about how the impersonal "one" is meant to act toward the impersonal "other." In regard to its emphasis on the radically situated self, Gilligan's view is akin to Alasdair MacIntyre's (*After Virtue*) and Michael Sandel's (*Liberalism and the Limits of Justice*).[7]

2. For Gilligan, not only is the self radically particularized, but so is the other, the person toward whom one is acting and with whom one stands in some relationship. The moral agent must understand the other person as the specific individual that he or she is, not merely as someone instantiating general moral categories such as friend or person in need. Moral action which fails to take account of this particularity is faulty and defective. While Kohlberg does not and need not deny that there is an irreducible particularity in our affective relationships with others, he sees this particularity only as a matter of personal attitude and affection, not relevant to morality itself. For him, as, implicitly, for a good deal of current moral philosophy, the moral significance of persons as the objects of moral concern is solely as bearers of morally significant but entirely general and repeatable characteristics.

Putting contrasts 1 and 2 together we can say that for Gilligan but not for Kohlberg moral action itself involves an irreducible particularity—a particularity of the agent, the other, and the situation.

3. Gilligan shares with Iris Murdoch (*The Sovereignty of Good*) the view that achieving knowledge of the particular other person toward whom one acts is an often complex and difficult moral task and one which draws on specifically moral capacities.[8] Understanding the needs, interests, and welfare of another person, and understanding the relationship between oneself and that other requires a stance toward that person informed by care, love, empathy, compassion, and emotional sensitivity. It involves, for example, the ability to see the other as different in important ways from

oneself, as a being existing in her own right, rather than viewing her through a simple projection of what one would feel if one were in her situation. Kohlberg's view follows a good deal of current moral philosophy in ignoring this dimension of moral understanding, thus implying that knowledge of individual others is a straightforwardly empirical matter requiring no particular moral stance toward the person.

4. Gilligan's view emphasizes the self as, in Michael Sandel's terms, "encumbered." She rejects the contrasting metaphor in Kohlberg, drawn from Kant, in which morality is ultimately a matter of the individual rational being legislating for himself and obeying laws or principles generated solely from within himself (i.e., from within his own reason). Gilligan portrays the moral agent as approaching the world of action bound by ties and relationships (friend, colleague, parent, child) which confront her as, at least to some extent, givens. These relationships, while subject to change, are not wholly of the agent's own making and thus cannot be pictured on a totally voluntarist or contractual model. In contrast to Kohlberg's conception, the moral agent is not conceived of as radically autonomous (though this is not to deny that there exists a less individualistic, less foundational, and less morality-generating sense of autonomy which does accord with Gilligan's conception of moral agency).

A contrast between Gilligan's and Sandel's conception of encumbrance, however, is that for Sandel the self's encumbrances are forms of communal identity, such as being a member of this or that nation, religious or ethnic group, class, neighborhood; whereas for Gilligan the encumbrances are understood more in terms of the concrete persons to whom one stands in specific relationships—being the father of Sarah, the teacher of Maureen, the brother of Jeff, the friend of Alan and Charles. In that way Sandel's "encumbrances" are more abstract than Gilligan's.

5. For Kohlberg the mode of reasoning which generates principles governing right action involves formal rationality alone. Emotions play at most a remotely secondary role in both the derivation and motivation for moral action.[9]

For Gilligan, by contrast, morality necessarily involves an intertwining of emotion, cognition, and action, not readily separable. Knowing what to do involves knowing others and being connected in ways involving both emotion and cognition. Caring action expresses emotion and understanding.

6. For Kohlberg principles of right action are universalistic, applicable to all. Gilligan rejects the notion that an action appropriate to a given individual is necessarily (or needs to be regarded by the agent as) universal, or generalizable to others. And thus she at least implicitly rejects, in favor of a wider notion of "appropriate response," a conception of "right action" which carries this universalistic implication. At the same time Gilligan's view avoids the individual subjectivism and relativism which is often seen as the only alternative to a view such as Kohlberg's; for Gilligan sees the notions of care and responsibility as providing nonsubjective standards by which appropriateness of response can be appraised in the particular case. It is a standard which allows one to say that a certain thing was the appropriate action for a particular individual to take, but not necessarily that it was the 'right' action for anyone in that situation.

7. For Gilligan morality is founded in a sense of concrete connection and direct response between persons, a direct sense of connection which exists prior to moral beliefs about what is right or wrong or which principles to accept. Moral action is meant to express and to sustain those connections to particular other people. For Kohlberg the ultimate moral concern is with morality itself—with morally right action and principle; moral responsiveness to others is mediated by adherence to principle.

## Impartialist Rejoinders to Gilligan

Faced with Gilligan's challenge to have found in her respondents a distinct moral orientation roughly defined by these seven contrasts, let us look at how Kohlberg, and defenders of impartialist morality more generally, do or might respond to this challenge. Eight alternative positions regarding the relation between impartial morality and a morality of care in personal relations suggest themselves.

1. Position 1 denies that the care orientation constitutes a genuinely distinct moral orientation from impartialism. Strictly speaking there is no such thing as a morality of care. Acting from care is actually acting on perhaps complex but nevertheless fully universalizable principles, generated ultimately from an impartial point of view.[10]

2. Position 2 says that, while care for others in the context of relationships may constitute a genuinely distinct set of concerns or mode of thought and motivation from that found in impartialist morality, and while these can be deeply important to individuals' lives, nevertheless such concerns are not moral but only personal ones. My caring for my friend David is important to me, but actions which flow directly from it are in that respect without moral significance.

Position 2 treats concerns with relationships as *personal* or *subjective* ones, in Nagel's and Williams's sense. Such a view is implied in Kohlberg's earlier and better-known work,[11] where impartialism was held to define the whole of (at least the highest and most mature form of) morality and to exclude, at least by implication, relational or care considerations. In his most recent work, replying to Gilligan, Kohlberg claims to have abandoned this consignment of care in personal relations to an entirely nonmoral status; but this view nevertheless continues to surface in his writing.[12]

In contrast to positions 1 and 2, the remaining views all accord, or at least allow for, some distinct moral significance to care.

3. Position 3 claims that concerns of care and responsibility in relationships are truly moral (and not merely personal) concerns and acknowledges them as genuinely distinct from impartiality, but it claims that they are nevertheless secondary to, parasitic on, and/or less significant a part of morality than considerations of impartiality, right, universal principle, and the like. Kohlberg makes three distinct suggestions falling under this rubric. (*a*) Our personal attachments to others intensify our sense of the dignity of other persons, a sense of dignity which is ultimately grounded in an impartialist outlook. Thus the husband's love for his wife intensifies and brings home to him more vividly her right to life, shared by all persons. (*b*) In a different vein, Kohlberg says that impartialism defines the central and most significant part of morality—what is obligatory and required—whereas the area of personal relationships is supererogatory, going beyond what is required. The demands of justice must be satisfied, but action on behalf of friends, family, and the like, while good and even perhaps admirable, is not required. Thus care is, so to speak, morally dependent on right and justice, whereas impartiality, right, and justice are not morally dependent on care. (*c*) The development of care is psychologically dependent on the sense of justice or right, but not vice versa.[13]

Position 3 differs from position 2 in granting some moral status to the concerns of relationship; care for friends is not only personally important but, given that one has satisfied all of one's impersonal demands, can be morally admirable as well.

4. Position 4 says that care is genuinely moral and constitutes a moral orientation distinct from impartiality, but it is an *inferior* form of morality precisely because it is not grounded in universal principle. On the previous view (3), the concerns of a care morality lie outside the scope of impartialist morality and are less significant for that very reason. In 4, by contrast, a care morality and an impartialist one cover, at least to some extent, the same territory; the same actions are prescribed by both. I may help out a friend in need out of direct concern for my friend; this action has some moral value, but the action is also prescribed by some principle, stemming ultimately from an impersonal perspective. And it is better to act from impartial principle than care because, for example, impartial morality ensures consistency and reliability more than care or because impartialism is (thought to be) wider in scope than is care morality (covering impersonal as well as personal situations). So on view 4, acting out of direct care for a friend has some moral value but not as much as if the action stems from a firm and general principle, say, one of aid to friends.

This view might naturally regard the morality of care as a stage along the way to a more mature impartialist morality, and such a construal is suggested in some of Kohlberg's earlier writings, where care responses are treated and scored as "conventional" morality (in contrast to the more developed "postconventional" morality)—as conforming to social expectations of "being good."

Position 4 is importantly different from positions 1 and 2. For position 4, even though all the demands of a care morality can be met by impartialist morality, still a moral agent could in general or in some set of circumstances be animated by care morality entirely independent of impartialist morality. For positions 1 and 2 there is no such thing as a morality of care independent of impartialist morality.

5. Position 5 acknowledges a difference between care and impartiality but sees this as a difference in the objects of moral assessment; care morality is concerned with evaluation of persons, motives, and character, while impartialist morality concerns the evaluation of acts.[14]

6. In position 6, considerations of an impartialist right set side constraints within which, but only within which, care considerations are allowed to guide our conduct. Considerations of impartiality trump considerations stemming from care; if the former conflict with the latter, it is care which must yield. If out of love for my daughter I want her to be admitted into a certain school, nevertheless, I may not violate just procedures in order to accomplish this. However, once I have satisfied impartialist moral requirements in the situation I am allowed to act from motives of care.

Such a view is found in recent defenses of a neo-Kantian position by Barbara Herman, Onora O'Neill, Stephen Darwall, and Marcia Baron.[15] And these writers generally see this view as implying view 3, that care is a less important element of morality than is impartiality. However, this implication holds only on the further assumption that considerations of impartial "rightness" are present in all situations. But many situations which involve care for friends, family, and the like seem devoid of demands of justice and impartiality altogether. In such situations care is the more significant consideration. And if such situations constitute a substantial part of our lives, then even if impartialist morality were a side constraint on care—even if it were granted that when the two conflict the claims of impartiality always take precedence—it would not follow from this that impartially derived rightness is more significant, important, or fundamental a part of morality than care. For in such situations care will be operating on its own, no considerations of impartiality being present to constrain it.[16]

Thus by itself the side-constraint view of the relation between impartiality and care seems to leave open the possibility that a morality of care is a central element in a morally responsible life. In this way, view 6 is weaker as a critique of Gilligan than the previous five views (except perhaps 5), all of which relegate care to an inferior, subsidiary, or nonexistent (moral) role. It is only with the additional, implausible, assumption that impartialist moral considerations apply in all situations that 6 implies 3.

But it might be thought that no defender of a Kantian-like view in ethics would accord such legitimacy and allow such importance to a non-rationalist, non-principle-based dimension of morality as I am construing in position 6. Let us examine this. As an interpretation of Kant, this neo-Kantian, side-constraint view (of O'Neill, Herman, and others) sees the categorical imperative essentially as a tester, rather than a generator, of maxims; the original source of maxims is allowed to lie in desires. This view rejects a traditional understanding of Kant in which moral principles of action are themselves derived from pure reason alone.

Nevertheless, such an interpretation leaves ambiguous the moral status accorded to the different desires which are to serve as the basis of maxims. The categorical imperative can, on this view, declare a desire only to be permissible or impermissible. But if we compare compassion for a friend or care for a child with a desire for an ice cream cone, or for food if one is hungry, then, even if both are permissible inclinations (in some particular situation), the compassion seems more morally significant in its own right than the desire for ice cream.

If the neo-Kantian admits this difference in the moral status of desires, she is then left with acknowledging a source of moral significance (the value of compassion compared with the desire for ice cream for oneself) which is not itself accounted for by the (neo-)Kantian perspective itself, but only bounded by it; and this is the position 6 discussed here—that care in personal relations does constitute a distinct dimension of morality, alongside, and subject to the constraints of, impartialist considerations of right.

To avoid this slide to position 6, the neo-Kantian can accept a moral distinction between types of permissible desires but attempt to account for this distinction in some kind of Kantian way—for example, by seeing the greater moral value of some desires (e.g., compassion) as a reflection of respect for rational agency, or of treating others as ends in themselves, or something along that line.[17] A different move would be to bite the bullet of denying, as Kant himself seems to have done (in the notion that "all inclinations are on the same level"), any moral difference between a permissible compassion and a permissible desire to eat ice cream. Whether either of these incompatible positions is itself persuasive is a question that I cannot take up here.

The point of this excursus is to suggest that if one sees the thrust of impartialist morality as setting side constraints on the pursuit of other concerns, such as care in personal relations, it will be difficult to avoid view 6, in which care in personal relationships is accorded some moral significance, and a moral significance which cannot be systematically relegated to a status inferior to that of impartiality.

7. Position 7 claims that, while care considerations are distinct from universal principle and impartiality and while they are genuinely moral, nevertheless their ultimate acceptability or justifiability rests on their being able to be validated or affirmed from an impartial perspective.

This view distinguishes the level of practical deliberation from that of ultimate justification and sees the level of deliberation (in this case, care in personal relationships) as taking a different form from that provided by the standard of justification (that is, impartiality). On view 7, from an impartial and universal standpoint one can see how it is appropriate and good that people sometimes act directly from care rather than from impartialist considerations.

This view is distinct from view 1 in that there care considerations were held to be really nothing but considerations of universal principle, perhaps with some nonmoral accoutrements, such as emotions and feelings. Unlike views 1 and 2, view 7 acknowledges that care is (part of) a genuinely distinct form of moral consciousness, stemming from a different source than does impartialism and not reducible to it. Impartiality gives its stamp of approval to care but does not directly generate it; care thus does not reflect impartiality.

View 7 is weaker than view 6 as an assertion of the priority of impartiality over care. It does not, for example, claim that impartialist considerations always trump care ones but allows the possibility that care might in some circumstances legitimately outweigh considerations of impartiality. It allows the possibility that, on the level of deliberation and of the agent's moral consciousness, care would play as central a role as impartiality. The superiority of impartiality to care is claimed to lie merely in the fact that, even when the claims of care are stronger than those of impartiality, it is ultimately only an impartial perspective which tells us this.

Position 7 sees impartiality as more fundamental to morality than care because it is impartiality which ultimately justifies or legitimizes care. Yet this view seems an extremely weak version of impartialism; for unlike positions 1 through 4 (and perhaps 5 and 6), it is compatible with Gilligan's own claim that the care mode of morality legitimately plays as significant and central a role in the morally mature adult's life as does the impartialist mode. View 7 does not even require the moral agent herself to be an impartialist, as long as the mixture of care and impartialist considerations which animate her life can in fact be approved of from an impartial point of view.[18]

8. A final position bears mentioning because it is prominent in Kohlberg's writings. This is that the final, most mature stage of moral reasoning involves an "integration of justice and care that forms a single moral principle."[19] This formulation taken in its own right—according care and justice equal status—does not really belong in our taxonomy, which is meant to cover only views which make impartiality in some way more fundamental to morality than care.[20] In fact, Kohlberg does not spell out this integration of care and justice, and the general tenor of his work makes it clear that he regards care as very much the junior partner in whatever interplay is meant to obtain between the two moral perspectives. So that, it seems fair to say, Kohlberg's understanding of the position mentioned here actually collapses it into one of the previous ones.[21]

In assessing both Gilligan's claim to have articulated a distinct voice within morality and the impartialist's response to this claim, it is important to know which counterclaim is being advanced. These eight views are by no means merely complementary to each other. The earlier views are much more dismissive of the moral claims of care in personal relationship than are the latter. It is an important confusion in Kohlberg's work that he attempts to occupy at least positions 2, 3, 4, 6, and 8, without seeming to be aware that these are by no means the same, or even compatible, philosophical positions. (On the other hand, there is a noteworthy tentativeness in some of Kohlberg's formulations in the volumes I have drawn on, which suggests that he was not certain that he had yet found an entirely satisfactory response to Gilligan.)

Before taking on some of these impartialist responses, the connections between such an inquiry and the controversy between virtue ethics and Kantian or utilitarian ethics bears some comment. Some of the seven contrasts drawn between Gilligan's and impartialist views characterize as well the contrast between a virtue-based ethic and its rivals; and some of the impartialist counterarguments against these contrasts are ones which are directed against virtue theory. Nevertheless, it should not be thought that all of the concerns of a moral outlook or sensibility grounded in care and relationship can be encompassed within what currently goes by the name of virtue theory. And the converse of this is true also; as Flanagan and Jackson point out,[22] attention to some of the concerns of virtue theory, for example, an exploration of some of the different psychological capacities contributing to a lived morality of care in relationships, would enrich the care approach.

Moreover, while Gilligan herself points to the existence of two distinct moral voices, once having questioned and rejected the notion of a single unitary account of the moral point of view, one might well question further why there need be only two psychologically and philosophically distinct moral voices. Why not three, or five? I would myself suggest that, even taken together, care and impartiality do not encompass all there is to morality. Other moral phenomena—a random selection might include community, honesty, courage, prudence—while perhaps not constituting full and comprehensive moral orientations, are nevertheless not reducible to (though also not necessarily incompatible with) care and impartiality. A satisfactory picture of moral maturity or moral excellence or virtue will have to go beyond the, admittedly large, territory encompassed by care and impartiality.

## The Moral Value of Care: Response to Impartialist Positions 1 and 2

The foregoing, largely taxonomic discussion is meant primarily to lay out the conceptual territory in which the various impartialist responses to the claims of personal care in morality can be evaluated. A full discussion of views 1 through 7 is impossible, and I would like to focus most fully on positions 1 and 2, which most forcefully and conclusively deny that there is anything morally and philosophically distinct in the morality of care. Building on these arguments, I will conclude with briefer discussions of views 3 through 7.

Position 1 denies the contrast, drawn in points 1 and 2, between the particularity involved in Gilligan's perspective and the universalism of Kohlberg's; position 2 asserts that, whatever there is to such a distinction, it is without moral significance. Position 1 claims that, when a moral agent acts from care for another, her action is governed by and generated from universal principle derived from an impartial point of view. This means more than that there merely exists some principle which prescribes the action in question as right; for that is the claim made in position 4 and will be discussed below. The mere existence of a governing principle would be compatible with the agent's action conforming to that principle by sheer accident; she could, for example, perform an action of aiding as prescribed by some duty of beneficence but do so for a wholly self-centered reason. There would be no moral value in such an action. What position 1 requires is that the agent who is acting from (what she regards as) care be drawing on, or making at least implicit use of, such an impartialist principle.

Both views 1 and 2 imply that what it is to be a morally responsible person—say, within the domain of personal relations—is captured by the conception of an agent coming to hold, and acting according to, universal principles. Let us approach this claim by considering some principles which might be considered universal and impartial and which might be thought to be applicable in the domain of personal relations, such as "Be loyal to friends," "Nurture one's children," and "Protect children from harm." Each particular morally right or good act within an agent's role (as friend, as parent) would be (according to this claim) prescribed by some such principle, which applies to anyone occupying the role and which is in that sense universal.[23] Benefiting the particular friend or child will then be an

application of universal principle to a specific situation governed by it.

Yet while it may be true that, say, a father will regard himself as accepting general principles of protecting and nurturing his children, it does not follow that applying those universal principles is all that is involved morally in protecting and nurturing his children. I want to argue that what it takes to bring such principles to bear on individual situations involves qualities of character and sensibilities which are themselves moral and which go beyond the straightforward process of consulting a principle and then conforming one's will and action to it. Specifically I will argue that knowing that the particular situation which the agent is facing is one which calls for the particular principle in question and knowing how to apply the principle in question are capacities which, in the domain of personal relations (and perhaps elsewhere too), are intimately connected with care for individual persons. Such particularized, caring understanding is integral to an adequate meeting of the agent's moral responsibilities and cannot be generated from universal principle alone.

Consider the general principle "Protect one's children from harm." Quite often it is only a parent's concerned and caring understanding of a particular child which tells her that the child's harm is at stake in a given situation and, thus, which tells her that the current situation is one in which the principle "Protect children from harm" is applicable. One adult viewing a scene of children playing in a park may simply not see that one child is being too rough with another and is in danger of harming the other child; whereas another adult, more attentive to the situation, and more sensitive about children's interaction, may see the potential danger and thus the need for intervention and protection. Both adults might hold the principle "Protect children from harm"; yet the second adult but not the first rightly sees the situation at hand as calling for that principle. Gilligan suggests that the sensitivity, caring, and attentiveness which leads the second adult to do so are moral qualities. This is supported by the foregoing argument, that such capacities are essential to the agent's being a morally responsible person in the way which the principles in question are meant to articulate.[24]

In addition, care for particular persons often plays a role in knowing *how* to apply a principle to a situation, even once one knows that the situation calls for it. In order to know what it is to nurture, to care, to protect (his children) from harm, a father must take into account the particular children that his children are, the particular relationships that have evolved between himself and them, and the particular understandings and expectations implicit in those relationships. For example, suppose a father has to decide whether and how to deal with a situation in which his daughter has hit her younger brother. He must take into account what various actions, coming from himself in particular, would mean to each of them. Would his intervention serve to undermine (either of) his children's ability to work out problems between themselves? Would punishing his daughter contribute to a pattern of seeming favoritism toward the son which she has complained of recently? How might each of the children's self-esteem and moral development be affected by the various options of action open to him?

The father's knowing the answers to these questions requires caring about his children in a way which appreciates and manifests an understanding of each one as an individual child and human being, and of each of their relationship to each other and to himself. Such a particularized caring knowledge of his children is required in order to recognize how the various courses of action available to the father will bear on their harm in the situation. Merely holding or averring the principles "Protect one's children from harm" or "Nurture one's children" does not by itself tell one what constitutes harm (and thus protection and nurturance) in regard to individual children and in a given situation.

So it is no support to the impartialist view to assert that the role of particularity in moral action lies in the application of general role-principles to the particular case; for, I have argued, that

process of application itself draws on moral capacities not accounted for by impartialism alone. Both knowledge of the situation and knowledge of what action the principle itself specifies in the situation are as much part of accomplishing the impartialist's own goal of acting according to the principle as is the intellectual task of generating or discovering the principle. Yet they are tasks which cannot be accounted for by an impartialist perspective alone.

I suggest then that both universality and particularistic care play a role in morally responsible action within personal relationships. Remember (see above) that it is no part of Gilligan's view to advocate *replacing* a concern for impartiality with care in personal relationships. If so, then acknowledging some role for universal principle even in the domain of personal relationships does not lead one to positions 1 or 2, which leave no distinct moral role for care in personal relations at all.[25]

Nevertheless, the foregoing argument should not be taken to imply that all morally good action within personal relationships does in fact involve application of universal principle; my argument has been only that even when it does it often requires some care for particular persons as well. But one can certainly imagine individually worthy actions of friendship or parenthood which are animated not by a sense of applying principle but by a direct care for the friend or child. This can even be (though it is not always) true of unreflective and spontaneous impulses of care. But in addition, care which is direct and unmediated by principle need not be unintelligent, impulsive, or unreflective; it can be guided by intelligent attention to the particular friend's or child's good, yet not be derived from universal principles regarding children or friends in general.[26]

If care in personal relations is granted to be of moral significance, both as an integral part of what it is for one's life to be informed by certain principles of responsible friendship, parenthood, and the like, as well as in its own right, then we must reject both position 1—that there is no difference between care and universal, impartial principle—and position 2—that while there may be a difference it is of no moral significance.[27]

## Is Care a Universal Principle?

One can imagine the following response to my argument against positions 1 and 2: "All right. One can acknowledge that specific relationships are central to the moral life of the individual and that, therefore, care for specific persons in its various modes of kindness, friendship, compassion, and the like are important human qualities which have a claim on being considered moral. Furthermore, one can admit that a moral decision procedure characterized by strict impartiality cannot be made to generate all the forms of moral response appropriate to this domain of morality.

"Nevertheless, in acting from love, care, compassion, is the moral agent not acting from some kind of 'principle'? Does not Gilligan want to say that everyone should be kind and caring, responsible to those to whom they are connected? Is she not saying we should all follow the principle, 'Be responsible within one's particular relationships,'" or even 'Be sensitive to particulars'? If so, is she not therefore proposing a morality which is meant to be universal, indeed to be based on universal principle?"

This objection is useful in bringing out that in one important sense a morality of care is meant to be a morality for all. It is not a relativistic morality in the sense of applying to some but not others or of being confined to one particular group.[28] However, the objection presents itself as if it were a defense of the strongest impartialist view, namely, position 1 (or perhaps position 2). Yet the notion of "universal principle" in the objection has moved entirely away from the sense in which universal principle is meant to *contrast* with a morality of personal care. It has become a notion which encompasses emotional response and which acknowledges that moral action—acting according to that principle—requires a care for particular persons which cannot be exhaustively codified

into universal principles. In that sense it is a notion of "universal principle" which has abandoned the pure rationalism, the pure impartiality, and the sense that adherence to universal principle alone (perhaps together with a strong will) is sufficient to characterize the moral psychology of Kohlberg's maturely moral agent. It acknowledges that other moral capacities, involving perception and sensitivity to particulars and care and concern for individual persons, are equally central to moral agency. Such a view no longer involves a critique of a particularistic morality of care in relationships.

## Response to Impartialist Views 3 through 7

Positions 3 through 7 will be considered more briefly. But first, one more point about position 2. Suppose it were replied to the argument of the previous section that the capacities of care, sensitivity to particular persons, and the like, may be good, and perhaps even necessary for the application of moral principle, but—precisely because they are not themselves a reflection of universal principle, impartiality, rationality, and the like—they are not themselves moral.

Naturally if 'moral' is defined in terms of impartiality, then anything outside of impartiality—even what is a necessary condition of it—is excluded. But then no independent argument will have been given as to why such a definition should be accepted.[29]

Let us consider position 3 in light of Kohlberg's suggestion that care in personal relations be seen as "supererogatory" and therefore secondary to or less significant than impartialist morality. 'Supererogatory' can mean different things. If supererogatory is taken to imply "having greater merit," then those who exemplify care would have greater merit than those who merely fulfilled obligations. In that case it would be hard to see why that which is supererogatory would have less importance than that which is merely obligatory.

On the other hand, if "supererogation" implies strictly "going beyond (impartial) duty" (with no implication of superior merit), then it seems implausible to see care in personal relations as supererogatory. For there would be no duties of the personal sort which acting from care within personal relations involves doing more of, since duties would all be impartialist. Yet if duties (or obligations) of personal relationship are countenanced, then, leaving aside questions about whether these can in fact be encompassed within an impartialist framework (see n. 25 above), it becomes implausible to regard all forms of care as going beyond these; for one thing, many caring actions can themselves be acts which are in fact obligatory. Out of care I may do something for a friend which I am in fact obliged to do anyway. But also many acts of friendship, familial care, and the like seem outside the territory of obligation altogether rather than involving more of the fulfillment of obligation.[30]

Finally, if supererogation is taken more generally to refer to that which is (morally) good but not required, with no implication either of superior merit or of going beyond duty, then it seems contentious to relegate that which is supererogatory to a less significant domain of morality than that governed by impartial obligations. That (on this view) impartialist obligations are *requirements* while the supererogatory would not be, would mean only that one needed to satisfy the former first. This is the position taken in 6, and, as argued in the discussion of that view, nothing follows about which domain or orientation within morality is the more significant or valuable. For it can plausibly be argued that that which is (morally) good but not required casts a much wider net than the merely obligatory, and is, at least in that regard, a much more significant part of a typical human life.

View 4 says that, while care is distinct from impartiality and does have moral significance, it has less moral value than impartiality, which can also fully encompass all of its demands. The picture here is of a range of morally bidden acts, which are prescribed by both care and impartiality (though impartiality extends beyond this range as well).

First of all, it can be doubted whether all of the actions bidden by care morality can be seen as generated by principles of right or duty; as mentioned above, many caring actions seem outside the obligation structure altogether. But leaving this point aside, actions stemming from principles of right and acts stemming from care are not simply identical acts prompted by different motives. Leaving aside the problems of recognizing the situation as calling for the principle and knowing how to apply it (see above), it is also true, as suggested in the fifth contrast between Gilligan and Kohlberg, that within personal relations actions grounded in principle or duty alone will often not be seen by their recipients as expressing an attitude or emotion thought to be proper to that relationship. Thus while I can, out of adherence to a principle of aiding friends, do something to aid my friend, that action will not have entirely fulfilled what a fuller notion of friendship bids of me, which is to perform the action of aiding as an action expressing my care for my friend.[31] If emotionally expressive action is an integral part of appropriate behavior within personal relationships, then a philosophy grounded in rational principle alone will be importantly deficient in this domain and cannot be seen as superior to one of care.

View 5 regards a morality of care as concerning the evaluation of persons and impartialist morality as involving the evaluation of acts. This seems unsatisfactory in both directions. Most important, care morality is meant to encompass not only inner motives but outward acts, specifically, as argued immediately above, emotion-expressing acts. Care involves a way of responding to other persons and does not merely provide standards for the evaluation of agents. What is true of a morality of care, which view 5 may be pointing to, is that it rejects a sharp distinction between act and motive which would allow for a standard of act evaluation wholly separate from one of agent evaluation.[32]

Apart from what has been said in the presentation of those views, positions 6 and 7 raise philosophical issues beyond the scope of this paper.[33]

Nevertheless, as we noted in those discussions, neither of these views, as they stand, put forth a strong challenge to Gilligan's views or to a morality of care.

Finally, it might be felt that the impartialist counterpositions discussed in this paper have served to push some of the contrasts 1–7, discussed earlier in the paper, into the background. This seems true. At the outset I claimed that Gilligan's work is of the first importance for moral philosophy, and that pursuing its implications for an adequate moral theory will take one into territory not readily encompassed within the categories of contemporary ethics. This paper is meant only as a preliminary to that enterprise, clearing out of the way some of the intellectual obstacles within contemporary ethics to pursuing some of these more radical directions.[34]

## Notes

1. See esp. Carol Gilligan, "Do the Social Sciences Have an Adequate Theory of Moral Development?" in *Social Science as Moral Inquiry*, ed. N. Haan, R. Bellah, P. Rabinow, and W. Sullivan (New York: Columbia University Press, 1983). *In a Different Voice* (Cambridge, Mass.: Harvard University Press, 1982), "Remapping the Moral Domain: New Images of the Self in Relationship," in *Reconstructing Individualism: Autonomy, Individuality, and the Self in Western Thought*, ed. T. Heller, M. Sosna, and D. Wellbery (Stanford, Calif.: Stanford University Press, 1986), and the paper cited above from the twentieth annual Chapel Hill colloquium, which is to be published in *The Emergence of Morality in Young Children*, ed. J. Kagan and S. Lamb (Chicago: University of Chicago Press, 1988). See also Nona Plessner Lyons, "Two Perspectives: On Self, Relationships, and Morality," *Harvard Educational Review* 53 (1983): 125–45.

2. The notion of an "impartialist" outlook is drawn front Stephen Darwall, *Impartial Reason* (Ithaca, N.Y.: Cornell University Press, 1983).

3. See B. Williams, "A Critique of Utilitarianism," in *Utilitarianism: For and Against*, ed. B. Williams and J. J. C. Smart (Cambridge: Cambridge University Press, 1973), *Moral Luck* (Cambridge: Cambridge University Press, 1980), and *Ethics and the Limits of Philosophy* (Cambridge, Mass.: Harvard University Press, 1985).

4. Thomas Nagel, *The View from Nowhere* (New York: Oxford University Press, 1986).

5. A detailed argument for this point is given in my "Iris Murdoch and the Domain of the Moral," in *Philosophical Studies* 50 (1986): esp. 357–459.

6. This is perhaps a slightly oversimplified picture of Gilligan's views, as there is also some suggestion in her writings that there is a deep flaw present in the impartialist/rationalist approach to morality which is not present in the care/responsibility approach. One possible construal of Gilligan's view in light of this seeming ambiguity is that she rejects any notion of justice as (morally and psychologically) *fundamental* or foundational to other virtues—especially to care, compassion, and the like. And that she rejects a conception of justice which is dependent on purely individualistic assumptions such as are sometimes seen as underlying more "foundational" views of justice. On this reading Gilligan would, e.g., reject any notion of justice generated from something like Rawls's original position (though Rawls has recently argued that this individualistic characterization does not apply to his view; see John Rawls, "Justice as Fairness: Political Not Metaphysical," *Philosophy and Public Affairs* 14 [1985]: 223–51). Yet on this construal of Gilligan's views, she *would* accept a notion of justice which exists as one virtue among others, interacting with and no more fundamental than they. It is not clear how this acceptable, nonfoundational notion of justice is to be characterized in Gilligan's work. In her paper at the Chapel Hill colloquium she suggests that it is to be conceived as something like "protection against oppression." It is not clear whether, or how, this characterization is meant to connect with a nonfoundational notion of "fairness," e.g. (such as Michael Walzer describes in *Spheres of Justice* [Oxford: Basil Blackwell, 1983]).

7. Alasdair MacIntyre, *After Virtue*, 2d ed. (Notre Dame, Ind.: University of Notre Dame Press, 1984); Michael Sandel, *Liberalism and the Limits of Justice* (Cambridge: Cambridge University Press, 1982).

8. Iris Murdoch, *The Sovereignty of Good* (London: Routledge & Kegan Paul, 1970).

9. In "The Current Formulation of the Theory," in his *Essays on Moral Development* (New York: Harper & Row, 1984), vol. 2, p. 291, Lawrence Kohlberg says that his view is distinguished from Kant's in including a role for "affect as an integral component of moral judgment or justice reasoning." Despite this remark, Kohlberg's more frequently rationalistic characterizations of his views do not bear out this contention. What is true of Kohlberg, as we will see below, is that he sometimes allows a legitimacy to care (as involving emotion) as a moral phenomenon, though, as we will also see, he is not consistent in this acknowledgment. But even when he thus acknowledges care, Kohlberg almost always relegates it to a secondary or derivative moral status. In this regard it is not clear that Kohlberg's view is significantly different from Kant's who, at least in some of his writings (especially the *Doctrine of Virtue*), allowed a secondary place for emotions in morality.

10. Kohlberg has himself taken such a position in his article "A Reply to Owen Flanagan," in *Ethics* 92 (1982): 513–28; however, this view appears hardly at all in his most recent writings—*Essays in Moral Development*, vol.

2, *The Psychology of Moral Development* (San Francisco: Harper & Row, 1984)—in which he attempts to answer Gilligan's and others' criticisms. There are several minor variations on the view that care *is* impartiality. One is to say that impartialist philosophies have all along been cognizant of the special moral ties and claims involved in particular personal relationships and have mustered their resources to deal with these. (George Sher's "Other Voices, Other Rooms? Women's Psychology and Moral Theory," in *Women and Moral Theory*, ed. E. Kittay and D. Meyers [Totowa, N.J.: Rowman & Littlefield, 1987], pp. 187–88, is an example.) Another is to acknowledge that, while care is an important aspect of the moral life which has been largely neglected by impartialist theories, care considerations are nevertheless able to be fully encompassed by impartialism without disturbance to its theoretical commitments.

11. For example, Lawrence Kohlberg, "From 'Is' to 'Ought': How to Commit the Naturalistic Fallacy and Get Away with It in the Study of Moral Development," and other essays in *Essays in Moral Development,* vol. 1, *The Philosophy of Moral Development* (New York: Harper & Row, 1981), and pt. 1 of *Essays in Moral Development,* vol. 2, *The Psychology of Moral Development.*

12. See, e.g., in "Synopses and Detailed Replies to Critics" (with C. Levine and A. Hewer), in *The Psychology of Moral Development*, p. 360, where Kohlberg says that many of the judgments in the care orientation are "personal rather than moral in the sense of a formal point of view."

13. The first two suggestions (*a* and *b*) are made on p. 229 of Kohlberg's "The Current Statement of the Theory," and the second (care as supererogatory) again on p. 307. The last, (*c*), is articulated by O. Flanagan and K. Jackson in "Justice, Care, and Gender: The Kohlberg–Gilligan Debate Revisited," in *Ethics* 97 (1987): 622–37.

14. I owe the delineation of this position to William Lycan (in personal correspondence).

15. Barbara Herman, "Integrity and Impartiality," *Monist* 66 (1983): 223–50; Onora O'Neill, *Acting on Principle* (New York: Columbia University Press, 1975), and "Kant after Virtue," *Inquiry* 26 (1984): 387–405; Darwall; Marcia Baron, "The Alleged Repugnance of Acting from Duty," *Journal of Philosophy* 81 (1984): 197–220.

16. It might be replied here that even if impartialist considerations do not arise in all situations, nevertheless, one must be concerned about them beyond those situations; for (on view 6) one must be committed beforehand to giving them priority over care considerations and so must be concerned with situations in which such considerations might arise, or in which one is not yet certain whether or not they are present. Yet even if this were so, it would not follow that one must be constantly on the lookout for impartialist strictures. An analogy: that considerations of life and death tend to trump or outweigh most other moral considerations does not mean that, in order to avoid causing death, one must in all situations be on the lookout for the

possibility that one might be doing so. I can not here consider the further impartialist rejoinder that even when there are no impartialist strictures or considerations anywhere on the horizon, a commitment to heeding them still permeates all situations, and this grounds the claim that the impartialist dimension of morality is more fundamental and significant than care, even in the sphere of personal relations. The conclusion does not seem to me to follow from the premise; the inference seems to go from a hypothetical concern to an actual one. But more needs to be said on this. (See the discussion by Michael Slote, "Morality and the Practical," in his *Common-Sense Morality and Consequentialism* [London: Routledge & Kegan Paul, 1985].)

17. This view is taken by Barbara Herman in "The Practice of Moral Judgment," *Journal of Philosophy* 82 (1985): 458.

18. I do not discuss position 7 in this paper, as I have attempted to do so in my "Iris Murdoch and the Domain of the Moral," esp. 351–53, where I argue that it is false. (For more on this, see n. 33 below.)

19. Kohlberg, "Synopses and Detailed Replies to Critics," p. 343.

20. For this reason I have omitted views which defend some role for impartiality merely by claiming that it is not incompatible with care in personal relations. (Such a view is suggested, e.g., by Jerome Schneewind in "The Uses of Autonomy in Ethical Theory," in Heller, Sosna, and Wellerby, eds., p. 73, though the argument there is about autonomy rather than impartiality.) For this view does not by itself grant impartiality any more significance than care; it simply says that the claims of impartiality do not get in the way of those of care. While such views are sometimes presented as if they constitute a defense of Kantian or some other impartialist ethical view, in fact by themselves (e.g., apart from views such as 1 through 7) they do not seem to me to do so.

21. Worthy of further exploration is the fact that, while Gilligan would agree with this formulation in its apparent granting of something like equal status to justice and care, Gilligan does not see the relation between the two voices as one of "integration" so much as the model of a full appreciation of the not readily integrated claims of both.

22. Flanagan and Jackson, p. 627.

23. There is another, somewhat more colloquial, sense of 'universal' which implies independence from particular roles. But for now I will adhere to the more formal, philosophical sense of 'universal' as implying applicability to anyone meeting a certain description (here, occupying a certain role within a personal relationship).

24. I do not mean to imply that every situation presents a significant issue of moral sensitivity or perception involved in knowing that a principle applies. If a child reaches to touch a hot stove, no one observing the situation could fail to see that here one needs to keep this from happening. But situations in life often do not come with their moral character so clearly declared to any and all beholders, a fact which is often masked in discussions of examples

in philosophy, where the moral character of the situation is already given in the description.

25. Note that the argument so far has been couched in terms of "universality." But universality is not the same as impartiality. A morality of personal relationship roles (such as father, friend) is not fully impartialist unless the precepts governing the role morality are derivable from the position of pure impartiality postulated by the impartialist view. For a criticism of this supposition, see my "Particularity and Responsiveness," in *The Emergence of Morality in Young Children,* ed. J. Kagan and S. Lamb (Chicago: University of Chicago Press, 1988), where it is argued that even if a role morality, such as that involved in parenthood, is applicable 'universally' to all parents, the content of the moral precepts involved in it cannot be derived, even indirectly, from the impartialistic moral standpoint in which, from the point of view of the agent, each individual is to count for one and no more than one. If this is so, the acceptance given in the argument of the present paper to (some role for) universality is not tantamount to an acceptance of the same role for impartiality. But the argument advanced therein to show that universal principle itself cannot cover the whole territory of morality will apply ipso facto to the narrower notion of impartiality.

26. For a more elaborate argument that care and concern can be intelligent and reflective without involving moral principle, see my *Friendship, Altruism, and Morality* (London: Routledge & Kegan Paul, 1980), esp. chap. 2.

27. There seems to be a range of different types of moral personalities, a range in which both universal principle and care for particular persons have varying degrees and kinds of involvement and interaction with one another. To some persons, responsible friendship and parenthood comes more naturally than to others; they find it easier to keep attentive to, to remain in touch with the needs of, to consistently care for friends and children. By contrast, others, also responsible as friends and parents, might find it more often necessary self-consciously to remind themselves of the general principles governing friendship and parenthood—to use their principles to get them to do what the others do without an even implicit recourse to principles. Of course, the operation of principle in a person's motivation does not always show itself in explicit consulting of that principle. One might have so internalized a principle that one acts on it almost automatically, without having to call it up in one's mind. Yet, as positions 2, 3, 4, 6, and 7 acknowledge, there is still a difference between acting from an internalized but universal principle and acting purely from care and concern for a specific individual, even if this difference is hard to make out in many specific instances. It is only position 1 which denies such a distinction entirely. That there can be a range of differences among persons in the degree to which universal principles animate their actions does not mean that one can imagine a fully responsible moral agent for whom they play no role at all. It would be difficult to imagine a person fully confronting the complex responsibilities of modern parenthood and friendship

without giving some thought to the general responsibilities, formulable as principles of some sort, attaching to the various roles which they inhabit. Yet at the same time it should not be forgotten that some people who are not especially reflective about their general responsibilities seem as if instinctively to know how to act well toward their particular friends, or toward their or others' children, much better in fact than some other people who are nevertheless quite articulate about the appropriate principles of responsible friendship and parenthood. To insist that seemingly unreflective persons must be acting according to general principles of action even when they are not able to articulate any such principles nor to recognize as their own ones suggested to them by others—to insist on this is to be blinded by rationalist prejudices.

28. This does not mean that Gilligan's view of morality is incompatible with all forms of relativism. Gilligan does not, I think, aspire, as Kohlberg does, to a timeless morality valid for all people in all historical times and cultures. It seems to me that Gilligan's view is compatible with the qualified relativism suggested in Williams's *Ethics and the Limits of Philosophy,* chap. 9—the view that, e.g., a care morality is appropriate for any culture which is a real historical option for us; but we cannot say that it either is or is not valid for ones which are not. Something like this view is suggested in Gilligan's article with J. Murphy, "Development from Adolescence to Adulthood: The Philosopher and the Dilemma of the Fact," in *Intellectual Development beyond Childhood,* ed. D. Kuhn (San Francisco: Jossey-Bass, Inc., 1979).

29. For a more detailed argument for not excluding considerations of care from the domain of the moral, see my "Particularity and Responsiveness," and "Iris Murdoch and the Domain of the Moral," esp. p. 361. See also the presentation above of position 6, in which the argument presented there has the force of shifting to the defender of Kant the burden of proof of denying moral worth to care and compassion and of restricting moral worth to that which is done from a sense of duty.

30. For an argument that many morally worthy acts of friendship, familial care, and the like, lie outside the structure of obligation or duty altogether, see my *Friendship, Altruism and Morality,* chap. 7.

31. See Michael Stocker, "Values and Purposes: The Limits of Teleology and the Ends of Friendship," *Journal of Philosophy* 78 (1981): 747–65.

32. For a sustained critique of the sharp separation between act and motive presupposed in view 5, see Stephen Hudson, *Human Character and Morality: Reflections from the History of Ideas* (London: Routledge & Kegan Paul, 1986), esp. chap. 3; and Blum, *Friendship, Altruism, and Morality,* chap. 7.

33. Some of the issues concerning view 7 are addressed in my "Iris Murdoch and the Domain of the Moral," esp. pp. 350–54 (see n. 18 above). There it is argued that the reflective point of view outside of the specific individual's caring for his friend, from which it can be

seen that the individual's caring action is a good one—or that compassion, concern for specific individuals' welfare, and similar traits and sentiments can be acknowledged as having moral value—cannot be identified with the specific standpoint of "impartiality" found in impartialist moral theories. Such impartiality is, it is argued, only one possible reflective viewpoint. If this is so, then it is no support for position 7 to argue that all rational beings would include principles of care, compassion, and the like, as part of an ultimately acceptable morality, for the standpoint from which these rational beings do so is not necessarily an impartialist one.

34. Some of this work can be found in recent writings of Annette Baier: "What Do Women Want in a Moral Theory?" *Nous* 19 (1985): 530–65, "Trust and Anti-Trust," *Ethics* 96 (1986): 231–60, "The Moral Perils of Intimacy," in *Pragmatism's Freud: The Moral Disposition of Psychoanalysis,* ed. Joseph Smith and W. Kerrigan (Baltimore: Johns Hopkins University Press, 1986), and "Hume: The Women's Moral Theorist," in E. Kittay and D Meyers, *Women and Moral Theory* (Totowa, N.J.: Rowman & Littlefield, 1987); and in Nel Noddings, *Caring: A Feminine Approach to Ethics (*Berkeley and Los Angeles: University of California Press, 1984).

# 27  Autonomy, Integrity, and Care

## VICTORIA DAVION

## 1. Introduction

In interviewing women, moral psychologist Carol Gilligan claims to have discovered a distinctive approach to moral deliberation which she refers to as the care perspective.[1] The care perspective in ethics involves seeing oneself as connected to others within a web of various relationships. Rather than seeing moral problems as conflicts of rights to be solved by ranking values, moral problems are seen as embedded in a contextual framework of others. Moral deliberation from within the care perspective aims to maintain these relations. "From within the care perspective, the relationship becomes the figure, defining self and others. Within the context of the relationship, the self as a moral agent perceives and responds to the perception of need. The shift in moral perspective is manifested by a shift in the moral question, from 'What is just?' to 'How do I respond?'"[2]

The care perspective in ethics can be contrasted with a more traditional rights-based approach. Adherents of rights-based ethics include John Locke, Immanuel Kant, and John Rawls. One central feature of this tradition is the importance of personal liberty. Each individual is seen as having certain basic rights, such as the right to life, liberty, and property. The self is seen as an autonomous individual, free to make choices that do not infringe upon the basic right of others. "From a justice perspective, the self as a moral agent stands as the figure against a ground of social relationships, judging the conflicting claims of others against a standard of equality or equal respect."[3]

I will not address questions concerning the accuracy of Gilligan's research. Rather, my discussion will focus on philosopher Nel Noddings's attempt to develop the care perspective into a fully developed ethical theory to serve as an alternative to ethics that treat justice as a basic concept and as an alternative to an ethic of principle.[4] On Noddings's analysis, caring requires actual encounters with actual individuals. One's ethical responsibility is to meet others as one-caring. For Noddings, caring is more than simply being concerned about others. It has three elements: (1) motivational engrossment and displacement in another, (2) feeling with the other, and (3) actual caretaking. Noddings tells us to "always meet the other as one caring" and to "maintain caring relations."

In this paper I will focus on Noddings's first component of caring—motivational displacement and engrossment in another. According to

Reprinted by permission of the publisher from *Social Theory and Practice,* 19, 2 (1993), 161–182.

Noddings, when one becomes engrossed in another, one suspends evaluation of the other and is transformed by the other. In motivational displacement, one allows the other's goals to become one's own. I will show that both of these involve a significant moral risk. If someone is evil, and one allows oneself to be transformed by that person, one risks becoming evil oneself. If the other's goals are immoral, and one makes those goals one's own, one becomes responsible for supporting immoral goals. This raises the issue of whether one can be in a caring relationship with someone who has immoral goals while avoiding moral responsibility for promoting those goals. I will argue that, in caring, one must nurture the other and, in doing this, one supports the other's goals in various ways. I will argue that because caring, as described by Noddings, involves supporting another's goals, the choice of whom to enter a caring relationship with, and choices about whether to continue a caring relationship, become significant moral issues. Therefore, we should not always meet the other as one-caring, and we can not always maintain caring relations. We must evaluate potential and ongoing relationships.

I will show that the evaluation of caring relationships requires knowledge of values more basic than care, because for any caring relationship to be morally good, it must not require parties to violate deeply held convictions in order to be in it. Each must be able to maintain moral integrity. Caring itself cannot be the most basic value in such an ethic. Therefore, I will argue that other values must be more basic than care, otherwise there is no basis for the evaluation of caring relationships.

In arguing that one must be able to maintain deeply held convictions in order for a caring relationship to be morally good, I do not mean to preclude the possibility that one could change one's deeply held convictions, but this raises interesting issues concerning self-deception. It is one thing to change deeply held convictions because one is honestly convinced they were misguided, and another to change merely to enter or maintain a caring relationship with someone.

Two related difficulties will be discussed in this paper: (1) We cannot expect to agree with all of a person's projects. To what extent is agreement necessary? (2) Is prejudice fueled by the suggestion that at least some agreement regarding moral convictions is necessary? And, does this suggestion, in fact, imply that we should avoid caring relationships with people different from ourselves? This is especially significant given the importance of respecting cultural differences in fighting against prejudices such as racism, xenophobia, homophobia, and so forth. I will argue that my suggestion neither implies that we should avoid people different from ourselves, nor encourages the making of unreflective judgments without considering such things as cultural differences. However, if after spending the time necessary to understand another person's values and projects one finds such values and projects reprehensible, and if one cannot see oneself supporting those values even indirectly, other things being equal, one should avoid a caring relationship with that person. Not to do this would be to sacrifice one's moral integrity, given that entering into a caring relationship involves engrossment and motivational displacement. This does not mean that one should not help that person in various ways, but one should avoid becoming engrossed or motivationally displaced, or both, in that person. Finally, I will argue that the process of evaluating ongoing and potential caring relationships can be seen as an exercise in moral autonomy. Diana T. Meyers presents an account of moral autonomy as a competency that can be exercised by responsibility reasoning. She suggests that in responsibility reasoning, "an individual's moral sense gains expression through an exercise in imaginative introjection by asking what choices are compatible with or reinforce desirable aspects of one's personal identity."[5] I will show that the evaluation of caring relationships can be seen as an exercise of moral autonomy using Meyers's account. Thus, I will show that the evaluation of caring relationships involves the concepts of moral integrity and moral autonomy. Their place within a care ethic has been an important question in the literature on this topic.

## 2. Caring

Although my focus will be on two particular components of caring—motivational displacement and engrossment—I shall begin with a general sketch of Noddings's ethic as a whole. This will allow us to see the risks involved in motivational displacement and engrossment more clearly. In developing the care perspective into a fully-blown ethical theory, Noddings attempts to offer an alternative to rule-based action-guiding ethical theories. The project of such theories is to generate universal moral rules, applicable to all moral agents in similar situations. These theories typically contend that there are objective facts in moral situations. Any moral agent can, in principle, "see" these facts. Once the facts are obtained, the theory provides a universal moral principle that tells the agent which actions are either permissible or obligatory in that particular situation. Because the facts are objective and available to all moral agents, and because the moral principles are universal, to be used by all moral agents, these theories prescribe the same actions for all moral agents in similar situations.

Noddings rejects these kinds of theories for important and interesting reasons. She claims that the idea of universality depends on an erroneous concept of sameness.

In order to act on principle we must establish that human predicaments exhibit sufficient sameness, and this we cannot do without abstracting away from concrete situations those qualities that seem to reveal sameness. In doing this we often lose the very qualities or factors that give rise to the moral question in the situation.[6]

Thus, while these theories may tell us that agents should behave the same way in similar situations, all things being equal, other things rarely, if ever, are equal.

The alternative offered by Noddings is an attempt to ground morality in the understanding of individual others with whom one interacts. Rather than seeking similarities between moral agents, this theory attends to differences. Before one can act morally in relation to another, one must attempt to understand the other's reality. This understanding is more than gaining an objective understanding of the facts. It involves attempting to see the other's reality as one's own. Only then can one act as one-caring towards another. Hence, for Noddings, morality is grounded in the experience of caring, to act as one-caring is the ethical ideal. She states "One must meet the other as one-caring. From this requirement there is no escape for one who would be moral."[7]

Noddings grounds her ethic in a relational ontology. Because human beings are constructed out of our relations with others, we must, in order to survive, remain in relation. She states: ". . . 'we' are the products of relation, not mere constituent parts."[8] The fact that the self is a product of relation is a central aspect of this ethic, and one which leads to many of the problems I shall discuss.

## 3. Some Problems with Caring

In this section I shall review some important criticisms of Noddings's ethic. My purpose in reviewing these is twofold: (1) I want to place my concerns and recommendations in the context of other discussions concerning Noddings, and (2) I hope to show that my suggestions for improvement speak not only to my own difficulties but address these other concerns as well. Noddings has been widely criticized for her position regarding the termination of caring relationships. For Noddings, the ethical ideal is to act as one-caring by meeting others as one caring and maintaining caring relationships. Whenever one cannot do this, one acts under a diminished ethical ideal. One may terminate a caring relationship when it threatens to prevent one's ability to act as one-caring towards others with whom one is also in caring relationships, but this seems to be the only justification for doing so. She states that although there are situations when there are no alternatives other than to cease caring when one does this one acts under a diminished ethical ideal. Thus:

The perceived lack of alternative induces minimal ethical functioning under the diminished ideal. The ethical agent accepts responsibility; it is she who is, personally, committed to caring . . . When the one-caring is driven to the point where she perceives only one solution, and that in opposition to the enhanced ideal, she is badly shaken and, in extreme cases, broken. For while she must still say, "It is I performing this act," it is clearly not the "I" she would have chosen. There can be no greater evil, then, than this: that the moral autonomy of the one-caring be so shattered that she acts against her own commitment to care.[9]

And:

When one intentionally rejects the impulse to care and deliberately turns her back on the ethical she is evil, and this evil cannot be redeemed.[10]

Thus, although someone may be justified in terminating a caring relationship, she still participates in evil and acts under a diminished ethical ideal. Several critics have argued this is a major flaw in Noddings's account. If one is justified in terminating the relationship, if one needs to do this in order to maintain oneself as one-caring, then surely one is not acting under a diminished ethical ideal. By doing the right thing one acts in accord with the ethical ideal; one does not somehow diminish it. In addition, some have argued that Noddings fails to value the one-caring sufficiently. Her discussion of when it is morally permissible to leave a caring relationship focuses on one's ability to continue caring for others. In discussing the case of a wife who kills her husband after many years of abuse, she cites the diminishment of the children's ethical ideals and their increasing fear and pain as reasons for the woman to act. "Assuming that her receptivity was adequate and that her motivational displacement was directed toward the needs of her children, she acted as one-caring but under a diminished ethical ideal."[11] Critics have argued that someone is also justified in ending a caring relationship for the sake of her or his own well-being and not only out of concern for others. This possibility is not even mentioned by Noddings.[12]

## 4. Caring and Moral Risk

I now turn to the two aspects of caring as described by Noddings that I wish to focus upon, motivational displacement and engrossment.

Using the mother-child relationship as a paradigm, she states:

My motive energy flows toward the other and perhaps, although not necessarily, toward his ends. I do not relinquish myself; I cannot excuse myself for what I do. But I allow my motive energy to be shared. I put it into the service of the other. . . . When this displacement occurs in the extreme form we sometimes hear parents speak of "living for" their children.

In such a mode we receive what is there as nearly as possible without evaluation or assessment. We are in a world of relation, having stepped out of the instrument world; we have either not yet established goals or we have suspended those we have established. We are not attempting to transform the world but we are allowing ourselves to be transformed.[13]

Noddings claims that there is reciprocity in a caring relationship. However, although she speaks of reciprocity, she states:

It is important to re-emphasize that this capacity is not contractual; that is, it is not characterized by mutuality. The cared-for contributes to the caring relation, as we have seen, by receiving the efforts of one-caring, and this receiving may be accomplished by a disclosure of his own subjective experience in direct response to the one caring or by a happy and vigorous pursuit of his own projects.[14]

Sarah Hoagland has objected that this model is unidirectional so that one person in a relationship can always be the one-caring and the other the cared-for.[15] In the case of mothering a small child, this seems fine. A small child cannot understand the projects of the mother and is not really in a position to help her try to pursue them. However, in adult relationships, or relationships between equals, something is wrong when one person does all the caretaking and the other receives all the care.

Reciprocity doesn't mean we play the same roles at the same time or even that we are cared-for and one-caring exactly one-half of the time. It means we are equally prepared to be ones-caring when it is necessary—that neither of us expects to be cared for all of the time. In what follows I will assume that Noddings is right in claiming that caring involves engrossment and motivational displacement, although I want to insist that between adults, other things being equal, for an ongoing caring relationship to be morally good, it must involve equal commitments on behalf of all parties to be the one-caring when this is at all possible.

The fact that the role of caregiver involves engrossment and motivational displacement, and the fact that reciprocity demands that one be willing to provide care for those who care for one, means that one's choice of caring relationships is an ethical matter. To see this, one need only look again at what is involved in engrossment and motivational displacement. When one is engrossed in another one receives what is there as fully as one can without judging what one sees. One is not trying to transform what is there but to let what is there transform oneself. In doing this if one becomes engrossed in someone who is morally corrupt, one risks being transformed into someone morally corrupt oneself. One risks character damage. To avoid this one must be critical before becoming engrossed. Becoming engrossed appears to involve a certain loss of control, and before one abdicates this control to another, one has an obligation to be sure that the changes in oneself will be changes one can support.

Engrossment leads to motivational displacement in which the other's goals become one's own. One's motive energy flows towards his or her ends. Again, a moral risk is involved, depending on what the cared-for's ends are. Here the issue is highly complex. In caring for others one sustains them providing them with energy to pursue their own projects. Even when one does not pursue their projects directly, one may contribute to the cared-for's ability to do so. A closer look at Noddings's model reveals this.

According to Noddings, caring involves putting one's motive energy into the service of another. This may involve directly working to promote the cared-for's goals. However, even in situations where one does not directly pursue the cared-for projects, one may indirectly support them by nurturing the cared-for. In caring for someone one may provide a generally nurturing atmosphere from which the cared-for gains energy to pursue his or her goals. If the cared-for gets strength from the caregiver and uses it to support the Ku Klux Klan, and if the caregiver knows this

is what is happening and continues to provide support, the caregiver is supporting the Ku Klux Klan, even if the caregiver regrets this. Thus, if one has dinner on the table every Thursday night at six o'clock sharp so that the other can get to the Klan meeting on time, one is indirectly supporting the activities of the Klan. In entering caring relationships one promotes the goals of the cared-for in various ways, even if that is not directly intended.

Obviously one is causally responsible for promoting the goals of the other in the situation described above. However, this does not yet settle the issue of moral responsibility. Noddings explicitly states that the caregiver can not excuse himself or herself for what he or she does in the service of the ends of the cared-for. In cases where nurturing involves directly promoting the goals of the other—by attending political meetings, for example—the question of moral responsibility is clear. One is morally responsible for one's choices. However, in cases where the promotion is indirect, questions of moral responsibility are more complex.

A look at Aristotle's analysis of moral responsibility is instructive here. According to Aristotle, one is morally responsible for actions which are (1) not done under compulsion, (2) done with knowledge of the circumstances, and (3) chosen. One is not morally responsible for actions done out of ignorance, or where the moving force is wholly outside the agent.[16]

Using Aristotle's framework, we can examine individual cases. Within the context of a caring relationship, it is possible that the caregiver does not know what the cared-for is doing with all the positive energy gotten out of the relationship, or does not know that the cared-for needs dinner at six-thirty sharp in order to make it to a Klan meeting. In these cases ignorance is involved, and so perhaps the caregiver is not morally responsible for promoting Klan activities. It is unclear whether these examples reflect true caring relationships as described by Noddings. In order for a caring relationship to be intimate, knowledge of the other's personal commitments is needed. However, relationships vary in degrees of intimacy. It is possible that one could make sure to have dinner on the table for a casual acquaintance at exactly six-thirty without knowing why she needs to leave by seven-thirty. In such a case, the caregiver would not be responsible for promoting the goals of the cared-for.

The interesting and more complex cases involve situations where the caregiver knows that her activities are helping the cared-for promote certain goals, but the caregiver does not believe in those goals. In such cases, the question of the caregiver's moral responsibility for promoting something wrong arises. We cannot simply assume moral responsibility here. The caregiver may be coerced into the service of the cared-for by the threat of physical violence. Domestic abuse cases are good examples. If the caregiver is acting out of the fear of battery, for example, she may not be morally responsible for her assistance. In such cases, I question whether these are genuine caring relationships rather than simple acts of self-preservation.

There are, however, cases where the caregiver is clearly morally responsible for supporting the goals of the cared-for, even when this support is only indirect. Suppose the caregiver is aware that the gun she is purchasing is to be used in Klan activities, and assume her choice to buy the gun is not made under coercive conditions. Her purpose in buying the gun is not to support the Klan but to support a loved-one who has asked her to run this errand. In this case she is morally responsible for providing the gun, and morally responsible for what the gun is used for, though perhaps to a lesser degree than the person who actually fires it. The caregiver voluntarily purchases the gun, is not ignorant of what it will be used for, and is not coerced into this choice. Even though her purpose in buying the gun was to support a loved one, she is partly responsible for what the gun is used for because she knew what it was to be used for when she bought it.

I have not attempted to offer a full account of moral responsibility in cases of caring relationships. There is a wide range of possible cases I have not discussed. However, I hope to have shown that there are at least some cases where caring is problematic from the standpoint of the

caregiver and therefore, a discussion of moral responsibility in such situations must be central to any ethic of care. It is dangerous to always meet the other as one-caring and to maintain caring relations. Critical evaluation prior to motivational displacement and engrossment is necessary for responsible action.[17]

Noddings misses these aspects of moral responsibility because she denies the absolute value of anything other than caring. This is shown in the passages discussed earlier where she insists that there is unredeemable evil in ending a caring relationship, even when doing so is necessary for the health and well being of the one-caring. It is also shown in the following example. She describes the situation of a person whose relatives are racist and involved in a violent battle against people of color. This person genuinely believes that her relatives are wrong. Yet she loves them for their past kindnesses to her personally. She is also acquainted with Jim, described as a black man fighting on the other side, against racists, for his basic human rights.

Noddings says of Ms. A:

She saw clearly what she would do, would really do. I could not, she said, ever—not ever—oppose my bigoted old father or my hysterical Aunt Phoebe with physical violence. I do not agree with either. Aunt Phoebe! Imagine a person in this day and age who would actually say (and demonstrate her statement by fainting at the thought), "Ah would just die if a niggah touched me!" Oh, she is wrong and my father is wrong. But there are years of personal kindness. They must count for something must they not? I know I could not fight on the other side. And what of the black man, Jim, who is after all "right"? If my sights picked him out, says Ms. A, I would note that it was Jim and move on to some other target.[18]

I find this example disturbing for several reasons. Jim is after all "right." But why is Jim "right" instead of RIGHT? The quotation marks around the word "right" indicate that in the mind of the thinker perhaps others think it is right, but the word "right" has lost its original meaning for her. Thus, she can put her relationships with her father and aunt before the rights of people to be treated with minimal human dignity. What about the other target at whom she aims instead of Jim? This person is also "right," yet she is killing him or her in order to fight on the same side as racists.

Perhaps the most telling aspect in this example is that she feels she cannot fight on the other side. Why not? Why can't she fight on the other side and aim at another target if her sights happen to fall on either her father or her aunt? If she did this she would be fighting on the right side while still refusing to use violence against her father and aunt. I think it is significant that not only can she not bear to use violence against her father and her aunt, neither can she join the other side. Her inability to join the other side somehow stems from her caring for her father and her aunt. The metaphor of standing with her father and aunt is important. When someone stands with someone else, or stands by someone else, they support those people. If she joins the other side this amounts to severing connections between herself and loved ones which she cannot bear to do. Therefore, she will stand with them in order to maintain certain ties, and will fight against what she really believes is right in order to do this. I think what she does is wrong. In "Caring and Evil," Claudia Card argues that because we cannot have caring relationships with most people in the world, we need other grounds for moral obligations towards them. In arguing that justice is necessary as well she states, "life can be worth living in the absence of caring from most people in the world, but in a densely populated world life is not apt to be worth living without justice from a great many people, including many whom we will never know."[19] Card is absolutely right about this. In fact, this point can be extended. Considerations of justice are necessary so that all decisions aren't made on the basis of whom one happens to care most about at a given time. Ms. A has chosen with whom to fight on the basis of loyalty to those she cares about. She has ignored considerations of justice completely. This includes ignoring justice in the case of someone she knows, namely Jim, and those she doesn't know, all the others fighting with Jim. The fact that she will not shoot at Jim does not mean she treats him justly, as she fails to fight for his basic human rights. With regard to the others whom she has chosen to kill, she becomes a murderer fighting for racism.

Noddings implies that Ms. A makes a morally acceptable choice in the example discussed above. She argues that the idea of someone willing to sacrifice loved ones for principles is frightening. I think she is right. However, it is also frightening to think about someone who will stand by their loved ones no matter what those people do. I find this kind of unconditional love problematic as well. Some middle ground is needed. I believe that in this case, the middle ground is to fight with the side one believes in, but not to aim directly at one's father or aunt. This doesn't involve sacrificing them, although it may involve sacrificing the relationship.[20]

Although I believe Ms. A reached the wrong decision in the dilemma stated above, I can also understand the emotional trauma involved in risking personal relationships for a cause. When loved ones take opposing sides in important moral struggles, relationships can he endangered. Thus, many will sacrifice their beliefs and values to remain in caring relationships. In the above example it is important that the people involved are family members. In some sense they didn't choose each other. Families are a kind of given. Under normal circumstances a child will grow to love caring (and even uncaring) adults well before she can judge their projects and commitments for herself. She may then find herself in a situation where she must choose between principles and loved ones. However, this case is instructive as we think about forming new relationships. Although we may find ourselves having to choose between principles and loved ones, we can work to minimize this by finding people whose basic principles we can support. This is like an insurance policy against being in the kinds of situations described above. In doing this we can take responsibility for who we are becoming by taking responsibility for who we allow into our transformative process. In becoming involved with someone whose projects one can not support, one sets oneself up to become like Ms. A, betraying one's own beliefs. If one chooses this path one is responsible for having put oneself into a position where one can not bear to do the right thing. This is not simply a matter of fate; one has, in an important sense, chosen it. Thus, it is not totally a matter of what Thomas Nagel and Bernard Williams refer to as "moral luck."[21] We can maintain at least some control in decisions about with whom we become involved. This is another reason why I believe literature on caring should avoid focusing on mother-child relationships as paradigm instances of caring. These relationships involve moral luck in ways that many other relationships may not.

## 5. Autonomy and Integrity in Caring Relationships

How can a care ethic provide guidance in evaluating caring relationships? In order to answer this question I shall first examine what is missing in Noddings's account, and then attempt to enrich the account to take care of the problems I shall discuss. As I have already stated, I believe the central problem is a failure to recognize absolute value in anything other than caring. Noddings privileges the caring relation because of her relational ontology: According to Noddings, we must maintain connections in order to survive. We do not have connections, we are connections. We naturally desire to care for others as a survival mechanism. Hence, Noddings, like Aristotle and many others, attempts to ground her ethic in an account of the type of beings humans are.

There are many problems in attempting such a project. I will focus on two. The first concerns the jump from the idea that maintaining caring relationships is necessary for human survival to the idea that all caring relationships are good. Even if Noddings's relational ontology is correct, it does not follow that all caring relations are good. One can consistently hold that caring is necessary for human survival and distinguish between morally desirable and morally undesirable instances of caring.

The second problem concerns the valuing of relationship more than the individuals who are relating. Sarah Hoagland points out that one cannot have a relation without having at least two beings to relate. Even if one is the product of one's relations, in making decisions about continuing caring relationships and about forming new ones, one acts out of a sense of oneself as a being separate from others. According to Hoagland:

Relation is central to ethics. However, there must be two beings, at least, to relate. Moving away from oneself is one aspect of the dynamic of caring, but it cannot be the only defining element. Otherwise, relationship is not ontologically basic, and the self ceases to exist in its own ethical right.[22]

Thus:

One who cares must perceive herself not just as both separate and related, but as ethically both separate and related. Otherwise, she can not acknowledge difference.[23]

Hoagland is correct. Furthermore, if one can not acknowledge difference, one can not evaluate the projects of others as the projects of others in order to make a responsible decision as to whether to promote those projects oneself.

I believe what is missing from Noddings's account is an account of the individuals within caring relations as important in themselves. This is reflected by the fact that the ethical ideal is to be one-caring and to maintain caring relations. What is needed is an enrichment of the ethical ideal to reflect not only the positive aspects of the self as one-caring, but also the self as a being with other important ethical commitments that make up its moral identity. One major problem in the example discussing Ms. A and Jim is that Ms. A must suffer a loss of moral integrity in order to maintain her relationships with her aunt and father. She must turn against important values which are part of her ethical ideal, her image of her best self. This indicates that there is more to her ethical ideal than merely maintaining certain relationships. Our account of the ethical ideal must be sensitive to this.

In order to enrich an account of the ethical ideal we need an account of moral integrity, a vision of a best self including more than an image of oneself as one-caring. Elsewhere I have argued that in order to have moral integrity, one must have at least one unconditional commitment.[24] This is the commitment to keep track of oneself, not to betray oneself. I argued that this kind of unconditional commitment, while highly abstract, doesn't imply a lack of attention to context. It requires that in each situation one pay careful attention to what one is doing and who one is becoming in doing it. It embraces the idea that we are dynamic beings, constantly growing and changing, but insists that we keep track of these changes rather than letting them happen randomly. Thus, monitoring who one allows into one's transformative process is essential in maintaining moral integrity. Seeing oneself as a being with moral integrity is part of seeing oneself as one's best self. Hence, it must be part of the ethical ideal. Thus, in order for caring to enhance the ethical ideal, it must not require a loss of moral integrity. At least one criterion for a caring relationship to be morally desirable is that all parties be able to maintain moral integrity within it. When a person must lose her integrity in order to care, caring does not enhance her ethical ideal, and therefore caring is undesirable.

Recently, Diana T. Meyers has suggested that an ethic of care can incorporate a sense of autonomy. This autonomy is different from the standard sense of autonomy based on allowing rules and principles to guide behavior. Meyers suggests that autonomy is a kind of competency. She states:

> . . . one asks what choices are compatible with or reinforce desirable aspects of one's personal identity. Questions like "What would it be like to have done that?" and "Could I bear to be the sort of person who can do that?" are foremost. To answer these questions satisfactorily, the individual must be able to envisage a variety of solutions, must be able to examine these solutions open-mindedly, must be able to imagine the likely results of carrying out these options, must be attuned to self-referential responses like shame and pride, must be able to critically examine these responses, and must be able to compare various possibilities systematically along sundry dimensions. Each of these abilities constitutes a complex skill, and, together, these skills equip the individual to make a choice by consulting her self. Thus, it is possible to say that people who deliberate in this way are self-governing.[25]

I want to suggest here that these are the kinds of questions one must ask oneself in order to determine whether a particular existing or potential relationship is morally desirable. One must ask what it would be like to support the others projects, whether one could live with oneself,

morally, if those projects were one's own. This is necessary in order to decide who one should allow into one's transformative process, which as I stated above, is necessary in order for an agent to maintain moral integrity.

## 6. Caring and Difference

The value of differences between people, and the importance of accepting difference as a way of overcoming such things as racism, anti-Semitism, and xenophobia, as well as enriching our lives by associating with people different from ourselves, has received much attention recently. It may appear that I am recommending close association only with people who are similar to ourselves as a way of insuring morally good associations. This could increase tendencies towards racism, anti-Semitism, homophobia, and xenophobia, and limit our associations with those different from us. I do not mean to encourage parochialism. In order to make in informed decision about entering into a caring relationship with another, one must get to know the other. If one makes snap decisions based on prejudice or superficial differences, or even on deep differences that one fails to try to understand, one acts too quickly. We may have a tendency, for example, to find certain cultural differences distasteful because they are unfamiliar. However, to refuse a relationship without really examining oneself and the other person, without trying to understand the difference would be a mistake, and this is not what I am suggesting. Yet, there are differences that make morally good, caring relationships impossible. If one finds certain deeply held values in the other to be truly wrong, if the person is committed to things that after searching oneself, being aware of aspects such as cultural differences into account, one finds morally reprehensible, one will be unable to maintain integrity within that relationship. Embracing difference is very important. However, not all differences are good simply because they are different. We still have important judgments to make.

One might wonder, at this point, about the possibility of attempting to change a person in order to make caring morally desirable. Once again, we must consider different cases. First, one might be in a caring relationship with another who has changed over the years, so that one can no longer support the other's projects, or one might be considering whether to enter into a relationship with someone whose projects one knows one cannot support, with the hope of changing that person.

Aristotle speaks to the first situation in his discussions of friendship. In discussing the question of ending friendships when a friend changes for the worse he states:

Must the friendship, then, be forthwith broken off? If they are capable of being reformed one should rather come to the assistance of their character or their property, inasmuch as this is better and more characteristic of friendship. But a man who breaks off such a friendship would seem to do nothing strange; for it was not to a man of this sort that he was a friend; when his friend has changed, therefore, and he is unable to save him, he gives him up.[26]

The issues involved in attempting to change another person are highly complex. When is someone incurable? Also, what are the ethics of attempting to change another's values? Once one is already in a caring relationship with another, one may incur an additional obligation to help the other that is the product of the relationship.

Because we may incur special obligations to help friends, it is important to learn about the character of a potential friend before becoming too intimately involved in a caring relationship. In attempting to change another, one must be aware that one might be changed in the process. If this occurs one bears some responsibility for whom one has become. Under certain circumstances ending a relationship may be the only ethical choice. I believe the kind of unconditional commitment that allows us to go against our important values is not a good thing. When we go against our most deeply held values for the sake of unconditional commitment to another person we do wrong. One can never be sure how another will

develop, thus unconditional commitment to another cannot be ethically acceptable. It amounts to the willingness to support anything a loved one is involved in, even things one finds morally outrageous. This is what makes the commitment unconditional. I believe that some things are wrong, no matter who does them. This is incompatible with an unconditional commitment to support another's goals, no matter what they are.

My analysis might strike some as chilling. Many of us were raised with the idea that the most important goal in our lives is to find unconditional love and support. It may seem as if I am advocating sacrificing loved ones for abstract ideas. However, this isn't so. I am not advocating sacrificing people, it is relationships I am recommending sacrificing under certain conditions. Many of us have been taught the value of unconditional commitment to other people. It is precisely this value that I am calling into question here.

## 7. Conclusion

This analysis demonstrates why a good caring relationship, one which allows both parties to maintain integrity, must incorporate values other than caring itself at a fundamental level. In order to know whether one can support another's projects one must have some knowledge of one's fundamental values. Answering to oneself that one could not live with oneself if one was involved in *that,* means knowing what one's values about *that* are. Thus, one's thoughts about justice, fairness, human rights and dignity, animal rights, environmental concerns, racism, sexism, and many other issues will play a part in guiding with whom one can have a morally desirable caring relationship.[27]

The ability of both parties to remain true to deeply held values within a relationship may not in itself make the relationship morally good. Two evil people can engage in horrendous things together, and their relationship would then be bad, however strong. Hence, while the ability of both parties to maintain integrity is not sufficient for caring to be good, it is necessary. I have not dealt with the problem of jointly held bad values. The aspect of integrity I have focused on involves not betraying oneself. There may indeed be other aspects. However, my analysis as it stands leaves room for the fact that while a certain two people may not be able to engage in a morally good caring relationship, each person might be able to do so with others who can support them. I have not unconditionally ruled out any particular values here (although there are some things I find unconditionally wrong).

I have suggested a strategy one might use to see if integrity can be maintained, one that involves the exercise of personal autonomy. Thus, the notions of integrity and autonomy have a central place within an ethic of care. While many of the recent discussions of the place of other values in an ethic of care have been concerned with obligations to those about whom one does not care, I have argued that values other than care determine whether a particular relationship between two people is itself a good instance of caring.

Although I have focused upon a particular example of an ethic of care in this analysis, I believe I have shown something that is important more generally. Any ethic of care that offers only caring itself as of absolute value can provide only an impoverished ethical ideal. There is more to ethical life than being one-caring, and sometimes it is wrong to be one-caring if this involves motivational displacement and engrossment in someone whose projects are wrong. What I want to say about caring is rather like what Kant says about happiness. He distinguishes between a thing's being good and useful, and a thing's being good without qualification. Thus, he claims that while happiness can be good it can also be bad when not under the direction of a good will.[28] I want to say something similar about caring relationships. Caring can be good when certain conditions are met. However, caring itself is not good without qualification as some instances of caring are bad. A viable ethical theory must provide an ethical ideal rich enough to distinguish between good and bad instances of caring, and therefore must incorporate moral integrity and autonomy into its ethical ideal.

## Notes

1. Carol Gilligan, *In A Different Voice* (Cambridge: Harvard University Press, 1982).
2. Carol Gilligan, "Moral Orientation and Moral Development," in Eva Kittay and Diana T. Meyers, eds., *Women and Moral Theory* (Maryland: Rowman and Littlefield Press, 1987), p. 23.
3. Gilligan, "Moral Orientation and Moral Development," p. 23.
4. Noddings, *Caring: A Feminine Approach to Moral Education* (Berkeley: University of California Press, 1984). For some interesting discussions on the philosophical implications of Gilligan's work see *Women and Moral Theory,* ed. Eva Kittay and Diana T. Meyers.
5. Diana T. Meyers, "The Socialized Self and Individual Autonomy: An Intersection Between Philosophy and Psychology," in *Women and Moral Theory,* pp. 129–38.
6. Nel Noddings, *Caring,* p. 85.
7. Nel Noddings, *Caring,*p. 201.
8. Nel Noddings, "A Response," in *Hypatia: A Journal of Feminist Philosophy* 5 (1990): 124.
9. Nel Noddings, *Caring,* p. 115.
10. Nel Noddings, *Caring,* p. 115.
11. Nel Noddings, *Caring,* p. 114.
12. This concern is addressed by the following authors in a symposium on Noddings's work in *Hypatia: A Journal of Feminist Philosophy* 5 (1990): Claudia Card, "Caring and Evil," 101–8, Sara Lucia Hoagland, "Some Concerns About Noddings' *Caring*": 109–14, Barbara Houston, "Caring and Exploitation": 115–19.
13. Nel Noddings, *Caring,* p. 34.
14. Nel Noddings, *Caring,* p. 151.
15. Sarah Lucia Hoagland, "Some Concerns About Noddings' *Caring,"* pp. 109–14.
16. Aristotle, *The Nicomachean Ethics,* trans. by David Ross (Oxford University Press, 1980), Book III, pp. 1–5.
17. In "Caring and Exploitation," Houston argues that Noddings places too much responsibility for the goodness of the cared-for on the one-caring, as part of the task of the ethical ideal. I agree with this criticism. I am making a different, though related, point here. The situations I am concerned with involve actions taken by the one-caring in order to promote the goals of the cared-for, where these goals are morally wrong.
18. Nel Noddings, *Caring,* p. 110.
19. Claudia Card, "Caring and Evil," pp. 101–7.
20. Hoagland questions Noddings's assumption that someone can be a racist and be an otherwise nice and decent person, an important assumption operating in this

example. Hoagland argues that one's attitude towards race cannot be isolated from one's moral character generally. One cannot be racist but otherwise fine. Sarah Lucia Hoagland, "Some Concerns About Noddings', *Caring,* p. 111.

21. Thomas Nagel and Bernard Williams, Symposium on Moral Luck in *Proceedings of the American Aristotelian Society,* Supp. Vol. L, (1976): 115–51. The concept of moral luck is tied into literature on caring in the following two pieces by Claudia Card: "Caring and Evil," 101–8 and "Gender and Moral Luck," in *Identity, Character and Morality,* ed., Owen Flanagan and Amelie Oksenberg Rorty, (Cambridge, MA: M.I.T. Press, 1990), pp. 199–217.

22. Nel Noddings, *Caring,* p. 111.

23. Nel Noddings, *Caring,* p. 111.

24. Davion, "Integrity and Radical Change," in *Feminist Ethics,* ed. by Claudia Card (Lawrence, KS: University of Kansas Press, 1991). In this paper I argue that one can

change greatly while maintaining moral integrity. However, in order to make sense of this idea, we must incorporate at least some notion of unconditional commitment into our account of moral integrity.

25. Diana T. Meyers, "The Socialized Self and Individual Autonomy: An Intersection Between Philosophy and Psychology," p. 151.

26. Aristotle, *The Nicomachean Ethics,* IX: 3.

27. Houston mentions the importance of knowing one's position on these issues so as to better act as one-caring. Barbara Houston, "Caring and Exploitation": 118. My point here is that one needs this in order to protect one's own well-being and not only the well-being of the cared-for.

28. Immanuel Kant, *Groundwork of the Metaphysic of Morals,* trans. by H.J. Paton (Harper & Row: New York, 1964), p. 61.

# 28   Is Care a Virtue for Health Care Professionals?

## HOWARD CURZER

*It is quite possible that the best soldiers may not be courageous.*

ARISTOTLE

## Introduction

*I am a very good man, but a very bad wizard.*

THE WIZARD OF OZ

This paper focuses on a point at which three of the most fashionable recent movements in ethics (virtue ethics, medical ethics, feminist ethics) intersect.

There are some moral rules which people generally should obey (Do not kill; do not steal; etc.). But different rules apply to people playing certain roles within the context of certain practices. (Soldiers generally should obey orders given by their commanding officers, but civilians have no such

duty; parents generally should try to save their own children from a burning house before they try to save other children; etc.). The set of rules which applies to people playing certain roles is sometimes called a role morality.

Role morality can be approached *via* virtue ethics, too. There are some character traits which, taken together, make someone a good person. A person lacking these virtues is morally deficient *qua* person. I shall call these *general virtues.* To be good at a role (to be a good lawyer or a good parent, for example), requires a collection of character traits which may be somewhat different from the general virtues. I shall call these character traits *role virtues.* I shall say with deliberate vagueness that role virtues are character traits which help the person achieve the goal(s) of the role. The constellation of virtues of a particular role is not always the same as the constellation of general virtues. To be good at a role might require all of the general virtues plus other character traits. Florence Nightingale suggests that this is true of nursing when she says that "A woman cannot be a good and intelligent nurse without being

Reprinted by permission of Kluwer Academic Publishers from *Journal of Medicine and Philosophy,* 18 (1993), 51–69.

a good and intelligent woman" (Benjamin and Curtis, 1985, p. 257). However, this is not true for all roles. Some role virtues might not be general virtues and some general virtues might not be role virtues. Indeed, role virtues might be general vices and vice verse. The competitiveness that makes people good businessmen might make them bad people, for example, and the general virtue of benevolence might be a marketplace vice.

There are further complexities. A character trait may occupy different places in the constellations of general virtues and role virtues. Courage, for example, has a higher priority as a military virtue than as a general virtue. Moreover role virtues are often narrower than general virtues of the same name. For example, military courage, unlike general courage, is predominantly courage in battle. Since roles are embedded in practices and associated with institutions, role virtues are sometimes relative to practices and institutions. The virtues of a teacher in a large state university, for example, differ significantly from the virtues of a teacher in a rural, one-room elementary school house.[1]

The practice with which I shall be concerned is medicine of the 1990's in major medical centers of industrialized countries. This is approximately the practice Veatch (1983, p. 188) calls "stranger medicine" because it is medicine practiced among people who are essentially strangers. I do not think that what I have to say can be applied in any straightforward way to third world medicine, 19th century American medicine, or small town modern medicine, for example.[2]

*I hate definitions.*

BENJAMIN DISRAELI

The first step in approaching medical ethics from the perspective of virtue is to ask, "What are the role virtues of physicians, nurses, and other health care professionals (HCPs)?" Feminism has prompted a partial answer to this question. Some feminists have recently claimed that care is a virtue which has been somewhat neglected, perhaps because it has been thought to be a feminine

virtue (Gilligan, 1982; Noddings, 1984). In particular, the following thesis has been advanced. (A) Care is a role virtue for HCPs (Fry, 1989, p. 99; Pellegrino, 1987, p. 22). A good HCP must have the character trait of care.

The word "care" is used in a variety of ways. Among other things "care" might mean "minister to" (take care of the sick), "to take an interest in" (care about freedom), or "to have a liking for" (care for chocolate).

Of course, "care" in thesis (A) does not mean merely "minister to." If thesis (A) is to be a non-trivial claim, then the character trait of care must include caring about as well as taking care of. I can take care of someone I do not care about, perhaps even someone I despise. HCPs should not only behave in certain ways toward patients, but HCPs should also care about patients.

Nor can "care" in thesis (A) mean merely "take an interest in." Heidegger uses the term "care" roughly this way. For Heidegger "care" refers to a morally neutral stance all people constantly have toward all sorts of things (Heidegger, 1962). In thesis (A), however, the term "care" refers to a morally positive relationship with people and perhaps animals. Thesis (A), moreover, presupposes that some people are more caring than others and some are uncaring.

Frankena's use of the term "care" meets these conditions. He defines care as non-indifference or respect for persons (Frankena, 1983, p. 71–75).[3] But one can be dispassionately non-indifferent. One can take an interest in people without liking them. One can act in ways which respect rather than violate the autonomy of people without wishing them well let alone being emotionally attached to them. But this cannot be what "care" means in thesis (A), and this is not what the feminists mean by "care." If "caring" meant merely respecting people's personhood, then there would be no different voice. The ethics of care would be no different from the ethics of justice. Feminists would merely be Kantians, and thesis (A) would be trivial.

Note that respect for persons is not the same as benevolence. A benevolent person not only respects the autonomy of others, but also wishes them well and tries to help them even on certain occasions when he or she has no duty to do so (Wallace, 1978, pp. 121–131). Note also that benevolent people need not "have a liking for" the objects of their benevolence. It is perfectly possible to be benevolent even toward people one dislikes.

As the feminists, the advocates of thesis (A), and I use the term, "care" means "have a liking for" a person, caring for that person. Care, unlike benevolence, involves emotional attachment. But what sort or level of emotional attachment?[4] Emotional attachments toward other people can be arranged roughly by degree ranging from dispassionateness through the attachment typically felt for mere acquaintances, the attachments typical of mild and close friendships, all the way to the attachment typical of love. As the feminists, the advocates of thesis (A), and I use the term, "care" involves not just the mild emotional attachment that we feel for the acquaintance, but considerably more emotional attachment. Care involves at least as much emotional attachment as is typical of mild friendships.[5]

Roughly speaking, the number of objects of attachment is inversely proportional to the degree of attachment. A person with the general virtue of care typically cares a lot for a small circle of intimate friends and family, somewhat less for a larger circle of ordinary friends, and does not care for everyone else. (The caring person may be non-indifferent or even benevolent toward everyone else since dispassionate non-indifference and even dispassionate benevolence is possible, but the caring person is not emotionally attached to everyone else.) The objects of the medical virtue of care are, however, a different group of people from the objects of the general virtue of care. Clearly, if care is a virtue for HCPs, then the objects of care for HCPs are predominately the patients.

Therefore, if care is a role virtue for HCPs, then in their professional capacity HCPs should not only minister to (take care of) and take an interest in (care about) their patients, but they should also have a liking for (care for) their patients. And not just any degree of liking. Thesis (A) implies that

HCPs should be significantly emotionally attached to their patients.

*General benevolence, but not general friendship, makes a man what he ought to be.*

JANE AUSTEN

"Caring" is a term so loaded with positive connotations that to criticize anything related to it is risky. No one wants to be perceived as "against caring" so I must proceed cautiously. Of course, I think that caring is a general virtue. Of course, I think that caring is a role virtue for some roles (e.g. parenting). Nevertheless, I think that thesis (A) is false. Care is not a role virtue for HCPs. Indeed, it is a vice. In their professional capacity, doctors, nurses, and other HCPs should not care for their patients.[6]

This is not the completely counterintuitive claim that HCPs should be uncaring brutes indifferent to the fate of their patients. Rather my claim is that they should not become significantly emotionally attached to their patients. Suppose, for example, that Anne is a doctor who does everything a doctor is supposed to do in the right way, at the right time, etc., except that she does not care for her patients. Her diagnoses are accurate. Her therapies are effective. Her manner is warm and friendly. She communicates well with her patients. And so on. In general, Anne wants to improve the overall length and quality of life of her patients and acts effectively to do so. But she does not regret the suffering and death of her patients any more than she regrets the suffering and death of other people's patients because she is not significantly emotionally attached to her patients. It would be very strange to say that Anne is not a good doctor. Yet that is what we would have to say if (A) care is a role virtue for HCPs.[7]

I shall argue for my claim in two stages. First, I shall show that care causes serious problems both for caring HCPs and for cared-for patients. Second, I shall argue that (B1) benevolence is a role virtue for HCPs and suggest that (B2) benevolence disposes HCPs to perform caring acts (acts typically performed by caring people). My argument for (B1) will consist in showing that benevolence causes fewer and less serious problems than care.

## Drawbacks of Care

*She loves you. And you know that can't be bad.*

THE BEATLES

Let me begin with a small but important point. Contrary to what is commonly believed, being cared for is not always intrinsically desirable.[8] In any given case, whether being cared for is intrinsically desirable depends on various factors within the situation. Anyone who has been the object of unrequited love can testify that being cared for can be a burden as well as a good. As feminists have emphasized, it is not always desirable to be cared for solely because of one's appearance. Finally, like other human emotions, care can assume twisted forms which torment the cared-for person. Some varieties of sadism, for example are really manifestations of care. The desirability of being cared for is a function of who is doing the caring, why one is cared for, and how the care is manifested. Moreover, even if the who, why, and how of caring are OK, being cared for can be an intrusive invasion of privacy. Some people may not want to become an object of significant emotional attachment by the members of a whole medical team overnight.

*It is not a great pleasure to bring pain to a friend.*

SOPHOCLES

Although caring usually benefits the person cared for in various ways, it has some straightforward, bad consequences, too. Caring makes some desirable actions more difficult and less frequent. Consider hurting someone for whom you care, causing intense physical pain. Consider communicating very bad news to someone for whom you care, causing intense mental anguish. Hurting patients and communicating very bad news to patients are things that HCPs frequently should do. They may be more reluctant to hurt patients for whom they care even when doing so is thera-

peutically indicated. They may be more reluctant to tell patients for whom they care very bad news even if the patients should know the truth. Similarly, caring usually makes it harder to withhold or withdraw treatment, deny patient's requests, etc. Yet these acts, too, are appropriate in some situations. Being cared for is, therefore, not always an unmitigated good.

*I love you. You belong to me.*

PAUL in *Breakfast at Tiffany's*

Caring also makes some undesirable actions easier and more frequent. Consider deceiving someone for his or her own good. People are more willing to deceive paternalistically those for whom they care than strangers. The caring relationship serves as a sort of justification. Some people sometimes think that caring for someone entitles the caring person to some control over the life of the cared-for person. The nurse who enters the room without knocking because she thinks herself entitled to a friend's liberties is a minor example. The doctor who prescribes a placebo for the patient's own good is a more serious example. In general, caring for a person seems to make paternalism easier and more frequent. Yet paternalism is seldom appropriate for HCPs.

Morse *et al.* (1990, p. 11) mention another common way in which caring yields undesirable consequences.

[The HCP] may relish a caring relationship and foster patient dependency to meet his or her own needs for caring, thus interfering with treatment goals that work toward patient autonomy and health.

Of course, all this is a long way from a demonstration that the disadvantages of being cared for outweigh the benefits. Indeed, what I have said so far suggests important ways in which care is beneficial. The cases where reluctance to hurt inspired by care saves patients from unnecessary pain probably far outnumber the cases where this reluctance deprives patients of painful, but overall beneficial therapy. So far I have merely shown that being cared for is not always purely good either intrinsically or instrumentally.[9]

*Love your neighbor as you love yourself.*

JESUS

The character trait of care involves emotional attachment to a person. We do not feel this attachment to others just because they are people. Instead, we feel it because of the particular people they are, because of particular facts about them. We care for others *qua* individual rather than *qua* person. Indeed, the injunction to care for patients often functions as a way of stressing that patients should be treated as individuals rather than mere numbers.

Since care requires an emotional investment based on particular facts, since we care for people as individuals, HCPs cannot care equally for all patients. A patient may be difficult for me to care for because he or she reminds me of an old flame who jilted me, has a sour personality, or has irritating mannerisms and bad breath. A patient may be easy to care for because he or she shares interests with me, is physically attractive, or has a great repertoire of jokes. It would require a saint to care for some really disgusting patients. Unrepentant child molesters, serial killers, highly manipulative sadists, etc. get sick and become patients just like the rest of us. As Downie and Telfer (1980, p. 91) observe "[S]ome things are clearly not psychologically possible. A caring worker cannot be in love with all his clients. Nor can he even like them all." The character trait of care requires us to care for people as individuals rather than merely as persons, and this, in turn, implies that we care for people unequally and that there are some people for whom we do not care (Noddings, 1984, p. 18). Of course, this is not an objection to the general virtue of care, but it is an objection to the thesis that (A) care is a role virtue for HCPs.

The fine talk of caring for patients as individuals conceals a nasty reality. To accept it is to endorse and encourage favoritism in health care. In practice, such talk encourages the HCP to take care of patients only insofar as the HCP likes the patient. The HCP, however, ought to be as impartial as possible toward patients. Note, moreover, that the patient's race, sex, and age are sometimes relevant to the ability of HCPs to care for the patient. Favoritism opens the door to even more unsavory practices such as racism, sexism, and ageism. These 'isms' have no place in the health care setting. Care is a problematic character trait for HCPs since it endorses and encourages these 'isms'.

*What would happen to me if I loved all of the children I said goodbye to?*

MARY POPPINS

One of the major problems facing HCPs is the problem of burnout. There are many causes of burnout, but one of them is surely getting significantly emotionally involved with patients, i.e. caring. Caring contributes to burnout in a variety of ways. First, the HCP can bring his or her patients' problems home only so long before giving up on the profession. People have only a limited tolerance for sharing sorrow and suffering. Emotional resources often get used up. Second, caring increases the vulnerability of the person who cares. To care for someone is to make an emotional investment which often becomes costly if the object of care dies, suffers, does not live up to expectations, rejects the care, recovers and departs, etc. Caring people get burned. Third, not only the practice of caring, but the very ideal of caring causes burnout. Some HCPs feel guilty about their inability to care for all of their patients equally. This guilt contributes to burnout. Thus, care causes burnout through emotional exhaustion, vulnerability, and self-recrimination (Maslach, 1982, pp. 2–14).

Burnout harms both HCPs and patients in direct and obvious ways. Burned out HCPs often suffer physical and psychological deterioration. Their patients, family, and friends also suffer. So do institutions and practices with which the burned out HCPs are associated. Emotional exhaustion leads people to quit. It thus exacerbates the shortage of HCPs (especially nurses), making the remaining staff more inadequate and overworked. Sometimes quitting is the lesser evil.

Emotionally exhausted HCPs who remain often unconsciously adopt various counter-productive coping strategies to minimize their emotional investments in their patients. These strategies undermine the ability of the HCP to deliver health care while exacerbating the original problem. Vulnerability leads to negative assessments of patients. "They are all trolls." It leads to detached, callous attitudes and responses to patients. Moreover, vulnerable people tend to strike back indiscriminately. They sometimes blame and punish not just the ones they cared for but also others. They often adopt vindictive attitudes toward people, in general. Self-recrimination, like emotional exhaustion, often leads to counterproductive coping strategies. Negative attitudes toward oneself take the joy out of one's own life and undermine the health care delivery process. Thus, ironically, caring for people often leads to burnout which often leads to treating people in uncaring or even hateful ways.

*A doctor who treats himself has a fool for a patient and a quack for a doctor.*

ANONYMOUS

Objectivity is a central virtue for every professional, especially for HCPs. Loss of objectivity decreases the accuracy of diagnosis, the correctness of treatment decisions, the success rate of procedures, etc. In general, objectivity is necessary to provide the best medical care.[10] Emotional ties to patients tend to compromise the objectivity of professionals. Other things being equal, the degree of objectivity about a patient is more or less inversely proportional to the degree of emotional attachment to the patient. Thus, doctors are warned not to treat themselves, their family members, or their friends as patients. They are too emotionally attached to self, family, and friends to be objective. Their caring prevents them from providing the best medical care to the ones for whom they care. Therefore, it seems bizarre to suggest that HCPs should care for their patients, for this

implies that they should abandon their objectivity, compromise their professional judgment, and, in general, decline to provide their patient with the best medical care.[11]

*The logic underlying an ethic of care is a psychological logic of relationships which contrasts with the formal logic of fairness that informs the justice approach.*

CAROL GILLIGAN

HCPs who care for their patients naturally tend to take their primary allegiance and duty to be toward their own patients rather than other people's patients or the community. Naturally, they try to get the best for their own patients. They tend to put their own patients first. This poses two problems in a situation of scarce resources. First, caring drives the cost of health care up. Second, caring impairs the ability of HCPs to allocate resources according to need. In other words, caring produces inefficiency and unfairness.

Consider the following oversimplified situation. The best therapy (BT) for a certain disease (D) is new, scarce, and very expensive. The second best therapy (SBT) is much cheaper, but not much worse except in a few cases. If doctors each care for their own patients, then they will tend to prescribe BT for their patients when the cost of BT is covered by third party payers. This will cause insurance or tax rates to go up, and therefore will cost many people a great deal. Overall, the community would be better off if doctors would prescribe SBT although the patients with D would usually be slightly worse off.[12]

If doctors each prescribed BT for their own patients, then the distribution of BT would be based on the access of physicians to BT rather than according to need, desert, etc. So a few people who desperately need BT (because they are allergic to SBT, for example) will not get it because the supply of BT will be exhausted. If doctors did not care for their patients, these all-too-common problems would arise less frequently. So these problems undermine the claim that care is a role virtue for HCPs.

## Alternatives to Care

*To bear the unbearable sorrow*

THE MAN OF LA MANCHA

It would be very odd if a character trait that led to burnout, bias, injustice, and inefficiency was a virtue. All of these drawbacks, however, do not, by themselves, show that care is a vice for HCPs. After all, in addition to these drawbacks, care has many obvious advantages which I have not mentioned. If all of the alternative character traits have worse drawbacks and/or fewer advantages, then care will turn out to be a virtue after all. So I must show that there is a better character trait for HCPs to have than care.

One way out of the problems of favoritism, burnout, objectivity loss, etc. is to say that HCPs should combine something like care with something like professional distance. Maslach (1982, pp. 147–148), for example, recommends the attitude of 'detached concern.'

This recommendation is ambiguous. It might mean that HCPs should adopt a watered down version of what I have been calling care. HCPs should have a positive emotional attachment to their patients, but that attachment should be much less than the emotional attachment associated with caring. If this is what "detached concern" means, then Maslach's recommendation is not significantly different from my own. (See below.)

However, Maslach's recommendation might be that HCPs should simply add a buffer of professional distance to undiluted care. HCPs should maintain a substantial emotional attachment to their patients, but somehow temper that attachment with detachment. If this is what "detached concern" means, then it is not a viable or even intelligible recommendation. It is an oxymoron. Like oil and water, detachment and concern do not mix. The recommended attitude is impossible to adopt because detachment and concern are incompatible.

*Hypocrisy is not generally a social sin, but a virtue.*

MISS MANNERS

My proposal replaces the thesis that (A) care is a role virtue for HCPs with the thesis that (B1) benevolence is a role virtue for HCPs, and since patients are generally best helped by caring actions, that (B2) benevolence disposes HCPs to perform caring acts. Benevolent behavior in the health care context is caring behavior. So I am advocating a shift from an ethics of care, to an ethics of care behavior. My suggestion is that HCPs should act *as if* they cared for patients as individuals, but it is not necessary or even desirable for them really to care for patients. HCPs should act *as if* they are significantly emotionally attached, but in fact should involve their feelings relatively little. They should be no more emotionally attached to their own patients than to someone else's patients or to the proverbial man on the street. HCPs should do the things that a person who really cared would do in the way that such a person would do them.[13] They should take special note of individual differences among patients, adopt an informal, friendly manner, take an interest in non-medical aspects of patients' lives, etc. (Downie and Telfer, 1980, p. 91) They should hug patients who need to be hugged. But they should not really care.

## Objections to My Proposal

*A good tree does not produce decayed fruit any more than a decayed tree produces good fruit.*

JESUS

Someone might object to my proposal by claiming that HCPs cannot consistently provide caring actions without actually caring. This objection is not without force. It must be conceded that, other things being equal, a person who really cares for patients will be able to treat patients in a caring manner more consistently than a person who does not really care for patients.

But other things are not equal. As I have mentioned above, caring HCPs are at higher risk of burnout, and burnout typically leads to treating patients in an uncaring manner. So although caring HCPs may act more caring at the beginning of their careers, benevolent but uncaring HCPs are more likely to act in a caring manner throughout the course of their careers.

Moreover, caring for patients is by no means the dominant factor in the ability to treat patients in a caring manner. If getting HCPs to treat patients in a caring manner is the goal, then it would be much more effective to train HCPs in certain techniques than to urge HCPs to care for their patients.

*Why Grumpy, you do care!*

SNOW WHITE

Another objection to my arguments is that they seem to imply that parents should not care for their children. Actually, however, my arguments do not really have this implication. Parents have many fewer children than HCPs have patients. And, of course, parents do not see their children rarely and only in institutional settings as HCPs see their patients. The dangers of favoritism, burnout, inefficiency, and unfairness are, therefore, much less for caring parents than for caring HCPs. The danger of objectivity loss is greater, but is compensated for by the fact that a parents have greater knowledge about their children than do HCPs about their patients. Thus, the drawbacks of care are much less for parents than for HCPs; so much so that the advantages of care outweigh the drawbacks for parents. Parents should care for their children although HCPs should not care for their patients. (Day-care workers seem to me to be a borderline case.)

*Men become gods by excess of virtue.*

ARISTOTLE *(NE vii 1)*

*But clearly the virtue we must study is human virtue.*

ARISTOTLE *(NE i 13)*

There is a sense in which courage is not a good character trait for an unjust person to have. It is better for an unjust person to be held back from robbery by cowardice than to go on to become a bold knave. Nevertheless, we call courage a virtue because it is a good character trait for a person with all of the other virtues to have. Similarly, perhaps care is not a good character trait for HCPs who are susceptible to burnout, bias, objectivity loss, etc. to have. But people are all not equally prone to these things. If the ideal HCP is well defended against the dangers of care so that its advantages outweigh its disadvantages, then is not care a virtue for HCPs?[14]

As usual when doing virtue ethics we must have recourse to the notion of a range of normal character traits. HCPs who are not susceptible to burnout, bias, objectivity loss, etc. while practicing modern medicine in major medical centers are vanishingly rare. There may well be a few extraordinary individuals for whom care is overall beneficial. But a character trait which is only good for a moral saint or superman to have is not a virtue. Instead a virtue is a character trait which is good for a normal good person to have. As I have shown, the character trait of care is not good for a normal HCP to have, so care is not a virtue for HCPs.

*[Ivan Ilych] wished most of all . . . for someone to pity him as a sick child is pitied.*

LEO TOLSTOY

My proposal seems to be open to an objection which has bedeviled Kant's theory of moral worth. Sometimes what a person wants and needs is to be cared for. Mere caring words and actions springing from some other character trait such as dutifulness or even disinterested benevolence will not do.

I shall not contest this claim here, though I do believe it is more controversial than some seem to think. Instead, I shall merely observe that it does not follow from the fact that patients have certain needs that it is the function of the HCP to meet these needs. After all, it is not the function of the HCP to meet all of the needs of the patient. To assume that providing emotional attachment to patients is part of the HCPs job description would beg the question of whether care is a medical virtue.

*Alienation appears not merely in the result but also in the process of production.*

KARL MARX

My theses that (B1) benevolence is a role virtue for HCPs, and that (B2) benevolence disposes HCPs to perform caring acts would solve the problems of favoritism, burnout, objectivity loss, etc. Of course my proposal has its own drawbacks. (a) From the HCPs point of view, the HCPs would be required to fake it on a regular basis, to live a lie. The peril of burnout would be replaced with the evils of alienation. (b) From the patient's point of view, patients might believe that HCPs care for them even though the HCPs do not really care. The perils of favoritism and objectivity loss would be replaced by the evils of deception. (c) Finally, there is a risk that HCPs will accept my rebuttal of the thesis that (A) care is a role virtue for HCPs while rejecting (B1) and (B2). Unscrupulous or incautious HCPs might use my arguments that HCPs should not care for their patients as rationalizations for acting in uncaring ways toward their patients.

Now these are real dangers, but I do not think that they are very serious. (a) People who meet the public (e.g. salespeople) are often required to smile when they feel surly, be helpful to people they despise, etc. This does not typically produce intolerable tension or psychic trauma. Nor is the performance of caring actions likely to cause

HCPs to become confused whether they care for certain patients.

(b) In our society caring acts are performed by a wide range of professionals and institutions. Customers and clients are well aware that these acts are often performed without attachment, that they are just part of the job. Indeed, people are often somewhat cynical about such acts. Patients will not leap to the conclusion that HCPs, whom they meet for relatively short blocks of time in professional contexts, care for them. HCPs will not typically deceive themselves or their patients by performing caring actions. In the relatively rare cases where there is a significant chance that patients might be misled by caring actions the HCPs may ward off misunderstandings by stating up front in a gentle way that they are not intending to befriend the patient, but are merely doing their jobs.

(c) Finally, almost any doctrine can be intentionally or accidentally twisted into a rationalization for something repulsive. I can only emphasize that my thesis does not justify or excuse HCPs who act in uncaring ways. HCPs *should* perform caring acts for patients. They just should not care for patients.

## Conclusion

*Money can't buy me love.*

THE BEATLES

Let us step back for a moment and look at the larger context. We have been discussing an aspect of the HCP/patient relationship. My suggestion is compatible with the consumerist, freemarket model of the HCP/patient relationship, but the thesis that (A) care is a role virtue for HCPs is not compatible with this model. According to the consumerist model it is unreasonable to expect the HCP to care for the patient for the same reason that it is unreasonable to expect the HCP to love the patient. Emotional attachment is not the sort of thing which can be bought and sold. Thesis (A) is compatible only with the paternalistic model, I think. So to advocate thesis (A) is indirectly to endorse the paternalistic model of the HCP/patient relationship. But the paternalistic model endorses some fairly unsavory practices. Thesis (A) is tarnished by the company it keeps.

Another aspect of the larger context is the enormous recent change in the nature of the health care delivery system. Most people's health care needs used to be met by the old family doctor who was also a family friend. (Or at least this is what most people "fondly remember.") *Qua* friend the old family doctors cared for their patients. These solo practitioners have now been replaced by health care teams within health care institutions. The HCP no longer sees the patient frequently in a variety of different settings as part of an ongoing multifaceted relationship. Instead HCPs typically see their patients only rarely, only professionally, and only within an institutional setting. This change of the institutions and practices of health care exacerbates most of the drawbacks of care mentioned above and tips care over the edge from virtue to vice for HCPs.

Expecting contemporary HCPs to care for their patients is as unreasonable as expecting love from a prostitute. In both cases the relationship seems intimate, but the exchange of money, the infrequency of contact, and the one-dimensionality of the relationship makes the relationship purely professional. Emotional attachment is incidental and destructive to the practice.

# NOTES

1. I take no position here on whether general virtues are relative to practices and/or institutions.

2. The importance of this qualification was suggested to me by Kai Wong.

3. The title of my paper gets its maximum shock value when "care" is understood in this sense. If the alternative to being a caring HCP is to be an uncaring, indifferent one, then of course HCPs should care for their patients.

4. A virtue is not merely a disposition to act in certain ways. It also involves having the right habits of passion, belief, desire, taste, and motive. To paraphrase Aristotle, a caring person, a person with the virtue of care, is a person who tends to form and maintain caring relationships with the right people, in the right way, with the right emotions,

etc.. So we must ask "What are the right emotions and who are the right people?"

5. Of course this does not imply that caring relationships *are* friendships. Friendships are two-way relationships, but caring relationships need not be two-way.

6. This claim implies that being a good HCP is incompatible with being a good person (and parent) or that it is possible to possess the general virtue of caring (and the parental virtue of caring) without caring for patients. I believe the latter implication to be correct.

7. Of course my opponent might say that people such as Anne do not exist. I shall try indirectly to show that they do.

8. The belief that being cared for is intrinsically desirable is often coupled with some fairly wild claims about the wonderful consequences of the caring relationship. Jean Watson, for example, claims that "In a transpersonal caring relationship, a spiritual union occurs between the two person where both are capable of transcending self, time, space, and the life history of each other" (Watson, 1988, p. 66). Lenninger claims that "[T]here can be no effective cure without care" (Lenninger, 1985, p. 210). I shall not bother to debunk these wild claims.

9. Of course, this is true for "being the object" of most virtues as well as vices. So far I have merely tried to raise the question of whether care is an overall good. I have merely tried to show that the answer is not obvious.

10. It sometimes said that objectivity is somehow antithetical to treating a patient as an individual. The idea is that an objective, scientific approach involves subsuming patients under general laws, classifying patients together with others with similar diseases and situations. It tends to put patients into pigeonholes and ignores the individuating details among patients. A subjective approach, on the other hand, focuses on what is unique about each patient. It tends to pick up important facts which the objective approach misses.

This is a mistake. What is actually going on here is that a sloppy objective approach is being contrasted with a careful objective approach. The former approach is called "objective" and the latter approach is called "subjective." But there is nothing subjective about carefully seeking all of the details about each patient. Indeed, a truly subjective approach tends to miss things, for a subjective approach takes the biases of the investigator to be central guides of the investigation rather than obstacles to be overcome.

11. It might be argued that nurses are different from other professionals in that objectivity is not central to or even part of nursing. This is a dangerous line of argument for it undermines the claims of nursing to be a profession. But it is also mistaken. Clearly, nursing includes tasks such as watching for particular symptoms and general changes in the overall health of the patient, administration of medication, performing and assisting in the performance of procedures, transmission of information between patient and doctor, etc. These are tasks for which objectivity is crucial.

12. In some cases the patients with D would be better off, too (perhaps because of economies of scale in the production of SBT). In these 'prisoner dilemmas' cases, if doctors each care for and prescribe BT for their own patients, the best interests of everyone, even the patients, are defeated.

13. Does this mean that benevolent, but uncaring doctors would prescribe BT rather than SBT for their patients? No. Unlike care, benevolence does not involve favoritism. Benevolent doctors will try to do what is best for all concerned rather than giving preference to the interests of their own patients. Thus, they will prescribe SBT.

14. This objection was suggested to me by Walter Schaller.

# References

Benjamin, M. and Curtis, J.: 1985, "Virtue and the practice of nursing," E. Shelp (ed.), *Virtue and Medicine,* D. Reidel Publ. Co., Dordrecht, pp. 257–273.

Downie, R. and Telfer, E.: 1980, *Caring and Curing,* Methuen and Co., London.

Frankena, W.: 1983, "Moral-point-of-view theories," in N. Bowie (ed.), *Ethical Theory in the Last Quarter of the Twentieth Century,* Hackett, Indianapolis, pp. 39–79.

Fry, S.: 1989, "The role of caring in a theory of nursing ethics," *Hypatia,* 4, 88–103.

Gilligan, C.: 1982, *In a Different Voice,* Harvard University Press, Cambridge.

Heidegger, M.: 1962, J. Macquarrie and E. Robinson (trans.), *Being and Time,* Harper & Row, New York.

Lenninger, M.: 1985, "Transcultural care diversity and university: A theory of nursing," *Nursing and Health Care,* 6, 209–212.

Maslach, C. 1982, *Burnout: The Cost of Caring,* Prentice-Hall, Englewood Cliffs.

Morse, J. *et al.*: 1990, "Concepts of caring and caring as a concept," *Advances in Nursing Science,* 13, 1–14.

Noddings, N.: 1984, *Caring,* University of California Press, Berkeley.

Pellegrino, E.: 1987, "The caring ethic: The relation of physician to patient," in A. Bishop and J. Scudder (ed.), *Caring, Curing, Coping: Nurse, Physician, Patient Relationships,* University of Alabama Press, Birmingham, pp. 8–30.

Veatch, R.: 1983, "The physician as stranger: The ethics of the anonymous patient-physician relationship," in E. Shelp (ed.), *The Clinical Encounter: The Moral Fabric of the Patient-Physician Relationship,* D. Reidel Publ. Co., Dordrecht, pp. 187–207.

Wallace, J.: 1978, *Virtues and Vices,* Cornell University Press, Ithaca.

Watson, J.: 1988, *Nursing: Human Science and Human Care,* National League for Nursing, New York.

# Questions

1. Compare and contrast Aristotle's account of the quasi-virtue of friendship with the Ethics of Care.

2. Aristotle says, "When men are friends they have no need of justice" (193, 1155a). However, he also says, "The demands of justice also seem to increase with the intensity of the friendship, which implies that friendship and justice exist between the same persons and have an equal extension" (208, 1160a). Is Aristotle being inconsistent? Explain Aristotle's view about the relationship between justice and friendship. Attack and/or defend Aristotle's view.

3. Discuss *one* of the following claims.

   a. Stephen King says, "Immorality proceeds from a lack of care." [S. King, "Notes on Horror," *Quest* 5 (1985), 31.]

   b. Noddings says, "An ethic built on caring is, I think, characteristically and essentially feminine."

   c. Just as Rawls and Nozick are, in their different ways, both Kantians, so Gilligan and Noddings are, in their different ways, both Aristotelians.

4. In her article, "Abortion and the 'Feminine Voice'" Wolf-Devine observes that abortion and its defenses fall on the masculine side of the masculine/feminine distinctions sketched by Gilligan and Noddings. Abortion is typically motivated by fear of attachment—the desire to avoid being tied down by a commitment to care. It severs the relationship between woman and fetus in order to preserve the separateness and autonomy of the woman. Abortion is typically defended in terms of rights: the rights of individual women to decline a relationship. Moreover,

abortion involves violence against the helpless. It is an expression of power justified by the claim that women should have control over their bodies. It is hardly a cooperative, egalitarian act. Instead, it is a subordination of the interests of one being to the interests of another.

Surely many feminists would argue against Wolf-Devine's view of abortion. Choose *one* of the following practices and describe it in *both* masculine and feminine terms. Which is a more accurate description of the practice you chose? What is the moral significance (if any) of your answer?

a. surrogate motherhood
b. imprisonment as punishment
c. sex with your spouse
d. prostitution
e. recycling
f. health care
g. politics
h. philosophy
i. euthanasia
j. welfare

5. Does the claim that the Ethics of Care is simply a description of the proto-virtue of natural care really solve all of the problems raised in the introduction to this section?

6. I have suggested that the Ethics of Care is an account of the natural virtue of care and that the Ethics of Justice is an account of the natural virtue of justice. Construct the Ethics of Courage. You might wish to refer to some work of literature, such as the *Iliad* by Homer.

7. Choose *one* of the following characters. Does your character typically employ the Ethics of Care, the Ethics of Justice, both, or neither? Explain your answer.

a. Huck in *Huckleberry Finn* by Mark Twain
b. Elizabeth in *Pride and Prejudice* by Jane Austin
c. Dorothea in *Middlemarch* by George Eliot
d. Raskolnikov in *Crime and Punishment* by Fyodor Dostoevsky

e. Nora in "A Doll's House" by Henrik Ibsen

8. Gilligan relates the Heinz dilemma that was originally used by Kohlberg to measure moral development in adolescence. "Heinz considers whether or not to steal a drug which he cannot afford to buy in order to save the life of his wife." She says that for Mainstream Ethics the question is whether Heinz should act or do nothing. Mainstream Ethics assumes that the only available action is to steal the drug. On the other hand, the Ethics of Care assumes that Heinz should act. The question is whether he should steal the drug or reason with the drug owner. But shouldn't a viable moral analysis of the dilemma consider both avenues?

Gilligan then uses the way in which two children, Jake and Amy, respond to the Heinz dilemma to illustrate proto-Mainstream Ethics and proto-Care Ethics. That is, she takes their responses as one bit of evidence that boys and girls develop along different paths toward different moral perspectives. Jake is insensitive to the needs of others, whereas Amy is insensitive to her own needs. Jake borders on selfishness, Amy on servility. But couldn't their responses merely indicate different paths toward (or failure modes of) a single morality that balances consideration for self and for others?

9. Suppose you are hiring a babysitter. Among the applicants is a man with good credentials who is, however, not known to you or to anyone you know well. According to Gilligan and Noddings, men are less likely to be caring, nurturing people than women and are more likely to be just, objective people. Does the Ethics of Care imply that you should reject the male applicant and hire a women with equally good credentials for the job? Does the Ethics of Care imply that when electing judges, you should vote for male candidates and reject female candidates, other things being equal? How would an advocate of the Ethics of Care defend that theory against the charge of gender bias?

# Economic Justice: Aristotle, Nozick, Mill, and Rawls

*"... with liberty and justice for all."*

PLEDGE OF ALLEGIANCE

Justice concerns everyone, of course, but it is of particular concern to women these days because women are often treated unjustly in a variety of different spheres (the workplace, the home, the courts, and so on). Justice is sometimes taken broadly to mean "respect for the rights of others" and is sometimes taken more narrowly to mean "fair distribution of goods and burdens." In this chapter I shall take justice narrowly and focus on justice in the distribution of income.

Clearly, what people earn from a job consists of more than merely money. The earnings of office workers include at least their benefits package as well as their salary. If the work is irritating, perhaps the irritation should be considered a negative part of their earnings. This can get fairly complicated. College professors, for example, earn their salary, plus a benefits package, plus flexibility of work schedule, minus administrative hassles, minus pre-tenure job insecurity, plus post-tenure job security, and so on. Thus let me define *income* to be salary plus job-related benefits minus job-related hardships.

There are difficulties. The extent to which something is a hardship seems to be relative to individual preferences. Some people abhor meeting the public or assuming a high degree of responsibility; others find these things merely irritating; still others enjoy them. If hardships are relative and people should be compensated for hardships, then compensation should be relative. This yields the paradoxical conclusion that the more people like their job, the less pay they deserve. Perhaps something is a hardship if a reasonable person would consider it to be a hardship. This yields the paradoxical conclusion that people with unreasonable tastes should be compensated for doing things they enjoy.

## Aristotle's Income Principle

When the Mikado declares that his object is "to make the punishment fit the crime,"[1] he is advocating a widely held approach toward the distribution of punishment. People who commit crimes of equal severity ought to receive equal punishments. People who commit crimes of unequal severity ought to receive proportionately unequal punishments.

$$\frac{\text{Severity of Anne's crime}}{\text{Severity of Bill's crime}} = \frac{\text{Anne's punishment}}{\text{Bill's punishment}}$$

Just as it seems unfair to punish people any other way than in proportion to their crime, so it seems unfair for two people who are equal in the relevant respects to receive unequal benefits or for two people who are unequal in the relevant respects to receive disproportionate benefits.

*Aristotle's Income Principle:* People with equal amounts of characteristic C ought to receive equal incomes. People with unequal amounts of C ought to receive proportionately unequal incomes.

$$\frac{\text{Anne's amount of C}}{\text{Bill's amount of C}} = \frac{\text{Anne's income}}{\text{Bill's income}}$$

Aristotle's Income Principle is merely a formal principle that must be supplemented with a material principle specifying characteristic C. It is, however, not at all clear what this material principle should be. What is the characteristic, C, according to which income should be distributed? People who claim to deserve high incomes because they work long, hard hours are implicitly supplementing Aristotle's Income Principle with the following principle.

*Principle of Effort:* C = the person's effort

That is, the harder people work at their jobs, the more money they should make. Similarly, people sometimes claim to deserve a high income because they are talented or because they contribute a great deal to society. Karl Marx's

**343**

famous slogan "From each according to his abilities; to each according to his needs"[2] is a proposal to distribute jobs according to talent and to distribute income according to need. So we have,

*Principle of Talent:* C = the person's talent
*Principle of Contribution:* C = the person's contribution to society
*Principle of Need:* C = the person's need

These material principles can, of course, be combined in various ways. Some might say, for example, that income ought to be distributed according to a weighted combination of effort and talent. [C = (constant$_1$) × (effort) + (constant$_2$) × (talent)] For the sake of brevity, I shall not discuss combinations of these principles.

Note that even after Aristotle's Income Principle has been combined with some material principle specifying C, the account of income distribution will remain incomplete. It may tell me that Bill deserves twice as much income as Anne, but I still do not know whether their yearly incomes should be, respectively, $10,000 and $20,000 or $50,000 and $100,000. Note also that although I have been talking about distribution, Aristotle's Income Principle does not presuppose a central distributor of income. This principle is a standard for the evaluation of patterns of income distribution no matter how these patterns are produced.

Each of these principles can be further specified in several different ways. For example, one version of the Principle of Need says that goods should be distributed in proportion to the needs of each person. That is, the more you need, the more you get. Each person's needs are ranked. After everyone's top-priority needs are satisfied, then the society satisfies everyone's second-priority needs, and then the third-priority needs, and so on until all goods are distributed among the people. The state of Oregon once planned to distribute health care in this way, although the plan was not actually put into effect.

Another version of the Principle of Need says that goods should be distributed in proportion to the *basic* needs of each person. That is, every-

one should get their basic needs (food, clothing, shelter, and perhaps life-saving health care) satisfied. In an affluent society like ours, the bulk of the goods will remain. These remaining goods should be distributed according to some other principle. Govier endorses this version of the Principle of Need and calls it the Permissive Principle. Our present welfare system is similar to, though not quite the same as, the Permissive Principle. Welfare aims not to satisfy *all* of the basic needs of *every* person, but rather to satisfy *some percentage* of the basic needs of *some* people—namely, the people who do not satisfy their own needs through the free market.

Yet another version of the Principle of Need says that everyone should have a *reasonable opportunity to satisfy* basic needs. That is, people who are unable to work should be provided with food, clothing, and other necessities whereas those who can work should be offered a job paying at least a subsistence wage (and perhaps they should be offered job training, day care services, and other assistance in working). Again, any remaining goods should be distributed through some other principle. Joel Feinberg advocates this version of the Principle of Need, which is sometimes called workfare. Trudy Govier calls it the Puritan Principle in "The Right to Eat and the Duty to Work." Feinberg and Govier disagree not only over whether we should have welfare or workfare but also over how the remaining goods should be distributed. Govier says the welfare system should supplement the free market, but Feinberg argues that the free market is an unjust economic system. He believes that workfare should supplement a system based on the Principle of Effort (and perhaps the Principle of Contribution).

"Doctors make three times as much money as professors, but they are not three times as smart; they do not work three times as hard; etc. Therefore, doctors make too much money." Feinberg formalizes this criticism of America's economic system in the following way.

*Argument (A)*

(1) There is no quality that most rich people share and most poor people lack. (You might

think that rich people are typically smart and/or industrious whereas poor people are not, but remember that many people are rich or poor simply through good or bad luck. A person may become rich, for example, by inheriting money or talent or simply by being in the right place at the right time.)

(2) If person X has more goodies than person Y, and person X is not different from person Y in some relevant way, then the state of affairs is unjust. (Aristotle's Income Principle)

(3) Therefore, America's economic system is unjust.

Presumably, the remedy for this sort of injustice would be state intervention in the marketplace either to control wages and fees or to redistribute income through taxes and transfer payments. Some people find this sort of intervention objectionable. Because argument (A) is valid and premise (1) is obviously true, people who disagree with argument (A) typically reject premise (2), Aristotle's Income Principle.

Combining Aristotle's Income Principle with the Principle of Effort yields counter-intuitive results. Because hard workers are found in every occupation, the Principle of Effort would require high incomes to cut across occupational lines. It would require hardworking mechanics to make just as much as equally hardworking physicians. Moreover, it says that the harder people work, the more money they should make whether or not they produce anything worthwhile. Suppose Calvin works twice as hard as Peter but produces only one-third as much (because he is clumsy, stupid, inefficient, or whatever). The Principle of Effort says that Calvin should make twice as much as Peter because he put in twice as much effort. This seems counter-intuitive. The Principle of Talent yields similar counter-intuitive results.

Why would anyone use effort as the basis for distribution of goods and burdens? Feinberg thinks that characteristics can be relevant to distributive justice only if their possessors can be responsible for those characteristics. If goods and burdens are distributed according to some characteristic, then everyone must have a fair opportunity to acquire that characteristic. Thus discrimination according to race or sex is wrong because some people do not have a fair opportunity to become white males. Using this *Fair Opportunity Requirement*, Feinberg suggests the following argument.

### Argument (B)

(1) It is not fair to reward and punish people on the basis of characteristics that are beyond their control. (Fair Opportunity Requirement)

(2) No plausible characteristic besides effort meets this requirement. The other characteristics all contain factors that people have no fair opportunity to acquire or avoid.

(3) Thus the Principle of Effort is the only principle that can be fairly combined with Aristotle's Income Principle.

Feinberg observes, however, that the motivation needed to exert oneself is also a function of heredity and circumstances. It seems that the Principle of Effort does not meet his Fair Opportunity Requirement, either.

The plausibility of the Principle of Talent probably arises from the notion that scarce resources should be maximally utilized. Excellent flutes should go to excellent flute players who can make full use of them, rather than to beginners who can get by just as well on mediocre flutes. Similarly, admission to medical school should go to people who have the talent to make good use of medical education, rather than to people on whom medical school will be wasted because they lack the appropriate learning skills.

Though this notion may incline us to use talent as a basis for distributing flutes, medical school admissions, and other resources that would otherwise be wasted, it is certainly not relevant to the distribution of goods such as income, which the talentless can use as well as the talented.

The Principle of Contribution is plausible when people are working together toward some common goal. Suppose Anne and Bill form a partnership (such as a marriage, a prospecting company, or whatever). Anne provides 1/3 of the capital and does 1/3 of the work. Bill provides 2/3 of the capital and does 2/3 of the work. Clearly, Anne deserves 1/3 of the profits and Bill deserves the other 2/3 of the profits.

Assessing contribution is usually difficult, however. For example, physicians in this society do not provide health care by themselves. They are part of a complex health care delivery system that includes nurses, technicians, drug companies, researchers, administrators, and equipment manufacturers. Without these other people, physicians could not do what they do. Separating the contribution of physicians to our society's common goal from the contribution of these other people seems a hopeless task. Indeed, the idea of a single social goal may be a mere fiction. Thus distributing income according to Aristotle's Income Principle + the Principle of Contribution is not a realistic option.

## Free Market Principle: Nozick

These days, the most common objection to Aristotle's Income Principle is simply that it is not the Free Market Principle. Aristotle's Income Principle says that distributions are just insofar as they conform to a certain pattern, no matter how the distributions came about. On the other hand, the free market approach to the issue of economic justice provides principles defining just acts and then says that "whatever [distribution] arises from a just situation by just steps is itself just." There is a range of views among free-marketeers about which acts are just. In general, the free-marketeer position can be characterized as follows.

> *Free Market Principle:* All acquisitions and transfers involving force, threat of force, or X are unjust. All other acquisitions and transfers are just. Distributions are just if and only if they arise from preceding just distributions through just acquisitions and transfers or if they arise from preceding unjust distributions through the appropriate rectifications.

Hard-core free-marketeers such as Robert Nozick and Ayn Rand say that $X = 0$. The moral theory underlying this position is quite simple. Hard-core free-marketeers define freedom as the absence of coercion (force or threat of force) against one's person or property, and they postulate that no other thing or combination of other things has higher value than freedom. Therefore, nothing is valuable enough to justify abridging the freedom of another person except the preservation of your own freedom or the freedom of some other person or the punishment of a rights violator. In particular, all acquisitions and transfers that abridge the freedom of other people are unjust. The elimination of poverty and racial discrimination are good things, for example, but they are not valuable enough to justify using coercion to redistribute the property of the wealthy or to require restaurant owners to serve blacks at their lunch counters. The hard-core free-marketeer's position might be put succinctly in terms of rights. All people have exactly three rights: the rights to life, freedom, and property. Acquisitions and transfers are just unless they violate someone's rights.

Soft-core free-marketeers do not think that $X = 0$, but they disagree among themselves about how to complete the Free Market Principle. For example some say, "$X = $ fraud." Others say, "$X = $ monopoly." Still others say, "$X = $ indoctrination and discrimination." Soft-core free-marketeers might be described as adding to the three familiar rights or as extending the right to freedom. For example, suppose some soft-core free-marketeers believe that "$X = $ fraud and monopoly." They might be taken as claiming that all people have exactly five rights: the rights to life, freedom, property, truth, and competition. Or they might be taken as claiming that all people have exactly three rights: the rights to life, freedom, and property, except that freedom is defined not as "freedom from coercion" but rather as "freedom to choose without coercion, deception, or monopoly."

The Free Market Principle says that whatever distribution arises from the operation of a free market is a just distribution. The dispute among the hard-core and soft-core free-marketeers is a dispute about what constitutes a *free* market.

Associated with the Free Market Principle is a political theory called *Libertarianism.* States use coercion to collect taxes. Some hard-core free-marketeers believe that this implies that no state is legitimate, but others accept the legitimacy of a "minimal state." They say that taxation is immoral unless the money is used to protect people's rights. Thus taxes that support an army, police force, and judiciary are justifiable, but if a government does more, it does so with stolen money. It is immoral for the state to use tax dollars to fund redistributive programs. It is wrong to steal from the rich even in order to give to the poor.

Feinberg and Nozick thus have opposite criticisms of America. Feinberg thinks the state does too little. It should be regulating and redistributing income more in order to produce some pattern conforming to Aristotle's Income Principle. Nozick thinks the state does too much. Nozick would oppose not only transfer programs (such as welfare, farm subsidies, social security) but also public services (such as parks, museums, libraries, roads, schools, public T.V.) regulatory agencies (such as FDA, FCC, FAA, OSHA), and research subsidies (such as NASA, NEH, NSF). All of these programs are illegitimate because they are not designed to protect rights, so collecting taxes to fund these programs is theft.

Soft-core free-marketeers have a different account of state legitimacy than hard-core free-marketeers because they have a different account of unjust transfers, people's rights, and free markets. In general, soft-core free-marketeers think that some more-than-minimal states are legitimate. Often they think that restrictions and redistributive programs are OK, especially when such programs penalize or compensate for illegitimate practices of the private sector. For example, a free-marketeer who believes that "X = fraud and monopoly" might think it legitimate to establish state agencies to discover and prosecute perpetrators of fraud and monopoly and perhaps to compensate victims.

Can Aristotle's Income Principle and the Free Market Principle be combined, then? In general, Aristotle's Income Principle says that some patterns of distribution are unjust no matter how they arise, whereas the Free Market Principle says that any pattern of distribution that arises without violations of rights is just. Nozick argues that no pattern conforming to Aristotle's Income Principle could persist in a free market. Massive rights violations would be required to establish and maintain such a pattern. One would have to prevent person A from giving goods to or trading goods with person B unless person B deserved the goods according to Aristotle's Income Principle. As Nozick says, one would have to prohibit "capitalist acts between consenting adults."

You might think that the Free Market Principle is roughly the same as Aristotle's Income Principle + Principle of Contribution. After all, doesn't the Law of Supply and Demand in a free market ensure that the more important someone's contribution is to society, the more that person will earn? Surprisingly, the answer is "no." Often there is a large demand for goods or services that are not helpful or are even harmful to society (such as cigarettes) and little demand for crucial goods or services (such as philosophy professors). Moreover, remember that because of gifts and other sorts of luck, many people acquire income in ways unrelated to the marketing of goods or services. Thus to establish and preserve a pattern of income distribution that conforms to Aristotle's Income Principle + Principle of Contribution, one would have to begin by prohibiting the purchase of goods or services that do not contribute to society and the giving of money to people who do not contribute to society.

*

There are quite a few objections to the Free Market Principle. Here is a smattering. Some people may find the minimal state to be too small. A political theory that calls a state unjust for banning discrimination and building public roads is a counter-intuitive political theory.

There seem to be just and unjust ways for people to distribute goods that they own. It was unjust, for example, for Jacob to play favorites among his children by giving only Joseph a "coat of many colors." (I do not mean to justify or excuse the response of Joseph's brothers, of course.) However, according to the Free Market Principle, people are entitled to dispose of their own goods in any way they like, so long as they violate no rights.

In a similar vein, some distributions within a society seem unfair no matter how they are arrived at. For example, it seems counter-intuitive to say that a society in which millions starve while a few incredibly wealthy people party gaily could be a just society.

Kant would certainly object to the idea that our only duties are to respect the rights of others, for Kant holds that we have a duty to help others who have no right to be helped. Of course, Nozick might maintain that a society that operated according to the Free-Market Principle was a just, but insufficiently benevolent, society. However, he might be hard pressed to explain why it is OK for a state to enforce justice but not benevolence.

Kantians might think that in order to be a just state, an affluent state must ensure that its citizens have certain opportunities. The morally significant sort of freedom is not *freedom from* coercion, fraud, monopoly, or anything else, but rather *freedom to* pursue one's own goals to a certain extent. However, to ensure this sort of freedom for its citizens, a state would have to interfere with the free market. Rights must be limited to prevent some people from having excessive control over others (for instance, through monopoly).

In a free market a person's freedom depends on his or her bargaining position. *Laissez faire,* the idea that the state should enforce rights but otherwise stay out of the marketplace, has some appeal if you picture the marketplace as a collection of more or less rational, adult, informed, roughly equal consumers and producers. However, if some people are already seriously and unjustly disadvantaged, non-interference merely perpetuates the situation and may allow it to degenerate. It is one thing to let two roughly

equal kids slug it out, but *laissez faire* is inappropriate when big kids with sticks gang up on a toddler. Similarly, the state needs to intervene to prevent white males from preserving and increasing their advantages, to protect irrational or uninformed consumers from exploitation, to protect ordinary people from coercive offers, and the like.

The Free Market Principle seems to ignore children. It assumes that all the members of society are autonomous adults. Most people would agree that the state has some duty to ensure that at least the basic needs of children are met. But once this is granted, the size of the state must increase substantially beyond the mere Libertarian, minimal state. For starters, public schools and welfare seem to be required.

## Utilitarian Income Principle

The Utilitarian Income Principle, whatever its content, will be a straightforward corollary of the Greatest Happiness Principle. It will be a very important rule in the Rule Utilitarian system. According to Utilitarianism, the just way of distributing income in a society is the way that will maximize happiness for the society.

At first glance an egalitarian distribution seems to maximize happiness for the society because of the phenomenon of diminishing marginal utility. If you take $100 away from a rich person and give it to a poor person, then the poor person will generally gain more happiness than the rich person will lose. The society will register a net gain of happiness.

If this phenomenon were the only factor, then a Utilitarian would favor taking money from the rich and giving it to the poor until an egalitarian distribution of wealth was achieved. But there are other factors, such as incentives. By paying different salaries for different jobs, society can encourage some people to work harder and can encourage some people to choose jobs that they would not otherwise choose. In these and other ways, inequalities may increase the efficiency of society. Of course, inequalities may introduce problems such as envy. But Utilitarianism aims at maximizing the total amount of happiness in society rather than the happiness of every individual. And it is quite likely that certain inequalities will increase the total amount of happiness of society more than enough to compensate for the phenomenon of marginal utility.

It is unclear which principle of economic justice Utilitarians should favor. Utilitarian arguments might be advanced for Aristotle's Income Principle, for the Free Market Principle, or for a number of other principles. Govier, for example, maintains that the free market should be modified by using taxation and transfer payments to make sure everyone's basic needs are satisfied. This is something like what we have now: capitalism plus a welfare safety net (Free Market Principle plus Aristotle's Income Principle + Principle of Need). Govier defends her proposal on Utilitarian and deontological grounds, not only against the bare Free Market Principle but also against what is now called workfare: capitalism plus a guarantee of a job to those who are willing to work (roughly, Free Market Principle plus Aristotle's Income Principle + Principle of Effort).

## Difference Principle: Rawls

In his famous book *A Theory of Justice,* John Rawls proposes a set of principles stipulating how the basic institutions of society should distribute certain goods. These *primary goods* are the goods that all rational people desire in order to carry out their life plans. They include rights and liberties, powers and opportunities, income and wealth, and self-respect. The following principle governs the distribution of income and wealth.

*Difference Principle:* Social and economic inequalities are to be arranged so that they are to the greatest benefit of the least advantaged and do not worsen the situation of others.

The Difference Principle says that an inequality is just if it improves the situation of the least-well-off class more than any other arrangement. For example, doctors make more money than many other people. Is this inequality just? Medicine clearly requires highly talented people, and it may be necessary to pay doctors well in order to induce highly talented people to become doctors. A good health care system benefits everyone in the society. In particular, the least-well-off class may be better off in a society where doctors have high incomes, because medical care is better in such a society. If so, then this is a just inequality according to the Difference Principle.

Rawls does not think that the Difference Principle is the only principle governing social justice, however. Society should also ensure that positions, such as the good jobs to which powers and opportunities attach, are "open to all." Of course there are several senses in which something can be open to all. Nozick thinks that a position is open to all if no one is prevented by coercion from attaining it. But Rawls thinks that it is not fair for society to provide advantages to some people, disadvantage others, and then let all of these people compete with each other for positions. Society must compensate for socially caused inequalities in order to make the competition for valuable positions fair. For example, if it takes education to get a good job, then society must ensure that not only the wealthy, but rather all of the people within society, can get an education. We might call this the *Fair Equality of Opportunity Principle.*

Rawls maintains that just as everyone should have equal opportunity, so everyone should have equal rights and liberties. No one should have more freedom of speech or freedom of movement, for example, than anyone else. Of course, rights and liberties may be equalized at a low level as well as a high level. Everyone has equal freedom of religion if all religions are banned or if all religions are tolerated. But Rawls' view is that everyone should have as much freedom as possible without making freedom unequal. That is, "each person is to have an equal right to the most extensive basic liberty compatible with a similar liberty for others." We might call this the *Maximal Equality of Liberty Principle.*

These three principles may conflict under certain circumstances. For example, it might be possible to enhance compliance with the Difference Principle by sacrificing certain liberties. Thus Rawls must set priorities. He maintains that the Maximal Equality of Liberty Principle has higher priority than the Fair Equality of Opportunity Principle, which, in turn, has higher priority than the Difference Principle. (For reasons that are opaque to me, Rawls calls these three principles, plus the priority rule, the *Two Principles*.) In order to be just, an inequality must not only benefit the least-well-off class without worsening the circumstances of the other classes; it must also do so without restricting the basic liberties and fair equality of opportunity within the society. This caveat indicates an important difference between the Utilitarian Income Principle and the Two Principles. In the unlikely event that enslaving half of the population would maximize happiness for the society, then *that* is what a Utilitarian would advocate. A Rawlsian, though, would stop short of this gruesome arrangement, for even if it somehow maximized happiness for everyone, it would not meet the other conditions.

*

How Rawls justifies the Two Principles is no less interesting than the statement of the principles themselves. Rawls has two basic lines of argument. One utilizes a vaguely Aristotelian method that purports to harmonize theory with refined common sense. Rawls calls this method *reflective equilibrium*. First, the theorist formulates a set of principles that apply to a range of cases. Then he or she attempts to match the principles to our considered judgments about the cases. If there is a mismatch, then the theorist modifies the judgments or the principles or both until a match is achieved. After all, our considered judgments might be wrong about this or that case, but if a single set of principles pulls together modified versions of our judgments

over a wide range of cases, then this match indicates that the principles are correct. Rawls claims that the Two Principles match our considered judgments about social justice.

Rawls' second line of argument is vaguely Kantian. Kant maintains that people act morally when they act on principles that could be adopted by any rational being no matter what his or her goals are. That is, people act morally when they act on universalizable maxims. Contrariwise, people act immorally when they make special exceptions for themselves, when they (a) act on principles that are based on particular desires or goals not shared with all other rational beings and (b) presuppose that other rational beings will not do so. That is, people act immorally when they act on non-universalizable maxims. If people could just bracket their own desires and goals and act only on principles derived from the reason that they share with all other rational beings, then they would act morally.

Like Kant, Rawls hopes to get substantive principles from formal constraints. He proposes a procedure for bracketing desires and goals and acting only on rational principles. Imagine a group of people who are ignorant of (a) their place in society, (b) their natural assets and abilities, (c) their conceptions of the good, (d) special features of their psychology, and (e) the particular circumstances of their society. Suppose that these people select principles to govern the major institutions of their own society. Rawls observes that people behind this *veil of ignorance* cannot tailor the principles of their society to fit their own special desires, goals, or circumstances for the simple reason that they are ignorant of these facts. They can only choose principles to which all rational beings would agree. The veil of ignorance rules out the possibility of making special exceptions for oneself. Thus whatever principles are chosen by people behind the veil of ignorance will not be selfishly immoral principles. (Of course, Rawls does not really expect to find such people or create them by inducing selective amnesia in actual individuals. The veil of ignorance is simply a thought experiment.)

Next Rawls combines this Kantian maneuver with the social contract tradition. He asks us to imagine that this group of people behind the veil of ignorance are (f) self-interested, (g) rational, (h) non-envious people, (i) with similar needs and abilities, (j) who are willing to commit themselves to obeying agreed-upon principles. Rawls says that people with these characteristics are in the *original position*. He claims that if people in the original position negotiate an agreement about the basic institutions of their society, they will end up adopting the true principles of justice. Why? The veil of ignorance precludes selfishly immoral principles. They will not end up with self-sacrificingly immoral principles because they are self-interested. Their similar needs and abilities will ensure that they will reach an agreement. They will not be deflected from rational choices by envy. And they will honor their commitments. Overall, Rawls believes that people in the original position will adopt the true principles of justice because the original position blocks all of the failure modes.

Because the people in the original position do not know what positions they actually hold in society, and because what is at stake is very important, when they work out the principles of justice for the basic institutions of society, they will choose conservatively. Recognizing that they might actually be at the bottom of the social ladder, they will choose principles that make the least-well-off class as well off as possible.

Rawls' final step is to argue that people using this strategy of *maximin* would choose the Two Principles to govern the basic institutions of society. Rawls takes it to be obvious that they will choose the Maximal Equality of Liberty Principle and the Fair Equality of Opportunity Principle because liberty and opportunity are crucial to everyone's life plan. Rawls must argue for the Difference Principle, however. An egalitarian distribution is *prima facie* just, he says, because a self-interested person would not agree to a smaller share than equality or let anyone else get away with a larger share. But equality may be inefficient. Sometimes inequalities produce a

greater amount by eliminating bottlenecks, providing incentives, and so on. Like some Utilitarians, Rawls is seeking a way to improve efficiency through inequalities without compromising justice. That is, Rawls is seeking efficiency-improving inequalities that would be agreed to by people in the original position using the maximin strategy. Now such people will agree to an inequality if and only if the surplus generated by the inequality benefits the least-well-off class without diminishing basic liberties and fair equality of opportunity within the society. That is, they will agree to the Difference Principle and to the priority rule that places the Difference Principle behind the other two principles.

Let us work through a simple example. Imagine a company of 10 people who are all paid equally. Sue and Sam could be terrific lathe operators, but they prefer their present jobs as bookkeepers. Tom and Tina could be bookkeepers and would enjoy it, but they are presently mediocre lathe operators. Sue and Sam could be persuaded to switch jobs with Tom and Tina for an extra $5000 per year. If they switch, a bottleneck would be eliminated and the company would make an extra $18,000 per year, enough to pay Sue and Sam $5000 each and to give everyone else a $1000 raise. Surely no rational, non-envious person would object to the inequality that would be introduced, for this inequality benefits everyone. Now imagine that another bottleneck could be eliminated if Dan and Diane work overtime. The company would make an extra $10,000, enough to pay Dan and Diane $2000 each in overtime pay and to give everyone else except Sue and Sam a $1000 raise. This inequality would not benefit everyone, but it would benefit the least-well-off class, which in this case would be everyone except Sue, Sam, Dan, and Diane. Again rational, non-envious people would prefer this situation to equality, for some would be better off and no one would be worse off.

In general, everyone will continue to prefer a new situation to the situation where everyone is paid equally as long as the least-well-off class benefits from each additional inequality, the other classes do not become worse off, and basic liberties and opportunities remain equal and maximal. Now if equality is just, then surely a situation that every rational, non-envious person prefers to equality is also just. Thus the Difference Principle provides a method for generating just inequalities.

## Notes

1. W.S. Gilbert and A. Sullivan, "The Mikado," *The Complete Plays of Gilbert and Sullivan* (Garden City, NY: Garden City Publishing Co., 1938), p. 382.

2. K. Marx, "Critique of the Gotha Programme," in *Karl Marx: A Reader,* ed. J. Elster (Cambridge, England: Cambridge University Press, 1986), pp. 162–167.

# 29    Economic Income and Social Justice

## JOEL FEINBERG

The term "distributive justice" traditionally applied to burdens and benefits directly distributed by political authorities, such as appointed offices, welfare doles, taxes, and military conscription, but it has now come to apply also to goods and evils of a nonpolitical kind that can be distributed by private citizens to other private citizens. In fact, in most recent literature, the term is reserved for economic distributions, particularly the justice of differences in economic income between classes, and of various schemes of taxation which discriminate in different ways between classes. Further, the phrase can refer not only to acts of distributing but also to de facto states of affairs, such as *the fact that* at present "the five percent at the top get 20 percent (of our national wealth) while the 20 percent at the bottom get about five percent."[1] There is, of course, an ambiguity in the meaning of "distribution." The word may refer to the *process* of distributing, or the product of some process of distributing, and either or both of these can be appraised as just or unjust. In addition, a "distribution" can be understood to be a "product" which is not the result of any deliberate distributing process, but simply a state of affairs whose production has been too complicated to summarize or to ascribe to any definite

group of persons as their deliberate doing. The present "distribution" of American wealth is just such a state of affairs.

Are the 5 percent of Americans "at the top" really different from the 20 percent "at the bottom" in any respect that would justicize the difference between their incomes? It is doubtful that there is any characteristic—relevant or irrelevant—common and peculiar to all members of either group. Some injustices, therefore, must surely exist. Perhaps there are some traits, however, that are more or less characteristic of the members of the privileged group, that make the current arrangements at least approximately just. What could (or should) those traits be? The answer will state a standard of relevance and a principle of material justice for questions of economic distributions, at least in relatively affluent societies like that of the United States.

At this point there appears to be no appeal possible except to basic attitudes, but even at this level we should avoid premature pessimism about the possibility of rational agreement. Some answers to our question have been generally discredited, and if we can see why those answers are inadequate, we might discover some important clues to the properties any adequate answer must possess. Even philosophical adversaries with strongly opposed initial attitudes may hope to come to eventual agreement if they share *some* relevant beliefs and standards and a common

From *Social Philosophy* by Joel Feinberg, copyright © 1973, 107–117, footnotes renumbered. Reprinted by permission of Prentice-Hall, Inc., Upper Saddle River, NJ.

commitment to consistency. Let us consider why we all agree (that is the author's assumption) in rejecting the view that differences in race, sex, IQ, or social "rank" are the grounds of just differences in wealth or income. Part of the answer seems obvious. People cannot by their own voluntary choices determine what skin color, sex, or IQ they shall have, or which hereditary caste they shall enter. To make such properties the basis of discrimination between individuals in the distribution of social benefits would be "to treat people differently in ways that profoundly affect their lives because of differences for which they have no responsibility."[2] Differences in a given respect are *relevant* for the aims of distributive justice, then, only if they are differences for which their possessors can be held responsible; properties can be the grounds of just discrimination between persons only if those persons had a *fair opportunity* to acquire or avoid them. Having rejected a number of material principles that clearly fail to satisfy the "fair opportunity" requirement, we are still left with as many as five candidates for our acceptance. (It is in theory open to us to accept two or more of these five as valid principles, there being no a priori necessity that the list be reduced to one.) These are: (1) the principle of perfect equality; (2) the principle[s] of need; (3) the principles of merit and achievement; (4) the principle of contribution (or due return); (5) the principle of effort (or labor). I shall discuss each of these briefly.

## (i) Equality

The principle of perfect equality obviously has a place in any adequate social ethic. Every human being is equally a human being, and . . . that minimal qualification entitles all human beings equally to certain absolute human rights: positive rights to noneconomic "goods" that by their very natures cannot be in short supply, negative rights not to be treated in cruel or inhuman ways, and negative rights not to be exploited or degraded even in "humane" ways. It is quite another thing, however, to make the minimal qualification of humanity the ground for an absolutely equal dis-

tribution of a country's *material wealth* among its citizens. A strict equalitarian could argue that he is merely applying Aristotle's formula of proportionate equality (presumably accepted by all parties to the dispute) with a criterion of relevance borrowed from the human rights theorists. Thus, distributive justice is accomplished between A and B when the following ratio is satisfied:

$$\frac{A's \ share \ of \ P}{B's \ share \ of \ P} = \frac{A's \ possession \ of \ Q}{B's \ possession \ of \ Q}$$

Where *P* stands for economic goods, *Q* must stand simply for "humanity" or "a human nature," and since every human being possesses *that Q* equally, it follows that all should also share a society's economic wealth (the *P* in question) equally.

The trouble with this argument is that its major premise is no less disputable than its conclusion. The standard of relevance it borrows from other contexts where it seems very little short of self-evident, seems controversial, at best, when applied to purely economic contexts. It seems evident to most of us that merely being human entitles *everyone*—bad men as well as good, lazy as well as industrious, inept as well as skilled—to a fair trial if charged with a crime, to equal protection of the law, to equal consideration of his interests by makers of national policy, to be spared torture or other cruel and inhuman treatment, and to be permanently ineligible for the status of chattel slave. Adding a right to an equal share of the economic pie, however, is to add a benefit of a wholly different order, one whose presence on the list of goods for which mere humanity is the sole qualifying condition is not likely to win wide assent without further argument.

It is far more plausible to posit a human right to the satisfaction of (better: to an opportunity to satisfy) one's *basic* economic needs, that is, to enough food and medicine to remain healthy, to minimal clothing, housing, and so on. As Hume pointed out,[3] even these rights cannot exist under conditions of extreme scarcity. Where there is not enough to go around, it cannot be true that everyone has a right to an equal share. But wherever there is moderate abundance or better—wherever a society produces more than enough to satisfy the *basic needs of everyone*—there it seems more plausible to say that mere possession of basic human needs qualifies a person for the opportunity to satisfy them. It would be a rare and calloused sense of justice that would not be offended by an affluent society, with a large annual agricultural surplus and a great abundance of manufactured goods, which permitted some of its citizens to die of starvation, exposure, or easily curable disease. It would certainly be *unfair* for a nation to produce more than it needs and not permit some of its citizens enough to satisfy their basic biological requirements. Strict equalitarianism, then, is a perfectly plausible material principle of distributive justice when confined to affluent societies and basic biological needs, but it loses plausibility when applied to division of the "surplus" left over after basic needs are met. To be sure, the greater the degree of affluence, the higher the level at which we might draw the line between "basic needs" and merely "wanted benefits," and insofar as social institutions create "artificial needs," it is only fair that society provide all with the opportunity to satisfy them.[4] But once the line has been drawn between what is needed to live a minimally decent life by the realistic standards of a given time and place and what is only added "gravy," it is far from evident that justice still insists upon absolutely equal shares of the total. And it is evident that justice does *not* require strict equality wherever there is reason to think that unequal distribution causally determines greater production and is therefore in the interests of everyone, even those who receive the relatively smaller shares.

Still, there is no way to *refute* the strict equalitarian who requires exactly equal shares for everyone whenever that can be arranged without discouraging total productivity to the point where everyone loses. No one would insist upon equal distributions that would diminish the size of the total pie and thus leave smaller slices for *everyone;* that would be opposed to reason. John Rawls makes this condition part of his "rational principle" of justice: "Inequalities are arbitrary unless it is reasonable to expect that they will work out to everyone's advantage. . . ."[5] We are left then with

a version of strict equalitarianism that is by no means evidently true and yet is impossible to refute. That is the theory that purports to apply not only to basic needs but to the total wealth of a society, and allows departures from strict equality when, *but only when,* they will work out to everyone's advantage. Although I am not persuaded by this theory, I think that any adequate material principle will have to attach great importance to keeping differences in wealth within reasonable limits, even after all basic needs have been met. One way of doing this would be to raise the standards for a "basic need" as total wealth goes up, so that differences between the richest and poorest citizens (even when there is no real "poverty") are kept within moderate limits.

## (ii) Need

The principle of need is subject to various interpretations, but in most of its forms it is not an independent principle at all, but only a way of mediating, the application of the principle of equality. It can, therefore, be grouped with the principle of perfect equality as a member of the equalitarian family and contrasted with the principles of merit, achievement, contribution, and effort, which are all members of the nonequalitarian family. Consider some differences in "needs" as they bear on distributions. Doe is a bachelor with no dependents; Roe has a wife and six children. Roe must satisfy the needs of eight persons out of his paycheck, whereas Doe need satisfy the needs of only one. To give Roe and Doe equal pay would be to treat Doe's interests substantially *more* generously than those of anyone in the Roe family. Similarly, if a small private group is distributing food to its members (say a shipwrecked crew waiting rescue on a desert island), it would not be fair to give precisely the same quantity to a one hundred pounder as to a two hundred pounder, for that might be giving one person all he needs and the other only a fraction of what he needs—a difference in treatment not supported by any relevant difference between them. In short, to distribute goods in proportion to basic needs is not really to depart from a standard of equality, but rather to bring those with some greater initial burden or deficit up to the same level as their fellows.

The concept of a "need" is extremely elastic. In a general sense, to say that $S$ needs $X$ is to say simply that if he doesn't have $X$ he will be harmed. A "basic need" would then be for an $X$ in whose absence a person would be harmed in some crucial and fundamental way, such as suffering injury, malnutrition, illness, madness, or premature death. Thus we all have a basic need for foodstuffs of a certain quantity and variety, fuel to heat our dwellings, a roof over our heads, clothing to keep us warm, and so on. In a different but related sense of need, to say that $S$ needs $X$ is to say that without $X$ he cannot achieve same specific purpose or perform some specific function. If they are to do their work, carpenters need tools, merchants need capital and customers, authors need paper and publishers. Some helpful goods are not strictly needed in this sense: an author with pencil and paper does not really need a typewriter to write a book, but he may need it to write a book speedily, efficiently, and conveniently. We sometimes come to rely upon "merely helpful but unneeded goods" to such a degree that we develop a strong habitual dependence on them, in which case (as it is often said) we have a "psychological" as opposed to a material need for them. If we don't possess that for which we have a strong psychological need, we may be unable to be happy, in which case a merely psychological need for a functional instrument may become a genuine need in the first sense distinguished above, namely, something whose absence is harmful to us. (Cutting across the distinction between material and psychological needs is that between "natural" and "artificial" needs, the former being those that can be expected to develop in any normal person, the latter being those that are manufactured or contrived, and somehow implanted in, or imposed upon, a person.) The more abundant a society's material goods, the higher the level at which we are required (by the force of psychological needs) to fix the distinction between "necessities" and "luxuries"; what *everyone* in a given

society regards as "necessary" tends to become an actual, basic need.

## (iii) Merit and Achievement

The remaining three candidates for material principles of distributive justice belong to the nonequalitarian family. These three principles would each distribute goods in accordance, not with need, but with *desert;* since persons obviously differ in their deserts, economic goods would be distributed unequally. The three principles differ from one another in their conceptions of the relevant *bases of desert* for economic distributions. The first is the principle of *merit.* Unlike the other principles in the nonequalitarian family, this one focuses not on what a person has *done* to deserve his allotment, but rather on what kind of person he is—what characteristics he has.

Two different types of characteristic might be considered meritorious in the appropriate sense: skills and virtues. Native skills and inherited aptitudes will not be appropriate desert bases, since they are forms of merit ruled out by the fair opportunity requirement. No one deserves credit or blame for his genetic inheritance, since no one has the opportunity to select his own genes. Acquired skills may seem more plausible candidates at first, but upon scrutiny they are little better. First, all acquired skills depend to a large degree on native skills. Nobody is born knowing how to read, so reading is an acquired skill, but actual differences in reading skill are to a large degree accounted for by genetic differences that are beyond anyone's control. Some of the differences are no doubt caused by differences in motivation afforded different children, but again the early conditions contributing to a child's motivation are also largely beyond his control. We may still have some differences in acquired skills that are to be accounted for solely or primarily by differences in the degree of practice, drill, and perseverance expended by persons with roughly equal opportunities. In respect to these, we can propitiate the requirement of fair opportunity, but only by nullifying the significance of acquired skill as such, for now skill is a relevant basis of desert only to the extent that it is a product of one's own effort. Hence, *effort* becomes the true basis of desert (as claimed by our fifth principle, discussed below), and not simply skill as such.

Those who would propose rewarding personal *virtues* with a larger than average share of the economic pie, and punishing defects of character with a smaller than average share, advocate assigning to the economic system a task normally done (if it is done at all) by noneconomic institutions. What they propose, in effect, is that we use retributive criteria of distributive justice. Our criminal law, for a variety of good reasons, does not purport to punish people for what they are, but only for what they do. A man can be as arrogant, rude, selfish, cruel, insensitive, irresponsible, cowardly, lazy, or disloyal as he wishes; unless he *does* something prohibited by the criminal law, he will not be made to suffer legal punishment. At least one of the legal system's reasons for refusing to penalize character flaws as such would also explain why such defects should not be listed as relevant differences in a material principle of distributive justice. The apparatus for detecting such flaws (a "moral police"?) would be enormously cumbersome and impractical, and its methods so uncertain and fallible that none of us could feel safe in entrusting the determination of our material allotments to it. We could, of course, give roughly equal shares to all except those few who have *outstanding* virtues—gentleness, kindness, courage, diligence, reliability, warmth, charm, considerateness, generosity. Perhaps these are traits that deserve to be rewarded, but it is doubtful that larger economic allotments are the appropriate vehicles of rewarding. As Benn and Peters remind us, "there are some sorts of 'worth' for which rewards in terms of income seem inappropriate. Great courage in battle is recognized by medals, not by increased pay."[6] Indeed, there is something repugnant, as Socrates and the Stoics insisted, in paying a man to be virtuous. Moreover, the rewards would offer a pecuniary motive for certain forms of excellence that require motives of a different kind, and would thus tend to be self-defeating.

The most plausible nonequalitarian theories are those that locate relevance not in meritorious traits and excellences of any kind, but rather in prior doings: not in what one is, but in what one has done. Actions, too, are sometimes called "meritorious," so there is no impropriety in denominating the remaining families of principles in our survey as "meritarian." One type of action-oriented meritarian might cite *achievement* as a relevant desert basis for pecuniary rewards, so that departures from equality in income are to be justicized only by distinguished achievements in science, art, philosophy, music, athletics, and other basic areas of human activity. The attractions and disadvantages of this theory are similar to those of theories which I rejected above that base rewards on skills and virtues. Not all persons have a fair opportunity to achieve great things, and economic rewards seem inappropriate as vehicles for expressing recognition and admiration of noneconomic achievements.

## (iv) Contribution or "Due Return"

When the achievements under consideration are themselves contributions to our general economic well-being, the meritarian principle of distributive justice is much more plausible. Often it is conjoined with an economic theory that purports to determine exactly what percentage of our total economic product a given worker or class has produced. Justice, according to this principle, requires that each worker get back exactly that proportion of the national wealth that he has himself created. This sounds very much like a principle of "commutative justice" directing us to give back to every worker what is really his own property, that is, the product of his own labor.

The French socialist writer and precursor of Karl Marx, Pierre Joseph Proudhon (1809–1865), is perhaps the classic example of this kind of theorist. In his book *What Is Property?* (1840), Proudhon rejects the standard socialist slogan, "From each according to his ability, to each according to his needs,"[7] in favor of a principle of distributive justice based on contribution, as interpreted by an economic theory that employed a pre-Marxist "theory of surplus value." The famous socialist slogan was not intended, in any case, to express a principle of distributive justice. It was understood to be a rejection of all considerations of "mere" justice for an ethic of human brotherhood. The early socialists thought it unfair, in a way, to give the great contributors to our wealth a disproportionately small share of the product. But in the new socialist society, love of neighbor, community spirit, and absence of avarice would overwhelm such bourgeois notions and put them in their proper (subordinate) place.

Proudhon, on the other hand, based his whole social philosophy not on brotherhood (an ideal he found suitable only for small groups such as families) but on the kind of distributive justice to which even some capitalists gave lip service:

The key concept was "mutuality" or "reciprocity." "Mutuality, reciprocity exists," he wrote, "when all the workers in an industry, instead of working for an entrepreneur who pays them and keeps their products, work for one another and thus collaborate in the making of a common product whose profits they share among themselves."[8]

Proudhon's celebrated dictum that "property is theft" did not imply that all *possession* of goods is illicit, but rather that the system of rules that permitted the owner of a factory to hire workers and draw profits ("surplus value") from *their* labor robs the workers of what is rightly theirs. "This profit, consisting of a portion of the proceeds of labor that rightfully belonged to the laborer himself, was 'theft.'"[9] The injustice of capitalism, according to Proudhon, consists in the fact that those who create the wealth (through their labor) get only a small part of what they create, whereas those who "exploit" their labor, like voracious parasites, gather in a greatly disproportionate share. The "return of contribution" principle of distributive justice, then, cannot work in a capitalist system, but requires a *fédération mutualiste* of autonomous producer-cooperatives in which those who create wealth by their work share it in proportion to their real contributions.

Other theorists, employing different notions of what produces or "creates" economic wealth, have used the "return of contribution" principle to support quite opposite conclusions. The contribution principle has even been used to justicize quite unequalitarian capitalistic status quos, for it is said that capital as well as labor creates wealth, as do ingenious ideas, inventions, and adventurous risk-taking. The capitalist who provided the money, the inventor who designed a product to be manufactured, the innovator who thought of a new mode of production and marketing, the advertiser who persuaded millions of customers to buy the finished product, the investor who risked his savings on the success of the enterprise—these are the ones, it is said, who did the most to produce the wealth created by a business, not the workers who contributed only their labor, and of course, these are the ones who tend, on the whole, to receive the largest personal incomes.

Without begging any narrow and technical questions of economics, I should express my general skepticism concerning such facile generalizations about the comparative degrees to which various individuals have contributed to our social wealth. Not only are there impossibly difficult problems of measurement involved, there are also conceptual problems that appear beyond all nonarbitrary solution. I refer to the elements of luck and chance, the social factors not attributable to any assignable individuals, and the contributions of population trends, uncreated natural resources, and the efforts of people now dead, which are often central to the explanation of any given increment of social wealth.

The difficulties of separating out causal factors in the production of social wealth might influence the partisan of the "return of contribution" principle in either or both of two ways. He might become very cautious in his application of the principle, requiring that deviations from average shares be restricted to very clear and demonstrable instances of unusually great or small contributions. But the moral that L. T. Hobhouse[10] drew from these difficulties is that *any* individual contribution will be very small relative to the immeasurably great contribution made by political, social, fortuitous, natural, and "inherited" factors. In particular, strict application of the "return of contribution" principle would tend to support a larger claim for the community to its own "due return," through taxation and other devices.

In a way, the principle of contribution is not a principle of mere *desert* at all, no matter how applied. As mentioned above, it resembles a principle of commutative justice requiring repayment of debts, return of borrowed items, or compensation for wrongly inflicted damages. If I lend you my car on the understanding that you will take good care of it and soon return it, or if you steal it, or damage it, it will be too weak to say that I "deserve" to have my own car, intact, back from you. After all, the car is mine or my due, and questions of ownership are not settled by examination of deserts; neither are considerations of ownership and obligation commonly outbalanced by considerations of desert. It is not merely "unfitting" or "inappropriate" that I should not have my own or my due; it is downright *theft* to withhold it from me. So the return of contribution is not merely a matter of merit deserving reward. It is a matter of a maker demanding that which he has created and is thus properly his. The ratio—*A*'s share of *X* is to *B*'s share of *X* as *A*'s contribution to *X* is to *B*'s contribution to *X*—appears, therefore, to be a very strong and plausible principle of distributive justice, whose main deficiencies, when applied to economic distributions, are of a practical (though severe) kind. If Hobhouse is right in claiming that there are social factors in even the most pronounced individual contributions to social wealth, then the principle of due return serves as a moral basis in support of taxation and other public claims to private goods. In any case, if *A*'s contribution, though apparently much greater than *B*'s, is nevertheless only the tiniest percentage of the total contribution to *X* (whatever that may mean and however it is to be determined), it may seem like the meanest quibbling to distinguish very seriously between *A* and *B* at all.

## (v) Effort

The principle of due return, as a material principle of distributive justice, does have some vulnerability to the fair opportunity requirement. Given unavoidable variations in genetic endowments and material circumstances, different persons cannot have precisely the same opportunities to make contributions to the public weal. Our final candidate for the status of a material principle of distributive justice, the *principle of effort*, does much better in this respect, for it would distribute economic products not in proportion to successful achievement but according to the degree of effort exerted. According to the principle of effort, justice decrees that hard-working executives and hard-working laborers receive precisely the same remuneration (although there may be reasons having nothing to do with justice for paying more to the executives), and that freeloaders be penalized by allotments of proportionately lesser shares of the joint products of everyone's labor. The most persuasive argument for this principle is that it is the closest approximation to the intuitively valid principle of due return that can pass the fair opportunity requirement. It is doubtful, however, that even the principle of effort fully satisfies the requirements of fair opportunity, since those who inherit or acquire certain kinds of handicap may have little opportunity to *acquire the motivation* even to do their best. In any event, the principle of effort does seem to have intuitive cogency giving it at least some weight as a factor determining the justice of distributions.

In very tentative conclusion, it seems that the principle of equality (in the version that rests on needs rather than that which requires "perfect equality") and the principles of contribution and effort (where nonarbitrarily applicable, and only *after* everyone's basic needs have been satisfied) have the most weight as determinants of economic justice, whereas all forms of the principle of merit are implausible in that role. The reason for the priority of basic needs is that, where there is economic abundance, the claim to life itself and to minimally decent conditions are, like other human rights, claims that all men make with perfect equality. As economic production increases, these claims are given ever greater consideration in the form of rising standards for distinguishing basic needs from other wanted goods. But no matter where that line is drawn, when we go beyond it into the realm of economic surplus or "luxuries," nonequalitarian considerations (especially contribution and effort) come increasingly into play.

## Notes

1. "T. R. B. from Washington" in *The New Republic,* Vol. CLX, No. 12 (March 22, 1969).

2. W. K. Frankena, "Some Beliefs About Justice," *The Lindley Lecture,* Department of Philosophy Pamphlet (Lawrence: University of Kansas, 1966), p. 10.

3. David Hume, *Enquiry Concerning the Principles of Morals* Part III (LaSalle, Ill.: The Open Court Publishing Company. 1947). Originally published in 1777.

4. This point is well made by Katzner, "An Analysis of the Concept of Justice," pp. 173–203.

5. John Rawls, "Justice as Fairness," *The Philosophical Review.* LXVII (1958), 165.

6. Benn and Peters, *Social Principles and the Democratic State,* p. 139.

7. Traced to Louis Blanc. For a clear brief exposition of Proudhon's view which contrasts it with that of other early socialists and also that of Karl Marx, see Robert Tucker's "Marx and Distributive Justice," in *Nomos VI: Justice,* ed. C. J. Friedrich and J. W. Chapman (New York: Aldine-Atherton Press, 1963), pp. 306–25.

8. Tucker, "Marx and Distributive Justice," p. 310.

9. Tucker, "Marx and Distributive Justice," p. 311.

10. L. T. Hobhouse, *The Elements of Social Justice* (London: George Allen and Unwin Ltd., 1922). See especially pp. 161–63.

# 30    Distributive Justice

## ROBERT NOZICK

The minimal state is the most extensive state that can be justified. Any state more extensive violates people's rights. Yet many persons have put forth reasons purporting to justify a more extensive state. It is impossible within the compass of this book to examine all the reasons that have been put forth. Therefore, I shall focus upon those generally acknowledged to be most weighty and influential, to see precisely wherein they fail. In this chapter we consider the claim that a more extensive state is justified, because necessary (or the best instrument) to achieve distributive justice; in the next chapter we shall take up diverse other claims.

The term "distributive justice" is not a neutral one. Hearing the term "distribution," most people presume that some thing or mechanism uses some principle or criterion to give out a supply of things. Into this process of distributing shares some error may have crept. So it is an open ques-

tion, at least, whether *re*distribution should take place; whether we should do again what has already been done once, though poorly. However, we are not in the position of children who have been given portions of pie by someone who now makes last minute adjustments to rectify careless cutting. There is no *central* distribution, no person or group entitled to control all the resources, jointly deciding how they are to be doled out. What each person gets, he gets from others who give to him in exchange for something, or as a gift. In a free society, diverse persons control different resources, and new holdings arise out of the voluntary exchanges and actions of persons. There is no more a distributing or distribution of shares than there is a distributing of mates in a society in which persons choose whom they shall marry. The total result is the product of many individual decisions which the different individuals involved are entitled to make. Some uses of the term "distribution," it is true, do not imply a previous distributing appropriately judged by some criterion (for example, "probability distribution"); nevertheless, despite the title of this chapter, it would be best to

From *Anarchy, State, and Utopia,* 149–182, with omissions. Copyright © 1974 by Basic Books, Inc. Reprinted by permission of Basic Books, a subsidiary of Perseus Books Group, LLC.

use a terminology that clearly is neutral. We shall speak of people's holdings; a principle of justice in holdings describes (part of) what justice tells us (requires) about holdings. I shall state first what I take to be the correct view about justice in holdings, and then turn to the discussion of alternate views.

## Section 1

### The Entitlement Theory

The subject of justice in holdings consists of three major topics. The first is the *original acquisition of holdings,* the appropriation of unheld things. This includes the issues of how unheld things may come to be held, the process, or processes, by which unheld things may come to be held, the things that may come to be held by these processes, the extent of what comes to be held by a particular process, and so on. We shall refer to the complicated truth about this topic, which we shall not formulate here, as the principle of justice in acquisition. The second topic concerns the *transfer of holdings* from one person to another. By what processes may a person transfer holdings to another? How may a person acquire a holding from another who holds it? Under this topic come general descriptions of voluntary exchange, and gift and (on the other hand) fraud, as well as reference to particular conventional details fixed upon in a given society. The complicated truth about this subject (with placeholders for conventional details) we shall call the principle of justice in transfer. (And we shall suppose it also includes principles governing how a person may divest himself of a holding, passing it into an unheld state.)

If the world were wholly just, the following inductive definition would exhaustively cover the subject of justice in holdings.

1. A person who acquires a holding in accordance with the principle of justice in acquisition is entitled to that holding.
2. A person who acquires a holding in accordance with the principle of justice in transfer, from someone else entitled to the holding, is entitled to the holding.
3. No one is entitled to a holding except by (repeated) applications of 1 and 2.

The complete principle of distributive justice would say simply that a distribution is just if everyone is entitled to the holdings they possess under the distribution.

A distribution is just if it arises from another just distribution by legitimate means. The legitimate means of moving from one distribution to another are specified by the principle of justice in transfer. The legitimate first "moves" are specified by the principle of justice in acquisition. Whatever arises from a just situation by just steps is itself just. The means of change specified by the principle of justice in transfer preserve justice. As correct rules of inference are truth-preserving, and any conclusion deduced via repeated application of such rules from only true premises is itself true, so the means of transition from one situation to another specified by the principle of justice in transfer are justice-preserving, and any situation actually arising from repeated transitions in accordance with the principle from a just situation is itself just. The parallel between justice-preserving transformations and truth-preserving transformations illuminates where it fails as well as where it holds. That a conclusion could have been deduced by truth-preserving means from premises that are true suffices to show its truth. That from a just situation a situation *could* have arisen via justice-preserving means does *not* suffice to show its justice. The fact that a thief's victims voluntarily *could* have presented him with gifts does not entitle the thief to his ill-gotten gains. Justice in holdings is historical; it depends upon what actually has happened. We shall return to this point later.

Not all actual situations are generated in accordance with the two principles of justice in holdings: the principle of justice in acquisition and the principle of justice in transfer. Some people steal from others, or defraud them, or enslave them, seizing their product and preventing them from living as they choose, or forcibly exclude others from competing in exchanges. None of these are permissible modes of transition from one situation to another. And some persons acquire holdings by means not sanctioned by the principle of justice in acquisition. The existence of past injustice (previous violations of the first two principles of justice in holdings) raises the third major topic under justice in holdings: the rectification of injustice in holdings. If past injustice has shaped present holdings in various ways, some identifiable and some not, what now, if anything, ought to be done to rectify these injustices? What obligations do the performers of injustice have toward those whose position is worse than it would have been had the injustice not been done? Or, than it would have been had compensation been paid promptly? How, if at all, do things change if the beneficiaries and those made worse off are not the direct parties in the act of injustice, but, for example, their descendants? Is an injustice done to someone whose holding was itself based upon an unrectified injustice? How far back must one go in wiping clean the historical slate of injustices? What may victims of injustice permissibly do in order to rectify the injustices being done to them, including the many injustices done by persons acting through their government? I do not know of a thorough or theoretically sophisticated treatment of such issues. Idealizing greatly, let us suppose theoretical investigation will produce a principle of rectification. This principle uses historical information about previous situations and injustices done in them (as defined by the first two principles of justice and rights against interference), and information about the actual course of events that flowed from these injustices, until the present, and it yields a description (or descriptions) of holdings in the society. The principle of rectification presumably will make use of its best estimate of subjunctive information about what would have occurred (or a probability distribution over what might have occurred, using the expected value) if the injustice had not taken place. If the actual description of holdings turns out not to be one of the descriptions yielded by the principle, then one of the descriptions yielded must be realized.

The general outlines of the theory of justice in holdings are that the holdings of a person are just if he is entitled to them by the principles of justice in acquisition and transfer, or by the principle of rectification of injustice (as specified by the first two principles). If each person's holdings are just, then the total set (distribution) of holdings is just. To turn these general outlines into a specific theory we would have to specify the details of each of the three principles of justice in holdings: the principle of acquisition of holdings, the principle of transfer of holdings, and the principle of rectification of violations of the first two principles. I shall not attempt that task here (Locke's principle of justice in acquisition is discussed below.). . . .

## How Liberty Upsets Patterns

It is not clear how those holding alternative conceptions of distributive justice can reject the entitlement conception of justice in holdings. For suppose a distribution favored by one of these non-entitlement conceptions is realized. Let us suppose it is your favorite one and let us call this distribution $D_1$; perhaps everyone has an equal share, perhaps shares vary in accordance with some dimension you treasure. Now suppose that Wilt Chamberlain is greatly in demand by basketball teams, being a great gate attraction. (Also suppose contracts run only for a year, with players being free agents.) He signs the following sort of contract with a team: In each home game, twenty-five cents from the price of each ticket of admission goes to him. (We ignore the question of whether he is "gouging" the owners, letting them look out for themselves.) The season starts, and people cheerfully attend his team's games; they buy their tickets, each time dropping a separate twenty-five cents of their admission price into a special box with Chamberlain's name on it. They are excited about seeing him play; it is worth the total admission price to them. Let us suppose that in one season one million persons attend his home games, and Wilt Chamberlain winds up with $250,000, a much larger sum than the average income and larger even than anyone else has.

Is he entitled to this income? Is this new distribution $D_2$, unjust? If so, why? There is *no* question about whether each of the people was entitled to the control over the resources they held in $D_1$; because that was the distribution (your favorite) that (for the purposes of argument) we assumed was acceptable. Each of these persons *chose* to give twenty-five cents of their money to Chamberlain. They could have spent it on going to the movies, or on candy bars, or on copies of *Dissent* magazine, or of *Monthly Review*. But they all, at least one million of them, converged on giving it to Wilt Chamberlain in exchange for watching him play basketball. If $D_1$ was a just distribution, and people voluntarily moved from it to $D_2$, transferring parts of their shares they were given under $D_1$ (what was it for if not to do something with?), isn't $D_2$ also just? If the people were entitled to dispose of the resources to which they were entitled (under $D_1$), didn't this include their being entitled to give it to, or exchange it with, Wilt Chamberlain? Can anyone else complain on grounds of justice? Each other person already has his legitimate share under $D_1$. Under $D_1$, there is nothing that anyone has that anyone else has a claim of justice against. After someone transfers something to Wilt Chamberlain, third parties *still* have their legitimate shares; *their* shares are not changed. By what process could such a transfer among two persons give rise to a legitimate claim of distributive justice on a portion of what was transferred, by a third party who had no claim of justice on any holding of the others *before* the transfer? To cut off objections irrelevant here, we might imagine the exchanges occurring in a socialist society after hours. After playing whatever basketball he does in his daily work, or doing whatever other daily work he does, Wilt Chamberlain decides to put in *overtime* to earn additional money. (First his work quota is set; he works time over that.) Or imagine it is a skilled juggler people like to see, who puts on shows after hours.

Why might someone work overtime in a society in which it is assumed their needs are satisfied? Perhaps because they care about things other than needs. I like to write in books that I read, and

to have easy access to books for browsing at odd hours. It would be very pleasant and convenient to have the resources of Widener Library in my back yard. No society, I assume, will provide such resources close to each person who would like them as part of his regular allotment (under $D_1$). Thus, persons either must do without some extra things that they want, or be allowed to do something extra to get some of these things. On what basis could the inequalities that would eventuate be forbidden? Notice also that small factories would spring up in a socialist society, unless forbidden. I melt down some of my personal possessions (under $D_1$) and build a machine out of the material. I offer you, and others, a philosophy lecture once a week in exchange for your cranking the handle on my machine, whose products I exchange for yet other things, and so on. (The raw materials used by the machine are given to me by others who possess them under $D_1$, in exchange for hearing lectures.) Each person might participate to gain things over and above their allotment under $D_1$. Some persons even might want to leave their job in socialist industry and work full time in this private sector. I shall say something more about these issues in the next chapter. Here I wish merely to note how private property even in means of production would occur in a socialist society that did not forbid people to use as they wished some of the resources they are given under the socialist distribution $D_1$. The socialist society would have to forbid capitalist acts between consenting adults.

The general point illustrated by the Wilt Chamberlain example and the example of the entrepreneur in a socialist society is that no end-state principle of distributional patterned principle of justice can be continuously realized without continuous interference with people's lives. Any favored pattern would be transformed into one unfavored by the principle, by people choosing to act in various ways; for example, by people exchanging goods and services with other people, or giving things to other people, things the transferrers are entitled to under the favored distributional pattern. To maintain a pattern one must either continually interfere to stop people from transferring resources as they wish to, or continually (or periodically) interfere to take from some persons resources that others for some reason chose to transfer to them. (But if some time limit is to be set on how long people may keep resources others voluntarily transfer to them, why let them keep these resources for *any* period of time? Why not have immediate confiscation?) It might be objected that all persons voluntarily will choose to refrain from actions which would upset the pattern. This presupposes unrealistically (1) that all will most want to maintain the pattern (are those who don't, to be "reeducated" or forced to undergo self-criticism"?), (2) that each can gather enough information about his own actions and the ongoing activities of others to discover which of his actions will upset the pattern, and (3) that diverse and far-flung persons can coordinate their actions to dovetail into the pattern. Compare the manner in which the market is neutral among persons' desires, as it reflects and transmits widely scattered information via prices, and coordinates persons' activities.

It puts things perhaps a bit too strongly to say that every patterned (or end-state) principle is liable to be thwarted by the voluntary actions of the individual parties transferring some of their shares they receive under the principle. For perhaps some *very* weak patterns are not so thwarted. Any distributional pattern with any egalitarian component is overturnable by the voluntary actions of individual persons over time; as is every patterned condition with sufficient content so as actually to have been proposed as presenting the central core of distributive justice. Still, given the possibility that some weak conditions or patterns may not be unstable in this way, it would be better to formulate an explicit description of the kind of interesting and contentful patterns under discussion, and to prove a theorem about their instability. Since the weaker the patterning, the more likely it is that the entitlement system itself satisfies it, a plausible conjecture is that any patterning either is unstable or is satisfied by the entitlement system. . . .

Taxation of earnings from labor is on a par with forced labor. Some persons find this claim obviously true: taking the earnings of *n* hours labor is like taking *n* hours from the person; it is like forcing the person to work *n* hours for another's purpose. Others find the claim absurd. But even these, *if* they object to forced labor, would oppose forcing unemployed hippies to work for the benefit of the needy. And they would also object to forcing each person to work five extra hours each week for the benefit of the needy. But a system that takes five hours' wages in taxes does not seem to them like one that forces someone to work five hours, since it offers the person forced a wider range of choice in activities than does taxation in kind with the particular labor specified. (But we can imagine a gradation of systems of forced labor, from one that specifies a particular activity, to one that gives a choice among two activities, to . . . ; and so on up.) Furthermore, people envisage a system with something like a proportional tax on everything above the amount necessary for basic needs. Some think this does not force someone to work extra hours, since there is no fixed number of extra hours he is forced to work, and since he can avoid the tax entirely by earning only enough to cover his basic needs. This is a very uncharacteristic view of forcing for those who *also* think people are forced to do something *whenever* the alternatives they face are considerably worse. However, *neither* view is correct. The fact that others intentionally intervene, in violation of a side constraint against aggression, to threaten force to limit the alternatives, in this case to paying taxes or (presumably the worse alternative) bare subsistence, makes the taxation system one of forced labor and distinguishes it from other cases of limited choices which are not forcings.

The man who chooses to work longer to gain an income more than sufficient for his basic needs prefers some extra goods or services to the leisure and activities he could perform during the possible nonworking hours; whereas the man who chooses not to work the extra time prefers the leisure activities to the extra goods or services he could acquire by working more. Given this, if it would be illegitimate for a tax system to seize some of a man's leisure (forced labor) for the purpose of serving the needy, how can it be legitimate for a tax system to seize some of a man's goods for that purpose? Why should we treat the man whose happiness requires certain material goods or services differently from the man whose preferences and desires make such goods unnecessary for his happiness? Why should the man who prefers seeing a movie (and who has to earn money for a ticket) be open to the required call to aid the needy, while the person who prefers looking at a sunset (and hence need earn no extra money) is not? Indeed, isn't it surprising that redistributionists choose to ignore the man whose pleasures are so easily attainable without extra labor, while adding yet another burden to the poor unfortunate who must work for his pleasures? If anything, one would have expected the reverse. Why is the person with the nonmaterial or nonconsumption desire allowed to proceed unimpeded to his most favored feasible alternative, whereas the man whose pleasures or desires involve material things and who must work for extra money (thereby serving whomever considers his activities valuable enough to pay him) is constrained in what he can realize? . . .

## Locke's Theory of Acquisition

Before we turn to consider other theories of justice in detail, we must introduce an additional bit of complexity into the structure of the entitlement theory. This is best approached by considering Locke's attempt to specify a principle of justice in acquisition. Locke views property rights in an unowned object as originating through someone's mixing his labor with it. This gives rise to many questions. What are the boundaries of what labor is mixed with? If a private astronaut clears a place on Mars, has he mixed his labor with (so that he comes to own) the whole planet, the whole uninhabited universe, or just a particular plot? Which plot does an act bring under ownership? The minimal (possibly disconnected) area such that an act

decreases entropy in that area, and not elsewhere? Can virgin land (for the purposes of ecological investigation by high-flying airplane) come under ownership by a Lockean process? Building a fence around a territory presumably would make one the owner of only the fence (and the land immediately underneath it).

Why does mixing one's labor with something make one the owner of it? Perhaps because one owns one's labor, and so one comes to own a previously unowned thing that becomes permeated with what one owns. Ownership seeps over into the rest. But why isn't mixing what I own with what I don't own a way of losing what I own rather than a way of gaining what I don't? If I own a can of tomato juice and spill it in the sea so that its molecules (made radioactive, so I can check this) mingle evenly throughout the sea, do I thereby come to own the sea, or have I foolishly dissipated my tomato juice? Perhaps the idea, instead, is that laboring on something improves it and makes it more valuable; and anyone is entitled to own a thing whose value he has created. (Reinforcing this, perhaps, is the view that laboring is unpleasant. If some people made things effortlessly, as the cartoon characters in *The Yellow Submarine* trail flowers in their wake, would they have lesser claim to their own products whose making didn't *cost* them anything?) Ignore the fact that laboring on something may make it less valuable (spraying pink enamel paint on a piece of driftwood that you have found). Why should one's entitlement extend to the whole object rather than just to the *added value* one's labor has produced? (Such reference to value might also serve to delimit the extent of ownership; for example, substitute "increases the value of" for "decreases entropy in" in the above entropy criterion.) No workable or coherent value-added property scheme has yet been devised, and any such scheme presumably would fall to objections (similar to those) that fell the theory of Henry George.

It will be implausible to view improving an object as giving full ownership to it, if the stock of unowned objects that might be improved is limited. For an object's coming under one person's ownership changes the situation of all others.

Whereas previously they were at liberty (in Hohfeld's sense) to use the object, they now no longer are. This change in the situation of others (by removing their liberty to act on a previously unowned object) need not worsen their situation. If I appropriate a grain of sand from Coney Island, no one else may now do as they will with *that* grain of sand. But there are plenty of other grains of sand left for them to do the same with. Or if not grains of sand, then other things. Alternatively, the things I do with the grain of sand I appropriate might improve the position of others, counterbalancing their loss of the liberty to use that grain. The crucial point is whether appropriation of an unowned object worsens the situation of others. . . .

Is the situation of persons who are unable to appropriate (there being no more accessible and useful unowned objects) worsened by a system allowing appropriation and permanent property? Here enter the various familiar social considerations favoring private property: it increases the social product by putting means of production in the hands of those who can use them most efficiently (profitably); experimentation is encouraged, because with separate persons controlling resources, there is no one person or small group whom someone with a new idea must convince to try it out; private property enables people to decide on the pattern and types of risks they wish to bear, leading to specialized types of risk bearing; private property protects future persons by leading some to hold back resources from current consumption for future markets; it provides alternate sources of employment for unpopular persons who don't have to convince any one person or small group to hire them, and so on. These considerations enter a Lockean theory to support the claim that appropriation of private property satisfies the intent behind the "enough and as good left over" proviso, *not* as a utilitarian justification of property. They enter to rebut the claim that because the proviso is violated no natural right to private property can arise by a Lockean process. The difficulty in working such an argument to show that the proviso is satisfied is in fixing the appropriate base line for comparison. Lockean

appropriation makes people no worse off than they would be *how?* This question of fixing the baseline needs more detailed investigation than we are able to give it here. It would be desirable to have an estimate of the general economic importance of original appropriation in order to see how much leeway there is for differing theories of appropriation and of the location of the baseline. Perhaps this importance can be measured by the percentage of all income that is based upon untransformed raw materials and given resources (rather than upon human actions), mainly rental income representing the unimproved value of land, and the price of raw material *in situ,* and by the percentage of current wealth which represents such income in the past.

We should note that it is not only persons favoring *private* property who need a theory of how property rights legitimately originate. Those believing in collective property, for example those believing that a group of persons living in an area jointly own the territory, or its mineral resources, also must provide a theory of how such property rights arise; they must show why the persons living there have rights to determine what is done with the land and resources there that persons living elsewhere don't have (with regard to the same land and resources).

## The Proviso

Whether or not Locke's particular theory of appropriation can be spelled out so as to handle various difficulties, I assume that any adequate theory of justice in acquisition will contain a proviso similar to the weaker of the ones we have attributed to Locke. A process normally giving rise to a permanent bequeathable property right in a previously unowned thing will not do so if the position of others no longer at liberty to use the thing is thereby worsened. It is important to specify *this* particular mode of worsening the situation of others, for the proviso does not encompass other modes. It does not include the worsening due to more limited opportunities to appropriate (the first way above, corresponding to the more stringent condition), and it does not include how I "worsen" a seller's position if I appropriate materials to make some of what he is selling, and then enter into competition with him. Someone whose appropriation otherwise would violate the proviso still may appropriate provided he compensates the others so that their situation is not thereby worsened; unless he does compensate these others, his appropriation will violate the proviso of the principle of justice in acquisition and will be an illegitimate one. A theory of appropriation incorporating this Lockean proviso will handle correctly the cases (objections to the theory lacking the proviso) where someone appropriates the total supply of something necessary for life.

A theory which includes this proviso in its principle of justice in acquisition must also contain a more complex principle of justice in transfer. Some reflection of the proviso about appropriation constrains later actions. If my appropriating all of a certain substance violates the Lockean proviso, then so does my appropriating some and purchasing all the rest from others who obtained it without otherwise violating the Lockean proviso. If the proviso excludes someone's appropriating all the drinkable water in the world, it also excludes his purchasing it all. (More weakly, and messily, it may exclude his charging certain prices for some of his supply.) This proviso (almost?) never will come into effect; the more someone acquires of a scarce substance which others want, the higher the price of the rest will go, and the more difficult it will become for him to acquire it all. But still, we can imagine, at least, that something like this occurs: someone makes simultaneous secret bids to the separate owners of a substance, each of whom sells assuming he can easily purchase more from the other owners; or some natural catastrophe destroys all of the supply of something except that in one person's possession. The total supply could not be permissibly appropriated by one person at the beginning. His later acquisition of it all does not show that the original appropriation violated the proviso (even by a reverse argument similar to the one above that tried to zip back from *Z* to *A*). Rather, it is the combination of the original appropriation *plus* all the later transfers and actions that violates the Lockean proviso.

Each owner's title to his holding includes the historical shadow of the Lockean proviso on appropriation. This excludes his transferring it into an agglomeration that does violate the Lockean proviso and excludes his using it in a way, in coordination with others or independently of them, so as to violate the proviso by making the situation of others worse than their baseline situation. Once it is known that someone's ownership runs afoul of the Lockean proviso, there are stringent limits on what he may do with (what it is difficult any longer unreservedly to call) "his property." Thus a person may not appropriate the only water hole in a desert and charge what he will. Nor may he charge what he will if he possesses one, and unfortunately it happens that all the water holes in the desert dry up, except for his. This unfortunate circumstance, admittedly no fault of his, brings into operation the Lockean proviso and limits his property rights. Similarly, an owner's property right in the only island in an area does not allow him to order a castaway from a shipwreck off his island as a trespasser, for this would violate the Lockean proviso. . . .

The fact that someone owns the total supply of something necessary for others to stay alive does *not* entail that his (or anyone's) appropriation of anything left some people (immediately or later) in a situation worse than the baseline one. A medical researcher who synthesizes a new substance that effectively treats a certain disease and who refuses to sell except on his terms does not worsen the situation of others by depriving them of whatever he has appropriated. The others easily can possess the same materials he appropriated; the researcher's appropriation or purchase of chemicals didn't make those chemicals scarce in a way so as to violate the Lockean proviso. Nor would someone else's purchasing the total supply of the synthesized substance from the medical researcher. The fact that the medical researcher uses easily available chemicals to synthesize the drug no more violates the Lockean proviso than does the fact that the only surgeon able to perform a particular operation eats easily obtainable food in order to stay alive and to have the energy to work. This shows that the Lockean proviso is not an "end-state principle"; it focuses on a particular way that appropriative actions affect others, and not on the structure of the situation that results.

Intermediate between someone who takes all of the public supply and someone who makes the total supply out of easily obtainable substances is someone who appropriates the total supply of something in a way that does not deprive the others of it. For example, someone finds a new substance in an out-of-the-way place. He discovers that it effectively treats a certain disease and appropriates the total supply. He does not worsen the situation of others; if he did not stumble upon the substance no one else would have, and the others would remain without it. However, as time passes, the likelihood increases that others would have come across the substance; upon this fact might be based a limit to his property right in the substance so that others are not below their baseline position; for example, its bequest might be limited. The theme of someone worsening another's situation by depriving him of something he

otherwise would possess may also illuminate the example of patents. An inventor's patent does not deprive others of an object which would not exist if not for the inventor. Yet patents would have this effect on others who independently invent the object. Therefore, these independent inventors, upon whom the burden of proving independent discovery may rest, should not be excluded from utilizing their own invention as they wish (including selling it to others). Furthermore, a known inventor drastically lessens the chances of actual independent invention. For persons who know of an invention usually will not try to reinvent it, and the notion of independent discovery here would be murky at best. Yet we may assume that in the absence of the original invention, sometime later someone else would have come up with it. This suggests placing a time limit on patents, as a rough rule of thumb to approximate how long it would have taken, in the absence of knowledge of the invention, for independent discovery.

I believe that the free operation of a market system will not actually run afoul of the Lockean proviso. . . .

# 31   A Theory of Justice

**JOHN RAWLS**

## The Main Idea of the Theory of Justice

My aim is to present a conception of justice which generalizes and carries to a higher level of abstraction the familiar theory of the social contract as found, say, in Locke, Rousseau, and Kant. In order to do this we are not to think of the original contract as one to enter a particular society

Reprinted by permission of the publisher from *Theory of Justice* by John Rawls, Cambridge MA: Harvard University Press. Copyright © 1971 by the President and Fellows of Harvard College.

or to set up a particular form of government. Rather, the guiding idea is that the principles of justice for the basic structure of society are the object of the original agreement. They are the principles that free and rational persons concerned to further their own interests would accept in an initial position of equality as defining the fundamental terms of their association. These principles are to regulate all further agreements; they specify the kinds of social cooperation that can be entered into and the forms of government that can be established. This way of regarding the principles of justice I shall call justice as fairness.

Thus we are to imagine that those who engage in social cooperation choose together, in one joint act, the principles which are to assign basic rights and duties and to determine the division of social benefits. Men are to decide in advance how they are to regulate their claims against one another and what is to be the foundation charter of their society. Just as each person must decide by rational reflection what constitutes his good, that is, the system of ends which it is rational for him to pursue, so a group of persons must decide once and for all what is to count among them as just and unjust. The choice which rational men would make in this hypothetical situation of equal liberty, assuming for the present that this choice problem has a solution, determines the principles of justice.

In justice as fairness the original position of equality corresponds to the state of nature in the traditional theory of the social contract. This original position is not, of course, thought of as an actual historical state of affairs, much less as a primitive condition of culture. It is understood as a purely hypothetical situation characterized so as to lead to a certain conception of justice. Among the essential features of this situation is that no one knows his place in society, his class position or social status, nor does any one know his fortune in the distribution of natural assets and abilities, his intelligence, strength, and the like. I shall even assume that the parties do not know their conceptions of the good or their special psychological propensities. The principles of justice are chosen behind a veil of ignorance. This ensures that no one is advantaged or disadvantaged in the choice of principles by the outcome of natural chance or the contingency of social circumstances. Since all are similarly situated and no one is able to design principles to favor his particular condition, the principles of justice are the result of a fair agreement or bargain. For given the circumstances of the original position, the symmetry of everyone's relations to each other, this initial situation is fair between individuals as moral persons, that is, as rational beings with their own ends and capable, I shall assume, of a sense of justice. The

original position is, one might say, the appropriate initial status quo, and thus the fundamental agreements reached in it are fair. This explains the propriety of the name "justice as fairness": it conveys the idea that the principles of justice are agreed to in an initial situation that is fair. The name does not mean that the concepts of justice and fairness are the same, any more than the phrase "poetry as metaphor" means that the concepts of poetry and metaphor are the same.

Justice as fairness begins, as I have said, with one of the most general of all choices which persons might make together, namely, with the choice of the first principles of a conception of justice which is to regulate all subsequent criticism and reform of institutions. Then, having chosen a conception of justice, we can suppose that they are to choose a constitution and a legislature to enact laws, and so on, all in accordance with the principles of justice initially agreed upon. Our social situation is just if it is such that by this sequence of hypothetical agreements we would have contracted into the general system of rules which defines it. Moreover, assuming that the original position does determine a set of principles (that is, that a particular conception of justice would be chosen), it will then be true that whenever social institutions satisfy these principles those engaged in them can say to one another that they are cooperating on terms to which they would agree if they were free and equal persons whose relations with respect to one another were fair. They could all view their arrangements as meeting the stipulations which they would acknowledge in an initial situation that embodies widely accepted and reasonable constraints on the choice of principles. The general recognition of this fact would provide the basis for a public acceptance of the corresponding principles of justice. No society can, of course, be a scheme of cooperation which men enter voluntarily in a literal sense; each person finds himself placed at birth in some particular position in some particular society, and the nature of this position materially affects his life prospects. Yet a society satisfying the principles of justice as fairness comes as close as a society can to being a voluntary scheme, for it meets the principles which free and equal persons would assent to under circumstances that are fair. In this sense its members are autonomous and the obligations they recognize self-imposed.

One feature of justice as fairness is to think of the parties in the initial situation as rational and mutually disinterested. This does not mean that the parties are egoists, that is, individuals with only certain kinds of interests, say in wealth, prestige and domination. But they are conceived as not taking an interest in one another's interests. They are to presume that even their spiritual aims may be opposed, in the way that the aims of those of different religions may be opposed. Moreover, the concept of rationality must be interpreted as far as possible in the narrow sense, standard in economic theory, of taking the most effective means to given ends. I shall modify this concept to some extent, but one must try to avoid introducing into it any controversial ethical elements. The initial situation must be characterized by stipulations that are widely accepted.

In working out the conception of justice as fairness one main task clearly is to determine which principles of justice would be chosen in the original position. To do this we must describe this situation in some detail and formulate with care the problem of choice which it presents. These matters I shall take up in the immediately succeeding chapters. It may be observed, however, that once the principles of justice are thought of as arising from an original agreement in a situation of equality, it is an open question whether the principle of utility would be acknowledged. Offhand it hardly seems likely that persons who view themselves as equals, entitled to press their claims upon one another, would agree to a principle which may require lesser life prospects for some simply for the sake of a greater sum of advantages enjoyed by others. Since each desires to protect his interests, his capacity to advance his conception of the good, no one has a reason to acquiesce in an enduring loss for himself in order to bring about a greater net balance of satisfaction. In the absence of strong and lasting benevolent impulses, a rational man would not accept a basic structure merely because it maximized the algebraic sum of advantages irrespective of its permanent effects on his own basic rights and interests. Thus it seems that the principle of utility is incompatible with the conception of social cooperation among equals for mutual advantage. It appears to be inconsistent with the idea of reciprocity implicit in the notion of a well-ordered society. Or, at any rate, so I shall argue.

I shall maintain instead that the persons in the initial situation would choose two rather different principles: the first requires equality in the assignment of basic rights and duties, while the second holds that social and economic inequalities, for example inequalities of wealth and authority, are just only if they result in compensating benefits for everyone, and in particular for the least advantaged members of society. These principles rule out justifying institutions on the grounds that the hardships of some are offset by a greater good in the aggregate. It may be expedient but it is not just that some should have less in order that others may prosper. But there is no injustice in the greater benefits earned by a few provided that the situation of persons not so fortunate is thereby improved. The intuitive idea is that since everyone's well-being depends upon a scheme of cooperation without which no one could have a satisfactory life, the division of advantages should be such as to draw forth the willing cooperation of everyone taking part in it, including those less well situated. Yet this can be expected only if reasonable terms are proposed. The two principles mentioned seem to be a fair agreement on the basis of which those better endowed, or more fortunate in their social position, neither of which we can be said to deserve, could expect the willing cooperation of others when some workable scheme is a necessary condition of the welfare of all. Once we decide to look for a conception of justice that nullifies the accidents of natural endowment and the contingencies of social circumstance as counters in quest for political and economic advantage, we are led to these principles. They express the result of leaving aside those aspects of the social world that seem arbitrary from a moral point of view.

The problem of the choice of principles, however, is extremely difficult. I do not expect the answer I shall suggest to be convincing to everyone. It is, therefore, worth noting from the outset that justice as fairness, like other contract views, consists of two parts: (1) an interpretation of the initial situation and of the problem of choice posed there, and (2) a set of principles which, it is argued, would be agreed to. One may accept the first part of the theory (or some variant thereof), but not the other, and conversely. . . .

## The Original Position and Justification

The concept of the original position, as I shall refer to it, is that of the most philosophically favored interpretation of this initial choice situation for the purposes of a theory of justice.

But how are we to decide what is the most favored interpretation? I assume, for one thing, that there is a broad measure of agreement that principles of justice should be chosen under certain conditions. To justify a particular description of the initial situation one shows that it incorporates these commonly shared presumptions. One argues from widely accepted but weak premises to more specific conclusions. Each of the presumptions should by itself be natural and plausible; some of them may seem innocuous or even trivial. The aim of the contract approach is to establish that taken together they impose significant bounds on acceptable principles of justice. The ideal outcome would be that these conditions determine a unique set of principles; but I shall be satisfied if they suffice to rank the main traditional conceptions of social justice.

One should not be misled, then, by the somewhat unusual conditions which characterize the original position. The idea here is simply to make vivid to ourselves the restrictions that it seems reasonable to impose on arguments for principles of justice, and therefore on these principles themselves. Thus it seems reasonable and generally acceptable that no one should be advantaged or disadvantaged by natural fortune or social circum-

stances in the choice of principles. It also seems widely agreed that it should be impossible to tailor principles to the circumstances of one's own case. We should insure further that particular inclinations and aspirations, and persons' conceptions of their good do not affect the principles adopted. The aim is to rule out those principles that it would be rational to propose for acceptance, however little the chance of success, only if one knew certain things that are irrelevant from the standpoint of justice. For example, if a man knew that he was wealthy, he might find it rational to advance the principle that various taxes for welfare measures be counted unjust; if he knew that he was poor, he would most likely propose the contrary principle. To represent the desired restrictions one imagines a situation in which everyone is deprived of this sort of information. One excludes the knowledge of those contingencies which sets men at odds and allows them to be guided by their prejudices. In this manner the veil of ignorance is arrived at in a natural way. This concept should cause no difficulty if we keep in mind the constraints on arguments that it is meant to express. At any time we can enter the original position, so to speak, simply by following a certain procedure, namely, by arguing for principles of justice in accordance with these restrictions.

It seems reasonable to suppose that the parties in the original position are equal. That is, all have the same rights in the procedure for choosing principles; each can make proposals, submit reasons for their acceptance, and so on. Obviously the purpose of these conditions is to represent equality between human beings as moral persons, as creatures having a conception of their good and capable of a sense of justice. The basis of equality is taken to be similarity in these two respects. Systems of ends are not ranked in value; and each man is presumed to have the requisite ability to understand and to act upon whatever principles are adopted. Together with the veil of ignorance, these conditions define the principles of justice as those which rational persons concerned to advance their interests would consent to as equals when none are known to be advantaged or disadvantaged by social and natural contingencies.

There is, however, another side to justifying a particular description of the original position. This is to see if the principles which would be chosen match our considered convictions of justice or extend them in an acceptable way. We can note whether applying these principles would lead us to make the same judgments about the basic structure of society which we now make intuitively and in which we have the greatest confidence; or whether, in cases where our present judgments are in doubt and given with hesitation, these principles offer a resolution which we can affirm on reflection. There are questions which we feel sure must be answered in a certain way. For example, we are confident that religious intolerance and racial discrimination are unjust. We think that we have examined these things with care and have reached what we believe is an impartial judgment not likely to be distorted by an excessive attention to our own interests. These convictions are provisional fixed points which we presume any conception of justice must fit. But we have much less assurance as to what is the correct distribution of wealth and authority. Here we may be looking for a way to remove our doubts. We can check an interpretation of the initial situation, then, by the capacity of its principles to accommodate our firmest convictions and to provide guidance where guidance is needed.

In searching for the most favored description of this situation we work from both ends. We begin by describing it so that it represents generally shared and preferably weak conditions. We then see if these conditions are strong enough to yield a significant set of principles. If not, we look for further premises equally reasonable. But if so, and these principles match our considered convictions of justice, then so far well and good. But presumably there will be discrepancies. In this case we have a choice. We can either modify the account of the initial situation or we can revise our existing judgments, for even the judgments we take provisionally as fixed points are liable to revision. By going back and forth, sometimes altering the conditions of the contractual circumstances, at others withdrawing our judgments and conforming them to principle, I assume that eventually we shall find a description of the initial situation that both expresses reasonable conditions and yields principles which match our considered judgments duly pruned and adjusted. This state of affairs I refer to as reflective equilibrium. It is an equilibrium because at last our principles and judgments coincide; and it is reflective since we know to what principles our judgments conform and the premises of their derivation. At the moment everything is in order. But this equilibrium is not necessarily stable. It is liable to be upset by further examination of the conditions which should be imposed on the contractual situation and by particular cases which may lead us to revise our judgments. Yet for the time being we have done what we can to render coherent and to justify our convictions of social justice. We have reached a conception of the original position.

I shall not, of course, actually work through this process. Still, we may think of the interpretation of the original position that I shall present as the result of such a hypothetical course of reflection. It represents the attempt to accommodate within one scheme, both reasonable philosophical conditions on principles as well as our considered judgments of justice. In arriving at the favored interpretation of the initial situation there is no point at which an appeal is made to self-evidence in the traditional sense either of general conceptions or particular convictions. I do not claim for the principles of justice proposed that they are necessary truths or derivable from such truths. A conception of justice cannot be deduced from self-evident premises or conditions on principles; instead, its justification is a matter of the mutual support of many considerations, of everything fitting together into one coherent view.

A final comment. We shall want to say that certain principles of justice are justified because they would be agreed to in an initial situation of equality. I have emphasized that this original position is purely hypothetical. It is natural to ask why, if this agreement is never actually entered into, we should take any interest in these principles, moral or otherwise. The answer is that the conditions embodied in the description of the original position are ones that we do in fact accept. Or if we do not, then perhaps we can be persuaded to do so by philosophical reflection. Each aspect of the contractual situation can be given supporting grounds. Thus what we shall do is to collect together into one conception a number of conditions on principles that we are ready upon due consideration to recognize as reasonable. These constraints express what we are prepared to regard as limits on fair terms of social cooperation. One way to look at the idea of the original position, therefore, is to see it as an expository device which sums up the meaning of these conditions and helps us to extract their consequences. . . .

## Two Principles of Justice

I shall now state in a provisional form the two principles of justice that I believe would be chosen in the original position. In this section I wish to make only the most general comments, and therefore the first formulation of these principles is tentative. As we go on I shall run through several formulations and approximate step by step the final statement to be given much later. I believe that doing this allows the exposition to proceed in a natural way.

The first statement of the two principles reads as follows.

> First: each person is to have an equal right to the most extensive basic liberty compatible with a similar liberty for others.
> Second: social and economic inequalities are to be arranged so that they are both (a) reasonably expected to be to everyone's advantage, and (b) attached to positions and offices open to all.

There are two ambiguous phrases in the second principle, namely "everyone's advantage" and "open to all." Determining their sense more exactly will lead to a second formulation of the principle.

By way of general comment, these principles primarily apply, as I have said, to the basic structure of society. They are to govern the assignment of rights and duties and to regulate the distribution of social and economic advantages. As their for-

mulation suggests, these principles presuppose that the social structure can be divided into two more or less distinct parts, the first principle applying to the one, the second to the other. They distinguish between those aspects of the social system that define and secure the equal liberties of citizenship and those that specify and establish social and economic inequalities. The basic liberties of citizens are, roughly speaking, political liberty (the right to vote and to be eligible for public office) together with freedom of speech and assembly; liberty of conscience and freedom of thought; freedom of the person along with the right to hold (personal) property; and freedom from arbitrary arrest and seizure as defined by the concept of the rule of law. These liberties are all required to be equal by the first principle, since citizens of a just society are to have the same basic rights.

The second principle applies, in the first approximation, to the distribution of income and wealth and to the design of organizations that make use of differences in authority and responsibility, or chains of command. While the distribution of wealth and income need not be equal, it must be to everyone's advantage, and at the same time, positions of authority and offices of command must be accessible to all. One applies the second principle by holding positions open, and then, subject to this constraint, arranges social and economic inequalities so that everyone benefits.

These principles are to be arranged in a serial order with the first principle prior to the second. This ordering means that a departure from the institutions of equal liberty required by the first principle cannot be justified by, or compensated for, by greater social and economic advantages. The distribution of wealth and income, and the hierarchies of authority, must be consistent with both the liberties of equal citizenship and equality of opportunity.

It is clear that these principles are rather specific in their content, and their acceptance rests on certain assumptions that I must eventually try to explain and justify. A theory of justice depends upon a theory of society in ways that will become evident as we proceed. For the present, it should be observed that the two principles (and this holds for all formulations) are a special case of a more general conception of justice that can be expressed as follows.

> All social values—liberty and opportunity, income and wealth, and the bases of self-respect—are to be distributed equally unless an unequal distribution of any, or all, of these values is to everyone's advantage.

Injustice, then, is simply inequalities that are not to the benefit of all. Of course, this conception is extremely vague and requires interpretation.

As a first step, suppose that the basic structure of society distributes certain primary goods, that is, things that every rational man is presumed to want. These goods normally have a use whatever a person's rational plan of life. For simplicity, assume that the chief primary goods at the disposition of society are rights and liberties, powers and opportunities, income and wealth. (Later the primary good of self-respect has a central place.) These are the social primary goods. Other primary goods such as health and vigor, intelligence and imagination, are natural goods; although their possession is influenced by the basic structure, they are not so directly under its control. Imagine, then, a hypothetical initial arrangement in which all the social primary goods are equally distributed: everyone has similar rights and duties, and income and wealth are evenly shared. This state of affairs provides a benchmark for judging improvements. If certain inequalities of wealth and organizational powers would make everyone better off than in this hypothetical starting situation, then they accord with the general conception.

Now it is possible, at least theoretically, that by giving up some of their fundamental liberties men are sufficiently compensated by the resulting social and economic gains. The general conception of justice imposes no restrictions on what sort of inequalities are permissible; it only requires that everyone's position be improved. We need not suppose anything so drastic as consenting to a condition of slavery. Imagine instead that men forgo certain political rights when the economic returns are significant and their capacity to influ-

ence the course of policy by the exercise of these rights would be marginal in any case. It is this kind of exchange which the two principles as stated rule out; being arranged in serial order they do not permit exchanges between basic liberties and economic and social gains. The serial ordering of principles expresses an underlying preference among primary social goods. When this preference is rational so likewise is the choice of these principles in this order.

In developing justice as fairness I shall, for the most part, leave aside the general conception of justice and examine instead the special case of the two principles in serial order. The advantage of this procedure is that from the first the matter of priorities is recognized and an effort made to find principles to deal with it. One is led to attend throughout to the conditions under which the acknowledgment of the absolute weight of liberty with respect to social and economic advantages, as defined by the lexical order of the two principles, would be reasonable. Offhand, this ranking appears extreme and too special a case to be of much interest; but there is more justification for it than would appear at first sight. Or at any rate, so I shall maintain. Furthermore, the distinction between fundamental rights and liberties and economic and social benefits marks a difference among primary social needs that one should try to exploit. It suggests an important division in the social system. Of course, the distinctions drawn and the ordering proposed are bound to be at best only approximations. There are surely circumstances in which they fail. But it is essential to depict clearly the main lines of a reasonable conception of justice; and under many conditions anyway, the two principles in serial order may serve well enough. When necessary we can fall back on the more general conception. . . .

## Interpretations of the Second Principle

I have already mentioned that since the phrases "everyone's advantage" and "equally open to all" are ambiguous, both parts of the second principle have two natural senses. Because these senses are independent of one another, the principle has four possible meanings. Assuming that the first principle of equal liberty has the same sense throughout, we then have four interpretations of the two principles. These are indicated in the table below.

In the system of natural liberty the principle of efficiency is constrained by certain background institutions; when these constraints are satisfied, any resulting efficient distribution is accepted as just. The system of natural liberty selects an efficient distribution roughly as follows. Let us suppose that we know from economic theory that under the standard assumptions defining a competitive market economy, income and wealth will be distributed in an efficient way, and that the particular efficient distribution which results in any period of time is determined by the initial distribution of assets, that is, by the initial distribution of income and wealth, and of natural talents and abilities. With each initial distribution, a definite efficient outcome is arrived at. Thus it turns out that if we are to accept the outcome as just, and not merely as efficient, we must accept the basis upon which over time the initial distribution of assets is determined.

In the system of natural liberty the initial distribution is regulated by the arrangement implicit in the conception of careers open to talents (as earlier defined). These arrangements presuppose a background of equal liberty (as specified by the first principle) and a free market economy. They require a formal equality of opportunity in that all have at least the same legal rights of access to all advantaged social positions. But since there is no effort to preserve an equality, or similarity, of social conditions, except insofar as this is necessary to preserve the requisite background institutions,

the initial distribution of assets for any period of time is strongly influenced by natural and social contingencies. The existing distribution of income and wealth, say, is the cumulative effect of prior distributions of natural assets—that is, natural talents and abilities—as these have been developed or left unrealized, and their use favored or disfavored over time by social circumstances and such chance contingencies as accident and good fortune. Intuitively, the most obvious injustice of the system of natural liberty is that it permits distributive shares to be improperly influenced by these factors so arbitrary from a moral point of view.

The liberal interpretation, as I shall refer to it, tries to correct for this by adding to the requirement of careers open to talents the further condition of the principle of fair equality of opportunity. The thought here is that positions are to be not only open in a formal sense, but that all should have a fair chance to attain them. Offhand it is not clear what is meant, but we might say that those with similar abilities and skills should have similar life chances. More specifically, assuming that there is a distribution of natural assets, those who are at the same level of talent and ability, and have the same willingness to use them, should have the same prospects of success regardless of their initial place in the social system, that is, irrespective of the income class into which they are born. In all sectors of society there should be roughly equal prospects of culture and achievement for everyone similarly motivated and endowed. The expectations of those with the same abilities and aspirations should not be affected by their social class.

The liberal interpretation of the two principles seeks, then, to mitigate the influence of social

| "Equally open" | "Everyone's advantage" | |
| --- | --- | --- |
| | Principle of efficiency | Difference principle |
| Equality as careers open to talents | System of Natural Liberty | Natural Aristocracy |
| Equality as equality of fair opportunity | Liberal Equality | Democratic Equality |

contingencies and natural fortune on distributive shares. To accomplish this end it is necessary to impose further basic structural conditions on the social system. Free market arrangements must be set within a framework of political and legal institutions which regulates the overall trends of economic events and preserves the social conditions necessary for fair equality of opportunity. The elements of this framework are familiar enough, though it may be worthwhile to recall the importance of preventing excessive accumulations of property and wealth and of maintaining equal opportunities of education for all. Chances to acquire cultural knowledge and skills should not depend upon one's class position, and so the school system, whether public or private, should be designed to even out class barriers.

While the liberal conception seems clearly preferable to the system of natural liberty, intuitively it still appears defective. For one thing, even if it works to perfection in eliminating the influence of social contingencies, it still permits the distribution of wealth and income to be determined by the natural distribution of abilities and talents. Within the limits allowed by the background arrangements, distributive shares are decided by the outcome of the natural lottery; and this outcome is arbitrary from a moral perspective. There is no more reason to permit the distribution of income and wealth to be settled by the distribution of natural assets than by historical and social fortune. Furthermore, the principle of fair opportunity can be only imperfectly carried out, at least as long as the institution of the family exists. The extent to which natural capacities develop and reach fruition is affected by all kinds of social conditions and class attitudes. Even the willingness to make an effort, to try, and so to be deserving in the ordinary sense is itself dependent upon happy family and social circumstances. It is impossible in practice to secure equal chances of achievement and culture for those similarly endowed, and therefore we may want to adopt a principle which recognizes this fact and also mitigates the arbitrary effects of the natural lottery itself. That the liberal conception fails to do this encourages one to look

for another interpretation of the two principles of justice.

Before turning to the conception of democratic equality, we should note that of natural aristocracy. On this view no attempt is made to regulate social contingencies beyond what is required by formal equality of opportunity, but the advantages of persons with greater natural endowments are to be limited to those that further the good of the poorer sectors of society. The aristocratic ideal is applied to a system that is open, at least from a legal point of view, and the better situation of those favored by it is regarded as just only when less would be had by those below, if less were given to those above. In this way the idea of *noblesse oblige* is carried over to the conception of natural aristocracy. . . .

## Democratic Equality and the Difference Principle

The democratic interpretation, as the table suggests, is arrived at by combining the principle of fair equality of opportunity with the difference principle. This principle removes the indeterminateness of the principle of efficiency by singling out a particular position from which the social and economic inequalities of the basic structure are to be judged. Assuming the framework of institutions required by equal liberty and fair equality of opportunity, the higher expectations of those better situated are just if and only if they work as part of a scheme which improves the expectations of the least advantaged members of society. The intuitive idea is that the social order is not to establish and secure the more attractive prospects of those better off unless doing so is to the advantage of those less fortunate.

. . . , The second principle is to read as follows.

Social and economic inequalities are to be arranged so that they are both (a) to the greatest benefit of the least advantaged and (b) attached to offices and positions open to all under conditions of fair equality of opportunity.

Finally, it should be observed that the difference principle, or the idea expressed by it, can easily be accommodated to the general conception of justice. In fact, the general conception is simply the difference principle applied to all primary goods including liberty and opportunity and so no longer constrained by other parts of the special conception. . . .

Thus although the difference principle is not the same as that of redress, it does achieve some of the intent of the latter principle. It transforms the aims of the basic structure so that the total scheme of institutions no longer emphasizes social efficiency and technocratic values. We see then that the difference principle represents, in effect, an agreement to regard the distribution of natural talents as a common asset and to share in the benefits of this distribution whatever it turns out to be. Those who have been favored by nature, whoever they are, may gain from their good fortune only on terms that improve the situation of those who have lost out. The naturally advantaged are not to gain merely because they are more gifted, but only to cover the costs of training and education and for using their endowments in ways that help the less fortunate as well. No one deserves his greater natural capacity nor merits a more favorable starting place in society. But it does not follow that one should eliminate these distinctions. There is another way to deal with them. The basic structure can be arranged so that these contingencies work for the good of the least fortunate. Thus we are led to the difference principle if we wish to set up the social system so that no one gains or loses from his arbitrary place in the distribution of natural assets or his initial position in society without giving or receiving compensating advantages in return. . . .

## The Reasoning Leading to the Two Principles of Justice

It will be recalled that the general conception of justice as fairness requires that all primary social goods be distributed equally unless an unequal distribution would be to everyone's advantage. No restrictions are placed on exchanges of these goods and therefore a lesser liberty can be compensated for by greater social and economic benefits. Now looking at the situation from the standpoint of one person selected arbitrarily, there is no way for him to win special advantages for himself. Nor, on the other hand, are there grounds for his acquiescing in special disadvantages. Since it is not reasonable for him to expect more than an equal share in the division of social goods, and since it is not rational for him to agree to less, the sensible thing for him to do is to acknowledge as the first principle of justice one requiring an equal distribution. Indeed, this principle is so obvious that we would expect it to occur to anyone immediately.

Thus, the parties start with a principle establishing equal liberty for all, including equality of opportunity, as well as an equal distribution of income and wealth. But there is no reason why this acknowledgment should be final. If there are inequalities in the basic structure that work to make everyone better off in comparison with the benchmark of initial equality, why not permit them? The immediate gain which a greater equality might allow can be regarded as intelligently invested in view of its future return. If, for example, these inequalities set up various incentives which succeed in eliciting more productive efforts, a person in the original position may look upon them as necessary to cover the costs of training and to encourage effective performance. One might think that ideally individuals should want to serve one another. But since the parties are assumed not to take an interest in one another's interests, their acceptance of these inequalities is only the acceptance of the relations in which men stand in the circumstances of justice. They have no grounds for complaining of one another's motives. A person in the original position would, therefore, concede the justice of these inequalities. Indeed, it would be shortsighted of him not to do so. He would hesitate to agree to these regularities only if he would be dejected by the bare knowledge or perception that others were better situated; and I have assumed that the parties decide as if they are not moved by envy. In order to make the principle regulating inequalities determinate, one looks at the system from the standpoint of the least advantaged representative man. Inequalities are permissible when they maximize, or at least all contribute to, the long-term expectations of the least fortunate group in society.

Now this general conception imposes no constraints on what sorts of inequalities are allowed, whereas the special conception, by putting the two principles in serial order (with the necessary adjustments in meaning), forbids exchanges between basic liberties and economic and social benefits. I shall not try to justify this ordering here. From time to time in later chapters this problem will be considered (§§ 39, 82). But roughly, the idea underlying this ordering is that if the parties assume that their basic liberties can be effectively exercised, they will not exchange a lesser liberty for an improvement in economic well-being. It is only when social conditions do not allow the effective establishment of these rights that one can concede their limitation; and these restrictions can be granted only to the extent that they are necessary to prepare the way for a free society. The denial of equal liberty can be defended only if it is necessary to raise the level of civilization so that in due course these freedoms can be enjoyed. Thus in adopting a serial order we are in effect making a special assumption in the original position, namely, that the parties know that the conditions of their society, whatever they are, admit the effective realization of the equal liberties. The serial ordering of the two principles of justice eventually comes to be reasonable if the general conception is consistently followed. This lexical ranking is the long-run tendency of the general view. For the most part I shall assume that the requisite circumstances for the serial order obtain.

It seems clear from these remarks that the two principles are at least a plausible conception of justice. The question, though, is how one is to argue for them more systematically. Now there are several things to do. One can work out their consequences for institutions and note their implications for fundamental social policy. In this way they are tested by a comparison with our considered judgments of justice. Part II is devoted to this. But one can also try to find arguments in their favor that are decisive from the standpoint of the original position. In order to see how this might be done, it is useful as a heuristic device to think of the two principles as the maximin solution to the problem of social justice. There is an analogy between the two principles and the maximin rule for choice under uncertainty. This is evident from the fact that the two principles are those a person would choose for the design of a society in which his enemy is to assign him his place. The maximin rule tells us to rank alternatives by their worst possible outcomes: we are to adopt the alternative the worst outcome of which is superior to the worst outcomes of the others. The persons in the original position do not, of course, assume that their initial place in society is decided by a malevolent opponent. As I note below, they should not reason from false premises. The veil of ignorance does not violate this idea, since an absence of information is not misinformation. But that the two principles of justice would be chosen if the parties were forced to protect themselves against such a contingency explains the sense in which this conception is the maximin solution. And this analogy suggests that if the original position has been described so that it is rational for the parties to adopt the conservative attitude expressed by this rule, a conclusive argument can indeed be constructed for these principles. . . . The person choosing has a conception of the good such that he cares very little, if anything, for what he might gain above the minimum stipend that he can, in fact, be sure of by following the maximin rule. It is not worthwhile for him to take a chance for the sake of a further advantage, especially when it may turn out that he loses much that is important to him. . . . The rejected alternatives have outcomes that one can hardly accept. The situation involves grave risks. Of course these features work most effectively in combination. The paradigm situation for following the maximin rule is when all three features are realized to the highest degree. This rule does not, then, generally apply, nor of course is it self-evident. Rather, it is a maxim, a rule of thumb, that comes into its own in special circumstances. Its application depends upon the qualitative structure of the possible gains and losses in relation to one's conception of the good, all this against a background in which it is reasonable to discount conjectural estimates of likelihoods. . . .

## The Kantian Interpretation of Justice as Fairness

Kant held, I believe, that a person is acting autonomously when the principles of his action are chosen by him as the most adequate possible expression of his nature as a free and equal rational being. The principles he acts upon are not adopted because of his social position or natural endowments, or in view of the particular kind of society in which he lives or the specific things that he happens to want. To act on such principles is to act heteronomously. Now the veil of ignorance deprives the persons in the original position of the knowledge that would enable them to choose heteronomous principles. The parties arrive at their choice together as free and equal rational persons knowing only that those circumstances obtain which give rise to the need for principles of justice.

To be sure, the argument for these principles does add in various ways to Kant's conception. For example, it adds the feature that the principles chosen are to apply to the basic structure of society; and premises characterizing this structure are used in deriving the principles of justice. But I believe that this and other additions are natural enough and remain fairly close to Kant's doctrine, at least when all of his ethical writings are viewed together. Assuming, then, that the reasoning in favor of the principles of justice is correct, we can say that when persons act on these principles they are acting in accordance with principles that they would choose as rational and independent persons in an original position of equality. The principles of their actions do not depend upon social or natural contingencies, nor do they reflect the bias of the particulars of their plan of life or the aspirations that motivate them. By acting from these principles persons express their nature as free and equal rational beings subject to the general conditions of human life. For to express one's nature as a being of a particular kind is to act on the principles that would be chosen if this nature were the decisive determining element. Of course, the choice of the parties in the original position is subject to the restrictions of that situation. But when we knowingly act on the principles of justice in the ordinary course of events, we deliberately assume the limitations of the original position. One reason for doing this, for persons who can do so and want to, is to give expression to one's nature.

The principles of justice are also categorical imperatives in Kant's sense. For by a categorical imperative Kant understands a principle of conduct that applies to a person in virtue of his nature as a free and equal rational being. The validity of the principle does not presuppose that one has a particular desire or aim. Whereas a hypothetical imperative by contrast does assume this: it directs us to take certain steps as effective means to achieve a specific end. Whether the desire is for a particular thing, or whether it is for something more general, such as certain kinds of agreeable feelings or pleasures, the corresponding imperative is hypothetical. Its applicability depends upon one's having an aim which one need not have as a condition of being a rational human individual. The argument for the two principles of justice does not assume that the parties have particular ends, but only that they desire certain primary goods. These are things that it is rational to want whatever else one wants. Thus given human nature, wanting them is part of being rational; and while each is presumed to have some conception of the good, nothing is known about his final ends. The preference for primary goods is derived, then, from only the most general assumptions about rationality and the conditions of human life. To act from the principles of justice is to act from categorical imperatives in the sense that they apply to us whatever in particular our aims are. This simply reflects the fact that no such contingencies appear as premises in their derivation.

We may note also that the motivational assumption of mutual disinterest accords with Kant's notion of autonomy, and gives another reason for this condition. So far this assumption has been used to characterize the circumstances of justice and to provide a clear conception to guide the reasoning of the parties. We have also seen that the concept of benevolence, being a second-order notion, would not work out well. Now we can add that the assumption of mutual disinterest is to allow for freedom in the choice of a system of final ends. Liberty in adopting a conception of the good is limited only by principles that are deduced from a doctrine which imposes no prior constraints on these conceptions. Presuming mutual disinterest in the original position carries out this idea. We postulate that the parties have opposing claims in a suitably general sense. If their ends were restricted in some specific way, this would appear at the outset as an arbitrary restriction on freedom. Moreover, if the parties were conceived as altruists, or as pursuing certain kinds of pleasures, then the principles chosen would apply, as far as the argument would have shown, only to persons whose freedom was restricted to choices compatible with altruism or hedonism. As the argument now runs, the principles of justice cover all persons with rational plans of life, whatever their content, and these principles represent the appropriate restrictions on freedom. Thus it is possible to say that the constraints on conceptions of the good are the result of an interpretation of the contractual situation that puts no prior limitations on what men may desire. There are a variety of reasons, then, for the motivational premise of mutual disinterest. This premise is not only a matter of realism about the circumstances of justice or a way to make the theory manageable. It also connects up with the Kantian idea of autonomy.

## Questions

1. Consider the following dialogue.

*Nozick:* A distribution is just if it arises from another just distribution by legitimate means. The legitimate means of moving from one distribution to another are specified by the principle of justice in transfer. The legitimate first "moves" are specified by the principle of justice in acquisition. Whatever arises from a just situation by just steps is itself just.

*Feinberg:* Your account of justice is inadequate because it does not handle the following case correctly. Mr. Miser legitimately acquired a lifeboat and enough food to last 5 people for 20 days. There are only 2 other people in the boat and land is only 10 days away. But Mr. Miser refuses to share his food with anyone. It is obvious that Mr. Miser is doing something wrong. My theory explains what Mr. Miser is doing wrong. He is violating the Fair Opportunity Requirement. But your theory does not explain what Mr. Miser is doing wrong. According to your theory Mr. Miser can do whatever he likes with the food because it is his food.

*Nozick:* OK. I'll modify my theory by adding the Lockean Proviso. "A process normally giving rise to a permanent bequeathable property right in a previously unowned thing will not do so if the position of others no longer at liberty to use the thing is thereby worsened." In other words, my modified theory is the same as my previous theory except that it is now wrong to make some unowned thing yours if doing so would worsen someone else's situation.

*Feinberg:* Your modified theory still cannot handle the lifeboat case.

*Nozick:* Yes it can! Yes it can!

*Feinberg:* Well, if the Lockean Proviso would enable your theory to handle Mr. Miser's lifeboat case, then the Lockean Proviso boils down to my own Fair Opportunity Requirement.

*Nozick:* No it doesn't! No it doesn't!

Can the modified theory handle Mr. Miser's lifeboat case satisfactorily? Is Nozick's modified theory equivalent to Feinberg's theory? Defend your answers.

2. Let us investigate the limits of the free market. Is there anything morally wrong with

any of the following practices? It is crucial to be consistent and non-arbitrary.

a. Selling sperm
b. Surrogate parenting
c. Selling babies
d. "Borrow-a-baby shops" (renting babies for a few years to people who enjoy raising babies but detest older children)
e. "Rent-a-kid shops" (renting children for a few hours to people who enjoy amusement parks more when accompanied by children)
f. "Escort services" (renting a date for an evening; sex is not included)
g. Prostitution
h. Selling blood
i. Modeling dresses

3. In what ways does Rawls argue that justice as fairness is an interpretation or extension of Kantian ideas? In what ways *is* justice as fairness an interpretation or extension of Kantian ideas? In what ways does justice as fairness *conflict with* Kantian ideas?

4. State Aristotle's Principle. State the Free Market Principle. Explain why Aristotle's Principle and the Free Market Principle are incompatible. Choose *one* of the following goods and answer *all* of the questions below.

a. Expensive health care (such as kidney transplants, major surgery, and long-term physical therapy)
b. Expensive legal care (such as good lawyers when one is on trial for murder, seeking a divorce, or defending oneself against a malpractice suit)
c. Expensive child care (such as a good pre-school, elementary school, and college)
d. Jobs (such as the job itself, job training, and unemployment compensation)
e. TA-ship awards (The Philosophy Department has $40,000 to distribute to TAs next year. Typically the department awards five TA-ships, but the amounts are not always equal.)
f. Payment for coffee, a negative good (The Philosophy Department provides coffee to faculty, philosophy graduate students,

philosophy undergraduate majors, and visitors. Typically, the faculty buy the coffee, but not everyone contributes equally.)
g. Library carrels (Presently, carrels at the library are distributed on a first-come, first-served basis to faculty. Faculty may renew carrels every year. There is a three-year waiting list.)
h. Children (Presently, children are distributed by adoption agencies to people who meet certain criteria.)

Would a Rule Utilitarian use Aristotle's Income Principle, or a modified version of the Free Market Principle, or neither principle to determine a just distribution of this good? Would a Kantian use Aristotle's Income Principle, or a modified version of the Free Market Principle, or neither principle to determine a just distribution of this good? In each case, if your answer is "Aristotle's Income Principle," specify which quality should be proportional to this good. If your answer is "Modified Free Market Principle," specify what the modification is. If your answer is "neither," specify which alternative principle you think should govern the distribution of this good.

5. Suppose that you are a parent with seven children. They were all born in one litter, which explains why they are the same age and also why they are dwarfs. You inherit $10,000.00 on the condition that you give it to (or spend it on) your children. Here is a partial description of your children. (You may find it useful to add further details.) *Sleepy* has MG, a disease that causes people to sleep most of the time. Naturally, his GPA is low, but his IQ is normal. Medication can cure him. *Sneezy* has terrible allergies, which can also be relieved by medication. *Doc* is pre-med. His IQ and GPA are higher than those of his brothers. *Grumpy* is simply a grouch. *Dopey* is retarded. His IQ and GPA are lower than those of his brothers. He would benefit from special education. *Happy* is a drug user. He has no intention of quitting. *Bashful* is a nerd. He would benefit from assertiveness training.

How would Nozick distribute the money? How would Feinberg distribute the money? How would Mill distribute the money? How would Govier distribute the money? How would Rawls distribute the money? How would you distribute the money? Explain and defend all of your answers.

6. Is Nozick's Free Market Principle + Lockean Proviso compatible with Aristotle's Income Principle + Principle of Need? If not, why not? If so, does one imply the other?

7. Feinberg, Govier, Marx, Mill, Nozick, Pojman, Rachels, and Rawls have been appointed regents of the university. Each has a different plan for paying faculty. Match the person to the plan. (There are some extra plans.) Which one of these plans is the most just? Explain why it is more just than the other plans.

   a. I suggest that we offer enormous salaries for football coaches. We will attract top coaching talent, which will improve the team. This will increase alumni contributions. After we pay the coaches, we will have enough money left over to give small raises to everyone else on the faculty. Even though coaches will be making much more than other professors, no one will be unhappy with this inequality because it benefits everyone.

   b. It is well known that members of the Astroarcheology Department work twice as hard as their colleagues in other departments, even though they are only half as talented and thus accomplish exactly the same amount. Because effort is the only criterion that everyone has a fair opportunity to meet, we ought to pay the members of the Astroarcheology Department twice as much as we pay the rest of the faculty.

   c. We should pay whatever it takes to attract good teachers to the university and not a penny more. The supply of philosophers far exceeds the demand for philosophers in this country, whereas the supply of engineers is much less than the demand for engineers. This means that we will end

up paying philosophy teachers much less than engineering teachers, but so what?

   d. I agree with plan (c), except that we ought to make sure that everyone on the faculty receives enough money to pay for food, clothing, shelter, and health care whether his or her teaching is great, mediocre, or awful before we start trying to match the market price in each discipline.

   e. Effort is important, but it is not the only factor. We ought to pay teachers somewhat less than the going rate and use the extra money to compensate the members of the Astroarcheology Department for their hard work.

   f. Effort is not important at all. The quantity and quality of teaching are what matters. The better the teacher is, the more we ought to pay him or her. All salaries should be based on merit. In particular, members of the Astroarcheology Department should be paid only half of what their colleagues in other departments are paid.

   g. Because teachers are members of the capitalist, war-mongering, exploitive, bourgeois class, and because they need no more filthy lucre to swell their already bloated moneybags, they should not be paid at all. Instead students of the working class, who are now forced to grovel and sweat for their meager crusts of stale bread, should be given whatever money they need to enable them to concentrate on their studies. Education is, after all, a necessity for anyone who lives in the modern world.

   h. Faculty parties tend to be dull, whereas parties thrown by the administrators are lively. Obviously, the administrators know how to enjoy themselves and the faculty do not. In fact, administrators get twice as much pleasure out of each dollar than faculty members. Thus we should pay administrators eight times as much as faculty members in order to maximize the total number of jollies at the university.

   i. Although administrators do get twice as much pleasure out of each dollar, there are ten faculty members for every administrator. Thus we should pay faculty members twice as much as administrators to maximize the total number of happy people at the university.

j. Prostitution and slavery are wrong because sexuality and people are not commodities. It degrades us as a society to treat people as sex objects or as things. Knowledge should not be a commodity either. Education, like sex and people, should not be bought and sold in the marketplace. Therefore, we should pay the faculty nothing and have all teaching be done by volunteers.

k. Everyone on the faculty ought to receive enough money to pay for food, clothing, shelter, and health care whether his or her teaching is great, mediocre, or awful. If there is extra money left over, give merit raises.

l. The purpose of the university is to educate students. The more information and skills you stuff into a student, the better educated the student is. I suggest that we give pre-tests and post-tests in every class and pay faculty members in proportion to the improvement of their students. This will attract talented student stuffers, and the university will be better able to achieve its purpose.

8. A band of dwarves seek to regain treasure stolen from their parents by a dragon named Smaug who also destroyed a town called Dale. The dwarves arrive in the town of Esgaroth penniless and desperate. The people of Esgaroth provide them with supplies. The dwarves go on to the mountain where the dragon lives and accidentally awaken the dragon. Smaug attacks and destroys Esgaroth. Bard (a bowman of Esgaroth and an heir of Girion, king of Dale) kills the dragon while trying to defend Esgaroth, and the dwarves seize the treasure in the dragon's lair. A few days later, Bard, at the head of an army, arrives at the mountain and, using the following arguments, asks the dwarves to turn over some of the treasure to him.

"I am Bard, and by my hand was the dragon slain and your treasure delivered. Moreover, I am by right descent the heir of Girion of Dale, and in your hoard is mingled much of the wealth of his halls and town, which of old Smaug stole. Further in his last battle Smaug destroyed the dwellings of the men of Esgaroth, and I am yet the servant of their mayor. I would speak for him and ask whether you have no thought for the sorrow and misery of his people. They aided you in your distress, and in recompense you have thus far brought ruin only, though doubtless undesigned."

Thorin, leader of the dwarves, replies,

"To the treasure of my people no man has a claim, because Smaug who stole it from us also robbed him of life or home. The price of the goods and the assistance that we received from Esgaroth we will fairly pay—in due time. But nothing will we give, not even a loaf's worth, under threat of force. While an armed host lies before our doors, we look on you as foes and thieves." [J. R. R. Tolkien, *The Hobbit* (New York: Ballantine Books, 1937), pp. 250–251 with omissions.]

Evaluate the justice of Bard's arguments and Thorin's arguments from the point of view of Nozick and from the point of view of Aristotle.

9. Rawls mentions the following General Conception of Justice: "All social values—liberty and opportunity, income and wealth, and the bases of self-respect—are to be distributed equally unless an unequal distribution of any, or all, of these values is to everyone's advantage." In what way does this General Conception of Justice differ from the Two Principles? Why does Rawls think that people in the Original Position would choose the Two Principles over the General Conception of Justice? Is Rawls right about this? Do you think that the Two Principles are closer to the truth about justice? Why or why not?

10. Feinberg says,

At present the 5 percent at the top get 20 percent of our national wealth while the 20 percent at the bottom get about 5 percent . . . Are the 5 percent of Americans at the top really different from the 20 percent at the bottom in any respect that would justicize the difference between their incomes? It is doubtful that there is any characteristic—relevant or irrelevant—common and peculiar to all members of either group. Some injustices, therefore, must surely exist.

Explain why Feinberg thinks that some injustices must surely exist. Would Nozick agree? Why or why not? Would you agree? Why or why not? Nozick says,

> A distribution is just if it arises from another just distribution by legitimate means. The legitimate means of moving from one distribution to another are specified by the principle of justice in transfer [and the principle of justice in rectification]. The legitimate first "moves" are specified by the principle of justice in acquisition. Whatever arises from a just situation by just steps is itself just.

Explain why Nozick thinks that a distribution is just if it arises from another just distribution by legitimate means. Would Feinberg agree? Why or why not? Would you agree? Why or why not?

11. On November 14, 1996, the U.S. policy for determining which patients get liver transplants changed. The former policy was that the *sickest* terminally ill patients were put at the top of the waiting list. The new policy is that the terminally ill patients with the *best prospects of survival* have top priority. Because children also do well with transplants, children who would suffer nerve damage without immediate liver transplant will also be put at the top of the waiting list, even if they are not terminally ill.

Here are some facts about liver transplanting. People who suffer liver failure because of a sudden illness do much better with transplants than people who have been ill for a long time. Thus people who face imminent death because of an unexpected liver failure will now have priority over those who are just as ill but who have a chronic disease. Typically, the longer you have the disease and the older you are, the sicker you get. Thus, under the old system, the longer your wait on the list, the better your odds of get-

ting a liver, but under the new system, your odds get worse as you wait. Patients who have a liver transplant that fails often do well with a second transplant, so they will now have priority over others, too. One common chronic disease that causes liver failure is alcoholic cirrhosis. However, no one even makes it onto the list who has not been alcohol-free for six months. Similarly, no one makes it onto the list if there is reason to believe that the patient will not follow the detailed regimen for caring for a transplanted liver. People of higher socio-economic class with a support system of relatives and friends are more likely to follow the regimen than people of lower socio-economic class without a support system.

Identify the various principles whose combination constitutes the old policy. Identify the principles whose combination constitutes the new policy. Do you agree with all of the aspects of either policy? Exactly what policy should be used to distribute livers for transplants? Justify your answer.

12. Rawls claims that the Two Principles match our considered judgments about social justice. Do they?

13. Most free-marketeers think it is OK to tax people in order to provide security against coercion. That is, they think it is OK for government to provide police and armed forces protection. Other people think it is OK to tax people in order to provide security against starvation and fatal illness. That is, they think it is OK for government to provide food stamps and life-saving health care. Still other people think it is OK to tax people in order to provide security against ignorance and fraud. That is, they think it is OK for government to provide high school education and certain sorts of regulation. In general, these three groups justify taxation in terms of the values of limited (a) freedom from coercion, (b) freedom from fear, (c) pursuit of happiness. Which of these positions would Kant accept? Which of these positions would Mill accept? Which of these positions do you accept? Explain your answers.

14. Would Act Utilitarians accept Aristotle's Income Principle? If not, why not? If so, with what principle of substantive justice would they supplement Aristotle's principle?

    Would Rule Utilitarians accept Aristotle's Income Principle? If not, why not? If so, with what principle of substantive justice would they supplement Aristotle's principle?

    Would Kant accept Aristotle's Income Principle? If not, why not? If so, with what principle of substantive justice would he supplement Aristotle's principle?

    Would you accept Aristotle's Income Principle? If not, why not? If so, with what principle of substantive justice would you supplement Aristotle's principle?

15. Rawls has been criticized in a variety of different ways. Select *one* of the following criticisms and explain how Rawls might rebut it.

    a. Hare: Reflective Equilibrium is nothing more than a sophisticated version of normative (ethical) relativism. It is merely a way of systematizing whatever beliefs you already hold. [R. M. Hare, "Rawls' Theory of Justice," in *Reading Rawls*, ed. N. Daniels (New York: Basic Books, 1974), pp. 81–107.]

    b. Feinberg: The people in the original position will prefer the Two Principles to the Principle of Utility if they adopt the maximin procedure. They will adopt the maximin procedure only if (i) they are not gamblers and only if (ii) the veil of ignorance excludes information about the probabilities of ending up in each class.

    However, it is not true that (i) gamblers are irrational or that (ii) the probabilities must be unknown to prevent bias. [J. Feinberg, "Rawls and Intuitionism," in *Reading Rawls*, ed. N. Daniels (New York: Basic Books, 1974), pp. 108–124.]

    c. Hart: The lexical ordering of the Two Principles gives liberty priority. But giving liberty priority is not a neutral move. It favors the best-off class because the state is typically a tool of the dominant class. [H. L. A. Hart, "Rawls on Liberty and its Priority," in *Reading Rawls*, ed. N. Daniels (New York: Basic Books, 1974), pp. 230–252.]

    d. Hart: People in the original position do not know enough about their preferences to know that they prefer not to trade off liberty for other goods. And it is not obvious that they should have this preference. Plato, for example, would not rate liberty so highly. [Hart, pp. 230–252.]

    e. Locke: Rawls believes that governments are legitimate if they would be consented to by rational people under certain conditions. But this is only a sham contract theory. No matter how wonderful a government is, it cannot be legitimate unless it has the actual consent of its citizens. [J. Locke, *Second Treatise of Government*, ed. C.B. Macpherson (Indianapolis, IN: Hackett, 1980), p. 52.]

    f. Plato: Rawls is trying to be neutral among various conceptions of the good. But justice is *not* neutral. Some conceptions of the good are less just than others.

# PART IV

# MORAL PROBLEMS

# Pornography and Sexual Harassment

*Poetry has a terrible power to corrupt even the best characters, with very few exceptions. . . . When it represents sex and anger, and the other desires and feelings of pleasure and pain which accompany all our actions, it waters them when they ought to be left to wither, and makes them control us when we ought to control them. . . . [Thus] the only poetry that should be allowed in a state is hymns to the gods and paeans in praise of good men. Once you go beyond that and admit the sweet lyric or epic muse, pleasure and pain become your rulers instead of law and reason.*

PLATO

Governments, like individuals, may act immorally in a variety of ways. They might attack innocent neighbors, oppress some of their citizens, refuse to honor their commitments, set up an unjust tax system, and so on. One important way in which a government may act immorally is by forbidding its citizens to perform acts that people should be free to perform. Something is wrong with a government that prohibits women from working, for example. What types of acts should be legal? That is, what types of acts are governments morally required to allow? (Of course, many acts may be either allowed or prohibited. Prohibiting one of these acts would itself be a morally neutral act. Thus the set of acts that should be legal is not simply the complement of the set of acts that should be illegal.) Here is a sample of controversial acts—acts that some people think should be legal, other people think should be illegal, and still others consider it optional whether to ban or legalize.

adultery
prostitution
premarital sex
peeping
public nudity
polygamy/polyandry
pornography
suicide
assisted suicide
active euthanasia
self-mutilation
helmetless cycling
seatbeltless driving
concealed weapons
cocaine use
heroin use
marijuana use
alcohol use
tobacco use
caffeine use
gambling
public flag burning
hate speech
satanic symbols
trashing your own yard
homosexual acts
homosexual marriage
homosexuals serving in the military

## Utilitarian Analysis

An Act Utilitarian would consider the question of which types of acts to allow on a case-by-case basis. What types of acts will it cause more jollies to allow than to prohibit? Will the society be happier if pornography is legal or illegal? Will prohibiting prostitution make the society better off? And so on. A Rule Utilitarian, on the other hand, would seek for a rule to cover all of these controversial acts—to stipulate which acts the government should allow. The right rule is the rule that, if followed, will produce more happiness (or less unhappiness) than any alternative rule. But what is the right rule? In his book *On Liberty*, Mill proposes the following principle.

*Harm Principle:* The government may prohibit acts of type X only if acts of type X directly harm others. If an act does not harm others directly, then the government should allow it. It is wrong for a government to prohibit acts that do not directly harm others. There should be no victimless crimes.

In the Harm Principle, *direct harm* does not mean "harm done without intermediaries." Mill is *not* saying anything like "If I push you through a window, then I have directly harmed you, but if I push Fred, who, in turn, knocks you through a window, then I have indirectly harmed you." Although Mill does not provide us with a definition of "direct harm," he does list types of acts that he says are *indirectly* harmful. Presumably, the rest of the harmful acts are directly harmful. The three sorts of indirect harms listed by Mill are wasting resources, wasting talent, and setting a bad example.[1] If I burn my books, refuse to get a job, or get drunk in the sight of my students, then I have indirectly harmed others. Note that some indirect harms are very serious and some direct harms trivial. If I slap you, I have directly harmed you a little bit, but if I cause you to become a drug addict by setting a bad example, I have indirectly harmed you severely. Two more sorts of harms should probably be added to Mill's list of indirect harms. Suppose I marry the woman you love or paint the house across from you a color you detest. I have harmed you, but only because of preferences you happen to have. This is a fourth sort of indirect harm. Finally, suppose I drive 90 m.p.h. in a school zone or dump toxic waste into the water supply. Even if I do not hit anyone or cause any disease, in some sense I have harmed people by putting them at serious risk. Of course, the government cannot prohibit *all* risky acts. The courts take the position that a risky act is directly harmful if and only if it poses a *clear and present danger*. Thus risky acts that do not pose a clear and present danger constitute a fifth sort of indirect harm.

Sometimes freedom must be restricted in order to achieve other goods, such as security from certain harms. We do need laws against murder, rape, and theft. These laws are clearly worth the cost. Society gains more jollies than it loses by prohibiting these acts. The point of the Harm Principle is to maximize freedom while still allowing the government to prohibit these acts. There are several reasons to do so. (a) People enjoy freedom for its own sake. Freedom itself is exhilarating. (b) Freedom also encourages progress through the operation of a "marketplace of ideas." Mill views society as an arena where a plethora of ideas compete for acceptance. In a free society, the good and true ideas will eventually outcompete the bad and false ones, because good and true ideas have more utility to society. (c) Moreover, freedom builds character by encouraging self-development, self-expression, and the like. (d) Finally, each law restricting people's freedom has a cost. The people who are prevented from doing what they want are less happy. The society that must pay for enforcing the law loses some happiness, too. After all, each new restriction requires more police, more judges, more prisons, and so on. Overall, the idea behind the Harm Principle is that the government should try to maximize freedom. The government should refrain from regulating the lives of its citizens as much as possible, because freedom is both intrinsically and instrumentally good.

Each of these claims is controversial. (a) The Existentialists remind us that people do not always enjoy freedom, for with freedom comes responsibility for choice. John Paul Sartre takes freedom to be an inescapable *burden*. He says, "man is condemned to be free."[2] (b) The history of ideas is not a succession of bricks being added to the temple of knowledge, but rather it is typically a three-steps-forward, two-steps-backward, and six-steps-sideways affair. Perhaps over hundreds of years, truth outcompetes falsehood, but in the short run, bet on the idea backed by the most power and the best rhetoric rather than on the best idea. (c) Plato warns that freedom easily becomes license, which destroys character. The best way to improve the character of most people is to expose them only to the right ideas. (If you find Plato's endorsement of censorship disturbing, ask yourself whether you intend to give your children an early, detailed, and impartial exposure to a variety of religions or to indoctrinate them thoroughly in the religion you believe to be correct before allowing them to study alternatives.) (d) Finally, although enforcing each law has a cost, the cost to society of not enforcing the law is often higher, even when the prohibited act does not directly harm others. Enforcing the seatbelt law, for example, is cheaper than paying the medical bills for injuries that could have been avoided by the wearing of seat belts. Despite these drawbacks, however, freedom does seem to be a very important good.

Arguments using the Harm Principle to justify the legality of controversial acts take the following form.

### Argument (A)

(1) If an act does not harm others directly, then the government should allow it. (Harm Principle)
(2) The activity or practice of [controversial act] does not directly harm others.
(3) Therefore, [controversial act] should be legal.

Under the Harm Principle, government would be able to ban only a few of the controversial acts listed above. Take cocaine use, for example. Cocaine causes serious physical and mental harm to the user, but does cocaine use directly harm others? Some people steal in order to obtain the money for cocaine, but this is probably a consequence of the present illegality of cocaine; the drug would be quite inexpensive if it were legal. Cocaine use may cause traffic accidents and damage fetuses, but this would justify merely a ban on driving under the influence of cocaine and on cocaine use during pregnancy, rather than a general ban on cocaine use. Overall, it is not obvious that cocaine use poses a clear and present danger to anyone other than the user. Take polygamy and polyandry. These practices have been illegal for many generations. They are widely thought to be immoral. Yet because they do not seem to harm others, the Harm Principle would require government to legalize them. Similarly, public nudity and seatbeltless driving seem impossible to prohibit on the basis of the Harm Principle, for neither act directly harms others. In general, the Harm Principle seems too permissive to many people. Feinberg considers the following alternatives to the Harm Principle.

*Harm + Offense Principle:* The government may prohibit acts of type X only if acts of type X directly harm others or are both very offensive to almost everyone and unreasonably difficult to avoid.

*Harm + Legal Moralism Principle:* The government may prohibit acts of type X only if acts of type X directly harm others or are seriously immoral.

*Harm + Paternalism Principle:* The government may prohibit acts of type X only if acts of type X directly harm others or severely harm the agent.

We would not want the government to prohibit harmless, rude remarks that are mildly offensive to most people, acts that are very offensive to only a few, or harmless acts performed in private, because such prohibitions would cost a lot of freedom. Thus the Harm + Offense Principle must contain the qualifications "very offensive" "to almost everyone," and "unreasonably difficult to avoid." For similar reasons, the Harm + Legal Moralism Principle must contain the qualification, "seriously," and the Harm + Paternalism Principle must contain the qualification "severely."

Each of these principles would allow government to prohibit some acts that (a) common sense wants prohibited but that (b) the bare Harm Principle requires government to allow. The Harm + Offense Principle would allow a ban on public nudity, for example. The Harm + Legal Moralism Principle would allow a ban on polygamy and polyandry. The Harm + Paternalism Principle would allow a ban on seatbeltless driving and cocaine use.

Unfortunately, each of these three principles seems to allow the government to prohibit too much. Not terribly long ago, a racially mixed couple publicly walking hand in hand was very offensive to almost everyone. Thus the Harm + Offense Principle would have allowed the government to prohibit such acts. Yet surely such a ban would be immoral. In general, the Harm +

Offense Principle subordinates the freedom of the few to the preferences of society and opens the way to a tyranny of the tastes of the (overwhelming) majority.

The Harm + Legal Moralism Principle does not share this problem. It does not allow the government to ban whatever acts the society *considers* immoral. It allows the government to ban only whatever acts *really are* immoral. This principle has a different drawback, however. Although the government should protect people from each other, when government tries to enforce morals beyond this, it quickly burgeons into a police state. For example, adultery is probably seriously immoral. Thus the Harm + Legal Moralism Principle would allow the government to prohibit adultery. Yet it would be grossly intrusive and counter-productive for the government to try to enforce laws against adultery.

The Harm + Paternalism Principle has a similar problem. Protecting individuals from themselves would require government to regulate every aspect of a person's life. For example, getting less than three hours of sleep per day is very self-destructive behavior, so the Harm + Paternalism Principle would allow the government to prohibit bad sleep habits. Yet only a totalitarian government could enforce laws against staying up all night.

## Virtue Ethics Analysis

The classical liberal conception of the role of government shared by John Locke, Thomas Hobbes, and our founding fathers is that government should provide people with the freedom to set their own goals, pursue their own plans, and develop their own character traits. Government should not impose on its citizens one way of life rather than another. Government should be value-neutral. On the other hand, some virtue theorists, including Aristotle, believe that government should endorse and even actively promote some goals, life plans, characters, and values rather than others. Some contemporary religious groups agree. They think that govern-

ment should impose a certain way of life and a certain set of values on its citizens. An intermediate position is that government should protect people from practices that tend to undermine good character traits or enhance bad character traits. But government should not promote one package of character traits rather than another. Government should ban acts that make people morally worse, but it should not sponsor acts that make people better.

> *Harm + Character Corruption Principle:* The government may prohibit acts of type X only if acts of type X are very likely to make the agent or others much less virtuous or more vicious.

Is this principle really different from the Harm Principle? Can acts of a certain type make a person much more vicious without resulting in actions directly harmful to others? Yes, it is possible to worsen a person's character dramatically without changing the person's behavior. For example, suppose that reading or viewing pornography transforms the sexual appetites of some people in the following way: They lose a taste for "ordinary" sex and acquire a taste for twisted sex through pornography, but they continue to believe that twisted sex is wrong, and they engage only in ordinary sex even after their tastes change. Before consuming pornography, these people had ordinary sex from desire with pleasure; after consuming pornography, they have ordinary sex from duty without pleasure. Pornography transforms these sexually temperate people into merely continent people. This is character degradation without harm to others. If pornography had no other effects, then the Harm + Character Corruption Principle would authorize government to ban pornography, whereas the bare Harm Principle would not. Of course, in order to determine whether pornography really does corrupt character in this way, we would need to distinguish virtuous and vicious sexual activity. [See the "Sexual Matters" section.]

One problem with the classical liberal conception of the role of government and with the bare Harm Principle (which is more or less the classical liberal conception's natural corollary) is that they seem to ignore the existence of children and child-like adults. They seem to assume that society consists of autonomous agents. The Harm + Character Corruption Principle, on the other hand, recognizes that vulnerable and developing characters require shielding from dangerous influences. It would allow the government to ban the use of narcotics but not the use of tobacco, for example, because narcotics undermine the user's character whereas tobacco undermines only the user's health. The Harm + Character Corruption Principle would allow the government to ban violence on prime-time T.V. if it makes children more prone to violence. On the other hand, like the other combination principles mentioned above, the Harm + Character Corruption Principle seems to allow the government to prohibit too much.

Because the other principles seem too strong, many people fall back on the Harm Principle, especially when it comes to government regulation of speech. Indeed, the First Amendment to the Constitution, "Congress shall make no law . . . abridging the freedom of speech . . ." has generally been interpreted in terms of the Harm Principle. That is, restrictions of the freedom of speech allowed by the courts (such as the "shouting 'fire' in a crowded theater" exception, the "fighting words" exception, and the "inciting to riot" exception) have all been justified on the grounds that they pose a clear and present danger of harm to others. Moreover, note that "speech" is understood very broadly to include not only the spoken or written word but also a wide range of non-verbal communication (such as flag burning). Pornography is considered to be speech and is therefore legally governed by the First Amendment.

## Pornography

Some people object to pornography and seek to ban or restrict it on the grounds that pornography is offensive. However, pornography is too popular to be "very offensive to almost every-

one." It is a multi-billion-dollar industry. Moreover, even if pornography were almost universally very offensive, the Harm + Offense Principle would not justify banning pornography. It would, at most, justify banning the *public display* of pornography. The Harm + Offense Principle does not allow the government to eliminate offensive practices; it merely allows the government to drive these practices underground.

Would the bare Harm Principle allow the government to ban pornography? Is pornography directly harmful to others? Until the last few decades, objections to pornography centered on the extent to which it undermines certain traditional values related to sex. For example, does pornography encourage promiscuity by portraying sex outside of marriage in a positive way? And does this constitute direct harm to someone? Although it might seem intuitively obvious that pornography does threaten traditional values, investigators have sought in vain for any evidence that pornography actually has this effect. Moreover, it is not obvious that undermining traditional values about sex would cause a loss of jollies. The traditional values do cause a fair amount of suffering, and multi-faceted effects of changes in attitudes and practices are notoriously unpredictable. Perhaps a less Victorian, sexually liberated society would be a happier one.

Recently, feminists have raised a different set of objections to pornography based on the fact that it subordinates women. Many women have spoken of being violated in the making of pornography and as a result of its use. Pornography not only defames women but also exacerbates sexist attitudes that, in turn, increase sex discrimination and other sexist practices. Thus reading or viewing pornography is not a victimless act. All women are victims—some more than others—because pornography increases the subordination of women. Moreover, some feminists argue that pornography marginalizes and silences women through socially constructing them in a certain way. That is, women cannot be seen or heard as they truly are, because men see women through the lens of pornography merely as trivial, sexual creatures who need not be respected or even taken seriously. As Kant might say, pornography encourages men to perceive and treat women as things rather than as persons—as sex *objects* rather than as free, rational beings.

Catharine MacKinnon argues that pornography also substantially increases the risk of violence against women because of the way male sexuality works in this society and the way in which women are already subordinated in this society. Pornography eroticizes hierarchy and coercion. It sexualizes male dominance, female submission, and violence against women. It tells consumers of pornography (who are overwhelmingly male) that rape, battery, harassment, and abuse are simply routine sex. Indeed, MacKinnon argues that in our society these acts *are* routine sex in two senses. Not only are these acts frighteningly commonplace, but also ordinary sex acts that do not get labeled as rape, battery, harassment, and abuse are actually quite similar to these acts. Ordinary sex often contains large components of dominance, submission, and violence. It occurs under conditions of inequality between women and men. Thus the common distinction between erotica (which is simply sexual) and pornography (which involves degradation of women) is misconceived because the simply sexual, when sold and often stolen, already involves degradation. Violence against and domination of women *is* erotic for men in the existing sexual paradigm. It turns men on. (But doesn't this show that all pornography is erotic rather than that all erotica is pornographic?)

Pornography socially constructs gender not only by trivializing women but also by telling men what women want and how men should act. Pornography's message is that women want to be violated and dominated and that men should go ahead and do so. This conditioning goes straight into the forebrain because it is delivered through arousal. It is a sort of brainwashing. This is why the research shows that exposure to pornography makes "normal men more closely resemble convicted rapists attitudinally," says MacKinnon. Pornography changes the attitudes and behavior of men toward women. In this way, as well as others, it directly harms women. Citing studies and testimony showing that men who view pornographic movies are more likely to rape and batter women, MacKinnon calls for pornography to be actionable as a civil rights violation by those who can prove it harms them. She maintains that this restriction is justified in order to reduce the harm that pornography causes. Indeed, MacKinnon and Andrea Dworkin co-authored such an ordinance for the city of Indianapolis making pornography actionable.

### Argument (B)

(1) If a type of act harms others directly, then the government may ban that type of act. (Harm Principle)
(2) Reading or viewing pornography directly harms women by defaming women, increasing sexist practices, marginalizing and silencing women, and increasing violence against and domination of women.
(3) Therefore, pornography may be banned.

Let us examine the several components of premise (2) of argument (B). Ronald Dworkin (no known relation to Andrea Dworkin) says that if pornography does not contribute to sexist practices or abuse, then pornography must be tolerated, not banned, even if it marginalizes and silences women. He says, "Every idea must be allowed to be heard, even those whose consequence is that other ideas will be misunderstood, or given little consideration, or even not be spoken at all. . . ." Freedom of speech is so important and so fragile that the government should not censor speech, even if that speech silences others.

This makes sense if the main threat to free speech is government censorship. But if one very serious threat to women's freedom of speech—not to mention equality—is pornography, then to refrain from censoring pornography is to stand by while women are silenced. Government should not only refrain from coercing its citizens but also prevent citizens from coercing each other. Similarly, government should not only avoid censoring but also prevent citizens from censoring each other. Just as government polices the economic marketplace, so government should police the marketplace of ideas. As Dworkin himself mentions, the First Amendment already allows the government to ban heckling and shouting that drowns out speakers. The courts have ruled that some speech must be restricted in order to maximize freedom of speech. Why does this principle not justify restricting pornography if pornography marginalizes and silences women?

Dworkin concedes that if pornography contributes to sexist practices and/or abuse, then banning it would be justified by the Harm Principle. However, Dworkin maintains that the studies and testimony suggest, but do not demonstrate, that pornography poses a clear and present danger. That is, the evidence that pornography is harmful is insufficient to justify a ban on pornography. Some of the evidence against pornography consists of anecdotes (garnered from rapists, victims, and police) of pornography triggering violent behavior. But anecdotal evidence is notoriously unreliable. Rapists typically have little insight into their own motives. They are also hungry for rationalizations. For example, in addition to blaming pornography, rapists also typically blame the victims for "leading them on." Because we reject the latter explanation, we should also give little credence to the former. Similarly, testimony from victims and police about what motivates abusers is suspect. Abusers may consume a lot of pornography, but that does not establish a causal link. Perhaps non-abusers consume lots of pornography, too. Moreover, even if we had evidence that more pornography consumers than non-consumers commit abuse, or that abusers use more pornography than non-abusers, this evidence would not be conclusive. Perhaps the pornography does not cause the abuse, but rather some third thing causes both abuse and the desire for pornography. Perhaps pornography even reduces abuse by providing a safety valve for the twisted tendencies of potential abusers. The rest of the evidence against pornography consists of studies that show that viewing violent pornography makes men more likely to believe that women enjoy rape, less willing to impose harsh punishments on rapists, and so on. However, this change in attitude is short-lived, and there is no evidence that it leads to a change in behavior. Overall, Dworkin would argue that pornography has not been shown to sustain or increase the level of discrimination or violence against women in our society. Thus the Harm Principle does not justify prohibiting pornography.

MacKinnon states that the empirical data do, in fact, prove harm, and she also objects that this reluctance to accept the data and this exclusive focus on an excessively narrow kind of causal link between pornography and abuse is quibbling and foot-dragging. Some women are raped to make pornography. It is OK to ban segregation, after all, even without much scientific evidence that segregation is directly harmful, because the harm associated with segregation is very great.

Dworkin might reply that this line of thought is too risky. It would justify the banning of too much speech and too many acts. For example, a plausible case can be made for the claim that romance novels directly harm women, too. Some women read large numbers of these novels and become dissatisfied with their humdrum lives. The novels seem to instill in these women a wildly unrealistic conception of happiness. This brainwashing leads some of these women to make irrational choices in life, such as neglecting their career ambitions to devote all of their time and energy to becoming more attractive to tall, dark, handsome, wealthy men. Yet it would clearly be wrong to ban romance novels on the basis of this argument. Substantiation, rather than suspicion, of harm should be the basis for limiting freedom of speech and action.

## Sexual Harassment

Sexual harassment falls into two categories. *Quid pro quo* sexual harassment is defined by Ellen Paul as "the extortion of sexual favors by a supervisor from a subordinate by threatening to penalize, fire, or fail to reward." Obviously this sort of sexual harassment may be banned under the Harm Principle. If your boss gives you the pseudo-choice "Have sex with me or I'll fire you," you are harmed by the threat in the same way (and perhaps just as seriously) as though you had been threatened with a beating. Often the threat is implicit. If your teacher simply asks you to have sex, the threat of retaliation if you refuse is probably present, even if unspoken. Indeed, it is difficult for a supervisor to express sexual interest in a subordinate without intentionally or unintentionally engaging in *quid pro quo* sexual harassment. Note that *quid pro quo* sexual harassment is not morally different from non-sexual *quid pro quo* harassment. It would be wrong for your boss to demand that you help him move his piano as a condition of continued employment (assuming that your job description does not include such things) for the same reason that it would be wrong for your boss to demand sex from you.

MacKinnon, who created the legal claim for sexual harassment and the *quid pro quo* harassment analysis, argues that *quid pro quo* sexual harassment is not very different from ordinary requests/demands for sex, either. *Quid pro quo* sexual harassment is wrong because it is an abuse of some sort of power (such as boss/worker, teacher/student). But ordinary sex involves a power hierarchy, too. In our society, men have power over women merely by being men. Just as a boss's mere request for sex from an employee carries with it an implicit threat, a man's request for sex from a woman also carries with it an implicit threat, even if he has no other sort of power over the woman. Even if the man lacks threatening dominance advantages over the woman, he has been socialized to aggress or at least to push and she to submit or at least to yield. MacKinnon says,

We are taught that we exist for men. We should be flattered or at least act as if we are—be careful about a man's ego because you never know what he can do to you. To flat out say to him, "You?" or "I don't want to" is not *in* most women's sex-role learning. To say it

is, is bravado. And that's because he's a man, not . . . because he's your boss . . . or your teacher or in some other hierarchy.

Under this analysis, it is rare and difficult for a man to express sexual interest in a woman without intentionally or unintentionally abusing his power over her.

The other sort of sexual harassment, *hostile-environment* sexual harassment, consists of annoying or violating verbal or physical behavior of a sexual sort creating a climate that impedes learning or job performance. Examples include inappropriate touching and comments. It can also include rape. At first glance, it seems that this sort of sexual harassment may not be banned under the bare Harm Principle. It seems offensive rather than harmful. Yet hostile-environment sexual harassment, like "fighting words," typically produces a visceral emotional response because of the relative powerlessness of the (typically female) victim and the history of sexism and sexual abuse in our society. It vividly reminds the victim of her vulnerability. She may think something like "If he can say that, what might he say or do next?" Hostile-environment sexual harassment may cause the victim to worry that she somehow "asked for it," or she may simply recoil with a "yuck!" Depending on the individual and the act, it may generate a powerful combination of fear, guilt, and revulsion. Therefore, some people argue that hostile-environment sexual harassment produces an immediate psychological injury. Indeed, if the harassment is severe and/or prolonged, it may yield stress-related illness. In part through offending, hostile-environment sexual harassment harms the victim.

Others argue that hostile-environment sexual harassment silences the victim, not by undermining the victim's credibility and/or personhood, as some say pornography silences women, but simply by preventing the victim from speaking. It operates as a preemptive strike, paralyzing the victim's ability to respond. Some say the same about pornography. Thus hostile-environment sexual harassment should not be protected by the First Amendment both because it is directly harmful and because it reduces, rather than increases, the overall amount of speech.

Most people agree that hostile-environment sexual harassment is directly harmful and should be actionable, but there is substantial disagreement on what should count as this sort of harassment. Paul maintains that an instance of annoying behavior should count as hostile-environment sexual harassment if and only if it is above a threshold of egregiousness determined by the reasonable-person standard. If a reasonable person would simply "shrug it off," then no matter how intimidating or irritating the actual victim finds it, the behavior is not hostile-environment sexual harassment. Paul also believes that this threshold turns out to be relatively high. The reasonable person classifies much annoying behavior as mere nuisance rather than as harassment. Paul maintains that instead of whining about minor irritations, women should develop a thick skin. Women should learn not to let such behavior get to them. Neither men nor women can expect always to be treated with kindness and respect. Paul thinks a low threshold would be patronizing to women because it would imply that women are too fragile to make it on their own. A low threshold would imply that women need always to be running to the government complaining, "Bobby said a rude word to me. Make him stop, daddy!"

MacKinnon might reply that although contemporary society has made some progress in combating the most blatant sexism, society's attitudes with respect to sex are still overwhelmingly male-supremacist. The line between harassment and mere nuisance is drawn neither too high nor too low, but can be simply skewed to women's concerns and needs. MacKinnon says, "Men have defined what can be called sexual about us. They say, 'I was just trying to be affectionate, flirtatious and friendly,' and we were just all felt up." According to MacKinnon, a reasonable-person/man standard might define hostile-environment sexual harassment in a way that allows men to get away with behavior that harms and silences women. Society may not perceive such behavior as harmful. It may also come to learn that a reasonable woman is reasonable, thus redefining reasonableness from the standpoint of the target of oppressive behaviors.

In addition to their disagreement about how hostile-environment sexual harassment should be defined, MacKinnon and Paul seem to be disagreeing on a rhetorical level. MacKinnon takes lack of awareness about sexual harassment to be a serious problem. She tries to sensitize people to sexual harassment. She urges people to recognize more behaviors as sexual harassment. Conversely, Paul takes oversensitivity to be a serious problem. She urges people to consider fewer behaviors as sexual harassment. (Parallels to other issues abound. For example, some people urge us to be more sensitive to the feelings of disadvantaged groups, whereas others deride this as excessive political correctness.) Perhaps both MacKinnon and Paul are right. Perhaps some people need their consciousness raised, whereas others need their boiling point lowered.

## Notes

1. J. S. Mill, *On Liberty* (Indianapolis, IN: Hackett, 1978), p. 78.
2. J. P. Sartre, "Existentialism Is a Humanism," in *Existentialism and Human Emotions,* trans. Bernard Frechtman (New York: Philosophical Library, 1985).

# 32   The Harm Principle

## JOHN STUART MILL

The object of this Essay is to assert one very simple principle, as entitled to govern absolutely the dealings of society with the individual in the way of compulsion and control, whether the means used be physical force in the form of legal penalties, or the moral coercion of public opinion. That principle is, that the sole end for which mankind are warranted, individually or collectively, in interfering with the liberty of action of any of their number, is self-protection. That the only purpose for which power can be rightfully exercised over any member of a civilized community, against his will, is to prevent harm to others. His own good, either physical or moral, is not a sufficient warrant. He cannot rightfully be compelled to do or forbear because it will be better for him to do so, because it will make him happier, because, in the opinions of others, to do so would be wise, or even right. These are good reasons for remonstrating with him, or reasoning with him, or persuading him, or entreating him, but not for compelling him, or visiting him with any evil in case he do otherwise. To justify that, the conduct from which it is desired to deter him, must be calculated to produce evil to some one else. The only part of the conduct of any one, for which he is amenable to society, is that which concerns others. In the part which merely concerns himself, his independence is, of right, absolute. Over himself, over his own body and mind, the individual is sovereign.

It is, perhaps, hardly necessary to say that this doctrine is meant to apply only to human beings in the maturity of their faculties. We are not speaking of children, or of young persons below the age which the law may fix as that of manhood and womanhood. Those who are still in a state to require being taken care of by others, must be protected against their own actions as well as against external injury. . . .

There is a sphere of action in which society, as distinguished from the individual, has, if any, only an indirect interest; comprehending all that portion of a person's life and conduct which affects only himself, or if it also affects others, only with their free, voluntary, and undeceived consent and participation. When I say only himself, I mean directly, and in the first instance: for whatever affects himself, may affect others *through* himself; and the objection which may be grounded on this contingency, will receive consideration in the sequel. This, then, is the appropriate region of human liberty. It comprises, first, the inward domain of consciousness; demanding liberty of conscience, in the most comprehensive sense; liberty of thought and feeling; absolute freedom of opinion and sentiment on all subjects, practical or speculative, scientific, moral, or theological. The liberty of expressing and publishing opinions may seem to fall under a different principle, since it belongs to that part of the conduct of an individual which concerns other people; but, being almost of as much importance as the liberty of thought itself, and resting in great part on the same reasons, is practically inseparable from it. Secondly, the principle requires liberty of tastes and pursuits; of framing the plan of our life to suit our own character; of doing as we like, subject to such consequences as may follow; without impediment from our fellow-creatures, so long as what we do does not harm them, even though they should think our conduct foolish, perverse, or wrong. Thirdly, from this liberty of each individual, follows the liberty, within the same limits, of combination among individuals; freedom to unite, for any purpose not involving harm to others: the persons combining being supposed to be of full age, and not forced or deceived.

Reprinted with permission of the publisher from *On Liberty* (Hackett, 1978), 9–12, with omissions.

No society in which these liberties are not, on the whole, respected, is free, whatever may be its form of government; and none is completely free in which they do not exist absolute and unqualified. The only freedom which deserves the name, is that of pursuing our own good in our own way, so long as we do not attempt to deprive others of theirs, or impede their efforts to obtain it. Each is the proper guardian of his own health, whether bodily, or mental and spiritual. Mankind are greater gainers by suffering each other to live as good to themselves, than by compelling each to live as seems good to the rest. . . .

# 33   The Harm Principle

## JOEL FEINBERG

## "No Man Is an Island"

Mill maintained in *On Liberty* that social interference is never justified in those of a man's affairs that concern himself only. But no man's affairs have effects on himself alone. There are a thousand subtle and indirect ways in which every individual act, no matter how private and solitary, affects others. It would therefore seem that society has a right, on Mill's own principles, to interfere in every department of human life. Mill anticipated this objection and took certain steps to disarm it. Let it be allowed that no human conduct is entirely, exclusively, and to the last degree self-regarding. Still, Mill insisted, we can distinguish between actions that are plainly other-regarding and those that are "directly," "chiefly," or "primarily" self-regarding. There will be a twilight area of cases difficult to classify, but that is true of many other workable distinctions, including that between night and day.

It is essential to Mill's theory that we make a distinction between two different kinds of consequences of human actions: the consequences *directly* affecting the interests of others, and those of primarily self-regarding behavior which only *indirectly* or *remotely* affect the interests of others. "No person ought to be punished simply for being

From *Social Philosophy* by Joel Feinberg. Copyright © 1973, 31–45, footnotes renumbered. Reprinted by permission of Prentice-Hall, Inc., Upper Saddle River, NJ.

drunk," Mill wrote, "but a soldier or policeman should be punished for being drunk on duty."[1] A drunk policeman directly harms the interests of others. His conduct gives opportunities to criminals and thus creates grave risk of harm to other citizens. It brings the police into disrepute, and makes the work of his colleagues more dangerous. Finally, it may lead to loss of the policeman's job, with serious consequences for his wife and children.

Consider, on the other hand, a hard working bachelor who habitually spends his evening hours drinking himself into a stupor, which he then sleeps off, rising fresh in the morning to put in another hard day's work. His drinking does not *directly* affect others in any of the ways of the drunk policeman's conduct. He has no family; he drinks alone and sets no direct example; he is not prevented from discharging any of his public duties; he creates no substantial risk of harm to the interests of other individuals. Although even his private conduct will have some effects on the interests of others, these are precisely the sorts of effects Mill would call "indirect" and "remote." First, in spending his evenings the way he does, our solitary tippler is *not* doing any number of other things that might be of greater utility to others. In not earning and spending more money, he is failing to stimulate the economy (except for the liquor industry) as much as he might. Second, he fails to spend his evening time improving his talents and making himself a better person. Perhaps he has a considerable native talent for painting or poetry, and his wastefulness is depriving the world of some valuable art. Third, he may make those of his colleagues who like him sad on his behalf. Finally, to those who know of his habits, he is a "bad example."[2] All of these "indirect harms" together, Mill maintained, do not outweigh the direct and serious harm that would result from social or legal coercion.

Mill's critics have never been entirely satisfied by this. Many have pointed out that Mill is concerned not only with political coercion and legal punishment but also with purely social coercion —moral pressure, social avoidance, ostracism. No responsible critic would wish the state to punish the solitary tippler, but social coercion is another matter. We can't prevent people from disapproving of an individual for his self-regarding faults or from expressing that disapproval to others, without undue restriction on *their* freedom. Such expressions, in Mill's view, are inevitably coercive, constituting a "milder form of punishment." Hence "social punishment" of individuals for conduct that directly concerns only themselves—the argument concludes—is both inevitable and, according to Mill's own principles, proper.

Mill anticipated this objection, too, and tried to cope with it by making a distinction between types of social responses. We cannot help but lower in our estimation a person with serious self-regarding faults. We will think ill of him, judge him to be at fault, and make him the inevitable and proper object of our disapproval, distaste, even contempt. We may warn others about him, avoid his company, and withhold gratuitous benefits from him—"not to the oppression of his individuality but in the exercise of ours."[3] Mill concedes that all of these social responses can function as "penalties"—but they are suffered "only in so far as they are the natural and, as it were, the spontaneous consequences of the faults themselves, not because they are purposely inflicted on him for the sake of punishment."[4] Other responses, on the other hand, add something to the "natural penalties"—pointed snubbing, economic reprisals, gossip campaigns, and so on. The added penalties, according to Mill, are

precisely the ones that are never justified as responses to merely self-regarding flaws—"if he displeases us, we may express our distaste; and we may stand aloof from a person as well as from a thing that displeases us, but we shall not therefore feel called on to make his life uncomfortable."[5]

## Other Proposed Grounds for Coercion

The distinction between self-regarding and other-regarding behavior, as Mill intended it to be understood, does seem at least roughly serviceable, and unlikely to invite massive social interference in private affairs. I think most critics of Mill would grant that, but reject the harm principle on the opposite ground that it doesn't permit enough interference. These writers would allow at least one, and as many as five or more, additional valid grounds for coercion. Each of these proposed grounds is stated in a principle listed below. One might hold that restriction of one person's liberty can be justified:

1. To prevent harm to others, either
   a. injury to individual persons (*The Private Harm Principle*), or
   b. impairment of institutional practices that are in the public interest (*The Public Harm Principle*);
2. To prevent offense to others (*The Offense Principle*);
3. To prevent harm to self (*Legal Paternalism*);
4. To prevent or punish sin, i.e., to "enforce morality as such" (*Legal Moralism*);
5. To benefit the self (*Extreme Paternalism*);
6. To benefit others (*The Welfare Principle*).

The liberty-limiting principles on this list are best understood as stating neither necessary nor sufficient conditions for justified coercion, but rather specifications of the *kinds* of reasons that are always relevant or acceptable in support of proposed coercion, even though in a given case they may not be conclusive."[6] Each principle states that interference might be permissible *if* (but not *only if*) a certain condition is satisfied. Hence the principles are not mutually exclusive; it is possible to hold two or more of them at once, even all of them together, and it is possible to deny all of them. Moreover, the principles cannot be construed as stating sufficient conditions for legitimate interference with liberty, for even though the principle is satisfied in a given case, the general presumption against coercion might not be outweighed. The harm principle, for example, does not justify state interference to prevent a tiny bit of inconsequential harm. Prevention of minor harm always counts in favor of proposals (as in a legislature) to restrict liberty, but in a given instance it might not count *enough* to outweigh the general presumption against interference, or it might be outweighed by the prospect of practical difficulties in enforcing the law, excessive costs, and forfeitures of privacy. A liberty-limiting principle states considerations that are always good reasons for coercion, though neither exclusively nor, in every case, decisively good reasons.

It will not be possible to examine each principle in detail here, and offer "proofs" and "refutations." The best way to defend one's selection of principles is to show to which positions they commit one on such issues as censorship of literature, "morals offenses," and compulsory social security programs. General principles arise in the course of deliberations over particular problems, especially in the efforts to defend one's judgments by showing that they are consistent with what has gone before. If a principle commits one to an antecedently unacceptable judgment, then one has to modify or supplement the principle in a way that does the least damage to the harmony of one's particular and general opinions taken as a group. On the other hand, when a solid, well-entrenched principle entails a change in a particular judgment, the overriding claims of consistency may require that the judgment be adjusted. This sort of dialectic is similar to the reasonings that are prevalent in law courts. When similar cases are decided in opposite ways, it is incumbent on the court to distinguish them in some respect that will reconcile the separate decisions with each other and with the common rule applied to each. Every effort is made to render current decisions consistent with past ones unless the precedents seem so disruptive of the overall internal harmony of the law that they must, reluctantly, be revised or abandoned. In social and political philosophy every person is on his own, and the counterparts to "past decisions" are the most confident judgments one makes in ordinary normative discourse. The philosophical task is to extract from these "given" judgments the principles that render them consistent, adjusting and modifying where necessary in order to convert the whole body of opinions into an intelligible, coherent system. There is no a priori way of refuting another's political opinions, but if our opponents are rational men committed to the ideal of consistency, we can always hope to show them that a given judgment is inconsistent with one of their own acknowledged principles. Then something will have to give.

## Morals Offenses and Legal Moralism

Immoral conduct is no trivial thing, and we should hardly expect societies to tolerate it; yet if men are *forced* to refrain from immorality, their own choices will play very little role in what they do, so that they can hardly develop critical judgment and moral traits of a genuinely praiseworthy kind. Thus legal enforcement of morality seems to pose a dilemma. The problem does not arise if we assume that all immoral conduct is socially harmful, for immoral conduct will then be prohibited by law not just to punish sin or to "force men to be moral," but rather to prevent harm to others. If, however, there are forms of immorality that do not necessarily cause harm, "the problem of the enforcement of morality" becomes especially acute.

The central problem cases are those criminal actions generally called "morals offenses." Offenses against morality and decency have long constituted a category of crimes (as distinct from offenses against the person, offenses against property, and so on). These have included mainly sex offenses, such as adultery, fornication, sodomy, incest, and prostitution, but also a miscellany of nonsexual offenses, including cruelty to animals, desecration of the flag or other venerated symbols, and mistreatment of corpses. In a useful article,[7]

Louis B. Schwartz maintains that what sets these crimes off as a class is not their special relation to morality (murder is also an offense against morality, but it is not a "morals offense") but the lack of an essential connection between them and social harm. In particular, their suppression is not required by the public security. Some morals offenses may harm the perpetrators themselves, but the risk of harm of this sort has usually been consented to in advance by the actors. Offense to other parties, when it occurs, is usually a consequence of perpetration of the offenses *in public,* and can be prevented by statutes against "open lewdness," or "solicitation" in public places. That still leaves "morals offenses" committed by consenting adults in private. Should they really be crimes?

In addition to the general presumption against coercion, other arguments against legislation prohibiting private and harmless sexual practices are drawn from the harm principle itself; laws governing private affairs are extremely awkward and expensive to enforce, and have side effects that are invariably harmful. Laws against homosexuality, for example, can only be occasionally and randomly enforced, and this leads to the inequities of selective enforcement and opportunities for blackmail and private vengeance. Moreover, "the pursuit of homosexuals involves policemen in degrading entrapment practices, and diverts attention and effort"[8] from more serious (harmful) crimes of aggression, fraud, and corruption.

These considerations have led some to argue against statutes that prohibit private immorality, but, not surprisingly, it has encouraged others to abandon their exclusive reliance on the harm and/or offense principles, at least in the case of morals offenses. The alternative principle of "legal moralism" has several forms. In its more moderate version it is commonly associated with the views of Patrick Devlin,[9] whose theory, as I understand it, is really an application of the public harm principle. The proper aim of criminal law, he agrees, is the prevention of harm, not merely to individuals, but also (and primarily) to society itself. A shared moral code, Devlin argues, is a necessary condition for the very existence of a community.

Shared moral convictions function as "invisible bonds" tying individuals together into an orderly society. Moreover, the fundamental unifying morality (to switch the metaphor) is a kind of "seamless web";[10] to damage it at one point is to weaken it throughout. Hence, society has as much right to protect its moral code by legal coercion as it does to protect its equally indispensable political institutions. The law cannot tolerate politically revolutionary activity, nor can it accept activity that rips asunder its moral fabric. "The suppression of vice is as much the law's business as the suppression of subversive activities; it is no more possible to define a sphere of private morality than it is to define one of private subversive activity."[11]

H. L. A. Hart finds it plausible that some shared morality is necessary to the existence of a community, but criticizes Devlin's further contention "that a society is identical with its morality as that is at any given moment of its history, so that a change in its morality is tantamount to the destruction of a society."[12] Indeed, a moral critic might admit that we can't exist as a society without some morality, while insisting that we can perfectly well exist without *this* morality (if we put a better one in its place). Devlin seems to reply that the shared morality *can* be changed even though protected by law, and, when it does change, the emergent reformed morality in turn deserves *its* legal protection.[13] The law then functions to make moral reform difficult, but there is no preventing change where reforming zeal is fierce enough. How does one bring about a change in prevailing moral beliefs when they are enshrined in law? Presumably by advocating conduct which is in fact illegal, by putting into public practice what one preaches, and by demonstrating one's sincerity by marching proudly off to jail for one's convictions:

there is . . . a natural respect for opinions that are sincerely held. When such opinions accumulate enough weight, the law must either yield or it is broken. In a democratic society . . . there will be a strong tendency for it to yield—not to abandon all defenses so as to let in the horde, but to give ground to those who are prepared to fight for something that they prize. To fight may be to suffer. A willingness to suffer is the most convincing proof of sincerity. Without the law there would be no proof. The law is the anvil on which the hammer strikes.[14]

In this remarkable passage, Devlin has discovered another argument for enforcing "morality as such," and incidentally for principled civil disobedience as the main technique for initiating and regulating moral change. A similar argument, deriving from Samuel Johnson and applying mainly to changes in religious doctrine, was well known to Mill. According to this theory, religious innovators deserve to be persecuted, for persecution allows them to prove their mettle and demonstrate their disinterested good faith, while their teachings, insofar as they are true, cannot be hurt, since truth will always triumph in the end. Mill held this method of testing truth, whether in science, religion, or morality, to be both uneconomical and ungenerous.[15] But if self-sacrificing civil disobedience is *not* the most efficient and humane remedy for the moral reformer, what instruments of moral change are available to him? This question is not only difficult to answer in its own right, it is also the rock that sinks Devlin's favorite analogy between "harmless" immorality and political subversion.

Consider the nature of subversion. Most modern law-governed countries have a constitution, a set of duly constituted authorities, and a body of statutes created and enforced by these authorities. The ways of changing these things will be well known, orderly, and permitted by the constitution. For example, constitutions are amended, legislators are elected, and new legislation is introduced. On the other hand, it is easy to conceive of various sorts of unpermitted and disorderly change— through assassination and violent revolution, or bribery and subornation, or the use of legitimately won power to extort and intimidate. Only these illegitimate methods of change can be called "subversion." But here the analogy between positive law and positive morality begins to break down. There is no "moral constitution," no well-known and orderly way of introducing moral legislation to duly constituted moral legislators, no clear convention of majority rule. Moral subversion, if there is such a thing, must consist in the employment of disallowed techniques of change instead of the officially permitted "constitutional" ones. It consists not simply of change as such, but of illegitimate change. Insofar as the notion of legitimately induced moral change remains obscure, illegitimate moral change is no better. Still, there is enough content to both notions to preserve some analogy to the political case. A citizen works *legitimately* to change public moral beliefs when he openly and forthrightly expresses his own dissent, when he attempts to argue, persuade, and offer reasons, and when he lives according to his own convictions with persuasive quiet and dignity, neither harming others nor offering counterpersuasive offense to tender sensibilities. A citizen attempts to change mores by *illegitimate* means when he abandons argument and example for force and fraud. If this is the basis of the distinction between legitimate and illegitimate techniques of moral change, then the use of state power to affect moral belief *one way or the other,* when harmfulness is not involved, is a clear ex-example of illegitimacy. Government enforcement of the conventional code is not to be called "moral subversion," of course, because it is used on behalf of the status quo; but whether conservative or innovative, it is equally in defiance of our "moral constitution" (if anything is).

The second version of legal moralism is the pure version, not some other principle in disguise. Enforcement of morality as such and the attendant punishment of sin are not justified as means to some further social aim (such as preservation of social cohesiveness) but are ends in themselves. Perhaps J. F. Stephen was expressing this pure moralism when he wrote that "there are acts of wickedness so gross and outrageous that . . . [protection of others apart], they must be prevented at any cost to the offender and punished if they occur with exemplary severity.[16] From his examples it is clear that Stephen had in mind the very acts that are called "morals offenses" in the law.

It is sometimes said in support of pure legal moralism that the world as a whole would be a better place without morally ugly, even "harmlessly immoral," conduct, and that our actual universe is intrinsically worse for having such conduct in it. The threat of punishment, the argument continues, deters such conduct. Actual instances of punishment not only back up the threat, and thus help keep future moral weeds out of the universe's garden, they also erase past evils from the universe's temporal record by "nullifying" them, or making it as if they never were. Thus punishment, it is said, contributes to the intrinsic value of the universe in two ways: by canceling out past sins and preventing future ones.[17]

There is some plausibility in this view when it is applied to ordinary harmful crimes, especially those involving duplicity or cruelty, which really do seem to "set the universe out of joint." It is natural enough to think of repentance, apology, or forgiveness as "setting things straight," and of punishment as a kind of "payment" or a wiping clean of the moral slate. But in cases where it is natural to resort to such analogies, there is not only a rule infraction, there is also a *victim*—some person or society of persons who have been harmed. Where there is no victim—and especially where there is no profit at the expense of another—"setting things straight" has no clear intuitive content.

Punishment may yet play its role in discouraging harmless private immoralities for the sake of "the universe's moral record." But if fear of punishment is to keep people from illicit intercourse (or from desecrating flags, or mistreating corpses) in the privacy of their own rooms, then morality shall have to be enforced with a fearsome efficiency that shows no respect for individual privacy. If private immoralities are to be deterred by threat of punishment, the detecting authorities must be able to look into the hidden chambers and locked rooms of anyone's private domicile. When we put this massive forfeiture of privacy into the balance along with the usual costs of coercion—loss of spontaneity, stunting of rational powers, anxiety, hypocrisy, and the rest—the price of securing mere outward conformity to the community's moral standards (for that is all that can be achieved by the penal law) is exorbitant.

Perhaps the most interesting of the nonsexual morals offenses, and the most challenging case for application of liberty-limiting principles, is cruelty to animals. Suppose that John Doe is an intelligent, sensitive person with one very severe neurotic trait—he loves to see living things suffer pain. Fortunately, he never has occasion to torture human beings (he would genuinely regret that), for he can always find an animal for the purpose. For a period he locks himself in his room every night, draws the blind, and then beats and tortures a dog to death. The sounds of shrieks and moans, which are music to his ears, are nuisances to his neighbors, and when his landlady discovers what he has been doing she is so shocked she has to be hospitalized. Distressed that he has caused harm to human beings, Doe leaves the rooming house, buys a five hundred acre ranch, and moves into a house in the remote, unpopulated center of his own property. There, in the perfect privacy of his own home, he spends every evening maiming, torturing, and beating to death his own animals.

What are we to say of Doe's bizarre behavior? We have three alternatives. First we can say that it is perfectly permissible since it consists simply in a man's destruction of his own property. How a man disposes in private of his own property is no concern of anyone else providing he causes no nuisance such as loud noises and evil smells. Second, we can say that this behavior is patently immoral even though it causes no harm to the interests of anyone other than the actor; further, since it obviously should *not* be permitted by the law, this is a case where the harm principle is inadequate and must be supplemented by legal moralism. Third, we can extend the harm principle to animals, and argue that the law can interfere with the private enjoyment of property not to enforce "morality as such," but rather to prevent harm to the animals. The third alternative is the most inviting, but not without its difficulties. We *must* control animal movements, exploit animal labor, and, in many cases, deliberately slaughter animals. All these forms of treatment would be "harm" if inflicted on human beings, but cannot be allowed to count as harm to animals if the harm principle is to be extended to them in a realistic way. The best compromise is to recognize one supreme interest of animals, namely the interest in freedom from cruelly or wantonly inflicted pain, and to count as "harm" all and only invasions of *that* interest.

## Obscenity and the Offense Principle

Up to this point we have considered the harm and offense principles together in order to determine whether between them they are sufficient to regulate conventional immoralities, or whether they need help from a further independent principle, legal moralism. Morals offenses were treated as essentially private so that the offense principle could not be stretched to apply to them. Obscene literature and pornographic displays would appear to be quite different in this respect. Both are materials deliberately published for the eyes of others, and their existence can bring partisans of the unsupplemented harm principle into direct conflict with those who endorse *both* the harm and offense principles.

In its untechnical, prelegal sense, the word "obscenity" refers to material dealing with nudity, sex, or excretion in an offensive manner. Such material becomes obscene in the legal sense when, because of its offensiveness or for some other reason [this question had best be left open in the definition], it is or ought to be without legal protection. The legal definition then incorporates the everyday sense, and essential to both is the requirement that the material *be offensive.* An item may offend one person and not another. "Obscenity," if it is to avoid this subjective relativity, must involve an interpersonal objective sense of "offensive." Material must be offensive by prevailing community standards that are public and well known, or be such that it is apt to offend virtually everyone.

Not all material that is generally offensive need also be harmful in any sense recognized by the harm principle. It is partly an empirical question whether reading or witnessing obscene material causes social harm; reliable evidence, even of a statistical kind, of causal connections between obscenity and antisocial behavior is extremely hard to find.[18] In the absence of clear and decisive evidence of harmfulness, the American Civil Liberties Union insists that the offensiveness of obscene material cannot be a sufficient ground for its repression:

> . . . [T]he question in a case involving obscenity, just as in every case involving an attempted restriction upon free speech, is whether the words or pictures are used in such circumstances and are of such a nature as to create a clear and present danger that they will bring about a substantial evil that the state has a right to prevent. . . . We believe that under the current state of knowledge, there is grossly insufficient evidence to show that obscenity brings about *any* substantive evil.[19]

The A.C.L.U. argument employs *only* the harm principle among liberty-limiting principles, and treats literature, drama, and painting as forms of expression subject to the same rules as expressions of opinion. In respect to both types of expression, "every act of deciding what should be barred carries with it a danger to the community."[20] The suppression itself is an evil to the author who is squelched. The power to censor and punish involves risks that socially valuable material will be repressed along with the "filth." The overall effect of suppression, the A.C.L.U. concludes, is almost certainly to discourage nonconformist and eccentric expression generally. In order to override these serious risks, there must be in a given case an even more clear and present danger that the obscene material, if not squelched, will cause even greater harm; such countervailing evidence is never forthcoming. (If such evidence were to accumulate, the A.C.L.U. would be perfectly willing to change its position on obscenity.)

The A.C.L.U. stand on obscenity seems clearly to be the position dictated by the unsupplemented harm principle and its corollary, the clear and present danger test. Is there any reason at this point to introduce the offense principle into the discussion? Unhappily, we may be forced to if we are to do justice to all of our particular intuitions in the most harmonious way. Consider an example suggested by Professor Schwartz. By the provisions of the new Model Penal Code, he writes, "a rich homosexual may not use a billboard on Times Square to promulgate to the general populace the techniques and pleasures of sodomy."[21] If the notion of "harm" is restricted to its narrow sense, that is, contrasted with "offense," it will be hard to reconstruct a rationale for this prohibition based on the harm principle. There is unlikely to be evidence that a lurid and obscene public poster in Times Square would create a clear and present danger of injury to those who fail to avert their eyes in time as they come blinking out of the subway stations. Yet it will be surpassingly difficult for even the most dedicated liberal to advocate freedom of expression in a case of this kind. Hence, if we are to justify coercion in this case, we will likely be driven, however reluctantly, to the offense principle.

There is good reason to be "reluctant" to embrace the offense principle until driven to it by an example like the above. People take perfectly genuine offense at many socially useful or harmless activities, from commercial advertisements to inane chatter. Moreover, widespread irrational prejudices can lead people to be disgusted, shocked, even morally repelled by perfectly innocent activities, and we should be loath to permit their groundless repugnance to override the innocence. The offense principle, therefore, must be formulated very precisely and applied in accordance with carefully formulated standards so as not to open the door to wholesale and intuitively unwarranted repression. At the very least we should require that the prohibited conduct or material be of the sort apt to offend almost everybody, and not just some shifting majority or special interest group.

It is instructive to note that a strictly drawn offense principle would not only justify prohibition of conduct and pictured conduct that is in its inherent character repellent, but also conduct and pictured conduct that is inoffensive in itself but offensive in inappropriate circumstances. I have in mind so-called indecencies such as public nudity. One can imagine an advocate of the unsupplemented harm principle arguing against the public nudity prohibition on the grounds that the sight of a naked body does no one any harm, and the state has no right to impose standards of dress or undress on private citizens. How one chooses to dress, after all, is a form of self-expression. If we do not permit the state to bar clashing colors or bizarre hair styles, by what right does it prohibit total undress? Perhaps the sight of naked people could at first lead to riots or other forms of antisocial behavior, but that is precisely the sort of contingency for which we have police. If we don't take away a person's right of free speech for the reason that its exercise may lead others to misbehave, we cannot in consistency deny his right to dress or undress as he chooses for the same reason.

There may be no answering this challenge on its own ground, but the offense principle provides a ready rationale for the nudity prohibition. The sight of nude bodies in public places is for almost everyone acutely *embarrassing*. Part of the explanation no doubt rests on the fact that nudity has an irresistible power to draw the eye and focus the thoughts on matters that are normally repressed. The conflict between these attracting and repressing forces is exciting, upsetting, and anxiety-producing. In some persons it will create at best a kind of painful turmoil, and at worst that experience of exposure to oneself of "peculiarly sensitive, intimate, vulnerable aspects of the self"[22] which is called *shame*. "One's feeling is involuntarily exposed openly in one's face; one is uncovered . . . taken by surprise . . . made a fool of."[23] The result is not mere "offense," but a kind of psychic jolt that in many normal people can be a painful wound. Even those of us who are better able to control our feelings might well resent the *nuisance* of having to do so.

If we are to accept the offense principle as a supplement to the harm principle, we must accept two corollaries which stand in relation to it similarly to the way in which the clear and present danger test stands to the harm principle. The first, the *standard of universality,* has already been touched upon. For the offensiveness (disgust, embarrassment, outraged sensibilities, or shame) to be sufficient to warrant coercion, it should be the reaction that could be expected from almost any person chosen at random from the nation as a whole, regardless of sect, faction, race, age, or sex. The second is the *standard of reasonable avoidability*. No one has a right to protection from the state against offensive experiences if he can effectively avoid those experiences with no unreasonable effort or inconvenience. If a nude person enters a public bus and takes a seat near the front, there may be no effective way for other patrons to avoid intensely shameful embarrassment (or other insupportable feelings) short of leaving the bus, which would be an unreasonable inconvenience. Similarly, obscene remarks over a loudspeaker, homosexual billboards in Times Square, and pornographic handbills thrust into the hands of passing pedestrians all fail to be reasonably avoidable.

On the other hand, the offense principle, properly qualified, can give no warrant to the suppression of *books* on the grounds of obscenity. When printed words hide decorously behind covers of books sitting passively on bookstore shelves, their offensiveness is easily avoided. The contrary view is no doubt encouraged by the common comparison of obscenity with "smut," "filth," or "dirt." This in turn suggests an analogy to nuisance law, which governs cases where certain activities create loud noises or terrible odors offensive to neighbors, and "the courts must weigh the gravity of the nuisance [substitute "offense"] to the neighbors against the social utility [substitute "redeeming social value"] of the defendant's conduct."[24] There is, however, one vitiating disanalogy in this comparison. In the case of "dirty books" the offense is easily avoidable. There is nothing like the evil smell of rancid garbage oozing right out through the covers of a book. When an "obscene" book sits on a shelf, who is there to be offended? Those who want to read it for the sake of erotic stimulation presumably will not be offended (or else they wouldn't read it), and those who choose not to read it will have no experience by which to be offended. If its covers are too decorous, some innocents may browse through it by mistake and be offended by what they find, but they need only close the book to escape the offense. Even this

offense, minimal as it is, could be completely avoided by prior consultation of trusted book reviewers. I conclude that there are no sufficient grounds derived either from the harm or offense principles for suppressing obscene literature, unless that ground be the protection of children; but I can think of no reason why restrictions on sales to children cannot work as well for printed materials as they do for cigarettes and whiskey.

## Notes

1. John Stuart Mill, *On Liberty* (New York: Liberal Arts Press, 1956), pp. 99–100.

2. Mill has a ready rejoinder to this last point: If the conduct in question is supposed to be greatly harmful to the actor himself, "the example, on the whole must be more salutary" than harmful socially, since it is a warning lesson, rather than an alluring model, to others. See Mill, *On Liberty*, p. 101.

3. Mill, *On Liberty*, p. 94.

4. Mill, *On Liberty*, p. 95.

5. Mill, *On Liberty*, p. 96.

6. I owe this point to Professor Michael Bayles. See his contribution to *Issues in Law and Morality*, ed. Norman Care and Thomas Trelogan (Cleveland: The Press of Case Western Reserve University, 1973).

7. Louis B. Schwartz, "Morals Offenses and the Model Penal Code," *Columbia Law Review*, LXIII (1963), 669 ff.

8. Schwartz, "Morals Offenses and the Model Penal Code," 671.

9. Patrick Devlin, *The Enforcement of Morals* (London: Oxford University Press, 1965).

10. The phrase is not Devlin's but that of his critic, H. L. A. Hart, In *Law, Liberty, and Morality* (Stanford: Stanford University Press, 1963), p. 51. In his rejoinder to Hart, Devlin writes: "Seamlessness presses the simile rather hard but apart from that, I should say that for most people morality is a web of beliefs rather than a number of unconnected ones." Devlin, *The Enforcement of Morals*, p. 115.

11. Devlin, *The Enforcement of Morals*, pp. 13–14.

12. Hart, *Law, Liberty, and Morality*, p. 51.

13. Devlin, *The Enforcement of Morals*, pp. 115 ff.

14. Devlin, *The Enforcement of Morals*, p. 116.

15. John Stuart Mill, *On Liberty*, pp. 33–34.

16. James Fitzjames Stephen, *Liberty, Equality, Fraternity* (London, 1873), p. 163.

17. Cf. C. D. Broad, "Certain Features in Moore's Ethical Doctrines," in P. A. Schilpp, *The Philosophy of G. E. Moore* (Evanston, Ill.: Northwestern University Press, 1942), pp. 48 ff.

18. There have been some studies made, but the results have been inconclusive. See the *Report of the Fed-*

eral Commission on Obscenity and Pornography (New York: Bantam Books, 1970), pp. 169–308.

19. *Obscenity and Censorship* (Pamphlet published by the American Civil Liberties Union, New York, March, 1963), p. 7.

20. *Obscenity and Censorship*, p. 4.

21. Schwartz, "Morals Offenses and the Penal Code," 680.

22. Helen Merrill Lynd, *On Shame and the Search for Identity* (New York: Science Editions, Inc., 1961), p. 33.

23. Lynd, *On Shame and the Search for Identity*, p. 32.

# 34 Pornography and Respect for Women

## ANN GARRY

*Pornography, like rape, is a male invention, designed to dehumanize women, to reduce the female to an object of sexual access, not to free sensuality from moralistic or parental inhibition. . . . Pornography is the undiluted essence of anti-female propaganda.*

> SUSAN BROWNMILLER,
> *Against Our Will: Men, Women and Rape*[1]

*It is often asserted that a distinguishing characteristic of sexually explicit material is the degrading and demeaning portrayal of the role and status of the human female. It has been argued that erotic materials describe the female as a mere sexual object to be exploited and manipulated sexually. . . . A recent survey shows that 41 percent of American males and 46 percent of the females believe that "sexual materials lead people to lose respect for women.". . . Recent experiments suggest that such fears are probably unwarranted.*

> Presidential Commission on Obscenity
> and Pornography[2]

The kind of apparent conflict illustrated in these passages is easy to find in one's own thinking as well. For example, I have been inclined to think that pornography is innocuous and to dismiss "moral" arguments for censoring it because many such arguments rest on an assumption I do not

share—that sex is an evil to be controlled. At the same time I believe that it is wrong to exploit or degrade human beings, particularly women and others who are especially susceptible. So if pornography degrades human beings, then even if I would oppose its censorship I surely cannot find it morally innocuous.

In an attempt to resolve this apparent conflict I discuss three questions: Does pornography degrade (or exploit or dehumanize) human beings? If so, does it degrade women in ways or to an extent that it does not degrade men? If so, must pornography degrade women, as Brownmiller thinks, or could genuinely innocuous, nonsexist pornography exist? Although much current pornography does degrade women, I will argue that it is possible to have nondegrading, nonsexist pornography. However, this possibility rests on our making certain fundamental changes in our conceptions of sex and sex roles. . . .

The . . . argument I will consider [here] is that pornography is morally objectionable, not because it leads people to show disrespect for women, but because pornography itself exemplifies and recommends behavior that violates the moral principle to respect persons. The content of pornography is what one objects to. It treats women as mere sex objects "to be exploited and manipulated" and degrades the role and status of women. In order to evaluate this argument, I will first clarify what it would mean for pornography itself to treat someone as a sex object in a degrading manner. I will then deal with three issues central to the discussion of pornography and respect

This article first appeared in *Social Theory and Practice* 4 (Summer 1978). It is reprinted here as it appears in Sharon Bishop and Marjorie Weinzweig, eds., *Philosophy and Women* (Wadsworth, 1979). Reprinted by permission of the author.

for women: how "losing respect" for a woman is connected with treating her as a sex object; what is wrong with treating someone as a sex object; and why it is worse to treat women rather than men as sex objects. I will argue that the current content of pornography sometimes violates the moral principle to respect persons. Then, in [the concluding part] of this paper, I will suggest that pornography need not violate this principle if certain fundamental changes were to occur in attitudes about sex.

To many people, including Brownmiller and some other feminists, it appears to be an obvious truth that pornography treats people, especially women, as sex objects in a degrading manner. And if we omit "in a degrading manner," the statement seems hard to dispute: How could pornography not treat people as sex objects?

First, is it permissible to say that either the content of pornography or pornography itself degrades people or treats people as sex objects? It is not difficult to find examples of degrading content in which women are treated as sex objects. Some pornographic films convey the message that all women really want to be raped, that their resisting struggle is not to be believed. By portraying women in this manner, the content of the movie degrades women. Degrading women is morally objectionable. While seeing the movie need not cause anyone to imitate the behavior shown, we can call the content degrading to women because of the character of the behavior and attitudes it recommends. The same kind of point can be made about films (or books or TV commercials) with other kinds of degrading, thus morally objectionable, content—for example, racist messages.

The next step in the argument is to infer that, because the content or message of pornography is morally objectionable, we can call pornography itself morally objectionable. Support for this step can be found in an analogy. If a person takes every opportunity to recommend that men rape women, we would think not only that his recommendation is immoral but that he is immoral too. In the case of pornography, the objection to making an inference from recommended behavior to the person who recommends is that we ascribe

predicates such as "immoral" differently to people than to films or books. A film vehicle for an objectionable message is still an object independent of its message, its director, its producer, those who act in it, and those who respond to it. Hence one cannot make an unsupported inference from "the content of the film is morally objectionable" to "the film is morally objectionable." Because the central points in this paper do not depend on whether pornography itself (in addition to its content) is morally objectionable, I will not try to support this inference. (The question about the relation of content to the work itself is, of course, extremely interesting; but in part because I cannot decide which side of the argument is more persuasive, I will pass.[3]) Certainly one appropriate way to evaluate pornography is in terms of the moral features of its content. If a pornographic film exemplifies and recommends morally objectionable attitudes or behavior, then its content is morally objectionable.

Let us now turn to the first of our three questions about respect and sex objects: What is the connection between losing respect for a woman and treating her as a sex object? Some people who have lived through the era in which women were taught to worry about men "losing respect" for them if they engaged in sex in inappropriate circumstances find it troublesome (or at least amusing) that feminists—supposedly "liberated" women—are outraged at being treated as sex objects, either by pornography or in any other way. The apparent alignment between feminists and traditionally "proper" women need not surprise us when we look at it more closely.

The "respect" that men have traditionally believed they have for women—hence a respect they can lose—is not a general respect for persons as autonomous beings; nor is it respect that is earned because of one's personal merits or achievements. It is respect that is an outgrowth of the "double standard." Women are to be respected because they are more pure, delicate, and fragile than men, have more refined sensibilities, and so on. Because some women clearly do not have these qualities, thus do not deserve respect, women must be divided into two groups—the good ones on the pedestal and the bad ones who have fallen from it. One's mother, grandmother, Sunday School teacher, and usually one's wife are "good" women. The appropriate behavior by which to express respect for good women would be, for example, not swearing or telling dirty jokes in front of them, giving them seats on buses, and other "chivalrous" acts. This kind of "respect" for good women is the same sort that adolescent boys in the back seats of cars used to "promise" not to lose. Note that men define, display, and lose this kind of respect. If women lose respect for women, it is not typically a loss of respect for (other) women as a class but a loss of self-respect.

It has now become commonplace to acknowledge that, although a place on the pedestal might have advantages over a place in the "gutter" beneath it, a place on the pedestal is not at all equal to the place occupied by other people (i.e., men). "Respect" for those on the pedestal was not respect for whole, full-fledged people but for a special class of inferior beings.

If a person makes two traditional assumptions —that (at least some) sex is dirty and that women fall into two classes, good and bad—it is easy to see how that person might think that pornography could lead people to lose respect for women or that pornography is itself disrespectful to women. Pornography describes or shows women engaging in activities inappropriate for good women to engage in—or at least inappropriate for them to be seen by strangers engaging in. If one sees these women as symbolic representatives of all women, then all women fall from grace with these women. This fall is possible, I believe, because the traditional "respect" that men have had for women is not genuine, whole-hearted respect for full-fledged human beings but half-hearted respect for lesser beings, some of whom they feel the need to glorify and purify.[4] It is easy to fall from a pedestal. Can we imagine 41 percent of men and 46 percent of women answering "yes" to the question, "Do movies showing men engaging in violent acts lead people to lose respect for men?"

Two interesting asymmetries appear. The first is that losing respect for men as a class (men with power, typically Anglo men) is more difficult than losing respect for women or ethnic minorities as a class. Anglo men whose behavior warrants disrespect are more likely to be seen as exceptional cases than are women or minorities (whose "transgressions" may be far less serious). Think of the following: women are temptresses; Blacks cheat the welfare system; Italians are gangsters; but the men of the Nixon administration are exceptions— Anglo men as a class did not lose respect because of Watergate and related scandals.

The second asymmetry concerns the active and passive roles of the sexes. Men are seen in the active role. If men lose respect for women because of something "evil" done by women (such as appearing in pornography), the fear is that men will then do harm to women—not that women will do harm to men. Whereas if women lose respect for male politicians because of Watergate, the fear is still that male politicians will do harm, not that women will do harm to male politicians. This asymmetry might be a result of one way in which our society thinks of sex as bad—as harm that men do to women (or to the person playing a female role, as in a homosexual rape). Robert Baker calls attention to this point in "'Pricks' and 'Chicks': A Plea for 'Persons.'"[5] Our slang words for sexual intercourse—"fuck," "screw," or older words such as "take" or "have"—not only can mean harm but have traditionally taken a male subject and a female object. The active male screws (harms) the passive female. A "bad" woman only tempts men to hurt her further.

It is easy to understand why one's proper grandmother would not want men to see pornography or lose respect for women. But feminists reject these "proper" assumptions: good and bad classes of women do not exist; and sex is not dirty (though many people believe it is). Why then are feminists angry at the treatment of women as sex objects, and why are some feminists opposed to pornography?

The answer is that feminists as well as proper grandparents are concerned with respect. However, there are differences. A feminist's distinction between treating a woman as a full-fledged person and treating her as merely a sex object does not correspond to the good-bad woman distinction. In the latter distinction, "good" and "bad" are properties applicable to groups of women. In the feminist view, all women are full-fledged people—some, however, are treated as sex objects and perhaps think of themselves as sex objects. A further difference is that, although "bad" women correspond to those thought to deserve treatment as sex objects, good women have not corresponded to full-fledged people; only men have been full-fledged people. Given the feminist's distinction, she has no difficulty whatever in saying that pornography treats women as sex objects, not as full-fledged people. She can morally object to pornography or anything else that treats women as sex objects.

One might wonder whether any objection to treatment as a sex object implies that the person objecting still believes, deep down, that sex is dirty. I don't think so. Several other possibilities emerge. First, even if I believe intellectually and emotionally that sex is healthy, I might object to being treated *only* as a sex object. In the same spirit, I would object to being treated *only* as a maker of chocolate chip cookies or *only* as a tennis partner, because only one of my talents is being valued. Second, perhaps I feel that sex is healthy, but it is apparent to me that you think sex is dirty; so I don't want you to treat me as a sex object. Third, being treated as any kind of object, not just as a sex object, is unappealing. I would rather be a partner (sexual or otherwise) than an object. Fourth, and more plausible than the first three possibilities, is Robert Baker's view mentioned above. Both (i) our traditional double standard of sexual behavior for men and women and (ii) the linguistic evidence that we connect the concept of sex with the concept of harm point to what is wrong with treating women as sex objects. As I said earlier, "fuck" and "screw," in their traditional uses, have taken a male subject, a female object, and have had at least two meanings: harm and have sexual intercourse with. (In addition, a prick is a man who harms people ruthlessly; and a motherfucker is so low that he would do something very harmful to his own dear mother.)[6] Because in our culture we connect sex with harm that men do to women, and because we think of

the female role in sex as that of harmed object, we can see that to treat a woman as a sex object is automatically to treat her as less than fully human. To say this does not imply that no healthy sexual relationships exist; nor does it say anything about individual men's conscious intentions to degrade women by desiring them sexually (though no doubt some men have these intentions). It is merely to make a point about the concepts embodied in our language.

Psychoanalytic support for the connection between sex and harm comes from Robert J. Stoller. Stoller thinks that sexual excitement is linked with a wish to harm someone (and with at least a whisper of hostility). The key process of sexual excitement can be seen as dehumanization (fetishization) in fantasy of the desired person. He speculates that this is true in some degree of everyone, both men and women, with "normal" or "perverted" activities and fantasies.[7]

Thinking of sex objects as harmed objects enables us to explain some of the first three reasons why one wouldn't want to be treated as a sex object: (1) I may object to being treated only as a tennis partner, but being a tennis partner is not connected in our culture with being a harmed object; and (2) I may not think that sex is dirty and that I would be a harmed object; I may not know what your view is; but what bothers me is that this is the view embodied in our language and culture.

Awareness of the connection between sex and harm helps explain other interesting points. Women are angry about being treated as sex objects in situations or roles in which they do not intend to be regarded in that manner—for example, while serving on a committee or attending a discussion. It is not merely that a sexual role is inappropriate for the circumstances; it is thought to be a less fully human role than the one in which they intended to function.

Finally, the sex-harm connection makes clear why it is worse to treat women as sex objects than to treat men as sex objects, and why some men have had difficulty understanding women's anger about the matter. It is more difficult for heterosexual men than for women to assume the role of "harmed object" in sex; for men have the self-concept of sexual agents, not of passive objects. This is also related to my earlier point concerning the difference in the solidity of respect for men and for women; respect for women is more fragile. Despite exceptions, it is generally harder for people to degrade men, either sexually or nonsexually, than to degrade women. Men and women have grown up with different patterns of self-respect and expectations regarding the extent to which they deserve and will receive respect or degradation. The man who doesn't understand why women do not want to be treated as sex objects (because he'd sure like to be) would not think of himself as being harmed by that treatment; a woman might.[8] Pornography, probably more than any other contemporary institution, succeeds in treating men as sex objects.

Having seen that the connection between sex and harm helps explain both what is wrong with treating someone as a sex object and why it is worse to treat a woman in this way, I want to use the sex-harm connection to try to resolve a dispute about pornography and women. Brownmiller's view, remember, was that pornography is "the undiluted essence of anti-female propaganda" whose purpose is to degrade women. Some people object to Brownmiller's view by saying that, since pornography treats both men and women as sex objects for the purpose of arousing the viewer, it is neither sexist, antifemale, nor designed to degrade women; it just happens that degrading of women arouses some men. How can this dispute be resolved?

Suppose we were to rate the content of all pornography from most morally objectionable to least morally objectionable. Among the most objectionable would be the most degrading—for example, "snuff" films and movies which recommend that men rape women, molest children and puppies, and treat nonmasochists very sadistically.

Next we would find a large amount of material (probably most pornography) not quite so blatantly offensive. With this material it is relevant to use the analysis of sex objects given above. As long as sex is connected with harm done to women, it will be very difficult not to see pornography as degrading to women. We can agree with

Brownmiller's opponent that pornography treats men as sex objects, too, but we maintain that this is only pseudoequality: such treatment is still more degrading to women.[9]

In addition, pornography often exemplifies the active/passive, harmer/harmed object roles in a very obvious way. Because pornography today is male-oriented and is supposed to make a profit, the content is designed to appeal to male fantasies. Judging from the content of the most popular legally available pornography, male fantasies still run along the lines of stereotypical sex roles— and, if Stoller is right, include elements of hostility. In much pornography the women's purpose is to cater to male desires, to service the man or men. Her own pleasure is rarely emphasized for its own sake; she is merely allowed a little heavy breathing, perhaps in order to show her dependence on the great male "lover" who produces her pleasure. In addition, women are clearly made into passive objects in still photographs showing only close-ups of their genitals. Even in movies marketed to appeal to heterosexual couples, such as *Behind the Green Door,* the woman is passive and undemanding (and in this case kidnapped and hypnotized as well). Although many kinds of specialty magazines and films are gauged for different sexual tastes, very little contemporary pornography goes against traditional sex roles. There is certainly no significant attempt to replace the harmer/harmed distinction with anything more positive and healthy. In some stag movies, of course, men are treated sadistically by women; but this is an attempt to turn the tables on degradation, not a positive improvement.

What would cases toward the least objectionable end of the spectrum be like? They would be increasingly less degrading and sexist. The genuinely nonobjectionable cases would be nonsexist and nondegrading; but commercial examples do not readily spring to mind.[10] The question is: Does or could any pornography have nonsexist, nondegrading content?

I want to start with the easier question: Is it possible for pornography to have nonsexist, morally acceptable content? Then I will consider whether any pornography of this sort currently exists.

Imagine the following situation, which exists only rarely today: Two fairly conventional people who love each other enjoy playing tennis and bridge together, cooking good food together, and having sex together. In all these activities they are free from hang-ups, guilt, and tendencies to dominate or objectify each other. These two people like to watch tennis matches and old romantic movies on TV, like to watch Julia Child cook, like to read the bridge column in the newspaper, and like to watch pornographic movies. Imagine further that this couple is not at all uncommon in society and that nonsexist pornography is as common as this kind of nonsexist sexual relationship. This situation sounds fine and healthy to me. I see no reason to think that an interest in pornography would disappear in these circumstances. People seem to enjoy watching others experience or do (especially do well) what they enjoy experiencing, doing, or wish they could do themselves. We do not morally object to people watching tennis on TV; why would we object to these hypothetical people watching pornography?

Can we go from the situation today to the situation just imagined? In much current pornography, people are treated in morally objectionable ways. In the scene just imagined, however, pornography would be nonsexist, nondegrading, morally acceptable. The key to making the change is to break the connection between sex and harm. If Stoller is right, this task may be impossible without changing the scenarios of our sexual lives—scenarios that we have been writing since early childhood. (Stoller does not indicate whether he thinks it possible for adults to rewrite their scenarios or for social change to bring about the possibility of new scenarios in future generations.) But even if we believe that people can change their sexual scenarios, the sex-harm connection is deeply entrenched and has widespread implications. What is needed is a thorough change in people's deep-seated attitudes and feelings about sex roles in general, as well as about sex and roles in sex (sexual roles). Although I cannot even sketch a general outline of such changes here, changes in pornography should be part of a comprehensive program. Television, children's educational material, and nonpornographic movies and novels may be far better avenues for attempting to change attitudes; but one does not want to take the chance that pornography is working against one.

What can be done about pornography in particular? If one wanted to work within the current institutions, one's attempt to use pornography as a tool for the education of male pornography audiences would have to be fairly subtle at first; nonsexist pornography must become familiar enough to sell and be watched. One should realize too that any positive educational value that nonsexist pornography might have may well be as short-lived as most of the effects of pornography. But given these limitations, what could one do?

Two kinds of films must be considered. First is the short film with no plot or character development, just depicted sexual activity in which nonsexist pornography would treat men and women as equal sex partners.[11] The man would not control the circumstances in which the partners had sex or the choice of positions or acts; the woman's preference would be counted equally. There would be no suggestion of a power play or conquest on the man's part, no suggestion that "she likes it when I hurt her." Sexual intercourse would not be portrayed as primarily for the purpose of male ejaculation—his orgasm is not "the best part" of the movie. In addition, both the man and woman would express their enjoyment; the man need not be cool and detached.

The film with a plot provides even more opportunity for nonsexist education. Today's pornography often portrays the female characters as playthings even when not engaging in sexual activity. Nonsexist pornography could show women and men in roles equally valued by society, and sex equality would amount to more than possession of equally functional genitalia. Characters would customarily treat each other with respect and consideration, with no attempt to treat men or women brutally or thoughtlessly. The local Pussycat Theater showed a film written and directed by a woman (*The Passions of Carol*), which exhibited a few of the features just mentioned. The main female character in it was the editor of a magazine parody of *Viva*. The fact that some of the characters treated each other very nicely, warmly, and tenderly did not detract from the pornographic features of the movie. This should not surprise us, for even in traditional male-oriented films, lesbian scenes usually exhibit tenderness and kindness.

Plots for nonsexist films could include women in traditionally male jobs (e.g., long-distance truckdriver) or in positions usually held in respect by pornography audiences. For example, a high-ranking female Army officer, treated with respect by men and women alike, could be shown not only in various sexual encounters with other people but also carrying out her job in a humane manner.[12] Or perhaps the main character could be a female urologist. She could interact with nurses and other medical personnel, diagnose illnesses brilliantly, and treat patients with great sympathy as well as have sex with them. When the Army officer or the urologist engages in sexual activities, [she] will treat [her] partners and be treated by them in some of the considerate ways described above.

In the circumstances we imagined at the beginning of [this part of the] paper, our nonsexist films could be appreciated in the proper spirit. Under these conditions the content of our new pornography would clearly be nonsexist and morally acceptable. But would the content of such a film be morally acceptable if shown to a typical pornography audience today? It might seem strange for us to change our moral evaluation of the content on the basis of a different audience, but an audience today is likely to see the "respected" urologist and Army officer as playthings or unusual prostitutes—even if our intention in showing the film is to counteract this view. The effect is that, although the content of the film seems morally acceptable and our intention in showing it is morally flawless, women are still degraded.[13] The fact that audience attitude is so important makes one wary of giving wholehearted approval to any pornography seen today.

The fact that good intentions and content are insufficient does not imply that one's efforts toward change would be entirely in vain. Of course, I could not deny that anyone who tries to change an institution from within faces serious difficulties. This is particularly evident when one is trying to change both pornography and a whole set of related attitudes, feelings, and institutions concerning sex and sex roles. But in conjunction with other attempts to change this set of attitudes, it seems preferable to try to change pornography instead of closing one's eyes in the hope that it will go away. For I suspect that pornography is here to stay.

## Notes

This article first appeared in *Social Theory and Practice*, vol. 4 (Summer 1978), pp. 395–421. It is reprinted here, by permission of the author, as it appears in *Philosophy and Women*, edited by Sharon Bishop and Majorie Weinzweig (Belmont, Calif.: Wadsworth, 1979).

1. New York: Simon and Schuster, 1975, p. 394.

2. *The Report of the Commission on Obscenity and Pornography* (Washington, D.C., 1970), p. 201.

3. In order to help one determine which position one feels inclined to take, consider the following statement: It is morally objectionable to write, make, sell, act in, use, and enjoy pornography; in addition, the content of pornography is immoral; however, pornography itself is not morally objectionable. If this statement seems extremely problematic, then one might well be satisfied with the claim that pornography is degrading because its content is.

4. Many feminists point this out. One of the most accessible references is Shulamith Firestone, *The Dialectic of Sex: The Case for the Feminist Revolution* (New York: Bantam, 1970), especially pp. 128–32.

5. In Richard Wasserstrom, ed., *Today's Moral Problems* (New York: Macmillan, 1975), pp. 152–71; see pp. 167–71. Also in Robert Baker and Frederick Elliston, eds., *Philosophy and Sex* (Buffalo, N.Y.: Prometheus Books, 1975).

6. Baker, in Wasserstrom, *Today's Moral Problems,* pp. 168–169.

7. "Sexual Excitement," *Archives of General Psychiatry* 3 (1976): 899–909, especially p. 903. The extent to which Stoller sees men and women in different positions with respect to harm and hostility is not clear. He often treats men and women alike, but in *Perversion: The Erotic Form of Hatred* (New York: Pantheon, 1975), pp. 89–91, he calls attention to differences between men and women especially regarding their responses to pornography and lack of understanding by men of women's sexuality. Given that Stoller finds hostility to be an essential element in male-oriented pornography, and given that women have not

responded readily to such pornography, one can speculate about the possibilities for women's sexuality: their hostility might follow a different scenario; they might not be as hostile, and so on.

8. Men seem to be developing more sensitivity to being treated as sex objects. Many homosexual men have long understood the problem. As women become more sexually aggressive, some heterosexual men I know are beginning to feel treated as sex objects. A man can feel that he is not being taken seriously if a woman looks lustfully at him while he is holding forth about the French judicial system or the failure of liberal politics. Some of his most important talents are not being properly valued.

9. I don't agree with Brownmiller that the purpose of pornography is to dehumanize women; rather it is to arouse the audience. The differences between our views can be explained, in part, by the points from which we begin. She is writing about rape; her views about pornography grow out of her views about rape. I begin by thinking of pornography as merely depicted sexual activity, though I am well aware of the male hostility and contempt for women that it often expresses. That pornography degrades women and excites men is an illustration of this contempt.

10. Virginia Wright Wexman uses the film *Group Marriage* (Stephanie Rothman, 1973) as an example of "more enlightened erotica." Wexman also asks the following questions in an attempt to point out sexism in pornographic films:

> Does it [the film] portray rape as pleasurable to women? Does it consistently show females nude but present men

fully clothed? Does it present women as childlike creatures whose sexual interests must be guided by knowing experienced men? Does it show sexually aggressive women as castrating viragos? Does it pretend that sex is exclusively the prerogative of women under twenty-five? Does it focus on the physical aspects of lovemaking, rather than the emotional ones? Does it portray women as purely sexual beings? ("Sexism of X-rated Films," *Chicago Sun-Times,* 28 March 1976.)

11. If it is a lesbian or male homosexual film, no one would play a caricatured male or female role. The reader has probably noticed that I have limited my discussion to heterosexual pornography, but there are many interesting analogies to be drawn with male homosexual pornography. Very little lesbian pornography exists, though lesbian scenes are commonly found in male-oriented pornography.

12. One should note that behavior of this kind is still considered unacceptable by the military. A female officer resigned from the U.S. Navy recently rather than be court-martialed for having sex with several enlisted men whom she met in a class on interpersonal relations.

13. The content may seem morally acceptable only if one disregards such questions as, "Should a doctor have sex with her patients during office hours?" More important is the propriety of evaluating content wholly apart from the attitudes and reactions of the audience; one might not find it strange to say that one film has morally unacceptable content when shown tonight at the Pussycat Theater but acceptable content when shown tomorrow at a feminist conference.

# 35    Liberty and Pornography

## RONALD DWORKIN

Through the efforts of Catharine MacKinnon, a professor of law at the University of Michigan, and other prominent feminists, Indianapolis, Indiana, enacted an antipornography ordinance. The ordinance defined pornography as "the graphic sexually explicit subordination of women, whether in pictures or words . . ." and it specified, as among pornographic materials falling within that definition, those that present women as

Reprinted with permission of the publisher from *The New York Review of Books.* Copyright © 1993 NYREV, Inc.

enjoying pain or humiliation or rape, or as degraded or tortured or filthy, bruised or bleeding, or in postures of servility or submission or display. It included no exception for literary or artistic value, and opponents claimed that applied literally it would outlaw James Joyce's *Ulysses,* John Cleland's *Memoirs of a Woman of Pleasure,* various works of D. H. Lawrence, and even Yeats's "Leda and the Swan." But the groups who sponsored the ordinance were anxious to establish that their objection was not to obscenity or indecency as such, but to the consequences for women of a particular kind of pornography, and they presumably thought that an exception for artistic value would undermine that claim.[1]

The ordinance did not simply regulate the display of pornography so defined, or restrict its sale or distribution to particular areas, or guard against the exhibition of pornography to children. Regulation for those purposes does restrain negative liberty, but if reasonable it does so in a way compatible with free speech. Zoning and display regulations may make pornography more expensive or inconvenient to obtain, but they do not offend the principle that no one must be prevented from publishing or reading what he or she wishes on the ground that its content is immoral or offensive.[2] The Indianapolis ordinance, on the other hand, prohibited any "production, sale, exhibition, or distribution" whatever of the material it defined as pornographic.

Publishers and members of the public who claimed a desire to read the banned material arranged a prompt constitutional challenge. The federal district court held that the ordinance was unconstitutional because it violated the First Amendment to the United States Constitution, which guarantees the negative liberty of free speech.[3] The Circuit Court for the Seventh Circuit upheld the district court's decision,[4] and the Supreme Court of the United States declined to review that holding. The Circuit Court's decision, in an opinion by Judge Easterbrook, noticed that the ordinance did not outlaw obscene or indecent material generally but only material reflecting the opinion that women are submissive, or enjoy being dominated, or should be treated as if they did. Easterbrook said that the central point of the First Amendment was exactly to protect speech from content-based regulation of that sort. Censorship may on some occasions be permitted if it aims to prohibit directly dangerous speech—crying fire in a crowded theater or inciting a crowd to violence, for example—or speech particularly and unnecessarily inconvenient—broadcasting from sound trucks patrolling residential streets at night, for instance. But nothing must be censored, Easterbrook wrote, because the message it seeks to deliver is a bad one, or because it expresses ideas that should not be heard at all.

It is by no means universally agreed that censorship should never be based on content. The British Race Relations Act, for example, forbids speech of racial hatred, not only when it is likely to lead to violence, but generally, on the grounds that members of minority races should be protected from racial insults. In America, however, it is a fixed principle of constitutional law that such regulation is unconstitutional unless some compelling necessity, not just official or majority disapproval of the message, requires it. Pornography is often grotesquely offensive; it is insulting, not only to women but to men as well. But we cannot consider that a sufficient reason for banning it without destroying the principle that the speech we hate is as much entitled to protection as any other. The essence of negative liberty is freedom to offend, and that applies to the tawdry as well as the heroic.

Lawyers who defend the Indianapolis ordinance argue that society does have a further justification for outlawing pornography: that it causes great harm as well as offense to women. But their arguments mix together claims about different types or kinds of harm, and it is necessary to distinguish these. They argue, first, that some forms of pornography significantly increase the danger that women will be raped or physically assaulted. If that were true, and the danger were clear and present, then it would indeed justify censorship of those forms, unless less stringent methods of control, such as restricting pornography's audience, would be feasible, appropriate, and effective. In fact, however, though there is some evidence that exposure to pornography weakens people's critical attitudes toward sexual violence, there is no persuasive evidence that it causes more actual incidents of assault. The Seventh Circuit cited a variety of studies (including that of the Williams Commission in Britain in 1979), all of which concluded, the court said, "that it is not possible to demonstrate a direct link between obscenity and rape. . . ."[5] A recent report based on a year's research in Britain said: "The evidence does not point to pornography as a cause of deviant sexual orientation in offenders. Rather, it seems to be used as part of that deviant sexual orientation."[6]

Some feminist groups argue, however, that pornography causes not just physical violence but a more general and endemic subordination of women. In that way, they say, pornography makes for inequality. But even if it could be shown, as a matter of causal connection, that pornography is in part responsible for the economic structure in which few women attain top jobs or equal pay for the same work, that would not justify censorship under the Constitution. It would plainly be unconstitutional to ban speech directly *advocating* that women occupy inferior roles, or none at all, in commerce and the professions, even if that speech fell on willing male ears and achieved its goals. So it cannot be a reason for banning pornography that it contributes to an unequal economic or social structure, even if we think that it does.

But the most imaginative feminist literature for censorship makes a further and different argument: that negative liberty for pornographers conflicts not just with equality but with positive liberty as well, because pornography leads to women's *political* as well as economic or social subordination. Of course pornography does not take the vote from women, or somehow make their votes count less. But it produces a climate, according to this argument, in which women cannot have genuine political power or authority because they are perceived and understood unauthentically—that is, they are made over by male fantasy into people very different from, and of much less consequence than, the people they really are. Consider, for example, these remarks from the work of the principal sponsor of the Indianapolis ordinance. "[Pornography] institutionalizes the sexuality of male supremacy, fusing the eroticization of dominance and submission with the social construction of male and female. . . . Men treat women as who they see women as being. Pornography constructs who that is. Men's power over women means that the way men see women defines who women can be."[7]

Pornography, on this view, denies the positive liberty of women; it denies them the right to be their own masters by recreating them, for politics and society, in the shapes of male fantasy. That is a powerful argument, even in constitutional terms, because it asserts a conflict not just between liberty and equality but within liberty itself, that is, a conflict that cannot be resolved simply on the ground that liberty must be sovereign. What shall we make of the argument understood that way? We must notice, first, that it remains a causal argument. It claims not that pornography is a consequence or symptom or symbol of how the identity of women has been reconstructed by men, but an important cause or vehicle of that reconstruction.

That seems strikingly implausible. Sadistic pornography is revolting, but it is not in general circulation, except for its milder, soft-porn manifestations. It seems unlikely that it has remotely the influence over how women's sexuality or character or talents are conceived by men, and indeed by women, that commercial advertising and soap operas have. Television and other parts of popular culture use sexual display and sexual innuendo to sell virtually everything, and they often show women as experts in domestic detail and unreasoned intuition and nothing else. The images they create are subtle and ubiquitous, and it would not be surprising to learn, through whatever research might establish this, that they indeed do great damage to the way women are understood and allowed to be influential in politics. Sadistic pornography, though much more offensive and disturbing, is greatly overshadowed by these dismal cultural influences as a causal force.

Judge Easterbrook's opinion for the Seventh Circuit assumed, for the sake of argument, however, that pornography did have the consequences the defenders of the ordinance claimed. He said that the argument nevertheless failed because the point of free speech is precisely to allow ideas to have whatever consequences follow from their dissemination, including undesirable consequences for positive liberty. "Under the First Amendment," he said, "the government must leave to the people the evaluation of ideas. Bald or subtle, an idea is as powerful as the audience allows it to be. . . . [The assumed result] simply demonstrates the power of pornography as speech. All of these unhappy effects depend on mental intermediation."

That is right as a matter of American constitutional law. The Ku Klux Klan and the American Nazi party are allowed to propagate their ideas in America, and the British Race Relations Act, so far as it forbids abstract speech of racial hatred, would be unconstitutional in the U.S. But does the American attitude represent the kind of Platonic absolutism Berlin warned against? No, because there is an important difference between the idea he thinks absurd, that all ideals attractive in themselves can be perfectly reconciled within a single utopian political order, and the different idea he thought essential, that we must, as individuals and nations, choose, among possible combinations of ideals, a coherent, even though inevitably and regrettably limited, set of these to define our own individual or national way of life. Freedom of speech, conceived and protected as a fundamental negative liberty, is the core of the choice modern democracies have made, a choice we must now honor in finding our own ways to combat the shaming inequalities women still suffer.

This reply depends, however, on seeing the alleged conflict within liberty as a conflict between the negative and positive senses of that virtue. We must consider yet another argument which, if successful, could not be met in the same way, because it claims that pornography presents a conflict within the negative liberty of speech itself. Berlin said that the character, at least, of negative liberty was reasonably clear, that although excessive claims of negative liberty were dangerous, they could at least always be seen for what they were. But the argument I have in mind, which has been offered by, among others, Frank Michelman of the Harvard Law School, expands the idea of negative liberty in an unanticipated way. He argues that some speech, including pornography, may be itself "silencing," so that its effect is to prevent other people from exercising their negative freedom to speak.

Of course it is fully recognized in First Amendment jurisprudence that some speech has the effect of silencing others. Government must

indeed balance negative liberties when it prevents heckling or other demonstrative speech designed to stop others from speaking or being heard. But Michelman has something different in mind. He says that a woman's speech may be silenced not just by noise intended to drown her out but also by argument and images that change her audience's perceptions of her character, needs, desires, and standing, and also, perhaps, change her own sense of who she is and what she wants. Speech with that consequence silences her, Michelman supposes, by making it impossible for her effectively to contribute to the process Judge Easterbrook said the First Amendment protected, the process through which ideas battle for the public's favor. "[It] is a highly plausible claim," Michelman writes, "[that] pornography [is] a cause of women's subordination and silencing. . . . It is a fair and obvious question why our society's openness to challenge does not need protection against repressive private as well as public action."[8]

He argues that if our commitment to negative freedom of speech is consequentialist—if we want free speech in order to have a society in which no idea is barred from entry—then we must censor some ideas in order to make entry possible for other ones. He protests that the distinction that American constitutional law makes between the suppression of ideas by the effect of public criminal law and by the consequences of private speech is arbitrary, and that a sound concern for openness would be equally worried about both forms of control. But the distinction the law makes is not between public and private power as such, but between negative liberty and other virtues, including positive liberty. It would indeed be contradictory for a constitution to prohibit official censorship while protecting the right of private citizens physically to prevent other citizens from publishing or broadcasting specified ideas. That would allow private citizens to violate the negative liberty of other citizens by preventing them from saying what they wish.

But there is no contradiction in insisting that every idea must be allowed to be heard, even those whose consequence is that other ideas will be misunderstood, or given little consideration, or even not be spoken at all because those who might speak them are not in control of their own public identities and therefore cannot be understood as they wish to be. These are very bad consequences, and they must be resisted by whatever means our Constitution permits. But acts that have these consequences do not, for that reason, deprive others of their negative liberty to speak, and the distinction, as Berlin insisted, is very far from arbitrary or inconsequential.

It is of course understandable why Michelman and others should want to expand the idea of negative liberty in the way they try to do. Only by characterizing certain ideas as themselves "silencing" ideas—only supposing that censoring pornography is the same thing as stopping people from drowning out other speakers—can they hope to justify censorship within the constitutional scheme that assigns a preeminent place to free speech. But the assimilation is nevertheless a confusion because it obscures the true political choice that must be made. [Isaiah Berlin] put the point with a striking combination of clarity and sweep:

I should be guilt-stricken, and rightly so, if I were not, in some circumstances, ready to make [some] sacrifice [of freedom]. But a sacrifice is not an increase in what is being sacrificed, namely freedom, however great the moral need or the compensation for it. Everything is what it is: liberty, not equality or fairness or justice or culture, or human happiness or a quiet conscience.[9]

## Notes

1. MacKinnon explained that "if a woman is subjected, why should it matter that the work has other value?" See her article "Pornography, Civil Rights, and Speech," in *Harvard Civil Rights–Civil Liberties Law Review,* Vol. 28, p. 21.

2. See my article "Do We Have a Right to Pornography?" reprinted as Chapter 17 in my book *A Matter of Principle* (Harvard University Press, 1985).

3. *American Booksellers Association, Inc. et al. v. William H. Hudnut, III, Mayor, City of Indianapolis, et al.,* 598 F. Supp. 1316 (S.D. Ind. 1984).

4. 771 F. 2d 323 (US Court of Appeals, Seventh Circuit).

5. That court, in a confused passage, said that it nevertheless accepted "the premises of this legislation," which included the claims about a causal connection with sexual violence. But it seemed to mean that it was accepting the rather different causal claim considered in the next paragraph, about subordination. In any case, it said that it accepted those premises only for the sake of argument, since it thought it had no authority to reject decisions of Indianapolis based on its interpretation of empirical evidence.

6. See the *Daily Telegraph,* December 23, 1990. Of course further studies might contradict this assumption. But it seems very unlikely that pornography will be found to stimulate physical violence to the overall extent that non-pornographic depictions of violence, which are much more pervasive in our media and culture, do.

7. See MacKinnon's article cited in note 1.

8. Frank Michelman, "Conceptions of Democracy in American Constitutional Argument: The Case of Pornography Regulation." *Tennessee Law Review,* Vol. 56, No. 291 (1989), pp. 303–304.

9. Isaiah Berlin, *Four Essays on Liberty* (Oxford University Press, 1968).

# 36   Pornography, Civil Rights and Speech

## CATHARINE MACKINNON

. . . There is a belief that this is a society in which women and men are basically equals. Room for marginal corrections is conceded, flaws are known

Reprinted with permission of the publisher from *Feminism Unmodified* by Catharine MacKinnon, Cambridge, MA: Harvard University Press, © 1987, 168–195, with omissions.

to exist, attempts are made to correct what are conceived as occasional lapses from the basic condition of sex equality. Sex discrimination law has concentrated most of its focus on these occasional lapses. It is difficult to overestimate the extent to which this belief in equality is an article of faith for most people, including most women, who wish to live in self-respect in an internal universe, even (perhaps especially) if not in the world. It is also partly an expression of natural law thinking: if we are inalienably equal, we can't "really" be degraded.

This is a world in which it is worth trying. In this world of presumptive equality, people make money based on their training or abilities or diligence or qualifications. They are employed and advanced on the basis of merit. In this world of just deserts, if someone is abused, it is thought to violate the basic rules of the community. If it doesn't, victims are seen to have done something they could have chosen to do differently, by exercise of will or better judgment. Maybe such people have placed themselves in a situation of vulnerability to physical abuse. Maybe they have done something provocative. Or maybe they were just unusually unlucky. In such a world, if such a person has an experience, there are words for it. When they speak and say it, they are listened to. If they write about it, they will be published. If certain experiences are never spoken about, if certain people or issues are seldom heard from, it is supposed that silence has been chosen. The law, including much of the law of sex discrimination and the First Amendment, operates largely within the realm of these beliefs.

Feminism is the discovery that women do not live in this world, that the person occupying this realm is a man, so much more a man if he is white and wealthy. This world of potential credibility, authority, security, and just rewards, recognition of one's identity and capacity, is a world that some people do inhabit as a condition of birth, with variations among them. It is not a basic condition accorded humanity in this society, but a prerogative of status, a privilege, among other things, of gender.

I call this a discovery because it has not been an assumption. Feminism is the first theory, the first practice, the first movement, to take seriously the situation of all women from the point of view of all women, both on our situation and on social life as a whole. The discovery has therefore been made that the implicit social content of humanism, as well as the standpoint from which legal method has been designed and injuries have been defined, has not been women's standpoint. Defin-

ing feminism in a way that connects epistemology with power as the politics of women's point of view, this discovery can be summed up by saying that women live in another world: specifically, a world of *not* equality, a world of inequality.

Looking at the world from this point of view, a whole shadow world of previously invisible silent abuse has been discerned. Rape, battery, sexual harassment, forced prostitution, and the sexual abuse of children emerge as common and systematic. We find that rape happens to women in all contexts, from the family, including rape of girls and babies, to students and women in the workplace, on the streets, at home, in their own bedrooms by men they do not know and by men they do know, by men they are married to, men they have had a social conversation with, and, least often, men they have never seen before. Overwhelmingly, rape is something that men do or attempt to do to women (44 percent of American women according to a recent study) at some point in our lives. Sexual harassment of women by men is common in workplaces and educational institutions. Based on reports in one study of the federal workforce, up to 85 percent of women will experience it, many in physical forms. Between a quarter and a third of women are battered in their homes by men. Thirty-eight percent of little girls are sexually molested inside or outside the family. Until women listened to women, this world of sexual abuse was *not spoken* of. It was the unspeakable. What I am saying is, if you *are* the tree falling in the epistemological forest, your demise doesn't make a sound if no one is listening. Women did not "report" these events, and overwhelmingly do not today, because no one is listening, because no one believes us. This silence does not mean nothing happened, and it does not mean consent. It is the silence of women of which Adrienne Rich has written, "Do not confuse it with any kind of absence."

Believing women who say we are sexually violated has been a radical departure, both methodologically and legally. The extent and nature of rape, marital rape, and sexual harassment itself, were discovered in this way. Domestic battery as a syndrome, almost a habit, was discovered through refusing to believe that when a woman is assaulted by a man to whom she is connected, that it is not an assault. The sexual abuse of children was uncovered, Freud notwithstanding, by believing that children were not making up all this sexual abuse. Now what is striking is that when each discovery is made, and somehow made real in the world, the response has been: it happens to men too. If women are hurt, men are hurt. If women are raped, men are raped. If women are sexually harassed, men are sexually harassed. If women are battered, men are battered. Symmetry must be reasserted. Neutrality must be reclaimed. Equality must be reestablished.

The only areas where the available evidence supports this, where anything like what happens to women also happens to men, involve children —little boys are sexually abused—and prison. The liberty of prisoners is restricted, their freedom restrained, their humanity systematically diminished, their bodies and emotions confined, defined, and regulated. If paid at all, they are paid starvation wages. They can be tortured at will, and it is passed off as discipline or as means to a just end. They become compliant. They can be raped at will, at any moment, and nothing will be done about it. When they scream, nobody hears. To be a prisoner means to be defined as a member of a group for whom the rules of what can be done to you, of what is seen as abuse of you, are reduced as part of the definition of your status. To be a woman is that kind of definition and has that kind of meaning.

Men *are* damaged by sexism. (By men I mean the status of masculinity that is accorded to males on the basis of their biology but is not itself biological.) But whatever the damage of sexism to men, the condition of being a man is not defined as subordinate to women by force. Looking at the facts of the abuses of women all at once, you see that a woman is socially defined as a person who, whether or not she is or has been, can be treated in these ways by men at any time, and little, if anything, will be done about it. This is what it means when feminists say that maleness is a form of power and femaleness is a form of powerlessness.

In this context, all of this "men too" stuff means that people don't really believe that the

things I have just said are true, though there really is little question about their empirical accuracy. The data are extremely simple, like women's pay figure of fifty-nine cents on the dollar. People don't really seem to believe that either. Yet there is no question of its empirical validity. This is the workplace story: what women do is seen as not worth much, or what is not worth much is seen as something for women to do. *Women* are seen as not worth much, is the thing. Now why are these basic realities of the subordination of women to men, for example, that only 7.8 percent of women have never been sexually assaulted, not effectively believed, not perceived as real in the face of all this evidence? Why don't *women* believe our own experiences? In the face of all this evidence, especially of systematic sexual abuse—subjection to violence with impunity is one extreme expression, although not the only expression, of a degraded status—the view that basically the sexes are equal in this society remains unchallenged and unchanged. The day I got this was the day I understood its real message, its real coherence: *This is equality for us.*

I could describe this, but I couldn't explain it until I started studying a lot of pornography. In pornography, there it is, in one place, all of the abuses that women had to struggle so long even to begin to articulate, all the *unspeakable* abuse: the rape, the battery, the sexual harassment, the prostitution, and the sexual abuse of children. Only in the pornography it is called something else: sex, sex, sex, sex, and sex, respectively. Pornography sexualizes rape, battery, sexual harassment, prostitution, and child sexual abuse; it thereby celebrates, promotes, authorizes, and legitimizes them. More generally, it eroticizes the dominance and submission that is the dynamic common to them all. It makes hierarchy sexy and calls that "the truth about sex" or just a mirror of reality. Through this process pornography constructs what a woman is as what men want from sex. This is what the pornography means.

Pornography constructs what a woman is in terms of its view of what men want sexually, such that acts of rape, battery, sexual harassment, prostitution, and sexual abuse of children become acts of sexual equality. Pornography's world of equality is a harmonious and balanced place. Men and women are perfectly complementary and perfectly bipolar. Women's desire to be fucked by men is equal to men's desire to fuck women. All the ways men love to take and violate women, women love to be taken and violated. The women who most love this are most men's equals, the most liberated; the most participatory child is the most grown-up, the most equal to an adult. Their consent merely expresses or ratifies these preexisting facts.

The content of pornography is one thing. There, women substantively desire dispossession and cruelty. We desperately want to be bound, battered, tortured, humiliated, and killed. Or, to be fair to the soft core, merely taken and used. This is erotic to the male point of view. Subjection itself, with self-determination ecstatically relinquished, is the content of women's sexual desire and desirability. Women are there to be violated and possessed, men to violate and possess us, either on screen or by camera or pen on behalf of the consumer. On a simple descriptive level, the inequality of hierarchy, of which gender is the primary one, seems necessary for sexual arousal to work. Other added inequalities identify various pornographic genres or subthemes, although they are always added through gender: age, disability, homosexuality, animals, objects, race (including anti-Semitism), and so on. Gender is never irrelevant.

What pornography *does* goes beyond its content: it eroticizes hierarchy, it sexualizes inequality. It makes dominance and submission into sex. Inequality is its central dynamic; the illusion of freedom coming together with the reality of force is central to its working. Perhaps because this is a bourgeois culture, the victim must look free, appear to be freely acting. Choice is how she got there. Willing is what she is when she is being equal. It seems equally important that then and there she actually be forced and that forcing be communicated on some level, even if only through still photos of her in postures of receptivity and access, available for penetration. Pornography in this view is a form of forced sex, a

practice of sexual politics, an institution of gender inequality.

From this perspective, pornography is neither harmless fantasy nor a corrupt and confused misrepresentation of an otherwise natural and healthy sexual situation. It institutionalizes the sexuality of male supremacy, fusing the erotization of dominance and submission with the social construction of male and female. To the extent that gender is sexual, pornography is part of constituting the meaning of that sexuality. Men treat women as who they see women as being. Pornography constructs who that is. Men's power over women means that the way men see women defines who women can be. Pornography is that way. Pornography is not imagery in some relation to a reality elsewhere constructed. It is not a distortion, reflection, projection, expression, fantasy, representation, or symbol either. It is a sexual reality.

In Andrea Dworkin's definitive work, *Pornography: Men Possessing Women,* sexuality itself is a social construct gendered to the ground. Male dominance here is not an artificial overlay upon an underlying inalterable substratum of uncorrupted essential sexual being. Dworkin presents a sexual theory of gender inequality of which pornography is a constitutive practice. The way pornography produces its meaning constructs and defines men and women as such. Gender has no basis in anything other than the social reality its hegemony constructs. Gender is what gender means. The process that gives sexuality its male supremacist meaning is the same process through which gender inequality becomes socially real.

In this approach, the experience of the (overwhelmingly) male audiences who consume pornography is therefore not fantasy or simulation or catharsis but sexual reality, the level of reality on which sex itself largely operates. Understanding this dimension of the problem does not require noticing that pornography models are real women to whom, in most cases, something real is being done; nor does it even require inquiring into the systematic infliction of pornography and its sexuality upon women, although it helps. What matters is the way in which the pornography itself provides what those who consume it want.

Pornography *participates* in its audience's eroticism through creating an accessible sexual object, the possession and consumption of which *is* male sexuality, as socially constructed; to be consumed and possessed as which, *is* female sexuality, as socially constructed; pornography is a process that constructs it that way.

The object world is constructed according to how it looks with respect to its possible uses. Pornography defines women by how we look according to how we can be sexually used. Pornography codes how to look at women, so you know what you can do with one when you see one. Gender is an assignment made visually, both originally and in everyday life. A sex object is defined on the basis of its looks, in terms of its usability for sexual pleasure, such that both the looking—the quality of the gaze, including its point of view—and the definition according to use become eroticized as part of the sex itself. This is what the feminist concept "sex object" means. In this sense, sex in life is no less mediated than it is in art. Men have sex with their image of a woman. It is not that life and art imitate each other; in this sexuality, they *are* each other.

To give a set of rough epistemological translations, to defend pornography as consistent with the equality of the sexes is to defend the subordination of women to men as sexual equality. What in the pornographic view is love and romance looks a great deal like hatred and torture to the feminist. Pleasure and eroticism become violation. Desire appears as lust for dominance and submission. The vulnerability of women's projected sexual availability, that acting we are allowed (that is, asking to be acted upon), is victimization. Play conforms to scripted roles. Fantasy expresses ideology, is not exempt from it. Admiration of natural physical beauty becomes objectification. Harmlessness becomes harm. Pornography is a harm of male supremacy made difficult to see because of its pervasiveness, potency, and, principally, because of its success in making the world a pornographic place. Specifically, its harm cannot be discerned, and will not be addressed, if viewed and approached neutrally, because it *is* so much of "what is." In other words, to the extent pornography succeeds in constructing social reality, it becomes invisible as harm. If we live in a world that pornography creates through the power of men in a male-dominated situation, the issue is not what the harm of pornography is, but how that harm is to become visible.

Obscenity law provides a very different analysis and conception of the problem of pornography. In 1973 the legal definition of obscenity became that which the average person, applying contemporary community standards, would find that, taken as a whole, appeals to the prurient interest: that which depicts or describes in a patently offensive way—you feel like you're a cop reading someone's *Miranda* rights—sexual conduct specifically defined by the applicable state law; and that which, taken as a whole, lacks serious literary, artistic, political or scientific value. Feminism doubts whether the average person genderneutral exists; has more questions about the content and process of defining what community standards are than it does about deviations from them; wonders why prurience counts but powerlessness does not and why sensibilities are better protected from offense than women are from exploitation; defines sexuality, and thus its violation and expropriation, more broadly than does state law; and questions why a body of law that has not in practice been able to tell rape from intercourse should, without further guidance, be entrusted with telling pornography from anything less. Taking the work "as a whole" ignores that which the victims of pornography have long known: legitimate settings diminish the perception of injury done to those whose trivialization and objectification they contextualize. Besides, and this is a heavy one, if a woman is subjected, why should it matter that the work has other value? Maybe what redeems the work's value is what enhances its injury to women, not to mention that existing standards of literature, art, science, and politics, examined in a feminist light, are remarkably consonant with pornography's mode, meaning, and message. And finally—first and foremost, actually—although the subject of these materials is overwhelmingly women, their contents almost entirely made up of women's bodies, our invisibility has been such, our equation as a sex *with* sex has been such, that the law of obscenity has never even considered pornography a women's issue.

Obscenity, in this light, is a moral idea, an idea about judgments of good and bad. Pornography, by contrast, is a political practice, a practice of power and powerlessness. Obscenity is ideational and abstract; pornography is concrete and substantive. The two concepts represent two entirely different things. Nudity, excess of candor, arousal or excitement, prurient appeal, illegality of the acts depicted, and unnaturalness or perversion are all qualities that bother obscenity law when sex is depicted or portrayed. Sex forced on real women so that it can be sold at a profit and forced on other real women; women's bodies trussed and maimed and raped and made into things to be hurt and obtained and accessed, and this presented as the nature of women in a way that is acted on and acted out, over and over; the coercion that is visible and the coercion that has become invisible—this and more bothers feminists about pornography. Obscenity as such probably does little harm. Pornography is integral to attitudes and behaviors of violence and discrimination that define the treatment and status of half the population. . . .

Now I'm going to talk about causality in its narrowest sense. Recent experimental research on pornography shows that the materials covered by our definition cause measurable harm to women through increasing men's attitudes and behaviors of discrimination in both violent and nonviolent forms. Exposure to some of the pornography in our definition increases the immediately subsequent willingness of normal men to aggress against women under laboratory conditions. It makes normal men more closely resemble convicted rapists attitudinally, although as a group they don't look all that different from them to start with. Exposure to pornography also significantly increases attitudinal measures known to correlate with rape and self-reports of aggressive acts, measures such as hostility toward women, propensity to rape, condoning rape, and predicting that one would rape or force sex on a woman if one knew one would not get caught. On this latter measure, by the way, about a third of all men predict that

they would rape, and half would force sex on a woman.

As to that pornography covered by our definition in which normal research subjects seldom perceive violence, long-term exposure still makes them see women as more worthless, trivial, non-human, and objectlike, that is, the way those who are discriminated against are seen by those who discriminate against them. Crucially, all pornography by our definition acts dynamically over time to diminish the consumer's ability to distinguish sex from violence. The materials work behaviorally to diminish the capacity of men (but not women) to perceive that an account of a rape is an account of a rape. The so-called sex-only materials, those in which subjects perceive no force, also increase perceptions that a rape victim is worthless and decrease the perception that she was harmed. The overall direction of current research suggests that the more expressly violent materials accomplish with less exposure what the less overtly violent—that is, the so-called sex-only materials—accomplish over the longer term. Women are rendered fit for use and targeted for abuse. The only thing that the research cannot document is which individual women will be next on that list. (This cannot be documented experimentally because of ethics constraints on the researchers—constraints that do not operate in life.) Although the targeting is systematic on the basis of sex, for individuals it is random. They are selected on a roulette basis. Pornography can no longer be said to be just a mirror. It does not just reflect the world or some people's perceptions. It *moves* them. It increases attitudes that are lived out, circumscribing the status of half the population.

What the experimental data predict will happen actually does happen in women's real lives. You know, it's fairly frustrating that women have known for some time that these things do happen. As Ed Donnerstein, an experimental researcher in this area, often puts it, "We just quantify the obvious." It is women, primarily, to whom the research results have been the obvious, because we live them. But not until a laboratory study predicts that these things *will* happen do people begin to believe you when you say they *did* happen to you. There is no—*not any*—inconsistency between the patterns the laboratory studies predict and the data on what actually happens to real women. Show me an abuse of women in society, I'll show it to you made sex in the pornography. If you want to know who is being hurt in this society, go see what is being done and to whom in pornography and then go look for them other places in the world. You will find them being hurt in just that way. We did in our hearings.

In our hearings women spoke, to my knowledge for the first time in history in public, about the damage pornography does to them. We learned that pornography is used to break women, to train women to sexual submission, to season women, to terrorize women, and to silence their dissent. It is this that has previously been termed "having no effect." The way men inflict on women the sex they experience through the pornography gives women no choice about seeing the pornography or doing the sex. Asked if anyone ever tried to inflict unwanted sex acts on them that they knew came from pornography, 10 percent of women in a recent random study said yes. Among married women, 24 percent said yes. That is a lot of women. A lot more don't know. Some of those who do testified in Minneapolis. One wife said of her ex-husband, "He would read from the pornography like a textbook, like a journal. In fact when he asked me to be bound, when he finally convinced me to do it, he read in the magazine how to tie the knots." Another woman said of her boyfriend, "[H]e went to this party, saw pornography, got an erection, got me . . . to inflict his erection on . . . There is a direct causal relationship there." One woman, who said her husband had rape and bondage magazines all over the house, discovered two suitcases full of Barbie dolls with rope tied on their arms and legs and with tape across their mouths. Now think about the silence of women. She said, "He used to tie me up and he tried those things on me." A therapist in private practice reported:

Presently or recently I have worked with clients who have been sodomized by broom handles, forced to have sex with over 20 dogs in the back seat of their car, tied up and then electrocuted on their genitals. These are children, [all] in the ages of 14 to 18, all of whom [have been directly affected by pornography,] [e]ither where the perpetrator has read the manuals and manuscripts at night and used these as recipe books by day or had the pornography present at the time of the sexual violence.

One woman, testifying that all the women in a group of ex-prostitutes were brought into prostitution as children through pornography, characterized their collective experience: "[I]n my experience there was not one situation where a client was not using pornography while he was using me or that he had not just watched pornography or that it was verbally referred to and directed me to pornography." "Men," she continued, "witness the abuse of women in pornography constantly and if they can't engage in that behavior with their wives, girl friends or children, they force a whore to do it." . . .

Pornography stimulates and reinforces, it does not cathect or mirror, the connection between one-sided freely available sexual access to women and masculine sexual excitement and sexual satisfaction. The catharsis hypothesis is fantasy. The fantasy theory is fantasy. Reality is: pornography conditions male orgasm to female subordination. It tells men what sex means, what a real woman is, and codes them together in a way that is behaviorally reinforcing. This is a real five-dollar sentence, but I'm going to say it anyway: pornography is a set of hermeneutical equivalences that work on the epistemological level. Substantively, pornography defines the meaning of what a woman is seen to be by connecting access to her sexuality with masculinity through orgasm. What pornography means *is* what it does. . . .

Power, as I said, is when you say something, it is taken for reality. If you talk about rape, it will be agreed that rape is awful. But rape is a conclusion. If a victim describes the facts of a rape, maybe she was asking for it or enjoyed it or at least consented to it, or the man might have thought she did, or maybe she had had sex before. It is now agreed that there is something wrong with sexual harassment. But describe what happened to you, and it may be trivial or personal or paranoid, or maybe you should have worn a bra that day. People are against discrimination. But describe the situation of a real woman, and they are not so sure she wasn't just unqualified. In law, all these disjunctions between women's perspective on our injuries and the standards we have to meet go under dignified legal rubrics like burden of proof, credibility, defenses, elements of the crime, and so on. These standards all contain a definition of what a woman is in terms of what sex is and the low value placed on us through it. They reduce injuries done to us to authentic expressions of who we are. Our silence is written all over them. So is the pornography. . . .

Women who charge men with sexual abuse are not believed. The pornographic view of them is: they want it; they all want it. When women bring charges of sexual assault, motives such as veniality or sexual repression must be invented, because we cannot really have been hurt. Under the trafficking provision, women's lack of credibility cannot be relied upon to negate the harm. There's no woman's story to destroy, no credibility-based decision on what happened. The hearings establish the harm. The definition sets the standard. The grounds of reality definition are authoritatively shifted. Pornography is bigotry, *period.* We are now—*in* the world pornography has decisively defined—having to meet the burden of proving, once and for all, for all of the rape and torture and battery, all of the sexual harassment, all of the child sexual abuse, all of the forced prostitution, *all* of it that the pornography is part of and that is part of the pornography, that the harm *does happen* and that when it happens it looks like this. Which may be why all this evidence never seems to be enough. . . .

The most basic assumption underlying First Amendment adjudication is that, socially, speech is free. The First Amendment says Congress shall not abridge the freedom of speech. Free speech, get it, *exists.* Those who wrote the First Amendment *had* speech—they wrote the Constitution. *Their* problem was to keep it free from the only power that realistically threatened it: the federal government. They designed the First Amendment to prevent government from constraining that which, if unconstrained by government, was free, meaning *accessible to them.* At the same time, we can't tell much about the intent of the framers with regard to the question of women's speech, because I don't think we crossed their minds. It is consistent with this analysis that their posture toward freedom of speech tends to presuppose that whole segments of the population are not systematically silenced socially, prior to government action. If everyone's power were equal to theirs, if this were a nonhierarchical society, that might make sense. But the place of pornography in the inequality of the sexes makes the assumption of equal power untrue.

This is a hard question. It involves risks. Classically, opposition to censorship has involved keeping government off the backs of people. Our law is about getting some people off the backs of other people. The risks that it will be misused have to be measured against the risks of the status quo. Women will never have that dignity, security, compensation that is the promise of equality so long as the pornography exists as it does now. The situation of women suggests that the urgent issue of our freedom of speech is not primarily the avoidance of state intervention as such, but getting affirmative access to speech for those to whom it has been denied.

# 37  Exaggerating the Extent of Sexual Harassment

**ELLEN FRANKEL PAUL**

Women in American society are victims of sexual harassment in alarming proportions. Sexual harassment is an inevitable corollary to class exploitation; as capitalists exploit workers, so do males in positions of authority exploit their female subordinates. Male professors, supervisors, and apartment managers in ever increasing numbers take advantage of the financial dependence and vulnerability of women to extract sexual concessions.

## Valid Assertions?

These are the assertions that commonly begin discussions of sexual harassment. For reasons that will be adumbrated below, dissent from the prevailing view is long overdue. Three recent episodes will serve to frame this disagreement.

Valerie Craig, an employee of Y & Y Snacks, Inc., joined several co-workers and her supervisor for drinks after work one day in July of 1978. Her supervisor drove her home and proposed that they become more intimately acquainted. She refused his invitation for sexual relations, whereupon he said that he would "get even" with her. Ten days after the incident she was fired from her job. She soon filed a complaint of sexual harassment with the Equal Employment Opportunity Commission (EEOC), and the case wound its way through the courts. Craig prevailed, the company was held liable for damages, and she received back pay, reinstatement, and an order prohibiting Y & Y from taking reprisals against her in the future.

Carol Zabowicz, one of only two female forklift operators in a West Bend Co. warehouse, charged that her co-workers over a four-year period from 1978–1982 sexually harassed her by such acts as: asking her whether she was wearing a bra; two of the men exposing their buttocks between ten and twenty times; a male co-worker grabbing his crotch and making obscene suggestions or growling; subjecting her to offensive and abusive language; and exhibiting obscene drawings with her initials on them. Zabowicz began to show symptoms of physical and psychological stress, necessitating several medical leaves, and she filed a sexual harassment complaint with the EEOC. The district court judge remarked that "the sustained, malicious, and brutal harassment meted out . . . was more than merely unreasonable; it was malevolent and outrageous." The company knew of the harassment and took corrective action only after the employee filed a complaint with the EEOC. The company was, therefore, held liable, and Zabowicz was awarded back pay for the period of her medical absence, and a judgment that her rights were violated under the Civil Rights Act of 1964.

On September 17, 1990, Lisa Olson, a sports reporter for the *Boston Herald*, charged five football players of the just-defeated New England Patriots with sexual harassment for making sexually suggestive and offensive remarks to her when she entered their locker room to conduct a post-game interview. The incident amounted to nothing short of "mind rape," according to Olson. After vociferous lamentations in the media, the National Football League fined the team and its players $25,000 each. The National Organization of Women called for a boycott of Remington electric shavers because the owner of the company, Victor Kiam, also owns the Patriots and . . . allegedly displayed insufficient sensitivity at the time when the episode occurred.

From "Bared Buttocks and Federal Cases," *Society* (1991). Reprinted by permission of Transaction Publishers. Copyright © 1991, all rights reserved.

## Utopian Treatment for Women

All these incidents are indisputably disturbing. In an ideal world—one needless to say far different from the one that we inhabit or are ever likely to inhabit—women would not be subjected to such treatment in the course of their work. Women, and men as well, would be accorded respect by co-workers and supervisors, their feelings would be taken into account, and their dignity would be left intact. For women to expect reverential treatment in the workplace is utopian, yet they should not have to tolerate outrageous, offensive sexual overtures and threats as they go about earning a living.

One question that needs to be pondered is: What kinds of undesired sexual behavior women should be protected against by law? That is, what kind of actions are deemed so outrageous and violate a woman's rights to such extent that the law should intervene, and what actions should be considered inconveniences of life, to be morally condemned but not adjudicated? A subsidiary question concerns the type of legal remedy appropriate for the wrongs that do require redress. Before directly addressing these questions, it might be useful to diffuse some of the hyperbole adhering to the sexual harassment issue.

## Harassment Surveys

Surveys are one source of this hyperbole. If their results are accepted at face value, they lead to the conclusion that women are disproportionately victims of legions of sexual harassers. A poll by the Albuquerque *Tribune* found that nearly 80 percent of the respondents reported that they or someone they knew had been victims of sexual harassment. The Merit Systems Protection Board determined that 42 percent of the women (and 14 percent of men) working for the federal government had experienced some form of unwanted sexual attention between 1985 and 1987, with unwanted "sexual teasing" identified as the most prevalent form. A Defense Department survey found that 64 percent of women in the military (and 17 percent of the men) suffered "uninvited and unwanted sexual attention" within the previous year. The United Methodist Church established that 77 percent of its clergywomen experienced incidents of sexual harassment, with 41 percent of these naming a pastor or colleague as the perpetrator, and 31 percent mentioning church social functions as the setting.

A few caveats concerning polls in general, and these sorts of polls in particular, are worth considering. Pollsters looking for a particular social ill tend to find it, usually in gargantuan proportions. (What fate would lie in store for a pollster who concluded that child abuse, or wife beating, or mistreatment of the elderly had dwindled to the point of negligibility!) Sexual harassment is a notoriously ill-defined and almost infinitely expandable concept, including everything from rape to unwelcome neck massaging, discomfiture upon witnessing sexual overtures directed at others, yelling at and blowing smoke in the ears of female subordinates, and displays of pornographic pictures in the workplace. Defining sexual harassment, as the United Methodists did, as "any sexually related behavior that is unwelcome, offensive or which fails to respect the rights of others," the concept is broad enough to include everything from "unsolicited suggestive looks or leers [or] pressures for dates" to "actual sexual assaults or rapes." Categorizing everything from rape to "looks" as sexual harassment makes us all victims, a state of affairs satisfying to radical feminists, but not very useful for distinguishing serious injuries from the merely trivial.

Yet, even if the surveys exaggerate the extent of sexual harassment, however defined, what they do reflect is a great deal of tension between the sexes. As women in ever increasing numbers entered the workplace in the last two decades, as the women's movement challenged alleged male hegemony and exploitation with ever greater intemperance, and as women entered previously all-male preserves from the board rooms to the coal pits, it is lamentable, but should not be surprising, that this tension sometimes takes sexual form. Not that sexual harassment on the job, in the university, and in other settings is a trivial or insignificant matter, but a sense of proportion needs to be restored and, even more important, distinctions need to be made. In other words, sexual harassment must be deideologized. Statements that paint nearly all women as victims and all men and their patriarchal, capitalist system as perpetrators, are ideological fantasy. Ideology blurs the distinction between being injured—being a genuine victim—and merely being offended. An example is this statement by Catharine A. MacKinnon, a law professor and feminist activist:

Sexual harassment perpetuates the interlocked structure by which women have been kept sexually in thrall to men and at the bottom of the labor market. Two forces of American society converge: men's control over women's sexuality and capital's control over employees' work lives. Women historically have been required to exchange sexual services for material survival, in one form or another. Prostitution and marriage as well as sexual harassment in different ways institutionalize this arrangement.

Such hyperbole needs to be diffused and distinctions need to be drawn. Rape, a nonconsensual invasion of a person's body, is a crime clear and simple. It is a violation of the right to the physical integrity of the body (the right to life, as John Locke or Thomas Jefferson would have put it). Criminal law should and does prohibit rape. Whether it is useful to call rape "sexual harassment" is doubtful, for it makes the latter concept overly broad while trivializing the former.

## Extortion of Sexual Favors

Intimidation in the workplace of the kind that befell Valerie Craig—that is, extortion of sexual favors by a supervisor from a subordinate by threatening to penalize, fire, or fail to reward—is what the courts term *quid pro quo* sexual harassment. Since the mid-1970s, the federal courts

have treated this type of sexual harassment as a form of sex discrimination in employment proscribed under Title VII of the Civil Rights Act of 1964. A plaintiff who prevails against an employer may receive such equitable remedies as reinstatement and back pay, and the court can order the company to prepare and disseminate a policy against sexual harassment. Current law places principal liability on the company, not the harassing supervisor, even when higher management is unaware of the harassment and, thus, cannot take any steps to prevent it.

*Quid pro quo* sexual harassment is morally objectionable and analogous to extortion: The harasser extorts property (i.e., use of the woman's body) through the leverage of fear for her job. The victim of such behavior should have legal recourse, but serious reservations can be held about rectifying these injustices through the blunt instrument of Title VII. In egregious cases the victim is left less than whole (for back pay will not compensate her for ancillary losses), and no prospect for punitive damages [is] offered to deter would-be harassers. Even more distressing about Title VII is the fact that the primary target of litigation is not the actual harasser, but rather the employer. This places a double burden on a company. The employer is swindled by the supervisor because he spent his time pursuing sexual gratification and thereby impairing the efficiency of the workplace by mismanaging his subordinates, and the employer must endure lengthy and expensive litigation, pay damages, and suffer loss to its reputation. It would be fairer to both the company and the victim to treat sexual harassment as a tort—that is, as a private wrong or injury for which the court can assess damages. Employers should be held vicariously liable only when they know of an employee's behavior and do not try to redress it.

## Defining Harassment Is Difficult

As for the workplace harassment endured by Carol Zabowicz—the bared buttocks, obscene portraits, etc.—that too should be legally redressable. Presently, such incidents also fall under the umbrella of Title VII, and are termed hostile environment sexual harassment, a category accepted later than *quid pro quo* and with some judicial reluctance. The main problem with this category is that it has proven too elastic: cases have reached the courts based on everything from off-color jokes to unwanted, persistent sexual advances by co-workers. A new tort of sexual harassment would handle these cases better. Only instances above a certain threshold of egregiousness or outrageousness would be actionable. In other words, the behavior that the plaintiff found offensive would also have to be offensive to the proverbial "reasonable man" of the tort law. That is, the behavior would have to be objectively injurious rather than merely subjectively offensive. The defendant would be the actual harasser, not the company, unless it knew about the problem and failed to act. Victims of scatological jokes, leers, unwanted offers of dates, and other sexual annoyances would no longer have their day in court.

A distinction must be restored between morally offensive behavior and behavior that causes serious harm. Only the latter should fall under the jurisdiction of criminal or tort law. Do we really want legislators and judges delving into our most intimate private lives, deciding when a look is a leer, and when a leer is a Civil Rights Act offense? Do we really want courts deciding, as one recently did, whether a school principal's disparaging remarks about a female school district administrator [were] sexual harassment and, hence, a breach of Title VII, or merely the act of a spurned and vengeful lover? Do we want judges settling disputes such as the one that arose at a car dealership after a female employee turned down a male co-worker's offer of a date and his colleagues retaliated by calling her offensive names and embarrassing her in front of customers? Or another case in which a female shipyard worker complained of an "offensive working environment" because of the prevalence of pornographic material on the docks? Do we want the state to prevent or compensate us for any behavior that someone might find offensive? Should people

have a legally enforceable right not to be offended by others? At some point, the price for such protection is the loss of both liberty and privacy rights.

## No Perfect Working Environment Exists

Workplaces are breeding grounds of envy, personal grudges, infatuation, and jilted loves, and beneath a fairly high threshold of outrageousness, these travails should be either suffered in silence, complained of to higher management, or left behind as one seeks other employment. No one, female or male, can expect to enjoy a working environment that is perfectly stress-free, or to be treated always and by everyone with kindness and respect. To the extent that sympathetic judges have encouraged women to seek monetary compensation for slights and annoyances, they have not done them a great service. Women need to develop a thick skin in order to survive and prosper in the workforce. It is patronizing to think that they need to be recompensed by male judges for seeing a few pornographic pictures on a wall. By their efforts to extend sexual harassment charges to even the most trivial behavior, the radical feminists send a message that women are not resilient enough to ignore the run-of-the-mill, churlish provocation from male co-workers. It is difficult to imagine a suit by a longshoreman complaining of mental stress due to the display of nude male centerfolds by female co-workers. Women cannot expect to have it both ways: equality where convenient, but special dispensations when the going gets rough. Equality has its price and that price may include unwelcome sexual advances, irritating and even intimidating sexual jests, and lewd and obnoxious colleagues.

Egregious acts—sexual harassment per se—must be legally redressable. Lesser but not trivial offenses, whether at the workplace or in other more social settings, should be considered moral lapses for which the offending party receives opprobrium, disciplinary warnings, or penalties, depending on the setting and the severity. Trivial offenses, dirty jokes, sexual overtures, and sexual innuendoes do make many women feel intensely discomfited, but, unless they become outrageous through persistence or content, these too should be taken as part of life's annoyances. The perpetrators should be either endured, ignored, rebuked, or avoided, as circumstances and personal inclination dictate. Whether Lisa Olson's experience in the locker room of the Boston Patriots falls into the second or third category is debatable. The media circus triggered by the incident was certainly out of proportion to the event.

As the presence of women on road gangs, construction crews, and oil rigs becomes a fact of life, the animosities and tensions of this transition period are likely to abate gradually. Meanwhile, women should "lighten up," and even dispense a few risque barbs of their own, a sure way of taking the fun out of it for offensive male bores.

## 38    Sex and Violence

### CATHARINE MACKINNON

I want to raise some questions about the concept of this panel's title, "Violence against Women," as a concept that may coopt us as we attempt to formulate our own truths. I want to speak specifically about four issues: rape, sexual harassment, pornography, and battery. I think one of the reasons we say that each of these issues is an example of violence against women is to reunify them. To say that aggression against women has this unity is to criticize the divisions that have been imposed on that aggression by the legal system. What I see to be the danger of the analysis, what makes it potentially cooptive, is formulating it— and it *is* formulated this way—these are the issues of violence, *not* sex: rape is a crime of violence, not sexuality; sexual harassment is an abuse of power, not sexuality; pornography is violence against women, it is not erotic. Although battering is not categorized so explicitly, it is usually treated as though there is nothing sexual about a man beating up a woman so long as it is with his fist. I'd like to raise some questions about that as well.

I hear in the formulation that these issues are violence against women, not sex, that we are in the shadow of Freud, intimidated at being called repressive Victorians. We're saying we're *op*pressed and they say we're *re*pressed. That is, when we say we're against rape, the immediate response is, "Does that mean you're against sex?" "Are you attempting to impose neo-Victorian prudery on sexual expression?" This comes up with sexual harassment as well. When we say we're against sexual harassment, the first thing people want to know is, "What's the difference between that and ordinary male-to-female sexual initiation?" That's a good question . . . The same is also true of criticizing pornography. "You can't be against erotica?" It's the latest version of the accusation that feminists are anti-male. To distinguish ourselves from this, and in reaction to it, we call these abuses violence. The attempt is to avoid the critique—we're not against sex—and at the same time retain our criticism of these practices. So we rename as violent those abuses that have been seen to be sexual, without saying that we have a very different perspective on violence and on sexuality and their relationship. I also think a reason we call these experiences violence is to avoid being called lesbians, which for some reason is equated with being against sex. In order to avoid that, yet retain our opposition to sexual violation, we put this neutral, objective, abstract word *violence* on it all.

To me this is an attempt to have our own perspective on these outrages without owning up to

Reprinted with permission of the publisher from *Feminism Unmodified* by Catharine MacKinnon, Cambridge, MA: Harvard University Press, © 1987, 85–92, with omissions.

having one. To have our point of view but present it as *not* a particular point of view. Our problem has been to label something as rape, as sexual harassment, as pornography in the face of a suspicion that it might be intercourse, it might be ordinary sexual initiation, it might be erotic. To say that these purportedly sexual events violate us, to be against them, we call them not sexual. But the attempt to be objective and neutral avoids owning up to the fact that women do have a specific point of view on these events. It avoids saying that from women's point of view, intercourse, sex roles, and eroticism can be and at times are violent to us as women.

My approach would claim our perspective; we are not attempting to be objective about it, we're attempting to represent the point of view of women. The point of view of men up to this time, called objective, has been to distinguish sharply between rape on the one hand and intercourse on the other; sexual harassment on the one hand and normal, ordinary sexual initiation on the other; pornography or obscenity on the one hand and eroticism on the other. The male point of view defines them by distinction. What women experience does not so clearly distinguish the normal, everyday things from those abuses from which they have been defined by distinction. Not just "Now we're going to take what *you* say as rape and call it violence"; "Now we're going to take what *you* say is sexual harassment and call it violence"; "Now we're going to take what *you* say is pornography and call it violence." We have a deeper critique of what has been done to women's sexuality and who controls access to it. What we are saying is that sexuality in exactly these normal forms often *does* violate us. So long as we say those things are abuses of violence, not sex, we fail to criticize what has been made of *sex,* what has been done to us *through* sex, because we leave the line between rape and intercourse, sexual harassment and sex roles, pornography and eroticism, right where it is.

I think it is useful to inquire how women and men (I don't use the term *persons,* I guess, because I haven't seen many lately) live through the meaning of their experience with these issues.

When we ask whether rape, sexual harassment, and pornography are questions of violence or questions of sexuality, it helps to ask, to whom? What is the perspective of those who are involved, whose experience it is—to rape or to have been raped, to consume pornography or to be consumed through it. As to what these things *mean* socially, it is important whether they are about sexuality to women and men or whether they are instead about "violence"—or whether violence and sexuality can be distinguished in that way, as they are lived out.

The crime of rape—this is a legal and observed, not a subjective, individual, or feminist definition—is defined around penetration. That seems to me a very male point of view on what it means to be sexually violated. And it is exactly what heterosexuality as a social institution is fixated around, the penetration of the penis into the vagina. Rape is defined according to what men think violates women, and that is the same as what they think of as the *sine qua non* of sex. What women experience as degrading and defiling when we are raped includes as much that is distinctive to us as is our experience of sex. Someone once termed penetration a "peculiarly resented aspect" of rape—I don't know whether that meant it was peculiar that it was resented or that it was resented with heightened peculiarity. Women who have been raped, often do resent having been penetrated. But that is not all there is to what was intrusive or expropriative of a woman's sexual wholeness.

I do think the crime of rape focuses more centrally on what men define as sexuality than on women's experience of our sexual being, hence its violation. A common experience of rape victims is to be unable to feel good about anything heterosexual thereafter—or anything sexual at all, or men at all. The minute they start to have sexual feelings or feel sexually touched by a man, or even a woman, they start to relive the rape. I had a client who came in with her husband. She was a rape victim, a woman we had represented as a witness. Her husband sat the whole time and sobbed. They couldn't have sex anymore because every time he started to touch her, she would flash to the rape scene and see his face change into the face of the man who had raped her. That, to me, is sexual. When a woman has been raped, and it is sex that she then cannot experience without connecting it to that, it was her sexuality that was violated.

Similarly, men who are in prison for rape think it's the dumbest thing that ever happened. . . . It isn't just a miscarriage of justice; they were put in jail for something very little different from what most men do most of the time and call it sex. The only difference is they got caught. That view is nonremorseful and not rehabilitative. It may also be true. It seems to me we have here a convergence between the rapist's view of what he has done and the victim's perspective on what was done to her. That is, for both, their ordinary experiences of heterosexual intercourse and the act of rape have something in common. Now this gets us into intense trouble, because that's exactly how judges and juries see it who refuse to convict men accused of rape. A rape victim has to prove that it was not intercourse. She has to show that there was force and she resisted, because if there was sex, consent is inferred. Finders of fact look for "more force than usual during the preliminaries." Rape is defined by distinction from intercourse— not nonviolence, intercourse. They ask, does this event look more like fucking or like rape? But what is their standard for sex, and is this question asked from the *woman's point of view?* The level of force is not adjudicated at her point of violation; it is adjudicated at the standard of the normal level of force. Who sets this standard?

In the criminal law, we can't put everybody in jail who does an ordinary act, right? Crime is supposed to be deviant, not normal. Women continue not to report rape, and a reason is that they believe, and they are right, that the legal system will not see it from their point of view. We get very low conviction rates for rape. We also get many women who believe they have never been raped, although a lot of force was involved. They mean that they were not raped in a way that is legally provable. In other words, in all these situations, there was not *enough* violence against them to take it beyond the category of "sex"; they were not

coerced enough. Maybe they were forced-fucked for years and put up with it, maybe they tried to get it over with, maybe they were coerced by something other than battery, something like economics, maybe even something like love.

What I am saying is that unless you make the point that there is much violence in intercourse, as a usual matter, none of that is changed. Also we continue to stigmatize the women who claim rape as having experienced a deviant violation and allow the rest of us to go through life feeling violated but thinking we've never been raped, when there were a great many times when we, too, have had sex and didn't want it. What this critique does that is different from the "violence, not sex" critique is ask a series of questions about normal, heterosexual intercourse and attempt to move the line between heterosexuality on the one hand— intercourse—and rape on the other, rather than allow it to stay where it is.

Having done that so extensively with rape, I can consider sexual harassment more briefly. The way the analysis of sexual harassment is sometimes expressed now (and it bothers me) is that it is an abuse of power, not sexuality. That does not allow us to pursue whether sexuality, as socially constructed in our society through gender roles, is *itself* a power structure. If you look at sexual harassment as power, not sex, what is power supposed to be? Power is employer/employee, not because courts are marxist but because this is a recognized hierarchy. Among men. Power is teacher/student, because courts recognize a hierarchy there. Power is on one side and sexuality on the other. Sexuality is ordinary affection, everyday flirtation. Only when ordinary, everyday affection and flirtation and "I was just trying to be friendly" come into the context of *another* hierarchy is it considered potentially an abuse of power. What is not considered to be a hierarchy is women and men—men on top and women on the bottom. That is not considered to be a question of power or social hierarchy, legally or politically. A feminist perspective suggests that it is.

When we have examples of coequal sexual harassment (within these other hierarchies), worker to worker on the same level, involving women and men, we have a lot of very interesting, difficult questions about sex discrimination, which is supposed to be about gender difference, but does not conceive of gender as a social hierarchy. I think that implicit in race discrimination cases for a brief moment of light was the notion that there is a social hierarchy between Blacks and whites. So that presumptively it's an exercise of power for a white person to do something egregious to a Black person or for a white institution to do something egregious systematically to many Black people. Situations of coequal power—among coworkers or students or teachers—are difficult to see as examples of sexual harassment unless you have a notion of male power. I think we lie to women when we call it not power when a woman is come onto by a man who is not her employer, not her teacher. What do we labor under, what do we feel, when a man—any man—comes and hits on us? I think we require women to feel fine about turning down male-initiated sex so long as the man doesn't have some *other* form of power over us. Whenever—every and any time—a woman feels conflicted and wonders what's wrong with her that she can't decline although she has no inclination, and she feels open to male accusations, whether they come from women or men, of "why didn't you just tell him to buzz off?" we have sold her out, not named her experience. We are taught that we exist for men. We should be flattered or at least act as if we are—be careful about a man's ego because you never know what he can do to you. To flat out say to him, "You?" or "I don't want to" is not *in* most women's sex-role learning. To say it is, is bravado. And that's because he's a man, not just because you never know what he can do to you because he's your boss (that's two things—he's a man and he's the boss) or your teacher or in some other hierarchy. It seems to me that we haven't talked very much about gender *as* a hierarchy, as a division of power, in the way that's expressed and acted out, primarily I think sexually. And therefore we haven't expanded the definition according to women's experience of sexuality, including our own sexual intimidation, of what things are sexual in this world. So men have also defined what can

be called sexual about us. They say, "I was just trying to be affectionate, flirtatious and friendly," and we were just all felt up. We criticize the idea that rape comes down to her word against his—but it really *is* her perspective against his perspective, and the law has been written from *his* perspective. If he didn't mean to be sexual, it's not sexual. If he didn't see it as forced, it wasn't forced. Which is to say, only male sexual violations, that is, only male ideas of what sexually violates us as women, are illegal. We buy into this when we say our sexual violations are abuses of power, not sex.

Just as rape is supposed to have nothing against intercourse, just as sexual harassment is supposed to have nothing against normal sexual initiation (men initiate, women consent—that's mutual?), the idea that pornography is violence against women, not sex, seems to distinguish artistic creation on the one hand from what is degrading to women on the other. It is candid and true but not enough to say of pornography, as Justice Stewart said, "I know it when I see it." *He* knows what he thinks it is when he sees it—but is that what *I* know? Is that the same "it"? Is he going to know what I know when I see it? I think pretty much not, given what's on the newsstand, given what is not considered hard-core pornography. Sometimes I think what is obscene is what does *not* turn on the Supreme Court—or what revolts them more. Which is uncommon, since revulsion is eroticized. We have to admit that pornography turns men on; it is therefore erotic. It is a lie to say that pornography is not erotic. When we say it is violence, not sex, we are saying, there is this degrading to women, over here, and this erotic, over there, without saying to whom. It is overwhelmingly disproportionately men to whom pornography is erotic. It is women, on the whole, to whom it is violent, among other things. And this is not just a matter of perspective, but a matter of reality.

Pornography turns primarily men on. Certainly they are getting something out of it. They pay incredible amounts of money for it; it's one of the largest industries in the country. If women got as much out of it as men do, we would buy it instead of cosmetics. It's a massive industry, cosmetics. We are poor but we have *some* money; we are some market. We spend our money to set ourselves up as the objects that emulate those images that are sold as erotic to men. What pornography says about us is that we enjoy degradation, that we are sexually turned on by being degraded. For me that obliterates the line, as a line at all, between pornography on one hand and erotica on the other, if what turns men on, what men find beautiful, is what degrades women. It is pervasively present in art, also, and advertising. But it is definitely present in eroticism, if that is what it is. It makes me think that women's sexuality as such is a stigma. We also sometimes have an experience of sexuality authentic somehow in all this. We are not allowed to have it; we are not allowed to talk about it; we are not allowed to speak of it or image it as from our own point of view. And, to the extent we try to assert that we are beings equal with men, we have to be either asexual or virgins.

To worry about cooptation is to realize that lies make bad politics. It is ironic that cooptation often results from an attempt to be "credible," to be strategically smart, to be "effective" on existing terms. Sometimes you become what you're fighting. Thinking about issues of sexual violation as issues of violence not sex could, if pursued legally, lead to opposing sexual harassment and pornography through morals legislation and obscenity laws. It is actually interesting that this theoretical stance has been widely embraced but these legal strategies have not been. Perhaps women realize that these legal approaches would not address the subordination of women to men, specifically and substantively. These approaches are legally as abstract as the "violence not sex" critique is politically abstract. They are both not enough and too much of the wrong thing. They deflect us from criticizing everyday behavior that is pervasive and normal and concrete and fuses sexuality with gender in violation and is not amenable to existing legal approaches. I think we need to think more radically in our legal work here.

Battering is called violence, rather than something sex-specific: this is done to women. I also think it is sexually done to women. Not only in where it is done—over half of the incidents are in the bedroom. Or the surrounding events—precipitating sexual jealousy. But when violence against women is eroticized as it is in this culture, it is very difficult to say that there is a major distinction in the level of sex involved between being assaulted by a penis and being assaulted by a fist, especially when the perpetrator is a man. If women as gender female are defined as sexual beings, and violence is eroticized, then men violating women has a sexual component. I think men rape women because they get off on it in a way that fuses dominance with sexuality. (This is different in emphasis from what Susan Brownmiller says.) I think that when men sexually harass women it expresses male control over sexual access to us. It doesn't mean they all want to fuck us, they just want to hurt us, dominate us, and control us, and that *is* fucking us. They want to be able to have that and to be able to say when they can have it, to *know* that. That is in itself erotic. The idea that opposing battering is about saving the family is, similarly, abstracted, gender-neutral. There are gender-neutral formulations of all these issues: law and order as opposed to derepression, Victorian morality as opposed to permissiveness, obscenity as opposed to art and freedom of expression. Gender-neutral, objective formulations like these avoid asking *whose* expression, from whose point of view? Whose law and whose order? It's not just a question of who is free to express ourselves; it's not just that there is almost no, if any, self-respecting women's eroticism. The fact is that what we do see, what we are allowed to experience, even in our own suffering, even in what we are allowed to complain about, is overwhelmingly constructed from the male point of view. Laws against sexual violation express what men see and do when they engage in sex with women; laws against obscenity center on the display of women's bodies in ways that men are turned on by viewing. To me, it not only makes us cooptable to define such abuses in gender-neutral terms like violence; when we fail to assert that we are fighting for the affirmative definition and control of our own sexuality, of our own lives as women, and that these experiences violate *that,* we have already been bought.

# Questions

1. Suppose you are a Rule Utilitarian legislator seeking a principle concerning which actions should be legal. Which of the following principles is the right one? Please state the right principle precisely and clearly. (*Hint:* The principle you choose should not be too restrictive or too permissive. It should force legislators to allow *all* of the activities that should be allowed, and it should enable legislators to ban *all* of the activities that should be banned.)

   a. Harm Principle
   b. Harm + Offense Principle
   c. Harm + Legal Moralism Principle
   d. Harm + Legal Paternalism Principle
   e. Harm + Character Corruption Principle
   f. your own principle

   Suppose that bills banning the following actions are being considered in the legislature.

   a. selling crack to adults
   b. selling low-quality handguns to adults
   c. discriminating by race when hiring
   d. discriminating by talent when hiring
   e. publicly displaying a Confederate flag
   f. public flag burning
   g. smoking marijuana in private
   h. smoking marijuana while on duty as a police officer

   How will you vote on each of these bills? Use the principle that you chose above to justify your answers. (*Hint:* If you want to prohibit an act because it has a certain characteristic, then you must show that the act actually has that characteristic. For example, if you use the Legal Moralism Principle to prohibit using opium, then you must show that using opium is immoral.)

2. Apply question 1 to the following list.
   a. putting porn onto the internet
   b. peeping with no possibility of discovery
   c. prostitution without coercion
   d. homosexual sex in private
   e. unprotected sex with an HIV-positive partner
   f. public nudity
   g. sex with chickens in private
   h. polygamy or polyandry without deception

3. Apply question 1 to the following list.
   a. making sexually explicit remarks to a crowd
   b. making sexually explicit remarks to a stranger in an elevator
   c. making sexually explicit remarks to a student in class
   d. smoking tobacco in class
   e. making communistic remarks in class
   f. urinating in class
   g. wearing satanic symbols on a T-shirt in class
   h. saying "Niggers are idiots" when teaching a class that includes blacks

4. Apply question 1 to the following list.
   a. sending sick children to elementary school
   b. rappelling down skyscrapers
   c. drinking lots of alcohol when pregnant
   d. allowing your dog to poop on the sidewalk
   e. underselling your competitor until he or she goes bankrupt
   f. posting the sign "Women are idiots" on campus
   g. carrying concealed weapons
   h. harassing pregnant women entering abortion clinics

5. The Harm Principle says that a state should not ban an act unless the act directly harms a person other than the agent. That is, there should be no victimless crimes. Mill endorses the Harm Principle. Why? Would Kant accept the Harm Principle? Why or why not? Would Rawls accept the Harm Principle? Why or why not? Would Aristotle accept the Harm Principle? Why or why not?

6. Paul distinguishes two types of sexual harassment: *quid pro quo* harassment and

hostile-environment harassment. Explain the difference. Answer *one* of the following questions.

   a. Would a Utilitarian consider both types of sexual harassment wrong? Why or why not?

   b. Would a Kantian consider both types of sexual harassment wrong? Why or why not?

   c. Would an Aristotelian consider both types of sexual harassment wrong? Why or why not?

7. With which of the statements in the following dialogue do you agree? With which of the statements do you disagree? Defend your answers while continuing the dialogue in a philosophically interesting way.

*A:* Hostile-environment sexual harassment and hate speech are similar. Both are harmless yet offensive. Thus, if the Harm Principle is right, both should be legal. But if the Offense Principle is right, the state may ban both.

*B:* Hostile-environment sexual harassment and hate speech are both psychologically harmful, especially when the comments are made by a person in authority (such as a boss or teacher) and aimed at a subordinate (such as a secretary or student). Thus both may be banned under the Harm Principle.

*A:* Women and minorities need to lighten up! Hostile-environment sexual harassment and hate speech are just words. A reasonable adult ought to be able to shrug them off and move on. (After all, white males can usually do that.) Thus they may not be banned under the Harm Principle.

*B:* Women and minorities are more vulnerable because of past and present oppression, so hostile-environment sexual harassment and hate speech are not just words. They are hurtful words. Just as flag burning is painful to veterans because of their military experience, so hostile-environment sexual harassment and hate speech are painful to women and minorities. All three may be banned under the Harm Principle.

*C:* It is insulting to say that veterans, women, and minorities are more vulnerable than reasonable adults. Hostile-environment sexual harassment and hate speech are not psychologically harmful. Instead, they are harmful because they encourage sexist and racist attitudes in white males. These attitudes, in turn, lead to harmful actions ranging from physical abuse to discrimination in hiring. This is why both hostile-environment sexual harassment and hate speech may be banned under the Harm Principle, but flag burning may not.

*A:* A few prejudiced people may become a tad more prejudiced, but overall, hostile-environment sexual harassment and hate speech do not pose a clear and present danger. Thus the Harm Principle demands that the state allow them.

*D:* You all need to reexamine your assumptions. Hostile-environment sexual harassment and hate speech are not similar. Hate speech is typically "fighting words," but the typical targets of hostile-environment sexual harassment are women who typically do not respond by fighting. Thus the Harm Principle allows us to ban hate speech but requires us to allow hostile-environment sexual harassment, because hate speech poses a clear and present danger of violence, but hostile-environment sexual harassment does not.

# Abortion

*". . . because a person's a person no matter how small."*

DR. SEUSS, *Horton Hears a Who*

Today's moral problems are hard. After more than 3000 years we have solved the easy ones. However, the abortion issue is even more complicated and multi-faceted than most other contemporary moral problems. This section will consider the issue of whether abortion is morally wrong, but not further issues such as whether the government should allow, regulate, or finance abortion.

## Do Fetuses Have a Right to Life?

Many people think that the abortion issue begins and ends with the question of whether fetuses have a right to life. This is a crucial question for the following, straightforward reason. Everyone grants that women have a right to determine what happens to their own bodies (though some people assign a higher priority to this right than do others, and some people assign it so low a priority that they seem merely to be paying it lip service). This right may be seen as a part of a right to liberty. However, this right is not unlimited. A woman has a right to do whatever she wants with her body so long as she does not violate the rights of others. Thus one cannot simply say, as some pro-choice advocates do, that abortion is justifiable because women have a right to their own bodies. One must ask whether abortion violates the rights of others. If fetuses have a right to life, then abortion seems to violate this right.

Do fetuses have a right to life? Some people draw the line at the point in fetal development where the fetus becomes able to feel pleasure and pain. That is, they say that the fetus gains a right to life when it reaches this developmental stage. Other people, of course, draw the line at conception or at birth. In *Roe v. Wade* the Supreme Court drew the line at the beginning of the third trimester because that is approximately when the fetus becomes viable (able to survive outside the womb).

This line-drawing approach obscures an important relationship. The question "Which fetuses have a right to life?" is actually part of a broader question: (a) "Which creatures have a right to life?" For example, do cows or computers or convicted murderers have a right to life? In order to answer this question according to principle rather than prejudice, we need to address a second question: (b) "What characteristics entitle a creature to a right to life?" What is it about ordinary adult humans, for example, that entitles them to a right to life? The trick is to find consistent, non-arbitrary, reasonable answers to these two questions. Unfortunately, all of the commonly proposed criteria for possession of a right to life seem to have some counterintuitive implications.

Many people say that we have a right to life because we *possess a soul*. However, lacking a soul detector, it is difficult to know which creatures have souls. The Catholic position is that because we do not know at what point in fetal development ensoulment occurs, we ought to err on the side of caution and abort no fetuses. However, wouldn't a similar argument say that we also ought to kill no animals? The advocates of the "possession of a soul" criterion often cite *Genesis* 1, where God gives man "dominion over" the animals, as evidence that animals lack souls and may therefore be killed. Yet in *Genesis* 3 God gives man "dominion over" women. In general, the *Bible* will not resolve our moral problems for us, because in order to understand what the *Bible* is saying about some moral problem, we already need a fair degree of insight into the problem.

Another common proposal is that we have a right to life because of our *humanity*, because we have human DNA. This criterion has very counter-intuitive implications. For example, the humanity criterion would grant a right to life to my tonsils but deny it to ET. More seriously, the humanity criterion seems arbitrary at best. The claim that whites have a right to life, but blacks do not, is racist because race is morally irrelevant. Similarly, the claim that humans have a right to life but non-humans do not seems suspiciously "speciesist." That is, the humanity criterion seems to reflect a prejudice against other creatures rather than a morally relevant feature. Advocates of the humanity criterion usually retreat to some other criterion when asked why humanity is relevant to the right to life.

According to Mill's Utilitarianism, morality is ultimately about pleasure and pain. Moreover, Utilitarianism is radically egalitarian in the sense that each bit of pleasure and pain (of the same quality) counts equally whether it is experienced by a saint or a sinner or even a dog. Every creature that can feel pleasure and pain—every *sentient* creature—has moral standing. This does not straightforwardly imply that killing saints, sinners, and dogs is equally wrong, because it might turn out that in the long run, killing a saint causes a loss of more jollies or higher-quality jollies for the universe. But it does imply that the pleasures of good people are not more important than the pleasures of bad people or canine pleasures just because they are pleasures of good people. Similarly, legalizing infanticide might have worse effects than legalizing abortion, but infants and sentient fetuses have equal moral standing. One way to express this is to say that all sentient creatures have a right to life, so killing any sentient creature, including a sentient fetus, is *prima facie* wrong. The sentience criterion is closer to common sense than the humanity criterion, for the sentience criterion gives a right to life to ET but not to tonsils. However, it also gives animals a right to life. Though this may please animal rights advocates, it clashes with common sense.

Kant maintains that morality applies only to rational beings. We have a right to life because of our *rationality*. But what does "rationality" mean? If the standard for rationality is *high*, then animals (with the possible exception of chimps and dolphins) will not qualify, but neither will some humans, including fetuses, infants, and psychotics. However, if the standard for rationality is *low* enough to include fetuses and infants, then many animals will also turn out to be rational. After all, cows are clearly more rational than neonates.

Kant's proposal might be modified to say that creatures have a right to life if they are *actually or potentially rational*. At first glance, this proposal has the advantage of harmonizing with common sense, for it seems to extend a right to life to infants and psychotics but not to animals. Unfortunately, the term "potentially" is vague. If we understand "potentially" *narrowly* so that a creature has the potential to reason if and only if it is *likely* to become rational naturally without high-tech intervention, then healthy people will have a right to life, but people who need antibiotics or respirators or some other product of modern medicine will lack a right to life. Surely, their need for treatment does not cost these people the right to life. On the other hand, if we understand "potentially" *broadly* so that a creature has the potential to reason if it is *possible* for the creature to become rational, perhaps with high-tech help, then cows will be potentially rational, and they will have a right to life because someone could invent an IQ-enhancing drug for cows. Worse yet, both interpretations have the following problem. Suppose that Jack and Jill do not yet know each other, but tonight they will meet at a singles bar, have sex, and produce a fetus. Even before Jack and Jill meet, the spatially disconnected entity consisting of Jack's sperm and Jill's egg is potentially rational. Thus it has a right to life, and preventing Jack and Jill from having sex would be murder!

Don Marquis maintains that killing is wrong because it deprives the victim of a *future like ours*. Because normal fetuses have such a future, abortion is normally wrong. But who is included in the reference group? If "ours" is interpreted *narrowly*, then many people (such as lunatics, the super rich, winos living in dumpsters, and Australian bushmen) do not have a future like ours. On the other hand, if "ours" is interpreted *broadly*, then some animals do have a future like ours and thus have a right to life. After all, animals experience sensual pleasure, adventure, attachment, and the like. Pampered pets may even live in houses, wear clothing, take daily walks, and do household chores. Moreover, the "future like ours" criterion seems just as "speciocentric" as the humanity criterion. After all, why can't a future that is very different from ours be equally (or more) valuable to its possessor? Depriving a creature of such a future would be a serious harm, so the creature might have a right not to be deprived of its future—that is, a right to life.

Susan Sherwin maintains that to be a creature with a right to life is to *fit into a network of relationships*. Because fetuses do not fit into networks, fetuses lack a right to life. They are valuable only insofar as pregnant women value them, so abortion is not wrong. Like all of the other criteria, Sherwin's criterion has some odd consequences. Hermits live outside of relationship networks, whereas pets are often "just like members of the family." Thus according to the network criterion, pets have a right to life but hermits do not. Sherwin might say that hermits have a right to life because they are potential network members, but this move leads to the problems of interpreting "potential" that I mentioned above. Moreover, why deny that fetuses are network members? Family and friends often think of fetuses as part of their relationship network and modify their lives to accommodate fetuses. Fetuses may not respond to caring, but neither do comatose people, and people do not lose their right to life when they lose consciousness.

Jane English and Rosalind Hursthouse object to this whole approach. English maintains that there is no characteristic or cluster of characteristics that all creatures with a right to life share. Instead there is a family resemblance among such creatures. Thus the attempt to find a criterion for a right to life is doomed. Hursthouse maintains that acting rightly does not require controversial, esoteric knowledge. Thus whether or not abortion is OK cannot depend on meta-physical discoveries about the criterion of the right to life.

## Utilitarian Analysis

English does not try to answer the questions "Which creatures have a right to life?" and "What characteristics entitle a creature to a right to life?" Instead she assumes, for the sake of argument, that fetuses lack a right to life and tries to show that some abortions are wrong anyway.

### Argument (A)

(1) People and whole societies are motivated to act morally by moral sentiments (such as sympathy and guilt).
(2) Babies have a right to life, but fetuses do not.
(3) Killing creatures that resemble creatures with a right to life undermines these moral sentiments. Over time, this reduces the motivation of people and societies to act morally.
(4) Reducing the motivation to act morally leads to immoral actions and thus causes enormous harm.
(5) Therefore, abortion is wrong.

This is a slippery slope argument. The idea is that if we allow abortions, then we will gradually lose the inhibitions that keep us from violating each others' rights. Thus even if we owe nothing to fetuses, abortion is wrong because the practice of abortion will produce a disastrous state of affairs.

Some Utilitarians might object to premise (3) of argument (A). They might deny that the slope is very slippery. That is, they might deny that abortion really would undermine the moral sentiments through which our ethical system operates. Other Utilitarians might maintain that denying abortions would result in lots of unwanted children, which is also an enormous harm. These Utilitarians would go on to say that it is not obvious which harm is greater. Abortion harms sentient fetuses, of course. Finally, non-Utilitarians might object to the whole idea of slippery slope arguments. Thus conclusion (5) of argument (A) does not follow without further argumentation. [For a more thorough Utilitarian analysis of abortion, see the "Utilitarianism" section.]

## Deontological Analysis

Judith Thomson assumes, for the sake of argument, that fetuses possess a right to life and tries to show that some abortions are morally OK. She points out that the assumption that fetuses have the same right to life as you and I does not settle the question of abortion. In a famous, action-packed, humorous article she discusses and rebuts several common arguments against abortion.

### Argument (B)

(1) Fetuses possess a right to life.
(2) Killing creatures with a right to life is always wrong.
(3) Therefore, abortion is wrong.

Thomson grants premise (1) of argument (B) for the sake of argument. She notes that because of premise (1), if argument (B) works for ordinary fetuses, then it works equally well for fetuses that result from rape or incest. Thus the popular position that "abortion is wrong because it is murder except in cases of rape or incest" is incoherent. (Abortion is an unusual moral problem because so many of the popular positions are not merely mistaken but wildly wrong. Consider the view, popular among politicians, that "Abortion is wrong because it is murder, but because there is no social consensus on this, abortion should be legal." If you think about this position for two minutes, you will see what is wrong with it.)

Premise (2) of argument (B) is false as it stands. Almost everyone acknowledges exceptions for self-defense, defense of others, just war, and the like. Thomson suggests an additional sort of exception.

*The Thomson Exception:* Removing a creature that possesses a right to life from life support to which the creature has no right is a kind of killing that constitutes a legitimate exception to the prohibition against killing.

For example, suppose Jack needs a certain drug to stay alive, but he cannot afford the drug. Jack steals it from the drugstore shelf. May the druggist take the drug back by force? The druggist would be dooming Jack, but nevertheless Thomson thinks that the druggist would not be violating his right to life by taking the drug, because it is the druggist's property. Jack's right to life does not give him a right to use the property of others in order to stay alive.

How is this relevant to abortion? Some methods of abortion directly destroy the fetus. Vacuum abortions pull the fetus apart, for example, and saline abortions poison the fetus. Other methods of abortion merely remove the fetus from the womb and allow it to die (withdraw its life support). The Thomson Exception suggests that there is a morally significant difference between these two classes of abortion methods. Removing the fetus from the womb is like removing the drug from Jack. It is a case of killing that is legitimized by the Thomson Exception. Hence, paradoxically, removing a non-viable fetus kills it but does not violate its right to life.

Look at the matter this way. A right is the flip side of a duty. What sort of right to life do people have? Here are two possibilities.

Fran has a *negative right to life* if everyone has a duty not to kill her except in cases of self-defense, defense of others, just war, and so on. Fran has a *positive right to life* if everyone has a duty not to kill her except in cases of self-defense, defense of others, just war, and so on, *and* everyone has a duty to provide her with at least the bare necessities for life except in cases where this is impossible, would violate the rights of others, and the like.

Suppose that people have a positive right to life. Presumably, society would then have a duty to provide people with the bare necessities for life. Individuals might give directly to others, or they could contribute their share to some social program for the assistance of others. Individuals might be able to choose the form of their contribution. Some would contribute money, others goods or services. In particular, if fetuses are people, then society would have a duty to provide fetuses with life support. But a pregnant woman who chose to contribute her share in money would not have to bear the additional burden of providing the fetus with a womb. Or at the very least, because she is the only one who is in a position to provide a womb to the fetus, society would have a duty to compensate her for her additional contribution—to rent her womb, presumably at market rates. Actually, very few people think that people have a positive right to life, because that would entail a high-priority obligation to feed not only famine victims but also lazy bums. Not feeding them would be a violation of their right to life; it would be murder. Most people think that a right to life does not include a right to life support. A Kantian, for example, might say that helping others is an imperfect duty. Thus everyone has a duty to help others, but no one has a right to be helped.

But if a fetus has only the negative right to life, then abortions that merely remove it from the womb do not violate its right to life (even if they are not done in self-defense). Such abortions are legitimate exceptions to the prohibition against killing. Thomson seems to have found a way of justifying abortions without denying that fetuses have a right to life! (Perhaps a pro-lifer would claim that fetuses have neither a positive nor a negative right to life but instead have some third sort of right to life.)

*

Some pro-lifers focus on the responsibilities of the pregnant woman rather than (or in addition to) the rights of the fetus. They make the following argument against abortion.

### Argument (C)

(1) Sex always constitutes an implicit promise by the woman to the fetus.
(2) Promise breaking is always wrong.
(3) Therefore, abortion is wrong.

Of course, a pregnant woman is responsible for the existence of the fetus in the purely causal sense that if the woman had not had sex, there would be no fetus. But causal responsibility is different from moral responsibility. The fact that a woman is causally responsible for a fetus does not imply that she has responsibilities to the fetus. Thus premise (1) of argument (C) is false. Clearly, a woman makes no promise to any fetus when she is raped. (Note that the thesis "Abortion is wrong except in cases of rape" makes much more sense if abortion is wrong because it is promise breaking than if abortion is wrong because it is murder.) In general, people are not morally responsible for the consequences of involuntary actions. Women have sex involuntarily more often than is usually thought. Sex is involuntary on the part of the woman when she has been brainwashed or indoctrinated. (Many women have been raised since childhood to believe that women have a duty to submit to the sexual desires of their husbands.) Similarly, sex is involuntary when a woman has sex in order to avoid physical or psychological abuse. Arguably, sex is involuntary when a woman has sex in order to avoid economic ruin. Sadly, cases like all of these are common. Thus, in many pregnancies the women make no promises to the fetus because the sex is involuntary.

People are not morally responsible for the consequences of voluntary actions when reasonable precautions are taken to prevent those consequences. For example, if the baby-sitter I hire eats the poisoned chocolate cake in my refrigerator even though I told her it was poisoned and put a DO NOT EAT sign on it, I am surely not morally responsible for her death. Similarly, a pregnant woman is not morally responsible for her pregnancy if she took reasonable precautions to prevent pregnancy. What counts as reasonable precautions? Some people might say that unless a woman does everything she can to avoid pregnancy, she is responsible for the pregnancy and has made a promise to the fetus. That is, they might interpret "reasonable precautions" to mean "all possible precautions." But this is too extreme because possible precautions range from occasional contraception all the way to hysterectomy. It would be counter-intuitive to say that a raped woman is responsible for her pregnancy because she neglected to get a hysterectomy. Similarly, although women can avoid date rape by avoiding dates, it would be counter-intuitive to say that a date-raped woman is responsible for her pregnancy because she agreed to go out on a date. Some people might take "reasonable precautions" to mean "regular contraception," whereas others might take "reasonable precautions" to mean "abstinence." In any event, it is clear that premise (1) stands in need of substantial qualification.

Premise (2) of argument (C) is also false. Almost everyone acknowledges various exceptions to the prohibition against promise breaking, just as they acknowledge exceptions to the prohibition against killing. Presumably, it is OK to kill or to break a promise in self-defense. But, asks English, what counts as self-defense? Clearly, I may kill or break a promise to save my life, so abortion to save the life of a woman would be OK even if the fetus has a right to life and if the woman has made a promise to the fetus. Would it be self-defense for a woman to kill or break a promise in order to save herself from serious physical or mental injury? massive pain or anguish? slavery or imprisonment? Probably so. What about loss of life prospects? Would it be self-defense for a woman to kill or break a promise to a fetus in order to save herself from serious loss of life prospects? If so, then a sixteen-year-old could have an abortion in order to avoid dropping out of high school, and she could justify breaking the promise to the fetus on grounds of self-defense.

English has probably justified too much. Suppose the dean is about to deny me tenure. Because of the extremely tight philosophy job market, I will be unable to get another philosophy teaching job. My life prospects will be seriously diminished. However, if the dean suddenly died, my friend would become interim dean and would grant me tenure. May I kill the present dean in self-defense? Perhaps a distinction between different sorts of life prospects would be helpful.

## Virtue Ethics Analysis

Violating rights and breaking promises are unjust actions, but injustice is only one kind of immorality. There are many moral vices besides injustice. Hursthouse draws the surprising conclusion that it is possible for a single act to be both a just act (even an act that the agent has a right to perform) and also a vicious, immoral act. I have a right to walk up to an ugly stranger and tell her bluntly that she is ugly, but doing so would be rude and uncaring, though just and honest. Similarly, says Hursthouse, even if a woman has a right to abortion on demand, choosing an abortion for trivial reasons is callous and light-minded (that is, vicious and immoral). On the other hand, the fact that abortion is a serious matter does not imply that abortion is always vicious. If pregnancy and birth will involve much suffering and little reward, then it is more than virtuous to refrain from abortion. Abortion is callous and light-minded when performed for trivial reasons but not when performed for important reasons.

If helping others involves substantial trouble or risk, then it is above and beyond the call of duty (supererogatory). We do not have a duty to be Splendid Samaritans or even Good Samaritans. However, the virtue of decency requires us to help others if we can do so with very little trouble and risk. We do have a duty to be Minimally Decent Samaritans. Suppose I can save a baby from drowning without even getting my shoes wet. If people have only the negative right to life, then justice does not require me to save the baby, but decency does. Thus Thomson and Hursthouse consider the following argument.

### Argument (D)

(1) Fetuses possess a right to life.
(2) Letting someone with a right to life die when I could help him or her with very little trouble and/or risk is indecent.
(3) Therefore, abortion is wrong.

Is argument (D) sound? Thomson is still granting premise (1) for the sake of argument. Premise (2) of argument (D) is true. Unfortunately, the conclusion does not follow. Carrying a fetus to term involves more than "very little trouble and/or risk." Contrary to what you might have heard, early abortion is typically safer than giving birth. Thus undergoing nine months of pregnancy typically involves some increased risk, not to mention substantial discomfort and inconvenience. Carrying a fetus to term is therefore not required by decency. It is charity, not duty. Thus, in general, abortion is not indecent. Even though the premises are true, argument (D) fails. On the other hand, Thomson thinks that carrying a fetus for a few weeks does not involve substantial trouble or risk and is, therefore, required by decency. She thinks this accounts for the fact that many people (even pro-choice people) believe that very late abortions performed for convenience are wrong. Thus Thomson's overall conclusion is this. *If* the fetus possesses a right to life, then abortion is morally permissible under the following conditions: (a) conception occurred because of involuntary sex or contraception failure, (b) the abortion does not kill the fetus directly but merely removes it from the womb, and (c) it would be too much trouble and/or risk to carry the fetus to term.

Thomson has underestimated the trouble and risk of delivering a baby. Even in uncomplicated deliveries, there is a small but significant risk of physical injury or death to the woman. Moreover, it is not uncommon for the woman to end up screaming in pain for hours during labor and to be physically and mentally exhausted for days after the delivery. (There are pain medications, but they have limitations and contraindications.) Thomson has also underestimated the psychological pain of giving a baby up for adoption. Abortion is not riskless or trouble-free, of course, but it is substantially less risky and troublesome than giving birth, so perhaps even late abortions are not indecent.

*

One Virtue Ethics approach to moral questions is to ask whether a certain act or practice could fit into the life of a good person. For example, striving to minimize sensual pleasure or risky actions may strike us as unappealing but morally acceptable projects. But Aristotle's conception of the moral sphere is somewhat larger than that of contemporary common

sense. He would observe that these projects are incompatible with a good life, and he would classify them as vicious (intemperate and cowardly). Now the fact that childbearing and parenting are intrinsically worthwhile and are, therefore, part of a good life implies that choosing abortion over parenthood may be manifesting a flawed grasp of happiness, suggests Hursthouse. She does allow that choosing not to have a child may be wise if one already has enough children, if having a child would harm one's life prospects, or if one's life is aimed at other equally good activities with which having a child would compete. But overall, Hursthouse maintains that opting for abortion is vicious unless one has a good reason.

Once one recognizes that this is an argument against childlessness rather than against abortion *per se*, Hursthouse's argument may lose some of its initial appeal. It is one thing to criticize someone for choosing to have an abortion, quite another to criticize someone for choosing to be childless. Although at different times it has been thought that people had a duty to state, family, God, or self to have children, common sense no longer accepts this claim. But perhaps Aristotle and Hursthouse would maintain that common sense has gone astray on this point.

## Feminist Analysis

Celia Wolf-Devine begins by summarizing several masculine/feminine distinctions drawn by feminists. She then argues that although feminists have almost universally been pro-choice, abortion is a rather masculine practice. Even more ironically, the justifications for abortion offered by feminists are based on masculine ways of thought. Of course, even if abortion and its defenses are masculine, this does not make abortion wrong.

Wolf-Devine goes on to apply the Ethics of Care to the issue of abortion. The Ethics of Care does not say that a person must care maximally for everyone and everything. Instead, the Ethics of Care says that people must balance conflicting responsibilities that arise from different relationships. Although one should generally strive to preserve relationships, sometimes one must temporarily or even permanently break off a relationship in order to preserve other relationships, to preserve one's own integrity, or to prevent exploitation or harm. Which relationships should one preserve, and which relationships should one discontinue? Wolf-Devine suggests several rules of thumb. Choose temporary break-ups over irremediable severing of relationships. Choose possible breaks over certain breaks. Choose breaks that cause mild, temporary harm over breaks that cause deep or lasting harm. Choose breaks that harm the wicked over breaks that harm the innocent. Choose breaks with strangers over breaks with immediate family. Wolf-Devine then observes that abortion turns out to be wrong according to any of these rules of thumb.

### Argument (E)

(1) Abortion causes an irremediable, inevitable severing of the relationship between fetus and pregnant woman that causes deep, lasting harm to an innocent member of the pregnant woman's immediate family.

(2) Carrying an unwanted fetus to term causes only temporary emotional harm to the pregnant woman.

(3) People should avoid irremediable, inevitable break-ups that cause deep, lasting harm to an innocent member of their immediate family.

(4) Therefore, abortion is wrong.

Sherwin would deny premise (1) of argument (E). She would deny that one can have a relationship with a fetus. And if no relationship is possible, then abortion does not sever a relationship. Nel Noddings takes a more moderate stance. She says that the pregnant woman can, but need not, have a relationship with a fetus. It follows that abortion can, but need not, break a relationship. Thus abortion might be wrong if the pregnant woman forms a relationship with the fetus be-

fore aborting. But if the pregnant woman does not vacillate, if she resolutely refrains from forming a relationship with the fetus, then abortion is OK.

Why, asks Wolf-Devine, do pregnant women have the option of forming or not forming a relationship with their fetuses? Why is forming a relationship not a duty? Noddings cannot maintain that I always have the option to form or not to form a relationship with someone I encounter, for then I need only avoid a relationship with someone in order to legitimize the exploitation of that person. Anyway, Noddings claims that we do have a *prima facie* duty to care for strangers we encounter. Now Noddings denies that we must form relationships with animals, for animals cannot increase their level of caring. (But wild animals do become pets.) Could Noddings use this denial to excuse pregnant women from forming relationships with fetuses? No. Fetuses clearly can increase their contributions to relationships over time. In just months they become infants, then children, and eventually adults. Noddings must acknowledge that pregnant women should form relationships with their fetuses and therefore that abortion breaks a relationship. Premise (1) of argument (E) stands.

Gilligan might deny that premise (3) of argument (E) is the whole story. The Ethics of Care does not require one to care for others while ignoring one's own needs and desires. People have a duty to care for themselves, if only to protect their own ability to care. Now this duty to care for oneself does not simply trump the duty to care for others. One must weigh and balance, taking into account the many details of the particular situation. But sometimes, says Gilligan, it turns out to be more important to save oneself from temporary emotional harm than it is to carry an unwanted fetus to term.

Wolf-Devine doubts that the choice to abort is a choice to care for oneself, because abortion is typically seen by pregnant women as a violation rather than a nurturing of self. But sometimes caring for oneself involves painful choices. For example, choosing certain medical treatments and choosing to divorce a person you still love can both be, in different ways, painful yet self-caring acts. Sometimes abortion is a painful, self-caring act, too. Thus perhaps the Ethics of Care does not unequivocally forbid abortion.

*

Sherwin suggests that traditional discussions of abortion, especially those discussions that focus on autonomy and rights, are problematic in at least three ways. First, traditional discussions take insufficient account of the actual subordination of women in contemporary society. For example, pro-lifers often maintain that women are responsible for their pregnancy because (except when raped) women could have avoided pregnancy by opting for abstinence or at least birth control. The pro-lifers go on to urge that women should "accept responsibility" by carrying the fetus to term. But Sherwin points out that women often have little control over their sexual lives because of explicit or implicit domination by men. Thus they are often unable to "just say 'No'" or even to use effective birth control methods. I am not morally responsible for a robbery I commit if you brainwash me into thinking that I should obey you in all things, or if you break my spirit by constant criticism, or if you threaten to impoverish my children, or if you threaten to beat me to a pulp unless I perform it. For similar reasons, women are often not morally responsible for their pregnancy.

Second, traditional discussions advance a gender-neutral approach to an issue where gender should not be ignored. After all, men do not get pregnant, and men are seldom substantially involved in child care. Moreover, the gender-neutral approach naturally focuses on the status of the fetus. But highlighting the fetus leaves the pregnant woman in shadow. While investigating the rights and interests of the fetus, it is easy to ignore those of the pregnant woman. But surely the rights and interests of all parties should be balanced against one another. For example, pro-lifers often glibly maintain that adoption is a better way of coping with unwanted pregnancy than abortion. But this not only ignores the

expense, hassle, pain, and risk of pregnancy, it also slides over the short- and long-term anguish that adoption often causes for women. (It also ignores the fact that at present, black or sickly babies are unlikely to be adopted in our society.) Similarly, pro-lifers tend to ignore or minimize the extent to which an unwanted child can disrupt a woman's life and reduce her educational, economic, and social options.

Third, traditional discussions ignore female perspectives and insights into the issue of abortion. Women may have ways of thinking about ethics that do not harmonize well with the individualistic assumptions of rights-based moral theories. For example, instead of thinking of abortion as an isolated act involving the rights of a fetus and perhaps the rights of a woman, it might be better to think of abortion as one practice among many others within a social context.

Sherwin tries to expose the hidden agenda of many pro-lifers. Pregnancy and child rearing often force women to become or remain economically, psychologically, and in other ways dependent on particular men. Sherwin notices that most opponents of abortion also oppose sex outside of marriage, favor patriarchal (husband-dominated) types of marriages, and oppose social programs to help the (predominantly female) poor. These practices also tend to subordinate women. She suggests that this is no coincidence. This pro-life constellation of views leads Sherwin to believe that the ultimate goal of many pro-lifers is to restrict and subordinate women. Consciously or unconsciously, they want to keep women barefoot and pregnant in the kitchen. That is, pro-lifers oppose abortion as part of a larger strategy, the goal of which is to keep women down.

Although some may dismiss this last suggestion as a paranoid *ad hominem* attack, others may find that Sherwin's suggestion crystallizes seemingly unrelated facts into a coherent picture. At any rate, we must all acknowledge the need to discuss abortion and other social issues not only in the focused, narrow way in which they are usually discussed but also in the broader context of related social practices.

# 39    A Defense of Abortion[1]

## JUDITH JARVIS THOMSON

Most opposition to abortion relies on the premise that the fetus is a human being, a person, from the moment of conception. The premise is argued for, but, as I think, not well. Take, for example, the most common argument. We are asked to notice that the development of a human being from conception through birth into childhood is continuous; then it is said that to draw a line, to choose a point in this development and say "before this point the thing is not a person, after this point it is a person" is to make an arbitrary choice, a choice for which in the nature of things no good reason can be given. It is concluded that the fetus is, or anyway that we had better say it is, a person from the moment of conception. But this conclusion does not follow. Similar things might be said about the development of an acorn into an oak tree, and it does not follow that acorns are oak trees, or that we had better say they are. Arguments of this form are sometimes called "slippery slope arguments" —the phrase is perhaps self-explanatory—and it is dismaying that opponents of abortion rely on them so heavily and uncritically.

I am inclined to agree, however, that the prospects for "drawing a line" in the development of the fetus look dim. I am inclined to think also that we shall probably have to agree that the fetus has already become a human person well before birth. Indeed, it comes as a surprise when one first learns how early in its life it begins to acquire human characteristics. By the tenth week, for example, it already has a face, arms and legs, fingers and toes; it has internal organs, and brain activity is detectable.[2] On the other hand, I think that the premise is false, that the fetus is not a person from the moment of conception. A newly fertilized ovum, a newly implanted clump of cells, is no more a person than an acorn is an oak tree. But I shall not discuss any of this. For it seems to me to be of great interest to ask what happens if, for the sake of argument, we allow the premise. How, precisely, are we supposed to get from there to the conclusion that abortion is morally impermissible? Opponents of abortion commonly spend most of their time establishing that the fetus is a person, and hardly any time explaining the step from there to the impermissibility of abortion. Perhaps they think the step too simple and obvious to require much comment. Or perhaps instead they are simply being economical in argument. Many of those who defend abortion rely on the premise that the fetus is not a person, but only a bit of tissue that will become a person at birth; and why pay out more arguments than you have to? Whatever the explanation, I suggest that the step they take is neither easy nor obvious, that it calls for closer examination than it is commonly given, and that when we do give it this closer examination we shall feel inclined to reject it.

I propose, then, that we grant that the fetus is a person from the moment of conception. How does the argument go from here? Something like this, I take it. Every person has a right to life. So the fetus has a right to life. No doubt the mother has a right to decide what shall happen in and to her body; everyone would grant that. But surely a person's right to life is stronger and more stringent than the mother's right to decide what happens in and to her body, and so outweighs it. So the fetus may not be killed; an abortion may not be performed.

It sounds plausible. But now let me ask you to imagine this. You wake up in the morning and find yourself back to back in bed with an unconscious violinist. A famous unconscious violinist. He has been found to have a fatal kidney ailment, and the Society of Music Lovers has canvassed all the available medical records and found that you alone have the right blood type to help. They have therefore kidnapped you, and last night the violin-

Judith Jarvis Thomson, "A Defense of Abortion," *Philosophy and Public Affairs*, 1, 1 (1971), 47–66. Copyright © 1971 by Princeton University Press. Reprinted by permission of Princeton University Press.

ist's circulatory system was plugged into yours, so that your kidneys can be used to extract poisons from his blood as well as your own. The director of the hospital now tells you, "Look, we're sorry the Society of Music Lovers did this to you—we would never have permitted it if we had known. But still, they did it, and the violinist now is plugged into you. To unplug you would be to kill him. But never mind, it's only for nine months. By then he will have recovered from his ailment, and can safely be unplugged from you." Is it morally incumbent on you to accede to this situation? No doubt it would be very nice of you if you did, a great kindness. But do you *have* to accede to it? What if it were not nine months, but nine years? Or longer still? What if the director of the hospital says, "Tough luck, I agree, but you've now got to stay in bed, with the violinist plugged into you, for the rest of your life. Because remember this. All persons have a right to life, and violinists are persons. Granted you have a right to decide what happens in and to your body, but a person's right to life outweighs your right to decide what happens in and to your body. So you cannot ever be unplugged from him." I imagine you would regard this as outrageous, which suggests that something really is wrong with that plausible-sounding argument I mentioned a moment ago.

In this case, of course, you were kidnapped; you didn't volunteer for the operation that plugged the violinist into your kidneys. Can those who oppose abortion on the ground I mentioned make an exception for a pregnancy due to rape? Certainly. They can say that persons have a right to life only if they didn't come into existence because of rape; or they can say that all persons have a right to life, but that some have less of a right to life than others, in particular, that those who came into existence because of rape have less. But these statements have a rather unpleasant sound. Surely the question of whether you have a right to life at all, or how much of it you have, shouldn't turn on the question of whether or not you are the product of a rape. And in fact the people who oppose abortion on the ground I mentioned do not make this distinction, and hence do not make an exception in case of rape.

Nor do they make an exception for a case in which the mother has to spend the nine months of her pregnancy in bed. They would agree that would be a great pity, and hard on the mother; but all the same, all persons have a right to life, the fetus is a person, and so on. I suspect, in fact, that they would not make an exception for a case in which, miraculously enough, the pregnancy went on for nine years. or even the rest of the mother's life.

Some won't even make an exception for a case in which continuation of the pregnancy is likely to shorten the mother's life: they regard abortion as impermissible even to save the mother's life. Such cases are nowadays very rare, and many opponents of abortion do not accept this extreme view. All the same, it is a good place to begin: a number of points of interest come out in respect to it.

*1.* Let us call the view that abortion is impermissible even to save the mother's life "the extreme view." I want to suggest first that it does not issue from the argument I mentioned earlier without the addition of some fairly powerful premises. Suppose a woman has become pregnant, and now learns that she has a cardiac condition such that she will die if she carries the baby to term. What may be done for her? The fetus, being a person, has a right to life, but as the mother is a person too, so has she a right to life. Presumably they have an equal right to life. How is it supposed to come out that an abortion may not be performed? If mother and child have an equal right to life, shouldn't we perhaps flip a coin? Or should we add to the mother's right to life her right to decide what happens in and to her body, which everybody seems to be ready to grant—the sum of her rights now outweighing the fetus' right to life?

The most familiar argument here is the following. We are told that performing the abortion would be directly killing[3] the child, whereas doing nothing would not be killing the mother, but only letting her die. Moreover, in killing the child, one would be killing an innocent person, for the child has committed no crime, and is not aiming at his mother's death. And then there are a variety of ways in which this might be continued. (1) But as directly killing an innocent person is always and absolutely impermissible, an abortion may not be performed. Or, (2) as directly killing an innocent person is murder, and murder is always and absolutely impermissible, an abortion may not be performed.[4] Or, (3) as one's duty to refrain from directly killing an innocent person is more stringent than one's duty to keep a person from dying, an abortion may not be performed. Or, (4) if one's only options are directly killing an innocent person or letting a person die, one must prefer letting the person die, and thus an abortion may not be performed.[5]

Some people seem to have thought that these are not further premises which must be added if the conclusion is to be reached, but that they follow from the very fact that an innocent person has a right to life.[6] But this seems to me to be a mistake, and perhaps the simplest way to show this is to bring out that while we must certainly grant that innocent persons have a right to life, the theses in (1) through (4) are all false. Take (2), for example. If directly killing an innocent person is murder, and thus is impermissible, then the mother's directly killing the innocent person inside her is murder, and thus is impermissible. But it cannot seriously be thought to be murder if the mother performs an abortion on herself to save her life. It cannot seriously be said that she *must* refrain, that she *must* sit passively by and wait for her death. Let us look again at the case of you and the violinist. There you are, in bed with the violinist, and the director of the hospital says to you, "It's all most distressing, and I deeply sympathize, but you see this is putting an additional strain on your kidneys, and you'll be dead within the month. But you *have* to stay where you are all the same. Because unplugging you would be directly killing an innocent violinist, and that's murder, and that's impermissible." If anything in the world is true, it is that you do not commit murder, you do not do what is impermissible, if you reach around to your back and unplug yourself from that violinist to save your life.

The main focus of attention in writings on abortion has been on what a third party may or may not do in answer to a request from a woman for an abortion. This is in a way understandable.

Things being as they are, there isn't much a woman can safely do to abort herself. So the question asked is what a third party may do, and what the mother may do, if it is mentioned at all, is deduced, almost as an afterthought, from what it is concluded that third parties may do. But it seems to me that to treat the matter in this way is to refuse to grant to the mother that very status of person which is so firmly insisted on for the fetus. For we cannot simply read off what a person may do from what a third party may do. Suppose you find yourself trapped in a tiny house with a growing child. I mean a very tiny house, and a rapidly growing child—you are already up against the wall of the house and in a few minutes you'll be crushed to death. The child on the other hand won't be crushed to death; if nothing is done to stop him from growing he'll be hurt, but in the end he'll simply burst open the house and walk out a free man. Now I could well understand it if a bystander were to say, "There's nothing we can do for you. We cannot choose between your life and his, we cannot be the ones to decide who is to live, we cannot intervene." But it cannot be concluded that you too can do nothing, that you cannot attack it to save your life. However innocent the child may be, you do not have to wait passively while it crushes you to death. Perhaps a pregnant woman is vaguely felt to have the status of house, to which we don't allow the right of self-defense. But if the woman houses the child, it should be remembered that she is a person who houses it.

I should perhaps stop to say explicitly that I am not claiming that people have a right to do anything whatever to save their lives. I think, rather, that there are drastic limits to the right of self-defense. If someone threatens you with death unless you torture someone else to death, I think you have not the right, even to save your life, to do so. But the case under consideration here is very different. In our case there are only two people involved, one whose life is threatened, and one who threatens it. Both are innocent: the one who is threatened is not threatened because of any fault, the one who threatens does not threaten because of any fault. For this reason we may feel that we bystanders cannot intervene. But the person threatened can.

In sum, a woman surely can defend her life against the threat to it posed by the unborn child, even if doing so involves its death. And this shows not merely that the theses in (1) through (4) are false; it shows also that the extreme view of abortion is false, and so we need not canvass any other possible ways of arriving at it from the argument I mentioned at the outset.

*2.* The extreme view could of course be weakened to say that while abortion is permissible to save the mother's life, it may not be performed by a third party, but only by the mother herself. But this cannot be right either. For what we have to keep in mind is that the mother and the unborn child are not like two tenants in a small house which has, by an unfortunate mistake, been rented to both: the mother *owns* the house. The fact that she does adds to the offensiveness of deducing that the mother can do nothing from the supposition that third parties can do nothing. But it does more than this: it casts a bright light on the supposition that third parties can do nothing. Certainly it lets us see that a third party who says "I cannot choose between you" is fooling himself if he thinks this is impartiality. If Jones has found and fastened on a certain coat, which he needs to keep him from freezing, but which Smith also needs to keep him from freezing, then it is not impartiality that says "I cannot choose between you" when Smith owns the coat. Women have said again and again "This body is *my* body!" and they have reason to feel angry, reason to feel that it has been like shouting into the wind. Smith, after all, is hardly likely to bless us if we say to him, "Of course it's your coat, anybody would grant that it is. But no one may choose between you and Jones who is to have it."

We should really ask what it is that says "no one may choose" in the face of the fact that the body that houses the child is the mother's body. It may be simply a failure to appreciate this fact. But it may be something more interesting, namely the sense that one has a right to refuse to lay hands on people, even where it would be just and fair to do so, even where justice seems to require that some-

body do so. Thus justice might call for somebody to get Smith's coat back from Jones, and yet you have a right to refuse to be the one to lay hands on Jones, a right to refuse to do physical violence to him. This, I think, must be granted. But then what should be said is not "no one may choose," but only "*I* cannot choose," and indeed not even this, but "*I* will not *act*," leaving it open that somebody else can or should, and in particular that anyone in a position of authority, with the job of securing people's rights, both can and should. So this is no difficulty. I have not been arguing that any given third party must accede to the mother's request that he perform an abortion to save her life, but only that he may.

I suppose that in some views of human life the mother's body is only on loan to her, the loan not being one which gives her any prior claim to it. One who held this view might well think it impartiality to say "I cannot choose." But I shall simply ignore this possibility. My own view is that if a human being has any just, prior claim to anything at all, he has a just, prior claim to his own body. And perhaps this needn't be argued for here anyway, since, as I mentioned, the arguments against abortion we are looking at do grant that the woman has a right to decide what happens in and to her body.

But although they do grant it, I have tried to show that they do not take seriously what is done in granting it. I suggest the same thing will reappear even more clearly when we turn away from cases in which the mother's life is at stake, and attend, as I propose we now do, to the vastly more common cases in which a woman wants an abortion for some less weighty reason than preserving her own life.

*3.* Where the mother's life is not at stake, the argument I mentioned at the outset seems to have a much stronger pull. "Everyone has a right to life, so the unborn person has a right to life." And isn't the child's right to life weightier than anything other than the mother's own right to life, which she might put forward as ground for an abortion?

This argument treats the right to life as if it were unproblematic. It is not, and this seems to me to be precisely the source of the mistake.

For we should now, at long last, ask what it comes to, to have a right to life. In some views having a right to life includes having a right to be given at least the bare minimum one needs for continued life. But suppose that what in fact *is* the bare minimum a man needs for continued life is something he has no right at all to be given? If I am sick unto death, and the only thing that will save my life is the touch of Henry Fonda's cool hand on my fevered brow, then all the same, I have no right to be given the touch of Henry Fonda's cool hand on my fevered brow. It would be frightfully nice of him to fly in from the West Coast to provide it. It would be less nice, though no doubt well meant, if my friends flew out to the West Coast and carried Henry Fonda back with them. But I have no right at all against anybody that he should do this for me. Or again, to return to the story I told earlier, the fact that for continued life that violinist needs the continued use of your kidneys does not establish that he has a right to be given the continued use of your kidneys. He certainly has no right against you that *you* should give him continued use of your kidneys. For nobody has any right to use your kidneys unless you give him such a right; and nobody has the right against you that you shall give him this right —if you do allow him to go on using your kidneys, this is a kindness on your part, and not something he can claim from you as his due. Nor has he any right against anybody else that *they* should give him continued use of your kidneys. Certainly he had no right against the Society of Music Lovers that they should plug him into you in the first place. And if you now start to unplug yourself, having learned that you will otherwise have to spend nine years in bed with him, there is nobody in the world who must try to prevent you, in order to see to it that he is given something he has a right to be given.

Some people are rather stricter about the right to life. In their view, it does not include the right to be given anything, but amounts to, and only to, the right not to be killed by anybody. But here a related difficulty arises. If everybody is to refrain from killing that violinist, then everybody must refrain from doing a great many different sorts of things. Everybody must refrain from slitting his throat, everybody must refrain from shooting him —and everybody must refrain from unplugging you from him. But does he have a right against everybody that they shall refrain from unplugging you from him? To refrain from doing this is to allow him to continue to use your kidneys. It could be argued that he has a right against us that *we* should allow him to continue to use your kidneys. That is, while he had no right against us that we should give him the use of your kidneys, it might be argued that he anyway has a right against us that we shall not now intervene and deprive him of the use of your kidneys. I shall come back to third-party interventions later. But certainly the violinist has no right against you that *you* shall allow him to continue to use your kidneys. As I said, if you do allow him to use them, it is a kindness on your part, and not something you owe him.

The difficulty I point to here is not peculiar to the right to life. It reappears in connection with all the other natural rights; and it is something which an adequate account of rights must deal with. For present purposes it is enough just to draw attention to it. But I would stress that I am not arguing that people do not have a right to life—quite to the contrary, it seems to me that the primary control we must place on the acceptability of an account of rights is that it should turn out in that account to be a truth that all persons have a right to life. I am arguing only that having a right to life does not guarantee having either a right to be given the use of or a right to be allowed continued use of another person's body—even if one needs it for life itself. So the right to life will not serve the opponents of abortion in the very simple and clear way in which they seem to have thought it would.

*4.* There is another way to bring out the difficulty. In the most ordinary sort of case, to deprive someone of what he has a right to is to treat him unjustly. Suppose a boy and his small brother are jointly given a box of chocolates for Christmas. If the older boy takes the box and refuses to give his brother any of the chocolates, he is unjust to him, for the brother has been given a right to half of them. But suppose that, having learned that otherwise it means nine years in bed with that violinist, you unplug yourself from him. You surely are not being unjust to him, for you gave him no right to use your kidneys, and no one else can have given him any such right. But we have to notice that in unplugging yourself, you are killing him; and violinists, like everybody else, have a right to life, and thus in the view we were considering just now, the right not to be killed. So here you do what he supposedly has a right you shall not do, but you do not act unjustly to him in doing it.

The emendation which may be made at this point is this: the right to life consists not in the right not to be killed, but rather in the right not to be killed unjustly. This runs a risk of circularity, but never mind; it would enable us to square the fact that the violinist has a right to life with the fact that you do not act unjustly toward him in unplugging yourself, thereby killing him. For if you do not kill him unjustly, you do not violate his right to life, and so it is no wonder you do him no injustice.

But if this emendation is accepted, the gap in the argument against abortion stares us plainly in the face: it is by no means enough to show that the fetus is a person, and to remind us that all persons have a right to life—we need to be shown also that killing the fetus violates its right to life, i.e., that abortion is unjust killing. And is it?

I suppose we may take it as a datum that in a case of pregnancy due to rape the mother has not given the unborn person a right to the use of her body for food and shelter. Indeed, in what pregnancy could it be supposed that the mother has given the unborn person such a right? It is not as if there were unborn persons drifting about the world, to whom a woman who wants a child says "I invite you in."

But it might be argued that there are other ways one can have acquired a right to the use of another person's body than by having been invited to use it by that person. Suppose a woman voluntarily indulges in intercourse, knowing of the chance it will issue in pregnancy, and then she does become pregnant; is she not in part responsible for the presence, in fact the very existence, of the unborn person inside her? No doubt she did

not invite it in. But doesn't her partial responsibility for its being there itself give it a right to the use of her body?[7] If so, then her aborting it would be more like the boy's taking away the chocolates, and less like your unplugging yourself from the violinist— doing so would be depriving it of what it does have a right to, and thus would be doing it an injustice.

And then, too, it might be asked whether or not she can kill it even to save her own life: If she voluntarily called it into existence, how can she now kill it, even in self-defense?

The first thing to be said about this is that it is something new. Opponents of abortion have been so concerned to make out the independence of the fetus, in order to establish that it has a right to life, just as its mother does, that they have tended to overlook the possible support they might gain from making out that the fetus is *dependent* on the mother, in order to establish that she has a special kind of responsibility for it, a responsibility that gives it rights against her which are not possessed by any independent person—such as an ailing violinist who is a stranger to her.

On the other hand, this argument would give the unborn person a right to its mother's body only if her pregnancy resulted from a voluntary act, undertaken in full knowledge of the chance a pregnancy might result from it. It would leave out entirely the unborn person whose existence is due to rape. Pending the availability of some further argument, then, we would be left with the conclusion that unborn persons whose existence is due to rape have no right to the use of their mothers' bodies, and thus that aborting them is not depriving them of anything they have a right to and hence is not unjust killing.

And we should also notice that it is not at all plain that this argument really does go even as far as it purports to. For there are cases and cases, and the details make a difference. If the room is stuffy, and I therefore open a window to air it, and a burglar climbs in, it would be absurd to say, "Ah, now he can stay, she's given him a right to the use of her house—for she is partially responsible for his presence there, having voluntarily done what enabled him to get in, in full knowledge that there are such things as burglars, and that burglars burgle." It would be still more absurd to say this if I had had bars installed outside my windows, precisely to prevent burglars from getting in, and a burglar got in only because of a defect in the bars. It remains equally absurd if we imagine it is not a burglar who climbs in, but an innocent person who blunders or falls in. Again, suppose it were like this: people-seeds drift about in the air like pollen, and if you open your windows, one may drift in and take root in your carpets or upholstery. You don't want children, so you fix up your windows with fine mesh screens, the very best you can buy. As can happen, however, and on very, very rare occasions does happen, one of the screens is defective; and a seed drifts in and takes root. Does the person-plant who now develops have a right to the use of your house? Surely not—despite the fact that you voluntarily opened your windows, you knowingly kept carpets and upholstered furniture, and you knew that screens were sometimes defective. Someone may argue that you are responsible for its rooting, that it does have a right to your house, because after all you *could* have lived out your life with bare floors and furniture, or with sealed windows and doors. But this won't do—for by the same token anyone can avoid a pregnancy due to rape by having a hysterectomy, or anyway by never leaving home without a (reliable!) army.

It seems to me that the argument we are looking at can establish at most that there are *some* cases in which the unborn person has a right to the use of its mother's body, and therefore *some* cases in which abortion is unjust killing. There is room for much discussion and argument as to precisely which, if any. But I think we should sidestep this issue and leave it open, for at any rate the argument certainly does not establish that all abortion is unjust killing.

5. There is room for yet another argument here, however. We surely must all grant that there may be cases in which it would be morally indecent to detach a person from your body at the cost of his life. Suppose you learn that what the violinist needs is not nine years of your life, but only one hour: all you need do to save his life is to spend one hour in that bed with him. Suppose also that letting him use your kidneys for that one hour would not affect your health in the slightest. Admittedly you were kidnapped. Admittedly you did not give anyone permission to plug him into you. Nevertheless it seems to me plain you *ought* to allow him to use your kidneys for that hour—it would be indecent to refuse.

Again, suppose pregnancy lasted only an hour, and constituted no threat to life or health. And suppose that a woman becomes pregnant as a result of rape. Admittedly she did not voluntarily do anything to bring about the existence of a child. Admittedly she did nothing at all which would give the unborn person a right to the use of her body. All the same it might well be said, as in the newly emended violinist story, that she *ought* to allow it to remain for that hour—that it would be indecent of her to refuse.

Now some people are inclined to use the term "right" in such a way that it follows from the fact that you ought to allow a person to use your body for the hour he needs, that he has a right to use your body for the hour he needs, even though he has not been given that right by any person or act. They may say that it follows also that if you refuse, you act unjustly toward him. This use of the term is perhaps so common that it cannot be called wrong; nevertheless it seems to me to be an unfortunate loosening of what we would do better to keep a tight rein on. Suppose that box of chocolates I mentioned earlier has not been given to both boys jointly, but was given only to the older boy. There he sits, stolidly eating his way through the box, his small brother watching enviously. Here we are likely to say "You ought not to be so mean. You ought to give your brother some of those chocolates." My own view is that it just does not follow from the truth of this that the brother has any right to any of the chocolates. If the boy refuses to give his brother any, he is greedy, stingy, callous—but not unjust. I suppose that the people I have in mind will say it does follow that the brother has a right to some of the chocolates, and thus that the boy does act unjustly if he refuses to give his brother any. But the effect of saying this is to obscure what we should keep distinct, namely the difference between the boy's refusal in this case and the boy's refusal in the earlier case, in which the box was given to both boys jointly, and in which the small brother thus had what was from any point of view clear title to half.

A further objection to so using the term "right" that from the fact that A ought to do a thing for B, it follows that B has a right against A that A do it for him, is that it is going to make the question of whether or not a man has a right to a thing turn on how easy it is to provide him with it: and this seems not merely unfortunate, but morally unacceptable. Take the case of Henry Fonda again. I said earlier that I had no right to the touch of his cool hand on my fevered brow, even though I needed it to save my life. I said it would be frightfully nice of him to fly in from the West Coast to provide me with it, but that I had no right against him that he should do so. But suppose he isn't on the West Coast. Suppose he has only to walk across the room, place a hand briefly on my brow —and lo, my life is saved. Then surely he ought to do it, it would be indecent to refuse. Is it to be said "Ah, well, it follows that in this case she has a right to the touch of his hand on her brow, and so it would be an injustice in him to refuse"? So that I have a right to it when it is easy for him to provide it, though no right when it's hard? It's rather a shocking idea that anyone's rights should fade away and disappear as it gets harder and harder to accord them to him.

So my own view is that even though you ought to let the violinist use your kidneys for the one hour he needs, we should not conclude that he has a right to do so—we should say that if you refuse, you are, like the boy who owns all the chocolates and will give none away, self-centered and callous, indecent in fact, but not unjust. And similarly, that even supposing a case in which a woman pregnant due to rape ought to allow the unborn person to use her body for the hour he needs, we should not conclude that he has a right to do so; we should conclude that she is self-centered, callous, indecent, but not unjust, if she refuses. The complaints are no less grave; they are just different. However, there is no need to insist on this point. If anyone does wish to deduce "he

has a right" from "you ought," then all the same he must surely grant that there are cases in which it is not morally required of you that you allow that violinist to use your kidneys, and in which he does not have a right to use them, and in which you do not do him an injustice if you refuse. And so also for mother and unborn child. Except in such cases as the unborn person has a right to demand it—and we were leaving open the possibility that there may be such cases—nobody is morally *required* to make large sacrifices, of health, of all other interests and concerns, of all other duties and commitments, for nine years, or even for nine months, in order to keep another person alive.

6. We have in fact to distinguish between two kinds of Samaritan: the Good Samaritan and what we might call the Minimally Decent Samaritan. The story of the Good Samaritan, you will remember, goes like this:

A certain man went down from Jerusalem to Jericho, and fell among thieves, which stripped him of his raiment, and wounded him, and departed, leaving him half dead.

And by chance there came down a certain priest that way; and when he saw him, he passed by on the other side.

And likewise a Levite, when he was at the place, came and looked on him, and passed by on the other side.

But a certain Samaritan, as he journeyed, came where he was; and when he saw him he had compassion on him.

And went to him, and bound up his wounds, pouring in oil and wine, and set him on his own beast, and brought him to an inn, and took care of him.

And on the morrow, when he departed, he took out two pence, and gave them to the host, and said unto him, "Take care of him; and whatsoever thou spendest more, when I come again, I will repay thee."

(*Luke 10:30–35*)

The Good Samaritan went out of his way, at some cost to himself, to help one in need of it. We are not told what the options were, that is, whether or not the priest and the Levite could have helped by doing less than the Good Samaritan did, but assuming they could have, then the fact they did nothing at all shows they were not even Minimally Decent Samaritans, not because they were not Samaritans, but because they were not even minimally decent.

These things are a matter of degree, of course, but there is a difference, and it comes out perhaps most clearly in the story of Kitty Genovese, who, as you will remember, was murdered while thirty-eight people watched or listened, and did nothing at all to help her. A Good Samaritan would have rushed out to give direct assistance against the murderer. Or perhaps we had better allow that it would have been a Splendid Samaritan who did this, on the ground that it would have involved a risk of death for himself. But the thirty-eight not only did not do this, they did not even trouble to pick up a phone to call the police. Minimally Decent Samaritanism would call for doing at least that, and their not having done it was monstrous.

After telling the story of the Good Samaritan, Jesus said "Go, and do thou likewise." Perhaps he meant that we are morally required to act as the Good Samaritan did. Perhaps he was urging people to do more than is morally required of them. At all events it seems plain that it was not morally required of any of the thirty-eight that he rush out to give direct assistance at the risk of his own life, and that it is not morally required of anyone that he give long stretches of his life—nine years or nine months—to sustaining the life of a person who has no special right (we were leaving open the possibility of this) to demand it.

Indeed, with one rather striking class of exceptions: no one in any country in the world is *legally* required to do anywhere near as much as this for anyone else. The class of exceptions is obvious. My main concern here is not the state of the law in respect to abortion, but it is worth drawing attention to the fact that in no state in this country is any man compelled by law to be even a Minimally Decent Samaritan to any person; there is no law under which charges could be brought against the thirty-eight who stood by while Kitty Genovese died. By contrast, in most states in this country women are compelled by law to be not merely Minimally Decent Samaritans, but Good Samaritans to unborn persons inside them. This doesn't by itself settle anything one way or the other, because it may well be argued that there should be laws in this country—as there are in many European countries—compelling at least Minimally Decent Samaritanism.[8] But it does show that there is a gross injustice in the existing state of the law. And it shows also that the groups currently working against liberalization of abortion laws, in fact working toward having it declared unconstitutional for a state to permit abortion, had better start working for the adoption of Good Samaritan laws generally, or earn the charge that they are acting in bad faith.

I should think, myself, that Minimally Decent Samaritan laws would be one thing, Good Samaritan laws quite another, and in fact highly improper. But we are not here concerned with the law. What we should ask is not whether anybody should be compelled by law to be a Good Samaritan, but whether we must accede to a situation in which somebody is being compelled—by nature, perhaps—to be a Good Samaritan. We have, in other words, to look now at third-party interventions. I have been arguing that no person is morally required to make large sacrifices to sustain the life of another who has no right to demand them, and this even where the sacrifices do not include life itself; we are not morally required to be Good Samaritans or anyway Very Good Samaritans to one another. But what if a man cannot extricate himself from such a situation? What if he appeals to us to extricate him? It seems to me plain that there are cases in which we can, cases in which a Good Samaritan would extricate him. There you are, you were kidnapped, and nine years in bed with that violinist lie ahead of you. You have your own life to lead. You are sorry, but you simply cannot see giving up so much of your life to the sustaining of his. You cannot extricate yourself, and ask us to do so. I should have thought that—in light of his having no right to the use of your body—it was obvious that we do not have to accede to your being forced to give up so much. We can do what you ask. There is no injustice to the violinist in our doing so.

7. Following the lead of the opponents of abortion, I have throughout been speaking of the fetus merely as a person, and what I have been asking is whether or not the argument we began with,

which proceeds only from the fetus' being a person, really does establish its conclusion. I have argued that it does not.

But of course there are arguments and arguments, and it may be said that I have simply fastened on the wrong one. It may be said that what is important is not merely the fact that the fetus is a person, but that it is a person for whom the woman has a special kind of responsibility issuing from the fact that she is its mother. And it might be argued that all my analogies are therefore irrelevant—for you do not have that special kind of responsibility for that violinist. Henry Fonda does not have that special kind of responsibility for me. And our attention might be drawn to the fact that men and women both *are* compelled by law to provide support for their children.

I have in effect dealt (briefly) with this argument in section 4 above; but a (still briefer) recapitulation now may be in order. Surely we do not have any such "special responsibility" for a person unless we have assumed it, explicitly or implicitly. If a set of parents do not try to prevent pregnancy, do not obtain an abortion, and then at the time of birth of the child do not put it out for adoption, but rather take it home with them, then they have assumed responsibility for it, they have given it rights, and they cannot *now* withdraw support from it at the cost of its life because they now find it difficult to go on providing for it. But if they have taken all reasonable precautions against having a child, they do not simply by virtue of their biological relationship to the child who comes into existence have a special responsibility for it. They may wish to assume responsibility for it, or they may not wish to. And I am suggesting that if assuming responsibility for it would require large sacrifices, then they may refuse. A Good Samaritan would not refuse—or anyway, a Splendid Samaritan, if the sacrifices that had to be made were enormous. But then so would a Good Samaritan assume responsibility for that violinist; so would Henry Fonda, if he is a Good Samaritan, fly in from the West Coast and assume responsibility for me.

*8.* My argument will be found unsatisfactory on two counts by many of those who want to regard abortion as morally permissible. First, while I do argue that abortion is not impermissible, I do not argue that it is always permissible. There may well be cases in which carrying the child to term requires only Minimally Decent Samaritanism of the mother, and this is a standard we must not fall below. I am inclined to think it a merit of my account precisely that it does *not* give a general yes or a general no. It allows for and supports our sense that, for example, a sick and desperately frightened fourteen-year-old schoolgirl, pregnant due to rape, may *of course* choose abortion, and that any law which rules this out is an insane law. And it also allows for and supports our sense that in other cases resort to abortion is even positively indecent. It would be indecent in the woman to request an abortion, and indecent in a doctor to perform it, if she is in her seventh month, and wants the abortion just to avoid the nuisance of postponing a trip abroad. The very fact that the arguments I have been drawing attention to treat all cases of abortion, or even all cases of abortion in which the mother's life is not at stake, as morally on a par ought to have made them suspect at the outset.

Secondly, while I am arguing for the permissibility of abortion in some cases, I am not arguing for the right to secure the death of the unborn child. It is easy to confuse these two things in that up to a certain point in the life of the fetus it is not able to survive outside the mother's body; hence removing it from her body guarantees its death. But they are importantly different. I have argued that you are not morally required to spend nine months in bed, sustaining the life of that violinist; but to say this is by no means to say that if, when you unplug yourself, there is a miracle and he survives, you then have a right to turn round and slit his throat. You may detach yourself even if this costs him his life; you have no right to be guaranteed his death, by some other means, if unplugging yourself does not kill him. There are some people who will feel dissatisfied by this feature of my argument. A woman may be utterly devastated by the thought of a child, a bit of herself, put out for adoption and never seen or heard of again. She may therefore want not merely that the child be detached from her, but more, that it die. Some opponents of abortion are inclined to regard this as beneath contempt—thereby showing insensitivity to what is surely a powerful source of despair. All the same, I agree that the desire for the child's death is not one which anybody may gratify, should it turn out to be possible to detach the child alive.

At this place, however, it should be remembered that we have only been pretending throughout that the fetus is a human being from the moment of conception. A very early abortion is surely not the killing of a person, and so is not dealt with by anything I have said here.

## Notes

1. I am very much indebted to James Thomson for discussion, criticism, and many helpful suggestions.

2. Daniel Callahan, *Abortion: Law, Choice and Morality* (New York, 1970), p. 373. This book gives a fascinating survey of the available information on abortion. The Jewish tradition is surveyed in David M. Feldman, *Birth Control in Jewish Law* (New York, 1968), Part 5; the Catholic tradition in John T. Noonan, Jr., "An Almost Absolute Value in History," in *The Morality of Abortion*, ed. John T. Noonan, Jr. (Cambridge, Mass., 1970).

3. The term "direct" in the arguments I refer to is a technical one. Roughly, what is meant by "direct killing" is either killing as an end in itself, or killing as a means of some end, for example, the end of saving someone else's life. See footnote 6 for an example of its use.

4. Cf. *Encyclical Letter of Pope Pius XI on Christian Marriage*, St. Paul Editions (Boston, n.d.), p. 32: "However much we may pity the mother whose health and even life is gravely imperiled in the performance of the duty allotted to her by nature, nevertheless what could ever be a sufficient reason for excusing in any way the direct murder of the innocent? This is precisely what we are dealing with here." Noonan (*The Morality of Abortion*, p. 43) reads this as follows: "What cause can ever avail to excuse in any way the direct killing of the innocent? For it is a question of that."

5. The thesis in (4) is in an interesting way weaker than those in (1), (2), and (3): they rule out abortion even in cases in which both mother *and* child will die if the abortion is not performed. By contrast, one who held the view expressed in (4) could consistently say that one needn't prefer letting two persons die to killing one.

6. Cf. the following passage from Pius XII, *Address to the Italian Catholic Society of Midwives:* "The baby in the maternal breast has the right to life immediately from God. —Hence there is no man, no human authority, no science, no medical, eugenic, social, economic or moral 'indication' which can establish or grant a valid juridical ground for a direct deliberate disposition of an innocent human life, that is a disposition which looks to its destruction either as an end or as a means to another end perhaps in itself not illicit.—The baby, still not born, is a man in the same degree and for the same reason as the mother." (quoted in Noonan, *The Morality of Abortion*, p. 45).

7. The need for a discussion of this argument was brought home to me by members of the Society for Ethical and Legal Philosophy, to whom this paper was originally presented.

8. For a discussion of the difficulties involved, and a survey of the European experience with such laws, see *The Good Samaritan and the Law*, ed. James M. Ratcliffe (New York, 1966).

# 40    Abortion and the Concept of a Person

## JANE ENGLISH

The abortion debate rages on. Yet the two most popular positions seem to be clearly mistaken. Conservatives maintain that a human life begins at conception and that therefore abortion must be wrong because it is murder. But not all killings of

humans are murders. Most notably, self defense may justify even the killing of an innocent person.

Liberals, on the other hand, are just as mistaken in their argument that since a fetus does not become a person until birth, a woman may do whatever she pleases in and to her own body. First, you cannot do as you please with your own body if it affects other people adversely.[1] Second,

Reprinted with permission of the publisher from *Canadian Journal of Philosophy*, 5, 2 (1975), 233–243.

if a fetus is not a person, that does not imply that you can do to it anything you wish. Animals, for example, are not persons, yet to kill or torture them for no reason at all is wrong.

At the center of the storm has been the issue of just when it is between ovulation and adulthood that a person appears on the scene. Conservatives draw the line at conception, liberals at birth. In this paper I first examine our concept of a person and conclude that no single criterion can capture the concept of a person and no sharp line can be drawn. Next I argue that if a fetus is a person, abortion is still justifiable in many cases; and if a fetus is not a person, killing it is still wrong in many cases. To a large extent, these two solutions are in agreement. I conclude that our concept of a person cannot and need not bear the weight that the abortion controversy has thrust upon it.

# I

The several factions in the abortion argument have drawn battle lines around various proposed criteria for determining what is and what is not a person. For example, Mary Anne Warren[2] lists five features (capacities for reasoning, self-awareness, complex communication, etc.) as her criteria for personhood and argues for the permissibility of abortion because a fetus falls outside this concept. Baruch Brody[3] uses brain waves. Michael Tooley[4] picks having-a-concept-of-self as his criterion and concludes that infanticide and abortion are justifiable, while the killing of adult animals is not. On the other side, Paul Ramsey[5] claims a certain gene structure is the defining characteristic. John Noonan[6] prefers conceived-of-humans and presents counterexamples to various other candidate criteria. For instance, he argues against viability as the criterion because the newborn and infirm would then be non-persons, since they cannot live without the aid of others. He rejects any criterion that calls upon the sorts of sentiments a being can evoke in adults on the grounds that this would allow us to exclude other races as non-persons if we could just view them sufficiently unsentimentally.

These approaches are typical: foes of abortion propose sufficient conditions for personhood which fetuses satisfy, while friends of abortion counter with necessary conditions for personhood which fetuses lack. But these both presuppose that the concept of a person can be captured in a strait jacket of necessary and/ or sufficient conditions.[7] Rather, "person" is a cluster of features, of which rationality, having a self concept and being conceived-of humans are only part.

What is typical of persons? Within our concept of a person we include, first, certain biological factors: descended from humans, having a certain genetic makeup, having a head, hands, arms, eyes, capable of locomotion, breathing, eating, sleeping. There are psychological factors: sentience, perception, having a concept of self and of one's own interests and desires, the ability to use tools, the ability to use language or symbol systems, the ability to joke, to be angry, to doubt. There are rationality factors: the ability to reason and draw conclusions, the ability to generalize and to learn from past experience, the ability to sacrifice present interests for greater gains in the future. There are social factors: the ability to work in groups and respond to peer pressures, the ability to recognize and consider as valuable the interests of others, seeing oneself as one among "other minds," the ability to sympathize, encourage, love, the ability to evoke from others the responses of sympathy, encouragement, love, the ability to work with others for mutual advantage. Then there are legal factors: being subject to the law and protected by it, having the ability to sue and enter contracts, being counted in the census, having a name and citizenship, the ability to own property, inherit, and so forth.

Now the point is not that this list is incomplete, or that you can find counter instances to each of its points. People typically exhibit rationality, for instance, but someone who was irrational would not thereby fail to qualify as a person. On the other hand, something could exhibit the majority of these features and still fail to be a person, as an advanced robot might. There is no single core of necessary and sufficient features which we can draw upon with the assurance that they constitute what really makes a person; there are only features that are more or less typical.

This is not to say that no necessary or sufficient conditions can be given. Being alive is a necessary condition for being a person, and being a U.S. Senator is sufficient. But rather than falling inside a sufficient condition or outside a necessary one, a fetus lies in the penumbra region where our concept of a person is not so simple. For this reason I think a conclusive answer to the question whether a fetus is a person is unattainable.

Here we might note a family of simple fallacies that proceed by stating a necessary condition for personhood and showing that a fetus has that characteristic. This is a form of the fallacy of affirming the consequent. For example, some have mistakenly reasoned from the premise that a fetus is human (after all, it is a human fetus rather than, say, a canine fetus) to the conclusion that it is *a* human. Adding an equivocation on "being," we get the fallacious argument that since a fetus is something both living and human, it is a human being.

Nonetheless, it does seem clear that a fetus has very few of the above family of characteristics, whereas a newborn baby exhibits a much larger proportion of them—and a two-year-old has even more. Note that one traditional anti-abortion argument has centered on pointing out the many ways in which a fetus resembles a baby. They emphasize its development ("It already has ten fingers . . .") without mentioning its dissimilarities to adults (it still has gills and a tail). They also try to evoke the sort of sympathy on our part that we only feel toward other persons ("Never to laugh . . . or feel the sunshine?"). This all seems to be a relevant way to argue, since its purpose is to persuade us that a fetus satisfies so many of the important features on the list that it ought to be treated as a person. Also note that a fetus near the time of birth satisfies many more of these factors than a fetus in the early months of development. This could provide reason for making distinctions among the different stages of pregnancy, as the U.S. Supreme Court has done.[8]

Historically, the time at which a person has been said to come into existence has varied widely. Muslims date personhood from fourteen days after conception. Some medievals followed Aristotle in placing ensoulment at forty days after conception for a male fetus and eighty days for a female fetus.[9] In European common law since the Seventeenth Century, abortion was considered the killing of a person only after quickening, the time when a pregnant woman first feels the fetus move on its own. Nor is this variety of opinions surprising. Biologically, a human being develops gradually. We shouldn't expect there to be any specific time or sharp dividing point when a person appears on the scene.

For these reasons I believe our concept of a person is not sharp or decisive enough to bear the weight of a solution to the abortion controversy. To use it to solve that problem is to clarify *obscurum per obscurius*.

## II

Next let us consider what follows if a fetus is a person after all. Judith Jarvis Thomson's landmark article, "A Defense of Abortion,"[10] correctly points out that some additional argumentation is needed at this point in the conservative argument to bridge the gap between the premise that a fetus is an innocent person and the conclusion that killing it is always wrong. To arrive at this conclusion, we would need the additional premise that killing an innocent person is always wrong. But killing an innocent person is sometimes permissible, most notably in self defense. Some examples may help draw out our intuitions or ordinary judgments about self defense.

Suppose a mad scientist, for instance, hypnotized innocent people to jump out of the bushes and attack innocent passersby with knives. If you are so attacked, we agree you have a right to kill the attacker in self defense, if killing him is the only way to protect your life or to save yourself from serious injury. It does not seem to matter here that the attacker is not malicious but himself an innocent pawn, for your killing of him is not done in a spirit of retribution but only in self defense.

How severe an injury may you inflict in self defense? In part this depends upon the severity of the injury to be avoided: you may not shoot someone merely to avoid having your clothes torn. This might lead one to the mistaken conclusion that the defense may only equal the threatened injury in severity; that to avoid death you may kill, but to avoid a black eye you may only inflict a black eye or the equivalent. Rather, our laws and customs seem to say that you may create an injury somewhat, but not enormously, greater than the injury to be avoided. To fend off an attack whose outcome would be as serious as rape, a severe beating or the loss of a finger, you may shoot; to avoid having your clothes torn, you may blacken an eye.

Aside from this, the injury you may inflict should only be the minimum necessary to deter or incapacitate the attacker. Even if you know he intends to kill you, you are not justified in shooting him if you could equally well save yourself by the simple expedient of running away. Self defense is for the purpose of avoiding harms rather than equalizing harms.

Some cases of pregnancy present a parallel situation. Though the fetus is itself innocent, it may pose a threat to the pregnant woman's well-being, life prospects or health, mental or physical. If the pregnancy presents a slight threat to her interests, it seems self defense cannot justify abortion. But if the threat is on a par with a serious beating or the loss of a finger, she may kill the fetus that poses such a threat, even if it is an innocent person. If a lesser harm to the fetus could have the same defensive effect, killing it would not be justified. It is unfortunate that the only way to free the woman from the pregnancy entails the death of the fetus (except in very late stages of pregnancy). Thus a self defense model supports Thomson's point that the woman has a right only to be freed from the fetus, not a right to demand its death.[11]

The self defense model is most helpful when we take the pregnant woman's point of view. In the pre-Thomson literature, abortion is often framed as a question for a third party: do you, a doctor, have a right to choose between the life of the woman and that of the fetus? Some have claimed that if you were a passer-by who witnessed a struggle between the innocent hypnotized attacker and his equally innocent victim,

you would have no reason to kill either in defense of the other. They have concluded that the self defense model implies that a woman may attempt to abort herself, but that a doctor should not assist her. I think the position of the third party is somewhat more complex. We do feel some inclination to intervene on behalf of the victim rather than the attacker, other things equal. But if both parties are innocent, other factors come into consideration. You would rush to the aid of your husband whether he was attacker or attackee. If a hypnotized famous violinist were attacking a skid row bum, we would try to save the individual who is of more value to society. These considerations would tend to support abortion in some cases.

But suppose you are a frail senior citizen who wishes to avoid being knifed by one of these innocent hypnotics, so you have hired a bodyguard to accompany you. If you are attacked, it is clear we believe that the bodyguard, acting as your agent, has a right to kill the attacker to save you from a serious beating. Your rights of self defense are transferred to your agent. I suggest that we should similarly view the doctor as the pregnant woman's agent in carrying out a defense she is physically incapable of accomplishing herself.

Thanks to modern technology, the cases are rare in which a pregnancy poses as clear a threat to a woman's bodily health as an attacker brandishing a switchblade. How does self defense fare when more subtle, complex and long-range harms are involved?

To consider a somewhat fanciful example, suppose you are a highly trained surgeon when you are kidnapped by the hypnotic attacker. He says he does not intend to harm you but to take you back to the mad scientist who, it turns out, plans to hypnotize you to have a permanent mental block against all your knowledge of medicine. This would automatically destroy your career, which would in turn have a serious adverse impact on your family, your personal relationships and your happiness. It seems to me that if the only way you can avoid this outcome is to shoot the innocent attacker, you are justified in so doing. You are defending yourself from a drastic injury to your life prospects. I think it is no exaggeration to claim that unwanted pregnancies (most obviously among teenagers) often have such adverse life-long consequences as the surgeon's loss of livelihood.

Several parallels arise between various views on abortion and the self defense model. Let's suppose further that these hypnotized attackers only operate at night, so that it is well known that they can be avoided completely by the considerable inconvenience of never leaving your house after dark. One view is that since you could stay home at night, therefore if you go out and are selected by one of these hypnotized people, you have no right to defend yourself. This parallels the view that abstinence is the only acceptable way to avoid pregnancy. Others might hold that you ought to take along some defense such as Mace which will deter the hypnotized person without killing him, but that if this defense fails, you are obliged to submit to the resulting injury, no matter how severe it is. This parallels the view that contraception is all right but abortion is always wrong, even in cases of contraceptive failure.

A third view is that you may kill the hypnotized person only if he will actually kill you, but not if he will only injure you. This is like the position that abortion is permissible only if it is required to save a woman's life. Finally we have the view that it is all right to kill the attacker, even if only to avoid a very slight inconvenience to yourself and even if you knowingly walked down the very street where all these incidents have been taking place without taking along any Mace or protective escort. If we assume that a fetus is a person, this is the analogue of the view that abortion is always justifiable, "on demand."

The self defense model allows us to see an important difference that exists between abortion and infanticide, even if a fetus is a person from conception. Many have argued that the only way to justify abortion without justifying infanticide would be to find some characteristic of personhood that is acquired at birth. Michael Tooley, for one, claims infanticide is justifiable because the really significant characteristics of a person are acquired some time after birth. But all such approaches look to characteristics of the developing

human and ignore the relation between the fetus and the woman. What if, after birth, the presence of an infant or the need to support it posed a grave threat to the woman's sanity or life prospects? She could escape this threat by the simple expedient of running away. So a solution that does not entail the death of the infant is available. Before birth, such solutions are not available because of the biological dependence of the fetus on the woman. Birth is the crucial point not because of any characteristics the fetus gains, but because after birth the woman can defend herself by a means less drastic than killing the infant. Hence self defense can be used to justify abortion without necessarily thereby justifying infanticide.

## III

On the other hand, supposing a fetus is not after all a person, would abortion always be morally permissible? Some opponents of abortion seem worried that if a fetus is not a full-fledged person, then we are justified in treating it in any way at all. However, this does not follow. Non-persons do get some consideration in our moral code, though of course they do not have the same rights as persons have (and in general they do not have moral responsibilities), and though their interests may be overridden by the interests of persons. Still, we cannot just treat them in any way at all.

Treatment of animals is a case in point. It is wrong to torture dogs for fun or to kill wild birds for no reason at all. It is wrong Period, even though dogs and birds do not have the same rights persons do. However, few people think it is wrong to use dogs as experimental animals, causing them considerable suffering in some cases, provided that the resulting research will probably bring discoveries of great benefit to people. And most of us think it all right to kill birds for food or to protect our crops. People's rights are different from the consideration we give to animals, then, for it is wrong to experiment on people, even if others might later benefit a great deal as a result of their suffering. You might volunteer to be a subject, but this would be supererogatory; you certainly have a right to refuse to be a medical guinea pig.

But how do we decide what you may or may not do to non-persons? This is a difficult problem, one for which I believe no adequate account exists. You do not want to say, for instance, that torturing dogs is all right whenever the sum of its effects on people is good—when it doesn't warp the sensibilities of the torturer so much that he mistreats people. If that were the case, it would be all right to torture dogs if you did it in private, or if the torturer lived on a desert island or died soon afterward, so that his actions had no effect on people. This is an inadequate account, because whatever moral consideration animals get, it has to be indefeasible, too. It will have to be a general proscription of certain actions, not merely a weighing of the impact on people on a case-by-case basis.

Rather, we need to distinguish two levels on which consequences of actions can be taken into account in moral reasoning. The traditional objections to Utilitarianism focus on the fact that it operates solely on the first level, taking all the consequences into account in particular cases only. Thus Utilitarianism is open to "desert island" and "lifeboat" counterexamples because these cases are rigged to make the consequences of actions severely limited.

Rawls' theory could be described as a teleological sort of theory, but with teleology operating on a higher level.[12] In choosing the principles to regulate society from the original position, his hypothetical choosers make their decision on the basis of the total consequences of various systems. Furthermore, they are constrained to choose a general set of rules which people can readily learn and apply. An ethical theory must operate by generating a set of sympathies and attitudes toward others which reinforces the functioning of that set of moral principles. Our prohibition against killing people operates by means of certain moral sentiments including sympathy, compassion and guilt. But if these attitudes are to form a coherent set, they carry us further: we tend to perform supererogatory actions, and we tend to feel similar compassion toward person-like non-persons.

It is crucial that psychological facts play a role here. Our psychological constitution makes it the case that for our ethical theory to work, it must prohibit certain treatment of non-persons which are significantly person-like. If our moral rules allowed people to treat some person-like non-persons in ways we do not want people to be treated, this would undermine the system of sympathies and attitudes that makes the ethical system work. For this reason, we would choose in the original position to make mistreatment of some sorts of animals wrong in general (not just wrong in the cases with public impact), even though animals are not themselves parties in the original position. Thus it makes sense that it is those animals whose appearance and behavior are most like those of people that get the most consideration in our moral scheme.

It is because of "coherence of attitudes," I think, that the similarity of a fetus to a baby is very significant. A fetus one week before birth is so much like a newborn baby in our psychological space that we cannot allow any cavalier treatment of the former while expecting full sympathy and nurturative support for the latter. Thus, I think that anti-abortion forces are indeed giving their strongest arguments when they point to the similarities between a fetus and a baby, and when they try to evoke our emotional attachment to and sympathy for the fetus. An early horror story from New York about nurses who were expected to alternate between caring for six-week premature infants and disposing of viable 24-week aborted fetuses is just that—a horror story. These beings are so much alike that no one can be asked to draw a distinction and treat them so very differently.

Remember, however, that in the early weeks after conception, a fetus is very much unlike a person. It is hard to develop these feelings for a set of genes which doesn't yet have a head, hands, beating heart, response to touch or the ability to move by itself. Thus it seems to me that the alleged "slippery slope" between conception and birth is not so very slippery. In the early stages of pregnancy, abortion can hardly be compared to murder for psychological reasons, but in the latest stages it is psychologically akin to murder.

Another source of similarity is the bodily continuity between fetus and adult. Bodies play a surprisingly central role in our attitudes toward persons. One has only to think of the philosophical literature on how far physical identity suffices for personal identity or Wittgenstein's remark that the best picture of the human soul is the human body. Even after death, when all agree the body is no longer a person, we still observe elaborate customs of respect for the human body; like people who torture dogs, necrophiliacs are not to be trusted with people.[13] So it is appropriate that we show respect to a fetus as the body continuous with the body of a person. This is a degree of resemblance to persons that animals cannot rival.

Michael Tooley also utilizes a parallel with animals. He claims that it is always permissible to drown newborn kittens and draws conclusions about infanticide.[14] But it is only permissible to drown kittens when their survival would cause some hardship. Perhaps it would be a burden to feed and house six more cats or to find other homes for them. The alternative of letting them starve produces even more suffering than the drowning. Since the kittens get their rights second-hand, so to speak, *via* the need for coherence in our attitudes, their interests are often overridden by the interests of full-fledged persons. But if their survival would be no inconvenience to people at all, then it is wrong to drown them, *contra* Tooley.

Tooley's conclusions about abortion are wrong for the same reason. Even if a fetus is not a person, abortion is not always permissible, because of the resemblance of a fetus to a person. I agree with Thomson that it would be wrong for a woman who is seven months pregnant to have an abortion just to avoid having to postpone a trip to Europe. In the early months of pregnancy when the fetus hardly resembles a baby at all, then, abortion is permissible whenever it is in the interests of the pregnant woman or her family. The reasons would only need to outweigh the pain and inconvenience of the abortion itself. In the middle months, when the fetus comes to resemble a person, abortion would be justifiable only when the continuation of the pregnancy or the birth of the child would cause harms—physical, psychological, economic or social—to the woman. In the late months of pregnancy, even on our current assumption that a fetus is not a person, abortion seems to be wrong except to save a woman from significant injury or death.

The Supreme Court has recognized similar gradations in the alleged slippery slope stretching between conception and birth. To this point, the present paper has been a discussion of the moral status of abortion only, not its legal status. In view of the great physical, financial and sometimes psychological costs of abortion, perhaps the legal arrangement most compatible with the proposed moral solution would be the absence of restrictions, that is, so-called abortion "on demand."

So I conclude, first, that application of our concept of a person will not suffice to settle the abortion issue. After all, the biological development of a human being is gradual. Second, whether a fetus is a person or not, abortion is justifiable early in pregnancy to avoid modest harms and seldom justifiable late in pregnancy except to avoid significant injury or death.[15]

# Notes

1. We also have paternalistic laws which keep us from harming our own bodies even when no one else is affected. Ironically, anti-abortion laws were originally designed to protect pregnant women from a dangerous but tempting procedure.

2. Mary Anne Warren, "On the Moral and Legal Status of Abortion," *Monist* 57 (1973), [*supra*, pp. 102–119].

3. Baruch Brody, "Fetal Humanity and the Theory of Essentialism," in Robert Baker and Frederick Elliston (eds.), *Philosophy and Sex* (Buffalo, N.Y., 1975).

4. Michael Tooley, "Abortion and Infanticide," *Philosophy and Public Affairs* 2 (1971). [Revised version *supra*, pp. 120–134.]

5. Paul Ramsey, "The Morality of Abortion," in James Rachels, ed., *Moral Problems* (New York, 1971).

6. John Noonan, "Abortion and the Catholic Church: A Summary History," *Natural Law Forum* 12 (1967), pp. 121–131.

7. Wittgenstein has argued against the possibility of so capturing the concept of a game, *Philosophical Investigations* (New York, 1958), § 66–71.

8. Not because the fetus is partly a person and so has some of the rights of persons, but rather because of the rights of person-like non-persons.

9. Aristotle himself was concerned, however, with the different question of when the soul takes form. For historical data, see Jimmye Kimmey, "How the Abortion Laws Happened," *Ms.* 1 (April, 1973), pp. 48ff, and John Noonan, *loc. cit.*

10. J. J. Thomson, "A Defense of Abortion," *Philosophy and Public Affairs* 1 (1971).[*Infra*, pp. 173–187.]

11. *Ibid.*, [p. 187].

12. John Rawls, *A Theory of Justice* (Cambridge, Mass., 1971), § 3–4.

13. On the other hand, if they can be trusted with people, then our moral customs are mistaken. It all depends on the facts of psychology.

14. *Op. cit.*, pp. 40, 60–61.

15. I am deeply indebted to Larry Crocker and Arthur Kuflik for their constructive comments.

# 41   Why Abortion Is Immoral

## DONALD MARQUIS

The view that abortion is, with rare exceptions, seriously immoral has received little support in the recent philosophical literature. No doubt most philosophers affiliated with secular institutions of higher education believe that the anti-abortion position is either a symptom of irrational religious dogma or a conclusion generated by seriously confused philosophical argument. The purpose of this essay is to undermine this general belief. This essay sets out an argument that purports to show, as well as any argument in ethics can show, that abortion is, except possibly in rare cases, seriously immoral, that it is in the same moral category as killing an innocent adult human being.

The argument is based on a major assumption. Many of the most insightful and careful writers on the ethics of abortion—such as Joel Feinberg, Michael Tooley, Mary Anne Warren, H. Tristram Engelhardt, Jr., L. W Sumner, John T. Noonan, Jr., and Philip Devine[1]—believe that whether or not abortion is morally permissible stands or falls on whether or not a fetus is the sort of being whose life it is seriously wrong to end. The argument of this essay will assume, but not argue, that they are correct.

Also, this essay will neglect issues of great importance to a complete ethics of abortion. Some anti-abortionists will allow that certain abortions, such as abortion before implantation or abortion when the life of a woman is threatened by a pregnancy or abortion after rape, may be morally permissible. This essay will not explore the casuistry of these hard cases. The purpose of this essay is to develop a general argument for the claim that the overwhelming majority of deliberate abortions are seriously immoral.

## I

A sketch of standard anti-abortion and pro-choice arguments exhibits how those arguments possess certain symmetries that explain why partisans of those positions are so convinced of the correctness of their own positions, why they are not successful in convincing their opponents, and why, to others, this issue seems to be unresolvable. An analysis of the nature of this standoff suggests a strategy for surmounting it.

Consider the way a typical anti-abortionist argues. She will argue or assert that life is present from the moment of conception or that fetuses look like babies or that fetuses possess a characteristic such as a genetic code that is both necessary and sufficient for being human. Anti-abortionists seem to believe that (1) the truth of all of these claims is quite obvious, and (2) establishing any of these claims is sufficient to show that abortion is morally akin to murder.

Reprinted with permission of the author and publisher from *Journal of Philosophy*, 68 (1989), 183–202.

A standard pro-choice strategy exhibits similarities. The pro-choicer will argue or assert that fetuses are not persons or that fetuses are not rational agents or that fetuses are not social beings. Pro-choicers seem to believe that (1) the truth of any of these claims is quite obvious, and (2) establishing any of these claims is sufficient to show that an abortion is not a wrongful killing.

In fact, both the pro-choice and the anti-abortion claims do seem to be true, although the "it looks like a baby" claim is more difficult to establish the earlier the pregnancy. We seem to have a standoff. How can it be resolved?

As everyone who has taken a bit of logic knows, if any of these arguments concerning abortion is a good argument, it requires not only some claim characterizing fetuses, but also some general moral principle that ties a characteristic of fetuses to having or not having the right to life or to some other moral characteristic that will generate the obligation or the lack of obligation not to end the life of a fetus. Accordingly, the arguments of the anti-abortionist and the pro-choicer need a bit of filling in to be regarded as adequate.

Note what each partisan will say. The anti-abortionist will claim that her position is supported by such generally accepted moral principles as "It is always prima facie seriously wrong to take a human life" or "It is always prima facie seriously wrong to end the life of a baby." Since these are generally accepted moral principles, her position is certainly not obviously wrong. The pro-choicer will claim that her position is supported by such plausible moral principles as "Being a person is what gives an individual intrinsic moral worth" or "It is only seriously prima facie wrong to take the life of a member of the human community." Since these are generally accepted moral principles, the pro-choice position is certainly not obviously wrong. Unfortunately, we have again arrived at a standoff.

Now, how might one deal with this standoff? The standard approach is to try to show how the moral principles of one's opponent lose their plausibility under analysis. It is easy to see how this is possible. On the one hand, the anti-abortionist will defend a moral principle concerning the wrongness of killing which tends to be broad in scope in order that even fetuses at an early stage of pregnancy will fall under it. The problem with broad principles is that they often embrace too much. In this particular instance, the principle "It is always prima facie wrong to take a human life" seems to entail that it is wrong to end the existence of a living human cancer-cell culture, on the grounds that the culture is both living and human. Therefore, it seems that the anti-abortionist's favored principle is too broad.

On the other hand, the pro-choicer wants to find a moral principle concerning the wrongness of killing which tends to be narrow in scope in order that fetuses will *not* fall under it. The problem with narrow principles is that they often do not embrace enough. Hence, the needed principles such as "It is prima facie seriously wrong to kill only persons" or "It is prima facie wrong to kill only rational agents" do not explain why it is wrong to kill infants or young children or the severely retarded or even perhaps the severely mentally ill. Therefore, we seem again to have a standoff. The anti-abortionist charges, not unreasonably, that pro-choice principles concerning killing are too narrow to be acceptable; the pro-choicer charges, not unreasonably, that anti-abortionist principles concerning killing are too broad to be acceptable.

Attempts by both sides to patch up the difficulties in their positions run into further difficulties. The anti-abortionist will try to remove the problems in her position by reformulating her principle concerning killing in terms of human beings. Now we end up with: "It is always prima facie seriously wrong to end the life of a human being." This principle has the advantage of avoiding the problem of the human cancer-cell culture counterexample. But this advantage is purchased at a high price. For although it is clear that a fetus is both human and alive, it is not at all clear that a fetus is a human *being*. There is at least something to be said for the view that something becomes a human being only after a process of development, and that therefore first trimester fetuses and perhaps all fetuses are not yet human beings. Hence, the anti-abortionist, by this move, has merely exchanged one problem for another.[2]

The pro-choicer fares no better. She may attempt to find reasons why killing infants, young children, and the severely retarded is wrong which are independent of her major principle that is supposed to explain the wrongness of taking human life, but which will not also make abortion immoral. This is no easy task. Appeals to social utility will seem satisfactory only to those who resolve not to think of the enormous difficulties with a utilitarian account of the wrongness of killing and the significant social costs of preserving the lives of the unproductive.[3] A pro-choice strategy that extends the definition of "person" to infants or even to young children seems just as arbitrary as an anti-abortion strategy that extends the definition of "human being" to fetuses. Again, we find symmetries in the two positions and we arrive at a standoff.

There are even further problems that reflect symmetries in the two positions. In addition to counterexample problems, or the arbitrary application problems that can be exchanged for them, the standard anti-abortionist principle "It is prima facie seriously wrong to kill a human being," or one of its variants, can be objected to on the grounds of ambiguity. If "human being" is taken to be a *biological* category, then the anti-abortionist is left with the problem of explaining why a merely biological category should make a moral difference. Why, it is asked, is it any more reasonable to base a moral conclusion on the number of chromosomes in one's cells than on the color of one's skin?[4] If "human being," on the other hand, is taken to be a *moral* category, then the claim that a fetus is a human being cannot be taken to be a premise in the anti-abortion argument, for it is precisely what needs to be established. Hence, either the anti-abortionist's main category is a morally irrelevant, merely biological category, or it is of no use to the anti-abortionist in establishing (noncircularly, of course) that abortion is wrong.

Although this problem with the anti-abortionist position is often noticed, it is less often noticed that the pro-choice position suffers from an analogous problem. The principle "Only persons have the right to life" also suffers from an ambiguity. The term "person" is typically defined in terms of psychological characteristics, although there will certainly be disagreement concerning which characteristics are most important. Supposing that this

matter can be settled, the pro-choicer is left with the problem of explaining why *psychological* characteristics should make a *moral* difference. If the pro-choicer should attempt to deal with this problem by claiming that an explanation is not necessary, that in fact we do treat such a cluster of psychological properties as having moral significance, the sharp-witted anti-abortionist should have a ready response. We do treat being both living and human as having moral significance. If it is legitimate for the pro-choicer to demand that the anti-abortionist provide an explanation of the connection between the biological character of being a human being and the wrongness of being killed (even though people accept this connection), then it is legitimate for the anti-abortionist to demand that the pro-choicer provide an explanation of the connection between psychological criteria for being a person and the wrongness of being killed (even though that connection is accepted).[5]

Feinberg has attempted to meet this objection (he calls psychological personhood "commonsense personhood"):

The characteristics that confer commonsense personhood are not arbitrary bases for rights and duties, such as race, sex or species membership; rather they are traits that make sense out of rights and duties and without which those moral attributes would have no point or function. It is because people are conscious; have a sense of their personal identities; have plans, goals, and projects; experience emotions; are liable to pains, anxieties, and frustrations; can reason and bargain, and so on—it is because of these attributes that people have values and interests, desires and expectations of their own, including a stake in their own futures, and a personal well-being of a sort we cannot ascribe to unconscious or nonrational beings. Because of their developed capacities they can assume duties and responsibilities and can have and make claims on one another. Only because of their sense of self, their life plans, their value hierarchies, and their stakes in their own futures can they be ascribed fundamental rights. There is nothing arbitrary about these linkages (*op. cit.*, p. 270).

The plausible aspects of this attempt should not be taken to obscure its implausible features. There is a great deal to be said for the view that being a psychological person under some description is a necessary condition for having duties. One cannot have a duty unless one is capable of behaving morally, and a being's capability of behaving morally will require having a certain psychology. It is far from obvious, however, that having rights entails consciousness or rationality, as Feinberg suggests. We speak of the rights of the severely retarded or the severely mentally ill, yet some of these persons are not rational. We speak of the rights of the temporarily unconscious. The New Jersey Supreme Court based their decision in the Quinlan case on Karen Ann Quinlan's right to privacy, and she was known to be permanently unconscious at that time. Hence, Feinberg's claim that having rights entails being conscious is, on its face, obviously false.

Of course, it might not make sense to attribute rights to a being that would never in its natural history have certain psychological traits. This modest connection between psychological personhood and moral personhood will create a place for Karen Ann Quinlan and the temporarily unconscious. But then it makes a place for fetuses also. Hence, it does not serve Feinberg's pro-choice purposes. Accordingly, it seems that the pro-choicer will have as much difficulty bridging the gap between psychological personhood and personhood in the moral sense as the anti-abortionist has bridging the gap between being a biological human being and being a human being in the moral sense.

Furthermore, the pro-choicer cannot any more escape her problem by making person a purely moral category than the anti-abortionist could escape by the analogous move. For if person is a moral category, then the pro-choicer is left without the resources for establishing (noncircularly, of course) the claim that a fetus is not a person, which is an essential premise in her argument. Again, we have both a symmetry and a standoff between pro-choice and anti-abortion views.

Passions in the abortion debate run high. There are both plausibilities and difficulties with the standard positions. Accordingly, it is hardly surprising that partisans of either side embrace with fervor the moral generalizations that support the conclusions they preanalytically favor, and reject with disdain the moral generalizations of their opponents as being subject to inescapable difficulties. It is easy to believe that the counterexamples to one's own moral principles are merely temporary difficulties that will dissolve in the wake of further philosophical research, and that the counterexamples to the principles of one's opponents are as straightforward as the contradiction between *A* and *O* propositions in traditional logic. This might suggest to an impartial observer (if there are any) that the abortion issue is unresolvable.

There is a way out of this apparent dialectical quandary. The moral generalizations of both sides are not quite correct. The generalizations hold for the most part, for the usual cases. This suggests that they are all *accidental* generalizations, that the moral claims made by those on both sides of the dispute do not touch on the *essence* of the matter.

This use of the distinction between essence and accident is not meant to invoke obscure metaphysical categories. Rather, it is intended to reflect the rather atheoretical nature of the abortion discussion. If the generalization a partisan in the abortion dispute adopts were derived from the reason why ending the life of a human being is wrong, then there could not be exceptions to that generalization unless some special case obtains in which there are even more powerful countervailing reasons. Such generalizations would not be merely accidental generalizations; they would point to, or be based upon, the essence of the wrongness of killing, what it is that makes killing wrong. All this suggests that a necessary condition of resolving the abortion controversy is a more theoretical account of the wrongness of killing. After all, if we merely believe, but do not understand, why killing adult human beings such as ourselves is wrong, how could we conceivably show that abortion is either immoral or permissible?

## II

In order to develop such an account, we can start from the following unproblematic assumption concerning our own case: it is wrong to kill *us*.

Why is it wrong? Some answers can be easily eliminated. It might be said that what makes killing us wrong is that a killing brutalizes the one who kills. But the brutalization consists of being inured to the performance of an act that is hideously immoral; hence, the brutalization does not explain the immorality. It might be said that what makes killing us wrong is the great loss others would experience due to our absence. Although such hubris is understandable, such an explanation does not account for the wrongness of killing hermits, or those whose lives are relatively independent and whose friends find it easy to make new friends.

A more obvious answer is better. What primarily makes killing wrong is neither its effect on the murderer nor its effect on the victim's friends and relatives, but its effect on the victim. The loss of one's life is one of the greatest losses one can suffer. The loss of one's life deprives one of all the experiences, activities, projects, and enjoyments that would otherwise have constituted one's future. Therefore, killing someone is wrong, primarily because the killing inflicts (one of) the greatest possible losses on the victim. To describe this as the loss of life can be misleading, however. The change in my biological state does not by itself make killing me wrong. The effect of the loss of my biological life is the loss to me of all those activities, projects, experiences, and enjoyments which would otherwise have constituted my future personal life. These activities, projects, experiences, and enjoyments are either valuable for their own sakes or are means to something else that is valuable for its own sake. Some parts of my future are not valued by me now, but will come to be valued by me as I grow older and as my values and capacities change. When I am killed, I am deprived both of what I now value which would have been part of my future personal life, but also what I would come to value. Therefore, when I die, I am deprived of all of the value of my future. Inflicting this loss on me is ultimately what makes killing me wrong. This being the case, it would seem that what makes killing *any* adult human being prima facie seriously wrong is the loss of his or her future.[6]

How should this rudimentary theory of the wrongness of killing be evaluated? It cannot be faulted for deriving an "ought" from an "is," for it does not. The analysis assumes that killing me (or you, reader) is prima facie seriously wrong. The point of the analysis is to establish which natural property ultimately explains the wrongness of the killing, given that it is wrong. A natural property will ultimately explain the wrongness of killing, only if (1) the explanation fits with our intuitions about the matter and (2) there is no other natural property that provides the basis for a better explanation of the wrongness of killing. This analysis rests on the intuition that what makes killing a particular human or animal wrong is what it does to that particular human or animal. What makes killing wrong is some natural effect or other of the killing. Some would deny this. For instance, a divine-command theorist in ethics would deny it. Surely this denial is, however, one of those features of divine-command theory which renders it so implausible.

The claim that what makes killing wrong is the loss of the victim's future is directly supported by two considerations. In the first place, this theory explains why we regard killing as one of the worst of crimes. Killing is especially wrong, because it deprives the victim of more than perhaps any other crime. In the second place, people with AIDS or cancer who know they are dying believe, of course, that dying is a very bad thing for them. They believe that the loss of a future to them that they would otherwise have experienced is what makes their premature death a very bad thing for them. A better theory of the wrongness of killing would require a different natural property associated with killing which better fits with the attitudes of the dying. What could it be?

The view that what makes killing wrong is the loss to the victim of the value of the victim's future gains additional support when some of its implications are examined. In the first place, it is incompatible with the view that it is wrong to kill only beings who are biologically human. It is possible that there exists a different species from another planet whose members have a future like ours. Since having a future like that is what makes killing someone wrong, this theory entails that it would be wrong to kill members of such a species. Hence, this theory is opposed to the claim that only life that is biologically human has great moral worth, a claim which many anti-abortionists have seemed to adopt. This opposition, which this theory has in common with personhood theories, seems to be a merit of the theory.

In the second place, the claim that the loss of one's future is the wrong-making feature of one's being killed entails the possibility that the futures of some actual nonhuman mammals on our own planet are sufficiently like ours that it is seriously wrong to kill them also. Whether some animals do have the same right to life as human beings depends on adding to the account of the wrongness of killing some additional account of just what it is about my future or the futures of other adult human beings which makes it wrong to kill us. No such additional account will be offered in this essay. Undoubtedly, the provision of such an account would be a very difficult matter. Undoubtedly, any such account would be quite controversial. Hence, it surely should not reflect badly on this sketch of an elementary theory of the wrongness of killing that it is indeterminate with respect to some very difficult issues regarding animal rights.

In the third place, the claim that the loss of one's future is the wrong-making feature of one's being killed does not entail, as sanctity-of-human-life theories do, that active euthanasia is wrong. Persons who are severely and incurably ill, who face a future of pain and despair, and who wish to die will not have suffered a loss if they are killed. It is, strictly speaking, the value of a human's future which makes killing wrong in this theory. This being so, killing does not necessarily wrong some persons who are sick and dying. Of course, there may be other reasons for a prohibition of active euthanasia, but that is another matter. Sanctity-of-human-life theories seem to hold that active euthanasia is seriously wrong even in an individual case where there seems to be good reason for it independently of public policy considerations. This consequence is most implausible, and it is a plus for the claim that the loss of a future of value is what makes killing wrong that it does not share this consequence.

In the fourth place, the account of the wrongness of killing defended in this essay does straightforwardly entail that it is prima facie seriously wrong to kill children and infants, for we do presume that they have futures of value. Since we do believe that it is wrong to kill defenseless little babies, it is important that a theory of the wrongness of killing easily account for this. Personhood theories of the wrongness of killing, on the other hand, cannot straightforwardly account for the wrongness of killing infants and young children.[7] Hence, such theories must add special ad hoc accounts of the wrongness of killing the young. The plausibility of such ad hoc theories seems to be a function of how desperately one wants such theories to work. The claim that the primary wrong-making feature of a killing is the loss to the victim of the value of its future accounts for the wrongness of killing young children and infants directly; it makes the wrongness of such acts as obvious as we actually think it is. This is a further merit of this theory. Accordingly, it seems that this value of a future-like-ours theory of the wrongness of killing shares strengths of both sanctity-of-life and personhood accounts while avoiding weaknesses of both. In addition, it meshes with a central intuition concerning what makes killing wrong.

The claim that the primary wrong-making feature of a killing is the loss to the victim of the value of its future has obvious consequences for the ethics of abortion. The future of a standard fetus includes a set of experiences, projects, activities, and such which are identical with the futures of adult human beings and are identical with the futures of young children. Since the reason that is sufficient to explain why it is wrong to kill human beings after the time of birth is a reason that also applies to fetuses, it follows that abortion is prima facie seriously morally wrong.

This argument does not rely on the invalid inference that, since it is wrong to kill persons, it is wrong to kill potential persons also. The category that is morally central to this analysis is the category of having a valuable future like ours; it is not the category of personhood. The argument to the conclusion that abortion is prima facie seriously morally wrong proceeded independently of the notion of person or potential person or any equivalent. Someone may wish to start with this analysis in terms of the value of a human future, conclude that abortion is, except perhaps in rare circumstances, seriously morally wrong, infer that fetuses have the right to life, and then call fetuses "persons" as a result of their having the right to life. Clearly, in this case, the category of person is being used to state the *conclusion* of the analysis rather than to generate the *argument* of the analysis.

The structure of this anti-abortion argument can be both illuminated and defended by comparing it to what appears to be the best argument for the wrongness of the wanton infliction of pain on animals. This latter argument is based on the assumption that it is prima facie wrong to inflict pain on me (or you, reader). What is the natural property associated with the infliction of pain which makes such infliction wrong? The obvious answer seems to be that the infliction of pain causes suffering and that suffering is a misfortune. The suffering caused by the infliction of pain is what makes the wanton infliction of pain on me wrong. The wanton infliction of pain on other adult humans causes suffering. The wanton infliction of pain on animals causes suffering. Since causing suffering is what makes the wanton infliction of pain wrong and since the wanton infliction of pain on animals causes suffering, it follows that the wanton infliction of pain on animals is wrong.

This argument for the wrongness of the wanton infliction of pain on animals shares a number of structural features with the argument for the serious prima facie wrongness of abortion. Both arguments start with an obvious assumption concerning what it is wrong to do to me (or you, reader). Both then look for the characteristic or the consequence of the wrong action which makes the action wrong. Both recognize that the wrong-making feature of these immoral actions is a property of actions sometimes directed at individuals other than postnatal human beings. If the structure of the argument for the wrongness of the wanton infliction of pain on animals is sound,

then the structure of the argument for the prima facie serious wrongness of abortion is also sound, for the structure of the two arguments is the same. The structure common to both is the key to the explanation of how the wrongness of abortion can be demonstrated without recourse to the category of person. In neither argument is that category crucial.

This defense of an argument for the wrongness of abortion in terms of a structurally similar argument for the wrongness of the wanton infliction of pain on animals succeeds only if the account regarding animals is the correct account. Is it? In the first place, it seems plausible. In the second place, its major competition is Kant's account. Kant believed that we do not have direct duties to animals at all, because they are not persons. Hence, Kant had to explain and justify the wrongness of inflicting pain on animals on the grounds that "he who is hard in his dealings with animals becomes hard also in his dealing with men."[8] The problem with Kant's account is that there seems to be no reason for accepting this latter claim unless Kant's account is rejected. If the alternative to Kant's account is accepted, then it is easy to understand why someone who is indifferent to inflicting pain on animals is also indifferent to inflicting pain on humans, for one is indifferent to what makes inflicting pain wrong in both cases. But, if Kant's account is accepted, there is no intelligible reason why one who is hard in his dealings with animals (or crabgrass or stones) should also be hard in his dealings with men. After all, men are persons: animals are no more persons than crabgrass or stones. Persons are Kant's crucial moral category. Why, in short, should a Kantian accept the basic claim in Kant's argument?

Hence, Kant's argument for the wrongness of inflicting pain on animals rests on a claim that, in a world of Kantian moral agents, is demonstrably false. Therefore, the alternative analysis, being more plausible anyway, should be accepted. Since this alternative analysis has the same structure as the anti-abortion argument being defended here, we have further support for the argument for the immorality of abortion being defended in this essay.

Of course, this value of a future-like-ours argument, if sound, shows only that abortion is prima facie wrong, not that it is wrong in any and all circumstances. Since the loss of the future to a standard fetus, if killed, is, however, at least as great a loss as the loss of the future to a standard adult human being who is killed, abortion, like ordinary killing, could be justified only by the most compelling reasons. The loss of one's life is almost the greatest misfortune that can happen to one. Presumably abortion could be justified in some circumstances, only if the loss consequent on failing to abort would be at least as great. Accordingly, morally permissible abortions will be rare indeed unless, perhaps, they occur so early in pregnancy that a fetus is not yet definitely an individual. Hence, this argument should be taken as showing that abortion is presumptively very seriously wrong, where the presumption is very strong—as strong as the presumption that killing another adult human being is wrong.

## III

How complete an account of the wrongness of killing does the value of a future-like-ours account have to be in order that the wrongness of abortion is a consequence? This account does not have to be an account of the necessary conditions for the wrongness of killing. Some persons in nursing homes may lack valuable human futures, yet it may be wrong to kill them for other reasons. Furthermore, this account does not obviously have to be the sole reason killing is wrong where the victim did have a valuable future. This analysis claims only that, for any killing where the victim did have a valuable future like ours, having that future by itself is sufficient to create the strong presumption that the killing is seriously wrong.

One way to overturn the value of a future-like-ours argument would be to find some account of the wrongness of killing which is at least as intelligible and which has different implications for the ethics of abortion. Two rival accounts possess at

least some degree of plausibility. One account is based on the obvious fact that people value the experience of living and wish for that valuable experience to continue. Therefore, it might be said, what makes killing wrong is the discontinuation of that experience for the victim. Let us call this the *discontinuation account*.[9] Another rival account is based upon the obvious fact that people strongly desire to continue to live. This suggests that what makes killing us so wrong is that it interferes with the fulfillment of a strong and fundamental desire, the fulfillment of which is necessary for the fulfillment of any other desires we might have. Let us call this the *desire account*.[10]

Consider first the desire account as a rival account of the ethics of killing which would provide the basis for rejecting the anti-abortion position. Such an account will have to be stronger than the value of a future-like-ours account of the wrongness of abortion if it is to do the job expected of it. To entail the wrongness of abortion, the value of a future-like-ours account has only to provide a sufficient, but not a necessary, condition for the wrongness of killing. The desire account, on the other hand, must provide us also with a necessary condition for the wrongness of killing in order to generate a pro-choice conclusion on abortion. The reason for this is that presumably the argument from the desire account moves from the claim that what makes killing wrong is interference with a very strong desire to the claim that abortion is not wrong because the fetus lacks a strong desire to live. Obviously, this inference fails if someone's having the desire to live is not a necessary condition of its being wrong to kill that individual.

One problem with the desire account is that we do regard it as seriously wrong to kill persons who have little desire to live or who have no desire to live or, indeed, have a desire not to live. We believe it is seriously wrong to kill the unconscious, the sleeping, those who are tired of life, and those who are suicidal. The value-of-a-human-future account renders standard morality intelligible in these cases; these cases appear to be incompatible with the desire account.

The desire account is subject to a deeper difficulty. We desire life, because we value the goods of this life. The goodness of life is not secondary to our desire for it. If this were not so, the pain of one's own premature death could be done away with merely by an appropriate alteration in the configuration of one's desires. This is absurd. Hence, it would seem that it is the loss of the goods of one's future, not the interference with the fulfillment of a strong desire to live, which accounts ultimately for the wrongness of killing.

It is worth noting that, if the desire account is modified so that it does not provide a necessary, but only a sufficient, condition for the wrongness of killing, the desire account is compatible with the value of a future-like-ours account. The combined accounts will yield an anti-abortion ethic. This suggests that one can retain what is intuitively plausible about the desire account without a challenge to the basic argument of this paper.

It is also worth noting that, if future desires have moral force in a modified desire account of the wrongness of killing, one can find support for an anti-abortion ethic even in the absence of a value of a future-like-ours account. If one decides that a morally relevant property, the possession of which is sufficient to make it wrong to kill some individual, is the desire at some future time to live —one might decide to justify one's refusal to kill suicidal teenagers on these grounds, for example —then, since typical fetuses will have the desire in the future to live, it is wrong to kill typical fetuses. Accordingly, it does not seem that a desire account of the wrongness of killing can provide a justification of a pro-choice ethic of abortion which is nearly as adequate as the value of a human-future justification of an anti-abortion ethic.

The discontinuation account looks more promising as an account of the wrongness of killing. It seems just as intelligible as the value of a future-like-ours account, but it does not justify an anti-abortion position. Obviously, if it is the continuation of one's activities, experiences, and projects, the loss of which makes killing wrong, then

it is not wrong to kill fetuses for that reason, for fetuses do not have experiences, activities, and projects to be continued or discontinued. Accordingly, the discontinuation account does not have the anti-abortion consequences that the value of a future-like-ours account has. Yet, it seems as intelligible as the value of a future-like-ours account, for when we think of what would be wrong with our being killed, it does seem as if it is the discontinuation of what makes our lives worthwhile which makes killing us wrong.

Is the discontinuation account just as good an account as the value of a future-like-ours account? The discontinuation account will not be adequate at all, if it does not refer to the *value* of the experience that may be discontinued. One does not want the discontinuation account to make it wrong to kill a patient who begs for death and who is in severe pain that cannot be relieved short of killing. (I leave open the question of whether it is wrong for other reasons.) Accordingly, the discontinuation account must be more than a bare discontinuation account. It must make some reference to the positive value of the patient's experiences. But, by the same token, the value of a future-like-ours account cannot be a bare future account either. Just having a future surely does not itself rule out killing the above patient. This account must make some reference to the value of the patient's future experiences and projects also. Hence, both accounts involve the value of experiences, projects, and activities. So far we still have symmetry between the accounts.

The symmetry fades, however, when we focus on the time period of the value of the experiences, etc., which has moral consequences. Although both accounts leave open the possibility that the patient in our example may be killed, this possibility is left open only in virtue of the utterly bleak future for the patient. It makes no difference whether the patient's immediate past contains intolerable pain, or consists in being in a coma (which we can imagine is a situation of indifference), or consists in a life of value. If the patient's future is a future of value, we want our account to make it wrong to kill the patient. If the patient's future is intolerable, whatever his or her immediate past, we want our account to allow killing the patient. Obviously, then, it is the value of that patient's future which is doing the work in rendering the morality of killing the patient intelligible.

This being the case, it seems clear that whether one has immediate past experiences or not does no work in the explanation of what makes killing wrong. The addition the discontinuation account makes to the value of a human future account is otiose. Its addition to the value-of-a-future account plays no role at all in rendering intelligible the wrongness of killing. Therefore, it can be discarded with the discontinuation account of which it is a part.

## IV

The analysis of the previous section suggests that alternative general accounts of the wrongness of killing are either inadequate or unsuccessful in getting around the anti-abortion consequences of the value of a future-like-ours argument. A different strategy for avoiding these anti-abortion consequences involves limiting the scope of the value of a future argument. More precisely, the strategy involves arguing that fetuses lack a property that is essential for the value-of-a-future argument (or for any anti-abortion argument) to apply to them.

One move of this sort is based upon the claim that a necessary condition of one's future being valuable is that one values it. Value implies a valuer. Given this one might argue that, since fetuses cannot value their futures, their futures are not valuable to them. Hence, it does not seriously wrong them deliberately to end their lives.

This move fails, however, because of some ambiguities. Let us assume that something cannot be of value unless it is valued by someone. This does not entail that my life is of no value unless it is valued by me. I may think, in a period of despair, that my future is of no worth whatsoever, but I may be wrong because others rightly see value—even great value—in it. Furthermore, my future can be valuable to me even I do not value

it. This is the case when a young person attempts suicide, but is rescued and goes on to significant human achievements. Such young people's futures are ultimately valuable to them, even though such futures do not seem to be valuable to them at the moment of attempted suicide. A fetus's future can be valuable to it in the same way. Accordingly, this attempt to limit the anti-abortion argument fails.

Another similar attempt to reject the anti-abortion position is based on Tooley's claim that an entity cannot possess the right to life unless it has the capacity to desire its continued existence. It follows that, since fetuses lack the conceptual capacity to desire to continue to live, they lack the right to life. Accordingly, Tooley concludes that abortion cannot be seriously prima facie wrong (*op. cit.*, pp. 46/7).

What could be the evidence for Tooley's basic claim? Tooley once argued that individuals have a prima facie right to what they desire and that the lack of the capacity to desire something undercuts the basis of one's right to it (*op. cit.*, pp. 44/5). This argument plainly will not succeed in the context of the analysis of this essay, however, since the point here is to establish the fetus's right to life on other grounds. Tooley's argument assumes that the right to life cannot be established in general on some basis other than the desire for life. This position was considered and rejected in the preceding section of this paper.

One might attempt to defend Tooley's basic claim on the grounds that because a fetus cannot apprehend continued life as a benefit, its continued life cannot be a benefit or cannot be something it has a right to or cannot be something that is in its interest. This might be defended in terms of the general proposition that, if an individual is literally incapable of caring about or taking an interest in some *X*, then one does not have a right to *X* or *X* is not a benefit or *X* is not something that is in one's interest.[11]

Each member of this family of claims seems to be open to objections. As John C. Stevens[12] has pointed out, one may have a right to be treated with a certain medical procedure (because of a health insurance policy one has purchased), even though one cannot conceive of the nature of the procedure. And, as Tooley himself has pointed out, persons who have been indoctrinated, or drugged, or rendered temporarily unconscious may be literally incapable of caring about or taking an interest in something that is in their interest or is something to which they have a right, or is something that benefits them. Hence, the Tooley claim that would restrict the scope of the value of a future-like-ours argument is undermined by counterexamples.[13]

Finally, Paul Bassen[14] has argued that, even though the prospects of an embryo might seem to be a basis for the wrongness of abortion, an embryo cannot be a victim and therefore cannot be wronged. An embryo cannot be a victim, he says, because it lacks sentience. His central argument for this seems to be that, even though plants and the permanently unconscious are alive, they clearly cannot be victims. What is the explanation of this? Bassen claims that the explanation is that their lives consist of mere metabolism and mere metabolism is not enough to ground victimizability. Mentation is required.

The problem with this attempt to establish the absence of victimizability is that both plants and the permanently unconscious clearly lack what Bassen calls "prospects" or what I have called "a future life like ours." Hence, it is surely open to one to argue that the real reason we believe plants and the permanently unconscious cannot be victims is that killing them cannot deprive them of a future life like ours; the real reason is not their absence of present mentation.

Bassen recognizes that his view is subject to this difficulty, and he recognizes that the case of children seems to support this difficulty for "much of what we do for children is based on prospects." He argues, however, that, in the case of children and in other such cases "potentiality comes into play only where victimizability has been secured on other grounds" (*ibid.,* p. 333).

Bassen's defense of his view is patently question-begging, since what is adequate to secure victimizability is exactly what is at issue. His examples do not support his own view against the thesis of this essay. Of course, embryos can be

victims: when their lives are deliberately terminated, they are deprived of their futures of value, their prospects. This makes them victims, for it directly wrongs them.

The seeming plausibility of Bassen's view stems from the fact that paradigmatic cases of imagining someone as a victim involve empathy, and empathy requires mentation of the victim. The victims of flood, famine, rape, or child abuse are all persons with whom we can empathize. That empathy seems to be part of seeing them as victims.[15]

In spite of the strength of these examples, the attractive intuition that a situation in which there is victimization requires the possibility of empathy is subject to counterexamples. Consider a case that Bassen himself offers: "Posthumous obliteration of an author's work constitutes a misfortune for him only if he had wished his work to endure" (*op cit.,* p. 318). The conditions Bassen wishes to impose upon the possibility of being victimized here seem far too strong. Perhaps this author, due to his unrealistic standards of excellence and his low self-esteem, regarded his work as unworthy of survival, even though it possessed genuine literary merit. Destruction of such work would surely victimize its author. In such a case, empathy with the victim concerning the loss is clearly impossible.

Of course, Bassen does not make the possibility of empathy a necessary condition of victimizability; he requires only mentation. Hence, on Bassen's actual view, this author, as I have described him, can be a victim. The problem is that the basic intuition that renders Bassen's view plausible is missing in the author's case. In order to attempt to avoid counterexamples, Bassen has made his thesis too weak to be supported by the intuitions that suggested it.

Even so, the mentation requirement on victimizability is still subject to counterexamples. Suppose a severe accident renders me totally unconscious for a month, after which I recover. Surely killing me while I am unconscious victimizes me, even though I am incapable of mentation during that time. It follows that Bassen's thesis fails. Apparently, attempts to restrict the value of a future-like-ours argument so that fetuses do not fall within its scope do not succeed.

# V

In this essay, it has been argued that the correct ethic of the wrongness of killing can be extended to fetal life and used to show that there is a strong presumption that any abortion is morally impermissible. If the ethic of killing adopted here entails, however, that contraception is also seriously immoral, then there would appear to be a difficulty with the analysis of this essay.

But this analysis does not entail that contraception is wrong. Of course, contraception prevents the actualization of a possible future of value. Hence, it follows from the claim that futures of value should be maximized that contraception is prima facie immoral. This obligation to maximize does not exist, however; furthermore, nothing in the ethics of killing in this paper entails that it does. The ethics of killing in this essay would entail that contraception is wrong only if something were denied a human future of value by contraception. Nothing at all is denied such a future by contraception, however.

Candidates for a subject of harm by contraception fall into four categories: (1) some sperm or other, (2) some ovum or other, (3) a sperm and an ovum separately, and (4) a sperm and an ovum together. Assigning the harm to some sperm is utterly arbitrary, for no reason can be given for making a sperm the subject of harm rather than an ovum. Assigning the harm to some ovum is utterly arbitrary, for no reason can be given for making an ovum the subject of harm rather than a sperm. One might attempt to avoid these problems by insisting that contraception deprives both the sperm and the ovum separately of a valuable future like ours. On this alternative, too many futures are lost. Contraception was supposed to be wrong, because it deprived us of one future of value, not two. One might attempt to avoid this problem by holding that contraception deprives the combination of sperm and ovum of a valuable future like ours. But here the definite article mis-

leads. At the time of contraception, there are hundreds of millions of sperm, one (released) ovum and millions of possible combinations of all of these. There is no actual combination at all. Is the subject of the loss to be a merely possible combination? Which one? This alternative does not yield an actual subject of harm either. Accordingly, the immorality of contraception is not entailed by the loss of a future-like-ours argument simply because there is no nonarbitrarily identifiable subject of the loss in the case of contraception.

# VI

The purpose of this essay has been to set out an argument for the serious presumptive wrongness of abortion subject to the assumption that the moral permissibility of abortion stands or falls on the moral status of the fetus. Since a fetus possesses a property, the possession of which in adult human beings is sufficient to make killing an adult human being wrong, abortion is wrong. This way of dealing with the problem of abortion seems superior to other approaches to the ethics of abortion, because it rests on an ethics of killing which is close to self-evident, because the crucial morally relevant property clearly applies to fetuses, and because the argument avoids the usual equivocations on "human life," "human being," or "person." The argument rests neither on religious claims nor on Papal dogma. It is not subject to the objection of "speciesism." Its soundness is compatible with the moral permissibility of euthanasia and contraception. It deals with our intuitions concerning young children.

Finally, this analysis can be viewed as resolving a standard problem—indeed, *the* standard problem—concerning the ethics of abortion. Clearly, it is wrong to kill adult human beings. Clearly, it is not wrong to end the life of some arbitrarily chosen single human cell. Fetuses seem to be like arbitrarily chosen human cells in some respects and like adult humans in other respects. The problem of the ethics of abortion is the problem of determining the fetal property that settles this moral controversy. The thesis of this essay is that the problem of the ethics of abortion, so understood, is solvable.

## Notes

1. Feinberg, "Abortion," in *Matters of Life and Death: New Introductory Essays in Moral Philosophy,* Tom Regan, ed. (New York: Random House, 1986), pp. 256–293; Tooley, "Abortion and Infanticide," *Philosophy and Public Affairs,* II, 1 (1972):37–65; Tooley, *Abortion and Infanticide* (New York: Oxford, 1984); Warren, "On the Moral and Legal Status of Abortion," *The Monist,* I.VII, 1 (1973):43–6I; Engelhardt, "The Ontology of Abortion," *Ethics,* I.XXXIV, 3 (1974):217–234; Sumner, *Abortion and Moral Theory* (Princeton: University Press, 1981); Noonan, "An Almost Absolute Value in History," in *The Morality of Abortion: Legal and Historical Perspectives,* Noonan, ed. (Cambridge: Harvard, 1970); and Devine, *The Ethics of Homicide* (Ithaca: Cornell, 1978).

2. For interesting discussions of this issue, see Warren Quinn, "Abortion: Identity and Loss," *Philosophy and Public Affairs,* XIII, 1 (1984):24–54; and Lawrence C. Becker, "Human Being: The Boundaries of the Concept," *Philosophy and Public Affairs,* IV, 4 (1975):334–359.

3. For example, see my "Ethics and the Elderly: Some Problems," in Stuart Spicker, Kathleen Woodward, and David Van Tassel, eds., *Aging and the Elderly: Humanistic Perspectives in Gerontology* (Atlantic Highlands, NJ: Humanities, 1978), pp. 341–355.

4. See Warren, *op. cit.,* and Tooley, "Abortion and Infanticide."

5. This seems to be the fatal flaw in Warren's treatment of this issue.

6. I have been most influenced on this matter by Jonathan Glover, *Causing Death and Saving Lives* (New York: Penguin, 1977), ch. 3; and Robert Young, "What Is So Wrong with Killing People?" *Philosophy,* I.IV, 210 (1979):515–528.

7. Feinberg, Tooley, Warren, and Engelhardt have all dealt with this problem.

8. "Duties to Animals and Spirits," in *Lectures on Ethics,* Louis Infeld, trans. (New York: Harper, 1963), p. 239.

9. I am indebted to Jack Bricke for raising this objection.

10. Presumably a preference utilitarian would press such an objection. Tooley once suggested that his account has such a theoretical underpinning. See his "Abortion and Infanticide," pp. 44/5.

11. Donald VanDeVeer seems to think this is self-evident. See his "Whither Baby Doe?" in *Matters of Life and Death,* p. 233.

12. "Must the Bearer of a Right Have the Concept of That to Which He Has a Right?" *Ethics,* XCV, 1 (1984):68–74.

13. See Tooley again in "Abortion and Infanticide," pp. 47–49.

14. "Present Sakes and Future Prospects: The Status of Early Abortion," *Philosophy and Public Affairs,* XI, 4 (1982):322–326.

15. Note carefully the reasons he gives on the bottom of p. 316.

## 42   Virtue Theory and Abortion

### ROSALIND HURSTHOUSE

Rosalind Hursthouse, "Virtue Theory and Abortion," *Philosophy and Public Affairs,* 20 (1991), 223–246, with omissions. Copyright © 1991 by Princeton University Press. Reprinted by permission of Princeton University Press.

Let us consider what a skeletal virtue theory looks like. It begins with a specification of right action:

> P.1. An action is right if it is what a virtuous agent would do in the circumstances.[1]

This . . . is a purely formal principle, giving one no guidance as to what to do, that forges the conceptual link between *right action* and *virtuous agent.* . . . [I]t must, of course, go on to specify what the latter is. The first step toward this may appear quite trivial, but is needed to correct a prevailing tendency among many critics to define the virtuous agent as one who is disposed to act in accordance with a deontologist's moral rules.

> P. 1a. A virtuous agent is one who acts virtuously, that is, one who has and exercises the virtues.

This subsidiary premise lays bare the fact that virtue theory aims to provide a nontrivial specification of the virtuous agent *via* a nontrivial specification of the virtues, which is given in its second premise:

P.2. A virtue is a character trait a human being needs to flourish or live well.

This premise forges a conceptual link between *virtue* and *flourishing* (or *living well* or *eudaimonia*). And, just as deontology, in theory, then goes on to argue that each favored rule meets its specification, so virtue ethics, in theory, goes on to argue that each favored character trait meets its.

These are the bare bones of virtue theory. . . .

## Abortion

As everyone knows, the morality of abortion is commonly discussed in relation to just two considerations: first, and predominantly, the status of the fetus and whether or not it is the sort of thing that may or may not be innocuously or justifiably killed; and second, and less predominantly (when, that is, the discussion concerns the *morality* of abortion rather than the question of permissible legislation in a just society), women's rights. If one thinks within this familiar framework, one may well be puzzled about what virtue theory, as such, could contribute. Some people assume the discussion will be conducted solely in terms of what the virtuous agent would or would not do. . . . Others assume that only justice, or at most justice and charity, will be applied to the issue, generating a discussion very similar to Judith Jarvis Thomson's.[2]

Now if this is the way the virtue theorist's discussion of abortion is imagined to be, no wonder people think little of it. It seems obvious in advance that in any such discussion there must be either a great deal of extremely tendentious application of the virtue terms *just, charitable,* and so on or a lot of rhetorical appeal to "this is what only the virtuous agent knows." But these are caricatures; they fail to appreciate the way in which virtue theory quite transforms the discussion of abortion by dismissing the two familiar dominating considerations as, in a way, fundamentally irrelevant. In what way or ways, I hope to make both clear and plausible.

Let us first consider women's rights. Let me emphasize again that we are discussing the *morality* of abortion, not the rights and wrongs of laws prohibiting or permitting it. If we suppose that women do have a moral right to do as they choose with their own bodies, or, more particularly, to terminate their pregnancies, then it may well follow that a *law* forbidding abortion would be unjust. Indeed, even if they have no such right, such a law might be, as things stand at the moment, unjust, or impractical, or inhumane: on this issue I have nothing to say in this article. But, putting all questions about the justice or injustice of laws to one side, and supposing only that women have such a moral right, *nothing* follows from this supposition about the morality of abortion, according to virtue theory, once it is noted (quite generally, not with particular reference to abortion) that in exercising a moral right I can do something cruel, or callous, or selfish, light-minded, self-righteous, stupid, inconsiderate, disloyal, dishonest—that is, act viciously.[3] Love and friendship do not survive their parties' constantly insisting on their rights, nor do people live well when they think that getting what they have a right to is of preeminent importance; they harm others, and they harm themselves. So whether women have a moral right to terminate their pregnancies is irrelevant within virtue theory, for it is irrelevant to the question "In having an abortion in these circumstances, would the agent be acting virtuously or viciously or neither?"

What about the consideration of the status of the fetus—what can virtue theory say about that? One might say that this issue is not in the province of any moral theory; it is a metaphysical question, and an extremely difficult one at that. Must virtue theory then wait upon metaphysics to come up with the answer?

At first sight it might seem so. For virtue is said to involve knowledge, and part of this knowledge consists in having the *right* attitude to things. "Right" here does not just mean "morally right" or "proper" or "nice" in the modern sense; it means "accurate, true." One cannot have the right or correct attitude to something if the attitude is based on or involves false beliefs. And this suggests that if the status of the fetus is relevant to the rightness or wrongness of abortion, its status must be known, as a truth, to the fully wise and virtuous person.

But the sort of wisdom that the fully virtuous person has is not supposed to be recondite; it does not call for fancy philosophical sophistication, and it does not depend upon, let alone wait upon, the discoveries of academic philosophers.[4] And this entails the following, rather startling conclusion: that the status of the fetus—that issue over which so much ink has been spilt—is, according to virtue theory, simply not relevant to the rightness or wrongness of abortion (within, that is, a secular morality).

Or rather, since that is clearly too radical a conclusion, it is in a sense relevant, but only in the sense that the familiar biological facts are relevant. By "the familiar biological facts" I mean the facts that most human societies are and have been familiar with—that, standardly (but not invariably), pregnancy occurs as the result of sexual intercourse, that it lasts about nine months, during which time the fetus grows and develops, that standardly it terminates in the birth of a living baby, and that this is how we all come to be.

It might be thought that this distinction—between the familiar biological facts and the status of the fetus—is a distinction without a difference. But this is not so. To attach relevance to the status of the fetus, in the sense in which virtue theory claims it is not relevant, is to be gripped by the conviction that we must go beyond the familiar biological facts, deriving some sort of conclusion from them, such as that the fetus has rights, or is not a person, or something similar. It is also to believe that this exhausts the relevance of the familiar biological facts, that all they are relevant to is the status of the fetus and whether or not it is the sort of thing that may or may not be killed.

These convictions, I suspect, are rooted in the desire to solve the problem of abortion by getting it to fall under some general rule such as "you ought not to kill anything with the right to life but may kill anything else." But they have resulted in what should surely strike any nonphilosopher as a most bizarre aspect of nearly all the current philosophical literature on abortion, namely, that, far from treating abortion as a unique moral problem,

markedly unlike any other, nearly everything written on the status of the fetus and its bearing on the abortion issue would be consistent with the human reproductive facts' (to say nothing of family life) being totally different from what they are. Imagine that you are an alien extraterrestrial anthropologist who does not know that the human race is roughly 50 percent female and 50 percent male, or that our only (natural) form of reproduction involves heterosexual intercourse, viviparous birth, and the female's (and only the female's) being pregnant for nine months, or that females are capable of childbearing from late childhood to late middle age, or that childbearing is painful, dangerous, and emotionally charged—do you think you would pick up these facts from the hundreds of articles written on the status of the fetus? I am quite sure you would not. And that, I think, shows that the current philosophical literature on abortion has got badly out of touch with reality.

Now if we are using virtue theory, our first question is not "What do the familiar biological facts show—what can be derived from them about the status of the fetus?" but "How do these facts figure in the practical reasoning, action and passions, thoughts and reactions, of the virtuous and the nonvirtuous? What is the mark of having the right attitude to these facts and what manifests having the wrong attitude to them?" This immediately makes essentially relevant not only all the facts about human reproduction I mentioned above, but a whole range of facts about our emotions in relation to them as well. I mean such facts as that human parents, both male and female, tend to care passionately about their offspring, and that family relationships are among the deepest and strongest in our lives—and, significantly, among the longest-lasting.

These facts make it obvious that pregnancy is not just one among many other physical conditions, and hence that anyone who genuinely believes that an abortion is comparable to a haircut or an appendectomy is mistaken.[5] The fact that the premature termination of a pregnancy is, in some sense, the cutting off of a new human life, and thereby, like the procreation of a new human life, connects with all our thoughts about human life and death, parenthood, and family relationships, must make it a serious matter. To disregard this fact about it, to think of abortion as nothing but the killing of something that does not matter, or as nothing but the exercise of some right or rights one has, or as the incidental means to some desirable state of affairs, is to do something callous and light-minded, the sort of thing that no virtuous and wise person would do. It is to have the wrong attitude not only to fetuses, but more generally to human life and death, parenthood and family relationships.

Although I say that the facts make this obvious, I know that this is one of my tendentious points. In partial support of it I note that even the most dedicated proponents of the view that deliberate abortion is just like an appendectomy or haircut rarely hold the same view of spontaneous abortion, that is, miscarriage. It is not so tendentious of me to claim that to react to people's grief over miscarriage by saying, or even thinking, "What a fuss about nothing!" would be callous and light-minded, whereas to try to laugh someone out of grief over an appendectomy scar or a botched haircut would not be. It is hard to give this point due prominence within act-centered theories, for the inconsistency is an inconsistency in attitude about the seriousness of loss of life, not in beliefs about which acts are right or wrong. Moreover, an act-centered theorist may say, "Well, there is nothing wrong with *thinking* 'What a fuss about nothing!' as long as you do not say it and hurt the person who is grieving. And besides, we cannot be held responsible for our thoughts, only for the intentional actions they give rise to." But the character traits that virtue theory emphasizes are not simply dispositions to intentional actions, but a seamless disposition to certain actions and passions, thoughts and reactions.

To say that the cutting off of a human life is always a matter of some seriousness at any stage is not to deny the relevance of gradual fetal development. Notwithstanding the well-worn point that clear boundary lines cannot be drawn, our emotions and attitudes regarding the fetus do change as it develops, and again when it is born, and

indeed further as the baby grows. Abortion for shallow reasons in the later stages is much more shocking than abortion for the same reasons in the early stages in a way that matches the fact that deep grief over miscarriage in the later stages is more appropriate than it is over miscarriage in the earlier stages (when, that is, the grief is solely about the loss of *this* child, not about, as might be the case, the loss of one's only hope of having a child or of having one's husband's child). Imagine (or recall) a woman who already has children; she had not intended to have more, but finds herself unexpectedly pregnant. Though contrary to her plans, the pregnancy, once established as a fact, is welcomed—and then she loses the embryo almost immediately. If this were bemoaned as a tragedy, it would, I think, be a misapplication of the concept of what is tragic. But it may still properly be mourned as a loss. The grief is expressed in such terms as "I shall always wonder how she or he would have turned out" or "When I took at the others, I shall think, 'How different their lives would have been if this other one had been part of them.'" It would, I take it, be callous and light-minded to say, or think, "Well, she has already *got* four children; what's the problem?"; it would be neither, nor arrogantly intrusive in the case of a close friend, to try to correct prolonged mourning by saying, "I know it's sad, but it's not a tragedy; rejoice in the ones you have." The application of *tragic* becomes more appropriate as the fetus grows, for the mere fact that one has lived with it for longer, conscious of its existence, makes a difference. To shrug off an early abortion is understandable just because it is very hard to be fully conscious of the fetus's existence in the early stages and hence hard to appreciate that an early abortion is the destruction of life. It is particularly hard for the young and inexperienced to appreciate this, because appreciation of it usually comes only with experience.

I do not mean "with the experience of having an abortion" (though that may be part of it) but, quite generally, "with the experience of life." Many women who have borne children contrast their later pregnancies with their first successful one, saying that in the later ones they were conscious of a new life growing in them from very early on. And, more generally, as one reaches the age at which the next generation is coming up close behind one, the counterfactuals "If I, or she, had had an abortion, Alice, or Bob, would not have been born" acquire a significant application, which casts a new light on the conditionals "If I or Alice have an abortion then some Caroline or Bill will not be born."

The fact that pregnancy is not just one among many physical conditions does not mean that one can never regard it in that light without manifesting a vice. When women are in very poor physical health, or worn out from childbearing, or forced to do very physically demanding jobs, then they cannot be described as self-indulgent, callous, irresponsible, or light-minded if they seek abortions mainly with a view to avoiding pregnancy as the physical condition that it is. To go through with a pregnancy when one is utterly exhausted, or when one's job consists of crawling along tunnels hauling coal, as many women in the nineteenth century were obliged to do, is perhaps heroic, but people who do not achieve heroism are not necessarily vicious. That they can view the pregnancy only as eight months of misery, followed by hours if not days of agony and exhaustion, and abortion only as the blessed escape from this prospect, is entirely understandable and does not manifest any lack of serious respect for human life or a shallow attitude to motherhood. What it does show is that something is terribly amiss in the conditions of their lives, which make it so hard to recognize pregnancy and childbearing as the good that they can be.

In relation to this last point I should draw attention to the way in which virtue theory has a sort of built-in indexicality. Philosophers arguing against anything remotely resembling a belief in the sanctity of life (which the above claims clearly embody) frequently appeal to the existence of other communities in which abortion and infanticide are practiced. We should not automatically assume that it is impossible that some other communities could be morally inferior to our own; maybe some are, or have been, precisely insofar as their members are, typically, callous or light-

minded or unjust. But in communities in which life is a great deal tougher for everyone than it is in ours, having the right attitude to human life and death, parenthood, and family relationships might well manifest itself in ways that are unlike ours. When it is essential to survival that most members of the community fend for themselves at a very young age or work during most of their waking hours, selective abortion or infanticide might be practiced either as a form of genuine euthanasia or for the sake of the community and not, I think, be thought callous or light-minded. But this does not make everything all right; as before, it shows that there is something amiss with the conditions of their lives, which are making it impossible for them to live really well.

The foregoing discussion, insofar as it emphasizes the right attitude to human life and death, parallels to a certain extent those standard discussions of abortion that concentrate on it solely as an issue of killing. But it does not, as those discussions do, gloss over the fact, emphasized by those who discuss the morality of abortion in terms of women's rights, that abortion, wildly unlike any other form of killing, is the termination of a pregnancy, which is a condition of a woman's body and results in *her* having a child if it is not aborted. This fact is given due recognition not by appeal to women's rights but by emphasizing the relevance of the familiar biological and psychological facts and their connection with having the right attitude to parenthood and family relationships. But it may well be thought that failing to bring in women's rights still leaves some important aspects of the problem of abortion untouched.

Speaking in terms of women's rights, people sometimes say things like, "Well, it's her life you're talking about too, you know; she's got a right to her own life, her own happiness." And the discussion stops there. But in the context of virtue theory, given that we are particularly concerned with what constitutes a good human life, with what true happiness or *eudaimonia* is, that is no place to stop. We go on to ask, "And is this life of hers a good one? Is she living well?"

If we are to go on to talk about good human lives, in the context of abortion, we have to bring in our thoughts about the value of love and family life, and our proper emotional development through a natural life cycle. The familiar facts support the view that parenthood in general, and motherhood and childbearing in particular, are intrinsically worthwhile, are among the things that can be correctly thought to be partially constitutive of a flourishing human life.[6] If this is right, then a woman who opts for not being a mother (at all, or again, or now) by opting for abortion may thereby be manifesting a flawed grasp of what her life should be, and be about—a grasp that is childish, or grossly materialistic or shortsighted, or shallow.

I said "*may* thereby": this *need* not be so. Consider, for instance, a woman who has already had several children and fears that to have another will seriously affect her capacity to be a good mother to the ones she has—she does not show a lack of appreciation of the intrinsic value of being a parent by opting for abortion. Nor does a woman who has been a good mother and is approaching the age at which she may be looking forward to being a good grandmother. Nor does a woman who discovers that her pregnancy may well kill her, and opts for abortion or adoption. Nor, necessarily, does a woman who had decided to lead a life centered around some other worthwhile activity or activities with which motherhood would compete.

People who are childless by choice are sometimes described as "irresponsible," or "selfish," or "refusing to grow up," or "not knowing what life is about." But one can hold that having children is intrinsically worthwhile without endorsing this, for we are, after all, in the happy position of there being more worthwhile things to do than can be fitted into one lifetime. Parenthood, and motherhood in particular, even if granted to be intrinsically worthwhile, undoubtedly take up a lot of one's adult life, leaving no room for some other worthwhile pursuits. But some women who choose abortion rather than have their first child, and some men who encourage their partners to choose abortion, are not avoiding parenthood for the sake of other worthwhile pursuits, but for the worthless one of "having a good time," or for the

pursuit of some false vision of the ideals of freedom or self-realization. And some others who say "I am not ready for parenthood yet" are making some sort of mistake about the extent to which one can manipulate the circumstances of one's life so as to make it fulfill some dream that one has. Perhaps one's dream is to have two perfect children, a girl and a boy, within a perfect marriage, in financially secure circumstances, with an interesting job of one's own. But to care too much about that dream, to demand of life that it give it to one and act accordingly, may be both greedy and foolish, and is to run the risk of missing out on happiness entirely. Not only may fate make the dream impossible, or destroy it, but one's own attachment to it may make it impossible. Good marriages, and the most promising children, can be destroyed by just one adult's excessive demand for perfection.

Once again, this is not to deny that girls may quite properly say "I am not ready for motherhood yet," especially in our society, and, far from manifesting irresponsibility or light-mindedness, show an appropriate modesty or humility, or a fearfulness that does not amount to cowardice. However, even when the decision to have an abortion is the right decision—one that does not itself fall under a vice-related term and thereby one that the perfectly virtuous could recommend—it does not follow that there is no sense in which having the abortion is wrong, or guilt inappropriate. For, by virtue of the fact that a human life has been cut short, some evil has probably been brought about,[7] and that circumstances make the decision to bring about some evil the right decision will be a ground for guilt if getting into those circumstances in the first place itself manifested a flaw in character.

What "gets one into those circumstances" in the case of abortion is, except in the case of rape, one's sexual activity and one's choices, or the lack of them, about one's sexual partner and about contraception. The virtuous woman (which here of course does not mean simply "chaste woman" but "woman with the virtues") has such character traits as strength, independence, resoluteness, decisiveness, self-confidence, responsibility, serious-mindedness, and self-determination—and no one, I think, could deny that many women become pregnant in circumstances in which they cannot welcome or cannot face the thought of having *this* child precisely because they lack one or some of these character traits. So even in the cases where the decision to have an abortion is the right one, it can still be the reflection of a moral failing—not because the decision itself is weak or cowardly or irresolute or irresponsible or light-minded, but because the lack of the requisite opposite of these failings landed one in the circumstances in the first place. Hence the common universalized claim that guilt and remorse are never appropriate emotions about an abortion is denied. They may be appropriate, and appropriately inculcated, even when the decision was the right one.

Another motivation for bringing women's rights into the discussion may be to attempt to correct the implication, carried by the killing-centered approach, that insofar as abortion is wrong, it is a wrong that only women do, or at least (given the preponderance of male doctors) that only women instigate. I do not myself believe that we can thus escape the fact that nature bears harder on women than it does on men,[8] but virtue theory can certainly correct many of the injustices that the emphasis on women's rights is rightly concerned about. With very little amendment, everything that has been said above applies to boys and men too. Although the abortion decision is, in a natural sense, the woman's decision, proper to her, boys and men are often party to it, for well or ill, and even when they are not, they are bound to have been party to the circumstances that brought it up. No less than girls and women, boys and men can in their actions, manifest self-centeredness, callousness, and light-mindedness about life and parenthood in relation to abortion. They can be self-centered or courageous about the possibility of disability in their offspring; they need to reflect on their sexual activity and their choices, or the lack of them, about their sexual partner and contraception; they need to grow up and take responsibility for their own actions and life in relation to fatherhood. If it is true, as I maintain, that insofar as motherhood is intrinsically worthwhile,

being a mother is an important purpose in women's lives, being a father (rather than a mere generator) is an important purpose in men's lives as well, and it is adolescent of men to turn a blind eye to this and pretend that they have many more important things to do.

## Conclusion

Much more might be said, but I shall end the actual discussion of the problem of abortion here, and conclude by highlighting what I take to be its significant features. . . .

The discussion does not proceed simply by our trying to answer the question "Would the perfectly virtuous agent ever have an abortion and, if so, when?"; virtue theory is not limited to considering "Would Socrates have had an abortion if he were a raped fifteen-year-old [girl]?" nor automatically stumped when we are considering circumstances into which no virtuous agent would have got herself. Instead, much of the discussion proceeds in the virtue- and vice-related terms whose applications, in several cases, yields practical conclusions. . . . These terms are difficult to apply correctly, and anyone might challenge my application of any one of them. So, for example, I have claimed that some abortions, done for certain reasons, would be callous or light-minded; that others might indicate an appropriate modesty or humility; that others would reflect a greedy and foolish attitude to what one could expect out of life. Any of these examples may be disputed; but what is at issue is, should these difficult terms be there, or should the discussion be couched in terms that all clever adolescents can apply correctly? . . .

Proceeding as it does in virtue- and vice-related terms, the discussion thereby, inevitably, also contains claims about what is worthwhile, serious and important, good and evil, in our lives. So, for example, I claimed that parenthood is intrinsically worthwhile, and that having a good time was a worthless end (in life, not on individual occasions); that losing a fetus is always a serious matter (albeit not a tragedy in itself in the first trimester) whereas acquiring an appendectomy scar is a trivial one; that (human) death is an evil. Once again, these are difficult matters, and anyone might challenge any one of my claims. But what is at issue is, as before, should these difficult claims be there, or can one reach practical conclusions about real moral issues that are in no way determined by premises about such matters? . . .

The discussion also thereby, inevitably, contains claims about what life is like (e.g., my claim that love and friendship do not survive their parties' constantly insisting on their rights; or the claim that to demand perfection of life is to run the risk of missing out on happiness entirely). What is at issue is, should those disputable claims be there, or is our knowledge (or are our false opinions) about what life is like irrelevant to our understanding of real moral issues?. . .

Naturally, my own view is that all these concepts should be there in any discussion of real moral issues and that virtue theory, which uses all of them, is the right theory to apply to them. I do not pretend to have shown this. I realize that proponents of rival theories may say that, now that they have understood how virtue theory uses the range of concepts it draws on, they are more convinced than ever that such concepts should not figure in an adequate normative theory, because they are sectarian, or vague, or too particular, or improperly anthropocentric. . . . Or, finding many of the details of the discussion appropriate, they may agree that many, perhaps even all, of the concepts should figure, but argue that virtue theory gives an inaccurate account of the way the concepts fit together (and indeed of the concepts themselves) and that another theory provides a better account; that would be interesting to see. . . .

## Notes

1. It should be noted that this premise intentionally allows for the possibility that two virtuous agents, faced with the same choice in the same circumstances, may act differently. For example, one might opt for taking her father off the life-support machine and the other for leaving her father on it. The theory requires that neither agent thinks that what the other does is wrong . . . , but it explicitly allows that no action is uniquely right in such a case—both are right. It also intentionally allows for the possibility that in some circumstances—those into which no virtuous agent could have got herself—no action is right. I explore this premise in greater length in "Applying Virtue Ethics," in a *festschrift* for Philippa Foot [Rosalind Hursthouse, Gavin Lawrence, and Warren Quinn, eds., *Virtues and Reasons, Philippa Foot and Moral Theory* (Oxford: Oxford University Press, 1996)].

2. Judith Jarvis Thomson, "A Defense of Abortion," *Philosophy & Public Affairs* 1, no. 1 (Fall 1971): 47–66. One could indeed regard this article as proto-virtue theory (no doubt to the surprise of the author) if the concepts of callousness and kindness were allowed more weight.

3. One possible qualification: if one ties the concept of justice very closely to rights, then if women do have a moral right to terminate their pregnancies it *may* follow that in doing so they do not act unjustly. (Cf. Thomson, "A Defense of Abortion.") But it is debatable whether even that much follows.

4. This is an assumption of virtue theory, and I do not attempt to defend it here. An adequate discussion of it would require a separate article, since, although most moral philosophers would be chary of claiming that intellectual sophistication is a necessary condition of moral wisdom or virtue, most of us, from Plato onward, tend to write as if this were so. Sorting out which claims about moral knowledge are committed to this kind of elitism and which can, albeit with difficulty, be reconciled with the idea that moral knowledge can be acquired by anyone who really wants it would be a major task.

5. Mary Anne Warren, in "On the Moral and Legal Status of Abortion," *Monist* 57 (1973) sec. 1, says of the opponents of restrictive laws governing abortion that "their conviction (for the most part) is that abortion is not a *morally* serious and extremely unfortunate, even though sometimes justified, act, comparable to killing in self-defense or to letting the violinist die, but rather is closer to being a *morally neutral* act, like cutting one's hair" (italics mine). I would like to think that no one *genuinely* believes this. But certainly in discussion, particularly when arguing against restrictive laws or the suggestion that remorse over abortion might be appropriate, I have found that some people say they believe it (and often cite Warren's article, albeit inaccurately, despite its age). Those who allow that it is morally serious, and far from morally neutral, have to argue against restrictive laws, or the appropriateness of remorse, on a very different ground from that laid down by the premise. "The fetus is just part of the woman's body (and she has a right to determine what happens to her body and should not feel guilt about anything she does to it)."

6. I take this as a premise here, but argue for it in some detail in my *Beginning Lives* (Oxford: Basil Blackwell, 1987). In this connection I also discuss adoption and the sense in which it may be regarded as "second best," and the difficult question of whether the good of parenthood may properly be sought, or indeed bought, by surrogacy.

7. I say "some evil has probably been brought about" on the ground that (human) life is (usually) a good and hence (human) death usually an evil. The exceptions would be (a) where death is actually a good or a benefit, because the baby that would come to be if the life were not cut short would be better off dead than alive, and (b) where death,

though not a good, is not an evil either, because the life that would be led (e.g., in a state of permanent coma) would not be a good.

8. I discuss this point at greater length in *Beginning Lives.*

# 43   Abortion and the "Feminine Voice"

## CELIA WOLF-DEVINE

A growing number of feminists now seek to articulate the "feminine voice," to draw attention to women's special strengths, and to correct the systematic devaluation of these by our male-dominated society. Carol Gilligan's book, *In a Different Voice,* was especially important to the emergence of this strain of feminist thought. It was her intention to help women identify more positively with their own distinctive style of reasoning about ethics, instead of feeling that there is something wrong with them because they do not think like men (as Kohlberg's and Freud's theories would imply). Inspired by her work, feminists such as Nel Noddings, Annette Baier, and the contributors to *Women and Moral Theory,*[1] have tried to articulate further the feminine voice in moral reasoning. Others such as Carol McMillan, Adrienne Rich, Sara Ruddick, and Nancy Hartsock agree that women have distinct virtues, and argue that these need not be self-victimizing.[2] When properly transformed by a feminist consciousness, women's different characteristics can, they suggest, be productive of new social visions.

Similar work is also being done by feminists who try to correct for masculine bias in other areas such as our conception of human nature, the way we view the relationship between people and nature, and the kinds of paradigms we employ in thinking about society.[3]

Some of those engaged in this enterprise hold that women *by nature* possess certain valuable traits that men do not, but more frequently, they espouse the weaker position that, on the whole, the traits they label "feminine" are more common among women (for reasons which are at least partly cultural), but that they also can be found in men, and that they should be encouraged as good traits for a human being to have, regardless of sex.[4]

Virtually all of those feminists who are trying to reassert the value of the feminine voice, also express the sort of unqualified support for free access to abortion which has come to be regarded as a central tenet of feminist "orthodoxy." What I wish to argue in this paper is that: (1) abortion is, by their own accounts, clearly a masculine response to the problems posed by an unwanted pregnancy, and is thus highly problematic for those who seek to articulate and defend the "feminine voice" as the proper mode of moral response, and that (2) on the contrary the "feminine voice" as it has been articulated generates a strong presumption against abortion as a way of responding to an unwanted pregnancy.[5]

These conclusions, I believe, can be argued without relying on a precise determination of the moral status of the fetus. A case at least can be made that the fetus is a person since it is biologically a member of the human species and will, in time, develop normal human abilities. Whether the burden of proof rests on those who defend the personhood of the fetus, or on those who deny it, is a matter of moral methodology, and for that reason will depend in part on whether one adopts a masculine or feminine approach to moral issues.

Reprinted with permission of the publisher from *Public Affairs Quarterly,* 3 (1989), 81–97.

# I. Masculine Voice/Feminine Voice

## A. Moral Reasoning

According to Gilligan, girls, being brought up by mothers, identify with them, while males must define themselves through separation from their mothers. As a result, girls have "a basis for empathy built into their primary definition of self in a way that boys do not."[6] Thus while masculinity is defined by separation and threatened by intimacy, femininity is defined through attachment and threatened by separation; girls come to understand themselves as imbedded within a network of personal relationships.

A second difference concerns attitudes toward general rules and principles. Boys tend to play in larger groups than girls, and become "increasingly fascinated with the legal elaboration of rules, and the development of fair procedures for adjudicating conflicts."[7] We thus find men conceiving of morality largely in terms of adjudicating fairly between the conflicting rights of self-assertive individuals.

Girls play in smaller groups, and accord a greater importance to relationships than to following rules. They are especially sensitive to the needs of the particular other, instead of emphasizing impartiality, which is more characteristic of the masculine perspective. They think of morality more in terms of having responsibilities for taking care of others, and place a high priority upon preserving the network of relationships which makes this possible. While the masculine justice perspective requires detachment, the feminine care perspective sees detachment and separation as themselves the moral problem.[8]

Inspired by Gilligan, many feminist philosophers have discovered a masculine bias in traditional ethical theories. Nel Noddings has written a book called *Caring: A Feminine Approach to Ethics*. Annette Baier has praised Hume for his emphasis on the role of the affections in ethics[9] and proposed that trust be taken as the central notion for ethical theory.[10] Christina Hoff Sommers has argued for giving a central role to special relationships in ethics."[11] And Virginia Held has suggested that the mother-child relationship be seen as paradigmatic of human relationships, instead of the economic relationship of buyer/seller (which she sees to be the ruling paradigm now).[12]

The feminine voice in ethics attends to the particular other, thinks in terms of responsibilities to care for others, is sensitive to our interconnectedness, and strives to preserve relationships. It contrasts with the masculine voice, which speaks in terms of justice and rights, stresses consistency and principles, and emphasizes the autonomy of the individual and impartiality in one's dealings with others.

## B. Human Nature: Mind and Body

Feminist writers have also discovered a masculine bias in the way we think of mind and body and the relationship between them. A large number of feminists, for example, regard radical mind/body dualism as a masculine way of understanding human nature. Alison Jaggar, for example, criticizes what she calls "normative dualism" for being "male biased,"[13] and defines "normative dualism" as "the belief that what is especially valuable about human beings is a particular "mental" capacity, the capacity for rationality."[14]

Another critic of dualism is Rosemary Radford Reuther, a theologian. Her book *New Woman, New Earth* is an extended attack upon what she calls transcendent hierarchical dualism, which she regards as a "male ideology."[15] By "transcendent dualism" she means the view that consciousness is "transcendent to visible nature"[16] and that there is a sharp split between spirit and nature. In the attempt to deny our own mortality, our essential humanity is then identified with a "transcendent divine sphere beyond the matrix of coming to be and passing away."[17] In using the term "hierarchical," she means that the mental or spiritual component is taken to be superior to the physical. Thus "the relation of spirit and body is one of repression, subjugation and mastery."[18]

Dodson Gray, whose views resemble Reuther's, poetically contrasts the feminine attitude with the masculine one as follows:

I see that life is not a line but a circle. Why do men imagine for themselves the illusory freedom of a soaring mind, so that the body of nature becomes a cage? 'Tis not true. To be human is to be circled in the cycles of nature, rooted in the processes that nurture us in life, breathing in and breathing out human life just as plants breathe in and out their photosynthesis.[19]

Feminists critical of traditional masculine ways of thinking about human nature also examine critically the conception of "reason" which has become engrained in our Western cultural heritage from the Greeks on. Genevieve Lloyd, for example, in *The Man of Reason: Male and Female in Western Philosophy*,[20] suggests that the very notion of reason itself has been defined in part by the exclusion of the feminine. And if the thing which makes us distinctively human namely our reason—is thought of as male, women and the things usually associated with them such as the body, emotion and nature, will be placed in an inferior position.

## C. Our Relationship with Nature

Many feminists hold that mind-body dualism which sees mind as transcendent to and superior to the body, leads to the devaluation of both women and nature. For the transcendent mind is conceived as masculine, and women, the body and nature assigned an inferior and subservient status.[21] As Rosemary Radford Reuther puts it:

The woman, the body and the world are the lower half of a dualism that must be declared posterior to, created by, subject to, and ultimately alien to the nature of (male) consciousness in whose image man made his God.[22]

Women are to be subject to men, and nature may be used by man in any way he chooses. Thus the male ideology of transcendent dualism sanctions unlimited technological manipulation of nature; nature is an alien object to be conquered.

Carolyn Merchant, in her book *The Death of Nature: Women, Ecology and the Scientific Revolution*,[23] focuses on the Cartesian version of dualism as particularly disastrous to our relationship with nature, and finds the roots of our present ecological crisis to lie in the 17th century scientific revolution—itself based on Cartesian dualism and the mechanization of nature. According to Merchant, both feminism and the ecology movement are egalitarian movements which have a vision of our interconnectedness with each other and with nature.

Feminists who stress the deep affinities between feminism and the ecology movement are often called "ecofeminists." Stephanie Leland, radical feminist and co-editor of a recent collection of ecofeminist writings, has explained that:

Ecology is universally defined as the study of the balance and interrelationship of all life on earth. The motivating force behind feminism is the expression of the feminine principle. As the essential impulse of the feminine principle is the striving towards balance and interrelationship, it follows that feminism and ecology are inextricably connected.[24]

The masculine urge is, she says, to "separate, discriminate and control," while the feminine impulse is "towards belonging, relationship and letting be."[25] The urge to discriminate leads, she thinks, to the need to dominate "in order to feel secure in the choice of a particular set of differences."[26] The feminine attitude springs from a more holistic view of the human person and sees us as imbedded in nature rather than standing over and above it. It entails a more egalitarian attitude, regarding the needs of other creatures as important and deserving of consideration. It seeks to "let be" rather than to control, and maintains a pervasive awareness of the interconnectedness of all things and the need to preserve this if all are to flourish.

Interconnectedness, which we found to be an important theme in feminist ethics, thus reappears in the writings of the ecofeminists as one of the central aspects of the feminine attitude toward nature.

## D. Paradigms of Social Life

Feminists' descriptions of characteristically masculine and feminine paradigms of social life center around two different focuses. Those influenced by Gilligan tend to stress the contrast between individualism (which they take to be characteristic of the masculine "justice tradition") and the view of society as "a web of relationships sustained by a process of communication"[27] (which they take to characterize the feminine "care perspective"). According to them, the masculine paradigm sees society as a collection of self-assertive individuals seeking rules which will allow them to pursue their own goals without interfering with each other. The whole contractarian tradition from Locke and Hobbes through Rawls is thus seen as a masculine paradigm of social life; we are only connected to others and responsible to them through our own choice to relinquish part of our autonomy in favor of the state. The feminine care perspective guides us to think about societal problems in a different way. We are already imbedded in a network of relationships, and must never exploit or hurt the other. We must strive to preserve those relationships as much as possible without sacrificing the integrity of the self.

The ecofeminists, pacifist feminists, and those whose starting point is a rejection of dualism, tend to focus more on the contrast between viewing social relationships in terms of hierarchy, power, and domination (the masculine paradigm) and viewing them in a more egalitarian and nonviolent manner (the feminine one). Feminists taking this position range from the moderate ones who believe that masculine social thought tends to be more hierarchical than feminine thought, to the extreme radicals who believe males are irredeemably aggressive and dominating, and prone to violence in order to preserve their domination.

The more moderate characterization of masculine social thought would claim that men tend to prefer a clear structure of authority; they want to know who is in control and have a clear set of procedures or rules for resolving difficult cases. The more extreme view, common among ecofeminists and a large number of radical feminists, is that males seek to establish and maintain patriarchy (systematic domination by males) and use violence to maintain their control. These feminists thus see an affinity between feminism (which combats male violence against women) and the pacifist movement (which does so on a more global scale). Mary Daly, for example, holds that

"the rulers of patriarchy—males with power—wage an unceasing war against life itself. . . . [F]emale energy is essentially biophilic."[28] Another radical feminist, Sally Miller Gearhart, says that men possess the qualities of objectification, violence, and competitiveness, while women possess empathy, nurturance, and cooperation.[29] Thus the feminine virtues must prevail if we are to survive at all, and the entire hierarchical power structure must be replaced by "horizontal patterns of relationship."[30]

Women are thus viewed by the pacifist feminists as attuned in some special way to the values and attitudes underlying a pacifist commitment. Sara Ruddick, for example, believes that maternal practice, because it involves "preservative love" and nurtures growth, involves the kinds of virtues which, when put to work in the public domain, lead us in the direction of pacifism.[31]

## II. Abortion

A person who had characteristically masculine traits, attitudes and values as defined above would very naturally choose abortion, and justify it ethically in the same way in which most feminists do. Conversely, a person manifesting feminine traits, attitudes and values would not make such a choice, or justify it in that way.

According to the ecofeminists, the masculine principle is insensitive to the interconnectedness of all life; it strives to discriminate, separate and control. It does not respect the natural cycles of nature, but objectifies it, and imposes its will upon it through unrestrained technological manipulation. Such a way of thinking would naturally lead to abortion. If the woman does not *want* to be pregnant, she has recourse to an operation involving highly sophisticated technology in order to defend her control of her body. This fits the characterization of the masculine principle perfectly.

Abortion is a separation—a severing of a life-preserving connection between the woman and the fetus. It thus fails to respect the interconnectedness of all life. Nor does it respect the natural cycles of nature. The mother and the developing child together form a delicately balanced ecosystem with the woman's entire hormonal system geared towards sustaining the pregnancy.[32] The abortionist forces the cervical muscles (which have become thick and hard in order to hold in the developing fetus) open and disrupts her hormonal system by removing it.

Abortion has something further in common with [what] the behavior ecofeminists and pacifist feminists take to be characteristically masculine; it shows a willingness to use violence in order to maintain control. The fetus is destroyed by being pulled apart by suction, cut in pieces, or poisoned. It is not merely killed inadvertently as fish might be by toxic wastes, but it is deliberately targeted for destruction. Clearly this is not the expression of a "biophilic" attitude. This point was recently brought home to me by a Quaker woman who had reached the conclusion that the abortion she had had was contrary to her pacifist principles. She said, "we must seek peaceableness both within and without."

In terms of social thought, again, it is the masculine models which are most frequently employed in thinking about abortion. If masculine thought is naturally hierarchical and oriented toward power and control, then the interests of the fetus (who has no power) would naturally be suppressed in favor of the interests of the mother. But to the extent that feminist social thought is egalitarian, the question must be raised of why the mother's interests should prevail over the child's.

Feminist thought about abortion has, in addition, been deeply pervaded by the individualism which they so ardently criticize. The woman is supposed to have the sole authority to decide the outcome of the pregnancy. But what of her interconnectedness with the child and with others? Both she and the unborn child already exist within a network of relationships ranging from the closest ones—the father, grandparents, siblings, uncles and aunts, and so on—to ones with the broader society—including the mother's friends, employer, employees, potential adoptive parents, taxpayers who may be asked to fund the abortion or subsidize the child, and all the numerous other people affected by her choice. To dismiss this already existing network of relationships as irrelevant to the mother's decision is to manifest the sort of social atomism which feminist thinkers condemn as characteristically masculine.

Those feminists who are seeking to articulate the feminine voice in ethics also face a *prima facie* inconsistency between an ethics of care and abortion. Quite simply, abortion is a failure to care for one living being who exists in a particularly intimate relationship to oneself. If empathy, nurturance, and taking responsibility for caring for others are characteristic of the feminine voice, then abortion does not appear to be a feminine response to an unwanted pregnancy. If, as Gilligan says, "an ethic of care rests on the premise of non-violence—that no one should be hurt,"[33] then surely the feminine response to an unwanted pregnancy would be to try to find a solution which does not involve injury to anyone, including the unborn.

"Rights" have been invoked in the abortion controversy in a bewildering variety of ways, ranging from the "right to life" to the "right to control one's body." But clearly those who defend unrestricted access to abortion in terms of such things as the woman's right to privacy or her right to control her body are speaking the language of an ethics of justice rather than an ethics of care. For example, Judith Jarvis Thomson's widely read article "A Defense of Abortion"[34] treats the moral issue involved in abortion as a conflict between the rights of the fetus and the mother's rights over her own body. Mary Anne Warren also sees the issue in terms of a conflict of rights, but since the fetus does not meet her criteria for being a person, she weighs the woman's rights to "freedom, happiness and self-determination" against the rights of other people in the society who would like to see the fetus preserved for whatever reason.[35] And, insofar as she appeals to consciousness, reasoning, self-motivated activity, the capacity to communicate, and the presence of self-concepts and self-awareness as criteria of personhood, she relies on the kind of opposition between mind and nature criticized by many feminists as masculine. In particular, she is committed to what Jaggar calls "normative dualism"—the view that what is especially valuable about humans is their mental capacity for rational thought.

It is rather striking that feminists defending abortion lapse so quickly into speaking in the masculine voice. Is it because they feel they must do so in order to be heard in our male dominated society, or is it because no persuasive defense of abortion can be constructed from within the ethics of care tradition? We now consider several possible "feminine voice" defenses of abortion.

## III. Possible Responses and Replies

Among the feminists seeking to articulate and defend the value of the feminine voice, very few have made any serious attempt to grapple with abortion. The writings of the ecofeminists and the pacifist feminists abound with impassioned defenses of such values as non-violence, a democratic attitude towards the needs of all living things, letting others be and nurturing them, and so on, existing side by side with impassioned defenses of "reproductive rights." They see denying women access to abortion as just another aspect of male domination and violence against women.

This will not do for several reasons. First, it is not true that males are the chief opponents of abortion. Many women are strongly opposed to it. The pro-life movement at every level is largely composed of women. For example, as of May 1988, 38 of the state delegates to the National Right to Life Board of Directors were women, and only 13 were men. Indeed as Jean Bethke Elshtain has observed,[36] the pro-life movement has mobilized into political action an enormous number of women who were never politically active before. And a Gallup poll in 1981 found that 51% of women surveyed believed a person is present at conception, compared with only 33% of the men. The pro-life movement, thus, cannot be dismissed as representing male concerns and desires only. Granted, a pro-choice feminist could argue that women involved in the pro-life movement suffer from "colonized minds," but this sort of argument

clearly can be made to cut both directions. After all, many of the strongest supporters of "reproductive rights" have been men—ranging from the Supreme Court in *Roe v. Wade* to the Playboy Philosopher.

Secondly, terms like violence and domination are used far too loosely by those who condemn anti-abortion laws. If there are laws against wife abuse, does this mean that abusive husbands are being subjected to domination and violence? One does not exercise violence against someone merely by crossing his or her will, or even by crossing his or her will and backing this up by threats of legal retribution.

Finally, those who see violence and domination in laws against abortion, but not in abortion itself, generally fail to look at the nature of the act itself, and thus fail to judge that act in light of their professed values and principles. This is not surprising; abortion is a bloody and distressing thing to contemplate. But one cannot talk about it intelligently without being willing to look concretely at the act itself.

One line of thought is suggested by Gilligan, who holds that at the highest level of moral development, we must balance our responsibility to care for others against our need to care for ourselves. Perhaps we could, then, see the woman who has an abortion as still being caring and nurturing in that she is acting out of a legitimate care for herself. This is an implausible view of the actual feelings of women who undergo abortions. They may believe they're "doing something for themselves" in the sense of doing what they must do to safeguard their legitimate interests. But the operation is more naturally regarded as a violation of oneself than as a nurturing of oneself. This has been noted, even by feminists who support permissive abortion laws. For example, Carolyn Whitbeck speaks of "the unappealing prospect of having someone scraping away at one's core,"[37] and Adrienne Rich says that "Abortion is violence: a deep, desperate violence inflicted by a woman upon, first of all, herself."[38]

We here come up against the problem that a directive to care, to nurture, to take responsibility for others, and so on, provides a moral orientation, but leaves unanswered many important questions and hence provides little guidance in problem situations. What do we do when caring for one person involves being uncaring toward another? How widely must we extend our circle of care? Are some kinds of not caring worse than others? Is it caring to give someone what they want even though it may be bad for them?

Thinking in terms of preserving relationships suggests another possible "feminine" defense of abortion—namely that the woman is striving to preserve her interconnectedness with her family, husband, or boyfriend. Or perhaps she is concerned to strengthen her relationship with her other children by having enough time and resources to devote to their care. To simply tell a woman to preserve *all* her existing relationships is not the answer. Besides the fact that it may not be possible (women *do* sometimes have to sever relationships), it is not clear that it would be desirable even if it were possible. Attempting to preserve our existing relationships has conservative tendencies in several unfortunate ways. It fails to invite us to reflect critically on whether those relationships are good, healthy or worthy of preservation.[39] It also puts the unborn at a particular disadvantage, since the mother's relationship with him or her is just beginning, while her relationships with others have had time to develop. And not only the unborn, but any needy stranger who shows up at our door can be excluded on the grounds that caring for them would disrupt our existing pattern of relationships. Thus the care perspective could degenerate into a rationalization for a purely tribal morality; I take care of myself and my friends.

But how are decisions about severing relationships to be made? One possibility is suggested by Gilligan in a recent article. She looks at the network of connections within which the woman who is considering abortion finds herself entangled, and says "to ask what actions constitute care or are more caring directs attention to the parameters of connection and the *costs of detachment* . . . (emphasis added)."[40] Thus, the woman considering abortion should reflect upon the comparative costs of severing various relationships. This

method of decision, however, makes her vulnerable to emotional and psychological pressure from others, by encouraging her to sever whichever connection is easiest to break (the squeaky wheel principle).[41]

But perhaps we can lay out some guidelines (or, at least, rules of thumb) for making these difficult decisions. One way we might reason, from the point of view of the feminine voice, is that since preserving interconnectedness is good, we should prefer a short term estrangement to an irremediable severing of relationship. And we should choose an action which *may* cause an irremediable break in relationship over one which is certain to cause such a break. By either of these criteria, abortion is clearly to be avoided.[42]

Another consideration suggested by Gilligan's work is that since avoiding hurt to others (or non-violence) is integral to an ethics of care, severing a relationship where the other person will be only slightly hurt would be preferable to severing one where deep or lasting injury will be inflicted by our action. But on this criterion, again, it would seem she should avoid abortion, since loss of life is clearly a graver harm than emotional distress.

Two other possible criteria which would also tell against abortion are: (1) that it is permissible to cut ties with someone who behaves unjustly and oppressively toward one, but not with someone who is innocent of any wrong against one, or (2) we have special obligations to our own offspring, and thus should not sever relationship with them.

Criteria can, perhaps, be found which would dictate severing relationship with the fetus rather than others, but it is hard to specify one which clearly reflects the feminine voice. Certainly the fight to control one's body will not do. The claim that the unborn is not a person and therefore does not deserve moral consideration can be faulted on several grounds. First, if the feminine voice is one which accepts the interconnectedness of all life and strives to avoid harm to nature and to other species, then the non-personhood of the fetus (supposing it could be proved) would not imply that its needs can be discounted. And secondly, the entire debate over personhood has standardly been carried on very much in the masculine voice.[43] One feminist, Janice Raymond,[44] has suggested that the question of when life begins is a masculine one, and if this is a masculine question, it would seem that personhood, with its juridical connotations, would be also. It is not clear that the care perspective has the resources to resolve this issue. If it cannot, then, one cannot rely on the non-personhood of the fetus in constructing a "feminine voice" defense of abortion. A care perspective would at least seem to place the burden of proof on those who would restrict the scope of care, in this case to those that have been born.

It seems that the only way open to the person who seeks to defend abortion from the point of view of the feminine voice is to deny that a relationship (or at least any morally significant relationship) exists between the embryo/fetus and the mother. The question of how to tell when a relationship (or a morally significant relationship) exists is a deep and important one, which has, as yet, received insufficient attention from those who are trying to articulate the feminine voice in moral reasoning. The whole ecofeminist position relies on the assumption that our relationship with nature and with other species is a real and morally significant one. They, thus, have no basis at all for excluding the unborn from moral consideration.

There are those, however, who wish to define morally significant relationships more narrowly—thus effectively limiting our obligation to extend care. While many philosophers within the "justice tradition" (for example, Kant) have seen moral significance only where there is some impact upon rational beings, Nel Noddings, coming from the "care perspective," tries to limit our obligation to extend care in terms of the possibility of "completion" or "reciprocity" in a caring relationship.[45] Since she takes the mother-child relationship to be paradigmatic of caring, it comes as something of a surprise that she regards abortion as a permissible response to an unwanted pregnancy.[46]

There are, on Noddings' view, two different ways in which we may be bound, as caring persons, to extend our care to one for whom we do not already have the sort of feelings of love and affection which would lead us to do the caring

action naturally. One is by virtue of being connected with our "inner circle" of caring (which is formed by natural relations of love and friendship) through "chains" of "personal or formal relations.[47] As an example of a person appropriately linked to the inner circle, she cites her daughter's fiancé. It would certainly *seem* that the embryo in one's womb would belong to one's "inner circle" (via natural caring), or at least be connected to it by a "formal relation" (that is, that of parenthood). But Noddings does not concede this. Who is part of my inner circle, and who is connected to it in such a way that I am obligated to extend care to him or her seems to be, for Noddings, largely a matter of my feelings toward the person and/or my choice to include him or her. Thus the mother *may* "confer sacredness" upon the "information speck"[48] in her womb, but need not if, for example, her relationship with the father is not a stable and loving one. During pregnancy "many women recognize the relation as established when the fetus begins to move about. It is not a question of when life begins, but of when relation begins."

But making the existence of a relation between the unborn and the mother a matter of her choice or feelings seems to run contrary to one of the most central insights of the feminine perspective in moral reasoning—namely that we already *are* interconnected with others, and thus have responsibilities to them. The view that we are connected with others only when we choose to be or when we *feel* we are, presupposes the kind of individualism and social atomism which Noddings and other feminists criticize as masculine.

Noddings also claims that we sometimes are obligated to care for "the proximate stranger." She says:

We cannot refuse obligation in human affairs by merely refusing to enter relation; we are, by virtue of our mutual humanity, already and perpetually in potential relation.[49]

Why, then, are we not obligated to extend care to the unborn? She gives two criteria for when we have an obligation to extend care: there must be "the existence of or potential for present relation" and the "dynamic potential for growth in relation, including the potential for increased reciprocity. . . ." Animals are, she believes, excluded by this second criterion since their response is nearly static (unlike a human infant).

She regards the embryo/fetus as not having the potential for present relationships of caring and reciprocity, and thus as having no claim upon our care. As the fetus matures, he or she develops increasing potential for caring relationships, and thus our obligation increases also. There are problems with her position, however.

First of all, the only relationships which can be relevant to *my* obligation to extend care, for Noddings, must be relationships with *me*. Whatever the criteria for having a relationship are, it must be that at a given time, an entity either has a relationship with me or it does not. If it does not, it may either have no potential for a morally significant relationship with me (for example, my word processor), or it may have such potential in several ways: (1) The relationship may become actual at the will of one or both parties (for example, the stranger sitting next to me on the bus). (2) The relationship may become actual only after a change in relative spatial locations which will take time, and thus can occur only in the future (for example, walking several blocks to meet a new neighbor, or traveling to Tibet to meet a specific Tibetan). Or (3) The relationship may become actual only after some internal change occurs within the other (for example by waiting for a sleeping drug to wear off, for a deep but reversible coma to pass, or for the embryo to mature more fully) and thus can also happen only in the future.

In all three of these cases there is present now in the other the potential for relations of a caring and reciprocal sort. In cases (1) and (2) this is uncontroversial, but (3) requires some defense in the case of the unborn. The human embryo differs now from a rabbit embryo in that it possesses potential for these kinds of relationships although neither of them is presently able to enter into relationships of any sort.[50] That potential becomes actualized only over time, but it can become actualized only because it is there to be actualized (as it is not in the rabbit embryo).[51] Noddings fails to give any reason why the necessity for some internal change to occur in the other before relation can become actual has such moral importance that we are entitled to kill the other in case (3), but not in the others, especially since my refraining from killing it is a sufficient condition for the actualization of the embryo's potential for caring relationships. Her criterion as it stands would also seem to imply that we may kill persons in deep but predictably reversible comas.

Whichever strand of Noddings' thought we choose, then, it is hard to see how the unborn can be excluded from being ones for whom we ought to care. If we focus on the narrow, tribal morality of "inner circles" and "chains," then an objective connection exists tying the unborn to the mother and other relatives. If we are to be open to the needy stranger because of the real potential for relationship and reciprocity, then we should be open to the unborn because he or she also has the real and present potential for a relationship of reciprocity and mutuality which comes with species membership.

Many feminists will object to my argument so far on the grounds that they do not, after all, consider abortion to be a *good* thing. They aren't pro-abortion in the sense that they encourage women to have abortions. They merely regard it as something which must be available as a kind of "grim option"—something a woman would choose only when the other alternatives are all immeasurably worse.[52]

First of all, the grim options view sounds very much like the "masculine voice"—we must grit our teeth, and do the distasteful but necessary deed (the more so where the deed involves killing).[53] Furthermore, it is in danger of collapsing into total subjectivism unless one is willing to specify some criteria for when an option is a genuinely grim one, beyond the agent's feeling that it is. What if she chooses to abort in order not to have to postpone her trip to Europe, or because she prefers sons to daughters? Surely these are not grim options no matter what she may say. Granted, the complicated circumstances surrounding her decision are best known to the woman herself. But this does not imply that no one is *ever* in a position to make judgments about whether her option is sufficiently grim to justify abortion. We do not generally concede that only the agent is in a position to judge the morality of his or her action.

Feminists standardly hold that absolutely no restrictions may be placed on a woman's right to choose abortion.[54] This position cannot be supported by the grim options argument. One who believes something is a grim option will be inclined to try to avoid or prevent it, and thus be willing, at least in principle, to place some restrictions on what counts as a grim option. Granted, practical problems exist about how such decisions are to be made and by whom. But someone who refuses in principle to allow any restrictions on women's right to abort cannot in good faith claim that they regard abortion only as a grim option.

Some feminists will say: yes, feminine virtues are a good thing for any person to have, and yes, abortion is a characteristically masculine way of dealing with an unwanted pregnancy, but in the current state of things we live in a male dominated society, and we must be willing to use now weapons which, ideally, in a good, matriarchal society, we would not use.[55] But there are no indications that an ideal utopian society is just around the corner; thus we are condemned to a constant violation of our own deepest commitments. If the traits, values and attitudes characteristic of the "feminine voice" are asserted to be good ones, we ought to act according to them. And such values and attitudes simply do not lend support to either the choice of abortion as a way of dealing with an unwanted pregnancy in individual cases, or to the political demand for unrestricted[56] access to abortion which has become so entrenched in the feminist movement. Quite the contrary.[57]

## Notes

1. See Nel Noddings, *Caring: A Feminine Approach to Ethics* (Berkeley: University of California Press, 1984), Annette Baier, "What Do Women Want in a Moral Theory?" *Nous,* vol. 19 (March, 1985), and "Hume, the Women's Moral Theorist?" in *Women and Moral Theory,* Kittay and Meyers (eds.) (Totowa, N.J.: Rowman & Littlefield, 1987).

2. Carol McMillan, *Women, Reason and Nature* (Princeton: Princeton University Press, 1982), Adrienne

Rich, *Of Woman Born* (N.Y.: Norton, 1976), Sara Ruddick, "Remarks on the Sexual Politics of Reason" in *Women and Moral Theory,* "Maternal Thinking" and "Preservative Love and Military Destruction: Some Reflections on Mothering and Peace" in Joyce Treblicot (ed.), *Mothering: Essays in Feminist Theory* (Totowa, N.J.: Rowman & Allanheld, 1983), and Nancy Hartsock "The Feminist Standpoint" in *Discovering Reality,* Harding (ed.) (Boston: D. Reidel, 1983).

3. Among them are such writers as Rosemary Radford Reuther, Susan Griffin, Elizabeth Dodson Gray, Brian Easla, Sally Miller Gearhart, Carolyn Merchant, Genevieve Lloyd, the pacifist feminists, and a number of feminists involved in the ecology movement.

4. In this paper I shall use the terms "masculine" and "feminine" only in this weaker sense, which is agnostic about the existence of biologically based differences.

5. A strong presumption against abortion is not, of course, the same thing as an absolute ban on all abortions. I do not attempt here to resolve the really hard cases; it is not clear that the feminine voice (at least as it has been articulated so far) is sufficiently fine-grained to tell us exactly where to draw the line in such cases.

6. See Carol Gilligan, *In a Different Voice* (Cambridge, MA: Harvard University Press, 1982), p. 8.

7. *Ibid.,* p. 10.

8. See Gilligan, "Moral Orientation and Moral Development" in *Women and Moral Theory,* p. 31.

9. Annette Baier, "Hume, the Woman's Moral Theorist?" in *Women and Moral Theory,* pp. 37–39.

10. Annette Baier, "What Do Women Want in a Moral Theory?" *Nous,* vol. 19 (March, 1985), p. 53.

11. Christina Hoff Sommers, "Filial Morality" in *Women and Moral Theory,* pp. 69–84.

12. Virginia Held, "Feminism and Moral Theory," in *Women and Moral Theory,* pp. 111–128.

13. Alison Jaggar, *Feminist Politics and Human Nature* (Totowa, N.J.: Rowman & Allanheld, 1983), p. 46.

14. *Ibid.,* p. 28.

15. Rosemary Radford Reuther, *New Woman, New Earth* (New York: The Seabury Press, 1975), p. 195.

16. *Ibid.,* p. 188.

17. *Ibid.,* p. 195.

18. *Ibid.,* p. 189.

19. Elizabeth Dodson Gray, *Why the Green Nigger* (Wellesley, MA: Roundtable Press, 1979), p. 54.

20. Genevieve Lloyd, *The Man of Reason: Male and Female in Western Philosophy* (Minneapolis: University of Minnesota Press, 1984).

21. See, e.g., Rosemary Radford Reuther, *New Woman, New Earth,* Elizabeth Dodson Gray, *Why the Green Nigger,* and Brian Easla, *Science and Sexual Oppression* (London: Weidenfeld and Nicolson, 1981).

22. Reuther, *op. cit.,* p. 195.

23. Carolyn Merchant, *The Death of Nature: Women, Ecology and the Scientific Revolution* (San Francisco: Harper & Row, 1980).

24. Stephanie Leland and Leonie Caldecott (eds.), *Reclaim the Earth: Women Speak out for Life on Earth* (London: The Women's Press, 1983), p. 72. For an overview of ecofeminist thought which focuses on the role of mind/body dualism, see Val Plumwood, "Ecofeminism: An Overview," *Australasian Journal of Philosophy,* Supplement to Vol. 64 (June, 1986), pp. 120–138.

25. Leland and Caldecott, *op. cit.,* p. 71.

26. *Ibid.,* p. 69.

27. Introduction to *Women and Moral Theory,* by Kittay and Meyers, p. 7.

28. Cited by Barbara Zanotti, "Patriarchy: A State of War," in *Reweaving the Web of Life,* Pam McAllister (ed.). (Philadelphia: New Society Publishers, 1982), p. 17.

29. See, e.g., Sally Miller Gearhart, "The Future—If There Is One—Is Female" in *Reweaving the Web of Life,* p. 266.

30. *Ibid.,* p. 272.

31. See Sara Ruddick, "Remarks on the Sexual Politics of Reason."

32. I owe the idea of regarding mother and child as an ecosystem to a conversation with Leonie Caldecott, co-editor of *Reclaim the Earth.*

33. Gilligan, *op. cit.,* p. 174.

34. Judith Jarvis Thomson, "A Defense of Abortion," *Philosophy and Public Affairs,* vol. 1 (1971), pp. 47–66.

35. Mary Anne Warren, "On the Moral and Legal Status of Abortion," *The Monist,* vol. 57 (January, 1973), reprinted in Wasserstrom, *Today's Moral Problems* (New York: Macmillan, 1985), p. 448.

36. Jean Bethke Elshtain, *Public Man, Private Woman* (Princeton, N.J.: Princeton University Press, 1981), p. 312.

37. Carolyn Whitbeck, "Women as People: Pregnancy and Personhood," in *Abortion and the Status of the Fetus,* W. B. Bondeson, et al. (eds.) (Boston: D. Reidel Publishing Co., 1983), p. 252.

38. Rich, *op. cit.,* p. 269.

39. Joan Tronto makes this point in "Beyond Gender Differences to a Theory of Care," *Signs,* vol. 22 (Summer, 1987), p. 666.

40. Carol Gilligan, "Moral Orientation and Moral Development" in *Women and Moral Theory,* p. 24.

41. This was evident in the reasoning of the women in Gilligan's case studies, many of whom had abortions in order to please or placate other significant persons in their lives.

42. Some post-abortion counselors find the sense of irremediable break in relationship to be one of the most painful aspects of the post-abortion experience, and try to urge the woman to imaginatively re-create a relationship with the baby in order to be better able to complete the necessary grieving process. Conversation with Teresa Patterson, post-abortion counselor at Crisis Pregnancy Center in Walnut Creek, California.

43. For an excellent "masculine voice" discussion of the personhood issues, see, e.g., Philip E. Devine, *The Ethics of Homicide* (Ithaca, NY: Cornell University Press, 1978).

44. Janice Raymond, *The Transsexual Empire* (Boston: Beacon Press, 1979), p. 114.

45. It would seem that in using the term "obligation," Noddings is blurring the distinction between the masculine and feminine voice, since obligations imply rights. When she speaks of obligations to extend care, however, these are not absolute, but relative to the individual's choice of being a caring person as an ethical ideal. They are binding on us only as a result of our own prior choice, and our care is not something the other can claim as a matter of justice.

46. Nodding's discussion of abortion occurs on pp. 87–90 of *Caring: A Feminine Approach to Ethics, op. cit.,* and all quotes are from these pages unless otherwise noted.

47. *Ibid.,* p. 47.

48. It is inaccurate to call even the newly implanted zygote an "information speck." Unlike a blueprint or pattern of information, it is alive and growing.

49. I realize that Noddings would not be happy with the extent to which I lean on her use of the term "criteria," since she prefers to argue by autobiographical example. However, since moral intuitions about abortion vary so widely, this sort of argument is not effective here.

50. I omit here consideration of such difficult cases as severe genetic retardation.

51. The notion of potentiality I am relying on here is roughly an Aristotelian one.

52. Carolyn Whitbeck articulates a view of this sort in "Women as People: Pregnancy and Personhood," *op. cit.*

53. Granted, this sort of judgment is, at least in part, an impressionistic one. It is supported, however, by Gilligan's findings about the difference between boys and girls in their response to the "Heinz dilemma" (where the man is faced with a choice between allowing his wife to die or stealing an expensive drug from the druggist to save her). Although the females she studies do not all respond to the dilemma in the same way (e.g. Betty at first sounds more like Hobbes than like what has been characterized as the feminine voice—pp. 75–76), some recurring patterns which she singles out as representative of the feminine voice are: resisting being forced to accept either horn of the dilemma, seeing all those involved as in relationship with each other, viewing the dilemma in terms of conflicting responsibilities rather than rights, and seeking to avoid or minimize harm to anyone (see, e.g., Sarah p. 95). Since the abortion decision involves killing and not merely letting die, it would seem that the impetus to find a way through the horns of the dilemma would be, if anything, greater than in the Heinz dilemma.

54. For example, one feminist, Roberta Steinbach, argues that we must not restrict a woman's rights to abort for reasons of sex selection *against females* because it might endanger our hard won "reproductive rights"! (See "Sex Selection: From Here to Fraternity" in Carol Gould (ed.), *Beyond Domination* (Totowa, NJ: Rowman & Allanheld, 1984), p. 280.)

55. For example, Annette Baier regards trust as the central concept in a feminine ethics, but speaks of "the principled betrayal of the exploiter's trust" (Baier, "What Do Women Want in a Moral Theory?" p. 62).

56. Restrictions can take many forms, including laws against abortion, mandatory counseling which includes information about the facts of fetal development and encourages the woman to choose other options, obligatory waiting periods, legal requirements to notify (and/or obtain the consent of) the father, or in the case of a minor the girl's parents, etc. To defend the appropriateness of any particular sort of restrictions goes beyond the scope of this paper.

57. I wish to thank the following for reading and commenting on an earlier draft of this paper: Edith Black, Tony Celano, Phil Devine, James Nelson, Alan Soble, and Michael Wreen.

# 44   Abortion: A Feminist Perspective

## SUSAN SHERWIN

Feminist reasoning in support of women's right to choose abortion is significantly different from the reasoning used by nonfeminist supporters of similar positions. For instance, most feminist accounts evaluate abortion policy within a broader framework, according to its place among the social institutions that support the subordination of women. In contrast, most nonfeminist discussions of abortion consider the moral or legal permissibility of abortion in isolation; they ignore (and thereby obscure) relevant connections with other social practices, including the ongoing power struggle within sexist societies over the control of women and their reproduction. Feminist arguments take into account the actual concerns that particular women attend to in their decision-making on abortion, such as the nature of a woman's feelings about her fetus, her relationships with her partner, other children she may have, and her various obligations to herself and others. In contrast, most nonfeminist discussions evaluate abortion decisions in their most abstract form (for example, questioning what sort of being a fetus is); from this perspective, specific questions of context are deemed irrelevant. In addition, nonfeminist arguments in support of choice about abortion are generally grounded in masculinist conceptions of freedom (such as privacy, individual choice, and individuals' property rights with respect to their own bodies), which do not meet the needs, interests, and intuitions of many of the women concerned.

Feminists also differ from nonfeminists in their conception of what is morally at issue with abortion. Nonfeminists focus exclusively on the morality and legality of performing abortions, whereas feminists insist that other issues, including the accessibility and delivery of abortion services, must also be addressed. . . .

## Women and Abortion

The most obvious difference between feminist and nonfeminist approaches to abortion lies in the relative attention each gives in its analysis to the interests and experiences of women. Feminist analysis regards the effects of unwanted pregnancies on the lives of women individually and collectively as the central element in the moral examination of abortion; it is considered self-evident that the pregnant woman is the subject of principal concern in abortion decisions. In many nonfeminist accounts, however, not only is the pregnant woman not perceived as central, she is often rendered virtually invisible. Nonfeminist theorists, whether they support or oppose women's right to choose abortion, generally focus almost all their attention on the moral status of the fetus.[1]

Reprinted with permission of the publisher from *No Longer Patient* (Temple University Press, 1992), 99–114, with omissions.

In pursuing a distinctively feminist ethics, it is appropriate to begin with a look at the role of abortion in women's lives. The need for abortion can be very intense; no matter how appalling and dangerous the conditions, women from widely diverse cultures and historical periods have pursued abortions. No one denies that if abortion is not made legal, safe, and accessible in our society women will seek out illegal and life-threatening abortions to terminate pregnancies they cannot accept. Antiabortion activists seem willing to accept this cost, although liberals definitely are not; feminists, who explicitly value women, judge the inevitable loss of women's lives that results from restrictive abortion policies to be a matter of fundamental concern.

Antiabortion campaigners imagine that women often make frivolous and irresponsible decisions about abortion, but feminists recognize that women have abortions for a wide variety of compelling reasons. Some women, for instance, find themselves seriously ill and incapacitated throughout pregnancy; they cannot continue in their jobs and may face insurmountable difficulties in fulfilling their responsibilities at home. Many employers and schools will not tolerate pregnancy in their employees or students, and not every woman is able to put her job, career, or studies on hold. Women of limited means may be unable to take adequate care of children they have already borne, and they may know that another mouth to feed will reduce their ability to provide for their existing children. Women who suffer from chronic disease, who believe themselves too young or too old to have children, or who are unable to maintain lasting relationships may recognize that they will not be able to care properly for a child when they face the decision. Some who are homeless, addicted to drugs, or diagnosed as carrying the AIDS virus may be unwilling to allow a child to enter the world with the handicaps that would result from the mother's condition. If the fetus is a result of rape or incest, then the psychological pain of carrying it may be unbearable, and the woman may recognize that her attitude to the child after birth will be tinged with bitterness. Some women learn that the fetuses that they carry have serious chromosomal anomalies and consider it best to prevent them from being born with a condition that is bound to cause them to suffer. Others, knowing the fathers to be brutal and violent, may be unwilling to subject a child to the beatings or incestuous attacks they anticipate; some may have no other realistic way to remove the child (or themselves) from the relationship.[2]

Finally, a woman may simply believe that bearing a child is incompatible with her life plans at the time. Continuing a pregnancy may have devastating repercussions throughout a woman's life. If the woman is young, then a pregnancy will likely reduce her chances of pursuing an education and hence limit her career and life opportunities. "The earlier a woman has a baby, it seems, the more likely she is to drop out of school; the less education she gets, the more likely she is to remain poorly paid, peripheral to the labor market, or unemployed, and the more children she will have" (Petchesky 1985, 150). In many circumstances, having a child will exacerbate the social and economic forces already stacked against a woman by virtue of her sex (and her race, class, age, sexual orientation, disabilities, and so forth). Access to abortion is necessary for many women if they are to escape the oppressive conditions of poverty.[3]

Whatever the specific reasons are for abortion, most feminists believe that the women concerned are in the best position to judge whether abortion is the appropriate response to a pregnancy. Because usually only the woman choosing abortion is properly situated to weigh all the relevant factors, most feminists resist attempts to offer general, abstract rules for determining when abortion is morally justified.[4] Women's personal deliberations about abortion involve contextually defined considerations that reflect their commitments to the needs and interests of everyone concerned, including themselves, the fetuses they carry, other members of their household, and so forth. Because no single formula is available for balancing these complex factors through all possible cases, it is vital that feminists insist on protecting each woman's right to come to her own conclusion and resist the attempts of other philosophers and moralists to set the agenda for these considerations. Feminists stress that women must be acknowledged as full moral agents, responsible for making moral decisions about their own pregnancies. Women may sometimes make mistakes in their moral judgments, but no one else can be assumed to have the authority to evaluate and overrule their judgments.[5]

. . . Because we live in a patriarchal society, it is especially important to ensure that women have the authority to control their own reproduction.[6] Despite the diversity of opinion found among feminists on most other matters, most feminists agree that women must gain full control over their own reproductive lives if they are to free themselves from male dominance.[7]

Moreover, women's freedom to choose abortion is linked to their ability to control their own sexuality. Women's subordinate status often prevents them from refusing men sexual access to their bodies. If women cannot end the unwanted pregnancies that result from male sexual dominance, then their sexual vulnerability to particular men may increase, because caring for an(other) infant involves greater financial needs and reduced economic opportunities for women.[8] As a result, pregnancy often forces women to become dependent on particular men. Because a woman's dependence on a man is assumed to entail her continued sexual loyalty to him, restriction of abortion serves to commit women to remaining sexually accessible to particular men and thus helps to perpetuate the cycle of oppression.

In contrast to most nonfeminist accounts, feminist analyses of abortion direct attention to how women get pregnant. Those who reject abortion seem to believe that women can avoid unwanted pregnancies "simply" by avoiding sexual intercourse. These views show little appreciation for the power of sexual politics in a culture that oppresses women. Existing patterns of sexual dominance mean that women often have little control over their sexual lives. They may be subject to rape by their husbands, boyfriends, colleagues, employers, customers, fathers, brothers, uncles, and dates, as well as by strangers. Often the sexual coercion is not even recognized as such by the participants but is the price of continued "good will"—popularity, economic survival, peace, or simple acceptance. Many women have found themselves in circumstances where they do not feel free to refuse a man's demands for intercourse, either because he is holding a gun to her head or because he threatens to be emotionally hurt if she refuses (or both). Women are socialized to be compliant and accommodating, sensitive to the feelings of others, and frightened of physical power; men are socialized to take advantage of every opportunity to engage in sexual intercourse and to use sex to express dominance and power. Under such circumstances, it is difficult to argue that women could simply "choose" to avoid heterosexual activity if they wish to avoid pregnancy. Catharine MacKinnon neatly sums it up: "The logic by which women are supposed to consent to sex [is]: preclude the alternatives, then call the remaining option 'her choice'" (MacKinnon 1989, 192).

Furthermore, women cannot rely on birth control to avoid pregnancy. No form of contraception that is fully safe and reliable is available, other than sterilization; because women may wish only to avoid pregnancy temporarily, not permanently, sterilization is not always an acceptable choice. The pill and the IUD are the most effective contraceptive means offered, but both involve significant health hazards to women and are quite dangerous for some.[9] No woman should spend the thirty to forty years of her reproductive life on either form of birth control. Further, both have been associated with subsequent problems of involuntary infertility, so they are far from optimal for women who seek to control the timing of their pregnancies.

The safest form of birth control involves the use of barrier methods (condoms or diaphragms) in combination with spermicidal foams or jelly. But these methods also pose difficulties for women. They are sometimes socially awkward to use. Young women are discouraged from preparing for sexual activity that might never happen and are offered instead romantic models of spontaneous passion; few films or novels interrupt scenes of seduction for a partner to fetch contraceptives. Many women find their male partners unwilling to use barrier methods of contraception, and they often find themselves in no position to insist. Further, cost is a limiting factor for many women. Condoms and spermicides are expensive and are not covered under most health care plans.[10] Only one contraceptive option offers women safe and fully effective birth control: barrier methods with the backup option of abortion.[11]

From a feminist perspective, the central moral feature of pregnancy is that it takes place in women's bodies and has profound effects on women's lives. Gender-neutral accounts of pregnancy are not available; pregnancy is explicitly a condition associated with the female body.[12] Because only women experience a need for abortion, policies about abortion affect women uniquely. Therefore, it is important to consider how proposed policies on abortion fit into general patterns of oppression for women. Unlike non-feminist accounts, feminist ethics demands that the effects of abortion policies on the oppression of women be of principal consideration in our ethical evaluations.

## The Fetus

In contrast to feminist ethics, most nonfeminist analysts believe that the moral acceptability of abortion turns entirely on the question of the moral status of the fetus. Even those who support women's right to choose abortion tend to accept the premise of the antiabortion proponents that abortion can be tolerated only if we can first prove that the fetus lacks full personhood.[13] Opponents of abortion demand that we define the status of the fetus either as a being that is valued in the same way as other humans, and hence is entitled not to be killed, or as a being that lacks in all value. Rather than challenging the logic of this formulation, many defenders of abortion have concentrated on showing that the fetus is indeed without significant value (Tooley 1972, Warren 1973); others, such as L. W. Sumner (1981), offer a more subtle account that reflects the gradual development of fetuses and distinguishes between early fetal stages, where the relevant criterion for personhood is absent, and later stages, where it is present. Thus the debate often rages between

abortion opponents, who describe the fetus as an "innocent," vulnerable, morally important, separate being whose life is threatened and who must be protected at all costs, and abortion supporters, who try to establish that fetuses are deficient in some critical respect and hence are outside the scope of the moral community. In both cases, however, the nature of the fetus as an independent being is said to determine the moral status of abortion.

The woman on whom the fetus depends for survival is considered as secondary (if she is considered at all) in these debates. The actual experiences and responsibilities of real women are not perceived as morally relevant to the debate, unless these women, too, can be proved innocent by establishing that their pregnancies are a result of rape or incest.[14] In some contexts, women's role in gestation is literally reduced to that of "fetal containers"; the individual women disappear or are perceived simply as mechanical life-support systems.[15]

The current rhetoric against abortion stresses that the genetic makeup of the fetus is determined at conception and the genetic code is incontestably human. Lest there be any doubt about the humanity of the fetus, we are assailed with photographs of fetuses at various stages of development that demonstrate the early appearance of recognizably human characteristics, such as eyes, fingers, and toes. Modern ultrasound technology is used to obtain "baby's first picture" and stimulate bonding between pregnant women and their fetuses (Petchesky 1987). That the fetus in its early stages is microscopic, virtually indistinguishable to the untrained eye from fetuses of other species, and lacking in the capacities that make human life meaningful and valuable is not deemed relevant by the self-appointed defenders of the fetus. The antiabortion campaign is directed at evoking sympathetic attitudes toward a tiny, helpless being whose life is threatened by its own mother; the fetus is characterized as a being entangled in an adversarial relationship with the (presumably irresponsible) woman who carries it (Overall 1987). People are encouraged to identify with the "unborn child," not with the woman whose life is also at issue.

In the nonfeminist literature, both defenders and opponents of women's right to choose abortion agree that the difference between a late-term fetus and a newborn infant is "merely geographical" and cannot be considered morally significant. Daniel Callahan (1986), for instance, maintains a pro-choice stand but professes increasing uneasiness about this position in light of new medical and scientific developments that increase our knowledge of embryology and hasten the date of potential viability for fetuses; he insists that defenders of women's right to choose must come to terms with the question of the fetus and the effects of science on the fetus's prospects apart from the woman who carries it. Arguments that focus on the similarities between infants and fetuses, however, generally fail to acknowledge that a fetus inhabits a woman's body and is wholly dependent on her unique contribution to its maintenance, whereas a newborn is physically independent, although still in need of a lot of care.[16] One can only view the distinction between being in or out of a woman's womb as morally irrelevant if one discounts the perspective of the pregnant woman; feminists seem to be alone in recognizing the woman's perspective as morally important to the distinction.[17]

In antiabortion arguments, fetuses are identified as individuals; in our culture, which views the (abstract) individual as sacred, fetuses qua individuals are to be honored and preserved. Extraordinary claims are made to establish the individuality and moral agency of fetuses. At the same time, the women who carry these fetal individuals are viewed as passive hosts whose only significant role is to refrain from aborting or harming their fetuses. Because it is widely believed that a woman does not actually have to do anything to protect the life of her fetus, pregnancy is often considered (abstractly) to be a tolerable burden to protect the life of an individual so like us.[18]

Medicine has played its part in supporting these attitudes. Fetal medicine is a rapidly expanding specialty, and it is commonplace in professional medical journals to find references to pregnant women as "the maternal environment." Fetal surgeons now have at their disposal a reper-toire of sophisticated technology that can save the lives of dangerously ill fetuses; in light of the excitement of such heroic successes, it is perhaps understandable that women have disappeared from their view. These specialists see the fetuses as their patients, not the women who nurture the fetuses. As the "active" agents in saving fetal lives (unlike the pregnant women, whose role is seen as purely passive), doctors perceive themselves as developing independent relationships with the fetuses they treat. Barbara Katz Rothman observes: "The medical model of pregnancy, as an essentially parasitic and vaguely pathological relationship, encourages the physician to view the fetus and mother as two separate patients, and to see pregnancy as inherently a conflict of interests between the two" (Rothman 1986, 25). . . .

In other words, some physicians have joined antiabortion campaigners in fostering a cultural acceptance of the view that fetuses are distinct individuals who are physically, ontologically, and socially separate from the women whose bodies they inhabit and that they have their own distinct interests. In this picture, pregnant women are either ignored altogether or are viewed as deficient in some crucial respect, and hence they can be subject to coercion for the sake of their fetuses. In the former case, the interests of the women concerned are assumed to be identical with those of the fetus; in the latter, the women's interests are irrelevant, because they are perceived as immoral, unimportant, or unnatural. Focus on the fetus as an independent entity has led to presumptions that deny pregnant women their roles as active, independent, moral agents with a primary interest in what becomes of the fetuses they carry. The moral question of the fetus's status is quickly translated into a license to interfere with women's reproductive freedom.

On a feminist account fetal development is examined in the context in which it occurs, within women's bodies, rather than in the isolation of imagined abstraction. Fetuses develop in specific pregnancies that occur in the lives of particular women. They are not individuals housed in generic female wombs or full persons at risk only because they are small and subject to the whims of women. Their very existence is relationally defined, reflecting their development within particular women's bodies; that relationship gives those women reason to be concerned about them. Many feminists argue against a perspective that regards the fetus as an independent being and suggest that a more accurate and valuable understanding of pregnancy would involve regarding the pregnant woman "as a biological and social unit" (Rothman 1986, 25). . . .

Most feminist views of what is valuable about persons reflect the social nature of individual existence. No human, especially no fetus, can exist apart from relationships; efforts to speak of the fetus itself, as if it were not inseparable from the woman in whom it develops, are distorting and dishonest. Fetuses have a unique physical status— within and dependent on particular women. That gives them also a unique social status. However much some might prefer it to be otherwise, no one other than the pregnant woman in question can do anything to support or harm a fetus without doing something to the woman who nurtures it. Because of this inexorable biological reality, the responsibility and privilege of determining a fetus's specific social status and value must rest with the woman carrying it. . . .

No absolute value attaches to fetuses apart from their relational status, which is determined in the context of their particular development. This is not the same, however, as saying that they have no value at all or that they have merely instrumental value, as some liberals suggest. The value that women place on their own fetuses is the sort of value that attaches to an emerging human relationship.

Nevertheless, fetuses are not persons, because they have not developed sufficiently in their capacity for social relationships to be persons in any morally significant sense (that is, they are not yet second persons). In this way they differ from newborns, who immediately begin to develop into persons by virtue of their place as subjects in human relationships; newborns are capable of some forms of communication and response. The moral status of fetuses is determined by the nature of their primary relationship and the value that is

created there. Therefore, feminist accounts of abortion emphasize the importance of protecting women's rights to continue or to terminate pregnancies as each sees fit.

## The Politics of Abortion

Feminist accounts explore the connections between particular social policies and the general patterns of power relationships in our society. . . . When we place abortion in the larger political context, we see that most of the groups active in the struggle to prohibit abortion also support other conservative measures to maintain the forms of dominance that characterize patriarchy (and often class and racial oppression as well). The movement against abortion is led by the Catholic church and other conservative religious institutions, which explicitly endorse not only fetal rights but also male dominance in the home and the church. Most opponents of abortion also oppose virtually all forms of birth control and all forms of sexuality other than monogamous, reproductive sex; usually, they also resist having women assume positions of authority in dominant public institutions. Typically, antiabortion activists support conservative economic measures that protect the interests of the privileged classes of society and ignore the needs of the oppressed and disadvantaged (Petchesky 1985). Although they stress their commitment to preserving life, many systematically work to dismantle key social programs that provide life necessities to the underclass. Moreover, some current campaigns against abortion retain elements of the racism that dominated the North American abortion literature in the early years of the twentieth century, wherein abortion was opposed on the grounds that it amounted to racial suicide on the part of whites.[19]

In the eyes of its principal opponents, then, abortion is not an isolated practice; their opposition to abortion is central to a set of social values that runs counter to feminism's objectives. Hence antiabortion activists generally do not offer alternatives to abortion that support feminist interests in overturning the patterns of oppression that confront women. Most deny that there are any legitimate grounds for abortion, short of the need to save a woman's life—and some are not even persuaded by this criterion (Nicholson 1977). They believe that any pregnancy can and should be endured. If the mother is unable or unwilling to care for the child after birth, then they assume that adoption can be easily arranged.

It is doubtful, however, that adoptions are possible for every child whose mother cannot care for it. The world abounds with homeless orphans; even in the industrialized West, where there is a waiting list for adoption of healthy (white) babies, suitable homes cannot always be found for troubled adolescents, inner-city AIDS babies, or many of the multiply handicapped children whose parents may have tried to care for them but whose marriages broke under the strain.

Furthermore, even if an infant were born healthy and could be readily adopted, we must recognize that surrendering one's child for adoption is an extremely difficult act for most women. The bond that commonly forms between women and their fetuses over the full term of pregnancy is intimate and often intense; many women find that it is not easily broken after birth. Psychologically, for many women adoption is a far more difficult response to unwanted pregnancies than abortion. Therefore, it is misleading to describe pregnancy as merely a nine-month commitment; for most women, seeing a pregnancy through to term involves a lifetime of responsibility and involvement with the resulting child and, in the overwhelming majority of cases, disproportionate burden on the woman through the child-rearing years. An ethics that cares about women would recognize that abortion is often the only acceptable recourse for them.

## Notes

1. Technically, the term "fetus" does not cover the entire period of development. Medical practitioners prefer to distinguish between differing stages of development with such terms as "conceptus," "embryo" (and, recently, "preembryo"), and "fetus." Because these distinctions are not relevant to the discussion here, I follow the course common to discussions in bioethics and feminism and use the term "fetus" to cover the entire period of development from conception to the end of pregnancy through either birth or abortion.

2. Bearing a child can keep a woman within a man's sphere of influence against her will. The Canadian news media were dominated in the summer of 1989 by the story of Chantel Daigle, a Quebec woman who faced injunctions granted to her former boyfriend by two lower courts against her choice of abortion before she was finally given permission for abortion by the Supreme Court of Canada. Daigle's explanation to the media of her determination to abort stressed her recognition that if she was forced to bear this child, she would never be free from the violent father's involvement in her life.

3. Feminists believe that it is wrong of society to make childbearing a significant cause of poverty in women, but the reality of our social and economic structures in North America is that it does. In addition to their campaigns for greater reproductive freedom for women, feminists also struggle to ensure that women receive greater support in child-rearing; in efforts to provide financial stability and support services to those who provide care for children, feminists would welcome the support of those in the anti-abortion movement who sincerely want to reduce the numbers of abortions.

4. Among the exceptions here, see Overall (1987), who seems willing to specify some conditions under which abortion is immoral (78–79).

5. Critics continue to base the debate on the possibility that women might make frivolous abortion decisions; hence they want feminists to agree to setting boundaries on acceptable grounds for choosing abortion. Feminists, however, should resist this injunction. There is no practical way of drawing a line fairly in the abstract; cases that may appear "frivolous" at a distance often turn out to be substantive when the details are revealed. There is no evidence to suggest that women actually make the sorts of choices worried critics hypothesize about: for example, the decision of a woman eight months pregnant to abort because she wants to take a trip or gets in "a tiff" with her partner. These sorts of fantasies, on which demands to distinguish between legitimate and illegitimate personal reasons for choosing abortion rest, reflect an offensive conception of women as irresponsible. They ought not to be perpetuated. Women seeking moral guidance in their own deliberations about choosing abortion do not find such hypothetical discussions of much use.

6. In her monumental historical analysis of the early roots of Western patriarchy, Lerner (1986) determined that patriarchy began in the period from 3100 to 600 B.C., when men appropriated women's sexual and reproductive capac-

ity; the earliest states entrenched patriarchy by institutionalizing the sexual and procreative subordination of women to men.

7. Some women claim to be feminist yet oppose abortion; some even claim to offer a feminist argument against abortion (see Callahan 1987). For reasons that I develop in this chapter, I do not believe a thorough feminist analysis can sustain a restrictive abortion policy, although I do acknowledge that feminists need to be wary of some of the arguments proposed in support of liberal policies on abortion.

8. The state could do a lot to ameliorate this condition. If it provided women with adequate financial support, removed the inequities in the labor market, and provided affordable and reliable child care, pregnancy need not so often lead to a woman's dependence on a particular man. That it does not [provide such support] is evidence of the state's complicity in maintaining women's subordinate position with respect to men.

9. The IUD has proven so hazardous and prone to lawsuits [that] it has been largely removed from the market in the United States (Pappert 1986). It is also disappearing from other Western countries but is still being purchased by population-control agencies for use in the developing world (LaCheen 1986).

10. For a more detailed discussion of the limitations of current contraceptive options, see Colodny (1989); for the problems of cost, see esp. 34–35.

11. See Petchesky (1985), esp. chap. 5, where she documents the risks and discomforts associated with Pill use and IUDs and the increasing rate at which women are choosing the option of diaphragm or condom, with the option of early, legal abortions as backup.

12. Eisenstein (1988) has developed an interesting account of sexual politics, which identifies the pregnant body as the central element in the cultural subordination of women. She argues that pregnancy (either actual or potential) is considered the defining characteristic of all women, and because it is not experienced by men, it is classified as deviance and considered grounds for different treatment.

13. Thomson (1971) is a notable exception to this trend.

14. Because she was obviously involved in sexual activity, it is often concluded that the noncoerced woman is not innocent but guilty. As such, she is judged far less worthy than the innocent being she carries within her. Some who oppose abortion believe that an unwanted pregnancy is a suitable punishment for "irresponsible" sex.

15. This seems reminiscent of Aristotle's view of women as flowerpots where men implant the seed with all the important genetic information and the movement necessary for development and the woman's job is that of passive gestation, like the flowerpot. See Whitbeck (1973) and Lange (1983).

16. Some are so preoccupied with the problem of fetuses being "stuck" in women's bodies that they seek to avoid this geographical complication altogether, completely severing the ties between woman and fetus. For example, Bernard Nathanson, an antiabortion activist with the zeal of a new convert, eagerly anticipates the prospect of artificial wombs as alternative means for preserving the lives of fetuses and "dismisses the traditional reverence for birth as mere 'mythology' and the act of birth itself as an 'insignificant event'" (cited in McDonnell 1984, 113).

17. Cf. Warren (1989) and Tooley (1972).

18. The definition of pregnancy as a purely passive activity reaches its ghoulish conclusion in the increasing acceptability of sustaining brain-dead women on life-support systems to continue their functions as incubators until the fetus can be safely delivered. For a discussion of this trend, see Murphy (1989).

19. See McLaren and McLaren (1986) and Petchesky (1985).

# References

Baier, Annette C. 1985. *Postures of the Mind: Essays on Mind and Morals.* Minneapolis: University of Minnesota Press.

Balasybrahmanyan, Vimal. 1986. "Finger in the Dike: The Fight to Keep Injectables Out of India." In *Adverse Effects: Women and the Pharmaceutical Industry,* ed. Kathleen McDonnell.

Callahan, Daniel. 1986. "How Technology is Reframing the Abortion Debate." *Hastings Center Report* 16 (1): 33–42.

Callahan, Sidney. 1987. "A Pro-Life Feminist Makes Her Case." *Utne Reader* (March/April): 104–14.

Colodny, Nikki. 1989. "The Politics of Birth Control in a Reproductive Rights Context." In *The Future of Human Reproduction,* ed. Christine Overall.

Eisenstein, Zillah R. 1988. *The Female Body and the Law.* Berkeley: University of California Press.

Harding, Sandra and Hintikka, Merrill, eds. 1983. *Discovering Reality: Feminist Perspectives on Epistemology, Metaphysics, Methodology, and Philosophy of Science.* Dordrecht, Holland: D. Reidel.

Held, Virginia. 1987. "Feminism and Moral Theory." In *Women and Moral Theory,* ed. Eva Feder Kittay and Diana Meyers.

Kittay, Eva Feder and Meyers, Diana T. 1987. *Women and Moral Theory.* Totowa, NJ: Rowman & Littlefield.

LaCheen, Cary. 1986. "Pharmaceuticals and Family Planning: Women Are the Target." In *Adverse Effects,* ed. Kathleen McDonnell.

Lange, Lynda. 1983. "Woman Is Not a Rational Animal: On Aristotle's Biology of Reproduction." In *Discovering Reality,* ed. Harding and Hintikka, 1983.

Lerner, Gerda. 1986. *The Creation of Patriarchy*. New York: Oxford University Press.

MacKinnon, Catharine. 1989. *Toward a Feminist Theory of the State*. Cambridge, MA: Harvard University Press.

McDonnell, Kathleen, ed. 1984. *Adverse Effects: Women and the Pharmaceutical Industry*. Toronto: Women's Press.

McLaren, Angus and McLaren, Arlene Tigar. 1986. *The Bedroom and the State: The Changing Practices and Politics of Contraception and Abortion in Canada, 1880–1980*. Toronto: McClelland & Stewart.

Murphy, Julien S. 1989. "Should Pregnancies Be Sustained in Brain-Dead Women? A Philosophical Discussion of Postmortem Pregnancy." In *Healing Technology*, ed. Kathryn Strother Ratcliff.

Nicholson, Susan T. 1977. "The Roman Catholic Doctrine of Therapeutic Abortion." In *Feminism and Philosophy*, ed. Mary Vetterling-Braggin, Frederick A. Elliston, and Jane English. Totowa, NJ: Littlefield, Adams & Co.

Overall, Christine. 1987. *Ethics and Human Reproduction: A Feminist Analysis*. Boston, MA: Allen & Unwin.

———, ed. 1989. *The Future of Human Reproduction*. Toronto: Women's Press.

Pappert, Ann. 1986. "The Rise and Fall of the IUD." In *Adverse Effects*, ed. Kathleen McDonnell.

Petchesky, Rosalind Pollack. 1985. *Abortion and Woman's Choice: The State, Sexuality, and Reproductive Freedom*. Boston, MA: Northeastern University Press.

———. 1987. "Foetal Images: The Power of Visual Culture in the Politics of Reproduction." In *Reproductive Technologies*, ed. Michelle Stanworth.

Ratcliff, Kathryn Strother, ed. 1989. *Healing Technology: Feminist Perspectives*. Ann Arbor: University of Michigan Press.

Rothman, Barbara Katz. 1986. "Commentary: When a Pregnant Woman Endangers Her Fetus." *Hastings Center Report* 16 (1): 25.

Stanworth, Michelle, ed. 1987. *Reproductive Technologies: Gender, Motherhood and Medicine*. Minneapolis: University of Minnesota Press.

Sumner, L. W. 1981. *Abortion and Moral Theory*. Princeton, NJ: Princeton University Press.

Thomson, Judith Jarvis. 1971. "A Defense of Abortion." *Philosophy and Public Affairs* 1(1): 47–66.

Tooley, Michael. 1972. "Abortion and Infanticide." *Philosophy and Public Affairs* 2(1): 37–65.

Warren, Mary Anne. 1973. "On the Moral and Legal Status of Abortion." *The Monist* 57: 43–61.

———. 1989. "The Moral Significance of Birth." *Hypatia* 4: 46–65.

Whitbeck, Carolyn. 1973. "Theories of Sex Difference." *Philosophical Forum* 5 (1, 2): 54–80.

# Questions

1. Moral philosophers sometimes use the word "person" in a technical sense. "Person" means "critter that has a right to life." Which of the following marginal organisms (if any) are persons?

   a. first-trimester fetuses
   b. third-trimester fetuses
   c. dolphins
   d. cows
   e. normal infants
   f. very defective infants
   g. my liver
   h. very psychotic people
   i. people with artificial hearts
   j. healthy 98-year-old people
   k. convicted murderers
   l. enemy civilians near factories
   m. Martians who do math and poetry
   n. corporations such as Exxon

   What criteria did you use to decide which of these critters are persons and which are not? That is, what is the essence of personhood? Is there an essence of personhood? On the basis of your classification, are there any changes that our society should make in the way it treats these organisms? [*Hint*: Remember to be consistent and non-arbitrary. If you claim that fetuses are persons because they have a high probability of being rational after 1 year, then you are committed (or are you?) to the claim that 98-year-olds are not persons because they do not have a high probability of being rational after 1 year. And this, in turn, commits you (or does it?) to the claim that abortion is wrong but killing healthy 98-year-olds who want to live is OK. On the other hand, if you claim that 98-year-olds are persons because they have a small chance of being rational after 1 year, then you are committed (or are you?) to the claim that cows are persons because (given that we might find a miracle drug that increases rationality of animals) they have a small chance of being rational after 1 year. And this, in turn, commits you (or does it?) to the claim that vegetarianism is morally required.]

2. Jane English considers the following claims.

(A) When attacked one may, of course, defend oneself. However, "the defense may only equal the threatened injury in severity; to avoid death you may kill, but to avoid a black eye you may only inflict a black eye or the equivalent."

(B) "[S]upposing a fetus is not after all a person, would abortion always be morally permissible? Some opponents of abortion seem worried that if a fetus is not a full-fledged person, then we are justified in treating it in any way at all."

Explain, in excruciating detail, what (if anything) English thinks is wrong with these claims. Use your own words. Do not merely repeat what she says. Do you agree with English's critique of these claims? If not, why not? If so, are you and English committed, by your rejection of these claims, to the view that it is morally OK (a) to kill deans who would vote against giving you tenure and (b) to provide abortion on demand?

3. Thomson considers three different arguments that might be put forth by a pro-life supporter.

a. "Every person has a right to life. So the fetus has a right to life. No doubt the mother has a right to decide what shall happen in and to her body; everyone would grant that. But surely a person's right to life is stronger and more stringent than the mother's right to decide what happens in and to her body, and so outweighs it. So the fetus may not be killed; an abortion may not be performed."

b. "Suppose a woman voluntarily indulges in intercourse, knowing of the chance it will issue in pregnancy, and then she does become pregnant; is she not in part responsible for the presence, in fact the very existence, of the unborn person inside her? No doubt she did not invite it in. But doesn't her partial responsibility for its being there itself give it a right to the use of her body?"

c. "We surely must all grant that there may be cases in which it would be morally indecent to detach a person from your body at the cost of his life. . . . Again suppose pregnancy lasted only an hour, and constituted no threat to life or health. And suppose that a woman . . . did nothing at all which would give the unborn person a right to the use of her body. All the same it might well be said . . . that she *ought* to allow it to remain for that hour—that it would be indecent of her to refuse."

Explain, in excruciating detail and in your own words, what (if anything) Thomson thinks is wrong with these arguments. Do you agree with Thomson's critique of these arguments? If not, why not? If so, are you and Thomson committed, by your rejection of these arguments, to the view that it is morally OK to let healthy but unwanted *infants* die?

4. Give a Kantian argument *for* the thesis that every person has a positive right to life. (*Hint:* See Kant's example 4, the duty to help others.) Give a Kantian argument *against* the thesis that every person has a positive right to life. (*Hint:* If Fred supports Bob, then Bob is treating Fred as a mere means.) Which is closer to Kant's real view? Which is closer to your view?

Give an Aristotelian argument *for* the thesis that every person has a positive right to life. Give an Aristotelian argument *against* the thesis that every person has a positive right to life. Which is closer to Aristotle's real view? Which is closer to your view?

Give a Utilitarian argument *for* the thesis that every person has a positive right to life. Give a Utilitarian argument *against* the thesis that every person has a positive right to life.

5. Thomson uses the following illustrations. Exactly what is each illustration supposed to show? Does it succeed? Why or why not?

a. plugged into a famous violinist with a kidney ailment

b. trapped in tiny house with a rapidly growing child

c. Smith, Jones, and Smith's coat in freezing weather

d. the touch of Henry Fonda's cool hand on a fevered brow

e. two boys and a box of chocolates given to both

f. a people-seed drifts through a defective screen

g. plugged into the violinist for 1 hour

h. two boys and a box of chocolates given to only one

i. Henry Fonda in the same room

j. Kitty Genovese murdered while 38 people watched

6. Choose *one* of the following pairs of scenarios. Compare and contrast the moral aspects of the actions.

   a. Fred and Joe are fifteen-year-old Siamese twins who share one heart. Fred drugs Joe and hires a doctor to separate the twins. The doctor is instructed to make sure that Fred gets the heart. Of course, Joe dies. Fred defends his actions by maintaining, "Joe had no more right to the heart than I did. And besides, it was self-defense. I had to separate myself from Joe in order to have a reasonable chance at a reasonable life."

   Sally is a fifteen-year-old, unmarried woman who becomes pregnant by being raped. She obtains an abortion that removes the non-viable fetus from the womb without damaging the fetus. Of course, the fetus dies. Sally defends her actions by maintaining, "The fetus had no right to the womb. And besides, it was self-defense. I had to separate myself from the fetus in order to have a reasonable chance at a reasonable life."

   (b) Helen and Lucy are fifteen-year-old Siamese twins who share one heart. Doctors determine that if they are not separated, they will soon die, but if they are separated, then only one will live. Therefore, the doctors separate them.

   Fran is a fifteen-year-old, pregnant woman. Doctors determine that if nothing is done, both Fran and her fetus will soon die, but that if the fetus is aborted, then Fran will live. Therefore, the doctors perform an abortion.

   (c) Tom and Bill step into a malfunctioning transporter together for fun, even though they are warned that there is a small chance that doing so will cause them to fuse together into a Siamese twin. Unluckily, they fuse in such a way that they now share one heart. Tom drugs Bill and hires a doctor to separate the twins. The doctor is instructed to make sure that Tom gets the heart. Of course, Bill dies. Tom defends his actions by maintaining, "I made no promises to Bill and he has no right to life support. Therefore, separation does not violate his right to life and breaks no promises."

   Betty is a fifteen-year-old, unmarried women who becomes pregnant by contraception failure. She obtains an abortion that removes the non-viable fetus from the womb without damaging the fetus. Of course, the fetus dies. Betty defends her actions by maintaining, "Because my pregnancy resulted in spite of my taking reasonable precautions, I have made no promise to the fetus. Therefore, abortion does not violate the fetus's right to life and breaks no promises."

7. One difficult moral question is whether acts and omissions are morally equivalent.

   Fred sees a small child carrying a $100 bill into a dark alley. He says to himself, "I'll have to kill the child in order to get away with stealing the money." Fred then enters the alley, kills the child, and takes the money.

   Ted receives a letter asking him to donate $100 to a charity dedicated to saving famine victims. He says to himself, "I am sure that I could keep a small child alive by donating the money." Ted then decides not to make the donation.

Would an Act Utilitarian consider these two acts morally equivalent? Why or why not?

Would a Rule Utilitarian consider these two acts morally equivalent? Why or why not?

Would a Kantian using CI#1 consider these two acts morally equivalent? Why or why not?

Would a Kantian using CI#2 consider these two acts morally equivalent? Why or why not?

Do you consider these two acts morally equivalent? Why or why not?

8. Ron holds the following beliefs.

(A) Welfare is morally wrong because it takes money from people who earned it and spends it on lazy bums.

(B) Passive euthanasia is morally OK because it is "letting Nature take its course," but active euthanasia is wrong because it is "playing God."

(C) Abortion is wrong because fetuses have a right to life and every abortion violates that right.

(D) People should try to do what Jesus wants us to do.

a. Because Ron thinks that we have no obligation to feed lazy bums, Ron must maintain that lazy bums do not have a positive right to life. It would be very nice of us to provide welfare to them, but we have no moral duty to do so. Charity is morally optional. On the other hand, everyone (even lazy bums) has a negative right to life. We have a moral duty not to kill them. Thus there is a large *moral* difference between killing people (who want to live) and letting those people die.

b. Because Ron thinks that passive and active euthanasia are morally different, Ron must maintain that killing and letting die are morally different even if the person wants to die. Again killing is morally wrong, but letting die is OK.

c. Thomson has pointed out that certain abortions do not kill the fetus but merely let the fetus die by removing the fetus from the mother's womb. These abortions do not violate the fetus's negative right to life. Because Ron thinks that *all* abortions violate the right to life of the fetus, Ron must maintain that the fetus has a positive right to life. That is, Ron must believe that there is no morally significant difference between killing and letting die.

d. In the Sermon on the Mount, Jesus says, "Love your enemy. Do good to those who hate you. Give to all who beg from you." Ron interprets this to mean at least that people should not let other people (who want to live) die, especially if they can be kept alive without much effort or risk. In other words, people have at least a right to rescue and perhaps even a positive right to life. Again Ron seems committed to the thesis that there is no morally significant difference between killing and letting die.

Ron's problem is that he wants to continue to believe (a), (b), (c), and (d) without being inconsistent about whether there is a morally significant difference between killing and letting die. Solve Ron's problem.

9. Choose *one* of the following tasks.

a. Defend the claim that the fetus *is* a person (that is, the fetus has a right to life) against Sherwin.

b. Defend the claim that the fetus *is not* a person (that is, the fetus lacks a right to life) against Marquis.

c. Defend the claim that it matters whether or not the fetus is a person (that is, the fetus has a right to life) against Hursthouse.

10. In his paper entitled "Active and Passive Euthanasia," Rachels argues that intentions are not relevant to the moral evaluation of an act, although they are relevant to the evaluation of a person's character. He says, "the intention is not relevant to deciding whether the act is right or wrong, but instead it is relevant to assessing the character of the person who does the act, which is very different."

Thomson says that a person can be condemned as indecent for not helping another, even if the person needing the help has no right to be helped. She says, "even supposing a case in which a woman pregnant due to rape ought to allow the unborn person to use her body for the hour he needs, we should not conclude that he has a right to do so; we should conclude that she is self-centered, callous, indecent, but not unjust, if she refuses."

Hursthouse agrees that intentions are relevant to the evaluation of a person's character. She argues that some acts are vicious (exhibit vices) even if the agent has a right to perform them. She says, "In exercising a moral right I can do something cruel, or callous, or selfish, light-minded, self-righteous, stupid, inconsiderate, disloyal, dishonest—that is, act viciously."

Are Rachels and Thomson disagreeing with each other here? If not, why not? If so, which of them is correct? Are Rachels and Hursthouse disagreeing with each other here? If not, why not? If so, which one of them is correct?

11. Choose and justify *one* of the following positions.

(A) Both animals and fetuses have a right to life.

(B) Neither animals nor fetuses have a right to life.

(C) Animals have a right to life but fetuses do not.

(D) Fetuses have a right to life but animals do not.

To which of the following beliefs are you committed by your chosen position and justification?

a. Abortion is wrong except in cases where the mother's life is endangered by continuation of the pregnancy.

b. We have a moral obligation to prevent animals from killing each other in the wild when doing so would involve little effort and little risk.

c. Active euthanasia is nearly always wrong.

d. Feeding starving dogs before starving children is morally equivalent to feeding starving children before starving dogs.

e. Brainless, soulless babies with the human genetic code lack a right to life.

# Sexual Matters:
# Exploitation, Perversion, and Prostitution

*Nichole: Boopsie, I wanted to have this little discussion because I don't think you understand how mistreated you are. B.D. treats you like a common household object! Do you know what you're doing? Do you want to be exploited?*

*Boopsie: Ooh! That sounds sexy!! What do I have to do to get "exploited"?! C'mon! Tell me, tell me! How do I get "exploited"?*

G. B. TRUDEAU

Common-sense beliefs about sexual matters undergo frequent, dramatic changes. For example, in Aristotle's Greece, homosexuality was the paradigm for sex and love, whereas heterosexuality was viewed with suspicion and disdain. Perhaps part of the reason was the assumption that people tend to acquire the character traits of their friends and lovers. It follows that lovers of women become effeminate like Paris in the *Iliad*, whereas lovers of men become manly like Achilles. Indeed, the best fighting force in Aristotle's time was a Spartan regiment consisting entirely of homosexual lovers. They were undefeated for decades until Alexander the Great, another homosexual warrior, wiped them out with superior firepower. Now, of course, the situation is reversed. Homosexuality is viewed with suspicion in some quarters and is thought to be linked with effeminacy, whereas heterosexuality is taken by most people to be the paradigm for sex and love. This shift has been brought about predominantly by Christianity's opposition to homosexuality, which arises from a certain view of the nature of sex.

Despite the fluctuations in common-sense beliefs about sexual matters, it may be possible to find some moral truths about various sexual practices. In this section I shall use adultery, homosexuality, prostitution, rape, and voyeurism as examples to explore the morality of sexuality.

## Natural and Unnatural

The distinction between natural and unnatural is central to the way in which many people think about sexual matters. (Indeed, the belief that "natural things are good and unnatural things are bad" is also central to many non-sexual matters. Think of all of the products touted as natural.) One common objection to homosexual activity, as well as to many other sorts of sexual acts, is that it is unnatural.

### Argument (A)

(1) Homosexuality is unnatural.
(2) If X is unnatural, then X is immoral.
(3) Therefore, homosexuality is immoral.

Unless the term "unnatural" has the same meaning in all three statements, this argument commits the fallacy of equivocation. But it is difficult to find a plausible meaning for "unnatural" that makes both premises true. If "unnatural" means "artificial" or "uncommon" or "not found among the animals," then premise (1) is false. Homosexual acts are neither artificial nor uncommon, nor are they rare among animals. Premise (2) also turns out to be false. Artificial hearts are not immoral even though they are unnatural in all three senses.

Some people take the term "unnatural" to mean "used in a way not intended by nature." On this definition the status of premise (1) is unclear, because we do not know what (or even whether) nature intends. But premise (2) is pretty clearly false. For example, necks were surely not intended by nature to hold up necklaces, yet the wearing of necklaces is not immoral.

Thomas Nagel deploys a more sophisticated attempt to distinguish natural from unnatural sex. He defines *natural sexual activity* as a rather complex interaction between persons "involving a desire that one's partner be aroused by the recognition of one's desire that he or she be aroused." That is, in natural sex person A wants person B to be sexually excited not just by anything but by a particular thing. Person A wants person B to be turned on by the awareness that person A wants person B to be turned on. Nagel then defines *unnatural or perverse sexual activity* as a severe deviation from this sort of interaction. On Nagel's account, sadism and masochism, voyeurism and exhibitionism, pederasty and bestiality, fetishism and pornography turn out to be perverse. However, homosexuality turns out to be natural. Premise (1) is false.

Nagel gives no argument for his account of natural sexual activity. He is implicitly appealing to our intuitions about sexuality. Moreover, his account may have no moral relevance. In order to show that some activity is morally wrong because it is unnatural, one must show *both* that the activity is unnatural and also that unnatural activity is immoral—that is, that premise (2) is true. But Nagel gives no reason to believe that sexual activity that fails to meet his definition of "natural" is immoral.

Some people maintain that although "unnatural" is hard to define, we all know it when we see it. However, the various things that previous generations have considered to be obviously unnatural suggest that we should not leave the unnaturalness question to our intuition or to common sense. It has not been long since our own culture considered educated women to be obviously unnatural, for example. People seem to project their own prejudices onto nature and call "unnatural" whatever they find abhorrent. Overall, as Richard Mohr suggests, argument (A) is better forgotten.

## Utilitarian Analysis

Rather than seeking a global account of sexual morality, Act Utilitarians deal with each sexual issue separately on a case-by-case basis. If a type of sexual act maximizes jollies, then it is morally acceptable. Igor Primoratz considers such an

analysis of prostitution. Obviously, the main advantage of prostitution is that it generates jollies for the customers and perhaps for the prostitutes. The hazards to the prostitute include physical and psychological diseases as well as maltreatment by customers and pimps. Hazards to society include the spread of disease as well as a debasement of the ideas and practice of sexuality within the society. Richard Wasserstrom suggests that moral censure of extramarital sex (including prostitution) helps to maintain the institution of marriage because people's desire for sex leads them to marry and stay married. On the other hand, Primoratz suggests that prostitution is a preserver of marriage, for many "married men who do not find complete sexual fulfillment within marriage are content to stay married provided that they can have extramarital commercial sex as well."

Overall, it is by no means clear whether the pros outweigh the cons. Moreover, the Act Utilitarian approach discounts the moral repugnance of certain acts by making the wrongness of an act contingent on its cost-benefit ratio. On this sort of approach, an act will turn out to be moral no matter how repugnant it is as long as its benefits turn out to be high enough to outweigh its drawbacks. If the pleasure gained by rapists turned out to be more than the suffering produced by rape, then according to Act Utilitarianism, rape would be moral.

\*

A Rule Utilitarian might subsume various sexual acts under very general rules that are not particularly designed with sexual matters in mind. For example, Wasserstrom argues that most adultery is wrong because it involves promise breaking or deception. Prostitution and homosexuality, of course, violate neither of these rules. Indeed, it is hard to find a general, non–sex-oriented rule that they do violate.

Alternatively, a Rule Utilitarian might seek some general rule about sex. The right rule is the rule that, if followed, would produce more happiness (or less unhappiness) than any alternative rule. Clearly, a Rule Utilitarian would reject the proposal that sexual acts are moral if and only if they are natural, for this proposal would hardly maximize jollies. Would a Rule Utilitarian accept the rule "Sex is wrong unless used for procreation" or the rule "Sex is wrong outside of marriage" or even the rule "Sex is wrong outside of long-term, loving relationships"? Because even casual sex typically yields great sensual pleasure, none of these proposals would seem very appealing to a Rule Utilitarian. Thus a Rule Utilitarian would probably end up sanctioning a larger variety of sexual acts than these rules would permit.

Daniel Nathan objects that Utilitarianism misses all of the wrongness of some sexual acts and some of the wrongness of others. For example, voyeurism produces psychological or social or financial harms when the victim becomes aware of the voyeurism or when the voyeur uses the information against the victim. According to Utilitarianism, most voyeurism is wrong because of the possibility of these harms. When the probability of these harms is very low, voyeurism seems OK according to Utilitarianism. The pleasure of the voyeur multiplied by its high likelihood outweighs the very unlikely suffering of the victim. However, although the victim does not experience a loss of jollies in such cases, he or she is harmed by being treated as less than a person, observes Nathan. This is why voyeurism is wrong even if it cannot be detected by or used against the victims. Moreover, even in cases where Utilitarianism labels voyeurism as wrong, this exploitation is present but unnoticed by Utilitarianism. Is being treated as a non-person intrinsically harmful?

## Deontological Analysis

Sometimes people (typically women) complain of being treated as sex objects. This complaint may be understood in at least two different ways. First, it may be an objection to overemphasizing one aspect of the total person while underemphasizing or even excluding the other aspects of a person. In this sense, treating someone as a sex object reduces a complex individual to a mere sexual being.

However, there is nothing wrong, in general, with treating people as two-dimensional. Indeed, we do this all the time. We treat clerks as commercial beings, teachers as pedagogical beings, and so on. It is morally acceptable to ignore most aspects of a total person even when engaging in intimate acts and relationships. Patients ignore the multi-facetedness of their doctors, for example. (Agreeing or pretending to value the whole person while actually valuing only the person's sexuality would be promise breaking or deception and would therefore be wrong. One party in a relationship may feel betrayed by the other party's attitude and actions.)

If the emphasis is placed upon "object" rather than "sex," then the phrase "sex object" expresses a different and deeper objection. "Sex object" may signify a tool or toy used to satisfy the sexual desires of others. Kant considers treating people as things to be the essence of evil. The second formulation of Kant's categorical imperative says that an act is immoral if the act treats someone as a mere means or thing rather than as an end or person. Ignoring the autonomy of a free, rational being is immoral. We bypass people's ability to make choices when we do something to them without their consent. Thus Kantians explicate the violation of autonomy, and in particular the treating of someone as a sex object, in terms of consent. But what sort of consent?

Onora O'Neill explores several notions of consent. First, she shows that *hypothetical consent* cannot serve as the criterion for moral acceptability of action. We cannot simply maintain that an act is OK if a rational person would consent to it. The fact that a rational person would consent to sex with Dick does not make it OK for Dick to have sex with Jane. It is Jane, not some hypothetical rational person, who must consent. Unless Jane consents, it is rape.

But Jane's *actual consent* is not enough. O'Neill points out that a mere "yes" may conceal various complexities. The consenter may not be fully competent to consent. For example, the consenter may be immature, irrational, or ignorant of crucial information. Thus if Jane is a minor, if she is drunk, or if she mistakenly thinks that Dick loves her, then her "yes" does not constitute meaningful consent. (The idea that minors cannot give meaningful consent is the justification of the statutory rape laws. Should we have laws against having sex with drunk or misled people?) Moreover, it is often difficult to know where consent starts and stops. Sexually charged situations are replete with ambiguous remarks and honest miscommunications as well as willful misunderstandings. It is tempting to think that clarity is always attainable. However, in some contexts (such as rape trials) the lack of a "no" (or even the lack of a repeated, forceful "NO") has sometimes been take to constitute consent. Furthermore, does a "yes" constitute consent only to the act or to the logical or likely developments or consequences of the act, too? For example, if Jane says "yes" to an invitation to go skinny-dipping by moonlight, is she tacitly consenting to sex afterwards?

Sometimes a threat or offer leaves room for some choice, but not enough. "Your money or your life," is a simple example. A person who "consents" to hand over his or her money is forced to make the choice. "Have sex with me or lose your job," is a parallel example. A person who "consents" to sex when the alternatives are bleak is not giving meaningful consent. Suppose Dick offers Jane a job on the condition that she sleep with him. If Jane can reasonably decline, then perhaps this is a moral, though crude, offer. But if Jane desperately needs the job, then Dick is making a coercive offer. Although he is not coercing Jane himself, he is taking advantage of her desperate situation. He is allowing her to be herded unwillingly into his bed. A coercive offer precludes meaningful consent. Thus the mere fact that prostitutes say "yes" to sex does not show that they meaningfully consent, for they may be saying "yes" to a coercer or to a coercive offer. Many prostitutes can choose whether to have sex with this or that customer, but they cannot choose to give up prostitution because they

are coerced by their pimp or by their desperate circumstances.

Of course, sometimes the alternatives one faces are undesirable but not so unsavory that a "yes" does not constitute consent. If I want to lose weight, I must choose between eating less and exercising more, yet no one would say that my "yes" to the exer-cycle salesperson is not meaningful consent. How shall we draw the line between desperate, coercive circumstances where consent is not meaningful and merely distasteful circumstances where consent to one of the options is meaningful? When a wife must choose between sex with her disgusting husband and a divorce that would leave her and her children impoverished, does her "yes" constitute consent?

Perhaps an act is OK if everyone involved gives *voluntary informed consent* to the act. That is, if the consenting parties are not significantly impaired and the situation is not desperate, then the act is not wrong. One of Nathan's explanations for the wrongness of voyeurism invokes this notion of consent. By definition, voyeurism precludes voluntary informed consent, so "showers are transformed into some sort of unintended striptease, . . . confidential discussions become public discourses, etc." By ignoring the wishes and choices of the victim, the voyeur treats the victim as a mere instrument for sexual pleasure. And this, of course, is a classic description of exploitation.

### Argument (B)

(1) It is wrong to treat persons as mere means.
(2) If a certain act disregards the choices of another person and thus transforms the other person's act into something he or she did not choose, then performing that act is treating the other person as a mere means.
(3) Voyeurism disregards the choices of the victim of voyeurism.
(4) Therefore, voyeurism is wrong.

Premise (2) of this argument seems to be false. We often disregard the choices of others and, without acting immorally, transform their acts into something they do not choose.

Kierkegaard describes a young man who ignores a serious older man's lecture and waits with amusement for a drop of sweat to fall from the older man's nose.[1] He transforms the older man into a clown just as the voyeur transforms a person preparing for a shower into a stripper. Yet the action of the young man, though frivolous, is hardly immoral. We are surely not required to see people as they want to be seen. The requirement that everyone involved in an act give voluntary informed consent is too strong. It prohibits too much. We are sometimes—even usually—entitled to do things despite the wishes of others. For example, Dick is surely entitled to marry Jane over the objections of jealous John.

O'Neill maintains that an act is OK if everyone involved could *possibly consent*. Dissent must be both possible and practical for all concerned. At first glance this condition seems too weak. After all, suppose Dick rapes Jane and then defends himself by saying, "Although Jane did not actually consent to have sex with me, it was possible for her to consent, so raping her was OK." Luckily, Dick's defense fails. Although Jane could have consented to sex with Dick, she could not have consented to be *forced* to have sex with Dick. And, of course, rape is forced sex.

As Aristotle points out, acts are nonvoluntary and certainly not chosen if they are performed under compulsion or from ignorance. Undesirable acts performed in order to avoid a disastrous outcome (Aristotle calls these "mixed acts") are also, in one sense, not chosen (48–49, 1110a). In a parallel way, it is impossible to consent to coercion, deception, and coercive offers. Of this section's sample acts, rape is obviously an example of coercion. Adultery usually (though not always) involves deception. Prostitution may involve a coercive offer if the prostitute's situation is desperate. And homosexual acts fall into none of these categories.

Nathan uses the notion of possible consent in his second explanation for the wrongness of voyeurism. Presumably the audience watching a stripper perform is not engaging in voyeurism, because the stripper knows that the audience is watching. By contrast, the victim of voyeurism is unaware of being spied on. Voyeurism is looking at someone without their knowledge. Thus, just as a person can consent to sex but not to rape (coerced sex), a person can consent to being looked at but not to voyeurism (secretly being looked at). Nathan takes this impossibility of consent to be the wrongness of voyeurism.

### Argument (C)

(1) It is wrong to treat persons as mere means.
(2) If the other person cannot possibly consent to a certain act, then performing that act is treating the other person as a mere means.
(3) Voyeurism is looking at someone without their knowledge.
(4) People cannot consent to being looked at without their knowledge.
(5) Therefore, voyeurism is wrong.

The difference between the stripper and the victim of voyeurism is not that the voyeur lies to the victim. The voyeur merely does not inform the victim that he or she is being spied on. Do we have a positive duty to provide people with certain information as well as a negative duty to avoid lying? Doctors have a duty to provide their patients with certain information, but the doctors' duty seems to arise from their relationship with their patients. Do strangers or even friends have a duty to provide each other with pertinent information? If I discover that my friend's child is suicidally depressed, I probably have a duty to notify my friend. On the other hand, if a stranger is about to purchase an ineffective bicycle helmet, I am probably not obligated to try to change the stranger's mind. What are the limits of this duty to provide pertinent information?

Perhaps the wrongness of voyeurism lies in the performing rather than in the not informing. Perhaps it is wrong to peep whether one notifies one's object or not. Aristotle might say that there is something wrong with peeping, itself, whether or not the person consents or could consent. If so, consent would not be the criterion of moral acceptability, and watching the stripper would turn out to be wrong.

\*

Could homosexuality, adultery, prostitution, or voyeurism be rejected on Kantian grounds, even if all of the involved parties give appropriate consent? One common objection to prostitution is that the prostitute sells her self. The assumption here is that sexuality is central to the identity of a person. By selling her sexual services, the prostitute is actually commodifying something that should have no price. She is commodifying a person, namely herself. To sell someone is to treat that person as thing. To sell oneself is to treat oneself as a thing. People should not be bought and sold, even if they consent. In particular, people should not sell themselves. Thus prostitution is wrong.

### Argument (D)

(1) It is wrong to treat persons as mere means.
(2) Sexuality is central to the identity of people.
(3) Thus selling sex is selling a person.
(4) Selling persons is treating persons as mere means.
(5) Therefore, prostitution is wrong.

Primoratz and Satz deny premise (2) of this argument. They maintain that sexuality is no more central to the identity of persons than many other things. Some people would rather sell their sexuality than their ideas or even their stamp collection, for example. Whatever the essence of identity is, it is not sexuality. Because we have no qualms about allowing people to sell their ideas or their stamps, we should have no objection to the sale of sexual services. Existentialists deny that there is any single thing that is central to the identity of every person. Different people make different things central to their selves by their different choices in life. Although sex may be central to the selves of some people, it may be peripheral to the selves of others. Thus selling sex is selling oneself only for some people, not for everyone.

One might also deny premise (4) of argument (D). Of course, selling persons into slavery without their consent violates Kant's categorical imperative, and this is what is usually meant by the phrase *selling persons*. But here the wrong-

ness may be the slavery rather than the selling. It is not so clear that selling persons *with* their consent is also a violation of Kant's categorical imperative. If, for a certain price, Sarah consents to do everything that Sally orders, then Sarah is simply Sally's employee. Working for someone else is not morally wrong, is it?

## Virtue Ethics Analysis

Just as Nathan and Satz point out that Utilitarianism does not capture the whole wrongness of certain sexual acts, Aristotelians might maintain that Kantianism also misses some of the wrongness. Oddly, the Kantian account ignores the sexual aspect of wrong sexual acts. Sexual acts may be bad even if they are not deceptive, coercive, etc. They may be bad *qua* sex. Or they may be bad both *qua* deceptive, coercive, etc. and *qua* sex. For example, it is often said that rape and battering are crimes of violence, not sex, and this is a Kantian view. But in her article "Sex and Violence," Catharine MacKinnon highlights the fact that the rape victim's sexuality is typically injured. These crimes can impair the ability to enjoy sex. Thus, following Aristotle, MacKinnon protests that rape and battering are crimes of sex as well as crimes of violence. A sexual act may be bad not just for Kantian reasons or *qua* sex but also for many other reasons. Sexual acts may be cowardly, unkind, and so on. The Kantian account ignores many failure modes. Aristotelians and Kantians disagree not only on which things are wrong but also on why certain things are wrong.

Aristotle considers sexual acts to fall into the sphere of sensual pleasure, which is governed by the virtue of temperance. We sometimes use the word "temperance" to mean enjoying moderate amounts of certain things, but Aristotle uses the term somewhat more broadly. A temperate person feels and acts rightly with respect to sensual pleasure. What counts as right varies from situation to situation and involves more than merely a moderate *amount*. Aristotle would say that a person who is temperate with respect to sex engages in sexual activity with the right people, to the right degree, on the right occasions, with the right goals.

Aristotle is sometimes accused of failing to provide a principle specifying the right way to act and feel for each virtue. Aristotle's account of the virtues is said to be empty because his account does not specify what counts as right for each virtue parameter. However, Aristotle does specify the right objects, amounts, and occasions for temperance. After narrowing the sphere of temperance to the pleasures of touch, he says,

> The things that, being pleasant, make for health or good condition, the temperate person will desire moderately and as he should, and also other pleasant things if they are not hindrances to these ends, or contrary to what is noble, or beyond his means. (76, 1119a)

Here Aristotle gives temperance a positive and wide content. Temperate people desire not only all tactile sensual pleasures conducive to health and good condition but also all other such pleasures except those that are unhealthy, deconditioning, unaffordable, or ignoble. That is, even if a certain sexual act does not improve one's health or get one into better physical condition, Aristotle would still say that the act is temperate as long as it does not make one's health or physical condition worse and as long as it is not ignoble or too expensive. Any object (or amount or occasion) of sexual desire or activity is right as long as it is not unhealthy, deconditioning, unaffordable, or ignoble. Accordingly, sex with your spouse is generally OK, but not while driving. That would be the wrong occasion because it is hazardous to your health. Viewing pornography moderately is OK.

But if the pornography precludes exercise or drives one into bankruptcy, then this would be an excessive amount and therefore intemperate. What does Aristotle mean by "ignoble"? Aristotle lived in a rather stratified society. His students were independently wealthy. His "ignoble" probably means something like "low-class" or "tacky." For example, whereas the present unregulated practice of prostitution would be intemperate because it is unhealthy, voyeurism would probably count as intemperate because it is ignoble. Aristotle also considers it ignoble for the well-off to use their superiority to exploit the needy. Thus if Dick offers Jane a job on the condition that she sleep with him, then Dick's offer is ignoble and therefore intemperate. In general, in a temperate person, each of the three temperance parameters meets all four criteria (see the table below).

Some of the desires and acts that fail to meet Aristotle's criteria are intemperate, but extreme failures are *brutish* or, as we would say, symptoms of mental illness rather than of vice. People who regularly have such desires and exhibit such behavior are to be pitied and treated rather than criticized and punished. For example, people who drink too much or too often are intemperate, but people who drink *way* too much or *way* too often are brutish or, as we would say, alcoholics. Pederasty is Aristotle's example of sexual brutishness (171, 1148b). Other brutish states might include satyrism, nymphomania, frigidity, and impotence, for these are sexual impairments where medical intervention rather than punishment is appropriate. Like Nagel, Aristotle begins with a picture of good sex and censures deviations from it. Unlike Nagel, however, Aristotle does not distinguish between

|  | Healthy | Conditioning | Affordable | Noble |
|---|---|---|---|---|
| Amount |  |  |  |  |
| Object |  |  |  |  |
| Occasion |  |  |  |  |

natural and unnatural but rather among temperance, vice, and disease. Aristotle's objection to pederasty is not that it is unnatural, but rather that it is sick.

Acts or passions may be temperate yet still be wrong because they violate the rules governing other virtues. Good sex is courageous, is just, and even exhibits a sense of humor when appropriate, as well as being temperate. Aristotle considers some adultery wrong because it is unjust (109–110, 1130a). He might denounce sex in which one partner is inconsiderate of the needs and desires of the other as lacking in benevolence. Exhibitionism is an interesting example of a sexual activity that is just and temperate but not fully virtuous. Exhibitionists (not just strippers but also people who dress in dramatically revealing ways) typically have low self-esteem, often caused by sexual abuse. Their conscious or subconscious belief is that they are worthless except as sex objects or that they can make something of themselves only through their sexuality. Now Aristotle lists pride as a virtue, and pride consists primarily in having a correct estimation of one's worth, one's abilities, and one's deserts. (Aristotelian pride is close to what we usually mean by self-respect rather than the sort of pride that "goeth before a fall.") Therefore, Aristotle might say that exhibitionism is wrong, not because of a lack of consent, but because it typically arises from insufficient pride. In general, to determine the moral status of an act, Aristotle would ask a series of questions. Is the act intemperate or brutish? (Do all three parameters meet the four criteria?) Is the act unjust? (Does it violate the principles of justice?) Is the act cowardly? And so on for each sphere of human life.

Of course, Utilitarians and Kantians might say that some of these are non-moral matters. Rape may be unfriendly and intemperate as well as coercive, but the *moral* wrongness is the coercion. Prostitution may be imprudent because of the health risk, but this does not make it immoral. Exhibitionism may arise from low self-esteem, but that is an error of knowledge rather than of morality. And so on. Clearly, Aristotle has a broader notion of morality than many modern philosophers. Certain matters are moral issues for Aristotle but not for Kant or Mill. Which is the better conception of the moral sphere?

## Feminist Analysis

Sexuality pervades all aspects of everyday life. Products from cars to coffee are advertised through sexual innuendo, for example. Some aspects and consequences of sexuality in our society are not immediately apparent to everyone. For example, many men and some women are oblivious to the way in which the very possibility of rape affects the emotions and actions of women. To get a sense of these effects, imagine that you are carrying a great deal of money, perhaps thousands of dollars, for a long period of time. Some people are willing to injure you in order to get the money if they think they can get away with it. They are bigger, stronger, and more experienced in fighting than you. Naturally, you take certain precautions and avoid certain situations. Your precautions become almost automatic. You may banish the danger from your mind most of the time. Yet naturally you are often afraid, and your movements, your behavior, and even your speech are circumscribed. This is the plight of most women.

Typically, rapists and batterers think that what they do is not much different from what most men do, observes MacKinnon in "Sex and Violence." Indeed, violence against women *is* erotic for men. It turns men on. Now in our culture, what counts as ordinary sex is defined from the man's point of view, and the ordinary man's sexual tastes are not very different from the tastes of rapists. MacKinnon draws the frightening conclusion that ordinary sex in our culture can be a lot like rape—rape for which the rapist is never convicted, like most rape! Put less provocatively, ordinary sex encompasses a range of behaviors, and that range includes quite a lot of violence against women. Although common sense does draw a line between rape and ordinary sex, MacKinnon claims that because common sense about sex in our society is really male-dominance-defined common sense, the line is misdrawn. A great deal of what is called ordinary sex should be classified as unacceptable sex because, like rape, it involves violence against women. MacKinnon is not saying that violent, abusive sex is natural or healthy, of course. She is saying that sexual abuse is common and, therefore, accepted in our society. How common? Reliable figures are notoriously difficult to obtain, but once one becomes sensitized, one sees it everywhere. Even in ordinary flirtation there is a fair amount of pushing, pulling, and twisting of women. Pornography teems with images of women being hurt or threatened with harm. Candid descriptions of what goes on in the bedrooms of ordinary people often include violence or fantasies of violence against women. Experiences, events witnessed, and remarks dropped by friends or even strangers are ignored by people whose consciousness has not been raised, but people who know what to look for recognize these things as indications of sexual violence against women.

On the other hand, one may see sexual abuse when it is not there. Just as a prejudiced person too quickly leaps to pejorative conclusions about the actions of blacks or women, just as a touchy person too quickly assumes that a setback is due to racism or sexism, and just as a naive person miscategorizes a rape or battering as mere "fooling around" or "she asked for it," so an oversensitized person construes something as sexual abuse when it is not. We tend to see what we expect to see.

\*

Feminists take different approaches to various sexual practices. One feminist approach urges the liberation of women from various patriarchal restrictions so that they may make their own choices about sex. On this view, extramarital sex has been censured and even banned by men in order to restrict the sexuality of women. The men who made society's moral code and laws limited women to sex within marriage in order to ensure that their daughters and

wives would remain theirs. Men saw women as livestock, so they made the sexuality laws match the property laws. It was wrong to take a daughter or wife for the same reason that it was wrong to take a horse. But women are not property. The moral and legal restrictions on extramarital sex should be lifted, according to this feminist stance.

On the other hand, feminists such as Satz have objected to certain sexual practices because these practices send a pernicious message about women. For example, Satz maintains that prostitution, together with our history of male domination, supports certain assumptions about women and that these assumptions, in turn, perpetuate the exploitation of women. Prostitution encourages people to perceive and treat women as the sexual servants of men. Therefore, although this practice might be innocuous in other contexts or if structured differently, prostitution as it presently exists in our society is immoral. [A similar argument may be made against pornography. See the "Pornography and Sexual Harassment" section.]

### Argument (E)

(1) Certain assumptions harm women by encouraging sexist attitudes.
(2) Prostitution perpetuates these assumptions.
(3) Therefore, prostitution is immoral.

Arguing for the immorality of practices on symbolic grounds is always tricky. Some people may deny premise (2) of argument (E). That is, they may maintain that prostitution sends a harmless message. After all, prostitutes are paid. Prostitutes are sellers rather than slaves. Thus the message sent by prostitution may be that women are in an enviable economic position. Women control the supply of a service for which there is substantial demand. Women's sexuality is a valuable commodity that they may use to gain money and power over men. More insidiously, women may bestow sexual favors as a reward or withhold them as a punishment to condition men—to make their husbands and lovers compliant. In other words, prostitution expresses the old cliché that women manipulate men through their sexuality.

But prostitutes do not see themselves this way. Instead, they tend to have low self-esteem, especially with regard to their sexuality. They see themselves as downtrodden sex servants rather than as well-off merchants of sex. Of course, prostitutes may think of prostitution in one way, whereas the practice of prostitution sends a very different message to society as a whole. Nevertheless, the way in which prostitutes see themselves seems to support Satz' view of the message of prostitution.

Other people may deny the validity of argument (E). That is, they may accept the truth of both premises and yet deny that conclusion (3) follows. The fact that a practice sends a bad message is not a sufficient reason for condemning the practice, for the practice may have advantages that outweigh the evil of its message. After all, many practices and institutions send messages deleterious to women. Christianity, for example, has long taught that women are morally inferior to men and should be ruled by their husbands. And, of course, the traditional family stars the father in the decision-making, catered-to role while the mother obeys and caters, and the children take their fathers and mothers as role models. Christianity and the traditional family have arguably done more to subordinate women than prostitution, yet common sense is not willing to condemn these two practices.

Perhaps common sense is wrong on this point. Some feminists maintain that if a practice symbolically (as well as actually) subordinates women, then this is a sufficient reason for condemning the practice. They then go on to condemn Christianity and the traditional family along with prostitution. After all, Karl Marx maintains that religion is "the opium of the people."[2] That is, religion lulls the exploited into contentment with their lot. It is a tool used by those with power (capitalists, colonialists, and men) to keep those who lack power (workers, natives, and women) from revolting. And Marx argues that the traditional marriage is simply a long-term prostitution relationship. The women exchange their sexual favors for economic and social goods.[3]

\*

How, then, do Utilitarianism, Deontology, and Virtue Ethics stand on the sample sexual acts of this section? Act Utilitarianism counter-intuitively allows unsavory acts such as voyeurism and rape if the attacker gains more than the victim loses. Rule Utilitarianism seems unable to find a rule prohibiting and allowing the right sorts of sexual acts. Kantian theory focuses on something Utilitarianism ignores, the fact that some sexual acts treat people as things rather than as persons by neglecting appropriate consent. Thus Kantians can easily reject rape and voyeurism, but adultery, prostitution, and homosexuality do not violate autonomy if all of the parties are candid with each other. Aristotelian Virtue Ethics, in turn, focuses on something Kantian theory ignores. Aristotle would condemn rape, voyeurism, and adultery not only as exploitive but also as bad sex. These acts are intemperate as well as unjust. Prostitution and homosexuality, on the other hand, are OK if practiced in moderation. Utilitarians would agree with feminists that practices, such as prostitution and voyeurism, that cause more harm than good by symbolically subordinating women are bad. Kantians, on the other hand, would condemn such practices only if they actually subordinated people. And Aristotelians would agree that subordination is bad, but for a different reason. Subordination is bad because it is ignoble on the part of the dominator rather than because of its effects on, or its disrespect for, the dominated.

## Notes

1. S. Kierkegaard, *Either Or*, vol. 1, trans. D. Swenson (Princeton, NJ: Princeton University Press, 1944), p. 295

2. K. Marx, "Contribution to the Critique of Hegel's Philosophy of Law," in *Karl Marx: A Reader*, ed. J. Elster (Cambridge, England: Cambridge University Press, 1986), p. 301.

3. K. Marx, "The Communist Manifesto," in *Karl Marx: A Reader*, ed. J. Elster (Cambridge, England: Cambridge University Press, 1986), p. 263.

# 45   Sexual Perversion

**THOMAS NAGEL**

There is something to be learned about sex from the fact that we possess a concept of sexual perversion. I wish to examine the idea, defending it against the charge of unintelligibility and trying to say exactly what about human sexuality qualifies it to admit of perversions. Let me begin with some general conditions that the concept must meet if it is to be viable at all. These can be accepted without assuming any particular analysis.

First, if there are any sexual perversions, they will have to be sexual desires or practices that are in some sense unnatural, though the explanation of this natural/unnatural distinction is of course the main problem. Second, certain practices will be perversions if anything is, such as shoe fetishism, bestiality, and sadism; other practices, such as unadorned sexual intercourse, will not be; about still others there is controversy. Third, if there are perversions, they will be unnatural sexual *inclinations* rather than just unnatural practices adopted not from inclination but for other reasons. Thus contraception, even if it is thought to be a deliberate perversion of the sexual and reproductive functions, cannot be significantly described as a *sexual* perversion. A sexual perversion must reveal itself in conduct that expresses an unnatural *sexual* preference. And although there might be a form of fetishism focused on the employment of contraceptive devices, that is not the usual explanation for their use.

The connection between sex and reproduction has no bearing on sexual perversion. The latter is a concept of psychological, not physiological, interest, and it is a concept that we do not apply to the lower animals, let alone to plants, all of which have reproductive functions that can go astray in various ways. (Think of seedless oranges.) Insofar as we are prepared to regard higher animals as perverted, it is because of their psychological, not

their anatomical, similarity to humans. Furthermore, we do not regard as a perversion every deviation from the reproductive function of sex in humans: sterility, miscarriage, contraception, abortion.

Nor can the concept of sexual perversion be defined in terms of social disapprobation or custom. Consider all the societies that have frowned upon adultery and fornication. These have not been regarded as unnatural practices, but have been thought objectionable in other ways. What is regarded as unnatural admittedly varies from culture to culture, but the classification is not a pure expression of disapproval or distaste. In fact it is often regarded as a *ground* for disapproval, and that suggests that the classification has independent content.

I shall offer a psychological account of sexual perversion that depends on a theory of sexual desire and human sexual interactions. To approach this solution I shall first consider a contrary position that would justify skepticism about the existence of any sexual perversions at all, and perhaps even about the significance of the term. The skeptical argument runs as follows:

"Sexual desire is simply one of the appetites, like hunger and thirst. As such it may have various objects, some more common than others perhaps, but none in any sense 'natural.' An appetite is identified as sexual by means of the organs and erogenous zones in which its satisfaction can be to some extent localized, and the special sensory pleasures which form the core of that satisfaction. This enables us to recognize widely divergent goals, activities, and desires as sexual, since it is conceivable in principle that anything should produce sexual pleasure and that a nondeliberate, sexually charged desire for it should arise (as a result of conditioning, if nothing else). We may fail to empathize with some of these desires, and some of them, like sadism, may be objectionable

From *Journal of Philosophy*, LXVI, 1 (Jan. 16, 1969):5–17 with omissions. Reprinted by permission.

on extraneous grounds, but once we have observed that they meet the criteria for being sexual, there is nothing more to be said on *that* score. Either they are sexual or they are not: sexuality does not admit of imperfection, or perversion, or any other such qualification—it is not that sort of affection."

This is probably the received radical position. It suggests that the cost of defending a psychological account may be to deny that sexual desire is an appetite. But insofar as that line of defense is plausible, it should make us suspicious of the simple picture of appetites on which the skepticism depends. Perhaps the standard appetites, like hunger, cannot be classed as pure appetites in that sense either, at least in their human versions.

Can we imagine anything that would qualify as a gastronomical perversion? Hunger and eating, like sex, serve a biological function and also play a significant role in our inner lives. Note that there is little temptation to describe as perverted an appetite for substances that are not nourishing: we should probably not consider someone's appetites *perverted* if he liked to eat paper, sand, wood, or cotton. Those are merely rather odd and very unhealthy tastes: they lack the psychological complexity that we expect of perversions. (Coprophilia, being already a sexual perversion, may be disregarded.) If on the other hand someone liked to eat cookbooks, or magazines with pictures of food in them, and preferred these to ordinary food—or if when hungry he sought satisfaction by fondling a napkin or ashtray from his favorite restaurant—then the concept of perversion might seem appropriate (it would be natural to call it gastronomical fetishism). It would be natural to describe as gastronomically perverted someone who could eat only by having food forced down his throat through a funnel, or only if the meal were a living animal. What helps is the peculiarity of the desire itself, rather than the inappropriateness of its object to the biological function that the desire serves. Even an appetite can have perversions if in addition to its biological function it has a significant psychological structure.

In the case of hunger, psychological complexity is provided by the activities that give it expression. Hunger is not merely a disturbing sensation that can be quelled by eating; it is an attitude toward edible portions of the external world, a desire to treat them in rather special ways. The method of ingestion: chewing, savoring, swallowing, appreciating the texture and smell, all are important components of the relation, as [are] the passivity and controllability of the food (the only animals we eat live are helpless mollusks). Our relation to food depends also on our size: we do not live upon it or burrow into it like aphids or worms. Some of these features are more central than others, but an adequate phenomenology of eating would have to treat it as a relation to the external world and a way of appropriating bits of that world, with characteristic affection. Displacements or serious restrictions of the desire to eat could then be described as perversions, if they undermined that direct relation between man and food which is the natural expression of hunger. This explains why it is easy to imagine gastronomical fetishism, voyeurism, exhibitionism, or even gastronomical sadism and masochism. Some of these perversions are fairly common.

If we can imagine perversions of an appetite like hunger, it should be possible to make sense of the concept of sexual perversion. I do not wish to imply that sexual desire is an appetite—only that being an appetite is no bar to admitting of perversions. Like hunger, sexual desire has as its characteristic object a certain relation with something in the external world; only in this case it is usually a person rather than an omelet, and the relation is considerably more complicated. This added complication allows scope for correspondingly complicated perversions.

The fact that sexual desire is a feeling about other persons may encourage a pious view of its psychological content—that it is properly the expression of some other attitude, like love, and that when it occurs by itself it is incomplete or subhuman. (The extreme Platonic version of such a view is that sexual practices are all vain attempts to express something they cannot in principle achieve: this makes them all perversions, in a sense.) But sexual desire is complicated enough without having to be linked to anything else as a condition for phenomenological analysis. Sex may serve various functions—economic, social, altruistic—but it also has its own content as a relation between persons.

The object of sexual attraction is a particular individual, who transcends the properties that make him attractive. When different persons are attracted to a single person for different reasons—eyes, hair, figure, laugh, intelligence—we nevertheless feel that the object of their desire is the same. There is even an inclination to feel that this is so if the lovers have different sexual aims, if they include both men and women, for example. Different specific attractive characteristics seem to provide enabling conditions for the operation of a single basic feeling, and the different aims all provide expressions of it. We approach the sexual attitude toward the person through the features that we find attractive, but these features are not the objects of that attitude.

This is very different from the case of an omelet. Various people may desire it for different reasons, one for its fluffiness, another for its mushrooms, another for its unique combination of aroma and visual aspect; yet we do not enshrine the transcendental omelet as the true common object of their affections. Instead we might say that several desires have accidentally converged on the same object: any omelet with the crucial characteristics would do as well. It is not similarly true that any person with the same flesh distribution and way of smoking can be substituted as object for a particular sexual desire that has been elicited by those characteristics. It may be that they recur, but it will be a new sexual attraction with a new particular object, not merely a transfer of the old desire to someone else. (This is true even in cases where the new object is unconsciously identified with a former one.)

The importance of this point will emerge when we see how complex a psychological interchange constitutes the natural development of sexual attraction. This would be incomprehensible if its object were not a particular person, but rather a person of a certain *kind.* Attraction is only the beginning, and fulfillment does not consist merely of behavior and contact expressing this attraction, but involves much more. . . .

Sexual desire involves a kind of perception, but not merely a single perception of its object, for in the paradigm case of mutual desire there is a complex system of superimposed mutual perceptions—not only perceptions of the sexual object, but perceptions of oneself. Moreover, sexual awareness of another involves considerable self-awareness to begin with—more than is involved in ordinary sensory perception. The experience is felt as an assault on oneself by the view (or touch, or whatever) of the sexual object.

Let us consider a case in which the elements can be separated. For clarity we will restrict ourselves initially to the somewhat artificial case of desire at a distance. Suppose a man and a woman, whom we may call Romeo and Juliet, are at opposite ends of a cocktail lounge, with many mirrors on the walls which permit unobserved observation, and even mutual unobserved observation. Each of them is sipping a martini and studying other people in the mirrors. At some point Romeo notices Juliet. He is moved, somehow, by the softness of her hair and the diffidence with which she sips her martini, and this arouses him sexually. Let us say that *X senses Y* whenever *X* regards *Y* with sexual desire. (*Y* need not be a person, and *X*'s apprehension of *Y* can be visual, tactile, olfactory, etc., or purely imaginary; in the present example we shall concentrate on vision.) So Romeo senses Juliet, rather than merely noticing her. At this stage he is aroused by an unaroused object, so he is more in the sexual grip of his body than she of hers.

Let us suppose, however, that Juliet now senses Romeo in another mirror on the opposite wall, though neither of them yet knows that he is seen by the other (the mirror angles provide three-quarter views). Romeo then begins to notice in Juliet the subtle signs of sexual arousal, heavy-lidded stare, dilating pupils, faint flush, etc. This of course intensifies her bodily presence, and he not only notices but senses this as well. His arousal is nevertheless still solitary. But now, cleverly calculating the line of her stare without actually looking her in the eyes, he realizes that it is directed at him through the mirror on the opposite wall. That is, he notices, and moreover senses, Juliet sensing him. This is definitely a new development, for it gives him a sense of embodiment not only through his own reactions but through the eyes and reactions of another. Moreover, it is separable from the initial sensing of Juliet; for sexual arousal might begin with a person's sensing that he is sensed and being assailed by the perception of the other person's desire rather than merely by the perception of the person.

But there is a further step. Let us suppose that Juliet, who is a little slower than Romeo, now senses that he senses her. This puts Romeo in a position to notice, and be aroused by, her arousal at being sensed by him. He senses that she senses that he senses her. This is still another level of arousal, for he becomes conscious of his sexuality through his awareness of its effect on her and of her awareness that this effect is due to him. Once she takes the same step and senses that he senses her sensing him, it becomes difficult to state, let alone imagine, further iterations, though they may be logically distinct. If both are alone, they will presumably turn to look at each other directly, and the proceedings will continue on another plane. Physical contact and intercourse are natural extensions of this complicated visual exchange, and mutual touch can involve all the complexities of awareness present in the visual case, but with a far greater range of subtlety and acuteness.

Ordinarily, of course, things happen in a less orderly fashion—sometimes in a great rush—but I believe that some version of this overlapping system of distinct sexual perceptions and interactions is the basic framework of any full-fledged sexual relation and that relations involving only part of the complex are significantly incomplete. The account is only schematic, as it must be to achieve generality. Every real sexual act will be psychologically far more specific and detailed, in ways that depend not only on the physical techniques employed and on anatomical details, but also on countless features of the participants' conceptions of themselves and of each other, which

become embodied in the act. (It is familiar enough fact, for example, that people often take their social roles and the social roles of their partners to bed with them.)

The general schema is important, however, and the proliferation of levels of mutual awareness it involves is an example of a type of complexity that typifies human interactions. Consider aggression, for example. If I am angry with someone, I want to make him feel it, either to produce self-reproach by getting him to see himself through the eyes of my anger, and to dislike what he sees—or else to produce reciprocal anger or fear, by getting him to perceive my anger as a threat or attack. What I want will depend on the details of my anger, but in either case it will involve a desire that the object of that anger be aroused. This accomplishment constitutes the fulfillment of my emotion, through domination of the object's feelings.

Another example of such reflexive mutual recognition is to be found in the phenomenon of meaning, which appears to involve an intention to produce a belief or other effect in another by bringing about his recognition of one's intention to produce that effect. . . . Sex has a related structure: it involves a desire that one's partner be aroused by the recognition of one's desire that he or she be aroused.

. . . Hunger leads to spontaneous interactions with food; sexual desire leads to spontaneous interactions with other persons, whose bodies are asserting their sovereignty in the same way, producing involuntary reactions and spontaneous impulses in *them*. These reactions are perceived, and the perception of them is perceived, and that perception is in turn perceived; at each step the domination of the person by his body is reinforced, and the sexual partner becomes more possessible by physical contact, penetration, and envelopment.

Desire is therefore not merely the perception of a pre-existing embodiment of the other, but ideally a contribution to his further embodiment which in turn enhances the original subject's sense of himself. This explains why it is important that the partner be aroused, and not merely aroused, but aroused by the awareness of one's desire. It also explains the sense in which desire has unity and possession as its object: physical possession must eventuate in creation of the sexual object in the image of one's desire, and not merely in the object's recognition of that desire, or in his or her own private arousal.

Even if this is a correct model of the adult sexual capacity, it is not plausible to describe as perverted every deviation from it. For example, if the partners in heterosexual intercourse indulge in private heterosexual fantasies, thus avoiding recognition of the real partner, that would, on this model, constitute a defective sexual relation. It is not, however, generally regarded as a perversion. Such examples suggest that a simple dichotomy between perverted and unperverted sex is too crude to organize the phenomena adequately.

Still, various familiar deviations constitute truncated or incomplete versions of the complete configuration, and may be regarded as perversions of the central impulse. If sexual desire is prevented from taking its full interpersonal form, it is likely to find a different one. The concept of perversion implies that a normal sexual development has been turned aside by distorting influences. I have little to say about this causal condition. But if perversions are in some sense unnatural, they must result from interference with the development of a capacity that is there potentially.

It is difficult to apply this condition, because environmental factors play a role in determining the precise form of anyone's sexual impulse. Early experiences in particular seem to determine the choice of a sexual object. To describe some causal influences as distorting and others as merely formative is to imply that certain general aspects of human sexuality realize a definite potential whereas many of the details in which people differ realize an indeterminate potential, so that they cannot be called more or less natural. What is included in the definite potential is therefore very important, although the distinction between definite and indeterminate potential is obscure. Obviously a creature incapable of developing the levels of interpersonal sexual awareness I have

described could not be deviant in virtue of the failure to do so. (Though even a chicken might be called perverted in an extended sense if it had been conditioned to develop a fetishistic attachment to a telephone.) But if humans will tend to develop some version of reciprocal interpersonal sexual awareness unless prevented, then cases of blockage can be called unnatural or perverted.

Some familiar deviations can be described in this way. Narcissistic practices and intercourse with animals, infants, and inanimate objects seem to be stuck at some primitive version of the first stage of sexual feeling. If the object is not alive, the experience is reduced entirely to an awareness of one's own sexual embodment. Small children and animals permit awareness of the embodment of the other, but present obstacles to reciprocity, to the recognition by the sexual object of the subject's desire as the source of his (the object's) sexual self-awareness. Voyeurism and exhibitionism are also incomplete relations. The exhibitionist wishes to display his desire without needing to be desired in return; he may even fear the sexual attentions of others. A voyeur, on the other hand, need not require any recognition by his object at all: certainly not a recognition of the voyeur's arousal.

On the other hand, if we apply our model to the various forms that may be taken by two-party heterosexual intercourse, none of them seem clearly to qualify as perversions. Hardly anyone can be found these days to inveigh against oral–genital contact, and the merits of buggery are urged by such respectable figures as D. H. Lawrence and Norman Mailer. In general, it would appear that any bodily contact between a man and a woman that gives them sexual pleasure is a possible vehicle for the system of multi-level interpersonal awareness that I have claimed is the basic psychological content of sexual interaction. Thus a liberal platitude about sex is upheld.

The really difficult cases are sadism, masochism, and homosexuality. The first two are widely regarded as perversions and the last is controversial. In all three cases the issue depends partly on causal factors: do these dispositions result only when normal development has been prevented? Even the form in which this question has been posed is circular, because of the word "normal." We appear to need an independent criterion for a distorting influence, and we do not have one.

It may be possible to class sadism and masochism as perversions because they fall short of interpersonal reciprocity. Sadism concentrates on the evocation of passive self-awareness in others, but the sadist's engagement is itself active and requires a retention of deliberate control which may impede awareness of himself as a bodily subject of passion in the required sense. De Sade claimed that the object of sexual desire was to evoke involuntary responses from one's partner, especially audible ones. The infliction of pain is no doubt the most efficient way to accomplish this, but it requires a certain abrogation of one's own exposed spontaneity. A masochist on the other hand imposes the same disability on his partner as the sadist imposes on himself. The masochist cannot find a satisfactory embodiment as the object of another's sexual desire, but only as the object of his control. He is passive not in relation to his partner's passion but in relation to his nonpassive agency. In addition, the subjection to one's body characteristic of pain and physical restraint is of a very different kind from that of sexual excitement: pain causes people to contract rather than dissolve. These descriptions may not be generally accurate. But to the extent that they are, sadism and masochism would be disorders of the second stage of awareness—the awareness of oneself as an object of desire.

Homosexuality cannot similarly be classed as a perversion on phenomenological grounds. Nothing rules out the full range of interpersonal perceptions between persons of the same sex. The issue then depends on whether homosexuality is produced by distorting influences that block or displace a natural tendency to heterosexual development. And the influences must be more distorting than those which lead to a taste for large breasts or fair hair or dark eyes. These also are contingencies of sexual preference in which people differ, without being perverted.

The question is whether heterosexuality is the natural expression of male and female sexual dis-

positions that have not been distorted. It is an unclear question, and I do not know how to approach it. There is much support for an aggressive–passive distinction between male and female sexuality. In our culture the male's arousal tends to initiate the perceptual exchange; he usually makes the sexual approach, largely controls the course of the act, and of course penetrates whereas the woman receives. When two men or two women engage in intercourse they cannot both adhere to these sexual roles. But a good deal of deviation from them occurs in heterosexual intercourse. Women can be sexually aggressive and men passive, and temporary reversals of role are not uncommon in heterosexual exchanges of reasonable length. For these reasons it seems to be doubtful that homosexuality must be a perversion, though like heterosexuality it has perverted forms.

Let me close with some remarks about the relation of perversion to good, bad, and morality. The concept of perversion can hardly fail to be evaluative in some sense, for it appears to involve the notion of an ideal or at least adequate sexuality which the perversions in some way fail to achieve. So, if the concept is viable, the judgment that a person or practice or desire is perverted will constitute a sexual evaluation, implying that better sex, or a better specimen of sex, is possible. This in itself is a very weak claim, since the evaluation might be in a dimension that is of little interest to us. (Though, if my account is correct, that will not be true.)

Whether it is a moral evaluation, however, is another question entirely—one whose answer would require more understanding of both morality and perversion than can be deployed here. Moral evaluation of acts and of persons is a rather special and very complicated matter, and by no means all our evaluations of persons and their activities are moral evaluations. We make judgments about people's beauty or health or intelligence which are evaluative without being moral. Assessments of their sexuality may be similar in that respect.

Furthermore, moral issues aside, it is not clear that unperverted sex is necessarily *preferable* to the perversions. It may be that sex which receives the highest marks for perfection *as sex* is less enjoyable than certain perversions; and if enjoyment is considered very important, that might outweigh considerations of sexual perfection in determining rational preference.

That raises the question of the relation between the evaluative content of judgments of perversion and the rather common *general* distinction between good and bad sex. The latter distinction is usually confined to sexual acts, and it would seem, within limits, to cut across the other: even someone who believed, for example, that homosexuality was a perversion could admit a distinction between better and worse homosexual sex, and might even allow that good homosexual sex could be better *sex* than not very good unperverted sex. If this is correct, it supports the position

that, if judgments of perversion are viable at all, they represent only one aspect of the possible evaluation of sex, even *qua sex*. Moreover it is not the only important aspect: sexual deficiencies that evidently do not constitute perversions can be the object of great concern.

Finally, even if perverted sex is to that extent not so good as it might be, bad sex is generally better than none at all. This should not be controversial: it seems to hold for other important matters, like food, music, literature, and society. In the end, one must choose from among the available alternatives, whether their availability depends on the environment or on one's own constitution. And the alternatives have to be fairly grim before it becomes rational to opt for nothing.

# 46    Gay Basics: Some Questions, Facts, and Values

RICHARD D. MOHR

## Who Are Gays Anyway?

A recent Gallup poll found that only one in five Americans reports having a gay or lesbian acquaintance.[1] This finding is extraordinary given the number of practicing homosexuals in America. Alfred Kinsey's 1948 study of the sex lives of 5,000 white males shocked the nation: 37 percent had at least one homosexual experience to orgasm in their adult lives; an additional 13 percent had homosexual fantasies to orgasm; 4 percent were exclusively homosexual in their practices; another 5 percent had virtually no heterosexual experience; and nearly one-fifth had at least as many homosexual as heterosexual experiences.[2]

Two out of five men one passes on the street have had orgasmic sex with men. Every second family in the country has a member who is essentially homosexual, and many more people regularly have homosexual experiences. Who are

homosexuals? They are your friends, your minister, your teacher, your bank teller, your doctor, your mail carrier, your secretary, your congressional representative, your sibling, parent, and spouse. They are everywhere, virtually all ordinary, virtually all unknown.

Several important consequences follow. First, the country is profoundly ignorant of the actual experience of gay people. Second, social attitudes and practices that are harmful to gays have a much greater overall harmful impact on society than is usually realized. Third, most gay people live in hiding—in the closet—making the "coming out" experience the central fixture of gay consciousness and invisibility the chief characteristic of the gay community.

## Ignorance, Stereotype, and Morality

Ignorance about gays, however, has not stopped people from having strong opinions about them. The void which ignorance leaves has been filled

Copyright © 1986. Reprinted with permission of the author.

with stereotypes. Society holds chiefly two groups of antigay stereotypes; the two are an oddly contradictory lot. One set of stereotypes revolves around alleged mistakes in an individual's gender identity: Lesbians are women that want to be, or at least look and act like, men—bulldykes, diesel dykes; while gay men are those who want to be, or at least look and act like, women—queens, fairies, limp-wrists, nellies. These stereotypes of mismatched genders provide the materials through which gays and lesbians become the butts of ethnic-like jokes. These stereotypes and jokes, though derisive, basically view gays and lesbians as ridiculous.

Another set of stereotypes revolves around gays as a pervasive sinister conspiratorial threat. The core stereotype here is the gay person as child molester and, more generally, as sex-crazed maniac. These stereotypes carry with them fears of the very destruction of family and civilization itself. Now, that which is essentially ridiculous can hardly have such a staggering effect. Something must be afoot in this incoherent amalgam.

Sense can be made of this incoherence if the nature of stereotypes is clarified. Stereotypes are not *simply* false generalizations from a skewed sample of cases examined. Admittedly, false generalizing plays some part in the stereotypes a society holds. If, for instance, one takes as one's sample homosexuals who are in psychiatric hospitals or prisons, as was done in nearly all early investigations, not surprisingly one will probably find homosexuals to be of a crazed and criminal cast. Such false generalizations, though, simply confirm beliefs already held on independent grounds, ones that likely led the investigator to the prison and psychiatric ward to begin with. Evelyn Hooker, who in the late '50s carried out the first rigorous studies to use nonclinical gays, found that psychiatrists, when presented with case files including all the standard diagnostic psychological profiles—but omitting indications of sexual orientation—were unable to distinguish gay files from straight ones, even though they believed gays to be crazy and supposed themselves to be experts in detecting craziness.[3] These studies proved a profound embarrassment to the psychiatric establishment, the financial well-being of

which has been substantially enhanced by "curing" allegedly insane gays. The studies led the way to the American Psychiatric Association finally dropping homosexuality from its registry of mental illnesses in 1973.[4] Nevertheless, the stereotype of gays as sick continues apace in the mind of America.

False generalizations *help maintain* stereotypes, they do not *form* them. As the history of Hooker's discoveries shows, stereotypes have a life beyond facts; their origin lies in a culture's ideology—the general system of beliefs by which it lives—and they are sustained across generations by diverse cultural transmissions, hardly any of which, including slang and jokes, even purport to have a scientific basis. Stereotypes, then, are not the products of bad science but are social constructions that perform central functions in maintaining society's conception of itself.

On this understanding, it is easy to see that the antigay stereotypes surrounding gender identification are chiefly means of reinforcing still powerful gender roles in society. If, as this stereotype presumes and condemns, one is free to choose one's social roles independently of gender, many guiding social divisions, both domestic and commercial, might be threatened. The socially gender-linked distinctions between breadwinner and homemaker, boss and secretary, doctor and nurse, protector and protected would blur. The accusations "fag" and "dyke" exist in significant part to keep women in their place and to prevent men from breaking ranks and ceding away theirs.

The stereotypes of gays as child molesters, sex-crazed maniacs, and civilization destroyers function to displace (socially irresolvable) problems from their actual source to a foreign (and so, it is thought, manageable) one. Thus, the stereotype of child molester functions to give the family unit a false sheen of absolute innocence. It keeps the unit from being examined too closely for incest, child abuse, wife battering, and the terrorism of constant threats. The stereotype teaches that the problems of the family are not internal to it, but external.[5]

One can see these cultural forces at work in society's and the media's treatment of current reports of violence, especially domestic violence.

When a mother kills her child or a father rapes his daughter—regular Section B fare even in major urban papers—this is never taken by reporters, columnists, or pundits as evidence that there is something wrong with heterosexuality or with traditional families. These issues are not even raised. But when a homosexual child molestation is reported, it is taken as confirming evidence of the way homosexuals are. One never hears of heterosexual murders, but one regularly hears of "homosexual" ones. Compare the social treatment of Richard Speck's sexually motivated mass murder of Chicago nurses with that of John Wayne Gacy's murders of Chicago youths. Gacy was in the culture's mind taken as symbolic of gay men in general. To prevent the possibility that "The Family" was viewed as anything but an innocent victim in this affair, the mainstream press knowingly failed to mention that most of Gacy's adolescent victims were homeless hustlers. That knowledge would be too much for the six o'clock news and for cherished beliefs.

Because "the facts" largely don't matter when it comes to the generation and maintenance of stereotypes, the effects of scientific and academic research and of enlightenment generally will be, at best, slight and gradual in the changing fortunes of lesbians and gay men. If this account of stereotypes holds, society has been profoundly immoral. For its treatment of gays is a grand scale rationalization, a moral sleight-of-hand. The problem is not that society's usual standards of evidence and procedure in coming to judgments of social policy have been misapplied to gays; rather, when it comes to gays, the standards themselves have simply been ruled out of court and disregarded in favor of mechanisms that encourage unexamined fear and hatred.

## Are Gays Discriminated Against? Does It Matter?

Partly because lots of people suppose they don't know any gay people and partly through willful ignorance of its own workings, society at large is unaware of the many ways in which gays are subject to discrimination in consequence of widespread fear and hatred. Contributing to this social ignorance of discrimination is the difficulty for gay people, as an invisible minority, even to complain of discrimination. For if one is gay, to register a complaint would suddenly target one as a stigmatized person, and so in the absence of any protections against discrimination, would simply invite additional discrimination. Further, many people, especially those who are persistently downtrodden and so lack a firm sense of self to begin with, tend either to blame themselves for their troubles or to view injustice as a matter of bad luck rather than as indicating something wrong with society. The latter recognition would require doing something to rectify wrong, and most people, especially the already beleaguered, simply aren't up to that. So for a number of reasons discrimination against gays, like rape, goes seriously underreported.

First, gays are subject to violence and harassment based simply on their perceived status rather than because of any actions they have performed. A recent extensive study by the National Gay Task Force found that over 90 percent of gays and lesbians had been victimized in some form on the basis of their sexual orientation.[6] Greater than one in five gay men and nearly one in ten lesbians had been punched, hit, or kicked, a quarter of all gays had had objects thrown at them, a third had been chased, a third had been sexually harassed, and 14 percent had been spit on—all just for being perceived as gay.

The most extreme form of antigay violence is queerbashing—where groups of young men target a person who they suppose is a gay man and beat and kick him unconscious and sometimes to death amid a torrent of taunts and slurs. Such seemingly random but in reality socially encouraged violence has the same social origin and function as lynchings of blacks—to keep a whole stigmatized group in line. As with lynchings of the recent past, the police and courts have routinely averted their eyes, giving their implicit approval to the practice.

Few such cases with gay victims reach the courts. Those that do are marked by inequitable procedures and results. Frequently judges will describe queerbashers as "just all-American boys." Recently a District of Columbia judge handed suspended sentences to queerbashers whose victim had been stalked, beaten, stripped at knife-point, slashed, kicked, threatened with castration, and pissed on, because the judge thought the bashers were good boys at heart—after all, they went to a religious prep school.[7]

Police and juries will simply discount testimony from gays; they typically construe assaults on and murders of gays as "justified" self-defense—the killer need only claim his act was a panicked response to a sexual overture. Alternatively, when guilt seems patent, juries will accept highly implausible "diminished capacity" defenses, as in the case of Dan White's 1978 assassination of openly gay San Francisco city [supervisor] Harvey Milk—Hostess Twinkies made him do it.[8]

These inequitable procedures and results collectively show that the life and liberty of gays, like those of blacks, simply count for less than the life and liberty of members of the dominant culture.

The equitable rule of law is the heart of an orderly society. The collapse of the rule of law for gays shows that society is willing to perpetrate the worst possible injustices against them. Conceptually there is only a difference in degree between the collapse of the rule of law and systematic extermination of members of a population simply for having some group status independently of any act an individual has performed. In the Nazi concentration camps, gays were forced to wear pink triangles as identifying badges, just as Jews were forced to wear yellow stars. In remembrance of that collapse of the rule of law, the pink triangle has become the chief symbol of the gay rights movement.[9]

Gays are subject to widespread discrimination in employment—the very means by which one puts bread on one's table and one of the chief means by which individuals identify themselves to themselves and achieve personal dignity. Governments are leading offenders here. They do a lot of discriminating themselves, require that others do it ([such as] government contractors), and set precedents favoring discrimination in the private sector. The federal government explicitly discriminates against gays in the armed forces, the CIA, FBI, National Security Agency, and the State Department. The federal government refuses to give security clearances to gays and so forces the country's considerable private-sector military and aerospace contractors to fire known gay employees. State and local governments regularly fire gay teachers, policemen, firemen, social workers, and anyone who has contact with the public. Further, states through licensing laws officially bar gays from a vast array of occupations and professions—everything from doctors, lawyers, accountants, and nurses to hairdressers, morticians, and used car dealers. The American Civil Liberties Union's handbook *The Rights of Gay People* lists 307 such prohibited occupations.[10]

Gays are subject to discrimination in a wide variety of other ways, including private-sector employment, public accommodations, housing, immigration and naturalization, insurance of all types, custody and adoption, and zoning regulations that bar "singles" or "nonrelated" couples. All of these discriminations affect central components of a meaningful life; some even reach to the means by which life itself is sustained. In half the states, where gay sex is illegal, the central role of sex to meaningful life is officially denied to gays.

All these sorts of discriminations also affect the ability of people to have significant intimate relations. It is difficult for people to live together as couples without having their sexual orientation perceived in the public realm and so becoming targets for discrimination. Illegality, discrimination, and the absorption by gays of society's hatred of them all interact to impede or block altogether the ability of gays and lesbians to create and maintain significant personal relations with loved ones. So every facet of life is affected by discrimination. Only the most compelling reasons could justify it.

## But Aren't They Immoral?

Many people think society's treatment of gays is justified because they think gays are extremely immoral. To evaluate this claim, a different sense of *moral* must be distinguished. Sometimes by *morality* is meant the overall beliefs affecting behavior in a society—its mores, norms, and customs. On this understanding, gays certainly are not moral: Lots of people hate them and social customs are designed to register widespread disapproval of gays. The problem here is that this sense of morality is merely a *descriptive* one. On this understanding *every* society has a morality—even Nazi society, which had racism and mob rule as central features of its "morality" understood in this sense. What is needed in order to use the notion of morality to praise or condemn behavior is a sense of morality that is *prescriptive* or *normative*—a sense of morality whereby, for instance, the descriptive morality of the Nazis is found wanting.

As the Nazi example makes clear, that something is descriptively moral is nowhere near enough to make it normatively moral. [The fact that] a lot of people in a society say something is good, even over eons, does not make it so. Our rejection of the long history of socially approved and state-enforced slavery is another good example of this principle at work. Slavery would be wrong even if nearly everyone liked it. So consistency and fairness require that we abandon the belief that gays are immoral simply because most people dislike or disapprove of gays or gay acts, or even because gay sex acts are illegal.

Furthermore, recent historical and anthropological research has shown that opinion about gays has been by no means universally negative. Historically, it has varied widely even within the larger part of the Christian era and even within the church itself.[11] There are even societies—current ones—where homosexuality is not only tolerated but a universal compulsory part of social maturation.[12] Within the last thirty years, American society has undergone a grand turnabout from deeply ingrained, near total condemnation to near total acceptance on two emotionally charged "moral" or "family" issues: contraception and divorce. Society holds its current descriptive morality of gays not because it has to, but because it chooses to.

If popular opinion and custom are not enough to ground moral condemnation of homosexuality, perhaps religion can. Such argument[s] proceed along two lines. One claims that the condemnation is a direct revelation of God, usually through the Bible; the other claims to be able to detect condemnation in God's plan as manifested in nature.

One of the more remarkable discoveries of recent gay research is that the Bible may not be as univocal in its condemnation of homosexuality as has been usually believed.[13] Christ never mention[ed] homosexuality. Recent interpreters of the Old Testament have pointed out that the story of Lot at Sodom is probably intended to condemn inhospitality rather than homosexuality. Further, some of the Old Testament condemnations of homosexuality seem simply to be ways of tarring those of the Israelites' opponents who happen to accept homosexual practices when the Israelites themselves did not. If so, the condemnation is merely a quirk of history and rhetoric rather than a moral precept.

What does seem clear is that those who regularly cite the Bible to condemn an activity like homosexuality do so by reading it selectively. Do ministers who cite what they take to be condemnations of homosexuality in Leviticus maintain in their lives all the hygienic and dietary laws of Leviticus? If they cite the story of Lot at Sodom to condemn homosexuality, do they also cite the story of Lot in the cave to praise incestuous rape? It seems then not that the Bible is being used to ground condemnations of homosexuality as much as society's dislike of homosexuality is being used to interpret the Bible.[14]

Even if a consistent portrait of condemnation could be gleaned from the Bible, what social significance should it be given? One of the guiding principles of society, enshrined in the [U.S.] Constitution as a check against the government, is that decisions affecting social policy are not made on religious grounds. If the real ground of the alleged immorality invoked by governments to discriminate against gays is religious (as it has explicitly been even in some recent court cases involving teachers and guardians), then one of the major commitments of our nation is violated.

## But Aren't They Unnatural?

The most noteworthy feature of the accusation of something being unnatural (where a moral rather than an advertising point is being made) is that the plaint is so infrequently made. One used to hear the charge leveled against abortion, but that has pretty much faded as antiabortionists have come to lay all their chips on the hope that people will come to view abortion as murder. Incest used to be considered unnatural but discourse now usually assimilates it to the moral machinery of rape and violated trust. The charge comes up now in ordinary discourse only against homosexuality. This suggests that the charge is highly idiosyncratic and has little, if any, explanatory force. It fails to put homosexuality in a class with anything else so that one can learn by comparison with clear cases of the class just exactly what it is that is allegedly wrong with it.

Though the accusation of unnaturalness looks whimsical, in actual ordinary discourse when applied to homosexuality, it is usually delivered with venom of forethought. It carries a high emotional charge, usually expressing disgust and evincing queasiness. Probably it is nothing but an emotional charge. For people get equally disgusted and queasy at all sorts of things that are perfectly natural—to be expected in nature apart from artifice—and that could hardly be fit subjects for moral condemnation. Two typical examples in current American culture are some people's responses to mothers' suckling in public and to women who do not shave body hair. When people have strong emotional reactions, as they do in these cases, without being able to give good reasons for them, we think of them not as operating morally, but rather as being obsessed and manic. So the feelings of disgust that some people have to gays will hardly ground a charge of immorality. People fling the term *unnatural* against gays in the same breath and with the same force as when they call gays "sick" and "gross." When they do this, they give every appearance of being neurotically fearful and incapable of reasoned discourse.

When *nature* is taken in *technical* rather than ordinary usage, it looks like the notion also will not ground a charge of homosexual immorality. When *unnatural* means "by artifice" or "made by humans," it need only be pointed out that virtually everything that is good about life is unnatural in this sense, that the chief feature that distinguishes people from other animals is their very ability to

make over the world to meet their needs and desires, and that their well-being depends upon these departures from nature. On this understanding of human nature and the natural, homosexuality is perfectly unobjectionable.

Another technical sense of *natural* is that something is natural, and so, good, if it fulfills some function in nature. Homosexuality on this view is unnatural because it allegedly violates the function of genitals, which is to produce babies. One problem with this view is that lots of bodily parts have lots of functions and just because some one activity can be fulfilled by only one organ (say, the mouth for eating) this activity does not condemn other functions of the organ to immorality (say, the mouth for talking, licking stamps, blowing bubbles, or having sex). So the possible use of the genitals to produce children does not, without more, condemn the use of the genitals for other purposes, say, achieving ecstasy and intimacy.

The functional view of nature will only provide a morally condemnatory sense to the unnatural if a thing which might have many uses has but one proper function to the exclusion of other possible functions. But whether this is so cannot be established simply by looking at the thing. For what is seen is all its possible functions. The notion of function seemed like it might ground moral authority, but instead it turns out that moral authority is needed to define proper function. Some people try to fill in this moral authority by appeal to the "design" or "order" of an organ, saying, for instance, that the genitals are designed for the purpose of procreation. But these people cheat intellectually if they do not make explicit *who* the designer and orderer is. If it is God, we are back to square one—holding others accountable for religious beliefs.

Further, ordinary moral attitudes about child-rearing will not provide the needed supplement, which, in conjunction with the natural function view of bodily parts, would produce a positive obligation to use the genitals for procreation. Society's attitude toward a childless couple is that of pity not censure—even if the couple could have children. The pity may be an unsympathetic one, that is, not registering a course one would choose *for oneself,* but this does not make it a course one would *require* of others. The couple who discovers it cannot have children is viewed not as having thereby had a debt canceled, but rather as having to forgo some of the richness of life, just as a quadriplegic is not viewed as absolved from some moral obligation to hop, skip, and jump, but is viewed as missing some of the richness of life. Consistency requires then that, at most, gays who do not or cannot have children are to be pitied rather than condemned. What is immoral is the willful preventing of people from achieving the richness of life. Immorality in this regard lies with those social customs, regulations, and statutes that prevent lesbians and gay men from establishing blood or adoptive families, not with gays themselves.

Sometimes people attempt to establish authority for a moral obligation to use bodily parts in a certain fashion simply by claiming that moral laws are natural laws and vice versa. On this account, inanimate objects and plants are good in that they follow natural laws by necessity, animals by instinct, and persons by a rational will. People are special in that they must first discover the laws that govern them. Now, even if one believes the view—dubious in the post-Newtonian, post-Darwinian world—that natural laws in the usual sense (e = mc², for instance) have some moral content, it is not at all clear how one is to discover the laws in nature that apply to people.

If, on the one hand, one looks to people themselves for a model—and looks hard enough—one finds amazing variety, including homosexuality as a social ideal (upper-class 5th-century Athenians) and even as socially mandatory (Melanesia today). When one looks to people, one is simply unable to strip away the layers of social custom, history, and taboo in order to see what's really there to any degree more specific than that people are the creatures that make over their world and are capable of abstract thought. That this is so should raise doubts that neutral principles are to be found in human nature that will condemn homosexuality.

On the other hand, if one looks to nature apart from people for models, the possibilities are stag-

gering. There are fish that change gender over their lifetimes: Should we "follow nature" and be operative transsexuals? Orangutans, genetically our next of kin, live completely solitary lives without social organization of any kind: Ought we to "follow nature" and be hermits? There are many species where only two members per generation reproduce: Shall we be bees? The search in nature for people's purpose—far from finding sure models for action—is likely to leave one morally rudderless.

## But Aren't Gays Willfully the Way They Are?

It is generally conceded that if sexual orientation is something over which an individual—for whatever reason—has virtually no control, then discrimination against gays is especially deplorable, as it is against racial and ethnic classes, because it holds people accountable without regard for anything they themselves have done. And to hold a person accountable for that over which the person has no control is a central form of prejudice.

Attempts to answer the question whether or not sexual orientation is something that is reasonably thought to be within one's own control usually appeal simply to various claims of the biological or "mental" sciences. But the ensuing debate over genes, hormones, twins, early childhood development, and the like is as unnecessary as it is currently inconclusive.[15] All that is needed to answer the question is to look at the actual experience of gays in current society, and it becomes fairly clear that sexual orientation is not likely a matter of choice. For coming to have a homosexual identity simply does not have the same sort of structure that decision-making has.

On the one hand, the "choice" of the gender of a sexual partner does not seem to express a trivial desire which might be as easily well fulfilled by a simple substitution of the desired object. Picking the gender of a sex partner is decidedly dissimilar, that is, to such activities as picking a flavor of ice cream. If an ice-cream parlor is out of one's flavor, one simply picks another. And if people were persecuted, threatened with jail terms, shattered careers, loss of family and housing and the like for eating, say, Rocky Road ice cream, no one would ever eat it; everyone would pick another easily available flavor. That gay people abide in being gay even in the face of persecution shows that being gay is not a matter of easy choice.

On the other hand, even if establishing a sexual orientation is not like making a relatively trivial choice, perhaps it is nevertheless relevantly like making the central and serious life choices by which individuals try to establish themselves as being of some type. Again, if one examines gay experience, this seems not to be the case. For one never sees anyone setting out to become a homosexual, in the way one does see people setting out to become doctors, lawyers, and bricklayers. One does not find gays-to-be picking some end—"At some point in the future, I want to become a homosexual"—and then set[ting] about planning and acquiring the ways and means to that end, in the way one does see people deciding that they want to become lawyers, and then sees them plan[ning] what courses to take and what sort of temperaments, habits, and skills to develop in order to become lawyers. Typically gays-to-be simply find themselves having homosexual encounters and yet at least initially resisting quite strongly the identification of being homosexual. Such a person even very likely resists having such encounters but ends up having them anyway. Only with time, luck, and great personal effort, but sometimes never, does the person gradually come to accept her or his orientation, to view it as a given material condition of life, coming as materials do with certain capacities and limitations. The person begins to act in accordance with his or her orientation and its capacities, seeing its actualization as a requisite for an integrated personality and as a central component of personal well-being. As a result, the experience of coming out to oneself has for gays the basic structure of a discovery, not the structure of a choice. And far from signaling immorality, coming out to others affords one of the few remaining opportunities in ever more bureaucratic, mechanistic, and socialistic societies to manifest courage.

## How Would Society at Large Be Changed If Gays Were Socially Accepted?

Suggestions to change social policy with regard to gays are invariably met with claims that to do so would invite the destruction of civilization itself: After all, isn't that what did Rome in? Actually Rome's decay paralleled not the flourishing of homosexuality, but its repression under the later Christianized emperors.[16] Predictions of American civilization's imminent demise have been as premature as they have been frequent. Civilization has shown itself rather resilient here, in large part because of the country's traditional commitments to a respect for privacy, to individual liberties, and especially to people minding their own business. These all give society an open texture and the flexibility to try out things to see what works. And because of this one now need not speculate about what changes reforms in gay social policy might bring to society at large. For many reforms have already been tried.

Half the states have decriminalized homosexual acts. Can you guess which of the following states still have sodomy laws? Wisconsin, Minnesota; New Mexico, Arizona; Vermont, New Hampshire; Nebraska, Kansas. One from each pair does and one does not have sodomy laws. And yet one would be hard pressed to point out any substantial difference between the members of each pair. (If you're interested: It is the second of each pair with them.) Empirical studies have shown that there is no increase in other crimes in states that have decriminalized [homosexual acts].[17] Further, sodomy laws are virtually never enforced. They remain on the books not to "protect society" but to insult gays and, for that reason, need to be removed.

Neither has the passage of legislation barring discrimination against gays ushered in the end of civilization. Some 50 counties and municipalities, including some of the country's largest cities (like Los Angeles and Boston) have passed such statutes and among the states and [counties] Wisconsin and the District of Columbia have model protective codes. Again, no more brimstone has fallen in these places than elsewhere. Staunchly antigay cities, like Miami and Houston, have not been spared the AIDS crisis.

Berkeley, California, has even passed domestic partner legislation giving gay couples the same rights to city benefits as married couples, and yet Berkeley has not become more weird than it already was.

Seemingly hysterical predictions that the American family would collapse if such reforms would pass proved false, just as the same dire predictions that the availability of divorce would lessen the ideal and desirability of marriage proved completely unfounded. Indeed, if current discriminations, which drive gays into hiding and into anonymous relations, were lifted, far from seeing gays raze American families, one would see gays forming them.

Virtually all gays express a desire to have a permanent lover. Many would like to raise or foster children—perhaps [from among the] alarming number of gay kids who have been beaten up and thrown out of their "families" for being gay. But currently society makes gay coupling very difficult. A life of hiding is a pressure-cooker existence not easily shared with another. Members of non-gay couples are here asked to imagine what it would take to erase every trace of their own sexual orientation for even just a week.

Even against oppressive odds, gays have shown an amazing tendency to nest. And those gay couples who have survived the odds show that the structure of more usual couplings is not a matter of destiny but of personal responsibility. The so-called basic unit of society turns out not to be a unique immutable atom but can adopt different parts, be adapted to different needs, and even be improved. Gays might even have a thing or two to teach others about divisions of labor, the relation of sensuality and intimacy, and stages of development in such relations.

If discrimination ceased, gay men and lesbians would enter the mainstream of the human community openly and with self-respect. The energies that the typical gay person wastes in the anxiety of leading a day-to-day existence of systematic disguise would be released for use in personal flourishing. From this release would be generated the many spin-off benefits that accrue to a society when its individual members thrive.

Society would be richer for acknowledging another aspect of human richness and diversity. Families with gay members would develop relations based on truth and trust rather than lies and fear. And the heterosexual majority would be better off for knowing that they are no longer trampling their gay friends and neighbors.

Finally and perhaps paradoxically, in extending to gays the rights and benefits it has reserved for its dominant culture, America would confirm its deeply held vision of itself as a morally progressing nation, a nation itself advancing and serving as a beacon for others—especially with regard to human rights. The words with which our national pledge ends—"with liberty and justice for all"—are not a description of the present but a call for the future. Ours is a nation given to a prophetic political rhetoric which acknowledges that morality is not arbitrary and that justice is not merely the expression of the current collective will. It is this vision that led the black civil rights movement to its successes. Those congressmen who opposed that movement and its centerpiece, the 1964 Civil Rights Act, on obscurantist grounds, but who lived long enough and were noble enough came in time to express their heartfelt regret and shame at what they had done. It is to be hoped and someday to be expected that those who now grasp at anything to oppose the extension of that which is best about America to gays will one day feel the same.

## Notes

1. "Public Fears—and Sympathies," *Newsweek,* August 12, 1985, p. 23.

2. Alfred C. Kinsey, *Sexual Behavior in the Human Male* (Philadelphia: Saunders, 1948), pp. 650–51. On the somewhat lower incidences of lesbianism, see Alfred C. Kinsey, *Sexual Behavior in the Human Female* (Philadelphia: Saunders, 1953), pp. 472–75.

3. Evelyn Hooker, "The Adjustment of the Male Overt Homosexual," *Journal of Projective Techniques* 21 (1957), pp. 18–31, reprinted in Hendrik M. Ruitenbeek, ed., *The Problem of Homosexuality* (New York: Dutton, 1963), pp. 141–61.

4. See Ronald Bayer, *Homosexuality and American Psychiatry* (New York: Basic Books, 1981).

5. For studies showing that gay men are no more likely —indeed, are less likely—than heterosexuals to be child molesters and that the largest classes and most persistent sexual abusers of children are the children's fathers, stepfathers, or mother's boyfriends, see Vincent De Francis, *Protecting the Child Victim of Sex Crimes Committed by Adults* (Denver: The American Humane Association, 1969), pp. vii, 38, 69–70; A. Nicholas Groth, "Adult Sexual Orientation and Attraction to Underage Persons," *Archives of Sexual Behavior* 7 (1978), pp. 175–81; Mary J. Spencer, "Sexual Abuse of Boys," *Pediatrics* 78:1 (July 1986), pp. 133–38.

6. See National Gay Task Force, *Antigay/Lesbian Victimization* (New York: NGTF, 1984).

7. "2 St. John's Students Given Probation in Assault on Gay," *The Washington Post,* May 15, 1984, p. 1.

8. See Randy Shilts, *The Mayor of Castro Street: The Life and Times of Harvey Milk* (New York: St. Martin's, 1982), pp. 308–25.

9. See Richard Plant, *The Pink Triangle: The Nazi War Against Homosexuals* (New York: Holt, 1986).

10. E. Carrington Boggan, *The Rights of Gay People: The Basic ACLU Guide to a Gay Person's Rights* (New York: Avon, 1975), pp. 211–35.

11. John Boswell, *Christianity, Social Tolerance, and Homosexuality: Gay People in Western Europe from the Beginning of the Christian Era to the Fourteenth Century* (Chicago: The University of Chicago Press, 1980).

12. See Gilbert Herdt, *Guardians of the Flute: Idioms of Masculinity* (New York: McGraw-Hill, 1981), pp.

232–39, 284–88; and see generally Gilbert Herdt, ed., *Ritualized Homosexuality in Melanesia* (Berkeley: University of California Press, 1984). For another eye-opener, see Walter J. Williams, *The Spirit and the Flesh: Sexual Diversity in American Indian Culture* (Boston: Beacon, 1986).

13. See especially Boswell, op. cit., Chap. 4.

14. For Old Testament condemnations of homosexual acts, see Leviticus 18:22, 21:3. For hygienic and dietary codes, see, for example, Leviticus 15:19–27 (on the uncleanliness of women) and Leviticus 11:1–47 (on not eating rabbits, pigs, bats, finless water creatures, legless creeping creatures, and so on). For Lot at Sodom, see Genesis 19:1–25. For Lot in the cave, see Genesis 19:30–38.

15. The preponderance of the scientific evidence supports the view that homosexuality is either genetically determined or a permanent result of early childhood development. See the Kinsey Institute's study by Alan Bell, Martin Weinberg, and Sue Hammersmith, *Sexual Preference: Its Development in Men and Women* (Bloomington: Indiana University Press, 1981); Frederick Whitam and Robin Mathy, *Male Homosexuality in Four Societies* (New York: Praeger, 1986), Chap. 7.

16. See Boswell, op. cit., Chapter 3.

17. See Gilbert Geis, "Reported Consequences of Decriminalization of Consensual Adult Homosexuality in Several American States." *Journal of Homosexuality* 1:4 (1976), pp. 419–26; Ken Sinclair and Michael Ross, "Consequences of Decriminalization of Homosexuality: A Study of Two Australian States," *Journal of Homosexuality* 12:1 (1985), pp. 119–27.

# 47   Just Looking: Voyeurism and the Grounds of Privacy

## DANIEL O. NATHAN

Soon after West Virginia coal mining companies began to employ women as miners in the 1970s the women became subject to a special sort of harassment. Male employees of Consolidation Coal were accused of spying on female co-workers while they used the showers and toilet facilities. Peepholes had been cut into the women's locker room from a supply room accessible to the men. The observation of the women purportedly went on for more than a year before the peepholes were finally discovered and legal action was initi-

ated against the company and the men involved. This case was one of the more notorious cases of voyeurism to occur in the past few years, having been reported in the *New York Times*[1] and on American television news in 1983. But voyeurism can hardly be considered an unusual phenomenon, and in its various forms it raises some morally interesting issues. There is in fact reason to ask generally what is wrong with acts of voyeurism even though we may believe that the answer is obvious in the particular case at hand. In the coal miner case, the women claimed that they were harmed in obvious and significant ways by the voyeurs. The eight women filing suit reported their

Reprinted with permission of the publisher from *Public Affairs Quarterly,* 4, 4 (1990), 365–386, with omissions.

feelings of humiliation and personal degradation, the long term effects on their ability to sleep, work and concentrate, and the damaging consequences on their personal relationships, including the dissolution of at least one of their marriages. The voyeurism occurred in the context of other purported sexual harassment, including some mine graffiti that made public the private conversations and activities that occurred in the women's locker room. It would seem that the implicit structure of the moral argument there is quite apparent. But, while on the surface the immorality of voyeurism might seem amenable to a straightforward analysis, there do remain some hidden moral complexities. And if so, certainly the relation of voyeurism to the broader issue of privacy also makes it worth asking whether some similar complexities arise there as well. This paper aims to explore the moral complexity of voyeurism and to see what that analysis tells us about certain moral and legal issues surrounding privacy.

Toward those ends, I first argue that it will not completely do to account for the immorality of voyeurism in terms of the understandings ordinarily given of its disutility. Typical utilitarian accounts simply do not adequately explain the immorality of voyeurism. Second, I examine an alternative and explicitly non-consequentialist account of what is morally objectionable about voyeurism, and show its implicit connection to the fundamental interests of moral agents. The upshot of these parts of the paper is that victims of voyeurs are harmed in special ways that are ignored by standard utilitarian accounts, and that these special harms must be considered as fundamental in any correct assessment of acts of voyeurism. The identification of these harms and their relation to deep-set interests provides the possibility of a fruitful consequentialist approach, though one that functions at a level deeper than ordinary accounts. In the third section, I turn to the larger question of privacy and explain how the consideration of these harms and their correlative deep-set interests provides a more satisfying framework for understanding certain crucial moral beliefs we have about privacy. Finally, in the same section I sketch some implications this picture has for analyzing any moral and legal right to privacy and the various puzzles that seem to confound attempts to define the notion of privacy itself.

## I

The most obvious and straightforward analysis of the morality of voyeurism is in terms of the production of overt harms. Thus, most often, philosophers demonstrate the wrongness of voyeurism in terms of the particular consequences of the act involved. They do this despite the fact that some of their views are consistent with, or are even eloquent defenses of non-consequentialism. Joel Feinberg, discussing the West Virginia mining case in *Offense to Others*,[2] focuses on the psychological pain caused to the women, their depression and sleeplessness, their feelings of shame and humiliation, their marital problems, all consequent upon their eventual discovery of the peephole. Feinberg does go on to say that "even in the possible cases where the threshold of actual harm had not been reached, a wrong was surely done them." But here again, the wrong is analyzed consequentially in terms of the depth of the offense experienced by the women on finding out they had been watched: Feinberg notes that it is an offense not fully captured by describing it merely as intense and longlasting "unpleasant states of mind."[3] Later he characterizes the offense as including both "a shocking affront to [the victim's] moral sensibilities" and the victim's sense of being "violated or threatened" by the affronting behaviors.[4] These conditions raise the possibility, on Feinberg's view, of criminal sanctions against the voyeurism based on the depth of the offense or psychological pain experienced by the women. It is worth noting here that, as will be apparent in later analyses as well, these overt harms and feelings of offense were uniformly consequences of *finding out* about the voyeurism. It seems reasonable to say that none of the consequences mentioned would have occurred had the peephole not been discovered by the women in this case. How, after all, could the women have felt humiliated if they had not found out about the spying?[5]

After a lengthy and eloquent defense of privacy rights in the non-consequentialist terms of "respect for persons,"[6] Stanley Benn treats voyeurism in more recent writings in what appears to be a consequentialist fashion, though the harms he cites are often more subtle than those specified above.[7] A voyeuristic intrusion can "constrain the easy intercourse of friends" and affront the self consciousness of its object. Benn explains that "one feels humiliated when one regards the image of oneself that another sees as despicable, and, whether or not one believes it to be just, one cannot help identifying with it." We are denied the "release from Mr. Prufrock's need to 'prepare a face to meet the faces that we meet.'"[8] Thus Benn identifies damaging consequences of voyeurism, and again the bad consequences are contingent on the *discovery* that one is being observed—for it clearly is upon that discovery that one is forced again to "prepare one's face," or to inhibit a conversation between friends, or to feel humiliated in the way Benn describes.

The discussion can be taken a step or two further, however, to show that a consequentialist analysis of the immorality of voyeurism does not necessarily rest on the consequences of the victim's *discovery* of the act. One of the outstanding fears about being observed in some private activity is that some information about one's activities which one desires to keep secret will become publicized. It is precisely that fear, of course, that lies behind the concerns that one would have to constrain private conversations if someone were eavesdropping. And some of the consequences (good or bad) of private information becoming public have absolutely nothing to do with whether the voyeur's victim knows about the act of voyeurism or not. Suppose a voyeur watches while his victim hides some money behind a book in his library, later breaks in and, using the knowledge gained through his observations, steals the money. The victim might never know that the theft was the result of the act of voyeurism, but he was harmed nonetheless. Or consider that a person's job prospects might be damaged should some details about his sex life become known to potential employers. In neither of these cases are the consequences at all dependent upon the victim's

coming to know about the voyeur. Certainly then it is possible that information acquired through covert observation could result in losses that count as very real and quite overt harms to the victim completely without the victim's knowledge of their cause.

However, when considering the previous examples, one must be struck by the fact that the harms produced are only what might be called "indirect" harms. It does not seem to be the act of voyeurism *itself* which in such cases harms the victim; it is the further use of the resulting information that is damaging. But if so, then what are we to make of an undetected act of voyeurism which does *not* result in such obvious harm to the victim's future interest? If the moral analysis of voyeurism rested only on harms contingent upon discovery or else on such other indirect harms as the publication or damaging use of the information involved, then we would really lack an analysis of the harmfulness of voyeurism *per se*. To see that this is so, we need only imagine an act of spying which always remained undetected and which never was used to damage the victim's future interests—in such a case, the voyeurism itself seems harmless. That is in fact how Benn and others refer to such a case. Perhaps there is some attraction to the conclusion that voyeurism *per se* is in this way harmless, but I wish to claim that such a conclusion is unsatisfactory.

Of course, to say that an act is harmless is not to say that it is therefore morally permissible. There remain both consequentialist and non-consequentialist analyses that could point toward a judgment that such an act is wrong after all. A consequentialist could point out that, prospectively, in the absence of certainty that no harm will come of the act, it would be wrong to engage in the act of spying because of the mere possibility of harmful consequences through discovery, publicity, etc. Alternatively, even an act that is itself harmless might influence others to become voyeurs in less "promising" contexts, or with worse results. From a non-consequentialist perspective, the wrongness could be analyzed somehow in terms of how the act violates a principle of right behavior, like that of the duty to show proper respect for one's fellow human beings. (The non-consequentialist analysis is developed in Section II below.)

As it stands, however, the basic consequentialist analysis[9] of the wrongness of undetected and unpublicized voyeurism remains disturbing: On that analysis, the more "careful" a spy one is, the less morally culpable one becomes. The voyeur who takes special precautions to ensure that his spying goes undetected is, on such a view, morally superior to one who is more careless about whether he is discovered. Yet, if we share any intuitions on this point, it is that the more subtle spy is also more reprehensible, much as we tend to see the skillful liar as more despicable than the clumsy one.[10] But even this important problem with standard consequentialist approaches does not quite capture the way in which such views mistake the immorality of voyeurism.

The crucial error, I think, lies in the starting point: the assumption that an act of undetected, unpublicized voyeurism is harmless. To address this, we need to shift from consequentially assessing the rightness or wrongness of the action to the more fundamental level of inquiring into the state of affairs that undetected voyeurism represents, that is, to determining whether the very state of affairs of being spied upon is itself a harmed state. From a disinterested perspective, I think that there is the sense that the victim of the voyeur is still every bit a victim, is harmed, whether she detects the voyeur or not.[11] Can any sense be made of this? What kind of harm after all could it be? How is the victimization to be understood? (Of course, the mere fact that we may agree here on the label "victim" in no way establishes the existence of a *harmed* state, since it makes sense to say that one may be a victim if one is merely wronged and not harmed.)

One way then to think of the present project is as an elucidation of the sense in which the undetected voyeur's victim is harmed. As such, it is part of a larger question of whether there can be harms that are never experienced. A consequence of the forthcoming account is that there would seem to be some harms which cannot be analyzed in terms of occurrent mental states.[12] If the claim that the voyeur's victim is harmed makes sense, it would thus have an impact on how we understand and assess the foundations of conse-

quentialist and in particular utilitarian theory. Another consequence, though one that cannot be apparent at this stage, is that it may give us a better grasp of a much larger class of moral theories, namely those that are "utility-based" though not necessarily utilitarian nor consequentialist in any thoroughgoing fashion.

*Do* we indeed share a sense that the object of the voyeur is harmed? It seems plausible to say that we feel sorry for the victim, but by itself this hardly points one way or another on the question of harm. There are certainly alternative explanations for our sympathy for the victim of the undiscovered voyeur. Perhaps we identify strongly enough with the victim that the factor of non-detection is muddied (*we* after all know about the spy), and our sympathy rests on how we imagine we would feel as the victim *knowing* about the voyeur. Or we might anticipate that the victim will become an object of derision sometime in the future, once again confusing the issue at hand. I cannot show that none of these alternative explanations would suffice as an account of our intuitions on this matter, but if a reasonable story of the possible harms inflicted on the voyeur's object can be told, a story that captures something central to our understanding of the voyeuristic intrusion itself, and to our understanding of privacy generally, then such a direct explanation should be preferred over its less direct alternatives.

## II

It may not even be obvious that a wrong occurs in acts of voyeurism in the absence of *overt* harms to the voyeur's object. Indeed, one might insist that, far from inquiring after a hidden harm done to the "victim," it is highly questionable that the individual has even been in *any* way wronged. Hence, before considering the more controversial issue of arcane harms (and also by way of setting a groundwork for that discussion), the moral wrongness of undetected and unpublicized voyeurism needs to be considered. The most direct case to be made for the wrongness of this sort of voyeurism appears to be a non-consequentialist one, and an obvious source for such an argument is Kant.

One can fashion at least two plausible Kantian arguments for the immorality of undetected voyeurism. Each argument arises from the Kantian notion of persons as ends in themselves, though the two differ in the more specific nature of the obligation seen as implied by treating someone as an end. On the one hand, we shall see that respect for persons as ends requires that in one's own actions one take into account every person's capacity for autonomous choice, and on the other hand, such respect requires an attitude of respect towards other persons as rational choosers *per se* through respect for their actual choices. So we must first actually insure that our action is such that the action does not itself make it impossible for the human "object(s)" of the action to assent to what is going on. When, for example, we purposely deceive another person we do precisely that, we make it *impossible* for him to agree with our action, and to so act is surely to disregard that person's ability to choose for himself. Even in the case of those "white" lies in which one could suppose that the person who is deceived might possibly otherwise assent to the action, the victim is by virtue of the deception (that is, not even knowing accurately what the action is) necessarily prevented from having the option of actually doing so. Thus, on Kantian grounds, such deception violates the obligation to treat humanity as an end in itself by failing to take seriously the victim's capacity for autonomous choice.[13]

Respect for persons entails, in Kant's view, not only ensuring the possibility that the other person assent to our actions, but also that we treat her actual choices as rational, and that we thus treat her as rationally in control of herself. In treating her as otherwise less then rational, she becomes for us a mere tool. Here is part of Christine Korsgaard's explanation of the Kantian view of what happens in cases of coercion or deception:

> Your reason is worked, like a machine: the deceiver tries to determine what levers to pull to get the desired results from you. Physical coercion treats someone's person as a tool; lying treats someone's *reason* as a tool . . . [A] tool has two essential characteristics: it is there to be used, and it does not control itself—its nature is to be directed by something else. To treat someone as a mere means is to treat her as if these things were true of her.[14]

Given a common sense knowledge of how people generally reason, the liar uses his victim's reasoning to produce the result the liar seeks, without any regard for the victim's own immediate goals. Thus, in Kant's example of the lying promise to repay a loan, the liar makes essential use of the lender's desire to be repaid (perhaps with interest), and in the process makes use of her reasoning that the promise is evidence that the loan shall be repaid. The liar does this in order to achieve the result he wishes, namely the simple acquisition of the money. So instead of treating the victim's actual reason as an end, he represents it only as a mediate cause, part of the causal chain he initiates for achievement of his own goal alone.[15] This is the case even if the lender might have been willing to give the money as a gift, without strings, for even here she is still deprived of the chance to *choose* that action, to control the features of the action that finally results. She lacks control in any sense over whether the money is treated as a gift; given the initial agreement, should it become a "gift" now, it is clearly without her say so. She is deprived of the very possibility of assent.

Clearly, treating someone as being less than rational in such cases does not require that the person ever be made aware of the treatment or suffer mental anguish as a result of the treatment. The wrongdoing can be understood at this point as a matter of the attitude reflected in [the] wrongdoer's action, namely a denial of the legitimacy of the other person's rationally chosen ends. Later, I suggest a way of understanding the wrongdoing in terms other than the attitude of the agent, in terms of actual and specific harms done by the voyeur. In the case of deception, there is a requirement that the victim be presently ignorant of the act of deception, and that she behave precisely consistently with this ignorance. This characterization has an obvious and direct parallel to the case of voyeurism.

The voyeur fails to show respect for persons in both respects delineated above: The undiscovered voyeur, through his use of deception, clearly makes it impossible for his victim to assent to being observed, and he furthermore treats his victim's actual choices only as means toward achievement of his own purposes. On the first point, the explanation follows quite the same lines as those indicated several paragraphs back. In the West Virginia mining case, the voyeurs took great pains to remain undetected, and so they clearly aimed to deceive their victims. As an act of deception, as we saw above, it disregards the women's very *capacity* to choose, and thus fails to respect them as persons. Never given the choice to assent, for example, to sharing their private conversations with others, the women were treated as though they lacked the very capacity to choose at all.

This link to purposeful deception of course is not special to the West Virginia case. Even setting aside that it is often psychologically important for the voyeur to believe that he has deceived his victim and that his observations are undetected, there seems to be a more important conceptual connection between voyeurism and deception. Consider a case in which, without coercion, the "victim" agrees in advance to being observed. Beyond the fact that it would likely change the moral assessment of the act, the prior agreement would raise serious doubts about even whether the action can be properly understood as voyeurism at all.

The other manner in which we can fail to respect others as persons is to ignore what we know to be their *actual* choices, not just their capacity to choose. Here again, it is fairly obvious how the voyeur shows disrespect toward his victim. In Kantian terms, reasons which should be treated as final causes are treated as mediate ones: the female mineworkers chose to be in the locker room to converse, to change clothes, etc. for *reasons* that could not be thought of as being treated with respect by the spies. More precisely, their reasoning was being used to serve the purposes of the spies, who must have believed that they could only be privy to such activities on the assumption that the women be allowed to reason that their actions would remain unobserved. This is clear given the confidential nature of some of the conversations reported, including ones concerning intimate relations and which later appeared as mine graffiti. The disrespect for the women's actions thus even goes beyond making essential use of the reasoning behind their actual choices; it also is found in the disregard of their actual choices. Here, not only because it is typically not

a victim's choice to be scrutinized at all, but because each of the victim's actions is itself *transformed* by the act of the voyeur into something of which the victim must be unaware and hence could not be understood to have chosen. The victim's actual choices are traded for a radically different set of actions. Thus, the miners' preparations for their showers are transformed into some sort of unintended striptease, their confidential discussions become public discourses, etc. That these transformations occur is once more entirely independent of any eventual discovery of the voyeur's act; it applies in as strict a fashion to the *undetected* voyeur as to any other, and it depends not at all on the victim's later experiencing humiliation or mental anguish of any sort.

Given that generally women in our society do not wish to be observed in such settings, the spies in the mining case explicitly disregard what they must assume to be their victims' actual choices in favor of choices preferred by the spies. The women, unaware that their acts have been changed in this situation, are in an important sense purposely deprived of rational control of their own actions. They are led to think that they have good reasons for their actions when in fact they have none.

Over possible objections from Kant, this apparently non-consequentialist analysis can be reconstructed so that the wrong may be understood in terms of the harm done to the victim, and hence in terms of bad consequences, but in a sufficiently subtle way that the harm remains regardless of the victim's awareness of being harmed. The following picture of the immorality of undetected voyeurism emerges: First, it is clear that the victim's desires are frustrated; the victim desires not merely to *believe* that she is not being observed, but not actually to *be* observed. The voyeur frustrates that desire whether discovered or not. Thus one could argue that because the frustration of certain actual desires (specifically reasonable, informed ones) is harmful, the voyeurism is harmful. On the face of it, we have seen there is no reason to believe that this actual desire of the victim is unreasonable or poorly grounded, or that a fully informed person would not make the same choice to be unobserved that, for example, the

West Virginia coal miners did. Nor, relatedly, is there reason to say that this particular object of desire is on balance bad for the victims or for other persons. Only if there were some reason to suspect that one or another of those alternatives obtains could one sensibly question whether some harm had been done. Consequently, there are no obvious grounds for denying that the frustration of desire here counts as a prima facie harm.

Also we have seen that one's autonomy is limited by the eyes of the voyeur, and not only when they are detected, because the choices that one thinks one has made are defeated through the action of the voyeur. Then, insofar as autonomy is in the interest of rational beings, the victim's interests are set back in this respect as well by the voyeur. Further, the victim's rational expectations about the nature and consequences of her actions are purposely defeated by the voyeur in the same way (contributing here to her loss of autonomy), and doing so damages her interest in protecting the usefulness of reason in deciding how to behave. More broadly speaking, by purposely interfering with the fulfillment of these reasonable expectations, the undetected voyeur sets back our interest in having a realistic understanding of the world and our situation within it with respect to other persons. This in turn defeats the ability to understand the context of our communications, and thus sets back the interest in being able to express and to do what we intend. None of these are trivial interests. In fact, they are interests that are absolutely essential to maximizing our ability to function as rational, moral agents in the world. Moreover, if a right to privacy can be seen to play a central role in the protection of such basic interests, it could itself be no trivial right.

Thus, a non-consequentialist analysis of the wrongness of acts of undetected voyeurism may point toward a deeper understanding of the intuition that closed the first section of this paper, the intuition that the victim of the voyeur is harmed in an important sense by the act of voyeurism itself. It does this through the explicit identification of a complex of deep-set interests that are not accessed by standard utilitarian approaches to the question of privacy. The special harms associated with undiscovered voyeurism I think turn out to be central to understanding the wrongfulness of voyeurism and invasions of privacy in general.

## III

The present analysis begins to explain what is otherwise unexplained on the typical consequentialist analyses of voyeurism. It makes sense of the moral disapproval of voyeurism even when the voyeurism remains undiscovered by its victim and suggests a way of understanding that in such situations the victim has been harmed in a tangible way. It also goes some distance toward explaining our reluctance to label as voyeurism those cases in which the victim has not been deceived, is instead aware of the "voyeur" and has nonetheless chosen to behave as he or she does regardless of being observed. Here it potentially grounds a moral distinction between cases of being a witting and willing object of observation and being an unwilling and unwitting object. It may also explain some of the special needs of the voyeur which are reflected in the voyeur's reliance/insistence on being undiscovered which go beyond merely the desire not to be caught and punished for his action. In this case, one might hypothesize that the voyeur desires more than merely to look at his victim but to wield power over her through undermining her autonomy. . . .

As we have seen, when there is a change in audience it changes the nature of the communication, and changes the very nature of the action itself. An act of beneficence can become hurtful, an act of self-interest can become self-destructive. Such changes could defeat a wide range of interests, ones as diverse as that of not harming others and of not harming ourselves. The action takes on new meaning with the intrusion of the secret observer; purposely deceived by another person, the agent consequently loses some degree of control and/or understanding of her own action. Insofar as the ability to make rational choices in such ordinary contexts is linked at all to our conception of autonomy, violations of privacy are violations of our autonomy—*not* in terms of our ability to control the behavior of others, but in terms of our ability to choose our own actions. It is that control that is disrupted by the voyeur, control of ourselves in some sense.

Understood in this fashion, the present analysis avoids some difficulties faced by the so-called "control" definitions of privacy that have been widely discussed in the privacy literature. A variety of illustrations have aimed to show that privacy could not amount to having control over access to oneself, or to information about oneself, or to one's sex life. The counterexamples show clearly that what produces a loss of privacy is not the absence of *control* over whether one is observed, but instead the act of observation itself. So Lois Lane maintains her privacy as long as Superman doesn't use his x-ray vision, but at no point does she *control* his use of that power. Still, the widespread temptation to locate the notion of control at the heart of privacy reflects what I think is the correct intuition that autonomy in some form or other is central to our interest in privacy. However, it is not the control of others' access to us that is pertinent, but rather our deep-set interest in the autonomy involved in our ability to control our own behavior and its proper interpretation. And so we have an interest in people not observing us without our knowledge or permission. That is a crucial interest because of how it factors into our ability to communicate with and behave toward one another. . . .

My claim is that we do have a right to privacy and that right arises from underlying and universal human interests. These centrally include the interests we have already discussed: interests in having a realistic understanding of the world and our situation within it, in having our reasonable expectations fulfilled, in having some grounds for being able to predict the consequences of our actions, in knowing the contexts of our communications so that we may express what we choose, etc. All of these interests are basic to our capacity to function as *rational choosers,* as persons in the world, as autonomous moral agents. Each of these interests can be jeopardized by invasions of privacy, even invasions of which we are unaware and will

never discover. So I wish to claim that our right to privacy is grounded most generally in these sorts of interests—that violations of privacy even in cases where they don't interfere with other interests, interfere with these. But one of the things that distinguishes my view from others is that I hold that there is a link between these interests and the consequent right.

What keeps this talk of interests from deteriorating into a straightforwardly consequentialist approach, vulnerable to standard objections, is that we still understand privacy as a moral *right.* As such, we cannot simply weigh the underlying interests against other competing interests in the particular case, like those of the voyeur or a nosy readership. The proper limitations on intrusive actions of the state or of other individuals do not depend on obvious and overt harms caused by the particular intrusive actions. Nor, on my view, do those limitations depend on the potential harm that general practices of intrusion would have on people, as rule consequentialist schemes might conceive it. What is instead being claimed is that persons have a right against intrusive actions *just because* we have so fundamental an interest in such things as those matters mentioned above. That we wish to claim a right here derives from . . . how essential we view those interests to be to our very ability to function as persons. We could not function as moral agents in the absence, for example, of being able to rely on our beliefs about the context of our actions. But this sort of foundational argument for rights hardly implies a consequentialist justification for safeguards against particular invasions of privacy, despite the fact that it invokes consideration of interests in a very fundamental fashion in the rational grounding of a general right to privacy. It is not for example a straightforwardly consequentialist view to argue, in the manner of the previous section, that any state which did not consider such basic interests of its citizens surely shows no respect for them as rational choosers, as persons.

None of this is meant to suggest that privacy rights are always very strong claims, or claims that may almost never be overridden. The interests which ground the right to privacy also ground other rights. Additionally, there are certainly other fundamental interests that we share as human beings. T. M. Scanlon has discussed, for example, the interests which underlie the right to freedom of expression.[16] These include the interest we have in bringing something to the attention of a wider audience, in changing our beliefs upon exposure to good reasons for such changes, in merely being exposed to ideas and attitudes different from our own. But when rights like those of free expression and privacy conflict with one another, we need not on the present view just weigh the consequences of the action on the interests involved. Instead, in order to take the rights seriously, we can ask at least two sorts of questions: (1) How important or fundamental is the interest that underlies the one right as opposed to the other? (2) How deeply entrenched is the relevant interest in this particular case; to what extent is it involved and threatened here? One should notice here in passing that the sorts of interests mentioned above as fundamental to privacy rights are as much involved in the voyeur case when undiscovered as when discovered. What distinguishes the two is that in the case where the invasion is discovered, a set of additional interests (like those of avoiding mental distress, or not being pressured to conform) are brought into consideration.

## IV

What are the more general implications of the present account? Some critics have urged that the right to privacy is fundamentally "the right to keep hidden from view" and as such it has a special connection to socially unacceptable and illegitimate actions. But, on the present view, privacy cannot be not grounded or even associated with any unjustified wish to manipulate or defraud. Nor does our interest in privacy seem in any essential way a reflection of human frailty or hypersensitivity, as other critics have claimed. It has been shown that the avoidance of mental distress is less central than an assortment of other interests that come into play in the defense of privacy.

Instead, the present construction suggests that privacy may be as basic a right as those of property and person. Certainly privacy appears to rest on interests that seem as basic and universal as those grounding the former. Further, in our starting point of tying privacy to the special and fundamental interests reflected in the undetected voyeur case, we see it to have a character that is different from and irreducible to those of property and person. We show it to rest on unique grounds in a way that can never be clear when thinking only of the "indirect" harms that have been the focus of other privacy studies. The identification of a unique and fundamental set of interests set back by even the most innocuous invasions of privacy is thus significant. It can serve both to ground a claim for a general right to privacy and to support those who have argued that this right to privacy is distinctive from other rights in a proper moral taxonomy. That there is a right is implied by the character of these interests and more particularly their role in establishing the conditions for moral personality itself. That privacy, if it is a right, is a distinctive one seems to follow from the unique combination of interests at work; interests which remain at risk even in the absence of concern over property and person. As a consequence, we may once more have to rethink the moral grounds of privacy.[17]

## Notes

1. April 29, 1982.
2. *Offense to Others,* pp. 51–52, the state is mislabelled "Kentucky," but it is clear that it is the same case.
3. *Ibid.,* p. 52.
4. *Ibid.,* pp. 59–60.
5. This is not to deny that they would have (and had already) experienced feelings of degradation associated with other aspects of the sexual harassment that took place. The suit alleges actions by the male coal miners that ranged from assaults and threats to insults and offensive graffiti.
6. "Privacy, Freedom, and Respect for Persons" (1971), reprinted in Ferdinand D. Schoeman (ed.), *Philosophical Dimensions of Privacy* (Cambridge, 1984).
7. "The Protection and Limitation of Privacy," *The Australian Law Journal,* vol. 52 (1978), pp. 601–12 and pp. 686–92.
8. *Ibid.,* p. 608.

9. By "basic" here I mean to exclude, for the time being, rule-consequentialist analyses.

10. It is possible that this is out of a sense that the subtlety reflects a more dangerous/harmful character, and thus a rule-consequentialist analysis could be attempted; but I do not think the appeal to rule consequentialism is necessary to explain such intuitions. Further, by resting its assessment on only an inference from the harmfulness of the general practice, the rule consequentialist could not explain our intuitions about the morality of the particular act.

11. Were this not so, then the undetected voyeur case would appear to reveal a fundamental conflict between our moral intuitions and consequentialism, a conflict that here I think only shows a misreading of the subtlety of possible harms and thus of consequentialism itself.

12. Cf. James Griffin, "Modern Utilitarianism," *Revue Internationale de Philosophie,* vol. 36 (1982), pp. 336–39. If the account to be given here is plausible, then it would appear that there are some harms which cannot be analyzed in terms of occurrent mental states. (The present account would lead us to drop what Griffin calls the "experience requirement.") Fully worked out, my view will need to distinguish such things as harms to the dead from those unexperienced but nonetheless real harms like those suffered by victims of successful covert invasions of privacy. Perhaps a line can be developed along which real harms will be divided from "unreal" ones in terms of whether or not the desires involved are those of actual (not former) moral agents. Obviously, this would have to be worked out. Griffin provides a solution, though not exactly along the lines I foresee, in *Well-Being* (Oxford: The Clarendon Press, 1986).

13. For a proper elucidation of the nature of this obligation and the one to follow, see Christine Korsgaard, "The Right to Lie: Kant on Dealing with Evil," *Philosophy and Public Affairs,* vol. 15 (1986), pp. 330ff.

14. *Ibid.,* p. 335.

15. Cf. *Ibid.,* p. 334.

16. Scanlon, "Freedom of Expression and Categories of Expression," *University of Pittsburgh Law Review,* vol. 40 (1979). My argument here draws on Scanlon's "two-tiered" view of rights as developed both in this article and in his "Rights, Goals, and Fairness," *Erkenntnis,* vol. 1 (1977), pp. 81–94.

17. This research grew out of work begun during Joel Feinberg's 1984 NEH Seminar on "The Moral Criticism of the Criminal Law." Two years later, a sabbatical spent at the University of Michigan in Ann Arbor permitted me time to resume work on the topic, and in the course of this extended period I have benefitted from discussions with James C. Anderson (sparking my initial interest in the topic), Marcia Baron, Richard Brandt, Howard Curzer, William Frankena, and Walter Schaller, as well as Joel Feinberg and the other members of the NEH seminar.

# 48   Between Consenting Adults

## ONORA O'NEILL

## The Personal Touch

One view of treating another as a person rather than using him or her is that it demands a certain tone and manner. If we show indifference to others, we do not treat them as persons; if our interactions are personal in tone, whether sympathetic or hostile, we treat them as persons. On this view employers who are cold or distant with their employees do not treat them as persons, but involved employers do so. A prostitute who does her or his job with uninvolved perfunctoriness is

From *Philosophy and Public Affairs,* 14, 3 (1985), 252–277 with omissions, footnotes renumbered. Copyright © 1985 by Princeton University Press. Reprinted by permission of Princeton University Press.

using the clients, and if their manner is similar, they use her or him, but if each had a personal manner the relationship would be personal and neither would use the other.

If this is what it is to treat others as persons and not to use them, neither notion can be fundamental for moral or political thought. We are familiar with uses of others that are cloaked by an involved and concerned manner. A planned seduction of someone less experienced treats him or her as means even when charmingly done. Employers who take paternalistic interest in employees' lives may yet both use them and fail to treat them as persons. Yet relationships without a personal tone may neither use others nor fail to treat them as persons. An impersonal relationship with a sales assistant may not use him or her in any morally objectionable way, nor fail in treating him or her as other than a person. A personal touch may, we shall see, be an important aspect of treating others as persons. But the notion entirely fails to capture the requirements for avoiding using others and provides a scanty account of treating others as persons.

## Actual Consent

A deeper and historically more important understanding of the idea of treating others as persons sees their consent to actions that affect them as morally significant. On this view it is morally objectionable to treat others in ways to which they do not consent. To do so treats another as a thing or tool, which cannot, so does not, consent to the ways in which it is used; such action fails to treat others as persons, who can choose, and may withhold consent from actions that affect them.

On this understanding of treating others as persons, rape and seduction are decisively unacceptable. The rapist's victim is coerced rather than consenting; and the seducer's victim lacks insight into what is proposed, and so neither can nor does consent to it. But many relationships between prostitutes and their clients are not, on this view, morally objectionable, since they are relationships between consenting adults. Similarly, slavery and forced labor and various forms of economic fraud use others and do not treat them as persons, but a contractual relationship like that between employer and employee does not use others or fail to treat them as persons.

This liberal understanding of avoiding using others and of treating them as persons encounters difficulties of various sorts when we consider what consent is.

An initial difficulty is that it is unclear what constitutes consent. In legal and institutional contexts the criteria are supposedly clearest. Here formal procedures supposedly show who consents to which actions by which others. But here too presumptions of consent are defeasible. Even the

clearest formulae of consent, such as signatures and formal oaths, may not indicate consent when there is ignorance, duress, misrepresentation, pressure or the like.[1] Such circumstances may void contracts and even nullify marriages. Formal procedures for consenting may reveal only spurious consent, and so cannot guarantee that everyone is treated as a person in this second sense.

Where formal procedures are lacking, the problem of determining what has been consented to is greater. Various debates about express and tacit consent reflect these difficulties. But the real problem here is not that consent is sometimes given in ways that are implicit rather than explicit, but that it is standardly unclear where consent—even the most explicit consent—stops. A nod to the auctioneer, though "implicit," conveys a quite precise consent to offering a price increased by a specified amount for a particular lot. At other times the boundaries of explicit consent are unclear. Like other propositional attitudes, consent is opaque. Consent may not extend to the logical implications, the likely results, or the indispensable presuppositions of that which is explicitly consented to. A classical and instructive example of this range of difficulties occurs in liberal political debates over how far consent to a particular constitution (explicitly or implicitly given) constitutes consent to particular governments formed under that constitution, and how far consent to a particular government or party constitutes consent to various components of government or party polity. The notion of loyal opposition is never more than contextually determinate.

A second range of difficulties arises when the consent given does not match the activities it supposedly legitimates. Marxist critics of capitalist economic forms suggest that workers do not consent to their employment despite its outwardly contractual form. For workers, unlike capitalists, cannot (at least in "ideal" capitalism) choose to be without work, on pain of starvation. Hence the outward contractual form masks an underlying coercion. Workers choose between employers (in boom times) but cannot choose or consent to non-employment. Analogously, women in most societies hitherto have not really consented to their restricted life possibilities. A choice between marriage partners does not show that the married life has been chosen. The outward forms of market economies and of unarranged marriages may mask how trivial the range of dissent and consent is. In a Marxist view bourgeois freedom is not the real thing, and men and women in bourgeois societies are still often treated as things rather than as persons. Bourgeois ideologies offer a fiction of freedom. They structure a false consciousness that obscures the extent to which human beings are used and not treated as persons.

A third range of difficulties with taking actual consent as pivotal for treating others as persons emerges when abilities to consent and dissent are impaired. Discussions in medical ethics show how hard it is to ensure that the consent that patients provide to their treatment is genuine. It is not genuine whenever they do not understand what they are supposedly consenting to or lack the independence to do anything other than "consent" to what they think the doctor wants or requires. Patients cannot easily understand complex medical procedures; yet if they consent only to a simplified account, they may not consent to the treatment proposed. And their peculiar dependence makes it hard even for those who are informed to make independent decisions about proposed treatment. Paradoxically, the case of severely impaired patients may seem easiest to handle. Patients too impaired to give any consent evidently cannot be treated as persons in this sense. Paternalism may then seem permissible, even required, for those who are, if temporarily, *only* patients. But with less impaired patients we are not so ready to set aside the ideal of treating others as persons. The difficult case is raised by those who are, as Mill would have put it, "in the maturity of their faculties." Even when we are mature we are seldom ideal rational patients! Here we confront the possibility that consent may be spurious even when based on average understanding and a standard ability to make decisions.

It is not only when we are subjects or employees or patients that we have only a partial understanding of ways in which others propose to act toward us and only an incomplete ability to make decisions for ourselves. Others' apparent consent, even their apparently informed consent, may *standardly* be insufficient to show that we treat them as persons when we interact with them. The problems of the defeasibility and indeterminacy of consent, of ideological distortions and self-deception, and of impaired capacities to consent are all forms of one underlying problem. The deeper problem in this area is simply a corollary of the opacity of intentionality. When we consent to another's proposals, we consent, even when "fully" informed, only to some specific formulation of what the other has it in mind to do. We may remain ignorant of further, perhaps equally pertinent, accounts of what is proposed, including some to which we would not consent. ("I didn't know I was letting myself in for that!" we may protest.) Even when further descriptions are inferable from the one consented to, the inference may not be made; and often we cannot infer which determinate action will enact some proposal. If we want to give an account of genuine, morally significant, consent, we need to explain *which* aspects of actions must be consented to if nobody is to be used or treated as less than a person. An account of genuine consent must then show how the morally significant aspects of plans, proposals and intentions are picked out as candidates for consent.

## Hypothetical Consent

Before considering how such an account might proceed, I shall look at an account of treating others as persons that does not require us to know what they consent to. This strategy explains treating others as persons not in terms of the consent actually given, but in terms of the hypothetical consent fully rational beings would give to the same proposal. The strategy has obvious merits.

One merit is that it suggests that at least sometimes actual consent is not morally decisive, even if well informed. Hence it allows for our strong intuitions that even a consensus may be iniquitous or irrelevant (perhaps it reflects false consciousness), and that not everything done between consenting adults treats the other as a person. This approach also deals readily with cases of impaired capacities to consent. Since it appeals to capacities that are standardly lacking, there is, in a way, no difference in its approach to those in "the maturity of their faculties" and to those more gravely impaired. By the standards of full rationality we are all impaired. But we can always ask whether the fully rational would consent.

But these merits are the acceptable face of a serious deficiency in this strategy. If treating others as persons requires only hypothetical rational consent, we may, as Berlin long ago pointed out, find ourselves overriding the actual dissent of others, coercing them in the name of higher and more rational selves who would consent to what is proposed. It seems implausible that treating others as persons should even sometimes be a matter of overriding what others as we know them actually choose.

Other difficulties with this strategy arise from the varied conceptions of rationality invoked. Many conceptions of rationality presuppose a given set of desires. If these are the actual desires of the consenter, appeal to hypothetical consent will not overcome the worry that a consensus may be iniquitous or reflect local ideology. Yet if there is no appeal to the consenter's actual desires, but only to some hypothetical set of rationally structured desires, then the theory may be too weak to determine what would rationally be consented to. Given that there are many rationally structured sets of hypothetical desires, rational structure alone cannot determine what would rationally be consented to. But there are difficulties in spelling out the content and grounds of a stronger (e.g., quasi-Platonic) account of rational desires that might determine hypothetical consent.

The appeal of hypothetical consent criteria of creating others as persons is that it overcomes the limitations of actual consent criteria by endowing hypothetical agents with cognitive capacities that extend their understanding of what is proposed. But it is just not clear how far the insight even of the ideally rational reaches. Do they, for example, have a more determinate insight into proposals

addressed to them than do those who make the proposals? What do they make of internally incoherent proposals? Which aspects of others' proposals are pivotal for the consent or dissent of the fully rational? A convincing account of hypothetical rational consent has to explain *which* aspects of others' actions must be hypothetically consented to if those actions are not to use others or to fail to treat them as persons. This approach cannot exempt us from the need to discover the morally significant aspects of plans, proposals and actions that are candidates for consent.

## Significant and Spurious Consent

If the notion of consent is to help explicate what it is to treat others as persons, we need an account of genuine, morally significant consent, and we need to distinguish it from spurious or morally trivial consent. Three preliminary points seem to me significant.

First, morally significant consent cannot be consent to all aspects of another's proposals that may affect me. Any complicated action will be performed under many descriptions, but most of them will be without moral significance. Morally significant consent will, I suggest, be consent to the deeper or more fundamental aspects of another's proposals. If I consent to be the subject for a medical experiment and the timing slips, I may have been inconvenienced, but not gravely misled. But my consent will have been spurious, and I will not have been treated as a person, but indeed used, if I consented to a seriously misleading account of the experiment and its risks.

Second, if another's consent is to be morally significant, it must indeed be his or her consent. To treat others as persons we must allow them the *possibility* either of consenting to or of dissenting from what is proposed. The initiator of action can ensure this possibility, but the consenting cannot be up to him or her. The morally significant aspect of treating others as persons may lie in making their consent or dissent *possible,* rather than in what they actually consent to or would hypothetically consent to if fully rational. A requirement that we ensure that others have this possibility cuts deep whenever they will be much affected by what we propose. There is not much difficulty in ensuring that those who will in any case be no more than spectators have a genuine possibility of dissent. They need only be allowed to absent themselves or to express disagreement, distaste or the like. But those closely involved in or affected by a proposal have no genuine possibility of dissent unless they can avert or modify the action by withholding consent and collaboration. If those closely affected have the possibility of dissent, they will be able to require an initiator of action either to modify the action or to desist or to override the dissent. But an initiator who presses on in the face of actively expressed dissent undercuts any genuine possibility of refusing the proposal and chooses rather to enforce it on others. Any "consent" the proposal receives will be spurious, and will not show that others have not been used, let alone that they have been treated as persons.

Third, we need to understand what makes genuine consent to the more fundamental aspects of action possible. But there is no guarantee that any one set of requirements makes genuine consent possible in all circumstances. There may be some necessary conditions, whose absence always makes genuine consent or dissent impossible, and other conditions that are needed to make consent possible only in some circumstances. It is plausible to think that when we act in ways that would *always* preclude genuine consent or dissent we will have used others. For example, if we coerce or deceive others, their dissent, and so their genuine consent, is in principle ruled out. Here we do indeed use others, treating them as mere props or tools in our own projects. Even the most rational and independent cannot genuinely consent to proposals about which they are deceived or with which they are compelled to comply. Even if a proposal would have been welcomed, and coercion or deception is otiose, its enforcement or surreptitious imposition precludes consent.

In other cases a proposal for action may not in principle preclude consent and dissent, but the particular others affected may be unable to dissent from it, or genuinely to consent to it. A full understanding of treating others as persons should, I suggest, take some account of the particularities of persons. It must allow that we take seriously the possibility of dissent and consent for others who, far from being ideally rational and independent beings, have their particular limitations that affect their abilities to dissent and to consent variously in varying circumstances. We are concerned not only to be treated as a person—any person—but to some extent to be treated as the particular persons we are. We are not merely possibly consenting adults, but particular friends, colleagues, clients, rivals, relations, lovers, neighbors; we have each of us a particular history, character, set of abilities and weaknesses, interests and desires. Even when others do not deceive or coerce us, or treat us in any way as tools, we may yet feel that they do not treat us as persons either. There is some point to the thought that being treated as a person needs a personal touch. Not being used may be enough for being treated as a person when somebody's particular identity and specific character are irrelevant, for example in commercial or other transactions with anonymous members of the public. (Even here we may think standards of courtesy must be met.) Still, in public contexts not being used may be the major part of being treated as a person; for if consent and dissent are in principle possible, we can refuse the opportunities, offers or activities that do not suit us. But where we have specific relations with particular others, being treated as persons may require far more. It may demand that we treat others not impersonally, but rather as the persons they are.

## Treating Others as Persons in Sexual Relationships

If this account of using others and treating them as persons is plausible, it should throw light on areas of life where such failures are thought common. One such area is sexual relationships and encounters. We might also hope to gain some understanding of *why* sexual relationships are thought peculiarly vulnerable to these sorts of failure.

Some sexual coercion is relatively straightforward. It is not hard to see why the victim of rape or of lesser sexual assault is used. However, rape differs from other forms of coercion in that, because of the implicit nature of much sexual communication and social traditions that encourage forms of sexual duplicity, it is unusually hard to be sure when there has been coercion. Also coercion of less straightforward sorts may occur in some sexual relationships and transactions, including relationships between prostitutes and their clients. Here the outward transaction may be an agreement between consenting adults. But when we remember the institutional context of much (at least contemporary, Western) prostitution, including the practice of pimping, brothel keeping and various forms of social ostracism and consequent dependence on a harsh subculture, we may come to think that not all transactions between prostitutes and clients are uncoerced; but it may not be the client who coerces.

Deception is a pervasive possibility in sexual encounters and relationships. There are not only well-known deceptions, such as seduction and breach of promise, but varied further possibilities as well. Many of these reflect the peculiarly implicit nature of sexual communication. Commercial and various distanced sexual encounters standardly use the very means of expression that deeper and longer-lasting attachments use. But when the endearments and gestures of intimacy are not used to convey what they standardly convey, miscommunication is peculiarly likely. Endearments standardly express not just momentary enthusiasm but affection; the contact of eyes, lips, skin, conveys some openness, acceptance and trust (often enough much more); embrace conveys a commitment that goes beyond a momentary clinging. These are potent gestures of human emotional life. If insufficient trust and commitment are present to warrant such expression, then those who use these endearments and gestures risk giving false messages about feelings, desires and even commitments. But perhaps, we may think, at least in sexual relationships that are commercial or very casual or largely formal, it is well understood by all concerned that these expressions have been decontextualized and no longer express the underlying intentions or attitudes or principles that they might express in a more

wholehearted relationship. But if such expressions are fully decontextualized, what part are they playing in an entirely casual or commercial or formalized encounter? If the expressions are taken at face value, yet what they would standardly express is lacking, each is likely to deceive the other. Relationships of prostitution, casual sexual encounters and the sexual aspect of faded marriages are not invariably deceptive. Such sexual relations may be either too crudely mechanical to use or misuse expressions of intimacy, or sufficiently informed by trust and concern for the language of intimacy to be appropriate. But relationships and encounters that standardly combine superficial expression of commitment with its underlying absence are peculiarly vulnerable to deception. Where too much is unexpressed, or misleadingly expressed, each risks duping the other and using him or her as means.

Avoiding deceit and coercion is only the core of treating others as persons in sexual relationships. In avoiding these we avoid clear and obvious ways of using as (mere) means. But to treat another as a person in an intimate, and especially an intimate sexual, relationship requires far more. These further requirements reflect the intimacy rather than the specifically sexual character of a relationship. However, if sexual relationships cannot easily be merely relationships between consenting adults, further requirements for treating another as a person are likely to arise in any sexual relationship. Intimate bodies cannot easily have separate lives.

Intimacy, sexual or not, alters relationships in two ways that are relevant here. First, those who are intimate acquire deep and detailed (but incomplete) knowledge of one another's lives, characters and desires. Secondly, each forms some desires that incorporate or refer to the other's desires, and consequently finds his or her happiness in some ways contingent upon the fulfillment of the other's desires.[2] Intimacy is not a merely cognitive relationship, but one where special possibilities for respecting and sharing (alternatively for disrespecting and frustrating) others' ends and desires develop. It is in intimate relationships that we are most able to treat others as persons—and most able to fail to do so.

Intimacy makes failures of respect and of love more possible. Lack of respect in intimate relationships may, for example, take both manipulative and paternalistic forms. The manipulator trades on the fact that the other is not just a possibly consenting adult, but one whose particular desires are known and may depend in part on the manipulator's desires. One who succumbs to so-called moral blackmail could have refused without suffering coercion and was not deceived, but was confronted with the dilemma of sacrificing something central to his or her life—perhaps career or integrity or relationships with others, or perhaps mainly the desire to accommodate the manipulator's desires—unless willing to comply. In intimate relationships it is all too easy to make the other an offer he or she cannot refuse; when we are close to others we can undercut their pursuit of ends without coercion or deceit. Modes of bargaining and negotiating with others that do not make dissent impossible for consenting adults in the abstract, and might be acceptable in public contexts, may yet undercut others' pursuit of their ends in intimate relationships. Here a great deal is demanded if we are to leave the other "space" for his or her pursuit of ends. To do so, and so maintain respect for those with whom we are intimate, requires not only that we take account of the particular interlock of desires, dependences and vulnerabilities that have arisen in a given relationship, but also that we heed any wider social context whose modes of discourse and received opinions may systematically undermine or belittle the other's ends and capacities to pursue them. Respect for others—the most basic aspect of sharing their ends—requires the greatest tact and insight when we are most aware of ways in which others' capacities to pursue ends are vulnerable.

Contexts that make manipulation hard to avoid also offer opportunities for paternalistic failures of respect. Unlike the manipulator, the paternalist does not deploy knowledge of the other and the other's ends to reduce his or her "space" for pursuit of those ends. The paternalist rather begins from a failure to acknowledge either *what* the other's ends are or that they are the *other's* ends. This failure of respect entails failures to share those ends, for to the paternalist they are either invisible or else not the other's ends but rather the ends to be sought for the other. The paternalist tries to express beneficence or love by imposing a conception of others' ends or interests. Lack of respect is then compounded by lack of love. Those who try to remake or control the lives of others with whom they are intimate do not merely fail in respect, however sincerely they may claim to seek the other's good. Paternalism toward those who have their own ends is not a form of love. However, since it is only fundamental principles of action (whether plans, proposals, policies or intentions) that must meet these standards, superficial departure from them when acting on morally acceptable fundamental principles may be acceptable, or even required. The jokes and surprises in which friendship may be expressed do not count as deceptions; but if they were incident to action or other maxims, they might constitute fraud or serious disrespect or unacceptable paternalism.[3]

Even in intimate relationships not all failures of love are consequent upon failures of respect. It is not only in manipulative and paternalistic action, where others' ends are respectively used and overlooked, that we may fail to share the ends of those with whom we are intimate. Failures of love also occur when the other's ends are indeed respected, and he or she is left the "space" in which to pursue them, yet no positive encouragement, assistance or support for their pursuit is given. Vulnerable, finite beings do not treat one another as ends merely by leaving each other an appropriate "space." Here again detailed knowledge of others and their desires, strengths and weaknesses offers wider possibilities. The support, concern and generosity we need from particular others if our pursuit of ends is to be not merely unprevented, but sufficiently shared to be a genuine possibility, are quite specific. If we are to treat others with whom we are intimate with love as well as respect, we must both see and (to some extent) support their ends.

Avoiding using others and treating them as persons both demand a great deal in intimate relationships. Only the avoidance of coercion demands no more than usual here, perhaps because coercion tends to destroy intimacy. Deception remains a possibility in any relationship, and more so where much is conveyed elliptically or by gesture. In brief sexual encounters as well as in commercial and formalized sexual relations the discrepancy of expression and underlying attitude offers many footholds for deception; even in sustained intimate relationships underlying attitudes and outlook can become, as it were, decoupled from the expression and gesture that convey them to the other, so that the language of intimacy is used deceptively. Intimate relationships also provide appropriate settings for manipulative and paternalistic failures of respect and of love. But the other side of these gloomy thoughts is that intimacy also offers the best chances for treating others as the particular persons they are.

## Notes

1. Excessive reliance on formal indicators of "consent" suggests doubts whether the consent is genuine. Consider the widespread European use of "treaties" to "legitimize"

acquisition of land or sovereignty by seeking the signature of barely literate native peoples with no understanding of European moral and legal traditions. See D. F. McKenzie's discussion of the treaty of Waitangi in "The Sociology of a Text: Orality, Print and Literacy in Early New Zealand."

2. By this I don't mean merely that sexual desire may include desires that refer to the other's sexual desires, but more broadly that at least some desires in intimate relationships are altruistic in the strict sense that they can be specified only by reference to the other's desires. This allows for nonsexual and even for hostile intimacy, where desire may be for the frustration rather than the fulfillment of the other's desires.

3. A sensitive element of the pattern of casuistry outlined here is determining which principles are the maxim(s) of a given action, and which ancillary. Here counterfactual considerations must always be introduced. We can rebut claims that some principle of action is the maxim of a given act if we have reason to believe that what was done would not have been done but for circumstances under which either maxim might have been expressed by that act. A claim to be acting out of friendship rather than disrespect in throwing a surprise party could be rebutted if the party would be thrown even when friendship would require other implementations (the friend is exhausted or ill or bereaved or shy).

## 49   Is Adultery Immoral?

### RICHARD WASSERSTROM

One argument for the immorality of adultery might go something like this: what makes adultery immoral is that it involves the breaking of a promise, and what makes adultery seriously wrong is that it involves the breaking of an important promise. For, so the argument might continue, one of the things the two parties promise each other when they get married is that they will abstain from sexual relationships with third persons. Because of this promise both spouses quite reasonably entertain the expectation that the other will behave in conformity with it. Hence, when one of the parties has sexual intercourse with a third person he or she breaks that promise about sexual relationships which was made when the marriage was entered into, and defeats the reason-

able expectations of exclusivity entertained by the spouse.

In many cases the immorality involved in breaching the promise relating to extramarital sex may be a good deal more serious than that involved in the breach of other promises. This is so because adherence to this promise may be of much greater importance to the parties than is adherence to many of the other promises given or received by them in their lifetime. The breaking of this promise may be much more hurtful and painful than is typically the case.

Why is this so? To begin with, it may have been difficult for the nonadulterous spouse to have kept the promise. Hence that spouse may feel the unfairness of having restrained himself or herself in the absence of reciprocal restraint having been exercised by the adulterous spouse. In

Reprinted with permission of the author.

addition, the spouse may perceive the breaking of the promise as an indication of a kind of indifference on the part of the adulterous spouse. If you really cared about me and my feelings—the spouse might say—you would not have done this to me. And third, and related to the above, the spouse may see the act of sexual intercourse with another as a sign of affection for the other person and as an additional rejection of the nonadulterous spouse as the one who is loved by the adulterous spouse. It is not just that the adulterous spouse does not take the feelings of the spouse sufficiently into account; the adulterous spouse also indicates through the act of adultery affection for someone other than the spouse. I will return to these points later. For the present, it is sufficient to note that a set of arguments can be developed in support of the proposition that certain kinds of adultery are wrong just because they involve the breach of a serious promise which, among other things, leads to the intentional infliction of substantial pain by one spouse upon the other.

Another argument for the immorality of adultery focusses not on the existence of a promise of sexual exclusivity but on the connection between adultery and deception. According to this argument, adultery involves deception. And because deception is wrong, so is adultery.

Although it is certainly not obviously so, I shall simply assume in this paper that deception is always immoral. Thus the crucial issue for my purposes is the asserted connection between extramarital sex and deception. Is it plausible to maintain, as this argument does, that adultery always does involve deception and is on that basis to be condemned?

The most obvious person on whom deceptions might be practiced is the nonparticipating spouse; and the most obvious thing about which the non-participating spouse can be deceived is the existence of the adulterous act. One clear case of deception is that of lying. Instead of saying that the afternoon was spent in bed with *A*, the adulterous spouse asserts that it was spent in the library with *B*, or on the golf course with *C*.

There can also be deception even when no lies are told. Suppose, for instance, that a person has sexual intercourse with someone other than his or her spouse and just does not tell the spouse about it. Is that deception? It may not be a case of lying if, for example, the spouse is never asked by the other about the situation. Still, we might say, it is surely deceptive because of the promises that were exchanged at marriage. As we saw earlier, these promises provide a foundation for the reasonable belief that neither spouse will engage in sexual relationships with any other persons. Hence the failure to bring the fact of extramarital sex to the attention of the other spouse deceives that spouse about the present state of the marital relationship.

Adultery, in other words, can involve both active and passive deception. An adulterous spouse may just keep silent or, as is often the fact, the spouse may engage in an increasingly complex way of life devoted to the concealment of the facts from the nonparticipating spouse. Lies, half-truths, clandestine meetings, and the like may become a central feature of the adulterous spouse's existence. These are things that can and do happen, and when they do they make the case against adultery an easy one. Still, neither active nor passive deception is inevitably a feature of an extramarital relationship.

It is possible, though, that a more subtle but pervasive kind of deceptiveness is a feature of adultery. It comes about because of the connection in our culture between sexual intimacy and certain feelings of love and affection. The point can be made indirectly at first by seeing that one way in which we can, in our culture, mark off our close friends from our mere acquaintances is through the kinds of intimacies that we are prepared to share with them. I may, for instance, be willing to reveal my very private thoughts and emotions to my closest friends or to my wife, but to no one else. My sharing of these intimate facts about myself is from one perspective a way of making a gift to those who mean the most to me. Revealing these things and sharing them with those who mean the most to me is one means by which I create, maintain, and confirm those inter-personal relationships that are of most importance to me.

Now in our culture, it might be claimed, sexual intimacy is one of the chief currencies through which gifts of this sort are exchanged. One way to tell someone—particularly someone of the opposite sex—that you have feelings of affection and love for them is by allowing to them or sharing with them sexual behaviors that one doesn't share with the rest of the world. This way of measuring affection was certainly very much a part of the culture in which I matured. It worked something like this. If you were a girl, you showed how much you liked someone by the degree of sexual intimacy you would allow. If you liked a boy only a little, you never did more than kiss—and even the kiss was not very passionate. If you liked the boy a lot and if your feeling was reciprocated, necking, and possibly petting, was permissible. If the attachment was still stronger and you thought it might even become a permanent relationship, the sexual activity was correspondingly more intense and more intimate, although whether it would ever lead to sexual intercourse depended on whether the parties (and particularly the girl) accepted fully the prohibition on non-marital sex. The situation for the boy was related, but not exactly the same. The assumption was that males did not naturally link sex with affection in the way in which females did. However, since women did, males had to take this into account. That is to say, because a woman would permit sexual intimacies only if she had feelings of affection for the male and only if those feelings were reciprocated, the male had to have and express those feelings, too, before sexual intimacies of any sort would occur.

The result was that the importance of a correlation between sexual intimacy and feelings of love and affection was taught by the culture and assimilated by those growing up in the culture. The scale of possible positive feelings toward persons of the other sex ran from casual liking at the one end to the love that was deemed essential to and characteristic of marriage at the other. The scale of possible sexual behavior ran from brief, passionless kissing or hand-holding at the one end to sexual intercourse at the other. And the correlation between the two scales was quite precise. As a result, any act of sexual intimacy carried substantial meaning with it, and no act of sexual intimacy was simply a pleasurable set of bodily sensations. Many such acts were, of course, more pleasurable to the participants because they were a way of saying what the participants' feelings were. And sometimes they were less pleasurable for the same reason. The point is, however, that in any event sexual activity was much more than mere bodily enjoyment. It was not like eating a good meal, listening to good music, lying in the sun, or getting a pleasant back rub. It was behavior that meant a great deal concerning one's feelings for persons of the opposite sex in whom one was most interested and with whom one was most involved. It was among the most authoritative ways in which one could communicate to another the nature and degree of one's affection. . . .

An additional rationale for the prohibition on extramarital sex can now be developed. For given this way of viewing the sexual world, extramarital sex will almost always involve deception of a deeper sort. If the adulterous spouse does not in fact have the appropriate feelings of affection for the extramarital partner, then the adulterous spouse is deceiving that person about the presence of such feelings. If, on the other hand, the adulterous spouse does have the corresponding feelings for the extramarital partner but not toward the nonparticipating spouse, the adulterous spouse is very probably deceiving the nonparticipating spouse about the presence of such feelings toward that spouse. Indeed, it might be argued, whenever there is no longer love between the two persons who are married to each other, there is deception just because being married implies both to the participants and to the world that such a bond exists. Deception is inevitable, the argument might conclude, because the feelings of affection that ought to accompany any act of sexual intercourse can only be held toward one other person at any given time in one's life. And if this is so, then the adulterous spouse always deceives either the partner in adultery or the nonparticipating spouse about the existence of such feelings. Thus extramarital sex involves deception of this sort and is for this reason immoral even if no deception *vis-à-vis* the occurrence of the act of adultery takes place.

What might be said in response to the foregoing arguments? The first thing that might be said is that the account of the connection between sexual intimacy and feelings of affection is inaccurate. Not inaccurate in the sense that no one thinks of things that way, but in the sense that there is substantially more divergence of opinion than that account suggests. For example, the view I have delineated may describe reasonably accurately the concepts of the sexual world in which I grew up, but it does not capture the sexual *weltanschauung* of today's youth at all. Thus, whether or not adultery implies deception in respect to feelings depends very much on the persons who are involved and the way they look at the "meaning" of sexual intimacy.

Second, the argument leaves to be answered the question of whether it is desirable for sexual intimacy to carry the sorts of messages described above. For those persons for whom sex does have these implications, there are special feelings and sensibilities that must be taken into account. But it is another question entirely whether any valuable end—moral or otherwise—is served by investing sexual behavior with such significance. That is something that must be shown and not just assumed. It might, for instance, be the case that substantially more good than harm would come from a kind of demystification of sexual behavior: one that would encourage the enjoyment of sex more for its own sake and one that would reject the centrality both of the association of sex with love and of love with only one other person.

I regard these as two of the more difficult, unresolved issues that our culture faces today in respect to thinking sensibly about the attitudes toward sex and love that we should try to develop in ourselves and in our children. Much of the contemporary literature that advocates sexual liberation of one sort or another embraces one or the other of two different views about the relationship between sex and love.

One view holds that sex should be separated from love and affection. To be sure sex is probably better when the partners genuinely like and enjoy each other. But sex is basically an intensive, exciting sensuous activity that can be enjoyed in a variety of suitable settings with a variety of suitable partners. The situation in respect to sexual pleasure is no different from that of the person who knows and appreciates fine food and who can have a very satisfying meal in any number of good restaurants with any number of congenial companions. One question that must be settled here is whether sex can be so demystified; another, more important question is whether it would be desirable to do so. What would we gain and what might we lose if we all lived in a world in which an act of sexual intercourse was no more or less significant or enjoyable than having a delicious meal in a nice setting with a good friend? The answer to this question lies beyond the scope of this paper.

The second view seeks to drive the wedge in a different place. It is not the link between sex and love that needs to be broken; rather, on this view, it is the connection between love and exclusivity that ought to be severed. For a number of the reasons already given, it is desirable, so this argument goes, that sexual intimacy continue to be reserved to and shared with only those for whom one has very great affection. The mistake lies in thinking that any "normal" adult will only have those feelings toward one other adult during his or her lifetime—or even at any time in his or her life. It is the concept of adult love, not ideas about sex, that, on this view, needs demystification. What are thought to be both unrealistic and unfortunate are the notions of exclusivity and possessiveness that attach to the dominant conception of love between adults in our and other cultures. Parents of four, five, six, or even ten children can certainly claim and sometimes claim correctly that they love all of their children, that they love them all equally, and that it is simply untrue to their feelings to insist that the numbers involved diminish either the quantity or the quality of their love. If this is an idea that is readily understandable in the case of parents and children, there is no necessary reason why it is an impossible or undesirable ideal in the case of adults. To be sure, there is probably a limit to the number of intimate, "primary" relationships that any person can maintain at any given time without the quality of the relationship being affected. But one adult ought surely be able to love two, three, or even six other adults at any one time without that love being different in kind or degree from that of the traditional, monogamous, lifetime marriage. And as between the individuals in these relationships, whether within a marriage or without, sexual intimacy is fitting and good.

The issues raised by a position such as this one are also surely worth exploring in detail and with care. Is there something to be called "sexual love" which is different from parental love or the non-sexual love of close friends? Is there something about love in general that links it naturally and appropriately with feelings of exclusivity and possession? Or is there something about sexual love, whatever that may be, that makes these feelings especially fitting here? Once again the issues are conceptual, empirical, and normative all at once: What is love? How could it be different? Would it be a good thing or a bad thing if it were different?

Suppose, though, that having delineated these problems we were now to pass them by. Suppose, moreover, we were to be persuaded of the possibility and the desirability of weakening substantially either the links between sex and love or the links between sexual love and exclusivity. Would it not then be the case that adultery could be free from all of the morally objectionable features described so far? To be more specific, let us imagine that a husband and wife have what is today sometimes characterized as an "open marriage." Suppose, that is, that they have agreed in advance that extramarital sex is—under certain circumstances—acceptable behavior for each to engage in. Suppose that as a result, there is no impulse to deceive each other about the occurrence or nature of any such relationships, and that no deception in fact occurs. Suppose, too, that there is no deception in respect to the feelings involved between the adulterous spouse and the extramarital partner. And suppose, finally, that one or the other or both of the spouses then has sexual intercourse in circumstances consistent with these understandings. Under this description, so the agreement might conclude, adultery is simply not immoral. At a minimum, adultery cannot very plausibly be condemned either on the ground that it involves deception or on the ground that it requires the breaking of a promise.

At least two responses are worth considering. One calls attention to the connection between marriage and adultery; the other looks to more instrumental arguments for the immorality of adultery. Both issues deserve further exploration.

One way to deal with the case of the "open marriage" is to question whether the two persons involved are still properly to be described as being married to each other. Part of the meaning of what it is for two persons to be married to each other, so this argument would go, is to have committed oneself to have sexual relationships only with one's spouse. Of course, it would be added, we know that that commitment is not always honored. We know that persons who are married to each other often do commit adultery. But there is a difference between being willing to make a commitment to marital fidelity, even though one may fail to honor that commitment, and not making the commitment at all. Whatever the relationship may be between the two individuals in the case described above, the absence of any commitment to sexual exclusivity requires the conclusion that their relationship is not a marital one. For a commitment to sexual exclusivity is a necessary although not a sufficient condition for the existence of a marriage.

Although there may be something to this suggestion, as it is stated it is too strong to be acceptable. To begin with, I think it is very doubtful that there are many, if any, *necessary* conditions for marriage; but even if there are, a commitment to sexual exclusivity is not such a condition.

To see that this is so, consider what might be taken to be some of the essential characteristics of a marriage. We might be tempted to propose that the concept of marriage requires the following: a formal ceremony of some sort in which mutual obligations are undertaken between two persons of the opposite sex; the capacity on the part of the persons involved to have sexual intercourse with each other; the willingness to have sexual intercourse only with each other; and feelings of love and affection between the two persons. The problem is that we can imagine relationships that are clearly marital and yet lack one or more of these features. For example, in our own society, it is possible for two persons to be married without going through a formal ceremony, as in the common-law marriages recognized in some jurisdictions. It is also possible for two persons to get married even though one or both lack the capacity to engage in sexual intercourse. Thus, two very elderly persons who have neither the desire nor the ability to have intercourse can, nonetheless, get married, as can persons whose sexual organs have been injured so that intercourse is not possible. And we certainly know of marriages in which love was not present at the time of the marriage, as, for instance, in marriages of state and marriages of convenience.

Counterexamples not satisfying the condition relating to the abstention from extramarital sex are even more easily produced. We certainly know of societies and cultures in which polygamy and polyandry are practiced, and we have no difficulty in recognizing these relationships as cases of marriages. It might be objected, though, that these are not counterexamples because they are plural marriages rather than marriages in which sex is permitted with someone other than with one of the persons to whom one is married. But we also know of societies in which it is permissible for married persons to have sexual relationships with persons to whom they [are] not married, for example, temple prostitutes, concubines, and homosexual lovers. And even if we knew of no such societies, the conceptual claim would still, I submit, not be well taken. For suppose all of the other indicia of marriage were present: suppose the two persons were of the opposite sex. Suppose they had the capacity and desire to have intercourse with each other, suppose they participated in a formal ceremony in which they understood themselves voluntarily to be entering into a relationship with each other in which substantial mutual commitments were assumed. If all these conditions were satisfied, we would not be in any doubt about whether or not the two persons were married even though they had not taken on a commitment of sexual exclusivity and even though they had expressly agreed that extramarital sexual intercourse was a permissible behavior for each to engage in.

A commitment to sexual exclusivity is neither a necessary nor a sufficient condition for the existence of a marriage. . . .

The remaining argument that I wish to consider—as I indicated earlier—is a more instrumental one. It seeks to justify the prohibition by virtue of the role that it plays in the development and maintenance of nuclear families. The argument, or set of arguments, might, I believe, go something like this.

Consider first a farfetched nonsexual example. Suppose a society were organized so that after some suitable age—say, 18, 19, or 20—persons were forbidden to eat anything but bread and water with anyone but their spouse. Persons might still choose in such a society not to get married. Good food just might not be very important to them because they have underdeveloped taste buds. Or good food might be bad for them because there is something wrong with their digestive system. Or good food might be important to them, but they might decide that the enjoyment of good food would get in the way of the attainment of other things that were more important. But most persons would, I think, be led to favor marriage in part because they preferred a richer, more varied diet to one of bread and water. And they might remain married because the family was the only legitimate setting within which good food was obtainable. If it is important to have society organized so that persons will both get married and stay married, such an arrangement would be well suited to the preservation of the family, and the prohibitions relating to food consumption could be understood as fulfilling that function.

It is obvious that one of the more powerful human desires is the desire for sexual gratification. The desire is a natural one, like hunger and thirst, in the sense that it need not be learned in order to be present within us and operative upon us. But there is in addition much that we do learn about what the act of sexual intercourse is like. Once we experience sexual intercourse ourselves—and in particular once we experience orgasm—we discover that it is among the most intensive, short-term pleasures of the body.

Because this is so, it is easy to see how the prohibition upon extramarital sex helps to hold marriage together. At least during that period of life when the enjoyment of sexual intercourse is one of the desirable bodily pleasures, persons will wish to enjoy those pleasures. If one consequence of being married is that one is prohibited from having sexual intercourse with anyone but one's spouse, then the spouses in a marriage are in a position to provide an important source of pleasure for each other that is unavailable to them elsewhere in the society.

The point emerges still more clearly if this rule of sexual morality is seen as of a piece with the other rules of sexual morality. When this prohibition is coupled, for example, with the prohibition on nonmarital sexual intercourse, we are presented with the inducement both to get married and to stay married. For if sexual intercourse is only legitimate within marriage, then persons seeking that gratification which is a feature of sexual intercourse are furnished explicit social directions for its attainment, namely marriage.

Nor, to continue the argument, is it necessary to focus exclusively on the bodily enjoyment that is involved. Orgasm may be a significant part of what there is to sexual intercourse, but it is not the whole of it. We need only recall the earlier discussion of the meaning that sexual intimacy has in our own culture to begin to see some of the more intricate ways in which sexual exclusivity may be connected with the establishment and maintenance of marriage as the primary heterosexual, love relationship. Adultery is wrong, in other words, because a prohibition on extramarital sex is a way to help maintain the institutions of marriage and the nuclear family.

Now I am frankly not sure what we are to say about an argument such as this one. What I am convinced of is that, like the arguments discussed earlier, this one also reveals something of the difficulty and complexity of the issues that are involved. So, what I want now to do—in the brief and final portion of this paper—is to try to delineate with reasonable precision what I take several of the fundamental, unresolved issues to be.

The first is whether this last argument is an argument for the *immorality* of extramarital sexual intercourse. What does seem clear is that there are differences between this argument and the ones considered earlier. The earlier arguments condemned adulterous behavior because it was

behavior that involved breaking of a promise, taking unfair advantage, or deceiving another. To the degree to which the prohibition on extramarital sex can be supported by arguments which invoke considerations such as these, there is little question but that violations of the prohibition are properly regarded as immoral. And such a claim could be defended on one or both of two distinct grounds. The first is that things like promise-breaking and deception are just wrong. The second is that adultery involving promise-breaking or deception is wrong because it involves the straightforward infliction of harm on another human being—typically the nonadulterous spouse—who has a strong claim not to have that harm so inflicted.

The argument that connects the prohibition on extramarital sex with the maintenance and preservation of the institution of marriage is an argument for the instrumental value of the prohibition. To some degree this counts, I think, against regarding all violations of the prohibition as obvious cases of immorality. This is so partly because hypothetical imperatives are less clearly within the domain of morality than are categorical ones, and even more because instrumental prohibitions are within the domain of morality only if the end they serve or the way they serve it is itself within the domain of morality.

What this should help us see, I think, is the fact that the argument that connects the prohibition on adultery with the preservation of marriage is at best seriously incomplete. Before we ought to be convinced by it, we ought to have reasons for believing that marriage is a morally desirable and just social institution. And this is not quite as easy or obvious a task as it may seem to be. For the concept of marriage is, as we have seen, both a loosely structured and a complicated one. There may be all sorts of intimate, interpersonal relationships which will resemble but not be identical with the typical marriage relationship presupposed by the traditional sexual morality. There may be a number of distinguishable sexual and loving arrangements which can all legitimately claim to be called *marriages*. The prohibitions of the traditional sexual morality may be effective ways to maintain some marriages and ineffective ways to promote and preserve others. The prohibitions of the traditional sexual morality may make good psychological sense if certain psychological theories are true, and they may be purveyors of immense psychological mischief if other psychological theories are true. The prohibitions of the traditional sexual morality may seem obviously correct if sexual intimacy carries the meaning that the dominant culture has often ascribed to it, and they may seem equally bizarre when sex is viewed through the perspective of the counterculture. Irrespective of whether instrumental arguments of this sort are properly deemed moral arguments, they ought not to fully convince anyone until questions like these are answered.

# 50   Markets in Women's Sexual Labor

## DEBRA SATZ

I will argue that the most plausible support for the thesis [that treating sexual capacities as commodities is worse than treating our other capacities as commodities] stems from the role of commercialized sex in sustaining a social world in which women form a subordinated group. Prostitution is wrong insofar as the sale of women's sexual labor reinforces broad patterns of sex discrimination. I argue that contemporary prostitution contributes to, and also instantiates, the perception of women as socially inferior to men. . . .

## Who Is a Prostitute?

While much has been written on the history of prostitution, and some empirical studies of prostitutes themselves have been undertaken, the few philosophers writing on this subject have tended to treat prostitution as if the term referred to something as obvious as "table." But it does not. Not only is it hard to draw a sharp line between prostitution and practices which look like prostitution, but as historians of the subject have emphasized, prostitution today is also a very different phenomenon from earlier forms of commercial sex. In particular, the idea of prostitution as a specialized

occupation of an outcast and stigmatized group is of relatively recent origin.

While all contemporary prostitutes are stigmatized as outsiders, prostitution itself has an internal hierarchy based on class, race, and gender. The majority of prostitutes—and all those who walk the streets—are poor. The majority of streetwalkers in the United States are poor black women. These women are a world apart from prostitution's upper tier. Consider three cases: a streetwalker in Boston, a call girl on Park Avenue, and a male prostitute in San Francisco's tenderloin district. In what way do these three lives resemble one another? Consider the three cases:

1. A fourteen-year-old girl prostitutes herself to support her boyfriend's heroin addiction. Later, she works the streets to support her own habit. She begins, like most teenage streetwalkers, to rely on a pimp for protection. She is uneducated and is frequently subjected to violence in her relationships and with her customers. She also receives no social security, no sick leave or maternity leave, and—most important—no control as to whether or not she has sex with a man. The latter is decided by her pimp.

2. Now imagine the life of a Park Avenue call girl. Many call girls drift into prostitution after "run of the mill promiscuity," led neither by material want nor lack of alternatives.[1] Some are young college graduates, who upon graduation earn money by prostitution while searching for other

Reprinted with permission of the publisher, University of Chicago Press, from *Ethics,* 106 (1995), 63–85, with omissions.

jobs. Call girls can earn between $30,000 and $100,000 annually. These women have control over the entire amount they earn as well as an unusual degree of independence, far greater than in most other forms of work. They can also decide whom they wish to have sex with and when they wish to do so.[2] There is little resemblance between their lives and that of the Boston street-walker.

3. Finally, consider the increasing number of male prostitutes. Most male prostitutes (but not all) sell sex to other men. Often the men who buy such sex are themselves married. Unfortunately, there is little information on male prostitutes; it has not been well studied as either a historical or a contemporary phenomenon. What we do know suggests that like their female counterparts, male prostitutes cover the economic spectrum. Two important differences between male and female prostitutes are that men are more likely to work only part time and that they are not generally subject to the violence of male pimps; they tend to work on their own.

Are these three cases distinct? Many critics of prostitution have assumed that all prostitutes were women who entered the practice under circumstances which included abuse and economic desperation. But that is a false assumption: the critics have mistaken a part of the practice for the whole.[3] For example, although women who walk the streets are the most visible, they constitute only about 20 percent of the prostitute population in the United States.[4]

The varying circumstances of prostitution are important because they force us to consider carefully what we think may be wrong with prostitution. For example, in the first case, the factors which seem crucial to our response of condemnation are the miserable background conditions, the prostitute's vulnerability to violence at the hands of her pimp or client, her age, and her lack of control over whether she has sex with a client. These conditions could be redressed through regulation without forbidding commercial sexual exchanges between consenting adults.[5] The second class of prostitution stands in sharp contrast. These women engage in what seems to be a voluntary activity, chosen among a range of decent alternatives. Many of these women sell their sexual capacities without coercion or regret. The third case rebuts arguments that prostitution has no other purpose than to subordinate women.

In the next section, I explore three alternative explanations of prostitution's wrongness, which I refer to respectively as economic, essentialist, and egalitarian.

## What Is Wrong with Prostitution?

. . .

### The Essentialist Approach

Essentialists hold that there is some intrinsic property of sex which makes its commodification wrong. Specific arguments differ, however, in what they take this property to be. I will consider two popular versions of essentialism: the first stresses the close connection between sex and the self; the second stresses the close connection between sex and human flourishing.

Some feminist critics of prostitution have argued that sexual and reproductive capacities are more crucially tied to the nature of our selves than our other capacities.[6] The sale of sex is taken to cut deeper into the self, to involve a more total alienation from the self. As Carole Pateman puts it, "When a prostitute contracts out use of her body she is thus selling *herself* in a very real sense. Women's selves are involved in prostitution in a different manner from the involvement of the self in other occupations."[7] The realization of women's selfhood requires, on this view, that some of the capacities embodied in their persons, including their sexuality, remain "market-inalienable."

Consider an analogous strategy for accounting for the value of bodily integrity in terms of its relationship to our personhood. It seems right to say that a world in which the boundaries of our bodies were not (more or less) secure would be a world in which our sense of self would be fundamentally shaken. Damage to, and violation of, our bodies affects us in a "deeper" way, a more significant way, than damage to our external property. Robbing my body of a kidney is a violation different in kind than robbing my house of a stereo, however expensive. Distributing kidneys from healthy people to sick people through a lottery is a far different act than using a lottery to distribute door prizes.[8]

But this analogy can only be the first step in an argument in favor of treating either our organs or sexual capacities as market-inalienable. Most liberals think that individual sovereignty over mind and body is crucial for the exercise of fundamental liberties. Thus, in the absence of clear harms, most liberals would reject legal bans on voluntary sales of body parts or sexual capacities. Indeed, the usual justification of such bans is harm to self: such sales are presumed to be "desperate exchanges" that the individual herself would reasonably want to foreclose. American law blocks voluntary sales of individual organs and body parts but not sales of blood on the assumption that only the former sales are likely to be so harmful to the individual that given any reasonable alternative, she herself would refrain from such sales.

Whatever the plausibility of such a claim with respect to body parts, it is considerably weaker when applied to sex (or blood). There is no strong evidence that prostitution is, at least in the United States, a desperate exchange. In part this reflects the fact that the relationship people have with their sexual capacities is far more diverse than the relationship they have with their body parts. For some people, sexuality is a realm of ecstatic communion with another, for others it is little more than a sport or distraction. Some people will find consenting to be sexually used by another person enjoyable or adequately compensated by a wage. Even for the same person, sex can be the source of a range of experiences.

Of course, the point cannot simply be that, as an empirical matter, people have differing conceptions of sexuality. The critics of prostitution grant that. The point is whether, and within what range, this diversity is desirable.

Let us assume, then, in the absence of compelling counterargument, that an individual can exercise sovereignty through the sale of her sexual capacities. Margaret Radin raises a distinct worry about the effects of widespread prostitution on human flourishing. Radin's argument stresses that widespread sex markets would promote inferior forms of personhood. She says that we can see this is the case if we "reflect on what we know now about human life and choose the best from among the conceptions available to us."[9] If prostitution were to become common, Radin argues, it would have adverse effects on a form of personhood which itself is intrinsically valuable. For example, if the signs of affection and intimacy were frequently detached from their usual meaning, such signs might well become more ambiguous and easy to manipulate. The marks of an intimate relationship (physical intimacy, terms of endearment, etc.) would no longer signal the existence of intimacy. In that case, by obscuring the nature of sexual relationships, prostitution might undermine our ability to apply the criteria for coercion and informational failure. Individuals might more easily enter into damaging relationships and lead less fulfilling lives as a result.

Radin is committed to a form of perfectionism which rules out the social practice of prostitution as incompatible with the highest forms of human development and flourishing. But why should perfectionists condemn prostitution while tolerating practices such as monotonous assembly line work where human beings are often mere appendages to machines? Monotonous wage labor, moreover, is far more widespread than prostitution. Can a consistent perfectionist give reasons for differentiating sexual markets from other labor markets?

It is difficult to draw a line between our various capacities such that only sexual and reproductive capacities are essential to the flourishing self. In a money economy like our own, we each sell the use of many human capacities. Writers sell the use of their ability to write, advertisers sell the use of their ability to write jingles, and musicians sell the use of their ability to write and perform symphonies. Aren't these capacities also closely tied to our personhood and its higher capacities? Yet the mere alienation of the use of these capacities, even when widespread, does not seem to threaten personal flourishing.

An alternative version of the essentialist thesis views the commodification of sex as an assault on personal dignity.[10] Prostitution degrades the prostitute. Elizabeth Anderson, for example, discusses the effect of commodification on the nature of sex as a shared good, based on the recognition of mutual attraction. In commercial sex, each party now values the other only instrumentally, not intrinsically. And, while both parties are thus prevented from enjoying a shared good, it is worse for the prostitute. The customer merely surrenders a certain amount of cash; the prostitute cedes her body: the prostitute is thus degraded to the status of a thing. Call this the degradation objection.

I share the intuition that the failure to treat others as persons is morally significant; it is wrong to treat people as mere things. But I am skeptical as to whether this intuition supports the conclusion that prostitution is wrong. Consider the contrast between slavery and prostitution. Slavery was, in Orlando Patterson's memorable phrase, a form of "social death": it denied to enslaved individuals the ability to press claims, to be—in their own right—sources of value and interest. But the mere sale of the use of someone's capacities does not necessarily involve a failure of this kind, on the part of either the buyer or the seller. Many forms of labor, perhaps most, cede some control of a person's body to others. Such control can range from requirements to be in a certain place at a certain time (e.g., reporting to the office), to requirements that a person (e.g., a professional athlete) eat certain foods and get certain amounts of sleep, or maintain good humor in the face of the offensive behavior of others (e.g., airline stewardesses). Some control of our capacities by others does not seem to be ipso facto destructive of our dignity. Whether the purchase of a form of human labor power will have this negative consequence will depend on background social macrolevel and microlevel institutions. Minimum wages, worker participation and control, health and safety regu-

lations, maternity and paternity leave, restrictions on specific performance, and the right to "exit" one's job are all features which attenuate the objectionable aspects of treating people's labor as a mere economic input. The advocates of prostitution's wrongness in virtue of its connection to selfhood, flourishing and degradation have not shown that a system of regulated prostitution would be unable to respond to their worries. In particular, they have not established that there is something wrong with prostitution irrespective of its cultural and historical context. . . .

## The Egalitarian Approach

Women's decisions to enter into prostitution must be viewed against the background of their unequal life chances and their unequal opportunities for income and rewarding work. The extent to which women face a highly constrained range of options will surely be relevant to whether, and to what degree, we view their choices as autonomous. Some women may actually loathe or judge as inferior the lives of prostitution they "choose." Economic inequality may thus shape prostitution. . . .

Prostitution makes an important and direct contribution to women's inferior social status. Prostitution shapes and is itself shaped by custom and culture, by cultural meanings about the importance of sex, about the nature of women's sexuality and male desire.[11]

If prostitution is wrong it is because of its effects on how men perceive women and on how women perceive themselves. In our society, prostitution represents women as the sexual servants of men. It supports and embodies the widely held belief that men have strong sex drives which must be satisfied—largely through gaining access to some woman's body. This belief underlies the mistaken idea that prostitution is the "oldest" profession, since it is seen as a necessary consequence of human (i.e., male) nature. It also underlies the traditional conception of marriage, in which a man owned not only his wife's property but her body as well. It should not fail to startle us that until recently, most states did not recognize the possibility of "real rape" in marriage.[12] (Marital rape remains legal in two states: North Carolina and Oklahoma.) . . .

My suggestion is that prostitution depicts an image of gender inequality, by constituting one class of women as inferior. Prostitution is a "theater" of inequality—it displays for us a practice in which women are subordinated to men. This is especially the case where women are forcibly controlled by their (male) pimps. It follows from my conception of prostitution that it need not have such a negative effect when the prostitute is male. More research needs to be done on popular images and conceptions of gay male prostitutes, as well as on the extremely small number of male prostitutes who have women clients.

The negative image of women who participate in prostitution, the image of their inferior status, is objectionable in itself. It constitutes an important form of inequality—unequal status—based on attitudes of superiority and disrespect. Unfortunately, this form of inequality has largely been ignored by political philosophers and economists who have focused instead on inequalities in income and opportunity. Moreover, this form of inequality is not confined to prostitutes. I believe that the negative image of women prostitutes has third party effects: it shapes and influences the way women as a whole are seen. This hypothesis is, of course, an empirical one. It has not been tested largely because of the lack of studies of men who go to prostitutes. Most extant studies of prostitution examine the behavior and motivations of the women who enter into the practice, a fact which itself raises the suspicion that prostitution is viewed as "a problem about the women who are prostitutes . . . [rather than] a problem about the men who demand to buy them."[13] In these studies, male gender identity is taken as a given. . . .

I can imagine hypothetical circumstances in which prostitution would not have a negative image effect, where it could mark a reclaiming of women's sexuality. Margo St. James and other members of Call Off Your Old Tired Ethics (COYOTE) have argued that prostitutes can function as sex therapists, fulfilling a legitimate social need as well as providing a source of experiment

and alternative conceptions of sexuality and gender. I agree that in a different culture, with different assumptions about men's and women's gender identities, prostitution might not have unequalizing effects. But I think that St. James and others have minimized the cultural stereotypes that surround contemporary prostitution and their power over the shape of the practice. Prostitution, as we know it, is not separable from the larger surrounding culture which marginalizes, stereotypes, and stigmatizes women. Rather than providing an alternative conception of sexuality, I think that we need to look carefully at what men and women actually learn in prostitution. I do not believe that ethnographic studies of prostitution would support COYOTE's claim that prostitution contributes to images of women's dignity and equal standing.

If, through its negative image of women as sexual servants of men, prostitution reinforces women's inferior status in society, then it is wrong. Even though men can be and are prostitutes, I think that it is unlikely that we will find such negative image effects on men as a group. Individual men may be degraded in individual acts of prostitution: men as a group are not.

Granting all of the above, one objection to the equality approach to prostitution's wrongness remains. Is prostitution's negative image effect greater than that produced by other professions in which women largely service men, for example, secretarial labor? What is special about prostitution?

The negative image effect undoubtedly operates outside the domain of prostitution. But there are two significant differences between prostitution and other gender-segregated professions.

First, most people believe that prostitution, unlike secretarial work, is especially objectionable. Holding such moral views of prostitution constant, if prostitution continues to be primarily a female occupation, then the existence of prostitution will disproportionately fuel negative images of women.[14] Second, and relatedly, the particular image of women in prostitution is more of an image of inferiority than that of a secretary. The image embodies a greater amount of objectification, of representing the prostitute as an object without a will of her own. Prostitutes are far more likely to be victims of violence than are secretaries: as I mentioned, the mortality rate of women in prostitution is forty times that of other women. Prostitutes are also far more likely to be raped: a prostitute's "no" does not, to the male she services, mean no.

## Should Prostitution Be Legalized?

It is important to distinguish between prostitution's wrongness and the legal response that we are entitled to make to that wrongness. Even if prostitution is wrong, we may not be justified in prohibiting it if that prohibition makes the facts in virtue of which it is wrong worse, or if its costs are too great for other important values, such as autonomy and privacy. For example, even if someone accepts that the contemporary division of labor in the family is wrong, they may still reasonably object to government surveillance of the family's division of household chores.

Suppose that we accept that gender equality is a legitimate goal of social policy. The question is whether the current legal prohibition on prostitution in the United States promotes gender equality. The answer I think is that it clearly does not. The current legal policies in the United States arguably exacerbate the factors in virtue of which prostitution is wrong.

The current prohibition on prostitution renders the women who engage in the practice vulnerable. First, the participants in the practice seek assistance from pimps in lieu of the contractual and legal remedies which are denied them. Male pimps may protect women prostitutes from their customers and from the police, but the system of pimp-run prostitution has enormous negative effects on the women at the lowest rungs of prostitution. Second, prohibition of prostitution raises the dilemma of the "double bind": if we prevent prostitution without greater redistribution of income, wealth, and opportunities, we deprive poor women of one way—in some circumstances the only way—of improving their condition.[15] Analogously, we do not solve the problem of homelessness by criminalizing it.

Furthermore, women are disproportionately punished for engaging in commercial sex acts. Many state laws make it a worse crime to sell sex than to buy it. Consequently, pimps and clients ("johns") are rarely prosecuted. In some jurisdictions, patronizing a prostitute is not illegal. The record of arrests and convictions is also highly asymmetric. Ninety percent of all convicted prostitutes are women. Studies have shown that male prostitutes are arrested with less frequency than female prostitutes and receive shorter sentences. One study of the judicial processing of 2,859 male and female prostitutes found that judges were more likely to find defendants guilty if they were female.[16]

Nor does the current legal prohibition on prostitution unambiguously benefit women as a class because the cultural meaning of current governmental prohibition of prostitution is unclear. While an unrestricted regime of prostitution—a pricing system in women's sexual attributes—could have negative external consequences on women's self-perceptions and perceptions by men, state prohibition can also reflect a view of women which contributes to their inequality. For example, some people support state regulation because they believe that women's sexuality is for purposes of reproduction, a claim tied to traditional ideas about women's proper role.

There is an additional reason why banning prostitution seems an inadequate response to the problem of gender inequality . . . Banning prostitution would not by itself—does not—eliminate it. . . . No city has eliminated prostitution merely through criminalization. Instead, criminalized prostitution thrives as a black market activity in which pimps substitute for law as the mechanism for enforcing contracts. It thereby makes the lives of prostitutes worse than they might otherwise be and without clearly counteracting prostitution's largely negative image of women.

If we decide to ban prostitution, these problems must be addressed. If we decide not to ban prostitution (either by legalizing it or decriminalizing it), then we must be careful to regulate the practice to address its negative effects. Certain restrictions on advertising and recruitment will be needed in order to address the negative image effects that an unrestricted regime of prostitution would perpetuate. . . .

## Conclusion

If the arguments I have offered here are correct, then prostitution is wrong in virtue of its contributions to perpetuating a pervasive form of inequality. In different circumstances, with different assumptions about women and their role in society, I do not think that prostitution would be especially troubling—no more troubling than many other labor markets currently allowed. . . . I believe that this intuition is itself bound up with well-entrenched views of male gender identity and women's sexual role in the context of that identity. If we are troubled by prostitution, as I think we should be, then we should direct much of our energy to putting forward alternative models of egalitarian relations between men and women.

## Notes

1. John Decker, *Prostitution: Regulation and Control* (Littleton, Colo.: Rothman, 1979), p. 191.

2. Compare Harold Greenwald, *The Elegant Prostitute: A Social and Psychoanalytic Study* (New York: Walker, 1970), p. 10.

3. Compare Kathleen Barry, *Female Sexual Slavery* (New York: Avon, 1979). If we consider prostitution as an international phenomenon, then a majority of prostitutes are desperately poor and abused women. Nevertheless, there is a significant minority who are not. Furthermore, if prostitution were legalized, it is possible that the minimum condition of prostitutes in at least some countries would be raised.

4. Priscilla Alexander, "Prostitution: A Difficult Issue for Feminists," in *Sex Work: Writings by Women in the Sex Industry,* ed. P. Alexander and F. Delacoste (Pittsburgh: Cleis, 1987).

5. Moreover, to the extent that the desperate background conditions are the problem it is not apparent that outlawing prostitution is the solution. Banning prostitution may only remove a poor woman's best option: it in no way eradicates the circumstances which led her to such a choice. See M. Radin, "Market-Inalienability," *Harvard Law Review* 100 (1987): 1849–1937, on the problem of the "double bind."

6. Prostitution is, however, an issue which continues to divide feminists as well as prostitutes and former prostitutes. On the one side, some feminists see prostitution as dehumanizing and alienating and linked to male domination. This is the view taken by the prostitute organization Women Hurt in Systems of Prostitution Engaged in Revolt (WHISPER). On the other side, some feminists see sex markets as affirming a woman's right to autonomy, sexual pleasure, and economic welfare. This is the view taken by the prostitute organization COYOTE.

7. Carole Pateman, *The Sexual Contract* (Stanford, Calif.: Stanford University Press, 1988), p. 207; emphasis added.

8. J. Harris, "The Survival Lottery," *Philosophy* 50 (1975): 81–87.

9. Radin, p. 1884.

10. Elizabeth Anderson, *Value in Ethics and Economics* (Cambridge, Mass.: Harvard University Press, 1993), p. 45.

11. Shrage ("Should Feminists Oppose Prostitution?") argues that prostitution perpetuates the following beliefs which oppress women: (1) the universal possession of a potent sex drive; (2) the "natural" dominance of men; (3) the pollution of women by sexual contact; and (4) the reification of sexual practice.

12. Susan Estrich, *Real Rape* (Cambridge, Mass.: Harvard University Press, 1987).

13. Carole Pateman, "Defending Prostitution: Charges against Ericsson," *Ethics* 93 (1983): 561–65, p. 563.

14. I owe this point to Arthur Kuflik.

15. Radin, pp. 1915 ff.

16. J. Lindquist et al., "Judicial Processing of Males and Females Charged with Prostitution," *Journal of Criminal Justice* 17 (1989): 277–91. Several state laws banning prostitution have been challenged on equal protection grounds. These statistics support the idea that prostitution's negative image effect has disproportionate bearing on male and female prostitutes.

# 51   What's Wrong with Prostitution?

**IGOR PRIMORATZ**

Over the last three decades the sexual morality of many Western societies has changed beyond recognition. Most of the prohibitions which made up the traditional, extremely restrictive outlook on sex that reigned supreme until the fifties—the prohibitions of masturbation, pre-marital and extra-marital sex, promiscuity, homosexuality—are no longer seen as very serious or stringent or, indeed, as binding at all. But one or two traditional prohibitions are still with us. The moral ban on prostitution, in particular, does not seem to have been repealed or radically mitigated. To be sure, some of the old arguments against prostitution are hardly ever brought up these days; but then, several new ones are quite popular, at least in certain circles. Prostitution is no longer seen as the most extreme moral depravity a woman is capable of; but the view that it is at least seriously morally flawed, if not repugnant and intolerable, is still widely held. In this paper I want to look into some of the main arguments in support of this view and try to show that none of them is convincing.[1]

## 1. Positive Morality

The morality of this society and of most other societies today condemns prostitution in no uncertain terms; the facts of the condemnation and its various, sometimes quite serious and far-reaching consequences for those who practice it, are too well known to need to be recounted here. But what do these facts prove? Surely not that prostitution *is* wrong, only that positive morality of this and many other societies *deems it* wrong.

## 2. Paternalism

One can argue that the wrongness of doing something follows from the fact that doing it has serious

From *Philosophy,* 68 (1993), 159–182 with omissions. Reprinted with the permission of Cambridge University Press.

adverse effects on the welfare, good, etc. of the agent and, having made that judgment, to exert the pressure of the moral sanction on the individuals concerned to get them to refrain from doing it. A popular way of arguing against prostitution is of this sort: it refers to such hazards of selling sex as (i) venereal diseases; (ii) unpleasant, humiliating, even violent behaviour of clients; (iii) exploitation by madams and pimps; (iv) the extremely low social status of prostitutes and the contempt and ostracism to which they are exposed. The facts showing that these are, indeed, the hazards of prostitution are well known; are they not enough to show that prostitution is bad and to be avoided?

A short way with this objection is to refuse to acknowledge the moral credentials of paternalism, and to say that what we have here is merely a prudential, not a moral, argument against prostitution.

However, we may decide to accept that paternalist considerations can be relevant to questions about what is morally right and wrong. In that case, the first thing to note about the paternalist argument is that it is an argument from *occupational* hazards and thus, if valid, valid only against prostitution as an *occupation*. For in addition to the professional prostitute, whose sole livelihood comes from mercenary sex, there is also the amateur, who is usually gainfully employed or married and engages in prostitution for additional income. The latter—also known as the secret prostitute—need not at all suffer from (iii) and (iv), and stands a much lower chance of being exposed to (i) and (ii). A reference to (iii) actually is not even an argument against professional prostitution, but merely against a particular, by no means necessary way of practicing it; if a professional prostitute is likely to be exploited by a madam or pimp, then she should pursue the trade on her own.

But it is more important to note that the crucial, although indirect, cause of all these hazards of professional prostitution is the negative attitude of society, the condemnation of prostitution by its morality and its laws. But for that, the prostitute could enjoy much better medical protection, much more effective police protection from abusive and aggressive behavior of clients and legal protection from exploitation by pimps and madams, and her social status would be quite different. Thus the paternalist argument takes for granted the conventional moral condemnation of prostitution, and merely gives an additional reason for not engaging in something that has already been established as wrong. But we can and should refuse to take that for granted, because we can and should refuse to submit to positive morality as the arbiter of moral issues. If we do so, and if a good case for morally condemning commercial sex has still not been made out, as I am trying to show in this paper, then all these hazards should be seen as reasons for trying to disabuse society of the prejudices against it and help to change the law and social conditions in general in which prostitutes work, in order radically to reduce, if not completely eliminate, such hazards.

However, there is one occupational hazard that has not been mentioned so far: one that cannot be blamed on unenlightened social morality, and would remain even if society were to treat prostitution as any other legitimate occupation. That is the danger to the sex life of the prostitute. As Lars Ericsson neatly puts it, "Can one have a well-functioning sexual life if sex is what one lives by?"[2]

One way of tackling this particular paternalist objection is to say, with David A. J. Richards, that perhaps one can. Richards claims that there is no evidence that prostitution makes it impossible for those who practice it to have loving relationships, and adds that "there is some evidence that prostitutes, as a class, are more sexually fulfilled than other American women."[3] The last claim is based on a study in which 175 prostitutes were systematically interviewed, and which showed that "they experienced orgasm and multiple orgasm more frequently in their personal, 'non-commercial' intercourse than did the normal woman (as defined by Kinsey norms)."[4] Another, probably safer response is to point out, as Ericsson does, that the question is an empirical one and that, since there is no conclusive evidence either way, we are not in a position to draw any conclusion.[5]

My preferred response is different. I would rather grant the empirical claim that a life of prostitution is liable to wreck one's sex life, i.e. the minor premise of the argument, and then look a bit more closely into the major premise, the principle of paternalism. For there are two rather different versions of that principle. The weak version prevents the individual from acting on a choice that is not fully voluntary, either because the individual is permanently incompetent or because the choice in question is a result of ignorance of some important facts or made under extreme psychological or social pressure. Otherwise the individual is considered the sole qualified judge of his or her own welfare, good, happiness, needs, interests and values, and the choice is ultimately his or hers. Moreover, when a usually competent individual is prevented from acting on a choice that is either uninformed or made under extreme pressure, and is therefore not fully voluntary, that individual will, when the choice-impairing conditions no longer obtain, agree that the paternalist interference was appropriate and legitimate, and perhaps even be grateful for it. Strong paternalism *is* meant to protect the individual from his or her voluntary choices, and therefore will not be legitimized by retrospective consent of the individual paternalized. The assumption is not that the individual is normally the proper judge of his or her own welfare, good, etc., but rather that someone else knows better where the individual's true welfare, good, etc. lie, and therefore has the right to force the individual to act in accordance with the latter, even though that means acting against his or her fully voluntary choice, which is said to be merely "subjective" or "arbitrary." Obviously, the weak version of paternalism does not conflict with personal liberty, but should rather be seen as its corollary; for it does not protect the individual from choices that express his or her considered preferences and settled values, but only against his or her "non-voluntary choices," choices the individual will subsequently disavow. Strong paternalism, on the other hand, is essentially opposed to individual liberty, and cannot be accepted by anyone who takes liberty seriously. Such paternalism smacks of intellectual and moral arrogance, and it is hard to see how it could ever be established by rational argument.[6]

Accordingly, if the argument from the dangers to the prostitute's sex life is not to be made rather implausible from the start, it ought to be put forward in terms of weak rather than strong paternalism. When put in these terms, however, it is not really an argument that prostitution is wrong because imprudent, but rather that it is wrong if and when it is taken up imprudently. It reminds us that persons permanently incompetent and those who still have not reached the age of consent should not (be allowed to) take up the life of prostitution and thereby most likely throw away the prospect of a good sex life. (They should not (be allowed to) become prostitutes for other reasons anyway.) As for a competent adult, the only legitimate paternalist interference with the choice of such a person to become a prostitute is to make sure that the choice is a free and informed one. But if an adult and sane person is fully apprised of the dangers of prostitution to the sex life of the prostitute and decides, without undue pressure of any sort, that the advantages of prostitution as an occupation are worth it, then it is neither imprudent nor wrong for that person to embark on the line of work chosen.[7] In such a case, as Mill put it, "neither one person, nor any number of persons, is warranted in saying to another human creature of ripe years that he shall not do with his life for his own benefit what he chooses to do with it."[8]

## 3. Some Things Just Are Not for Sale

In the eyes of many, by far the best argument against prostitution is brief and simple: some things just are not for sale, and sex is one of them.

[Consider] two views of sex that are both historically and theoretically different: the traditional view, which originated in religion, that sex is legitimate only within marriage and as a means to procreation, and the more modern, secular, "romantic" view that sex is to be valued only when it expresses and enhances a loving relationship. Let me look briefly into these two views in order to see whether a commitment to either does, indeed, commit one to favoring a ban on prostitution.

The first views sex as intrinsically inferior, sinful and shameful, and accepts it only when, and in so far as, it serves an important extrinsic purpose which cannot be attained by any other means: procreation. Moreover, the only proper framework for bringing up children is marriage; therefore sex is permissible only within marriage. These two statements make up the core of the traditional Christian understanding of sex, elaborated in the writings of St. Augustine and St. Thomas Aquinas, which has been by far the most important source of Western sexual ethics.

Do those who are committed to this view of sex—and in contemporary Western societies, I suppose, only practicing Catholics are—have to endorse the ban on prostitution? At a certain level, they obviously must think ill of it. . . .

But then, even the legitimacy of marital and procreative sex is of a rather low order: as sex, it is intrinsically problematic; as marital and procreative, it is accepted as a necessary evil, an inevitable concession to fallen human nature. As St. Augustine says, "any friend of wisdom and holy joys who lives a married life" would surely prefer to beget children without "the lust that excites the indecent parts of the body," if it only were possible.[9] Therefore, if it turns out that accepting sex within marriage and for the purpose of procreation only is not concession enough, that human sexuality is so strong and unruly that it cannot be confined within these bounds and that attempts to confine it actually endanger the institution of marriage itself, the inevitable conclusion will be that further concession is in order. That is just the conclusion reached by many authors with regard to prostitution: it should be tolerated, for it provides a safety valve for a force which will otherwise subvert the institution of marriage and destroy all the chastity and decency this institution makes possible. My favorite quotation is from Mandeville, who, of course, sees that as but another instance of the general truth that private vices are public benefits:

If Courtezans and Strumpets were to be prosecuted with as much Rigour as some silly people would have it, what Locks or Bars would be sufficient to preserve the Honour of our Wives and Daughters? For 'tis not only that the Women in general would meet with far greater Temptations, and the Attempts to ensnare the Innocence of Virgins would seem more excusable to the sober part of Mankind than they do now: But some Men would grow outrageous, and Ravishing would become a common Crime. Where six or seven Thousand Sailors arrive at once, as it often happens at *Amsterdam,* that have seen none but their own Sex for many Months together, how is it to be suppos'd that honest Women should walk the Streets unmolested, if there were no Harlots to be had at reasonable Prices? . . . There is a Necessity of sacrificing one part of Womankind to preserve the other, and prevent a Filthiness of a more heinous Nature.[10]

That prostitution is indispensable for the stability and the very survival of marriage has not been pointed out only by cynics like Mandeville, misanthropes like Schopenhauer,[11] or godless rationalists like Lecky[12] and Russell;[13] it was acknowledged as a fact, and as one that entails that prostitution ought to be tolerated rather than suppressed, by St. Augustine and St. Thomas themselves.[14] Moreover, it has been confirmed by sociological study of human sexual behavior, which shows that the majority of clients of prostitutes are married men who do not find complete sexual fulfillment within marriage, but are content to stay married provided they can have extramarital commercial sex as well.[15] Accordingly, even if one adopts the most conservative and restrictive view of sex there is, the view which ties sex to marriage and procreation, one need not, indeed should not, condemn prostitution too severely. One should rather take a tolerant attitude to it, knowing that it is twice removed from the ideal state of affairs, but that its demise would bring about something incomparably worse.

Another view which would seem to call for the condemnation of prostitution is the "romantic" view of sex as essentially tied to love; for mercenary sex is normally as loveless as sex can ever get. The important thing to note is that whatever unfavorable judgment on prostitution is suggested by this view of sex, it will not be a judgment unfavorable to prostitution as such, but rather to prostitution as a type of loveless sex. It is the lovelessness, not the commercial nature of the practice that the "romantic" objects to.

One response to this kind of objection would be to take on squarely the view of sex that generates it. One could, first, take a critical look at the arguments advanced in support of the view that sex should always be bound up with love; second, bring out the difficulties of the linkage, the tensions between love and sex which seem to make a stable and fruitful combination of the two rather unlikely; finally, argue for the superiority of loveless, noncommittal, "plain sex" over sex that is bound up with love. All this has already been done by philosophers such as Alan Goldman and Russell Vannoy,[16] and probably by innumerable non-philosophers as well.

Another response would be to grant the validity of the "romantic" view of sex, but only as a personal ideal, not a universally binding moral standard. This is the tack taken by Richards,[17] who points out that it would be signally misguided, indeed absurd, to try to enforce this particular ideal, based as it is "on the cultivation of spontaneous romantic feeling."[18] My preferred response to the "romantic" objection is along these lines, but I would like to go a bit further, and emphasize that it is possible to appreciate the "romantic" ideal and at the same time not only grant that sex which falls short of it need not be wrong, but also allow that it can be positively good (without going as far as to claim that it is actually better than sex with love).

The "romantic" typically points out the difference between sex with and without love. The former is a distinctively human, complex, rich and fruitful experience, and a matter of great importance; the latter is merely casual, a one-dimensional, barren experience that satisfies only for a short while and belongs to our animal nature. These differences are taken to show that sex with love is valuable, while loveless sex is not. This kind of reasoning has the following structure:

A is much better than B.
Therefore, B is no good at all.

In addition to being logically flawed, this line of reasoning, if it were to be applied in areas other than sex, would prove quite difficult to follow. For one thing, all but the very rich among us would die of hunger; for only the very rich can afford to take *all* their meals at the fanciest restaurants.[19]

Of course, B can be good, even if it is much less good than A. Loveless sex is a case in point. Moreover, other things being equal, it is better to be able to enjoy both loving and loveless sex than only the former. A person who enjoyed sex as part of loving relationships but was completely incapable of enjoying plain sex would seem to be missing out on something. To be sure, the "romantic" rejection of plain sex often includes the claim that other things are not equal: that a person who indulges in plain sex thereby somehow damages, and ultimately destroys, his or her capacity for experiencing sex as an integral part of a loving relationship. This is a straightforward empirical claim about human psychology; and it is clearly false.

All this has to do with plain sex in general, rather than with its mercenary variety in particular. That is due to the general character of the "romantic" objection to prostitution: prostitution is seen as flawed not on account of its commercial nature, but rather because it has nothing to do with love. Accordingly, as far as the "romantic" view of sex is concerned, by exonerating plain sex, one also exonerates its commercial variety.

## 4. The Feminist Critique (a): Degradation of Women

In this section and the next I deal with what I have termed the "feminist" objections to prostitution. This should not be taken to suggest that these objections are put forward only by feminists, nor that they are shared by all feminists. . . .

*Just why* should prostitution be considered degrading? There are four main answers: (i) because it is utterly impersonal; (ii) because the prostitute is reduced to a mere means; (iii) because of the intimate nature of the acts she performs for money; (iv) because she actually sells her body, herself. Let me look into each of these claims in turn.

(i) Prostitution is degrading because the relation between the prostitute and the client is com-

pletely impersonal. The client does not even perceive, let alone treat, the prostitute as the person she is; he has no interest, no time for any of her personal characteristics, but relates to her merely as a source of sexual satisfaction, nothing more than a sex object.

One possible response to this is that prostitution need not be impersonal. There is, of course, the streetwalker who sells sex to all comers (or almost); but there is also the prostitute with a limited number of steady clients, with whom she develops quite personal relationships. So if the objection is to the impersonal character of the relation, the most that can be said is that a certain kind of prostitution is degrading, not that prostitution as such is. I do not want to make much of this, though. For although in this, as in many other services, there is the option of personalized service, the other, impersonal variety is typical.

My difficulty with the argument is more basic: I cannot see why the impersonal nature of a social transaction or relation makes that transaction or relation degrading. After all, the personal relations we have with others—with our family, friends and acquaintances—are just a small part (although the most important part) of our social life. The other part includes the overwhelming majority of our social transactions and relations which are, and have to be, quite impersonal. I do not have a personal relationship with the newspaper vendor, the bus driver, the shop assistant, and all those numerous other people I interact with in the course of a single day; and, as long as the basic decencies of social intercourse (which are purely formal and impersonal) are observed, there is nothing wrong with that. There is nothing wrong for me to think of and relate to the newspaper vendor as just that and, as far as I am concerned, nothing more. . . .

(ii) Prostitution is said to degrade the prostitute because she is used as a means by the client. The client relates to the prostitute in a purely instrumental way: she is no more than a means to his sexual satisfaction. If so, is he not reducing her to a mere means, a thing, a sex object, and thereby degrading her?

If he were to rape her, that would indeed amount to treating her without regard to her desires, and thus to reducing, degrading her to a mere means. But as a customer rather than a rapist, he gets sexual satisfaction from her for a charge, on the basis of a mutual understanding, and she does her part of the bargain willingly. It is not true that he acts without regard to her desires. He does not satisfy her sexual desire; indeed, the prostitute does not desire that he should do so. But he does satisfy the one desire she has with regard to him: the desire for money. Their transaction is not "a mutual delight, entered into from the spontaneous impulse of both parties," but rather a calculated exchange of goods of different order. But it does not offend against the principle of respect for human beings as such as long as it is free from coercion and fraud, and both sides get what they want.

Most of our social transactions and relations are impersonal, and most are instrumental. There is nothing wrong with either impersonal or instrumental ways, of relating to others as such. Just as the fact that A relates to B in a completely impersonal way is not tantamount to a violation of B's personhood, B's status as a person, so the fact that A relates to B in a purely instrumental way is not equivalent to A's reducing B to a mere means. In both cases B's informed and freely given consent absolves the relation of any such charge, and thereby also of the charge of degradation.

(iii) Sex is an intimate, perhaps the most intimate, part of our lives. Should it not therefore be off limits to commercial considerations and transactions? And is it not degrading to perform something so intimate as a sex act with a complete stranger and for money?

It is not. As Ericsson points out,

we are no more justified in devaluating the prostitute, who, for example, masturbates her customers, than we are in devaluating the assistant nurse, whose job it is to take care of the intimate hygiene of disabled patients. Both help to satisfy important human needs, and both get paid for doing so. That the harlot, in distinction to the nurse, intentionally gives her client pleasure is of course nothing that should be held against her![20]

(iv) Prostitution is degrading because what the prostitute sells is not simply and innocuously a service, as it may appear to a superficial look;

actually, there is much truth in the old-fashioned way of speaking of her as a woman who "sells herself." And if *that* is not degrading, what is?

This point has been made in two different ways.

David Archard has recently argued that there is a sense in which the prostitute sells herself because of the roles and attitudes involved in the transaction:

Sexual pleasure is not . . . an innocent commodity. Always implicated in such pleasure is the performance of roles, both willing and unwilling. These roles range from the possibly benign ones of doer and done-to, through superior and subordinate to abaser and abased. Thus, when a man buys "sex" he also buys a sexual role from his partner, and this involves the prostitute in being something more than simply the neutral exchanger of some commodity.

More specifically,

if I buy (and you willingly sell) your allegiance, your obsequiousness, your flattery or your servility there is no easy distinction to be made between you as "seller" and the "good" you choose to sell. Your whole person is implicated in the exchange. So it is too with the sale of sex.[21]

However, commercial sex need not involve obsequiousness, flattery or servility, let alone allegiance, on the part of the prostitute. These attitudes, and the "role" they might be thought to make up, are not its constitutive parts; whether, when, and to what degree they characterize the transaction is an empirical question that admits of no simple and general answer. Indeed, those who, knowingly or not, tend to approach the whole subject of sex from a "romantic" point of view often say that sex with prostitutes is an impoverished, even sordid experience because of the impersonal, quick, mechanical, blunt way in which the prostitute goes about her job.

Moreover, some services that have nothing to do with sex tend to involve and are expected to involve some such attitudes on the part of the person providing the service. Examples would vary from culture to culture; the waiter and the hairdresser come to mind in ours. Now such attitudes are undoubtedly morally flawed; but that does not tell against any particular occupation in which they may be manifested, but rather against the attitudes themselves, the individuals who, perhaps unthinkingly, come to adopt them, and the social conventions that foster such attitudes.

Another way to try to show that the prostitute sells herself, rather than merely a service like any other, is to focus on the concept of self-identity. This is the tack taken by Carole Pateman. She first points out that the service provided by the prostitute is related in a much closer way to her body than is the case with any other service, for sex and sexuality are constitutive of the body, while the labor and skills hired out in other lines of work are not. "Sexuality and the body are . . . integrally connected to conceptions of femininity and masculinity, and all these are constitutive of our individuality, our sense of self-identity."[22] Therefore, when sex becomes a commodity, so do bodies and selves.

But if so, what of our ethnic identity? When asked to say who they are, do not people normally bring up their ethnic identity as one of the most important things they need to mention? If it is granted that one's ethnic identity is also constitutive of one's individuality, one's sense of self-identity, what are we to say of a person who creates an item of authentic folk art and then sells it, or of a singer who gives a concert of folk music and charges for attendance? Are they also selling themselves, and thus doing something degrading and wrong?

The likely response will be to refuse to grant our ethnic identity the same significance for our self-identity that is claimed for gender. Although people typically refer to their ethnic identity when explaining who they are, there are also many exceptions. There are individuals who used to think of themselves in such terms, but have come to repudiate, not merely their particular ethnic affiliation, but the very idea that ethnicity should be part of one's sense of who one is. There are also persons who have always felt that way (perhaps because that is how they were brought up to feel). They do not think of their own sense of self-identity as somehow incomplete, and neither should we. There are no analogous examples with regard to gender; we all think of ourselves as either men or women, and whatever particular

conception one has of one's gender, the conception is closely connected with one's sexuality. Gender is much more basic than ethnicity, much more closely related to our sense of self-identity than ethnicity and anything else that may be thought relevant.

Perhaps it is. But if that is reason enough to say that the prostitute sells her body and herself, and thus does something degrading and wrong, will not we have to say the same of the wet nurse and the surrogate mother? Their bodies and gender are no less involved in what they do than the body and gender of the prostitute; and they charge a fee, just as the prostitute does. I do not know that anybody has argued that there is something degrading, or otherwise morally wrong, in what the wet nurse does, nor that what she does is selling her body or herself, so I think she is a good counterexample to Pateman's argument.

The surrogate mother might be thought a less compelling one, for there has been considerable debate about the nature and moral standing of surrogacy. I do not need to go into all that, though. The one objection to surrogacy relevant in the present context is "that it is inconsistent with human dignity that a woman should use her uterus for financial profit and treat it as an incubator for someone else's child."[23] However, it is not explained just why it should be thought inconsistent with human dignity to do that. Indeed, it is not clear how it could be, if it is not inconsistent with human dignity that a woman should use her breasts for financial profit and treat them as a source of nourishment for someone else's child. And if it is not, why should it be inconsistent with human dignity that a woman should use her sex organs and skills for financial profit and treat them as a source of pleasure for someone else?

## 5. The Feminist Critique (b): Oppression of Women

The other main feminist objection to prostitution is that it exemplifies and helps to maintain the oppression of women. This objection is much more often made than argued. It is frequently made by quoting the words of Simone de Beauvoir that the prostitute "sums up all the forms of feminine slavery at once";[24] but de Beauvoir's chapter on prostitution, although quite good as a description of some of its main types, is short on argument and does nothing to show that prostitution as such must be implicated in the oppression of women.

An argument meant to establish that with regard to our society has recently been offered by Laurie Shrage. She expressly rejects the idea of discussing commercial sex in a "cross-cultural" or "trans-historical" way, and grants that it need not be oppressive to women in every conceivable or, indeed, every existing society. What she does claim is that in our society prostitution epitomizes and perpetuates certain basic cultural assumptions about men, women and sex which provide justification for the oppression of women in many domains of their lives, and in this way harm both prostitutes and women in general.[25]

There are four such cultural assumptions, which need not be held consciously but may be implicit in daily behavior. A strong sex drive is a universal human trait. Sexual behavior defines one's social identity, makes one a particular "kind" of person: one is "a homosexual," "a prostitute," "a loose woman." Men are "naturally" dominant. In this connection, Shrage points out that the sex industry in our society caters almost exclusively to men, and "even the relatively small number of male prostitutes at work serve a predominantly male consumer group."[26] Finally, sexual contact pollutes and harms women.

The last claim is supported by a three-pronged argument. (i) In a woman, a history of sexual activity is not taken to suggest experience in a positive sense, expertise, high-quality sex. On the contrary, it is seen as a negative mark that marks off a certain kind of woman; women are valued for their "innocence." (ii) That sex with men is damaging to women is implicit in the vulgar language used to describe the sex act: "a woman is 'fucked,' 'screwed,' 'banged,' 'had,' and so forth, and it is a man (a 'prick') who does it to her."[27] (iii) The same assumption is implicit in "the metaphors we use" for the sex act. Here Shrage draws on

Andrea Dworkin's book *Intercourse,* which invokes images of physical assault and imperialist domination and describes women having sexual intercourse with men as being not only entered or penetrated, but also "split," "invaded," "occupied" and "colonized" by men.

These cultural assumptions define the meaning of prostitution in our society. By tolerating prostitution, our society implies its acceptance of these assumptions, which legitimize and perpetuate the oppression of women and their marginality in all the main areas of social life. As for prostitutes and their clients, whatever their personal views of sex, men and women, they imply by their actions that they accept these assumptions and the practice they justify.

Now this argument is unobjectionable as far as it goes; but it does not go as far as Shrage means it to. In order to assess its real scope, we should first note that she repeatedly speaks of "our" and "our society's" toleration of prostitution, and refers to this toleration as the main ground for the conclusion that the cultural assumptions prostitution is said to epitomize in our society are indeed generally accepted in it. But toleration and acceptance are not quite the same; actually, toleration is normally defined as the putting up with something we *do not* accept. Moreover, prostitution is not tolerated at all. It is not tolerated legally: in the United States it is legal only in Nevada and illegal in all other states, while in the United Kingdom and elsewhere in the West, even though it is not against the law as such, various activities practically inseparable from it are. Some of these restrictions are quite crippling; for instance, as Marilyn G. Haft rightly says, "to legalize prostitution while prohibiting solicitation makes as much sense as encouraging free elections but prohibiting campaigning."[28] It is certainly not tolerated morally; as I pointed out at the beginning, the condemnation of prostitution is one of the very few prohibitions of the traditional sexual morality that are still with us. It is still widely held that prostitution is seriously morally wrong, and the prostitute is subjected to considerable moral pressure, including the ultimate moral sanction, ostracism from decent society. That the practice is still with us is not for want of trying to suppress it, and therefore should not be taken as a sign that it is being tolerated.

Furthermore, not all the cultural assumptions prostitution in our society allegedly epitomizes and reinforces are really generally accepted. The first two—that human beings have a strong sex drive, and that one's sexual behavior defines one's social identity—probably are. The other two assumptions—that men are "naturally" dominant, and that sex with men harms women—are more important, for they make it possible to speak of oppression of women in this context. I am not so sure about the former; my impression is that at the very least it is no longer accepted quite as widely as it used to be a couple of decades ago. And I think it is clear that the latter is not generally accepted in our society today. The evidence Shrage brings up to show that it is is far from compelling.

(i) It is probably true that the fact that a woman has a history of sexual activity is not generally appreciated as an indicator of experience and expertise, analogously to other activities. But whatever the explanation is—and one is certainly needed—I do not think that entails the other half of Shrage's diagnosis, namely that women are valued for their "innocence." That particular way of valuing women and the whole "Madonna or harlot" outlook to which it belongs are well behind us as a society, although they characterize the sexual morality of some very traditional communities. A society which has made its peace with nonmarital sex in general and adolescent sex in particular to the extent that ours has could not possibly have persisted in valuing women for their "innocence."

(ii) Shrage draws on Robert Baker's analysis of the language used to refer to men, women and sex. Baker's point of departure is the claim that the way we talk about something reflects our conception of it; he looks into the ways we talk about sex and gender in order to discover what our conceptions of these are. With regard to sexual intercourse, it turns out that the vulgar verbs used to refer to it such as "fuck," "screw," "lay," "have"

etc. display an interesting asymmetry: they require an active construction when the subject is a man, and a passive one when the subject is a woman. This reveals that we conceive of male and female roles in sex in different ways: the male is active, the female passive. Some of these verbs—"fuck," "screw," "have"—are also used metaphorically to indicate deceiving, taking advantage of, harming someone. This shows that we conceive of the male sexual role as that of harming the person in the female role, and of a person who plays the female sexual role as someone who is being harmed.[29]

This is both interesting and revealing, but what is revealed is not enough to support Shrage's case. Why is "the standard view of sexual intercourse"[30] revealed not in the standard, but in the vulgar, i.e. sub-standard, way of talking about it? After all, everybody, at least occasionally, talks about it in the standard way, while only some use the vulgar language too. Baker justifies his focusing on the latter by pointing out that the verbs which belong to the former, and are not used in the sense of inflicting harm as well, "can take both females and males as subjects (in active constructions) and thus *do not pick out the female role. This demonstrates that we conceive of sexual roles in such a way that only females are thought to be taken advantage of in intercourse.*"[31] It seems to me that the "we" is quite problematic, and that all that these facts demonstrate is that some of us, namely those who speak of having sex with women as fucking or screwing them, also think of sex with them in these terms. Furthermore, the ways of talking about sex may be less fixed than Baker's analysis seems to suggest. According to Baker, sentences such as "Jane fucked Dick," "Jane screwed Dick" and "Jane laid Dick," if taken in the literal sense, are not sentences in English. But the usage seems to have changed since his article was published; I have heard native speakers of English make such sentences without a single (linguistic) eyebrow being raised. The asymmetry seems to have lost ground. So the import of the facts analyzed by Baker is much more limited than he and Shrage take it to be, and the facts themselves are less clear-cut and static too.

(iii) Shrage's third argument for the claim that our society thinks of sex with men as polluting and harmful to women is the weakest. Images of physical assault and imperialist domination certainly are not "the metaphors we use for the act of sexual intercourse"; I do not know that anyone except Andrea Dworkin does. The most likely reason people do not is that it would be silly to do so.

What all this shows, I think, is that there is no good reason to believe that our society adheres to a single conception of heterosexual sex, the conception defined by the four cultural assumptions Shrage describes, claims to be epitomized in, and reinforced by, prostitution, and wants to ascribe to every single case of commercial sex in our society as its "political and social meaning," whatever the beliefs and values of the individuals concerned. Some members of our society think of heterosexual sex in terms of Shrage's four assumptions and some do not. Accordingly, there are in our society two rather different conceptions of prostitution, which in this context are best termed (a) prostitution as commercial screwing, and (b) prostitution as commercial sex *simpliciter*. What is their relative influence on the practice of prostitution in our society is a question for empirical research. Shrage rightly objects to the former being implicated in the oppression of women in our society, and one need not be a feminist in order to agree. But that objection is not an objection to prostitution in our society as such.

## 6. Conclusion

I have taken a critical look at a number of arguments advanced to support the claim that prostitution stands morally condemned. If what I have been saying is right, none of these arguments is convincing. Therefore, until some new and better ones are put forward, the conclusion must be that there is nothing morally wrong with it. Writing about pornography—another practice which has been condemned and suppressed by traditional morality and religion, and has recently come under attack from feminist authors as well—G. L. Simons said that in a society which values liberty, "social phenomena are, like individuals, innocent until proven guilty."[32] So is prostitution.[33]

## Notes

1. I am concerned only with prostitution in its primary, narrow sense of "commercial" or "mercenary sex," "sex for money," and not with prostitution in the derived sense of "use of one's ability or talent in a base or unworthy way." The question I am asking is whether prostitution in the former, original sense is a case of prostitution in the latter, secondary sense.

2. L. Ericsson, "Charges against Prostitution: An Attempt at a Philosophical Assessment," *Ethics* 90 (1979/80), 357.

3. D. A. J. Richards, *Sex, Drugs, Death, and the Law: An Essay on Human Rights and Overcriminalization* (Totowa, NJ: Rowman and Littlefield, 1982), 113.

4. Ibid., 146 n. 251. The study referred to is described in W. B. Pomeroy, "Some Aspects of Prostitution," *Journal of Sex Research* 1 (1965).

5. L. Ericsson, loc. cit.

6. For an analysis of the two kinds of paternalism, see J. Feinberg, "Legal Paternalism," *Canadian Journal of Philosophy* 1 (1971).

7. Many authors who have written on prostitution as a "social evil" have claimed that it is virtually never a freely chosen occupation, since various social conditions (lack of education, poverty, unemployment) force innumerable women into it. This argument makes it possible for Mrs. Warren (and many others) to condemn prostitution, while absolving the prostitute. But even if the empirical claim were true, it would not amount to an argument against prostitution, but only against the lack of alternatives to it.

8. J. S. Mill, *On Liberty*, C. V. Shields (ed.) (Indianapolis: Bobbs-Merrill, 1956), 93.

It was clear to Mill that his rejection of paternalism applied in the case of prostitution just as in any other case, but the way he says that is somewhat demure; see ibid., 120–122.

9. Augustine, *Concerning the City of God*, trans. H. Bettenson (Harmondsworth: Penguin, 1972), Bk. 14, Ch. 16, 577.

10. B. Mandeville, *The Fable of the Bees*, F. B. Kaye (ed.) (Oxford University Press, 1957), Remark (II.), I, 95–96, 100.

Mandeville discusses prostitution in detail in *A Modest Defence of Publick Stews: or, an Essay upon Whoring, As it is now practis'd in these Kingdoms* (London: A. Moore, 1724) (published anonymously). The argument I have quoted from the *Fable* is elaborated on pp. ii–iii, xi–xii, 39–52.

11. A. Schopenhauer, "On Women," *Parerga and Paralipomena,* trans. E. F. J. Payne (Oxford: Oxford University Press, 1974), I, 623.

12. W. E. H. Lecky, *History of European Morals* (London: Longmans, Green & Co., 1869), II, 299–300.

13. B. Russell, *Marriage and Morals* (London: George Allen & Unwin, 1958), 116.

14. St. Augustine, *De ordine,* II, 4; St. Thomas Aquinas, *Summa theologiae,* 2a2ae, q. 10, art. 11.

15. H. Benjamin and R. E. L. Masters, *Prostitution and Morality* (London: Souvenir Press, 1965), 201.

16. See A. Goldman, "Plain Sex," *Philosophy of Sex,* A. Soble (ed.) (Totowa, NJ: Littlefield, Adams & Co., 1980); R. Vannoy, *Sex without Love: A Philosophical Exploration* (Buffalo: Prometheus Books, 1980).

17. Op. cit., 99–104.

18. Ibid., 103–104.

19. For examples of this kind of reasoning and a detailed discussion of its structure, see J. Wilson, *Logic and Sexual Morality* (Harmondsworth: Penguin, 1965), 59–74.

20. L. Ericsson, op. cit., 342.

21. D. Archard, "Sex for Sale: The Morality of Prostitution," *Cogito* 3 (1989), 49–50.

22. C. Pateman, "Defending Prostitution: Charges against Ericsson," *Ethics* 93 (1982/3), 562.

23. *Report,* 45.

24. S. de Beauvoir, *The Second Sex,* trans. and ed. H. M. Parshley (London: Pan Books, 1988), 569.

25. By "our society" Shrage most of the time seems to mean contemporary American society, but toward the end of the paper claims to have discussed "the meaning of commercial sex in modern Western culture" (L. Shrage, "Should Feminists Oppose Prostitution?" *Ethics* 99 (1989/90), 361).

26. Ibid. 354.

27. Ibid. 355.

28. M. G. Haft, "Hustling for Rights," *The Civil Liberties Review* 1 (1973/4), 20, quoted in A. M. Jaggar, "Prostitution," *Philosophy of Sex,* A. Soble (ed.), 350.

29. See R. Baker, "'Pricks' and 'Chicks': A Plea for 'Persons,'" *Philosophy and Sex,* R. Baker and F. Elliston (eds.) (Buffalo: Prometheus Books, 1975).

30. Ibid. 50.

31. Ibid. 61.

32. G. L. Simons, *Pornography without Prejudice: A Reply to Objectors* (London: Abelard-Schuman, 1972), 96.

33. I have benefited from conversations on the subject of this paper with Carla Freccero and Bernard Gert, and from critical reponses from audiences at Hull, Liverpool, Newcastle, St. Andrews and York, where I read this paper in December 1990/January 1991.

My greatest debt is to Antony Duff, Sandra Marshall, and Walter Sinnott-Armstrong, who read an earlier version of the paper and made a number of critical comments and suggestions for clarification and revision.

The paper was written during my stay at the Morrell Studies in Toleration project, Department of Politics, University of York, in the Winter and Spring terms of 1990/91. I would like to acknowledge with gratitude a research grant from the British Academy, which made that possible.

# Questions

1. One difficult moral question is whether acts and omissions are morally equivalent. Stan is married, but he is sexually attracted to a co-worker who is not his wife and who would like to have an affair with him. One day, after working late at the office with her, Stan kisses her passionately. Dan is married, but he is sexually attracted to a co-worker who is not his wife and who would like to have an affair with him. One day, after working late at the office with her, she kisses him passionately. Dan savors the kiss and makes no effort to hinder her.

   Would an Act Utilitarian consider these two acts morally equivalent? Why or why not?

   Would a Rule Utilitarian consider these two acts morally equivalent? Why or why not?

   Would a Kantian using the first formulation of the Categorical Imperative consider these two acts morally equivalent? Why or why not?

   Do you consider these two acts morally equivalent? Why or why not?

2. Most sophisticated Kantians, Utilitarians, and Aristotelians believe that it is generally wrong to commit adultery. What exceptions to the rule against committing adultery would sophisticated Kantians accept? What exceptions to the rule against committing adultery would sophisticated Utilitarians accept? What exceptions to the rule against committing adultery would sophisticated

Aristotelians accept? List as many different sorts of exceptions as you can think of. How would sophisticated Kantians, Utilitarians, and Aristotelians justify these exceptions?

3. Choose *one* of the following sexual practices and answer the questions that follow the list.

a. modeling for T.V. or magazine ads (not pornography)

b. modeling for pornography (consenting adults only)

c. marriage counseling (including improving the sex lives of couples)

d. adultery (when the spouse knows about and consents to the affair)

e. peeping at nude people in their own homes (when the chances of discovery are low)

f. surrogate motherhood (when the baby will be raised by the biological father and his infertile wife)

g. prostitution (when prostitution is legal and prostitutes are inspected regularly for sexually transmitted diseases)

h. promiscuous premarital sex (averaging two or more different partners per week)

i. homosexual sex (when both partners are unmarried)

j. sex with an employee (when the employee consents to the affair)

k. sex when HIV+ (when both partners are aware of the risks)

l. ordinary sex (in a public place where children almost never go)

m. sex with your own sixteen-year-old child (when the child consents)

n. repeated sexual jokes and innuendoes directed by a boss at a secretary (when the secretary expresses displeasure about it)

o. viewing pornography in private

Would a Kantian (using CI#1 and/or CI#2) consider this practice moral or immoral? Explain your answer.

Would an Aristotelian (using Aristotle's account of temperance and/or other virtues) consider this practice moral or immoral? Explain your answer.

Would a Utilitarian (Act or Rule) consider this practice moral or immoral? Explain your answer.

4. Belliotti offers the following Kantian explanation for the wrongness of bestiality and necrophilia. [R. Belliotti, "A Philosophical Analysis of Sexual Ethics," *Journal of Social Philosophy*, 10 (1979), 8–11.]

(A) It is wrong to treat persons as mere means.

(B) Ignoring the interests of sentient beings is treating persons as mere means.

(C) Bestiality and necrophilia involve the involuntary participation of the animals and corpses. Their interests are ignored.

(D) Therefore, bestiality and necrophilia are wrong.

Premise (B) seems false. To be a person requires more than mere sentience. Animals and corpses are not persons, so we need not respect their interests. Moreover, premise (C) is sometimes false. The animals may not mind the sex, and the corpses do not care, so their interests are not ignored. Neither the animals nor the corpses are harmed. How could Belliotti rebut these objections? What, if anything, is wrong with bestiality and necrophilia?

5. Throughout most of the 1970s, the residents of a certain women's dormitory at Gotham University spent quite a bit of time sunbathing nude on the roof of their dorm. They believed that no one could possibly see them. (No nearby buildings were high enough; helicopters did not get low enough.) However, certain faculty members and graduate students permanently trained an Astronomy Department telescope on the roof of that dormitory from a distance of about a mile and spent their free time looking through this telescope. None of the sunbathers ever knew about this peeping. Which of the following philosophers would think that this peeping was immoral? Why?

a. Act Utilitarian

b. Rule Utilitarian

c. Aristotelian

d. Kantian using CI#1

e. Kantian using CI#2

f. you

6. Suppose Bruce is a closet homosexual. He tells no lies, but he volunteers no information, either, for he knows that some of his friends are homophobes who would feel polluted by friendship with a homosexual. Of course, his friends cannot consent to Bruce's keeping his homosexuality a secret from them. One cannot consent to not being informed. Just as the victim of voyeurism cannot consent to unknowingly being looked at, so the "victim" of homosexual friendship cannot consent to unknowingly being friends with a homosexual.

Does Bruce have a duty to inform his friends of his sexual preferences? Does the voyeur have a duty to inform the victim?

7. Alice is desperately in need of money because she is unable to earn enough to support her two children on her own. Although she finds Bob repulsive, she accepts his offer of marriage because he is rich. Carol finds her husband Ted repulsive, but she remains married to him because she is unable to earn enough to support her two children on her own.

Are Alice's consent and Carol's consent equally legitimate, or is one more legitimate than the other? Explain your answer.

# Affirmative Action

*A girl should not expect special privileges because of her sex, but neither should she "adjust" to prejudice and discrimination. She must learn to compete...not as a woman, but as a human being.*

BETTY FRIEDAN

Our society has responded in a variety of different ways to past and present discrimination on the basis of sex, race, national origin, religion, and so on. (Louis Pojman's article provides a nice description and chronology.) Some government policies simply require non-discrimination. Other policies require organizations and individuals to make a special effort to recruit minority and female applicants for jobs, education, and the like. Other policies go even further and give *preferential treatment* to minority and/or female applicants with or without specific numerical goals or *quotas*. In this section I shall focus on policies that require organizations and individuals to choose qualified minorities and/or women over more qualified white men. I shall use the term "affirmative action" to refer to just these policies, even though the term is sometimes used more broadly to refer to all policies aimed at rectifying unjust discrimination. The arguments I shall discuss are all applications of four principles of justice that can, in turn, be seen as applications of Mill's Utilitarianism, Kant's Deontology, and Aristotle's Virtue Ethics. [Refer to the "Economic Justice" section throughout this section.] Naturally, the arguments for and against affirmative action differ somewhat depending on whether one is talking about hiring applicants for jobs, admitting applicants to educational programs, renting apartments to applicants, or other sorts of choices. Indeed, the issues vary substantially within these large categories. The arguments concerning busing in K–12 are different from the arguments concerning admission to college, which are different from the arguments concerning admission to medical school. In this section I shall focus on hiring decisions. Again the arguments for and against affirmative action differ somewhat depending on whether one is considering giving preference to women, blacks, hispanics, native Americans, or people with disabilities. In this section I shall focus on affirmative action for women and blacks.

One more preliminary remark: Often a person's stand on a moral issue does not derive from an evaluation of an argument or arguments. Instead, it is an unreflective parroting of some authority figure's view, a knee-jerk emotional reaction to a perceived threat, or a result of some other, even less rational process. For example, now that racist and sexist statements are increasingly socially unacceptable, opposition to affirmative action is becoming a way to express or encode racism and sexism. On the other hand, endorsement of affirmative action is sometimes simply an expression of rage and revulsion at perceived past and present injustices rather than a reasoned conclusion about what should be done. As you proceed through this section, try to root out or least bracket any unsavory grounds for your views.

## Utilitarian Analysis

Some people say that we should end affirmative action because it is not working or even because it is counter-productive. In order to assess the success or failure of affirmative action, we need to know its goals. What would count as success and what as failure? Of course, it would be unreasonable to dismiss affirmative action on the grounds that it has not solved *all* of our social problems. That was never affirmative action's goal and should not be used as its criterion of evaluation. Perhaps we should say that affirmative action is a success if it is beneficial, overall, to society. Of course, when a society undergoes rapid, multi-faceted change, as ours has in recent years, it is almost impossible to determine the causes and effects of these changes with any precision. Yet in order to work out a hedonistic calculation, we would need to know which of the many changes that have taken place in our society since affirmative action began are the result (wholly or partially) of affirmative action. Thus even the best empirical analysis of affirmative action will be speculative and approximate. A hedonistic calculation with jolly counts and probabilities is beyond hope.

It is important to keep in mind that Utilitarian considerations cannot be used in isolation from each other. Pojman blames affirmative action for contributing to falling standards and decreasing efficiency. But even if this is true, there may well be positive effects of affirmative action that outweigh this drawback. For example, Pojman neglects to credit affirmative action with breaking the virtual lock that white men used to have on high- and middle-income jobs. Nor does he credit affirmative action with changing social attitudes to the point where the exclusionary practices and derisive remarks that used to be common and accepted are now rare and are widely recognized to be wrong. (Perhaps he believes that these changes could have been accomplished without preferential treatment by enforcement of non-discrimination and rigorous recruitment of minorities and women.) All of the positive and negative effects of affirmative action must be bundled together to form one overall Utilitarian assessment. Here are *some* of the factors that should be taken into account when using the hedonistic calculus to determine the moral status of affirmative action.

**Some Drawbacks of Affirmative Action.** Affirmative action leads people to believe (falsely) that many blacks and women obtain jobs *regardless* of their qualifications. This belief has several demoralizing effects. (1) It undermines the motivation of blacks and women. (2) It also undermines the self-respect of blacks and women who get jobs and have nagging doubt about *how* they

got these jobs. (3) The belief that unqualified blacks and women get jobs undermines the confidence and respect that white men place in black and female job holders. (4) Moreover, this belief encourages white men to feel that they are being treated unfairly and thus leads to resentment and backlash. (5) Finally, affirmative action may cause a drop in productivity.

**Some Advantages of Affirmative Action.** One factor that obstructs the entry and advancement of blacks and women in certain jobs is the lack of black and female role models and mentors in that field. (1) Affirmative action increases the number of such role models and mentors and hence makes it easier for blacks and women to enter and advance in these fields. (2) Affirmative action also undermines stereotypes. People who believe that blacks and women cannot perform certain tasks well reject this prejudice when they actually see blacks and women performing these tasks well. (3) By allowing blacks and women to assume decision-making roles in various institutions, affirmative action increases diversity and allows these institutions to incorporate the special insights that blacks and women may contribute. (4) Finally, by changing social attitudes and increasing the percentage of blacks and women in the better-paying jobs, affirmative action plays a role in reducing the tensions and divisions within our society.

Unfortunately, it is not at all clear what weight to give to these factors. Some people give great weight to equalizing and little weight to efficiency, whereas Pojman assigns great weight to efficiency and little weight to equalizing. However, this list of pros and cons clearly shows that affirmative action has diminishing returns. As more and more blacks and women get good jobs, the need for additional role models, mentors, counter-examples to stereotypes, and contributors of special insight decreases. But the resentment, backlash, and undermining of motivation, respect, and self-respect increases. Thus even if affirmative action was justified at its inception according to Utilitarianism, it will eventually cease to be justified when the cons come to outweigh the pros. Perhaps we have already reached that point or are about to reach it.

## Deontological Analysis: Free Market

President Johnson introduced affirmative action with a metaphor. Suppose two runners, one white and one black, are about to run a race. The starting gun sounds and the white runner takes off down the track, but the black runner goes nowhere because he or she has been chained to the starting line by the white runner's grandparents. The referee unchains the black runner. Obviously, the referee cannot simply let the race continue, because the white runner now has a substantial lead. Obviously, the fair thing to do is hold the white runner back until the black runner catches up. The white runner objects, "I am being punished for a wrong done by my grandparents." But the referee replies, "No one is being punished. I am merely removing an advantage to which you were not entitled in the first place." This is the familiar argument that affirmative action is compensation for past wrongs.

### Argument (A)

(1) Taking goods or their equivalents from people who have unjustly acquired them, and restoring these goods or their equivalents to people who have been unjustly deprived of them, is just.
(2) Present-day blacks and women have been deprived of various goods by past unjust practices. Present-day white men have benefited from these same unjust practices.
(3) Affirmative action removes from present-day white men the equivalent of some unjustly acquired goods and restores the equivalent of these goods to present-day blacks and women.
(4) Therefore, affirmative action is just.

Every theory of justice accepts premise (1). In Robert Nozick's version of the Free Market Principle, premise (1) is simply the Principle of Recti-

fication. Objections to argument (A) focus on premises (2) and (3). Perhaps the most common objection is this. Previous generations of blacks and women have been wronged, of course, but slavery, segregation, sexism, and similar injustices are practices of the past. Thus present-day blacks and women are not entitled to restitution because they have not been wronged. Affirmative action simply punishes present-day white men who have done no wrong and gives undeserved handouts to blacks and women. Affirmative action punishes some children for the sins of their parents and rewards other children because their parents deserved to be rewarded.

This objection is seriously mistaken about the extent to which blacks and women are still subordinated. But even if we grant, for purposes of argument, that all unjust practices have been completely eliminated, the effects of unjust treatment of past people live on in the disadvantages of their descendants. Suppose your grandparents enslaved my grandparents for 40 years. Your grandparents stole from each of my grandparents the value of 40 years of labor (say, $20,000 per year × 40 years × 4 grandparents = $32,000,000). Suppose further that through no fault of their own, my grandparents and parents were unable to recover this money from your grandparents and parents. Now you grow up in a rich household while I grow up in a poor household. You go to good neighborhood schools, hire tutors if you need them, have leisure time in which to study, go to an expensive college, get good health care, live in a nice house, take refreshing vacations, and so on, whereas I have none of these advantages. Now when you and I compete for good jobs, you have a significant advantage over me even if all unjust practices have been completely eliminated from society. If the state takes advantages worth up to $32,000,000 (plus interest) away from you, the state is not punishing you for crimes you did not commit. It is merely taking away advantages to which you were never entitled, the equivalent of stolen property. And if the state gives the advantages to me, it is not giving me a handout that I did nothing to deserve. It is merely returning the equivalent of stolen property to which I was always entitled. Similarly, even if present-day whites have done nothing wrong, they still owe restitution to present-day blacks because the whites have profited from (and the blacks have been penalized by) wrongs done by previous generations.

Why should we use affirmative action rather than some other practice to compensate blacks? Other practices might indeed do equally well, but it seems appropriate that restitution take the form of preference in hiring because the disadvantages caused by past injustice make it more difficult for blacks to compete for jobs. Many blacks are trapped in a poverty cycle, for example, because their ancestors were victims of slavery and discrimination. And growing up poor puts them at a disadvantage when seeking jobs. Thus affirmative action roughly balances these unjust disadvantages and allows blacks to obtain the jobs that they would have obtained had the initial injustice not occurred.

Although Pojman acknowledges that we have duties to compensate people for certain sort of wrongs, he objects that in the case of affirmative action it is unclear exactly who is owed restitution and who owes it to them—who are the victims and who the beneficiaries of injustice. Some blacks are well off; some whites are impoverished. Some blacks are not descendants of slaves; some whites (such as immigrants) are not descendants of slave owners or discriminators. In general, Pojman's claim is that the vagueness of premise (2) vitiates argument (A). After all, the conclusion of a sound argument can be no more precise than the vaguest of its premises.

But we *do* know who has lost and who has gained by slavery and discrimination. All blacks are owed restitution, for all have suffered great losses. Some blacks have prospered, of course, but they have prospered *despite* unjust disadvantages. And all whites owe restitution, for all have benefited greatly. All have had a better start in life and less competition for the good things in life. Of course, some have not prospered, but they have not prospered *despite* unjust advantages. Suppose Fred steals all of my money and

gives it to you. If I nevertheless go on to become a millionaire while you become a pauper, my success and your failure do not nullify your duty to compensate me because of my unjust loss and your unjust gain.

Of course, many whites are not descendants of slave owners or discriminators. But affirmative action is not unfairly penalizing these whites, for they have also benefited from past injustice, though not so directly or so greatly as the descendants of slave owners or discriminators. Past injustices have undermined the ability of blacks to compete for jobs. *All* whites, then, face fewer and less qualified black competitors for jobs than they would have faced if blacks had not been disadvantaged by past injustice. Thus whites have better odds of getting better jobs. Similarly, patterns of stereotyping and discrimination have disadvantaged not only descendants of slaves but also other blacks who have arrived here since then. Thus *all* whites owe restitution to *all* blacks.

Other people object to premise (3). Should it be *only* blacks and women who receive restitution? Don't other groups who have suffered injustice (such as Asians and native Americans) also deserve restitution? And should it be *only* white men who are looking for jobs who bear the burden of restitution? Shouldn't all white men somehow surrender their unjust advantages? Affirmative action is unfair, according to this objection, because it forces only some of the beneficiaries of injustice to provide restitution to only some of the victims of injustice. The problem with affirmative action is that it does too little.

On the other hand, some people think affirmative action does too much. Surely there should be a statute-of-limitations clause on the Principle of Rectification, says this objection. If we try to provide restitution to all unjustly treated groups, we will end up taking everything away from everyone and giving it to someone else. For example, we will begin by giving America back to the native Americans. Because this is obviously absurd, we ought to give up on the idea of restitution. We should concentrate on preventing present and future injustice rather than spending our energies providing restitution for past injustice.

One reply to this pair of objections is that even though affirmative action does not compensate and burden exactly the right people, affirmative action is a workable practice that *approximates* perfect justice. Adding affirmative action to our present economic system brings us closer to perfect justice. More people get approximately what they deserve with affirmative action.

Even if argument (A) is sound with respect to blacks, the argument seems not to apply to women because injustice to women in one generation does not produce disadvantages for women in the next generation. Women in the 1970s were denied good jobs in favor of men. Thus job-seeking women of the 1990s are disadvantaged insofar their mothers had worse jobs than justice required. However, job-seeking women of the 1990s also benefited insofar as their fathers had better jobs than justice required. The injustice evens out, so women of the 1990s are not owed restitution.

However, injustice to women in one generation *does* produce disadvantages for women in the next generation through the following mechanism. Practices that are in themselves not exactly unjust, but that resulted from unjust practices in the past, live on into the present, placing women at an unjust disadvantage. For example, for generations women were almost completely blocked from obtaining good jobs. Instead, they were shunted into doing the bulk of the housework and child care. This was unjust, of course. Recently, the blockade has been lifted and women are now permitted to compete equally with men for the good jobs. At least they can compete equally in the formal sense that women's applications may no longer legally be rejected out of hand but must be given equal consideration. However, the expectation that women should do the bulk of the housework and child care remains widespread. Girls are encouraged to learn homemaking and child-raising skills, whereas boys are discouraged from these "sissy" pursuits. This is not exactly

unjust, but look at the result. Wives find themselves competent, eager, and expected to undertake the housework and child care, whereas husbands find themselves unprepared, reluctant, and expected not to undertake these tasks. Naturally, the lion's share of the housework and child care typically becomes the responsibility of the wife. Here is another example that reinforces this same distribution of labor. Until recently, when women did find jobs, they were paid rather little because they were "only women." It remains true that jobs performed predominantly by women (such as nurse and elementary school teacher) pay much less than jobs done predominantly by men (such as doctor and college professor). Thus when a typical couple sits down to decide who will work full-time outside of the home, and who will work part-time or not at all in order to keep the house and raise the kids, there are large financial incentives for the high-earning husband to be the breadwinner and the low-earning wife to be the homemaker. The result of these and other social factors is that even though women are now eligible for good jobs, they tend not to apply for them, and when they do apply, they find themselves at a competitive disadvantage because they are burdened with a disproportionate share of the housework and child care. (I do not mean to suggest that housework and child care are unrewarding, but they do require a surprising amount of time, energy, and attention. It is obviously easier to get a career as an executive, lawyer, doctor, or professor off the ground if one *has* a spouse doing the housework and child care than if one *is* a spouse doing the housework and child care.) These examples of past, sexist, unjust practices generating disadvantages for present-day women undermine the objection to argument (A). Like present-day blacks, present-day women seem to be owed restitution for past injustices that deprive them of goods they deserve.

Practices that arise from injustice and disadvantage contemporary women do seem to be dwindling. Eventually, this argument will no longer justify affirmative action. Is this argument nearly obsolete? If you think so, stand outside any elementary school at dismissal time and watch who picks up the kids.

\*

Affirmative action is often called *reverse discrimination* by its opponents. This pejorative term suggests the following argument.

### Argument (B)

(1) Discrimination on the basis of race or sex is wrong.

(2) Affirmative action (reverse discrimination) is simply one variety of discrimination on the basis of race or sex.

(3) Therefore, affirmative action (reverse discrimination) is wrong.

As it stands, premise (1) is false. Killing is wrong, but we allow exceptions for self-defense, defense of others, and the like. Presumably, we would also allow exceptions to the principle that discrimination on the basis of race or sex is wrong. But what exceptions are legitimate? In order to answer this question, we need to determine *why* discrimination against blacks and women is wrong even though some sorts of discrimination (such as discrimination against lazy and incompetent people) are OK. Joal Feinberg says that "Properties can be the grounds of just discrimination between persons only if those persons had a fair opportunity to acquire or avoid those properties." Because blacks and women do not have a fair opportunity to change their race or sex (leaving aside difficult and expensive medical procedures), it follows from Feinberg's *Fair Opportunity Requirement* that discrimination against blacks and women is wrong. White men do not have the option of becoming blacks or women, either, so Feinberg's view supports argument (B).

I do not think Feinberg's Fair Opportunity Requirement is the correct explanation of the wrongness of discrimination against blacks and women. Suppose someone invents a simple, inexpensive way to change one's race or sex so that everyone would have a fair opportunity to become a white man. Would discrimination against blacks and women become OK? Presumably not. People should not have to make this sort of change in order to avoid discrimination.

After all, people can change their religion, yet religious discrimination is still wrong. Moreover, stupid people do not have a fair opportunity to become smart, and yet it is presumably OK to discriminate on the basis of intelligence.

Pojman argues that discrimination against blacks and women is wrong because (a) jobs should be distributed only according to characteristics that are relevant to the performance of the job, and (b) race and sex are irrelevant characteristics. Pojman's view supports argument (B) because affirmative action, like discrimination against blacks and women, distributes jobs according to race and sex.

I shall postpone discussion of Pojman's claim that (a) jobs should be distributed only according to relevant characteristics. Unfortunately, it is not true that (b) race and sex are always irrelevant characteristics. Singer describes an all-too-common situation. Suppose you own a bakery and your customers include a large number of racists who will not patronize stores that employ blacks. If you hire a black clerk, your business will suffer. Here race is a very relevant characteristic. An important part of a clerk's job is to please the customers, and blacks (through no fault of their own) just cannot do it in such situations. Yet presumably even in this case, you should not refuse to hire blacks. After all, to refuse to hire blacks in situations like this is to compound the injustice of the customers' bigotry. Moreover, if people refuse to hire blacks in such situations, discrimination will remain with us forever. Thus the irrelevance of race or sex is not what makes discrimination against blacks and women morally wrong.

Richard Wasserstrom maintains that discrimination against blacks and women is wrong because it is part of a larger pattern of oppression. Although things are better than they used to be, blacks and women are still paid less, on the average, than white men for the same performance on the same type of job, and they are subject to more harassment and fear in day-to-day life, and so on. This pattern of injustice hinders some blacks and women from obtaining the jobs they would otherwise obtain. Because white men are not oppressed, affirmative action is not part of a larger pattern of oppression. Thus discrimination against blacks and women is wrong, but discrimination against white men is OK. (Or rather, if affirmative action is wrong, it is not wrong for the same reason that discrimination against blacks and women is wrong.) If Wasserstrom is right, then argument (B) fails.

Indeed, Wasserstrom's view suggests another rationale for affirmative action. We fight fire with fire, so why not fight discrimination against blacks and women with affirmative action (reverse discrimination)? Here the point of affirmative action is to combat present injustice rather than to provide restitution for past injustice.

### Argument (C)

(1) The ability of blacks and women to obtain good jobs is presently impaired by unjust practices.

(2) Affirmative action balances these unjust practices so that blacks and women end up getting approximately the job that they would have got if contemporary society were just.

(3) Therefore, affirmative action is just.

Some people will simply deny premise (1) and maintain that society has completely purged its former racism and sexism. But if there is no discrimination against blacks or women, why are blacks and women under-represented in the good jobs and underpaid in all jobs? One explanation that has recently slithered from the hate-mongering fringe to the borders of respectability is that blacks are genetically inferior and women are hormonally inferior. The data "supporting" this claim are dubious at best, but even if the data were solid, we should not jump to conclusions about how to interpret them. It is well established that first-born children have higher IQs, on the average, than later-born children. Does this imply a genetic or hormonal difference? The usual explanation is environmental rather than organic. Perhaps first-born children have higher IQs because they get more positive attention from their parents, and/or less negative attention from siblings, for example. Similarly, if there really is an ability difference between white men and blacks and women, then the most likely explanation is that white men have advantages in upbringing that blacks and women lack. Perhaps teachers tend to give white boys more and/or better sorts of attention. But this suggests not only that racism and sexism are still with us but also that racism and sexism are doing damage to blacks and women themselves as well as reducing their opportunities in life.

Many people will reject both the idea of racial and gender inferiority and the claim that racist and sexist practices persist in our society. An alternative explanation for the under-representation and underpayment of blacks and women is that there are practices within our society that disadvantage blacks and women even though they are not unjust practices. I shall explore this alternative below.

## Deontological Analysis: Rawls

Everyone agrees that rigid caste societies are unjust because the good things in life, such as good jobs, should be open to all. But what is implied by the phrase "open to all"? Nozick thinks good jobs are open to everyone if no one is blocked from these jobs by coercion. On this minimal interpretation, good jobs are open to all even if employers are discriminating on the basis of race and sex. Most people think this level of openness is insufficient and that society should prohibit racial and sexual discrimination as well as coercion. John Rawls thinks that even this further level of openness is insufficient. To be just, a society must also ensure that no one is blocked from the good jobs by socially caused inequalities, according to Rawls. For example, most good jobs require education. If education were available only to the wealthy, then children of poor people would not have a shot at these good jobs. Children of poor people would be doomed to poverty, and we would have a *de facto* caste society. Thus to be just, a society must not only prohibit racial and sexual discrimination and coercion but also make an adequate level of education available to all, rich and poor. Our society does this by furnishing public schooling for grades K–12, subsidizing state universities, and providing financial aid for college students, medical students, and so on. Note that Rawls does not think that everyone is entitled to an equally good job. Instead, he thinks everyone should have an equal opportunity to obtain a good job, where "equal opportunity" is understood as compensation for socially caused inequalities.

Is prohibiting coercion and discrimination according to race and sex, along with providing an adequate level of education, enough to ensure the creation of a society where the good jobs are open to all? Many people believe that this is enough and, therefore, that affirmative action is superfluous or counter-productive. After all, if we eliminate race and sex discrimination and compensate for the disadvantages of poverty, haven't we leveled the playing field? How could any socially caused inequalities remain?

Mary Ann Warren argues that even this is insufficient. We need affirmative action to achieve just hiring practices. This is because there are practices that would not be sexist in a perfect society (they can be described in gender-neutral terms) but that unfairly disadvantage women because of certain features of our present society. For example, the practice of rejecting applicants who have primary child-care responsibilities does not directly discriminate against anyone on the basis of sex. In principle, men as well as women can be primary caregivers. However, in our society the primary caregivers are overwhelmingly female, so this hiring practice has the effect of discriminating against women. Warren calls such practices *secondary sexism*. These practices create socially caused inequalities in our society and prevent the good jobs from being open to all. Merely eliminating discrimination according to race and sex would leave secondary sexist practices in place. Thus we need to do more than eliminate discrimination according to race and sex.

Some secondary sexist practices (such as the seniority system) are so deeply entrenched that eliminating them would be immoral or impractical. Because we cannot eliminate these secondary sexist practices in the near future, we must somehow compensate for them in order to ensure that we give every applicant roughly the same chance of being hired as they would have in a just society. Warren's suggested method is for each employer to hire women in proportion to the percentage of qualified female candidates in the applicant pool. This is a type of affirmative action because it would sometimes require the employer to pass over better-qualified men in order to hire enough women. But the chances of the typical male candidate would not fall below what his chances would be in a just society. What men would lose through this type of affirmative action is what they presently gain through secondary (and primary) sexist practices. For example, if 70 qualified men and 30 qualified women apply for 10 jobs, the odds in a just society are that the top 10 applicants will be 7 men and 3 women. But in our society the top 10 applicants might be 9 men and 1 woman, because the careers of some of the women who would otherwise have made it into the top 10 have been crippled by the fact that these women have been raising children and doing housework or by some other residue from more sexist times. Warren says the employer should hire the top 7 men and the top 3 women because that is what would happen in a just society. If her suggestion is implemented, 2 men will be passed over in favor of 2 less-qualified women. But these men are not being unjustly treated, for by this hypothesis, in a just society they would not have got the job, anyway.

### Argument (D)

(1) A hiring practice in our present society is just if and only if this practice gives every applicant the same chance of being hired that the applicant would have in a just society.
(2) Affirmative action compensates for secondary (and primary) sexism and thus brings our society closer to a just society.
(3) Therefore, affirmative action is just.

Naturally, as primary and secondary sexism dwindle, affirmative action should become less and less severe, in Warren's view. However, because primary and secondary sexism are clearly not about to vanish, affirmative action will remain necessary for the foreseeable future.

One problem with Warren's line of thought is the difficulty of determining the extent to which women are disadvantaged and therefore how much to reverse-discriminate. Warren's proposal of looking to the percentage of qualified female candidates in the applicant pool is flawed because sexist practices and sexist socialization of men and women skew the applicant pools. It might be that in a just society the applicant pool would be 50–50 rather than 70–30. If so, the employer should hire 5 men and 5 women. On the other hand, we cannot assume that men and women in a perfectly just society would be equally likely to opt for every career. Maybe some careers just do not appeal equally to men and to women because of natural differences. Perhaps the fact that 3/10 of the applicants for a certain type of job are women and 7/10 of the applicants are men reflects real differences in preference and not sexist practices. But if we cannot know even approximately what our targets should be, then how can we decide when affirmative action is justified and when it is not?

## Aristotelian Analysis

Like many opponents of affirmative action, Pojman maintains that affirmative action violates the rights of the white applicants. Now according to the strict Free Market Principle, no one has a right to any particular job or even to be considered for a particular job. As long as the employer is using no coercion, he or she is free to offer the job to anyone. It is OK to give veterans preference (that is, to discriminate against nonveterans), after all. It is OK to hire people simply because you like them. Thus, according to the strict Free Market Principle, affirmative action does not violate the rights of white male applicants. (If any rights are violated by affirmative action, it is the rights of employers to hire whom they please. But there may well be no such right. After all, if there were such a right, the policy of prohibiting discrimination against blacks and women would also violate it.) Pojman's claim that affirmative action violates rights cannot be based on the Free Market Principle. Instead, it is based on a rival principle, Aristotle's Principle plus the Principle of Talent. Pojman's argument is this.

### Argument (E)

(1) The best-qualified applicant for a particular job deserves the job.
(2) Affirmative action distributes jobs to people who are not the best-qualified applicants.
(3) Therefore, affirmative action is unjust.

Although it is often thought that most contemporary employers try to hire the best-qualified applicant because it pays to do so, this is a compound misconception. First, it is often *not* good business to try to hire the best-qualified applicant. It may be not worth the trouble to find the best-qualified applicant, for example, or the best-qualified applicant may not be content with the job. Hiring the lazy, incompetent son of your company's best client may be an excellent move. And so on. Second, contemporary employers are aware that trying to hire the best-qualified applicant often is not advisable, so they often do *not* try to hire the best-qualified applicant. America is not a meritocracy. The idea that actual employers typically hire on the basis of talent is a myth. Many other factors skew hiring decisions. Sometimes employers hire the least threatening applicant or the applicant who "fits in" best. Perhaps employers morally *should* hire the best-qualified applicant, but they do not presently do so because it is often not good business to do so. Thus Pojman's argument is an attack on the status quo rather than a defense of the status quo.

Because the Free Market Principle and Aristotle's Principle are incompatible, Pojman's argument will not appeal to hard-core free-marketeers. It will not appeal to all advocates of Aristotle's Principle, either, for not all advocates of Aristotle's Principle combine it with the Principle of Talent. Like Feinberg, James Rachels thinks that goods such as jobs should, at least partially, be distributed according to Aristotle's

Principle together with the Principle of Effort. Desert is based on effort because, unlike talent, effort meets the Fair Opportunity Requirement. People are responsible for how hard they work but not for how talented they are. Thus the most talented person probably does not deserve the job because people typically do not deserve their talents and so do not deserve anything on the basis of their talents.

Pojman replies that even if people do not deserve their talents, they must deserve what they procure through the use of their talents. Otherwise, no one would deserve anything.

\*

Because our present economic system incorporates aspects of both the Free Market Principle and Aristotle's Principle, perhaps we should evaluate affirmative action on the basis of combinations of these principles. Rachels combines the Free Market Principle with Aristotle's Principle plus the Principle of Effort and then applies the combination to the issue of affirmative action in the following way.

### Argument (F)

(1) In our society, blacks and women generally face more obstacles than do white men.

(2) Suppose that a white male applicant is slightly better qualified for a job than a black or female applicant. The black or female applicant probably worked substantially harder than the white male to achieve roughly the same level of qualification.

(3) Although no one has a right to a job (Free Market Principle), the harder a person works, the more he or she deserves a job (Aristotle's Principle plus the Principle of Effort).

(4) Thus the black or female applicant deserves the job more than the white male.

(5) Therefore, affirmative action is just.

The quasi-Calvinist premise (3) is troubling. Hard-core free-marketeers will not accept premise (3)'s amendment to the Free Market Principle, of course. But even people open to combining the Free Market Principle with Aristotle's Principle may object that we are probably no more responsible for our effort than for our talent. As Feinberg himself says, our willingness and ability to exert ourselves are a function of our heredity and environment. So according to Feinberg's own Fair Opportunity Requirement, distribution should not be based on effort. Moreover, argument (F) suggests the counter-intuitive thesis that stupid or impoverished applicants with slightly worse qualifications than those of smart or rich applicants are more deserving of jobs because they have probably worked much harder to achieve these lower qualifications.

Let us take stock. From a Utilitarian perspective, affirmative action seems justified, but only for a limited period of time. The drawbacks of affirmative action are increasing while its benefits are decreasing. From a Free Market perspective, affirmative action is also justified only for a limited period of time. It is justified until appropriate compensation for past and present injustice has been made. From a Rawlsian perspective, affirmative action is justified only until primary and secondary racist and sexist practices wither away. Finally, the Aristotelian analysis of affirmative action seems inconclusive.

# 52   The Moral Status of Affirmative Action

## LOUIS P. POJMAN

*"A ruler who appoints any man to an office, when there is in his dominion another man better qualified for it, sins against God and against the State."* (The Koran)

*"[Affirmative Action] is the meagerest recompense for centuries of unrelieved oppression."* (quoted by Shelby Steele as the justification for Affirmative Action)

Hardly a week goes by . . . that the subject of Affirmative Action does not come up. Whether in the guise of reverse discrimination, preferential hiring, non-traditional casting, quotas, goals and time tables, minority scholarships, or race-norming, the issue confronts us as a terribly perplexing problem. During the last general election (November 7, 1996) California voters by a 55% to 45% vote approved Proposition 209 (called the "California Civil Rights Initiative") which would have made it illegal to discriminate on the basis of race or gender, hence ending affirmative action in California. A federal judge subsequently prohibited the bill from going into effect, arguing that it may violate the equal protection clause of the 14th amendment. Both sides have reorganized for a renewed battle. The Supreme Court is likely to decide the issue in the near future. Affirmative action was one of the issues that divided the Democratic and Republican parties during the 1996 election, the Democrats supporting it ("Mend it don't end it") and the Republicans opposing it ("affirmative action is reverse racism"). Other illustrations of the debate are Chicago's Mayor Daley's decision (in May 1995) to bypass the results of a Chicago police exam in order to promote minority officers, Administration Assistant

Secretary of Education Michael Williams' judgment that Minority Scholarships are unconstitutional (which was overruled); the demand that Harvard Law School hire a black female professor; the revelations of race-norming in state employment agencies; as well as debates over quotas, underutilization guidelines, and diversity in employment; all testify to the importance of this subject for contemporary society.

There is something salutory as well as terribly tragic inherent in this problem. The salutory aspect is the fact that our society has shown itself committed to eliminating unjust discrimination. Even in the heart of Dixie there is a recognition of the injustice of racial discrimination. Both sides of the affirmative action debate have good will and appeal to moral principles. Both sides are attempting to bring about a better society, one which is color blind, but they differ profoundly on the morally proper means to accomplish that goal.

And this is just the tragedy of the situation: good people on both sides of the issue are ready to tear each other to pieces over a problem that has no easy or obvious solution. And so the voices become shrill and the rhetoric hyperbolic. The same spirit which divides the pro-choice movement from the right-to-life movement on abortion divides liberal pro-Affirmative Action advocates from liberal anti-Affirmative Action advocates. This problem, more than any other, threatens to destroy the traditional liberal consensus in our society. I have seen family members and close friends who until recently fought on the same side of the barricades against racial injustice divide in enmity over this issue. The anti-affirmative liberals ("liberals who've been mugged") have tended toward a form of neo-conservatism, and the pro-affirmative liberals have tended to side with the radical left to form the "politically correct ideology" movement.

In this paper I will confine myself primarily to Affirmative Action policies with regard to race,

Reprinted with permission of the publisher from *Public Affairs Quarterly*, 6, 2 (1992), 181–206 with slight modifications by the author.

but much of what I say can be applied to the areas of gender and ethnic minorities.

# I. Definitions

First let me define my terms:

*Discrimination* is simply judging one thing to differ from another on the basis of some criterion. "Discrimination" is a good quality, having reference to our ability to make distinctions. As rational and moral agents we need to make proper distinctions. To be rational is to discriminate between good and bad arguments, and to think morally is to discriminate between reasons based on valid principles and those based on invalid ones. What needs to be distinguished is the difference between rational and moral discrimination, on the one hand, and irrational and immoral discrimination, on the other hand.

*Prejudice* is a discrimination based on irrelevant grounds. It may simply be an attitude which never surfaces in action, or it may cause prejudicial actions. A prejudicial discrimination in action is immoral if it denies someone a fair deal. So discrimination on the basis of race or sex where these are not relevant for job performance is unfair. Likewise, one may act prejudicially in applying a relevant criterion on insufficient grounds, as in the case where I apply the criterion of being a hard worker but then assume, on insufficient evidence, that the black man who applies for the job is not a hard worker.

There is a difference between prejudice and bias. *Bias* signifies a tendency toward one thing rather than another where the evidence is incomplete or is based on non-moral factors. For example, you may have a bias toward blondes and I toward redheads. But prejudice is an attitude (or action) where unfairness is present—where one *should* know or do better—as in the case where I give people jobs simply because they are redheads. Bias implies ignorance or incomplete knowledge, whereas prejudice is deeper, involving a moral failure—usually a failure to pay attention to the evidence. But note that calling people

racist or sexist without good evidence is also an act of prejudice.

*Equal opportunity* exists when everyone has a fair chance at the best positions that society has at its disposal. Only native aptitude and effort should be decisive in the outcome, not factors of race, sex, or special favors.

*Affirmative Action* is the effort to rectify the injustice of the past as well as to produce a situation closer to the ideal of equal opportunity by special policies. Put this way, it is Janus-faced or ambiguous, having both a backward-looking and a forward-looking feature. The backward-looking feature is its attempt to correct and compensate for past injustice. This aspect of Affirmative Action is strictly deontological. The forward-looking feature is its implicit ideal of a society free from prejudice, where one's race or gender is irrelevant to basic opportunities. This is both deontological and utilitarian: deontological in that it aims at treating people according to their merits or needs, utilitarian in that a society perceived as fair will be a happier society.

When we look at a social problem from a backward-looking perspective, we need to determine who has committed or benefited from a wrongful or prejudicial act and to determine who deserves compensation for that act.

When we look at a social problem from a forward-looking perspective, we need to determine what a just society (one free from prejudice) would look like and how to obtain that kind of society. The forward-looking aspect of Affirmative Action is paradoxically race-conscious, because it uses race to bring about a society that is not race-conscious—that is color blind (in the morally relevant sense of this term).

It is also useful to distinguish two versions of Affirmative Action. *Weak Affirmative Action* involves such measures as the elimination of segregation (namely the idea of "separate but equal"), widespread advertisement of job opportunities to groups not previously represented in certain privileged positions, special scholarships for the disadvantaged classes (such as the poor), using under-representation or a history of past discrimination as a tie breaker when candidates are relatively equal, and the like.

*Strong Affirmative Action* involves more positive steps to eliminate past injustice, such as reverse discrimination, hiring candidates on the basis of race and gender in order to reach equal or nearly equal results, and proportionate representation in each area of society.

## II. A Brief History of Affirmative Action

1. After a long legacy of egregious racial discrimination the forces of civil justice came to a head during the decade of 1954–1964. In the 1954 U.S. Supreme Court decision, *Brown* v. *Board of Education,* racial segregation was declared inherently and unjustly discriminatory, a violation of the constitutional right to equal protection, and in 1964 Congress passed the Civil Rights Act which banned all forms of racial discrimination.

During this time the goal of the Civil Rights Movement was Equal Opportunity. The thinking was that if only we could remove the hindrances to progress, invidious segregation, discriminatory laws, and irrational prejudice against blacks, we could free our country from the evils of past injustice and usher in a just society in which the grandchildren of the slave could play together and compete with the grandchildren of the slave owner. We were after a color-blind society in which every child had an equal chance to attain the highest positions based not on his skin color but on the quality of his credentials. In the early 60's when the idea of reverse discrimination was mentioned in Civil Rights groups, it was usually rejected as a new racism. The Executive Director of the NAACP, Roy Wilkins, stated this position unequivocally during congressional consideration of the 1964 civil rights law. "Our association has never been in favor of a quota system. We believe the quota system is unfair whether it is used for [blacks] or against [blacks]. . . . [We] feel people ought to be hired because of their ability, irrespective of their color. . . . We want equality, equality of opportunity and employment on the basis of ability."[1]

So the Civil Rights Act of 1964 was passed outlawing discrimination on the basis of race or sex.

Title VII, Section 703(a) Civil Rights Act of 1964: It shall be an unlawful practice for an employer—(1) to fail or refuse to hire or to discharge any individual or otherwise to discriminate against any individual with respect to his compensation, terms, conditions, or privileges of employment, because of such individual's race, color, sex, or national origin; or

(2) to limit, segregate, or classify his employees or applicants for employment in any way which would deprive or tend to deprive any individual of employment opportunities or otherwise adversely affect his status as an employee because of such individual's race, color, religion, sex, or national origin. [42 U.S.C. 2000e-2(a).]

. . . Nothing contained in this title shall be interpreted to require any employer . . . to grant preferential treatment to any individual or to any group . . . on account of an imbalance which may exist with respect to the total numbers or percentage of persons of any race . . . employed by any employer . . . in comparison with the total or percentage of persons of such race . . . in any community, State, section, or other areas, or in the available work force in any community, State, section, or other area. [42 U.S.C.2000e-2(j)]

The Civil Rights Act of 1964 espouses a meritocratic philosophy, calling for equal opportunity and prohibiting reverse discrimination as just another form of prejudice. The Voting Rights Act (1965) was passed and Jim Crow laws throughout the South were overturned. Schools were integrated and public accommodations opened to all. Branch Rickey's promotion of Jackie Robinson from the minor leagues in 1947 to play for the Brooklyn Dodgers was seen as the paradigm case of this kind of equal opportunity—the successful recruiting of a deserving person.

2. But it was soon noticed that the elimination of discriminatory laws was not producing the fully integrated society that leaders of the civil rights movement had envisioned. Eager to improve the situation, in 1965 President Johnson went beyond equal opportunity to Affirmative Action. He issued the famous Executive Order 11246 in which the Department of Labor was enjoined to issue government contracts with construction companies on the basis of race. That is, it would engage in reverse discrimination in order to make up for the

evils of the past. He explained the act in terms of the shackled runner analogy.

> Imagine a hundred yard dash in which one of the two runners has his legs shackled together. He has progressed 10 yds., while the unshackled runner has gone 50 yds. How do they rectify the situation? Do they merely remove the shackles and allow the race to proceed? Then they could say that "equal opportunity" now prevailed. But one of the runners would still be forty yards ahead of the other. Would it not be the better part of justice to allow the previously shackled runner to make-up the forty yard gap; or to start the race all over again? That would be affirmative action towards equality. (President Lyndon Johnson 1965 inaugurating the Affirmative Action Policy of Executive Order 11246).

In 1967 President Johnson issued Executive Order 11375 extending Affirmative Action (henceforth "AA") to women. Note here that AA originates in the executive branch of government. Until the Kennedy-Hawkins Civil Rights Act of 1990, AA policy was never put to a vote or passed by Congress. Gradually, the benefits of AA were extended to Hispanics, native Americans, Asians, and handicapped people.[2]

The phrase "An Equal Opportunity/Affirmative Action Employer" ("AA/EO") began to appear as official public policy. But few noticed an ambiguity in the notion of "AA" which could lead to a contradiction in juxtaposing it with "EO," for there are two types of AA. At first AA was interpreted as what I have called "Weak Affirmative Action," in line with equal opportunity, signifying wider advertisement of positions, announcements that applications from blacks would be welcomed, active recruitment and hiring blacks (and women) over *equally* qualified men. While few liberals objected to these measures, some expressed fears of an impending slippery slope towards reverse discrimination.

However, except in professional sports—including those sponsored by universities—Weak Affirmative Action was not working, so in the late 60's and early 70's a stronger version of Affirmative Action was embarked upon—one aimed at equal results, quotas (or "goals"—a euphemism for "quotas"). In *Swann v. Charlotte-Mecklenburg* (1971), regarding the busing of children out of their neighborhood in order to promote integration, the Court, led by Justice Brennan, held that Affirmative Action was implied in *Brown* and was consistent with the Civil Right Act of 1964. The NAACP now began to support reverse discrimination.

Thus began the search for minimally qualified blacks in college recruitment, hiring, and the like. Competence and excellence began to recede into second place as the quest for racial, ethnic, and gender diversity became the dominant goals. The slogan "We have to become race conscious in order to eliminate race consciousness" became the paradoxical justification for reverse discrimination.

3. In 1968 the Department of Labor ordered employers to engage in utilization studies as part of its policy of eliminating discrimination in the work place. The office of Federal Contract Compliance of the U.S. Department of Labor (Executive Order 11246) stated that employers with a history of *underutilization* of minorities and women were required to institute programs that went beyond passive nondiscrimination through deliberate efforts to identify people of "affected classes" for the purpose of advancing their employment. Many employers found it wise to adopt policies of preferential hiring in order to preempt expensive government suits.

Employers were to engage in "utilization analysis" of their present work force in order to develop "specific and result-oriented procedures" to which the employer commits "*every good-faith effort*" in order to provide "relief for members of an '*affected class,*' who by virtue of *past discrimination* continue to suffer the present effects of that discrimination." This self-analysis is supposed to discover areas in which such affected classes are underused, considering their availability and skills. "*Goals and timetables* are to be developed to guide efforts to correct deficiencies in the employment of affected classes people in each level and segment of the work force." Affirmative Action also calls for "rigorous examination" of standards and criteria for job performance, not so as to "dilute necessary standards" but in order to ensure that "arbitrary and

*the unshackled man will be weak - not used to freedom*
*how have shackles affected them - what scares*

discriminatory employment practices are eliminated" and to eliminate unnecessary criteria which "have had the effect of eliminating women and minorities" either from selection or promotion.[3]

4. In 1969 two important events occurred. (a) The Philadelphia Plan—The Department of Labor called for "goals and time tables" for recruiting minority workers. In Philadelphia area construction industries, where these companies were all white, family run, businesses, the contractor's union took the case to court on the grounds that Title VII of the Civil Rights Act prohibits quotas. The Third Circuit Court of Appeals upheld the Labor Department, and the Supreme Court refused to hear it. This case became the basis of the EEOC's aggressive pursuit of "goals and time tables" in other business situations.

(b) In the Spring of 1969 James Forman disrupted the service of Riverside Church in New York City and issued the Black Manifesto to the American Churches, demanding that they pay blacks $500,000,000 in reparations. The argument of the Black Manifesto was that for three and a half centuries blacks in America have been "exploited and degraded, brutalized, killed and persecuted" by whites; that this was part of the persistent institutional patterns of first, legal slavery and then, legal discrimination and forced segregation; and that through slavery and discrimination whites had procured enormous wealth from black labor with little return to blacks. These facts were said to constitute grounds for reparations on a massive scale. The American churches were but the first institutions to be asked for reparations.[4]

5. The Department of Labor issued guidelines in 1970 calling for hiring representatives of *underutilized* groups. "*Nondiscrimination* requires the elimination of all existing discriminatory conditions, whether purposeful or inadvertent . . . *Affirmative action* requires . . . the employer to make additional efforts to recruit, employ and promote qualified members of groups formerly excluded" (HEW Executive Order 22346, 1972). In December of 1971 Guidelines were issued to eliminate underutilization of minorities, aiming at realignment of job force at every level of society.

6. In *Griggs v. Duke Power Company* (1971) the Supreme Court interpreted Title VII of the Civil Rights Act as forbidding use of aptitude tests and high school diplomas in hiring personnel. These tests were deemed presumptively discriminatory, employers having the burden of proving such tests relevant to performance. The notion of *sufficiency* replaced that of excellence or best qualified, as it was realized (though not explicitly stated) that the social goal of racial diversity required compromising the standards of competence.

7. In 1977, the EEOC called for and *expected* proportional representation of minorities in every area of work (including universities).

8. In 1978 the Supreme Court addressed the Bakke case. Alan Bakke had been denied admission to the University of California at Davis Medical School even though his test scores were higher than the 16 blacks who were admitted under the Affirmative Action quota program. He sued the University of California and the U.S. Supreme Court ruled (*University of California v. Bakke*, July 28, 1978) in a 5 to 4 vote that reverse discrimination and quotas are illegal except (as Justice Powell put it) when engaged in for purposes of promoting diversity (interpreted as a means to extend free speech under the First Amendment) and restoring a situation where an institution has had a history of prejudicial discrimination. The decision was greeted with applause from anti-AA quarters and dismay from pro-AA quarters. Ken Tollett lamented, "The affirmance of Bakke would mean the reversal of affirmative action; it would be an officially sanctioned signal to turn against blacks in this country. . . . Opposition to special minority admissions programs and affirmative action is anti-black."[5]

But Tollett was wrong. The Bakke case only shifted the rhetoric from "quota" language to "goals and time tables" and "diversity" language. In the 80's affirmative action was alive and well, with preferential hiring, minority scholarships, and "race norming" prevailing in all walks of life. No other white who has been excluded from admission to college because of his race has even won his case. In fact only a year later, Justice Brennan was to write in *U.S. Steel v. Weber* that prohibition of racial discrimination against "any individual" in Title VII of the Civil Rights Act did not apply to discrimination against whites.[6]

9. Perhaps the last step in the drive towards equal results took place in the institutionalization of grading applicants by group related standards, race norming. Race norming is widely practiced but most of the public is unaware of it, so let me explain it.

Imagine that four men come into a state employment office in order to apply for a job. One is black, one Hispanic, one Asian and one white. They take the standard test (a version of the General Aptitude Test Battery or VG-GATB). All get a composite score of 300. None of them will ever see that score. Instead the numbers will be fed into a computer and the applicants' percentile ranking emerges. The scores are group-weighted. Blacks are measured against blacks, whites against whites, Hispanics against Hispanics. Since blacks characteristically do less well than other groups, the effect is to favor blacks. For example, a score of 300 as an accountant will give the black a percentile score of 87, an Hispanic a percentile score of 74 and a white or oriental a score of 47. The black will get the job as the accountant. See the accompanying table.

This is known as race norming. Until an anonymous governmental employee recently blew the whistle, this practice was kept a secret in several state employment services. Prof. Linda Gottfredson of the University of Delaware, one of the social scientists to expose this practice, has since had her funding cut off. In a recent letter published in the New York Times she writes:

One of America's best-kept open secrets is that the Employment Service of the Department of Labor has unabashedly promulgated quotas. In 1981 the service recommended that state employment agencies adopt a race-conscious battery to avoid adverse impact when referring job applicants to employers. . . . The score adjustments are not trivial. An unadjusted score that places a job applicant at the 15th percentile among whites would, after race-norming, typically place a black near the white 50th percentile. Likewise, unadjusted scores at the white 50th percentile would, after race-norming, typically place a black near the 85th percentile for white job applicants. . . . [I]ts use by 40 states in the last decade belies the claim that *Griggs* did not lead to quotas.[7]

10. In the *Ward Cove, Richmond,* and *Martin* decisions of the mid-80's the Supreme Court limited preferential hiring practices, placing a greater burden of proof on the plaintiff, now required to prove that employers have discriminated. The Kennedy-Hawkins Civil Rights Act of 1990, which was passed by Congress last year, sought to reverse these decisions by requiring employers to justify statistical imbalances not only in the employment of racial minorities but also that of ethnic and religious minorities. Wherever underrepresentation of an "identified" group exists, the employer bears the burden of proving he is innocent of prejudicial behavior. In other words, the bill would make it easier for minorities to sue

## Percentile Conversion Tables

Jobs are grouped into five broad families: Family I includes, for example, machinists, cabinet makers, and tool makers; Family II includes helpers in many types of agriculture, manufacturing, and so on; Family III includes professional jobs such as accountant, chemical engineer, nurse, editor; Family IV includes bus drivers, bookkeepers, carpet layers; Family V includes exterminators, butchers, file clerks. A raw score of 300 would convert to the following percentile rankings:

|          | I  | II | III | IV | V  |
|----------|----|----|-----|----|----|
| Black    | 79 | 59 | 87  | 83 | 73 |
| Hispanic | 62 | 41 | 74  | 67 | 55 |
| Other    | 39 | 42 | 47  | 45 | 42 |

Sources: Virginia Employment Commission: U.S. Department of Labor. Employment and Training Administration, Validity Generalization Manual (Section A: Job Family Scoring).

employers. President Bush vetoed the bill, deeming it a subterfuge for quotas. A revised bill is now in Congressional committee.

Affirmative Action in the guise of underutilized or "affected groups" now extends to American Indians, Hispanics—Spaniards (including Spanish nobles) but not Portuguese, Asians, the handicapped, and in some places Irish and Italians. Estimates are that 75% of Americans may obtain AA status as minorities: everyone except the white non-handicapped male. It is a strange policy that affords special treatment to the children of Spanish nobles and illegal immigrants but not the children of the survivors of Russian pogroms or Nazi concentration camps.

Of course, there is nothing new about the notions of racial discrimination and preferential treatment. The first case of racial discrimination is the fall of man, as standardly interpreted, in which the whole race is held accountable and guilty of Adam's sin. The notion of collective responsibility also goes way back in our history. The first case of preferential treatment is God's choosing Abel's sacrifice of meat and rejecting Cain's vegetarian sacrifice—which should give all Jewish-Christian vegetarians something to think about! The first case of preferential treatment in Greek mythology is that of the Achaian horse race narrated in the 23rd book of the Iliad. Achilles had two prizes to give out. First prize went to the actual winner. Antilochus, son of Nestor, came in second, but Achilles decided to give second prize to Eumelius because he was of a nobler rank, even though he had come in last. Antilochus complained, saying in effect, "If it is preordained that some other criterion than merit is to count for the award, why should we have a race at all?" Achilles was moved by this logic and gave the prize to Antilochus, offering Eumelius a treasure of his own.

Neither is Affirmative Action primarily an American problem. Thomas Sowell has recently written a book on the international uses of preferential treatment, *Preferential Policies: An International Perspective* in which he analyzes government mandated preferential policies in India, Nigeria, Malaysia, Sri Lanka, and the United States.[8] We will consider Sowell's study towards the end of this paper.

## III. Arguments for Affirmative Action

Let us now survey the main arguments typically cited in the debate over Affirmative Action. I will briefly discuss seven arguments on each side of the issue.

### 1. Need for Role Models

This argument is straightforward. We all have need of role models, and it helps to know that others like us can be successful. We learn and are encouraged to strive for excellence by emulating our heroes and role models.

However, it is doubtful whether role models of one's own racial or sexual type are necessary for success. One of my heroes was Gandhi, an Indian Hindu, another was my grade school science teacher, one Miss DeVoe, and another was Martin Luther King. More important than having role models of one's own type is having genuinely good people, of whatever race or gender, to emulate. Furthermore, even if it is of some help to people with low self-esteem to gain encouragement from seeing others of their particular kind in leadership roles, it is doubtful whether this need is a sufficient condition to justify preferential hiring or reverse discrimination. What good is a role model who is inferior to other professors or business personnel? Excellence will rise to the top in a system of fair opportunity. Natural development of role models will come more slowly and more surely. Proponents of preferential policies simply lack the patience to let history take its own course.

### 2. The Need of Breaking the Stereotypes

Society may simply need to know that there are talented blacks and women, so that it does not automatically assign them lesser respect or status. We need to have unjustified stereotype beliefs replaced with more accurate ones about the talents of blacks and women. So we need to engage in preferential hiring of qualified minorities even when they are not the most qualified.

Again, the response is that hiring the less qualified is neither fair to those better qualified who are passed over nor an effective way of removing inaccurate stereotypes. If competence is accepted as the criterion for hiring, then it is unjust to override it for purposes of social engineering. Furthermore, if blacks or women are known to hold high positions simply because of reverse discrimination, then they will still lack the respect due to those of their rank. In New York City there is a saying among doctors, "Never go to a black physician under 40," referring to the fact that AA has affected the medical system during the past fifteen years. The police use "Quota Cops" and "Welfare Sergeants" to refer to those hired without passing the standardized tests. (In 1985 180 black and hispanic policemen, who had failed a promotion test, were promoted anyway to the rank of sergeant.) The destruction of false stereotypes will come naturally as qualified blacks rise naturally in fair competition (or if it does not—then the stereotypes may be justified). Reverse discrimination sends the message home that the stereotypes are deserved—otherwise, why do these minorities need so much extra help?

## 3. Equal Results Argument

Some philosophers and social scientists hold that human nature is roughly identical, so that on a fair playing field the same proportion from every race and gender and ethnic group would attain to the highest positions in every area of endeavor. It would follow that any inequality of results itself is evidence for inequality of opportunity. John Arthur, in discussing an intelligence test, Test 21, puts the case this way.

History is important when considering governmental rules like Test 21 because low scores by blacks can be traced in large measure to the legacy of slavery and racism: segregation, poor schooling, exclusion from trade unions, malnutrition, and poverty have all played their roles. Unless one assumes that blacks are naturally less able to pass the test, the conclusion must be that the results are themselves socially and legally constructed, not a mere given for which law and society can claim no responsibility.

The conclusion seems to be that genuine equality eventually requires equal results. Obviously blacks have been treated unequally throughout US history, and just as obviously the economic and psychological effects of that inequality linger to this day, showing up in lower income and poorer performance in school and on tests than whites achieve. Since we have no reason to believe that difference in performance can be explained by factors other than history, equal results are a good benchmark by which to measure progress made toward genuine equality.[9]

The result of a just society should be equal numbers in proportion to each group in the work force.

However, Arthur fails even to consider studies that suggest that there are innate differences between races, sexes, and groups. If there are genetic differences in intelligence and temperament within families, why should we not expect such differences between racial groups and the two genders? Why should the evidence for this be completely discounted?

Perhaps some race or one gender is more intelligent in one way than another. At present we have only limited knowledge about genetic differences, but what we do have suggests some difference besides the obvious physiological traits.[10] The proper use of this evidence is not to promote discriminatory policies but to be *open* to the possibility that innate differences may have led to an over-representation of certain groups in certain areas of endeavor. It seems that on average blacks have genetic endowments favoring them in the development of skills necessary for excellence in basketball.

Furthermore, on Arthur's logic, we should take aggressive AA against Asians and Jews since they are over-represented in science, technology, and medicine. So that each group receives its fair share, we should ensure that 12% of the philosophers in the United States are black, reduce the percentage of Jews from an estimated 15% to 2% —firing about 1,300 Jewish philosophers. The fact that Asians are producing 50% of Ph.D's in science and math and blacks less than 1% clearly shows, on this reasoning, that we are providing special secret advantages to Asians.

But why does society have to enter into this results game in the first place? Why do we have to decide whether all difference is environmental or genetic? Perhaps we should simply admit that we lack sufficient evidence to pronounce on these issues with any certainty—but if so, should we not be more modest in insisting on equal results? Here is a thought experiment. Take two families of different racial groups, Green and Blue. The Greens decide to have only two children, to spend all their resources on them, to give them the best education. The two Green kids respond well and end up with achievement test scores in the 99th percentile. The Blues fail to practice family planning. They have 15 children. They can only afford 2 children, but lack of ability or whatever prevents them from keeping their family down. Now they need help for their large family. Why does society have to step in and help them? Society did not force them to have 15 children. Suppose that the achievement test scores of the 15 children fall below the 25th percentile. They cannot compete with the Greens. But now enters AA. It says that it is society's fault that the Blue children are not as able as the Greens and that the Greens must pay extra taxes to enable the Blues to compete. No restraints are put on the Blues regarding family size. This seems unfair to the Greens. Should the Green children be made to bear responsibility for the consequences of the Blues' voluntary behavior?

My point is simply that Arthur needs to cast his net wider and recognize that demographics and childbearing and -rearing practices are crucial factors in achievement. People have to take some responsibility for their actions. The equal results argument (or axiom) misses a greater part of the picture.

## 4. The Compensation Argument

The argument goes like this: blacks have been wronged and severely harmed by whites. Therefore white society should compensate blacks for the injury caused them. Reverse discrimination in terms of preferential hiring, contracts, and scholarships is a fitting way to compensate for the past wrongs.

This argument actually involves a distorted notion of compensation. Normally, we think of compensation as owed by a specific person $A$ to another person $B$ whom $A$ has wronged in a spe-

cific way $C$. For example, if I have stolen your car and used it for a period of time to make business profits that would have gone to you, it is not enough that I return your car. I must pay you an amount reflecting your loss and my ability to pay. If I have only made $5,000 and only have $10,000 in assets, it would not be possible for you to collect $20,000 in damages—even though that is the amount of loss you have incurred.

Sometimes compensation is extended to groups of people who have been unjustly harmed by the greater society. For example, the United States government has compensated the Japanese-Americans who were interred during the Second World War, and the West German government has paid reparations to the survivors of Nazi concentration camps. But here a specific people have been identified who were wronged in an identifiable way by the government of the nation in question.

On the face of it the demand by blacks for compensation does not fit the usual pattern. Perhaps Southern States with Jim Crow laws could be accused of unjustly harming blacks, but it is hard to see that the United States government was involved in doing so. Furthermore, it is not clear that all blacks were harmed in the same way or whether some were *unjustly* harmed or harmed more than poor whites and others (e.g. short people). Finally, even if identifiable blacks were harmed by identifiable social practices, it is not clear that most forms of Affirmative Action are appropriate to restore the situation. The usual practice of a financial payment seems more appropriate than giving a high level job to someone unqualified or only minimally qualified, who, speculatively, might have been better qualified had he not been subject to racial discrimination. If John is the star tailback of our college team with a promising professional future, and I accidentally (but culpably) drive my pick-up truck over his legs, and so cripple him, John may be due compensation, but he is not due the tailback spot on the football team.

Still, there may be something intuitively compelling about compensating members of an oppressed group who are minimally qualified. Suppose that the Hatfields and the McCoys are enemy clans and some youths from the Hatfields go over and steal diamonds and gold from the McCoys, distributing it within the Hatfield economy. Even though we do not know which Hatfield youths did the stealing, we would want to restore the wealth, as far as possible, to the McCoys. One way might be to tax the Hatfields, but another might be to give preferential treatment in terms of scholarships and training programs and hiring to the McCoys.[11]

This is perhaps the strongest argument for Affirmative Action, and it may well justify some weak versions of AA, but it is doubtful whether it is sufficient to justify strong versions with quotas and goals and time tables in skilled positions. There are at least two reasons for this. First, we have no way of knowing how many people of group *G* would have been at competence level *L* had the world been different. Secondly, the normal criterion of competence is a strong prima facie consideration when the most important positions are at stake. There are two reasons for this: (1) society has given people expectations that if they attain certain levels of excellence they will be awarded appropriately and (2) filling the most important positions with the best qualified is the best way to insure efficiency in job-related areas and in society in general. These reasons are not absolutes. They can be overridden. But there is a strong presumption in their favor so that a burden of proof rests with those who would override them.

At this point we get into the problem of whether innocent non-blacks should have to pay a penalty in terms of preferential hiring of blacks. We turn to that argument.

## 5. Compensation from Those Who Innocently Benefited from Past Injustice

White males as innocent beneficiaries of unjust discrimination of blacks and women have no grounds for complaint when society seeks to rectify the tilted field. White males may be innocent of oppressing blacks and minorities (and women), but they have unjustly benefited from that oppression or discrimination. So it is perfectly proper that less qualified women and blacks be hired before them.

The operative principle is: He who knowingly and willingly benefits from a wrong must help pay for the wrong. Judith Jarvis Thomson puts it this way. "Many [white males] have been direct beneficiaries of policies which have down-graded blacks and women . . . and even those who did not directly benefit . . . had, at any rate, the advantage in the competition which comes of the confidence in one's full membership [in the community], and of one's right being recognized as a matter of course."[12] That is, white males obtain advantages in self respect and self-confidence deriving from a racist system which denies these to blacks and women.

*Objection.* As I noted in the previous section, compensation is normally individual and specific. If *A* harms *B* regarding *x*, *B* has a right to compensation from *A* in regards to *x*. If *A* steals *B*'s car and wrecks it, *A* has an obligation to compensate *B* for the stolen car, but *A*'s son has no obligation to compensate *B*. Furthermore, if *A* dies or disappears, *B* has no moral right to claim that society compensate him for the stolen car—though if he has insurance, he can make such a claim to the insurance company. Sometimes a wrong cannot be compensated, and we just have to make the best of an imperfect world.

Suppose my parents, divining that I would grow up to have an unsurpassable desire to be a basketball player, bought an expensive growth hormone for me. Unfortunately, a neighbor stole it and gave it to little Lew Alcindor, who gained the extra 18 inches—my 18 inches—and shot up to an enviable 7 feet 2 inches. Alias Kareem Abdul Jabbar, he excelled in basketball, as I would have done had I had my proper dose.

Do I have a right to the millions of dollars that Jabbar made as a professional basketball player—the unjustly innocent beneficiary of my growth hormone? I have a right to something from the neighbor who stole the hormone, and it might be kind of Jabbar to give me free tickets to the Laker basketball games, and perhaps I should be remembered in his will. As far as I can see, however, he does not *owe* me anything, either legally or morally.

Suppose further that Lew Alcindor and I are in high school together and we are both qualified to play basketball, only he is far better than I. Do I deserve to start in his position because I would have been as good as he is had someone not cheated me as a child? Again, I think not. But if being the lucky beneficiary of wrong-doing does not entail that Alcindor (or the coach) owes me anything in regards to basketball, why should it be a reason to engage in preferential hiring in academic positions or highly coveted jobs? If minimal qualifications are not adequate to override excellence in basketball, even when the minimality is a consequence of wrongdoing, why should they be adequate in other areas?

## 6. The Diversity Argument

It is important that we learn to live in a pluralistic world, learning to get along with those of other races and cultures, so we should have fully integrated schools and employment situations. Diversity is an important symbol and educative device. Thus preferential treatment is warranted to perform this role in society.

But, again, while we can admit the value of diversity, it hardly seems adequate to override considerations of merit and efficiency. Diversity for diversity's sake is moral promiscuity, since it obfuscates rational distinctions, and unless those hired are highly qualified the diversity factor threatens to become a fetish. At least at the higher levels of business and the professions, competence far outweighs considerations of diversity. I do not care whether the group of surgeons operating on me reflect racial or gender balance, but I do care that they are highly qualified. And likewise with airplane pilots, military leaders, business executives, and, may I say it, teachers and professors. Moreover, there are other ways of learning about other cultures besides engaging in reverse discrimination.

## 7. Anti-Meritocratic (Desert) Argument to Justify Reverse Discrimination: "No One Deserves His Talents"

According to this argument, the competent do not deserve their intelligence, their superior character, their industriousness, or their discipline; therefore they have no right to the best positions in society; therefore society is not unjust in giving these positions to less (but still minimally) qualified blacks and women. In one form this argument holds that since no one deserves anything, society may use any criteria it pleases to distribute goods. The criterion most often designated is social utility. Versions of this argument are found in the writings of John Arthur, John Rawls, Bernard Boxill, Michael Kinsley, Ronald Dworkin, and Richard Wasserstrom. Rawls writes, "No one deserves his place in the distribution of native endowments, any more than one deserves one's initial starting place in society. The assertion that a man deserves the superior character that enables him to make the effort to cultivate his abilities is equally problematic; for his character depends in large part upon fortunate family and social circumstances for which he can claim no credit. The notion of desert seems not to apply to these cases."[13] Michael Kinsley is even more adamant:

Opponents of affirmative action are hung up on a distinction that seems more profoundly irrelevant: treating individuals versus treating groups. What is the moral difference between dispensing favors to people on their "merits" as individuals and passing out society's benefits on the basis of group identification?

Group identifications like race and sex are, of course, immutable. They have nothing to do with a person's moral worth. But the same is true of most of what comes under the label "merit." The tools you need for getting ahead in a meritocratic society—not all of them but most: talent, education, instilled cultural values such as ambition—are distributed just as arbitrarily as skin color. They are fate. The notion that people somehow "deserve" the advantages of those characteristics in a way they don't "deserve" the advantage of their race is powerful, but illogical.[14]

It will help to put the argument in outline form.

1. Society may award jobs and positions as it sees fit as long as individuals have no claim to these positions.
2. To have a claim to something means that one has earned it or deserves it.
3. But no one has earned or deserves his intelligence, talent, education or cultural values which produce superior qualifications.
4. If a person does not deserve what produces something, he does not deserve its products.
5. Therefore better qualified people do not deserve their qualifications.
6. Therefore, society may override their qualifications in awarding jobs and positions as it sees fit (for social utility or to compensate for previous wrongs).

So it is permissible if a minimally qualified black or woman is admitted to law or medical school ahead of a white male with excellent credentials or if a less qualified person from an "underutilized" group gets a professorship ahead of a far better qualified white male. Sufficiency and underutilization together outweigh excellence.

*Objection.* Premise 4 is false. To see this, reflect that just because I do not deserve the money that I have been given as a gift (for instance) does not mean that I am not entitled to what I get with that money. If you and I both get a gift of $100 and I bury mine in the sand for 5 years while you invest yours wisely and double its value at the end of five years, I cannot complain that you should split the increase 50/50 since neither of us deserved the original gift. If we accept the notion of responsibility at all, we must hold that persons deserve the fruits of their labor and conscious choices. Of course, we might want to distinguish moral from legal desert and argue that, morally speaking, effort is more important than outcome, whereas, legally speaking, outcome may be more important. Nevertheless, there are good reasons in terms of efficiency, motivation, and rough justice for holding a strong prima facie

principle of giving scarce high positions to those most competent.

The attack on moral desert is perhaps the most radical move that egalitarians like Rawls and company have made against meritocracy, but the ramifications of their attack are far reaching. The following are some of its implications. Since I do not deserve my two good eyes or two good kidneys, the social engineers may take one of each from me to give to those needing an eye or a kidney—even if they have damaged their organs by their own voluntary actions. Since no one deserves anything, we do not deserve pay for our labors or praise for a job well done or first prize in the race we win. The notion of moral responsibility vanishes in a system of levelling.

But there is no good reason to accept the argument against desert. We do act freely and, as such, we are responsible for our actions. We deserve the fruits of our labor, reward for our noble feats and punishment for our misbehavior.

We have considered seven arguments for Affirmative Action and have found no compelling case for Strong AA and only one plausible argument (a version of the compensation argument) for Weak AA. We must now turn to the arguments against Affirmative Action to see whether they fare any better.[15]

# IV. Arguments against Affirmative Action

## 1. Affirmative Action Requires Discrimination against a Different Group

Weak Affirmative Action weakly discriminates against new minorities, mostly innocent young white males, and Strong Affirmative Action strongly discriminates against these new minorities. As I argued in III.5, this discrimination is unwarranted, since, even if some compensation to blacks were indicated, it would be unfair to make innocent white males bear the whole brunt of the payments. In fact, it is poor white youth who become the new pariahs on the job market. The children of the wealthy have no trouble getting into the best private grammar schools and, on the basis of superior early education, into the best universities, graduate schools, managerial and professional positions. Affirmative Action simply shifts injustice, setting blacks and women against young white males, especially ethnic and poor white males. It does little to rectify the goal of providing equal opportunity to all. If the goal is a society where everyone has a fair chance, then it would be better to concentrate on support for families and early education and decide the matter of university admissions and job hiring on the basis of traditional standards of competence.

## 2. Affirmative Action Perpetuates the Victimization Syndrome

Shelby Steele admits that Affirmative Action may seem "the meagerest recompense for centuries of unrelieved oppression" and that it helps promote diversity. At the same time, though, notes Steele, Affirmative Action reinforces the spirit of victimization by telling blacks that they can gain more by emphasizing their suffering, degradation and helplessness than by discipline and work. This message holds the danger of blacks becoming permanently handicapped by a need for special treatment. It also sends to society at large the message that blacks cannot make it on their own.

Leon Wieseltier sums up the problem this way.

The memory of oppression is a pillar and a strut of the identity of every people oppressed. It is no ordinary marker of difference. It is unusually stiffening. It instructs the individual and the group about what to expect of the world, imparts an isolating sense of aptness. . . . Don't be fooled, it teaches, there is only repetition. For that reason, the collective memory of an oppressed people is not only a treasure but a trap.

In the memory of oppression, oppression outlives itself. The scar does the work of the wound. That is the real tragedy: that injustice retains the power to distort long after it has ceased to be real. It is a posthumous victory for the oppressors, when pain becomes a tradition. And yet the atrocities of the past must never be forgotten. This is the unfairly difficult dilemma of the newly emancipated and the newly enfranchised: an honorable life is not possible if they remember too little

and a normal life is not possible if they remember too much.[16]

With the eye of recollection, which does not "remember too much," Steele recommends a policy which offers "educational and economic development of disadvantaged people regardless of race and the eradication from our society—through close monitoring and severe sanctions—of racial and gender discrimination."[17]

## 3. Affirmative Action Encourages Mediocrity and Incompetence

Last spring Jesse Jackson joined protesters at Harvard Law School in demanding that the Law School faculty hire black women. Jackson dismissed Dean of the Law School, Robert C. Clark's standard of choosing the best qualified person for the job as "Cultural anemia." "We cannot just define who is qualified in the most narrow vertical academic terms," he said. "Most people in the world are yellow, brown, black, poor, non-Christian and don't speak English, and they can't wait for some White males with archaic rules to appraise them."[18] It might be noted that if Jackson is correct about the depth of cultural decadence at Harvard, blacks might be well advised to form and support their own more vital law schools and leave places like Harvard to their archaism.

At several universities, the administration has forced departments to hire members of minorities even when far superior candidates were available. Shortly after obtaining my Ph.D. in the late 70's I was mistakenly identified as a black philosopher (I had a civil rights record and was once a black studies major) and was flown to a major university, only to be rejected for a more qualified candidate when it discovered that I was white.

Stories of the bad effects of Affirmative Action abound. The philosopher Sidney Hook writes that "At one Ivy League university, representatives of the Regional HEW demanded an explanation of why there were no women or minority students in the Graduate Department of Religious Studies. They were told that a reading knowledge of Hebrew and Greek was presupposed. Whereupon the representatives of HEW advised orally: 'Then end those old fashioned programs that require irrelevant languages. And start up programs on relevant things which minority group students can study without learning languages.'"[19]

Nicholas Capaldi notes that the staff of HEW itself was one-half women, three-fifths members of minorities, and one-half black—a clear case of racial over-representation.

In 1972 officials at Stanford University discovered a proposal for the government to monitor curriculum in higher education: the "Summary Statement . . . Sex Discrimination Proposed HEW Regulation to Effectuate Title IX of the Education Amendment of 1972" to "establish and use internal procedure for reviewing curricula, designed both to ensure that they do not reflect discrimination on the basis of sex and to resolve complaints concerning allegations of such discrimination, pursuant to procedural standards to be prescribed by the Director of the office of Civil Rights." Fortunately, Secretary of HEW Caspar Weinberger when alerted to the intrusion, assured Stanford University that he would never approve of it.[20]

Government programs of enforced preferential treatment tend to appeal to the lowest possible common denominator. Witness the 1974 HEW Revised Order No. 14 on Affirmative Action expectations for preferential hiring: "Neither minorities nor female employees should be required to possess higher qualifications than those of the lowest qualified incumbents."

Furthermore, no tests may be given to candidates unless it is *proved* to be relevant to the job.

No standard or criteria which have, by intent or effect, worked to exclude women or minorities as a class can be utilized, unless the institution can demonstrate the necessity of such standard to the performance of the job in question.

Whenever a validity study is called for . . . the user should include . . . an investigation of suitable alternative selection procedures and suitable alternative methods of using the selection procedure which have as little adverse impact as possible. . . . Whenever the user is shown an alternative selection procedure with evidence of less adverse impact and substantial evidence of validity for the same job in similar circumstances, the user should investigate it to determine the appropriateness of using or validating it in accord with these guidelines.[21]

At the same time Americans are wondering why standards in our country are falling and the Japanese are getting ahead. Affirmative Action with its twin idols, Sufficiency and Diversity, is the enemy of excellence. I will develop this thought below (IV.6).

## 4. Affirmative Action Policies Unjustly Shift the Burden of Proof

Affirmative Action legislation tends to place the burden of proof on the employer who does not have an "adequate" representation of "underutilized" groups in his work force. He is guilty until proven innocent. I have already recounted how in the mid-eighties the Supreme Court shifted the burden of proof back onto the plaintiff, while Congress is now attempting to shift the burden back to the employer. Those in favor of deeming disproportional representation "guilty until proven innocent" argue that it is easy for employers to discriminate against minorities by various subterfuges, and I agree that steps should be taken to monitor against prejudicial treatment. But being prejudiced against employers is not the way to attain a just solution to discrimination. The principle: innocent until proven guilty, applies to employers as well as criminals. Indeed, it is clearly special pleading to reject this basic principle of Anglo-American law in this case of discrimination while adhering to it everywhere else.

## 5. An Argument from Merit

Traditionally, we have believed that the highest positions in society should be awarded to those who are best qualified—as the Koran states in the quotation at the beginning of this paper. Rewarding excellence both seems just to the individuals in the competition and makes for efficiency. Note that one of the most successful acts of integration, the recruitment of Jackie Robinson in the late 40's, was done in just this way, according to merit. If Robinson had been brought into the major league as a mediocre player or had batted .200 he would have been scorned and sent back to the minors where he belonged.

Merit is not an absolute value. There are times when it may be overridden for social goals, but there is a strong prima facie reason for awarding positions on its basis, and it should enjoy a weighty presumption in our social practices.

In a celebrated article Ronald Dworkin says that "Bakke had no case" because society did not owe Bakke anything. That may be, but then why does it owe anyone anything? Dworkin puts the matter in Utility terms, but if that is the case, society may owe Bakke a place at the University of California/Davis, for it seems a reasonable rule-utilitarian principle that achievement should be rewarded in society. We generally want the best to have the best positions, the best qualified candidate to win the political office, the most brilliant and competent scientist to be chosen for the most challenging research project, the best qualified pilots to become commercial pilots, only the best soldiers to become generals. Only when little is at stake do we weaken the standards and content ourselves with sufficiency (rather than excellence) —there are plenty of jobs where "sufficiency" rather than excellence is required. Perhaps we now feel that medicine or law or university professorships are so routine that they can be performed by minimally qualified people—in which case AA has a place.

But note, no one is calling for quotas or proportional representation of *underutilized* groups in the National Basketball Association where blacks make up 80% of the players. But if merit and merit alone reigns in sports, should it not be valued at least as much in education and industry?

## 6. The Slippery Slope

Even if Strong AA or Reverse Discrimination could meet the other objections, it would face a tough question: once you embark on this project, how do you limit it? Who should be excluded from reverse discrimination? Asians and Jews are over-represented, so if we give blacks positive quotas, should we place negative quotas to these other groups? Since white males, "WMs," are a minority which is suffering from reverse discrimination, will we need a New Affirmative Action policy in the 21st century to compensate for the discrimination against WMs in the late 20th century?

Furthermore, Affirmative Action has stigmatized the *young* white male. Assuming that we accept reverse discrimination, the fair way to make sacrifices would be to retire *older* white males who are more likely to have benefited from a favored status. Probably the least guilty of any harm to minority groups is the young white male —usually a liberal who has been required to bear the brunt of ages of past injustice. Justice Brennan's announcement that the Civil Rights Act did not apply to discrimination against whites shows how the clearest language can be bent to serve the ideology of the moment.[22]

## 7. The Mounting Evidence against the Success of Affirmative Action

Thomas Sowell of the Hoover Institute has shown in his book *Preferential Policies: An International Perspective* that preferential hiring almost never solves social problems. It generally builds in mediocrity or incompetence and causes deep resentment. It is a short term solution which lacks serious grounding in social realities.

For instance, Sowell cites some disturbing statistics on education. Although twice as many blacks as Asians students took the nationwide Scholastic Aptitude Test in 1983, approximately fifteen times as many Asian students scored above 700 (out of a possible 800) on the mathematics half of the SAT. The percentage of Asians who scored above 700 in math was also more than six times higher than the percentage of American Indians and more than ten times higher than that of Mexican Americans—as well as more than double the percentage of whites. As Sowell points out, in all countries studied, "intergroup performance disparities are huge" (108).

There are dozens of American colleges and universities where the median combined verbal SAT score and mathematics SAT score total 1200 or above. As of 1983 there were less than 600 black students in the entire US with combined SAT scores of 1200. This meant that, despite widespread attempts to get a black student "representation" comparable to the black percentage of the population (about 11%), there were not enough black students in the entire country for the Ivy League alone to have such a "representation" without going beyond this pool—even if the entire pool went to the eight Ivy League Colleges.[23]

Often it is claimed that a cultural bias is the cause of the poor performance of blacks on SAT (or IQ tests), but Sowell shows that these test scores are actually a better predictor of college performance for blacks than for Asians and whites. He also shows the harmfulness of the effect on blacks of preferential acceptance. At the University of California, Berkeley, where the freshman class closely reflects the actual ethnic distribution of California high school students, more than 70% of blacks fail to graduate. All 312 black students entering Berkeley in 1987 were admitted under "Affirmative Action" criteria rather than by meeting standard academic criteria. So were 480 out of 507 Hispanic students. In 1986 the median SAT score for blacks at Berkeley was 952, for Mexican Americans 1014, for American Indians 1082 and for Asian Americans 1254. (The average SAT for all students was 1181.)

The result of this mismatching is that blacks who might do well if they went to a second tier or third tier school where their test scores would indicate they belong, actually are harmed by preferential treatment. They cannot compete in the institutions where high abilities are necessary.

Sowell also points out that Affirmative Action policies have mainly assisted the middle class black, those who have suffered least from discrimination. "Black couples in which both husband and wife are college-educated overtook white couples of the same description back in the early

1970's and continued to at least hold their own in the 1980's" (115).

Sowell's conclusion is that similar patterns of results obtained from India to the USA wherever preferential policies exist. "In education, preferential admissions policies have led to high attrition rates and substandard performances for those preferred students . . . who survived to graduate." In all countries the preferred tended to concentrate in less difficult subjects which lead to less remunerative careers. "In the employment market, both blacks and untouchables at the higher levels have advanced substantially while those at the lower levels show no such advancement and even some signs of retrogression. These patterns are also broadly consistent with patterns found in countries in which majorities have created preferences for themselves. . . ." (116).

The tendency has been to focus at the high level end of education and employment rather than on the lower level of family structure and early education. But if we really want to help the worst off improve, we need to concentrate on the family and early education. It is foolish to expect equal results when we begin with grossly unequal starting points—and discriminating against young white males is no more just than discriminating against women, blacks or anyone else.

## Conclusion

Let me sum up. The goal of the Civil Rights movement and of moral people everywhere has been equal opportunity. The question is: how best to get there. Civil Rights legislation removed the legal barriers to equal opportunity, but did not tackle the deeper causes that produced differential results. Weak Affirmative Action aims at encouraging minorities in striving for the highest positions without unduly jeopardizing the rights of majorities, but the problem of Weak Affirmative Action is that it easily slides into Strong Affirmative Action where quotas, "goals," and equal results are forced into groups, thus promoting mediocrity, inefficiency, and resentment. Furthermore, Affirmative Action aims at the higher levels of society—universities and skilled jobs—yet if we want to improve our society, the best way to do it is to concentrate on families, children, early education, and the like. Affirmative Action is, on the one hand, too much, too soon and on the other hand, too little, too late.

Martin Luther said that humanity is like a man mounting a horse who always tends to fall off on the other side of the horse. This seems to be the case with Affirmative Action. Attempting to redress the discriminatory iniquities of our history, our well-intentioned social engineers engage in new forms of discriminatory iniquity and thereby think that they have successfully mounted the horse of racial harmony. They have only fallen off on the other side of the issue.[24]

## Notes

1. Quoted in William Bradford Reynolds, "Affirmative Action is Unjust" in D. Bender and B. Leone (eds.), *Social Justice* (St. Paul, MN, 1984), p. 23.

2. Some of the material in this section is based on Nicholas Capaldi's *Out of Order: Affirmative Action and the Crisis of Doctrinaire Liberalism* (Buffalo, NY, 1985), chapters 1 and 2. Capaldi, using the shackled runner analogy, divides the history into three stages: a *platitude stage* "in which it is reaffirmed that the race is to be fair, and a fair race is one in which no one has either special disadvantages or special advantages (equal opportunity)"; a *remedial stage* in which victims of past discrimination are to be given special help overcoming their disadvantages; and a *realignment stage* "in which all runners will be reassigned to those positions on the course that they would have had if the race had been fair from the beginning" (p. 18f).

3. Wanda Warren Berry, "Affirmative Action is Just" in D. Bender, *op. cit.*, p. 18.

4. Robert Fullinwider, *The Reverse Discrimination Controversy* (Totowa, NJ, 1970), p. 25.

5. Quoted in Fullinwider, *op. cit.*, p. 4f.

6. See Lino A. Graglia, "'Affirmative Action,' the Constitution, and the 1964 Civil Rights Act," *Measure*, no. 92 (1991).

7. Linda Gottfredson, "Letters to the Editor," *New York Times*, Aug. 1, 1990 issue. Gender-norming is also a feature of the proponents of Affirmative Action. Michael Levin begins his book *Feminism and Freedom* (New Brunswick, 1987) with federal court case *Beckman v. NYFD* in which 88 women who failed the New York City Fire Department's

entrance exam in 1977 filed a class-action sex discrimination suit. The court found that the physical strength component of the test was not job-related, and thus a violation of Title VII of the Civil Rights Act, and ordered the city to hire 49 of the women. It further ordered the fire department to devise a special, less-demanding physical strength exam for women. Following EEOC guidelines if the passing rate for women is less than 80% that of the passing rate of men, the test is presumed invalid.

8. Thomas Sowell, *Preferential Policies: An International Perspective* (New York, 1990).

9. John Arthur, *The Unfinished Constitution* (Belmont, CA, 1990), p. 238.

10. See Phillip E. Vernon's excellent summary of the literature in *Intelligence: Heredity and Environment* (New York, 1979) and Yves Christen "Sex Differences in the Human Brain" in Nicholas Davidson (ed.) *Gender Sanity* (Lanham, 1989) and T. Bouchard, *et al.*, "Sources of Human Psychological Differences: The Minnesota Study of Twins Reared Apart," *Science*, vol. 250 (1990).

11. See Michael Levin, "Is Racial Discrimination Special?" *Policy Review*, Fall issue (1982).

12. Judith Jarvis Thomson, "Preferential Hiring" in Marshall Cohen, Thomas Nagel and Thomas Scanlon (eds.), *Equality and Preferential Treatment* (Princeton, 1977).

13. John Rawls, *A Theory of Justice* (Cambridge, 1971), p. 104; See Richard Wasserstrom "A Defense of Programs of Preferential Treatment," *National Forum* (Phi Kappa Phi Journal), vol. 58 (1978). See also Bernard Boxill, "The Morality of Preferential Hiring," *Philosophy and Public Affairs*, vol. 7 (1978).

14. Michael Kinsley, "Equal Lack of Opportunity," *Harper's*, June issue (1983).

15. There is one other argument which I have omitted. It is one from precedence and has been stated by Judith Jarvis Thomson in the article cited earlier:

> "Suppose two candidates for a civil service job have equally good test scores, but there is only one job available. We could decide between them by coin-tossing. But in fact we do allow for declaring for A straightaway, where A is a veteran, and B is not. It may be that B is a non-veteran through no fault of his own. . . . Yet the fact is that B is not a veteran and A is. On the assumption that the veteran has served his country, the country owes him something. And it is plain that giving him preference is not an unjust way in which part of that debt of gratitude can be paid" (p. 379f).

The two forms of preferential hiring are analogous. Veteran's preference is justified as a way of paying a debt of gratitude; preferential hiring is a way of paying a debt of compensation. In both cases innocent parties bear the burden of the community's debt, but it is justified.

My response to this argument is that veterans should not be hired in place of better qualified candidates, but that benefits like the GI scholarships are part of the contract with veterans who serve their country in the armed services. The notion of compensation only applies to individuals who have been injured by identifiable entities. So the analogy between veterans and minority groups seems weak.

16. Quoted in Jim Sleeper, *The Closest of Strangers* (New York, 1990), p. 209.

17. Shelby Steele, "A Negative Vote on Affirmative Action." *New York Times,* May 13, 1990 issue.

18. *New York Times,* May 10, 1990 issue.

19. Nicholas Capaldi, *op. cit.,* p. 85.

20. Cited in Capaldi, *op. cit.,* p. 95.

21. *Ibid.*

22. The extreme form of this New Speak is incarnate in the Politically Correct Movement ("PC" ideology) where a new orthodoxy has emerged, condemning white, European culture and seeing African culture as the new savior of us all. Perhaps the clearest example of this is Paula Rothenberg's book *Racism and Sexism* (New York, 1987) which asserts that there is no such thing as black racism; only whites are capable of racism (p. 6). Ms. Rothenberg's book has been scheduled as required reading for all freshmen at the University of Texas. See Joseph Salemi, "Lone Star Academic Politics," no. 87 (1990).

23. Thomas Sowell, *op. cit.,* p. 108.

24. I am indebted to Jim Landesman, Michael Levin, and Abigail Rosenthal for comments on a previous draft of this paper. I am also indebted to Nicholas Capaldi's *Out of Order* for first making me aware of the extent of the problem of Affirmative Action.

# 53   One Way to Understand and Defend Programs of Preferential Treatment

## RICHARD A. WASSERSTROM

Programs of preferential treatment make relevant the race or sex of individuals in the sense that the race or sex of an applicant for admission, a job, or a promotion constitutes a relevant, although not a decisive, reason for preferring that applicant over others. In my discussion of these programs I will consider only preferential treatment programs concerned with preferring a person who is black over one who is white, but what I have to say will be illustrative of a way to approach and assess comparable programs in which members of other ethnic or minority groups, or women, are concerned.

My thesis is a twofold one. First, such programs can very plausibly be seen to be good programs for us to have in our society today because they help to make the social conditions of life less racially oppressive and thereby more just, and because they help to distribute important social goods and opportunities more equally and fairly. Second, these programs can be seen to help to realize these desirable aims without themselves being in any substantial respect unjust—without, that is, taking an impermissible characteristic into account, violating persons' rights, failing to give individuals what they deserve, or treating them in some other way that is unfair.

The positive case for such programs begins with the following claim about our own society: we are still living in a society in which a person's race, his or her blackness rather than whiteness, is a socially significant and important category. Race is not, in our culture, like eye color. Eye color is an irrelevant category in that eye color is not an important social or cultural fact about individuals; nothing of substance turns on what eye color they have. To be black rather than white is not like that at all. To be black is to be at a disadvantage in terms of most of the measures of success or satisfaction—be they economic, vocational, political, or social. To see, in a very crude and rough way, that this is so one could conduct a thought experiment. If one wanted to imagine maximizing one's chances of being satisfied with one's employment or career, politically powerful rather than powerless, secure from arbitrary treatment within the

Reprinted with permission of the publisher from *The Moral Foundations of Civil Rights,* ed. Robert Fullinwider and Claudia Mills (Rowman and Littlefield, 1986).

social institutions, reasonably well off economically, and able to pursue one's own goals and develop one's own talents in ways that would be satisfying to oneself, and if one could choose whether to be born either white or black, wouldn't one choose to be born white rather than black?

If this claim about the existing social reality of race is correct, then two further claims seem plausible. The first is that there is in place what can correctly be described as a system of racial oppression. It is a racial system in that the positions of political, economic, and social power and advantage are concentrated and maintained largely in the hands of those who are white rather than black. It is an oppressive one in that some of these inequalities in social burdens and lessened opportunities are unjust because of the nature of the disadvantages themselves—they are among those that no one ought fairly be required to confront or combat in any decent society. And it is an oppressive one in that others of these inequalities are tied to race in contexts and ways that make such a connection itself manifestly unfair and unjust. But the primary and fundamental character of the oppression is in what results from these and related features and is not reducible to them. The oppression has to do, first, with the *systemic nature* of the unequal and maldistributed array of social benefits, opportunities, and burdens, and it has to do, as well, with *how* things are linked together to constitute an interlocking, mutually reinforcing system of social benefits and burdens, ideology, and the like which, when tied to race as they are, make it a system of *racial* disadvantage and oppression—and, for all of these reasons, a decidedly unjust one.

Now, if this be granted, the next claim is that even if it is assumed that the intentions and motivations of those occupying positions of relative power and opportunity are wholly benign and proper with respect to the pursuit of the wrongful perpetuation of any unjust racial oppression toward blacks, it is likely that the system will perpetuate itself unless blacks come to occupy substantially more of the positions within the major social institutions than they have occupied in the past and now do. Thus, to have it occur that blacks do come to occupy more of these positions of power, authority, and the like is *a* way, if not *the* way, to bring about the weakening, if not the destruction, of that interlocking system of social practices, structures, and ideology that still plays a major if not fundamental role in preventing persons who are black from being able to live the kinds of lives that all persons ought to be able to live—lives free from the burdens of an existing, racially oppressive system.

If this is so, then the case for programs of preferential treatment can be seen to rest upon the truth of the claim that they are designed specifically to accomplish this end, and upon the truth of the claim that they do accomplish it. They do succeed in introducing more blacks into the kinds of vocations, careers, institutional positions, and the like than would have been present if these programs had not been in place. In this respect there is, I believe, little question but that the programs have worked and do work to produce, for example, black judges and lawyers where few if any existed before, and to produce, more generally, black employees in businesses and in places within the other major structures and hierarchies where few if any were present before. And this can be seen to be especially important and desirable because changes of this sort in the racial composition of these institutions have mutually reinforcing consequences that can reasonably be thought to play an important role in bringing about the dismantling of the existing system of racial disadvantage and oppression.

They do so, first, by creating role models for other black persons to identify with and thereby come to see as realizable in their own lives. They do so, second, by bringing members of this historically excluded and oppressed group into relationships of equality of power, authority, and status with members of the dominant group. This is important because when relationships of this kind are nonexistent or extremely infrequent, as they are in the system of racial oppression, the system tends most easily and regularly to sustain itself. Third, changes in the racial composition of the major social institutions work, as well, to make it possible for blacks, with their often different and distinctive but no less correct views of the nature of the complex social world in which we all live, to participate in such things as the shaping of academic programs and disciplines and to participate in the definition, focus, and direction of significant social, legal, economic, and related institutional policies, and in deliberations and debates concerning their supporting justifications. And they do so, finally, by making it more likely that there will be the more immediate and meaningful provision of important services and benefits to other members of that group who have up until now been denied fair and appropriate access to them.

Thus, the primary claim in support of these programs is that, in what they do and how they work, they can be seen to play a substantial role in weakening the system of racial oppression that is still in place and that makes a person's blackness have the kind of pervasively deleterious social meaning and significance that it ought not. The aim of these programs is to eliminate this system and to produce a society in which race will cease to matter in this way, and on this view of things it may be superficially paradoxical but is, nonetheless, more deeply plausible to believe that such can be significantly accomplished by taking race into account in the way these programs do.

What should be apparent is that, in some large measure, there are empirical claims involved here, and to the degree to which there are, disagreements about the justifiability of preferential treatment programs can be located and settled by attending to their truth or falsity. Thus, if such programs produce or exacerbate racial hostility, or if they lead to a reduced rather than an enhanced sense of self-respect on the part of blacks, then these are matters that count against the overall case for these programs. But I do not, myself, think the case against them can be rested very easily upon such grounds, and I do not think that, when it is, the evidence is very convincing and the arguments very plausible. Nor are such programs typically opposed on grounds of this sort. Instead, the main ground of principled opposition has to do with what is thought to be fundamentally wrong with them: with the fact that they are unjust, inconsistent with important ideals and principles,

and violative of persons' basic rights. In what follows, I will seek very briefly to indicate why this is not so and how my way of understanding and justifying these programs can help to bring these matters, too, into a different and more proper focus.

The first argument that is both common and close to the core of the cluster of objections to these programs is this: if it was wrong to take race into account when blacks were the objects of racial policies of exclusion, then it is wrong to take race into account when the objects of the policies differ only in their race. Simple considerations of intellectual consistency—of what it means to have had a good reason for condemning those social policies and practices—require that what was a good reason then be a good reason now.

The right way to answer this objection is, I think, to agree that the practices of racial exclusion that were an integral part of the fabric of our culture, and which still are, to some degree, were and are pernicious. Yet, one can grant this and also believe that the kinds of racial preferences and quotas that are a part of contemporary preferential treatment programs are commendable and right. There is no inconsistency involved in holding both views. The reason why depends upon a further analysis of the social realities. A fundamental feature of programs that discriminated against blacks was that these programs were a part of a larger social universe in which the network of social institutions concentrated power, authority, and goods in the hands of white individuals. This same social universe contained a complex ideology that buttressed this network of institutions and at the same time received support from it. Practices that prevented or limited the access of blacks to the desirable social institutions, places, and benefits were, therefore, wrong both because of their direct consequences on the individuals most affected by them, and because the system of racial superiority that was constituted by these institutions and practices was an immoral one, in that it severely and unjustifiably restricted the capacities, autonomy, and happiness of those who were members of the less favored category.

Whatever may be wrong with today's programs of preferential treatment, even those with quotas, it should be clear that the evil, if any, is simply not the same. Blacks do not constitute the dominant social group. Nor is the prevailing ideological conception of who is a fully developed member of the moral and social community one of an individual who is black rather than white. Programs that give a preference to blacks do not add to an already comparatively overabundant supply of resources and opportunities at the disposal of members of the dominant racial group in the way in which exclusionary practices of the past added to the already overabundant supply of resources and opportunities at the disposal of whites. Thus, if preferential treatment programs are to be condemned or abandoned, it cannot be either because they seek to perpetuate an unjust society in which the desirable options for living are husbanded by and for those who already have the most, or because they realize and maintain a morally corrupt ideal of distinct grades of political, social, and moral superiority and inferiority— in this case grades or classes of superiority and inferiority tied to and determined by one's race.

A related objection that fares no better, I believe, has to do with the identification of what exactly was wrong, say, with the system of racial discrimination in the South, or with what is wrong with any system of racial discrimination. One very common way to think about the wrongness of racial discrimination is to see the essential wrongness as consisting in the use of an irrelevant characteristic, namely race, to allocate social benefits and burdens of various sorts, for, given this irrelevance, individuals end up being treated in an arbitrary manner. On this view, the chief defect of the system of racial segregation and discrimination that we had and still have is to be located in its systemic capriciousness. Hence, on this view, what is wrong and unjust about any practice or act of taking any individual's race into account is the irrational and arbitrary character of the interest in and concern with race.

I am far less certain that that is the central flaw at all—especially with our own historical system of racial segregation and discrimination. Consider, for instance, the most hideous of the practices, human slavery. The primary thing that was wrong, I think, with that institution was not that the partic-

ular individuals who were assigned the place of slaves were assigned there arbitrarily by virtue of an irrelevant characteristic, i.e., their race. Rather, the fundamental thing that was and is wrong with slavery is the practice itself—the fact that some human beings were able to own other human beings—and all that goes with the acceptance of that practice and that conception of permissible interpersonal relationships. A comparable criticism can be made of many of the other discrete practices and institutions that comprised the system of racial discrimination even after human slavery was abolished.

The fundamental wrongness in taking race into account in this way has to do, perhaps, with arbitrariness, but it is the special arbitrariness attendant upon using race in the constitution and maintenance of any system of oppression so as to make that system a system of racial oppression. The irrationality, arbitrariness, and deep injustice of taking race into account cannot, I think, be isolated or severed from the place of a racial criterion in the very constitution of that system which becomes both a system of *oppression* and a system of *racial* oppression in and through the regular systematic use of that criterion. Whatever may be said about the appropriateness of regarding race as relevant in other contexts, the arbitrariness of taking race into account has a special and distinctive bite of injustice when race becomes the basis for fixing persons' unequal positions, opportunities, and status in this kind of systemically pervasive fashion. When viewed in the light of existing social realities and in the light of this conception of the wrongness of a racially oppressive system, the central consideration is that contemporary programs of preferential treatment, even when viewed as a system of programs, cannot plausibly be construed in either their design or effects as consigning whites to the kind of oppressed status systematically bestowed upon blacks by the dominant social institutions.

A third very common objection is that, when used in programs of preferential treatment, race is too broad a category for programs designed to promote, in a legitimate way in our present society, conditions of fair equality of opportunity and full equality with respect to political and social status. The objection presupposes that whatever the appropriate or relevant characteristic, it is not race. Instead, almost always it is taken to be disadvantaged socio-economic status.

This objection, too, helps to bring into focus the mistaken conception of the social realities upon which a number of the central objections to preferential treatment programs depend. While socio-economic status unquestionably affects in deep and pervasive ways the kinds of lives persons can and will be able to fashion and live, it is, I think, only a kind of implausible, vulgar Marxism, or socio-economic reductionism of some other type, that ultimately, underlies the view that, in our society, socio-economic status is the sole, or even the primary, locus of systemic oppression. Given my analysis of the social realities, blackness is as much a primary locus of oppression as is socio-economic status. And if so, it is implausible to insist, as this objection does, that socio-economic status is central while race is not. Race is just the appropriate characteristic to make directly relevant if the aim is to alter the existing system of racial oppression and inequality, or otherwise to mitigate its effects. Socio-economic status is an indirect, imperfect, unduly narrow, and overly broad category with which to deal with the phenomena of *racial* oppression and disadvantage, in precisely the same way in which race is an indirect, imperfect, unduly narrow, and overly broad category to take on the phenomena of *socio-economic* oppression and disadvantage.

The final objection I wish to introduce concerns the claim that these programs are wrong because they take race into account rather than taking into account the only thing that does and should matter: an individual's qualifications. And qualifications, it is further claimed, have nothing whatsoever to do with race. Here, I can mention only very briefly some of the key issues that seem to me to be at stake in understanding and assessing such an objection.

First, it is important to establish what the argument is for making selections solely on the basis of who is the most qualified among the applicants, candidates, and the like. One such argument for the exclusive relevance of qualifications—although it is seldom stated explicitly—is that the most qualified persons should always be selected for a place or position because the tasks or activities connected with that place or position will then be done in the most economical and efficient manner. Now, there is nothing wrong in principle with an argument based upon the good results that will be produced by a social practice of selection based solely upon the qualifications of the applicant. But there is a serious problem that many opponents of preferential treatment programs must confront. The nature and magnitude of their problem is apparent if their objection to my way of justifying these programs is that any appeal to good and bad results is the wrong *kind* of justification to offer. For if that is the basis of their objection, then it is simply inconsistent for them to rest their case for an exclusive preoccupation with qualifications upon a wholly analogous appeal to the good results alleged to follow upon such a practice. In any event, what is central is that this reason for attending only to qualifications fails to shift inquiry to that different kind of analysis having to do with justice that was originally claimed to be decisive.

Second, given the theses offered earlier concerning how the increased presence of blacks in the positions of the major social institutions changes the workings of those institutions, it is anything but obvious why a person's blackness cannot or should not appropriately be taken into account as one of the characteristics which, in any number of contexts, genuinely should count as an aspect of one's qualifications for many positions or places at this time in our social life. And preferential treatment programs can, therefore, often be plausibly construed as making just the judgment that a person's blackness is indeed one of the relevant characteristics helping to establish his or her overall qualifications.

Third, even if this way of looking at qualifications is rejected, a further question must still be addressed with respect to any or all of the characteristics of the more familiar sort that are thought to be the ones that legitimately establish who is the most qualified for a position: is the person who possesses these characteristics, and who is, hence, the most qualified, to be selected because that is what he or she deserves, or for some other reason? If persons do truly deserve to be selected by virtue of the possession of the characteristics that make them the most qualified, then to fail to select them is to treat them unjustly. But I am skeptical that a connection of the right sort can be established between being the most qualified in this sense and deserving to be selected. The confusion that so often arises in thinking about this issue comes about, I think, because of a failure to distinguish two very different ways in which the linkage between qualifications and desert might be thought to be a sound one.

The first way is this. If there is a system of selection in place with rules and criteria that specify how to determine who is the most qualified and therefore is to be selected, then there is, of course, a sense in which the most qualified, as defined by those criteria, do deserve to be selected by virtue of their relationship to those rules and criteria. But this sense of desert is a surface one, and any resulting desert claim is very weak because it derives its force and significance wholly from the existing criteria and rules for selection. In this same sense, once preferential treatment programs are established and in place, as many now are, these new programs can also be understood to establish alternative grounds and criteria for selection; as such, they stand on the same footing as more conventional systems of qualification and selection. In the identical manner, therefore, these new programs also give rise to surface claims of desert, founded now upon the respect in which those who best satisfy those criteria have a claim that they deserve to be selected because that is what the rules of these programs provide should happen.

What this suggests, I believe, is that the real and difficult question about the possible linkage between qualifications and desert has to be sought elsewhere, for that question has to do with whether those who possess certain characteristics deserve, in virtue of their possession of those characteristics, to have a selection procedure in place which makes selections turn on the possession of those characteristics. If they do, then those who

possess those characteristics do deserve in a deep, nonsurface way to be selected because of their qualifications. But now the problem is that being the best at something, or being the most able in respect to some task or role, does not, by itself at least, seem readily convertible into a claim about what such persons thereby genuinely deserve in virtue of things such as these being true of them. Perhaps a theory of desert of the right sort can be developed and adequately defended to show how and why those who are most able deserve (in a deep sense) selection criteria that will make them deserving of selection (in a surface sense); however, given the difficulty of connecting in any uniform way the mere possession of abilities with things that the possessor can claim any credit or responsibility for, and given the alternative plausibility of claims of desert founded upon attributes such as effort or need, the intellectual task at hand is a formidable one, and one that opponents of preferential treatment programs have not yet, I think, succeeded in coming to terms with in a convincing fashion.

Nonetheless, as was suggested earlier, there may be good reasons of other sorts for being interested in persons' qualifications—reasons which have to do, for example, with how well a predefined job or role will be performed and with the relative importance of having it done as well as possible. These reasons point directly to the good that will be promoted by selecting the most able. Still, a concern for having some predetermined job or role performed *only* by the person who will be *the best* at performing it is something that itself must be defended, given the good that is otherwise done by programs of preferential treatment (construed, as they must be within this objection, as programs which make race a relevant, but non-qualification-related criterion for selection). And the plausibility of that exclusive concern with performance will vary greatly with the position and its context. Sometimes this concern will be of decisive, or virtually decisive, importance; when it legitimately is, preferential treatment of the sort I have been defending should play a very minor or even nonexistent role in the selections to be made. But in many contexts, and most of them are the ones in which preferential treatment programs operate, no such exclusive concern seems defensible. In the case of admission to college or professional school, of selection to a faculty, or of selection for training or employment, the good that is secured in selecting the most qualified person, in this restricted sense, is at most only one of the goods to be realized and balanced against those other, quite substantial ones whose realization depends upon the implementation of such programs. In sum, therefore, preferential treatment programs are presumptively justifiable insofar as they work to dismantle the system of racial oppression that is still in place, although it should not be; and their justifiability is rendered more secure once it can be seen, as I think it should be, that they are not unjust either in themselves or as constitutive elements of any larger system of racial oppression.

# 54   Secondary Sexism and Quota Hiring

## MARY ANNE WARREN

I want to call attention to a pervasive form of discrimination against women, one which helps to explain the continuing male monopoly of desirable jobs in the universities, as elsewhere. Discrimination of this sort is difficult to eliminate or even, in some cases, to recognize, because (1) it is not explicitly based on sex, and (2) it typically *appears* to be justified on the basis of plausible moral or practical considerations. The recognition of this form of discrimination gives rise to a new argument for the use of numerical goals or quotas in the hiring of women for college and university teaching and administrative positions.

I shall argue that because of these de facto discriminatory hiring practices, minimum numerical quotas for the hiring and promotion of women are necessary, not (just) to compensate women for past discrimination or its results, or to provide women with role models, but to counteract this *ongoing* discrimination and thus make the competition for such jobs more nearly fair. Indeed, given the problems inherent in the compensatory justice and role-model arguments for reverse discrimina-

tion, this may well be the soundest argument for the use of such quotas.

## I. Primary and Secondary Sexism

Most of us try not to be sexists; that is, we try not to discriminate unfairly in our actions or attitudes toward either women or men. But it is not a simple matter to determine just which actions or attitudes discriminate unfairly, and a sincere effort to avoid unfair discrimination is often not enough. This is true of both of the forms of sexism that I wish to distinguish.

In its primary sense, "sexism" means *unfair discrimination on the basis of sex*. The unfairness may be unintentional; but the cause or reason for the discrimination must be the sex of the victim, not merely some factor such as size or strength that happens to be correlated with sex. Primary sexism may be due to dislike, distrust, or contempt for women, or, in less typical cases, for men or hermaphrodites. Or it may be due to sincerely held but objectively unjustified beliefs about women's properties or capacities. It may also be due to beliefs about the properties women *tend* to have, which are objectively justified but inappro-

Mary Anne Warren, "Secondary Sexism and Quota Hiring," *Philosophy and Public Affairs*, 6, 3 (1977), 240–261, with omissions. Copyright © 1977 by Princeton University Press. Reprinted by permission of Princeton University Press.

priately applied to a particular case, in which the woman discriminated against does not have those properties.

For instance, if members of a philosophy department vote against hiring or promoting a woman logician because they dislike women (logicians), or because they think that women cannot excel in logic, or because they know that most women do not so excel and wrongly conclude that this one does not, then they are guilty of primary sexism. This much, I think, is noncontroversial.

But what should we say if they vote to hire or promote a man rather than a woman because he has a wife and children to support, while she has a husband who is (capable of) supporting her? Or because they believe that the woman has child-care responsibilities which will limit the time she can spend on the job? What if they hire a woman at a lower rank and salary than is standard for a man with comparable qualifications, for one of the above reasons? These actions are not sexist in the primary sense because there is no discrimination on the basis of sex itself. The criteria used *can* at least be applied in a sex-neutral manner. For instance, it might be asserted that if the woman candidate had had a spouse and children who depended upon her for support, this would have counted in her favor just as much as it would in the case of a man.

Of course, appeals to such intrinsically sex-neutral criteria may, in some cases, be mere rationalizations of what is actually done from primary sexist motives. In reality, the criteria cited may not be applied in a sex-neutral manner. But let us assume for the sake of argument that the application of these criteria *is* sex-neutral, not merely a smoke screen for primary sexism. On this assumption, the use of such criteria discriminates against women only because of certain contingent features of this society, such as the persistence of the traditional division of labor in marriage and child-rearing.[1]

Many people see nothing morally objectionable in the use of such intrinsically sex-neutral yet de facto discriminatory criteria. For not only may employers who use such criteria be free of pri-

mary sexism, but their actions may appear to be justified on both moral and pragmatic grounds. It might, for instance, be quite clear that a department will really do more to alleviate economic hardship by hiring or promoting a man with dependents rather than a woman with none, or that a particular woman's domestic responsibilities will indeed limit the time she can spend on the job. And it might seem perfectly appropriate for employers to take account of such factors.

Nevertheless, I shall argue that the use of such considerations is unfair. It is an example of secondary sexism, which I define as comprising all those actions, attitudes and policies which, while not using sex itself as a reason for discrimination, do involve sex-correlated factors or criteria and do result in an unfair impact upon (certain) women. In the case of university hiring policies, secondary sexism consists in the use of sex-correlated selection criteria which are not valid measures of academic merit, with the result that women tend to be passed over in favor of men who are not, in fact, better qualified. I call sexism of this sort *secondary,* not because it is any less widespread or harmful than primary sexism, but because (1) it is, in this way, indirect or covert, and (2) it is typically parasitic upon primary sexism, in that the injustices it perpetuates—for example, those apparent from the male monopoly of desirable jobs in the universities—are usually due in the first instance to primary sexism.

Two points need to be made with respect to this definition. First, it is worth noting that, although in the cases we will be considering the correlations between sex and the apparently independent but de facto discriminatory criteria are largely due to past and present injustices against women, this need not always be the case. The discriminatory impact of excluding pregnancy-related disabilities from coverage by employee health insurance policies, for example, probably makes this an instance of secondary sexism. Yet it is certainly not (human) injustice which is responsible for the fact that it is only women who become pregnant. The fact that the correlation is due to biology rather than prior injustice does not show that the exclusion is not sexist. Neither does the fact that pregnancy is often undertaken voluntarily. If such insurance programs fail to serve the needs of women employees as well as they serve those of men, then they can escape the charge of sexism only if—as seems unlikely—it can be shown that they cannot possibly be altered to include disabilities related to pregnancy without ceasing to serve their mutually agreed upon purposes, and/or producing an even greater injustice.

This brings us to the second point. It must be stressed that on the above definition the use of valid criteria of merit in hiring to university positions is not an instance of secondary sexism. Some might argue that merit criteria discriminate unfairly against women, because it is harder for women to earn the advanced degrees, to write the publications, and to obtain the professional experience that are the major traditional measures of academic merit. But it would be a mistake to suppose that merit criteria as such are therefore sexist. They are sexist only to the extent that they understate women's actual capacity to perform well in university positions; and to that extent, they are invalid as criteria of merit. To the extent that they are valid, that is, the most reliable available measurements of capacities which are indeed crucial for the performance of the job, they are not unjust, even though they may result in more men than women being hired.

If this seems less than obvious, the following analogy may help. It is surely not unjust to award first prize in a discus throwing contest to the contestant who actually makes the best throw (provided, of course, that none of the contestants have been unfairly prevented from performing up to their capacity on this particular occasion), even if some of the contestants have in the past been wrongly prevented from developing their skill to the fullest, say by sexist discrimination in school athletic programs. Such contestants may be entitled to other relevant forms of compensation, for example, special free training programs to help them make up for lost time, but they are not entitled to win this particular contest. For the very *raison d'être* of an athletic contest dictates that prizes go to the best performers, not those who perhaps

*could* have been the best, had past conditions been ideally fair.

So too, a university's central reasons for being dictate that positions within it be filled by candidates who are as well qualified as can be found. Choosing less qualified candidates deprives students of the best available instruction, colleagues of a more intellectually productive environment, and—in the case of state-funded universities—the public of the most efficient use of its resources.[2] To appoint inferior candidates defeats the primary purposes of the university, and is therefore wrongheaded, however laudable its motivations. It is also, as we shall see, a weapon of social change which is apt to backfire against those in whose interest it is advocated. . . .

## II. Secondary Sexism in University Hiring

Consider the following policies, which not infrequently influence hiring, retention, and promotion decisions in American colleges and universities:

1. Antinepotism rules, proscribing the employment of spouses of current employees.
2. Giving preference to candidates who (are thought to) have the greater financial need, where the latter is estimated by whether someone has, on the one hand, financial dependents, or, on the other hand, a spouse capable of providing financial support.
3. The "last hired-first fired" principle, used in determining who shall be fired or not rehired as a result of staffing cutbacks.
4. Refusing promotions, tenure, retention seniority, or pro-rata pay to persons employed less than full time, where some are so employed on a relatively long-term basis and where there is no evidence that such persons are (all) less well qualified than full time employees.
5. Hiring at a rank and salary determined primarily by previous rank and salary rather than by more direct evidence of a candidate's competence, for example, degrees, publications, and student and peer evaluations.

6. Counting as a negative factor the fact that a candidate has or is thought to have, or to be more likely to have, childcare or other domestic responsibilities which may limit the time s/he can spend on the job.

7. Giving preference to candidates with more or less uninterrupted work records over those whose working careers have been interrupted (for example, by raising children) in the absence of more direct evidence of a present difference in competence.

8. Not hiring, especially to administrative or supervisory positions, persons thought apt to encounter disrespect or lack of cooperation from peers or subordinates, without regard for whether this presumed lack of respect may be itself unjustified, for example, as the result of primary sexism.

9. Discriminating against candidates on the grounds of probable mobility due to the mobility of a spouse, present or possible.

Each of these practices is an example of secondary sexism, in that while the criterion applied does not mention sex, its use nevertheless tends to result in the hiring and promotion of men in preference to women who are not otherwise demonstrably less well qualified. I suggest that in seeking to explain the continuing underrepresentation of women in desirable jobs in the universities, we need to look not only toward primary sexist attitudes within those institutions, and certainly not toward any intrinsic lack of merit on the part of women candidates,[3] but toward covertly, and often unintentionally, discriminatory practices such as these.

Of course, none of these practices operates to the detriment of women in every case; but each operates against women much more often than against men, and the cumulative effect is enormous. No doubt some of them are more widespread than others and some (for example, the use of antinepotism rules) are already declining in response to pressures to remove barriers to the employment of women. Others, such as policies 3 and 4, are still fairly standard and have barely begun to be seriously challenged in most places.

Some are publicly acknowledged and may have been written into law or administrative policy, for example, policies 1, 3, 4, and 5. Others are more apt to be private policies on the part of individual employers, to which they may not readily admit or of which they may not even be fully aware, for example, policies 2, 6, 7, and 8. It is obviously much more difficult to demonstrate the prevalence of practices of the latter sort. Nevertheless, I am certain that all of these practices occur, and I strongly suspect that none is uncommon, even now.

This list almost certainly does not include all of the secondary sexist practices which influence university hiring. But these examples are typical, and an examination of certain of their features will shed light on the way in which secondary sexism operates in the academic world and on the reasons why it is morally objectionable.

In each of these examples, a principle is used in choosing between candidates that in practice acts to discriminate against women who may even be better qualified intrinsically than their successful rivals, on any reliable and acceptable measure of merit.[4] Nevertheless, the practice may *seem* to be justified. Nepotism rules, for instance, act to exclude women far more often than men, since women are more apt to seek employment in academic and/or geographical areas in which their husbands are already employed than vice versa. Yet nepotism rules may appear to be necessary to ensure fairness to those candidates and appointees, both male and female, who are *not* spouses of current employees and who, it could be argued, would otherwise be unfairly disadvantaged. Similarly, giving jobs or promotions to those judged to have the greatest financial need may seem to be simple humanitarianism, and the seniority system may seem to be the only practical way of providing job security to *any* portion of the faculty. For policies 5 through 9, it could be argued that, although the criteria used are not entirely reliable, they may still have *some* use in predicting job performance.

Thus each practice, though discriminatory in its results, may be defended by reference to principles which are not intrinsically sexbiased. In the context of an otherwise sexually egalitarian society, these practices would probably not result in de facto discrimination against either sex. In such a society, for instance, men would not hold a huge majority of desirable jobs, and women would be under no more social or financial pressure than men to live where their spouses work rather than where they themselves work; thus they would not be hurt by nepotism rules any more often, on the average, than men.[5] The average earning power of men and women would be roughly equal, and no one could assume that women, any more than men, ought to be supported by their spouses, if possible. Thus the fact that a woman has an employed spouse would not be thought to reduce her need for a job any more—or any less—than in the case of a man. We could proceed down the list; in a genuinely nonsexist society, few or none of the conditions would exist which cause these practices to have a discriminatory impact upon women.

Of course, there may be other reasons for rejecting these practices, besides their discriminatory impact upon women. Nepotism rules might be unfair to married persons of both sexes, even in a context in which they were not *especially* unfair to women. My point is simply that these practices would not be instances of sexism in a society which was otherwise free of sexism and its results. Hence, those who believe that the test of the justice of a practice is whether or not it would unfairly disadvantage any group or individual *in the context of an otherwise just society* will see no sexual injustice whatever in these practices.

But surely the moral status of a practice, as it operates in a certain context, must be determined at least in part by its actual consequences, in that context. The fact is that each of these practices acts to help preserve the male monopoly of desirable jobs, in spite of the availability of women who are just as well qualified on any defensible measure of merit. This may or may not suffice to show that these practices are morally objectionable. It certainly shows that they are inconsistent with the "straight merit" principle, that is, that jobs

should go to those best qualified for them on the more reliable measures of merit. Hence, it is ironic that attempts to counteract such de facto discriminatory practices are often interpreted as attacks on the "straight merit" principle.

## III. Why Secondary Sexism Is Unfair

Two additional points need to be stressed in order to show just why these practices are unfair. In the first place, the contingent social circumstances which explain the discriminatory impact of these practices are themselves morally objectionable, and/or due to morally objectionable practices. It is largely because men *are* more able to make good salaries, and because married women are still expected to remain financially dependent upon their husbands, if possible, that the fact that a woman has an employed husband can be seen as evidence that she doesn't "need" a job. It is because a disproportionate number of women must, because of family obligations and the geographical limitations these impose, accept part-time employment even when they would prefer full time, that the denial of tenure, promotion and pro-rata pay to part-time faculty has a discriminatory impact upon women. That women accept such obligations and limitations may seem to be their own free choice; but, of course, that choice is heavily conditioned by financial pressures—for example, the fact that the husband can usually make more money—and by sexually stereotyped social expectations.

Thus, the effect of these policies is to compound and magnify prior social injustices against women. When a woman is passed over on such grounds, it is rather as if an athlete who had without her knowledge been administered a drug to hamper her performance were to be disqualified from the competition for failing the blood-sample test. In such circumstances, the very least that justice demands is that the unfairly imposed handicap not be used as a rationale for the imposition of further handicaps. If the unfair handicaps that society imposes upon women cause them to be passed over by employers because of a lack of straight merit, that is one thing, and it is unfortunate, but it is not obvious that it involves unfairness on the part of the employers. But if those handicaps are used as an excuse for excluding them from the competition regardless of their merit, as all too often happens, this is quite another thing, and it is patently unfair.

In the second place, practices such as these often tend to perpetuate the very (unjust) circumstances which underlie their discriminatory impact, thus creating a vicious circle. Consider the case of a woman who is passed over for a job or promotion because of her childcare responsibilities. Given a (better) job, she might be able to afford day care, or to hire someone to help her at home, or even to persuade her husband to assume more of the responsibilities. Denying her a job because of her domestic responsibilities may make it almost impossible for her to do anything to lessen those responsibilities. Similarly, denying her a job because she has a husband who supports her may force him to continue supporting her and her to continue to accept that support.

Both of these points may be illustrated by turning to a somewhat different sort of example. J. R. Lucas has argued that there are cases in which women may justifiably be discriminated against on grounds irrelevant to their merit. He claims, for example, that it is "not so evidently wrong to frustrate Miss Amazon's hopes of a military career in the Grenadier Guards on the grounds not that she would make a bad soldier, but that she would be a disturbing influence in the mess room."[6]

But this is a paradigm case of secondary, and perhaps also primary, sexism; it is also quite analogous to practice 8. To exclude women from certain jobs or certain branches of the military on the grounds that certain third parties are not apt to accept them, when that nonacceptance is itself unreasonable and perhaps based on sexual bigotry, is to compound the injustice of that bigotry. If it is inappropriate for soldiers to be disturbed or to make a disturbance because there are women in the mess room, then it is wrong to appeal to those

soldiers' attitudes as grounds for denying women the opportunities available to comparably qualified men. It is also to help ensure the perpetuation of those attitudes, by preventing male soldiers from having an opportunity to make the sorts of observations which might lead to their eventually accepting women as comrades.

Thus, these practices are morally objectionable because they compound and perpetuate prior injustices against women, penalizing them for socially imposed disadvantages which cannot be reliably shown to detract from their actual present capacities. We may conclude that the hiring process will never be fair to women, nor will it be based on merit alone, so long as such practices persist on a wide scale. But it remains to be seen whether numerical hiring quotas for women are a morally acceptable means of counteracting the effects of sexist hiring practices.

## IV. Weak Quotas

I shall discuss the case for mandatory hiring quotas of a certain very minimal sort: those based on the proportion of women, not in the population as a whole, but among qualified and available candidates in each academic field. Such a "weak" quota system would require that in each institution, and ideally within each department and each faculty and administrative rank and salary, women be hired and promoted at least in accordance with this proportion. If, for instance, a tenured or tenure-track position became available in a given department on an average of every other year, and if women were twenty percent of the qualified and available candidates in that field, then such a quota system would require that the department hire a woman to such a position at least once in ten years.[7] . . .

Under such a quota system, even if (some) employers do use weak discrimination in favor of women to meet their quota, this will not render the job competition especially unfair to men. For, as I will argue, unfairness would result only if the average male candidate's chances of success were reduced to below what they would be in an ongoing, just society, one in which men and women had complete equality of opportunity and the competition was based on merit alone; and I will argue that the use of weak reverse discrimination to meet proportional hiring quotas will not have this effect.

## V. Quotas and Fairness

Now one way to support this claim would be to argue that in an ongoing, just society women would constitute a far higher proportion of the qualified candidates in most academic fields and that therefore the average male candidate's chances would, other things being equal, automatically be reduced considerably from what they are now. Unfortunately, however, the premise of this argument is overly speculative. It is possible that in a fully egalitarian society women would still tend to avoid certain academic fields and to prefer others, much as they do now, or even that they would fail to (attempt to) enter the academic profession as a whole in much greater numbers than at present.

But whatever the proportion of male and female candidates may be, it must at least be the case that in a just society the chances of success enjoyed by male candidates must be no greater, on the average, and no less than those enjoyed by comparably qualified women. Individual differences in achievement, due to luck or to differences in ability, are probably inevitable; but overall differences in the opportunities accorded to comparably qualified men and women, due to discrimination, would not be tolerated.

The question, then, is: Would the use of weak discrimination in favor of women, to a degree just sufficient to offset continuing sexist discrimination against women and thus to meet minimum quotas, result in lowering the average chances of male candidates to below those of comparably qualified women? The answer, surely, is that it would not, since by hypothesis men would be passed over, in order to fill a quota, in favor of women no better qualified only as often as women continue to be passed over, because of primary or secondary sexism, in favor of men no better qualified.

In this situation, individual departures from the "straight merit" principle might be no less frequent than at present; indeed, their frequency might even be doubled. But since it would no longer be predominantly women who were repeatedly disadvantaged by those departures, the overall fairness of the competition would be improved. The average long-term chances of success of *both* men and women candidates would more closely approximate those they would enjoy in an ongoing just society. If individual men's careers are temporarily set back because of weak reverse discrimination, the odds are good that these same men will have benefited in the past and/or will benefit in the future—not necessarily in the job competition, but in *some* ways—from sexist discrimination against women. Conversely, if individual women receive apparently unearned bonuses, it is highly likely that these same women will have suffered in the past and/or will suffer in the future from primary or secondary sexist attitudes. Yet, the primary purpose of a minimum quota system would not be to compensate the victims of discrimination or to penalize its beneficiaries, but rather to increase the overall fairness of the situation—to make it possible for the first time for women to enjoy the same opportunity to obtain desirable jobs in the universities as enjoyed by men with comparable qualifications.

It is obvious that a quota system implemented by weak reverse discrimination is not the ideal long-term solution to the problem of sexist discrimination in academic hiring. But it would be a great improvement over the present situation, in which the rate of unemployment among women Ph.D.'s who are actively seeking employment is still far higher than among men with Ph.D.'s, and in which women's starting salaries and chances of promotion are still considerably lower than those of men.[14] Strong reverse discrimination is clearly the least desirable method of implementing quotas. Not only is it unfair to the men who are passed over, and to their potential students and colleagues, to hire demonstrably less well qualified women, but it is very apt to reinforce primary sexist attitudes on the part of all concerned, since it appears to presuppose that women cannot measure up on their merits. But to presume that proportional hiring quotas could not be met without strong reverse discrimination is also to make that discredited assumption. If, as all available evidence indicates, women in the academic world are on the average just as hard-working, productive, and meritorious as their male colleagues, then there can be no objection to hiring and promoting them at least in accordance with their numbers, and doing so will increase rather than decrease the extent to which success is based upon merit.

## VI. Are Quotas Necessary?

I have argued that minimum proportional quotas such as I have described would not make the job competition (especially) unfair to men. But it might still be doubted that quotas are necessary to make the competition fair to women. Why not simply attack sexist practices wherever they exist and then let the chips fall as they may? . . .

Even if primary sexism were to vanish utterly from the minds of all employers, secondary sexist practices such as those we have considered would in all likelihood suffice to perpetuate the male monopoly of desirable jobs well beyond our lifetimes. Such practices cannot be expected to vanish quickly or spontaneously; to insist that affirmative action measures stop short of the use of quotas is to invite their continuation and proliferation.

## Notes

1. I mean, of course, the tradition that the proper husband earns (most of) the family's income, while the proper wife does (most of) the housekeeping and childrearing.

2. It might be argued that the hiring process ought no to be based on merit alone, because there are cases in which being a woman, or being black, might itself be a crucial job qualification. As Michael Martin points out, this might well be the case in hiring for, say, a job teaching history in a previously all white-male department which badly needs to provide its students with a more balanced perspective. See "Pedagogical Arguments for Preferential Hiring and Tenuring of Women Teachers in the University," *The Philosophical Forum* 5, no. 2: 325–333. I think it is preferable, however, to describe such cases, not as instances requiring a departure from the merit principle, but as instances in which sex or race itself, or rather certain interests and abilities that are correlated with sex or race, constitutes a legitimate qualification for a certain job, and hence a measure of merit, vis-à-vis that job.

3. With respect to one such measure, books and articles published, married women Ph.D.'s published as much or slightly more than men, and unmarried women only slightly less. See "The Woman Ph.D.: A Recent Profile," by R. J. Simon, S. M. Clark, and K. Galway, in *Social Problems* 15, no. 2 (Fall 1967): 231.

4. I am assuming that whether a candidate is married to a current employee, or has dependents, or a spouse capable of supporting her, whether she is employed on a part-time or a full-time basis, her previous rank and salary, the continuity of her work record, and so on, are not in themselves reliable and acceptable measures of merit. As noted in example 5, more direct and pertinent measures of merit can be obtained. Such measures as degrees, publications, and peer and student evaluations have the moral as well as pragmatic advantage of being based on the candidate's actual past performance, rather than on unreliable and often biased conjectures of various sorts. Furthermore, even if there is or were *some* correlation (it would surely not be a *reliable* one) between certain secondary sexist criteria and job performance, it could still be argued that employers are not morally entitled to use such criteria, because of the unfair consequences of doing so. As Mary Vetterling has observed, there might well be some correlation between having "a healthy and active sex life" and "the patience and good humor required of a good teacher"; yet employers are surely not entitled to take into account the quality of a person's sex life in making hiring and promotion decisions. "Some Common Sense Notes on Preferential Hiring," *The Philosophical Forum* 5, no. 2: 321.

5. Unless, perhaps, a significant average age difference between wives and husbands continued to exist.

6. J. R. Lucas, "Because You Are a Woman," *Moral Problems,* ed. James Rachels (New York: Harper & Row, 1975), p. 139.

7. In practice problems of statistical significance will probably require that quotas be enforced on an institution-wide basis rather than an inflexible department-by-department basis. Individual departments, especially if they are small and if the proportion of qualified women in the field is low, may fail to meet hiring quotas, not because of primary or secondary sexism, but because the best qualified candidates happen in fact to be men. But if no real discrimination against women is occurring, then such statistical deviations should be canceled out on the institutional level, by deviations in the opposite direction.

## 55 What People Deserve

**JAMES RACHELS**

I shall discuss the concept of desert, and argue that what people deserve always depends on their own past actions. In order to illustrate the practical consequences of my analysis, I will consider its application to the problem of reverse discrimination.

## The Relation between Justice and Desert

It is an important point of logic that if a value-judgment is true, there must be good reasons in support of it. Suppose you are told that you ought to do a certain action, or that so-and-so is a good man. You may ask *why* you ought to do it, or *why* he is a good man, and if no reasons can be given, you may reject those judgments as arbitrary. Claims of justice have this in common with other value-judgments; an action or social policy is just, or unjust, only if there is some reason why it is so. The attempt to decide questions of justice is, therefore, largely a matter of assessing the reasons that can be offered in support of the competing judgments.

Judgments of justice may be distinguished from other sorts of value-judgments by the kinds of reasons that are relevant to supporting them. The fact that an action would make someone unhappy may be a reason why that action *ought not* be done, but it is not a reason why the action would be *unjust*. On the other hand, the fact that an action would violate someone's rights is a reason why the act would be unjust. Questions of justice are narrower than questions of what should be done, in this sense: Any reason why an act would be unjust is also a reason why it should not be done; but not every reason why an act should not be done is a reason for thinking it unjust.

Reprinted by permission of the author.

The fact that people are, or are not, treated as they deserve to be treated is one kind of reason why an action or social policy may be just or unjust. I say "one kind of reason" because there are also other sorts of reasons relevant to supporting claims of justice. Besides requiring that people be treated as they deserve, justice may also require that people's rights be respected, which is different, and, as Nozick emphasizes, historical backgrounds may also be relevant to determining justice. A complete theory of justice would provide, among other things, an exhaustive account of the different kinds of reasons relevant to supporting such judgments. I will not attempt to construct a complete theory; instead, I will only sketch that part of the theory having to do with desert. As a preliminary, I want to cite two instances from recent philosophical writing on justice in which the neglect of desert, as one consideration among others, has caused difficulty.

(a) The problem of reverse discrimination is one aspect of the more general problem of distributive justice, having to do with justice in the distribution of jobs and educational opportunities. Black people, women, and members of other groups have often been denied access to jobs and educational opportunities. It is easy enough to say that this is wrong, but it is not so easy to say exactly what should now be done about it. Some believe it is enough that we simply stop discriminating against them. Others think we ought to go further and give such persons preferential treatment, at least temporarily, in order to help rectify the past injustices. And in many cases this is already being done. The problem is whether this sort of preferential treatment is itself unjust to the whites, males, or others who are disadvantaged by it.

The term "distributive justice" is commonly used by philosophers, but as Nozick points out, it can be misleading.[1] It suggests that there is a central supply of things which some authority has to dole out; but for most goods, there is no such supply and no such authority. Goods are produced by diverse individuals and groups who then have rights with respect to them, and the "distribution" of holdings at any particular time will depend, at least in part, on the voluntary exchanges and agreements those people have made. Jobs, for example, do not come from some great stockpile, to be handed out by a master "distributor" who may or may not follow principles of "justice." Jobs are created by the independent decisions of countless business people, who are entitled, within some limits of course, to operate their own businesses according to their own judgments. In a free society those people get to choose with whom they will make what sorts of agreements, and this means, among other things, that they get to choose who is hired from among the various job applicants.

These observations suggest an argument in defense of reverse discrimination: If private business people have a right to hire whomever they please, don't they have a right to hire blacks and women in preference to others? In her paper on "Preferential Hiring" Judith Jarvis Thomson[2] advances an argument based on exactly this idea. The argument begins with this principle:

No perfect stranger has a right to be given a benefit which is yours to dispose of; no perfect stranger even has a right to be given an equal chance at getting a benefit which is yours to dispose of.[3]

Since many jobs are benefits which private employers have a right to dispose of, those employers violate no one's rights in hiring whomever they wish. If they choose to hire blacks, or women, rather than other applicants, they have a perfect right to do so. Therefore, she concludes, "there is no problem about preferential hiring," at least in the case of private businesses.

Thomson's principle is plausible. If something is *yours,* then no one else has a right to it—at least, no perfect stranger who walks in off the street wanting it. Suppose you have a book which you don't need and decide to give away as a gift. Smith and Jones both want it, and you decide to give it to Smith. Is Jones entitled to complain? Apparently not, since *he* had no claim on it in the

first place. If it was your book, you were entitled to give it to whomever you chose; you violated no right of Jones in giving it to Smith. Why shouldn't the same be true of jobs? If you start a business, on your own, why shouldn't you be free to hire whomever you please to work with you? You violate no one's rights in hiring whomever you please, since no one had a right to be hired by you in the first place.

This is an important and powerful argument because it calls attention to a fact that is often overlooked, that people do not naturally have claims of right to jobs and other benefits which are privately produced. However, the argument also depends on another assumption which is false, namely, the assumption that people are treated unjustly *only if* their rights are violated. In fact, a person may be treated unjustly even though no right of his is violated, because he is not treated as he deserves to be treated. Suppose one applicant for a job has worked very hard to qualify himself for it; he has gone to night-school, at great personal sacrifice, to learn the business, and so on. Another applicant could have done all that, but chose not to; instead, he has frittered away his time and done nothing to prepare himself. In addition, the first applicant has worked hard at every previous job he has held, making a good record for himself, whereas the second is a notorious loafer—and it's his own fault; he has no good excuse. Now it may be true that neither applicant has a *right* to the job, in the sense that the employer has the right to give the job to whomever he pleases. However, the first man is clearly more deserving, and if the employer is concerned to treat job applicants fairly he will not hire the second man over the first.

*(b)* Now let me return briefly to Nozick.[4] In Part II of *Anarchy, State and Utopia* he defends capitalism, not merely as efficient or workable, but as the only moral economic system, because it is the only such system which respects individual rights. Under capitalism people's holdings are determined by the voluntary exchanges (of services and work as well as goods) they make with others. Their right to liberty requires that they be allowed to make such exchanges, provided that

they violate no one else's rights in doing so. Having acquired their holdings by such exchanges, they have a right to them; so it violates their rights for the government (or anyone else) to seize their property and give it to others. It is impermissible, therefore, for governments to tax some citizens in order to provide benefits for others.

The obvious objection is that such an arrangement could produce a disastrously unfair distribution of goods. Some lucky entrepreneurs could become enormously rich, while other equally deserving people are poor, and orphans starve. In reply Nozick contends that even if unmodified capitalism did lead to such a distribution, that would not necessarily be unjust. The justice of a distribution, he says, can be determined only by considering the historical process which led to it. We cannot tell whether a distribution is just simply by checking whether it conforms to some nonhistorical pattern, for example the pattern of everyone having equal shares, or everyone having what he or she needs. To show this Nozick gives a now-famous argument starring the basketball player Wilt Chamberlain. First, he says, suppose the goods in a society are distributed according to some pattern which you think just. Call this distribution $D_1$. Since you regard $D_1$ as a just distribution, you will agree that under it each person has a right to the holdings in his or her possession. Now suppose a million of these people each decide to give Wilt Chamberlain twenty-five cents to watch him play basketball. Chamberlain becomes rich, and the original pattern is upset. But if the original distribution was just, mustn't we admit that the new distribution ($D_2$) is also just?

Each of these persons *chose* to give twenty-five cents of their money to Chamberlain. They could have spent it on going to the movies, or on candy bars, or on copies of *Dissent* magazine, or of *Monthly Review.* But they all, at least one million of them, converged on giving it to Wilt Chamberlain in exchange for watching him play basketball. If $D_1$ was a just distribution, and people voluntarily moved from it to $D_2$, transferring parts of their shares they were given under $D_1$ (what was it for if not to do something with?), isn't $D_2$ also just? . . . Can anyone else complain on grounds of justice? . . . After someone transfers something to Wilt Chamberlain,

third parties *still* have their legitimate shares; *their* shares are not changed.[5]

The main argument here seems to depend on the principle that *If $D_1$ is a just distribution, and $D_2$ arises from $D_1$ by a process in which no one's rights are violated, then $D_2$ is also just.* Now Nozick is surely right that the historical process which produces a situation is one of the things that must be taken into account in deciding whether it is just. But that need not be the only relevant consideration. The historical process *and* other considerations, such as desert, must be weighed together to determine what is just. Therefore, it would not follow that a distribution is just *simply* because it is the result of a certain process, even a process in which no one's rights are violated. So this argument cannot answer adequately the complaint against unmodified capitalism.

To make the point less abstract, consider the justice of inherited wealth. A common complaint about inherited wealth is that some people gain fortunes which they have done nothing to deserve, while others, of equal merit, have nothing. This seems unjust on the face of it. Nozick points out that if the testators legitimately own their property —if it is *theirs*—then they have a right to give it to others as a gift. (The holdings of third parties will not be changed, etc.) Bequests are gifts; therefore property owners have a right to pass on their property to their heirs. This is fair enough, but at most it shows only that there is more than one consideration to be taken into account here. That some people have more than others, without deserving it, counts against the justice of the distribution. That they came by their holdings in a certain way may count in favor of the justice of the same distribution. It should come as no surprise that in deciding questions of justice competing claims must often be weighed against one another, for that is the way it usually is in ethics.

## Desert and Past Actions

Deserts may be positive or negative, that is, a person may deserve to be treated well or badly; and they may be general or specific, that is, a person may deserve to be treated in a generally good or bad way, or he may deserve some specific kind of good or bad treatment. An example may make the latter distinction clear. Suppose a woman has always been kind and generous with others. As a general way of dealing with her, she deserves that others be kind and generous in return. Here we need not specify any *particular* act of kindness to say what she deserves, although of course treating her kindly will involve some particular act or other. What she deserves is that people treat her decently in *whatever* situation might arise. By way of contrast, think of someone who has worked hard to earn promotion in his job. He may deserve, *specifically*, to be promoted.

I wish to argue that the basis of all desert is a person's own past actions. In the case of negative desert, this is generally conceded. In order for a person to deserve punishment, for example, he must have *done something* to deserve it. More-over, he must have done it "voluntarily," in Aristotle's sense, without any excuse such as ignorance, mistake, or coercion. In allowing these excuses and others like them, the law attempts to restrict punishment to cases in which it is deserved.

But not every negative desert involves punishment, strictly speaking. They may involve more informal responses to other people's misconduct. Suppose Adams and Brown work at the same factory. One morning Adams' car breaks down and he calls Brown to ask for a ride to work. Brown refuses, not for any good reason, but simply because he won't be bothered. Later, Brown finds himself in the same fix: his car won't start, and he can't get to work; so he calls Adams to ask for a lift. Now if Adams is a kind and forgiving person, he may grant Brown's request. And perhaps we all ought to be kind and forgiving. However, if Adams does choose to help Brown, he will be treating Brown better than Brown deserves. Brown deserves to be left in the lurch. Here I am not arguing that we ought to treat people as they deserve—although I do think there are reasons for so treating people, which I will mention presently—here I am only describing what the concept of desert involves. What Brown *deserves,* as opposed to what kindness or any other value might decree, is

to be treated as well, *or as badly,* as he himself chooses to treat others.

If I am right, then the familiar lament "What did I do to deserve this?," asked by a victim of misfortune, is more than a mournful cliché. If there is no satisfactory answer, then in fact one does *not* deserve the misfortune. And since there is always a presumption against treating people badly, if a person does not deserve bad treatment it is likely to be wrong to treat him in that way. On the other side, in the case of positive deserts, we may notice a corresponding connection between the concept of desert and the idea of *earning* one's way, which also supports my thesis.

To elaborate an example I used earlier, think of an employer who has to decide which of two employees to give a promotion. One has worked very hard for the company for several years. He has always been willing to do more than his share of work; he has put in a lot of overtime when no one else would; and so on. The other has always done the least he could get by with, never taking on any extra work or otherwise exerting himself beyond the necessary minimum. Clearly, if the choice is between these two candidates, it is the first who deserves the promotion. It is important to notice that this conclusion does not depend on any estimate of how the two candidates are likely to perform in the future. Even if the second candidate were to reform, so that he would work just as hard (and well) in the new position as the first candidate, the first is still more deserving. What one deserves depends on what one has done, not on what one will do.

Of course there may be any number of reasons for not giving the promotion to the most deserving candidate: perhaps it is a family business, and the second candidate is the boss's son, and he will be advanced simply because of who he is. But that does not make him the most deserving candidate; it only means that the promotion is to be awarded on grounds other than desert. Again, the boss might decide to give the position to the second candidate because he is extraordinarily smart and talented, and the boss thinks for that reason he will do a better job (he has promised to work harder in the future). This is again to award the job on grounds other than desert, for no one deserves anything *simply* in virtue of superior intelligence and natural abilities. As Rawls emphasizes, a person no more deserves to be intelligent or talented than he deserves to be the boss's son—or, than he deserves to be born white in a society prejudiced against nonwhites. These things are all matters of chance, at least as far as the lucky individual himself is concerned.

Three questions naturally arise concerning this view. First, aren't there bases of desert *other than* a person's past actions, and if not, why not? Second, if a person may not deserve things in virtue of being naturally talented or intelligent or fortunate in some other way, how can he deserve things by working for them? After all, isn't it merely a matter of luck that one person grows up to be industrious—perhaps as the result of a rigorous upbringing by his parents—while another person is not encouraged, and ends up lazy for reasons beyond his control? And finally, even if I am right about the basis of desert, what reason is there actually to treat people according to their deserts? Why should desert matter? I will take up these questions in order. The answers, as we shall see, are interrelated.

*(a)* In his important article "Justice and Personal Desert" Joel Feinberg says that "If a person is deserving of some sort of treatment, he must, necessarily, be so in virtue of *some possessed characteristic* or prior activity."[6] Among the characteristics that may be the basis of desert he includes abilities, skills, physical attributes, and so on. In a tennis game, for example, the most skillful player deserves to win, and in a beauty contest the prettiest or most handsome deserves to win.

Does the most skillful player deserve to win an athletic competition? It seems a natural enough thing to say. But suppose the less skilled player has worked very hard, for weeks, to prepare himself for the match. He has practiced nine hours a day, left off drinking, and kept to a strict regimen. Meanwhile, his opponent, who is a "natural athlete," has partied, stayed drunk, and done nothing in the way of training. *But he is still the most skilled,* and as a result can probably beat the other guy anyway. Does he *deserve* to win the game,

simply because he is better endowed by nature? Does he *deserve* the acclaim and benefits which go with winning? Of course, skills are themselves usually the product of past efforts. People must work to sharpen and develop their natural abilities; therefore, when we think of the most skillful as the most deserving, it may be because we think of them as having worked hardest. (Ted Williams practiced hitting more than anyone else on the Red Sox.) But sometimes that assumption is not true.

Do the prettiest and most handsome deserve to win beauty contests? Again, it seems a natural enough thing to say. There is no doubt that the *correct* decision for the judges of such a competition to make is to award the prize to the best-looking. But this may have little to do with the contestants' deserts. Suppose a judge were to base his decision on desert; we might imagine him reasoning like this: "Miss Montana isn't the prettiest, but after all, she's done her best with what nature provided. She's studied the use of make-up, had her teeth and nose fixed, and spent hours practicing walking down runways in high-heeled shoes. That smile didn't just happen; she had to learn it by spending hours before a mirror. Miss Alabama, on the other hand, is prettier, but she just entered the contest on a lark—walked in, put on a bathing suit, and here she is. Her make-up isn't even very good." If all this seems ridiculous, it is because the point of such contests is *not* to separate the more deserving from the less (and maybe because beauty contests are themselves a little ridiculous, too). The criterion is beauty, not desert, and the two have little to do with one another. The same goes for athletic games: the purpose is to see who is the best player, or at least who is able to defeat all the others, and not to discover who is the most deserving competitor.

There is a reason why past actions are the only bases of desert. A fair amount of our dealings with other people involves holding them responsible, formally or informally, for one thing or another. It is unfair to hold people responsible for things over which they have no control. People have no control over their native endowments—over how smart, or athletic, or beautiful they naturally are—

and so we may not hold them responsible for those things. They are, however, in control of (at least some of) their own actions, and so they may rightly be held responsible for the situations they create, or allow to exist, by their voluntary behavior. But those are the *only* things for which they may rightly be held responsible. The concept of desert serves to signify the ways of treating people that are appropriate responses to them, *given that* they are responsible for those actions or states of affairs. That is the role played by desert in our moral vocabulary. And, as ordinary-language philosophers used to like to say, if there weren't such a term, we'd have to invent one. Thus the explanation of why past actions are the only bases of desert connects with the fact that *if* people were never responsible for their own conduct—if hard determinism were true—no one would ever deserve anything, good or bad.

*(b)* According to the view I am defending, we may deserve things by working for them, but not simply by being naturally intelligent or talented or lucky in some other way. Now it may be thought that this view is inconsistent, because whether someone is willing to work is just another matter of luck, in much the same way that intelligence and talent are matters of luck. Rawls takes this position when he says:

Perhaps some will think that the person with greater natural endowments deserves those assets and the superior character that made their development possible.
Because he is more worthy in this sense, he deserves the greater advantages that he could achieve with them. This view, however, is surely incorrect. It seems to be one of the fixed points of our considered judgments that no one deserves his place in the distribution of nature endowments, any more than one deserves one's initial starting place in society. The assertion that a man deserves the superior character that enables him to make the effort to cultivate his abilities is equally problematic; for his character depends in large part upon fortunate family and social circumstances for which he can claim no credit. The notion of desert seems not to apply to these cases.[7]

So if a person does not deserve anything on account of his intelligence or natural abilities, how can he deserve anything on account of his industriousness? Isn't willingness to work just another matter of luck?

The first thing to notice here is that people do not deserve things on account of their *willingness* to work, but only on account of their actually having worked. The candidate for promotion does not deserve it because he has been willing to work hard in his old job, or because he is willing to work hard in the new job. Rather he deserves the promotion because he actually *has* worked hard. Therefore it is no objection to the view I am defending to say that willingness to work is a character trait that one does not merit. For, on this view, the basis of desert is not a character trait of any kind, not even industriousness. The basis of desert is a person's past actions.

Now it may be that some people have been so psychologically devastated by a combination of poor native endowment and unfortunate family and social circumstances that they no longer have the capacity for making anything of their lives. If one of these people has a job, for example, and doesn't work very hard at it, it's no use blaming him because, as we would say, he just hasn't got it in him to do any better. On the other hand, there are those in whom the capacity for effort has not been extinguished. Among these, some choose to work hard, and others, who *could* so choose, do not. It is true of everyone in this latter class that he is *able,* as Rawls puts it, "to strive conscientiously." The explanation of why some strive, while others don't, has to do with their own choices. When I say that those who work hard are more deserving of success, promotions, etc., than those who don't, I have in mind comparisons made among people in this latter class, in whom the capacity for effort has not been extinguished.[8]

There is an important formal difference between industriousness, considered as a lucky asset and other lucky assets such as intelligence. For only by exercising this asset—i.e., by working—can one utilize his other assets, and achieve anything with them. Intelligence alone produces nothing; intelligence plus work can produce something. And the same relation holds between industriousness and every other natural talent or asset. Thus "willingness to work," if it is a lucky asset, is a sort of super-asset which enables one's other assets to be utilized. Working is simply the way one uses whatever else one has. This point may help to explain why the concept of desert is tied to work in a way in which it is not tied to intelligence or talents. And at the same time it may also provide a rationale for the following distinction: if a person displays intelligence and talent in his work, and earns a certain benefit by it, then he deserves the benefit *not* because of the intelligence or talent shown, but only on account of the work done.

*(c)* Finally, we must ask why people ought to be treated according to their deserts. Why should desert matter? In one way, it is an odd question. The reason why the conscientious employee ought to be promoted is precisely that he has earned the promotion by working for it. That is a full and sufficient justification for promoting him, which does not require supplementation of any sort. If we want to know why he should be treated in that way, that is the answer. It is not easy to see what else, by way of justification, is required.

Nevertheless, something more may be said. Treating people as they deserve is one way of treating them as autonomous beings, responsible for their own conduct. A person who is punished for his misdeeds is *held responsible* for them in a concrete way. He is not treated as a mindless automaton, whose defective performances must be "corrected," or whose good performance promoted, but as a responsible agent whose actions merit approval or resentment.[9] The recognition of deserts is bound up with this way of regarding people. Moreover, treating people as they deserve *increases* their control over their own lives and fortunes, for it allows people to determine, through their own actions, how others will respond to them. It can be argued on grounds of kindness that people should not always be treated as they deserve, when they deserve ill. But this should not be taken to imply that deserts count for nothing. They can count for something, and still be overridden in some cases. To deny categorically that desert matters would not only excuse the malefactors; it would leave all of us impotent to earn the good treatment and other benefits which others have to bestow, and thus would

deprive us of the ability to control our own destinies as social beings.

## Reverse Discrimination

Is it right to give preferential treatment to blacks, women, or members of other groups who have been discriminated against in the past? I will approach this issue by considering the deserts of the individuals involved. "Reverse Discrimination" is not a particularly good label for the practices in question because the word "discrimination" has come to have such unsavory connotations. Given the way that word is now used, to ask whether reverse *discrimination* is justified already prejudices the question in favor of a negative answer. But in other ways the term is apt: the most distinctive thing about reverse discrimination is that it *reverses* past patterns, so that those who have been discriminated against are now given preferential treatment. At any rate, the label is now part of our common vocabulary, so I will stay with it.

The following example incorporates the essential elements of reverse discrimination. The admissions committee of a certain law school assesses the qualifications of applicants by assigning numerical values to their college grades, letters of recommendation, and test scores, according to some acceptable formula. (The better the grades, etc., the higher the numerical values assigned.) From past experience the committee judges that a combined score of 600 is necessary for a student to have a reasonable chance of succeeding in the school's program. Thus in order to be minimally qualified for admission an applicant must score at least 600. However, because there are more qualified applicants than places available, many who score over 600 are nevertheless rejected.

Against this background two students, one black and one white, apply for admission. The black student's credentials are rated at 700, and the white student's credentials are rated at 720. So although both exceed the minimum requirement by a comfortable margin, the white student's qualifications are somewhat better. But the white applicant is rejected and the black applicant is accepted. The officials of the school explain that this decision is part of a policy designed to bring more blacks into the legal profession. The scores of the white applicants are generally higher than those of the blacks; so, some blacks with lower scores must be admitted in order to have a fair number of black students in the entering class.

I should point out that this example is patterned after an actual case. In 1971 a student named Marco DeFunis applied for admission to the University of Washington Law School, and was rejected. He then learned that one-fourth of those accepted were minority-group students with academic records inferior to his own. The law school conceded that DeFunis had been passed over to make room for the minority students, and DeFunis brought suit charging that his rights had been violated. A lower court ruled in his favor; the Supreme Court of the state of Washington reversed this decision. The United States Supreme Court heard the case, but then declined to rule on the substance since the specific issue involved—DeFunis' admission to the University of Washington Law School—had become a moot point. DeFunis had been enrolled in the School when he filed suit, and by the time the case reached the highest court he had already graduated! So the example is not merely a philosopher's invention.

Now a number of arguments can be given in support of the law school's policy, and other policies like it. Black people have been, and still are, the victims of racist discrimination. One result is that they are poorly represented in the professions. In order to remedy this it is not enough that we simply stop discriminating against them. For, so long as there are not enough "role models" available—i.e., black people visibly successful in the professions, whom young blacks can recognize as models to emulate—young blacks cannot be expected to aspire to the professions and prepare for careers in the way that young whites do. It is a vicious cycle: while there are relatively few black lawyers, relatively few young blacks will take seriously the possibility of becoming lawyers, and so they will not be prepared for law school. But if relatively few young blacks are well-prepared for law school, and admissions committees hold them to the same high standards as the white applicants, there will be relatively few black lawyers. Law school admissions committees may try to help set things right, and break this cycle, by temporarily giving preferential treatment to black applicants.

Moreover, although many people now recognize that racist discrimination is wrong, prejudice against blacks is still widespread. One aspect of the problem is that a disproportionate number of blacks are still poor and hold only menial jobs, while the most prestigious jobs are occupied mostly by whites. So long as this is so, it will be easy for the white majority to continue with their old stereotyped ideas about black people. But if there were more black people holding prestigious jobs, it would be much more difficult to sustain the old prejudices. So in the long run law school admissions policies favoring black applicants will help reduce racism throughout the society.

I believe these arguments, and others like them, show that policies of reverse discrimination can be socially useful, although this is certainly a debatable point. For one thing, the resentment of those who disapprove of such policies will diminish their net utility. For another, less qualified persons will not perform as well in the positions they attain. However, I will not discuss these issues any further. I will concentrate instead on the more fundamental question of whether policies of reverse discrimination are unjust. After all, the rejected white student may concede the utility of such policies and nevertheless still complain that he has been treated unjustly. He may point out that he has been turned down simply because of his race. If he had been black, and had had exactly the same qualifications, he would have been accepted. This, he may argue, is equally as unjust as discriminating against black people on account of their race. Moreover, he can argue that, even if black people have been mistreated, he was not responsible for it, and so it is unfair to penalize him for it now. These are impressive arguments and, if they cannot be answered, the rightness of reverse discrimination will remain in doubt regardless of its utility.

I will argue that whether the white applicant has been treated unjustly depends on *why* he has better credentials than the black, that is, it depends on what accounts for the 20-point difference in their qualifications.

Suppose, for example, that his higher qualifications are due entirely to the fact that he has worked harder. Suppose the two applicants are equally intelligent, and have had the same opportunities. But the black student has spent a lot of time enjoying himself, going to the movies, and so forth, while the white student has passed by such pleasures to devote himself to his studies. If *this* is what accounts for the difference in their qualifications, then it seems that the white applicant really has been treated unjustly. For he has earned his superior qualifications; he deserves to be admitted ahead of the black student because he has worked harder for it.

But now suppose a different explanation is given as to why the white student has ended up with a 20-point advantage in qualifications. Suppose the applicants are equally intelligent *and* they have worked equally hard. However, the black student has had to contend with obstacles which his white competitor has not had to face. For example, his early education was at the hands of ill-trained teachers in crowded, inadequate schools, so that by the time he reached college he was far behind the other students and despite his best efforts he never quite caught up. If *this* is what accounts for the difference in qualifications, things look very different. For now the white student has not earned his superior qualifications. He has done nothing to deserve them. His record is, of course, the result of things he's done, just as the black student's record is the result of things the black student has done. But the fact that he has a *better* record than the black student is not due to anything he has done. That difference is due only to his good luck in having been born into a more advantaged social position. Surely he cannot

deserve to be admitted into law school ahead of the black simply because of *that.*

Now in fact black people in the United States have been, and are, systematically discriminated against, and it is reasonable to believe that this mistreatment does make a difference to black people's ability to compete with whites for such goods as law school admission. Therefore, at least some actual cases probably do correspond to the description of my example. Some white students have better qualifications for law school only because they have not had to contend with the obstacles faced by their black competitors. If so, their better qualifications do not automatically entitle them to prior admission.

Thus it is not the fact that the applicant is black that matters. What is important is that, as a result of past discriminatory practices, he has been unfairly handicapped in trying to achieve the sort of academic standing required for admission. If he has a claim to "preferential" treatment now, it is for *that* reason.

It follows that, even though a system of reverse discrimination might involve injustice for some whites, in many cases no injustice will be done. In fact the reverse is true: If no such system is employed—if, for example, law school admissions are granted purely on the basis of "qualifications" —*that* may involve injustice for the disadvantaged who have been unfairly handicapped in the competition for qualifications.

It also follows that the most common arguments against reverse discrimination are not valid. The white student in our example cannot complain that he is being rejected simply because he is white. The effect of the policy is only to *neutralize an advantage* that he has had because he is white, and that is very different.[10] Nor will it do any good for the white to complain that, while blacks may have suffered unjust hardships, *he* is not responsible for it and so should not be penalized for it. The white applicant is not being penalized, or being made to pay reparations, for the wrongs that have been done to blacks. He is simply not being allowed to *profit* from the fact that those wrongs were done, by now besting the black in a competition that is "fair" only if we ignore the obstacles which one competitor, but not the other, has had to face.

## Notes

1. Robert Nozick, *Anarchy, State and Utopia* (New York: Basic Books, 1974), pp. 149–150.

2. Judith Jarvis Thomson, "Preferential Hiring," *Philosophy and Public Affairs,* vol. 2, no. 4 (Summer 1973), pp. 364–384.

3. *Ibid.,* p. 369.

4. The following is from my review of *Anarchy, State and Utopia* in *Philosophia,* vol. 7 (1977).

5. Nozick, p. 161.

6. Joel Feinberg, *Doing and Deserving* (Princeton: Princeton University Press, 1970), p. 58 (italics added).

7. John Rawls, *A Theory of Justice* (Cambridge, Mass.: Harvard University Press, 1971), pp. 103–104.

8. What I am resisting—and what I think Rawls' view leads us towards—is a kind of determinism that would make all moral evaluation of persons meaningless. On this tendency in Rawls, see Nozick, pp. 213–214.

9. This point is elaborated by Herbert Morris in his illuminating paper "Persons and Punishment," *The Monist,* vol. 52 (1968), pp. 475–501.

10. Cf. George Sher, "Justifying Reverse Discrimination in Employment," *Philosophy and Public Affairs,* vol. 4, no. 2 (Winter 1975), pp. 159–170. Sher also argues that "reverse discrimination is justified insofar as it neutralizes competitive disadvantages caused by past privations" (p. 165). I have learned a lot from Sher's paper.

## Questions

1.    *Nozick:* "The principle of rectification will make use of its best estimate of subjunctive information about what would have occurred . . . if the injustice had not taken place. If the actual description of holdings turns out not to be the description yielded by the principle then [we should try to achieve] the description yielded by the principle."

   *Johnson:* Because the ancestors of most of the white population treated the ancestors of most of the black population unjustly, your theory implies that present-day whites owe reparations to present-day blacks. Something

like affirmative action seems like a good way of paying those reparations, so your theory implies that affirmative action is required by justice.

   *Nozick:* No it doesn't! No it doesn't!

   Does Nozick's theory imply that present-day whites owe reparations to present-day blacks? If not, why not? If so, is affirmative action the most appropriate way of making these reparations according to Nozick's theory? Why or why not?

   Construct a parallel argument whose conclusion is that present-day men owe reparations to present-day women. Is this parallel argument better or worse than the original argument? Explain. If you think this parallel argument works, do you think that affirmative action is the most appropriate way of making these reparations according to Nozick's theory? Why or why not?

2.    *Warren:* We need affirmative action to compensate for present unjust practices. "Would the use of weak discrimination in favor of women [be unjust to men]? The answer, surely, is that it would not, since by hypothesis men would be passed over, in order to fill a quota, in favor of women no better qualified only as often as women continue to be passed over, because of primary or secondary sexism, in favor of men no better qualified." That is, we should figure out how many women would be hired for the job if hiring decisions were not tainted with primary or secondary sexism and then make sure to hire that many women. Of course, to do this, we will have to give preference to women over men sometimes, but this will not reduce the chances of success of male candidates below what they would be in a just society.

   *Wasserstrom:* Even though I favor affirmative action, I object to your whole approach because it accords too much importance to the principle of talent.

*Warren:* No it doesn't! No it doesn't!

Would Rachels agree that the use of weak discrimination in favor of women would not be unjust to men? If not, why not? If so, would this undermine his combination of the Free Market Principle with Aristotle's Principle?

Construct a parallel argument whose conclusion is that the use of weak discrimination in favor of blacks would not be unjust to whites. Is this parallel argument better or worse than the original argument? Explain. In what ways (if any) is this parallel argument different from Rachels' argument for affirmative action?

3. Using Hursthouse's article "Virtue Theory and Abortion" as a model, apply Aristotle's virtue theory to the problem of affirmative action. You will have to consider the virtue of justice, of course, but you should consider other virtues as well.

4. Sophisticated Utilitarians and Kantians believe that it is generally wrong to discriminate on the basis of sex or race when hiring. They also believe that this principle can be deduced from more general moral principles. Answer any *two* of the following questions.

   a. Why does a sophisticated Utilitarian think that it is generally wrong to discriminate on the basis of sex or race when hiring? What exceptions to this moral principle would a sophisticated Utilitarian accept? (List as many different sorts of exceptions as you can think of.) How would a sophisticated Utilitarian justify these exceptions? (You may use Act or Rule Utilitarianism.)

   b. Why does a sophisticated Kantian think that it is generally wrong to discriminate on the basis of sex or race when hiring? What exceptions to this moral principle would a sophisticated Kantian accept? (List as many different sorts of exceptions as you can think of.) How would a sophisticated Kantian justify these exceptions? (You may use CI#1 or CI#2.)

   c. Why do you think that it is generally wrong to discriminate on the basis of sex or race when hiring? What exceptions to this moral principle would you accept? (List as many different sorts of exceptions as you can think of.) How would you justify these exceptions?

5. Choose *two* of the following philosophers: Rachels, Pojman, Warren, Wasserstrom, Mill, Kant, Aristotle, Rawls, Nozick, Gilligan, yourself. [See the "Economic Justice" section and the "Ethics of Care" section.] How would each of your two chosen philosophers answer the following questions? Explain your philosophers' rationale for their answers.

   a. Is it wrong to give preference to whites when hiring?

   b. Is it wrong to give preference to whites when admitting to college?

   c. Is it wrong to give preference to pretty women when hiring?

   d. Is it wrong to give preference to pretty women when admitting to college?

   e. Is it wrong to give preference to blacks when hiring?

   f. Is it wrong to give preference to blacks when admitting to college?

6. Suppose that Fred is hiring a sales clerk at a department store. Answer *all* of the following questions.

   a. Is it morally wrong for Fred to discriminate against blacks? (That is, if Fred must choose between a qualified white person and a somewhat more qualified black person, is it morally wrong for Fred to hire the white person because he or she is white?) Why or why not?

   b. Is it morally wrong for Fred to discriminate against Jews? Why or why not?

   c. Is it morally wrong for Fred to discriminate against non-veterans? Why or why not?

   d. Is it morally wrong for Fred to discriminate against non-citizens? Why or why not?

   e. Is it morally wrong for Fred to discriminate against strangers? Why or why not?

Be consistent! If you say that discrimination against blacks is wrong because race is irrelevant to the job, then you are committed (or are you?) to the claim that discrimination against non-veterans is wrong. Or if you say that discrimination against blacks is wrong because people do not have a fair opportunity to become white, then you are committed (or are you?) to the claim that discrimination against Jews is OK, because Jews have a fair opportunity to become Christian. Or if you say that discrimination against strangers is OK, because people ought to be able to hire whomever they like with their own money, then you are committed (or are you?) to the claim that discrimination against blacks is OK. And so on.

7. Continue the following dialogue in a philosophically interesting way.

*Lyndon Johnson:* Affirmative action is justified because today's blacks are worse off than they would have been, because their ancestors were enslaved by the ancestors of today's whites. Therefore, today's whites owe a debt to today's blacks.

*David Duke:* Are today's blacks really worse off? If you mean *particular* blacks, consider that their ancestors would never have met if not for slavery, so they would never have existed. If you mean blacks *in general*, consider that American blacks are much better off than African blacks.

*Feinberg:* Justice does not depend on historical circumstances, but present injustices require present solutions regardless of how they came about. Otherwise we would have to begin by giving America back to the native Americans, and this is plainly impractical. Moreover, some disadvantaged groups (such as homosexuals) tend not to leave descendants, whereas other disadvantaged groups (such as women) leave non-disadvantaged descendants.

*Nozick:* But this assumes some ideal pattern of distribution. As a free-marketeer I cannot accept this.

*Pojman:* Affirmative action would actually punish some innocent people. For example, recent Russian immigrants would be treated as oppressive whites even though neither they nor their ancestors enslaved American blacks. Moreover, affirmative action would worsen the oppression of some disadvantaged groups (children of alcoholics, for example).

*Johnson:* Certainly any affirmative action program will be imperfect, but the crucial question is this. Would society be more just with or without such a program?

*Pojman:* It is possible for legitimate claims of justice to conflict. For example, there are more legitimate claims to Palestine than there is land. Similarly, although blacks deserve to be helped, whites deserve not to be discriminated against.

8. Suppose that we begin with Rachels's idea of combining the Free Market Principle with Aristotle's Principle and then add Pojman's idea of combining the Principle of Talent with Aristotle's Principle. What are the pros and cons of the following argument?

(A) Although no one has a right to a job (Free Market Principle), the more talent a person has, the more he or she deserves a job (Aristotle's Principle + Principle of Talent).

(B) Affirmative action distributes jobs to people who are not the most qualified applicants.

(C) Therefore, affirmative action is unjust.

9. Choose *one* of the following philosophers: (a) Kant, (b) Nozick, (c) Feinberg. Using the ideas of your chosen philosopher, perform *all* of the following tasks. Construct an argument *favoring* laws that require affirmative action with respect to race in hiring. Construct an argument *opposing* laws that require affirmative action with respect to race in hiring. Construct an argument *favoring* laws that ban racial discrimination in hiring. Construct an argument *opposing* laws that ban racial

discrimination in hiring. Which of these arguments would your chosen philosopher probably endorse? Which of these arguments would you endorse?

10. State *one* argument in favor of or against affirmative action for blacks. Does your chosen argument work? Why or why not? State a parallel version of your chosen argument that applies to affirmative action for women. Does your parallel argument work? Why or why not?

11. Sam owns an apartment building. He does not rent to blacks. He says that he himself has nothing against blacks but that if he rents an apartment to a black person, some of his other tenants will move out and he will have a tough time renting future vacant apartments. Why is Sam's sort of racial discrimination morally wrong? There are several different ways to answer this question. The answer you give will make some of the following questions difficult and others easy. That is, it will be hard to answer some of the following questions in ways that are consistent with your judgment about Sam. Answer what are, in your case, the *two hardest* of the following questions.

a. Is it OK to discriminate against atheists when renting? Why or why not?

b. Is it OK to discriminate against pet owners when renting? Why or why not?

c. Is it OK to discriminate against animals by eating them? Why or why not?

d. Is it OK to discriminate against fetuses by aborting them? Why or why not?

e. Is it OK to discriminate against very defective infants by euthanizing them? Why or why not?

f. Is it OK to discriminate against homosexuals by making homosexual marriage illegal? Why or why not?

g. Is it OK to discriminate against homophobes (people who are offended by homosexuals) by legalizing homosexual marriage? Why or why not?

# Poverty and Marriage

*Blessed are you who are poor, for the kingdom of God is yours. . . . But woe to you who are rich for you have received your consolation.*

JESUS

**A** person's response to the problem of poverty usually depends on his or her view of the principal cause of poverty. Some people blame the poor; they think that poverty results primarily from vices such as laziness. Other people blame no one; they think that poverty results from the natural forces of the marketplace. Yet other people blame the rich; they think that poverty results from injustice.

The major government response to poverty is called welfare. Welfare is not a single program. Rather, the term "welfare" refers to a large collection of different programs, such as food stamps, subsidized housing, and Medicaid. The largest of these programs is Aid to Families with Dependent Children (AFDC). Eligibility requirements for these programs differ somewhat, although many people qualify for several programs. For years America's policy was that if you were poor enough, you qualified for these programs no matter why you were poor and no matter how long you had been poor. In 1996 Congress passed, and President Clinton signed, a bill transforming welfare from entitlements to programs of limited assistance by imposing a time limit on welfare benefits. A person may now remain on welfare for no more than two years at a time and no more than five years over a lifetime.

## Utilitarian Analysis

In his notorious book *Losing Ground: American Social Policy 1950–1980*, Charles Murray blames the poor for their poverty. He insinuates that poverty results primarily from laziness and irresponsibility. He also claims that welfare makes things worse, largely by rewarding dysfunctional behavior. Murray maintains that if welfare were eliminated, then most welfare recipients would be pressured into getting jobs and unwed teenagers would be discouraged from having babies. This would be better for them and for the country. Of course, some people would be unable to go to work because they are disabled, because no jobs are available, because they have young children and no day care, or for some other reason. But Murray claims that local charities would pick up most of the slack. A few deserving people would fall through the cracks, but overall, the advantages of eliminating welfare would outweigh the disadvantages.

Does poverty result primarily from the vices of the poor? Like many people, Murray is obsessed by the images of the welfare cheater (the person who could work but pretends to be unable to work in order to continue to collect welfare checks), the welfare dependent (the person who stays on welfare for a lifetime), and the welfare winner (the person who garners a high income from welfare). Yet studies show that welfare cheaters, dependents, and winners are rare. To begin with, in 1995 two-thirds of the AFDC recipients were children. Half of the AFDC recipients remained on AFDC less than four years; two-thirds left AFDC after eight years. The amount families received from AFDC varies from state to state, but the average monthly benefit was $373.00 from AFDC plus $88.00 from food stamps per family. Average family size for AFDC was about three people. Thus the 1995 welfare rolls were not filled with able-bodied adults collecting big money from the government for their whole lives.

Does welfare makes things worse? Murray speaks as though eliminating welfare were an untried measure. Now that a policy of governmental support of the poor has failed, we should try not supporting the poor. (Has welfare failed?) However, America has tried leaving the poor to fend for themselves before. We had no governmental safety net until AFDC became a federal program in 1935 under President Roosevelt. Before that, a fair number of people were dying in the streets and many others lived in excruciating poverty. History suggests that if we eliminate welfare, then some people will starve and others will become very poor, homeless, and malnourished. Moreover, when poverty increases, crime increases. Murray might claim that things would be different now, but he gives us no reason to think so.

On the other hand, it cannot be denied that our welfare system has fostered some dysfunctional attitudes and behavior. Perhaps this is a result of rewarding these behaviors, as Murray suggests. Or perhaps it is a consequence of society's portrayal of welfare as charity. This characterization stigmatizes welfare recipients as parasites both in the eyes of others and in their own eyes. This loss of self-respect makes the stereotype self-fulfilling. To accomplish anything, a person must have some self-confidence. Society's fear of welfare cheaters, dependents, and winners may also be a self-fulfilling prophecy. To avoid "being taken in," society established an expensive and intrusive bureaucracy to check up on welfare recipients. However, as any parent knows, both trust and mistrust are self-fulfilling. When you trust people, they often try to be worthy of your trust, but when you are suspicious of people, they feel they have nothing to lose by deceit. But is it possible to structure a welfare program in a way that avoids stigmatizing and scrutinizing welfare recipients?

## Deontological Analysis: Nozick

Robert Nozick blames no one for poverty. Some may become poor through vice or injustice, but most are poor simply because there is little demand for their goods and services. They are manual laborers after automation, slide rule salespeople in the computer age, dare devils in a safety-conscious world. They are simply unlucky. Suppose Paula is poor and Ricky is rich not because of violations of rights but simply because of luck. According to Nozick's Free Market Principle, Ricky owes Paula nothing. Ricky is entitled to all of his money because, after all, he earned it. It would be nice of Ricky to help Paula, of course, but he is not morally required to do so and should not be forced to do so. Giving to the poor is supererogatory. People cannot be faulted for not giving; recipients are expected to be grateful. Thus if the government taxes Ricky in order to pay for a welfare program that supports Paula, the government is treating Ricky unjustly. It is forcing him to do something he has no moral duty to do. Government programs such as welfare that transfer funds from the rich to the poor violate the property rights of the rich, according to Nozick. [See the "Economic Justice" section.]

Trudy Govier denies that Ricky is entitled to all of his money. She points out that Ricky's earning power is partially a function of society. Ricky did not accumulate his wealth on his own, for he made use of society's schools, libraries, roads, previous discoveries, and so on. Govier concludes that society has a legitimate claim to some of Ricky's earnings. Society has the right to take its share of Ricky's wealth and give it to people like Paula. Thus transfer programs such as welfare do not victimize the rich.

This is too simple, however. Nozick would concede that Ricky made use of society's resources in order to become wealthy. But if society provided those resources to Ricky without first obtaining his agreement to pay, then the resources were a gift. Gifts do not entitle the giver to anything (except possibly gratitude). Thus, to find out whether transfer programs are legitimate, we must determine what Ricky agreed to pay. It may turn out that the rich have made no commitment to society or to the poor.

Nozick's Free Market Principle seems to assume that society consists of able-bodied adults. It ignores the existence of children and the disabled. At least it denies that they have any special claims. Suppose we add to Nozick's Free Market Principle the plausible claim that children should not be allowed to starve. Naturally, parents bear the primary responsibility for meeting the basic needs of children, but some parents are unable or unwilling to provide for their children. Society could provide for these children by removing them from the custody of their parents and placing them in orphanages and foster homes. Or society could leave the children in the custody of their parents and help the parents to care for the children with money, goods, and services. The latter policy has been shown to be cheaper for society and better for the children. Thus AFDC seems to be a justified program according to the supplemented Free Market Principle. Moreover, food stamps and housing subsidies are also justified when they go to households with children. In other words, if Nozick acknowledges that society should ensure that children's basic needs are met, then he must concede that the bulk of welfare is legitimate.

## Deontological Analysis: Rawls

Everyone knows that Liberals and Conservatives differ over how the government should respond to poverty. But what is the difference between Liberals and Conservatives? Some people describe a Liberal as a person willing to sacrifice liberty in order to increase equality, whereas a Conservative is a person willing to sacrifice equality in order to increase liberty. Ronald Dworkin rejects this characterization. He says that neither Liberals nor Conservatives want people to have equal shares of social goods and that both Liberals and Conservatives want all people be treated with equal concern and respect. However, Liberals seek to achieve this goal in one way, Conservatives in another. According to Dworkin, Liberals believe that the state should be neutral with respect to different conceptions of the good life. Political decisions should not presuppose some set of values. Government should merely ensure that the people

allow each other the opportunity to pursue their own life plans. By contrast, non-Liberals believe that the state should apply some particular conception of the good life impartially to all people. Non-Liberals differ from each other by endorsing different conceptions of the good life. Marxists think that the government should enforce one set of values; Platonists would enforce a different set; the Religious Right would enforce yet another set; and so on.

Perhaps Conservatives may be distinguished from some other Non-Liberals in the following way. A Liberal is a person willing to allow substantial government interference in the public/economic sphere in order to promote equal concern and respect but reluctant to trade liberty for anything in the private/personal sphere. On the other hand, a Conservative is a person willing to allow substantial government interference in the private/personal sphere but reluctant to trade liberty for anything in the public/economic sphere. To round out the picture, Libertarians are willing to sacrifice liberty in neither sphere, whereas Totalitarians are willing to sacrifice liberty in both spheres (see the table on page 630).

Dworkin takes the Liberal view that the state should be neutral between competing ideals to imply that everyone should begin with an equal opportunity to prosper. To allow some people to have a better shot at happiness than others would be to favor some conceptions of the good life—some set of values—over others. As the *Declaration of Independence* says,

We hold these Truths to be self-evident, that all men are created equal, that they are endowed by their Creator with certain inalienable Rights, that among these are Life, Liberty, and the Pursuit of Happiness—That to secure these Rights, Governments are instituted among Men. . . .

Thus the state should take steps to equalize everyone's opportunity to pursue happiness. At least, says John Rawls, we should eliminate or nullify socially caused inequalities. Now some inequalities we can do little or nothing about, but we have some control over wealth distribution. Liberals do not seek total equality of wealth. Instead, Liberals believe that all people ought to have enough resources so that they have an equal opportunity to prosper. Rawls maintains that the good jobs ought to be *open to all*, not in the absurd sense that "everyone is entitled to a good job" or in the minimal, Nozickian sense that "no one will be stopped from seeking a good job," but rather in the sense that all individuals should have an *equal opportunity* to obtain a good job whether they are poor or rich. [See the "Economic Justice" section.] Rawls does not describe the implementation of this equal opportunity principle, but presumably, in addition to public schooling and anti-discrimination laws, and the like, equality of opportunity would require the government to redistribute wealth a bit. We should tax the well off in order to supplement the income of the poor so that they will be able to compete for good jobs. The government might do this in several different ways.

The simplest way would be for the government to provide enough money, goods, and services to bring the poor up to a certain minimum standard of living—a set of benefits that would satisfy a person's basic needs. Before providing this benefit package to you, the government would check to be sure that you really need it but would not ask why you are poor, how you intend to use the money, or whether you are seeking employment. This is the principle behind the idea of welfare as entitlement. Govier calls it the *Permissive Principle*.

Do not mistake the Permissive Principle for Communism or Socialism. (Many people are quite confused about Communism and Socialism, presumably because of the myths spread about these doctrines during the cold war.) *Communism* says that there should no private property and no government. All society members should simply contribute whatever they can to society and take from the common pot whatever they require. "From each according to his ability; to each according to his need," says Marx. *Socialism* says that there should be private property and government. But the government, rather than private individuals, should own and run the "means of production"—the factories, farms, and so on. Under socialism, there would be not only public roads, schools, and libraries but also public steel mills, auto plants, and oil refineries. Govier is endorsing neither of these systems. Her Permissive Principle is simply the Free Market Principle plus a comprehensive safety net. It says all goods and services should be distributed according to the Free Market Principle except that government should meet the basic needs of all society members who are unable or unwilling to provide for themselves.

Under the Permissive Principle everyone is entitled to government support. The Permissive Principle sanctions *freeriders*—people who could work but choose to be supported by the government instead. Many people consider this a decisive drawback. Freeriding is unfair to those who support the freerider, of course. There are also a number of Utilitarian objections to the Permissive Principle. For example, being supported actually harms the freeriders. It erodes self-respect while positively reinforcing dysfunctional character traits. Moreover, the option to decline work and be supported undermines the motivation to work throughout the society.

| | Government intervention in the private/personal sphere is justified. | Government intervention in the public/economic sphere is justified. |
|---|---|---|
| Libertarians | seldom | seldom |
| Liberals | seldom | often |
| Conservatives | often | seldom |
| Totalitarians | often | often |

Our judicial system provides suspects with many rights. We could convict a higher percentage of guilty people if suspects had fewer rights, but we take safeguarding the innocent from wrongful punishment to be a higher priority than punishing the guilty. Perhaps we should err on the side of caution in our welfare system, too. Perhaps it is more important to ensure that the truly needy are helped than it is to eliminate freeriders. If so, the Permissive Principle may be our best bet, for any system that filters out freeriders will also filter out some of the truly needy.

A popular alternative lies between the stern Free Market Principle and the generous Permissive Principle. The *Puritan Principle* says that the government should ensure that people who wish to work can obtain decent jobs that pay enough to yield a minimal standard of living. To do this the government should provide job training, financial support during the training period, transportation, day care, and various other goods and services to those who cannot work without them. Indeed, the government might have to provide the poor with jobs if suitable jobs are unavailable in the private sector; it might have to be the employer of last resort. Of course, the government might provide all of this under the Permissive Principle, too. But the difference between the Permissive Principle and the Puritan Principle is this: Under the Puritan Principle, people who, despite all of this help and encouragement from the government, choose not to work would receive no benefits. This is roughly the principle behind the 1996 welfare bill. It is sometimes called *workfare*.

The Puritan Principle would not allow freeriders, and it would encourage and empower people to work, but it has drawbacks. Although workfare is sometimes touted as a money-saving policy, studies and pilot programs suggest that workfare is more expensive than welfare. Providing people who have fallen through society's cracks with the skills and means to find and hold a job is no trivial task. Surprisingly, it is cheaper to support these people than to enable them to support themselves. Moreover, in order to block freeriders, the government must establish a bureaucracy to check up on workfare recipients to make sure that they are trying to work. This bureaucracy is expensive, and it has demoralizing and humiliating effects on the recipients. Finally, children of people who choose not to work would be supported under the Permissive Principle, but under the Puritan Principle they would suffer for the vices of their parents.

## Ethics of Care

When we look at who is actually poor, we discover that poverty is a women's issue as well as a children's issue. The overwhelming majority of poor adults are women. The Puritan Principle and the Free Market Principle are too abstract, says the Ethics of Care. They are unfair to women because they ignore the concrete relationships that are central to women's lives. If we look carefully at these relationships, we see that most women are poor because of injustice.

The Puritan Principle or workfare presupposes that poor people are poor because they are not working. It does not exactly blame the poor, but it says, in a fatherly way, "Some of you need a job and the rest need a swift kick." However, this ignores the fact that adult welfare recipients typically *are* working. Their work is child care. Their problem is not finding work but rather obtaining credit for the work they are already doing. After all, had they chosen to surrender or abort their children, they would not be on welfare. It is their decision to fulfill their responsibilities and perform the work of child care that impoverishes them.

Moreover, workfare presupposes that once women find paid work, they can make it. But this ignores the fact that women are disadvantaged by the need to do child care and housework (not to mention the obstacle of sex discrimination). Their problem is not finding paid work; rather, it is finding time and energy to do paid work. Unless you have actually attempted it, it is difficult to understand how much of an obstacle child care presents to working outside of the home. Suppose you are a single mom with two young children trying to hold down an office job. You have to get the kids up, fed, dressed, and dropped off at day care or school in time to get to work by, say, 8:00 A.M. After work you pick up the kids, feed them, play with them a bit, put them to sleep, and then do housework. Weekends are for errands. Moreover, you miss a lot of work staying home to care for sick kids. Single parenting can be done, but it is harder than it looks.

Nozick's Free Market Principle assumes that, in general, people who are well off have no duties to the poor because they have made no commitments to the poor. It does not exactly blame the poor, but it says, "Hey, we didn't make you poor, so don't expect us to help you." But this ignores the implicit commitments that society makes to women. The typical adult welfare recipient is a single mother who is dependent on welfare because she does not have enough savings or marketable job skills. She lacks these because she did not plan to support herself. Instead, she anticipated being supported by a husband. Unfortunately, she is divorced or she never married. But society fosters this sort of dependence by socializing women to rely on husbands. These women are impoverished because they did what they were expected to do—because they trusted the commitment society made to them. Being members of society, well-off people have participated in fostering this expectation in women. Thus they have made an implicit commitment to these women.

According to the Ethics of Care, we have a duty to try to meet the needs of those to whom we are related, at least when the relationships are not corrupt. Thus the Ethics of Care blames those (primarily men) who shirk their responsibility by abandoning their children, instead of wrongly praising them for their independence as other theories do. And the Ethics of Care praises those (primarily women) who accept their responsibility by caring for their children (especially when this choice leads to poverty and prejudice), instead of wrongly blaming them for their dependence as other theories do.

Presumably, the Ethics of Care would endorse Govier's Permissive Principle, not for Utilitarian or Deontological reasons, but rather because a caring society, like a caring parent, would not abandon its own. Mainstream Ethics loses sight of this because it works with abstract relationships between abstract individuals in a hypothetical society instead of with the concrete relationships that constitute an actual society. [See the "Ethics of Care" section.]

\*

Onora O'Neill disagrees with this Ethics of Care analysis. Mainstream accounts of justice are not too abstract, says O'Neill. Instead, they are idealized. They might be accurate accounts of some ideal world, but they do not depict the real world correctly. The problem is not that Rawls's and Nozick's claims about people, institutions, and practices are too general. Instead, the problem is that some of their general claims are false. Rawls assumes, for example, that justice is a matter only for the public sphere—that justice need not cross the public/private boundary. Thus Rawls ignores injustice within the family. (Similarly, most accounts of international justice assume that justice need not cross national boundaries. They assume that the principal agents are sovereign states and ignore multinational corporations, international agencies, and so on.) Analogously, Nozick relies on the fiction that all people are roughly equal, fully autonomous agents. He ignores important differences of power and autonomy among individuals and thus misses the ways in which the powerful pressure the powerless. Nozick fails to notice that because of their weak bargaining position, some people have no choice but to agree to practices and promises that cause them to become and remain impoverished.

A natural reaction to idealized abstraction is to seek the concreteness of Ethical Relativism or the Ethics of Care. Both of these theories emphasize the need to focus on particular facts. Relativism says that we must study the customs and values of a culture in order to determine what is considered right within that culture. The Ethics of Care says that we must study the networks of relationships and emotions in order to determine what is right in a given situation. However, O'Neill urges us to avoid Relativism and the Ethics of Care because both tend to reinforce the status quo and thus undermine attempts to secure justice for the exploited. A relativistic account of justice will enable one to criticize a culture or individuals within the culture for violating the culture's values, but it will not enable one to challenge the values of a culture. It will damn hypocrisy but not moral blindness. The Ethics of Care does not have this problem. But insofar as the Ethics of Care assigns to women the tasks of caring for others, it acquiesces in (or even ratifies) the traditional division of labor along gender lines that feminists have sought to overthrow. The Ethics of Care can easily "end up endorsing rather than challenging social and economic structures that marginalize women and confine them to a private sphere, . . . to the nursery and the kitchen, to purdah and to poverty."

## Deontological Analysis: Kant

So far we have been taking poverty as a given and wondering whether and how to reduce or eliminate it. However, another way to respond to poverty is to try to prevent it. Naturally, the first step is to determine the causes of poverty. O'Neill takes injustice to be one of the main causes of poverty, and she sketches an account that spotlights this injustice.

O'Neill's account is unapologetically abstract but strives to avoid idealization. Following Kant, O'Neill rejects principles and practices insofar as they are not universalizable. She proposes that justice consists in following principles that could be adopted by any group of rational beings. Such a group could not rationally adopt a principle that deception or coercion is acceptable, for the victims could not accede to such principles. Of course, they can utter the word "yes." But assent does not count as legitimate if the agent is ignorant of crucial information. For example, impoverished people who are unaware of the possibility of a better life are often satisfied with the life they have. Assent obtained by force or threats or because the agent is in a desperate sit-

uation is not legitimate, either. For example, impoverished people, especially those who must support children, elderly parents, or other dependents often accept exploitive offers because they are desperate. The "yes" to the meager life or the exploitive offer is not true consent, because "no" was not a viable option. As O'Neill puts it,

> They are vulnerable not only to low wages, low standards of industrial safety, endemic debt, and disadvantageous dependence on those who provide credit, but also to disadvantageous patterns of entitlement within the family. . . . Family structures can enable, even impose, forms of deception and domination. . . . A woman who has no adequate entitlements of her own, and insecure rights to a share in family property or income, will not always be coerced, but is always vulnerable to coercion.

In general, no acts, practices, or institutions are just unless they *are accepted* and *could have been rejected* by those they constrain. Both actual assent and possible dissent are necessary.

\*

Just as the Ethics of Care criticizes Nozick and Rawls for being too abstract, Martha Nussbaum complains that O'Neill's Kantianism is too abstract—too far from the content of people's lives. She thinks O'Neill cannot deduce principles that adequately address the problem of poverty from the thin premise that acceptable acts and practices must be universalizable. True, a group of people could not consistently endorse principles of deception and coercion, but there are unjust principles that they could consistently endorse.

Rather than asking what rational beings *could* agree to, Nussbaum's alternative proposal requires participants in a practice to determine what they actually *do* agree to. First, participants should ask themselves what they take to be the essential aspects of humanity and of a flourishing human life. Second, participants should make sure that they apply these aspects honestly and consistently to an evaluation of the practice. If you acknowledge that blacks are human beings and that freedom is an essential aspect of a good human life, then you should oppose black slavery. If you acknowledge that poor people are human beings and that humans have basic needs, then you should oppose economic systems that leave some humans without the resources to satisfy these needs. In general, Nussbaum seeks to stamp out double standards.

Nussbaum's account faces two objections. First, even if a practice denies people something essential to a flourishing human life, it does not follow that the practice is wrong. People may not be entitled to what they need. Imprisoning certain criminals is not wrong, for example, because they are not entitled to a flourishing human life. Similarly, killing in self-defense is not wrong (because attackers forfeit their right to life?). Nozick would acknowledge that poor people are people and that they need food to flourish, yet Nozick would deny that the poor are thereby owed food.

Second, Nussbaum's account exhibits a sort of Relativism. She asks people to apply *their own* views about humanity to practices. But their views may be false. If you do not acknowledge that blacks are human beings, or if you do not recognize the value of freedom, then you will find nothing wrong with black slavery.

# Marriage

Susan Okin argues that the traditional institution of marriage is a major cause of poverty and injustice. Okin shows in detail how marriage, as it presently exists within our society, makes women much more likely to become impoverished and victimized. The expectations and assumptions concerning marriage, the laws and customs surrounding marriage—all conspire to reduce the earning power of women. This, in turn, makes women dependent on husbands or the state. And this makes women vulnerable to exploitation during marriage and to poverty after divorce.

Let us focus on one piece of this progression. Women end up doing the bulk of the housework and child care for three interrelated reasons. First, powerful social assumptions about gender roles channel women toward these tasks and channel men away from them. For example, girls are socialized to be more willing to make compromises and sacrifices than boys, so when it comes time to divide the household tasks, husbands tend to stand firm and wives tend to compromise and sacrifice by picking up these tasks. Moreover, girls are much more likely than boys to learn housework skills and child-care skills, so after marriage wives are better able and more willing to perform these tasks than husbands. These gender role assumptions contribute to the second reason why women end up doing more than their share of the housework and child care. Encouraged by society to plan for being a mother with primary child-care responsibilities and a (at least partially supported) wife with primary housework responsibilities, women are less inclined to make serious preparations for high-paying careers. Instead, many women choose low-paying, dead-end careers because these are the jobs that offer fewer and flexible hours. For this reason, and also because of sex discrimination in the workplace, women after marriage have lower earning power than men. Now it often happens that one spouse's career must be compromised or sacrificed because someone must handle child care or because of the need to relocate or for a variety of other reasons. Naturally, it makes financial sense to compromise or sacrifice the lower earnings of the wife rather than the higher earnings of the husband. Therefore, the woman gives up or cuts back on her paid work and assumes the housework and child-care tasks. This course of action is self-perpetuating, because it further reduces the woman's earning power. The lower earning power of women also leads to the third reason why women end up doing the bulk of the housework and child care. Typically, neither husband nor wife wants to do these tasks, but the wife has more incentive to capitulate because her bargaining position is worse. The break-up of the marriage would be a financial disaster for her, but not for him. The man's standard of living tends to rise dramatically after divorce, but the woman's standard of living often drops precipitously. One reason is that the woman has lower earning power, but there are other reasons, too. Typically, women end up with custody of the children, which reduces their income potential further, while increasing their need. Child support awards are woefully inadequate and often go unpaid, anyway. Finally, when the family's assets are divided, the most important asset, the husband's earning power, is left out of consideration.

These and other patterns produce not only a disproportionate division of housework and child care within the family but a host of other effects as well, including the impoverishment of many women and children after divorce. But let us use the disproportionate division of housework and child care as a touchstone for comparing the accounts of justice that we have mentioned so far. Let us see what Nozick, Rawls, the Ethics of Care, O'Neill, and Nussbaum are able to say about this complex issue.

Nozick's response is simple. Sometimes domestic violence or threats lie behind the disproportionate division, and Nozick (like everyone else) would consider that to be unjust. But otherwise there is no injustice here. Although women end up with the short end of the stick, their rights are not violated.

Rawls does not explicitly apply his theory to issues of justice within families, so I shall extrapolate. Rawls's Difference Principle says that social and economic inequalities must not worsen the situation of others and must maximally benefit the least advantaged class if the inequalities are to be just. Roughly speaking, it is OK for some people to have more goodies than others, but only if this harms no one and helps the impoverished. Now after divorce, men's standard of living typically rises whereas the women's and children's standard of living typically falls. This inequality clearly fails Rawls's Difference Principle test, so Rawlsians would condemn this aspect of traditional marriage and require that the standard of living of both households be equal after divorce. Rawls also maintains that desirable positions within society must be "open to all," not just in the weak sense that

no one should be blocked from these positions but also in the strong sense that the society should compensate for socially caused inequalities between competitors. Everyone should have an equal opportunity to gain desirable positions. It follows that not only must society prevent anything from blocking women from good jobs (by banning sex discrimination, subsidizing day care, and so on), but society must also compensate women for disadvantages caused by gender-related expectations, and socialization (perhaps by affirmative action). But Rawls's decision to give liberty a higher priority than equality of opportunity and the Difference Principle requires that gender-based distribution of labor within marriage be tolerated by society, even while society strives to minimize the resulting injustice. [See the "Economic Justice" section.]

The Ethics of Care is not surprised that wives tend to be more willing and better able to do the housework and child care. And the Ethics of Care considers men who do not keep up with women in this respect to be lacking. However, there is nothing wrong with the choice to prepare for careers that accommodate these tasks. Nor is there anything problematic about the decision to cut back on the lower-paying career when someone's career needs pruning in order to nurture the family. Paying inadequate or no child support is an uncaring thing to do, of course. But the Ethics of Care has nothing to say about whether to divide the husband's earning power in the event of a divorce, for that is an issue of justice rather than of care.

O'Neill might find deception in society's tendency to encourage women to make career plans on the assumption of eventually being supported by a husband. O'Neill might also find it illegitimate for the husband to improve his bargaining position by taking advantage of the wife's fear of divorce. But the other matters are not morally problematic in her view, and even these two objections seem rather strained and artificial. After all, it is common knowledge in our society that divorce is prevalent and that women typically end up with the children. Society does not mislead women about these facts.

These days, moreover, the supported wife is not presented as the only role model for women. Thus the claim that society deceives women is somewhat tenuous. Second, in O'Neill's view there is nothing wrong with bargaining from unequal positions so long as neither person is menaced with a desperate situation. Now in many cases, divorce does not reduce women to destitution but merely lowers their standard of living. In these cases, the husbands are not exploiting a desperate situation by not compromising on the housework and child care. Even in cases where the wife is at risk of destitution, the threat of divorce may not be explicitly or even implicitly invoked by the husband. In such cases, the husband is arguably benefiting from the situation but is not exploiting it.

Nussbaum might find a double standard in the facts that (a) girls are socialized to be more willing to make compromises and sacrifices than boys, (b) women's careers rather than men's careers are typically compromised or sacrificed after marriage, and (c) women gain custody without adequate support.

## Virtue Ethics Analysis: Aristotle

Overall, none of these responses to the disproportionate division of housework and child care seems completely adequate. Aristotle would say that they are all too abstract. Understanding injustice requires a preliminary determination of the essential aspects of humanity and the essential aspects of a flourishing human life (not what participants take these aspects to be). Perceiving injustice clearly depends on having the right facts and the right values. Thus, according to Dworkin's definition, Aristotle is not a Liberal. He does not think that the state should be neutral with respect to different views of the good life. (Aristotle is not a Conservative either.)

Aristotle might begin his analysis by observing that between friends there must be reciprocity. Both partners must contribute equally to the friendship (although they need not contribute the same things), or else the relationship is ex-

ploitive. Justice requires that each partner have an equal share of the burdens as well as of the benefits. This seems to be an obvious and crucial fact about marriages that the other theories miss. Of course, determining whether two different sorts of contributions are equivalent is tricky. If the husband has a job at which he works 40 hours a week and the wife does all of the housework and child care but does not work outside the home, are the partners contributing equally? If the husband and wife are both working outside the home, but the husband's job requires many more hours or pays much better, is it fair for the wife to do all of the housework and child care? Although some cases are difficult to decide, many others are clear. Aristotle would probably have no trouble labeling many contemporary marriages "unjust."

Justice is not the only Aristotelian consideration. An Aristotelian (though probably not Aristotle himself) might assert that child care and housework are both central components of the good life, so both men and women should engage fully in these activities. By avoiding these activities, the husband is missing out on a great good. Anyone who has raised a child will acknowledge that child care is an invaluable experience (notwithstanding its aggravations), for it makes your life richer as it makes your character better. It is more difficult to see why washing dishes is an important component of a good life. But if housework is thought of as making family life run smoothly amid an environment of comfort and beauty, then perhaps the Aristotelian has a point. If both husband and wife do substantial amounts of child care and housework, won't the family's standard of living be lower? Perhaps, the Aristotelian would reply, but equal participation in child care and housework is more valuable than a high standard of living to the good human life.

Finally, Aristotle would assert that part of the good life is being just and even magnanimous to others, especially to one's friends and former friends. Thus husbands are wrong to capitalize on their wives' fear of divorce in order to get their way in domestic disputes. And they are also wrong to accept a higher standard of living than their wives enjoy after divorce. That is just not the way nice guys behave.

*

Okin comes to the same conclusions as Aristotle about what is wrong with the traditional marriage and how it should be modified. First, men and women should have equal responsibility for housework and child care. Okin points out that some of our social institutions should be modified to facilitate this equal responsibility. For example, decent day care facilities, parental leaves, and flexible schedules should be widely available to workers with small children so that women are not under pressure to (a) put their careers on hold in order to stay home with the kids, or (b) choose careers with flexible hours

(typically lower-paying careers), or (c) lose sleep, and jeopardize health and sanity trying to manage full-time careers along with child care.

Second, Okin claims that both resultant households should have the same standard of living in cases of divorce. One reason for this is to reduce the likelihood that the wife will have to choose between drudgery within the marriage and poverty after divorce. Okin's proposal would level the playing field somewhat by making the negotiating positions of the husband and wife more nearly equal. Justice provides another justification for Okin's proposal. Because the husband's earning potential is an asset that the wife as well as the husband has nurtured, so it should not belong only to the husband after divorce.

# 56   The Right to Eat and the Duty to Work

## TRUDY GOVIER

Although the topic of welfare is not one with which philosophers have often concerned themselves, it is a topic which gives rise to many complex and fascinating questions—some in the area of political philosophy, some in the area of ethics, and some of a more practical kind. The variety of issues related to the subject of welfare makes it particularly necessary to be clear just which issue one is examining in a discussion of welfare. In a recent book on the subject, Nicholas Rescher asks:

In what respects and to what extent is society, working through the instrumentality of the state, responsible for the welfare of its members? What demands for the promotion of his welfare can an individual reasonably make upon his society? These are questions to which no answer can be given in terms of some *a priori* approach with reference to universal ultimates. Whatever answer can appropriately be given will depend,

in the final analysis, on what the society decides it should be.[1]

Rescher raises this question only to avoid it. His response to his own question is that a society has all and only those responsibilities for its members that it thinks it has. Although this claim is trivially true as regards legal responsibilities, it is inadequate from a moral perspective. If one imagines the case of an affluent society which leaves the blind, the disabled, and the needy to die of starvation, the incompleteness of Rescher's account becomes obvious. In this imagined case one is naturally led to raise the question as to whether those in power ought to supply those in need with the necessities of life. Though the needy have no legal right to welfare benefits of any kind, one might very well say that they ought to have such a right. It is this claim which I propose to discuss here.[2]

I shall approach this issue by examining three positions which may be adopted in response to it. These are:

From Trudy Govier, *Philosophy of the Social Sciences,* 5 (1975), 125–143, with omissions. Copyright © 1975 by Sage Publications. Reprinted by permission of Sage Publications, Inc.

1. *The Individualist Position:* Even in an affluent society, one ought not to have any legal right to state-supplied welfare benefits.
2. *The Permissive Position:* In a society with sufficient resources, one ought to have an unconditional legal right to receive state-supplied welfare benefits. (That is, one's right to receive such benefits ought not to depend on one's behaviour; it should be guaranteed.)
3. *The Puritan Position:* In a society with sufficient resources one ought to have a legal right to state-supplied welfare benefits; this right ought to be conditional, however, on one's willingness to work.

But before we examine these positions, some preliminary clarification must be attempted. . . .

Welfare systems are state-supported systems which supply benefits, usually in the form of cash income, to those who are in need. Welfare systems thus exist in the sort of social context where there is some private ownership of property. If no one owned anything individually (except possibly his own body), and all goods were considered to be the joint property of everyone, then this type of welfare system could not exist. A state might take on the responsibility for the welfare of its citizens, but it could not meet this responsibility by distributing a level of cash income which such citizens would spend to purchase the goods essential for life. The welfare systems which exist in the western world do exist against the background of extensive private ownership of property. It is in this context that I propose to discuss moral questions about having a right to welfare benefits. By setting out my questions in this way, I do not intend to endorse the institution of private property, but only to discuss questions which many people find real and difficult in the context of the social organization which they actually do experience. The present analysis of welfare is intended to apply to societies which (*a*) have the institution of private property, if not for means of production, at least for some basic good; and (*b*) possess sufficient resources so that it is at least possible for every member of the society to be supplied with the necessities of life.

## 1. The Individualist View

It might be maintained that a person in need has no legitimate moral claim on those around him and that the hypothetical inattentive society which left its blind citizens to beg or starve cannot rightly be censured for doing so. This view, which is dramatically at odds with most of contemporary social thinking, lives on in the writings of Ayn Rand and her followers.[3] The Individualist sets a high value on uncoerced personal choice. He sees each person as a responsible agent who is able to make his own decisions and to plan his own life. He insists that with the freedom to make decisions goes responsibility for the consequences of those decisions. A person has every right, for example, to spend ten years of his life studying Sanskrit— but if, as a result of this choice, he is unemployable, he ought not to expect others to labour on his behalf. No one has a proper claim on the labour of another, or on the income ensuing from that labour, unless he can repay the labourer in a way acceptable to that labourer himself. Government welfare schemes provide benefits from funds gained largely by taxing earned income. One cannot "opt out" of such schemes. To the Individualist, this means that a person is forced to work part of his time for others.

Suppose that a man works forty hours and earns two hundred dollars. Under modern-day taxation, it may well be that he can spend only two-thirds of that money as he chooses. The rest is taken by government and goes to support programmes which the working individual may not himself endorse. The beneficiaries of such programmes—those beneficiaries who do not work themselves—are as though they have slaves working for them. Backed by the force which government authorities can command, they are able to exist on the earnings of others. Those who support them do not do so voluntarily, out of charity; they do so on government command.

Someone across the street is unemployed. Should you be taxed extra to pay for his expenses? Not at all. You have not injured him, you are not responsible for the fact that he is unemployed (unless you are a senator or bureaucrat who agitated for further curtailing of business which legislation passed, with the result that your neighbour was laid off by the curtailed business). You may voluntarily wish to help him out, or better still, try to get him a job to put him on his feet again; but since you have initiated no aggressive act against him, and neither purposefully nor accidentally injured him in any way, you should not be legally penalized for the fact of his unemployment.[4]

The Individualist need not lack concern for those in need. He may give generously to charity; he might give more generously still, if his whole income were his to use, as he would like it to be. He may also believe that, as a matter of empirical fact, existing government programmes do not actually help the poor. They support a cumbersome bureaucracy and they use financial resources which, if untaxed, might be used by those with initiative to pursue job-creating endeavours. The thrust of the Individualist's position is that each person owns his own body and his own labour; thus each person is taken to have a virtually unconditional right to the income which that labour can earn him in a free market place.[5] For anyone to pre-empt part of a worker's earnings without that worker's voluntary consent is tantamount to robbery. And the fact that the government is the intermediary through which this deed is committed does not change its moral status one iota.

On an Individualist's view, those in need should be cared for by charities or through other schemes to which contributions are voluntary. Many people may wish to insure themselves against unforeseen calamities and they should be free to do so. But there is no justification for non-optional government schemes financed by taxpayers' money. . . .

## 2. The Permissive View

Directly contrary to the Individualist view of welfare is what I have termed the Permissive view. According to this view, in a society which has sufficient resources so that everyone could be supplied with the necessities of life, every individual ought to be given the legal right to social security, and this right ought not to be conditional in any way upon an individual's behavior. *Ex hypothesi*

the society which we are discussing has sufficient goods to provide everyone with food, clothing, shelter and other necessities. Someone who does without these basic goods is scarcely living at all, and a society which takes no steps to change this state of affairs implies by its inaction that the life of such a person is without value. It does not execute him; but it may allow him to die. It does not put him in prison; but it may leave him with a life of lower quality than that of some prison inmates. A society which can rectify these circumstances and does not can justly be accused of imposing upon the needy either death or lifelong deprivation. And those characteristics which make a person needy—whether they be illness, old age, insanity, feeblemindedness, inability to find paid work, or even poor moral character—are insufficient to make him deserve the fate to which an inactive society would in effect condemn him. One would not be executed for inability or failure to find paid work; neither should one be allowed to die for this misfortune or failing.

A person who cannot or does not find his own means of social security does not thereby forfeit his status as a human being. If other human beings, with physical, mental and moral qualities different from his, are regarded as having the right to life and to the means of life, then so too should he be regarded. A society which does not accept the responsibility for supplying such a person with the basic necessities of life is, in effect, endorsing a difference between its members which is without moral justification. . . .

The adoption of a Permissive view of welfare would have significant practical implications. If there were a legal right, unconditional upon behaviour, to a specified level of state-supplied benefits, then state investigation of the prospective welfare recipient could be kept to a minimum. Why he is in need, whether he can work, whether he is willing to work, and what he does while receiving welfare benefits are on this view quite irrelevant to his right to receive those benefits. A welfare recipient is a person who claims from his society that to which he is legally entitled under a morally based welfare scheme. The fact that he makes this claim licenses no special state or societal interference with his behaviour. If the Permissive view of welfare were widely believed, then there would be no social stigma attached to being on welfare. There is such a stigma, and many long-term welfare recipients are considerably demoralized by their dependent status.[6] These facts suggest that the Permissive view of welfare is not widely held in our society.

## 3. The Puritan View

This view of welfare rather naturally emerges when we consider that no one can have a right to something without someone else's, or some group of other persons', having responsibilities correlative to this right. In the case in which the right in question is a legal right to social security, the correlative responsibilities may be rather extensive. They have been deemed responsibilities of "the state." The state will require resources and funds to meet these responsibilities, and these do not emerge from the sky miraculously, or zip into existence as a consequence of virtually effortless acts of will. They are taken by the state from its citizens, often in the form of taxation on earned income. The funds given to the welfare recipient and many of the goods which he purchases with these funds are produced by other members of society, many of whom give a considerable portion of their time and their energy to this end. If a state has the moral responsibility to ensure the social security of its citizens then all the citizens of that state have the responsibility to provide state agencies with the means to carry out their duties. This responsibility, in our present contingent circumstances, seems to generate an obligation to *work*.

A person who works helps to produce the goods which all use in daily living and, when paid, contributes through taxation to government endeavours. The person who does not work, even though able to work, does not make his contribution to social efforts towards obtaining the means of life. He is not entitled to a share of the goods produced by others if he chooses not to take part in their labours. Unless he can show that there is a moral justification for his not making the sacrifice

of time and energy which others make, he has no legitimate claim to welfare benefits. If he is disabled or unable to obtain work, he cannot work; hence he has no need to justify his failure to work. But if he does choose not to work, he would have to justify his choice by saying "others should sacrifice their time and energy for me; I have no need to sacrifice time and energy for them." This principle, a version of what Rawls refers to as a free-rider's principle, simply will not stand up to criticism.[7] To deliberately avoid working and benefit from the labours of others is morally indefensible.

Within a welfare system erected on these principles, the right to welfare is conditional upon one's satisfactorily accounting for his failure to obtain the necessities of life by his own efforts. Someone who is severely disabled mentally or physically, or who for some other reason cannot work, is morally entitled to receive welfare benefits. Someone who chooses not to work is not. The Puritan view of welfare is a kind of compromise between the Individualist view and the Permissive view. . . .

The Puritan view of welfare, based as it is on the inter-relation between welfare and work, provides a rationale for two connected principles which those establishing welfare schemes in Canada and in the United States seem to endorse. First of all, those on welfare should never receive a higher income than the working poor. Secondly, a welfare scheme should, in some way or other, incorporate incentives to work. These principles, which presuppose that it is better to work than not to work, emerge rather naturally from the contingency which is at the basis of the Puritan view: the goods essential for social security are products of the labour of some members of society. If we wish to have a continued supply of such goods, we must encourage those who work to produce them. . . .

# Appraisal of Policies: Social Consequences and Social Justice

In approaching the appraisal of prospective welfare policies under these two aspects I am, of course, making some assumptions about the moral appraisal of suggested social policies. Although these cannot possibly be justified here, it may be helpful to articulate them, at least in a rough way.

Appraisal of social policies is in part teleological. To the extent that a policy, P, increases the total human welfare more than does an alternative policy, P', P is a better social policy than P'. Or, if P leaves the total human welfare as it is, while P' diminishes it, then to that extent, P is a better social policy than P'. Even this skeletal formulation of the teleological aspect of appraisal reveals why appraisal cannot be entirely teleological. We consider total consequences—effects upon the total of "human well-being" in a society. But this total is a summation of consequences on different individuals. It includes no judgements as to how far we allow one individual's well-being to decrease while another's increases, under the same policy. Judgements relating to the latter problems are judgements about social justice.

In appraising social policies we have to weigh up considerations of total well-being against considerations of justice. Just how this is to be done, precisely, I would not pretend to know. However, the absence of precise methods does not mean that we should relinquish attempts at appraisal: some problems are already with us, and thought which is necessarily tentative and imprecise is still preferable to no thought at all.

## 1. Consequences of Welfare Schemes

First, let us consider the consequences of the non-scheme advocated by the Individualist. He would have us abolish all non-optional government programmes which have as their goal the improvement of anyone's personal welfare. This rejection extends to health schemes, pension plans and education, as well as to welfare and unemployment insurance. So following the Individualist would lead to very sweeping changes.

The Individualist will claim (as do Hospers and Ayn Rand) that on the whole his non-scheme will bring beneficial consequences. He will admit, as he must, that there are people who would suffer

tremendously if welfare and other social security programmes were simply terminated. Some would even die as a result. We cannot assume that spontaneously developing charities would cover every case of dire need. Nevertheless the Individualist wants to point to benefits which would accrue to businessmen and to working people and their families if taxation were drastically cut. It is his claim that consumption would rise, hence production would rise, job opportunities would be extended, and there would be an economic boom, if people could only spend all their earned income as they wished. This boom would benefit both rich and poor.

There are significant omissions which are necessary in order to render the Individualist's optimism plausible. Either workers and businessmen would have insurance of various kinds, or they would be insecure in their prosperity. If they did have insurance to cover health problems, old age and possible job loss, then they would pay for it; hence they would not be spending their whole earned income on consumer goods. Those who run the insurance schemes could, of course, put this money back into the economy—but government schemes already do this. The economic boom under Individualism would not be as loud as originally expected. Furthermore the goal of increased consumption-increased productivity must be questioned from an ecological viewpoint: many necessary materials are available only in limited quantities.

Finally, a word about charity. It is not to be expected that those who are at the mercy of charities will benefit from this state, either materially or psychologically. Those who prosper will be able to choose between giving a great deal to charity and suffering from the very real insecurity and guilt which would accompany the existence of starvation and grim poverty outside their padlocked doors. It is to be hoped that they would opt for the first alternative. But, if they did, this might be every bit as expensive for them as government-supported benefit schemes are now. If they did not give generously to charity, violence might result. However one looks at it, the consequences of Individualism are unlikely to be good.

Welfare schemes operating in Canada today are almost without exception based upon the principles of the Puritan view. To see the consequences of that type of welfare scheme we have only to look at the results of our own welfare programmes. Taxation to support such schemes is high, though not so intolerably so as to have led to widescale resentment among taxpayers. Canadian welfare programmes are attended by complicated and often cumbersome bureaucracy, some of which results from the interlocking of municipal, provincial and federal governments in the administration and financing of welfare programmes. The cost of the programmes is no doubt increased by this bureaucracy; not all the tax money directed to welfare programmes goes to those in need. Puritan welfare schemes do not result in social catastrophe or in significant business stagnation—this much we know, because we already live with such schemes. Their adverse consequences, if any, are felt primarily not by society generally nor by businessmen and the working segment of the public, but rather by recipients of welfare.

Both the Special Senate Committee Report on Poverty and the Real Poverty Report criticize our present system of welfare for its demoralization of recipients, who often must deal with several levels of government and are vulnerable to arbitrary interference on the part of administering officials. Welfare officials have the power to check on welfare recipients and cut off or limit their benefits under a large number of circumstances. The dangers to welfare recipients in terms of anxiety, threats to privacy and loss of dignity are obvious. According to the Senate Report, the single aspect shared by all Canada's welfare systems is "a record of failure and insufficiency, of bureaucratic rigidities that often result in the degradation, humiliation and alienation of recipients."[8] The writers of this report cite many instances of humiliation, leaving the impression that these are too easily found to be "incidental aberrations."[9] Concern that a welfare recipient either be unable to work or be willing to work (if unemployed) can easily turn into concern about how he spends the income supplied him, what his plans for the future

are, where he lives, how many children he has. And the rationale underlying the Puritan scheme makes the degradation of welfare recipients a natural consequence of welfare institutions. Work is valued and only he who works is thought to contribute to society. Welfare recipients are regarded as parasites and spongers—so when they are treated as such, this is only what we should have expected. Being on welfare in a society which thinks and acts in this fashion can be psychologically debilitating. Welfare recipients who are demoralized by their downgraded status and relative lack of personal freedom can be expected to be made less capable of self-sufficiency. To the extent that this is so, welfare systems erected on Puritan principles may defeat their own purposes.

In fairness, it must be noted here that bureaucratic checks and controls are not a feature only of Puritan welfare systems. To a limited extent, Permissive systems would have to incorporate them too. Within those systems, welfare benefits would be given only to those whose income was inadequate to meet basic needs. However, there would be no checks on "willingness to work," and there would be no need for welfare workers to evaluate the merits of the daily activities of recipients. If a Permissive guaranteed income system were administered through income tax returns, everyone receiving the basic income and those not needing it paying it back in taxes, then the special status of welfare recipients would fade. They would no longer be singled out as a special group within the population. It is to be expected that living solely on government-supplied benefits would be psychologically easier in that type of situation.

Thus it can be argued that for the recipients of welfare, a Permissive scheme has more advantages than a Puritan one. This is not a very surprising conclusion. The Puritan scheme is relatively disadvantageous to recipients, and Puritans would acknowledge this point; they will argue that the overall consequences of Permissive schemes are negative in that these schemes benefit some at too great a cost to others. (Remember, we are not yet concerned with the *justice* of welfare policies, but solely with their consequences as regards *total* human well-being within the society in question.)

The concern which most people have regarding the Permissive scheme relates to its costs and its dangers to the "work ethic." It is commonly thought that people work only because they have to work to survive in a tolerable style. If a guaranteed income scheme were adopted by the government, this incentive to work would disappear. No one would be faced with the choice between a nasty and boring job and starvation. Who would do the nasty and boring jobs then? Many of them are not eliminable and they have to be done somehow, by someone. Puritans fear that a great many people—even some with relatively pleasant jobs—might simply cease to work if they could receive non-stigmatized government money to live on. If this were to happen, the permissive society would simply grind to a halt.

In addressing these anxieties about the consequences of Permissive welfare schemes, we must recall that welfare benefits are set to ensure only that those who do not work have a bearable existence, with an income sufficient for basic needs, and that they have this income regardless of why they fail to work. Welfare benefits will not finance luxury living for a family of five! If jobs are adequately paid so that workers receive more than the minimum welfare income in an earned salary, then there will still be a financial incentive to take jobs. What guaranteed income schemes will do is to raise the salary floor. This change will benefit the many non-unionized workers in service and clerical occupations.

Furthermore it is unlikely that people work solely due to (i) the desire for money and the things it can buy and (ii) belief in the Puritan work ethic. There are many other reasons for working, some of which would persist in a society which had adopted a Permissive welfare system. Most people are happier when their time is structured in some way, when they are active outside their own homes, when they feel themselves part of an endeavour whose purposes transcend their particular egoistic ones. Women often choose to work outside the home for these reasons as much as for financial ones. With these and other factors operating I cannot see that the adoption of a Permissive welfare scheme would be followed by a level

of slothfulness which would jeopardize human well-being.

Another worry about the Permissive scheme concerns cost. It is difficult to comment on this in a general way, since it would vary so much from case to case. Of Canada at the present it has been said that a guaranteed income scheme administered through income tax would cost less than social security payments administered through the present bureaucracies. It is thought that this saving would result from a drastic cut in administrative costs. The matter of the work ethic is also relevant to the question of costs. Within a Puritan framework it is very important to have a high level of employment and there is a tendency to resist any reorganization which results in there being fewer jobs available. Some of these proposed reorganizations would save money; strictly speaking we should count the cost of keeping jobs which are objectively unnecessary as part of the cost of Puritanism regarding welfare.

In summary, we can appraise Individualism, Puritanism and Permissivism with respect to their anticipated consequences, as follows: Individualism is unacceptable; Puritanism is tolerable, but has some undesirable consequences for welfare recipients; Permissivism appears to be the winner. Worries about bad effects which Permissive welfare schemes might have due to high costs and (alleged) reduced work-incentives appear to be without solid basis.

## 2. Social Justice under Proposed Welfare Schemes

We must now try to consider the merits of Individualism, Puritanism and Permissivism with regard to their impact on the distribution of the goods necessary for well-being. [Robert] Nozick has argued against the whole conception of a distributive justice on the grounds that it presupposes that goods are like manna from heaven: we simply get them and then have a problem—to whom to give them. According to Nozick we know where things come from and we do not have the problem of to whom to give them. There is not really a problem of distributive justice, for there is no central distributor giving out manna from heaven! It is necessary to counter Nozick on this point since his reaction to the (purported) problems of distributive justice would undercut much of what follows.[10]

There is a level at which Nozick's point is obviously valid. If A discovers a cure for cancer, then it is A and not B or C who is responsible for this discovery. On Nozick's view this is taken to imply that A should reap any monetary profits which are forthcoming; other people will benefit from the cure itself. Now although it cannot be doubted that A is a bright and hardworking person, neither can it be denied that A and his circumstances are the product of many co-operative endeavours: schools and laboratories, for instance. Because this is so, I find Nozick's claim that "we know where things come from" unconvincing at a deeper level. Since achievements like A's presuppose extensive social co-operation, it is morally permissible to regard even the monetary profits accruing from them as shareable by the "owner" and society at large.

Laws support existing income levels in many ways. Governments specify taxation so as to further determine net income. Property ownership is a legal matter. In all these ways people's incomes and possibilities for obtaining income are affected by deliberate state action. It is always possible to raise questions about the moral desirability of actual conventional arrangements. Should university professors earn less than lawyers? More than waitresses? Why? Why not? Anyone who gives an account of distributive justice is trying to specify principles which will make it possible to answer questions such as these, and nothing in Nozick's argument suffices to show that the questions are meaningless or unimportant.

Any human distribution of anything is unjust insofar as differences exist for no good reason. If goods did come like manna from heaven and the Central Distributor gave A ten times more than B, we should want to know why. The skewed distribution might be deemed a just one if A's needs were objectively ten times greater than B's, or if B refused to accept more than his small portion of goods. But if no reason at all could be given for it, or if only an irrelevant reason could be given (e.g.,

A is blue-eyed and B is not), then it is an unjust distribution. All the views we have expounded concerning welfare permit differences in income level. Some philosophers would say that such differences are never just, although they may be necessary, for historical or utilitarian reasons. Whether or not this is so, it is admittedly very difficult to say just what would constitute a good reason for giving A a higher income than B. Level of need, degree of responsibility, amount of training, unpleasantness of work—all these have been proposed and all have some plausibility. We do not need to tackle all this larger problem in order to consider justice under proposed welfare systems. For we can deal here solely with the question of whether everyone should receive a floor level of income; decisions on this matter are independent of decisions on overall equality or principles of variation among incomes above the floor. The Permissivist contends that all should receive at least the floor income; the Individualist and the Puritan deny this. All would claim justice for their side.

The Individualist attempts to justify extreme variations in income, with some people below the level where they can fulfill their basic needs, with reference to the fact of people's actual accomplishments. This approach to the question is open to the same objections as those which have already been raised against Nozick's non-manna-from-heaven argument, and I shall not repeat them here. Let us move on to the Puritan account. It is because goods emerge from human efforts that the Puritan advances his view of welfare. He stresses the unfairness of a system which would permit some people to take advantage of others. A Permissive welfare system would do this, as it makes no attempt to distinguish between those who choose not to work and those who cannot work. No one should be able to take advantage of another under the auspices of a government institution. The Puritan scheme seeks to eliminate this possibility, and for that reason, Puritans would allege, it is a more just scheme than the Permissive one.

Permissivists can best reply to this contention by acknowledging that any instance of free-riding would be an instance where those working were done an injustice, but by showing that any justice which the Puritan preserves by eliminating free-riding is outweighed by *injustice* perpetrated elsewhere. Consider the children of the Puritan's free-riders. They will suffer greatly for the "sins" of their parents. Within the institution of the family, the Puritan cannot suitably hurt the guilty without cruelly depriving the innocent. There is a sense, too, in which Puritanism does injustice to the many people on welfare who are not free-riders. It perpetuates the opinion that they are non-contributors to society and this doctrine, which is over-simplified if not downright false, has a harmful effect upon welfare recipients.

Social justice is not simply a matter of the distribution of goods, or the income with which goods are to be purchased. It is also a matter of the protection of rights. Western societies claim to give their citizens equal rights in political and legal contexts; they also claim to endorse the larger conception of a right to life. Now it is possible to interpret these rights in a limited and formalistic way, so that the duties correlative to them are minimal. On the limited, or negative, interpretation, to say that A has a right to life is simply to say that others have a duty not to interfere with A's attempts to keep himself alive. This interpretation of the right to life is compatible with Individualism as well as with Puritanism. But it is an inadequate interpretation of the right to life and of other rights. A right to vote is meaningless if one is starving and unable to get to the polls; a right to equality before the law is meaningless if one cannot afford to hire a lawyer. And so on.

Even a Permissive welfare scheme will go only a very small way towards protecting people's rights. It will amount to a meaningful acknowledgement of a right to life, by ensuring income adequate to purchase food, clothing and shelter—at the very least. These minimum necessities are presupposed by all other rights a society may endorse in that their possession is a precondition of being able to exercise these other rights. Because it protects the rights of all within a society better than do Puritanism and Individualism, the

Permissive view can rightly claim superiority over the others with regard to justice.

## Notes

1. Nicholas Rescher, *Welfare: Social Issues in Philosophical Perspective*, p. 114.

2. One might wish to discuss moral questions concerning welfare in the context of natural rights doctrines. Indeed, Article 22 of the United Nations Declaration of Human Rights states, "Everyone, as a member of society, has the right to social security and is entitled, through national effort and international cooperation and in accordance with the organization and resources of each State, to the economic, social and cultural rights indispensable for his dignity and the free development of his personality." I make no attempt to defend the right to welfare as a natural right. Granting that rights imply responsibilities or duties and that "ought" implies "can," it would only be intelligible to regard the right to social security as a natural right if all states were able to ensure the minimum well-being of their citizens. This is not the case. And a natural right is one which is by definition supposed to belong to all human beings simply in virtue of their status as human beings. The analysis given here in the permissive view is compatible with the claim that all human beings have a *prima facie* natural right to social security. It is not, however, compatible with the claim that all human beings have a natural right to social security if this right is regarded as one which is so absolute as to be inviolable under any and all conditions.

3. See, for example, Ayn Rand's *Atlas Shrugged*, *The Virtue of Selfishness*, and *Capitalism: the Unknown Ideal*.

4. John Hospers, *Libertarianism: A Political Philosophy for Tomorrow*, p. 67.

5. I say virtually unconditional, because an Individualist such as John Hospers sees a legitimate moral role for government in preventing the use of force by some citizens against others. Since this is the case, I presume that he would also regard as legitimate such taxation as was necessary to support this function. Presumably that taxation would be seen as consented to by all, on the grounds that all "really want" government protection.

6. Ian Adams, William Cameron, Brian Hill, and Peter Penz, *The Real Poverty Report*, pp. 167–187.

7. See *A Theory of Justice*, pp. 124, 136. Rawls defines the free-rider as one who relies on the principle "everyone is to act justly except for myself, if I choose not to," and says that his position is a version of egoism which is eliminated as a morally acceptable principle by formal constraints. This conclusion regarding the tenability of egoism is one which I accept and which is taken for granted in the present context.

8. *Senate Report on Poverty*, p. 73.

9. The Hamilton Public Welfare Department takes automobile licence plates from recipients, making them available again only to those whose needs meet with the Department's approval. (*Real Poverty Report,* p. 186.) The *Globe and Mail* for 12 January 1974 reported that welfare recipients in the city of Toronto are to be subjected to computerized budgeting. In the summer of 1973, the two young daughters of an Alabama man on welfare were sterilized against their own wishes and without their parents' informed consent. (See *Time,* 23 July 1973.)

10. Robert Nozick, "Distributive Justice," *Philosophy and Public Affairs,* Fall 1973.

# 57  Liberalism

## RONALD DWORKIN

. . . Is there a thread of principle that runs through the core liberal positions, and that distinguishes these from the corresponding conservative positions? There is a familiar answer to this question that is mistaken, but mistaken in an illuminating way. The politics of democracies, according to this answer, recognizes several independent constitutive political ideals, the most important of which are the ideals of liberty and equality. Unfortunately, liberty and equality often conflict: sometimes the only effective means to promote equality require some limitation of liberty, and sometimes the consequences of promoting liberty are detrimental to equality. In these cases, good government consists in the best compromise between the competing ideals, but different politicians and citizens will make that compromise differently. Liberals tend relatively to favor equality more and liberty less than conservatives do, and the core set of liberal positions I described is the result of striking the balance that way.

This account offers a theory about what liberalism is. Liberalism shares the same constitutive principles with many other political theories, including conservatism, but is distinguished from these by attaching different relative importance to different principles. The theory therefore leaves room, on the spectrum it describes, for the radical who cares even more for equality and less for liberty than the liberal, and therefore stands even farther away from the extreme conservative. The liberal becomes the man in the middle, which explains why liberalism is so often now considered wishy-washy, an untenable compromise between two more forthright positions.

No doubt this description of American politics could be made more sophisticated. It might make room for other independent constitutive ideals shared by liberalism and its opponents, like stability or security, so that the compromises involved in particular decisions are made out to be more complex. But if the nerve of the theory remains the competition between liberty and equality as constitutive ideals, then the theory cannot succeed. . . . It seems to apply, at best, to only a limited number of the political controversies it tries to explain. It is designed for economic controversies, but is either irrelevant or misleading in the case of censorship and pornography, and indeed, in the criminal law generally.

But there is a much more important defect in this explanation. It assumes that liberty is measurable so that, if two political decisions each invades the liberty of a citizen, we can sensibly say that one decision takes more liberty away from him than the other. That assumption is necessary, because otherwise the postulate, that liberty is a constitutive ideal of both the liberal and conservative political structures, cannot be maintained. Even firm conservatives are content that their liberty to drive as they wish (for example, to drive uptown on Lexington Avenue) may be invaded for the sake, not of some important competing political ideal, but only for marginal gains in convenience or orderly traffic patterns. But since

Reprinted by permission of the author from *A Matter of Principle* (Harvard University Press, 1985), 188–212, with omissions.

traffic regulation plainly involves some loss of liberty, the conservative cannot be said to value liberty as such unless he is able to show that, for some reason, less liberty is lost by traffic regulation than by restrictions on, for example, free speech, or the liberty to sell for prices others are willing to pay, or whatever other liberty he takes to be fundamental.

That is precisely what he cannot show, because we do not have a concept of liberty that is quantifiable in the way that demonstration would require. He cannot say, for example, that traffic regulations interfere less with what most men and women want to do than would a law forbidding them to speak out in favor of Communism, or a law requiring them not to fix their prices as they think best. Most people care more about driving than speaking for Communism, and have no occasion to fix prices even if they want to. I do not mean that we can make no sense of the idea of fundamental liberties, like freedom of speech. But we cannot argue in their favor by showing that they protect more liberty, taken to be an even roughly measurable commodity, than does the right to drive as we wish; the fundamental liberties are important because we value something else that they protect. But if that is so, then we cannot explain the difference between liberal and conservative political positions by supposing that the latter protect the commodity of liberty, valued for its own sake, more effectively than the former.

It might now be said, however, that the other half of the liberty–equality explanation may be salvaged. Even if we cannot say that conservatives value liberty, as such, more than liberals, we can still say that they value equality less, and that the different political positions may be explained in that way. Conservatives tend to discount the importance of equality when set beside other goals, like general prosperity or even security; while liberals value equality relatively more, and radicals more still. Once again, it is apparent that this explanation is tailored to the economic controversies, and fits poorly with the noneconomic controversies. Once again, however, its defects are more general and more important. We must

identify more clearly the sense in which equality could be a constitutive ideal for either liberals or conservatives. Once we do so, we shall see that it is misleading to say that the conservative values equality, in that sense, less than the liberal. We shall want to say, instead, that he has a different conception of what equality requires.

We must distinguish between two different principles that take equality to be a political ideal. The first requires that the government treat all those in its charge *as equals,* that is, as entitled to its equal concern and respect. That is not an empty requirement: most of us do not suppose that we must, as individuals, treat our neighbor's children with the same concern as our own, or treat everyone we meet with the same respect. It is nevertheless plausible to think that any government should treat all its citizens as equals in that way. The second principle requires that the government treat all those in its charge *equally* in the distribution of some resource of opportunity, or at least work to secure the state of affairs in which they all are equal or more nearly equal in that respect. It is conceded by everyone that the government cannot make everyone equal in every respect, but people do disagree about how far government should try to secure equality in some particular resource, for example, in monetary wealth.

If we look only at the economic–political controversies, then we might well be justified in saying that liberals want more equality in the sense of the second principle than conservatives do. But it would be a mistake to conclude that they value equality in the sense of the first and more fundamental principle any more highly. I say that the first principle is more fundamental because I assume that, for both liberals and conservatives, the first is constitutive and the second derivative. Sometimes treating people equally is the only way to treat them as equals; but sometimes not. Suppose a limited amount of emergency relief is available for two equally populous areas injured by floods; treating the citizens of both areas as equals requires giving more aid to the more seriously devastated area rather than splitting the available funds equally. The conservative believes that in many other, less apparent, cases treating citizens equally amounts to not treating them as equals. He might concede, for example, that positive discrimination in university admissions will work to make the two races more nearly equal in wealth, but nevertheless maintain that such programs do not treat black and white university applicants as equals. If he is a utilitarian, he will have a similar, though much more general, argument against any redistribution of wealth that reduces economic efficiency. He will say that the only way to treat people as equals is to maximize the average welfare of all members of community, counting gains and losses to all in the same scales, and that a free market is the only, or best, instrument for achieving that goal. This is not (I think) a good argument, but if the conservative who makes it is sincere, he cannot be said to have discounted the importance of treating all citizens as equals.

So we must reject the simple idea that liberalism consists in a distinctive weighting between constitutive principles of equality and liberty. But our discussion of the idea of equality suggests a more fruitful line. I assume (as I said) that there is broad agreement within modern politics that the government must treat all its citizens with equal concern and respect. I do not mean to deny the great power of prejudice in, for example, American politics. But few citizens, and even fewer politicians, would now admit to political convictions that contradict the abstract principle of equal concern and respect. Different people hold, however, as our discussion made plain, very different conceptions of what that abstract principle requires in particular cases.

What does it mean for the government to treat its citizens as equals? That is, I think, the same question as the question of what it means for the government to treat all its citizens as free, or as independent, or with equal dignity. In any case, it is a question that has been central to political theory at least since Kant.

It may be answered in two fundamentally different ways. The first supposes that government must be neutral on what might be called the question of the good life. The second supposes that

government cannot be neutral on that question, because it cannot treat its citizens as equal human beings without a theory of what human beings ought to be. I must explain that distinction further. Each person follows a more-or-less articulate conception of what gives value to life. The scholar who values a life of contemplation has such a conception; so does the television-watching, beer-drinking citizen who is fond of saying "This is the life," though he has thought less about the issue and is less able to describe or defend his conception.

The first theory of equality supposes that political decisions must be, so far as is possible, independent of any particular conception of the good life, or of what gives value to life. Since the citizens of a society differ in their conceptions, the government does not treat them as equals if it prefers one conception to another, either because the officials believe that one is intrinsically superior, or because one is held by the more numerous or more powerful group. The second theory argues, on the contrary, that the content of equal treatment cannot be independent of some theory about the good for man or the good of life, because treating a person as an equal means treating him the way the good or truly wise person would wish to be treated. Good government consists in fostering or at least recognizing good lives; treatment as an equal consists in treating each person as if he were desirous of leading the life that is in fact good, at least so far as this is possible.

This distinction is very abstract, but it is also very important. I shall now argue that liberalism takes, as its constitutive political morality, the first conception of equality. I shall try to support that claim in this way. In the next section of this essay I shall show how it is plausible, and even likely, that a thoughtful person who accepted the first conception of equality would, given the economic and political circumstances of the United States in the last several decades, reach the positions I identified as the familiar core of liberal positions. . . . It is plausible and even likely that someone who held a particular version of the second theory of equality would reach what are normally regarded as the core of American conservative positions. I say "a particular version of" because American conservatism does not follow automatically from rejecting the liberal theory of equality. The second (or nonliberal) theory of equality holds merely that the treatment government owes citizens is at least partly determined by some conception of the good life. Many political theories share that thesis, including theories as far apart as, for example, American conservatism and various forms of socialism or Marxism, though these differ in the conception of the good life they adopt, and hence in the political institutions and decisions they endorse. In this respect, liberalism is decidedly not some compromise or halfway house between more forceful positions, but stands on one side of an important line that distinguishes it from all competitors taken as a group. . . .

I now define a liberal as someone who holds the first, or liberal, theory of what equality requires. Suppose that a liberal is asked to found a new state. He is required to dictate its constitution and fundamental institutions. He must propose a general theory of political distribution, that is, a theory of how whatever the community has to assign, by way of goods or resources or opportunities, should be assigned. He will arrive initially at something like this principle of rough equality: resources and opportunities should be distributed, so far as possible, equally, so that roughly the same share of whatever is available is devoted to satisfying the ambitions of each. Any other general aim of distribution will assume either that the fate of some people should be of greater concern than that of others, or that the ambitions or talents of some are more worthy, and should be supported more generously on that account.

Someone may object that this principle of rough equality is unfair because it ignores the fact that people have different tastes, and that some of these are more expensive to satisfy than others, so that, for example, the man who prefers champagne will need more funds if he is not to be frustrated than the man satisfied with beer. But the liberal may reply that tastes as to which people differ are, by and large, not afflictions, like diseases, but are rather cultivated, in accordance

with each person's theory of what his life should be like. The most effective neutrality, therefore, requires that the same share be devoted to each, so that the choice between expensive and less expensive tastes can be made by each person for himself, with no sense that his overall share will be enlarged by choosing a more expensive life, or that, whatever he chooses, his choice will subsidize those who have chosen more expensively.

But what does the principle of rough equality of distribution require in practice? If all resources were distributed directly by the government through grants of food, housing, and so forth; if every opportunity citizens have were provided directly by the government through the provisions of civil and criminal law; if every citizen had exactly the same talents; if every citizen started his life with no more than what any other citizen had at the start; and if every citizen had exactly the same theory of the good life and hence exactly the same scheme of preferences as every other citizen, including preferences between productive activity of different forms and leisure, then the principle of rough equality of treatment could be satisfied simply by equal distributions of everything to be distributed and by civil and criminal laws of universal application. Government would arrange for production that maximized the mix of goods, including jobs and leisure, that everyone favored, distributing the product equally.

Of course, none of these conditions of similarity holds. But the moral relevance of different sorts of diversity are very different, as may be shown by the following exercise. Suppose all the conditions of similarity I mentioned did hold except the last: citizens have different theories of the good and hence different preferences. They therefore disagree about what product the raw materials and labor and savings of the community should be used to produce, and about which activities should be prohibited or regulated so as to make others possible or easier. The liberal, as lawgiver, now needs mechanisms to satisfy the principles of equal treatment in spite of these disagreements. He will decide that there are no better mechanisms available, as general political institutions, than the two main institutions of our own political economy: the economic market, for decisions about what goods shall be produced and how they shall be distributed, and representative democracy, for collective decisions about what conduct shall be prohibited or regulated so that other conduct might be made possible or convenient. Each of these familiar institutions may be expected to provide a more egalitarian division than any other general arrangement. The market, if it can be made to function efficiently, will determine for each product a price that reflects the cost in resources of material, labor, and capital that might have been applied to produce something different that someone else wants. That cost determines, for anyone who consumes that product, how much his account should be charged in computing the egalitarian division of social resources. It provides a measure of how much more his account should be charged for a house than a book, and for one book rather than another. The market will also provide, for the laborer, a measure of how much should be credited to his account for his choice of productive activity over leisure, and for one activity rather than another. It will tell us, through the price it puts on his labor, how much he should gain or lose by his decision to pursue one career rather than another. These measurements make a citizen's own distribution a function of the personal preferences of others as well as of his own, and it is the sum of these personal preferences that fixes the true cost to the community of meeting his own preferences for goods and activities. The egalitarian distribution, which requires that the cost of satisfying one person's preferences should as far as is possible be equal to the cost of satisfying another's, cannot be enforced unless those measurements are made.

We are familiar with the anti-egalitarian consequences of free enterprise in practice; it may therefore seem paradoxical that the liberal as lawgiver should choose a market economy for reasons of equality rather than efficiency. But, under the special condition that people differ only in preferences for goods and activities, the market is more egalitarian than any alternative of comparable generality. The most plausible alternative would be to allow decisions of production, investment, price, and wage to be made by elected offi-

cials in a socialist economy. But what principles should officials use in making those decisions? The liberal might tell them to mimic the decisions that a market would make if it was working efficiently under proper competition and full knowledge. This mimicry would be, in practice, much less efficient than an actual market would be. In any case, unless the liberal had reason to think it would be much more efficient, he would have good reason to reject it. Any minimally efficient mimicking of a hypothetical market would require invasions of privacy to determine what decisions individuals would make if forced actually to pay for their investment, consumption, and employment decisions at market rates, and this information gathering would be, in many other ways, much more expensive than an actual market. Inevitably, moreover, the assumptions officials make about how people would behave in a hypothetical market reflect the officials' own beliefs about how people should behave. So there would be, for the liberal, little to gain and much to lose in a socialist economy in which officials were asked to mimic a hypothetical market.

But any other instructions would be a direct violation of the liberal theory of what equality requires, because if a decision is made to produce and sell goods at a price below the price a market would fix, then those who prefer those goods are, *pro tanto,* receiving more than an equal share of the resources of the community at the expense of those who would prefer some other use of the resources. Suppose the limited demand for books, matched against the demand for competing uses for wood pulp, would fix the price of books at a point higher than the socialist managers of the economy will charge; those who want books are having less charged to their account than the egalitarian principle would require. It might be said that in a socialist economy books are simply valued more, because they are inherently more worthy uses of social resources, quite apart from the popular demand for books. But the liberal theory of equality rules out that appeal to the inherent value of one theory of what is good in life.

In a society in which people differed only in preferences, then, a market would be favored for its egalitarian consequences. Inequality of monetary wealth would be the consequence only of the fact that some preferences are more expensive than others, including the preference for leisure time rather than the most lucrative productive activity. But we must now return to the real world. In the actual society for which the liberal must construct political institutions, there are all the other differences. Talents are not distributed equally, so the decision of one person to work in a factory rather than a law firm, or not to work at all, will be governed in large part by his abilities rather than his preferences for work or between work and leisure. The institutions of wealth, which allow people to dispose of what they receive by gift, means that children of the successful will start with more wealth than the children of the unsuccessful. Some people have special needs, because they are handicapped; their handicap will not only disable them from the most productive and lucrative employment, but will incapacitate them from using the proceeds of whatever employment they find as efficiently, so that they will need more than those who are not handicapped to satisfy identical ambitions.

These inequalities will have great, often catastrophic, effects on the distribution that a market economy will provide. But, unlike differences in preferences, the differences these inequalities make are indefensible according to the liberal conception of equality. It is obviously obnoxious to the liberal conception, for example, that someone should have more of what the community as a whole has to distribute because he or his father had superior skill or luck. The liberal lawgiver therefore faces a difficult task. His conception of equality requires an economic system that produces certain inequalities (those that reflect the true differential costs of goods and opportunities) but not others (those that follow from differences in ability, inheritance, and so on). The market produces both the required and the forbidden inequalities, and there is no alternative system that can be relied upon to produce the former without the latter.

The liberal must be tempted, therefore, to a reform of the market through a scheme of redistribution that leaves its pricing system relatively intact but sharply limits, at least, the inequalities

in welfare that his initial principle prohibits. No solution will seem perfect. The liberal may find the best answer in a scheme of welfare rights financed through redistributive income and inheritance taxes of the conventional sort, which redistributes just to the Rawlsian point, that is, to the point at which the worst-off group would be harmed rather than benefited by further transfers. In that case, he will remain a reluctant capitalist, believing that a market economy so reformed is superior, from the standpoint of his conception of equality, to any practical socialist alternative. Or he may believe that the redistribution that is possible in a capitalist economy will be so inadequate, or will be purchased at the cost of such inefficiency, that it is better to proceed in a more radical way, by substituting socialist for market decisions over a large part of the economy, and then relying on the political process to ensure that prices are set in a manner at least roughly consistent with his conception of equality. In that case he will be a reluctant socialist, who acknowledges the egalitarian defects of socialism but counts them as less severe than the practical alternatives. In either case, he chooses a mixed economic system—either redistributive capitalism or limited socialism—not in order to compromise antagonistic ideals of efficiency and equality, but to achieve the best practical realization of the demands of equality itself.

Let us assume that in this manner the liberal either refines or partially retracts his original selection of a market economy. He must now consider the second of the two familiar institutions he first selected, which is representative democracy. Democracy is justified because it enforces the right of each person to respect and concern as an individual; but in practice the decisions of a democratic majority may often violate that right, according to the liberal theory of what the right requires. Suppose a legislature elected by a majority decides to make criminal some act (like speaking in favor of an unpopular political position, or participating in eccentric sexual practices), not because the act deprives others of opportunities they want, but because the majority disapproves of those views or that sexual morality. The political decision, in other words, reflects not just some accommodation of the *personal* preferences of everyone, in such a way as to make the opportunities of all as nearly equal as may be, but the domination of one set of *external* preferences, that is, preferences people have about what others shall do or have. The decision invades rather than enforces the right of citizens to be treated as equals.

How can the liberal protect citizens against that sort of violation of their fundamental right? It will not do for the liberal simply to instruct legislators, in some constitutional exhortation, to disregard the external preferences of their constituents. Citizens will vote these preferences in electing their representatives, and a legislator who chooses to ignore them will not survive. In any case, it is sometimes impossible to distinguish, even by introspection, the external and personal components of a political position: this is the case, for example, with associational preferences, which are the preferences some people have for opportunities, like the opportunity to attend public schools—but only with others of the same "background."

The liberal, therefore, needs a scheme of civil rights whose effect will be to determine those political decisions that are antecedently likely to reflect strong external preferences and to remove those decisions from majoritarian political institutions altogether. The scheme of rights necessary to do this will depend on general facts about the prejudices and other external preferences of the majority at any given time, and different liberals will disagree about what is needed at any particular time. But the rights encoded in the Bill of Rights of the United States Constitution, as interpreted (on the whole) by the Supreme Court, are those that a substantial number of liberals would think reasonably well suited to what the United States now requires (though most would think that the protection of the individual in certain important areas, including sexual publication and practice, are much too weak).

The main parts of the criminal law, however, present a special problem not easily met by a scheme of civil rights that disable the legislature from taking certain political decisions. The liberal knows that many of the most important decisions required by an effective criminal law are not made by legislators at all, but by prosecutors deciding whom to prosecute for what crime, and by juries and judges deciding whom to convict and what sentences to impose. He also knows that these decisions are antecedently very likely to be corrupted by the external preferences of those who make these decisions because those they judge, typically, have attitudes and ways of life very different from their own. The liberal does not have available, as protection against these decisions, any strategy comparable to the strategy of civil rights that merely remove a decision from an institution. Decisions to prosecute, convict, and sentence must be made by someone. But he has available, in the notion of procedural rights, a different device to protect equality in a different way. He will insist that criminal procedure be structured to achieve a margin of safety in decisions, so that the process is biased strongly against the conviction of the innocent. It would be a mistake to suppose that the liberal thinks that these procedural rights will improve the *accuracy* of the criminal process, that is, the probability that any particular decision about guilt or innocence will be the right one. Procedural rights intervene in the process, even at the cost of inaccuracy, to compensate in a rough way for the antecedent risk that a criminal process, especially if it is largely administered by one class against another, will be corrupted by the impact of external preferences that cannot be eliminated directly. This is only the briefest sketch of how various substantive and procedural civil rights follow from the liberal's initial conception of equality; it is meant to suggest, rather than demonstrate, the more precise argument that would be available for more particular rights.

So the liberal, drawn to the economic market and to political democracy for distinctly egalitarian reasons, finds that these institutions will produce inegalitarian results unless he adds to his scheme different sorts of individual rights. These rights will function as trump cards held by individuals; they will enable individuals to resist particular decisions in spite of the fact that these decisions are or would be reached through the normal workings of general institutions that are not themselves challenged. The ultimate justification for these rights is that they are necessary to protect equal concern and respect; but they are not to be understood as representing equality in contrast to some other goal or principle served by democracy or the economic market. The familiar idea, for example, that rights of redistribution are justified by an ideal of equality that overrides the efficiency ideals of the market in certain cases, has no place in liberal theory. For the liberal, rights are justified, not by some principle in competition with an independent justification of the political and economic institutions they qualify, but in order to make more perfect the only justification on which these other institutions may themselves rely. If the liberal arguments for a particular right are sound, then the right is an unqualified improvement in political morality, not a necessary but regrettable compromise of some other independent goal, like economic efficiency.

. . . This form of liberalism insists that government must treat people as equals in the following sense. It must impose no sacrifice or constraint on any citizen in virtue of an argument that the citizen could not accept without abandoning his sense of his equal worth. This abstract principle requires liberals to oppose the moralism of the New Right, because no self-respecting person who believes that a particular way to live is most valuable for him can accept that this way of life is base or degrading. No self-respecting atheist can agree that a community in which religion is mandatory is for that reason finer, and no one who is homosexual that the eradication of homosexuality makes the community purer.

So liberalism as based on equality justifies the traditional liberal principle that government should not enforce private morality of this sort. But it has an economic as well as a social dimension. It insists on an economic system in which no citizen has less than an equal share of the community's resources just in order that others may have more of what he lacks. I do not mean that liberalism insists on what is often called "equality of result," that is, that citizens must each have the same wealth at every moment of their lives. A government bent on the latter ideal must constantly redistribute wealth, eliminating whatever inequalities in wealth are produced by market transactions. But this would be to devote *unequal* resources to different lives. Suppose that two people have very different bank accounts, in the middle of their careers, because one decided not to work, or not to work at the most lucrative job he could have found, while the other single-mindedly worked for gain. Or because one was willing to assume especially demanding or responsible work, for example, which the other declined. Or because one took larger risks which might have been disastrous but which were in fact successful, while the other invested conservatively. The principle that people must be treated as equals provides no good reason for redistribution in these circumstances; on the contrary, it provides a good reason *against* it.

For treating people as equals requires that each be permitted to use, for the projects to which he devotes his life, no more than an equal share of the resources available for all, and we cannot compute how much any person has consumed, on balance, without taking into account the resources he has contributed as well as those he has taken from the economy. The choices people make about work and leisure and investment have an impact on the resources of the community as a whole, and this impact must be reflected in the calculation equality demands. If one person chooses work that contributes less to other people's lives than different work he might have chosen, then, although this might well have been the right choice for him, given his personal goals, he has nevertheless added less to the resources available for others, and this must be taken into account in the egalitarian calculation. If one person chooses to invest in a productive enterprise rather than spend his funds at once, and if his investment is successful because it increases the stock of goods or services other people actually want, without coercing anyone, his choice has added more to social resources than the choice of someone who did not invest, and this, too, must be reflected in any calculation of whether he has, on balance, taken more than his share.

This explains, I think, why liberals have in the past been drawn to the idea of a market as a method of allocating resources. An efficient market for investment, labor, and goods works as a kind of auction in which the cost to someone of what he consumes, by way of goods and leisure, and the value of what he adds, through his productive labor or decisions, is fixed by the amount his use of some resource costs others, or his contributions benefit them, in each case measured by their willingness to pay for it. Indeed, if the world were very different from what it is, a liberal could accept the results of an efficient market as *defining* equal shares of community resources. If people start with equal amounts of wealth, and have roughly equal levels of raw skill, then a market allocation would ensure that no one could properly complain that he had less than others, over his whole life. He could have had the same as they if he had made the decisions to consume, save, or work that they did.

But in the real world people do not start their lives on equal terms; some begin with marked advantages of family wealth or of formal and informal education. Others suffer because their race is despised. Luck plays a further and sometimes devastating part in deciding who gains or keeps jobs everyone wants. Quite apart from these plain inequities, people are not equal in raw skill or intelligence or other native capacities; on the contrary, they differ greatly, through no choice of their own, in the various capacities that the market tends to reward. So some people who are perfectly willing, even anxious, to make exactly the choices about work and consumption and savings that other people make end up with fewer resources, and no plausible theory of equality can accept this as fair. This is the defect of the ideal fraudulently called "equality of opportunity": fraudulent because in a market economy people do not have equal opportunity who are less able to produce what others want.

So a liberal cannot, after all, accept the market results as defining equal shares. His theory of economic justice must be complex, because he accepts two principles which are difficult to hold in the administration of a dynamic economy. The first requires that people have, at any point in their lives, different amounts of wealth insofar as the genuine choices they have made have been more or less expensive or beneficial to the community, measured by what other people want for their lives. The market seems indispensable to this principle. The second requires that people not have different amounts of wealth just because they have different inherent capacities to produce what others want, or are differently favored by chance. This means that market allocations must be corrected in order to bring some people closer to the share of resources they would have had but for these various differences of initial advantage, luck, and inherent capacity.

Obviously any practical program claiming to respect both these principles will work imperfectly and will inevitably involve speculation, compromise, and arbitrary lines in the face of ignorance. For it is impossible to discover, even in principle, exactly which aspects of any person's economic position flow from his choices and which from advantages or disadvantages that were not matters of choice; and even if we could make this determination for particular people, one by one, it would be impossible to develop a tax system for the nation as a whole that would leave the first in place and repair only the second. There is therefore no such thing as the perfectly just program of redistribution. We must be content to choose whatever programs we believe bring us closer to the complex and unattainable ideal of equality, all things considered, than the available alternatives, and be ready constantly to reexamine that conclusion when new evidence or new programs are proposed.

Nevertheless, in spite of the complexity of that ideal, it may sometimes be apparent that a society falls far short of any plausible interpretation of its requirements. It is, I think, apparent that the United States falls far short now. A substantial minority of Americans are chronically unemployed or earn wages below any realistic "poverty line" or are handicapped in various ways or burdened with special needs; and most of these people would do the work necessary to earn a decent living if they had the opportunity and capacity. Equality of resources would require more rather than less redistribution than we now offer.

This does not mean, of course, that we should continue past liberal programs, however inefficient these have proved to be, or even that we should insist on "targeted" programs of the sort some liberals have favored—that is, programs that aim to provide a particular opportunity or resource, like education or medicine, to those who need it. Perhaps a more general form of transfer, like a negative income tax, would prove on balance more efficient and fairer, in spite of the difficulties in such schemes. And whatever devices are chosen for bringing distribution closer to equality of resources, some aid undoubtedly goes to those who have avoided rather than sought jobs. This is to be regretted, because it offends one of the two principles that together make up equality of resources. But we come closer to that ideal by tolerating this inequity than by denying aid to the far greater number who would work if they could. If equality of resources were our only goal, therefore, we could hardly justify the present retreat from redistributive welfare programs.

. . . If people are asked to sacrifice for their community, they must be offered some reason why the community which benefits from that sacrifice is their community; there must be some reason why, for example, the unemployed blacks of Detroit should take more interest in either the public virtue or the future generations of Michigan than they do in those of Mali.

We must ask in what circumstances someone with the proper sense of his own independence and equal worth can take pride in a community as being his community, and two conditions, at least, seem necessary to this. He can take pride in its present attractiveness—in the richness of its culture, the justice of its institutions, the imagination of its education—only if his life is one that in some way draws on and contributes to these public virtues. He can identify himself with the future of the community and accept present deprivation as sacrifice rather than tyranny, only if he has

some power to help determine the shape of that future, and only if the promised prosperity will provide at least equal benefit to the smaller, more immediate communities for which he feels special responsibilities, for example, his family, his descendants, and, if the society is one that has made this important to him, his race.

These seem minimal conditions, but they are nevertheless exigent. Together they impose serious restraints on any policy that denies any group of citizens, however small or politically negligible, the equal resources that equal concern would otherwise grant them. Of course no feasible program can provide every citizen with a life valuable in his own eyes. But these constraints set a limit to what a government that respects equality may deliberately choose when other choices are available. People must not be condemned, unless this is unavoidable, to lives in which they are effectively denied any active part in the political, economic, and cultural life of the community. So if economic policy contemplates an increase in unemployment, it must also contemplate generous public provision for retraining or public employment. The children of the poor must not be stinted of education or otherwise locked into positions at the bottom of society. Otherwise their parents' loyalty to them acts not as a bridge but as a bar to any identification with the future these parents are meant to cherish.

If this is right, then it suggests an order of priorities which any retrenchment in welfare programs should follow. Programs like food stamps, Aid to Families with Dependent Children, and those using federal funds to make higher education available for the poor are the last programs that should be curtailed, or (what amounts to the same thing) remitted to the states through some "new federalism." If "targeted" programs like these are thought to be too expensive, or too inefficient, then government must show how alternative plans or programs will restore the promise of participation in the future that these programs offered. In any case, cutbacks in the overall level of welfare provided to the poor should be accompanied by efforts to improve the social integration and political participation of blacks and other minorities who suffer most, in order to assure them a more prominent role in the community for which they sacrifice. Reductions in welfare should not be joined to any general retreat from affirmative action and other civil rights programs, or to any effort to repeal or resist improvements in the Voting Rights Act. . . .

. . . If government pushes people below the level at which they can help shape the community and draw value from it for their own lives, or if it holds out a bright future in which their own children are promised only second-class lives, then it forfeits the only premise on which its conduct might be justified. . . .

# 58 Justice, Gender, and International Boundaries

## ONORA O'NEILL

## 1. Justice for Impoverished Providers

Questions about justice to women and about international justice are often raised in discussions of development. Yet the most influential theories of justice have difficulty in handling either topic. I shall first compare some theoretical difficulties that have arisen in these two domains, and then sketch an account of justice that may be better suited to handling questions of gender and international justice.

I begin by distinguishing *idealized* from *relativized* theories of justice. Idealized accounts of justice stress the need to abstract from the particularities of persons. They paint justice as blind to gender and nationality. Its principles are those that would regulate the action of idealized "abstract individuals." They take no account of differences between men and women; they transcend international boundaries. Relativized accounts of justice acknowledge the variety and differences among humankind; they ground principles of justice in the discourse and traditions of actual communities. Since nearly all of these relegate (varying portions of) women's lives to a "private" sphere,

within which the political virtue of justice has no place, and see national boundaries as the limits of justice, appeals to actual traditions tend both to endorse institutions that exclude women from the "public" sphere, where justice is properly an issue, and to insulate one "public" sphere from another.

Both idealized and relativized accounts of justice look inadequate from the perspective of those whom they marginalize. Women, in particular poor women, will find that neither approach takes account of the reality of performing both reproductive and productive tasks, while having relatively little control over the circumstances of one's life. Women's lives are not well conceived just as those of abstract individuals. A world of abstract individuals assumes away relations of dependence and interdependence; yet these are central to most lives actually available to women. Nor are women's lives well conceived solely in terms of traditions that relegate them to a "private" sphere. The productive contributions and the cognitive and practical independence of actual women are too extensive, evident, and economically significant to be eclipsed by ideologies of total domesticity and dependence.

The awkward fit of theory to actuality is most vivid for poor women in poor economies. These women may depend on others, but lack the supposed securities of dependence. They are impoverished, but are often providers. They are powerless, yet others who are yet more vulnerable

Copyright © The United Nations University 1993. Reprinted from *The Quality of Life* edited by Martha Nussbaum and Amartya Sen (1993), 303–323, by permission of Oxford University Press.

I would particularly like to thank Deborah Fitzmaurice, James Griffin, Barbara Harriss, Martha Nussbaum, and Sara Ruddick for help with various problems that arose in writing this paper.

depend on them for protection.[1] Their vulnerability reflects heavy demands as much as slender resources. They may find that they are relegated to and subordinated within a domestic sphere, whose separate and distinctive existence is legitimated not by appeals to justice but by entrenched views of family life and honour. They may also find that this domestic sphere is embedded in an economy that is subordinate to distant and richer economies. They not only raise children in poverty; they raise crops and do ill-paid and insecure work whose rewards fluctuate to the beat of distant economic forces. This second subordination, too, is legitimated in varied discourses which endorse an internationalized economic order but only national regimes of taxation and welfare. A serious account of justice cannot gloss over the predicaments of impoverished providers in marginalized and developing economies.

## 2. Preview: Abstraction and Contextualization

Both idealized and relativized approaches to justice make seemingly legitimate demands. Idealized approaches insist that justice must *abstract* from the particularities of persons. Blindness to difference is a traditional image of justice and guarantees impartiality. Yet principles of justice that are supposedly blind to differences of power and resources often seem to endorse practices and policies that suit the privileged. Hence a demand that justice take account of *context* can seem equally reasonable. Justice, it is argued, needs more than abstract principles: it must guide judgements that take account of actual contexts and predicaments and of the differences among human beings. Relativized principles of justice meet this demand: but since they are rooted in history, tradition, or local context, they will endorse traditional sexism or nationalism. Any relativism tends to prejudice the position of the weak, whose weakness is mirrored and partly constituted by their marginalization in received ways of thought and by their subordination and oppression in established orders. Yet idealizing

approaches do no better. Where relativist approaches are uncritical of established privilege, idealized approaches are uncritical of the privileges from which they abstract.

If idealized and relativized accounts of justice were the only possibilities we would have to choose between demands for abstraction from difference and for sensitivity to difference. If there are other possibilities, an account of justice may be able to meet demands both for abstract principles and for contextualized judgements. I shall try to sketch a third possibility, which gives both abstraction and contextualization their due—but only their due. This can be done by meeting the demands for abstract and contextual reasoning in two distinct, successive moves.

The first move is to argue for abstract principles of universal scope, while rejecting the supposed link between abstraction and positions that not merely abstract but (in a sense to be explained) idealize. Much contemporary moral reasoning, and in particular "abstract liberalism" (whether "deontological" or utilitarian), handles issues of gender and international justice badly not because it abstracts (e.g. from sex, race, nationality), but because it almost always idealizes specific conceptions of the human agent and of national sovereignty which are often more admired and more (nearly) feasible for developed rather than developing societies and in men rather than in women. Genuine abstraction, without idealization, is, however, the route rather than the obstacle to broad scope and is unobjectionable in *principles* of justice.

The second move answers demands that we take account of the context and particularities of lives and societies, but does not endorse established ideals of gender and of national sovereignty. Abstract principles of justice are not rejected, but viewed as intrinsically incomplete and indeterminate, a guide rather than an algorithm for judging cases. The second move insists that justice can take account of *certain* differences by applying abstract principles to determinate cases without either tacitly reintroducing restricted ideals (e.g. by privileging certain views of gender and sovereignty) or relativizing principles of justice to accepted beliefs, traditions, or practices. Abstract principles can guide contextualized judgements without lapsing into relativism.

## 3. Feminist Critiques of Abstract Justice

Discussions of gender justice have been structured by disagreements over the extent and import of differences between men and women. For liberals who defend abstract principles of justice it has been embarrassing that the Rights of Man were taken for so long and by so many of their predecessors as the rights of men, and that liberal practice failed for so long to end male privilege.[2] (Socialist feminists suffer analogous embarrassments.) Starting with Wollstonecraft and J. S. Mill, liberal feminists argued against the different treatment of women, and claimed that women's rationality entitled them to equal rights.

Later liberal feminists noted that even when women had equal political and legal rights, their political participation and economic rewards remained less than those of men—and less than those of men whose qualifications and labour force participation women matched. Supposedly gender-neutral and neutralizing institutions, such as democratic political structures and markets, turned out to be remarkably bad at reducing gender differentials.[3] Approximations to political and legal justice in various domains of life evidently will not close the radical gap between men's and women's paths and prospects.[4]

In response many liberal feminists argued that justice demands more thorough equal treatment. It may, for example, require forms of affirmative action and reverse discrimination in education and employment, as well as welfare rights to social support for the poor and those with heavy family responsibilities. *Some* differences are to be acknowledged in principles of justice. This move has two difficulties. First, many liberals deny that justice demands compensatory redistribution, especially of positional goods. They think these should be allocated by competitive and merito-

cratic procedures. This debate is of particular importance in the developed world.

The second problem arises even where the goods to be distributed are not positional, and is particularly significant in the Third World. Where resources are scarce, non-positional goods such as basic health care, income support, children's allowances, or unemployment insurance will not be fundable out of a slender national tax base. If social justice demands basic welfare provision, justice has to reach across boundaries. An account of gender justice would then have to be linked to one of international distributive justice.[5]

This liberal debate continues, but its terms have been increasingly questioned by feminists in the last decade, many of whom claim that, despite its aspirations, gender bias is integral to liberal justice.[6] Their suspicions focus on the very abstraction from difference and diversity which is central to liberal justice. Some feminist critics of abstract liberalism have highlighted respects in which particular supposedly gender-neutral theories covertly assume or endorse gendered accounts of the human subject and of rationality. Many aspects of this critique are convincing.

However, the most fundamental feminist challenge to abstract liberalism impugns reliance on abstraction itself. Gilligan's influential work claims that an emphasis on justice excludes and marginalizes the "other voice" of ethical thought. "Abstract liberalism" simply and unacceptably devalues care and concern for particular others, which are the core of women's moral life and thought, seeing them as moral immaturity.[7] The voice of justice is intrinsically "male" in its refusal to grasp the actualities of human difference, in its supposed agnosticism about the good for man, and in its resulting disregard of the virtues, and specifically of love and care. On this account the problem is not to secure like treatment for women, but to secure differentiated treatment for all.

In locating the distinction between justice and care (and other virtues) in a disagreement over the legitimacy of relying on abstract principles, some feminist critics of abstract liberalism construe concern for care as opposing concern for justice. They can end up endorsing rather than challenging social and economic structures that marginalize women and confine them to a private sphere. Separatism at the level of ethical theory can march with acceptance of the powers and traditions that be. The cost of a stress on caring and relationships to the exclusion of abstract justice may be relegation to the nursery and the kitchen, to purdah and to poverty. In rejecting "abstract liberalism" such feminists converge with traditions that exclude and marginalize women. Even when they appeal to "women's experience," rather than to established traditions and discourses, as the clue to understanding the other "voice," they agree that differences are taken seriously only when actual differences are endorsed.[8]

The disputes that divide liberal feminists and their contextualist critics pose an unwelcome dilemma about gender justice. If we adopt an abstract account of justice, which is blind to differences between people—and so to the ways in which women's lives in the developed and in the undeveloped world differ from men's lives—we commit ourselves (it is said) to uniform treatment regardless of difference. If we acknowledge the ethical importance of differences, we are likely to endorse traditional social forms that sustain those differences, including those that subordinate and oppress women.

## 4. The Communitarian Critique of Abstract Justice

This dilemma recurs in certain discussions of international justice. Abstract liberalism proclaims the Rights of Man. As Burke was quick to complain, this is quite a different matter from proclaiming the rights of Englishmen, or of Frenchmen, or of any coherent group. Abstraction was the price to be paid for ethical discourse that could cross the boundaries of states and nations and have universal appeal; and Burke found the price unacceptable. The internationalist, cosmopolitan commitments that were implicit in the ideals of liberalism have repeatedly been targets of conservative and communitarian criticism.

Liberal practice has, however, once again been embarrassingly different. It has not been universalistic, but clearly subordinated to the boundaries and demands of nation states. This is evident in relations between rich and poor states. Like treatment for like cases is partially secured by laws and practices within many democratic states; only a few enthusiasts argue for world government, or think that rights of residence, work, and welfare, as well as burdens of taxation, should be global. Such enthusiasm is often dismissed by practical people who hold that a plurality of national jurisdictions provides the framework within which liberal ideals can be pursued. Liberals may not be generally willing to take differences seriously; but they have taken differences between sovereign states remarkably seriously.

Their communitarian critics take differences and boundaries seriously in theory as well as in practice.[9] When boundaries are taken wholly seriously, however, international justice is not just played down, but wiped off the ethical map. Walzer's work is a good case in point. He holds that the largest sphere of justice is the political community and that the only issues not internal to such communities are about membership in them and conflicts between them. The issues of membership concern the admission of individual aliens; rights and duties do not go beyond borders.[10] A commitment to community is a commitment to the historical boundaries of political communities, whatever these happen to be and whatever injustices their constitution and their preservation entail. Communitarians cannot easily take any wider view of ethical boundaries since their critique of abstraction is in part a demand for ethical discourse that takes "our" language, "our" culture, and "our" traditions seriously.[11]

Like current debates on gender justice, discussions of international justice apparently pose an unwelcome choice. Either we can abstract from the reality of boundaries, and think about principles of justice that assume an ideal cosmopolitan world, in which justice and human rights do not stop at the boundaries of states. Or we can acknowledge the reality of boundaries and construe the principles of justice as subordinate to those of national sovereignty. Cosmopolitan ideals are evident in the discourse of much of the human rights movement; but recent liberal theorists have shifted towards the relativism of their communitarian critics, and even come to regard liberal principles of justice as no more than the principles of liberal societies. Rawls in particular now[12] hinges his theory of justice not on an abstract and idealized construction of an original position but on the actual ideals of citizens of liberal democratic societies. Here we see a surprising and perhaps unstable convergence between abstract liberal theorists and their communitarian critics.

## 5. Abstraction with and without Idealization

Debates about gender and international justice are not merely similar in that each is structured by a confrontation between advocates of abstract and of contextualized justice. In each debate many advocates of supposedly abstract approaches to justice go far beyond abstraction. What these debates term "abstraction" is often a set of specific, unargued *idealizations* of human agency, rationality, and life, and of the sovereignty and independence of states. And in each debate what is said to be attention to actual situations and contexts in judging is in fact *relativism* about principles. These conflations are avoidable.

Abstraction, taken strictly, is simply a matter of detaching certain claims from others. Abstract reasoning hinges nothing on the satisfaction or non-satisfaction of predicates from which it abstracts. All uses of language must abstract more or less: the most detailed describing cannot dent the indeterminacy of language. Indeed it is not obvious that there is anything to object to in very abstract principles of justice. Highly abstract ways of reasoning are often admired (mathematics, physics), and frequently well paid (accountancy, law). What is different about abstract ethical reasoning? When we look at objections to "abstract" ethical principles and reasoning in detail, it appears that they are often objections not to detachment from certain predicates, but to the inclusion of predi-

cates that are false of the objects of the domain to which a theory is then applied. Reasoning that abstracts from some predicate makes claims that do not hinge on the objects to which the reasoning is applied satisfying that predicate. Reasoning that idealizes does make claims that hinge on the objects to which it is applied satisfying certain predicates. Where those predicates are unsatisfied the reasoning simply does not apply.

The principles and theories of justice to which the critics of "abstract liberalism" object are indeed abstract. They take no account of many features of agents and societies. However, these principles and theories not only abstract but idealize. They assume, for example, accounts of rational choice whose claims about information, coherence, capacities to calculate, and the like are not merely not satisfied by some deficient or backward agents, but are actually satisfied by no human agents (perhaps they are approximated, or at least admired, in restricted shopping and gambling contexts!). They also assume idealized accounts of the mutual independence of persons and their opportunities to pursue their individual "conceptions of the good"; and of the sovereignty and independence of states, that are false of all human beings and all states. Such idealizations no doubt have theoretical advantages: above all they allow us to construct models that can readily be manipulated. However, they fail to apply to most, if not all, practical problems of human choice and foreign policy.

If idealized descriptions are not abstracted from those that are true of actual agents, they are not innocuous ways of extending the scope of reasoning. Each idealization posits "enhanced" versions of the objects of the domain to which the model is applied. They may privilege certain sorts of human agent and life and certain sorts of society by covertly presenting (enhanced versions of) their specific characteristics as the ideal for all human action and life. In this way covert gender chauvinism and exaggerated respect for state power can be combined with liberal principles. Idealization masquerading as abstraction produces theories that appear to apply widely, but which covertly exclude those who do not match a certain ideal, or match it less well than others. Those who are excluded are then seen as defective or inadequate. A review of the debates about gender and international justice shows that the feminist and communitarian critique of liberal justice can legitimately attack spurious idealizations without impugning abstraction that eschews idealization.

## 6. Gender and Idealized Agents

Liberal discussions of justice ostensibly hinge nothing on gender differences. They apply to individuals, considered in abstraction from specific identities, commitments, and circumstances. Recent critics insist that liberal theories of justice are far from being as gender-blind as their advocates claim. An instructive example is Rawls's *A Theory of Justice.* Rawls was particularly concerned not to rely on an extravagant model of rational choice. His principles of justice are those that would be chosen by agents in an "original position" in which they know *less* rather than *more* than actual human agents. He conceives his work as carrying the social contract tradition to "a higher level of abstraction." In particular, agents in the original position do not know their social and economic position, their natural assets, or their conceptions of the good.[13] The original position operationalizes the image of justice as blind to difference.

However, Rawls has at a certain point to introduce grounds for those in the original position to care about their successors. He suggests that we may think of them as heads or at other times as representatives of families, "as being so to speak deputies for an everlasting moral agent or institution"[14] and that some form of family would be just. Yet in doing so he pre-empts the question of intrafamilial justice. He pre-empts the question not by crude insistence that heads of families must be men, but by taking it as read that there is some just form of family which allows the interests of some to be justly represented by others. The shift from individuals to heads of families as agents of construction is not an innocent abstraction; it

*assumes* a family structure which secures identity of interests between distinct individuals. It takes for granted that there is some just "sexual contract,"[15] that justice can presuppose a legitimate separation of "private" from "public" domains. This is idealization indeed: it buries the question of gender justice rather than resolving it. Rawls's text leaves it surprisingly obscure whether women are to be relegated to a "private" sphere and represented by men in the construction of justice, whether both "public" and "private" realms are to be shared by all on equal terms, or whether women alone are to carry the burdens of both spheres.[16]

The more radical feminist critique of abstract liberalism rejects not merely the suppressed gendering of the subject which Pateman and Okin detect in classical and contemporary liberal writers, but abstraction itself. In advocating an ethic of care these critics, we have seen, come close both to traditional misogynist positions and to ethical relativism. When the "voices" of justice and of care are presented as alternatives between which we must choose, each is viewed as a complete approach to moral issues. However, the two in fact focus on different aspects of life. Justice is concerned with institutions, care and other virtues with character, which is vital in unmediated relationships with particular others. The central difference between the "voices" of justice and care is not that they reason in different ways. Justice requires judgements about cases as well as abstract principles; care is principled as well as responsive to differences. Justice matters for impoverished providers because their predicament is one of institutionally structured poverty which cannot be banished by idealizing an ethic of care.

## 7. Idealized Boundaries

A comparable slide from abstraction to idealization can be found in discussions of international justice. Discussions of global economic and political issues often take it for granted that the principal actors are states. Traditionally the main divide in these discussions has been between realists, who contend that states, although agents, are exempt from moral obligations and criticism, and idealists, who insist that states are not merely agents but accountable agents who must meet the demands of justice.[17]

In discussions of distributive justice, however, the salient issue has not been the conflict between idealists and realists, but their agreement that state boundaries define the main actors in international affairs. These shared terms of debate endorse an exaggerated, idealized view of the agency and mutual independence of sovereign states, which is now often criticized as obsolete. The common ground on which realists and idealists traditionally debated international relations is being eroded as other actors, including international agencies, regional associations, and above all transnational corporations, play a more and more significant role in world affairs.[18] A world that is partitioned into discrete and mutually impervious sovereign states is not an abstraction from our world, but an idealized version of it, or perhaps an idealized version of what it once was. Realists as well as idealists idealize the sovereignty of states.

Idealized conceptions both of state sovereignty and of state boundaries limit discussions of international distributive justice. Although long subject to theoretical questioning from advocates of human rights, who deny that states can be sovereign in determining the fates of individuals, many liberals are coy about criticizing rights violations elsewhere. They limit criticism to violations of liberty rights, and offer little account of the agency or responsibilities of institutions; they find it hard to see how justice could require that state boundaries be breached to reduce the poverty that lies beyond them. Even those liberals who defend welfare rights are often concerned with welfare in one (rich) country. It is commonplace to view economic development of poorer regions as optional "aid," not obligatory justice. Those who have tried to argue for global welfare rights within a liberal framework have to show who bears the obligations that correspond to these rights, and this has proved uphill work.[19] Meanwhile liberals, like communitarians, confine jus-

tice within national boundaries. Liberals do so self-consciously and provisionally; communitarians on principle and unapologetically; others tacitly and without discussion.

## 8. Abstraction without Idealization

The only way to find theories that have wide scope is to abstract from the particularities of agents; but when abstraction is displaced by idealization we are not led to theories with wide scope, but to theories that apply only to idealized agents.

This suggests that if we are interested in international or gender justice we should resist the temptation to rely on idealizing models of human agency or national sovereignty. We should instead consider what sort of theory of justice we would have if we abstracted but refused to idealize any one conception of rationality or independence, and so avoided marginalizing or excluding those who do not live up to specific ideals of rationality or of independence from others. Abstraction without idealization may allow us to consider a wide range of human agents and institutional arrangements without hinging anything on the specific features of agents' traditions, ideologies, and capacities to act. If we could do this we might avoid idealized accounts of agency and sovereignty without following feminist and communitarian critics of abstract liberalism into relativism.

Recent discussions may simply have been mistaken in treating appeals to idealized and relativized standards of rationality and agency as the only options. There are other possibilities. We do not have to hinge liberal arguments for rights or for the limits of government power either on the *hypothetical* consent of those who meet some *ideal* standard of rationality and mutual independence, or on the *actual* acceptance of an outlook and its categories that *relativizes* consent to an established order. We could instead begin simply by abstracting from existing social orders. We could consider what principles of action must be adopted by agents who are numerous, diverse, and *neither* ideally rational *nor* ideally independent of one another, and yet avoid specific assumptions about these agents. We can bracket both idealizations and the status quo. The issue then becomes: how powerful and convincing an account of justice can we offer if we appeal neither to fictions of ideal rationality and independence nor to the contingencies of actual agents and institutions? What happens if we abstract without idealizing?

## 9. Plurality and Justice: Who Counts?

Let us begin with the thought of a plurality of potentially interacting and diverse agents. This rules out two cases. First, it rules out the case where justice is not a problem because there is no plurality, or no genuine plurality, of agents, hence no potential for conflict between agents. (The action of agents in such a degenerate plurality would be automatically or necessarily coordinated, e.g. by instinct or by a pre-established harmony.) Second, it rules out hinging an account of justice on an assumed, contingent, and determinate limit to the diversity of its members, which provides a common ground between them and permits a contingent, socially guaranteed convergence and co-ordination. The two cases that are ruled out are once again those which would base principles of justice on an assumed ideal convergence or an assumed actual historical or social convergence.

What does justice require of such a plurality? At least we can claim that their most basic principles must be ones that *could* be adopted by all. If they were not, at least some agents would have to be excluded from the plurality for whom the principles can hold, whose boundaries would have to be drawn more narrowly.

Such a redrawing of boundaries is, of course, the very move often used to exclude women and foreigners, let alone foreign women, from the domain of justice. Those who exclude simply refuse to count certain others as members of a plurality of potentially interacting agents. An account of justice which hinges on the sharability

of principles can be preempted by excluding some from the domain of justice without argument. So it is important to see the move for what it is. This can best be done by asking *who* makes the move.

The move is not made by idealized genderless theorists who live outside state and society. It is made by people who generally expect women to interact with them, to follow language and reason, to understand and take part in elaborate traditions and institutions, perhaps even to love, honour, and obey. It is made by people who expect ordinary processes of translation, trade, and negotiation to work with foreigners. To deny the agency of others with whom we plan to interact in complex ways reeks of bad faith. Bad faith can be avoided only by counting as members of the plurality for whom principles of justice are to hold *anybody* with whom interaction is to be attempted or held possible. The question then becomes: are there any principles which must be adopted by all members of a plurality of potentially interacting agents? We cannot simply stipulate that such principles are irrelevant for interactions with certain others on whose (no doubt imperfect) capacities to reason and (no doubt limited) abilities to act independently we know we depend.

If women were all transported to Betelgeuse, and so beyond all interaction with the remaining men on Earth, neither men nor women would have to see the other as falling within the domain of justice. Less fancifully, since the ancient inhabitants of the Andes and their contemporaries in Anglo-Saxon England could not and did not interact, neither would have acted in bad faith if they had excluded the other from the domain of justice. Neither could practise either justice or injustice towards the other. Things are different for the actual men and women who inhabit the earth now: the potential for interaction cannot be assumed away, and others cannot be arbitrarily excluded from the domain of justice. We rely on global economic and political processes, so cannot consistently insist that justice (conveniently for the developed world) stops at state frontiers, any more than we can rely on women's rationality and their productive contribution and then argue that justice (conveniently for some men) stops at the edge of a supposed "private" sphere, whose existence and demarcation is in fact presupposed in defining a "public" sphere.

## 10. Plurality and Justice: What Principles?

Justice is then in the first place a matter of keeping to principles that can be adopted by any plurality of potentially interacting beings. But if we eschew both idealization and relativism, and rely on mere abstraction, will we have strong enough premises to identify those principles? Does a universalizability test cut any ice? Granted that universalizability is not uniformity (as some critics of abstract liberalism suppose), is it not too weak a demand to ground an account of justice? In particular, will not any internally coherent principle for individual action be a universalizable principle?[20]

We have, however, to remember that we are considering the case of a plurality of *potentially interacting* beings, that is of beings who share a world. Any principle of action that is adopted by all members of such pluralities alters the world that they share and becomes a background condition of their action. This is why certain principles of action which can coherently be held by some cannot be coherently held by all. Examples of non-universalizable principles can illustrate the point. A principle of deception, which undermines trust, would, if universally adopted, make all trusting, hence all projects of deception, incoherent. Selective deception is on the cards: universal deception is impossible. Since a principle of deception cannot be a fundamental one for any plurality, justice requires that it be rejected. Equally, a policy of coercion which seeks to destroy or undercut the agency and independence of at least some others for at least some time cannot be universally held. Those who are victims of coercion cannot (while victims) also act on the principles on which their coercers act.[21] Equally, a principle of violence which damages the agency

of some others cannot be universally acted on. Put quite generally, principles of action that hinge on victimizing some, so on destroying, paralysing, or undercutting their capacities for action for at least some time and in some ways, can be adopted by some but cannot be adopted as fundamental principles by any plurality.[22]

To keep matters under control, let us imagine only that justice demands (at least) that action and institutions should not be based on principles of deception and victimization. (There may be other principles of justice.) We are still far from showing just what justice demands, since we do not know what refusing to deceive or to coerce may demand in specific circumstances. These guidelines are highly indeterminate. We seem to have paid the classic price of abstraction. Highly abstract principles do not tell us what to do in a specific context.

Abstract principles are only part of practical, or specifically of ethical, reasoning, however. Principles never determine their own applications; even the culturally specific principles that relativists favour do not determine their own applications. All practical reasoning requires judgement and deliberation by which principles are applied to particular cases. An account of gender and international justice is no exception. We need in particular to be able to judge what specific institutions and action are needed if poor women in poor economies are to be accorded justice.

## 11. Plurality and Justice: Deliberation without Relativism

Two background issues must be dealt with summarily before considering moves from abstract basic principles to determinate judgements. First, we have no reason to expect that principles of justice will provide any algorithm of rational choice. Nor do we need any algorithm for principles to be important. Even principles that provide only a set of side constraints on action may exert a powerful influence. Second, we have no reason to think that principles of justice are relevant only to the action of individuals. A full account of the agency of institutions would be a complex matter. I shall not go into it here, but will assume that it can be given and that institutions and practices, like individuals, must meet the demands of justice.

These moves, however, are preliminary to the main task of giving a more determinate account of what may be required if principles of deception or victimization are rejected. How, for example, can we judge whether specific types of family or economic activity are based on deception or victimization? Are all forms of hierarchy and subordination coercive? If not, how do we discern the boundaries of deceit and coercion in actual contexts? It is not hard to see that certain categories of individual action—for example, fraud or wife burning or battering—deceive or victimize, but other cases of deception and coercion by individuals are hard to adjudicate. It may also be hard to judge whether social traditions that isolate or exclude women, or economic and familial arrangements that ensure their acute economic vulnerability, amount to modes of deceit and coercion.

In this paper the task cannot be to reach determinate judgements about particular cases, but only to see that reasoned moves from very abstract principles towards more specific principles, whose relevance and application to particular cases may be easier to assess, may be possible. It will not be enough to lean on the received criteria by which "our" tradition or nation picks out ethically significant "cases" or "options" for approaching them. We beg questions if we assume that categories of thought that have been hospitable to male dominance and imperialism can be decisive for discerning or judging justice to those whose problems have been marginalized and whose agency and capacities have been formed, perhaps deformed, by unjust institutions. We cannot rely uncritically on the categories of established discourse, including the discourse of social scientists and the "helping" professions, to pick out the significant problems. These categories are themselves matters for ethical concern and criticism.[23] We have, after all, no more reason to trust relativized discussions of justice, gender, or boundaries than to trust idealized approaches unequivocally. Those discussions are no

more free of theory and ideology than are idealized discussions of justice. Their ways of individuating typical problem cases may be familiar; but familiarity may mask contentious and unjust delimitations. If the received views of a society or tradition are taken as defining the domain of problems to which abstract principles of justice are applied, unvindicated ideals will be introduced and privileged, just as they are in idealized approaches to justice.

Some confirmation of the ways in which received descriptions of social relations reflect larger and disputed ideals is suggestive. Consider, for example, how issues of gender are passed over as if invisible. We find an enormous amount of shifting around in the choice of basic units of social analysis. In the shifts between descriptions that focus on individuals, wage-earners, and heads of families, there is enough flexibility for the blunt facts of economic and other subordination of women to be veiled. Women's low wages can seem unworrying if they are wives for whom others provide; their dependence on husbands and fathers can seem acceptable if they are after all wage-earning individuals, so not invidiously dependent. Reproductive labour may (with convenient ambiguity!) be thought of as priceless.[24] Wage-earning women's low pay can be seen as fitting their low skills and vindicating their domestic subordination to wage-earning men, who as "heads of families" are entitled to discretionary expenditure and leisure which wage-earning women must do without because they (unlike men!) have family commitments. The gloomy evidence of social structures that classify women's contributions as less valuable even when more onerous or more skilled is evident enough. We continually find ourselves "thinking about men as individuals who direct households and about women as family members."[25]

There are equally serious reasons to mistrust the move from abstract principles to determinate judgements in discussions of individual motivation. These too are shaped by received views, and in milieux which are strongly individualist are easily diverted into attempts to pin blame for injustices on individuals. Women, after all, commonly acquiesce in their social and economic subordination. Are they then to be blamed for servility? Or are men to be blamed for oppressing or exploiting women?[26] Or do these individualist approaches to assigning blame lead no further than the higher bickering? It can seem that we have reasons to mistrust not only relativist approaches to gender justice but even the attempt to apply an abstract, non-idealized principle of justice. But we do not inhabit an ideal world. Idealized conceptions of justice simply do not apply to international relations, social relations, or individual acts in a world in which states, men, and women *always* lack the capacities and the opportunities of idealized agents. States are not really sovereign—even superpowers have limited powers; and men and women are always more or less vulnerable, ignorant, insecure, lacking in confidence or means to challenge or oppose the status quo. In a world of agents with finite capacities and opportunities, poor women in poor economies differ not in kind but in degree in their dependence on others and in others' demands on them.

## 12. Just Deliberation in a World of Vulnerable Agents

If we are to apply principles of justice that are neither idealized, nor merely relative to actual societies, to vulnerable lives and their predicaments, we must see how to move towards determinate judgements about actual cases. The principles of justice for which I have argued take us in this direction because they focus neither on the arrangements to which ideally rational and mutually independent beings would consent, nor on the arrangements to which others in possibly oppressive situations do consent. Rather they ask which arrangements a plurality of interacting agents with finite capacities *could* consent to. I have suggested, provisionally, that this non-idealizing construction identifies the rejection of deception, coercion, and other ways of victimizing others as principles of justice.

But principles are not enough. Non-idealizing abstraction avoids some problems, but not others.

If we are to move from abstract principles to determinate judgements we need to operationalize the idea of avoiding acting on unsharable principles, without subordinating it to the categories and views of the status quo. One reasonable way of doing so might be to ask to what extent the arrangements that structure vulnerable lives are ones that *could have been refused or renegotiated by those whom they actually constrain*. If those affected by a given set of arrangements could have refused or renegotiated them, their consent is no mere formality, but genuine, legitimating consent. If they could not but "accept" those institutions, their "consent" will not legitimate. The point of this way of operationalizing the notion of possible consent is that it neither ascribes ideal reasoning capacities and ideal independence from others nor hinges legitimation on an actual "consent" that may reflect injustice. On this account justice requires that institutions, like acts, allow those on the receiving end, even if frail and dependent, to refuse or renegotiate the roles and tasks assigned to them.

Dissent becomes harder when capacities to act are less developed and more vulnerable, and when opportunities for independent action are restricted. Capacities to act are constrained both by lack of abilities and by commitments to others. Institutional arrangements can disable agency both by limiting capacities to reason and act independently and by increasing the demands to meet the needs and satisfy the desires of others. Apparent consent to such arrangements does not show that they are just. Whenever "consent" reflects lack of capacity or opportunity to do anything else, it does not legitimate. Thinking in this way about justice, we can see that *it demands more, not less, to be just to the vulnerable*. The vulnerable are much easier to deceive and to victimize than the strong. If we are to judge proposals for action by seeing whether they involve serious deception or victimization (coercion or violence), *more* will be demanded when others are vulnerable than when they are secure, and most when they are most vulnerable.[27] By contrast both idealized and relativized accounts of justice tend to conceal the fact that justice to the weak demands more than justice to the strong. Idealized accounts of justice tend to ignore vulnerability and relativized accounts to legitimate it.

# 13. Achieving Justice for Impoverished Providers

The lives of poor women in poor economies illustrate these points well. Consider, for example, daily commercial transactions and practices. Their justice, it is usually said, lies in the fact that arrangements are mutually agreed. But where there are great disparities of knowledge and vulnerability between agents, the "agreement" of the weak may be spurious. They may have been duped by offers they did not understand or overwhelmed by "offers" they dared not refuse. Within national jurisdictions these facts are well recognized, and commercial practice is regulated to prevent pressure and fraud. Contracts can be voided for fraud; there are "truth in lending" provisions; debt and bankruptcy lead not to loss of liberty but to loss of property; those with dependents can rely on a safety net of welfare rights. International economic transactions take place in a far less regulated space, yet link agents with far greater disparities in power and resources. The weak can suffer both from particular others who take advantage of their ignorance and vulnerability, and because nothing informs them about or shields them from the intended or unintended consequences either of distant or of local economic forces. The poor, and above all women who are impoverished providers, cannot refuse or renegotiate economic structures or transactions which hurt them. They are vulnerable not only to low wages, low standards of industrial safety, endemic debt, and disadvantageous dependence on those who provide credit, but also to disadvantageous patterns of entitlement within the family. Debtors who need further loans for survival, for example, cannot make much fuss about the terms creditors offer for purchasing their crops.[28] Market "imperfections" are neither avoidable nor trivial for vulnerable agents with many dependents;

equally, "perfect" markets can magnify vulnerability to distant economic forces.

Idealized pictures of justice have tended to overlook the import of economic power: by idealizing the capacities and the mutual independence of those involved in market transactions they obscure the reasons why the weak may be unable to dissent from arrangements proposed by the strong. They also tend to distinguish sharply between intended and unintended consequences, and to view the latter as unavoidable "forces." Yet these forces are themselves the outcome of institutional arrangements and could be changed or modified, as they have been within many jurisdictions. The problem of shielding the weak from these forces has nothing to do with "natural" processes, and everything to do with the weakness of the voices that call for change. This is hardly surprising. Market institutions magnify the security and so the voices of the haves. Formal democracy provides only slender and partial redress for the weak, and is often lacking.

Typical family structures illustrate the gulf between ideally independent agents (whom "ideal" market structures might suit) and actual powerlessness. These structures often draw a boundary between "public" and "private" domains, assign women (wives and daughters) to the "private" domain, and leave them with slender control of resources, but heavy commitments to meet others' needs. They may lack adequate economic entitlements, effective enfranchisement, or access to sources of information or debate by which to check or challenge the proposals and plans of the more powerful. Women in this predicament lack security, and must meet the demands of others (often fathers and husbands) who dominate them. Family structures can enable, even impose, forms of deception and domination. Where women are isolated, secluded, barred from education or wage earning, or have access to information only via the filter of more powerful family members, their judgement is weakened, and their independence stunted. Often this vulnerability may be shielded by matching concern and restraint; often it will not. A rhetoric of familial concern and protective paternalism can easily camouflage a callous lack of concern and legitimate deceptive acts and practices.

Similar points can be made about victimization. A principle of non-coercion, for example, basically demands that action should not undercut others' agency. If agents were all ideally independent of one another, they might find little difficulty in dissenting from many forms of attempted domination. However, family structures always limit independence, and usually limit women's independence more. A woman who has no adequate entitlements of her own, and insecure rights to a share in family property or income, will not always be coerced, but is always vulnerable to coercion.[29] When her independence is also restricted by family responsibilities she will be even easier to coerce. In these circumstances ostensible consent reveals little; it certainly does not legitimate forms of domination and subordination. Relations of dependence are not always or overtly coercive; but they provide structures of subordination within which it is all too easy to silence or trivialize the articulation of dissent. To guarantee that action is not based on principles which others cannot share, it is necessary to ensure that proposals that affect others are ones from which *they* can dissent. Institutionalized dependence tends to make dissent hard or impossible. Those who cannot secure economic independence or who cannot rely on others to take a share in caring for genuine dependents (children, the elderly) cannot easily say "no" or set their own terms. They must go along with the proposals of the more powerful.

*Genuine, legitimating consent is undermined by the very institutions which most readily secure an appearance of consent.* Institutionalized dependence may ensure that the weak provide a spurious "consent" to the action of the strong, while remaining at their mercy. If the strong reliably show restraint, there may *in fact* be no injustice within relationships which institutionalize dependence; but institutions that rely too heavily on the self-restraint of the stronger cannot reliably avoid injustice. Whether the proposals of the strong are economic or sexual, whether they rely on the ignorance and isolation of the weak to

deceive them, or on their diminished opportunities for independent action, or on the habits of deference and appeasement which become second nature for the weak, they ride on unjust social practices. *The weak risk recurrent injustice unless institutions are structured to secure the option of refusal or renegotiation for those whose capacities and opportunities are limited.*

A woman who has no entitlements of her own lives at the discretion of other family members who have them, so is likely to have to go along even with proposals she greatly dislikes or judges imprudent. If she were an ideally independent agent, or even had the ordinary independence and opportunities of those who have entitlements adequate for themselves and their dependents, she could risk dissent from or at least renegotiate proposals put by those who control her means of life. Being powerless and vulnerable she cannot readily do either. Hence any consent that she offers is compromised and does not legitimate others' proposals. Just as we would find it absurd to hinge legitimating consent to medical treatment on procedures geared to the cognitive capacities and independence of a notional "ideal rational patient," so we should find it absurd to hinge legitimating consent to others' plans on the cognitive capacities and independence of a notional ideal rational impoverished provider for others.

This is not to say that impoverished providers are irrational or wholly dependent or cannot consent. It is, however, a matter of taking seriously the ways in which their capacities and opportunities for action constrain their possibilities for refusal and negotiation. If they are to be treated with justice, others who interact with them must not rely on these reduced capacities and opportunities to impose their will. Those who do so rely on unjust institutional structures that enable deceit, coercion, and forms of victimization.

In applying abstract, non-idealizing principles we have to take account not indeed of the actual beliefs, ideals, or categories of others, which may reflect unjust traditions, but of others' actual *capacities* and *opportunities* to act—and their incapacities and lack of opportunities. This move does not lead back to relativism: no principle is endorsed because it is actually accepted. Put in general terms we can use modal notions to identify principles, but indicative ones to apply them. The principles of justice can be determined for any possible plurality: for they demand only the rejection of principles that cannot be shared by all members of a plurality. Judgements about the justice of actual situations are regulated but not entailed by these principles. The most significant features of actual situations that must be taken into account in judgements about justice are the security or vulnerability that allow actual others to dissent from and to seek change in the arrangements which structure their lives.

# Notes

1. Cf. Ruddick (1989). Her account of women's predicament stresses that it reflects heavy demands as much as meagre resources. To be preferred, I think, because it does not take for granted that the lack of resources is significant because "public" while the press of others' demands is less so because merely "private."

2. Okin (1979); Charvet (1982); Pateman (1988); Jaggar (1983).

3. Scott (1986).

4. The differences run the gamut of social indicators. Most dramatically in some Third World countries women and girls do worse on a constellation of very basic social indicators: they die earlier, have worse health, eat less than other family members, earn less, and go to school less. See Sen (1987), Harriss (1988 and 1991).

5. The problem is not merely one of resources. Where funds have been adequate for publicly funded welfare provision, this too has been inadequate to eliminate the differences between the economic and political prospects of men and of women. Many women in the formerly socialist countries, for example, find that they have secured greater equality in productive labour with no reduction in reproductive tasks. This is a reason for doubting that arguments establishing welfare rights—e.g. a right to food—take a broad enough view of disparities between men's and women's prospects.

6. E.g. Pateman (1988); Okin (1987).

7. Gilligan (1982); Kittay and Meyers (1987); Lloyd (1984); MacMillan (1982); Ruddick (1987); Noddings (1984); Chodorow (1978).

8. Many of those who urge respect for the "other" voice insist that they do not reject the demands of justice, and that they see the two "voices" as complementary rather than alternative. The positions taken by different writers, and by the same writers at different times, vary. The protests must be taken in context: those who appeal to "women's experience" or "women's thinking" appeal to a source that mirrors the traditional relegation of women to a "private" sphere, and cannot readily shed those commitments. It is important to remember that those who care have traditionally been thought to have many cares.

9. Such approaches can be found in Walzer (1983); Sandel (1982); MacIntyre (1981 and 1984); Williams (1985), and, perhaps most surprisingly, Rawls (1985). For some discussion of the implications of these works for international justice see O'Neill (1988b).

10. Walzer acknowledges that this means that he can "only begin to address the problems raised by mass poverty in many parts of the globe" (1983: 30). Critics may think that his approach in fact pre-empts answers to questions of global justice.

11. Communitarians can, however, take lesser loyalties seriously: where a state is divided into distinct national and ethical communities, those distinct traditions may in fact be the widest boundaries within which issues of justice can be debated and determined. They could argue for secession from a multinational state; but they cannot say anything about what goes on beyond the boundaries of "our" community. Cf. Walzer (1983: 319).

12. Rawls (1985).

13. Rawls (1970:11–12).

14. Rawls (1970: 128).

15. Cf. Pateman (1988); Nicholson (1987).

16. See Okin (1987: 46–7). She considers whether the original position abstracts from knowledge of one's sex. Even if she is right in thinking that Rawls relies on a covertly gendered account of the subject, this idealization may have little effect on his theory of justice if the thought experiment of the original position has so relentlessly suppressed difference that the supposed plurality of voices is a fiction. In that case we should read the work as taking an idealized rather than a merely abstract view of rational choice from the very start, and as appealing to a single ideally informed and dispassionate figure as the generator of the principles of justice.

17. See Beitz (1979) for an account of debates between realists and idealists.

18. Keohane and Nye (1970); Luper-Foy (1988).

19. See Shue (1980, 1984); Alston and Tomasevski (1984); Brown and Shue (1977); Gewirth (1982); Luper-Foy (1988); O'Neill (1986).

20. This is the hoary problem of formalism in Kantian ethics. For recent discussions of aspects of the problem see Bittner (1974); Höffe (1977); O'Neill (1989: Part II).

21. It does not follow that every coercive act is unjust; some coercion, e.g. the use of sanctions to enforce law, may be the condition of any reliable space for uncoerced action. In such cases the appropriate expression of an underlying principle of rejecting coercion is, surprisingly, and crucially for political argument, one that, taken out of context, might express an underlying principle of coercion.

22. I have put these matters briefly. For more extended treatment see the references given in n. 20 and O'Neill (1988*a*).

23. Edelman (1984).

24. Nicholson (1987).

25. Stiehm (1983); Scott (1986); Sen (1987).

26. Postow (1978–9); Hill (1979); Pfeffer (1985); Sen (1987).

27. I focus here on the obligations of the strong rather than the rights of the weak. This is not to deny that agitation and resistance by the weak can help remind and persuade the strong of their obligations and make it more difficult for them to repudiate them. However, to focus primarily on rights falsifies the predicament of the weak, who are in no position to ensure that others meet their obligations.

28. Shue (1984); Harriss (1987 and 1991).

29. See Sen (1987) for a fuller account of entitlements. While I have chosen to stress *vulnerabilities* that must not be exploited, rather than *capabilities* that ought to be secured, I believe this account of justice to the powerless is fully compatible with Sen's.

# References

Alston, P. (1984). "International Law and the Human Right to Food," in P. Alston and K. Tomasevski (eds.), *The Right to Food*. Dordrecht: Nijhoff.

—— and Tomasevski, K. (eds.) (1984). *The Right to Food*. Dordrecht: Nijhoff.

Beitz, Charles (1979). *Political Theory and International Relations*. Princeton, NJ: Princeton University Press.

Bittner, Rüdiger (1974). "Maximen," in G. Funke (ed.), *Akten des 4. Internationalen Kant-Kongresses*. Berlin: De Gruyter.

Brown, Peter, and Shue, Henry (eds.) (1981). *Boundaries: National Autonomy and its Limits*. New Jersey: Rowman & Littlefield.

Charvet, John (1982). *Feminism*. London: Dent.

Chodorow, Nancy (1978). *The Reproduction of Mothering*. Berkeley, Calif.: University of California Press.

Edelman, Murray (1984). "The Political Language of the Helping Professions," in Michael J. Shapiro (ed.), *Language and Politics*. New York: NYU Press.

Gewirth, Alan (1982). "Starvation and Human Rights," in his *Human Rights: Essays on Justification and Applications*. Chicago: Chicago University Press.

Gilligan, Carol (1982). *In a Different Voice: Psychological Theory and Women's Dependence*. Cambridge, Mass.: Harvard University Press.

Harriss, Barbara (1987). "Merchants and Markets of Grain in South Asia," in Teodor Shanin (ed.), *Peasants and Peasant Societies*. Oxford: Blackwell.

—— (1988). *Differential Female Mortality and Health Care in South Asia*, Working Paper 13. Oxford:

Queen Elizabeth House, and *Journal of Social Studies*, 41, Dhaka University.

—— (1991). "Intrafamily Distribution of Hunger in South Asia," in J. Drèze and A. K. Sen (eds.), *The Political Economy of Hunger*, i. Oxford: Clarendon Press.

Hill, Thomas (1973). "Servility and Self Respect," *Monist*, 57, 87–104.

Höffe, Otfried (1977). "Kants kategorischer Imperativ als Kriterium des Sittlichen," *Zeitschrift für Philosophische Forschung*, 31, 354–84.

Hoffman, Stanley (1981). *Duties Beyond Borders: On the Limits and Possibilities of Ethical International Politics*. Syracuse, New York: Syracuse University Press.

Jaggar, Alison M. (1983). *Feminist Politics and Human Nature*. Brighton: Harvester Press.

Keohane, Robert O., and Nye, Joseph S. (eds.) (1970). *Transnational Relations and World Politics*. Cambridge, Mass.: Harvard University Press.

Kittay, Eva Feders, and Meyers, Diane T. (eds.) (1987). *Women and Moral Theory*. New York: Rowman and Littlefield.

Lloyd, Genevieve (1984). *The Man of Reason: "Male" and "Female" in Western Philosophy*. London: Methuen.

Luper-Foy, Stephen (ed.) (1988). *Problems of International Justice*. Boulder and London: Westview Press.

MacIntyre, Alasdair (1981). *After Virtue*. London: Duckworth.

—— (1984). *Is Patriotism a Virtue?* University of Kansas, Lawrence: Philosophy Department.

MacMillan, Carol (1982). *Women, Reason and Nature*. Oxford: Blackwell.

Nicholson, Linda (1987). "Feminism and Marx: Integrating Kinship with the Economic," in Seyla Benhabib and Drucilla Cornell (eds.), *Feminism as Critique*. Cambridge: Polity Press.

Noddings, Nel (1984). *Caring*. Berkeley, Calif.: University of California Press.

Okin, Susan Miller (1979). *Women in Political Thought*. Princeton, NJ: Princeton University Press.

—— (1987). "Justice and Gender," *Philosophy and Public Affairs*, 16, 42–72.

O'Neill, Onora (1986). *Faces of Hunger: An Essay on Poverty, Justice and Development*. London: George Allen and Unwin.

—— (1988*a*). "Children's Rights and Children's Lives," *Ethics*, 98, 445–63.

—— (1988*b*). "Ethical Reasoning and Ideological Pluralism," *Ethics*, 98, 705–22.

—— (1989). *Constructions of Reason: Explorations of Kant's Practical Philosophy*. Cambridge: Cambridge University Press.

Pateman, Carole (1988). *The Sexual Contract*. Cambridge: Polity Press.

Pfeffer, Raymond, (1985). "The Responsibility of Men for the Oppression of Women," *Journal of Applied Philosophy*, 2, 217–29.

Postow, B. C. (1978–9). "Economic Dependence and Self-respect," *Philosophical Forum*, 10, 181–201.

Rawls, John (1970). *A Theory of Justice.* Cambridge, Mass.: Harvard University Press.

——— (1985). "Justice as Fairness: Political not Metaphysical," *Philosophy and Public Affairs*, 14, 223–51.

Ruddick, Sara (1987). "Remarks on the Sexual Politics of Reason," in Kittay and Meyers (1987).

——— (1989). "Maternal Thinking," in her *Maternal Thinking: Towards a Politics of Peace.* Boston, Mass: Beacon Press.

Sandel, Michael (1982). *Liberalism and the Limits of Justice.* Cambridge: Cambridge University Press.

Scott, Alison MacEwen (1986). "Industrialization, Gender Segregation and Stratification Theory," in Rosemary Crompton and Michael Mann (eds.), *Gender and Stratification.* Cambridge: Polity Press.

Sen, Amartya K. (1981). *Poverty and Famines: An Essay on Entitlement and Deprivation.* Oxford: Clarendon Press.

——— (1987). *Gender and Cooperative Conflicts.* WIDER Working Paper. Helsinki: World Institute for Development Economics Research.

Shue, Henry (1980). *Basic Rights: Subsistence, Affluence and U.S. Foreign Policy.* Princeton, NJ: Princeton University Press.

——— (1981). "Exporting Hazard," in Brown and Shue (1991).

——— (1984). "The Interdependence of Duties," in Alston and Tomasevski (1984).

Singer, Peter (1972). "Famine, Affluence and Morality," *Philosophy and Public Affairs*, 3, 229–43.

Stiehm, Judith Hicks (1983). "The Unit of Political Analysis: Our Aristotelian Hangover," in Sandra Harding and Merrill B. Hintikka (eds.), *Discovering Reality: Feminist Perspectives on Epistemology, Metaphysics, Methodology and Philosophy of Science.* Dordrecht: Reidel.

Walzer, Michael (1983). *Spheres of Justice: A Defence of Pluralism and Equality.* Oxford: Martin Robertson.

Williams, Bernard (1985). *Ethics and the Limits of Philosophy.* London: Fontana.

# 59   Commentary on Onora O'Neill's "Justice, Gender, and International Boundaries"

## MARTHA NUSSBAUM

Copyright © The United Nations University 1993. Reprinted from *The Quality of Life* edited by Martha Nussbaum and Amartya Sen (1993), 324–335 with omissions, by permission of Oxford University Press.

. . . [A]t least two different general accounts of gender justice seem to be available: an account based, as is O'Neill's, on the test of universalizability of principles, and the question about the consistency of the imagined result; and . . . an approach based on the concept of human functioning and an idea of the human being.

O'Neill's Kantian approach asks us to abstract more or less totally from the content of the lives of the individuals we are asked to imagine, and then to think what universally sharable principles would have to govern their lives with one another, given that they are "numerous, diverse, and nei-

ther ideally rational *nor* ideally independent of one another." By applying the test of universalizability, O'Neill, following Kant, is able to rule out principles that could not consistently be held by all of a plurality of potentially interacting beings. Among these will be various forms of deception and victimization. And if we then look at the actual lives of women in many societies, we will discover, O'Neill argues, that these lives exhibit the bad effects of these non-universalizable principles.

I think that O'Neill puts the case for the Kantian approach as well as it can be put; and she does well in showing how a certain amount of very important ethical content can be generated out of the formal interest in consistency and universalizability. I am impressed by her discussions of exploitation and deception. But I have doubts in the end about how far we can go in moral argument on this issue through an approach so thin on content. (An approach that discourages us from asking some of our most basic and ordinary questions, such as "Who *are* these people? What are they trying to do? What general abilities and circumstances do they have?") These doubts will perhaps be clearer when I have described the other approach, as I understand it.

The approach through an idea of the human being and human functioning urges the parties involved in the argument to ask themselves what aspects of living they consider so fundamental that they could not regard a life as a fully human one without them. Put this way, it is not a request for a matter of metaphysical or biological fact, but a request for a particularly deep and searching kind of evaluative inquiry. This inquiry does abstract, certainly, from many concrete features of actual lives, for it asks us to consider what are the most important things that must turn up in any life that we will be willing to recognize as human. Asking this requires us to abstract from many local features of our lives that are more dispensable, and to explore those areas of life, those functions, that are the basis for our sense of recognition and affiliation, for our judgements of humanness, when we meet other humans from ways of life that are in many respects very different. Frequently this inquiry will be carried on by myth-making and story-telling, in which we imagine beings who are like us in some ways and not in others, asking whether they count for us as human; or in which we imagine transformations, and ask whether the life in question is still a human life or some other sort of life. Several remarks can now be made about the differences between this approach and the Kantian approach.

1. Here, in contrast to the Kantian's focus on the formal characteristics of principles, we are all along talking about content, and the actual living of lives—though at a very general level. This inquiry is, in fact, continuous with a more general inquiry into the quality of life, or what the ancient Greeks (who did much to develop this approach) would have called the question of human flourish-

ing, or the good life for a human being. It provides some parameters for such an inquiry, by showing us which lives fall altogether beyond the pale of humanness.

2. In this inquiry, much of the important moral work is done by the imagination, and by our deepest emotions about what our imagination produces; in the Kantian approach, by contrast, the work is supposed to be done by the formal notion of consistency, a notion the consideration of which involves the intellect, far more than the imagination or emotions. Kant himself was certainly rather hostile to the role played by emotions in practical judgement; although this may not be a necessary feature of the Kantian approach, it has certainly had a great deal of influence on many modern Kantians.[1]

3. In the approach through the idea of human functioning, we are learning about how we understand ourselves, about our deepest attachments and commitments and the reasons for them. In the Kantian approach, by contrast, we are learning certain things about what rational consistency requires of all rational beings, but (deliberately) not much about the specific sort of rational being we are, or about why we care about what we do care about, consistency included.

4. The approach through human functioning makes it very easy to apprehend the fact that lives may contain conflicting obligations or values. For the stories of human life on which such an approach frequently relies show us how progress in one area of life can bring tensions, and even deficiencies, in other areas—and in general how full the world is of things we care about and ought to honour in action. They lead us, then, to expect that in the course of living well we will face some difficult dilemmas. The Kantian insistence on ethical consistency avoids, and even denies, this. I shall later return to this question.

But so far I have said little about how I think an approach in terms of human functioning would handle the question of women. For many believers in some such approach have been far from feminist. Indeed, they frequently just left women out, claiming that they were not fully-fledged human beings and did not have the capacity for fully human functioning. How, then, does my version of the approach propose to deal with that problem?

I believe that by directing us, first, to look at what is deepest and also most broadly shared in human life in many times and places, and, second, by urging us to do so by using our imaginations, the human functioning approach provides valuable resources for the defender of women's equality. In order to make this clearer I want to offer two examples of such arguments, taken from ancient Greek thought. The two are really, I think, complementary parts of what would be a single process of argument, the one part being more schematic, the other involving a fuller and more concrete exercise of imagination. The examples are an argument from the Stoic treatise "Should Women Too Do Philosophy?" written by Musonius Rufus at Rome in the first century AD; and Aristophanes' great comic play *Lysistrata,* written at Athens in the fifth century BC. It is important to mention at the start that both are radical arguments, in that their conclusions go enormously beyond and dramatically against the norms that were actually recognized by their societies.

The Musonius argument is marvellously simple. It goes like this. Women (he asserts) have, as anyone can see, exactly the same basic faculties as men. Let's go through the list, he now says. Women, as you cannot deny, can see, hear, taste, smell, feel. Furthermore, they can also reason. And on top of this they plainly display a sensitivity to ethical distinctions. So: if you believe that getting a "higher education" that includes some training in philosophical reflection is a good thing for someone with those basic human abilities, then, if you are consistent, you must grant that it is a good thing for women. Musonius now imagines the male interlocutor raising various objections about the consequences of this educational proposal— for example, that it will lead women to sit around talking philosophy rather than getting the house-work done. He dismisses such points as special

pleading. Nobody, he says, should neglect practical duties for philosophical conversation; but this applies as much to men as to women, and cannot therefore be used as the basis for an educational difference.

What this argument does is to get the unreflective interlocutor to look closely at various features of his daily dealings with women, and to admit that he implicitly recognizes, in those dealings, the presence of the list of basic abilities that he believes to be both necessary and sufficient for humanness. He talks to his wife as a reasoning being, and a being sensitive to ethical norms; so how can he consistently deny her what would be good for a reasoning being? By looking at the actual content of her life, with imagination and responsive feeling—and at a rather general level —he comes to recognize what he himself values. Notice that this approach relies on an interest in consistency too, but in a different place: for it asks the interlocutor to examine himself—his statements, his actions, his relations with others—for consistency, thus treating consistency as a regulative part of a larger inquiry into content.[2]

The *Lysistrata* performs a similar job, I think, far more concretely. In Aristophanes' famous comedy about how women end the Peloponnesian War by refusing sex to their husbands,[3] the first thing that happens to the male member of the audience is that he is taken inside the women's quarters of the house, somewhere that might have seemed to him altogether alien and different. (Athenian women rarely left the house, so there were relatively few opportunities for the type of interaction that would have prompted the recognition of female rationality.) What he now finds is that here inside the house, far from the market-place and the assembly with which he would tend to associate the (male) world of reason, practical reasoning is going on, including reasoning about central public issues. This reasoning is carried on with much spirit, and in a morally resourceful way. By the end of the play, it is difficult to see how a sincere member of the audience can have failed to accept the remarkable heroine as a reasoning political being similar to himself, and to grant that such a being has a substantial role to play in the city's political life. The charm and verbal resourcefulness of the drama play a large part in luring the audience in, so that they will recognize what the drama wants them to recognize. As with Musonius, this argument focuses on some very general features of human life, depicting the rest in a fanciful way: it gets us to abstract from other contingencies of current arrangements. Thus it leads us to ask which features are the most essential, to focus on those features, and to realize that women share them.

Of course, like any other sort of moral argument, this sort might not work. This one plainly did not, as any rate not on a large scale, since Athenian women went on living as they had lived, and the war went on as well, with disastrous results. But the failure of a single argument to overcome entrenched resistance does not seem to me to count against it. And on the whole I am inclined to believe that arguments of this sort will get us further, where women are concerned, than formal arguments of the Kantian type. I believe that, with respect to the four differences I have mentioned, the human function arguments probably come out ahead, both in terms of efficacy and in terms of philosophical power.

First, it seems essential to focus on *content* as these arguments do—because the actual doings and beings of people seem to be what we have to talk about here, not just what traffic rules will police their doings and beings. Indeed, it seem hard to say anything meaningful about traffic rules until we know who the parties are and what they are doing. Second, we need to rely upon the faculties on which these arguments rely—for the imagination of ways of life seems to be a faculty absolutely indispensable for the full and fully rational investigation of these and other questions concerning deprived people. Both imagination and emotions are necessary to the full recognition of what, in the end, we need to recognize in these cases: that this is a human life before me, and not merely a thing.[4] Third, it seems vital to promote self-understanding as these arguments do. At the conclusion of this sort of argument, we understand more than we do at the conclusion of a for-

mal argument, for we understand why certain things matter to us, how much they matter, how this grounds our relations with others, and so forth. Finally, this approach, and not the other, prepares us for a just appreciation of the problem of conflict among values.

But before I turn to that problem, I want to mention that I think O'Neill herself actually uses what I would call a human function argument at certain crucial points in her paper: for example, when she asks us to recognize our mutual interdependence, our vulnerability, and our general situation as beings "whose agency and capacities have been formed, perhaps deformed, by unjust institutions." Much of the force in her application of principles to situations comes from such rich though general description of features of human life; and I doubt that the paper would have had the power it does without them. In fact, at one point she insists that one *must* take account of capacities and forms of life in this very general way: "In applying abstract, non-idealizing principles we have to take account not indeed of the actual beliefs, ideals, or categories of others, which may reflect unjust traditions, but of others' actual *capacities* and *opportunities* to act—and their incapacities and lack of opportunities." She suggests that this sort of reflection is necessary only in applying principles and not in formulating them. But in some of her concrete arguments it seems an important part of her scrutiny of principles. So I conclude that her approach is actually a mixed approach, which, as such, may be able to surmount many of the difficulties I have raised here for the Kantian approach. . . .

It seems plain that when you value a plurality of different goods, all of which are taken to make a non-homogeneous contribution to the goodness of a life, then you will discover, either more or less often, depending on how you live, that you are faced with a situation in which you cannot satisfy the demands of all the things to which you are committed. This is not just a women's problem, of course; but it is a problem that has been recognized and felt more prominently, on the whole (in certain areas of life at least), by women than by men.

There seem to be two reasons for this. First, women frequently try to combine a plurality of commitments—especially commitments to both work and family—that men less frequently try to combine. If we put the problem that way, it is, I think, a plus for women. For if you believe, as I do, that caring for your family and/or children and doing some form of valued work are both important functions in most human lives, male and female, then it is better to recognize that fact and to feel the associated conflicts than to deny the fact (for example, by simply neglecting your children) and to have an apparently conflict-free existence (one that avoids recognition of the conflicts).

The second reason such conflicts are an especially acute problem for women is, however, a negative one: societies have, on the whole, given women relatively little help in managing the conflicts they face, and men far more help. A good system of public child care would simply eliminate some, though not all, of the conflicts women face in this sphere. (And of course this would also be a great advantage for *men* who face those conflicts.) While I do think that some level of conflict, or at any rate the permanent risk of conflict, is an inevitable concomitant of any human life that is plainly rich in value,[5] there is no reason why society should not alleviate this situation by arranging things so that conflict-producing situations arise more rarely.

A serious difficulty I have with O'Neill's Kantian approach is that it gives us no direction as to how to face such conflicts. Kant himself famously, or infamously, invoked his own idea of practical consistency in order to deny that there are any such conflicts.[6] O'Neill is far too sensitive, and sensible, to do this. But to test the acceptability of an arrangement as she does, by testing for consistency, does raise a problem. What sort of consistency are we looking for, and what guidance do we get about what sort is the right sort, and how much enough? I think the human function approach does far better, by instructing us to imagine the various components of a life, both singly and in various combinations, so that we will naturally come to understand how richness of life brings dilemmas and tensions, how the distinct-

ness of each valuable thing imports a possibility of disharmony.

. . . Living well as a human being has a plurality of distinct components, none of them reducible to the others—a fact that any approach in terms of a single quantitative scale simply obscures from view. This aspect of human life is well represented in the polytheism of ancient Greek religion. For this religion tells us, in effect, that there are many spheres of human living that claim our commitment, and commitment to which makes us the beings we are; we ought to honour all of those spheres—including political life, the arts, love, reasoning, the earth on which we live. And it tells us, as well, that these gods, so to speak, do not always agree; that frequently a devotion to one will risk offence against another, so we are faced with many difficult choices.[7] That, none the less, the quality of any individual life, and also of any city or country's life, will be measured by and on all of these distinct dimensions, so that we can neither simply leave some out nor treat them as commensurable by some single quantitative scale.

This is a human problem, not just a women's problem. But right now it is in most societies particularly a women's problem, both because of the institutional neglect of which I have spoken, and also because women have been insisting that there are, for human life, more "gods," so to speak, than anyone might have thought—affiliation as well as autonomy, the care of the family as well as independent work. My own view is that the resulting conception, while more prone to conflict, is a richer and more adequate conception of the quality of life. Richer because the components are more numerous and more diverse; richer, too, because, while the diverse component activities sometimes get in one another's way, they equally or more often provide mutual illumination and enhancement—as the love of individuals in the family gives citizenship a new depth of understanding, as personally satisfying work gives new vitality to the care of the family. In this way, the experience of women should be viewed not simply as a source of many bad examples of social injustice and difficult problems of social arrangement—though of course we must continue to stress that aspect—but also as a source of certain sorts of insight and aspiration, as we try to arrive at an adequate conception of the quality of life.

## Notes

1. This is especially clear in Rawls (1971), where a conception of "considered judgement" is employed that rules out judgements made under emotional influence. For discussion and criticism of this, see Nussbaum (1990*a*); Richardson (forthcoming).

2. For further discussion of Musonius, see Nussbaum (1987*a*); the treatise is not generally available in translation. For further discussion of Stoic views of women, see Foucault (1984) and de Sainte Croix (1981). On the relationship of arguments of this type of the Socratic elenchus, see my comment on Charles Taylor, with references.

3. For an authoritative discussion of the play, see Henderson (1987); on the position of women in ancient Athens, see Pomeroy (1975), Lefkowitz and Fant (1982).

4. In this connection, Seneca (Moral Epistle 108) makes a spirited defence of literature as an essential source of ethical reflection. He argues that literary language and the structures of dramatic plots make ethical meanings more vivid and forceful, so that they appeal to the imagination, producing moral progress through self-recognition. (Note that like most Stoic thinkers Seneca, with great plausibility, thinks of the emotions as cognitive and selective, not merely animal urges. For discussion and defence of this view, see Nussbaum (1987*b*, 1990*a*).)

5. See Nussbaum (1986*a*: chs. 2–3; 1989).

6. Kant's views are presented in the introduction to the *Metaphysics of Morals:* see Kant (1797).

7. See Nussbaum (1986*a*: chs. 2–3).

## References

Chen, M. (1987). *A Quiet Revolution: Women in Transition in Rural Bangladesh* (Dhaka: BRAC).

De Sainte Croix, G.E.M. (1981). *The Class Struggle in the Ancient Greek World.* London: Duckworth.

Foucault, M. (1984). *The History of Sexuality,* iii, trans. R. Hurley. New York: Pantheon.

Gilligan, C. (1982). *In a Different Voice: Psychological Theory and Women's Dependence.* Cambridge, Mass.: Harvard University Press.

Henderson, J. (1987). *Aristophanes: Lysistrata* (edition and commentary). Oxford: Clarendon Press.

Kant, Immanuel. (1797). *The Metaphysical Elements of Justice.* Part I of *The Metaphysics of Morals,* trans. J. Ladd. Indianapolis: Bobbs Merrill, 1965.

Lefkowitz, M., and Fant, M. (eds.) (1982). *Women's Life in Greece and Rome.* Baltimore, Md.: Johns Hopkins University Press.

Martin, Jane Roland (1985). *Reclaiming a Conversation.* New Haven: Yale University Press.

Nussbaum, M. (1986*a*). *The Fragility of Goodness: Luck and Ethics in Greek Tragedy and Philosophy.* Cambridge: Cambridge University Press.

—— (1986*b*). Review of Martin (1985). *New York Review of Books,* 30 Jan.

—— (1987*a*). "Undemocratic Vistas." Review of Allan Bloom, *The Closing of the American Mind. New York Review of Books,* 5 Nov.

—— (1987*b*). "The Stoics on the Extirpation of the Passions," *Apeiron,* 20, 129–77.

—— (1988*a*). "Nature, Function, and Capability: Aristotle on Political Distribution," *Oxford Studies in Ancient Philosophy,* suppl. vol., 145–84.

—— (1988*b*). "Non-Relative Virtues: An Aristotelian Approach," *Midwest Studies in Philosophy,* 13. A revised and expanded version appears in this volume.

—— (1989). "Tragic Dilemmas," *Radcliffe Quarterly* (Mar.).

—— (1990*a*). *Love's Knowledge: Essays on Philosophy and Literature.* New York and Oxford: Oxford University Press.

—— (1990*b*). "Aristotelian Social Democracy," in G. Mara and H. Richardson (eds.), *Liberalism and the Good.* New York: Routledge, Chapman, and Hall, 203–52.

—— (1995). "Aristotle on Human Nature and the Foundations of Ethics," in a *World, Mind, and Ethics,* volume in honour of Bernard Williams, ed. J. Altham and P. Harrison Cambridge: Cambridge University Press.

O'neill, O. (Onora Nell) (1975). *Acting on Principle: An Essay on Kantian Ethics.* New York: Columbia University Press.

—— (1986). *Faces of Hunger. An Essay on Poverty, Justice, and Development.* London: George Allen and Unwin.

—— (1990). *Collected Essays on Moral Philosophy.* Cambridge: Cambridge University Press.

Pomeroy, S. (1975). *Goddesses, Whores, Wives, and Slaves: Women in Classical Antiquity.* New York: Schocken Books.

Putnam, H. (1987). *The Many Faces of Realism.* LaSalle, Ill.: Open Court.

Rawls, J. (1971). *A Theory of Justice.* Cambridge, Mass.: Harvard University Press.

Richardson, H. (forthcoming). "The Emotions of Reflective Equilibrium."

Sen, A. (1980). "Equality of What?" in S. McMurrin (ed.), *Tanner Lectures on Human Values,* i. Cambridge: Cambridge University Press. Repr. in Sen (1982).

——— (1982). *Choice, Welfare, and Measurement.* Oxford: Basil Blackwell.

——— (1984). *Resources, Value, and Development.* Oxford: Basil Blackwell.

——— (1985). *Commodities and Capabilities.* Amsterdam: North-Holland.

——— (1987a). *The Standard of Living. Tanner Lectures on Human Values 1985,* ed. G. Hawthorne. Cambridge: Cambridge University Press.

——— (1987b). "Gender and Cooperative Conflicts." WIDER Working Paper. Helsinki: World Institute for Development Economics Research; published in I. Tinker, ed., *Women and World Development* (Oxford 1990).

——— (1992). *Inequality Reexamined.* Oxford, Cambridge, MA, and New York: Clarendon Press, Harvard University Press, and Russell Sage Foundation.

Seneca, L.A. *On Anger (De Ira),* in *L.A. Senecae Dialogorum Libri Duodecim,* ed. L. D. Reynolds. Oxford: Clarendon Press.

——— *Moral Epistles (Epistulae Morales),* ed. L. D. Reynolds. Oxford: Clarendon Press.

# 60  Justice, Gender, and the Family

## SUSAN MOLLER OKIN

## Vulnerability by Marriage

Here, I present and analyze the facts of contemporary gender-structured marriage in the light of theories about power and vulnerability and the issues of justice they inevitably raise. I argue that marriage and the family, as currently practiced in our society, are unjust institutions. They constitute the pivot of a societal system of gender that renders women vulnerable to dependency, exploitation, and abuse. When we look seriously at the distribution between husbands and wives of such critical social goods as work (paid and unpaid), power, prestige, self-esteem, opportunities for self-development, and both physical and economic security, we find socially constructed inequalities between them, right down the list. . . .

Nevertheless, as we shall see, in crucial respects gender-structured marriage *involves women in a cycle of socially caused and distinctly asymmetric vulnerability.* The division of labor within marriage (except in rare cases) makes wives far more likely than husbands to be exploited both within the marital relationship and in the world of work outside the home. To a great extent and in numerous ways, contemporary women in our society are *made* vulnerable by marriage itself. They are first set up for vulnerability during their developing years by their personal (and socially reinforced) expectations that they will be the primary caretakers of children, and that in fulfilling this role they will need to try to attract and to keep the economic support of a man, to whose work life they will be expected to give priority. They are rendered vulnerable by the actual division of labor within almost all current marriages. They are disadvantaged at work by the fact that the world of wage work, including the professions, is still largely structured around the assumption that "workers" have wives at home. They are rendered far more vulnerable if they become the primary caretakers of children, and their vulnerability peaks if their marriages dissolve and they become single parents. . . .

## Vulnerability by Anticipation of Marriage

As the women Kathleen Gerson recently studied looked back on their girlhood considerations about the future, virtually all of them saw themselves as confronting a choice: *either* domesticity and motherhood *or* career.[1] Given the pervasiveness of sex-role socialization (including the mixed or negative messages that girls are often given about their future work lives), the actual obstacles

Reprinted with permission of the publisher from *Justice, Gender, and the Family* by Susan Moller Okin, 135–186, with omissions. Copyright © 1989 by Basic Books, Inc. a subsidiary of Perseus Books Group, LLC.

that our social structures place in the way of working mothers, and the far greater responsibility, both psychological and practical, that is placed on mothers than on fathers for their children's welfare, it is not surprising that these women perceived a conflict between their own work interests and the interests of any children they might have.[2] While many reacted against their own mothers' domestic lives, very few were able to imagine successfully combining motherhood with a career. And those who did generally avoided confronting the dilemmas they would have to face.[3] But most grew up with the belief that "a woman can have either a career or children, but not both."[4] Not surprisingly, many of them, assuming that they would want to have children, followed educational and work paths that would readily accommodate the demands of being a primary parent. The only way that those who were career-oriented came to believe that they might avoid the difficult choice, and even attempt to combine their work with mothering, was by deciding to be trailblazers, rejecting strongly ingrained beliefs about the incompatibility of the two.

Needless to say, such a choice does not confront boys in their formative years. *They* assume—reasonably enough, given our traditions and present conditions and beliefs—that what is expected of them as husbands and fathers is that, by developing a solid work life, they will provide the primary financial support of the family. Men's situation can have its own strains, since those who feel trapped at work cannot opt for domesticity and gain as much support for this choice as a woman can.[5] For those who become unemployed, the conflict of their experience with society's view of the male as provider can be particularly stressful. But boys do not experience the dilemma about work and family that girls do as they confront the choices that are crucial to their educations, future work lives and opportunities, and economic security.

When women envisage a future strongly influenced by the demands on them as wives and particularly as mothers, they are likely to embark on traditionally female fields of study and/or occupational paths. The typical route for women is still to finish their education with high school and to marry and have children in their early twenties, though a growing minority are continuing their education, establishing themselves in careers, and marrying later.[6] Some of those who are primarily family-oriented foresee their wage work as temporary or intermittent, while some envisage trying to combine some continued work in the marketplace with traditionally female family responsibilities. But whether such women enter clerical, sales, or service work, or train for one of the predominantly female professions such as teaching or nursing, they are heading not only for the relatively more flexible hours or greater replaceability that most of these jobs afford but also for low pay, poor working conditions, and, above all, blocked mobility. In 1987, women who worked year-round at full-time jobs earned a median wage of $15,704—71 percent of the $22,204 earned by full-time working men.[7] The fact that women's educational achievement is becoming equal to men's, through the level of master's degrees, is clearly affecting women's *participation* in the work force).[8] But, though it could also potentially affect their earnings relative to men's, it has done so very little up to now, in part because the professional and service occupations that are more than two-thirds female—such as education, humanities, home economics, library science, and health science—are far worse paid than those that are still more than two-thirds male—such as science and engineering.[9] Occupational sex segregation cancels out women's educational advances: in 1985, the average full-time working white woman with a college degree or higher earned $2,000 less than the average white man who had only a high-school diploma; and the average black woman with some college education earned slightly less than the average white man who had only an elementary school education.[10]

Regardless of educational achievement, women are far more likely than men to work in administrative support jobs, as a secretary, typist, or bookkeeper, for example, which in most cases hold no prospects for advancement. Almost 30 percent of employed women worked in this category in 1985, compared with fewer than 6 percent of men.[11] . . . It is no wonder, then, that most women are, even before marriage, in an economic position that sets them up to become more vulnerable during marriage, and most vulnerable of all if their marriage ends and—unprepared as they are —they find themselves in the position of having to provide for themselves and their children.

## Vulnerability within Marriage

Marriage continues the cycle of inequality set in motion by the anticipation of marriage and the related sex segregation of the workplace. Partly because of society's assumptions about gender, but also because women, on entering marriage, tend already to be disadvantaged members of the work force, married women are likely to start out with less leverage in the relationship than their husbands. As I shall show, answers to questions such as whose work life and work needs take priority, and how the unpaid work of the family will be allocated—if they are not simply assumed to be decided along the lines of sex difference, but are live issues in the marriage—are likely to be strongly influenced by the differences in earning power between husbands and wives. In many marriages, partly because of discrimination at work and the wage gap between the sexes, wives (despite initial personal ambitions and even when they are full-time wage workers) come to perceive themselves as benefiting from giving priority to their husbands' careers. Hence they have little incentive to question the traditional division of labor in the household. This in turn limits their own commitment to wage work and their incentive and leverage to challenge the gender structure of the workplace. Experiencing frustration and lack of control at work, those who thus turn toward domesticity, while often resenting the lack of respect our society gives to full-time mothers, may see the benefits of domestic life as greater than the costs.[12] . . .

**Predominantly Houseworking Wives.**  When a woman is a full-time housewife—as are about two-fifths of married women in the United States who live with their husbands—she does less total work, on average, than her employed husband: 49.3 hours per week, compared with his 63.2. This is also true of couples in which the wife works part-time (defined as fewer than thirty hours per week, including commuting time), though the average difference per week is reduced to eight hours in this case.[13] This is, of course, partly because housework is less burdensome than it was before the days of labor-saving devices and declining fertility. Not surprisingly, however, during the early years of child rearing, a nonemployed wife (or part-time employed wife) is likely to work about the same total number of hours as her employed husband. But the *quantity* of work performed is only one of a number of important variables that must be considered in order for us to assess the justice or injustice of the division of labor in the family, particularly in relation to the issue of the cycle of women's vulnerability.

In terms of the quality of work, there are considerable disadvantages to the role of housewife.[14] One is that much of the work is boring and/or unpleasant. Surveys indicate that most people of both sexes do not like to clean, shop for food, or do laundry, which constitute a high proportion of housework. Cooking rates higher, and child care even higher, with both sexes, than other domestic work.[15] In reality, this separation of tasks is strictly hypothetical, at least for mothers, who are usually cleaning, shopping, doing laundry, and cooking at the same time as taking care of children. Many wage workers, too, do largely tedious and repetitive work. But the housewife-mother's work has additional disadvantages. One is that her hours of work are highly unscheduled; unlike virtually any other worker except the holder of a high political office, she can be called on at any time of the day or night, seven days a week. Another is that she cannot, nearly as easily as most other workers, change jobs. Her family comes to depend on *her* to do all the things she does. Finding substitutes is difficult and expensive, even if the housewife is not discouraged or forbidden by her husband to seek paid work. The skills and experience she has gained are not valued by prospective employers. Also, once a woman has taken on the role of housewife, she finds it extremely difficult, for reasons that will be explored, to shift part of this burden back onto her husband. Being a housewife thus both impairs a woman's ability to support herself and constrains her future choices in life.[16]

Many of the disadvantages of being a housewife spring directly or indirectly from the fact that all her work is unpaid work, whereas more than four-fifths of her husband's total work is paid work. This may at first seem a matter of little importance. If wives, so long as they stay married, usually share their husbands' standards of living for the most part, why should it matter who earns the income? It matters a great deal, for many reasons. In the highly money-oriented society we live in, the housewife's work is devalued. In fact, in spite of the fact that a major part of it consists of the nurturance and socialization of the next generation of citizens, it is frequently not even acknowledged as work or as productive, either at the personal or at the policy level. This both affects the predominantly houseworking wife's power and influence within the family and means that her social status depends largely upon her husband's, a situation that she may not consider objectionable so long as the marriage lasts, but that is likely to be very painful for her if it does not.[17]

Also, although married couples usually share material well-being, a housewife's or even a part-time working wife's lack of access to much money of her own can create difficulties that range from the mildly irritating through the humiliating to the devastating, especially if she does not enjoy a good relationship with her husband. Money is the subject of most conflict for married couples, although the issue of housework may be overtaking it.[18] Bergmann reports that in an informal survey, she discovered that about 20 percent of the housewife-mothers of her students were in the position of continually having to appeal to their husbands for money. The psychological effects on an adult of economic dependence can be great. As Virginia Woolf pointed out fifty years ago, any man who has difficulty estimating them should simply imagine himself depending on his wife's income.[19] The dark side of economic dependence is also indicated by the fact that, in the serious predivorce situation of having to fight for their

future economic well-being, many wives even of well-to-do men do not have access to enough cash to pay for the uncovering and documentation of their husband's assets.

At its (not so uncommon) worst, the economic dependence of wives can seriously affect their day-to-day physical security. As Linda Gordon has recently concluded: "The basis of wife-beating is male dominance—not superior physical strength or violent temperament . . . but social, economic, political, and psychological power. . . . Wife-beating is the chronic battering of a person of inferior power who for that reason cannot effectively resist."[20] Both wife abuse and child abuse are clearly exacerbated by the economic dependence of women on their husbands or cohabiting male partners. Many women, especially full-time housewives with dependent children, have no way of adequately supporting themselves, and are often in practice unable to leave a situation in which they and/or their children are being seriously abused. In addition to increasing the likelihood of the more obvious forms of abuse—physical and sexual assault—the fear of being abandoned, with its economic and other dire consequences, can lead a housewife to tolerate infidelity, to submit to sexual acts she does not enjoy, or experience psychological abuse including virtual desertion.[21] The fact that a predominantly houseworking wife has no money of her own or a small paycheck is not necessarily significant, but it can be very significant, especially at crucial junctures in the marriage.

Finally, as I shall discuss, the earnings differential between husband and housewife can become devastating in its significance for her and for any dependent children in the event of divorce (which in most states can now occur without her consent). This fact, which significantly affects the relative potential of wives and husbands for exit from the marriage, is likely to influence the distribution of power, and in turn paid and unpaid work, *during* the marriage as well.

**Predominantly Wage-Working Wives and Housework.** Despite the increasing labor force participation of married women, including mothers, "working wives still bear almost all the responsibility for housework." They do less of it than housewives, but "they still do the vast bulk of what needs to be done," and the difference is largely to be accounted for not by the increased participation of men, but by lowered standards, the participation of children, purchased services such as restaurant or frozen meals, and, in elite groups, paid household help. Thus, while the distribution of paid labor between the sexes is shifting quite considerably onto women, that of unpaid labor is not shifting much at all, and "the couple that shares household tasks equally remains rare."[22] The differences in total time spent in all "family work" (housework and child care plus yard work, repairs, and so on) vary considerably from one study to another, but it seems that fully employed husbands do, *at most,* approximately half as much as their fully employed wives, and some studies show a much greater discrepancy.

Bergmann reports that "husbands of wives with full-time jobs averaged about two minutes more housework per day than did husbands in housewife-maintaining families, hardly enough additional time to prepare a soft-boiled egg."[23] Even unemployed husbands do much less housework than wives who work a forty-hour week. Working-class husbands are particularly vocal about not being equal partners in the home, and do little housework. In general, however, a husband's income and job prestige are *inversely* related to his involvement in household chores, unless his wife is employed in a similarly high-paid and prestigious job. Many husbands who profess belief in sharing household tasks equally actually do far less than their wives, when time spent and chores done are assessed. In many cases, egalitarian attitudes make little or no difference to who actually does the work, and often "the idea of shared responsibility turn[s] out to be a myth."[24]

Some scholars are disinclined to perceive these facts as indicating unequal power or exploitation. They prefer to view them as merely embodying adherence to traditional patterns, or to justify them as efficient in terms of the total welfare of the family (the husband's time being too valuable to spend doing housework).[25] There are clear indications, however, that the major reason

that husbands and other heterosexual men living with wage-working women are not doing more housework is that *they do not want to, and are able, to a very large extent, to enforce their wills.* How do we know that the unequal allocation of housework is not equally women's choice? First, because most people do not like doing many of the major household chores. Second, because almost half of wage-working wives who do more than 60 percent of the housework say that they would prefer their husbands to do more of it.[26] Third, because husbands with higher salaries and more prestigious jobs than their wives (the vast majority of two-job couples) are in a powerful position to resist their wives' appeal to them to do more at home, and it is husbands with the highest prestige who do the least housework of all. Even when there is little conflict, and husbands and wives seem to agree that the woman should do more of the housework, they are often influenced by the prevailing idea that whoever earns less or has the less prestigious job should do more unpaid labor at home. But since the maldistribution of wages and jobs between the sexes in our society is largely out of women's control, even *seemingly nonconflictual* decisions made on this basis cannot really be considered fully voluntary on the part of wives.[27] Finally, the resistance of most husbands to housework is well documented, as is the fact that the more housework men do, the more it becomes a cause of fighting within couples. . . .

The constraints placed on wives as workers are strengthened by the fact that many full-time employers assume, in innumerable ways, that "someone" is at home at least part-time during the day to assume primary responsibility for children. The traditional or quasi-traditional division of labor is clearly assumed in the vast discrepancy between normal full-time working hours and children's school hours and vacations. It is assumed by the high degree of geographical mobility required by many higher-level management positions. It is also implicit in the structure of the professions, in which the greatest demands are placed on workers at the very peak of the child-rearing years. Academia and the law are two clear examples; both tenure and partnership decisions are typically made for a person between the ages of thirty and thirty-five, with obvious discriminatory implications for the professional parent (almost always a woman) who does not have a partner willing to assume the major responsibility for children.

Because the structure of most wage work is inconsistent with the parenting responsibilities chiefly borne by women, far fewer women (especially married women) than men *do* work full-time. Only 27 percent of all wives in families with children worked full-time year-round in 1984, compared with 77 percent of husbands.[28] Some mothers conclude that, given the demands of their work, the only reasonable answer to the needs of their children is to take time out of the workplace altogether. Others work part-time. But the repercussions of either of these choices, given the current structure and attitudes of the workplace, are often serious and long-lasting. The investment in career assets is by far the most valuable property owned by most couples. To the extent that wives work part-time or intermittently, their own career potential atrophies, and they become deeply dependent on their husbands' career assets. Even when a wife maintains her career, her husband's work needs—in terms of time, freedom from other preoccupations, education and training, and geographical mobility—usually take priority. . . .

Blumstein and Schwartz's study establishes quite decisively that "in three out of four of the types of couples . . . studied [all types except lesbian couples], . . . the amount of money a person earns—in comparison with a partner's income—establishes relative power."[29] Given that even the 26 percent of all wives who work full-time earn, on average, only 63 percent as much as the average full-time working husband, and the average wife who works for pay (full- or part-time) earns only 42 percent as much, it is therefore not at all surprising that male dominance is far more common than female dominance in couples who deviate from a relatively egalitarian distribution of power.[30] When women are employed, and especially when their earnings approach those of their husbands, they are more likely to share decision-making power equally with their husbands and to have greater financial autonomy. In marriages in

which the husband earned over $8,000 more than the wife (more than half the marriages in the Blumstein and Schwartz sample), the husband was rated as more powerful (as opposed to an equal sharing of power or to the wife's being more powerful) in 33 percent of cases. In marriages in which the incomes of husband and wife were approximately equal, only 18 percent of the husbands were rated as more powerful. The workplace success of wives, then, helps considerably to equalize the balance of power within their marriages and gains them greater respect from their husbands, who often have little respect for housework. Success at work, moreover, can reduce the expectation that a wife will do the vast bulk of family work.[31] Nevertheless, the full-time employment, and even the equal or greater earnings, of wives do not guarantee them equal power in the family, for the male-provider *ideology* is sometimes powerful enough to counteract these factors.[32]

Given these facts about the way power is distributed in the family, and the facts brought out earlier about the typical contentiousness of the issue of housework, it is not difficult to see how the vulnerability of married women in relation to the world of work and their inequality within the family tend to form part of a vicious cycle. Wives are likely to start out at a disadvantage, because of both the force of the traditions of gender and the fact that they are likely to be already earning less than their husbands at the time of marriage. In many cases, the question of who is responsible for the bulk of the unpaid labor of the household is probably not raised at all, but *assumed,* on the basis of these two factors alone. Because of this "nondecision" factor, studies of marital power that ask only about the respective influence of the partners over *decisions* are necessarily incomplete, since they ignore distributions of burdens and benefits that may not be perceived as arising from decisions at all.[33]

However, there *is* often conflict about how much time each partner should devote to wage work and how much to family work. This may include disagreement over the issue of whether the wife should have a job at all, whereas this is almost always taken for granted (a "nondecision") in the case of the husband. Since the partner whose wage work is given priority and who does far less unpaid family work is likely to increase the disparity between his and his spouse's earnings, seniority, and work status, his power in the family will tend to grow accordingly. Hence if, as is likely, he wishes to preserve a traditional or semi-traditional division of labor in the family, he is likely to be able to do so. This need not involve constant fighting, with the man always winning; his "man" power and his earning power combined may be so preeminent that the issue is never even raised. Either way, his wife is likely to find it difficult to reallocate the family work so as to make him responsible for more of it so that she can take a job or expend more time and energy on the one she has. In addition, the weight of tradition and of her own sex-role socialization will contribute to her powerlessness to effect change. . . .

## Vulnerability by Separation or Divorce

There is now little doubt that, while no-fault divorce does not appear to have caused the increasing rate of divorce, it has considerably affected the economic outcome of divorce for both parties.[34] Many studies have shown that whereas the average economic status of men improves after divorce, that of women and children deteriorates seriously. Nationwide, the per-capita income of divorced women, which was only 62 percent that of divorced men in 1960, decreased to 56 percent by 1980.[35] The most illuminating explanation of this is Lenore Weitzman's recent pathbreaking study, *The Divorce Revolution*. Based on a study of 2,500 randomly selected California court dockets between 1968 and 1977 and lengthy interviews with many lawyers, judges, legal experts, and 228 divorced men and women, the book both documents and explains the differential social and economic impact of current divorce law on men, women, and children. Weitzman presents the striking finding that in the first year after divorce, the average standard of living of divorced men, adjusted for household

size, increases by 42 percent while that of divorced women falls by 73 percent. . . .

The basic reason for this is that the courts are now treating divorcing men and women more or less as equals. Divorcing men and women are not, of course, equal, both because the two sexes are not treated equally in society and, as we have seen, because typical, gender-structured marriage makes women socially and economically vulnerable. The treatment of unequals as if they were equals has long been recognized as an obvious instance of injustice. In this case, the injustice is particularly egregious because the inequality is to such a large extent the result of the marital relationship itself. Nonetheless, that divorce as it is currently practiced in the United States involves such injustice took years to be revealed. There are various discrete parts of this unjust treatment of unequals as if they were equals, and we must briefly examine each of them.

The first way in which women are unequally situated after divorce is that they almost always continue to take day-to-day responsibility for the children. The increased rate of divorce has especially affected couples between the ages of twenty-five and thirty-nine—those most likely to have dependent children. And in approximately 90 percent of cases, children live with mothers rather than fathers after divorce. This is usually the outcome preferred by both parents. Relatively few fathers seek or are awarded sole custody, and in cases of joint custody, which are increasing in frequency, children still tend to live mainly with their mothers. Thus women's postdivorce households tend to be larger than those of men, with correspondingly larger economic needs, and their work lives are much more limited by the needs of their children.[36]

Second, as Weitzman demonstrates, no-fault divorce laws, by depriving women of power they often exerted as the "innocent" and less willing party to the divorce, have greatly reduced their capacity to achieve an equitable division of the couple's tangible assets. Whereas the wife (and children) typically used to be awarded the family home, or more than half of the total tangible assets of the marriage, they are now doing much worse in this respect. . . . Whether what is supposed to be happening is the "equal" division of property, as in the community property states, or the "equitable" division, as in the common law states, what is in fact happening is neither equal nor equitable. This is partly because even when the division of *tangible* property is fairly equal, what is in fact most families' principal asset is largely or entirely left out of the equation. This leads us to the third component of injustice in the current practice of divorce.[37]

As we have seen, most married couples give priority to the husband's work life, and wives, when they work for wages, earn on average only a small fraction of the family income, and perform the great bulk of the family's unpaid labor. The most valuable economic asset of a typical marriage is not any tangible piece of property, such as a house (since, if there is one, it is usually heavily mortgaged). In fact, "the average divorcing couple has less than $20,000 in net worth." By far the most important property acquired in the average marriage is its career assets, or human capital, the vast majority of which is likely to be invested in the husband. As Weitzman reports, it takes the average divorced man only about *ten months* to earn as much as the couple's entire net worth.[38] The importance of this marital asset is hard to overestimate, yet it has only recently begun to be treated in some states as marital property for the purposes of divorce settlements.[39] Even if "marital property" as traditionally understood is divided evenly, there can be no equity so long as this crucial piece is left in the hands of the husband alone. Except for the wealthy few who have significant material assets, "support awards that divide income, especially future income, are the most valuable entitlements awarded at divorce."[40] . . .

But, particularly now that one in two marriages is expected to end in divorce, it is simply unrealistic to suggest that the threat of exit is absent, especially at times of marital conflict, or that the different abilities of spouses implicitly or explicitly to call on this threat are not likely to affect power and influence in the relationship. Ending a marriage usually causes pain and dislocation for both adults as well as for any children involved. However, the argument presented in this chapter has demonstrated clearly that, in all the ways that are affected by economic deprivation, women and children are likely to suffer considerably more than men from marital dissolution. It is highly probably that most wives, well aware of this fact, take it into consideration in deciding how firm a stand to take on, or even whether to raise, important issues that are likely to be conflictual. We cannot adequately understand the distribution of power in the family without taking this factor into account, and the idea that marriage is a just relationship of mutual vulnerability cannot survive this analysis.

If we are to aim at making the family, our most fundamental social grouping, more just, we must work toward eradicating the socially created vulnerabilities of women that stem from the division of labor and the resultant division of power within it. . . .

## Toward a Humanist Justice

I shall argue here that any just and fair solution to the urgent problem of women's and children's vulnerability must encourage and facilitate the equal sharing by men and women of paid and unpaid work, of productive and reproductive labor. We must work toward a future in which all will be likely to choose this mode of life. A just future would be one without gender. In its social structures and practices, one's sex would have no more relevance than one's eye color or the length of one's toes. No assumptions would be made about "male" and "female" roles; childbearing would be so conceptually separated from child rearing and other family responsibilities that it would be a cause for surprise, and no little concern, if men and women were not equally responsible for domestic life or if children were to spend much more time with one parent than the other. It would be a future in which men and women participated in more or less equal numbers in every sphere of life, from infant care to different kinds of paid work to high-level politics. Thus it would no longer be the case that having no experience of raising children would be the practical prerequisite for attaining positions of the greatest social influence. Decisions about abortion and rape, about divorce settlements and sexual harassment, or about any other crucial social issues would not be made, as they often are now, by legislatures and benches of judges overwhelmingly populated by men whose power is in large part due to their advantaged position in the gender structure. If we are to be at all true to our democratic ideals, moving away from gender is essential. Obviously, the attainment of such a social world requires major changes in a multitude of institutions and social settings outside the home, as well as within it. . . .

## Moving Away from Gender

First, public policies and laws should generally assume no social differentiation of the sexes. Shared parental responsibility for child care would be both assumed and facilitated. Few people outside of feminist circles seem willing to acknowledge that society does not have to choose between a system of female parenting that renders women and children seriously vulnerable and a system of total reliance on day care provided outside the home. While high-quality day care, subsidized so as to be equally available to all children, certainly constitutes an important part of the response that society should make in order to provide justice for women and children, it is only one part.[41] If we start out with the reasonable assumption that women and men are equally parents of their children, and have equal responsibility for both the unpaid effort that goes into caring for them and their economic support, then we must rethink the demands of work life throughout the period in which a worker of either sex is a parent of a small child. We can no longer cling to the by now largely mythical assumption that every worker has "someone else" at home to raise "his" children.

The facilitation and encouragement of equally shared parenting would require substantial changes.[42] It would mean major changes in the

workplace, all of which could be provided on an entirely (and not falsely) gender-neutral basis. Employers must be required by law not only completely to eradicate sex discrimination, including sexual harassment. They should also be required to make positive provision for the fact that most workers, for differing lengths of time in their working lives, are also parents, and are sometimes required to nurture other family members, such as their own aging parents. Because children are borne by women but can (and, I contend, should) be raised by both parents equally, policies relating to pregnancy and birth should be quite distinct from those relating to parenting. Pregnancy and childbirth, to whatever varying extent they require leave from work, should be regarded as temporarily disabling conditions like any others, and employers should be mandated to provide leave for all such conditions.[43] Of course, pregnancy and childbirth are far *more* than simply "disabling conditions," but they should be treated as such for leave purposes, in part because their disabling effects vary from one woman to another. It seems unfair to mandate, say, eight or more weeks of leave for a condition that disables many women for less time and some for much longer, while *not* mandating leave for illnesses or other disabling conditions. Surely a society as rich as ours can afford to do both.

Parental leave during the postbirth months must be available to mothers and fathers on the same terms, to facilitate shared parenting; they might take sequential leaves or each might take half-time leave. All workers should have the right, without prejudice to their jobs, seniority, benefits, and so on, to work less than full-time during the first year of a child's life, and to work flexible or somewhat reduced hours at least until the child reaches the age of seven. Correspondingly greater flexibility of hours must be provided for the parents of a child with any health problem or disabling condition. The professions whose greatest demands (such as tenure in academia or the partnership hurdle in law) coincide with the peak period of child rearing must restructure their demands or provide considerable flexibility for those of their workers who are also participating parents. Large-scale employers should also be required to provide high-quality on-site day care for children from infancy up to school age. And to ensure equal quality of day care for all young children, *direct government subsidies* (not tax credits, which benefit the better-off) should make up the difference between the cost of high-quality day care and what less well paid parents could reasonably be expected to pay.

There are a number of things that schools, too, must do to promote the minimization of gender. As Amy Gutmann has recently noted, in their present authority structures (84 percent of elementary school teachers are female, while 99 percent of school superintendents are male), "schools do not simply reflect, they perpetuate the social reality of gender preferences when they educate children in a system in which men rule women and women rule children." She argues that, since such sex stereotyping is "a formidable obstacle" to children's rational deliberation about the lives they wish to lead, sex should be regarded as a relevant qualification in the hiring of both teachers and administrators, until these proportions have become much more equal.[44]

An equally important role of our schools must be to ensure in the course of children's education that they become fully aware of the politics of gender. This does not only mean ensuring that women's experience and women's writing are included in the curriculum, although this in itself is undoubtedly important.[45] Its political significance has become obvious from the amount of protest that it has provoked. Children need also to be taught about the present inequalities, ambiguities, and uncertainties of marriage, the facts of workplace discrimination and segregation, and the likely consequences of making life choices based on assumptions about gender. They should be discouraged from thinking about their futures as *determined* by the sex to which they happen to belong. For many children, of course, personal experience has already "brought home" the devastating effects of the traditional division of labor between the sexes. But they do not necessarily come away from this experience with positive

ideas about how to structure their own future family lives differently. As Anita Shreve has recently suggested, "the old home-economics courses that used to teach girls how to cook and sew might give way to the new home economics: teaching girls *and boys* how to combine working and parenting."[46] Finally, schools should be required to provide high-quality after-school programs, where children can play safely, do their homework, or participate in creative activities.

## Protecting the Vulnerable

The pluralism of beliefs and modes of life is fundamental to our society, and the genderless society I have just outlined would certainly not be agreed upon by all as desirable. Thus when we think about constructing relations between the sexes that could be agreed upon in the original position, and are therefore just from all points of view, we must also design institutions and practices acceptable to those with more traditional beliefs about the characteristics of men and women, and the appropriate division of labor between them. It is essential, if men and women are to be allowed to so divide their labor, as they must be if we are to respect the current pluralism of beliefs, that society protect the vulnerable. Without such protection, the marriage contract seriously exacerbates the initial inequalities of those who entered into it, and too many women and children live perilously close to economic disaster and serious social dislocation; too many also live with violence or the continual threat of it. It should be noted here that the rights and obligations that the law would need to promote and mandate in order to protect the vulnerable need not—and should not—be designated in accordance with sex, but in terms of different functions or roles performed. There are only a minute percentage of "househusbands" in this country, and a very small number of men whose work lives take second priority after their wives'. But they can quite readily be protected by the same institutional structures that can protect traditional and quasi-traditional wives, so long as these are designed without reference to sex.

Gender-structured marriage, then, needs to be regarded as a currently necessary institution (because still chosen by some) but one that is socially problematic. It should be subjected to a number of legal requirements, at least when there are children.[47] Most important, there is no need for the division of labor between the sexes to involve the economic dependence, either complete or partial, of one partner on the other. Such dependence can be avoided if both partners have *equal legal entitlement* to all earnings coming into the household. The clearest and simplest way of doing this would be to have employers make out wage checks equally divided between the earner and the partner who provides all or most of his or her unpaid domestic services. In many cases, of course, this would not change the way couples actually manage their finances; it would simply codify what they already agree on—that the household income is rightly shared, because in a real sense jointly earned. Such couples recognize the fact that the wage-earning spouse is no more supporting the homemaking and child-rearing spouse than the latter is supporting the former; the form of support each offers the family is simply different. Such couples might well take both checks, deposit them in a joint account, and really share the income, just as they now do with the earnings that come into the household.

In the case of some couples, however, altering the entitlement of spouses to the earned income of the household as I have suggested *would* make a significant difference. It would make a difference in cases where the earning or higher-earning partner now directly exploits this power, by refusing to make significant spending decisions jointly, by failing to share the income, or by psychologically or physically abusing the nonearning or low-earning partner, reinforced by the notion that she (almost always the wife) has little option but to put up with such abuse or to take herself and her children into a state of destitution. It would make a difference, too, in cases where the higher-earning partner indirectly exploits this earning power in order to perpetuate the existing division of labor in the family. In such instances considerable

changes in the balance of power would be likely to result from the legal and societal recognition that the partner who does most of the domestic work of the family contributes to its well-being just as much, and therefore rightly *earns* just as much, as the partner who does most of the workplace work. . . .

The same fundamental principle should apply to separation and divorce, to the extent that the division of labor has been practiced within a marriage. Under current divorce laws, as we have seen, the terms of exit from marriage are disadvantageous for almost all women in traditional or quasi-traditional marriages. Regardless of the consensus that existed about the division of the family labor, these women lose most of the income that has supported them and the social status that attached to them because of their husband's income and employment, often at the same time as suddenly becoming single parents, and prospective wage workers for the first time in many years. This combination of prospects would seem to be enough to put most traditional wives off the idea of divorcing even if they had good cause to do so. In addition, since divorce in the great majority of states no longer requires the consent of both spouses, it seems likely that wives for whom divorce would spell economic and social catastrophe would be inhibited in voicing their dissatisfactions or needs within marriage. The terms of exit are very likely to affect the use and the power of voice in the ongoing relationship. At worst, these women may be rendered virtually defenseless in the face of physical or psychological abuse. . . .

. . . [I]t seems wholly reasonable to expect a person whose career has been largely unencumbered by domestic responsibilities to support financially the partner who undertook these responsibilities. This support, in the form of combined alimony and child support, should be far more substantial than the token levels often ordered by the courts now. *Both postdivorce households should enjoy the same standard of living.* Alimony should not end after a few years, as the (patronizingly named) "rehabilitative alimony" of today does; it should continue for at least as long as the traditional division of labor in the marriage did and, in the case of short-term marriages that produced children, until the youngest child enters first grade and the custodial parent has a real chance of making his or her own living. After that point, child support should continue at a level that enables the children to enjoy a standard of living equal to that of the noncustodial parent. There can be no reason consistent with principles of justice that some should suffer economically vastly more than others from the breakup of a relationship whose asymmetric division of labor was mutually agreed on. . . .

For those whose response to what I have argued here is the practical objection that it is unrealistic and will cost too much, I have some answers and some questions. Some of what I have suggested would not cost anything, in terms of public spending, though it would redistribute the costs and other responsibilities of rearing children more evenly between men and women. Some policies I have endorsed, such as adequate public support for children whose fathers cannot contribute, may cost more than present policies, but may not, depending on how well they work.[48] Some, such as subsidized high-quality day care, would be expensive in themselves, but also might soon be offset by other savings, since they would enable those who would otherwise be full-time child carers to be at least part-time workers.

All in all, it seems highly unlikely that the *long-term* costs of such programs—even if we count only monetary costs, not costs in human terms—would outweigh the long-term benefits. In many cases, the cycle of poverty could be broken —and children enabled to escape from, or to avoid falling into, it—through a much better early start in life.[49] But even if my suggestions would cost, and cost a lot, we have to ask: How much do we care about the injustices of gender? How much do we care that women who have spent the better part of their lives nurturing others can be discarded like used goods? How ashamed are we that one-quarter of our children, in one of the richest countries in the world, live in poverty? How much do we care that those who raise chil-

dren, *because* of this choice, have restricted opportunities to develop the rest of their potential, and very little influence on society's values and direction? How much do we care that the family, our most intimate social grouping, is often a school of day-to-day injustice? How much do we *want* the just families that will produce the kind of citizens we need if we are ever to achieve a just society?

## Notes

1. Gerson, *Hard Choices,* esp. pp. 136–38.

2. On female socialization, see Nancy Chodorow, *The Reproduction of Mothering* (Berkeley: University of California Press, 1978); Lenore J. Weitzman, "Sex-Role Socialization," in *Women: A Feminist Perspective,* 2nd ed., ed. Jo Freeman (Palo Alto: Mayfield, 1979). On the practical conflicts faced by wage-working mothers, see, for example, Linda J. Beckman, "The Relative Rewards and Costs of Parenthood and Employment for Employed Women," *Psychology of Women Quarterly* 2, no. 3 (1978); Mary Jo Frug, "Securing Job Equality for Women: Labor Market Hostility to Working Mothers," *Boston University Law Review* 59, no. 1 (1979).

3. In Gerson's sample, only 14 percent of the respondents' own mothers had worked during their preschool years, and 46 percent had mothers who had never worked outside the home until their children left (p. 45). On avoidance of the conflict between wage work and motherhood, see Gerson, *Hard Choices,* pp. 64–65.

4. Ibid., p. 137.

5. Moreover, the support that *women* can expect for this choice is now waning. See, for example, Gerson, *Hard Choices,* pp. 77–80, 212.

6. Bianchi and Spain, *American Women,* chaps. 1 and 4.

7. As recently as 1984, full-time working women earned on average $14,780, only 64 percent of men's $23,220. Thus the very recent closing of the gap was as much due to the approximate $1,000 *drop* in the average man's annual wage as to the $1,000 rise in the average woman's. (Sources: *Employment and Earnings,* U.S. Department of Labor, Bureau of Labor Statistics, (Washington D.C.: Government Printing Office, July 1987); U.S. Bureau of the Census, Current Population Reports, Series P–60, no. 149, *Money Income and Poverty Status of Families and Persons in the United States: 1984* (Washington, D.C.: Government Printing Office, 1985), p. 2.

8. In May 1987, 87.7 percent of all women with a college degree were employed, compared with 33.7 percent of women who had not completed high school. Of women

with a college degree, 81.6 percent were employed *full-time,* compared with only 23.6 percent of those who did not complete high school (*Employment and Earnings*).

9. In 1987 (second quarter), men in "service" occupations had an average salary of $15,912, compared with an average of $10,244 for women in "service" occupations; the average man in a "professional specialty" earned $32,552, compared with the average "professional" woman's $23,348 (*Employment and Earnings*).

10. *Women in the American Economy,* Current Population Reports, Special Studies, U.S. Department of Commerce, Bureau of the Census (Washington, D.C.: Government Printing Office, 1986).

11. *Current Population Reports,* Population Profile of the United States 1984–85, U.S. Department of Commerce, Bureau of the Census. Samuel Cohn's recent study of occupational sex-typing examines in detail the feminization of clerical work within two large British firms. He concludes that the discrepancy in job status and rates of pay between the sexes is largely the result of the concentration of women in clerical jobs from which there is virtually no possibility of promotion, and their exclusion from supervisory positions. *The Process of Occupational Sex-Typing* (Philadelphia: Temple University Press, 1985).

12. Gerson, *Hard Choices,* chap. 5 and pp. 130–31.

13. Bergmann, *Economic Emergence,* p. 263, table 11-2, using University of Michigan 1975–76 data. Note that, given Fuch's findings, these figures may well have changed, since women working part-time are likely to be working longer hours.

14. See Bergmann, *Economic Emergence,* chap. 9, "The Job of Housewife." One indicator that the homemaker role involves considerable disadvantages is the extremely small number of men who choose it. Blumstein and Schwartz say that despite recent media interest in house-husbands, "try as we might, . . . we could not find a significant number" of them. "Only 4 of 3,632 husbands describe their work as taking care of the house full-time" (*American Couples,* pp. 146, 561*n*11). Bergmann reports: "In January 1986, 468,000 men were estimated to be out of the workforce because they were 'keeping house,' 22 percent more than in 1980" (*Economic Emergence,* p. 259, citing U.S. Bureau of Labor Statistics, *Employment and Earnings* (February 1986), p. 15. Another factor influencing this, however, as both Blumstein and Schwartz and Gerson note, may be the fact that few married women wish to undertake the full provider role.

15. Bergmann, *Economic Emergence,* p. 267.

16. See Weitzman, *The Divorce Revolution,* esp. pp. xi, 35.

17. See Gerson, *Hard Choices,* pp. 211–12, for a good summary of how "work associated with child rearing and the private sphere has been systematically devalued," and the current effects of this on domestically oriented women. See also Polatnick, "Why Men Don't Rear Children." Studies such as Blumstein and Schwartz's cite examples of husbands using in arguments the fact that their wives do not earn money: "if you're so smart, how come you don't earn anything?" (*American Couples,* pp. 58–59). See Weitzman, *The Divorce Revolution,* pp. 315–16, on divorcing housewives' devaluing of their work, and pp. 334–36, on how their identification by their husbands' social status can lead to a loss of sense of identity by wives after divorce. At the public policy level, the lack of recognition of the economic value of housewives' work is indicated by the fact that housework is included in the GNP only if it is paid work done by a housekeeper. The old story about the parson who lowers the GNP by marrying his housekeeper still holds true, in spite of the fact that it has been estimated that, if it *were* included, unpaid housework done in the industrialized countries would constitute between 25 and 40 percent of the GNP. Debbie Taylor et al., *Women: A World Report* (Oxford: Oxford University Press, 1985).

18. Blumstein and Schwartz say: "Money matters are the most commonly discussed issues among married couples. In study after study, going back several decades, between one quarter and one third of all married couples ranked money as their primary problem" (*American Couples,"* p. 52). Fuchs reports that, according to Morton H. Shaevitz, an expert on gender relations, "Arguments about housework are the leading cause of domestic violence in the United States" (*Women's Quest,* p. 74, citing *Healthcare Forum* 1987, p. 27).

19. Bergmann, *Economic Emergence,* pp. 211–12; Virginia Woolf, *Three Guineas* (London: Harcourt Brace, 1938), p. 110; see also pp. 54–57.

20. Linda Gordon, *Heroes of Their Own Lives* (New York: Viking, 1988), p. 251.

21. Bergmann, *Economic Emergence,* pp. 205–6; Sidel, *Women and Children,* pp. 40–46. See also Lenore Walker, *The Battered Woman* (New York: Harper & Row, 1979). Fears stemming from economic dependence seem to be just beneath the surface, with many housewives, and ready to emerge at the hint of a sympathetic ear. Gerson occasionally reports this (e.g., p. 115), and I have heard the same fears of being left, expressed by acquaintances who are economically dependent wives, since I told them of my work on this book. Chapter 8 of Lillian Rubin's *Worlds of Pain* (New York: Basic Books, 1976) is an excellent source on the effects of the relative powerlessness and dependence of working-class housewives on their unwilling compliance with their husbands' sexual demands. Blumstein and Schwartz discuss at some length the relationship between power and sexual initiation, refusal, consideration of each partner's needs, and satisfaction (*American Couples,* pp. 206–306 passim).

22. See Bergmann, *Economic Emergence,* chap. 11; Bianchi and Spain, *American Women,* pp. 231–40; Blumstein and Schwartz, *American Couples,* pp. 144–48; Gerson, *Hard Choices,* p. 170. Quotations are from Blumstein and Schwartz, p. 144, and Gerson, p. 170. There is broad agreement on this issue, though some studies find that, in

very recent years, male participation in housework and child care appears to be slightly on the rise. Bergmann reports that when some of the couples who participated in the 1975–76 University of Michigan Study were resurveyed in 1981–82, it appeared that "these husbands had increased their contributions by about an hour per week over the six-year interval" (p. 266). On the other hand, she finds that "younger husbands appear to do even less housework than their older counterparts, although neither group of men averages as much as half an hour per day" (p. 264).

23. Bergmann, *Economic Emergence,* p. 263. She defines as "housewife-maintaining" "those families in which the wives devoted five or fewer hours a week to paid employment" (p. 62n). Sharon Y. Nickols and Edward Metzen, in "Impact of Wife's Employment upon Husband's Housework," *Journal of Family Issues* 3 (June 1982), found on the basis of a time-allocation study from 1968 to 1973 that when wives became employed their average hours per week spent in housework dropped from thirty-five to twenty-three, but that their husbands' average contribution stayed at two hours per week.

24. Blumstein and Schwartz, *American Couples,* p. 145. They find that, among full-time employed married couples who profess strongly egalitarian attitudes about housework, 44 percent of wives compared with 28 percent of husbands do more than ten hours of housework per week. Also, some of the examples they cite suggest that the "egalitarianism" of these professed attitudes may be rather superficial; as one wife says of her husband's cleaning the floors and oven: "He takes care of that *for me*" (p. 142, emphasis added). See also Shelley Coverman, "Explaining Husbands' Participation in Domestic Labor," *The Sociological Quarterly* 26, no. 1 (1985); Bianchi and Spain, *American Women,* p. 233.

25. For recent examples, see Becker, *A Treatise on the Family;* and Jonathan Gershuny, *Social Innovation and the Division of Labour* (Oxford: Oxford University Press, 1983), p. 156.

26. Bergmann, *Economic Emergence,* pp. 267–68 and refs., p. 350n9.

27. Blumstien and Schwartz, *American Couples,* pp. 139–54, esp. 151–54. See below on the importance of "nondecisions" in studying power.

28. Ellwood, *Poor Support,* table 5.1, p. 33 (tabulated from U.S. Bureau of the Census Current Population Survey, March 1985).

29. Blumstein and Schwartz, *American Couples,* pp. 53, 52.

30. Bianchi and Spain, *American Women,* p. 202. In 1986, working wives contributed about 28 percent to family income. Congressional Caucus for Women's Issues: *Selected Statistics on Women,* July 1988, p. 3.

31. Blumstein and Schwartz, *American Couples,* pp. 53–93 passim and 139–44. See also Polatnick, "Why Men Don't Rear Children," esp. pp. 23–25.

32. Blumstein and Schwartz, *American Couples,* pp. 56–57.

33. See Peter Bachrach and Morton S. Baratz, "The Two Faces of Power," *American Political Science Review* 56 (1962): 947–52, on the importance of taking account of "nondecisions" when studying the distribution of power. Unfortunately, the phrasing of the question about power that Blumstein and Schwartz posed to their respondents does not allow us to look at nondecisions. It seems very likely, given the strongly gendered traditions of marriage, that many married couples would not have regarded "Who will be the primary parent?" or "Who will do the housework?" as "important decision[s] affecting [the] relationship," since they would not have regarded them as things to be decided at all. An ongoing study includes a question that addresses this issue: *Study of First Years of Marriage* (Survey Research Center, Institute for Social Research, University of Michigan, Ann Arbor; 1986), question D6, p. 28.

34. Bianchi and Spain, *American Women,* p. 26, citing numerous studies. See also James B. McLindon, "Separate But Unequal: The Economic Disaster of Divorce for Women and Children," *Family Law Quarterly* 21, no. 3 (1987). However, cf. Herbert Jacob's dissenting argument in "Another Look at No-Fault Divorce and the Post-Divorce Finances of Women," *Law and Society Review* 23, no. 1 (1989). Beginning with California in 1970, all states except South Dakota now have some form of no-fault divorce law. Twenty-two states still have fault-based divorce as well as no-fault. Most of the pure no-fault states allow unilateral divorce by one party without the consent of the other. Weisman, *The Divorce Revolution,* pp. 41–43, 417–19.

35. Bianchi and Spain, *American Women,* pp. 30–32 and refs., 205–7, 216–18; Gerson, *Hard Choices,* pp. 221–22 and refs. As Bianchi and Spain comment, "although female-maintained families have become more middle-class—at least as indexed by the educational attainment of the householder—their income situation relative to husband-wife households has deteriorated" (p. 207).

36. Weitzman, *The Divorce Revolution,* pp. xiii–xiv and chaps. 8, 9; Blumstein and Schwartz, *American Couples,* pp. 33–34. Gerson says: "Although joint custody arrangements are on the rise, Hacker (1982) reports that the number of divorced fathers with sole custody of their children has actually decreased in the last decade" (*Hard Choices,* p. 221). See also Clair Vickery, "The Time-Poor: A New Look at Poverty," *Journal of Human Resources* 12 (Winter 1977), on the extra time demands on custodial mothers.

37. Weitzman, *The Divorce Revolution,* chap. 4.

38. Ibid., pp. 53, 60.

39. Some changes have been occurring; most states now regard pensions and other retirement benefits as marital assets, but far fewer are viewing other career assets, such as professional degrees, training, or goodwill, this way. Weitzman, *The Divorce Revolution,* p. 47 and chap. 5. See also Doris Jonas Freed and Timothy B. Walker, "Family Law in the Fifty States: An Overview," *Family Law Quarterly* 28, no. 4 (1985): 411–26.

40. Weitzman, *The Divorce Revolution,* p. 61; see also pp. 68–69.

41. It seems reasonable to conclude that the effects of day care on children are probably just as variable as the effects of parenting—that is to say, very widely variable depending on the quality of the day care and of the parenting. There is no doubt that good out-of-home day care is expensive—approximately $100 per full-time week in 1987, even though child-care workers are now paid only about two-thirds as much per hour as other comparably educated women workers (Victor Fuchs, *Women's Quest for Economic Equality* [Cambridge: Harvard University Press, 1988], pp. 137–38). However, it is undoubtedly easier to control its quality than that of informal "family day care." In my view, based in part on my experience of the excellent day-care center that our children attended for a total of seven years, good-quality day care must have small-scale "home rooms" and a high staff-to-child ratio, and should pay staff better than most centers now do. For balanced studies of the effects of day care on a poor population, see Sally Provence, Audrey Naylor, and June Patterson, *The Challenge of Daycare* (New Haven: Yale University Press, 1977); and, most recently, Lisbeth B. Schorr (with Daniel Schorr), *Within Our Reach—Breaking the Cycle of Disadvantage* (New York: Anchor Press, Doubleday, 1988), chap. 8.

42. Much of what I suggest here is not new; it has formed part of the feminist agenda for several decades, and I first made some of the suggestions I develop here in the concluding chapter of *Women in Western Political Thought* (Princeton: Princeton University Press, 1979). Three recent books that address some of the policies discussed here are Fuchs, *Women's Quest*, chap. 7; Philip Green, *Retrieving Democracy: In Search of Civic Equality* (Totowa, N.J.: Rowman and Allanheld, 1985), pp. 96–108; and Anita Shreve, *Remaking Motherhood: How Working Mothers Are Shaping Our Children's Future* (New York: Fawcett Columbine, 1987), pp. 173–78. In Fuchs's chapter he carefully analyzes the potential economic and social effects of alternative policies to improve women's economic status, and concludes that "child-centered policies" such as parental leave and subsidized day care are likely to have more of a positive impact on women's economic position than "labor market policies" such as antidiscrimination, comparable pay for comparable worth, and affirmative action have had and are likely to have. Some potentially very effective policies, such as on-site day care and flexible and/or reduced working hours for parents of young or "special needs" children, seem to fall within both of his categories.

43. The dilemma faced by feminists in the recent California case *Guerra v. California Federal Savings and Loan Association,* 107 S. Ct. 683 (1987) was due to the fact that state law mandated leave for pregnancy and birth and that it did *not* mandate for other disabling conditions. Thus to defend the law seemed to open up the dangers of discrimination that the earlier protection of women in the workplace had resulted in. (For a discussion of this general issue of equality versus difference, see, for example, Wendy W. Williams, "The Equality Crisis: Some Reflections on Culture, Courts, and Feminism," *Women's Rights Law Reporter* 7, no. 3

[1982].) The Supreme Court upheld the California law on the grounds that it treated workers equally in terms of their rights to become parents.

44. Amy Gutmann, *Democratic Education* (Princeton: Princeton University Press, 1987), pp. 112–15; quotation from pp. 113–14. See also Elisabeth Hansot and David Tyack, "Gender in American Public Schools: Thinking Institutionally," *Signs* 13, no. 4 (1988).

45. A classic text on this subject is Dale Spender, eds., *Men's Studies Modified: The Impact of Feminism on the Academic Disciplines* (Oxford: Pergamon Press, 1981).

46. Shreve, *Remaking Motherhood,* p. 237.

47. Mary Ann Glendon has set out a "children first" approach to divorce (Glendon, *Abortion and Divorce,* pp. 94ff.); here I extend the same idea to ongoing marriage, where the arrival of a child is most often the point at which the wife becomes economically dependent.

48. David Ellwood estimates that "if most absent fathers contributed the given percentages, the program would actually save money" (*Poor Support,* p. 169).

49. Schorr's *Within Our Reach* documents the ways in which the cycle of disadvantage can be effectively broken, even for those in the poorest circumstances.

# Questions

1. Govier argues that the Permissive View of welfare is better than the Individualist View and the Puritan View. She uses both Utilitarian and non-Utilitarian arguments. State her arguments. If you disagree with her, explain what is wrong with her arguments.

   If you agree with her, take her view a step further. Govier considers the question of how income should be distributed in an affluent society. Consider now the problem of distributing goods in a non-affluent society. If there are not enough resources to satisfy the basic needs of everyone, what principle should be used to distribute the available resources? That is, what is the fair way of distributing goods in a situation where someone must starve?

2. Compare and contrast any *three* of the following statements. Focus on explaining how each differs from the other two. Describe cases where the principles would prescribe different actions.

   a. Singer: "If it is in our power to prevent something very bad from happening, without thereby sacrificing anything morally significant, we ought, morally, to do it." [P. Singer, "Famine, Affluence, and Morality," *Philosophy and Public Affairs* 1 (1972).]

b. Nozick: "The holdings of a person are just if he is entitled to them by the principles of justice in acquisition and transfer, or by the principle of rectification of injustice."

c. Aristotle: Equals should be treated equally; unequals should be treated proportionately unequally. The virtuous person "will refrain from giving to anybody and everybody, in order that he may have something to give the right amounts to the right people, at the right time, and where it is noble to do so" (81, 1120b).

d. Jesus: "If any one would sue you and take your coat, let him have your cloak as well; and if any one forces you to go one mile, go with him two miles. Give to him who begs from you, and do not refuse him who would borrow from you."

e. O'Neill: "In Kantian moral reasoning, the basis for beneficent action is that we cannot, without it, treat others of limited rationality and autonomy as ends in themselves. This is not to say that Kantian beneficence won't make others happier . . . but that happiness secured by purely paternalistic means, or at the cost of manipulating others' desires, will not count as beneficent in the Kantian picture. . . . Clearly, the alleviation of need must rank far ahead of the furthering of happiness in the Kantian picture. I might make my friends very happy by throwing extravagant parties; but this would probably not increase anybody's possibility for autonomous action to any great extent." [O. O'Neill, "Perplexities of Famine and World Hunger," *Matters of Life and Death*, 2d. ed., ed. T. Regan (New York: Random House, 1980), pp. 326–327.]

f. Mill: "The readiness to [sacrifice one's own happiness in order to serve the happiness of others] is the highest virtue which can be found in man. . . . The utilitarian morality refuses to admit that the sacrifice is itself a good. . . . The happiness which forms the utilitarian standard of what is right in conduct is not the agent's own happiness but that of all concerned. As between his own happiness and that of others, utilitarianism requires him to be as strictly impartial as a disinterested and benevolent spectator" (16).

g. Feinberg: "It seems that the principle of equality (in the version that rests on needs rather than that which requires 'perfect equality') and the principles of contribution and effort (where nonarbitrarily applicable, and only after everyone's basic needs have been satisfied) have the most weight as determinants of economic justice. . . . The reason for the priority of basic needs is that, where there is economic abundance, the claim to life itself and to minimally decent conditions are, like other human rights, claims that all men make with perfect equality."

h. Kant: Every person has an imperfect duty to help others. (32 and 37, A 423 and 430)

i. Thomson: "In some views having a right to life includes having a right to be given at least the bare minimum one needs for continued life. [But these views are wrong.] . . . The right to life consists in . . . the right not to be killed unjustly. [The right to life is negative, not positive.]" "[However,] there may well be cases in which carrying the child to term requires only Minimally Decent Samaritanism of the mother, and this is a standard we must not fall below."

j. Rachels: "The bare difference between killing and letting die does not, in itself, make a moral difference." And by a similar argument, the bare difference between harming a person and allowing a person to come to harm does not, in itself, make a moral difference.

k. Govier: "*The Permissive Position:* In a society with sufficient resources, one ought to have an unconditional legal right to receive state-supplied welfare benefits. (That is, one's right to receive such benefits ought not to depend on one's behavior; it should be guaranteed.)"

l. Govier: *"The Puritan Position:* In a society with sufficient resources, one ought to have a legal right to state-supplied welfare benefits; this right ought to be conditional, however, on one's willingness to work."

3. Nussbaum says, "It seems plain that when you value a plurality of different goods, all of which are taken to make a non-homogeneous contribution to the goodness of a life, then . . . you cannot satisfy the demands of all the things to which you are committed. This is not just a women's problem, of course; but it is a problem that has been recognized and felt more . . . by women than by men . . . A serious difficulty I have with O'Neill's Kantian approach is that it gives us no direction as to how to face such conflicts."

What sort of conflicts is Nussbaum talking about? Give some examples. Has this problem been recognized and felt more by women than by men? Why does Nussbaum believe that O'Neill's approach gives us no direction as to how to face such conflicts? How might O'Neill defend her approach against Nussbaum's criticism?

4. Workfare programs are touted as achieving two goals. First, workfare makes it easier for the poor to get and hold jobs by teaching job skills and building self-esteem, work habits, and motivation. Second, workfare deters people from taking government assistance by requiring them to work at unappealing jobs. Are these objectives incompatible? Why or why not?

5. A defender of the traditional institution of marriage might maintain that Okin has neglected the benefits women reap from marriage. First of all, women have the option not to work outside of the home. This is not a trivial choice like the decision to wear pants or a skirt. It is a very valuable option. Second, if the husband supports the family and the wife does the housework and child care, then he is contributing more to the marriage than she. After all, the monetary value of housework and child care must be rather low, because these services are available in the marketplace at a low cost. Third, women who seek custody of the children in a divorce almost always succeed. This is no negligible advantage. Write a dialogue between Okin and this defender on the topic of justice in marriage.

6. Dworkin claims that Liberals would opt for a market economy. Conservatives would also opt for a market economy. In what ways would Dworkin and Conservatives disagree about the economy?

7. Compare and contrast welfare and workfare from a Utilitarian point of view.

8. Choose *one* of the following practices, and answer the questions that follow the list.

   a. welfare tax (taxing the well off in order to support people who cannot support themselves)

   b. the 1996 welfare law (discontinuing welfare benefits to single mothers after two years)

   c. freeriding (choosing to be supported by the government when you could work)

   d. traditional wife (choosing to be supported by your husband when you could work)

Would a Kantian (using CI#1 or CI#2) consider this practice morally required, morally optional, or morally wrong? Explain your answer. Would a Rule Utilitarian consider this practice morally required, morally optional, or morally wrong? Explain your answer. Describe the similarities and differences between the Kantian analysis and the Rule Utilitarian analysis.

9. Nussbaum maintains that there are unjust principles that a group of people could consistently endorse. Do you agree? If so, list some such principles and explain how a group of people could consistently endorse them. If not, explain how O'Neill might rebut Nussbaum's claim.

10. A critic of Dworkin's brand of liberalism might say, "Liberals are not really value-neutral. Liberals favor using government to enforce the values of tolerance and equality. They oppose conceptions of the good life that require people to coerce other people. For example, they would ban lives based on violence or sadism. Liberals are not even neutral with respect to religions. They would prohibit militant religions that convert people by force for their own good and religions that deem some people to be inferior to others, for example." How might Dworkin reply to this criticism? Do you agree with Dworkin or with the critic?

# Euthanasia, Suicide, and Futility

*Do not go gentle into that good night*
*Old age should burn and rave at close of day;*
*Rage, rage against the dying of the light.*

DYLAN THOMAS

*E*uthanasia (literally "good death," colloquially "mercy killing") has recently become a pressing moral issue. It is fashionable, but false, to attribute this to technological advances that enable us to prolong lives past the point when they are worth living. Actually, there have always been a fair number of people who longed for death. Pneumonia used to be called "the old man's friend" because it ended so many misery-filled lives. The weakening of a taboo rather than medical progress is the cause of increasing demand for euthanasia. Increasingly, euthanasia is also becoming a moral issue because of the drive to reduce the runaway costs of health care. If a patient would be better off dead, why pay for lifesaving therapy?

Until the 1970s biomedical ethics discussions were more or less dominated by Catholic theologians. One of their beliefs was (approximately) that harmful acts are morally wrong if and only if the harm is intentional. It follows from this belief that if an act has both an intended, good effect and an unintended, harmful effect, then the harmful effect does not make the act wrong, even if the harm is foreseen (as long as the good effect is not produced by the harmful effect, the benefits outweigh the drawbacks, and the act is not intrinsically wrong). This *Doctrine of Double Effect* implies that intentionally causing death is wrong but performing an act that results in death is OK as long as the death was not the intended effect of the act (and the other conditions are met). Thus, according to the Doctrine of Double Effect, it is OK to bomb an enemy munitions plant next to a school as long as your goal is to destroy the plant and not to kill the children. Similarly, is OK to administer morphine even if death is likely to result as long as your goal is to relieve pain. Because *active euthanasia*—directly killing someone—is always intentional, the Doctrine of Double Effect implies that active euthanasia is always wrong. On the other hand, *passive euthanasia*—allowing someone to die when you could keep the person alive—might be intentional or unintentional. It is clearly intentional, and therefore wrong, if the person's life could be saved with cheap, low-tech, *ordinary* therapy. Passive euthanasia might be unintentional if sustaining the person's life required expensive, high-tech, *extraordinary* therapy. The A.M.A. seemed to be expressing this position in its policy statement of 1973:

The intentional termination of the life of one human being by another—mercy killing—is contrary to that for which the medical profession stands and is contrary to the policy of the American Medical Association. The cessation of the employment of extraordinary means to prolong the life of the body when there is irrefutable evidence that biological death is imminent is the decision of the patient and/or his immediate family.

At that time, the big question was this: Is it morally OK to stop providing already ongoing, expensive, high-tech life support to patients—to turn off respirators, for example? From one perspective, *withdrawal of life support* looks like active euthanasia, because you do something. You pull the plug. From another perspective, withdrawal of life support looks like passive euthanasia, because you opt not to sustain the life anymore. The consensus seems to be that withdrawal of life support is morally acceptable. It is more like passive euthanasia than like active euthanasia.

When large numbers of non-Catholic philosophers joined the discussion, they rejected the belief that underlies the Doctrine of Double Effect, the belief that intentions determine the rightness and wrongness of acts. Instead, as Rachels says, the newcomers held that intentions determine whether a person is deserving of praise or blame, but not whether an act is right

**695**

or wrong. After all, if two people perform the same act with different intentions (for example, a saint donates to charity in order to help people, whereas a con artist donates to charity in order to set up a scam), then the different intentions cannot make the act right in one case and wrong in the other, because in both cases it is *the same act*. When intentions were no longer seen as relevant to the evaluation of action and the Doctrine of Double Effect was rejected, the distinction between ordinary and extraordinary therapy became irrelevant, although the distinction between active and passive euthanasia remained important. Allowing people to die by withholding ordinary therapy became accepted, and the controversial question was this: Is it morally OK to allow the patient to die by *withholding food and water?* From one perspective, withholding food and water looks like withholding ordinary therapy and thus like passive euthanasia, for it is almost always a matter of declining to install a naso-gastric tube rather than declining to raise a spoon to the patient's lips. From another perspective, withholding nutritional support looks like active euthanasia. Whenever you withhold therapy there is always a chance, however small, that the patient will recover anyway. However, without food and water, patients always die. The emerging consensus is that withholding nutritional support is morally acceptable. It, too, is more like passive euthanasia than like active euthanasia.

Recently, Jack Kevorkian dramatically refocused the public debate by helping a number of people kill themselves. From one perspective, *assisted suicide* looks like passive euthanasia, for the doctor does nothing to the patient. The patient, not the doctor, pulls the trigger. From another perspective, assisted suicide looks like active euthanasia, for the doctor contributes to the death of the patient. No consensus on the morality of assisted suicide is in sight.

In 1975 James Rachels published an article arguing that the active/passive euthanasia distinction is morally irrelevant—that active and passive euthanasia are morally equivalent. Either both are OK or both are equally wrong.

He describes two scenarios. Smith drowns a child for the sake of an inheritance. Jones, who has the same intentions and motives, lets a child drown when he could easily have saved the child. Because these acts are morally equivalent, and because the only difference between these acts is the bare difference between killing and letting die, there must be no moral difference between killing and letting die. Hence there must be no moral difference between active and passive euthanasia.

### Argument (A)

(1) The only difference between active euthanasia and passive euthanasia is the bare difference between killing and letting die.

(2) The only difference between the acts of Smith and Jones is the bare difference between killing and letting die.

(3) The acts of Smith and Jones are equally immoral.

(4) Thus killing and letting die are morally equivalent. (from premises 2 and 3)

(5) Therefore, active euthanasia and passive euthanasia are morally equivalent. (from premises 1 and 4)

Note that Rachels is *not* saying that the acts of Smith and Jones are morally equivalent to the acts of active and passive euthanizers. In fact, Rachels thinks that the acts of Smith and Jones are wicked whereas euthanasia is good. Instead, Rachels is saying that because the acts of Smith and Jones are equally bad, it follows that the acts of active and passive euthanasia are morally equal.

Daniel Callahan argues that when a doctor allows a patient to die, the disease is the cause of death, so the doctor does not bear the moral responsibility for the death. Of course, if the doctor omitted a life-saving treatment that should have been provided, then the doctor is responsible for omitting that treatment. But that responsibility for the omission is not the same as responsibility for the death. Thus there is a moral difference between killing and letting die.

Dan Brock argues that the action/omission distinction will not bear the weight that Callahan wishes to place upon it. If a greedy heir unplugs a respirator required to sustain the life of a wealthy relative or refuses to give a life-sustaining oxygen treatment, we would say that the greedy heir rather than the disease is responsible for the death of the wealthy relative. Indeed, cutting the hose of a scuba diver is not morally different from smothering someone with a pillow. In all of these cases, one person is responsible for the asphyxiation of another.

One troubling consequence of the moral equivalence of killing and letting die is that being a good Samaritan turns out to be a high-priority moral duty rather than a supererogatory act. We have a duty to help others who want to live stay alive (at least, if we can do so with very little trouble and very little risk), because allowing them to die is just as bad as murder. Some people may embrace this consequence, but many people do not think our duties to others are so extensive or weighty. A person who takes a European vacation instead of donating the money to feed ten starving people in the Third World may not be generous, but this person is not the moral equivalent of a mass murderer, either.

Overall, one trend in the last few decades has been a progressive acceptance of more sorts of euthanasia. We seem to be moving from controversy over passive euthanasia involving extraordinary therapy closer and closer to blithe acceptance of active euthanasia.

\*

Another trend in the last few decades has been the increasing clamor for control over one's own health care. Until the 1970s doctors tended to have rather paternalistic relationships with their patients, but for a variety of reasons, more and more people found such relationships less and less acceptable. "Doctor's orders" became recommendations. Patients stopped saying, "Whatever you think, doc" and started formulating and expressing their own treatment preferences, including their preferences concerning euthanasia. Some medically competent patients requested immediate euthanasia of one sort or another, but many others stipulated that they wished to be euthanized if certain conditions

came to pass when they became unconscious, senile, or otherwise medically incompetent. This raised the following question: Is there a morally significant difference between euthanizing people of sound mind at their own request (*voluntary euthanasia*) and euthanizing medically incompetent people on the basis of statements and requests made before they became incompetent (*expressed-wishes euthanasia*)? The consensus seems to be that people do not lose their rights when they lose their competence. They still have their rights, although these rights can be exercised only by a proxy. Thus whatever sorts of euthanasia are morally acceptable when voluntary are also acceptable when based on previously expressed wishes.

Some people, however, do not express wishes about any sort of euthanasia before becoming medically incompetent. Infants, for example, never formulate preferences about euthanasia, yet sometimes it seems clear that a terribly impaired infant (such as brainless infants so fragile that they hemorrhage when touched) would be better off dead. Once we agree that euthanasia on the basis of previously expressed wishes is morally OK, it seems natural to extend the privilege (privilege?) of euthanasia to patients with no previously expressed wishes. Instead of euthanizing them on the basis of what they actually said, we might euthanize them on the basis of what they would say (if they were medically competent and reasonable). In other words, we might euthanize patients with no previously expressed wishes when it is in their best interest to be euthanized. Is this *best-interest euthanasia* also morally equivalent to voluntary euthanasia?

Taken together, the two trends involving eighteen different types of euthanasia (exhibited in the table on page 698) constitute a progressive acceptance of more and more sorts of euthanasia for more and more sorts of people. We have moved from controversy over voluntary euthanasia to acceptance of euthanizing people without their consent. Will the next step be to deny life-saving therapy to certain people who want it? We already deny futile therapy to those who request it, and more and more therapies are being designated as futile. Are we rationing life-saving therapy covertly?

## Utilitarian Analysis

Although the types of euthanasia differ substantially from each other, the utilitarian considerations for and against each type are surprisingly similar. The advantages of euthanasia are straightforward. First, euthanasia reduces the pain and suffering of patients and that of their families, friends, doctors, and nurses. Although physical pain may be well controlled by medicine these days, we are not yet able to control psychological suffering effectively. Thus there is still a demand for euthanasia. Second, euthanasia increases the autonomy of patients. It gives people more control over when and how they exit from life. Third, many people who do not actually use euthanasia feel more secure throughout their lives knowing that euthanasia is an available option. Finally, euthanasia conserves the resources of society. As health care costs spiral upward, this consideration assumes increasing importance.

The disadvantages of euthanasia are also straightforward. First, some patients mistakenly opt for euthanasia because of severe yet temporary pain, depression, fear, shock, effects of medication, or financial pressure, when they could go on living lives that are well worth living. If euthanasia were not considered a morally ac-

ceptable option, such patients would be forced to tolerate their tough times and go on to lead rewarding lives. Similarly, in cases of expressed-wishes and best-interest euthanasia, some proxies make the wrong decisions because of greed, jealousy, confusion about patients' preferences, or mistakes about what counts as a worthwhile life. Again, if euthanasia were not considered acceptable, people with lives worth living would not be doomed by proxy error. Third, some doctors wrongly recommend euthanasia because of mistaken diagnosis. Perhaps Kevorkian has assisted the suicides of some people who could have flourished with the aid of anti-depressant drugs. For all three of these reasons, some people who would have lived happily if euthanasia were still taboo die instead because euthanasia is sanctioned.

It is easy to overstate the impact of these factors. With the reasonably effective painkillers and anti-depressants currently available, with advance directives, and with required counseling and waiting periods before the euthanizing of patients, the number of patients and proxies making wrong decisions is dwindling. The problem of physician error is also small. People sometimes say, for example, "Doctors can't be certain that any person is terminally ill." If this means, "In practice, predictions are unreliable," then it is simply false. Errors do occur, of course, but they are rare. If this means, "In theory, certainty is unobtainable," then it is true but irrelevant. Whether a patient is terminally ill or not, we must choose a treatment plan on the basis of

|  | Passive Extraordinary | Passive Ordinary | Food and Water | Withdraw Life Support | Assisted Suicide | Active Direct Killing |
|---|---|---|---|---|---|---|
| Voluntary |  |  |  |  |  |  |
| Expressed Wishes |  |  |  |  |  |  |
| Best Interest |  |  |  |  |  |  |

the best available data. We do not have the option of avoiding this choice, because doing nothing is also a treatment plan.

The fourth disadvantage is that euthanasia may be just the first step on a slippery slope. Euthanizing people may cause medical professionals to become more and more callous and uncaring. This would cause the quality of medical care to decline. More important, in conjunction with other trends that are contributing to the devaluation of life in our society, euthanasia might lead to horrible practices. We might end up killing people who wish to live simply because someone (such as proxies, doctors, government, or the establishment) does not like them. Thus Weisbard and Siegler maintain that we have a duty to try to avoid horrible practices like this by providing symbolically significant care. In particular, they maintain that we should not euthanize patients by starvation and dehydration. Food and water have great symbolic significance.

This slippery-slope worry might seem extreme, even hysterical. After all, many things are possible but so unlikely that they are not worth worrying about. On the other hand, it is worth noting two things. First, a social policy of euthanasia has already slid down this slope once. The Nazis' policy of extermination grew out of their euthanasia program. Second, our society has already slipped, in just a few decades, from controversy over the mildest sort of euthanasia to clear acceptance of some of the more extreme versions of euthanasia. Indeed, both overtreatment *and* undertreatment are big problems at the end of life.

## Deontological Analysis

By giving competent people more control over the timing and manner of their death, euthanasia increases their options and enhances their autonomy. Can this argument justify euthanasia of the incompetent, too? Can proxies really exercise the autonomy of medically incompetent people? Weisbard and Siegler argue that it is impossible

to know what incompetent patients would choose if they were competent, even if they have previously expressed preferences. After all, what people say they would want in some hypothetical scenario often differs significantly from what the same people choose when they actually find themselves in that scenario. Thus others should not decide whether life-saving treatment is worth it for the patient. We should not actively or even passively euthanize medically incompetent patients.

Although we cannot be certain of what medically incompetent patients would choose, we often have pretty good evidence. In such cases, respect for the patient's autonomy requires the proxy to honor the patient's probable preferences. Expressed-wishes euthanasia can be deontologically justified. However, best-interest euthanasia seems to require a different justification. Without previous choice or possibility of choice, there is no autonomy to respect.

Killing incompetent people who have not requested death seems to many to be going too far. Even if they *would* think that their lives are not worth living, do we really have a right to kill such people? Should we really kill people when we have *no idea* what they would think, just because *we* think that, objectively speaking (whatever that means), their life is not worth living? This concern assumes that we should not allow people to die without a good reason. Keeping people alive is considered the default option. Weisbard and Siegler utilize this common-sense view in the following argument against withholding food and fluids.

### Argument (B)

(1) It is OK to let nature take its course, but playing God is immoral.
(2) Withholding food and fluids goes beyond letting nature take its course. It is really playing God.
(3) Therefore, withholding food and fluids is immoral.

Premise (1) sounds good, but like most slogans, it does not withstand much scrutiny. First, playing God presumably means making decisions that we do not have the knowledge and/or right to make *when we do not have to make them.* However, we do have to decide whether to withhold food and fluids, because choosing to give food and fluids is also a choice. There is no default option. Withholding food and fluids is a life-or-death decision, but so is giving food and fluids. Choosing to keep someone alive when the person would otherwise die is just as much playing God as choosing to allow someone to die when otherwise she or he would live. Second, letting nature take its course is neither good nor bad in any of the usual meanings of the word "natural." Even if withholding food and fluids is unnatural, it does not follow that it is immoral. Many practices, including medicine, are moral but unnatural. Similarly, even if withholding food and fluids is natural, it does not follow that it is moral. Many practices, including infanticide and polygamy, are natural but immoral.

\*

Obviously, enslaving another person is a gross violation of that person's autonomy. For the same reason, people may not ask others to enslave them, either. Similarly, Callahan maintains that killing others, killing oneself, and asking to be killed are all violations of autonomy. Like the right to liberty, the right to life is an inalienable right.

Kant is often thought to have opposed suicide, and by extension all types of euthanasia, with a similar argument. He says that we have a duty to ourselves not to commit suicide when continued life is likely to be worse than death. Just as killing another person in order to advance one's own happiness is wrong because it treats the other as a mere means, so committing suicide is wrong because it treats oneself as a mere means to one's own happiness. In both cases, the autonomy of the victim is violated.

These arguments use odd senses of rights and autonomy. Just as we can give away our property without surrendering our right to property, so we can give away our liberty or life without surrendering our right to liberty or life. That is why people can become soldiers and why soldiers can accept "suicide missions." Patients who request euthanasia are giving up their life, not their right to life. They are exercising their autonomy, not surrendering it. The idea of treating oneself as a mere means just does not make sense.

Thomas Hill's reconstruction of Kant's argument is more plausible. According to Hill, Kant first identifies a cluster of character traits that endows us with moral significance. These traits, which Kant sometimes calls "humanity," make us responsible for certain duties and entitled to certain rights. These traits make us persons rather than things. Our humanity is the basis of our autonomy. The second formulation of Kant's categorical imperative says that you should "treat humanity, whether in your own person or in the person of another, always at the same time as an end and never simply as a means." Here Kant demands not only that we respect the humanity of others but also that we respect our own humanity. As Kant says, humanity has dignity rather than price. It should not be exchanged for anything else, for that would be to rank autonomy below another good—to treat it as a mere means for obtaining something else. Killing others is wrong not because their lives are valuable or because they do not want to be killed but rather because killing violates autonomy. For the same reason one should not kill oneself. So far, we have the following argument.

### Argument (C)

(1) Always treat humanity as an end and never simply as a means. Never exchange humanity for anything else.

(2) Suicide is an exchange of humanity for something else (such as the absence of pain). It involves ranking something else above autonomy.

(3) Therefore, suicide is an immoral act.

The most common reason why people commit suicide is to avoid a life where pain outweighs pleasure. This places pleasure (or the absence of pain) above autonomy. However, not all suicides are exchanges of humanity for something else. Suicide chosen to avoid an imminent, unpleasant death does not subordinate autonomy to anything but merely chooses among exit modes. Similarly, Kant would probably allow suicide when the alternative is the loss of autonomy through mental degeneration, great pain, or the like. Presumably, Kant would say that suicide is OK when the alternative is to perform a wicked act or lead an evil life. In such conflict-of-duty situations, suicide may be the lesser evil. Perhaps suicide would also be OK in order to help others (for example, to avoid revealing secrets that would compromise national security), although helping others must be understood as helping others maintain or enhance their autonomy rather than as increasing their pleasure or decreasing their burden. In such cases suicide would be understood as an exchange of autonomy for autonomy rather than as an exchange of autonomy for something else. Overall, argument (C) fails because premise (2) is false.

Hill suggests that suicide is OK when the alternative is to lose one's integrity. This suggestion assumes that humanity may be sacrificed for the sake of integrity—that integrity is more important than humanity. Thus Hill denies premise (1) as well as premise (2). Of course, if premise (1) of argument (C) is false and autonomy is commensurable with other values—that is, if autonomy may be traded for other things—then perhaps it is OK to relinquish one's autonomy in exchange for release from suffering, too.

## Virtue Ethics Analysis

I have already alluded to the Utilitarian concern that the practice of euthanasia might lead down a slippery slope from character corruption to moral disaster. But suppose that although euthanasia tends to corrupt the characters of doctors and even to corrupt society in general, nevertheless the practice of euthanasia does not lead to mass murder or any other terrible acts because that outcome is somehow blocked by institutional safeguards. Alternatively, suppose that euthanasia does not corrupt people at all but

instead that to carry euthanasia out on a regular basis requires people who are already corrupt. From a Utilitarian point of view, euthanasia might then turn out to be a justifiable practice. However, from a virtue ethics point of view, a practice that corrupts character or requires corrupt characters is an immoral practice. Thus euthanasia would not be sanctioned.

### Argument (D)

(1) Practices that require or produce vices are immoral practices.
(2) Euthanasia requires or produces uncaring, callous people.
(3) Uncaringness and callousness are vices.
(4) Therefore, euthanasia is an immoral practice.

One might object to premise (2) of argument (D). After all, doctors inflict a great deal of pain in their work, yet this does not generally make doctors sadistic or even require them to be insensitive to the suffering of others. Presumably this is because the pain is not sought for its own sake but is merely a necessary evil on the way to the patient's best interest. Similarly, euthanasia will probably not make doctors uncaring or even callous or require them to be so, because in the practice of euthanasia, death is not sought for its own sake but is merely a necessary evil on the way to the patient's best interest.

In the paper "Is Care a Virtue for Health Care Professionals?" I object to premise (3) of argument (D). I deny that care is a virtue for doctors. I argue that significant emotional attachment to patients is problematic because it leads to favoritism, burnout, inefficiency, and unfairness on the part of the doctor. Doctors should perform caring actions but should preserve a professional distance and avoid emotional attachment to patients. Thus a medical practice that undermines care or that must be performed by uncaring people is not producing or requiring a vice.

\*

Many virtue theorists say that self-respect is a virtue. For Aristotle, proper pride is the mean between the vices of vanity and excessive humility. Now some people attempt suicide out of a lack of self-esteem, from feelings of worthlessness or worse. People may feel that they are a burden to their family, to society, even to the universe. They find themselves contemptible and disgusting. Is this lack of self-esteem the vice of excessive humility?

Virtue ethics must distinguish between vice and mental illness, for the vicious and the mentally ill deserve and respond to different treatment. The vicious should be blamed, but they typically do not improve; the mentally ill should be treated with compassion, and they improve with therapy. Roughly speaking, Aristotle distinguishes between vice and mental illness by the extent of the deviation from virtue. Occasional liars are dishonest; constant liars are compulsive. People who wash their hands 20 times per day are fastidious; people who wash their hands 100 times per day have a phobia. And so on. The level of self-loathing that leads to suicide is so severe that it must be classified as mental illness rather than vice. The medically competent person who rationally chooses death over life even though he or she is not terminally ill or in excruciating pain is a character in some Romantic and Existentialist literature. However, this figure is a myth. Serious suicide in such situations is simply a symptom of the dangerous, deadly disease of depression.

*

Sometimes euthanasia and suicide are contemptuously described as "taking the easy way out." In general, there is nothing wrong with doing things the easy way. People who tend to do things the hard way are not admired as highly virtuous; rather, they are disdained as dullards. When euthanasia and suicide are criticized as "taking the easy way out" the implication is that they are cowardly acts. A courageous person would endure the suffering rather than give up on life.

This is a rather ironic reversal of the Roman view, which was that *not* committing suicide in certain situations is cowardly. Aristotle would certainly not make the blanket statement that euthanasia and suicide are cowardly. For Aristotle, courage does not consist in facing all things, taking all risks, and enduring all suffering.

Instead, Aristotle's view is that the courageous person takes risks that are worth taking and endures suffering when necessary. That is, when the goal of an act is worth the risk and the chances of failure are not too high, then the act is courageous; otherwise the act is foolhardy. The courageous person retreats from a hopeless or worthless struggle. Extrapolating, Aristotle might concede that euthanasia and suicide are cowardly when there is a reasonable chance of pushing through some suffering in order to achieve a reasonably good, reasonably long life. But declining euthanasia or suicide would be foolhardy when the alternative is enduring great suffering with little chance of obtaining a worthwhile life. In general, Aristotle would say that seeking futile treatment is a vicious act.

## Futility

Whereas the currently sanctioned forms of euthanasia begin with decisions made by patients or their proxies to end life by withholding or withdrawing treatment, doctors, hospitals, managed-care organizations, insurance companies, and the government are all seeking ways to save money by withholding or withdrawing treatment *despite* the desires of patients. Cases of doctors imposing undesired treatment are dwindling, and cases of doctors refusing requested treatment are on the rise. One way to deny treatment is to label the therapy "futile." A therapy is *strictly futile* it has no chance of doing any good. Strictly futile therapy is useless therapy. It has always been clear that doctors have no obligation to provide therapy that is futile in this strict sense. Recently, it has become increasingly popular to recognize a looser sense of futility. A therapy is *loosely futile* if it has little chance of achieving a worthwhile goal. This loose sense of futility is needed in order to justify the rejection of ridiculous requests for fad medications and nostrums. After all, few therapies, no matter how wacky, can be said to have *no* chance of achieving anything good. Totally unexpected things do happen. Powdered rhinoceros horn might cure something, or have a placebo effect, or simply make the patient feel heeded. Is any therapy strictly futile?

Lawrence Schneiderman, Nancy Jecker, and Albert Jonsen plausibly propose that a therapy should be considered loosely futile if it has failed in the last 100 cases to improve "the patient's prognosis, comfort, well-being or general state of health." Moreover, "any treatment that merely preserves permanent unconsciousness or that fails to end total dependence on intensive medical care should be regarded as nonbeneficial and, therefore, futile." They believe that denying therapy to patients is morally acceptable if the treatment meets either of these criteria.

Anne Epstein disagrees. Because of its strict sense the term "futility" has objective, scientific, clinical connotations. Whether a treatment is futile seems to be a determination that a doctor is best qualified to make. However, as Epstein argues, the judgment that a certain treatment is loosely futile rests on value judgments. Doctors can make the objective determination that "Treatment T has probability $P$ of achieving goal $G$," but doctors are neither trained nor particularly qualified to judge whether $G$ is a worthwhile goal or whether $P$ is high enough. Schneiderman, Jecker, and Jonsen seem to assume that everyone's top priority is to "live long and prosper." However Epstein observes that patients often attach a higher priority to other goals. They may want to conserve the family fortune or punish themselves for past sins, for example. Similarly, some patients are willing to take much higher risks than others. Why should patients with different goals and/or risk-taking priorities be discriminated against? Epstein argues that because futility judgments are based on value judgments, they should be made by the patients. It may be reasonable to refuse to provide harmful, immoral, strictly futile, or unpaid therapy. However, a patient should not be denied a certain therapy merely because the doctor thinks the therapy is loosely futile. Such denials violate patient autonomy by wrenching the decision of whether to "go for it" away from the patient and bestowing responsibility for that decision on the doctor.

Doctors are increasingly subject to conflicts of interest. On the one hand, they are pulled by their commitment to the patient to try everything, even low-probability shots, for some chance is better than nothing. On the other hand, doctors are pressured by their third-party payers and perhaps by their social conscience to reduce the cost of medical care. Under these conditions, the determination that such-and-such a therapy is futile is a tempting way for doctors to reduce costs without violating their obligations to patients. However, because the distinction between the strict and loose senses of futility is seldom explicit, doctors may call a therapy futile because it meets the criterion of loose futility, but they may then go on to think and act as though the therapy were strictly futile. That is, although doctors are actually using the looser sense of futility, they seem to be making objective judgments rather than value judgments because the two senses of "futility" are conflated. This conflation creates several problems.

The need and desire to save money yield a temptation and a tendency for doctors to declare more and more therapies futile. Thus even if there is nothing wrong with our present standard of futility, contemporary medical practice may already be on the road to something colder, darker, and more mercantile. And the conflation of the two senses of "futility" makes the slope more slippery.

This conflation also raises a virtue ethics worry about honesty and trust. Doctors who deny therapy because it is futile are often concealing from their patients (and perhaps from themselves) the fact that they are making value judgments. The doctor says, "No, I shall not provide therapy T because it won't do any good." The doctor is thinking, "Well, actually therapy T does have an itsy-bitsy chance of working, but it's not worth it." This deception may erode the honesty of the doctor-deceivers and the trust of patient-victims. Once people allow themselves to tell small lies, it quickly becomes easier to tell worse lies for less benevolent reasons. Moreover, deceptive practices require obfuscation to keep them hidden, compounding inadvertent deception with a cover-up. Yet without high levels of honesty and trust, people become worse.

Perhaps the most important problem is that denying therapy on the grounds of futility becomes covert rationing as soon as the strict sense of "futility" is exchanged for the loose sense. Covert rationing is dangerous because it leads to an unjust distribution of important goods. Because public *consensus* is absent, the rationing is not uniformly applied. Different doctors applying different principles end up making different decisions about which treatments to deny to which patients. Moreover, because public *scrutiny* is absent, prejudice plays a larger role. Discrimination flourishes when allocation decisions are not open to public inspection. This is a matter of particular concern for women (and minorities). Studies show that doctors take men substantially more seriously than women in several ways. Women's complaints are more often casually dismissed. Less research is devoted to diseases that primarily afflict women. And so on. Futility adds another worrisome piece to this pattern of prejudice against women in the delivery of health care. Women are more likely to be denied requests for treatment on the grounds of futility, even when the odds and effects of the treatment are the same for men and women.

Gatter and Moskop suggest that the problems that arise from the practice of denying futile therapy may be avoided by replacing the covert rationing of loose futility with explicit rationing.[1] If we must reduce the overall cost of medical care, then the priorities should be set by society in an open, democratic, and principled manner, rather than covertly and idiosyncratically by individual doctors labeling some therapies futile. Explicit rationing will reduce equivocation with respect to the term "futility," deception of patients, and injustice in distribution. Moreover, instead of the yes or no of a futility determination, explicit rationing allows for a range of priority rankings.

## Feminist Analysis

Standard approaches portray the issue of suicide as a clash between the rights of individuals to choose the time and manner of their own death and the duties of individuals and/or states to uphold the value of life by opposing the temptation to take life, even one's own. This statement of the problem is abstract and gender-neutral. A feminist analysis might begin with the observation that suicide is an issue of particular importance to women because many attempted suicides are performed by young women. Most of these suicide attempts would be dismissed as irrelevant by the standard approaches, for when examined concretely rather than abstractly, these suicide attempts turn out to be calls for help rather than expressions of a desire for death. Instead of dismissing these call-for-help suicide attempts, feminists might take them as a starting point to go beyond the question of whether to help or hinder attempts to satisfy a death wish. As is often the case, feminists can bring a new perspective to light by focusing on a hitherto underinvestigated set of (mostly women's) experiences.

Call-for-help suicide attempts typically arise out of a perceived lack of caring. These suiciders feel unloved, unwanted, and excluded from various webs of caring relationships. This perception may be accurate or mistaken or even delusional. Nevertheless, the perception should not be ignored. When your young child screams, "I'm running away from home because no one here loves me," you do not reply, "Good luck; write when you get work." You certainly do not offer, "Would you like a lift to the bus station?" Responses such as these simply confirm the child's perception that he or she is unloved. Instead, recognizing a crisis, your first step is to prevent the child from leaving. Moreover, you do not simply lock the door and then consider the matter resolved. The child will still feel unloved. You must go on to express your love for the child. Of course, those who make call-for-help suicide attempts are not young children. No matter. They share the same goals and needs. They hope for rescue because rescue indicates that someone cares. Permission to commit suicide would simply confirm the fear that no one even cares enough to stop them. Assisted suicide is even worse, for that sends the same message as a ride to the bus station. Thus it is symbolically important for society not to endorse suicide and assisted suicide.

Moreover, merely blocking these acts, like merely locking the door, just forces those who feel excluded to endure hopeless loneliness. Positive expressions of care are also necessary. The medical profession already does some of this. Doctors not only thwart suicide attempts but also follow up with counseling and/or medication. Suicide attempts are treated as symptoms of a serious problem or disease. The symptoms are blocked while the disease is diagnosed and treated. Indeed, people who have attempted suicide are often cured (cured!) with medication and surprising other therapy. Hearing aids are often an effective treatment of depression, for example. Expressions of care must also come from parents, children, spouses, and friends but this often piles an additional burden on already overburdened caregivers. In general, these caregivers are another mostly female group whose toil is largely ignored by the standard philosophical approaches to suicide, euthanasia, and other health care issues (although they are no longer completely unsung heroes and heroines in the popular press). Arguably, these caregivers should not assume the whole burden unaided by social programs, for that would be neither a just nor a caring response on the part of society. Moreover, these caregivers may also need care themselves.

Should we extrapolate from this analysis of suicide to the conclusion that society should not endorse any sort of euthanasia? Such an extrapolation ignores important differences between typical suicide attempts and typical requests for euthanasia. Requests for euthanasia are usually true expressions of a wish for death rather than symptoms that someone feels unloved. Yet some who attempt suicide really seek death, and some euthanasia requests are really calls for help. Just enjoining suicide and endorsing euthanasia is too simple. Somehow we must accommodate the care claims of different groups. Perhaps a requirement for waiting periods and psychiatric evaluations before euthanasia would suffice.

## Note

1. R. Gatter and J. Moskop, "From Futility to Triage," *The Journal of Medicine and Philosophy* 20 (1995), pp. 191–204.

# 61   Active and Passive Euthanasia

## JAMES RACHELS

The distinction between active and passive euthanasia is thought to be crucial for medical ethics. The idea is that it is permissible, at least in some cases, to withhold treatment and allow a patient to die, but it is never permissible to take any direct action designed to kill the patient. This doctrine seems to be accepted by most doctors, and it is endorsed in a statement adopted by the House of Delegates of the American Medical Association on December 4, 1973:

The intentional termination of the life of one human being by another—mercy killing—is contrary to that for which the medical profession stands and is contrary to the policy of the American Medical Association.

The cessation of the employment of extraordinary means to prolong the life of the body when there is irrefutable evidence that biological death is imminent is the decision of the patient and/or his immediate family.

Reprinted with permission of the publisher from *New England Journal of Medicine*, 292, 2 (1975), 78–80. Copyright © 1975 Massachusetts Medical Society. All rights reserved.

The advice and judgment of the physician should be freely available to the patient and/or his immediate family.

However, a strong case can be made against this doctrine. In what follows, I will set out some of the relevant arguments, and urge doctors to reconsider their views on this matter.

To begin with a familiar type of situation, a patient who is dying of incurable cancer of the throat is in terrible pain, which can no longer be satisfactorily alleviated. He is certain to die within a few days, even if present treatment is continued, but he does not want to go on living for those days since the pain is unbearable. So he asks the doctor for an end to it, and his family joins in the request.

Suppose the doctor agrees to withhold treatment, as the conventional doctrine says he may. The justification for his doing so is that the patient is in terrible agony, and since he is going to die anyway, it would be wrong to prolong his suffering needlessly. But now notice this. If one simply withholds treatment, it may take the patient longer to die, and so he may suffer more than he would if more direct action were taken and a lethal injection given. This fact provides strong reason for thinking that, once the initial decision not to prolong his agony has been made, active euthanasia is actually preferable to passive euthanasia, rather than the reverse. To say otherwise is to endorse the option that leads to more suffering rather than less, and is contrary to the humanitarian impulse that prompts the decision not to prolong his life in the first place.

Part of my point is that the process of being "allowed to die" can be relatively slow and painful, whereas being given a lethal injection is relatively quick and painless. Let me give a different sort of example. In the United States about one in 600 babies is born with Down's syndrome. Most of these babies are otherwise healthy—that is, with only the usual pediatric care, they will proceed to an otherwise normal infancy. Some, however, are born with congenital defects such as intestinal obstructions that require operations if they are to live. Sometimes, the parents and the doctor will decide not to operate, and let the

infant die. Anthony Shaw describes what happens then:

> . . . When surgery is denied [the doctor] must try to keep the infant from suffering while natural forces sap the baby's life away. As a surgeon whose natural inclination is to use the scalpel to fight off death, standing by and watching a salvageable baby die is the most emotionally exhausting experience I know. It is easy at a conference, in a theoretical discussion, to decide that such infants should be allowed to die. It is altogether different to stand by in the nursery and watch as dehydration and infection wither a tiny being over hours and days. This is a terrible ordeal for me and the hospital staff—much more so than for the parents who never set foot in the nursery.[1]

I can understand why some people are opposed to all euthanasia, and insist that such infants must be allowed to live. I think I can also understand why other people favor destroying these babies quickly and painlessly. But why should anyone favor letting "dehydration and infection wither a tiny being over hours and days?" The doctrine that says that a baby may be allowed to dehydrate and wither, but may not be given an injection that would end its life without suffering, seems so patently cruel as to require no further refutation. The strong language is not intended to offend, but only to put the point in the clearest possible way.

My second argument is that the conventional doctrine leads to decisions concerning life and death made on irrelevant grounds.

Consider again the case of the infants with Down's syndrome who need operations for congenital defects unrelated to the syndrome to live. Sometimes, there is no operation, and the baby dies, but when there is no such defect, the baby lives on. Now, an operation such as that to remove an intestinal obstruction is not prohibitively difficult. The reason why such operations are not performed in these cases is, clearly, that the child has Down's syndrome and the parents and doctor judge that because of that fact it is better for the child to die.

But notice that this situation is absurd, no matter what view one takes of the lives and potentials of such babies. If the life of such an infant is worth preserving, what does it matter if it needs a simple operation? Or, if one thinks it better that such a baby should not live on, what difference does it make that it happens to have an unobstructed intestinal tract? In either case, the matter of life and death is being decided on irrelevant grounds. It is the Down's syndrome, and not the intestines, that is the issue. The matter should be decided, if at all, on that basis, and not be allowed to depend on the essentially irrelevant question of whether the intestinal tract is blocked.

What makes this situation possible, of course, is the idea that when there is an intestinal blockage, one can "let the baby die," but when there is no such defect there is nothing that can be done, for one must not "kill" it. The fact that this idea leads to such results as deciding life or death on irrelevant grounds is another good reason why the doctrine should be rejected.

One reason why so many people think that there is an important moral difference between active and passive euthanasia is that they think killing someone is morally worse than letting someone die. But is it? Is killing, in itself, worse than letting die? To investigate this issue, two cases may be considered that are exactly alike except that one involves killing whereas the other involves letting someone die. Then, it can be asked whether this difference makes any difference to the moral assessments. It is important that the cases be exactly alike, except for this one difference, since otherwise one cannot be confident that it is this difference and not some other that accounts for any variation in the assessments of the two cases. So, let us consider this pair of cases:

In the first, Smith stands to gain a large inheritance if anything should happen to his six-year-old cousin. One evening while the child is taking his bath, Smith sneaks into the bathroom and drowns the child, and then arranges things so that it will look like an accident.

In the second, Jones also stands to gain if anything should happen to his six-year-old cousin. Like Smith, Jones sneaks in planning to drown the child in his bath. However, just as he enters the bathroom Jones sees the child slip and hit his head and fall face down in the water. Jones is delighted; he stands by, ready to push the child's head back

under if it is necessary, but it is not necessary. With only a little thrashing about the child drowns all by himself, "accidentally," as Jones watches and does nothing.

Now Smith killed the child, whereas Jones "merely" let the child die. That is the only difference between them. Did either man behave better, from a moral point of view? If the difference between killing and letting die were in itself a morally important matter, one should say that Jones's behavior was less reprehensible than Smith's. But does one really want to say that? I think not. In the first place, both men acted from the same motive, personal gain, and both had exactly the same end in view when they acted. It may be inferred from Smith's conduct that he is a bad man, although that judgment may be withdrawn or modified if certain further facts are learned about him—for example, that he is mentally deranged. But would not the very same thing be inferred about Jones from his conduct? And would not the same further considerations also be relevant to any modification of this judgment? Moreover, suppose Jones pleaded, in his own defense, "After all, I didn't do anything except just stand there and watch the child drown. I didn't kill him; I only let him die." Again, if letting die were in itself less bad than killing, this defense should have at least some weight. But it does not. Such a "defense" can only be regarded as a grotesque perversion of moral reasoning. Morally speaking, it is no defense at all.

Now, it may be pointed out, quite properly, that the cases of euthanasia with which doctors are concerned are not like this at all. They do not involve personal gain or the destruction of normally healthy children. Doctors are concerned only with cases in which the patient's life is of no further use to him, or in which the patient's life has become or will soon become a terrible burden. However, the point is the same in these cases: the bare difference between killing and letting die does not, in itself, make a moral difference. If a doctor lets a patient die, for humane reasons, he is in the same moral position as if he had given the patient a lethal injection for humane reasons. If his decision was wrong—if, for example, the patient's illness was in fact curable—the decision would be equally regrettable no matter which method was used to carry it out. And if the doctor's decision was the right one, the method used is not in itself important.

The AMA policy statement isolates the crucial issue very well; the crucial issue is "the intentional termination of the life of one human being by another." But after identifying this issue, and forbidding "mercy killing," the statement goes on to deny that the cessation of treatment is the intentional termination of a life. This is where the mistake comes in, for what is the cessation of treatment, in these circumstances, if it is not "the intentional termination of the life of one human being by another?" Of course, it is exactly that, and if it were not, there would be no point to it.

Many people will find this judgment hard to accept. One reason, I think, is that it is very easy to conflate the question of whether killing is, in itself, worse than letting die, with the very different question of whether most actual cases of killing are more reprehensible than most actual cases of letting die. Most actual cases of killing are clearly terrible (think, for example, of all the murders reported in the newspapers), and one hears of such cases every day. On the other hand, one hardly ever hears of a case of letting die, except for the actions of doctors who are motivated by humanitarian reasons. So one learns to think of killing in a much worse light than of letting die. But this does not mean that there is something about killing that makes it in itself worse than letting die, for it is not the bare difference between killing and letting die that makes the difference in these cases. Rather, the other factors—the murderer's motive of personal gain, for example, contrasted with the doctor's humanitarian motivation—account for different reactions to the different cases.

I have argued that killing is not in itself any worse than letting die; if my contention is right, it follows that active euthanasia is not any worse than passive euthanasia. What arguments can be given on the other side? The most common, I believe, is the following:

"The important difference between active and passive euthanasia is that, in passive euthanasia, the doctor does not do anything to bring about the patient's death. The doctor does nothing, and the patient dies of whatever ills already afflict him. In active euthanasia, however, the doctor does something to bring about the patient's death: he kills him. The doctor who gives the patient with cancer a lethal injection has himself caused his patient's death; whereas if he merely ceases treatment, the cancer is the cause of the death."

A number of points need to be made here. The first is that it is not exactly correct to say that in passive euthanasia the doctor does nothing, for he does do one thing that is very important: he lets the patient die. "Letting someone die" is certainly different, in some respects, from other types of action—mainly in that it is a kind of action that one may perform by way of not performing certain other actions. For example, one may let a patient die by way of not giving medication, just as one may insult someone by way of not shaking his hand. But for any purpose of moral assessment, it is a type of action nonetheless. The decision to let a patient die is subject to moral appraisal in the same way that a decision to kill him would be subject to moral appraisal: it may be assessed as wise or unwise, compassionate or sadistic, right or wrong. If a doctor deliberately let a patient die who was suffering from a routinely curable illness, the doctor would certainly be to blame for what he had done, just as he would be to blame if he had needlessly killed the patient. Charges against him would then be appropriate. If so, it would be no defense at all for him to insist that he didn't "do anything." He would have done something very serious indeed, for he let his patient die.

Fixing the cause of death may be very important from a legal point of view, for it may determine whether criminal charges are brought against the doctor. But I do not think that this notion can be used to show a moral difference between active and passive euthanasia. The reason why it is considered bad to be the cause of someone's death is that death is regarded as a great evil—and so it is. However, if it has been decided that euthanasia—even passive euthanasia—is desirable in a given case, it has also been decided that in this instance death is no greater an evil than the patient's continued existence. And if this is true, the usual reason for not wanting to be the cause of someone's death simply does not apply.

Finally, doctors may think that all of this is only of academic interest—the sort of thing that philosophers may worry about but that has no practical bearing on their own work. After all, doctors must be concerned about the legal consequences of what they do, and active euthanasia is clearly forbidden by the law. But even so, doctors should also be concerned with the fact that the law is forcing upon them a moral doctrine that may well be indefensible, and has a considerable effect on their practices. Of course, most doctors are not now in the position of being coerced in this matter, for they do not regard themselves as merely going along with what the law requires. Rather, in statements such as the AMA policy statement that I have quoted, they are endorsing this doctrine as a central point of medical ethics. In that statement, active euthanasia is condemned not merely as illegal but as "contrary to that for which the medical profession stands," whereas passive euthanasia is approved. However, the preceding considerations suggest that there is really no moral difference between the two, considered in themselves (there may be important moral differences in some cases in their *consequences,* but, as I pointed out, these differences may make active euthanasia, and not passive euthanasia, the morally preferable option). So, whereas doctors may have to discriminate between active and passive euthanasia to satisfy the law, they should not do any more than that. In particular, they should not give the distinction any added authority and weight by writing it into official statements of medical ethics.

## Note

1. A. Shaw: "Doctor, Do We Have a Choice?" *The New York Times Magazine,* Jan. 30, 1972, p. 54.

# 62   Active and Passive Euthanasia: An Impertinent Distinction?

## THOMAS D. SULLIVAN

Because of recent advances in medical technology, it is today possible to save or prolong the lives of many persons who in an earlier era would have quickly perished. Unhappily, however, it often is impossible to do so without commiting the patient and his or her family to a future filled with sorrows. Modern methods of neurosurgery can successfully close the opening at the base of the spine of a baby born with severe myelomeningocoele, but do nothing to relieve the paralysis that afflicts it from the waist down or to remedy the patient's incontinence of stool and urine. Antibiotics and skin grafts can spare the life of a victim of severe and massive burns, but fail to eliminate the immobilizing contractions of arms and legs, the extreme pain, and the hideous disfigurement of the face. It is not surprising, therefore, that physicians and moralists in increasing number recommend that assistance should not be given to such patients, and that some have even begun to advocate the deliberate hastening of death by medical means, provided informed consent has been given by the appropriate parties.

The latter recommendation consciously and directly conflicts with what might be called the "traditional" view of the physician's role. The traditional view, as articulated, for example, by the House of Delegates of the American Medical Association in 1973, declared:

The intentional termination of the life of one human being by another—mercy killing—is contrary to that for

Reprinted with permission of the author from *Human Life Review,* 3, 3 (1977), 40–46.

which the medical profession stands and is contrary to the policy of the American Medical Association.

The cessation of the employment of extra-ordinary means to prolong the life of the body when there is irrefutable evidence that biological death is imminent is the decision of the patient and/or his immediate family. The advice and judgment of the physician should be freely available to the patient and/or his immediate family.

Basically this view involves two points: (1) that it is impermissible for the doctor or anyone else to terminate intentionally the life of a patient, but (2) that it is permissible in some cases to cease the employment of "extraordinary means" of preserving life, even though the death of the patient is a foreseeable consequence.

Does this position really make sense? Recent criticism charges that it does not. The heart of the complaint is that the traditional view arbitrarily rules out all cases of intentionally acting to terminate life, but permits what is in fact the moral equivalent, letting patients die. This accusation has been clearly articulated by James Rachels in a widely-read article that appeared in a recent issue of the *New England Journal of Medicine,* entitled "Active and Passive Euthanasia."[1] By "active euthanasia" Rachels seems to mean *doing something* to bring about a patient's death, and by "passive euthanasia," not doing anything, i.e., just letting the patient die. Referring to the A.M.A. statement, Rachels sees the traditional position as always forbidding active euthanasia, but permitting passive euthanasia. Yet, he argues, passive euthanasia may be in some cases morally indistinguishable from active euthanasia, and in other cases even worse. To make his point he asks his readers to consider the case of a Down's syndrome baby with an intestinal obstruction that easily could be remedied through routine surgery. Rachels comments:

I can understand why some people are opposed to all euthanasia and insist that such infants must be allowed to live. I think I can also understand why other people favor destroying these babies quickly and painlessly. But why should anyone favor letting "dehydration and infection wither a tiny being over hours and days"? The doctrine that says that a baby may be allowed to dehydrate and wither, but may not be given an injection that

would end its life without suffering, seems so patently cruel as to require no further refutation.[2]

Rachels' point is that decisions such as the one he describes as "patently cruel" arise out of a misconceived moral distinction between active and passive euthanasia, which in turn rests upon a distinction between killing and letting die that itself has no moral importance.

One reason why so many people think that there is an important difference between active and passive euthanasia is that they think killing someone is morally worse than letting someone die. But is it? . . .To investigate this issue two cases may be considered that are exactly alike except that one involves killing whereas the other involves letting someone die. Then, it can be asked whether this difference makes any difference to the moral assessments. . . .

In the first, Smith stands to gain a large inheritance if anything should happen to his six-year-old cousin. One evening while the child is taking his bath, Smith sneaks into the bathroom and drowns the child, and then arranges things so that it will look like an accident.

In the second, Jones also stands to gain if anything should happen to his six-year-old cousin. Like Smith, Jones sneaks in planning to drown the child in his bath. However, just as he enters the bathroom Jones sees the child slip and hit his head, and fall face down in the water. Jones is delighted; he stands by, ready to push the child's head back under if it is necessary, but it is not necessary. With only a little thrashing about, the child drowns all by himself, "accidentally," as Jones watches and does nothing.[3]

Rachels observes that Smith killed the child, whereas Jones "merely" let the child die. If there's an important moral distinction between killing and letting die, then, we should say that Jones's behavior from a moral point of view is less reprehensible than Smith's. But while the law might draw some distinctions here, it seems clear that the acts of Jones and Smith are not different in any important way, or, if there is a difference, Jones's action is even worse.

In essence, then, the objection to the position adopted by the A.M.A. of Rachels and those who argue like him is that it endorses a highly questionable moral distinction between killing and letting die, which, if accepted, leads to indefensible medical decisions. Nowhere does Rachels quite come out and say that he favors active euthanasia in some cases, but the implication is clear. Nearly everyone holds that it is sometimes pointless to prolong the process of dying and that in those cases it is morally permissible to let a patient die even though a few hours or days could be salvaged by procedures that would also increase the agonies of the dying. But if it is impossible to defend a general distinction between letting people die and acting to terminate their lives directly, then it would seem that active euthanasia also may be morally permissible.

Now what shall we make of all this? It *is* cruel to stand by and watch a Down's baby die an agonizing death when a simple operation would remove the intestinal obstruction, but to offer the excuse that in failing to operate we didn't *do* anything to bring about death is an example of moral evasiveness comparable to the excuse Jones would offer for his action of "merely" letting his cousin die. Furthermore, it is true that if someone is trying to bring about the death of another human being, then it makes little difference from the moral point of view if his purpose is achieved by action or by malevolent omission, as in the cases of Jones and Smith.

But if we acknowledge this, are we obliged to give up the traditional view expressed by the A.M.A. statement? Of course not. To begin with, we are hardly obliged to assume the Jones-like role Rachels assigns the defender of the traditional view. We have the option of operating on the Down's baby and saving its life. Rachels mentions that possibility only to hurry past it as if that is not what his opposition would do. But, of course, that is precisely the course of action most defenders of the traditional position would choose.

Secondly, while it may be that the reason some rather confused people give for upholding the traditional view is that they think killing someone is always worse than letting them die, nobody who gives the matter much thought puts it that way. Rather they say that killing someone is clearly morally worse than not killing them, and killing them can be done by acting to bring about their death or by refusing ordinary means to keep them alive in order to bring about the same goal.

What I am suggesting is that Rachels's objections leave the position he sets out to criticize untouched. It is worth noting that the jargon of active and passive euthanasia—and it is jargon—does not appear in the resolution. Nor does the resolution state or imply the distinction Rachels attacks, a distinction that puts a moral premium on overt behavior—moving or not moving one's parts—while totally ignoring the intentions of the agent. That no such distinction is being drawn seems clear from the fact that the A.M.A. resolution speaks approvingly of ceasing to use extraordinary means in certain cases, and such withdrawals might easily involve bodily movement, for example unplugging an oxygen machine.

In addition to saddling his opposition with an indefensible distinction it doesn't make, Rachels proceeds to ignore one that it does make—one that is crucial to a just interpretation of the view. Recall the A.M.A. allows the withdrawal of what it calls extra-ordinary means of preserving life; clearly the contrast here is with ordinary means. Though in its short statement those expressions are not defined, the definition Paul Ramsey refers to as standard in his book, *The Patient as Person,* seems to fit.

Ordinary means of preserving life are all medicines, treatments, and operations, which offer a reasonable hope of benefit for the patient and which can be obtained and used without excessive expense, pain, and other inconveniences.

Extra-ordinary means of preserving life are all those medicines, treatments, and operations which cannot be obtained without excessive expense, pain, or other inconvenience, or which, if used, would not offer a reasonable hope of benefit.[4]

Now with this distinction in mind, we can see how the traditional view differs from the position Rachels mistakes for it. The traditional view is that the intentional termination of human life is impermissible, irrespective of whether this goal is brought about by action or inaction. Is the action or refraining *aimed at* producing a death? Is the termination of life *sought, chosen or planned?* Is the intention deadly? If so, the act or omission is wrong.

But we all know it is entirely possible that the unwillingness of a physician to use extra-ordinary means for preserving life may be prompted not by a determination to bring about death, but by other motives. For example, he may realize that further treatment may offer little hope of reversing the dying process and/or be excruciating, as in the case when a massively necrotic bowel condition in a neonate is out of control. The doctor who does what he can to comfort the infant but does not submit it to further treatment or surgery may foresee that the decision will hasten death, but it certainly doesn't follow from that fact that he intends to bring about its death. It is, after all, entirely possible to foresee that something will come about as a result of one's conduct without intending the consequence or side effect. If I drive downtown, I can foresee that I'll wear out my tires a little, but I don't drive downtown with the intention of wearing out my tires. And if I choose to forgo my exercises for a few days, I may think that as a result my physical condition will deteriorate a little, but I don't omit my exercise with a view to running myself down. And if you have to fill a position and select Green, who is better qualified for the post than her rival Brown, you needn't appoint Mrs. Green with the intention of hurting Mr. Brown, though you may foresee that Mr. Brown will feel hurt. And if a country extends its general education programs to its illiterate masses, it is predictable the suicide rate will go up, but even if the public officials are aware of this fact, it doesn't follow that they initiate the program with a view to making the suicide rate go up. In general, then, it is not the case that all the foreseeable consequences and side effects of our conduct are necessarily intended. And it is because the physician's withdrawal of extra-ordinary means can be otherwise motivated than by a desire to bring about the predictable death of the patient that such action cannot categorically be ruled out as wrong.

But the refusal to use ordinary means is an altogether different matter. After all, what is the point of refusing assistance which offers reasonable hope of benefit to the patient without involving excessive pain or other inconvenience? How could it be plausibly maintained that the refusal is not motivated by a desire to bring about the death of the patient? The traditional position, therefore, rules out not only direct actions to bring about death, such as giving a patient a lethal injection, but malevolent omissions as well, such as not providing minimum care for the newborn.

The reason the A.M.A. position sounds so silly when one listens to arguments such as Rachels's is that he slights the distinction between ordinary and extraordinary means and then drums on cases where *ordinary* means are refused. The impression is thereby conveyed that the traditional doctrine sanctions omissions that are morally indistinguishable in a substantive way from direct killings, but then incomprehensibly refuses to permit quick and painless termination of life. If the traditional doctrine would approve of Jones's standing by with a grin on his face while his young cousin drowned in a tub, or letting a Down's baby wither and die when ordinary means are available to preserve its life, it would indeed be difficult to see how anyone could defend it. But so to conceive the traditional doctrine is simply to misunderstand it. It is not a doctrine that rests on some supposed distinction between "active" and "passive euthanasia," whatever those words are supposed to mean, nor on a distinction between moving and not moving our bodies. It is simply a prohibition against intentional killing, which includes both direct actions and malevolent omissions.

To summarize—the traditional position represented by the A.M.A. statement is not incoherent. It acknowledges, or more accurately, insists upon the fact that withholding ordinary means to sustain life may be tantamount to killing. The traditional position can be made to appear incoherent only by imposing upon it a crude idea of killing held by none of its more articulate advocates.

Thus the criticism of Rachels and other reformers, misapprehending its target, leaves the traditional position untouched. That position is simply a prohibition of murder. And it is good to remember, as C. S. Lewis once pointed out:

No man, perhaps, ever at first described to himself the act he was about to do as Murder, or Adultery, or Fraud, or Treachery. . . .And when he hears it so described by other men he is (in a way) sincerely shocked and surprised. Those others "don't understand." If they knew what it had really been like for him, they would not use those crude "stock" names. With a wink or a titter, or a cloud of muddy emotion, the thing has slipped into his will as something not very extraordinary, something of which, rightly understood in all of his peculiar circumstances, he may even feel proud.[5]

I fully realize that there are times when those who have the noble duty to tend the sick and the dying are deeply moved by the sufferings of their patients, especially of the very young and the very old, and desperately wish they could do more than comfort and companion them. Then, perhaps, it seems that universal moral principles are mere abstractions having little to do with the agony of the dying. But of course we do not see best when our eyes are filled with tears.

## Notes

1. *New England Journal of Medicine,* 292; 78–80. Jan. 9, 1975.
2. Ibid., pp. 78–79.
3. Ibid., p. 79.
4. Paul Ramsey, *The Patient As Person* (New Haven and London: Yale University Press, 1970), p. 122. Ramsey abbreviates the definition first given by Gerald Kelly, S.J., *Medico-Moral Problems* (St. Louis, Missouri: The Catholic Hospital Association, 1958), p. 129.
5. C. S. Lewis, *A Preface to Paradise Lost* (London and New York: Oxford University Press, 1970), p. 126.

# 63  On Killing Patients with Kindness: An Appeal for Caution

## ALAN J. WEISBARD AND MARK SIEGLER

The powerful rhetoric of "death with dignity" has gained much intellectual currency and increasing practical import in recent years.[1] Beginning as a plea for more humane and individualized treatment in the face of the sometimes cold and impersonal technological imperatives of modem medicine, this rhetoric brought needed attention to the plight of dying patients not wishing to "endure the unendurable."[2] It has prompted legal and clinical changes empowering such patients (and sometimes their representatives) to assert some control over the manner, if not the fact, of their dying. The "death with dignity" movement has now advanced to a new frontier: the termination or withdrawal of fluids and nutritional support.

The increasing acceptability in respected forums of proposals to permit avoidable deaths by dehydration or malnutrition—proposals which, a few years ago, would almost certainly have been repudiated by the medical community as medically objectionable, legally untenable, and morally unthinkable—is evidenced by a slew of recent contributions to the medical and bioethics literatures,[3] by a sprinkling of court decisions,[4] and, indeed, by the existence of the very conference that led to this volume. This new stream of emerging opinion, supporting the explicit ethical and legal legitimation of this practice, is typically couched in comforting language of caution and compassion, by persons of undoubted sincerity and good faith. But the underlying analysis is, we fear, unlikely to long remain within these cautious bounds.

Careful scrutiny suggests what is ultimately at stake in this controversy: that for an increasing number of incompetent patients, the benefits of continued life are perceived as insufficient to justify the burden and cost of care; that death is seen as the desired outcome; and—critically—that the role of the health care professional is to participate in bringing this outcome about. Fearful that this development bodes ill for patients, health care professionals, the patient-physician relationship,

Reprinted with permission of the publisher from *By No Extraordinary Means,* ed. Joanne Lynn (Indiana University Press, 1986), 108–116.

and other vital societal values, we feel compelled to speak out against the all-too-rapid acceptance of withdrawal of fluids or nutritional support as accepted or standard medical practice. While recognizing that particular health care professionals, for reasons of compassion and conscience and with full knowledge of the personal legal risks involved, may on occasion elect to discontinue fluids and nutritional support, we nonetheless believe that such actions should generally be proscribed, pending much fuller debate and discussion than has yet taken place.

## Qualifications

We do not intend to address here the deep philosophic issues posed by the moral status of the permanently unconscious. There is much philosophic dispute concerning whether the permanently unconscious are living persons who possess rights and interests, whether the obligation of care fully extends to such patients, and whether such patients should and eventually will be encompassed within a broadened understanding of brain death. The present authors take somewhat different views on these questions and present no joint position here on the withdrawal of fluids and nutritional support from patients reliably diagnosed as permanently unconscious.

Nor is our principal concern with decisions by competent, adult, terminally ill patients who contemporaneously or through advance directives (living wills, durable powers of attorney, or carefully considered, reliably witnessed, oral statements) direct that their process of dying not be prolonged through such techniques as those required to maintain life-sustaining nourishment and hydration. We encourage fuller discussion of these issues among patients, families, and medical professionals at a time the patient is able to participate in an informed and thoughtful fashion. We caution only that patients should be made aware that some "artificial" techniques may be useful in making them more comfortable and in easing the dying process, and should not be rejected unthinkingly by those seeking a more "natural"

death. Further, as the much publicized case of Elizabeth Bouvia[5] reminds us, neither physicians nor health care institutions may be compelled to assist in, or to preside over, the suicides of patients, especially those who are not terminally ill.

Nor, finally, do we mean to be understood as necessarily advocating the use of that modality of providing hydration or nutritional support considered most likely to extend survival time maximally without regard to other relevant factors, including the intrusiveness of the technology to the patient in comparison with the plausible alternatives, or the nature and likelihood of serious side effects. Our position is intended as neither vitalist nor absolutist, except with regard to our insistence on providing sufficient assistance to preclude painful hunger or thirst and to avoid directly causing death (as perceived by health care professionals and the wider society) by failing to provide food and water minimally necessary to preclude death by starvation or dehydration.

## Critique

Our focus, then, is primarily on the withdrawal of fluids and nutrition from patients possessing the capacity for consciousness who have not competently rejected such support. While concerns may seem premature in light of the qualifications and thoughtful discussions of both substantive and procedural safeguards expressed in several recent contributions to the literature,[6] we remain troubled that the underlying analysis, once accepted by clinicians and courts, will not long be confined within the limits initially set forth.

What, then, is the underlying analysis, and why do we find it so potentially troubling? The argument rests on the dual propositions that, first, the provision of fluids and nutritional support by "artificial" means constitutes "medical interventions guided by considerations similar to those governing other treatment methods,"[7] and that, second, judgments regarding the withdrawal of such interventions should be based on calculations of the "burdens and benefits" associated with the treatment (sometimes also referred to as "proportionality"). These propositions are rooted in the work of the President's Commission for the Study of Ethical Problems in Medicine,[8] were adopted by the California appellate court in the *Barber* and *Nejdl*[9] case, and play a central role in the analyses set forth by several recent commentators.[10]

We do not dispute that the "benefits and burdens" formulation is useful in a number of contexts and marks a clear analytic improvement over unconsidered references to "extraordinary measures" or "artificial means," terms which have introduced much unnecessary confusion and provide little real assistance in decision-making. What we find troublesome is the assertion that physicians, families, courts, or other third parties can properly conclude that the "burdens" of [providing] fluids and nutrition—a generally unconvincing catalogue of potential "complications" or "side effects"—outweigh the benefit, sustaining life. (We recognize that, in rare cases, the provision of fluids and, particularly, nutritional support may be medically futile or counterproductive in sustaining life, and we do not here recommend that such futile or counterproductive steps be mandated.)

Advocates of withdrawing fluids and nutritional support that are effective in, and necessary for, sustaining life justify their position by arguing that a speedy and painless death is in the patient's "best interests" (a claim with little foundation in existing law, which has traditionally viewed the preservation of life, at least for noncomatose patients, as a core component of "best interests"). While the argument is compassionately made, and may be persuasive in certain cases, it fails to acknowledge explicitly that its objective may be attained more swiftly, more directly, more honestly, through the administration of lethal injections. Homicide is, in this setting, the ultimate analgesic. But to the extent active euthanasia is rejected—we think wisely—by existing law and medical ethics, we believe a similar conclusion is generally mandated for withdrawal of fluids and nutrition, and for much the same reasons.

If active euthanasia has found little support thus far in either medical or legal circles, the rea-

sons are not confined to an exclusive concern with prolonging the life of the patient. The courts have made clear that respirators and dialysis machines are not legally mandated in all cases of respiratory or renal failure, even where their withdrawal is thought likely to result in death. In this sense, the withdrawal of fluids and nutrition is subject to a similar analysis. But in another and—we believe—more powerful sense, the result is quite different, at least in terms of our society's moral perceptions and self-image.

Withdrawal of respirators and dialysis machines can be seen, and *is* seen and emotionally understood, as the removal of artificial impediments to "letting nature take its course." Death can be understood in such cases as the natural result of the disease process. In cases where death may indeed be the desired (and ultimately unavoidable) outcome, it can be allowed to come without imposing a heavy burden of guilt and moral responsibility on physicians or family members for acting to bring it about, and without challenging important social barriers against killing.[11] And sometimes, as in the case of Karen Quinlan, nature can surprise us: the patient can survive despite some experts' predictions to the contrary.

The case of withdrawing fluids and nutritional supports is different in critical respects. Although the techniques for providing such supports may be medical, and thus logically associated with other medical interventions, the underlying obligations of providing food and drink to those who hunger or thirst transcend the medical context, summoning up deep human responses of caring, of nurturing, of human connectedness, and of human community. Social scientists and humanists have only begun to explore the deeper social meanings and ramifications of depriving patients of "food and water," of permitting deaths from starvation or dehydration. While sophisticated observers may argue that the image of "starvation" or "thirst" may be misleading in the cases of some patients, particularly the unconscious, or that limited nutritional intake may slow the progress of a cancer, it is far from clear that such explanations will be compelling to the public, or even, perhaps, to many members of the health professions, particularly if the practice of withholding fluids and nutritional supports takes root and is applied to an ever broader class of patients.

Further, unlike withdrawal of respirators or dialysis machines, withdrawal of fluids and nutrition cannot so readily be seen as "letting nature take its course." Dehydration or lack of nutrition become the direct cause of death for which moral responsibility cannot be avoided. The psychological and social ramifications of bringing death about in this fashion will, in our view, be difficult or impossible to distinguish from those accompanying lethal injections or other modes of active euthanasia. There will be no surprises: withdrawal of all food and water from helpless patients must necessarily result in their deaths.

Given the demographic trends in our society—the dramatically increasing pool of those characterized as the "superannuated, chronically ill, physically marginal elderly," those Daniel Callahan has labeled "the biologically tenacious"—denial of fluids and nutrition may well become "the nontreatment of choice."[12] The process is tellingly illustrated by two recent court cases. Clarence Herbert, the patient whose death gave rise to the homicide prosecution in *Barber,* was initially understood, at least by his wife, to be brain dead. In fact, Herbert was comatose but not brain dead, although the quickness of diagnosis and the subsequent nontreatment decisions led to some troubling questions of the adequacy of both diagnosis and prognosis. The sequence of decisions is instructive. First the respirator was removed. When Herbert failed to succumb as predicted, intravenous feeding was discontinued. Only then—a week later—did Herbert "comply" with the course desired, and expire.[13]

Similarly, in the *Conroy* case, the patient's nephew had previously refused to authorize surgery for his aunt's gangrene.[14] When that condition proved not to be terminal, the nephew apparently expressed his disinclination to authorize other life-extending measures.[15] Only when this decision failed to bring about the desired result—death—did the nephew and physicians contemplate the next step: termination of fluids and nutrition supplied by nasogastric tube.

Both these cases illustrate a troubling dynamic, one much like a self-fulfilling prophecy. Once a determination has been reached—perhaps for understandable and humanitarian reasons—that death is the desired outcome, decision-makers become increasingly less troubled by the choice of means to be employed to achieve that outcome. The line between "allowing to die" and "actively killing" can be elusive, and we are skeptical that any logical or psychological distinction between "allowing to die" by starvation and actively killing, as by lethal injection, will prove viable. If we as a society are to retain the prohibition against active killing, the admittedly wavering line demarcating permissible "allowing to die" must exclude death by avoidable starvation. We frankly acknowledge that our concern here extends beyond a solicitude for the outcome for the patient to include our fears for the impact of decisions and actions on family members, health care professionals, and societal values, which will survive the death of the patient. If these separate and additional concerns are to be discounted, we are hard-pressed to understand the remaining justifications for prohibition of active euthanasia in the perceived "best interests" of the incompetent patient.

We have witnessed too much history to disregard how easily society disvalues the lives of the "unproductive"—the retarded, the disabled, the senile, the institutionalized, the elderly—of those who in another time and place were referred to as "useless eaters."[16] The confluence of the emerging stream of medical and ethical opinion favoring legitimation of withholding fluids and nutrition with the torrent of public and governmental concern over the costs of medical care (and the looming imposition of cost-containment strategies which may well impose significant financial penalties on the prolonged care of the impaired elderly) powerfully reinforces our discomfort. In the current environment, it may well prove convenient—and all too easy—to move from recognition of the individual's "right to die" (to us, an unfortunate rephrasing of the legally more limited right to refuse medical treatment) to a climate enforcing a socially obligatory "duty to die," preferably quickly and cheaply.[17] The recent suggestions that all new applicants for Medicare be provided copies of "living wills" or similar documents illustrate how this process may unfold.[18] Our concern here is not with the encouragement of patient self-determination regarding medical care, including decisions about dying, which we vigorously support, but rather with the incorporation of such strategies *as a method of cost control.*

Finally, we would urge that efforts in this field be rechanneled from demonstrating that some patients' quality of life is too poor, too "meaningless," to justify the burdens of continued life, toward the challenge of finding better ways to improve the comfort and quality of life of such patients. In particular, we hope the current debate will stimulate further discussion of the merits of different modalities of providing fluids and nutrition. For example, with the development of endoscopic placement techniques for gastronomy tubes, this superficially more invasive "surgical" procedure may prove safer and more comfortable for many patients than the nonsurgical insertion of nasogastric tubes, which are sometimes a source of continuing discomfort for patients and are more likely to elicit the use of restraints to prevent the deliberate or accidental removal of the tubes. More attention must be paid to the clinical, institutional, economic, and legal implications of these and other alternatives.

## Conclusion

When coupled with powerful economic forces and with the disturbing tendency, both among professionals and in the broader society, to disvalue the lives of the "unproductive," the compassionate call for withdrawing or withholding fluids and nutrition in a few, selected cases bears the seeds of great potential abuse. Little is to be lost, and much potentially gained, by slowing down the process of legitimation, taking stock of where we have come and where we are going, improving our methods of comforting and caring for the dying without necessarily hurrying to dispatch them on their way, and deferring any premature legal, ethical, or professional approval and legitimation of this new course. The movement for "death with dignity" arose in response to deficiencies on the caring side of medicine; it would be sadly ironic if this latest manifestation served to undercut the image of physician as caring and nurturing servant and to undermine deep human values of caring and nurturance throughout society.

## Notes

1. Portions of this paper appeared, in a somewhat different form, in Mark Siegler and Alan J. Weisbard, "Against the Emerging Stream: Should Fluids and Nutritional Support Be Discontinued?" *Arch. Intern. Med.* 145:129–132 (January 1985).

2. *In re Quinlan,* 70 N.J. 10, 355 A.2d 647, *cert. denied,* 429 U.S. 922, 97 S. Ct. 319, 50 L. Ed. 2d 289 (1976).

3. See, e.g., David W. Meyers, "Legal Aspects of Withdrawing Nourishment from an Incurably Ill Patient," *Arch. Intern. Med.* 145:125–128 (January 1985); Rebecca S. Dresser and Eugene V. Boisaubin, Jr., "Ethics, Law and Nutritional Support," *Arch. Intern. Med.* 145:122–124 (January 1985); Joanne Lynn and James F. Childress, "Must Patients Always Be Given Food and Water?" *Hastings Cent. Rep.* 13:17–21 (October 1983); S. H. Wanzer et al., "The Physician's Responsibility Toward Hopelessly Ill Patients," *N. Engl. J. Med.* 310:955–959 (1984).

4. *Barber v. Superior Court of the State of California,* 195 Cal. Rptr. 484 (Cal. App. 2 Dist. 1983); *In re Conroy,* 98 N.J. 321, 486 A.2d 1209 (1985). *In the Matter of Mary Hier,* 18 Mass. App. 200, 464 N.E.2d 959, *app. den.,* 392 Mass. 1102 (1984).

5. *Bouvia v. County of Riverside,* Superior Ct. of St. of Calif., Riverside County, No. 159780 (1984).

6. See note 3, *supra.*

7. Lynn and Childress, *supra* note 3, at 18.

8. President's Commission for the Study of Ethical Problems in Medicine and Biomedical and Behavioral Research, *Deciding to Forgo Life-Sustaining Treatment,* Washington, D.C.: U.S. Government Printing Office (1983).

9. See note 4, *supra.*

10. See note 3, *supra.*

11. See generally, Alan J. Weisbard, "On the Bioethics of Jewish Law: The Case of Karen Quinlan," *Israel L. Rev.* 14:337–368 (1979); Robert A. Burt, "Authorizing Death for Anomalous Newborns," in Aubrey Milunsky and George J. Annas (eds.), *Genetics and the Law,* New York: Plenum Press (1975); Robert A. Burt, "The Ideal of Community in the Work of the President's Commission," *Cardozo L. Rev.* 6:267–286 (1985).

12. Daniel Callahan, "On Feeding the Dying," *Hastings Cent. Rep.* 13:22 (October 1983).

13. See *Barber, supra* note 4, and Bonnie Steinbock, "The Removal of Mr. Herbert's Feeding Tube," *Hastings Cent. Rep.* 13:13–116 (October 1983).

14. *Conroy, supra* note 4.

15. Personal communications to author.

16. The reference is to the Nazi euthanasia program. While the authors have been unable to locate an explicit reference to "useless eaters," Nazi usage of the phrase "useless mouths" is documented by Nora Levin, *The Holocaust:*

*The Destruction of European Jewry: 1933–1945,* New York: Schocken (1968), 302.

17. Recent remarks on "the duty to die" attributed to Colorado Governor Richard Lamm are illustrative. *New York Times,* March 29, 1984 at A16, col. 5.

18. Proceedings of the House of Delegates, American Medical Association 133rd Annual Meeting, June 1984 at 177 (commenting on recommendations of Advisory Council on Social Security).

# 64   Voluntary Active Euthanasia

## DAN W. BROCK

. . . In the recent bioethics literature some have endorsed physician-assisted suicide but not euthanasia. Are they sufficiently different that the moral arguments for one often do not apply to the other? A paradigm case of physician-assisted suicide is a patient's ending his or her life with a lethal dose of a medication requested of and provided by a physician for that purpose. A paradigm case of voluntary active euthanasia is a physician's administering the lethal dose, often because the patient is unable to do so. The only difference that need exist between the two is the person who actually administers the lethal dose—the physician or the patient. In each, the physician plays an active and necessary causal role.

In physician-assisted suicide the patient acts last (for example, Janet Adkins herself pushed the button after Dr. Kevorkian hooked her up to his suicide machine), whereas in euthanasia the physician acts last by performing the physical equivalent of pushing the button. In both cases, however, the choice rests fully with the patient. In both the patient acts last in the sense of retaining the right to change his or her mind until the point at which the lethal process becomes irreversible. How could there be a substantial moral difference between the two based only on this small difference in the part played by the physician in the

causal process resulting in death? Of course, it might be held that the moral difference is clear and important—in euthanasia the physician kills the patient whereas in physician-assisted suicide the patient kills him- or herself. But this is misleading at best. In assisted suicide the physician and patient together kill the patient. To see this, suppose a physician supplied a lethal dose to a patient with the knowledge and intent that the patient will wrongfully administer it to another. We would have no difficulty in morality or the law recognizing this as a case of joint action to kill for which both are responsible.

If there is no significant, intrinsic moral difference between the two, it is also difficult to see why public or legal policy should permit one but not the other; worries about abuse or about giving anyone dominion over the lives of others apply equally to either. As a result, I will take the arguments evaluated below to apply to both and will focus on euthanasia.

My concern here will be with *voluntary* euthanasia only—that is, with the case in which a clearly competent patient makes a fully voluntary and persistent request for aid in dying. Involuntary euthanasia, in which a competent patient explicitly refuses or opposes receiving euthanasia, and nonvoluntary euthanasia, in which a patient is incompetent and unable to express his or her wishes about euthanasia, will be considered here only as potential unwanted side-effects of permit-

Reproduced by permission. Copyright © The Hastings Center. *Hastings Center Report,* 22, 2 (1992), 10–12 with omissions.

ting voluntary euthanasia. I emphasize as well that I am concerned with *active* euthanasia, not withholding or withdrawing life-sustaining treatment, which some commentators characterize as "passive euthanasia." . . .

## The Central Ethical Argument for Voluntary Active Euthanasia

The central ethical argument for euthanasia is familiar. It is that the very same two fundamental ethical values supporting the consensus on patient's rights to decide about life-sustaining treatment also support the ethical permissibility of euthanasia. These values are individual self-determination or autonomy and individual well-being. By self-determination as it bears on euthanasia, I mean people's interest in making important decisions about their lives for themselves according to their own values or conceptions of a good life, and in being left free to act on those decisions. Self-determination is valuable because it permits people to form and live in accordance with their own conception of a good life, at least within the bounds of justice and consistent with others doing so as well. In exercising self-determination people take responsibility for their lives and for the kinds of persons they become. A central aspect of human dignity lies in people's capacity to direct their lives in this way. The value of exercising self-determination presupposes some minimum of decisionmaking capacities or competence, which thus limits the scope of euthanasia supported by self-determination; it cannot justifiably be administered, for example, in cases of serious dementia or treatable clinical depression.

Does the value of individual self-determination extend to the time and manner of one's death? Most people are very concerned about the nature of the last stage of their lives. This reflects not just a fear of experiencing substantial suffering when dying, but also a desire to retain dignity and control during this last period of life. Death is today increasingly preceded by a long period of significant physical and mental decline, due in part to the technologi-

cal interventions of modern medicine. Many people adjust to these disabilities and find meaning and value in new activities and ways. Others find the impairments and burdens in the last stage of their lives at some point sufficiently great to make life no longer worth living. For many patients near death, maintaining the quality of one's life, avoiding great suffering, maintaining one's dignity, and insuring that others remember us as we wish them to become of paramount importance and outweigh merely extending one's life. But there is no single, objectively correct answer for everyone as to when, if at all, one's life becomes all things considered a burden and unwanted. If self-determination is a fundamental value, then the great variability among people on this question makes it especially important that individuals control the manner, circumstances, and timing of their dying and death.

The other main value that supports euthanasia is individual well-being. It might seem that individual well-being conflicts with a person's self-determination when the person requests euthanasia. Life itself is commonly taken to be a central good for persons, often valued for its own sake, as well as necessary for pursuit of all other goods within a life. But when a competent patient decides to forgo all further life-sustaining treatment then the patient, either explicitly or implicitly, commonly decides that the best life possible for him or her with treatment is of sufficiently poor quality that it is worse than no further life at all. Life is no longer considered a benefit by the patient, but has now become a burden. The same judgment underlies a request for euthanasia: continued life is seen by the patient as no longer a benefit, but now a burden. Especially in the often severely compromised and debilitated states of many critically ill or dying patients, there is no objective standard, but only the competent patient's judgment of whether continued life is no longer a benefit. . . .

Most opponents do not deny that there are some cases in which the values of patient self-determination and well-being support euthanasia. Instead, they commonly offer two kinds of arguments against it that on their view outweigh or override this support. The first kind of argument is that in any individual case where considerations of the patient's self-determination and well-being do support euthanasia, it is nevertheless always ethically wrong or impermissible. The second kind of argument grants that in some individual cases euthanasia may *not* be ethically wrong, but maintains nonetheless that public and legal policy should never permit it. The first kind of argument focuses on features of any individual case of euthanasia, while the second kind focuses on social or legal policy. In the next section I consider the first kind of argument.

## Euthanasia Is the Deliberate Killing of an Innocent Person

. . . Consider the case of a patient terminally ill with ALS disease. She is completely respirator dependent with no hope of ever being weaned. She is unquestionably competent but finds her condition intolerable and persistently requests to be removed from the respirator and allowed to die. Most people and physicians would agree that the patient's physician should respect the patient's wishes and remove her from the respirator, though this will certainly cause the patient's death. The common understanding is that the physician thereby allows the patient to die. But is that correct?

Suppose the patient has a greedy and hostile son who mistakenly believes that his mother will never decide to stop her life-sustaining treatment and that even if she did her physician would not remove her from the respirator. Afraid that his inheritance will be dissipated by a long and expensive hospitalization, he enters his mother's room while she is sedated, extubates her, and she dies. Shortly thereafter the medical staff discovers what he has done and confronts the son. He replies, "I didn't kill her, I merely allowed her to die. It was her ALS disease that caused her death." I think this would rightly be dismissed as transparent sophistry—the son went into his mother's room and deliberately killed her. But, of course, the son performed just the same physical actions, did just the same thing, that the physician would

have done. If that is so, then doesn't the physician also kill the patient when he extubates her? . . .

Killing is often understood, especially within medicine, as unjustified causing of death; in medicine it is thought to be done only accidentally or negligently. It is also increasingly widely accepted that a physician is ethically justified in stopping life support in a case like that of the ALS patient. But if these two beliefs are correct, then what the physician does cannot be killing, and so must be allowing to die. Killing patients is not, to put it flippantly, understood to be part of physicians' job description. What is mistaken in this line of reasoning is the assumption that all killings are *unjustified* causings of death. Instead, some killings are ethically justified, including many instances of stopping life support.

Another reason for resisting the conclusion that stopping life support is often killing is that it is psychologically uncomfortable. Suppose the physician had stopped the ALS patient's respirator and had made the son's claim, "I didn't kill her, I merely allowed her to die. It was her ALS disease that caused her death." The clue to the psychological role here is how naturally the "merely" modifies "allowed her to die." The characterization as allowing to die is meant to shift felt responsibility away from the agent—the physician—and to the lethal disease process. Other language common in death and dying contexts plays a similar role; "letting nature take its course" or "stopping prolonging the dying process" both seem to shift responsibility from the physician who stops life support to the fatal disease process. However psychologically helpful these conceptualizations may be in making the difficult responsibility of a physician's role in the patient's death bearable, they nevertheless are confusions. Both physicians and family members can instead be helped to understand that it is the patient's decision and consent to stopping treatment that limits their responsibility for the patient's death and that shifts that responsibility to the patient. . . .

Suppose both my arguments are mistaken. Suppose that killing is worse than allowing to die and that withdrawing life support is not killing, although euthanasia is. Euthanasia still need not for that reason be morally wrong. To see this, we need to determine the basic principle for the moral evaluation of killing persons. What is it that makes paradigm cases of wrongful killing wrongful? One very plausible answer is that killing denies the victim something that he or she values greatly—continued life or a future. Moreover, since continued life is necessary for pursuing any of a person's plans and purposes, killing brings the frustration of all of these plans and desires as well. In a nutshell, wrongful killing deprives a person of a valued future, and of all the person wanted and planned to do in that future.

A natural expression of this account of the wrongness of killing is that people have a moral right not to be killed. But in this account of the wrongness of killing, the right not to be killed, like other rights, should be waivable when the person makes a competent decision that continued life is no longer wanted or a good, but is instead worse than no further life at all. In this view, euthanasia is properly understood as a case of a person having waived his or her right not to be killed. . . .

## Potential Good Consequences of Permitting Euthanasia

What are the likely good consequences? First, if euthanasia were permitted it would be possible to respect the self-determination of competent patients who want it, but now cannot get it because of its illegality. We simply do not know how many such patients and people there are. In the Netherlands, with a population of about 14.5 million (in 1987), estimates in a recent study were that about 1,900 cases of voluntary active euthanasia or physician-assisted suicide occur annually. No straightforward extrapolation to the United States is possible for many reasons, among them, that we do not know how many people here who want euthanasia now get it, despite its illegality. Even with better data on the number of persons who want euthanasia but cannot get it, significant moral disagreement would remain about how much weight should be given to any instance of failure to respect a person's self-determination in this way. . . .

A second good consequence of making euthanasia legally permissible benefits a much larger group. Polls have shown that a majority of the American public believes that people should have a right to obtain euthanasia if they want it.[1] No doubt the vast majority of those who support this right to euthanasia will never in fact come to want euthanasia for themselves. Nevertheless, making it legally permissible would reassure many people that if they ever do want euthanasia they would be able to obtain it. This reassurance would supplement the broader control over the process of dying given by the right to decide about life-sustaining treatment. Having fire insurance on one's house benefits all who have it, not just those whose houses actually burn down, by reassuring them that in the unlikely event of their house burning down, they will receive the money needed to rebuild it. Likewise, the legalization of euthanasia can be thought of as a kind of insurance policy against being forced to endure a protracted dying process that one has come to find burdensome and unwanted, especially when there is no life-sustaining treatment to forgo. The strong concern about losing control of their care expressed by many people who face serious illness likely to end in death suggests that they give substantial importance to the legalization of euthanasia as a means of maintaining this control.

A third good consequence of the legalization of euthanasia concerns patients whose dying is filled with severe and unrelievable pain or suffering. When there is a life-sustaining treatment that, if forgone, will lead relatively quickly to death, then doing so can bring an end to these patients' suffering without recourse to euthanasia. For patients receiving no such treatment, however, euthanasia may be the only release from their otherwise prolonged suffering and agony. This argument from mercy has always been the strongest argument for euthanasia in those cases to which it applies.[2] . . .

Specialists in pain control, as for example the pain of terminally ill cancer patients, argue that there are very few patients whose pain could not be adequately controlled, though sometimes at the cost of so sedating them that they are effectively unable to interact with other people or their environment. Thus, the argument from mercy in cases of physical pain can probably be met in a large majority of cases by providing adequate measures of pain relief. . . .

Dying patients often undergo substantial psychological suffering that is not fully or even principally the result of physical pain.[3] The knowledge about how to relieve this suffering is much more limited than in the case of relieving pain, and efforts to do so are probably more often unsuccessful. If the argument from mercy is extended to patients experiencing great and unrelievable psychological suffering, the numbers of patients to which it applies are much greater.

One last good consequence of legalizing euthanasia is that once death has been accepted, it is often more humane to end life quickly and peacefully, when that is what the patient wants. Such a death will often be seen as better than a more prolonged one. People who suffer a sudden and unexpected death, for example by dying quickly or in their sleep from a heart attack or stroke, are often considered lucky to have died in this way. We care about how we die in part because we care about how others remember us, and we hope they will remember us as we were in "good times" with them and not as we might be when disease has robbed us of our dignity as human beings. As with much in the treatment and care of the dying, people's concerns differ in this respect, but for at least some people, euthanasia will be a more humane death than what they have often experienced with other loved ones and might otherwise expect for themselves. . . .

## Potential Bad Consequences of Permitting Euthanasia

Some of the arguments against permitting euthanasia are aimed specifically against physicians, while others are aimed against anyone being permitted to perform it. I shall first consider one argument of the former sort. Permitting physicians to perform euthanasia, it is said, would be incompatible with their fundamental moral and professional commit-

ment as healers to care for patients and to protect life. Moreover, if euthanasia by physicians became common, patients come to fear that a medication was intended not to treat or care, but instead to kill, and would thus lose trust in their physicians. This position was forcefully stated in a paper by Willard Gaylin and his colleagues:

> The very soul of medicine is on trial . . . This issue touches medicine at its moral center; if this moral center collapses, if physicians become killers or are even licensed to kill, the professional—and, therewith, each physician—will never again be worthy of trust and respect as healer and comforter and protector of life in all its frailty.

These authors go on to make clear that, while they oppose permitting anyone to perform euthanasia, their special concern is with physicians doing so:

> We call on fellow physicians to say that they will not deliberately kill. We must also say to each of our fellow physicians that we will not tolerate killing of patients and that we shall take disciplinary action against doctors who kill. And we must say to the broader community that if it insists on tolerating or legalizing active euthanasia, it will have to find non-physicians to do its killing.[4]

If permitting physicians to kill would undermine the very "moral center" of medicine, then almost certainly physicians should not be permitted to perform euthanasia. But how persuasive is this claim? Patients should not fear, as a consequence of permitting *voluntary* active euthanasia, that their physicians will substitute a lethal injection for what patients want and believe is part of their care. If active euthanasia is restricted to cases in which it is truly voluntary, then no patient should fear getting it unless she or he has voluntarily requested it. (The fear that we might in time also come to accept nonvoluntary, or even involuntary, active euthanasia is a slippery slope worry I address below.) Patients' trust of their physicians could be increased, not eroded, by knowledge that physicians will provide aid in dying when patients seek it.

Might Gaylin and his colleagues nevertheless be correct in their claim that the moral center of medicine would collapse if physicians were to become killers? . . . In spelling out above what I called the positive argument for voluntary active euthanasia, I suggested that two principal values —respecting patients' self-determination and promoting their well-being—underlie the consensus that competent patients, or the surrogates of incompetent patients, are entitled to refuse any life-sustaining treatment and to choose from among available alternative treatments. It is the commitment to these two values in guiding physicians' actions as healers, comforters, and protectors of their patients' lives that should be at the "moral center" of medicine, and these two values support physicians' administering euthanasia when their patients make competent requests for it.

What should not be at that moral center is a commitment to preserving patients' lives as such, without regard to whether those patients want their lives preserved or judge their preservation a benefit to them. . . .

A second bad consequence that some foresee is that permitting euthanasia would weaken society's commitment to provide optimal care for dying patients. We live at a time in which the control of health care costs has become, and is likely to continue to be, the dominant focus of health care policy. If euthanasia is seen as a cheaper alternative to adequate care and treatment, then we might become less scrupulous about providing sometimes costly support and other services to dying patients. Particularly if our society comes to embrace deeper and more explicit rationing of health care, frail, elderly, and dying patients will need to be strong and effective advocates for their own health care and other needs, although they are hardly in a position to do this. We should do nothing to weaken their ability to obtain adequate care and services.

This second worry is difficult to assess because there is little firm evidence about the likelihood of the feared erosion in the care of dying patients. There are at least two reasons, however, for skepticism about this argument. The first is that the same worry could have been directed at recognizing patients' or surrogates' rights to forgo life-sustaining treatment, yet there is no persuasive evidence that recognizing the right to refuse treatment has caused a serious erosion in the quality of care of dying patients. The second reason for skepticism about this worry is that only a very small proportion of deaths would occur from euthanasia if it were permitted. In the Netherlands, where euthanasia under specified circumstances is permitted by the courts, though not authorized by statute, the best estimate of the proportion of overall deaths that result from it is about 2 percent.[5] Thus, the vast majority of critically ill and dying patients will not request it, and so will still have to be cared for by physicians, families, and others. Permitting euthanasia should not diminish people's commitment and concern to maintain and improve the care of these patients.

A third possible bad consequence of permitting euthanasia (or even a public discourse in which strong support for euthanasia is evident) is to threaten the progress made in securing the rights of patients or their surrogates to decide about and to refuse life-sustaining treatment.[6] This progress has been made against the backdrop of a clear and firm legal prohibition of euthanasia, which has provided a relatively bright line limiting the dominion of others over patients' lives. It has therefore been an important reassurance to concerns about how the authority to take steps ending life might be misused, abused, or wrongly extended. . . .

As with the second potential bad consequence of permitting euthanasia, this third consideration too is speculative and difficult to assess. The feared erosion of patients' or surrogates' rights to decide about life-sustaining treatment, together with greater court involvement in those decisions, are both possible. However, I believe there is reason to discount this general worry. The legal rights of competent patients and, to a lesser degree, surrogates of incompetent patients to decide about treatment are very firmly embedded in a long line of informed consent and life-sustaining treatment cases, and are not likely to be eroded by a debate over, or even acceptance of, euthanasia. It will not be accepted without safeguards that reassure the public about abuse, and if that debate shows the need for similar safeguards for some life-sustaining treatment decisions they should be adopted there as well. In neither case are the only possible safeguards greater court involvement, as the recent growth of institutional ethics committees shows.

The fourth potential bad consequence of permitting euthanasia has been developed by David Velleman and turns on the subtle point that making a new option or choice available to people can sometimes make them worse off, even if once they have the choice they go on to choose what is best for them.[7] Ordinarily, people's continued existence is viewed by them as given, a fixed condition with which they must cope. Making euthanasia available to people as an option denies them the alternative of staying alive by default. If people are offered the option of euthanasia, their continued existence is now a choice for which they can be held responsible and which they can be asked by others to justify. We care, and are right to care, about being able to justify ourselves to others. To the extent that our society is unsympathetic to justifying a severely dependent or impaired existence, a heavy psychological burden of proof may be placed on patients who think their terminal illness or chronic infirmity is not a sufficient reason for dying. Even if they otherwise view their life as worth living, the opinion of others around them that it is not can threaten their reason for living and make euthanasia a rational choice. Thus the existence of the option becomes a subtle pressure to request it.

This argument correctly identifies the reason why offering some patients the option of euthanasia would not benefit them. Velleman takes it not as a reason for opposing all euthanasia, but for restricting it to circumstances where there are "unmistakable and overpowering reasons for persons to want the option of euthanasia," and for denying the option in all other cases. But there are at least three reasons why such restriction may not be warranted. First, polls and other evidence support that most Americans believe euthanasia should be permitted (though the recent defeat of

the referendum to permit it in the state of Washington raises some doubt about this support). Thus, many more people seem to want the choice than would be made worse off by getting it. Second, if giving people the option of ending their life really makes them worse off, then we should not only prohibit euthanasia, but also take back from people the right they now have to decide about life-sustaining treatment. The feared harmful effect should already have occurred from securing people's right to refuse life-sustaining treatment, yet there is no evidence of any such widespread harm or any broad public desire to rescind that right. Third, since there is a wide range of conditions in which reasonable people can and do disagree about whether they would want continued life, it is not possible to restrict the permissibility of euthanasia as narrowly as Velleman suggests without thereby denying it to most persons who would want it; to permit it only in cases in which virtually everyone would want it would be to deny it to most who would want it.

A fifth potential bad consequence of making euthanasia legally permissible is that it might weaken the general legal prohibition of homicide. This prohibition is so fundamental to civilized society, it is argued, that we should do nothing that erodes it. . . .

Permitting euthanasia would require qualifying, at least in effect, the legal prohibition against homicide, a prohibition that in general does not allow the consent of the victim to justify or excuse the act. Nevertheless, the very same fundamental basis of the right to decide about life-sustaining treatment—respecting a person's self-determination—does support euthanasia as well. Individual self-determination has long been a well-entrenched and fundamental value in the law, and so extending it to euthanasia would not require appeal to novel legal values or principles. That suicide or attempted suicide is no longer a criminal offense in virtually all states indicates an acceptance of individual self-determination in the taking of one's own life analogous to that required for voluntary active euthanasia. The legal prohibition (in most states) of assisting in suicide and the refusal in the law to accept the consent of the victim as a possible justification of homicide are both arguably a result of difficulties in the legal process of establishing the consent of the victim after the fact. If procedures can be designed that clearly establish the voluntariness of the person's request for euthanasia, it would under those procedures represent a carefully circumscribed qualification on the legal prohibition of homicide. Nevertheless, some remaining worries about this weakening can be captured in the final potential bad consequence, to which I will now turn.

This final potential bad consequence is the central concern of many opponents of euthanasia and, I believe, is the most serious objection to a legal policy permitting it. According to this "slippery slope" worry, although active euthanasia may be morally permissible in cases in which it is unequivocally voluntary and the patient finds his or her condition unbearable, a legal policy permitting euthanasia would inevitably lead to active euthanasia being performed in many other cases in which it would be morally wrong. To prevent those other wrongful cases of euthanasia we should not permit even morally justified performance of it.

Slippery slope arguments of this form are problematic and difficult to evaluate.[8] From one perspective, they are the last refuge of conservative defenders of the status quo. When all the opponent's objections to the wrongness of euthanasia itself have been met, the opponent then shifts ground and acknowledges both that it is not in itself wrong and that a legal policy which resulted only in its being performed would not be bad. Nevertheless, the opponent maintains, it should still not be permitted because doing so would result in its being performed in other cases in which it is not voluntary and would be wrong. In this argument's most extreme form, permitting euthanasia is the first and fateful step down the slippery slope to Nazism. Once on the slope we will be unable to get off.

Now it cannot be denied that it is *possible* that permitting euthanasia could have these fateful consequences, but that cannot be enough to warrant prohibiting it if it is otherwise justified. A sim-

ilar *possible* slippery slope worry could have been raised to securing competent patients' rights to decide about life support, but recent history shows such a worry would have been unfounded. It must be relevant how likely it is that we will end with horrendous consequences and an unjustified practice of euthanasia. How *likely* and *widespread* would the abuses and unwarranted extensions of permitting it be? By abuses, I mean the performance of euthanasia that fails to satisfy the conditions required for voluntary active euthanasia, for example, if the patient has been subtly pressured to accept it. By unwarranted extensions of policy, I mean later changes in legal policy to permit not just voluntary euthanasia, but also euthanasia in cases in which, for example, it need not be fully voluntary. Opponents of voluntary euthanasia on slippery slope grounds have not provided the data or evidence necessary to turn their speculative concerns into well-grounded likelihoods.

It is at least clear, however, that both the character and likelihood of abuses of a legal policy permitting euthanasia depend in significant part on the procedures put in place to protect against them. I will not try to detail fully what such procedures might be, but will just give some examples of what they might include:

1. The patient should be provided with all relevant information about his or her medical condition, current prognosis, available alternative treatments, and the prognosis of each.
2. Procedures should ensure that the patient's request for euthanasia is stable or enduring (a brief waiting period could be required) and fully voluntary (an advocate for the patient might be appointed to ensure this).
3. All reasonable alternatives must have been explored for improving the patient's quality of life and relieving any pain or suffering.
4. A psychiatric evaluation should ensure that the patient's request is not the result of a treatable psychological impairment such as depression.[9]

These examples of procedural safeguards are all designed to ensure that the patient's choice is fully informed, voluntary, and competent, and so a true exercise of self-determination. . . .

## The Slip into Nonvoluntary Active Euthanasia

I believe slippery slope worries can largely be limited by making necessary distinctions both in principle and in practice, one slippery slope concern is legitimate. There is reason to expect that legalization of voluntary active euthanasia might soon be followed by strong pressure to legalize some nonvoluntary euthanasia of incompetent patients unable to express their own wishes. Respecting a person's self-determination and recognizing that continued life is not always of value to a person can support not only voluntary active but nonvoluntary euthanasia as well. . . . The very same logic that has extended the right to refuse life-sustaining treatment from a competent patient to the surrogate of an incompetent patient (acting with or without a formal advance directive from the patient) may well extend the scope of active euthanasia. The argument will be, Why continue to force unwanted life on patients just because they have now lost the capacity to request euthanasia from us? . . .

Making nonvoluntary active euthanasia legally permissible, however, would greatly enlarge the number of patients on whom it might be performed and substantially enlarge the potential for misuse and abuse. As noted above, frail and debilitated elderly people, often demented or otherwise incompetent and thereby unable to defend and assert their own interests, may be especially vulnerable to unwanted euthanasia.

For some people, this risk is more than sufficient reason to oppose the legalization of voluntary euthanasia. But while we should in general be cautious about inferring much from the experience in the Netherlands to what our own experience in the United States might be, there may be one important lesson that we can learn from them. One commentator has noted that in the Netherlands families of incompetent patients have less authority than do families in the United States to act as surrogates for incompetent patients in making decisions to forgo life-sustaining treatment.[10]

From the Dutch perspective, it may be we in the United States who are *already* on the slippery slope in having given surrogates broad authority to forgo life-sustaining treatment for incompetent persons. In this view, the more important moral divide, and the more important with regard to potential for abuse, is not between forgoing life-sustaining treatment and euthanasia, but instead between voluntary and nonvoluntary performance of either. If this is correct, then the more important issue is ensuring the appropriate principles and procedural safeguards for the exercise of decision-making authority by surrogates for incompetent persons in *all* decisions at the end of life. This may be the correct response to slippery slope worries about euthanasia. . . .

## Notes

1. P. Painton and E. Taylor, "Love or Let Die," *Time,* 19 March 1990. pp. 62–71; *Boston Globe/*Harvard University Poll. *Boston Globe.* 3 November 1991.

2. James Rachels, *The End of Life* (Oxford: Oxford University Press, 1986).

3. Eric Cassell, *The Nature of Suffering and the Goals of Medicine* (New York: Oxford University Press, 1991).

4. Willard Gaylin, Leon R. Kass, Edmund D. Pellegrino, and Mark Siegler, "Doctors Must Not Kill," *JAMA* 259 (1988): 2139–40.

5. Paul J. Van der Maas et al., "Euthanasia and Other Medical Decisions Concerning the End of Life," *Lancet* 338 (1991): 669–674.

6. Susan M. Wolf, "Holding the Line on Euthanasia," Special Supplement, *Hastings Center Report* 19, no. 1 (1989): 13–15.

7. My formulation of this argument derives from David Velleman's statement of it in his commentary on an earlier version of this paper delivered at the American Philosophical Association Central Division meetings; a similar point was made to me by Elisha Milgram in discussion on another occasion.

8. Frederick Schauer, "Slippery Slopes." *Harvard Law Review* 99 (1985): 361–83; Wibren van der Burg, "The Slippery Slope Argument," *Ethics* 102 (October 1991): 42–65.

9. There is evidence that physicians commonly fail to diagnose depression. See Robert I. Misbin, "Physicians Aid in Dying," *NEJM* 325 (1991): 1304–7.

10. Margaret P. Battin, "Seven Caveats Concerning the Discussion of Euthanasia in Holland," *American Philosophical Association Newsletter on Philosophy and Medicine* 89, no. 2 (1990).

# 65   When Self-Determination Runs Amok

## DANIEL CALLAHAN

The euthanasia debate is not just another moral debate, one in a long list of arguments in our pluralistic society. It is profoundly emblematic of three important turning points in Western thought. The first is that of the legitimate conditions under which one person can kill another. The acceptance of voluntary active euthanasia would morally sanction what can only be called "consenting adult killing." By that term I mean the killing of one person by another in the name of their mutual right to be killer and killed if they freely agree to play those roles. This turn flies in the face of a longstanding effort to limit the circumstances under which one person can take the life of another, from efforts to control the free flow of guns and arms, to abolish capital punishment, and to more tightly control warfare. Euthanasia would add a whole new category of killing to a society that already has too many excuses to indulge itself in that way.

The second turning point lies in the meaning and limits of self-determination. The acceptance of euthanasia would sanction a view of autonomy holding that individuals may, in the name of their own private, idiosyncratic view of the good life, call upon others, including such institutions as medicine, to help them pursue that life, even at the risk of harm to the common good. This works against the idea that the meaning and scope of our own right to lead our own lives must be conditioned by, and be compatible with, the good of the community, which is more than an aggregate of self-directing individuals.

The third turning point is to be found in the claim being made upon medicine: it should be prepared to make its skills available to individuals to help them achieve their private vision of the good life. This puts medicine in the business of

promoting the individualistic pursuit of general human happiness and well-being. It would overturn the traditional belief that medicine should limit its domain to promoting and preserving human health, redirecting it instead to the relief of that suffering which stems from life itself, not merely from a sick body.

I believe that, at each of these three turning points, proponents of euthanasia push us in the wrong direction. Arguments in favor of euthanasia fall into four general categories, which I will take up in turn: (1) the moral claim of individual self-determination and well-being; (2) the moral irrelevance of the difference between killing and allowing to die; (3) the supposed paucity of evidence to show likely harmful consequences of legalized euthanasia; and (4) the compatibility of euthanasia and medical practice.

## Self-Determination

Central to most arguments for euthanasia is the principle of self-determination. People are presumed to have an interest in deciding for themselves, according to their own beliefs about what makes life good, how they will conduct their lives. That is an important value, but the question in the euthanasia context is, What does it mean and how far should it extend? If it were a question of suicide, where a person takes her own life without assistance from another, that principle might be pertinent, at least for debate. But euthanasia is not that limited a matter. The self-determination in that case can only be effected by the moral and physical assistance of another. Euthanasia is thus no longer a matter only of self-determination, but of a mutual, social decision between two people, the one to be killed and the other to do the killing.

How are we to make the moral move from my right of self-determination to some doctor's right to kill me—from *my* right to *his* right? Where does

Reprinted with permission of the publisher from *Hastings Center Report*, 22, 2, (1992), 52–55. Copyright © The Hastings Center.

the doctor's moral warrant to kill come from? Ought doctors to be able to kill anyone they want as long as permission is given by competent persons? Is our right to life just like a piece of property, to be given away or alienated if the price (happiness, relief of suffering) is right? And then to be destroyed with our permission once alienated?

In answer to all those questions, I will say this: I have yet to hear a plausible argument why it should be permissible for us to put this kind of power in the hands of another, whether a doctor or anyone else. The idea that we can waive our right to life, and then give to another the power to take that life, requires a justification yet to be provided by anyone.

Slavery was long ago outlawed on the ground that one person should not have the right to own another, even with the other's permission. Why? Because it is a fundamental moral wrong for one person to give over his life and fate to another, whatever the good consequences, and no less a wrong for another person to have that kind of total, final power. Like slavery, dueling was long ago banned on similar grounds: even free, competent individuals should not have the power to kill each other, whatever their motives, whatever the circumstances. Consenting adult killing, like consenting adult slavery or degradation, is a strange route to human dignity.

There is another problem as well. If doctors, once sanctioned to carry out euthanasia, are to be themselves responsible moral agents—not simply hired hands with lethal injections at the ready—then they must have their own *independent* moral grounds to kill those who request such services. What do I mean? As those who favor euthanasia are quick to point out, some people want it because their life has become so burdensome it no longer seems worth living.

The doctor will have a difficulty at this point. The degree and intensity to which people suffer from their diseases and their dying, and whether they find life more of a burden than a benefit, has very little directly to do with the nature or extent of their actual physical condition. Three people can have the same condition, but only one will find the suffering unbearable. People suffer, but

suffering is as much a function of the values of individuals as it is of the physical causes of that suffering. Inevitably in that circumstance, the doctor will in effect be treating the patient's values. To be responsible, the doctor would have to share those values. The doctor would have to decide, on her own, whether the patient's life was "no longer worth living."

But how could a doctor possibly know that or make such a judgment? Just because the patient said so? I raise this question because, while in Holland at the euthanasia conference reported by Maurice de Wachter elsewhere in this issue, the doctors present agreed that there is no objective way of measuring or judging the claims of patients that their suffering is unbearable. And if it is difficult to measure suffering, how much more difficult to determine the value of a patient's statement that her life is not worth living?

However one might want to answer such questions, the very need to ask them, to inquire into the physician's responsibility and grounds for medical and moral judgment, points out the social nature of the decision. Euthanasia is not a private matter of self-determination. It is an act that requires two people to make it possible, and a complicit society to make it acceptable.

## Killing and Allowing to Die

Against common opinion, the argument is sometimes made that there is no moral difference between stopping life-sustaining treatment and more active forms of killing, such as lethal injection. Instead I would contend that the notion that there is no morally significant difference between omission and commission is just wrong. Consider in its broad implications what the eradication of the distinction implies: that death from disease has been banished, leaving only the actions of physicians in terminating treatment as the cause of death. Biology, which used to bring about death, has apparently been displaced by human agency. Doctors have finally, I suppose, thus genuinely become gods, now doing what nature and the deities once did.

What is the mistake here? It lies in confusing causality and culpability, and in failing to note the way in which human societies have overlaid natural causes with moral rules and interpretations. Causality (by which I mean the direct physical causes of death) and culpability (by which I mean our attribution of moral responsibility to human actions) are confused under three circumstances.

They are confused, first, when the action of a physician in stopping treatment of a patient with an underlying lethal disease is construed as *causing* death. On the contrary, the physician's omission can only bring about death on the condition that the patient's disease will kill him in the absence of treatment. We may hold the physician morally responsible for the death, if we have morally judged such actions wrongful omissions. But it confuses reality and moral judgment to see an omitted action as having the same causal status as one that directly kills. A lethal injection will kill both a healthy person and a sick person. A physician's omitted treatment will have no effect on a healthy person. Turn off the machine on me, a healthy person, and nothing will happen. It will only, in contrast, bring the life of a sick person to an end because of an underlying fatal disease.

Causality and culpability are confused, second, when we fail to note that judgments of moral responsibility and culpability are human constructs. By that I mean that we human beings, after moral reflection, have decided to call some actions right or wrong, and to devise moral rules to deal with them. When physicians could do nothing to stop death, they were not held responsible for it. When, with medical progress, they began to have some power over death—but only its timing and circumstances, not its ultimate inevitability—moral rules were devised to set forth their obligations. Natural causes of death were not thereby banished. They were, instead, overlaid with a medical ethics designed to determine moral culpability in deploying medical power.

To confuse the judgments of this ethics with the physical causes of death—which is the connotation of the word *kill*—is to confuse nature and human action. People will, one way or another, die of some disease; death will have dominion over all of us. To say that a doctor "kills" a patient by allowing this to happen should only be understood as a moral judgment about the licitness of his omission, nothing more. We can, as a fashion of speech only, talk about a doctor *killing* a patient by omitting treatment he should have provided. It is a fashion of speech precisely because it is the underlying disease that brings death when treatment is omitted; that is its cause, not the physician's omission. It is a misuse of the word *killing* to use it when a doctor stops a treatment he believes will no longer benefit the patient—when, that is, he steps aside to allow an eventually inevitable death to occur now rather than later. The only deaths that human beings invented are those that come from direct killing—when, with a lethal injection, we both cause death and are morally responsible for it. In the case of omissions, we do not cause death even if we may be judged morally responsible for it.

This difference between causality and culpability also helps us see why a doctor who has omitted a treatment he should have provided has "killed" that patient while another doctor—performing precisely the same act of omission on another patient in different circumstances—does not kill her, but only allows her to die. The difference is that we have come, by moral convention and conviction, to classify unauthorized or illegitimate omissions as acts of "killing." We call them "killing" in the expanded sense of the term: a culpable action that permits the real cause of death, the underlying disease, to proceed to its lethal conclusion. By contrast, the doctor who, at the patient's request, omits or terminates unwanted treatment does not kill at all. Her underlying disease, not his action, is the physical cause of death; and we have agreed to consider actions of that kind to be morally licit. He thus can truly be said to have "allowed" her to die.

If we fail to maintain the distinction between killing and allowing to die, moreover, there are some disturbing possibilities. The first would be to confirm many physicians in their already too-powerful belief that, when patients die or when physicians stop treatment because of the futility of continuing it, they are somehow both morally and physically responsible for the deaths that follow. That notion needs to be abolished, not strengthened. It needlessly and wrongly burdens the physician, to whom should not be attributed the powers of the gods. The second possibility would be that, in every case where a doctor judges medical treatment no longer effective in prolonging life, a quick and direct killing of the patient would be seen as the next, most reasonable step, on grounds of both humaneness and economics. I do not see how that logic could easily be rejected.

## Calculating the Consequences

When concerns about the adverse social consequences of permitting euthanasia are raised, its advocates tend to dismiss them as unfounded and overly speculative. On the contrary, recent data about the Dutch experience suggests that such concerns are right on target. From my own discussions in Holland, and from the articles on that subject in this issue and elsewhere, I believe we can now fully see most of the *likely* consequences of legal euthanasia.

Three consequences seem almost certain, in this or any other country: the inevitability of some abuse of the law; the difficulty of precisely writing, and then enforcing, the law; and the inherent slipperiness of the moral reasons for legalizing euthanasia in the first place.

Why is abuse inevitable? One reason is that almost all laws on delicate, controversial matters are to some extent abused. This happens because not everyone will agree with the law as written and will bend it, or ignore it, if they can get away with it. From explicit admissions to me by Dutch proponents of euthanasia, and from the corroborating information provided by the Remmelink Report and the outside studies of Carlos Gomez and John Keown, I am convinced that in the Netherlands there are a substantial number of cases of nonvoluntary euthanasia, that is, euthanasia undertaken without the explicit permission of the person being killed. The other reason abuse is inevitable is that the law is likely to have a low enforcement priority in the criminal justice system. Like other laws of similar status, unless there is an unrelenting and harsh willingness to pursue abuse, violations will ordinarily be tolerated. The worst thing to me about my experience in Holland was the casual, seemingly indifferent attitude toward abuse. I think that would happen everywhere.

Why would it be hard to precisely write, and then enforce, the law? The Dutch speak about the requirement of "unbearable" suffering, but admit that such a term is just about indefinable, a highly subjective matter admitting of no objective standards. A requirement for outside opinion is nice, but it is easy to find complaisant colleagues. A requirement that a medical condition be "terminal" will run aground on the notorious difficulties of knowing when an illness is actually terminal.

Apart from those technical problems there is a more profound worry. I see no way, even in principle, to write or enforce a meaningful law that can guarantee effective procedural safeguards. The reason is obvious yet almost always overlooked. The euthanasia transaction will ordinarily take place within the boundaries of the private and confidential doctor-patient relationship. No one can possibly know what takes place in that context unless the doctor chooses to reveal it. In Holland, less than 10 percent of the physicians report their acts of euthanasia and do so with almost complete legal impunity. There is no reason why the situation should be any better elsewhere. Doctors will have their own reasons for keeping euthanasia secret, and some patients will have no less a motive for wanting it concealed.

I would mention, finally, that the moral logic of the motives for euthanasia contain within them the ingredients of abuse. The two standard motives for euthanasia and assisted suicide are said to be our right of self-determination, and our claim upon the mercy of others, especially doctors, to relieve our suffering. These two motives are typically spliced together and presented as a single justification. Yet if they are considered independently—and there is no inherent reason why they must be linked—they reveal serious problems. It is said that a competent, adult person should have a right to euthanasia for the relief of suffering. But why must the person be suffering? Does not that stipulation already compromise the principle of self-determination? How can self-determination have any limits? Whatever the person's motives may be, why are they not sufficient?

Consider next the person who is suffering but not competent, who is perhaps demented or mentally retarded. The standard argument would deny euthanasia to that person. But why? If a person is suffering but not competent, then it would seem grossly unfair to deny relief solely on the grounds of incompetence. Are the incompetent less entitled to relief from suffering than the competent? Will it only be affluent, middle-class people, mentally fit and savvy about working the medical system, who can qualify? Do the incompetent suffer less because of their incompetence?

Considered from these angles, there are no good moral reasons to limit euthanasia once the principle of taking life for that purpose has been legitimated. If we really believe in self-determination, then any competent person should have a right to be killed by a doctor for any reason that suits him. If we believe in the relief of suffering, then it seems cruel and capricious to deny it to the incompetent. There is, in short, no reasonable or logical stopping point once the turn has been made down the road to euthanasia, which could soon turn into a convenient and commodious expressway.

## Euthanasia and Medical Practice

A fourth kind of argument one often hears both in the Netherlands and in this country is that euthanasia and assisted suicide are perfectly compatible with the aims of medicine. I would note at the very outset that a physician who participates in another person's suicide already abuses medicine. Apart from depression (the main statistical cause of suicide), people commit suicide because they find life empty, oppressive, or meaningless. Their judgment is a judgment about the value of continued life, not only about health (even if they are sick). Are doctors now to be given the right to make judgments about the kinds of life worth living and to give their blessing to suicide for those they judge wanting? What conceivable competence, technical or moral, could doctors claim to play such a role? Are we to medicalize suicide, turning judgments about its worth and value into one more clinical issue? Yes, those are rhetorical questions.

Yet they bring us to the core of the problem of euthanasia and medicine. The great temptation of modern medicine, not always resisted, is to move beyond the promotion and preservation of health into the boundless realm of general human happiness and well-being. The root problem of illness and morality is both medical and philosophical or religious. "Why must I die" can be asked as a technical, biological question or as a question about the meaning of life. When medicine tries to respond to the latter, which it is always under pressure to do, it moves beyond its proper role.

It is not medicine's place to lift from us the burden of that suffering which turns on the meaning we assign to the decay of the body and its eventual death. It is not medicine's place to determine when lives are not worth living or when the burden of life is too great to be borne. Doctors have no conceivable way of evaluating such claims on the part of patients, and they should have no right to act in response to them. Medicine should try to relieve human suffering, but only that suffering which is brought on by illness and dying as biological phenomena, not that suffering which comes from anguish or despair at the human condition.

Doctors ought to relieve those forms of suffering that medically accompany serious illness and the threat of death. They should relieve pain, do what they can to allay anxiety and uncertainty, and be a comforting presence. As sensitive human beings, doctors should be prepared to respond to patients who ask why they must die, or die in pain. But here the doctor and the patient are at the same level. The doctor may have no better an answer to those old questions than anyone else; and certainly no special insight from his training as a physician. It would be terrible for physicians to forget this, and to think that in a swift, lethal injection, medicine has found its own answer to the riddle of life. It would be a false answer, given by the wrong people. It would be no less a false answer for patients. They should neither ask medicine to put its own vocation at risk to serve their private interests, nor think that the answer to suffering is to be killed by another. The problem is precisely that, too often in human history, killing has seemed the quick, efficient way to put aside that which burdens us. It rarely helps, and too often simply adds to one evil still another. That is what I believe euthanasia would accomplish. It is self-determination run amok.

# 66   Self-Regarding Suicide: A Modified Kantian View

## THOMAS E. HILL

Moral debates about suicide typically focus on the questions of whether suicide is immoral and whether we should interfere with suicide attempts. These questions naturally turn attention to matters such as conflicting rights, social consequences, religious belief, and the difficulty of drawing a sharp line between right and wrong in complex cases. My concern will be somewhat different. I want to consider what ideals of attitude toward human life and death may lie behind the common intuition that some suicides are morally objectionable, to some degree, even though not harmful to others and not a violation of anyone's rights.

The puzzling cases arise when the suicide is not failing in his obligations to others, but lacks any overriding moral reason to take his life. He is within his rights and yet his decision still seems morally significant. The issue is not whether suicide is strictly immoral, still less how a sharp line can be drawn between the permissible and the impermissible. The question, rather, is how an ideal person would view such choices. Or, in other words, what sort of attitudes toward life and death do we, from a moral point of view, want to encourage and see present in those who are moved to consider suicide?

My suggestion will be that to explain certain common intuitive beliefs on this question we need to move beyond consideration of rights and utility

to a qualified Kantian principle about the value of life as a rational autonomous agent. Though I find Kant's rigoristic opposition to suicide untenable, the spirit of his idea of humanity as an end in itself, I think, leads to a more tenable position. This idea, appropriately qualified, opposes attitudes which sometimes motivate suicide, but it does not condemn, in fact it encourages, suicide from other motives in special circumstances. The Kantian idea accords with a view which I believe is widely held in popular thought, though currently unfashionable in philosophy, namely, that moral considerations are not all other-regarding. Though Kant went too far in saying that suicide is always a violation of a duty to oneself, there is more that a moral person considering suicide needs to think about than his relations to other people.

My discussion will be divided as follows. First, I state some intuitive beliefs about the sort of cases in which suicide falls short of the morally ideal, as well as other cases in which suicide seems unobjectionable. These are the intuitions which need to be explained and which prompt us to look beyond rights and utility. Second, I sketch some main points pertinent to suicide in Kant's ethics and indicate ways in which I believe Kant's theory needs modification. Third, I propose a qualified Kantian principle and contrast its perspective on the value of life with some alternatives. Fourth, I consider the application of the principle to suicide, indicating how it would support the initial intuitive beliefs about when suicide is objectionable and when it is not. Finally, I close with brief

From Thomas E. Hill, *Suicide and Life-Threatening Behavior*, 13,4, 1983. Reprinted by permission of Plenum Publishing Corp.

remarks on the possibility of employing Kantian arguments to make the principle more persuasive.

# I

Real life is admittedly more complex than any of our philosophical categories, but to further discussion, I want to focus attention on four specially defined types of suicide. Pure instances are at least conceivable, though real cases doubtless contain a mixture of elements.

In each case, we are to imagine that the persons contemplating suicide are free from obligations to others which would be violated or neglected if they choose suicide. For example, there are no outstanding promises to be kept, no children to care for, no institutional obligations to be met, and so on. Moreover, unlike most actual cases, there are none who will grieve or feel guilt-ridden when they learn of the suicide. As far as anyone can, the persons who choose suicide have already paid their debt of gratitude to the individuals and society who have benefited them, and they have made constructive contributions to charity and other good causes. Perhaps some will say that no one ever discharges his obligation to others, but for present purposes let us suppose that this is not so. The point of setting aside obligations to others in this way is not, of course, to deny their importance in real, typical cases, but simply to isolate other moral considerations which may be relevant.

To further simplify, let us imagine that in the cases we shall consider, there is an absence of the sort of altruistic motives which are often thought to make suicide morally commendable. For example, suicide is not a necessary means to save one's family from disastrous financial costs involved in lingering illness; it is not the only way a spy can keep from betraying his country under torture; it is not a dramatic protest against an unjust war; and so on. So far as others are concerned, there is no reason for, or against, suicide.

## (1) Impulsive Suicide

A suicide might be called impulsive if it is prompted by a temporarily intense, yet passing

desire or emotion out of keeping with the more permanent character, preferences, and emotional state of the agent. We need not suppose that the agent is "driven" or "blinded" or momentarily insane, but his act is not the sort that coheres with what he most wants and values over time. In calmer, more deliberative moments he would have wished that he would not respond as he did. If he had survived, he would have come to regret his decision. Examples might include cases of lovers who take their lives in moments of intense grief, wealthy businessmen who experience sudden financial disaster and are frightened of facing the world without money, and active, life-loving hedonists enraged at fate when first learning that they have contracted a crippling disease. Some suicides in these circumstances might be rational, but when I refer to suicides as impulsive, I have in mind only those which would have been avoided if the agent had been in full rational control of himself.

## (2) Apathetic Suicide

Sometimes a suicide might result not so much from intense desire or emotion as from apathy. The problem is not overwhelming passion, but absence of passion, lack of interest in what might be done or experienced in a continued life. One can imagine, for example, an extremely depressed person who simply does not care about the future. The causes of his emotional state may lie in personal failure, rejected love, and so on. But what he experiences is not intense shame, anger, fear, etc., but rather emptiness. He may acknowledge that after time, perhaps with psychotherapy and antidepressive drugs, he would again take joy in living. But the thought arouses no current desire to continue living. If his suicide is irrational, it is not because his mind is unclear or his reason swayed by intense emotion.

## (3) Self-Abasing Suicide

I call a suicide self-abasing if it results from a sense of worthlessness or unworthiness, which expresses itself not in apathy, but rather in a desire to manifest self-contempt, to reject oneself, to "put oneself down." The motivating attitude is more than an intellectual judgment about one's merits, relative to others or absolutely, according to various standards of morality, social utility, intelligence, etc., though such judgments may be among the causes of the attitude. Particular rejections, failures, and violations of conscience might contribute to the attitude, but it need not be a merely momentary or passing feeling. One's life is seen as having a negative value, not just devoid of things to enjoy, like an empty cupboard, but contemptible, like a despised insect one wants to swat or turn away from in disgust. Such suicide carries a symbolic message, even if only expressed to oneself: "This creature is worth less than nothing." The agent does not irrationally miscalculate whether continued life will bring more joy than misery, for he is not involved in any such calculation. In effect, he denies that he deserves such consideration, even from himself. This is more than self-punishment, which can be a way of acknowledging oneself as a responsible agent and alleviating particular guilt feelings. The self-abasing attitude, on the contrary, says "punishment is too good for me—I should be discarded."

### (4) Hedonistic Calculated Suicide

By this I mean suicide that is decided upon as the result of a certain sort of cost/benefit calculation. Seeing that others will be unaffected by his decision (our simplifying hypothesis), the hedonistic calculator regards his choice as determined by his best estimate of the balance of pleasures and pain he expects to receive under each option. Immediate suicide by a painless method will result in a short, fairly predictable list of pleasures and pains. Continued life will produce a more complex series of experiences more difficult to calculate. Uncertainties cloud the picture and disparate pleasures and pains are hard to weigh against one another with anything like mathematical precision. But, in theory, the problem is seen as simple. One chooses the course that results in the best balance of expected pain and pleasure, taking into account intensity, duration, certainty, etc. More sophisticated calculators may think in terms of preferences and ordinal comparisons, rather than

cardinal rankings of sensations, but the central point remains that the value of continued life is seen as a function of the joys and miseries, delights and discomforts, etc., that one is likely to experience. Long life *per se* has no value. But, as long as the pleasure/pain balance is above a certain threshold, the more life the better. When, in one's best estimate, the balance falls irretrievably below the threshold, it is time to end the game. The reason for ending it, like the reason for continuing to live, is to obtain the best balance, over time, of pleasure over pain.

Although these four types of suicide are significantly different, I think that they all reflect an attitude towards life that is less than ideal. This is not to say that suicides of these sorts are *wrong* or *immoral*. However, it is meant to imply more than that they are "unfortunate" or that benevolent people would wish that they not occur. My sense is that, though condemnation and blame seem inappropriate, a person's life story would be morally better if it did not end in one of these ways. One would not select for emulation a biography which concluded with impulsive, apathetic, self-abasing, or hedonistic calculating suicide. Insofar as one wanted to admire the principal character, one would want to rewrite the ending. . . .

. . . [T]here are several sorts of suicide which I especially want to distinguish from our four previous paradigms, because the objectionable features of our paradigm cases seem absent in these other cases. Prominent among these will be heroic, self-sacrificial suicides, done for the welfare of others. For present purposes, however, we are setting aside altruistic motives. Quite aside from these other-regarding suicides, there remain at least three important sorts of cases which, except when prohibited by religion, are widely regarded as unobjectionable. For example, I expect many would agree with me that there is little or nothing objectionable about the following.

### (1) Suicide When Human Life Is No Longer Possible

Suppose that progressive disease is inevitably destroying one's capacities to function as more than a lower animal or vegetable. One's body might remain alive for some time, yet life as a human being is all but over. If one does not choose suicide while still having lucid moments with a capacity for rational choice, one's life will continue as a vegetable, since others, let us imagine, will be unwilling to terminate it. Suicide in such a case need not be from impulse, apathy, self-abasement, or pleasure/pain calculation. One may simply see that human life is over and prefer not to continue to live as a subhuman being. Different people will draw the line between human life and subhuman life at somewhat different places, no doubt. However, at some extreme point, few will deny that the line has been crossed.

### (2) Suicide to End Gross Irremediable Pain

Even those of us who reject hedonistic calculation as the test of the value of life may concede that there is a point at which a person's pain is so horrible, so persistent, and so irremediable that suicide is thoroughly understandable and unobjectionable. It is not that pain and pleasure in general determine the value of life, but rather that gross, unavoidable, continuous pain can override other considerations. Living as a human being is valuable, one might say, not just *because* it has pleasures and only minimal pains, but it may be valuable to the agent *on condition that* continuing pain does not exceed some tolerable threshold.

### (3) Suicides Based on Self-Regarding Moral Beliefs

The suicides probably most often accepted as justifiable are those motivated by strong moral convictions. In the most familiar and least controversial instances, the moral considerations are other-regarding, for example, saving another's life or trying to avert a war. Yet suicide can sometimes be motivated by moral convictions not concerned with one's obligations to others, the welfare of others, etc. For example, people have sometimes found themselves trapped with no apparent options but suicide or a life they regard as base,

degrading, and utterly contrary to their deepest values concerning how one should live (aside from effects on others). They cannot see how, even to a minimal degree, they can be "true to themselves" and live as they would be forced to. Some have viewed prostitution this way; others, life as a beggar, an addict, a cannibal, a boot-licking slave. Hopefully, in real life, suicide is rarely, if ever, the only alternative, and everyone does not share the same view about the comparative value of death and these ways of life. But if the choice were forced and the agent felt deeply that the only possible life for him was contrary to his most basic personal ideals, then to many surely suicide would seem the most admirable course.[1]

## II

Taking these intuitive inflections for now as given, let us consider what general moral principle, or principles, might underlie them, accounting for our objections to the first four sorts of cases and our acceptance of the latter three. Principles regarding human rights are unlikely candidates to account for these cases, because the intuitions we wish to explain concern attitudes falling short of an ideal, not wrongs done to others. Utilitarian considerations might be cited in several cases (for example, impulsive and apathetic suicide), but seem not to be the whole story. The self-abaser, for example, seems to have a less than ideal attitude, quite aside from whether he or others would be happier if he changed. The calculated suicide seems to miss something, just because he considers nothing but utility. Even if (as seems doubtful) utilitarian reflection would always oppose the objectionable attitudes in (1)–(4), I think it is implausible that this adequately reflects our *reasons* for opposing those attitudes; for I suspect we sense the defects in the attitudes while still uncertain about the consequences (for example, whether the depressed person will really be happier if he continues to live). Sophisticated utilitarians may yet come up with explanations,[2] but my doubts are sufficient to lead me to explore in another direction.

An obvious alternative is Kant's moral theory.[3] My suggestion will be that, though inadequate as it stands, Kant's theory points towards a principle which could ground the intuitive beliefs about suicide which we have just considered.

The tenets of Kant's moral theory which I think are particularly important to the topic of suicide can be summarized as follows:

(1) In trying to decide whether one should do something, it is extremely important to determine what one's intentions and policies would be in doing it. These, together with one's underlying motive for having those intentions and policies, are what determine the kind of moral worth one's action will have.

(2) An essential feature of our humanity is that we are rational agents with autonomy of the will. This does not mean that we always act rationally or that we always manifest our autonomy, but it does imply that we have certain capacities and predispositions. These include the following: (a) practical reason applied to the satisfaction of our desires: that is, a capacity and disposition to pursue our ends in accord with "hypothetical imperatives," to set ourselves goals and follow informed policies about the best means to achieve them; (b) negative freedom: that is, the ability to act in accord with principles or policies without being fully determined to do so by desires or any external causal factors; (c) positive freedom or autonomy: that is, setting oneself principles and values which stem purely from one's nature as a rational being uncaused and unmotivated by one's desires or any external factors; (d) a predisposition to value one's humanity, or one's nature as a rational and free being, as an "end in itself": that is, to value the preservation, development, exercise, and honoring of one's rational nature independently of benefits and costs measured in terms of pleasure and pain or desire satisfaction.

(3) All moral considerations are ultimately grounded in our nature as rational beings with autonomy. For example, we are unconditionally obligated to follow the principles and values which we set ourselves as rational and positively

free (see (2) c); and nothing else, such as tradition, religious or secular authority, natural instinct, etc., can be the ultimate ground of obligation.

(4) A fundamental moral principle, one to which any rational being with autonomy would commit himself, is: always act so that you treat humanity (that is, autonomy and rationality) never simply as a means, but always as an end in itself (that is, as something with "unconditional and incomparable worth").[4] This applies to "humanity" in oneself as well as in others. The arguments for this are several, but none appeals to the ideas of social utility or maximum satisfaction for the agent.

On the basis of these claims, Kant draws a double conclusion concerning the moral character of suicide.

(5) Suicide (at least suicide for the reasons Kant imagined) is opposed to the principle of humanity as an end in itself stated in (4) above because it "throws away" and degrades humanity in oneself. Thus, suicide expresses an attitude that one's nature as a rational, autonomous person is not of "incomparable worth" and "above all price." Suicide to end pain, for example, places cessation of pain, which is a mere "relative" and "conditioned" value, above rationality and autonomy, which (Kant says) have worth that "admits no equivalent."

(6) Suicide, therefore, is always, or nearly always, wrong. In fact, it is contrary to a "perfect ethical duty to oneself." This duty is a stringent prohibition, concerned with motives and attitudes and not merely intentional "external acts," which is grounded in the value of one's own humanity rather than in regard for others.[5]

These views of Kant's—both the tenets of his moral theory and the conclusions he draws concerning suicide—have provoked much controversy. I believe that the best of his ideas can be retained after much is conceded to his critics. Some prominent objections are the following:

Re (1): Kant is often thought to have exaggerated the role of the agent's intentions and policies and underrated the role of consequences in determining what a person should do. A more modest Kantian view would insist on the importance of the agent's intentions and policies, but not deny the relevance of other factors.

Re (2): Kant is also criticized for exaggerating the degree to which actual human beings have autonomy and rationality. There is more variation in rational capacities than Kant imagined, it is argued, and the most autonomy we can aspire to is relative freedom from determination by unthinking impulse and narrow, selfish desires, unchecked by impartial reasoning. Adoption of pure rational principles, uninfluenced by any (even impartial) human desires, is generally thought impossible. Though Kant himself would never have yielded on this point, one might argue that the value of rationality and autonomy is not wholly dependent on Kant's extreme, otherworldly interpretation of them.

Re (3): Kant's attempt to derive all moral principles from the idea of rational free will has been far from universally persuasive. Even those who doubt Kant's attempt can grant that more is needed to ground morality than tradition, authority, instinct, etc., and that at least a part of taking a moral point of view is readiness to attribute value impartially to rational, autonomous human life within the bounds of certain other principles.

Re (4): Kant's principle that humanity should be treated as an end in itself has been variously interpreted and criticized, but the objection most persuasive to me is that it places an absolutely overriding value on the rational side of human life as opposed to the feeling, experiencing side. That is, Kant's principle not only declares that our rationality and freedom have a special intrinsic value, independent of pleasure and pain; it also implies that the preservation, development, etc., of rationality and freedom *override* any consideration of pleasure and pain with which they might conflict.[6] This means, for example, not only that one must avoid taking brain-damaging drugs for pleasure, but also that one must never neglect or damage one's rational capacities to alleviate *any* amount of pain, in oneself *or* others. However, a more qualified version of Kant's principle is possible and, in fact, in line with modifications already suggested. That is, one should treat humanity (or rational, autonomous human living) as a special

intrinsic value, independent of but not always overriding considerations of pleasure and pain. As such, the principle would belong to a more pluralistic ethic than Kant's, one which requires weighing and balancing competing considerations. But that, in the end, may be the only sort of theory we can conscientiously live with.[7]

Re the conclusions concerning suicide, (5) and (6): Kant's view that suicide is always, or nearly always, contrary to a perfect duty to oneself provokes objections on at least two counts. First, that suicide is often justified (for example, in situations mentioned in the last section). Second, that, because a person cannot violate his own rights, duties *to* oneself, in a strict sense, are impossible. Both objections, however, would be met if we accepted a qualified position, which remains in line with (5) above yet is consonant with previous modifications of Kant's view. One might hold, for example, that suicide *from certain attitudes* is always, or nearly always, objectionable, at least a falling short of a moral ideal, and that this is not solely because it is contrary to the welfare or rights of others. This would allow that some suicides are justified and even commendable, but suicides rooted in certain attitudes (for example, undervaluation of rational, autonomous human life) would be opposed. They would be opposed, not strictly condemned as immoral; and they would be opposed as out of line with an ideal moral attitude toward one's life, not as a violation of a strict duty to oneself.

## III

Suppose, then, that we accepted the spirit of Kant's theory but adopted the qualifications mentioned above. What sort of principle might remain, and how would it apply to important choices aside from matters of life and death?

The principle I propose to consider is this: *A morally ideal person will value life as a rational, autonomous agent for its own sake, at least provided that the life does not fall below a certain threshold of gross, irremediable, and uncompensated pain and suffering.*

The main task in explaining the principle is to give some sense to the idea of "life as a rational, autonomous agent," but first some preliminary comments are in order.

First, the principle expresses an ideal rather than a duty. Thus questions of blame, censure, and enforcement associated with violations of duty are not at issue here. Also the principle is not meant to be absolute or unconditional. Other moral considerations, even other ideals, might override it in some circumstances. It is intended as at least one consideration in a pluralistic ethics which admits the need for judgment in weighing considerations of quite different sorts.

In the same spirit the "certain threshold" of pain and suffering is admittedly left indeterminate. At extreme points, one hopes, there will be agreement, but no precise guidelines can be given to settle borderline cases. This indeterminacy, however, should not be confused with vacuousness. Nor should it be supposed that this qualification regarding extreme circumstances implies that in normal circumstances rational, autonomous living should be valued for the sake of pleasure (or a favorable pleasure/pain ratio). The qualification is meant to reflect the idea that although the value of rational, autonomous living is not a function of the pleasure and pain it brings, a sufficiently gross level of suffering can undermine that value, making the sufferer incapable of finding that life meaningful or even tolerable.

The principle is not meant to suggest more than it says. In particular, it does not imply that life has value *only* when rational and autonomous. Nor does the qualification strictly imply that life has *no* value when consumed with gross, irremediable, and uncompensated pain. These matters are left open.

To say that rational, autonomous living is ideally valued for its own sake is to say that, ideally, it is seen as valuable independently of various ends to which it might serve as a means or necessary condition: for example, the general welfare, the greater enjoyment of the agent, the development of culture, or the maintenance of democratic institutions. What is not implied, once again, is that rational, autonomous living is the only good, the complete good, or an unconditional good.

The principle holds that one should value all rational, autonomous life, not simply one's own. Typically, perhaps, a person comes to value his own rational, autonomous life first and foremost, but ideally identification with others and the spirit of a moral point of view will in time lead him to value for others what he has come to prize for himself. Whether an ideal person is completely impartial, valuing the lives of all rational autonomous agents to exactly the same degree, is not determined, one way or the other, by our principle. The point is that all such lives are to be valued independently of various consequences, not that they are always to be prized equally.

The more thoroughly Kantian adherents of the principle will regard it as basic, nonderivative, and morally comprehensive. But for present purposes it need not be so viewed. That is, those who want to more nearly approximate Kant's theory will hold that the principle itself is not derived from any further moral principles (such as rule-utilitarian or divine command principles). Further, they will view the principle as a guide for moral decision in all areas of life, not just for specific problems such as drug use, moral education, capital punishment, or suicide. However, the principle could also have a more modest place in an ethical theory; that is, as an important but derivative and noncomprehensive ideal.

These preliminaries aside, the more difficult task is to say what is meant by "life as a rational, autonomous agent." Here I can only sketch the beginnings of an account that obviously needs further development.

First, following Kant, I think of rationality and autonomy as capacities and dispositions which belong to virtually all adult and nearly adult, human beings. Though they may be developed and exercised to greater or lesser degrees, basic rationality and autonomy are not special characteristics of an educated elite. They are features which distinguish virtually all human beings from lower animals.

Second, rational autonomy includes some minimum capacity and disposition to see causal connections (for example, to understand what will happen if one does this or that); to be aware of a variety of wants, for both future states of affairs as well as present ones; to set oneself ends and adopt policies and plans to achieve them; to revise ends and policies in the light of new information; to form and alter goals and policies in response to one's own deepest wants and values, to some extent independent of blind adherence to tradition, authority, and the opinions of others; and to resist immediate temptation in the pursuit of adopted ends, values, and policies.

Third, in saying that an agent is autonomous, I mean in part that he can, within a wide area of life, choose what to value and what not to value without contravening any fixed, objective, preset order of values in the world. As Kant, Sartre, and others have maintained, an autonomous person is a "creator of values," not merely a discoverer of values, at least within a wide range of morally permissible choice.[8] Within that range, we may choose to value some things, and to disvalue others, for their own sakes. Contrary to Moorean intuitionists, intrinsic values do not exist as properties in the world. They are not so much perceived as chosen.

Fourth, an autonomous agent is not restricted to pleasure and pain in what he can value. This is not a point about the causes of valuing, but rather about its scope. That is, human beings, so far as they are autonomous, have the capacity and disposition to care for things other than pleasant and painful experiences. This is not simply a denial of psychological egoism, as traditionally conceived. It is also a denial of psychological hedonism, that is, the view that human beings, whether egoistic or altruistic, can attribute intrinsic value only to pleasure and intrinsic disvalue only to pain. This idea of autonomy, which is found in such diverse thinkers as Kant, Sartre, and Nietzsche, is not so much an assertion of the high-mindedness of human beings as their wide-ranging capacity to form values. It is illustrated not merely in moral commitment and single-minded pursuit of truth, but also in more mundane concerns about what others are saying behind our backs and what is happening to our favorite forest flowers when no one is there to see them. To care about such matters is not the same as caring about their possible consequences or even about the pleasure or pain we may get in contemplating them.

Finally, it should be noted that rational autonomy, as conceived here, is *not* possession of rights to control one's life, *not* Sartrean freedom from all objective moral constraints, and *not* a pure Kantian will independent of all causation and desire. What is intended is a more modest set of capacities, which contrast not with causally explainable moral choices or objective moral constraints, but rather with being governed completely by instinct, being a creature of impulse without goals or policies, having an utterly incoherent set of goals and policies, being unable to follow through on one's own policies and principles, being blindly obedient to the commands or expectations of others, being rigidly bound to unrevisable self-commands, being bound in all one's choices to values one sees as fixed apart from oneself, and being unable to care about anything for its own sake except pleasure and pain.

The attitude towards life expressed by our modified Kantian principle may be contrasted with two other extreme views. The first is what I call the *Consumer Perspective*. This is exemplified most dramatically in Bentham's remarks about rational prudence. Intrinsic values are fixed: pleasure on the positive side, pain on the negative. When all is taken into account, the prudent person measures the value of his life by what he expects to receive, the number, duration, intensity and probability of pleasant and painful sensations. More time is better if one is still receiving more of the good than the bad, just as longer time at a party is better, until boredom outweighs the pleasure. The value of one's life from now on does not depend essentially on anything that has gone before; unless it happens that the past comes back to haunt one (for example, with bad memories, angry bill collectors, or hangovers), the past is irrelevant to whether continued life is worthwhile. This perspective is primarily forward-looking. To evaluate a stretch of life, one pictures oneself standing at the beginning trying to imagine what it will feel like to live through it. One's existence as valuer is only derivately important. It is needed, as it were, to receive and register the goods, which are the only things valued for their own sakes.

At the opposite extreme is what I call the *Obituarist Perspective*.[9] This looks at life as one might from life's end, preparing to summarize its salient features for the world. The focus is on the record, or story line, not how it felt to experience that life. Pleasures and pains tend to diminish in importance, as we typically weigh these more heavily in anticipation than in retrospect. "Was the result worth the pain?" considered after the fact, is more likely to invoke an affirmative response than "Will the result be worth the pain?" asked before an undertaking. Like the Consumer Perspective, the Obituarist Perspective sees the value of a stretch of life as determined by its content. But the value is measured by its contribution to the whole biography, not by a summation of discrete experiences. A principle of organic unities may be invoked. The value of the whole may exceed the sum of the value of the parts. The existence of the agent as chooser and valuer is again derivative, but now it is derived from the value of the whole life that is finally created rather than from the amount of good experiences received. If it was good that someone was alive at a time, this is because it was a necessary condition for the unfolding of a life of a certain sort.

Contrast these perspectives with what I shall call the *Author Perspective*. As I imagine a working novelist might, this looks both forward and backward, wondering what it would be to experience each stretch of life, but ever mindful of how this fits into a meaningful whole. To some extent what makes the life worthwhile is not seen as fixed or predetermined—by either hedonistic or aesthetic standards. Not only what the agent will do, but also what will be the salient features, good and bad, is a matter of choice, within some limits at least. The author, in part, writes the criteria of evaluation as well as the story line. The value of the life as author, when the story is one's own, is not seen as entirely derivative from the final content of the story, once finished, nor from the feelings experienced in living through it. Rather, living as the author, making the crucial choices, deciding what to count meaningful and what trivial, these are valued for their own sakes. This is not simply to say that one enjoys being the author and so values living derivatively as a necessary condition of such enjoyment; that puts the focus in the wrong place. Even if it is true that one *enjoys* liv-

ing as author, one enjoys it partly because this expresses what one is and wants to be. This is quite different from wanting enjoyment and so, for this reason, valuing the prerequisite life as author.

Probably no one assumes any of these perspectives on life exclusively, nor would I suggest that one should. The point of contrasting the metaphors is simply to make more vivid the ideal we have been considering. For to value one's life as a rational autonomous agent for its own sake means to some extent shifting from the Consumer and Obituarist perspectives to that of the Author. The crucial feature of this shift is that one values oneself as a potential maker of a meaningful life. The value of living is not entirely determined by the content of the life one makes; rather, that life acquires value in part because it is the expression of one's choices as its author.[10]

## IV

The modified Kantian principle we have been considering has obvious implications regarding issues in everyday life quite aside from suicide. For example, it tends to oppose drug use which seriously impairs a healthy person's capacities to think and take charge of his life. It commends the development of one's capacities for rational self-control, not simply for the results, but because this is a natural expression of valuing for their own sake one's capacities as a rational autonomous agent.[11] The principle would urge self-respect in the sense of keeping our day-to-day choices in line with the personal standards we set for ourselves, for we are not fully self-governing when our actions fail to match the values we profess to ourselves. In dealing with others, we would be urged to respect their own choices within a range of morally permissible conduct. To place their comfort or happiness above their own declared values (as is often done in benevolent lies) would not be to value them as autonomous agents. There would be a strong presumption against killing human beings in most circumstances. But euthanasia for those who have lost the capacity for even minimally rational, autonomous living would not be ruled out.

Regarding suicide, the Kantian principle, I think, distinguishes cases in just the way I initially proposed. The impulsive suicide, for example, falls short of the ideal in two ways. He places comparatively little value on his continued existence as an autonomous agent, as shown by his willingness to give this up to satisfy a momentary impulse. Further, he makes his choice in an irrational manner, being guided by a passing feeling out of keeping with the more enduring features of his character and personality. He both loses self-control and destroys his potentially controlling self. The apathetic suicide may not reach his decision in an irrational manner, but he chooses to treat his continuing potential to make a life as if it were virtually worthless—he throws it away even in the absence of strong impulses and concerns about his future. The deficiency is not in his feelings (lack of a felt wish to live), but in his policies. His act says, "Others aside, I stand for nothing. My potential to author a life means nothing to me, given that I see no future states that I now feel a desire for."

The self-abasing suicide even more dramatically undervalues his capacities for rational, autonomous living, for he views his life as worth less than nothing. He takes the Obituarist Perspective that the worth of life is measured entirely by one's record and, even more, he denies the possibility that he can make the whole story meaningful by future action; he attributes no value to living as the author of his life. Given his value assumptions, his decision may be rational; but it is not a decision that counts his being rational and autonomous as valuable. For him, all personal worth must be earned, and this attitude is incompatible with valuing life as an autonomous agent for its own sake.

Finally, the hedonistic, calculating suicide is opposed to our Kantian principle because he treats life as a rational, autonomous agent as a derivative value, good only because and so long as it is needed to achieve the ultimate end of maximum pleasure/pain balance. The Consumer Perspective is operative here. The ultimate values are fixed, not chosen. The prospective content of continued life entirely determines whether it is worthwhile. The pertinent question is, "What will I get?" not "What can I make of it?"

Contrast these cases with the suicides initially mentioned as intuitively unobjectionable. Suicides to avoid living in a subhuman condition do not contravene our principle, because the life that is ended lacks the potential for rational, autonomous agency. Troublesome questions may arise about what exact point in a gradual decline marks the end of "human" life, but, though practically difficult, these present no objections to the main point of the Kantian principle, which is that ideally what is valued is life with certain human potential, not merely being alive. Suicides to end gross, irremediable pain are not opposed to the principle, if the pain is such that it renders a person incapable of making any significant use of his human capacities. To end one's life in these conditions need not express the attitude that rational, autonomous living has no value in itself. It may simply show that one does not hold this value unconditionally and above all else.

Finally, suicide as the only way to avoid a life seen as demeaning and contrary to one's personal standards does not express an attitude inconsistent with the Kantian principle. To be sure, one cuts short the time one could live as a rational, autonomous agent; but doing so can be a manifestation of autonomy, an ultimate decision of the author of a life story to conclude it with a powerful expression of ideals he autonomously chose to live by. The principle affirms a presumption in favor of continued life as long as one's capacities are intact. But we cannot consistently maintain the value of autonomous living without admitting that, under some conditions, autonomously chosen values require one to make the choice that excludes all further choices. If you value being an author and have just one story to write, you should not hurry to conclude it. But sometimes, to give it the meaning you intend, you must end it before you spoil it.

## V

My aim has been to explain a certain ideal and some of its implications, not to argue for it. Some, I know, will object that moral considerations must be other-regarding. Others may object that the author-metaphor suggests elitist standards remote from the life of ordinary people. Many will demand further reasons for accepting the ideal. These are legitimate concerns which I will not pretend to answer here. Instead, I conclude with a brief mention of two Kantian lines of argument that may merit consideration.

Kant spent little effort in constructing explicit arguments for his principle that humanity is an end in itself, perhaps because he regarded this idea as so basic and immediately persuasive. Nevertheless, he suggests at least two arguments on its behalf. The first, liberally reconstructed, is this.[12] There is, contrary to Hume, one (but only one) substantive value or "end" that can be attributed to every rational being, independently of the particular desires that he, as an individual, may have. This is "humanity," or "rational nature," itself, that is, one's existence as a being with reason, the capacity to set ends, and the ability to make choices with at least a degree of independence from impulse and given, nonrational desire. By virtue of being a rational agent, a person necessarily values rationality in himself. The impartiality implicit in the moral point of view requires him to acknowledge *in principle* the same value in others. The practical effect of valuing rational agency is implicit commitment to preserving it, developing it, making use of it, and "honoring" it symbolically. Since each individual also has other particular desires by virtue of not being a rational agent alone, the commitment to the value of rational agency is not always honored in practice. Sometimes we choose to destroy our rational capacities in pursuit of our special individual desires. Yet, taking a moral point of view involves adopting the principles and values of rational agents when thinking independently of their individual desires, in fact placing these above all other considerations. Therefore, taking the moral point of view requires valuing "humanity," or rational, free agency, for its own sake, not merely as a means to satisfying particular individual desires. In fact, it requires placing rational, free agency above all else.

There are, of course, many points at which the argument may be challenged, but it shows, at least, how valuing rational agency for its own sake can be deeply imbedded in a basic theory about what morality is. The argument does not lose interest, I think, merely because we take a more limited view of rational free agency than Kant. Its conclusion will be more modest if we reject the view that morality requires placing the value of rational agency *above all else* in favor of the view that a moral point of view requires giving it at least some independent value. But this more modest conclusion would be in line with our modified Kantian principle. Critics may still doubt that rational beings necessarily value their rational agency for its own sake or that a moral point of view involves adopting the principles and values of rational agents. But to challenge Kant on these points is to place the controversy where it belongs, at the heart of moral theory.

The second argument is roughly this:[13] Most valuable things have value only because valued by human beings. Their value is derivative from the fact that they serve our interests and desires. Even pleasure, which we value for its own sake, has only derivative value, that is, value dependent on the contingent fact that human beings want it. Now if valuers confer derivative value on things by their preferences and choices, those valuers must themselves have value. In fact, they must have value independent of, and superior to, the derivative values which they create.

The guiding analogy is how we value *ends.* We value certain means because they serve certain intermediate ends, which in turn we value because they contribute finally to our ultimate ends, that is, what we value for its own sake. The value of the means and the intermediate ends is derivative from the value of the ultimate ends; unless we value the ultimate end, the means and intermediate ends would be worthless to us. So, it seems, the source of derivative value must itself be valuable for its own sake. Since the ultimate source of the value of our contingent ends, such as health, wealth, and even pleasure, is their being valued by human beings, human beings, as valuers, must be valued for their own sakes.

Now there are a number of ways of reading this argument which render it quite implausible. If

Midas could make worthless objects valuable by touching them, he would be a valuable fellow to have around. But we do not necessarily value him for his own sake. Again, if I admit that a sleazy film has market value derived from the preferences of a certain class of viewers, I am not thereby committed to valuing those viewers, as valuers, for their own sakes. One can admit that persons are a source of derivative values in these ways and yet consistently refuse to value them for their own sakes.

Nevertheless, the argument suggests an idea worth considering. Suppose we grant that, at least from a moral point of view, we should value individuals' satisfactions of their particular ends (within some limits) and, further, that these ends are to be valued *because* chosen by the various individuals. For example, we should care about Peter's athletic achievement and Paul's enjoyment of art not because athletic prowess and aesthetic enjoyment are objectively good in themselves or because *we* like these things. Rather, we should care about them because Peter and Paul chose them (within moral limits). The Kantian argument would simply remind us that, in conceding this basic point, we are committed to valuing Peter, Paul, and others, as valuers, for their own sakes. That is, from a moral point of view, their value to us as choosers does not stem entirely from a prior independent value of what they, or we, choose. Valuing the valuers for their own sakes is implicit in giving weight to their ends independent of our own likes and the content of those ends.

The application of this idea to one's own life would be this: The value of one's ends and life-projects from a moral point of view does not entirely depend upon how they serve others' wants or upon any fixed, objective intrinsic values; they have value because one chooses them (within certain moral limits). This implies that one's life as a chooser, or creator of value is to be valued for its own sake. This does not mean that one may never choose to end that life, but only that to end it *because of an attitude* which denies that value, is to fail to identify fully with a moral point of view.

Some will object, I am sure, that a moral point of view is only concerned with the value of others'

ends or that the reconstructed Kantian argument begins with a premise that is still controversial. These objections cannot be lightly dismissed. But, again, debate about them is at least debate at the heart of moral theory, not at the fringes.

## Notes

1. This category could include some cases which look like self-abasing suicides but may be significantly different. For example, a man who has just killed his wife and children in a jealous rage may feel that to continue to live would be dishonorable, that only taking his own life could begin to acknowledge his remorse. If so, the suicide could be seen as a grasp for a shred of dignity, not self-abasement in my sense.

2. Modifications in classic utilitarianism include G. E. Moore's "ideal utilitarianism" in *Principia Ethica* (1960) and *Ethics* (1967), Mill's introduction of "qualities" of pleasure in *Utilitarianism*, and rule-utilitarianism of several types.

3. Here I draw from several of Kant's works, especially the *Groundwork of the Metaphysics of Morals* (tr. H. J. Paton, Harper & Row, 1909, pp. 80–116) and *The Metaphysical Principles of Virtue: Part II of the Metaphysics of Morals* (tr. James Ellington, Bobbs Merrill, 1981, pp. 82–85). Suicide is also discussed in Kant's *Lectures on Ethics* (tr. Louis Infield, Harper & Row, 1930, pp. 147–159). My summary concerns less the details of his remarks about suicide than the aspects of his general theory that have important implications regarding suicide. I intentionally omit Kant's unpersuasive argument from the first formula of the Categorical Imperative, *Groundwork*, p. 89.

4. My understanding of this principle is explained in "Humanity as an End in Itself," *Ethics* 91 (October 1980), pp. 84–99.

5. In the *Metaphysics of Morals*, Kant leaves open "casuistical questions" about whether taking one's life is wrong in certain extreme cases (for example, anticipation of an unjust death sentence or of madness and death from the bite of a rabid dog). In the *Lectures on Ethics* (tr. Louis Infield, Harper & Row, 1930), he says only Cato's heroic suicide has given the world opportunity to defend suicide. But even that was a violation of himself and so not really noble (pp. 149, 153). In the *Lectures*, Kant also remarks that "life is not to be highly regarded for its own sake" (p. 150), which seems paradoxical. But a close reading, I think, shows that the point is that mere life (including life contrary to duty, life as a beast, etc.) is not what one should value highly. It is rather life as a rational, autonomous, and moral agent.

6. See my "Humanity as an End in Itself," *Ethics* 91 (October 1980).

7. This view of ethical theory is nicely expressed in Stuart Hampshire's *Two Theories of Morality* (Oxford University Press, 1977, pp. 1–55).

8. Sartre and Kant differ, of course, on the sense in which we "create values." Kant held that moral principles are self-imposed by our nature as free *rational* beings, while the value of nonmoral "relative ends," within the limits of these principles, stems from the personal preferences of individuals. Sartre sees all values as created by individual choices, free from all objective rational constraints.

9. I take the term from Hampshire's remark (*op. cit.,* p. 95) that Aristotle leads the reader "to view a human life, and particularly his own, from the standpoint of his eventual obituarist." But I would not pretend to reduce Aristotle's theory to my oversimple model.

10. In Sartrean terms, one might say that ideally one values *being-for-itself* independently of one's *being-in-itself*.

11. Sometimes we value a capacity solely because its employment produces results we like. But sometimes the results of employing a capacity are valued simply as manifestations of an admired capacity. Kant's view of rational autonomy in persons is more nearly the latter attitude, I think. We honor the capacity in all, even those who neglect it. We want all to use it, not to achieve some independently valued result, but because it is too splendid a thing to leave unused (or to misuse or abuse).

12. This argument is reconstructed from the *Groundwork,* especially pp. 96, 115–116.

13. See the *Groundwork,* pp. 95–96.

# 67    Should Cancer Patients Be Dialyzed?

## ANNE C. EPSTEIN

Dialysis is a life-saving, lifelong (in the absence of transplant) treatment that requires large investments of the patient's time and Medicare's money. We are currently in an era where vast monetary expenditures for health care are being questioned and may not be forthcoming. The major reasons for withholding potentially effective medical treatment to date has been to respect the right of the patient to refuse care and to improve quality of life for the individual patient. We are also seeing the emergence of other justifications for withholding care, justifications that consider certain broad social goods (or needs) as being more important than the good (or need) of the individual patient. This is the line of thought involved in the rationing of health care resources.

There are several reasons that dialysis might not be offered in general to patients with advanced cancer. First, dialysis might be thought to be futile. Second, dialysis might be thought to result in a poor quality of life for patients with cancer. Finally, it might be thought that dialysis

should be withheld from patients with advanced cancer because of cost.

## Is It Futile to Dialyze Patients with Widespread Cancer and End-Stage Renal Disease?

### The Importance of the "Futility" Judgment

Today the ethics of treatment or nontreatment strongly embrace the principle of patient self-determination. This approach has largely replaced the approach of medical paternalism. I believe this shift in medical decision-making is proper and appropriate. The major exception to this trend concerns the question of whether treatment is futile. It is the physician, not the patient, who determines that treatment is futile, and that determination often drives critical treatment decisions. For example, if a physician decides, without consultation with the patient, that dialysis would be futile in a particular case, the physician is likely to not even offer the treatment and thus allow the patient to die.

Reprinted by permission of the author and the publisher from *Seminars in Nephrology,* 13, 3 (1993), 315–323. Copyright © 1993 by W. B. Saunders.

The judgment that a treatment is futile has a host of important consequences. Many thinkers believe that physicians have no ethical obligation to offer futile treatment.[1–7] Physicians have never been compelled to offer futile treatment by law and patients who request futile treatments might even be refused.[8–10] Declaring a therapeutic intervention to be futile halts almost all other ethical, social, or legal discussions about its appropriateness.

If it could be established that dialysis was futile treatment in patients with widespread cancer, then it could be strongly argued that dialysis should not even be offered to these patients. Needless to say, third party payers would likely take notice of interventions that have been declared futile and drastically curtail reimbursement for them.

### Futility Is Supposed to Be Scientifically Objective

What is it about "futility" that yields such profound ethical implications? The answer is that futility is believed to be a scientifically objective judgment that does not incorporate any value judgments.[1, 11, 12] Because it is objective, it avoids all the messy ethical problems associated with patient values and self-determination. The judgment is properly made by the physician, not by the patient.

I will argue that the judgment of medical futility often involves important value judgments and that its apparent objectivity is an illusion—a view supported by others.[10, 13, 14] Therefore, I will suggest that only in a limited number of circumstances can the judgment that treatment is futile be made on objective grounds.

### Futile toward What End?

A futile effort is one that is very unlikely to produce the intended goal, yet we must clearly establish the goal of treatment before we can estimate the likelihood of achieving it. A treatment could be said to be futile in and of itself if there were universally accepted treatment goals. Possible candidates include: saving life in the short run (e.g. success of resuscitation in establishing spontaneous heartbeat); saving life long enough to leave the hospital (1-, 3-, 6-, or 12-month survival, etc.); achieving an acceptable quality of life; or achieving a combination of length and quality of life. Each of these outcomes has been invoked at various times to measure the effectiveness of medical therapy. There exists no uniformly established goal of treatment according to which medical efficacy or futility can be established.

"Futility" requires an objective judgment that does not incorporate patient values. Given the lack of uniformity regarding treatment goals, and the need for patient input to establish them, is it still possible to find a legitimate use for the term?

### Futility as Failure to Influence the Disease Process or Affect Symptoms

The most objective medical futility judgment is that the treatment does not favorably alter the disease process or its symptoms. For example, pacemaker placement in electromechanical dissociation is probably futile, as is penicillin in influenza.

Even in this case one could argue that treatments that are devoid of any medical efficacy may nevertheless not be futile by virtue of their psychological benefit. Sometimes family members harbor long-lasting guilt in cases where they feel that "everything" was not done for the patient. In cases where an emergency life-saving treatment is totally ineffective, there seems little reason to object to giving that treatment if the patient or family desire it, as long as the patient does not suffer, and the treatment adds little to the overall cost. The family will feel that "everything possible was done," which may greatly aid the process of grieving and healing.

### Are There Any Universal Treatment Goals?

Even if the goals of medical treatment are not scientifically objective, except that therapy alter the disease or its symptoms in some way, perhaps all patients have the same goals. In that case, the physician can assume the existence of a particular treatment goal and judge whether treatment is futile based on that goal. Therefore a judgment of "futility" could be made objectively. Let us consider various treatment goals to see if some of them are so universally held by patients that we can use them as if they were "objective."

## Quality of Life Is Neither an Objective Nor a Universal Treatment Goal

An apparently universal goal of medical therapy is to maximize the patient's overall quality of life. We could say that a treatment is futile if it will fail to maximize the patient's quality of life.[1] However, it is not true that quality of life is always the patient's goal for treatment; the patient may have other goals that he or she considers to be more important. For example, some patients believe that saving a large amount of money for their families takes higher priority than quality of life. Some patients may want to hang on to life long enough to see a loved one or to finish an important project, and some patients have the goal of prolonging life at all costs.

In addition, there are no universal standards for what constitutes an acceptable quality of life. There appears to be general agreement that quality of life is unacceptable if the patient will never be able to interact with his or her environment in any meaningful way. On the other hand, many of us would rather not live with major brain injury that still permitted some interaction, yet some patients still want everything done to preserve such a life. Patients also differ considerably in their approach to risk-taking. Some will not give up until the doctor declares that death is "certain," whereas others will flinch at much shorter odds. Some will always wait for a miracle.

It is apparent that the (competent, informed) patient (or proxy), not the physician, is the one who should judge what is overall in his or her own best interests. Therefore quality of life is necessarily a value judgment to be determined by the patient. Thus quality of life fails to be a useful yardstick by which to judge futility of treatment on two grounds: it is neither universal nor objective.

## No Universal Goal for Quantity of Life Saved

It would be nice if there were general agreement about the value of life expectancy. We could then determine that if treatment were unable to produce a life expectancy of X amount, it would be universally acknowledged to be futile. But is there such a universal goal for life expectancy? One candidate might be the goal of "hospital discharge." Treatment that has no reasonable chance of producing survival to hospital discharge has generally been forgone. However, we are seeing a trend toward shorter hospitalizations and more treatment at home or as an outpatient. Fifteen years ago it would have been difficult to imagine going home on a ventilator, which now is an acceptable option for some patients. It is apparent that the criteria of "hospital discharge" is highly dependent on technology and custom. Perhaps patients do not value life if it be permanently within the confines of the hospital, or perhaps "hospital discharge" is actually a surrogate marker for other length and quality of life considerations. The length of life implied in the phrase "until hospital discharge" requires further clarification before it might be a useful marker. Regarding other length of life decisions, I have seen an intelligent, informed, and competent patient choose to be mechanically ventilated for the sake of 2 days of sentient life in the intensive care unit, and I expect that other physicians have similar stories. Jewish law suggests that treatment can be forgone when life expectancy is less than 72 hours.[8] I find this reasonable and suspect that it would be widely supported, but I note that it is not universal. It is simply not clear that there exists a cutoff time below which all patients would choose to forgo treatment and be permitted to die.

There appears to be no widespread agreement regarding the length of life that is important to achieve or what relative risks to take to achieve that goal. Because such decisions are highly subjective and, even within a single patient, highly influenced by a variety of factors, they represent value judgments best made by the patient.

## How Unlikely Must Effectiveness Be before We Call Treatment Futile?

Even if the goal of medical therapy could be stipulated for a definition of futility, there is still the problem of determining the probability of effectiveness. Just how unlikely must it be that the treatment will work before we declare it futile?[1, 10] Is a 1% or .1% or .01% chance of effectiveness too little? How about 5% or 10%? In addition, there is the difficulty of determining probabilities of treatment effectiveness when clinical trials involve small numbers of patients or when the patients' characteristics do not match those of the patients included in clinical trials.

Patients as well as physicians vary in the degree of risk each is willing to assume for the sake of any given goal. It has been said that, overall, most people are not very good at assessing the meaning of probability. Schneiderman et al[1] have proposed that treatment that was not effective in the previous 100 cases be considered futile, although they offer no justification for choosing this number. Although I find their proposal interesting, I am not persuaded. I am not sure that a search for "objective" parameters of probability will be any more rewarding than a search for "objective" goals of medical therapy. At present, it seems more reasonable to acknowledge the value judgments inherent in risk-taking decisions. Such value judgments are best made by the competent and informed patient.

## Futility as Relative to the Treatment Goal

The scientific objectivity of a futility judgment could be salvaged by stating medical efficacy conclusions in clearly relative terms, such as: "Given the limitations of the current data, treatment X appears to be Y% effective in achieving 6-month survival in patients of Z type." This is in fact the form used in the conclusions of most published studies. Using the judgment of medical futility in this context is accurate and not misleading in its implication of objectivity. Such cautious conclusions do not, on their own, carry ethical weight because the scientific judgment of effectiveness is clearly divorced from any value judgment. Whether or not such a goal is desirable, given the burdens it carries, is a matter for the patient to decide.

## Some Conclusions about Judgments of Medical Futility

The judgment that a treatment is futile should be medically objective for it to justify the ethical ramifications that it has carried. However, I have found only a limited sense in which this judgment can be applied objectively, and therefore properly be made by the physician instead of the patient: the treatment has X probability of achieving a particular goal. I have tried to show that there are no universally accepted goals of treatment and that the determination of the goal of medical treatment is heavily value-laden. Therefore it seems to me that we should abandon the search for "objective" goals of medical therapy. The goal of medical therapy is best established individually by each patient according to his or her own values.[14] In other words, the determination of the goal toward which medical treatment aims is in fact a value judgment best made by the patient. Any judgment of the efficacy of a proposed treatment is a function of this value judgment. Medical judgments of futility properly are limited to assessments of probability of achieving a certain outcome.

It is important to note that determining probability of any given outcome is not a trivial feat. It involves all sorts of judgments regarding statistical inferences, adequacy of data, the nature of the clinical trial, and applicability to the patient at hand. Some of these judgments are issues for the philosophy of science and the social sciences. Thus it may be argued that even apparently "simple" judgments of medical probability in fact involve complex value judgments.

## Is Dialysis Futile?

Let us try now to answer the question, "Is dialysis futile in cancer patients?" Dialysis is clearly an effective treatment in modifying the course and symptoms of end-stage renal disease (ESRD) in cancer patients. To answer the question of whether dialysis is futile in the relative sense, we must first establish what the goals of treatment are. This we cannot do in general, so we must do it on a case-by-case basis in conference with our patients. Then we can hope to discover how effective dialysis might be in achieving those goals. A better question is, "What are the relative burdens and benefits of dialysis treatment in this particular patient with cancer and ESRD?"

## Is Dialysis Likely to Further the Treatment Goals of the Cancer Patient?

### Quality of Life in the Terminally Ill

In otherwise healthy individuals with curable illnesses, obviously quality of life is best enhanced by treatment and cure of the disease. Patients with cancer are no exception, and no one would argue that cure, if possible and if not unduly burdensome, should be the oncologist's goal.

Quality of life becomes an issue when there is a conflict between the value of prolonging life and the value of enhancing quality of life, as frequently occurs in decisions close to the end of life. This occurs when treatment may worsen overall quality of life for the patient. I take the ethical position that it is the patient who should choose which of these two values are more important in any particular treatment decision. Then the problem in the care of patients with terminal illness who opt for quality over quantity becomes the problem of choosing treatment modalities that overall will benefit the patient and disregarding those that will not.

### Quality of Life for the Patient with Cancer

Because often the physician's goal for the terminally ill patient ought to be to maximize the qual-

ity of life for that patient, it should be clear that all people with the same diagnosis should not be treated in the same way. To speak in general about what is good for "cancer patients" would ignore the vast differences among them that are critical for decision-making. Cancer patients are an extraordinarily heterogeneous group. For many cure is a realistic expectation, and many others live long periods of high-quality life before the terminal stages of illness supervene. Some will suffer a rapid demise following diagnosis, but for many there will be a prolonged period of disability and suffering before death. A number will die with their cancer but not of it. Some will never be diagnosed, and for some the disease will not significantly alter their life expectancy or quality of life. How can we confront such a diverse group of patients and say anything at all in general about their treatment?

Even if we speak only of patients with widespread cancer, there are still enough critical differences among them so that no single type of therapy suits all. Some will have days or weeks to live; some may have many months. Some will be in pain; others comfortable. Some will have suffered other losses that render their lives meaningless; some will be intellectually intact and functional except perhaps for weakness. Some will want desperately to finish a task before they die; some will want desperately to save their families' money. Some will have suffered enough already; some will be willing to suffer more for the sake of an outside chance at remission. Some will face painful exit modes; some are likely to die gently of the first serious complication. Each of these factors will influence whether any given treatment such as dialysis for ESRD will be more likely to help or to harm.

### Life-Prolonging Treatment in the Terminally Ill

Now it is a mistake to think that no treatment that prolongs life will benefit the terminally ill. Of course anyone would like to live as long as his or her quality of life is acceptable: this statement is a tautology. Therefore, ignoring for a moment questions of cost, life-prolonging treatments should he used when treatment results in adequate quality of life and probably should be forgone when they do not.

Although this strategy seems obvious, it seems to me that it is sometimes ignored. There may be several reasons for this.

First of all, quality of life for the terminally ill patient may be better than the physician realizes. Given modern methods of pain control, a reasonably clear sensorium, and a supportive environment, patients in advanced stages of disease may enjoy their lives despite their physical limitations. Such people participate in family gatherings, read or watch TV, and communicate with loved ones. These activities are compatible with a rewarding existence that the patient is in no hurry to leave. When such a patient comes down with an intercurrent treatable illness, such as pneumonia or a pleural effusion, it may well be worth it to the patient to put up with the discomforts of hospitalization and treatment to salvage several months of a good life.

Second, the patient with a short amount of life remaining, but with an acceptable quality of life, may value that time more than the physician realizes. It is up to the patient, and no one else, to determine that life-prolonging treatment is not worthwhile solely because the time gained is too short. For some patients with good qualities of life, even unpleasant treatments may be worthwhile if they prolong a brief but enjoyable existence. There is no reason to welcome death until life becomes unbearable. Again, modern methods of pain control and consideration for the patient's quality of life may make such scenarios more common in the future.

Third, the public may romanticize the idea of a "natural death." Sometimes the public seems to believe that life-prolonging treatment for the terminally ill is necessarily worse than being allowed to die. In fact, being allowed to die of a treatable disease, such as pneumonia, often is far more miserable than being treated with intravenous (IV) antibiotics and oxygen and continuing to live. For each individual patient, the risks and benefits of each proposed treatment must be weighed against the alternatives to see if overall the treatment is

worth the price. There are in fact few foregone conclusions. Of course it is the physician's responsibility to absolutely minimize suffering associated with either curative treatment or its absence.

Fourth, even on occasions when death is welcomed, the physician may be able to "choose" for the patient a relatively pleasant death instead of an unpleasant one.[15] For example, the physician could drain the massive pleural effusions that would have produced a respiratory death but then allow the patient to die of exsanguination a short time later. In this setting it is right to prolong life by draining the effusions, because overall it will be more beneficial to the patient. Even for those with poor qualities of life there are still degrees of suffering. It may well be better to live a short while longer while suffering to a mild degree than to die right now and suffer much more.

## Does Dialysis Treatment Result in a Poor Quality of Life?

People without ESRD widely believe that life on dialysis is of poor quality.[16] Proposals to withhold dialysis from certain large groups of patients, such as the elderly, have been justified on the grounds that life on dialysis merely prolongs misery. However, patients with ESRD on dialysis rate their own quality of life almost as well as does the general populations.[17, 18] Patients on CAPD overall were more satisfied with their lives than were patients on in-center hemodialysis. Therefore, it appears that quality of life on dialysis is clearly acceptable and is not in itself a source of misery from which death is sought as an escape. On the other hand, life may be a source of misery for other reasons. For example, a patient in the end stage of metastatic breast cancer with superior vena cava obstruction and difficulty breathing may decide death is preferable to continuing to live under such circumstances. In such cases, patients may elect to stop dialysis to expedite death, but the method of demise should not be confused with the motivation for death. The patient in the example above decided to stop dialysis because the superior vena cava obstruction and its complications made life miserable, not because of the burdens of dialysis treatment.

## Should We Withhold Dialysis from Patients with Advanced Cancer as Part of a Program of Rationing Health Care Resources?

### Is Dialysis Too Expensive?

Recently the Medicare ESRD program has received a great deal of attention because of its cost, and some have questioned its widespread use. It is especially vulnerable to this attack because it is a separate line item in the federal budget, it costs much more than originally anticipated, and it is funded by federal dollars. It is truly an example of a nationalized health program for a single disease.

But is the ESRD program really that expensive for the benefit gained? At the time of this writing in Lubbock, Texas, Medicare approves a charge of $119.32 per in-center dialysis treatment and pays 80% of that. In addition, Medicare approves of professional fees of $197.40 per month, 80% of which is paid.[19] Thus for a patient receiving in-center dialysis treatment 3 times a week, Medicare currently pays a total of $16,786 per year, 80% of the approved fee of $20,982 per year. Compared with the cost of controlling metastatic cancer with chemotherapy or radiotherapy for a year, this cost seems like a fairly good deal. The gain is clear: without treatment for ESRD, everybody dies within a few weeks. Dialysis is a surprisingly cost-effective form of therapy.

It seems that saving the lives of people with ESRD has lost its romance. Perhaps this is because of public misperceptions that life on dialysis is hell. Perhaps it is because of the changing demographics of ESRD patients who are now predominantly elderly and have associated chronic illnesses. Perhaps it is because saving lives requires ongoing treatment rather than being a quick and dramatic cure. Perhaps it is because saving a patient with ESRD is easy and routine. Perhaps it is because there are a lot of ESRD patients, and we notice the cost. Whatever the reason, it is a mistake to devalue the dramatic role that dialysis plays in saving life.

### How Might Medical Care Be Rationed If Rationing Becomes Necessary?

It seems likely that in the United States we soon must make difficult public decisions about how to ration health care resources. If so, we will have to decide on what basis we wish to limit medical care. In the absence of such decisions, most medical care currently is rationed according to ability to pay, which is approximately equivalent to one's insurance status. There is increasing consensus that this default rationing principle is morally unacceptable. Therefore, we should seek morally acceptable rationing principles. Dialysis treatment in patients with advanced cancer may seem like a good candidate for rationing. It is a moderately costly treatment in patients with limited life expectancy. The Medicare ESRD program in particular has been the target of budget cuts because it is a high-profile, expensive, federally funded program.

Can we come up with morally acceptable rationing principles that would justify limiting care to patients with cancer and ESRD? There are a variety of principles for distribution of scarce resources. Here I wish to consider some of those distribution principles that might have a bearing on rationing of medical resources to cancer patients with ESRD.

### Rationing According to Medical Benefit

First, health care might be rationed according to the degree of medical benefit. In other words, treatment that is likely to benefit patients a great deal would he given priority over treatment that would benefit patients less. This principle seems highly reasonable and objective. Certainly this principle would work well when goals were clearly specified. For example, the value of angioplasty versus coronary artery bypass grafting in various anatomical and functional situations could be established with reference to the goals of improving functional class and prolonging life. If one mode of treatment is clearly more effective than the other, it should be clearly preferred.

However, we get into trouble if we try to determine medical benefit in an "objective" way, outside of the direct reference to treatment goals. For example, it would be a mistake to try to stipulate that patients with congestive heart failure and coronary artery disease benefit more from treatment than do patients with cancer and ESRD. This is because such general stipulations of who benefits more than another involve inescapable value judgments. It would first have to be determined which values are more important than others so that different types of benefits could be compared. Thus, the attempt to determine an "objective" value for medical benefit suffers from the same problems as does the problem of determining an "objective" definition of futility, which I have addressed above. When not linked to specified treatment goals, medical benefit, like medical futility, is a value-laden judgment masquerading as an objective scientific fact.

It is possible for society to declare what goals of medical treatment we are willing to finance.[13] We may decide that we as a society do not value unconscious life and decide not to treat patients in that state except to maintain comfort and dignity, or we might decide that treatment unlikely to extend life more than 72 hours should not be funded. But these decisions should be made openly and in a way accountable to the public and to the medical profession and should be applied universally. The British National Health Service never had a universal or accountable system for rationing of resources,[20] with the result that rationing happened in a sometimes profoundly unjust fashion.[21, 22] The British rationing system is one whose flaws we should not wish to emulate.

## Rationing According to Life-Years Saved

Second, health care resources might be rationed according to life-years saved. That is, treatments that result in longer life expectancies would be funded in preference to treatments that resulted in a shorter life expectancy. This rationing principle would very often focus on the patient substrate rather than on the effectiveness of treatment. After all, life-saving treatment to a young adult would result in far more life-years saved than the same treatment applied to an older adult. Thus, this system frequently rations according to the patient's life expectancy that predates the current illness.

There are profound problems with rationing according to "life-years saved." Using this principle, if it is good to save a life for 5 years, then it is doubly good to save a life for 10 years. Therefore, assuming a life expectancy of 80 years, it is twice as good to save the life of a 40-year-old as it is to save the life of a 60-year-old. In other words, the life of a 40-year-old is twice as valuable as that of a 60-year-old.

I have serious difficulty accepting the moral legitimacy of this claim. Common law always has held that all (adult) lives are of equal value under the law. We do not give the murderer of a 60-year-old half the jail sentence of the murderer of a 40-year-old, and I doubt that, all else being equal, a 60-year-old values his or her life only half as much as does a 40-year-old. The mere fact of a shorter life expectancy does not otherwise seem to imply that life is of less value.

Now I am willing to believe that, when close to the end of life, many individuals no longer will value their lives as much as they did previously, merely because of the brevity of remaining time. And I am also willing to accept the principle that saving the life of a child is a higher moral priority than saving the life of an older adult. That is, it seems reasonable to me to think that at the extremes of life, value of life may be related to life expectancy. But it does not seem true that the value of life is proportional to the expected time remaining for the broad middle spectrum of life expectancies. However, it is unclear where the line is drawn between "the middle range" and "the end" of life. Such decisions are for the patient to determine.

What moral value should we place on the length of expected life, independent of the value we place on quality of life? In other words, would we be willing to withhold treatment from a patient who had a relatively short life expectancy but whose quality of life was very good and who wanted to live? After all, we are all familiar with patients who have long life expectancies but terrible qualities of life, such as patients in chronic vegetative states or those with a variety of brain injuries or chronic pain syndromes. We also are familiar with patients who live short but high-quality lives: those who are physically comfortable, mentally intact, and surrounded by loved ones, and who continue with their life's work as long as possible.

## Rationing According to Quality of Life

We might try to ration according to quality of life. That is, we might preferably fund treatments that resulted in a good quality of life compared with treatments that resulted in worse qualities of life. There are obvious problems in objectively determining quality of life. As I have tried to show, quality of life is a highly subjective parameter that only the patient can determine reliably. Notwithstanding, a scale has been developed that adjusts "life-years saved" according to quality of life parameters: this has been dubbed "quality-adjusted life-years saved."[23] This scale was developed by assigning objective values to quality of life associated with a specific illness. This objective value was determined by a survey of college students when asked to rate their anticipated quality of life if they were to come down with particular diseases. Not surprisingly, these young, healthy people estimated their quality of life with ESRD as being much poorer than did people who actually had the disease. Yet this is just the sort of calculation on which cost-benefit analyses are sometimes made. It is evident that neither accountants nor college students are better at coming up with objective values for quality of life than are the rest of us. On the other hand, it might be possible to use instruments that already have been developed to directly ask patients to rate their own qualities of life. If proper patient categories (a big *if!*) and techniques were established, it might be possible to find a reasonable scale for quality of life associated with a particular illness or treatment.

As I have tried to show, patients with short life expectancies frequently do benefit from life-prolonging treatment. Life with cancer usually is not merely a prolongation of misery, and patients on dialysis usually rate their quality of life as being quite good. An argument against treating all cancer patients with ESRD, as a class, cannot be made on humanitarian grounds. Of course there are many individual cases where the patient's benefit would be best served by withholding dialysis. What I object to is a public policy that would divert funds away from a whole class of patients on morally shaky grounds.

## Rationing According to Productivity

Cost-benefit analysis, which reduces all factors to dollars, implicitly values life according to productivity.[23] Grossly, this could consist in a calculation of future earning potential. In a more humanitarian fashion, "benefit" could be calculated according to some formula that considered other contributions as well as purely financial ones. Obviously productivity plummets when a person retires, when children leave home, or when a person becomes disabled. Productivity increases with better-paying jobs, longer times in the work force, or having many children. Past contribution is not taken into account. Clearly, low productivity is a criterion that can be applied to patients who are disabled because of cancer.

This value of productivity has no reasonable moral basis. It is the nonmoral consideration that we give to machines: they are valuable only insofar as they perform useful service for us. When they are no longer useful, they should be discarded. But people are not things, and it would be immoral to treat them as if they were things. Therefore I think that productivity is not a just basis for allocating resources.

## Is There a Moral Basis for Rationing Dialysis to Cancer Patients?

One might be tempted to suggest rationing dialysis to patients with advanced cancer on the grounds of limited life expectancy. However, I have tried to show that short lives still may be valuable to the patient. In addition, note that the shorter the duration of treatment, the less expensive the treatment; therefore, it would be less urgent to ration treatment. One might be tempted to ration dialysis to cancer patients on the grounds that such patients have poor qualities of life. However, I have tried to show that neither cancer patients nor dialysis patients necessarily have a poor quality of life. One might be tempted to ration dialysis to cancer patients on the grounds that dialysis offers no medical benefit. However, I have tried to show that what counts as medical benefit is best determined by the patient, and that dialysis clearly is effective in ameliorating the uremic syndrome and saving life in cancer patients with ESRD. Finally, one might be tempted to ration dialysis to cancer patients on the grounds that patients with advanced cancer are not productive member of society, and that medical dollars should be directed towards those who contribute to the economy. However, I have tried to show that such a value system is at odds with other important values that we hold about the worth of people.

If we as a society choose eventually to ration according to some of the principles that I have described above, then we will have to specify openly what we do or do not value. For example, we might choose not to fund treatment that has less than a 1% chance of effectiveness at favorably altering disease process or symptoms. We might choose not to fund life-prolonging treatment for patients who cannot interact meaningfully with their environment or for whom treatment would result in less than 72-hour survival. If such decisions eventually are made, then we can apply them to patients with advanced cancer and ESRD, but it would make no sense to ration dialysis according to the diagnosis of advanced cancer. Patients with the same diagnosis are just too different regarding what makes their life valuable to them and perhaps to society.

## Conclusions

In this essay I have searched for reasons that might justify withholding dialysis from patients with incurable cancer. I have considered the arguments that dialysis in such patients is futile; that it will result in poor quality of life; and that dialysis should be restricted to patients with advanced cancer according to principles of rationing health care resources. I have tried to show that none of these arguments can withstand close scrutiny. Dialysis in cancer patients with ESRD is a reasonably cost-effective treatment whose benefits outweigh its burdens in many cases. Therefore, decisions about dialysis should not be treated differently from decisions about the benefits and burdens of any other medical treatment. Dialysis should be a therapeutic option available to all people, including people with cancer, to be used when the benefit to the patient exceeds the burdens of treatment. In general, this will include all but those near death. Each case must be decided on its own merits, and it is the competent and informed patient or proxy who ultimately should make the decision.

In the event that we as a society decide to overtly ration health care resources, it will be vital to establish rationing principles in a publicly accountable way. Rationing decisions should be made on the basis of sound moral principles and some difficult decisions about social values. Diagnosis alone is not a sound moral principle on which to base rationing decisions.

## Notes

1. Schneiderman LJ, Jecker NS, Jonson AR: Medical futility: Its meaning and ethical implications. *Ann Intern Med* 112:949–954, 1990

2. Jecker NS: Knowing when to stop: The limits of medicine. *Hastings Cent Rep* 21(3):5–8, 1991

3. Chervenak FA, McCullough LB: Justified limits on refusing intervention. *Hastings Cent Rep* 21(2): 12–18, 1991

4. Tomlinson T, Brody H: Futility and the ethics of resuscitation. *JAMA* 264:1276–1280, 1990

5. Miles SH: Informed demand for "non-beneficial" medical treatment. *N Engl J Med* 325:512–515, 1991

6. Brett AS, McCullough LB: When patients request specific interventions: Defining the limits of the physician's obligation. *N Engl J Med* 315:1347–1351, 1986

7. President's Commission for the Study of Ethical Problems in Medicine and Biomedical and Behavioral Research: *Deciding to Forgo Life-Sustaining Treatment.* Washington, DC. US Government Printing Office, 1983, pp. 197–229

8. Wilde JA, Pedroni AT: When must you provide "futile care?". *Contemp Pediatr* 8(11)35–40, 1991

9. Hackler C, Hiller FC: Family consent to orders not to resuscitate: reconsidering hospital policy. *JAMA* 264:1281–1283. 1990

10. Lantos JD, Singer PA, Walker RM, et al: The illusion of futility in clinical practice. *Am J Med* 87:81–84, 1989

11. Murphy DJ: Do-not-resuscitate orders: time for reappraisal in long-term-care institutions. *JAMA* 260:2098–2101, 1988

12. Tomlinson T, Brody H: Ethics and communication in do-not-resuscitate orders. *N Engl J Med* 318:43–46, 1988

13. Callahan D: Medical futility, medical necessity: The problem-without-a-name. *Hastings Cent Rep* 21(4):30–35, 1991

14. Yougner SJ: Who defines futility? *JAMA* 260:2094–5, 1988

15. Battin MP: The least worst death. *Hastings Cent Rep* 13(2):13–19, 1983

16. Sackett DL, Torrance GW: The utility of different health states as perceived by the general public. *J Chronic Dis* 31:697–704, 1978

17. Johnson JP, McCauley CR, Copley JB: The quality of life of hemodialysis and transplant patients. *Kidney Int* 22: 286–291, 1982

18. Evans RW, Manninen DL, Garrison LP, et al: The quality of life of patients with end-stage renal disease. *N Engl J Med* 312:553–559, 1985

19. Ehrenfeld CL: Personal communication

20. Simmons RG, Marine SK: The regulation of high cost technology medicine: the case of dialysis and transplantation in the United Kingdom. *J Health Soc Behav* 25:320–334, 1984

21. Ward ED: Dialysis or death? Doctors should stop covering up for an inadequate health service. *J Med Ethics* 12: 61–63, 1986

22. Challah S, Wing AJ, Bauer R, et al: Negative selection of patients for dialysis and transplantation in the United Kingdom. *BMJ* 288:1119–1122, 1984

23. Avorn J: Benefit and cost analysis in geriatric care: Turning age discrimination into health policy. *N Engl J Med* 310:1294–1301, 1984

# 68    Medical Futility: Its Meaning and Ethical Implications

LAWRENCE J. SCHNEIDERMAN, NANCY S. JECKER, AND ALBERT R. JONSEN

A 62-year-old man with irreversible respiratory disease is in the intensive care unit. He is severely obtunded. During 3 weeks in the unit, repeated efforts to wean him from ventilatory support have been unsuccessful. There is general agreement among his physicians that he could not survive outside of an intensive care setting. They debate whether therapy should include cardiopulmonary resuscitation if the patient has a cardiac arrest or antibiotics if he develops infection. The patient gave no previous indication of his wishes nor executed an advance directive. Some physicians argue that a "do not resuscitate" order may be written without consulting the family, because resuscitation would be futile. Other physicians object, pointing out that resuscitation cannot be withheld on grounds of medical futility, because the patient could survive indefinitely in the intensive care

unit. They agree to consult the family on this matter. At first there is considerable disagreement within the family until a son asks whether there is any hope at all that his father might recover. The physicians look at each other. There is always hope. This unites the family. They insist that if the situation is not hopeless, the physicians should continue all measures including resuscitation.

How should these physicians deal with this family's demands? The answer depends on both how the physicians define futility and the weight they give it when patients or surrogates strongly express treatment preferences. Are these issues perhaps too complex or ambiguous to resolve (1, 2)? We submit that they are not, and we offer both a theoretical and practical approach to the concept of futility, an approach that we believe serves in this case and more generally in similar cases by restoring a common sense notion of medical duty. We recognize that if futility is held to be nothing more than a vague notion of physician discretion,

From *Annals of Internal Medicine*, 112 (1990), 949–954. Reprinted by permission of the American College of Physicians.

it is subject to abuse: therefore, we propose specific standards by which this idea can be appropriately invoked. In our view, judgments of futility emerge from either quantitative or qualitative evaluations of clinical situations. Such evaluations determine whether physicians are obligated to offer an intervention. If an intervention is judged to be futile, the duty to present the intervention as an option to the patient or the patient's family is mitigated or eliminated. We recognize—indeed invite—examination and challenge of our proposal.

## The Glare of Autonomy

Less than a few decades ago, the practice of medicine was characterized by a paternalism exemplified in the expression, "doctor's orders." Physicians determined by themselves or in consultation with colleagues the usefulness of courses of treatment. The art of medicine was considered to include selectively withholding as well as disclosing information in order to maintain control over therapy. The dramatic shift toward patient self-determination that has taken place in recent decades almost certainly received much of its momentum from society's backlash to this paternalism. In addition, philosophical and political concerns about the rights of individuals and respect for persons elevated the principle of autonomy to a position in ethics that it had not previously held. Today, ethics and the law give primacy to patient autonomy, defined as the right to be a fully informed participant in all aspects of medical decision making and the right to refuse unwanted, even recommended and life-saving, medical care. So powerful has this notion of autonomy become that its glare often blinds physicians (and ethicists) to the validity of earlier maxims that had long defined the range of physicians' moral obligations toward patients. Among these was the maxim, respected in ethics and law, that futile treatments are not obligatory. No ethical principle or law has ever required physicians to offer or accede to demands for treatments that are futile (3, 4). Even the so-called Baby Doe regula-

tions, notorious for their advocacy of aggressive medical intervention, permit physicians to withhold treatment that is "futile in terms of the survival of the infant" or "virtually futile" (5). Even when this maxim is accepted in theory, however, physicians frequently practice as though every available medical measure, including absurd and overzealous interventions, must be used to prolong life unless patients give definitive directions to the contrary (6, 7). Some physicians allow patients (or surrogates) to decide when a treatment is futile, thereby overriding medical judgment and potentially allowing the patient (or surrogate) to demand treatment that offers no benefit (8).

## Comparison of Effect and Benefit

In the early nineteenth century, all medications were, by definition, effective: They inevitably brought about the effect that their names described. Emetics could be counted on to cause vomiting; purgatives to cause laxation; sudorifics, sweating; and so on (9). These effects, given the medical theories of the times, were presumed always to be beneficial. Failure to heal was a defect of nature, not of the physician or the treatment. However, one advance of modern medicine, particularly with the introduction of controlled clinical trials, was to clarify by empiric methods the important distinction between effect and benefit. In examining the notion of futility, physicians sometimes fail to keep this distinction in mind.

For example, a recent discussion of futility includes the following: "[Physicians] may acknowledge that therapy is effective, in a limited sense, but believe that the goals that can be achieved are not desirable, as when considering prolonged nutritional support for patients in a persistent vegetative state. Physicians should acknowledge that, in such situations, potentially achievable goals exist. Therapy is not, strictly speaking, futile" (2). On the contrary, we believe that the goal of medical treatment is not merely to cause an effect on some portion of the patient's anatomy, physiology, or chemistry, but to benefit the patient as a whole. No physician would feel obligated to yield to a patient's demand to treat pneumonia with insulin. The physician would rightly argue that (in the absence of insulin-requiring diabetes) such treatment is inappropriate; insulin might have a physiologic effect on the patient's blood sugar, but would offer no benefit to the patient with respect to the pneumonia. Similarly, nutritional support could effectively preserve a host of organ systems in a patient in persistent vegetative state, but fail to restore a conscious and sapient life. Is such nutritional treatment futile or not? We argue that it is futile for the simple reason that the ultimate goal of any treatment should be improvement of the patient's prognosis, comfort, well-being, or general state of health. A treatment that fails to provide such a benefit—even though it produces a measurable effect—should be considered futile.

## Approaching a Definition

The word futility comes from the Latin word meaning leaky (*futilis*). According to the *Oxford English Dictionary,* a futile action is "leaky, hence untrustworthy, vain, failing of the desired end through intrinsic defect." In Greek mythology, the daughters of Danaus were condemned in Hades to draw water in leaky sieves. Needless to say, their labors went for nought. The story conveys in all its fullness the meaning of the term: A futile action is one that cannot achieve the goals of the action, no matter how often repeated. The likelihood of failure may be predictable because it is inherent in the nature of the action proposed, and it may become immediately obvious or may become apparent only after many failed attempts.

This concept should be distinguished from etymologic neighbors. Futility should not be used to refer to an act that is, in fact, impossible to do. Attempting to walk to the moon or restore cardiac function in an exsanguinated patient would not be futile acts; they would be physically and logically impossible. Nor should futility be confused with acts that are so complex that, although theoretically possible, they are implausible. The production of a human infant entirely outside the womb,

from in-vitro combination of sperm and egg to physiologic viability, may be theoretically possible but, with current technology, is implausible.

Further, futile, because the term is not merely descriptive, but also operational, denoting an action that will fail and that ought not be attempted, implies something more than simply rare, uncommon, or unusual. Some processes that are quite well understood and quite probable may occur only occasionally, perhaps because of their complexity and the need for many circumstances to concur at the same time. For example, successful restoration to health of a drug addict with bacterial endocarditis might require a combination of medical, psychological, social, and educational efforts. These interventions could work but, due to various factors (including limited societal resources), they rarely work. However, they are not futile.

Futility should also be distinguished from hopelessness. Futility refers to the objective quality of an action; hopelessness describes a subjective attitude. Hope and hopelessness bear more relation to desire, faith, denial, and other psychological responses than to the objective possibility or probability that the actions being contemplated will be successful. Indeed, as the chance for success diminishes, hope may increase and replace reasonable expectation. Something plausible is hardly ever hopeless, because hope is what human beings summon up to seek a miracle against overwhelming odds. It is possible then to say in the same breath, "I know this is futile, but I have hope." Such a statement expresses two facts, one about the objective properties of the situation, the other about the speaker's psychological state.

Futility refers to an expectation of success that is either predictably or empirically so unlikely that its exact probability is often incalculable. Without specific data, one might predict futility from closely analogous experience. (For example, one might avoid a trial of a particular chemotherapy for one type of cancer based on failures seen when used for treating similar forms of cancer.) Or one may have accumulated empiric experience insufficient to state precisely the likelihood of success, but sufficient to doubt the likelihood of success. (For example, physicians have had only a few years of experience with a currently popular medication to cure baldness, but sufficient experience to be dubious of its long-term success.)

Reports of one or two "miraculous" successes do not counter the notion of futility, if these successes were achieved against a background of hundreds or thousands of failures. Such rare exceptions are causally inexplicable, because any clinical situation contains a multitude of factors—in addition to treatment—that might affect outcome. As Wanzer and colleagues (10) stated, "The rare report of a patient with a similar condition who survived is not an overriding reason to continue aggressive treatment."

## Quantitative and Qualitative Aspects

The futility of a particular treatment may be evident in either quantitative or qualitative terms. That is, futility may refer to an improbability or unlikelihood of an event happening, an expression that is quasi-numeric, or to the quality of the event that treatment would produce. Thus, determining futility resembles using decision analysis—with one important distinction. In decision analysis, the decision to use a procedure is based on the joint product of the probability of success and the quality (utility) of the outcome (11). Thus, very low probability might be balanced by very high utility. In our proposal of futility, however, we treat the quantitative and qualitative aspects as independent thresholds, as minimal cutoff levels, either of which frees the physician from the obligation to offer a medical treatment.

This independence of futility determinants can be traced back to medical antiquity (12, 13). The perception of futility derived from the Hippocratic corpus might be considered, in modern terms, to be quantitative or probabilistic. A book titled "The Art" (14) enjoins physicians to acknowledge when efforts will probably fail: "Whenever therefore a man suffers from an ill which is too strong for the means at the disposal of medicine, he surely must not even expect that it can be overcome by medicine." The writer further admonishes the physi-

cian that to attempt futile treatment is to display an ignorance which is "allied to madness."

Plato's *Republic* (15), on the other hand, has a qualitative notion of futility, one that emphasizes the inappropriateness of efforts that result in patients surviving, but leading literally useless lives. According to Plato, the kind of medicine "which pampers the disease" was not used by the Asclepian physicians:

> Asclepius . . . taught medicine for those who were healthy in their nature but were suffering from a specific disease; he rid them of it . . . then ordered them to live as usual. . . . For those however, whose bodies were always in a state of inner sickness he did not attempt to prescribe a regimen . . . to make their life a prolonged misery. . . . Medicine was not intended for them and they should not be treated even if they were richer than Midas.

Thus, both the quantitative and qualitative aspects of futility are recognized in the most ancient traditions. Hippocrates rejects efforts that are quantitatively or probabilistically unlikely to achieve a cure; Plato objects to a cure consummating (qualitatively) in a life that "isn't worth living." Both quantitative and qualitative aspects relate to a single underlying notion: The result is not commensurate to the effort. The effort is, on the part of the agent, a repeated expenditure of energy that is consistently nonproductive or, if productive, its outcome is far inferior to that intended.

## Defining Futility

We propose that, on the basis of these considerations, the noun "futility" and the adjective "futile" be used to describe any effort to achieve a result that is possible but that reasoning or experience suggests is highly improbable and that cannot be systematically produced. The phrase, "highly improbable," implies that a statistical statement about probability might be applicable. In the strict sense, such a statement cannot be made, as proper conditions for determining probability (that is, prospective comparisons of precisely controlled treatment and nontreatment on identically matched subjects) will never be present. We introduce the concept of "systematic" to point out that if a rare "success" is not explicable or cannot be predictably repeated, its causality is dubious, because it is uncertain whether treatment, some extraneous influence, or random variation caused the result.

## Quantitative Aspects

In keeping with the quantitative approach to futility, we propose that when physicians conclude (either through personal experience, experiences shared with colleagues, or consideration of reported empiric data) that in the last 100 cases, a medical treatment has been useless, they should regard that treatment as futile. Technically, we cannot say that observing no successes in 100 trials means that the treatment never works. However, such an observation serves as a point estimate of the probability of treatment success. Although we cannot say with certainty that the point estimate is correct, statistical methods can be used to estimate a range of values that include the true success rate with a specified probability. For example, if there have been no successes in 100 consecutive cases, the clinician can be 95% confident that no more than 3 successes would occur in each 100 comparable trials (3 successes per 100 trials is the upper limit of the 95% CI). This confidence range would narrow as the number of observations increased. If no successes were seen in 200 cases, the upper limit of the 95% CI would be 1.5 successes per 100 cases and, for no successes in 1000 observations, the upper limit would be approximately 0.3 successes per 100 cases. In practical terms, because data from controlled clinical trials can only rarely be called on and applied to a specific case, practitioners usually use their extended experience as the source of their conclusions. Here, specialty practice contributes an essential element: for example, an intensive care pulmonary specialist who sees several hundred patients who have similar disease conditions and receive similar therapy can often group together "futility characteristics"

better than a generalist who does not see cases in so focused a manner.

Without systematic knowledge of the various factors that cause a therapy to have less than a 1% chance of success—knowledge that would allow the physician to address these factors—we regard it as unreasonable to require that the physicians offer such therapy. To do so forces the physician to offer any therapy that may have seemed to work or that may conceivably work. In effect, it obligates the physician to offer a placebo. Only when empirically observed (though not understood) outcomes rise to a level higher than that expected by any placebo effect (16), can a specific therapy be considered to be "possibly helpful" in rare or occasional cases and its appropriateness evaluated according to rules of decision analysis. In the clinical setting, such judgments also would be influenced, of course, by considering such tradeoffs as how cheap and simple the intervention is and how serious or potentially fatal the disease (*see* Exceptions and Cautions).

Although our proposed selection of proportions of success is admittedly arbitrary, it seems to comport reasonably well with ideas actually held by physicians. For example, Murphy and colleagues (17) invoked the notion of futility in their series of patients when survival after cardiopulmonary resuscitation was no better than 2% (upper limit of 95% CI as calculated by authors), and Lantos and colleagues (18) when survival was no better than 7% (upper limit of 95% CI as calculated by authors).

Obviously, as medical data on specific situations are gathered under appropriate experimental conditions, empiric uncertainty can be replaced with empiric confidence (19). Admittedly, some disorders may be too rare to provide sufficient experience for a confident judgment of futility, even when efforts are made to pool data. We acknowledge this difficulty but adhere to our conservative standard to prevent arbitrary abuse of power. In judging futility, as in other matters, physicians should admit uncertainty rather than impose unsubstantiated claims of certainty. Therefore, our view of futility should be considered as encouraging rather than opposing well conducted clinical trials. Important examples of such work in progress include studies of survival after cardiopulmonary resuscitation (17–24) and use of prognostic measures in patients requiring intensive medical care (25, 26).

Already, data on burn patients (27) and on patients in persistent vegetative state with abnormal neuroophthalmic signs (28) are sufficient to help with decision making. The latter group of patients present a particular challenge to presently confused notions of futility, perhaps accounting in part for why an estimated 5000 to 10,000 patients in persistent vegetative state are now being maintained in medical institutions (29). The mythologic power of the coma patient who "wakes up" apparently overrides the rarity of documented confirmation of such miraculous recoveries (which have resulted, moreover, in incapacitating mental impairment or total dependence) (28). This point bears on the frequently heard excuse for pushing ahead with futile therapies: "It is only by so doing that progress is made and the once futile becomes efficacious. Remember the futility of treating childhood leukemia or Hodgkin lymphoma." These statements hide a fallacy. It is not through repeated futility that progress is made, but through careful analysis of the elements of the "futile case," followed by well designed studies, that advances knowledge. We also point out that our proposal is intended for recognized illness in the acute clinical setting. It does not apply to preventive treatments, such as immunizations, estrogen prophylaxis for hip fractures, or penicillin prophylaxis for rheumatic heart disease and infectious endocarditis, all of which appear to have lower rates of efficacy because they are purposely administered to large groups of persons, many of whom will never be at risk for or identified with the particular diseases that their treatments are intended to prevent.

## Qualitative Aspects

In keeping with the qualitative notion of futility we propose that any treatment that merely preserves permanent unconsciousness or that fails to end total dependence on intensive medical care should be regarded as nonbeneficial and, therefore, futile. We do not regard futility as "an elusive concept" (2). It is elusive only when effects on the patient are confused with benefits to the patient or when the term is stretched to include either considerations of 5-year survival in patients with cancer (not at all pertinent to the notion of futility) or the "symbolic" value to society of treating handicapped newborns or patients in persistent vegetative state (which rides roughshod over patient-centered decision making) (2).

Here is the crux of the matter. If futility is qualitative, why should the patient not always decide whether the quality achieved is satisfactory or not? Why should qualitatively "futile" results not be offered to the patient as an option? We believe a distinction is in order. Some qualitatively poor results should indeed be the patient's option, and the patient should know that they may be attainable. We believe, however, that other sorts of qualitatively poor results fall outside the range of the patient's autonomy and need not be offered as options. The clearest of these qualitatively poor results is continued biologic life without conscious autonomy. The patient has no right to be sustained in a state in which he or she has no purpose other than mere vegetative survival; the physician has no obligation to offer this option or services to achieve it. Other qualitatively poor results are conditions requiring constant monitoring, ventilatory support, and intensive care nursing (such as in the example at the beginning of our paper) or conditions associated with overwhelmingly suffering for a predictably brief time. Admittedly, these kinds of cases fall along a continuum, and there are well known examples of the most remarkable achievements of life goals despite the most burdensome handicaps. However, if survival requires the patient's entire preoccupation with intensive medical treatment, to the extent that he or she cannot achieve any other life goals (thus obviating the goal of medical care), the treatment is effective but not beneficial; it need not be offered to the patient, and the patient's family has no right to demand it.

Specifically excluded from our concept of futility is medical care for patients for whom such care offers the opportunity to achieve life goals, however limited. Thus, patients whose illnesses are severe enough to require frequent hospitalization, patients confined to nursing homes, or patients with severe physical or mental handicaps are not, in themselves, objects of futile treatments. Such patients (or their surrogates) have the right to receive or reject any medical treatment according to their own perceptions of benefits compared with burdens.

Some observers might object, as a matter of principle, to excluding patient input from assessments of qualitative futility. Others might be concerned that such exclusion invites abuse, neglect, and a retreat to the paternalistic "silent world" of the past in which doctors avoided communication with their patients (30). In response to the latter objection, we acknowledge that potential for abuse is present and share this concern. We would deplore the use of our proposal to excuse physicians from engaging patients in ongoing informed dialogue. Nonetheless, the alternative is also subject to abuse (for example, when legal threats made by patients and surrogates cow hospitals into providing excessive care). We reiterate that the distinction between medical benefit and effect justifies excluding patients from determination of qualitative futility. Physicians are required only to provide medical benefits to patients. Physicians are permitted, but not obligated, to offer other, non-medical benefits. For example, a physician is not obligated to keep a patient alive in an irreversible vegetative state, because doing so does not medically benefit the patient. However, as noted below, a physician may do so on compassionate grounds, when temporary continuance of biologic life achieves goals of the patient or family.

## Exceptions and Cautions

We have attempted to provide a working definition of futility. We also have drawn attention to the ethical notion that futility is a professional judgment that takes precedence over patient autonomy and permits physicians to withhold or withdraw care deemed to be inappropriate without subjecting such a decision to patient approval. Thus, we regard our proposal as representing the ordinary duties of physicians, duties that are applicable where there is medical agreement that the described standards of futility are met. We recognize, however, that the physician's duty to serve the best interests of the patient may require that exceptions to our approaches be made under special circumstances.

An exception could well be made out of compassion for the patient with terminal metastatic cancer who requests resuscitation in the event of cardiac arrest to survive long enough to see a son or daughter who has not yet arrived from afar to pay last respects. Such an exception could also be justified to facilitate coping and grieving by family members, a goal the patient might support (32–36). Although resuscitation may be clearly futile (that is, would keep the patient alive in the intensive care unit for only 1 or 2 more days), complying with the patient's wishes would be appropriate, provided such exceptions do not impose undue burdens on other patients, health care providers, and the institution, by directly threatening the health care of others. We hasten to add, however, that our notion of futility does not arise from considerations of scarce resources. Arguments for limiting treatments on grounds of resource allocation should proceed by an entirely different route and with great caution in our present open system of medical care, as there is no universally accepted value system for allocation (31) and no guarantee that any limits a physician imposes on his or her patients will be equitably shared by other physicians and patients in the same circumstances (37, 38).

Admittedly, in cases in which treatment has begun already, there may be an emotional bias to continue, rather than withdraw, futile measures (10). If greater attention is paid at the outset to indicating futile treatments, these situations would occur less frequently; however, the futility of a given treatment may not become clear until it has been implemented. We submit that physicians are entitled to cease futile measures in such cases, but should do so in a manner sensitive to the emotional investments and concerns of caretakers.

What if a hospitalized patient with advanced cancer demands a certain medication (for example, a particular vitamin), a treatment that the physician believes to be futile? Several aspects of this demand support its overriding the physician's invocation of futility. Certain death is expected and, although an objective goal such as saving the patient's life or even releasing the patient from the hospital might be unachievable, the subjective goal of patient well-being might be enhanced (a placebo-induced benefit). In this particular situation, the effort and resources invested to achieve this goal impose a negligible burden on the health care system and do not threaten the health care of others. Thus, although physicians are not obligated to offer a placebo, they occasionally do. For example, Imbus and Zawacki (27) allowed burn patients to opt for treatment even when survival was unprecedented. In this clinical situation, compassionate yielding imposes no undue burden, because survival with or without treatment is measured in days. In contrast, yielding to a surrogate's demand for unlimited life-support for a patient in persistent vegetative state may lead to decades of institutional care.

*Acknowledgements:* The authors thank two anonymous reviewers and Robert M. Kaplan, PhD, for their helpful comments.

## Notes

1. Younger SJ. Who defines futility? *JAMA.* 1988:260: 2094–5.

2. Lantos JD, Singer PA, Walker RM, et al. The illusion of futility in clinical practice. *Am J Med.* 1989:87:81–4.

3. President's Commission for the Study of Ethical Problems in Medicine and Biomedical and Behavioral Research. *Deciding to Forego Life-Sustaining Treatment: A Report on the Ethical, Medical, and Legal Issues in Treatment Decisions.* Washington DC: U.S. Government Printing Office: 1983:60–89.

4. Jonsen AR. What does life support support? *Pharos.* 1987:50(1):4-7.

5. *Child Abuse and Neglect Prevention and Treatment.* Washington, DC: U.S. Department of Health and Human Services, Office of Human Development Services; 1985: Federal Register 50:14887–8.

6. Blackhall LJ. Must we always use CPR? *N Engl J Med.* 1987:317:1281–5.

7. Tomlinson T, Brody H. Ethics and communication in do-not-resuscitate orders. *N Engl J Med.* 1988:318:43–6.

8. Lo B. Life-sustaining treatment in patients with AIDS: challenge to traditional decision-making. In: Juengst ET, Koenig BA, eds. *The Meaning of AIDS.* v 1. New York: Praeger: 1989:86–93.

9. Rosenberg CE. The therapeutic revolution: medicine, meaning, and social change in nineteenth-century America. *Perspect Biol Med.* 1977;20:485–506.

10. Wanzer SH, Adelstein SJ, Cranford RE, et al. The physician's responsibility toward hopelessly ill patients. *N Engl J Med.*1984: 310:955–9.

11. Weinstein MC, Fineberg HV. *Clinical Decision Analysis.* Philadelphia: W.B. Saunders: 1980.

12. Amundsen DW. The physician's obligation to prolong life: a medical duty without classical roots. *Hastings Cent Rep.* 1978;8:23–30.

13. Jonsen AR. *The Old Ethics and the New Medicine.* Cambridge: Harvard University Press: 1990.

14. Hippocratic corpus, the art. In: Reiser SJ, Dyck AJ, Curran WJ, eds. *Ethics in Medicine: Historical Perspectives and Contemporary Concerns.* Cambridge, Massachusetts: MIT Press: 1977:6–7.

15. Plato. In: Grube GM, transl. *Republic.* Indianapolis: Hackett Publishing: 1981:76–7.

16. Beecher HK. The powerful placebo. *JAMA.* 1955: 159:1602–6.

17. Murphy DJ, Murray AM, Robinson BE, Campion EW. Outcomes of cardiopulmonary resuscitation in the elderly. *Ann Intern Med.* 1989: 111:199–205.

18. Lantos JD, Miles SH, Silverstein MD, Stocking CB. Survival after cardiopulmonary resuscitation in babies of very low birth weight. *N Engl J Med.* 1988:318:91–5.

19. Freiman JA, Chalmers TC, Smith H Jr, Koehler RR. The importance of beta, the type II error and sample size in the design and interpretation of the randomized control trial. Survey of 71 "negative" trials. *N Engl J Med.* 1978:299:690–4.

20. Bedell SE, Delbanco TL, Cook EF, Epstein FH. Survival after cardiopulmonary resuscitation in the hospital. *N Engl J Med.* 1983:309:569–76.

21. Gordon M, Horowitz E. Cardiopulmonary resuscitation of the elderly. *J Am Geriatr Soc.* 1984:32:930–4.

22. *Life-Sustaining Technologies and the Elderly.* Washington, DC: U.S. Congress. Office of Technology Assessment: 1987: publication OTA-BA-306, 167–201.

23. Johnson AL, Tanser PH, Ulan RA, Wood TE. Results of cardiac resuscitation in 552 patients. *Am J Cardiol.* 1967:20:831–5.

24. Taffet GE, Teasdale TA, Luchi RJ. In-hospital cardiopulmonary resuscitation. *JAMA.* 1988:260:2069–72.

25. Knaus WA, Draper EA, Wagner DP, Zimmerman JD. APACHE II: a severity of disease classification system. *Crit Care Med.* 1985: 13:818–29.

26. Knaus WA, Draper EA, Wagner DP, Zimmerman JE. An evaluation of outcome from intensive care in major medical centers. *Ann Intern Med.* 1986:104:410–8.

27. Imbus SH, Zawacki BE. Autonomy for burned patient when survival is unprecedented. *N Engl J Med.* 1977:297:308–11.

28. Plum F, Posner JB. *The Diagnosis of Stupor and Coma.* 3d ed. Philadelphia: F.A. Davis: 1980.

29. Cranford RE. The persistent vegetative state: the medical reality (getting the facts straight). *Hastings Cent Rep.* 1988: 18:27–32.

30. Katz J. *The Silent World of Doctor and Patient.* New York: Free Press: 1984.

31. Emery DD, Schneiderman LJ. Cost-effectiveness analysis in health care. *Hastings Cent Rep.* 1989:19:8–13.

32. Yarborough M. Continued treatment of the fatally ill for the benefit of others. *J Am Geriatr Soc.*1988:36:63–7.

33. Perkins HS. Ethics at the end of life: practical principles for making resuscitation decisions. *J Gen Intern Med.* 1986:1:170–6.

34. Miles SH. Futile feeding at the end of life: family virtues and treatment decisions. *Theor Med.* 1987:8:293–302.

35. Jecker NS. Anencephalic infants and special relationships. *Theor Med.* 1990.

36. Jecker NS. The moral status of patients who are not strict persons. *J Clin Med.* 1990.

37. Schneiderman LJ, Spragg RG. Ethical decisions in discontinuing mechanical ventilation. *N Engl J Med.* 1988: 318:984–8.

38. Daniels N. Why saying no to patients in the United States is so hard: cost containment justice, and provider autonomy. *N Engl J Med.* 1986:314:1380–3.

# Questions

1. Choose any *one* of the following tasks. Do not vary the facts between the two arguments or ignore factors in one argument while using them in the other.

   a. Give an argument based on the Sermon on the Mount showing that active, voluntary euthanasia is immoral, *and* give an argument based on the Sermon on the Mount showing that active, voluntary euthanasia is moral.

   b. Give a Utilitarian argument showing that active, voluntary euthanasia is immoral, *and* give a Utilitarian argument showing that active, voluntary euthanasia is moral.

   c. Give a Kantian argument showing that active, voluntary euthanasia is immoral, *and* give a Kantian argument showing that active, voluntary euthanasia is moral. (*Hint:* Consider Kant's discussion of suicide and of helping others.)

2. State the best argument you can think of against active euthanasia. State a parallel argument against capital punishment. Do you find either of these arguments persuasive? Why or why not?

   State the best argument you can think of in favor of active euthanasia. State a parallel argument in favor of capital punishment. Do you find either of these arguments persuasive? Why or why not?

   Is it possible to be in favor of capital punishment and opposed to active euthanasia without inconsistency? Is it possible to be opposed to capital punishment and in favor of active euthanasia without inconsistency?

3. Note that the question "Is euthanasia of such-and-such a type practiced upon such-and-such a person moral?" is very different from the question "Should euthanasia of such-and-such a type practiced upon such-and-such a person be legal?" This section has examined the morality of euthanasia from Utilitarian, Kantian, and Aristotelian perspectives. Using Utilitarian, Kantian, *or* Aristotelian arguments, discuss the *legality* of euthanasia.

4. Ned, Fred, and Jed are all terminally ill and in intractable pain. Ned kills himself by taking poison. Fred stops taking the life-prolonging medication he has been taking for the last few months and promptly dies. Jed does not seek treatment of intercurrent pneumonia and promptly dies of it. Answer any *one* of the following questions.

a. Would an Act Utilitarian consider these three acts morally equivalent? Why or why not?

b. Would a Rule Utilitarian consider these three acts morally equivalent? Why or why not?

c. Would a Kantian using CI#1 consider these three acts morally equivalent? Why or why not?

d. Would a Kantian using CI#2 consider these three acts morally equivalent? Why or why not?

e. Do you consider these three acts morally equivalent? Why or why not?

5. Consider the following claims.

(A) Active euthanasia is OK, but suicide is immoral.

(B) Active euthanasia is immoral, but suicide is OK.

Perform any *two* of the following tasks.

a. Provide a Kantian argument for claim (A).

b. Provide a Kantian argument for claim (B).

c. Provide a Utilitarian argument for claim (A).

d. Provide a Utilitarian argument for claim (B).

e. Explain why it is impossible to do task (a).

f. Explain why it is impossible to do task (b).

g. Explain why it is impossible to do task (c).

h. Explain why it is impossible to do task (d).

6. Choose *one* of the following tasks.

a. Using Hursthouse's article on abortion as a guide, analyze the practice of active euthanasia from a virtue ethics point of view. That is, determine whether the practice of active euthanasia exhibits the vice of injustice, or cowardice, or intemperance, or foolishness, or any other vice.

b. Using Thomson's article "A Defense of Abortion" as a guide, analyze the practice of active euthanasia. Be sure to fill your answer with cute but accurate illustrations. Start with the observation that, just as the right to life does not include the right to be given the bare necessities for life, so the right to life does not include the right to take one's own life.

7. Schneiderman, Jecker, and Jonsen propose absolute standards for judging a therapy to be futile and then refusing to provide that therapy. Epstein maintains that the standards for refusing to provide a therapy should be relative to the individual. What arguments does Epstein advance against Schneiderman, Jecker, and Jonsen? How might Schneiderman, Jecker, and Jonsen reply to Epstein's arguments?

8. As things stand now, people with no previously expressed wishes about treatment who are found to be medically incompetent are *forced* to undergo whatever medical treatment (or non-treatment) their proxy decides upon, *whether they want to or not*. We do not test people for financial, personal, or career competence and *force* those that are found financially incompetent to make or not to make certain investments, those that are found personally incompetent to make or not to make certain marriages, and those that are found to have little career competence to take or not to take certain jobs *whether they want to or not*. However, we do not allow minors to marry without the consent of a proxy, and we do not let people practice certain professions without passing a licensing test. Should we continue to force medically incompetent people to do things they don't want to do?

9. If a patient asks a doctor to provide a therapy that the doctor believes to be harmful, the doctor is expected to refuse. Naturally, the determination that a certain therapy is harmful involves a value judgment. Yet if we believe that doctors can and should determine which therapies are harmful, are we not also committed to the belief that doctors can and should determine which therapies are futile, even if this determination involves value judgments?

10. The courts use the "reasonable-person" standard to decide many issues. For example, they use this standard to determine how to

treat medically incompetent people who have expressed no preferences. Why not use the reasonable-person standard to decide which therapies are futile? That is, why not say that a therapy is loosely futile (and therefore deniable to patients) if and only if a reasonable person would consider the therapy to have little chance of achieving a worthwhile goal?

11. It is presently illegal and arguably immoral to damage an early fetus that will not be aborted, but it is presently legal and arguably morally permissible to abort the fetus. By analogy, one might expect that it would be wrong to mutilate oneself or ask someone else to do it, but it would be morally permissible to kill oneself or request euthanasia. Do the arguments against damaging fetuses show that self-mutilation and mutilation by others upon request are immoral? Do the arguments in favor of suicide and euthanasia also justify self-mutilation and mutilation by others upon request?

12. Is there a morally significant distinction between active and passive euthanasia? If so, explain what is wrong with Rachels's argument.

    If not, explain why there seems to be a morally significant distinction between stealing a car and allowing a car to be stolen by someone else when you could stop them. Explain why there seems to be a morally significant distinction between vandalizing a building and allowing a building to be damaged when you could prevent it.

    Apply your analysis to the following question. Is there a morally significant distinction between lying to a patient and allowing the patient to retain false beliefs when you could tell the patient the truth?

13. If you believe that active and passive euthanasia are morally equivalent, are you necessarily committed to the view that people have a right to life-extending health care? If you believe that people have a right to life-

extending health care, are you necessarily committed to the view that active and passive euthanasia are morally equivalent?

14. If you believe that the doctor-patient relationship should be paternalistic, are you necessarily committed to the view that the doctor should decide which therapies are futile and withhold these therapies despite patient requests for them? If you believe that the doctor should decide which therapies are futile and withhold these therapies despite patient requests for them, are you necessarily committed to the view that the doctor-patient relationship should be paternalistic?

15. Mr. Jones is in a deep coma. As far as the doctors can determine, he has no friends, no relatives, no money, and no brain function. He has essentially no hope of ever waking up. Keeping him alive would cost about $1000 per day for an indefinite length of time (perhaps 30 days, perhaps 30 years). Is it moral to kill Mr. Jones or to let him die?

    If you think it is *not* moral to kill him or let him die, who should pay for his care? That is, what principle of distributive justice should be used to determine which people should bear the financial burden of keeping Mr. Jones alive? Defend your answer.

    If you think it *is* moral to kill him or let him die, consider the following slightly different case. Mr. Smith has no friends, no money, and no brain function, but he has a sister who says, "I will pay $1000 per day for the next 30 years, if necessary, to keep my dear brother alive. Doing this will, of course, prevent me from sending my kids to college. Susie, who dreams of becoming a doctor, will never be able to go to medical school. Tom will have to postpone his marriage. And so on. But never mind about them. The important thing is to keep Mr. Smith alive." Should Mr. Smith's sister *be allowed* to spend her money keeping Mr. Smith alive, or is it OK to let him die *in spite of* her wishes? Defend your answer.